The Princeton Encyclopedia of the World Economy

The Princeton

PRINCETON REFERENCE

Encyclopedia of the World Economy

Volume II

EDITORS IN CHIEF

Kenneth A. Reinert

Ramkishen S. Rajan

ASSOCIATE EDITORS

Amy Jocelyn Glass

Lewis S. Davis

PRINCETON UNIVERSITY PRESS

PRINCETON AND OXFORD

Copyright © 2009 by Princeton University Press

Published by Princeton University Press, 41 William Street,
Princeton, New Jersey 08540

In the United Kingdom: Princeton University Press, 6 Oxford Street,
Woodstock, Oxfordshire 0X20 1TW

The findings, interpretations, and conclusions expressed in this book
are entirely those of the authors writing in their personal capacities.
They do not necessarily represent the views or positions of the institutions with which the authors are affiliated, or of any other person
associated with those institutions.

Library of Congress Cataloging-in-Publication Data
The Princeton encyclopedia of the world economy / editors in chief,
Kenneth A. Reinert, Ramkishen S. Rajan ; associate editors, Amy
Jocelyn Glass, Lewis S. Davis.

    p. cm.

  Includes bibliographical references and index.

  ISBN 978-0-691-12812-2 (hbk. : alk. paper)   1. International
trade—Encyclopedias.   2. International finance—
Encyclopedias.   3. International business enterprises—
Encyclopedias.   4. International economic relations—
Encyclopedias.   I. Reinert, Kenneth A.   II. Rajan, Ramkishen S.
III. Glass, Amy Jocelyn.   IV. Davis, Lewis S.

  HF1373.P75 2009

  337.03—dc22   2008020573

This book has been composed in Adobe Garamond and Myriad

Printed on acid-free paper.

press.princeton.edu
Printed in the United States of America
10 9 8 7 6 5 4 3 2 1

Contents

Alphabetical List of Entries

Topical List of Entries

2. Models and Theory

International Trade
economies of scale
foreign direct investment under monopolistic
    competition
foreign direct investment under oligopoly
Heckscher-Ohlin model
monopolistic competition
New Economic Geography
New Trade Theory
nontraded goods
oligopoly models
political economy of trade policy
Ricardian model
specific-factors model

International Finance
Balassa-Samuelson effect
Feldstein-Horioka puzzle
forward premium puzzle
interest parity conditions
J-curve effect
Marshall-Lerner condition
Mundell-Fleming model
New Open Economy Macroeconomics
optimum currency area (OCA) theory
primary products trade
quantity theory of money
Swan diagram
Triffin dilemma

International Production
foreign direct investment: the OLI framework
foreign direct investment under monopolistic
    competition
foreign direct investment under oligopoly
internalization theory
knowledge-capital model of the multinational
    enterprise
location theory
pollution haven hypothesis
proximity-concentration hypothesis

International Economic Development
aid, international, and political economy
dependency theory
evolution of development thinking
growth in open economies, neoclassical models
growth in open economies, Schumpeterian
    models
infant industry argument
North-South trade
South-South trade

3. Institutions and Agreements

International Trade
African Caribbean Pacific–European Union
    partnership agreements (ACP-EU)
African Union
Agreement on Agriculture
Agreement on Trade-Related Aspects of
    Intellectual Property Rights (TRIPS)
agricultural trade negotiations
Andean Community
Asia Pacific Economic Cooperation (APEC)
Association of Southeast Asian Nations (ASEAN)
Basel Convention
Central American Common Market (CACM)
Central American–Dominican Republic Free
    Trade Area (CAFTA-DR)
Common Agricultural Policy
Common Market for Eastern and Southern Africa
    (COMESA)
Convention on Biological Diversity
Convention on International Trade in
    Endangered Species (CITES)
Doha Round
Economic Community of West African States
    (ECOWAS)
European Union
Free Trade Area of the Americas (FTAA)
General Agreement on Tariffs and Trade (GATT)
General Agreement on Trade in Services (GATS)
Global Environment Facility
Group of Seven/Eight (G7/G8)

financial services
gender
illegal drugs trade
information and communication technology
labor standards
pharmaceuticals
shipping
smuggling
steel
textiles and clothing
trade and the environment
trade and wages

International Finance

balance sheet approach/effects
capital flows to developing countries
carry trade
debt deflation
dollar standard
euro
Eurocurrencies
financial services
global imbalances
hedge funds
international financial architecture
international financial centers
monetary versus fiscal dominance
money laundering

offshore financial centers
sequencing of financial sector reforms
sovereign wealth funds

International Production

foreign direct investment and exit of local
    firms
foreign direct investment and export
    performance
foreign direct investment and innovation,
    imitation
foreign direct investment and international
    technology transfer
foreign direct investment and labor markets
foreign direct investment and tax revenues

International Economic Development

access to medicines
child labor
corruption
democracy and development
digital divide
global income inequality
global public goods
health and globalization
poverty, global
textiles and clothing
transition economies

Directory of Contributors

Rajat Acharyya
Reader, Department of Economics, Jadavpur University, Calcutta
   trade and wages (coauthor)

Charles Adams
Visiting Professor, Lee Kuan Yew School of Public Policy, National University of Singapore
   carry trade

Joshua Aizenman
Professor of Economics, University of California, Santa Cruz
   financial crisis; international reserves

Mark Allen
Director, Policy and Development Review Department, International Monetary Fund
   balance sheet approach/effects (coauthor)

Kym Anderson
George Gollin Professor of Economics, University of Adelaide
   distortions to agricultural incentives

Klaus Armingeon
Professor of Political Science and Director, Institute of Political Science, University of Berne
   Organisation for Economic Co-operation and Development (OECD)

Sven W. Arndt
Charles M. Stone Professor of Money, Credit, and Trade, Claremont McKenna College
   fragmentation

Nancy Neiman Auerbach
Associate Professor of International Political Economy, Scripps College
   financial liberalization; Latin American debt crisis; petrodollars, recycling of (coauthor)

Marc Bacchetta
Counselor, Economic Research and Statistics Division World Trade Organization
   tariff escalation; tariffs

Christopher M. Bacon
Lecturer, Departments of Latin American and Latino Studies, Sociology and Environmental Studies, University of California, Santa Cruz
   fair trade

Jennifer Bair
Assistant Professor of Sociology, Yale University
   commodity chains

King Banaian
Professor of Economics, St. Cloud State University
   currency substitution and dollarization

Subhayu Bandyopadhyay
Research Officer, Federal Reserve Bank of St. Louis

    common market (coauthor)

Frank Barry
Lecturer, School of Economics,
University College Dublin

    foreign direct investment and labor markets

Andrew L. Beath
PhD Candidate in Government, Harvard
University

    migration, international (coauthor)

Hamid Beladi
Professor of Economics, College of Business,
University of Texas at San Antonio

    nontraded goods (coauthor)

Paul Bergin
Associate Professor of Economics, University
of California, Davis

    Balassa-Samuelson effect

Pradip Bhatnagar
Economist, Technical Support Facility of the Group
of Fifteen (G-15), Geneva

    temporary movement of natural persons

Richard Blackhurst
Professor of International Economics,
The Fletcher School, Tufts University

    General Agreement on Tariffs and Trade (GATT);
    World Trade Organization

Robert A. Blecker
Professor of Economics, American University

    steel

Clemens F. J. Boonekamp
Director, Trade Policies Review Division,
World Trade Organization

    Trade Policy Review Mechanism

James M. Boughton
Historian, International Monetary Fund

    International Monetary Fund surveillance

François Bourguignon
Director, Paris School of Economics

    global income inequality (coauthor)

Paul Bowles
Professor of Economics, University of Northern British
Columbia

    beggar-thy-neighbor policies; mercantilism

Russell S. Boyer
Professor of Economics, University of Western
Ontario

    Mundell-Fleming model

Carlos A. Primo Braga
Senior Advisor, International Policy and Partnerships
Group, World Bank

    World Trade Organizaton, accession to
    (coauthor)

Mark R. Brawley
Professor of Political Science, McGill University

    globalization

Drusilla K. Brown
Associate Professor of Economics, Tufts University

    labor standards

Richard C. K. Burdekin
Jonathan B. Lovelace Professor of Economics,
Claremont McKenna College

    commodity-price pegging; debt deflation;
    quantity theory of money; seigniorage

Kenneth Button
Professor of Public Policy and Director, Center for
Transportation Policy, Operations, and Logistics,
George Mason University

    air transportation; shipping

Fang Cai
Economist, Division of International Finance, Federal Reserve

    home country bias

Rui Castro
Associate Professor of Economics, Université de Montréal

    growth in open economies, neoclassical models

Tony Cavoli
Lecturer, School of Commerce, University of South Australia

    capital mobility (coauthor); inflation targeting; monetary policy rules

Avik Chakrabarti
Associate Professor of Economics, University of Wisconsin–Milwaukee

    nontraded goods (coauthor)

Maggie Xiaoyang Chen
Assistant Professor of Economics and International Affairs, George Washington University

    fixed costs and foreign direct investment; market access

Yin-Wong Cheung
Professor of Economics, University of California, Santa Cruz

    exchange rate forecasting; purchasing power parity

Menzie D. Chinn
Professor of Economics and Public Affairs, Robert M. La Follette School of Public Affairs, University of Wisconsin

    effective exchange rate; forward premium puzzle; interest parity conditions

Eric M. P. Chiu
Assistant Professor, Institute of National Policy and Public Affairs, National Chung Hsing University

    currency crisis (coauthor)

Christopher K. Clague
Emeritus Professor of Economics, University of Maryland

    democracy and development

Jennifer Clapp
CIGI Chair in International Governance and Professor, Faculty of Environmental Studies, University of Waterloo

    Basel Convention

Kimberly A. Clausing
Professor of Economics, Reed College

    intrafirm trade

Paul Collier
Professor of Economics and Director, Center for the Study of African Economies, University of Oxford

    aid, military (coauthor)

Brian R. Copeland
Professor of Economics, University of British Columbia

    pollution haven hypothesis

Germán Creamer
Center for Computational Learning Systems, Columbia University

    Andean Community

Edward Crenshaw
Associate Professor of Sociology, Ohio State University

    digital divide

Michael R. Curtis
Adjunct Professor of Public Policy, George Mason University

    petroleum

Lewis S. Davis
Assistant Professor of Economics, Union College

    development

Harry de Gorter
Associate Professor, Department of Applied Economics and Management, Cornell University

    tariff rate quotas

James W. Dean
Ross Distinguished Professor, Department of Economics, Western Washington University

    Eurocurrencies; exorbitant privilege; money supply

Alan V. Deardorff
John W. Sweetland Professor of International Economics and Professor of Economics and Public Policy, University of Michigan

    Ricardian model

Gelaye Debebe
Assistant Professor of Organizational Sciences, George Washington University

    brain waste

Sirathorn Dechsakulthorn
PhD Candidate in Economics, Claremont Graduate University

    discipline (coauthor)

Robert Dekle
Professor of Economics, University of Southern California

    banking crisis

Desmond Dinan
Jean Monnet Professor, School of Public Policy, George Mason University

    European Union

Elias Dinopoulos
Professor of Economics, University of Florida

    growth in open economies, Schumpeterian models

Jonathan P. Doh
Associate Professor of Management and Operations, Herbert G. Rammrath Endowed Chair in International Business, and Director, Center for Global Leadership, Villanova School of Business, Villanova University

    nongovernmental organizations (NGOs)

Kathryn M. E. Dominguez
Professor of Public Policy and Economics, University of Michigan, and Research Associate, National Bureau of Economic Research

    sterilization

Brian Doyle
Senior Economist, International Finance Division, Federal Reserve Board

    New Open Economy Macroeconomics

Graham Dutfield
Professor of International Governance, School of Law, University of Leeds

    Agreement on Trade-Related Aspects of Intellectual Property Rights (TRIPS); World Intellectual Property Organization

Eric V. Edmonds
Associate Professor of Economics, Dartmouth College; Director, Child Labor Network, Institute for the Study of Labor (IZA); Faculty Research Fellow, National Bureau of Economic Research

    child labor

Andrew Elek
Independent Scholar

    Asia Pacific Economic Cooperation (APEC) (coauthor)

Kimberly Ann Elliott
Senior Fellow, Center for Global Development and Peter G. Peterson Institute for International Economics

    International Labor Organization

Korkut A. Erturk
Professor of Economics, University of Utah

   bubbles; speculation

Wilfred J. Ethier
Professor of Economics, University of Pennsylvania

   economies of scale

Simon J. Evenett
Professor of International Trade and Economic Development, Swiss Institute for International Economics and Applied Economic Research, University of St. Gallen; Research Fellow, Center for Economic Policy Research (CEPR)

   competition policy; government procurement; World Trade Organization, accession to (coauthor)

David Favre
Professor of Law, Michigan State University College of Law

   Convention on International Trade In Endangered Species (CITES)

Robert C. Feenstra
C. Bryan Cameron Distinguished Chair in International Economics and Director, Center for International Data, University of California, Davis; Director, International Trade and Investment Program, National Bureau of Economic Research

   outsourcing/offshoring (coauthor)

Richard Feinberg
Professor of International Political Economy and Director, APEC Study Center, University of California, San Diego

   Free Trade Area of the Americas (FTAA)

Susan Feinberg
Associate Professor of International Business, Rutgers Business School

   location theory

Michael Ferrantino
International Economist, U.S. International Trade Commission

   appropriate technology and foreign direct investment

Francisco Ferreira
Development Research Group, World Bank

   global income inequality (coauthor)

Ben Ferrett
Research Fellow, Leverhulme Center for Research on Globalization and Economic Policy, School of Economics, University of Nottingham

   foreign direct investment under oligopoly

Christopher Findlay
Professor of Economics, University of Adelaide

   Asia Pacific Economic Cooperation (APEC) (coauthor)

Lionel Fontagné
Professor of Economics, Paris School of Economics, Université de Paris 1 Panthéon-Sorbonne

   South-South trade

Joseph F. Francois
Professor of Economics, Johannes Kepler Universität Linz

   partial equilibrium models (coauthor)

Michele Fratianni
Professor of Business Economics and Public Policy Emeritus, Indiana University, and Professor of Economics, Università Politecnica delle Marche, Ancona

   Bank for International Settlements (BIS); dominant currency; Feldstein-Horioka puzzle; gold standard, international

Francis Fukuyama
Bernard L. Schwartz Professor of International Political Economy and Director, International

Development Program, Paul H. Nitze School of Advanced International Studies, Johns Hopkins University

    international institutional transfer

Andrea K. Gerlak
Visiting Professor, Department of Political Science, University of Arizona

    Global Environment Facility (coauthor)

Chetan Ghate
Assistant Professor of Economics, Indian Statistical Institute, New Delhi

    time inconsistency problem

Amit Ghosh
Assistant Professor, Department of Economics, Illinois Wesleyan University

    exchange rate pass-through

Christopher L. Gilbert
Professor of Econometrics, University of Trento

    World Bank (coauthor)

Kate Gillespie
Research Associate Professor, Department of Marketing, McCombs School of Business, University of Texas at Austin

    smuggling

Amy Jocelyn Glass
Associate Professor of Economics, Texas A&M University

    foreign direct investment and innovation, imitation (coauthor); infrastructure and foreign direct investment; vertical versus horizontal foreign direct investment

Linda S. Goldberg
Federal Reserve Bank of New York and National Bureau of Economic Research

    exchange rates and foreign direct investment

Ian Goldin
Director, James Martin 21st Century School, and Professorial Fellow, Balliol College, University of Oxford

    aid, international; evolution of development thinking; migration, international (coauthor)

Holger Görg
Associate Professor and Reader, School of Economics, University of Nottingham

    foreign direct investment and exit of local firms; linkages, backward and forward

Ashima Goyal
Professor of Economics, Indira Gandhi Institute of Development Research, Mumbai, India

    assignment problem; hedging; hot money and sudden stops (coauthor); Swan diagram

Ilene Grabel
Professor of International Economics, Graduate School of International Studies, University of Denver

    Tobin tax

Jean-Christophe Graz
Assistant Professor, Institute of Political and International Studies, University of Lausanne

    World Economic Forum

Duncan Green
Head of Research for Oxfam GB

    anti-globalization (coauthor)

Joshua Greene
Deputy Director, IMF-Singapore Regional Training Institute

    black market premium; dual exchange rate

Matt Griffith
Senior Advisor, Commission for Rural Communities in London

    anti-globalization (coauthor)

Stephany Griffith-Jones
Executive Director of the Initiative for Policy Dialogue, Columbia University

　capital flows to developing countries

Nigel Grimwade
Principal Lecturer of Economics and Finance, Department of Business, Computing, and Information Management, London South Bank University

　competitive advantage

Alfred V. Guender
Associate Professor, Department of Economics, University of Canterbury

　monetary conditions index

Morley Gunderson
Professor, Center for Industrial Relations and Human Resources and Department of Economics, University of Toronto; CIBC Chair in Youth Employment

　social policy in open economies

Markus Haacker
Economist, African Department, International Monetary Fund

　health and globalization; HIV/AIDS; Millennium Development Goals

David M. Hart
Associate Professor, School of Public Policy, George Mason University

　brain gain

C. Randall Henning
Professor, School of International Service at American University and Visiting Fellow, Peter G. Peterson Institute for International Economics

　exchange rate weapon

Almas Heshmati
Professor of Economics and Head of Department of Economics and Finance, University of Kurdistan

Hawler; Research Fellow, Techno-Economics, Management and Policy Program, Seoul National University

　information and communications technology (coauthor)

Jack High
Professor, School of Public Policy, George Mason University

　balance of payments

Anke Hoeffler
Research Officer, Center for the Study of African Economics, Department of Economics, St. Antony's College, University of Oxford

　aid, military (coauthor)

Bernard Hoekman
Senior Advisor, Development Research Group, World Bank and Researcher, Center for Economic Policy Research (CEPR)

　Doha Round; Uruguay Round

Henrik Horn
Senior Research Fellow, Research Institute of Industrial Economics (IFN), Stockholm, and Research Fellow, Center for Economic Policy Research (CEPR)

　nondiscrimination (coauthor)

Brett House
Economist, Policy and Development Review Department, International Monetary Fund

　balance sheet approach/effects (coauthor)

Andrew Hughes Hallett
Professor, School of Public Policy, George Mason University

　Bonn Summit; international policy coordination; Smithsonian Agreement

Michael Hutchison
Professor of Economics, University of California, Santa Cruz

　Bank of Japan; exchange rate regimes

Barry W. Ickes
Professor of Economics, Pennsylvania State University

    political economy of policy reform

Asif Islam
Research Associate, Department of Agricultural and Resource Economics, University of Maryland

    trade and the environment (coauthor)

Hiro Ito
Associate Professor, Department of Economics, Portland State University

    expenditure changing and expenditure switching; financial repression; liquidity trap, the

J. Bradford Jensen
Associate Professor of Economics and International Business, McDonough School of Business, Georgetown University; Senior Fellow at Peter G. Peterson Institute for International Economics; Research Associate at National Bureau of Economic Research

    outsourcing/offshoring (coauthor)

Omotunde E. G. Johnson
Retiree, International Monetary Fund, and Adjunct Professor, School of Public Policy, George Mason University

    African Union

R. Barry Johnston
Assistant Director, Monetary and Capital Markets Department, International Monetary Fund

    international financial centers; money laundering; offshore financial centers; sequencing of financial sector reform

Ronald W. Jones
Xerox Professor of Economics, University of Rochester

    specific-factors model

Philippe Jorion
Chancellor's Professor of Finance, The Paul Merage School of Business, University of California at Irvine

    hedge funds

Tim Josling
Senior Fellow, Freeman Spogli Institute for International Studies, Stanford University, and Visiting Professor, Imperial College, London

    Agreement on Agriculture; agricultural trade negotiations

Joseph P. Joyce
Professor of Economics, Wellesley College

    International Monetary Fund (IMF); International Monetary Fund conditionality

William H. Kaempfer
Vice Provost and Professor of Economics, University of Colorado, Boulder

    sanctions (coauthor)

Inge Kaul
Special Advisor, United Nations Development Program

    global public goods

Sydney J. Key
Lecturer, Graduate Program in Banking and Financial Law, Boston University School of Law

    financial services

Christopher Kilby
Associate Professor of Economics, Vassar College

    aid, bilateral

John Kirton
Associate Professor of Political Science, University of Toronto

    Group Of Seven/Eight (G7/G8)

Jörn Kleinert
Professor of Economics, Eberhard-Karls-University Tübingen

    market size and foreign direct investment

Vladimir Klyuev
Economist, Western Hemisphere Department, International Monetary Fund

    capital accumulation in open economies

Ulrich Koester
Professor of Agricultural Economics, University of Kiel, Germany

    Common Agricultural Policy

Michel Kostecki
Professor of Marketing, Enterprise Institute, University of Neuchâtel

    trade-related capacity building

Jan Kregel
Distinguished Research Professor in the Center for Full Employment and Price Stability, University of Missouri, Kansas City; Senior Scholar, Levy Economics Institute, Bard College

    Bretton Woods system; Triffin dilemma

Kala Krishna
Professor of Economics, Pennsylvania State University

    free trade area; rules of origin

Pravin Krishna
Chung Ju Yung Distinguished Professor of International Economics and Business, Paul H. Nitze School of Advanced International Studies, and Professor of Economics, Johns Hopkins University

    multilateralism; regionalism

Maurice Kugler
Center for International Governance Innovation Chair in International Public Policy and Professor of Economics, Wilfrid Laurier University, and Visiting Professor of Public Policy, John F. Kennedy School of Government, Harvard University

    factor endowments and foreign direct investment

Philip R. Lane
Professor of Economics, and Director, Institute for International Integration Studies, Trinity College, Dublin

    transfer problem

Minkyu Lee
PhD Candidate, Technology Management Economics and Policy Program, Seoul National University

    information and communications technology (coauthor)

James Lehman
Professor of Economics, Pitzer College

    Federal Reserve Board

Priscilla Liang
Assistant Professor of Business and Economics, California State University, Channel Islands

    contagion (coauthor)

Ramón López
Professor of Economics, Department of Agriculture and Resource Economics, University of Maryland

    trade and the environment (coauthor)

Eduardo Lora
Principal Advisor, Research Department, Inter-American Development Bank

    Washington consensus

Mary E. Lovely
Associate Professor of Economics, Syracuse University

    agglomeration and foreign direct investment

Anton D. Lowenberg
Professor of Economics, California State University, Northridge

    sanctions (coauthor)

Rodney Ludema
Associate Professor of Economics, Georgetown University

    multilateral trade negotiations

Ronald MacDonald
Adam Smith Chair of Political Economy and Director of PhD Programs, Department of Economics, University of Glasgow

equilibrium exchange rate; exchange rate
volatility

Alex Mandilaras
Lecturer in Economics, University of Surrey

early warning systems; exchange market
pressure

Andrea Maneschi
*Professor of Economics and Director, Graduate
Program in Economic Development, Vanderbilt
University*

comparative advantage; gains from trade

Sugata Marjit
*Director and Reserve Bank of India Professor,
Center for Studies in Social Sciences,
Calcutta*

trade and wages (coauthor)

Stephen Marks
Professor of Economics, Pomona College

asymmetric information

James R. Markusen
*Professor of International Economics, University of
Colorado*

foreign direct investment (FDI);
internalization theory

Antoine Martin
*Senior Economist, Federal Reserve Bank of
New York*

currency competition; multiple currencies

Philip Martin
*Professor of Agricultural and Resource Economics
and Chair, UC Comparative Immigration and
Integration Program, University of California, Davis*

migration governance

Will Martin
*Lead Economist, Trade and Development Research
Group, World Bank*

tariff-cutting formulas

Catherine Matraves
*Visiting Assistant Professor of Economics, Michigan
State University*

pharmaceuticals

Xenia Matschke
*Assistant Professor of Economics, University
of Connecticut*

New Trade Theory

Aaditya Mattoo
*Lead Economist, Development Research Group,
World Bank*

General Agreement on Trade in Services (GATS);
trade in services

Petros C. Mavroidis
*Edwin B. Barker Professor of Law, Columbia
Law School; Professor of Law, University
of Neuchâtel*

nondiscrimination (coauthor)

Daniel Maxwell
*Associate Professor, The Fletcher School, Tufts
University*

aid, food; aid, humanitarian

Joseph A. McCahery
*Professor of Corporate Governance, Center
for Law and Economics, University
of Amsterdam*

corporate governance

Ronald I. McKinnon
*William D. Eberle Professor of International
Economics, Stanford University*

conflicted virtue; dollar standard

Niall P. Meagher
*Senior Counsel, Advisory Center on World Trade
Organization Law, Geneva*

World Trade Organization dispute settlement
(coauthor)

Jose Mendez
Professor of Economics, W. P. Carey School of Business, Arizona State University

Central American Common Market (CACM); Central American–Domincan Republic Free Trade Area (CAFTA-DR)

Mokhtar M. Metwally
Professor of Economics, University of Wollongong

Gulf Cooperation Council

Klaus Meyer
Professor of Strategy and International Business, School of Management, University of Bath

foreign market entry

Constantine Michalopoulos
Independent Consultant

special and differential treatment

Branko Milanovic
Economist, Development Research Group, World Bank

global income inequality (coauthor)

Chris Milner
Assistant Professor, School of Economics and Leverhulme Center for Research in Globalization and Economic Policy (GEP), University of Nottingham

effective protection; export promotion

Eugenio J. Miravete
Associate Professor of Economics, University of Texas

infant industry argument

Ajit Mishra
Senior Lecturer, Department of Economics and International Development, University of Bath

corruption

Andrew Mitchell
Senior Lecturer, Melbourne Law School

electronic commerce

Devashish Mitra
Professor of Economics and Gerald B. and Daphna Cramer Professor of Global Affairs, Maxwell School, Syracuse University

trade and economic development, international

Pradeep K. Mitra
Chief Economist, Europe and Central Asia Region, World Bank

transition economies

José G. Montalvo
Professor, Department of Economics, Universitat Pompeu Fabra

aid, international, and political economy

Michael O. Moore
Professor of Economics and International Affairs and Director, Institute for Economic Policy, Elliott School of International Affairs, George Washington University

anti-dumping

C. W. Morgan
Associate Professor and Research Fellow, Center for Economic Development and International Trade (CREDIT), School of Economics, University of Nottingham

African Caribbean Pacific–European Union (ACP-EU) partnership agreements

Arijit Mukherjee
Associate Professor and Reader in Economics, University of Nottingham

technology licensing

Jacob Wanjala Musila
Associate Professor of Economics, Athabasca University

Common Market for Eastern and Southern Africa (COMESA); Economic Community of West African States (ECOWAS)

Ethan C. Myers
Teaching Associate, Department of Social Thought and Political Economy, University of Massachusetts

Global Environment Facility (coauthor)

Usha Nair-Reichert
Associate Professor of Economics and Undergraduate Director, School of Economics, Georgia Institute of Technology

proximity-concentration hypothesis

Rajneesh Narula
Professor of International Business Regulation, Department of Economics, University of Reading

multinational enterprises

Léonce Ndikumana
Associate Professor of Economics, University of Massachusetts at Amherst

capital flight

J. Peter Neary
Professor of Economics, University of Oxford and Research Fellow, Center for Economic Policy Research (CEPR)

foreign direct investment: the OLI framework

Douglas Nelson
Professor of Economics, Tulane University

political economy of trade policy

Richard Newfarmer
Economic Advisor, International Trade and Department and Prospects Group, World Bank

international investment agreements

Hildegunn Kyvik Nordås
Senior Economist, Organisation for Economic Co-operation and Development (OECD)

textiles and clothing

Ilan Noy
Associate Professor of Economics, University of Hawai'i, Manoa

capital controls (coauthor); hot money and sudden stops (coauthor); special drawing rights

Gianmarco I. P. Ottaviano
Professor of Economics, University of Bologna

New Economic Geography

David Palmeter
Senior Counsel, Sidley Austin LLP, Washington, DC

World Trade Organization dispute settlement (coauthor)

Alberto Paloni
Senior Lecturer, Department of Economics, and Director, Center for Development Studies, Glasgow University

structural adjustment

Arvind Panagariya
Professor of Economics and Jagdish Bhagwati Professor of Indian Political Economy, School of International and Public Affairs, Columbia University

Heckscher-Ohlin model

Letizia Paoli
Professor, Leuven Institute of Criminology, K.U. Leuven Faculty of Law, Belgium

illegal drugs trade

Giovanni Peri
Associate Professor of Economics, University of California, Davis

techonology spillovers

Emile-Robert Perrin
High Council on International Co-operation (HCCI), French Prime Minister's Office

regional development banks (coauthor)

Richard Pomfret
Professor of Economics, University of Adelaide

common currency; optimum currency area (OCA) theory

Helen Popper
Associate Professor of Economics, Santa Clara University

foreign exchange intervention; real exchange rate

Susan Pozo
Professor of Economics, Western Michigan University

remittances

Thitima Puttitanun
Assistant Professor of Economics, San Diego State University

intellectual property rights and foreign direct investment

Horst Raff
Professor of Economics, Christian-Albrechts University of Kiel

joint ventures; mergers and acquisitions

Ramkishen S. Rajan
Associate Professor, School of Public Policy, George Mason University

capital controls (coauthor); capital mobility (coauthor); exchange rate pass-through (coauthor); fear of floating (coauthor); hot money and sudden stops (coauthor); sovereign wealth funds (coauthor)

Carlos D. Ramirez
Associate Professor of Economics, George Mason University

convertibility; original sin

Priya Ranjan
Associate Professor of Economics, University of California, Irvine

trade costs and foreign direct investment

Martin Ravallion
Director, Development Research Group, World Bank

global income inequality (coauthor)

Kenneth A. Reinert
Professor, School of Public Policy, George Mason University

applied general equilibrium models; gravity models; migration, international (coauthor); partial equilibrium models (coauthor)

Nola Reinhardt
Professor of Economics, Smith College

primary products trade

Kara M. Reynolds
Assistant Professor of Economics, American University

countervailing duties

Francisco Rivera-Batiz
Professor of Economics and Education, Teachers College, Columbia University

economic development

Donna Roberts
Senior Economist, Economic Research Service, U.S. Department of Agriculture

sanitary and phytosanitary measures

G. Chris Rodrigo
Independent Consultant

revealed comparative advantage

Riordan Roett
Sarita and Don Johnston Professor of Political Science and Director of Western Hemisphere Studies, Paul H. Nitze School of Advanced International Studies (SAIS), Johns Hopkins University

Mercosur

Christoph Rosenberg
Senior Regional Representative for Central Europe and the Baltics, European Department, International Monetary Fund

balance sheet approach/effects (coauthor)

G. Kristin Rosendal
Senior Research Fellow, Fridtjof Nansen Institute

Convention on Biological Diversity

Roy J. Ruffin
*Anderson Professor of Economics,
University of Houston*

monopolistic competition; oligopoly

C. Ford Runge
*Distinguished McKnight University Professor of
Applied Economics and Law and Director, Center for
International Food and Agricultural Policy, University
of Minnesota*

multilateral environmental agreements

Kamal Saggi
*Dedman Distinguished Collegiate Professor
of Economics, Southern Methodist University*

foreign direct investment and innovation,
imitation (coauthor); foreign direct investment
and international technology transfer

Dominick Salvatore
*Distinguished Professor and Director of the PhD
Program, Department of Economics, Fordham
University*

euro; global imbalances; international liquidity;
reserve currency; vehicle currency

Carlos Santiso
*Governance and Public Finance Adviser, Department
for International Development (DFID),
United Kingdom*

regional development banks (coauthor)

John Sargent
*Assistant Professor of Management, College of
Business, University of Texas-Pan American*

export processing zones

Prabirjit Sarkar
*Professor of Economics, Jadavpur University,
Calcutta*

terms of trade

Frederic M. Scherer
*Aetna Professor of Public Policy Emeritus,
John F. Kennedy School of Government, Harvard
University*

access to medicines

Nicolas Schmitt
*Professor of Economics, Simon Fraser University;
Research Fellow, Center for Economic Studies, Ifo
Institute for Economic Research, Munich*

parallel imports

Patricia Higino Schneider
*Assistant Professor of Economics, Mount Holyoke
College*

intellectual property rights

Jeffrey J. Schott
*Senior Fellow, Peter G. Peterson Institute for
International Economics*

North American Free Trade Agreement
(NAFTA)

M. Fuat Sener
Associate Professor of Economics, Union College

technological progress in open economies

Brad Setser
*Fellow for Geoeconomics, Council on Foreign
Relations*

bail-ins; bailouts; international financial
architecture

Pierre L. Siklos
*Professor of Economics and Director, Viessmann
European Research Center, Wilfrid Laurier
University*

European Central Bank; European Monetary
Union; impossible trinity; Maastricht Treaty

Keith Sill
*Senior Economist, Federal Reserve Bank
of Philadelphia*

peso problem; sovereign risk

Slavi Slavov
Assistant Professor of Economics,
Pomona College

    currency board arrangement (CBA); fear of floating (coauthor)

James L. Smith
Cary M. Maguire Chair in Oil and Gas
Management, Department of Finance,
Edwin L. Cox School of Business,
Southern Methodist University

    Organization of the Petroleum Exporting Countries (OPEC)

Pamela J. Smith
Associate Professor, Department of Applied
Economics, University of Minnesota

    trade-related investment measures (TRIMs)

Servaas Storm
Faculty of Technology, Policy and Management,
Department of Economics, Delft University of
Technology

    import substitution industrialization

Deborah L. Swenson
Associate Professor of Economics, University of
California, Davis

    domestic content requirements; transfer pricing

Alan O. Sykes
Professor of Law, Stanford Law School

    safeguards

Wendy Takacs
Professor of Economics, University of Maryland,
Baltimore County

    nontariff measures; quotas

Evan Tanner
Senior Economist, Western Hemisphere Division,
International Monetary Fund

    monetary versus fiscal dominance

Vito Tanzi
Former Director of the Fiscal Affairs Department,
International Monetary Fund

    subsidies and financial incentives to foreign direct investment

David G. Tarr
Consultant and former Lead Economist,
Development Research Group, World Bank

    customs unions

Jonathan R. W. Temple
Professor of Economics, University of Bristol

    international income convergence

Willem Thorbecke
Associate Professor of Economics, George Mason
University; Senior Fellow, Research Institute
of Economy, Trade, and Industry, Tokyo

    Louvre Accord; Plaza Accord; twin deficits

Jose L. Tongzon
Associate Professor of Economics, National University
of Singapore

    Association of Southeast Asian Nations (ASEAN)

Farid Toubal
Assistant Professor, Paris School of Economics,
University of Paris I, Panthéon-Sorbonne, CNRS,
France

    intangible assets

John Toye
Visiting Professor of Economics, St. Antony's College,
University of Oxford

    United Nations Conference on Trade and Development

Dieter M. Urban
Professor, Department of Business and Economics,
Johannes Gutenberg-Universität

    knowledge-capital model of the multinational enterprise

Diego E. Vacaflores
Assistant Professor, Department of Finance and Economics, Texas State University

    foreign direct investment and tax revenues

Hylke Vandenbussche
Professor of International Economics, Université Catholique de Louvain

    footloose production

Charles van Marrewijk
Professor of Economics, Erasmus University Rotterdam

    absolute advantage; intraindustry trade

Irene van Staveren
Associate Professor of Feminist Development Economics, Institute of Social Studies, The Hague; Professor of Economics and Christian Ethics, Institute for Management Research, Radboud University Nijmegen

    gender

Anthony J. Venables
Professor of Economics, University of Oxford

    foreign direct investment under monopolistic competition

Matias Vernengo
Assistant Professor of Economics, University of Utah

    dependency theory

David Vines
Professor of Economics, Oxford University

    World Bank (coauthor)

Peter Walkenhorst
Senior Economist, International Trade Group, World Bank

    foreign equity restrictions

Howard J. Wall
Vice President and Regional Economics Advisor, Federal Reserve Bank of St. Louis

    common market (coauthor)

Stefanie Walter
Researcher, Center for Comparative and International Studies, Swiss Federal Institute of Technology, Zurich

    currency crisis (coauthor)

Joshua C. Walton
PhD Candidate, School of Politics and Economics, Claremont Graduate University

    currency crisis (coauthor)

Howard White
Fellow, Institute of Development Studies, University of Sussex

    poverty, global

Clas Wihlborg
Fletcher Jones Chair in International Business, Argyros School of Business and Economics, Chapman University

    deposit insurance; lender of last resort

Thomas D. Willett
Director of the Claremont Institute for Economic Studies and Horton Professor of Economics, Claremont Graduate University and Claremont McKenna College

    contagion (coauthor); currency crisis (coauthor); discipline (coauthor); petrodollars, recycling of (coauthor); sovereign wealth funds (coauthor)

John Williamson
Senior Fellow, Peter G. Peterson Institute for International Economics

    band, basket, and crawl (BBC)

John S. Wilson
Lead Economist, Development Research Group, International Trade, World Bank

    technical barriers to trade; trade facilitation

Peter Wilson
Independent Scholar

    J-curve effect; Marshall-Lerner condition

L. Alan Winters
*Professor of Economics, University of Sussex;
Research Fellow and former Program Director of
the Center for Economic Policy Research (CEPR)*

North-South trade

Paul Winters
*Associate Professor of Economics, American
University*

agriculture

Kar-yiu Wong
*Professor of Economics and Director, Research Center
for International Economics, University
of Washington*

brain drain

Jon Wongswan
*Emerging Markets Researcher, International Active
Equities Group, Barclays Global Investors,
San Francisco*

spillovers

Kevin Honglin Zhang
*Associate Professor of Economics, Illinois State
University*

foreign direct investment and export
performance

Laixun Zhao
*Professor, Research Institute for Economics and
Business, Kobe University*

unions and foreign direct investment

The Princeton Encyclopedia of the World Economy

■ illegal drugs trade

Despite the lack of reliable estimates on other illegal markets, the trade in prohibited narcotics and other psychoactive drugs is generally considered to be the illegal activity with the largest turnover worldwide. The *2005 World Drug Report* of the United Nations Office on Drugs and Crime (UNODC) includes a systematic effort to produce a comprehensive set of estimates. For illicit drugs as a whole, the UNODC estimates a total of almost $322 billion in retail sales in 2003; $94 billion in wholesale revenues; and $13 billion in producer sales (UNODC 2005).

The largest market, according to the UN calculations, is cannabis herb (normally called marijuana), which has a retail market size of $113 billion. Marijuana is followed by cocaine ($71 billion), the opiates ($65 billion), and cannabis resin (popularly called hashish, with $29 billion). The markets for synthetic drugs (properly called amphetamine-type stimulants and including methamphetamine, amphetamine, and ecstasy) total about $44 billion. Though derived from an economic model, these figures are in reality guesstimates and have to be treated with great caution. The basis inputs that are needed for such calculations—data on production, prices, and quantities exported, imported, and consumed—are themselves often estimates and frequently based on deficient data.

If compared to global licit exports or global gross domestic product (GDP) (respectively, $7,503 billion and $35,765 billion in 2003), the estimated size of the global illicit drug market may not appear to be very large. Total retail drug expenditures correspond to 0.9 percent of global GDP and drug wholesale revenues represent only 1.3 percent of global exports measures. The size of the global illicit drug market is not insubstantial, however. Illicit drug wholesale revenues account for 14 percent of global agricultural products and are much higher than the export value of most licit agricultural commodities (UNODC 2005).

The global drug market also involves a considerable number of people. According to the 2006 UNODC estimates, about 200 million people currently use illicit drugs at least once a year (about 5 percent of the world population age 15–64). Cannabis is by far the most popular and widespread illegal drug: out of the 200 million total, 162 million are cannabis users. Cannabis is followed by synthetic drugs (some 35 million people), which include amphetamines (used by 35 million people) and ecstasy (almost 10 million people). The number of opiate users is estimated at some 16 million people, of which 11 million are heroin users. Some 13 million people use cocaine at least once a year. A large proportion of drug users can be found in Asia. More than 60 percent of the world's amphetamine users and more than half of opiate users reside there (UNODC 2006; Paoli, Greenfield, and Reuter 2008). Asia accounts only for a small portion of total retail expenditures, however: $35 billion or 11 percent. With $142 billion (or 44 percent) and $106 billion (or 33 percent), respectively, North America and Europe account for the bulk of total retail expenditure estimates (UNODC 2005), simply because retail drug prices are much higher there than in developing nations.

Drugs and Source Countries The two most dangerous plant-based drugs, heroin and cocaine, are produced in a small number of poor countries, which are often thousands of miles away from many end-users. Virtually all the cultivation of the coca bush (from which cocaine is made) is concentrated in three Andean countries: Colombia, Peru, and Bolivia, accounting for 63, 25, and 11 percent respectively of world production in 2005. Most cocaine hydrochloride is processed in Colombia and from there is exported into the United States and Europe (UNODC 2006).

From the late 1980s on, Afghanistan and Burma effectively "owned" world opium production, with a fringe of second- and third-tier producers contributing only modestly. Together, Afghanistan and Burma (or Myanmar, as it was renamed by the military dictatorship in 1989) accounted for more than 95 percent of world production in 2005. After 2001, however, the two-country dominance began shifting to one-country dominance, with Afghanistan accounting for an increasing share of world production—Afghanistan's share of the total was more than 88 percent in 2005. Although it accounted in 2005 for less than 1 percent of world's heroin production, Colombia has since the mid-1990s become one of the major suppliers of the U.S. market. With slightly higher figures (1.5 percent of total production), Mexico is also an important source of heroin for the U.S. market (UNODC 2006; Paoli, Greenfield, and Reuter 2008).

The cultivation of cannabis is much more decentralized than that of opium and coca—so much so that in 2006 the UNODC identified 176 countries or territories where cannabis is produced. This spread is primarily due to the great adaptability of the cannabis plant, which grows well in virtually every inhabited region of the world and can be cultivated with little maintenance in small plots or even indoors. In addition, unlike most other illicit drugs, cannabis products can be consumed with little processing after harvesting. Thanks to these two char-

acteristics, users can feasibly cultivate their own supply even in countries that rigorously apply the world prohibition regime. The U.S. authorities, for example, report that about two-thirds of the cannabis consumed in the country, predominantly in the form of marijuana, is domestically produced. The main foreign supplier of marijuana in the United States is Mexico. Hashish, the cannabis resin that is particularly popular in Europe, predominantly comes from Morocco (UNODC 2006).

Even more than cannabis, synthetic drugs are rarely trafficked across long distances because they can be easily manufactured in small and mobile laboratories in, or close to, areas of consumption. Hence, for example, the majority of the ecstasy pills consumed in Europe is produced in the Netherlands and, to a much lesser extent, in Belgium and some Eastern European countries. Likewise, the U.S. demand for methamphetamine is traditionally supplied by clandestine laboratories in California, several Midwestern states, and Mexico. Reflecting Asia's lion's share of the synthetic drug market, Burma is the world largest producer of methamphetamine (UNODC 2006).

Evolution of Drug Markets and Variable Characteristics of Suppliers Notwithstanding the large number of illegal drug users worldwide and the magnitude of the world drug economy, the illegal drug trade is a relatively new phenomenon. In fact, only in the last three decades of the 20th century did it assume mass proportions. Until about the beginning of the 20th century, all psychoactive drugs could be freely produced and consumed not only in Asia and Latin America, but also in Western countries. The production, trade, and consumption of opium, coca, and their derivatives began to be severely regulated and then largely prohibited (except for limited medical purposes) only after the first International Opium Convention was concluded in The Hague in 1912. The new international drug control regime, whose enforcement was entrusted after World War I to the League of Nations and after World War II to the United Nations, seemed quite successful at first. During the 1920s, 1930s, and 1940s the consumption of all prohibited substances rapidly declined in the United States, Europe, and many Asian nations (scholars debate the extent to which the interwar decline is attributable to increasing prohibition rather than other factors, above all, changing medical and public attitudes toward drugs; see Courtwright 2001; Berridge 1999). Under pressure from the United States, cannabis trade and possession were also increasingly restricted and, finally, subjected to the international drug control regime in the early 1960s.

From the 1960s onward, the demand for heroin, cocaine, and cannabis rose again, first in the United States and then in Western Europe. At the end of the 20th century, it also grew in the second (former communist) and third-world countries. The postwar expansion of illicit drug use was caused by contingent events—such as the Vietnam War, which brought thousands of young American soldiers into contact with heroin—and macrosocial changes. Among the latter, two are most important: (1) the rise of a youth mass subculture, which resorted to illegal psychoactive substances to distinguish itself from the mainstream culture, and (2) technological progress, which made communication, travel, and trade in both legal and illegal commodities easier and faster.

From the 1960s onward, the rising demand for illicit drugs fostered the development of drug distribution systems able to transfer drugs from producers to consumers. In the beginning, illegal drugs were imported by the consumers themselves, who used some of them and sold the rest within a close circle of friends. It was a sort of "ants trafficking." Soon, however, in both the United States and Western Europe the professional role of the drug dealer began to consolidate. In a few years, the development of a large-scale drug market fostered the progressive entry of professional criminals into the drug business.

In source countries, where the state authorities are often unable or unwilling to enforce the international prohibition regime, large organizations have sometimes emerged to coordinate opium poppy and coca cultivation and to process heroin and cocaine. In northern Burma, for example, the refinement and export of heroin were first organized by the nationalist Chinese Kuomintang Army and, more recently, by several armies representing local ethnic minorities. Much of the coca cultivation in Colombia also takes place in the inland areas controlled by guerrilla and paramilitary movements, particularly the FARC (Fuerzas Armadas Revolucionarias de Colombia).

In developed countries, the constraints deriving from the illegal status of the drugs have so far prevented the consolidation of large-scale, hierarchically organized drug-trafficking enterprises. These constraints arise from two facts: all illegal market actors—particularly drug traffickers and dealers—are obliged to operate (1) without the state and (2) against the state.

Since the goods and services they provide are prohibited, illegal market suppliers operate without the state; they cannot resort to state institutions to enforce contracts and have the violations of contracts prosecuted. As a result, property rights are poorly protected, employment contracts can hardly be formalized, and the development of large, formally organized, enduring companies is strongly discouraged.

All suppliers of illegal commodities—specifically drugs—are also required to operate against the state, that is, under the constant threat of being arrested and having their assets confiscated by law enforcement institutions. They therefore try to organize their activities to assure that the risk of police detection is minimized. Incorporating drug transactions into kinship and friendship networks and reducing the number of customers and employees are two of the strategies that drug entrepreneurs most often employ to reduce their vulnerability to law enforcement efforts (Reuter 1985).

Empirical research confirms these insights. In Europe and North America, the great majority of drug deals, even those involving large quantities, are carried out by numerous, relatively small, and often ephemeral enterprises. Especially at the intermediate and lower levels, many dealers work alone, either to finance their own drug habits or, more rarely, to earn fast money. Many drug distributors are members of ethnic minorities who either exploit direct connections to source countries or are pushed into dealing by lack of rewarding alternatives in the legitimate economy. At the retail level and in closed settings, drugs are also often distributed by inconspicuous persons who have no contact with the underworld.

For the same reasons, the relationships among illegal drug enterprises generally involve competition rather than collusion. The best evidence against control is simply the ease with which new sellers enter and the speed with which dealers depart. There may be rents for various capacities, but certainly no power to exclude. Throughout Europe and North America, moreover, drug-dealing firms are price-takers rather than price-givers: that is, none of them is able to influence the commodity's price appreciably by varying the quantity of the output it sells. The continuing decline of prices during the 20-year period 1985–2005 at all levels of the market in heroin and most other drugs suggests that, if markets power ever existed, it has by now been dissipated.

The danger that the contemporary illegal drugs industry represents for the world economy is not limited to its turnover and the number of people it involves as producers, traffickers, and users. Two further aspects need to be considered. The industry is a major source of corruption, violence, and instability in a number of drug-producing and transit countries—its collateral effects being occasionally reinforced by the war on drugs itself. Moreover, the international routes and networks that have been developed for the transportation of illegal drugs from source countries to the final consumer nations (and for bringing back the money the other way round) can be used for a plurality of other illicit goals, ranging from human smuggling and trafficking to terrorism financing.

See also globalization; primary products trade; smuggling

FURTHER READING

Berridge, Virginia. 1999. *Opium and the People: Opiate Use and Drug Control Policy in Nineteenth and Early Twentieth Century England*. London: Free Association Books. The only empirical account of the history of opiate use and drug control policy in a European nation.

Courtwright, David T. 2001. *Dark Paradise: A History of Opiate Addiction in America*. Cambridge: Harvard University Press. The standard work on the history of opiate use in the United States from the mid-nineteenth century to the 1990s.

Paoli, Letizia, Victoria Greenfield, and Peter Reuter. 2008. *The World Heroin Market: Can Its Supply Be Reduced?* New York: Oxford University Press. A seminal analysis of the evolution, composition, and behavior of the world opiate market and an objective assessment of what nations and the international community can achieve in drug control.

Reuter, Peter. 1985. *The Organization of Illegal Markets: An Economic Analysis*. Washington, DC: National Institute of Justice. A compact but very insightful analysis of the organization of illegal markets in developed countries.

Thoumi, Francisco E. 2003. *Illegal Drugs, Economy, and Society in the Andes*. Washington, DC: Woodrow Wilson Center. A seminal analysis of the cocaine industry in three main producing countries—Colombia, Bolivia, and Peru—and its impact upon the local legitimate economy and society.

UNODC (United Nations Office on Drugs and Crime). Annual. *World Drug Report*. Vienna: UNODC. Downloadable from http://www.unodc.org/unodc/en/world_drug_report.html. The most comprehensive annual description of the world illicit drug markets.

LETIZIA PAOLI

■ **illiquidity**
See banking crisis

■ **import substitution industrialization**
Import substitution industrialization (ISI) is a trade and economic policy based on the premise that a developing country should attempt to substitute products it imports with domestically produced substitutes. The policy has three major tenets: (1) an active industrial policy to promote a domestic industrial base producing strategic substitutes, often involving strong public sector investment in infrastructure and in "strategic" sectors, and the establishment of development banks to support these ac-

tivities; (2) protective barriers to trade (namely, tariffs and quotas to protect new or infant industries) and changes in the internal terms of trade against traditional primary exports; and (3) a monetary policy that rations foreign exchange, with multiple exchange rates to channel it preferentially to the imports of noncompetitive intermediate and capital goods. Generally, a distinction is made between a first "easy" phase of ISI, during which mostly nondurable goods are produced, and later more "mature" phases in which import substitution deepens, producing nondurable consumer as well as intermediate and capital goods, and (in some cases) more emphasis is given to export promotion (by the imposition of export incentives on old layers of import protection).

Historical Origins The first experiments with ISI were launched and sustained by the industrializing countries of Europe, North America, and Russia in the 19th century in order to overcome their relative economic (and political) backwardness vis-à-vis the industrial leader, then the United Kingdom (Gerschenkron 1962; Chang 2002). Early theoretical justifications for ISI include List (1841) and Manoïlesco (1928). The most coherent post–World War II formulations of and justifications for ISI appear in Prebisch (1950), Nurkse (1959), and Gerschenkron (1962). Important reviews of the evolution of ideas about ISI are Bruton (1998) and Waterbury (1999).

The Rationale for ISI Import substitution policies were adopted by many low-income developing nations during the early 1950s as a means to escape from the primary commodity specialization trap and to promote industrial diversification. Specialization in labor-intensive primary commodities was considered undesirable because of declining world markets for primary products, the limited scope for technological progress in primary production, and the long-term deteriorating terms of trade of primary commodities, which caused low-income countries to have to pay relatively more for manufactured goods imported from industrialized countries. Further motivation for ISI was provided by the lack of adequate external financing, in combination with a reluctance to devalue the exchange rate (for fear of its inflationary effects), and the high levels of (agricultural) protection in the industrialized countries.

Industrialization of the developing world was considered imperative: only by the transformation of productive structures toward manufacturing could average labor productivity be raised so as to generate a higher standard of living (through increased real wages) and to reduce the incidence of poverty and destitution. Crucial to the generation of increased (manufacturing) productivity growth was the development of substantial technological capabilities, including technical knowledge, quality control practices, entrepreneurial and managerial skills, and work habits (Amsden 2001). The buildup of such technological capabilities is a path-dependent process in which accumulated experience plays the crucial role; it involves learning by doing, adaptation, and induced technological change as well as the development of manufacturing entrepreneurial and working classes. ISI was regarded as essential in kick-starting the development of such technological capabilities. While the initial costs of industrial production are higher than former import prices, the economic rationale for ISI is that, given time, (1) the industry will eventually be able to reap the benefits of large-scale production, technological learning, manufacturing experience (learning by doing), and lower production costs (the so-called infant industry argument for tariff protection), and (2) the balance of payments will be improved as fewer manufactured goods are imported.

ISI Policy Instruments The typical strategy is first to erect tariff barriers or quotas on the importation of strategic commodities and then to try to set up a domestic industry to produce the goods imported; often, this involves cooperation with foreign companies encouraged to set up their plants behind the wall of tariff protection and given various tax and investment incentives. Tariff protection is supplemented by numerous quantitative and direct controls on the availability of foreign exchange. The other major policy instrument is the exchange rate, which is generally overvalued (relative to a free trade situation) in order to keep the domestic price of capital goods low. Often, *multiple* exchange rate systems are used instead of trade policy to implicitly tax competitive imports and traditional exports and subsidize complementary imports. Domestically, ISI policies include strong public-sector investment in infrastructure and in strategic sectors, including energy and irrigation, the establishment of development banks to support these activities, industrial policy regulating domestic investment, and price and fiscal policies to change the domestic terms of trade against agriculture and traditional primary exports (Bruton 1998; Amsden 2001).

The Logic behind ISI In theory, there is no presumption that ISI will unambiguously reduce or accelerate economic growth in relation to openness in trade. The main complications are twofold.

First, in traditional (static) trade theory, assuming that no market imperfections and other imposed distortions exist, the effect of import protection (as under ISI) is to reduce the level of real gross domestic product (GDP) at world prices; however, simple Harberger triangles from a competitive model rarely identify welfare losses from trade restrictions larger than 1.5–2 percent of GDP, which is far too small to produce significant changes in growth (Ocampo and Taylor 1998; Winters 2004). But in the presence of market failures (such as positive production externalities in import-competing sectors), traditional trade theory shows that real GDP can be higher under protection than under free trade (Bhagwati 1958).

Second, in models of endogenous growth, generated by nondiminishing returns to reproducible factors of production or by learning by doing and other variants of technological progress, the forces of comparative advantage may push an economy's resources in the direction of dynamic activities that generate long-run growth (via externalities in research and development, expanding product variety, learning by doing, increasing returns to scale, agglomeration effects, the creation of forward and backward linkages, and so on) *or divert* them from such activities into traditional, nondynamic ones. Free trade can thus be detrimental to a country's economic growth prospects, especially when it lacks

adequate technological capabilities and (given its initial factor endowments) has a comparative advantage in nondynamic sectors. Import protection may lead to higher long-run growth of real GDP if the trade restrictions promote technologically more dynamic sectors over others (Ocampo and Taylor 1998; Rodríguez and Rodrik 2001).

Experience with ISI The voluminous empirical literature evaluating the benefits and costs of ISI can be classified into two categories: cross-country regression-based studies investigating the impact of import protection (often under ISI) on economic growth (Rodríguez and Rodrik 2001; Srinivasan and Bhagwati 2001; Winters 2004), and in-depth (comparative) analyses of historical country experiences (Little et al. 1970; Balassa et al. 1971; Bhagwati 1978; Krueger 1978; Cardénas et al. 2000; Amsden 2001; Wade 2004). From these two strands of literature, no general, unambiguous conclusion about the *net* impact of ISI policies on growth (and economic performance in general) emerges, but only *contingent* conclusions pointing to a large number of country-specific, often political-economy, and external characteristics.

Cross-Country Regression Studies Surveys of cross-national econometric studies of the relationship between trade policy regimes (including ISI trade policy regimes) and growth, including Edwards (1993), Rodríguez and Rodrik (2001), and Winters (2004), conclude that much of the cross-country (linear) regression studies have been plagued by conceptual and empirical shortcomings, lack of relevant control variables, problems of causality and endogeneity, multicollinearity, lack of appropriate control variables, and measurement errors. As a result, no robust systematic conclusions about the impact on growth of ISI trade policies can be drawn from this literature (Srinivasan and Bhagwati 2001).

Comparative Country Studies The effects of ISI have been analyzed in a number of influential studies under the auspices of the Organisation for Economic Co-operation and Development, the National Bureau of Economic Research, and the World Bank (e.g., Little et al. 1970; Balassa et al. 1971; Bhagwati 1978; Krueger 1978). These identified substantial macroeconomic costs of ISI. First, ISI led to inefficiencies in resource allocation, because—through an overvalued exchange rate—it introduced a bias against exports and in favor of (capital-intensive sectors in) the home market, thus leading to underutilization of capital stock (in capital-scarce economies), declining capital productivity, and a failure of high investment rates to significantly reduce widespread unemployment and underemployment (Bruton 1998). In addition, ISI generally gave rise to a wide and nontransparent dispersion of effective exchange rates, which served to make the protectionist regime more complex, distorting the structure of incentives that ISI itself required. Second, imports generally rose faster than expected due to the demand for capital goods and intermediate goods to support the new industries; as a result, balance of payments problems were widespread—the more so because (agricultural) exports were penalized by the broad strategy of ISI (Little et al. 1970; Balassa et al. 1971). Rather than reducing dependence on imported inputs (energy) and technology, the strategy may have significantly increased it. Third, IS regimes have been argued to induce directly unproductive profit-seeking (DUP) activities (Bhagwati 1982), diverting resources from productive use into unproductive but profitable lobbying to change or evade policies or to seek the revenues they generate; this, in turn, reduced investment and productivity growth and hence long-term growth (Winters 2004). Fourth, in countries where the home market is relatively small, ISI created less competitive markets, which in some cases reduced aggregate efficiency, productivity growth, and innovativeness. Taken together, these tendencies suggest that the trade and exchange rate policies of ISI became self-defeating in terms of its objectives: to increase capital accumulation and generate a more diversified productive structure of production.

During the 1990s, however, the impact of ISI on economic performance was reconsidered (Bruton 1998; Rodrik 1999)—particularly within the context of the rapidly growing East Asian economies (Storm and Naastepad 2005). According to this "revisionist" literature, ISI worked well during the period 1950–73, bringing unprecedented economic growth to many developing countries in Latin America (Cárdenas et al. 2000; Rodrik 1998) and (East) Asia (Amsden 1989, 2001; Wade 2004). Along with GDP growth came labor productivity increases (through rapid capital accumulation), which translated into higher real wages of those employed, rising standards of living, and the development of substantial technological capabilities in manufacturing. The "revisionists" argue that ISI preceded exporting in almost all industries in almost all late-industrializing countries and in fact was a prerequisite for export-led growth, because it would not have been possible without the technological capabilities accumulated during the ISI effort that preceded it. The revisionist account emphasizes that countries pursued radically different strategies during the "mature" stage of ISI. One group of countries, including many Latin American ones, began to deepen import substitution in intermediate and capital goods. In conjunction with inappropriate monetary and fiscal policies (which led to frequent periods of high domestic inflation), this contributed to significant exchange rate instability, with large adverse effects on nontraditional exports growth and export diversification. The result was unsustainable external balances, growing international indebtedness, and collapse in response to negative external shocks (Cárdenas et al. 2000). The other group of countries, including most East Asian newly industrializing economies (NIEs), began to place substantially more emphasis on export promotion, tying incentives to export performance, while continuing with ISI. This "mixed" model of ISI became a success, unlike the "deepened" model, because NIEs' governments (1) were able to discipline private-sector firms by means of monitorable performance standards (e.g., export targets) in exchange for subsidies to make private manufacturing activities profitable (Amsden 2001); (2) avoided external imbalances by promoting exports and maintaining competitive exchange rates; and (3) succeeded in designing protection and export-promotion measures that induced indigenous technological learning and knowledge accumulation (Bruton 1998). From the revisionist literature follow important, still unresolved political-economy questions related to the nature of government, the main one of which is how NIEs' governments could induce the technological learning in private-sector firms that is usually assumed to be the consequence of market competition.

See also dependency theory; export promotion; infant industry argument; linkages, backward and forward; trade and economic development, international

FURTHER READING

Amsden, Alice H. 1989. *Asia's Next Giant: South Korea and Late Industrialization*. New York: Oxford University Press. Informative examination of Korea's industrialization in both a comparative and historical context, which challenges much conventional economic thinking on development.

———. 2001. *The Rise of "The Rest": Challenges to the West from Late-Industrializing Economies*. Oxford: Oxford University Press. A masterful analysis of major late-industrializing countries in which the accumulation of industrial knowledge-based assets assumes center stage.

Balassa, Bela, Joel Bergsman, Pedro Malan, Teresa Jean-neret, Gerardo Bueno, John Power, Stephen Lewis, Stephen Guisinger, and Preben Munthe. 1971. *The Structure of Protection in Developing Countries*. Baltimore: Johns Hopkins University Press. Influential World Bank study of the welfare impact of protection in seven developing countries.

Bhagwati, Jagdish N. 1958. "Immiserizing Growth: A Geometric Note." *Review of Economic Studies* 25 (3): 201–5. Examines circumstances in which declines in the (barter) terms of trade outweigh the welfare benefits of trade-induced growth.

———. 1978. *Foreign Trade Regimes and Economic Development: Anatomy and Consequences of Exchange Control Regimes*. Cambridge, MA: Ballinger. First synthesis volume of an influential NBER project on trade policy regimes and development, highlighting the downside of ISI.

———. 1982. "Directly Unproductive, Profit-seeking (DUP) Activities." *Journal of Political Economy* 90 (5): 988–1002. Pioneering contribution to the political economy of (endogenous) trade policy.

Bruton, Henry J. 1998. "A Reconsideration of Import Substitution." *Journal of Economic Literature* 36 (2): 903–36. Balanced evaluation of ISI, which emphasizes technological learning and knowledge accumulation as the prime sources of growth.

Cardénas, Enrique, José Antonio Ocampo, and Rosemary Thorp. 2000. *An Economic History of Twentieth-Century Latin America. Industrialization and the State in Latin America: The Postwar Years*. London: Palgrave Macmillan. Useful essays on Latin-American state-led industrialization from the early 1940s to the 1990s.

Chang, Ha-Joon. 2002. *Kicking Away the Ladder. Development Strategies in Historical Perspective*. London: Anthem Press. An original historical analysis of the interventionist trade and industrial policies followed by the now-developed countries during the 19th century.

Edwards, Sebastian. 1993. "Openness, Trade Liberalization and Growth in Developing Countries." *Journal of Economic Literature* 31 (3): 1358–93. Provides a comprehensive review of the literature up to the early 1990s.

Gerschenkron, Alexander. 1962. *Economic Backwardness in Historical Perspective*. Cambridge, MA: Harvard University Press. Pioneering and very influential formulation of the specific problems facing late-industrializing nations.

Krueger, Anne O. 1978. *Foreign Trade Regimes and Economic Development: Liberalization Attempts and Consequences*. Cambridge, MA: Ballinger. Second synthesis volume of the NBER project on trade policy regimes and development, which supports export orientation and reliance on price incentives rather than ISI policies.

List, Friedrich. 1909 [1841]. *The National System of Political Economy*. Book 4. Translated by Sampson S. Lloyd. London: Longman, Green. Original protest against the principle of absolute free trade, emphasizing the importance of interventionist (ISI) policies for development.

Little, I.M.D., T. Scitovsky, and M. Scott. 1970. *Industry and Trade in Some Developing Countries: A Comparative Study*. New York: Oxford University Press. One of the first studies to estimate the effective rates of protection associated with ISI and to highlight negative developmental effects.

Manoïlesco, Mihaïl. 1928. *Théorie du Protectionisme*. Paris: Marcel Giaud. Intense advocacy of ISI policies, which was further developed by Raúl Prebisch.

Nurkse, Ragnar. 1959. *Patterns of Trade and Development*. Stockholm: Almquist and Wicksell. Masterful combination of history and economic theory arguing that trade could not be an engine of growth for post–World War II late-industrializing countries.

Ocampo, José Antonio, and Lance Taylor. 1998. "Trade Liberalization in Developing Countries: Modest Benefits but Problems with Productivity Growth, Macro Prices and Income Distribution." *Economic Journal* 108 (453): 1523–46. Substantive critique of the argument that trade is good for growth from a modern structuralist perspective.

Prebisch, Raúl. 1950. *The Economic Development of Latin America and Its Principal Problems*. New York: United Nations. A classic treatise that argues for ISI as a means to escape from poverty and primary production specialization.

Rodríguez, Francisco, and Dani Rodrik. 2001. "Trade Policy and Economic Growth: A Skeptic's Guide to the Cross-National Evidence." In *NBER Macroeconomics Annual 2000*, edited by Ben S. Bernanke and Kenneth Rogoff. Cambridge: MIT Press, 261–25. Offers a well-argued and empirically grounded critique of major studies investigating the link between trade policy and growth.

Rodrik, Dani. 1998. "Globalization, Social Conflict, and Economic Growth." *World Economy* 21 (2): 143–58. Well-argued defense of ISI policies.

———. 1999. *Making Openness Work: The New Global Economy and the Developing Countries*. Washington, DC: The Overseas Development Council. Careful analysis of the negative effects on development of openness to trade and finance, highlighting the scope for government action in promoting development under globalization.

Srinivasan, T. N., and Jagdish Bhagwati. 2001. "Outward-Orientation and Development: Are Revisionists Right?" In *Trade, Development and Political Economy: Essays in Honor of Anne O. Krueger*, edited by D. Lal and R. H. Snape. New York: Palgrave, 3–26. Substantive review of the cross-country regression studies on trade policy and growth in defense of the virtues of trade openness.

Storm, Servaas, and C.W.M. Naastepad. 2005. "Strategic Factors in Economic Development: East Asian Industrialization 1950–2003." *Development and Change* 36 (6): 1059–94. Useful review of the role of ISI in East Asian economic development.

Wade, Robert. 2004. *Governing the Market: Economic Theory and the Role of Government in East Asian Industrialization*. Princeton, NJ: Princeton University Press. A skillful analytical account of Taiwan's governed economic development in which ISI played a key part.

Waterbury, John. 1999. "The Long Gestation and Brief Triumph of Import-substituting Industrialization." *World Development* 27 (2): 323–41. Examines the highly diverse origins of what became known as ISI.

Winters, L. Alan. 2004. "Trade Liberalization and Economic Performance: An Overview." *Economic Journal* 114 (February): F4–F21. Useful survey emphasizing the serious methodological problems that arise when trying to assess the impact of trade policy on economic performance.

SERVAAS STORM

■ impossible trinity

The impossible trinity describes an apparently inescapable constraint faced by policymakers, namely the impossibility of simultaneously fixing an exchange rate, permitting full capital mobility, and implementing a monetary policy with only domestic goals in mind. A fixed exchange rate implies, by the law of purchasing power parity (PPP), an inexorable link between domestic and foreign price levels. A less restrictive interpretation of PPP implies that domestic inflation is completely determined by foreign inflation. Clearly, if this is the case then a monetary policy geared toward purely domestic objectives cannot succeed. Similarly, a fixed exchange rate that operates in a world where capital is perfectly mobile must lead to a loss of control over domestic monetary policy.

Imagine an exchange rate that is undervalued—that is, the domestic price of the foreign currency (i.e., the exchange rate) is above what is perceived to be the equilibrium exchange rate. If interest rates happen to be the same in the two countries then, other things being equal, foreign investors will find domestic investments more attractive since, assuming the present situation does not persist, and the exchange rate returns to equilibrium, in the future foreign investors will be able to buy more of the foreign currency when their investment matures. As a result, the mere fixing of an exchange rate out of equilibrium creates forces that influence domestic interest rates. The important point is that a fixed exchange rate and full capital mobility can be incompatible with an independently determined domestic monetary policy (Obstfeld and Rogoff 1995).

Some economists have argued that the unwillingness to accept the existence of this trinity led many emerging economies (middle-income countries with some access to global financial markets) to adopt "soft" pegs instead of the "hard" peg assumed in the foregoing description of the impossible trinity phenomenon (Calvo and Reinhart 2002). Essentially, a hard peg establishes a rigidly fixed exchange rate that leaves relatively little room for change in the event of some unexpected event. In contrast, a soft peg is a fixed exchange rate system where the policy authorities, either explicitly or implicitly, leave room for adjustments or changes in the exchange rate as circumstances warrant. Others have pointed out that the existence of an impossible trinity is confirmed by the failure of the so-called soft pegs as demonstrated by the currency crises in emerging markets, such as Mexico in 1994; Thailand, Indonesia, and Korea in 1997; Russia and Brazil in 1998; and Argentina and Turkey in 2000 (Fischer 2001). The consequence is that exchange rate systems throughout the world have become bipolar in nature: they gravitate toward fixed or floating exchange rates. Intermediate exchange rate regimes are, therefore, a vanishing breed.

Not all interested observers agree with the notion that the impossible trinity is an immutable economic force. An understanding of these different positions requires an exploration of the proposition of the so-called vanishing middle.

The Vanishing Middle? The vanishing middle phenomenon is a corollary of the impossible trinity. Since it not possible to simultaneously fix an exchange rate, permit full capital mobility, and implement a monetary policy with only domestic goals in mind, economies will either gravitate toward a pegged exchange rate or permit their exchange rate to freely float. In order to understand the significance of the impossible trinity it is necessary to briefly examine how exchange rate classifications are made. Until approximately 2000, the long-standing practice of the International Monetary Fund (IMF) was to report exchange rate regimes according to each member country's own view of how its exchange rate is set. As such, the resulting classification can be likened to a type of de jure classification.

By 2000, the IMF was confronting the fact that de jure and de facto definitions of the exchange rate need not be the same. Several academics (e.g., Levy-Yeyati and Sturzenegger 2005) were beginning to modify official classifications. They were dissatisfied with how governments interpreted the type of exchange rate regime they had in place when they reported their view to the IMF. However, the classification used by the economist Fischer (2001) in making the case for the impossible trinity continued to distinguish among pegged rates in a horizontal band, a crawling peg, and managed floating regimes with no preannounced exchange rate path. This suggests that a managed float differs from certain types of pegged exchange rate regimes only because the desired exchange rate is not preannounced. However, if one were also to classify exchange rate regimes based on their credibility, transparency, or durability, then it is difficult to see what sets these types of exchange rate regimes apart from one another. The soft versus hard peg classification permits a more subtle distinction between types of pegged exchange rate regimes though again, based on the historical record, or using the metric of central bank transparency, the distinction is more a matter of convenience than one with meaningful economic implications. In general, whether central banks manage international reserves owned by the government, or own them outright, they are almost always responsible for initiating intervention.

The economists Reinhart and Rogoff (2004) take a different approach to setting up an exchange rate regime classification scheme according to five categories: pegged, limited flexibility, managed float, freely floating, and freely falling. The authors conclude that far fewer countries than previously thought actually chose either one of the corner solutions of the peg and the free float. More important is their finding that floating regimes deliver relatively lower inflation, but possibly at the cost of a lower average per capita economic growth rate than less flexible exchange rate regimes. The point is that the difficulty of defining a true peg suggests, as noted earlier, that a variety of managed floating regimes exists. Nevertheless, classifications still rely on whether the central bank and/or the government have a particular exchange rate regime in mind and how much variability is permitted in the exchange rate. No consideration is given to the possibility that an exchange rate regime in which intervention is used to influence uncertainty in exchange rate movements is, in some sense, also a type of managed regime.

Also absent from the discussion so far is whether it makes any difference whether the economies in question are advanced, emerging, or developing. It could be argued that one's interpretation of whether in fact exchange rate regimes are evolving to one corner of the exchange rate regime type spectrum or the other, namely, whether countries are increasingly adopting either fixed or floating regimes, is strongly related to restrictions placed on capital movements (Eichengreen and Razo-Garcia 2006). More advanced countries are much more likely to permit the free movement of capital than developing countries and, therefore, are more likely to adopt a floating exchange rate regime.

Can a Country Escape the Impossible Trinity?
The concept of a trinity immediately brings to mind the notion of an inescapable constraint in the menu of policies available to sovereign nations. Of course, the arguments are expressed in purely economic terms. However, when political dimensions are considered the policy choice dilemma facing the authorities can become even more complicated. After all, governments typically choose the exchange rate regime while the monetary policy strategy, at least in short run, is often the responsibility of the central bank. Rodrik (2000) refers to a "political trilemma," which is a variant on the impossible trinity concept. The trilemma seeks to reconcile the influence of economic integration on the nation-state. The latter

is arguably less "independent" the greater the influence of globalization. Whereas globalization involves the internationalization of economic forces, international agreements such as the Bretton Woods arrangement after World War II link nation-states through formal international political structures. Finally, at the other end of the trilemma are attempts to create a global form of federalism wherein nation-states relax the divisions created by national borders for some greater political or economic goal. The European Union immediately comes to mind.

Perhaps the best way to summarize the state of the debate is to quote from Cooper (1999, 16–17):

> What is less obvious is that floating rates, independent monetary policy and freedom of capital movement may also be incompatible, at least for countries with small and poorly developed capital markets, i.e., for most countries. That would leave a more limited menu of choice for such countries: between floating rates with capital account restrictions and some monetary autonomy, or fixed rates free of capital restrictions but with loss of monetary autonomy. Put bluntly, two prescriptions regularly extended to developing countries by the international community, including the IMF and the US Treasury, namely to move toward greater exchange rate flexibility and to liberalize international capital movements, may be in deep tension, even deep contradiction.

See also band, basket, and crawl (BBC); Bretton Woods system; capital mobility; carry trade; currency board arrangement (CBA); currency crisis; discipline; European Monetary Union; exchange rate regimes; exchange rate volatility; fear of floating; interest parity conditions; International Monetary Fund (IMF); international reserves; purchasing power parity

FURTHER READING
Calvo, Guillermo, and Carmen Reinhart. 2002. "Fear of Floating." *Quarterly Journal of Economics* 117: 379–408. A technical article that makes the case that countries that act as if they have a floating exchange rate actually try to manipulate exchange rate movements.

Cooper, Richard. 1999. "Exchange Rate Choices." Harvard Institute for Economic Research Discussion Paper No. 1877 (July). Cambridge, MA: Harvard University. Summarizes the views, pro and con, of the choice between a fixed or flexible exchange rate regime.

Eichengreen, Barry, and Raul Razo-Garcia. 2006. "The International Monetary System in the Last and Next 20 Years." *Economic Policy* 47 (July): 393–442. Written for the well-informed general reader and provides an overview of the difficulties and consequences of alternative ways of defining different types of exchange rate regimes.

Fischer, Stanley. 2001. "Exchange Rate Regimes: Is the Bipolar View Correct?" *Journal of Economic Perspectives* 15: 3–24. Argues that countries around the world are choosing either a peg or a pure float.

Levi-Yeyati, Eduardo, and Federico Sturzenegger. 2005. "Classifying Deeds versus Words." *European Economic Review* 49 (August): 1603–35. Proposes a new way of classifying exchange rate regimes for a large number of countries around the world. More than one classification type is proposed.

Obstfeld, Maurice, and Kenneth S. Rogoff. 1995. "The Mirage of Fixed Exchange Rates." *Journal of Economic Perspectives* 9 (fall): 73–96. Fairly accessible to readers with some economics training that essentially amounts to a critique of fixed exchange rates.

Reinhart, Carmen, and Kenneth S. Rogoff. 2004. "The Modern History of Exchange Rate Arrangements: A Reinterpretation." *Quarterly Journal of Economics* 199: 1–48. An alternative classification to the one by Levy-Yeyati and Sturzenegger, based on an exhaustive analysis of exchange rate policies in a large sample of countries around the world and over the past few decades.

Rodrik, Dani. 2000. "How Far Will International Economic Integration Go?" *Journal of Economic Perspectives* 14 (winter): 177–86. Ties in the phenomenon of globalization with the constraints implied by the impossible trinity.

PIERRE L. SIKLOS

■ infant industry argument

The infant industry argument suggests that an industry may be developed under the umbrella of the government's temporary protection. Such a policy must weigh the future cost savings of an industry in which dynamic economies of scale are present with the current consumers' foregone rents due to higher domestic prices as well as higher imported prices of similar products. By establishing an import tariff that is somewhat related to the efficiency level of the domestic industry relative to the foreign one, the government articulates a rent redistribution mechanism, from domestic consumers to local producers, that may help the local industry to overcome the initial cost disadvantage and thus survive in the long run.

The argument that local industry can develop only if given a chance to reduce costs has been around for a long time. During the first Washington administration (1788–92), the first U.S. secretary of the treasury, Alexander Hamilton, favored the temporary protection of the American industry to facilitate its full and fast development as an effective way for the United States to become less dependent on English manufactures. Import substitution can certainly be welfare enhancing if learning is fast enough so that near-future cost savings overcome current consumer losses. It should be pointed out that an import duty not only makes imports more expensive. It also allows domestic producers of similar products to charge higher prices, thus softening domestic competition. This is perhaps the reason why Thomas Jefferson, then secretary of state of the Washington administration and representative of the rural South, bitterly opposed Hamilton's protection plan. Import duties immediately made consumption of all products more expensive for southerners while the North reaped the gains through an increase in jobs and industrial capability. Hamilton's policy—as later Friedrich List's proposals for Germany—was intended to be temporary but it was still around more than a half century after it was first implemented, and the issue of protection was second only to slavery in the contentious relations between the North and the South in the period leading up to the Civil War.

The academic debate surrounding the infant industry argument focuses on whether this policy can be effective and on analyzing whether the future gains offset current costs. But this is a debate that is not alien to the influence of political ideology. Left-leaning parties traditionally favor the involvement of governments in economic activity and as a consequence they traditionally favor a protectionist policy based on the infant industry or any other argument. Conservative parties favor promarket policies, lately favor free-trade agreements, and commonly have denounced the infant industry argument based on failed experiences or have pointed out how easily a projected temporary protection can become permanent.

Infant industry tariff protection was successfully implemented in Japan after World War II, establishing the principle that has inspired the import-substitution policy of many Latin American and Asian countries for many decades with varying degrees of success. Despite many promises of an imminent opening to trade, successive governments repeatedly renewed tariff protection. Japan succeeded in developing its industry and some other countries later moved toward a policy of export promotion in order to ensure fast learning and the development of the domestic industry. The Latin American experience was less positive. Domestic industries failed to take off despite repeated renewals of protection, while locals felt impoverished as imports and related domestic products became more expensive. Furthermore, as domestic producers felt that their respective governments would renew protection, they had little interest in innovating and becoming more efficient. If the dynamic gains of protection are never realized because domestic producers do not believe that protection is temporary, the effects of the infant-industry protection can be analyzed within a static setup with a domestic industry with market power. In the case of Latin America a well-intended but poorly designed policy led to a massive transfer of rents from consumers to producers, who saw their market power significantly increased and the incentives to innovate reduced.

As noted earlier, an import duty does more than just increase the price of imports. Local producers of similar products can charge higher markups as foreign competitors lose at least part of their cost advantage. These are not the only costs of protection. In addition, protection induces a loss of competitiveness of industries that use the output of the infant industry as inputs. These "collateral costs" of protection are ignored in the partial equilibrium analysis commonly used to evaluate the welfare implications of the infant industry argument. However, since governments commonly fail to lift protection, these additional costs of establishing a "temporary" import duty confirm the current negative opinion that the overwhelming majority of economists share regarding any tariff protection based on potential learning effects.

The temporal trade-off of cost and benefits motivates the research question surrounding the infant industry argument. Could the infant industry have been developed without protection? If so, what is the cost of this development? Will the infant industry ever be able to compete with developed foreign firms? In welfare terms, can protection lead to a higher total surplus than simply allowing imports at competitive prices? And last, will protection ever end or is the infant industry argument just another excuse to prolong protection indefinitely?

Perhaps the most important criticism of the infant industry argument is that governments lack any incentive to lift such protection in the future. If that is the case, any incentive that protection may introduce for firms to invest and take advantage of this temporary protection will disappear, and thus the country will end up, as many undeveloped economies nowadays, with high import duties but without dynamic industrial development.

The practical implementation of the infant industry argument is certainly difficult. Governments must be able to accurately predict the learning dynamics of each particular industry to be protected as well as the cost that such protection generates to domestic consumers and firms. From a theoretical point of view, the question is a different one: Is infant industry tariff protection "logically" time-inconsistent? Should we oppose such protection on the basis of a theoretical result or just because from a practical perspective we believe that its effectiveness is quite implausible?

A majority of economists have argued against infant industry protection mostly from ideological premises rather than based on an appropriate theoretical model. Thus the infant industry argument is frequently dismissed by pointing out that free trade is Pareto dominant, that is, it would be mutually beneficial to all countries involved. Neither Hamilton nor the protectionists ever claimed such a global viewpoint. The infant industry argument therefore needs to be addressed within the partial equilibrium framework of a small country and evaluated on the basis of whether a temporary protection policy can effectively help develop a domestic infant industry that otherwise would never have taken off.

The academic debate on infant industry protection has recently focused on precisely the issue of whether tariff protection will ever end after successfully helping the domestic industry to develop. To summarize the results described in the rest of this entry: infant industry protection may be effective and temporary when the level of protection is linked to the efficiency level of the domestic industry. However, it will commonly fail if it sets a future liberalization date that is independent of the degree of development of the domestic industry, or if cost reduction requires specific investments that are not directly linked to the production decisions of domestic firms.

A Framework for the Analysis of Infant Industry Protection Consider a small country where an early industry suffers from such cost disadvantage relative to foreign producers that it will have to shut down in the event that the domestic government enforces a free trade policy. The domestic and foreign industries produce similar, but not necessarily identical products. The foreign industry is assumed to behave competitively and to have exhausted all its dynamic economies of scale. A single infant monopolist is assumed to produce all domestic production. This firm enjoys significant learning by doing and marginal cost will fall as production takes place. The demand for differentiated domestic and imported products depends on the decision variables of the two players: government chooses the import tariff to maximize the discounted sum of consumer surplus, profits, and tax revenues while the monopolist chooses the relative price of the domestic good that maximizes the net present value of future profits. Marginal cost reduces at a certain rate with current production and experience depreciates as a fraction of the current level of marginal cost. Therefore, learning is a reversible process that requires some positive output to induce cost savings while at the stationary equilibrium, once learning is exhausted, current production only impedes marginal cost from increasing.

The monopolist and the government engage in a dynamic game where the former chooses the price and the latter the tariff level. Both players discount the future at a common rate. The game is dynamic because each player's action affects the state of the game, that is, the level of marginal cost through the direct or indirect effect on the domestic production and accumulation of experience. This setup is essentially a capital accumulation game World such as the one studied by Reynolds (1987). If we further restrict our attention to a system of linear demands for domestic products and imports, this dynamic model becomes a linear-quadratic differential game that allows us to obtain a closed-form solution and thus easily characterize the features of the equilibrium strategies.

Alternative Assumptions The foregoing description is based on Miravete (2003). Melitz (2005) departs from this framework in two main aspects: the domestic industry is assumed to be competitive and the government behaves as a social planner.

The earlier framework could be easily generalized to an *n*-firm symmetric oligopoly industry without changing qualitative results other than learning would now be slower as each firm would only count for one *n*th of accumulated experience. Thus the more firms in the domestic industry, the faster learning needs to be in order to achieve higher welfare than the default scenario where domestic firms just shut down and consumers only purchase from foreign firms. An additional issue that may arise when several firms compete in the domestic market is the existence of learning spillovers. As Stokey (1986) shows, this introduces additional reasons to protect an industry.

By assuming the existence of a social planner rather than a noncooperative solution, Melitz eliminates the dynamic interaction between government and firms. This corresponds to a situation in the above framework when the government and the monopolist collude in choosing the tariff and price strategies, which may be important for state-owned industries or when the industry in question has significant political influence. In a dynamic strategic environment firms would charge higher prices and the government lower rates than in Melitz's case.

This framework presents another important advantage: an infinite horizon game rules out the possibility of any other future rent after the formal end of the game, and the equilibrium strategies are thus robust to the existence of any other unaccounted rent. This is not the case of Leahy and Neary (1999), Miyagiwa and Ohno (1999), and most explicitly Tornell (1991), who considers the possibility of a third period where wages are renegotiated when the initial protection of the industry was planned only for two periods. Considering extraneous elements after the planning horizon of the game as formally ended turns protection, by definition, into a time-inconsistent policy.

Markov versus Non-Markov Strategies The basic criticism to the infant industry argument is that governments lack the ability to commit to taking particular policy actions in the future. In particular, a government cannot commit to reducing protection if the protected industry fails to make the anticipated productivity gains. Although this may be true in practice, it cannot be defended with models that by construction make reneging from the announced policy the dominant government's strategy. A more interesting distinction is the use of strategies that are linked to the level of efficiency of the domestic industry. The effect of learning is reducing the marginal cost of production simply by means of producing in the past. A protection strategy linked to this marginal cost (or alternatively to the related level of output or price) of the domestic industry is called a Markov strategy.

A way to help governments renege from announced liberalization is by using non-Markov strategies such as in the case of Staiger and Tabellini (1987) or Matsuyama (1990). Protection eases domestic production, and thus, through learning, marginal costs get reduced. In these models, however, cost reduction depends on investments that are not linked to the state of the game, that is, the level of marginal cost. Therefore there is no source of commitment for the government either. In the framework described earlier such policies can indeed be computed when both the government and the domestic producer can commit to a sequence of tariffs and prices over time. But most generally, a Markov perfect equilibrium can be constructed when both tariffs and prices are made contingent on the evolving level of marginal cost. The interesting added result of taking this approach is that if such strategies are employed, the best response of the government to the pricing of firms is to reduce tariff protection as the level of marginal cost decreases. Thus there is no need to renege and time-consistent equilibrium strategies lead to future trade liberalization. The government simply allows the domestic firm to earn the minimum markup to induce them to reduce costs beyond the static equilibrium. As this process takes place, marginal cost gets reduced, and the required level of protection needed is also lower. But this result also confirms Hamilton's intuition, that protection based on the infant industry argument would be only temporary despite sometimes surviving for a long time.

See also import substitution industrialization; trade and economic development, international

FURTHER READING

Leahy, Dermot, and Peter J. Neary. 1999. "Learning by Doing, Precommitment and Infant-industry Promotion." *Review of Economic Studies* 66 (2): 447–74. A model of tariff protection with a finite horizon.

Matsuyama, Kiminori. 1990. "Perfect Equilibria in a Trade Liberalization Game." *American Economic Review* 80

(3): 480–92. A game-theoretical model that shows that permanent protection may arise from the lack of commitment of tariff protection policies.

Melitz, Marc J. 2005. "When and How Should Infant Industries Be Protected?" *Journal of International Economics* 66 (1): 177–96. An elegant model of learning by doing that points out how the speed of learning determines the length of protection needed by an industry.

Miravete, Eugenio J. 2003. "Time-consistent Protection with Learning by Doing." *European Economic Review* 47 (5): 761–90. A differential game model that shows that time-consistent protection is possible in an infinite-horizon differential game where firms' and the government's strategies are contingent on the level of marginal cost of the industry.

Miyagiwa, Kaz, and Yuka Ohno. 1999. "Credibility of Protection and Incentives to Innovate." *International Economic Review* 40 (1): 143–63. A dynamic model of industry protection with policies that are not linked to industry performance.

Reynolds, Stanley S. 1987. "Capacity Investment, Preemption, and Commitment in an Infinite Horizon Model." *International Economic Review* 28 (1): 69–88. A differential game-theoretical framework that studies capital accumulation games.

Staiger, Robert W., and Guido Tabellini. 1987. "Discretionary Trade Policy and Excessive Protection." *American Economic Review* 77 (5): 823–37. A model of non-Markov protection strategies that shows how the lack of commitment leads to high tariffs.

Stokey, Nancy L. 1986. "The Dynamics of Industrywide Learning." In *Equilibrium Analysis: Essays in Honor of Kenneth J. Arrow*, vol. 2, edited by W. P. Heller, R. M. Starr, and D. A. Starret. New York: Cambridge University Press, 81–104. An elegant dynamic model of industry performance where learning occurs in the early stages of development through spillover effects.

Tornell, Aaron. 1991. "Time Inconsistency of Protectionist Programs." *Quarterly Journal of Economics* 106 (3): 963–74. A model of finite-horizon protection where time inconsistency arises by extending the length of the game once the strategies have been defined.

EUGENIO J. MIRAVETE

■ inflation targeting

Since the early 1990s, inflation targeting has become the predominant monetary policy choice for central banks in industrial and developing economies alike. New Zealand, the United Kingdom, Canada, Australia, Norway, Sweden, and Israel were among the first countries to adopt this policy. Since then, many emerging market economies have also adopted it, including Chile, Brazil, South Africa, Korea, Indonesia, Thailand, and the Philippines. Inflation targeting is currently regarded as best practice monetary policy for countries operating flexible exchange rate regimes.

At its core, inflation targeting is a monetary policy system that manipulates a policy instrument (usually a short-term nominal interest rate, but sometimes the nominal effective exchange rate) according to available information with the objective of controlling inflation. The rate of inflation is the primary objective of this regime but is not the sole objective; the system permits the pursuit of secondary objectives such as smoothing changes in output, interest rates, or even the exchange rate.

The successful implementation of inflation targeting depends on a checklist of features:

1. A binding commitment to price stability as the primary policy objective. This is normally presented in a central bank act or similar piece of legislation that sets the objectives and operational rules for the functioning of a central bank.

2. Transparency. This takes the form of announced inflation targets, published minutes of meetings of the monetary policy committee, and the publication of periodic inflation reports.

3. An independent and accountable central bank.

4. A floating exchange rate. In a world of high capital mobility, having an exchange rate target compromises the efficacy of inflation targeting. Nonetheless, central banks in emerging markets often have a strong desire to manage exchange rate movements while maintaining an inflation targeting regime.

5. A monetary policy rule (MPR). The MPR is a policy rule that guides the instrument of the inflation targeting policy. If the nominal interest rate is the policy instrument, the MPR states how it should react to key economic variables such that the policy objective is attained (see Taylor 2001).

Inflation targeting has several advantages. First, it enables policymakers to focus on domestic policy considerations and to respond to those shocks affecting the domestic economy. Second, inflation targeting does not require a stable relationship between the money supply and inflation but uses all available information deemed useful in achieving the target. Third, inflation targeting is transparent and easily understood by the public (Mishkin 2000). Inflation targeting also has two notable disadvantages. The first is that, owing to the long and variable lags between the time a policy is instigated and point it begins to take effect, inflation is inherently difficult to control. The second, which is pertinent to emerging market economies, is that the exchange rate flexibility associated with inflation targeting may lead to financial instability.

A strict inflation target provides that inflation is the *sole* objective of monetary policy. In other words the only variable the central bank cares about is inflation. Flexible inflation targeting essentially targets inflation but allows for a secondary objective. The usual secondary objective is output, where the central bank seeks to minimize the gap between the current growth rate of output and some steady-state value. Other secondary objectives may include dampening the growth of asset prices, reducing the volatility of the exchange rate, or minimizing potential disruptions in domestic financial markets caused by sharp changes in interest rates. It is commonly held and demonstrated in simulation studies (see Svensson 1997) that output variability is lower under flexible inflation targeting and that the inflation target is attained more quickly under strict inflation targeting. Central banks are often under pressure to take output conditions into account, however, and in this situation, flexible inflation targeting is a viable option.

There are several other analytical and operational dimensions to inflation targeting that are significant in its construction. These include the central bank's selection of a strict versus flexible inflation target, whether it should target domestic inflation (inflation in the price of those goods produced and consumed domestically) or consumer price index inflation (domestic inflation plus inflation in the price of tradable goods), whether the central bank should target current inflation or an inflation forecast, and the extent to which the central bank should respond to the exchange rate and asset prices.

See also exchange rate regimes; monetary policy rules; money supply; seigniorage

FURTHER READING

Ball, L. 1997. "Efficient Rules for Monetary Policy." NBER Working Paper No. 5952. Cambridge, MA: National Bureau of Economic Research. Presents the basic analytics for a closed-economy strict and flexible inflation targeting system and the specification of the rule(s) required to reach the inflation objective.

Cavoli, T., and R. Rajan. 2006. "Inflation Targeting in East Asia: Exploring the Role of the Exchange Rate." *Briefing Notes in Economics*, No. 74 (September-October). Similar to Ball (1997) but for open economies where the role of the exchange rate as a policy objective is examined.

Debelle, G. 2001. "The Case for Inflation Targeting in East Asian Countries." In *Future Directions for Monetary Policy in East Asia*, edited by D. Gruen. Canberra: Reserve Bank of Australia, 65–82. Examines the issues regarding the appropriateness of inflation targeting in developing economies—particularly in Asia.

Mishkin, F. S. 2000. "Inflation Targeting in Emerging Market Countries." *American Economic Review Papers and Proceedings* 90 (2): 105–9. Evaluates the checklist for inflation targeting for developing economies.

Svensson, L.E.O. 1997. "Inflation Forecast Targeting: Implementing and Monitoring Inflation Targets." *European Economic Review* 41 (6): 1111–46. Presents a technical treatment of the trade-offs inherent in strict versus flexible inflation targeting and examines whether central banks should target actual current inflation or a forecast of future inflation.

Taylor, J. B. 2001. "The Role of the Exchange Rate in Monetary Policy Rules." *American Economic Review Papers and Proceedings* 91: 263–67. Examines the issues of fitting the exchange rate in an inflation targeting framework.

TONY CAVOLI

■ information and communications technology

Information and communications technology (ICT) refers to all technologies and devices used in managing and processing information systems. In contrast to the manufacturing industries such as shipbuilding, steel, automobiles, and textiles, which create value directly, ICT in the form of computers, software, the Internet, multimedia, and management of information services creates value indirectly. ICT includes data for business use, voice communication, images, multimedia, and many types of technologies for the purpose of development and exchange of information. The definition of the ICT sector differs among industrialized countries. The U.S. and Organisation for Economic Co-operation and Development (OECD) definitions are presented in table 1.

The introduction of increased processing power of hardware along with complementary software and telecommunications infrastructure have enhanced the ability to store, retrieve, analyze, and communicate data and information within and between organizations and their partners and suppliers, and ultimately to the consumer. In particular, ICT deals with the use of electronics, computers, and computer software to convert, store, protect, process, transmit, and retrieve information. For that reason, computer professionals are often called information technology (IT) specialists or business process consultants, and the division of a company or university that deals with software technology is often called the IT department. Other names for the latter are information services, management information services, or managed service providers.

As a general rule, capital and labor as important elements in the growth of an economy lead to decreasing returns to scale. Therefore, even though these factor inputs of production may increase, the growth of an economy over a certain level cannot be expected. Information may produce increasing returns to scale and become an important factor for sustainable growth, however. Thus, in recent years, ICT has been considered an input in the production of goods and services and a factor affecting total factor productivity growth at both the micro- and the macro levels (see Shiu and Heshmati 2006).

Review of the ICT Literature ICT is considered one of the three major technological breakthroughs of the modern era (see Edquist and Henrekson 2007), the others being steam power and electricity. ICT includes some of the wider information technology innovations and applications, and their commercialization and transfer have been quite rapid. These enhance the communication of more accurate and value-added information to workers, managers, and consumers, thus reducing uncertainty and time use in conducting many types of businesses.

There has been great interest among researchers in investigating how some countries were able to take advantage of ICT to accelerate their rates of growth and productivity. In these studies one examines the contribution of IT investment to economic growth and finds that the returns on IT investment are significantly positive. In the transitional countries of Central and Eastern Europe (CEE), one observes a chronic underinvestment in telecommunications infrastructure. The result suggests that improving investment may ultimately improve the channel between aggregate investment and growth economywide (see also Zhu 1996; Madden and Savage 1998).

Return on IT differs by the country's development level. Results from intercountry studies relating IT and non-IT inputs to gross domestic product (GDP) over time suggest that for developed countries, returns from IT capital investments are positive, while returns from non-IT capital investments are not commensurate with relative factor shares. The situation is reversed for developing countries, where

Table 1
An industrial sector–based definition of ICT

U.S. Department of Commerce IT-producing industries	OECD ICT industry
Hardware industries	Manufacturing
Computers and equipment	Manufacture of office, accounting, and computing machinery
Wholesale trade of computers and equipment	Manufacture of insulated wire and cable
Retail trade of computers and equipment	Manufacture of electronic valves, tubes, and other electronic components
Calculating and office machines	Manufacture of television and radio transmitters and apparatus for line telephony and line telegraphy
Magnetic and optical recording media	
Electron tubes	
Printed circuit boards	Manufacture of television and radio receivers, sound or video recording or reproducing apparatus, and associated goods
Semiconductors	
Passive electronic components	
Industrial instruments for measurement	Manufacture of instruments and appliances for measuring, checking, testing, navigating, and other purposes, except industrial process control equipment
Instruments for measuring electricity	
Laboratory analytical instruments	
	Manufacture of industrial process control equipment
Communications equipment industries	
Household audio and video equipment	Services: Goods related
Telephone and telegraph equipment	Wholesale of machinery, equipment, and supplies
Radio and TV communications equipment	Renting of office machinery and equipment (including computers)
Software/services industries	Services: Intangible
Computer programming	Telecommunications
Prepackaged software	Computer and related activities
Wholesale trade of software	
Retail trade of software	
Computer-integrated system design	
Computer processing, data preparation	
Information retrieval services	
Computer services management	
Computer rental and leasing	
Computer maintenance and repair	
Computer related services, NEC	
Communications services industries	
Telephone and telegraph communications	
Cable and other TV services	

Sources: U.S. Department of Commerce (2003), OECD (2000).

returns from non-IT capital are quite substantial, but those from IT capital investments are not statistically significant. The impacts of IT investment on economic growth in a cross section of countries shows that the relative contribution of IT to GDP growth in developing counties between 1980 and 1995 was less than 2 percent, compared to more than 10 percent in developed countries (see Dewan and Kraemer 2000; Pohjola 2001).

Investment in ICT and Its Diffusion Evidence on the role of ICT investment is primarily available at the macroeconomic level. It has been observed that ICT has been a very dynamic area of investment, due to the steep decline in ICT prices, which has encouraged investment in ICT and expansion of production at the same time shifting investment away from other assets. The capital deepening that results from investment in ICT is considered an important driver of economic growth. It establishes the infrastructure for the use of ICT networks and provides productive equipment and software to businesses. Measures of ICT investment are therefore of considerable interest in examining growth performance in many countries. Investment is usually estimated by using business surveys. These surveys usually allow the total investment to be disaggregated into a number of well-defined asset groups, including ICT. There is a broad understanding in the statistical community about the definition of ICT products. The pace of investment differs widely by country. The lowest levels of the share of investment in ICT are found in low-income nations, while the highest are in high-income nations.

Generally, network products, including telephone, e-mail, Internet, computer hardware, and software, have distinct features such as network effect, critical mass, lock-in, and path dependency, which affect late takeoff in their diffusion. A positive direct network effect means a positive utility gain for consumers when the number of users operating the same system increases. For example, the first e-mail message was sent in 1969, but the adoption did not take off until 1990. Since then, Internet traffic has been doubling every year. This example raises an important question, which is when to expect a new technology to diffuse and what should be the minimum number of users (the critical mass) needed for inducing potential consumers to adopt it.

At the global level, the diffusion of key ICTs such as the Internet, mobile phones, and personal computers in accordance with the World Bank's classifications are shown in figures 1, 2, and 3. To judge from these graphs, which are based on data published in OECD (2000; 2004), United Nations Conference on Trade and Development (2003), U.S. Department of Commerce (2003), and World Bank (2006), we observed that high-income countries show a high level of diffusion. In addition, in the case of the diffusion of the Internet and personal com-

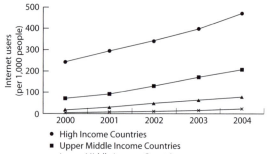

Figure 1

The diffusion of the Internet

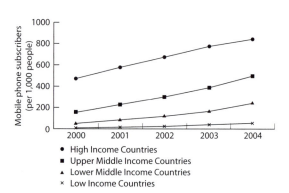

Figure 2

The diffusion of mobile phones

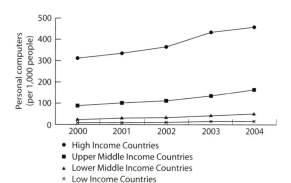

Figure 3

The diffusion of personal computers

puters, the gap between high-income and low-income countries measured in Internet users per 1,000 people increases over time.

The "digital divide" is the socioeconomic difference between communities with access to computers and the Internet and those without such access. At the microlevel, it refers to the gap between individuals, households, businesses, and geographical areas with regard to their opportunities and abilities to access and to use IT services for a wide variety of activities. The gap is due to differing literacy and technical skills, and the gap in availability of useful digital content. The digital divide at the aggregate level is often discussed in conjunction with the gap between rich and poor, and developed and underdeveloped nations concerning access to and use of digital communication. In an international context, the divide indicates that developed countries are far better equipped than developing countries to use the advantages of rapidly expanding Internet technology. The more rapidly the rate at which Internet technology is developed and spread, the more the quality-of-life differences between developed and underdeveloped countries become evident. Despite the productivity, connectivity, and many other recognized and measurable positive effects associated with Internet use, the international digital divide is widening.

Given the gradually decreasing number of fixed (land-line) telephone subscribers per 1,000 people in contrast to mobile subscribers, it is highly probable that the traditional fixed phone is being supplanted by the mobile phone as telecommunications services develop. Consumers show increasing preference for data-based communication instead of voice-based, and new communications services such as voice-over-Internet protocol have entered the market through the development of Internet technology. Given the Internet's high rate of growth and the emergence of broadband services, the difference between Internet telephony and traditional voice telephony has begun to erode. Such changes are dynamically transforming the traditional communications industry structure. The diffusion into the marketplace of telephone, mobile phone, and Internet services has

progressed differently in different places, determined mainly by local and regional economic conditions.

The Effects of ICT on Economic Growth Much attention has been given to how much IT affects the growth of an economy (see Jorgenson 2001). As is well known, IT can transform our economic system by increasing productivity and stimulating economic growth. At the firm level, there are four mechanisms or channels through which IT investment affects the growth of an economy. The first channel is that the IT industry itself grows dramatically, and the nations where the IT industry occupies a leading position may have more than one leading growth sector. In the decade between 1995 and 2005, many nations' portion of revenue derived from the IT sector in their total GDP increased. For example, even in the case of China achieving an 8 percent annual growth rate during that decade, the growth of the IT sectors was faster than the overall economic growth. Accordingly, the expansion of IT sectors affects the growth of the economy positively. By the second channel, IT can facilitate the catch-up process by activating the diffusion process of technologies. According to Antonelli (1990), developing countries can take advantage of the opportunity of catch-up by overcoming asymmetry and disequilibrium of information through the diffusion of IT. The third relation between IT and economic growth is that developed IT affects the integration and efficiency of markets and it stimulates economic growth. This is called the market integration effect. In the final mechanism, IT improves the management and decision-making processes of companies. Additionally, ICT helps firms gain market share, raise overall productivity, expand their product range, customize the services offered, respond better to client demand, and reduce inefficiency.

Economies that successfully implement new ICT may be able to overcome barriers that have long held them back in their contribution to the global trade. The rapid spread of the Internet has opened up previously unavailable commercial and political information. In particular, ICT has reduced many of the transaction costs of participating in subcontracting through business-to-business interaction, and it facilitates the operations of low-cost suppliers of IT services based in developing countries. In other words, IT can increase total output eventually through reduced transaction costs. Enough constructed IT infrastructure decreases the cost of information, and in the long run it makes the market more effective. Less-developed countries face a higher cost to obtain information because their information market is less efficient than in developed countries.

IT investments have specific features. A decreased telecommunications cost can be used to decrease costs associated with decisions to distribute resources between cities and rural communities. The decreased telecommunications costs make the use of a larger quantity of information possible, which contributes to better decision making. It increases the opportunity for arbitrage and makes the financial market more efficient. Finally, decreased cost can provide more information about market prices. Even if ICT spread in similar ways in different places, one would not expect similar economic benefits from it. Only with a regulatory environment, the availability of appropriate skills, the ability to change organizational setups, and the strength of accompanying innovations in ICT applications can the benefits of IT be maximized. The magnitude of complementary policies for IT investment must be expanded. Such policies aim to enhance the conditions for developing the economy, through provision of infrastructure, prohibition of monopoly in the telecommunications market, allowing for new entrants, enacting efficient laws and regulations, and providing a high-quality education system.

Edquist and Henrekson (2007) examined productivity growth following the three major technological breakthroughs: the steam power revolution, electrification, and the ICT revolution. The authors distinguish between sectors producing and sectors using the new technology and find a long lag from the time of the original invention until a substantial increase in the rate of productivity growth can be observed, as well as strong evidence of rapid product price decreases over time. The highest productivity growth rates are found in the ICT-producing industries, which may be explained by the ICTs'

more rapid rate of technological development compared with previous breakthroughs.

New Economy and the Productivity Paradox

The extraordinary performance of the U.S. economy in the late 1990s and the associated economic growth were referred to as the "new economy." The computing power of microchips, which underlies the rapid progress in productivity of ICT, has doubled every 18–24 months since 1965, as Moore's Law predicted. Contrary to mainstream economists' theoretical models, inflation and unemployment were low at the same time, particularly following 1992, and the economy experienced sustained growth and the stock market boomed throughout the 1990s.

The new economy phenomenon happened because of a number of factors. First, increased efficiency in firms' management though ICT adoption affected productivity growth at the firm level and connected productivity growth in each industry through spillover effects. As a consequence, productivity in the total economy increased. In other words, since the middle of the 1980s, more intensive competition between companies contributed to high investment in IT and the introduction of innovative management, which in turn affected productivity gains.

Second, productivity gains led to a low inflation rate. When productivity continues to grow, the inflation rate becomes lower because inflation is offset by productivity increases. Furthermore, low inflation coexists with low interest rates, and it increases the investment rate. Finally, it can link productivity growth and sustained economic growth in an interconnected cycle of investment, productivity, and economic growth.

Third, the wide-ranging diffusion of IT and Internet use made it possible for the new economy to evolve. The spread of IT and the Internet due to price reductions stimulated the network effect, and it induced sustained economic growth by creating increasing returns to scale in the whole economy. Furthermore, continuous strong productivity growth since the 2001 recession made it likely that some of the gains of the late 1990s may endure.

In disagreement with the widespread view about productivity gains through ICT adoption, Robert Solow commented in 1987 on the IT productivity paradox that the productivity of the workforce had not risen as IT had extended through Western industry. It was widely believed that office automation was boosting labor or total factor productivity, but the growth accounts did not seem to confirm this, because the "computer era" from the early 1970s to the time that Solow spoke about the paradox included a massive slow-down in growth as the machines were becoming ubiquitous.

The causes of the productivity paradox are the following. First, a portion of the benefit from ICT is not included in productivity statistics. Productivity statistics of service sectors with a high rate of investment in ICT correspond to this case. For example, the increased benefit of financial services such as ATMs (automated teller machines) is not included in productivity statistics. Insurance, business services, and health services show the same phenomenon of the benefits of ICT not being fully reflected in productivity statistics.

Second, there may be a lag in productivity improvements. The lag is because computers did not enhance productivity until things such as software, the Internet, and handhelds became prevalent. It takes a long time for a new technology to become popular and companies to adopt it. Given that ICT increases multifactor productivity through networks, and building a network requires a long time, productivity growth will lag behind the initial introduction of new technology. Productivity growth originating from IT may already be occurring, but a flaw in the measurement tools available may be hiding it.

Third, previously much research aimed at identifying the effect of ICT at the company level was based on small samples. If the early impact of ICT is trivial, research in the early stage will not capture the contribution of ICT. In addition, some research shows that the ICT impact differs by industrial sector. These days, there are more detailed data on ICT investment available to measure the impacts of ICT.

In the search for explanations of the productivity paradox, Oliner and Sichel (2000) deny the significance of the IT sector by arguing that IT accounted for no more than 2 percent of the capital stock in any country in the world. Other economists have made more controversial statements about the utility of computers: that they pale into insignificance as a source of productivity advantage when compared to the first industrial revolution or the adoption of motorcars.

The Role of ICT in the World Economy The OECD (2004) report on the impact of ICT provides two important messages. First, ICT continued to have a strong impact on performance. Productivity growth in the United States, the main example of ICT-led growth and productivity improvements, continued to be strong. ICT networks had spread throughout much of the OECD business sector and would spread further to enhance business performance. The release of increasingly powerful microprocessors was projected to continue for the foreseeable future. These factors were expected to encourage ICT investment and support further productivity growth.

Second, the impact of ICT differed markedly across OECD economies. Many OECD countries lagged in the diffusion of ICT and had scope for greater uptake. It was expected that the largest economic benefits of ICT would be observed in countries with high levels of ICT diffusion. Having the equipment or network is not sufficient to derive economic benefits, however. Other factors, such as the regulatory environment, skills, ability to change organizational setups, and the strength of innovations in ICT applications all affect the ability of firms to seize the benefits of ICT. Consequently, the impact of ICT on economic growth and performance of countries with equal ICT diffusion will not be the same.

IT makes a positive although small contribution to economic growth, but its impact is positively related to the level of development. Studies of the relationships between IT and economic performance suggest that the impact of IT diffusion can differ even among developed countries with similar level of development. The limited existing empirical evidence shows that developing counties that did not adopt complementary policies have gained little benefit from IT investment. In general, for developing countries it is rather difficult to catch any systematic evidence about such relationships. While the evidence suggests that IT contributes to the growth of developed countries, this relationship is less clear in the case of developing countries.

A long time period is required to link IT investment to economic growth and establish a causal relationship between the two. For IT to be effective, its spread needs to reach a critical threshold. To obtain high returns from IT investment, developing countries must adopt complementary policies that fulfill conditions for economic development such as building up the basic infrastructure, creating a non-monopoly telecommunications market, opening the market, enacting effective laws and regulations, and building a high-quality educational system. For developing countries, diffusion and application of IT can play an important role in the growth of the economy, but for IT to have a full impact, more fundamental complementary investments are essential.

See also digital divide; electronic commerce; globalization

FURTHER READING

Antonelli, Cristiano. 1990. "Information Technology and the Derived Demand for Telecommunications Services in the Manufacturing Industry." *Information Economics and Policy* 4: 45–55. An empirical examination of the factors that influence the growth in demand for telecommunication services in the Italian manufacturing sector.

Dewan, Sanjeen, and Kenneth L. Kraemer. 2000. "Information Technology and Productivity: Evidence from Country-level Data." *Management Science* 46: 548–62. An empirical analysis of significant differences between developed and developing countries with respect to their structure of returns from capital investments.

Edquist, Harald, and Magnus Henrekson. 2007. "Technological Breakthroughs and Productivity Growth." *Research in Economic History* 24: 1–53. An examination of productivity growth following three major technological breakthroughs: the steam power revolution, electrification, and the ICT revolution.

Jorgenson, Dale W. 2001. "Information Technology and the U.S. Economy." *American Economic Review* 91 (1): 1–32. An important study of the link between IT and the fundamental change in the U.S. economy leading to a permanent improvement in the U.S. growth prospects.

Madden, Gary, and Scott J. Savage. 1998. "CEE Telecommunications Investment and Economic Growth." *Information Economics and Policy* 10: 173–95. An empirical examination of the relationship between gross fixed investment, telecommunications infrastructure investments, and economic growth.

Oliner, Stephen D., and Daniel E. Sichel. 2000. "The Resurgence of Growth in the Late 1990s: Is Information Technology the Story." *Journal of Economic Perspectives* 14 (4): 3–22. An empirical examination of the influence of ICT on productivity growth.

Organisation for Economic Co-operation and Development (OECD). 2000. *Information Technology Outlook 2000*. Paris: OECD. A thorough review of trends and prospects in the ICT industry.

———. 2004. *The Economic Impact of ICT: Measurement, Evidence, and Implication*. Paris: OECD. A comprehensive overview of the impacts of ICT on economic performance, and the ways through which these impacts can be measured.

Pohjola, Matti. 2001. "Information Technology and Economic Growth: A Cross-Country Analysis." In *Information Technology, Productivity, and Economic Growth: International Evidence and Implications for Economic Development*, edited by Matti Pohjola. Oxford: Oxford University Press, 242–56. An exploration of impacts of information technology investment on economic growth in a cross-section of countries.

Shiu, Alice, and Almas Heshmati. 2006. "Technical Change and Total Factor Productivity for Chinese Province: A Panel Data Analysis." IZA Discussion Paper 2133. Bonn: The Institute for the Study of Labor. An empirical analysis of the variables that affect total factor productivity growth in China.

United Nations Conference on Trade and Development. 2003. *E-Commerce and Development Report 2003*. New York: UNCTAD. A thorough overview of the implications of the growth of digital economy for developing countries.

U.S. Department of Commerce. 2003. *Digital Economy 2003*. Washington, DC: U.S. Department of Commerce. A comprehensive review of conditions in U.S. information technology industries and the effects of IT on national economic performance.

World Bank. 2006. *World Development Indicators 2006*. Washington, DC: World Bank. World Bank's premier annual compilation of data about development, including more than 900 indicators in over 80 tables organized in 6 sections: World View, People, Environment, Economy, States and Markets, and Global Links.

Zhu, Ji. 1996. "Comparing the Effects of Mass Media and Telecommunications on Economic Development: A Pooled Time Series Analysis." *Gazette* 57: 17–28. An empirical study of the contribution of telecommunications to economic development.

ALMAS HESHMATI AND MINKYU LEE

■ infrastructure and foreign direct investment

Foreign direct investment (FDI), acquiring a controlling share of a foreign firm, is more likely to occur in countries with good physical infrastructure such as bridges, ports, and highways. Therefore, especially for countries with poor infrastructure, investing in improvements in infrastructure may be important for attracting FDI. Nonetheless, some countries with poor infrastructure may be unattractive hosts for FDI for a variety of other reasons, and even substantial investments in infrastructure might not bring FDI pouring in. But all else being equal, a country with better infrastructure would be expected to attract more FDI (as well as more domestic investment).

The positive effect of infrastructure on FDI has been found to be quite robust to time periods and countries considered, other control variables included, the measure of infrastructure used, and the like. Examining the determinants of FDI into U.S. states for 1981–83, Coughlin, Terza, and Arromdee (1991) find that more extensive transportation infrastructures were associated with increased FDI.

Wheeler and Mody (1992) find that infrastructure quality is an important variable for developing countries seeking to attract FDI from the United States, but is less important for developed countries that already have high-quality infrastructures.

Using a self-reinforcing model of FDI, Cheng and Kwan (2000) find support for good infrastructure (density of roads) as a determinant of FDI into 29 Chinese regions from 1985 to 1995. The quality of the roads, however, did not seem to matter much: high-grade paved roads did not perform any better than all roads in determining which regions hosted the most FDI.

Infrastructure Broadly Defined Fung et al. (2005) examine whether hard infrastructure, in the form of more highways and railroads, or soft infrastructure, in the form of more transparent institutions and deeper reforms, leads to more FDI. Their analysis controls for other determinants of FDI such as regional market sizes, human capital, and tax policies. Their data are on FDI from the United States, Japan, Korea, Hong Kong, and Taiwan to regions of China. They find that soft infrastructure is a more important determinant of FDI than hard infrastructure.

Government infrastructure is used to refer to a country's political, institutional, and legal environment. It captures aspects of legislation, regulation, and legal systems that condition freedom of transacting, security of property rights, and transparency of government and legal processes (Globerman and Shapiro 2003). Government infrastructure is an important determinant of both inflows and outflows of FDI. Not only does government infrastructure attract FDI, but the proper conditions can also stimulate the creation of home-grown multinational enterprises (MNEs) that invest abroad. The biggest gains from improving government infrastructure appear to arise for small developing countries—the benefits of further enhancements may be less for countries already enjoying good governance.

Globerman and Shapiro (2003) examine the effect of government infrastructure on both the probability that a country receives FDI and on the amount of FDI received (for countries receiving any FDI). They find that countries failing to achieve a minimum threshold of effective governance are unlikely to receive any U.S. FDI. Thus ineffective governments that fail to promote transparent markets and whose legal systems are not rooted in English law are apt to be excluded from FDI. Globerman and Shapiro's second analysis examines the determinants of the amount of FDI, for those countries receiving FDI. They find government infrastructure, including aspects of the legal system, to be an important determinant of the amount of FDI received, for countries that do receive FDI.

As richer data become available, the influence of more types of institutions can be examined and for a wider range of countries. Given the likelihood that the impact of institutions on FDI drops off once a certain level has been achieved, most interest has focused on examining the role of institutions on FDI into developing countries. Most estimates suggest that institutions are very important. Improving institutional quality from a low level to a high level could have as much of an impact on FDI as if suddenly the country shared a border with the investing country—a big change. It may be important to properly control for the correlation between per capita gross domestic product and FDI and for potential endogeneity of institutions (that FDI creates pressure for better institutions). In addition to institutions affecting FDI, some researchers have argued that FDI affects institutions, as will be discussed for the case of corruption in the next section.

Corruption Corruption is the misuse of public power or authority for private gain. Corruption tends to arise when governments control access to markets, so naturally corruption can matter for FDI. Wei (2000) established corruption's deterrent effect on FDI. Using data on bilateral investment from 12 source countries to 45 host countries, Wei finds that an increase in the corruption level in the host country leads to a reduction in inward FDI. An increase in the corruption level from that of Singapore to that of Mexico is estimated to have the same effect of deterring inward FDI as raising the tax rate by 50 percent. Additionally Wei finds that

U.S. investors are no more averse to corruption than average for investors from member countries of the Organisation for Economic Co-operation and Development (OECD).

Not just the level of corruption in a host country, but the degree to which it differs from the level in the source country, may matter for FDI. Habib and Zurawicki (2002) provide support for the negative impact on FDI of both the level of corruption in the host country and the absolute difference in the corruption level between the host and the source country. MNEs from a country with high degrees of corruption may be better able to deal with high levels of corruption in a host country than firms from a country with little corruption. The former firms are experienced in dealing with corruption, whereas the latter are accustomed to transparency. Of course, corruption may take many forms, and thus experience from one country may not fully translate to another. On the other hand, firms accustomed to dealing with bribery might be able to operate well in less corrupt environments, but even they may undergo some adjustment to the different environment. Especially when there is still some corruption, it may be hard for foreign firms to learn just where bribes are needed and where rules must be followed.

While many papers operate on the notion that corruption deters FDI, the opposite can be argued as well. In fast-growing countries with substantial bureaucracies, the ability of corruption to "grease the wheel" may be more important than the amount of the bribe required. In such situations, the bribe may be considered a small price to pay for cutting through many layers of red tape and speeding up approval. When weighing costs versus benefits, how big a bribe is required must be compared to how much improvement in speed or likelihood of approval is gained. The terms "helping hand" versus "grabbing hand" corruption have been used to distinguish corruption that positively affects FDI from that which negatively affects FDI (see Egger and Winner 2006). The fact that corruption on the whole seems to deter FDI suggests that corruption does more grabbing than helping.

In addition to the question of how corruption affects FDI there is also the question of how FDI might affect corruption. Under the U.S. Foreign Corrupt Practices Act of 1977, U.S. firms are not allowed to bribe (or give gifts to) foreign governments to gain favor in contracts, so FDI from the United States might be expected to push toward less corruption. Kwok and Tadesse (2006) propose three avenues through which MNEs may affect institutions in host countries. First, the regulatory pressure effect describes implications of the fact that foreign firms may be constrained to not pay bribes. Bribes may be against company norms, rules set by the source government, or conventions set by the global businesses community. Second, the demonstration effect is based on the notion that, like productivity, the tendency of MNEs to avoid corruption may spill over to other firms. When local firms deal with MNEs or hire some of their former workers, they can observe how business decisions are made in MNEs. The presence of MNEs should counter existing norms by demonstrating an alternative method of conducting business that can be more efficient. Finally, the professionalization effect relates to the likelihood that leaders (or future leaders) of host firms will acquire training in professional business practices (which discourage corrupt practices) and that these new practices will become socialized in younger generations.

One should recognize that the effect of corruption may be difficult to separate from other aspects of government infrastructure such as bureaucracy, as corruption and bureaucracy tend to be linked (corruption arises to cut through the bureaucracy). In addition to affecting whether a country receives FDI and how much FDI it receives, corruption could also affect the value foreign (or even domestic) firms are willing to pay when acquiring local firms. In general, corruption may be one of many dimensions a country may seek to improve in the hope of becoming a more attractive location for FDI.

Remaining Questions More work needs to be done on how firms adapt to environments plagued by corruption. Some evidence suggests that more firms may opt for joint ventures in the face of corruption. A local partner may be more experienced at dealing with corruption and the host government in general. What other strategies do (or should) firms use when operating in a corrupt environment? Similar to joint ventures, are firms more likely to opt for acquiring a local firm over greenfield investment (building a new plant) in corrupt environments? Is there evidence that firms adopt an expansion strategy in which experience in moderately corrupt countries helps prepare them to begin operations in more severely corrupt regimes? Do firms hire a larger proportion of local workers in more corrupt environments?

More work should also be done to address the variation in types of corruption. All corruption is not created equal. Are some forms of corruption more damaging to FDI than others? Some forms of corruption may act more like fixed costs, such as a bribe for approval to enter the market. Such corruption could be less distorting (as long as it is not prohibitive) than a bribe that is set in relation to number of employees, production, or profits. What evidence is there that bigger or more profitable firms are expected to pay larger bribes? In which situations are foreign firms especially exposed to corruption, and when are domestic firms just as bad off?

Kellenberg (2007) compares a policy of public input provision to a policy of subsidy incentives for attracting FDI. More analysis of this kind is needed, such as comparing a reduction in corruption or an improvement in government infrastructure to use of subsidies. One might like to know, due to corruption (alone), how much of a subsidy would Mexico have to pay to make it as attractive to FDI as Singapore? The next decade of research should bring us answers to such questions, and many more.

See also corruption; location theory

FURTHER READING

Cheng, Leonard K., and Yum K. Kwan. 2000. "What Are the Determinants of the Location of Foreign Direct Investment? The Chinese Experience." *Journal of International Economics* 51 (2): 379–400. Evidence that good infrastructure, measured as density of all roads, matters for FDI into Chinese regions.

Coughlin, Cletus C., Joseph V. Terza, and Vachira Arromdee. 1991. "State Characteristics and the Location of Foreign Direct Investment within the United States." *Review of Economics and Statistics* 73 (4): 675–83. Finds that more extensive transportation infrastructures were associated with increased FDI into U.S. states.

Egger, Peter, and Hannes Winner. 2006. "How Corruption Influences Foreign Direct Investment: A Panel Data Approach." *Economic Development and Cultural Change* 54 (2): 459–86. Argues that corruption deters FDI in developing but not developed countries and that the importance of corruption has declined over time.

Fung, K. C., Alicia Garcia-Herrero, Hitomi Iizaka, and Alan Siu. 2005. "Hard or Soft? Institutional Reforms and Infrastructure Spending as Determinants of Foreign Direct Investment." *Japanese Economic Review* 56 (4): 408–16. Demonstrates that soft infrastructure can be more important than hard infrastructure for attracting FDI to Chinese regions.

Globerman, Steven, and Daniel Shapiro. 2003. "Governance Infrastructure and U.S. Foreign Direct Investment." *Journal of International Business Studies* 34 (1): 19–39. Finds government infrastructure matters for whether a country receives any FDI and also for the amount of FDI received.

Habib, Mohsin, and Leon Zurawicki. 2002. "Corruption and Foreign Direct Investment." *Journal of International Business Studies* 33 (2): 291–307. Considers both the level of corruption and the absolute difference in the levels across countries.

Kellenberg, Derek K. 2007. "The Provision of Public Inputs and Foreign Direct Investment." *Contemporary Economic Policy* 25 (2): 170–84. Compares investment in public infrastructure to subsidies as methods for attracting FDI.

Kwok, Chuck C. Y., and Solomon Tadesse. 2006. "The MNC as an Agent of Change for Host-country Institutions: FDI and Corruption." *Journal of International Business Studies* 37 (6): 767–85. Considers three avenues through which FDI can deter corruption.

Wei, Shang-Jin. 2000. "How Taxing Is Corruption on International Investors?" *Review of Economics and Statistics* 82 (1): 1–11. Compares the deterrent effect of corruption to that of higher taxes, and compares the response of FDI from the United States to corruption to that typical for the OECD.

Wheeler, David, and Ashoka Mody 1992. "International Investment Location Decisions: The Case of U.S. Firms." *Journal of International Economics* 33 (1–2): 57–76. Finds that the quality of infrastructure is quite important for U.S. firms locating in developing countries, but not for developed country hosts.

AMY JOCELYN GLASS

■ **intangible assets**

The integration of the world economy has underlined the need for firms to exploit their intangible assets on a global scale. Firms' intangible assets include their stock of knowledge, which is related to ideas, research and development (R&D), patent and blueprints, scientific and technical workers, and management techniques. In addition, intangible assets consist of their stock of goodwill, which is associated with product quality reputation, trademarks, and brand names.

The empirical evidence shows that the growth in intangible assets has been a recent phenomenon. As emphasized by Griliches (1994), the source of economic growth and wealth lies no longer in the investment of physical, tangible assets but in the creation and use of intangible assets. The contribution of the latter is hard to measure due to lack of data and uniform definition concerning its measurement. There is, however, substantial anecdotal evidence that enterprises have increased their relative investment in intangible assets. The pace of intangible investment by U.S. private firms has risen sharply in recent decades. By the late 1990s, their investments in intangible assets were around 1 trillion dollars a year, which was about the same as expenditure on tangible assets (Nakamura 2001).

The traditional explanation of multinational enterprises (MNEs) rests on the existence of firm-specific intangible assets. These assets give MNEs offsetting advantages over foreign producers because they have the property of *joint inputs*. Relative to physical tangible assets, intangible assets are easier and cheaper to transfer to foreign subsidiaries. For instance, blueprints and patents are very costly to produce but once they are created, they can be supplied to any foreign subsidiaries without reducing their value or productivity. Investing in tangible assets typically involves fixed costs at the plant level, whereas investing in intangible assets involves fixed costs at the level of the firm.

The empirical evidence confirms that MNEs have a larger value of intangible assets relative to their market value (compared to other firms). Industries with a high proportion of multinational firms tend to be characterized by high levels of intangible assets (evidenced as substantial R&D and advertising expenditures relative to sales), new or sophisticated products, and high shares of skilled employment (Markusen 1995). Since the early 1990s, for instance, the stock of business services has risen ninefold, to reach 26 percent of total inward foreign direct investment (FDI) stock in services in 2002 (UNCTAD 2004).

Understanding the importance of intangible assets for FDI requires investigating their transferability to local firms and their impact on host economies.

Transferability of Knowledge-Based Assets
Transferring knowledge-based assets to local firms is quite different from transferring other intermediate inputs. Knowledge is not necessarily easily transferred, especially across firms. The reason is that knowledge-based assets are usually deeply embedded in the institutional and organizational contexts of their origins. Moreover, knowledge-based assets have a tacit component that is not codified and therefore is imperfectly transferable to local firms. For instance, production processes requiring highly specialized workers are usually transferred to subsidiaries rather than to other firms since licensing would entail costly training of local employees (Teece 1986).

The transmission of knowledge-based assets is subject to market failures such as the dilution of property rights. Product reengineering, for example, may allow the local firm to discover the tacit knowledge embedded in the new product and to start

a rival firm. In addition, the MNE might break the terms of the license and transfer the knowledge-based asset to a different local firm. The problem for the MNE is to design an optimal contract that preserves the value of its knowledge-based assets. This contract usually includes rent sharing with the local firm. If defection cannot be avoided, the MNE will prefer to internalize its assets in spite of higher setup costs.

The empirical evidence presented by Smith (2001) on U.S. firms' foreign operations shows that licensing is a more likely entry mode in markets characterized by stronger protection of intellectual property rights.

Transferability of Goodwill Assets The stock of knowledge is not the only intangible asset that is difficult to transfer to local firms. The transfer of goodwill assets such as reputation for quality can face severe problems if the local firm does not fully appropriate the returns from maintaining the MNE's brand reputation. Examples of industries where reputation is important include hotels and restaurants, consulting, and financial services. The reputation problem faced by MNEs is as follows. Consumers value quality and are willing to pay more if they believe that the firm is supplying high-quality products or services. The local firm may be tempted to compromise on products' quality to reduce costs. This strategy leads to higher short-term profit, but once consumers become disappointed with their purchases, the MNE may retaliate and purchase products from other suppliers.

The fact that foreign parties do not fully appropriate the returns from maintaining the MNE's reputation gives rise to FDI. The local firm does not internalize the costs to the global reputation of the MNE when it provides low-quality goods. This problem is why the MNE should design contracts that specify much more than prices. In practice, the usual method to achieve such a result is a franchise contract in which the local firm agrees on a complete business concept. The contract needs to ensure that the local firm provides a level of quality sufficient to maintain the reputation of the MNE. However, the franchising agreement will still not be sufficient to solve the reputation problem when efforts to maintain the quality of products and/or services are not fully verifiable. In this case, the MNE may prefer to set up its own subsidiary, which allows more effective incentive and control systems.

Intangible Assets and Spillovers to Foreign Economies Researchers have attempted to identify and empirically measure spillovers from MNEs' transfer of intangible assets to local firms. These spillovers may be positive or negative. On the one hand, MNEs may enable local firms to upgrade their technology, to the extent that they bring better business practices, technology, or management. On the other hand, MNEs may increase competition by attracting demand away from local firms. If economies of scale are important, the loss of demand will reduce the productivity of local firms by reducing the scale of their production.

Positive or negative spillovers may be direct, from firm to firm, through imitation of technology, managerial and organizational innovations, or competition. They can also be indirect through the labor market when specialized skilled workers from the MNE are complementary to workers in the local firm or when they move to rival firms. In either case, the ability of local firms to assimilate or value new knowledge, the so-called *absorptive capacity*, is crucial for obtaining significant benefits from FDI.

There is weak evidence for spillovers from MNEs. Positive spillovers from multinational firms are supported by casual evidence from many countries, but their existence and magnitude are difficult to establish empirically (UNCTAD 2001). Several studies have emphasized the role of local firms' absorptive capacity in explaining the lack of spillovers from multinational activities. This reasoning suggests that spillovers may not affect firms equally but may benefit only firms with high levels of absorptive capacity. The lack of strong empirical evidence for spillovers suggests also that multinational firms have succeeded in protecting their intangible assets.

In sum, intangible assets are vital to the incentives for MNEs to form and vital to the ability of MNEs to continue to prosper. Successful MNEs have valuable intangible assets, transfer the benefits of these in-tangibles to subsidiaries producing abroad, and protect their intangible assets by limiting the degree that the benefits spill over to rival firms.

See also foreign direct investment: the OLI framework; technology spillovers

FURTHER READING

Griliches, Zvi. 1994. "Productivity, R&D, and the Data Constraint." *American Economic Review* 84 (1): 1–23. An empirical analysis that questions the determinants of growth in light of the increase of investment in intangible assets such as R&D.

Markusen, James. 1995. "The Boundaries of Multinational Enterprises and the Theory of International Trade." *Journal of Economic Perspectives* 9 (2): 169–89. Survey of the ownership, location, and internalization advantage of MNEs that incorporates new theories of international trade.

Nakamura, Leonard. 2001. "What Is the U.S. Gross Investment in Intangibles? (At Least) One Trillion Dollars a Year!" Working Paper No. 01-15. Federal Reserve Bank of Philadelphia. Suggest an estimation of U.S. investment in intangible assets.

Smith, Pamela. 2001. "How Do Foreign Patent Rights Affect U.S. Exports, Affiliate Sales, and Licenses?" *Journal of International Economics* 55 (2): 411–39. An empirical study finding that stronger intellectual property rights protection leads to more licensing.

Teece, David. 1986. *The Multinational Corporation and the Resource Cost of International Technology Transfer.* Cambridge, MA: Ballinger. Analysis of knowledge transfer costs, market externalities, and the internalization of knowledge assets.

United Nations Conference on Trade and Development (UNCTAD). 2001. "Should Countries Promote Foreign Direct Investment?" G24 Discussion Paper Series No. 9. Geneva: UNCTAD. Determinants and impacts of spillovers from FDI and their policies implications.

———. 2004. "The Shift toward Services." *World Investment Report.* Geneva. UNCTAD. Available at http://www.unctad.org/en/docs/wir2004_en.pdf. Annual overview of trends in FDI, including a detailed analysis of FDI in intangible assets.

FARID TOUBAL

■ **integrated framework**
See trade-related capacity building

■ **intellectual property rights**

Intellectual property rights are legal devices designed to protect intellectual property, which can be broadly defined as a recognized ownership over the ideas, designs, inventions, or concepts created by a person or organization. Intellectual property rights are therefore instruments intended to ensure that the originators of intellectual property have control over its use.

Intellectual property rights relate to two broad categories of intellectual property: industrial property, and literary and artistic property. Industrial property can be protected by patents, utility models, industrial designs, trademarks, and geographical indications. Literary and artistic property protection may be provided by copyrights. Intellectual property rights may also be granted in the form of sui generis protection. Additionally, trade secrets offer an alternative way of providing protection to intellectual property.

Types of Intellectual Property Rights *Patents* allow an inventor to exclude all others from commercially exploiting his or her invention for a fixed period of time, usually 20 years. They apply both to novel products (such as new drugs) and to novel processes (such as a new method of producing an existing drug).

Utility models are also used to protect inventions in certain countries but are usually sought for less technically complex devices. The requirements for achieving protection under utility models are less stringent than the ones for achieving protection under patents, and the length of protection is also shorter for utility models.

Industrial designs protect the ornamental or aesthetic features (shape, pattern, color) of a useful article that is reproduced by industrial means.

Trademarks and service marks are used to protect a distinctive mark or name that identifies a product, service, or company.

Geographical indications are signs used on goods that originate from a particular geographical location and possess qualities or a reputation that are due to that location.

Copyrights protect the rights of creators of literary and artistic works (such as books, poems, music, paintings and sculptures, films) to communicate, display, perform, and make or sell copies of those works. The length of protection is usually the lifetime of the creator plus 50 to 70 years. Copyrights may also apply to technology-based works such as computer programs, electronic databases, and multimedia productions.

Sui generis protection refers to new categories of intellectual property rights that apply to forms of creative activities resulting from recent technology advances that do not fit into the standard categories of intellectual property. Computer software, layout design of integrated circuits, plant breeder's rights, and electronic transmission of databases or broadcasts are some examples.

Trade secrets are not intellectual property rights in the traditional sense. They provide protection to industrial property through legislation that deems it illegal to disclose or use proprietary information about production practices and processes that is considered commercially valuable for a company (ranging from a list of secret ingredients to customer lists). Trade secrets have no statutory time limit but the protection they offer may expire through learning by fair means, such as reverse engineering or reading public documents.

National and International Dimensions of Intellectual Property Rights Intellectual property rights are national in scope: legislation regarding intellectual property rights is enacted at the national level and is part of a country's legal system. Countries face a fundamental trade-off when designing a system of intellectual property rights. On the one hand, intellectual property rights should generate a sufficient incentive for invention and creation to occur by providing an effective means of protection to the rights of the originators of intellectual property. On the other hand, intellectual property rights should ensure proper diffusion and access to intellectual property, so that society as a whole benefits from public access to new ideas. For instance, by offering intellectual property protection through a patent, society has opted to create a temporary monopoly (or exclusive market) for the product protected under that patent. The presence of such monopoly imposes societal costs in terms of high prices and lower efficiency, but it also generates the incentives for invention to occur by guaranteeing higher profits to patent holders. Once a patent is granted, however, all technical information pertaining to that new product (or process) becomes publicly available for others to use in their own research activities. In this sense, intellectual property rights restrict the use of proprietary ideas in production, but patenting may foster their use by others in research. Therefore, the societal benefits derived from having access to this information may outweigh the costs imposed on society by the presence of a monopoly.

Economists explain this basic trade-off by thinking about intellectual property rights in terms of the provision of a public good. First, intellectual property is nonrivalrous, that is, one person's use of it does not reduce another person's use. Therefore the marginal cost of providing access to the information embodied in intellectual property to another user is very small and has the potential to generate benefits to society as a whole. For example, the patenting of a plasma display panel can generate positive benefits (or externalities) through technological spillovers, since all the technical details pertaining to such invention can now be accessed by other researchers at a negligible cost. Second, intellectual property may be nonexcludable by private means. That is, it may be impossible to preclude others from using the information without authorization. This generates what economists refer to as a free-rider problem: without protection of intellectual property, no one will wish to bear the costs of generating it.

Most legal systems try to balance these two goals of providing financial incentives for innovation and providing society with access to new ideas and inventions, which is a challenging task. If intellectual property rights were too weak, plasma display panels might have never been created. If intellectual property rights were too strong, the spillover benefits associated with such an invention might never sufficiently spread across society. Note that this basic trade-off presents static and dynamic considerations. By bearing the static costs of protecting intellectual property today, society may enjoy the dynamic gains of faster innovation and growth in the future.

Each form of intellectual property right is designed with these goals in mind. When patents are granted, society gains full access to the technical information regarding a new product or process, and the fixed length of protection minimizes the costs of providing access to this product or process at prices higher than marginal costs. Copyright protection allows exceptions under the "fair use doctrine," which defines activities that can make use of protected works in the interests of educational, scientific, and technical advances. It is less clear how trade secrets can provide net benefits to society since they generate market power without divulging information. Economists have started to recognize, however, that protecting trade secrets may also generate important incentives for innovation, for example, by reducing incentives for research and development patent races or by facilitating reverse engineering.

Additional considerations about designing a system of intellectual property protection are relevant to the case of an open economy. For countries that are net exporters of intellectual property, large losses can occur from the imitation and use of their innovations in foreign countries with weak intellectual property rights. For countries that are net importers of products subject to intellectual property protection, the decision to provide or even strengthen intellectual property rights generates static costs such as higher prices for imported goods or technology, transfer of monopoly rents to foreign firms or foreign countries, and loss of employment in local firms whose production is imitative in nature. And to the extent that imitative activities may generate technological spillovers and affect a country's growth rate, intellectual property protection may impose dynamic costs in terms of reduced access to international technologies and slower growth in the long run.

Stronger intellectual property rights may also result in dynamic welfare gains. For instance, the transfer of monopoly rents to foreign firms may result in innovation that is better suited to domestic needs than to foreign needs. Additionally, stronger intellectual property rights can facilitate technological diffusion, innovation, and growth by generating incentives for trade in knowledge-intensive goods, foreign direct investment (FDI), and licensing agreements. A key issue in evaluating the net impact of these trade-offs for an open economy is a country's overall technical potential. If the local economy does not possess the infrastructure and know-how to reproduce new technologies through imitation or reverse engineering, weaker intellectual property protection would not generate the positive effects of technological diffusion. In this case, stronger intellectual property rights might be more desirable since they provide better opportunities for formal technology transfer through access to knowledge-intensive goods, foreign patents, joint ventures, and licensing agreements. Another important consideration is market size; foreign firms may not have enough incentives to engage in production targeted to domestic needs if the size of the local market is relatively small.

Since intellectual property rights are national in scope, the level of protection provided by such instruments (and the level of enforcement of such protection) can vary widely across countries, with the largest variations occurring between developed and developing countries. These discrepancies exist not only with respect to the de jure level of protection, but also with respect to the de facto enforcement of the existing legislation. This issue becomes especially important and controversial as owners of intellectual property seek to exploit international markets. The debate is relevant not only for individuals or organizations that possess ownership of intellectual property but also for national policy, since a country's level of intellectual property rights may affect its volumes of international trade and FDI flows and its levels of innovation and economic growth.

The International Debate Regarding Intellectual Property Rights The need to protect industrial property at the international level was first recognized in the Paris Convention for the Protection of Industrial Property in 1883, and later extended to literary and artistic property in the Berne Convention for the Protection of Literary and Artistic Works in 1886. These treaties, which constitute the core foundation of the World Intellectual Property Organization (WIPO), established a system in which inventors or artists could seek protection for their work in other countries on terms no less favorable than the terms available to the nationals of those countries. Note that this would imply that a U.S. patent holder, seeking to extend protection of her intellectual property to other countries, would still need to apply for a patent in each country separately. The treaties, however, guaranteed that she would be treated just like any other citizen of that country. Since then, the international legislation regarding intellectual property rights has undergone several changes primarily driven by two important forces: technological progress and globalization. First, technological progress has required the adaptation of intellectual property rights instruments in key areas such as integrated circuits, computer software, and biotechnology inventions. Second, the globalization process has facilitated the diffusion of intellectual property across international borders, increasing the controversy over discrepancies in intellectual property rights across countries.

The current system of global intellectual property rights encompasses various intergovernmental treaties administered by the WIPO, as well as intellectual property rights legislation that is part of bilateral, regional, or international trade agreements. The most important and controversial of such agreements is the Agreement on Trade-Related Aspects of Intellectual Property Rights (TRIPS), which came into effect in 1995 under the auspices of the World Trade Organization. In contrast to the Paris Convention, the TRIPS agreement imposes minimum standards of protection, which are either in line with or exceed the practices of most industrialized countries, and establishes a dispute settlement mechanism to enforce these minimum standards.

As intellectual property rights become a standard feature in many international trade agreements, the need for a better understanding of how these rules will affect countries becomes a pressing issue in economic research. Recent theoretical and empirical research has focused on trying to better understand the specific channels through which intellectual property rights might affect innovation and economic growth, such as international trade flows, FDI, and licensing.

Economic theory suggests an ambiguous relationship between intellectual property rights and international trade flows. On the one hand, stronger intellectual property rights raises demand for the protected goods and could lead to increased sales. On the other hand, stronger intellectual property protection also augments the market power of foreign patent holders, allowing them to charge higher prices, which could generate reduced sales. Empirical studies in this area are therefore needed to settle this question.

Research undertaken so far suggests that stronger intellectual property rights have a positive impact on overall trade volumes, but are not relevant to trade in high-technology goods. Several explanations have been offered for this puzzle. It is possible that high-technology trade flows are less responsive to intellectual property rights because those products are simply harder to imitate than low-tech products. It is also conceivable that intellectual property rights matter the most to middle-income large developing countries, which are more likely to possess the technical capabilities to undertake reverse engineering. Finally, high-technology firms may decide to serve foreign markets through FDI and licensing.

The theoretical ambiguity with respect to the impact of intellectual property rights also extends to FDI and licensing. Empirical studies suggest that intellectual property rights are less important in attracting FDI than other factors, such as a country's infrastructure or overall business climate. Stronger intellectual property rights, however, are important in stimulating formal transfers of technology, especially in the case of large developing countries with strong abilities to absorb technology. This result also holds for international licensing flows, since stronger intellectual property rights reduce the costs of establishing and monitoring licensing contracts.

Economic research in all these areas relies on national rankings of intellectual property rights, mainly the Ginarte and Park (1997) index. This is a time-varying index of intellectual property rights protection based on five categories of patent law: extent of coverage, membership in international patent agreements, provisions for loss of protection, de jure enforcement mechanisms, and the duration of protection. The index provides extensive coverage in terms of countries and years; however, one of its main drawbacks is the fact that it does not account for the de facto enforcement of the legislation.

Other Controversial Issues The debate over intellectual property rights is further complicated by ongoing deliberations regarding such critical issues as parallel imports, compulsory licensing, and traditional knowledge.

Parallel Imports Parallel imports occur when price differences between countries, generated by disparities in intellectual property protection, allow international arbitrage to take place. Consider a situation in which legitimate goods (as opposed to knock-offs) are placed in circulation in a certain market under legislation that protects intellectual property. If the wholesale price of such goods is low enough and transportation costs are not prohibitive, it may be possible for an independent trader to profit by selling those goods in other markets in which intellectual property rights are weaker. Parallel imports are not prohibited under international legislation (TRIPS), and their legality depends on whether or not national laws confine protection to the country in which the protected goods are first sold. If protection is exhausted at the international level, firms fully lose control over a product's distribution once the product has been put for sale in any location. In that case, markets are open to parallel imports from foreign countries. Economists have shown that the effects of limiting parallel imports on a country's welfare are theoretically ambiguous and depend on the underlying motivations to pursue parallel trading in the first place.

Compulsory Licensing Compulsory licensing refers to a situation in which the government of the importing country has the legal authority to force the foreign holder of a patent to license production to a local firm as a condition of patent protection. This practice is allowed by international legislation (TRIPS) only under extreme circumstances, such as public health emergencies.

The regulation of parallel imports and the use of compulsory licensing have been critical issues in various international forums on providing access to medicines in developing countries.

Traditional Knowledge Most research in economics has focused on patents and copyrights, ignoring questions related to traditional knowledge. Traditional knowledge generally refers to the wisdom, knowledge, and teachings that are long-standing traditions of certain regional, indigenous, or local communities. These traditions can be expressed through various means, such as stories, folklore, rituals, and songs. The controversy over the protection of traditional knowledge has its roots in the 1992 Convention on Biological Diversity, which recognized the value of traditional knowledge in protecting species, ecosystems, and landscapes in language that contradicts international intellectual property agreements, especially the TRIPS agreement. Protecting traditional knowledge requires a sui generis type of protection and is a particularly important issue in developing countries, which have objected, for example, to patenting of traditional uses of medicinal plants.

Future Concerns The scope and pace of globalization, as well as technological progress, will ensure that intellectual property rights continue to play an important role in negotiations regarding international trade agreements. Intellectual property rights will also remain an important issue in designing domestic policies, especially in developing countries, since they have the potential to affect important macroeconomic variables such as a country's growth rate, volume of international trade, or FDI and licensing flows. Economists' efforts to better understand the precise mechanisms through which intellectual property rights affect these variables are therefore essential in facilitating the resolution of international disputes over intellectual property protection. But this research effort should also try to improve existing measures of cross-country comparisons involving intellectual property rights, and focus on less explored issues, such as whether and how to provide intellectual property protection to traditional knowledge.

See also access to medicines; Agreement on Trade-Related Aspects of Intellectual Property Rights (TRIPS); Convention on Biological Diversity; foreign direct investment (FDI); intellectual property rights and foreign direct investment; World Intellectual Property Organization; World Trade Organization

FURTHER READING

Finger, J. Michael, and Philip Schuler. 2003. *Poor People's Knowledge: Promoting Intellectual Properties in Developing Countries.* Washington, DC: World Bank and Oxford University Press. Addresses questions of traditional knowledge, access to genetic resources, and other topics that are increasingly relevant to policymakers in developing countries.

Fink, Carsten, and Keith Maskus, eds. 2005. *Intellectual Property and Development: Lessons from Recent Economic Research.* Washington, DC: World Bank and Oxford University Press. This book provides a compilation of articles on various controversial issues related to intellectual property rights.

Ginarte, Juan Carlos, and Walter G. Park. 1997. "Determinants of Patent Rights: A Cross-National Study." *Research Policy* 26 (3): 283–301. Provides details on the criteria used to construct the Ginarte-Park index.

Maskus, Keith. 2000. *Intellectual Property Rights in the Global Economy.* Washington, DC: Institute for International Economics. Even though the main focus of this book is the TRIPS agreement, chapters 3, 4, and 5 offer a broad overview of the economics of intellectual property rights and their impact on the world economy.

Owen, Lippert. 1999. *Competitive Strategies for the Protection of Intellectual Property.* Vancouver, Canada: Fraser

Institute. Provides a compilation of articles that relate to the many facets of designing a system of intellectual property rights.

PATRICIA HIGINO SCHNEIDER

■ intellectual property rights and foreign direct investment

The impact of intellectual property rights (IPRs) on foreign direct investment (FDI) plays a central role in the debate between developed and developing countries over intellectual property rights protection. Many developing countries have begun to reform their IPR regimes in response to the Agreement on Trade-Related Aspects of Intellectual Property Rights (TRIPS) and pressure from developed countries. As multinational enterprises (MNEs) strive to make use of their knowledge assets beyond national borders, they have made IPRs an issue of multilateral negotiations. Governments of developing countries also believe that agreeing to TRIPS ultimately would allow them wider access to agricultural and textile markets in developed countries. In addition, business interests within many developing countries have encouraged their governments to adopt stronger IPR protection in order to protect their own innovations tailored to the domestic market. Some observers also argue that stronger IPRs protection can encourage imports, inward FDI, and technology licensing, all of which can lead to an increase in technology transfer.

Effect of IPRs on Technology Transfer and Innovation Technology is fundamental to economic development, and its importance for raising productivity and living standards has long been recognized. Innovation and technological progress can raise productivity through the introduction of new goods, the improvement of existing goods, and reduction in the costs of production. Resources for innovations tend to be highly concentrated in a small number of advanced countries, however. For developing countries whose firms are not at the technological frontier, international technology transfer is important for promoting development. Some transfers occur between willing partners in formal trans-actions, but much comes through informal non-market transactions or spillovers. One of the transfer channels is trade in goods and services, with imports of goods having the potential to transfer knowledge through reverse engineering and cross-border learning of production methods and product design. Another channel is FDI, particularly inward FDI, where MNEs deploy advanced technology to their subsidiaries that may be diffused to host-country firms. Licensing, which involves the purchase of production and distribution rights for a product and the knowledge required to make effective use of these rights, is another channel for technology diffusion. Joint ventures combine many of the properties of FDI and licensing, and hence will also involve technology transfer. Informal channels of technology diffusion include imitation, movement of personnel from one firm to another taking with them specific knowledge of their original firm's technologies, data in patent applications, and the migration of people. There is no formal compensation to the original owner of the technology transferred. In this case, IPRs clearly play a role.

Intellectual properties have the characteristic of a public good: they are available on a nonexclusive basis. It is not possible to prevent others from applying knowledge even without the authorization of its creator. They are also nonrivalrous in use (additional parties can benefit from them at zero additional cost). Once an innovation has been created, its nonrival character suggests that benefits will be maximized if its use is free to all at marginal cost. Although a policy of free access might yield benefits in the short run, it will damage the incentive for further innovation. When the new technology is imitated, it reduces the potential profits of the original inventor and potentially removes the incentive to engage in innovative activities. Since imitation has lower costs than innovation, imitators have the advantage over innovators unless the latter can restrict access to their innovation. This characteristic provides the argument for strong IPRs protection. In the absence of IPRs, the market for intellectual properties would fail or yield an inefficient supply of output. As to the connection to FDI and trade, many producers of intellectual output are engaged in both domestic and foreign markets. Risks of unauthorized copying and imitation exist both at home and abroad. Thus in regions where IPRs are weak, incentives to market via trade or FDI might be weak since the innovating firm's ability to appropriate rents is threatened. Moreover, an infringement of IPRs may adversely affect incentives to innovate and produce and thereby affect the potential to export and invest abroad.

Effect of IPRs on Imports, FDI, and Licensing
In determining the impact of IPRs on FDI, it is useful to rely on the widely accepted ownership-location-internalization (OLI) framework by Dunning (1993). When selling its products abroad, a firm is at least initially disadvantaged relative to local producers. Thus, to compete effectively with indigenous firms, a foreign producer must possess some advantages. Ownership advantage explains that MNEs must have assets that are unique to the firms, which usually take the form of new technologies, know-how, reputation for quality, or brand name. Ownership advantages assure a firm's ability to enter the host country's market. Location advantages are needed for firms to locate business abroad. This could be in the form of lower transportation cost, avoiding tariffs, lower input prices, lower standards and regulations, and access to the distribution markets. Internalization advantage gives the incentive to the MNEs to retain full control over the production process rather than to license their knowledge assets to local firms in a foreign country. This advantage covers the costs from license contract breaching, as well as control over the quality and reputation of the MNEs' products.

As mentioned earlier, MNEs have several options to exploit their knowledge assets. Apart from FDI, international trade and cross-border licensing represent the most important channels to transfer technology to the host countries. Hence, according to the OLI framework, IPRs protection should have an impact on the relative attractiveness of the three modes. Weak IPRs protection increases the probability of imitation, which erodes a firm's ownership advantages and makes a host country a less attractive location for foreign investors. An inadequate IPRs regime, therefore, deters FDI and encourages exporting. At the same time, a weak IPRs system increases the benefits of internalization since it is associated with a greater risk of the licensee's breaching the contract and acting in direct competition with the seller; this improves the attractiveness of FDI while discouraging licensing. Thus the overall relationship between the level of IPRs protection and FDI can be ambiguous.

Other theories conclude that the impact of IPRs protection on FDI varies by industries. MNEs are more likely to undertake FDI rather than licensing when they have a complex technology and highly differentiated products and when the costs of transferring technology through licensing are high (Horstmann and Markusen 1987). In such circumstances stronger IPRs, by reducing the risks of technology leakage, may increase the extent of licensing (Yang and Maskus 2001), thus reducing the need for FDI. For industries where technologies are relatively easy to imitate, however, we would expect more attention to be paid to the strength of IPRs protection. As such, the IPRs regime is likely to be important for sectors such as drugs, cosmetics, and health care products; chemicals; machinery, and equipment; and electrical equipment (Smarzynska 2004).

The concern about the IPRs regime also depends on the purpose of an investment project, being the highest in the case of R&D facilities and the lowest for projects focusing exclusively on sales and distribution (Mansfield 1994). This difference is expected given the nature and function of IPRs, which center on the ability to appropriate. In industries where firms have alternative means to appropriate the returns to their investments, the firms may forgo seeking IPRs and rely on other forms of protection. Other methods of protecting their knowledge assets include: (1) education and incubation of local innovators: for example, Microsoft is helping China develop its local software industry; (2) R&D strategies: firms increase their R&D to increase their lead time, sales, and services because litigation is slow, costly, and uncertain (some of them add anticounterfeiting features to prevent imitation); (3) other business strategies: working with the imitators, lower prices on products in developing countries, and bundling products with services. These possibilities might explain why FDI in certain industries is found to be insignificantly affected by IPRs.

Empirical evidence on the relationship between IPRs protection and FDI is mixed. Lee and Mansfield (1996) find positive relationship between the two in 14 developing host countries, while Primo Braga and Fink (1998) do not obtain statistically significant results. When considering the simultaneous effects of IPRs on three entry modes (export, FDI, and licensing), Smith (2001) found that strong IPRs promote licensing more than FDI but have no impact on exports, while Maskus, Saggi, and Puttitanun (2005) found that strong IPRs result in a higher probability of FDI relative to licensing.

The inconsistency of empirical results might be due to the crude measure of IPRs protection. The measurement problems are common in proxy for the IPRs protection such as national patent indexes of Rapp and Rozek (1990) or Ginarte and Park (1997). While it might be relatively easy to classify relevant laws and regulations on the books (such as coverage and patent length), actual enforcement is very difficult to judge objectively. Moreover these measures capture only overall countrywide variations in the protection of intellectual property in a single national index, ignoring the cross-industry differences in effective protection.

Conflicts between Developed and Developing Countries over IPRs Strengthening the IPRs regime has been pushed aggressively by the United States and other major industrialized countries. These developed countries tend to opt for relatively strong IPRs systems, with the aim of encouraging creative activities and innovations that are seen as an important source of long-run economic growth.

Developing countries, on the other hand, argue that stronger IPRs could limit the local imitation of new technologies, reduce the supplies of products, and increase the prices of new goods. Hence the majority of developing countries have opted for weak IPRs protection, if any, as a way of allowing the rapid diffusion of knowledge through imitation as a sig-

nificant source of technological development. Providing stronger IPRs protection is seen as shifting profits from domestic imitative firms to foreign firms and reducing outputs of new technologies to the monopoly level, and hence increasing prices in the domestic economy rather than encouraging domestic innovative activity.

The counterargument is that stronger IPRs protection can help reward creativity and risk-taking even in developing economies, while weak IPRs protection can keep developing countries dependent on dynamically inefficient firms that rely on counterfeiting and imitation. It is also argued that the lack of technology transfers to the developing countries via FDI is due to the inadequacy of the IPRs protection and that such protection would promote FDI.

Nevertheless, economics studies showed that the net welfare effect of the host country depends on the host country's characteristics. In a small country where production and innovation capabilities are limited, higher IPRs standard likely will improve welfare through higher access to products that would not be available otherwise. If a country has greater production and imitation capability, but limited innovative capacity, higher standards of protection will hurt local producers and result in lower welfare for the economy. However, as innovative capacity improves, a country will gain from higher IPRs standard (Chen and Puttitanun 2006). In sum, strengthening IPRs protection has different welfare implication depending on the characteristics of each country.

See also Agreement on Trade-Related Aspects of Intellectual Property Rights (TRIPS); foreign direct investment (FDI); foreign direct investment and innovation, imitation; foreign direct investment and international technology transfer; foreign market entry; fragmentation; internalization theory; international investment agreements; location theory; multinational enterprises; technology licensing; technology spillovers; trade-related investment measures (TRIMs)

FURTHER READING

Chen, Yongmin, and Thitima Puttitanun. 2005. "Intellectual Property Rights and Innovation in Developing

Countries." *Journal of Development Economics* 78: 474–93. The first formalized model showing a U-shaped relationship between development level and IPRs.

Dunning, John H. 1993. *Multinational Enterprises and the Global Economy.* Suffolk, UK: Addison-Wesley. This seminal work explains advantages needed to become a successful MNE.

Ginarte, Juan C., and Walter Park. 1997. "Determinants of Patent Rights: A Cross National Study." *Research Policy* 26: 283–301. Developed a widely used IPRs index that expanded on the work by Rapp and Rozek.

Horstmann, Ignatius, and James R. Markusen. 1987. "Licensing versus Direct Investment: A Model of Internalization by the Multinational Enterprise." *Canadian Journal of Economics* 20: 464–81. First paper to formalize the notion of internalization incentives for multinational firms.

Lee, Jeoung-Yeon, and Edwin Mansfield. 1996. "Intellectual Property Protection and U.S. Foreign Direct Investment." *The Review of Economics and Statistics* 78: 181–86. Uses data from a survey of 100 U.S. firms in 1991 to assess the importance of IPRs for investment in 14 countries.

Mansfield, Edwin. 1994. "Intellectual Property Protection, Foreign Direct Investment, and Technology Transfer." Discussion Paper No. 19. Washington, DC: International Finance Corporation. Survey evidence from 100 U.S. firms showing that IPRs influence FDI decisions only for certain industries.

Maskus, Keith E., Kamal Saggi, and Thitima Puttitanun. 2005. "Patent Rights and International Technology Transfer through Direct Investment and Licensing." In *International Public Goods and Transfer of Technology under a Globalized Intellectual Property Regime,* edited by Keith E. Maskus and Jerome H. Reichman. Cambridge: Cambridge University Press, 265–81. A theoretical model and empirical evidence showed the tradeoff between FDI and licensing.

Primo Braga, Carlos A., and Carsten Fink. 1998. "The Relationship between Intellectual Property Rights and Foreign Direct Investment." *Duke Journal of Comparative and International Law* 9: 163–87. An often-cited article reviewed implications of IPRs on FDI and presented empirical analysis that showed no significant relationship between the two.

Rapp, Richard, and Richard Rozek. 1990. "Benefits and Costs of Intellectual Property Protection in Developing Countries." *Journal of World Trade* 24: 75–102. The first paper to develop an IPRs index rating the patent laws.

Smarzynska, Beata. 2004. "The Composition of Foreign Direct Investment and Protection of Intellectual Property Rights: Evidence from Transition Economies." *European Economic Review* 48: 39–62. Examines whether IPRs affect composition of FDI flows for 24 transition countries in 1995.

Smith, Pamela J. 2001. "How Do Foreign Patent Rights Affect U.S. Exports, Affiliate Sales, and Licenses?" *Journal of International Economics* 55: 411–40. First empirical analysis that takes into account the simultaneous decision of multinational firms in choosing an entry mode.

Yang, Guifang, and Keith E. Maskus. 2001. "Intellectual Property Rights, Licensing, and Innovation in an Endogenous Product-Cycle Model." *Journal of International Economics* 53: 169–87. The theoretical model showed importance of patent laws in reducing the licensing cost.

THITIMA PUTTITANUN

■ Inter-American Development Bank

See regional development banks

■ interest parity conditions

Interest parity conditions are no-arbitrage profit conditions for financial capital. When such conditions hold, it is infeasible for investors to obtain higher returns by borrowing or lending. Hence, in principle, interest parity conditions define theoretical linkages between interest rates and exchange rates between countries.

The easiest way to understand parity conditions is to consider how a typical investor can save in different locations. Suppose the home currency is a dollar, and the foreign currency is a euro. Further assume that a forward market exists. A forward contract allows an investor to enter into an agreement this period to exchange currencies k periods hence at a forward rate F known today. Then the investor can either save at home, receiving interest rate i, or save abroad, converting by the exchange rate S, receiving the foreign interest rate i^*, and then converting back to home currency by the forward rate F obtaining at time t for a trade at time $t+1$.

$$(1+i) \qquad versus \qquad (1+i_t^*) \times \frac{F_{t,t+1}}{S_t}$$

If the gross return on the left is greater than that on the right, then investors will place their capital in the home country; if it is less, then investors will place their capital abroad. With infinite amounts of capital moving in search of the highest return (and in this example, there is no risk in nominal terms), these returns will be equalized.

$$(1+i) = (1+i_t^*) \times \frac{F_{t,t+1}}{S_t} \qquad (1)$$

After manipulation,

$$\frac{(i-i^*)}{(1+i_t^*)} = \frac{F_{t,t+1} - S_t}{S_t} \qquad (2)$$

This condition is called "covered interest rate parity," reflecting the fact that investors are "covered" against nominal uncertainty by way of the forward market.

If the forward rate is equal to the future spot rate, such that $F_{t,t+1} = S_{t,t+1}^e$, then (2) becomes:

$$\frac{(i-i^*)}{(1+i_t^*)} = \frac{S_{t,t+1}^e - S_t}{S_t} \qquad (3)$$

where the e superscript denotes "expected." Equation (3) is termed *uncovered interest rate parity*. This expression holds when investors do not require compensation for the uncertainty associated with trading currencies in the future. It states that *expected* nominal returns are equalized across borders in common currency terms.

When interest rates are low, the following log approximations are often used for equations (2) and (3).

$$(i_t - i_t^*) = f_{t,t+1} - s_t \qquad (2')$$
$$(i_t - i_t^*) = s_{t,t+1}^e - s_t \qquad (3')$$

where f and s are the logs of the forward and spot rates, respectively.

Frankel (1991) has labeled condition (2) holding as characterizing perfect capital mobility, while condition (3) is associated with perfect capital substitutability. These terms arise from the view that if (2) does not hold, there must be some sort of impediment—capital controls or the threat thereof—to the free flow of financial capital. But even if capital is free to move, investors may still respond to risk; that response to risk might drive a wedge between the expected spot and forward rates. When investors are risk-neutral in nominal terms, then investors will treat capital (say debt instruments issued in different currencies) as perfectly substitutable.

The conditions just discussed pertain to financial capital. In order to consider the mobility of physical capital, one has to bring into play the prices of commodities. Integration of goods markets are often defined as relative purchasing power parity (PPP) holding. Ex ante relative PPP can be written as:

$$s_{t,t+1}^e - s_t = (p_{t,t+1}^e - p_t) - (p_{t,t+1}^{*e} - p_t^*) \qquad (4)$$

where p is the log price level. Equation 4 states that expected depreciation equals the expected inflation differential. Combining (4) with the uncovered interest rate parity condition (3′) leads to real interest parity.

$$i_t - (p_{t,t+1}^e - p_t) = i_t^* - (p_{t,t+1}^{*e} - p_t^*) \qquad (5)$$

This says that the expected rate of return on capital, expressed in physical units, is equalized across borders. To the extent that in neoclassical models the marginal product of capital equals the real interest rate, this condition is equivalent to the equalization of marginal product of capital equalized across borders.

Covered Interest Parity Assessed For developed economies since the dismantling of capital controls, covered interest parity holds fairly well. It should be noted that most tests are conducted using offshore rates, in which case (2) is sometimes termed *closed interest parity*, although the term *covered interest parity* is often used to encompass this concept.

Early tests were conducted by Frenkel and Levich (1975). They found that, after accounting for transactions costs, covered interest parity held for three-month horizons. Offshore rates sometimes diverge from onshore rates, so that the findings of covered interest parity are somewhat weaker.

The question of whether covered interest parity holds for longer horizons is an open one. Popper (1993) concludes that covered interest differentials at long maturities are not appreciably greater than those for short (up to one year) maturities. This is a surprising result given that there are likely a number of regulatory impediments that would tend to introduce frictions into the arbitrage process.

Prior to the dismantling of capital controls, and in many emerging markets today, covered interest parity is unlikely to hold. In other words, covered interest differentials could be interpreted as political risk, associated with the possibility of governmental authorities placing restrictions on deposits located in different jurisdictions (clearly this is not relevant when all the deposits are offshore). Aliber (1973) is credited with this interpretation, while Dooley and Isard (1980) provided empirical estimates for the deutsche mark/dollar rate.

The Empirical Evidence for Uncovered Interest Parity Uncovered interest parity (UIP) is a more difficult condition to test, essentially because expected exchange rate changes are unobservable. In the literature, most tests of UIP are actually joint tests of UIP and the rational expectations hypothesis, that is, that ex post realizations of the exchange rate are an unbiased measure of the ex ante exchange rate, namely, $s^e_{t,t+1} = E(s_{t+1}|I_t)$. This assumption combined with equation (2′) yields this standard regression equation, sometimes called the Fama equation (Fama 1984):

$$s_{t+1} - s = \beta_0 + \beta_1(f_{t,t+1} - s_t) + v_{t+1} \qquad (6)$$

Or by virtue of covered interest parity holding,

$$s_{t+1} - s = \beta_0 + \beta_1(i_t - i^*_t) + v_{t+1} \qquad (7)$$

where under the joint null hypothesis v_{t+1} is a mean zero error unpredictable using past information, and $\beta_1 = 1$.

The evidence in favor of this joint hypothesis of UIP and rational expectations is quite weak. The regression of the ex post change of the spot exchange rate on either the forward discount (in equation 6) or the interest differential (in equation 7) typically yields a slope coefficient estimate that is not only different from unity, but in fact negative and different from zero at conventional levels of statistical significance. This is true for reserve currencies (the U.S. dollar, the yen, the Swiss franc, the deutschemark, the franc, or the euro) at horizons up to a year. It is also true for some emerging market currencies (see Frankel and Poonawala 2006). One interesting characteristic of these regressions is that, although the coefficients are typically different from zero in a statistical sense, the proportion of total variation explained is typically very small.

At longer horizons (3, 5, and 10 years) the evidence is more supportive of the combined UIP–rational expectations hypothesis. Chinn and Meredith (2004) document that estimates of the β_1 coefficient are usually not significantly different from the posited value of unity at 5- and 10-year horizons. The finding that the joint hypothesis of UIP and rational expectations holds better at long horizons than at short appears to be robust. Nonetheless, some caution is necessary here. Consider regressions involving 10-year interest differentials; by 2003, there would be only three nonoverlapping observations available per currency. Interestingly, Chaboud and Wright (2005) find that UIP also holds at extremely short horizons of a few minutes.

Other interesting results pertain to periods of extreme market turmoil. Flood and Rose (2002), following their 1996 work, find that UIP holds better in recent times when the sample encompasses successful attacks on currency pegs. Nonetheless, they still find lots of heterogeneity in experiences with UIP.

A different perspective on UIP is provided by dropping the rational expectations hypothesis.

A new area of research involves an investigation of whether UIP holds for emerging markets. Bansal and Dahlquist (2000) found that there was a basic asymmetry in whether UIP holds. In particular, they find that when the U.S. interest rate is lower than foreign country rates, UIP holds, while UIP fails to hold when the U.S. rate is higher. They also find that idiosyncratic factors, such as the gross domestic product per capita of the foreign country, are important in determining the degree of failure of UIP to hold.

Using the forward discount instead of interest differentials, Frankel and Poonawala (2006) find that there is substantial heterogeneity in the results. What matters importantly is the exchange rate regime: highly managed exchange rate regimes are associated with currencies that exhibit greater deviations from UIP.

Real Interest Parity Measured If UIP does not seem to hold at short horizons, it seems unlikely that real interest parity, described as exact equalization of real interest rates, would hold. One could, however, still test the weaker condition that movements in real rates in one country would be met by one-for-one real movements in other countries.

The key difficulty with testing this condition, like that with testing UIP, is that market expectations are not directly observable. Hence, one can conduct only joint tests for real interest parity. In Fujii and Chinn (2001), real interest rates are calculated using a variety of proxy measures of expected inflation: ex post inflation, and inflation predicted using lagged values of inflation models. Both approaches are consistent with rational expectations. They find that the real interest parity holds with different strength at different horizons. As in numerous previous studies (Cumby and Obstfeld 1984; Mark 1985), the real interest parity (RIP) hypothesis is decisively rejected with short horizon data. At 5- to 10-year horizons, however, the empirical evidence becomes far more supportive and in some cases the RIP hypothesis is not rejected. In general, RIP, *up to a constant*, holds better at long horizons than at short horizons. These results are robust to alternative ways of modeling expected inflation rates.

In recent years, several countries, including the United Kingdom, the United States, France, and Canada, have begun issuing inflation-indexed debt securities. These are marketable securities whose principal is adjusted by changes in the price level (usually the consumer price index). The principal increases with the inflation rate so that the real return can be directly observed. A cursory investigation re-

veals that there is no evidence of equalization. Moreover, although there is some covariation, it is not anywhere near one for one. The thinness of the markets and the differences in the maturities of the relevant debt instruments, however, make strong conclusions in either direction difficult.

See also capital mobility; exchange rate regimes; exchange rate volatility; forward premium puzzle; peso problem; purchasing power parity; reserve currency; sovereign risk; speculation

FURTHER READING

Aliber, Robert. 1973. "The Interest Parity Theorem: A Reinterpretation." *Journal of Political Economy* 81: 1451–59. An early formalization of the idea that political risk—the possibility of the imposition of capital controls or regulations—might drive a wedge between observed returns.

Bansal, Ravi, and Magnus Dahlquist. 2000. "The Forward Premium Puzzle: Different Tales from Developed and Emerging Economies." *Journal of International Economics* 51: 115–44. Documents some stylized facts regarding interest rate differentials and changes in exchange rates for a wide set of currencies.

Chaboud, Alain, and Jonathan Wright. 2005. "Uncovered Interest Parity: It Works, but Not for Long." *Journal of International Economics* 66 (2): 349–62. Demonstrates that uncovered interest rate parity holds at extremely short horizons of several minutes.

Chinn, Menzie D. 2006. "The (Partial) Rehabilitation of Interest Rate Parity: Longer Horizons, Alternative Expectations and Emerging Markets." *Journal of International Money and Finance* 25 (1) (February): 7–21. Surveys the empirical literature regarding uncovered interest rate parity.

Chinn, Menzie D., and Guy Meredith. 2004. "Monetary Policy and Long Horizon Uncovered Interest Parity." *IMF Staff Papers* 51 (3) (November): 409–30. Documents the tendency for interest rate differentials to be better predictors of subsequent exchange rate movements at longer horizons, and to provide a theoretical model based on central bank behavior.

Cumby, Robert E., and Maurice Obstfeld. 1984. "International Interest Rate and Price Level Linkages under Flexible Exchange Rates: A Review of Recent Evidence."

In *Exchange Rate Theory and Practice*, edited by J. F. O. Bilson and R. C. Marston. Chicago: University of Chicago Press, 121–51. Provides an early test of real interest parity, using the rational expectations methodology.

Dooley, Michael, and Peter Isard. 1980. "Capital Controls, Political Risk, and Deviations from Interest-rate Parity." *Journal of Political Economy* 88 (2): 370–84. Gives empirical estimates in support of the proposition that deviations from interest rate parity may be caused by the presence of capital controls.

Fama, Eugene F. 1984. "Forward and Spot Exchange Rates." *Journal of Monetary Economics* 14 (3): 319–38. Provides early estimates of canonical regressions of exchange rate changes on the forward discount.

Flood, Robert, and Andrew Rose. 1996. "Fixes: Of the Forward Discount Puzzle." *Review of Economics and Statistics* 78 (4): 748–52. Documents the fact that when there are expectations of large exchange rate changes—as during currency crises—interest differentials do predict the direction of subsequent exchange rate changes.

———. 2002. "Uncovered Interest Parity in Crisis." *IMF Staff Papers* 49: 252–66. Documents the fact that when there are expectations of large exchange rate changes—as during currency crises—interest differentials do predict the direction of subsequent exchange rate changes.

Frankel, Jeffrey A. 1991. "Quantifying International Capital Mobility in the 1980s." NBER Working Paper No. W2856. Available at http://ssrn.com/abstract= 284049. Systematically measures the extent of capital mobility and makes a distinction between perfect capital mobility and perfect capital substitutability.

Frankel, Jeffrey, and Jumana Poonawala. 2006. "The Forward Market in Emerging Currencies: Less Biased Than in Major Currencies." NBER Working Paper No. 12496 (August). Cambridge, MA: National Bureau of Economic Research. Shows the predictive characteristics of the forward discount for emerging market currencies.

Frenkel, Jacob, and Richard Levich. 1975. "Covered Interest Arbitrage: Unexploited Profits?" *Journal of Political Economy* 83 (2): 325–38. Examines a transactions cost-based explanation for why covered interest parity does not hold exactly.

Froot, Kenneth, and Jeffrey Frankel. 1989. "Forward Discount Bias: Is It an Exchange Risk Premium?" *Quarterly Journal of Economics* 104 (1) (February): 139–61. Uses survey data on exchange rate expectations to determine whether a risk premium or biased expectations explain the forward premium puzzle.

Fujii, Eiji, and Menzie D. Chinn. 2001. "Fin de Siècle Real Interest Parity." *Journal of International Financial Markets, Institutions and Money* 11 (3/4): 289–308. Uses several methods of measuring expected inflation to test whether real interest rates are equalized across borders.

Mark, N. C. 1985. "Some Evidence on the International Inequality of Real Interest Rates." *Journal of International Money and Finance* 4: 189–208. Provides an early test of real interest parity.

Popper, Helen. 1993. "Long-Term Covered Interest Parity—Evidence from Currency Swaps." *Journal of International Money and Finance* 12 (4): 439–48. Examines whether covered interest parity holds at multi-year horizons.

MENZIE D. CHINN

■ internalization theory

Internalization refers to the decision by a multinational firm producing abroad whether to own a foreign production facility or to license or contract with a foreign firm to produce a good or service on behalf of the multinational. Specifically, internalization refers to production internal to the ownership boundaries of the firm. This topic has a long history in the international business literature, but has more recently emerged under the converse name of outsourcing. This is merely a change in name: the firm must decide whether to internalize or outsource. Other terms used to refer to this decision include *mode choice* and *boundaries of the firm.*

This entry focuses on relatively recent papers that offer alternative formal models of the internalization decision. Nevertheless, it is important for researchers in this field to acknowledge the substantial contributions of earlier writers in the international business tradition, including John Dunning, Mark Casson, Alan Rugman, Oliver Williamson, and others. An excellent review of this literature is provided in Caves (2007) and in a somewhat more circumscribed fashion in Markusen (2002).

Firms make mode choices, such as among exports, subsidiary production, and outsourcing, in response to the conditions and constraints they experience. A typical starting point in the theory of the multinational is that the firm possesses proprietary assets that give it a motive for expanding abroad in the first place. These assets could include product or process technology, a brand name or trademark, or a reputation for product quality. But in moving or using these assets abroad, the firm runs certain risks of asset dissipation or holdup through opportunistic behavior of foreign licensees, contractors, or even by the firm's own managers in the case of an owned subsidiary. Asset dissipation is therefore a motive for internalization. But this must be balanced against other competing forces, such as giving the local manager or licensee strong incentives to engage in efficient investment and effort levels. Internalization theory explores the tension among these alternative factors and derives the optimal mode choice for firms subject to various assumptions about contracting and other constraints.

The Internalization Decision and Opportunistic Behavior Some of the first formal models of the internalization decision were published in the late 1980s and 1990s and draw their empirical motivation from the strong association of multinationality with knowledge-based assets such as those described in the previous paragraph (again, see Caves 2007 and Markusen 2002). On the one hand, these assets (or the services thereof) are easily transferred overseas, such as providing a blueprint, chemical formula, or procedure to a foreign plant. On the other hand, the same characteristics that make it easy to transfer these assets make them easily learned by foreign managers, agents, or licensees. Once the agent sees the blueprint or license he or she could defect to produce the product in a new firm.

Horstmann and Markusen (1987) have a model in which the intangible or knowledge-based asset is a reputation for product quality. This quality can only be observed by a consumer after purchase and use of the product. The difficulty is that, if the firm extracts all of the rents from a local licensee, that licensee has an incentive to product a cheap, low-quality substitute and earn positive profits for one period before being fired. The multinational risks asset dissipation

through agent opportunism, a theme that occurs repeatedly in subsequent papers.

The Horstmann-Markusen (1987) paper tends to focus on a firm's decision to export versus produce abroad. It is less well suited to explicitly considering the decision to create an owned subsidiary versus using a foreign licensee; after all, the local manager has much the same incentives as a licensee. Two 1996 papers made some further progress on this issue. Ethier and Markusen (1996) have a model in which a firm introduces a new product every second period. During the first period of a product's life, the local agent or manager absorbs all relevant aspects of the technology and is capable of producing the product on his or her own in the second period. At the end of the second period, the product is obsolete and the manager's knowledge is of no further use.

Under certain parameterizations of this model, the multinational can extract all rents with a single-product licensing contract, and so this is of course optimal. For other parameterizations, this cannot be done. The alternative is for the multinational to offer a contract that shares some rents with the local manager, and this can be credible and incentive-compatible for both parties over the long term in which the contract and rent sharing is repeated with every new product. This long-term incentive-compatible sharing arrangement is thought of as a subsidiary relationship, not limited to one product but continuing indefinitely into the future.

Horstmann and Markusen (1996) have quite a different approach, introducing asymmetric information along with moral hazard. The potential local agent or manager possesses local information on market demand or costs that is not known to the multinational. The market could actually be large, but the agent has an incentive to pretend it is small and shirk on effort so that sales are consistent with high effort in a small market. The best feasible licensing contract forces the multinational to share rents, termed information rents, with the agent. The alternative is for the firm to establish an owned subsidiary from the beginning, which is more costly, but the firm learns the true state of demand or costs without having to share rents to extract this information. In the vernacular, an owned subsidiary gives the multinational a larger share of a smaller pie, another theme that occurs repeatedly in the internalization/outsourcing literature.

Three later papers followed in the tradition of the Ethier and Markusen (1996) model: Fosfuri, Motta, and Rønde (2001); Glass and Saggi (2002); and Markusen (2001). All share the idea that knowledge is absorbed by workers in the course of production, and they are then at least potentially able to defect and start rival firms after some period of time. The Fosfuri, Motta, and Rønde model has a richer technological structure than the original Ethier and Markusen model. In particular, the managers or licensees who absorb the knowledge from the multinational may later enter into a complementary relationship with their former employer rather than a competitive one, supplying goods or services to the multinational. This is a valuable development insofar as there are many examples of former employees, in Taiwan, for example, becoming contractors in a cooperative relationship with their old firms.

Glass and Saggi (2002) focus on workers in general and not managers or licensees specifically. Workers absorb knowledge and can be hired away by local firms. The multinational has two options to prevent the dissipation of its technology, termed a transfer of technology (i.e., the term *technology transfer* in this model refers to transfer from the multinational to the host-country firm, not to whether or not the multinational uses or "transfers" its technology to the host-country plant). The firm can pay its workers a wage premium, or it can choose an alternative, more costly location (e.g., export to the host country). Glass and Saggi solve for parameters under which the multinational prevents technology transfer by paying sufficiently high wages and under which the multinational's best option is to pay minimal wages and accommodate the technology transfer through worker mobility. The welfare consequences of these alternatives are analyzed. There is no explicit modeling of a licensing or outsourcing alternative to establishing a subsidiary.

Markusen (2001) follows in the Ethier-Markusen tradition as just noted. He extends this model to include an explicit analysis of intellectual properties rights and provides a welfare analysis. Tighter intellectual property protection and contract enforcement raise the costs to the local manager of defecting, but also raise the costs to the multinational of firing and replacing the manager after one period. Tighter enforcement means that the incentive-compatible contract allows the multinational to share fewer rents with the local manager or licensee. This presents a trade-off for the host country in setting policy. Tighter enforcement means that the multinational may now enter the country whereas before the optimal policy was to export, and this is welfare improving for the host. On the other hand, for a firm that is entering anyway, tighter enforcement transfers rents from the local manager to the firm and hence is welfare reducing.

Property Rights Approach and the Holdup Problem About the same time as this last set of papers, an important advancement to the internalization question was being developed by Antrás, Grossman, and Helpman (Antrás 2003, 2005; Antrás and Helpman 2004; Grossman and Helpman 2004). All of these authors substitute the term *outsourcing* for the term *internalization*. Their approach is sometimes termed the "property-rights" approach to the firm after contributions by Grossman and Hart (1986) and Hart and Moore (1990), following earlier contributions of Williamson (1985) and others in the international business literature.

The new literature combines a number of separate elements that together produce a coherent model that offers clear empirical predictions. The first element (in no particular order) is the assumption that production requires "relation-specific investments," meaning that a multinational and a foreign individual or firm must incur sunk investments prior to production that have no outside value if the relationship breaks down. The second element is the assumption of incomplete contracting: certain things are simply not contractible or alternatively any contract on these items is not enforceable. The papers just mentioned focus on the idea of noncontractibility, in particular they assume that certain things either cannot be observed and/or are not verifiable by third parties rather than focusing on institutional failures such that contracts cannot be enforced. These two elements of the newer theory are shared with the older literature reviewed above.

The assumptions of sunk investments and noncontractibility lead to a third problem, which is ex-post "holdup." What happens after production occurs cannot be contracted ex ante, and so each party has some ability to negotiate ex post and to prevent the other party from fully utilizing the output. As is generally assumed in this approach to the firm, the Antrás-Grossman-Helpman papers assume that the multinational and the local manager or firm engage in ex post Nash bargaining over the surplus. The final element of this approach is the notion of ownership, necessary in order to distinguish an owned subsidiary from an arm's-length supplier. The property rights approach defines the owner of the foreign production facility as the party that has residual rights of control; that is, the party that owns any output or other assets of the firm in the event that bargaining breaks down.

The difficulty for the multinational is that the choice between an owned subsidiary and an arm's-length licensee both entail some inefficiency again due to incomplete contracting. Antrás (2003), in an elegant model and exposition, assumes that the multinational chooses the quantity of capital to be used in production and the local manager or licensee chooses the quantity of labor. In the Nash bargaining phase, the problem is that each party will receive only a fraction of the marginal return to its ex ante investment, and thus there will be investment in both capital and labor (in Antrás's model) in equilibrium. Ownership of the local supplier entitles the multinational to residual rights of control and thus improves the ex post bargaining position, but reduces the local manager's incentive to make an efficient ex ante investment.

Antrás assumes that there are many potential host-country licensees or managers and that the multinational can impose an up-front fee and so competition among suppliers will lead the up-front fee to adjust so that the local supplier will just break even. Let X be the output that is produced. Because X is assumed to be a component that is specific to the multinational firm, it also follows that the local manager/licensee has no ability to use X outside the relationship even if he or she

has residual ownership rights, and so the manager/licensee's outside option is zero under either the subsidiary or licensing relationship. But the multinational's outside option is higher with residual rights of control. The firm can use at least part of the X when the multinational is the owner, but neither party can use X in the licensing relationship when bargaining breaks down. Thus the multinational will capture a larger share of the surplus in ex post bargaining under a subsidiary arrangement.

The consequence when combining these various elements is that, while both a subsidiary and a licensing relationship suffer from underinvestment, the subsidiary relationship suffers more from an underinvestment in labor relative to capital: the licensee has less incentive to invest due to a smaller marginal share. The licensing arrangement suffers more from an underinvestment in capital, since the multinational receives a smaller share in the ex post bargaining outcome. The next step becomes straightforward: the subsidiary is the more profitable option for a capital-intensive industry while the arm's-length contract is more profitable for a labor-intensive industry. This clear prediction is successfully taken to the data.

A conceptually related model is found in Antrás (2005). A product-cycle model is developed, in which a high-tech input that can be produced only in the North is combined with a low-tech input that can be produced either in the North or South. As time passes, the technology shifts so that the high-tech input is less important. The theory predicts that, as time passes, production first shifts to the South within firm boundaries and only later to independent foreign firms.

Various extensions and refinements of this approach are found in other Antrás-Grossman-Helpman papers noted above. These are an advance on the earlier literature discussed above, insofar as the difference between an owned subsidiary and an arm's-length relationship is sharper and better defined. Empirical predictions are similarly sharper and then have so far stood up under empirical investigation such as in Feenstra and Hanson (2005) in addition to Antrás's own results.

Chen, Horstmann, and Markusen (2007) have produced a new model in which there is both knowledge capital and physical capital. As in the earlier literature, the knowledge capital is absorbed by the workers over the first period and hence there is no clear ownership issue: knowledge is nonexcludable. The physical capital is fully excludable as in the newer property-rights papers and belongs to the residual claimant, the owner of the production facility. They obtain the prediction that the owned subsidiary is more likely to be chosen in an industry in which the ratio of knowledge capital to physical capital is high. They suggest that this could be proxied by a Tobin's Q statistic in subsequent empirical analysis. The results seem consistent with the extensive empirical analysis surveyed in Caves (2007).

Areas Needing More Research All of these models are helpful in understanding the internalization versus outsourcing decision, and they seem to be standing up well to empirical analysis as noted. They are, however, very specific models. The international business literature, while less formal and analytic, identifies a far broader range of factors influencing a firm's entry mode choice in serving a foreign market. Judging by the references contained in most of the papers surveyed here, the international business literature under the term *internalization* is generally being ignored in the literature under the name *outsourcing*. This is surely a mistake, and researchers in the more formal economics tradition are missing out on the richness of detail, ideas, and empirical evidence found in the international business literature. Again, Caves (2007) is an excellent background for any scholar interested in this field.

We can conclude then with a brief listing of some of the other factors that seem important and which are ripe pickings for more formal analysis. Complex tax systems influence firms' mode choices. Formal barriers to majority-owned affiliates, often indirect and hard to measure, corrupt observations from developing countries and suggest more joint ventures and arm's-length arrangements than would actually be observed in less-regulated markets. A broad range of institutions including legal systems, contract enforcement, corrupt practices, host government hold-up, and intellectual property protection influence the relative attractiveness of owned affiliates versus licensing and other hybrid mode forms.

Some disconnect with empirical evidence is also evident. While many of the newer formal models surveyed here assume the foreign partner is providing an intermediate for the multinational, empirical evidence consistently shows that the major motive for foreign direct investments is to serve local markets, with production for regional third countries coming in second. Production for export back to the parent country amounts to only about 10 percent of sales for foreign affiliates of U.S. manufacturing multinationals and even then, much of this small amount is final goods assembled in labor-intensive factories abroad. Examinations of lengthy, complex outsourcing contracts apparently cast some doubt on convenient assumptions that a whole range of things are noncontractible since they appear very explicitly in these real-world contracts, but there is little published evidence on this point.

Other even more intangible but no doubt very real considerations are often mentioned in the international business literature. Dissimilar corporate cultures and conflicts between the global objectives of the multinational and the more circumscribed and short-run objectives of the potential local contracting firm are just two of many examples. Multinationals are not trying to maximize local profits, and the task of inducing a local affiliate, much less a licensee, to respond to the firm's global strategy is a difficult contracting complication. All of these factors suggest that there is still much to be done.

See also foreign direct investment: the OLI framework

FURTHER READING

Antrás, Pol. 2003. "Firms, Contracts, and Trade Structure." *Quarterly Journal of Economics* 118 (4): 1375–1418. Shows that the subsidiary option is more profitable for capital-intensive industries, whereas arm's-length contracting is more profitable for labor-intensive industries.

———. 2005. "Incomplete Contracts and the Product Cycle." *American Economic Review* 95 (3): 1054–71. Product cycle model in which manufacturing is shifted abroad first within firm boundaries, and at a later stage to independent foreign firms.

Antrás, Pol, and Elhanan Helpman. 2004. "Global Sourcing." *Journal of Political Economy* 112 (3): 552–80. Extension/refinement of Antrás (2003) to include varying degrees of contractibility across inputs and countries in a model of whether to integrate into the production of intermediate inputs or outsource them, and from which country to source the inputs.

Caves, Richard E. 2007. *Multinational Enterprise and Economic Analysis*. 3d ed. Cambridge: Cambridge University Press. Excellent background reading on international business approach.

Chen, Yongmin, Ignatius J. Horstmann, and James R. Markusen. 2007. "Physical versus Knowledge Capital as Determinants of Multinational Firms' Mode Choices for Foreign Production." University of Colorado Working Paper. Boulder, CO. Predicts that subsidiaries should be more likely in industries with a high ratio of knowledge capital to physical capital.

Ethier, Wilfred J., and James R. Markusen. 1996. "Multinational Firms, Technology Diffusion and Trade." *Journal of International Economics* 41 (1–2): 1–28. Model of contracting issues, division of rents, and mode choice when manager/licensee learns all about technology and becomes potential rival.

Feenstra, Robert C., and Gordon H. Hanson. 2005. "Ownership and Control in Outsourcing to China: Estimating the Property-Rights Theory of the Firm." *Quarterly Journal of Economics* 120 (2): 729–61. Studies factory ownership and input control for trade processing in China, where foreign firms contract out assembly of intermediates into final products.

Fosfuri, Andrea, Massimo Motta, and Thomas Rønde. 2001. "Foreign Direct Investments and Spillovers through Workers' Mobility." *Journal of International Economics* 53 (1): 205–22. Studies conditions under which technology spillovers occur to workers trained with a superior technology leaving to work for a local competitor.

Glass, Amy J., and Kamal Saggi. 2002. "Multinational Firms and Technology Transfer." *Scandinavian Journal of Economics* 104 (4): 495–513. Model of host country policy toward FDI when firms may decide to pay a wage premium or to produce elsewhere, in order to protect their technology from leaving to rival rivals through the movement of workers.

Grossman, Gene M., and Elhanan Helpman. 2004. "Managerial Incentives and the International Organization of Production." *Journal of International Economics* 63 (2): 237–62. Extension/refinement of Antrás (2003): models location and organization choices of heterogeneous firms and how these are affected by falling trade costs.

Grossman, Sanford J., and Oliver D. Hart. 1986. "The Costs and Benefits of Ownership: A Theory of Vertical and Lateral Integration." *Journal of Political Economy* 94 (4): 691–719. A first paper developing the property rights approach to the firm.

Hart, Oliver D., and John Moore. 1990. "Property Rights and the Nature of the Firm." *Journal of Political Economy* 98 (6): 1119–58. A second paper, drawing on Grossman and Hart (1986), on the property rights approach to the firm.

Horstmann, Ignatius J., and James R. Markusen. 1987. "Licensing Versus Direct Investment: A Model of Internalization by the Multinational Enterprise." *Canadian Journal of Economics* 20 (3): 464–81. Models contracting issues related to product quality—rents must be shared to provide licensee incentive not to defect by selling low quality.

———. 1996. "Exploring New Markets: Direct Investment, Contractual Relations, and the Multinational Enterprise." *International Economic Review* 37 (1): 1–20. Model of mode choice emphasizing the trade-off between information rents under licensing versus higher costs of establishing a subsidiary.

Markusen, James R. 2001. "Contracts, Intellectual Property Rights, and Multinational Investment in Developing Countries." *Journal of International Economics* 53 (1): 189–204. Captures how intellectual property rights and contract enforcement affect the division of profits between a multinational and local manager/licensee.

———. 2002. *Multinational Firms and the Theory of International Trade*. Cambridge, MA: MIT Press. Formal theory and empirical estimation of MNE models; concentrates somewhat on defining, developing, and estimating the knowledge-capital model.

Williamson, Oliver E. 1985. *The Economic Institutions of Capitalism*. New York: Free Press. A classic work on the boundaries of the firm.

JAMES R. MARKUSEN

■ international financial architecture

The international financial architecture is the set of institutions and norms—both international and domestic—that shape the international financial system. The institutional relations among industrial economies are clearly part of the international financial architecture. The policy debate that followed the currency crises in Asia and other emerging market crises in the late 1990s focused on reforms that could help make the integration of emerging economies into the international financial system less disruptive.

The resulting debate rested on two assumptions. First, private capital should normally flow from advanced economies to emerging economies—at least to those with sound economic fundamentals and solid policy frameworks. Second, the integration of emerging economies into global financial markets—a process that was catalyzed by the 1989–90 Brady plan, which transformed bad loans left over from the 1980s debt crisis into bonds—had not proceeded as smoothly as many had hoped. The "architects" consequently sought to create an institutional structure that would sustain private financial flows to emerging economies while reducing the risk that sudden interruptions in these flows would lead to painful crises and also increasing the international community's ability to manage crises that could not be avoided.

Background U.S. treasury secretary Robert Rubin first used the term *international financial architecture* in a speech in April 1998. The resulting debate culminated in the Cologne communiqué in 1999. It emphasized the need for a higher standard of transparency, stronger financial systems in emerging economies, changes in financial regulation in industrial economies to help make capital flows less cyclical, "corner" exchange rate regimes, and greater efforts to involve private creditors in the provision of crisis financing. This agenda informed much of the work of the International Monetary Fund (IMF) over the next few years.

It would be a mistake, however, to limit analysis of the architecture reforms solely to the specific proposals that followed from Rubin's speech: the debate over the need to reform the international financial architecture started well before Rubin coined the term *architecture* and did not end when the term disappeared from the official sector's formal lexicon in 2001. After Mexico's crisis of 1994–95, the Group of Seven (G7) called for the development of new facilities designed to allow the IMF to lend larger sums, but for shorter periods and at higher rates, as well an expansion of the IMF's lending capacity. These reforms were implemented in 1997 and 1998 with the creation of the Supplemental Reserve Facility and congressional approval of an IMF quota increase. The substantive debate over many key issues continued through 2003, when Mexico's decision to introduce collective action clauses (CACs)—provisions that allowed a supermajority of bondholders to amend a bond's financial terms—ended the debate over IMF's proposal for a new international sovereign bankruptcy regime. The intensity of the debate over the right scale of IMF lending waned in the absence of any major crises. New topics, notably a surge in the U.S. current account deficit largely financed by a rise in the current account surplus of the emerging world, moved to the top of the international economic and financial policy agenda.

During the peak of the debate over financial crises in emerging economies, many complained that talk of architecture was too grand and that "plumbing" would be a more appropriate metaphor. Such arguments came from two directions: those who thought better plumbing was all that the international financial system needed, and those who thought the G7 was making a mistake by just fiddling with the plumbing when a truly new architecture was needed.

Ambitious Proposals The Asian crisis certainly generated a host of ambitious proposals. The IMF's first deputy managing director Anne Krueger proposed radically changing the institutions for debt restructuring by amending the IMF's Articles of Agreement to provide sovereign governments in default with bankruptcy-style protections (the sovereign debt restructuring mechanism, or SDRM). The economist Joseph Stiglitz suggested a "super" Chapter 11 regime to facilitate an across-the-board restructuring of private borrowers' debts in the event of macroeconomic shocks.

Anne Krueger's predecessor, Stanley Fischer, focused more on the institutional structure for crisis lending than on the institutional structure for debt restructuring. Fischer argued that the IMF should be transformed into a lender of last resort, able to lend in quantities that would be sure to end cross-border runs. The International Financial Institutions Advisory Committee (2000), more commonly called the Meltzer Commission, suggested that the IMF get out of the business of lending to countries that promise to deliver sound macroeconomic policies only when they are close to default and instead lend large sums to countries that qualified in advance for extra protection by maintaining good policies. The International Financial Institutions Advisory Committee (IFIAC) specifically recommended that the IMF lend large sums for short-term loans—120 days with only one possible rollover—to countries that prequalified for support. The IFIAC also suggested that the strength of a country's banking system be the key criterion for determining eligibility. Others have proposed less draconian forms of prequalification.

Proposed changes in governance of the major international financial institutions were equally dramatic, with proposals tabled to merge the IMF and the World Bank, to eliminate both institutions, and to create a new global financial regulator.

More Modest Results In the end, calls for major reforms generally were rejected in favor of more incremental changes. The IMF toyed with a facility based on prequalification (the contingent credit line, or CCL) but never gave up its traditional crisis lending. A new forum that brought regulators together with finance ministries, central banks, and the IMF (the Financial Stability Forum) and the development of new international codes and standards substituted for the creation of an international superregulator. No major reforms were made to the IMF's voting structure after the Asian crisis—though in 2006, the IMF did increase the quota of four underrepresented emerging economies: China, Korea, Mexico, and Turkey. The membership of informal clubs such as the G7 that often influenced IMF policy did not change, but a new forum, the G20, was created to bring the G7 together with major emerging markets.

Modest Reforms In the end, though, the architects did more than just clean up the plumbing. Some of the most consequential changes were adopted early on. After the crisis in Mexico, the United States decided to strengthen multilateral institutions for crisis financing. This led, in time, to important changes in the architecture. A bigger IMF was combined with facilities designed to allow the IMF to put more money on the table faster. In principle, exceptional IMF financing came with an expectation that those funds could be repaid more quickly than a typical IMF loan. In practice, the IMF's major shareholders did lend large sums to some countries that did not have a realistic chance of repaying the fund quickly; the large short-term loans provided to Turkey, Brazil, and Argentina in 2001 and 2002 all had to be refinanced. Large-scale crisis financing from the IMF effectively became the norm—despite claims by the G7 to the contrary—when major emerging economies encountered financial difficulties.

The institutions for debt restructuring evolved organically. The large international banks generally stopped providing medium- to long-term syndicated loans to the governments of emerging economies after the debt crisis of the 1980s, instead lending for shorter terms to private banks (some of which then lent to their local government) or private firms. Nonetheless, the architecture for coordinating the major international banks that was inherited from the sovereign debt crisis of the 1980s was adapted in Korea to help coordinate a rescheduling of interbank credit lines. New institutions for bond restructuring emerged, though not without some birth pangs. Negotiations between a distressed sovereign borrower and a coordinating committee of banks gave way to exchange offers. Distressed debtors, often advised by a major international bank, offered to exchange old bonds for new bonds with different payment terms. The success of these exchanges—participation was high and litigation proved less troublesome than initially anticipated—eliminated much of the pressure for more dramatic changes to the institutions for debt restructuring.

Arguably of most importance, the policies of most of the world's emerging economies changed dramatically. Emerging market economies embraced central bank independence and inflation targeting. Indeed, their inflation rates began to converge with those of the advanced countries. Local currency bond markets took off. Emerging economies concluded that they needed to hold far more reserves than they had held in the past; most now hold reserves well in excess of their short-term external debts. Many emerging economies began to allow their exchange rate to float, though most still intervene far more heavily than advanced economies. Transparency increased dramatically—at least for those emerging economies that felt compelled to live up to the IMF's revised standards.

Compared to the changes made in emerging markets, the changes in regulatory structure in industrial economies were quite modest. Concerns that capital flows from the industrial world to emerging economies were procyclical, with too much money flowing into emerging economies in good times and too much flowing out in bad times, did not prompt major policy changes. A revised set of Basel capital standards was in the process of being implemented as of 2007. Although hedge funds and the regulators of the banks that provide hedge funds with leverage were temporarily chastened by the 1998 implosion of a major U.S. hedge fund, Long-term Capital Management, the formal regulatory structure changed little. After a brief down period, hedge funds entered a new phase of phenomenal growth.

The debate on architecture ended with a broad consensus on the steps emerging economies needed to take to reduce the probability of crises, but with few tools that could force an emerging economy to follow these recommendations. A comparable consensus on the core issue of crisis resolution never truly emerged. The G7 was comfortable with an IMF that had the capacity to make big loans, and policy statements that claimed—without much credibility—that this capacity would not be used in the future. The G7—and for that matter the world's major emerging economies—never could define

when a debt restructuring should be an integral part of efforts to resolve a crisis.

Changes in the global economy, though, gradually shifted the focus of policy markets away from emerging market crises and reduced the pressure to find real consensus on difficult issues. Worries about too much demand for IMF lending gave way to concerns that the IMF might earn too little from its lending to cover its expenses. Concerns that the IMF was too reluctant to criticize emerging economies that clung too tenaciously to exchange rate pegs in the face of current account deficits gave way to concerns that the IMF was too reluctant to criticize emerging economies that intervened heavily to maintain undervalued exchange rates. Concerns that emerging economies had too few reserves gave way to concerns that they held too many—and were adding even more every year.

By 2005, private capital flows to emerging economies matched their pre–Asian crisis peak. Eastern Europe, in part because of its institutional tie to the rest of Europe, relied on these capital inflows to cover significant current account deficits. But most other emerging economies used this surge in private capital flows, along with the windfall from rising commodity prices, to add to their reserves. In aggregate, the emerging world ran a large current account surplus, financing deficits in many of the world's advanced economies. This system, which has been labeled a new Bretton Woods system, represented a real change in the international financial architecture, even if it did not emerge from the debate that occupied policymakers in the 1990s, let alone a new Bretton Woods conference.

The debate over the architecture for managing financial crises in emerging economies has been superseded by a different architecture debate focused on finding new ways to facilitate macroeconomic policy coordination between the world's new creditor countries and its major debtor countries to help reduce global imbalances. This debate covers a very different set of topics than the previous debate—from the optimal use of emerging economies' vast reserves to strengthening the IMF's surveillance of surplus countries in the emerging world and deficit countries in the G7. One topic, though, has stayed constant: the continuing need to adapt the international financial world's governing institutions, both formal and informal, to better reflect the growing role emerging economies play in the international financial system.

Also see bail-ins; bailouts; banking crisis; Bretton Woods system; capital flows to developing countries; currency crisis; exchange rate regimes; financial crisis; global imbalances; hedge funds; hot money and sudden stops; inflation targeting; International Monetary Fund (IMF); International Monetary Fund conditionality; International Monetary Fund surveillance; international policy coordination; international reserves; Latin American debt crisis; lender of last resort; original sin; twin deficits

FURTHER READING

Group of Seven. 1999. *Strengthening the International Financial Architecture: Report of G-7 Finance Ministers to the Cologne Economic Summit.* Cologne, Germany: G7. A comprehensive statement of the G7's agreed approach to the architecture reform.

International Financial Institutions Advisory Commission (IFIAC). 2000. *Report.* Washington, DC: United States Congress. Downloadable from http://www.house.gov/jec/imf/meltzer.htm. More commonly called the Report of the Meltzer Commission. It proposed that the IMF lend for very short terms only to countries that prequalified for support.

Kenen, Peter B. 2001. *The International Financial Architecture: What's New? What's Missing?* Washington, DC: Institute for International Economics. A retrospective assessment of the initial round of reforms from an influential academic voice.

King, Mervyn. 2006. "Reform of the International Monetary Fund." (February). A key speech that helped to define the current "architecture" debate.

Krueger, Anne. 2001a. "International Financial Architecture for 2002: A New Approach to Sovereign Debt Restructuring." Speech at the National Economists' Club Annual Members' Dinner, American Enterprise Institute, November 26. Washington, DC. Downloadable from http://www.imf.org/external/np/speeches/2001/112601.htm. The case for a new international bankruptcy regime.

Rubin, Robert E., and Jacob Weisberg. 2003. *In an Uncertain World: Tough Choices from Wall Street to Washington.* New York: Random House. Rubin's thinking on the international financial architecture.

Task Force on the Future International Financial Architecture (CFR Task Force). 1999. *Safeguarding Prosperity in a Global Financial System.* New York: Council on Foreign Relations. An agenda for reform that both parallels and differs from the reforms the G7 embraced at Cologne.

Truman, Edwin. 2006. *A Strategy for IMF Reform.* Washington, DC: Institute for International Economics. A comprehensive review of current proposals for IMF reform.

BRAD SETSER

■ international financial centers

International financial centers (IFCs) are global hubs for banking, insurance, capital, money, and foreign exchange transactions. A large share of global trade and management of financial wealth and debt instruments is conducted in these centers. By virtue of the volume of transactions and the depth of their markets, they are leaders in setting the price of financial instruments. Such instruments are used to channel (intermediate) capital between savers and borrowers and to transfer financial risk.

The predominant IFCs are London and New York. Other key centers include Tokyo and Frankfurt. A number of financial centers are important in a regional context, including Singapore and Hong Kong. Offshore financial centers are important domiciles for international financial transactions with the pricing and trading of the financial instruments keyed off the markets in the major IFCs. The term *international financial center* is also used as a signal by some centers that a preferential tax and/or flexible regulatory regime will apply to financial entities/transactions domiciled there. Competition among the financial centers is intense, and successful centers offer comparative advantage for market participants.

Growth and Evolution of IFCs The major IFCs have evolved in response to underlying economic circumstances. The initial importance of both London and New York can be traced to their geographical and historical locations as centers of trade and commerce and to the use, respectively, of British pounds and U.S. dollars for the denomination of international trade and investment transactions. Through a series of financial innovations, London has remained a dominant IFC notwithstanding the post–World War II decline in the importance of sterling and the UK economy. Since the 1960s, for example, London has been the principal host of an international market in money, credit, and debt instruments denominated in U.S. dollars (the so-called Eurodollar market). Other innovations include deregulation of its stock market in the mid-1980s, elimination of exchange controls, and a market-friendly approach to regulation. The volume of international transactions in London is now several times that of domestic transactions. A similar balance of transactions can be found in centers such as Hong Kong, Singapore, Luxembourg, Ireland, and Switzerland, for example. By contrast, domestic transactions still dominate in centers such as New York and Tokyo, reflecting the size of their domestic economies.

Several factors have promoted the development of IFCs. The growth of international trade and investment in the period following World War II was accompanied by a rapidly expanding volume of international capital flows. The global increase in capital movements has responded to and helped finance the emergence of substantial imbalances between countries with surpluses and those with deficits in their balance of payments. A significant part of these international capital flows has been intermediated by the institutions and markets in the IFCs as they adapted their financial institutions and instruments to the global financing needs. Large deficits in the U.S. current accounts have been matched by increases in purchases of U.S. dollar assets, primarily through the major IFCs.

During the 1970s, a succession of increases in oil prices resulted in significant balance of payment surpluses among oil-producing countries. These surpluses were "recycled" through the IFCs, initially largely through the placement of surplus funds in bank deposits in those centers. At the same time, a number of advanced, developing, and emerging market economies looked to the international financial markets to finance their foreign-exchange reserve positions or their programs of economic growth and development. The facilities and instruments to mobilize the capital transfers, such as syndicated loans and international bonds, were provided by institutions based in the IFCs. Large corporations also tapped the international markets to finance investment.

A theoretical explanation of why certain financial centers have become dominant can be found in the literature on central place theory, which is used to explain why cities tend to be of unequal size. The underlying idea is that there is a trade-off between economies of scale that lead to concentration of activities, spurring centers of activity to grow, and the costs of accessing these centers of activity, which places a limit on the size of the center and allows other centers to grow. In the case of financial transactions, potentially significant benefits of concentration include the pooling of expertise and the bringing together of a large number of buyers and sellers of financial instruments. The ability to trade with a financial center can also be limited, for example, by the time zone where the financial center is located. The central-place theory has limitations when it comes to financial centers, which are in intense competition. No center can remain dominant as an IFC relying solely on its location. In the first decade of the 21th century New York started falling behind, losing traditional businesses to London, while new centers sprang up, as in Dubai, for example, which captured business from Europe, Asia, and the Middle East.

IFCs are characterized by mature financial markets that are deep (have a capacity to handle a range of transactions of different tenor and in large volumes), liquid (have a capacity to trade in and out of positions with reasonable certainty about the prices at which the trades will take place), and relatively efficient (have pricing that reflects current market information). The legal foundation for financial contracts is well developed, providing reasonable legal certainty in the execution of the transactions, combined with sufficient flexibility to accommodate rapid innovation in financial instruments. The technical and institutional infrastructures for the financial markets are advanced and include a highly skilled and specialized labor force, ease of communications, efficient and low-cost trading platforms, and payments systems that help to mitigate financial systems risks. These systems are supported by regulatory structures and supervisory systems directed to customer protection, the prevention/mitigation of market and institution failures, and the prevention of financial abuse. The concentration of financial activity in the major centers places a significant responsibility on the host countries to ensure that the financial markets and institutions meet the highest regulatory standards, not least to protect their reputations, and regulators and central banks have proved quite adept at intervening at critical moments to maintain the stability and reputation of their centers.

The importance of the major business lines varies among the different financial centers, and they have also been evolving rapidly under intense competition and financial innovation. These business lines include (1) international banking (intermediating between international borrowers and depositors), investment banking (e.g., underwriting of equities and fixed-income investments, underwriting and brokering securitized streams of payments obligations [e.g., from credit cards, mortgages] and advisory services in mergers and acquisitions), and private banking (investment and advisory services for private wealth management); (2) foreign-exchange trading in spot, forward, and swap markets covering all the major currencies as well as nondeliverable forward markets in less convertible currencies; (3) insurance activities of various forms (e.g., life, marine, property, and casualty) and reinsurance; (4) securities dealing in equities, primarily through organized exchanges, and bonds in domestic and international currencies; (5) fund and asset management and administration such as mutual funds, pension funds,

and hedge funds; (6) derivatives trading (e.g., swaps, options, interest rate equities, commodities, and credit contracts) both in over-the-counter markets and on organized exchanges; and (7) commodities trading (e.g., precious and other metals, agricultural and energy products) in spot, futures, and options transactions.

Consequences of Growth of IFCs IFCs are important both to the economies where they are located and internationally. They have direct importance to the local economies as sources of employment, contributors to foreign earnings and the balance of payments, and to gross domestic product. Internationally their importance derives from the provision of a range of financial services more efficiently than would be possible in local financial markets, reflecting the volume of transactions and the sophistication of the supporting infrastructure. The major banking and financial groups, which have a large international presence, are also headquartered in these centers. The management of a large share of global financial activity is therefore directed through these centers. The institutions in the IFCs have traditionally been at the forefront of innovations in financial instruments and techniques, adapting rapidly to changes in the global financial environment.

The global consequences of IFCs have not been without controversy. The growth of the Eurocurrency market was associated with concerns that it would undermine monetary policy and result in an uncontrolled expansion in global credit. These concerns abated as the authorities moved from monetary control that relied on direct instruments (such as credit ceiling and high, non-interest-bearing reserve requirements)—which were not applied to transactions through the euro markets—to indirect monetary instruments that relied on the market's adjustment of interest rates. The latter has a global impact, including in the euro markets. From time to time there are concerns that competition in the IFCs leads to an underpricing of risk, threatening the stability of financial institutions, and the global financial system. Credit spreads have tended to follow patterns of decline associated with financial innovation, only to face sudden reversals when the assumptions and instruments on which the declines were based are tested by worsening economic conditions. Examples include the decline in spreads in the 1970s and 1980s on credits to developing countries with the growth of the market in syndicated credits that preceded the first international debt crisis; and the expansion of securitization to a broader range of debt payment flows, including subprime mortgages that preceded a sharp loss of confidence in the international credit markets in 2007. Rapid innovation in financial centers has posed, and continues to pose, a major challenge for financial regulators as they seek to understand and mitigate potential and emerging risks. As the underlying transactions have become less transparent, the rating agencies have grown to play an increasingly important role in the pricing of credits and the functioning of markets. The IFCs have provided global benefits, but they are not without risk, and history has shown that the markets and their regulators will be tested.

See also Eurocurrencies; offshore financial centers; petrodollars, recycling of; trade in services

FURTHER READING

Johnston, R. B. 1983. *The Economics of the Euro-Market: History, Theory, and Policy.* London: Macmillan Press. Surveys the reasons for the development of IFCs, their role in global finance, and the policy debates on regulation of these centers.

R. BARRY JOHNSTON

■ international income convergence

Observers of the world economy often ask whether poorer countries are catching up with the rich countries. Put differently, are average living standards converging? This fundamental question has been much studied, especially since the development of new models and data in the mid-1980s. The answers help to shed light on the effects of globalization and development policies and provide a way of thinking about long-run predictions for the world economy. In principle, they also help to discriminate between models of the growth process. For all these reasons, the convergence question is central to the study of growth and development and also plays a role in international economics.

In popular commentary, it is common to hear claims such as "the rich countries are getting richer and the poor are getting poorer." It is well known that, after the mid-19th century, income levels diverged as some countries grew faster than others, but whether the poor countries became even poorer is open to debate. For more recent decades, the pattern is more complicated. Some poor countries have grown rapidly, notably many of those in East and Southeast Asia. Others have not, and some of the worst performers, predominantly in sub-Saharan Africa, have seen their gross domestic product (GDP) per capita decline even in absolute terms.

The diversity of experience implies that detailed studies of convergence may have an informative role to play. These studies are usually based on comparisons in relative terms, using ratios (rather than absolute gaps) to assess inequality in living standards or labor productivity at different points in time. Measurement should allow for differences in price levels across countries, and this can be achieved using version 6.2 of the Penn World Table developed by Heston, Summers, and Aten (2006). Using the standard deviation of the logarithm of output per capita to measure inequality, and excluding countries with populations below 250,000 in 1960, reveals a modest but steady increase in dispersion between 1960 and 2003 for a sample of 93 countries. The standard deviation rose by around 25 percent over the period as a whole.

The pattern is more complicated if we concentrate on the developed countries. For the countries above the 80th percentile of output per capita in 1960, there is some convergence until the late 1970s, but divergence later. There is clearer evidence for convergence if we restrict the sample to the Western European economies. In summary, there is no general tendency for convergence, unless we consider subgroups of similar economies, such as those of Western Europe. These findings will be one theme of what follows.

Convergence and the Solow Model Our understanding of convergence and divergence needs to be guided by theoretical models. Much of the literature, especially in its empirical guise, starts from the one-sector neoclassical growth model of Solow (1956). An aggregate production function is used to relate a country's output to a set of inputs, which would typically include capital equipment and labor. In this view of the world, international differences in labor productivity arise from differences in inputs per worker, or from differences in how efficiently inputs are combined. Convergence then requires stocks of inputs per worker, or efficiency levels, to move closer together. If GDP per capita is the yardstick, rather than output per worker hour, we should also consider changes in labor force participation rates and average working hours.

Models of this kind embody a view of living standards that is very different from the accounts found in popular commentary. In those accounts, development is often seen as a competitive process, in which wealth in one country is said to require poverty elsewhere. In contrast, in many theoretical models, productivity is determined independently of the productivity levels of other countries. If countries abroad are growing rapidly, this does not undermine domestic living standards.

In exploring the other predictions of growth models, the literature has distinguished between two different ways in which countries might be said to converge. *Absolute convergence* is the form that most commentators have in mind, namely whether inequality across countries in average living standards is tending to diminish. As we have seen, the overall tendency in recent decades has been one of gradual divergence.

We can learn more about this using a second idea, that of *conditional convergence*. The central hypothesis is that convergence is only to be expected within groups of economies that share similar structural characteristics. Within such groups, we should expect the countries that are initially poorer to grow more quickly, but this tendency is still compatible with divergence overall, given that there may be important differences across groups.

For this idea to be more than a truism, we need to be specific about the characteristics that are similar within groups. Consider a simple version of the Solow model, in which technical efficiency grows at the same rate in all countries. In this case, countries will converge to parallel equilibrium growth paths. Along these paths, capital and output will grow at the same rate, which is the equilibrium outcome, or steady-state, implied by the model. We can now consider what the model predicts about relative levels of output per worker in the long-run equilibrium—in other words, the extent of dispersion of the equilibrium paths. The highest levels of output per worker will be associated with countries that have high rates of investment, high levels of efficiency, and low rates of population growth. If two countries are alike in these various respects, the country that is initially poorer will grow relatively quickly, and living standards in the two countries will converge. But this convergence is only conditional, because it relies on the two countries looking alike in terms of the variables that influence the level of the steady-state growth path. This can explain why we might observe absolute convergence only within subgroups of countries, such as those of Western Europe, that are likely to share similar steady-state paths.

Even when conditional convergence is a good description of the data, whether or not countries converge in the absolute sense will depend on a range of factors. These include not only the dispersion of the equilibrium growth paths, but also the starting point of each country relative to its own equilibrium path. A further complication is that variables such as investment rates or population growth rates may be changing over time. In this case, the equilibrium paths of the different countries will move gradually apart or closer together, and this too will influence the observed extent of convergence.

The same basic analysis can easily be extended in other directions. For example, the quality of a country's institutions may be an important determinant of the level of the steady-state growth path. Other candidates include the education and skills of a country's workforce and the extent of government-provided infrastructure. The explicit specification of steady-state determinants is central to the Solow model's empirical content and the testing of its predictions.

Convergence predictions become more complicated in models where there is more than one equilibrium outcome. For example, the Solow model can be adapted to make the population growth rate a declining function of the level of income per capita. In that case, there may be one equilibrium with high living standards and slow population growth, and another equilibrium with low living standards and faster population growth. Although models with more than one equilibrium outcome are inherently difficult to test, they support the idea that income dispersion is not the only relevant issue. We might also be interested in whether there is any mobility within the distribution of living standards and whether the distribution changes shape over time. The work of Quah (for example, 1996) represents the major contribution along these lines.

There are several other limitations to the analysis sketched above. One is that we have assumed that the rate of technical progress is the same across countries, so that all countries grow at the same rate in the long run. This assumption is unrealistic, but less so than it first appears. Imagine that, other things equal, countries with a low initial level of efficiency are more likely to show rapid improvements in efficiency, perhaps because there is greater scope for easily adopting existing technologies from abroad. In that case, there may still be an equilibrium in which all countries grow at the same rate in the long run. In this long-run equilibrium, differences in the speed of adoption will be reflected in equilibrium "technology gaps" between leading and following countries, so that countries differ in relative income levels rather than long-run growth rates.

Convergence among Interdependent Economies The simplicity of the Solow model can be useful, not least in developing some intuition about where and when convergence should be expected. It is clear that absolute convergence is far from inevitable and that, even in a simple model, a wide range of outcomes is possible. The model is also a useful corrective to the view that economic development is essentially a competitive process and helps to explain why that view is less popular with economists than with noneconomists. Nevertheless, it is obvious that much of interest has been omitted. In practice, countries exchange goods and services; capital and labor sometimes move between countries; and ideas and technologies may spread beyond national borders in complex ways. These interactions are worth considering in more detail.

Many observers see the international trade of goods and services as central to the convergence process. It is true that, in principle, trade can lead to convergence in factor prices such as real wages and the returns to capital. In this case, differences in living standards will arise only when inputs per capita differ. If capital and labor are the only inputs used in production, factor price equalization implies that differences in living standards are driven entirely by differences in capital-labor ratios.

There are two problems with this story. First, it is false even at the level of casual observation, because real wages are readily seen to vary widely across countries. Second, the theoretical conditions under which factor price equalization occurs are extremely strict. Typically, production technologies are required to be the same across countries, but recent empirical work usually concludes that levels of technical efficiency vary widely. In this case, trade may still equalize factor prices, but only once we adjust them for international differences in the productivity of the different factors. The required adjustment makes this more general prediction harder to test.

Even in the absence of factor price equalization, trade in goods and services may still contribute to the convergence process. One view is that trade helps to encourage the transfer of technology across countries. These "dynamic" gains from trade are less well understood than the static gains of conventional trade theory. Their possible importance is highlighted by countries that have grown rapidly while becoming more integrated with the world economy. Separating this process of integration and growth into cause and effect is not straightforward, and empirical researchers seem to be divided on the extent to which trade flows promote technology diffusion and convergence. It is also worth noting that introducing dynamic considerations can overturn some of the predictions of textbook models of trade. For example, firms and countries may become more productive as they gain experience in producing a particular good or service. If this process of "learning-by-doing" has an important role in productivity improvement, then sometimes trade can even lead to divergence (see Helpman 2004 for more discussion).

Since the relationship between trade and convergence is potentially ambiguous, empirical evidence becomes especially important. One of the best-known studies is that by Sachs and Warner (1995). They classify most of the world's economies as either closed or open to trade. Over the period 1970–89, they find evidence for convergence within the group of open economies, but not within the group of closed economies. Open economies are also found to grow more quickly on average. The results are hardly conclusive, however. A high proportion of the open economies in the sample are members of the Organisation for Economic Co-operation and Development, and perhaps these countries converged because they are alike in other ways. Moreover, when Sachs and Warner distinguish between closed and open economies, their criteria can be interpreted as reflecting several broader dimensions of economic policy, and not simply trade policy.

Another approach asks whether specific episodes of trade liberalization have been followed by convergence among the liberalizing countries. Slaughter (1997) provides a summary and critique of some of this work. An ever-present constraint is the small number of countries available to empirical researchers, which makes it difficult to establish whether trade liberalization promotes convergence in practice.

If the effects of trade on convergence are uncertain, those of international capital flows are even more so. As is well known, these flows increased over the 1980s and 1990s, as many countries dismantled capital controls. The move to open capital accounts means that domestic investment is no longer constrained by domestic saving, and capital will tend to move to wherever the return is highest. Countries that are initially poor, with low saving rates, could be among those to benefit from this process. In textbook models, the marginal product of capital will be especially high in these countries, and capital will flow into them until the returns are driven down to the level available elsewhere in the world. Output and wages have the potential to increase rapidly. Although profits associated with the new investment will be returned to the foreign owners of capital, national income will also increase over time.

This mechanism only works, however, if foreign investors are not deterred by high risks. Moreover, countries that receive large-scale capital flows have the potential to be destabilized by, for example, changes in investor sentiment. This argument gained increased prominence with the East Asian financial crisis of 1997–98. To the extent that capital flows are destabilizing, their effects on convergence must be regarded as ambiguous.

Such problems may be less serious for long-term capital flows, notably foreign direct investment (FDI). It is often suggested that FDI encourages the international diffusion of technology, promoting convergence. The effects of FDI on productivity in recipient countries, and the extent of spillover benefits for domestic firms, have been a focus of recent empirical research.

This introduction only skims the surface of the theory and evidence on convergence. In this respect, one final point is worth making. In popular commentary on issues such as globalization, or development policies, the outcomes are sometimes assessed primarily in terms of inequality between countries. This is not without its associated dangers. In principle, it is conceivable for some events or policies to raise incomes everywhere, while leading to overall divergence in living standards, if some countries benefit more than others. This suggests that the analysis of convergence—development in relative terms—should often be supplemented with consideration of the level of development in absolute terms. It is the latter that is likely to have more influence on the everyday lives of the world's poor.

See also capital accumulation in open economies; capital mobility; foreign direct investment and international technology transfer; growth in open economies, neoclassical models; trade and economic development, international

FURTHER READING

Dowrick, Steve, and J. Bradford De Long. 2003. "Globalization and Convergence." In *Globalization in Historical Perspective*, edited by Michael D. Bordo, Alan M. Taylor, and Jeffrey G. Williamson. Chicago: NBER and University of Chicago Press, 191–220. Takes a wide, historical view of convergence.

Galor, Oded. 1996. "Convergence? Inferences from Theoretical Models." *Economic Journal* 106 (437): 1056–69. Examines the convergence implications of models with more than one equilibrium outcome.

Helpman, Elhanan. 2004. *The Mystery of Economic Growth*. This book, especially chapter 5, is one of the best introductions to these issues.

Heston, Alan, Robert Summers, and Bettina Aten. 2006. "Penn World Table Version 6.2." Data set available at the Center for International Comparisons of Production, Income, and Prices, at the University of Pennsylvania (September).

Jones, Charles I. 2002. *An Introduction to Economic Growth*. 2d ed. New York: Norton. An excellent introduction to a range of growth models.

Mankiw, N. Gregory, David Romer, and David Weil. 1992. "A Contribution to the Empirics of Economic Growth." *Quarterly Journal of Economics* 107 (2): 407–37. A classic paper in growth economics, partly because it gives new empirical content to the Solow model and clarifies the role of conditional convergence.

Obstfeld, Maurice, and Kenneth Rogoff. 1996. *Foundations of International Macroeconomics*. Cambridge, MA: MIT Press. Chapter 7 provides an illuminating discussion of many aspects of convergence, with a focus on open economies.

Quah, Danny T. 1996. "Twin Peaks: Growth and Convergence in Models of Distribution Dynamics." *Economic Journal* 106 (437): 1045–55. One of several classic studies by Quah on the world's distribution of income per capita across countries.

Sachs, Jeffrey D., and Andrew W. Warner. 1995. "Economic Reform and the Process of Global Integration." *Brookings Papers on Economic Activity* 1: 1–118. An influential but controversial study of the links between national policies and convergence.

Sala-i-Martin, Xavier. 2006. "The World Distribution of Income: Falling Poverty and . . . Convergence, Period." *Quarterly Journal of Economics* 121 (2): 351–97. A study of income inequality and convergence across the world's individuals, rather than across countries.

Slaughter, Matthew J. 1997. "Per Capita Income Convergence and the Role of International Trade." *American Economic Review* 87 (2): 194–99. A useful overview of some of the convergence mechanisms that arise when countries trade with one another.

Solow, Robert M. 1956. "A Contribution to the Theory of Economic Growth." *Quarterly Journal of Economics* 70: 65–94. Introduced Solow's classic model of national economic growth.

JONATHAN R. W. TEMPLE

■ international institutional transfer

There is by now a substantial literature on the importance of institutions to economic development. Institutions are formal or informal rules that constrain individual choice and reduce transaction costs, thereby facilitating collective action (North 1990). Governments that can credibly commit to the enforcement of property rights and a rule of law that can adjudicate conflicting property rights claims are seen as particularly important in facilitating long-term investment and therefore growth (de Soto 1989). In addition, political institutions that mitigate social conflict and provide public goods are also critical. There is substantial empirical evidence that institutions are strongly correlated with growth (see Knack and Keefer 1995; Easterly and Levine 2002); there is a debate, however, as to whether institutions are endogenous or exogenous to the economic system (see Sachs 2005).

Colonialism One of the most common exogenous sources of institutions are foreign actors, in the form of colonial powers, occupation authorities, industrialized great powers, multilateral organizations such as the World Bank or the International

Monetary Fund, or other international donors. There is considerably less empirical understanding of possibilities for institutional transfer across international boundaries than there is for the endogenous creation of institutions within a single society.

One important source of information concerning institutional transfer comes from the history of colonialism, where mostly European great powers exercised formal sovereignty over territories in what is now the developing world. There is, unfortunately, a relatively small comparative literature that systematically analyzes the long-term institutional impact of different colonial regimes. This is, of course, a morally fraught subject, since most colonial relationships were exploitative and destructive of indigenous institutions and cultures. It is clear that there is a huge variance in colonial experiences, even within individual empires. The British, for example, left relatively durable institutions in the Indian subcontinent and in their settler colonies in southern Africa, but in other places such as West Africa they relied largely on local elites and left behind considerably weaker institutions. The Japanese were relatively more successful in creating durable economic institutions in their Korean, Taiwanese, and Manchurian colonies (Woo 1991) than the Americans were in the Philippines. Acemoglu, Robinson, and Johnson (2001) suggest that European colonialists left strong institutions in territories where environmental conditions (particularly disease burdens) allowed them to settle, such as North America and South Africa. In other places, such as Latin America and West Africa, they created extractive regimes that were not conducive to securing property rights or rule of law. In a similar vein, Engerman and Sokoloff (2002) have suggested that initial factor endowments—the nature of cash crops, mineral resources, and labor—predisposed institutions in North and South America and the Caribbean to greater or lesser degrees of inequality, differences that have persisted over time.

The Governance Agenda in International Development Decolonization and the emergence of the developing world in the 1950s, 1960s, and 1970s created new conditions for institutional transfer. In the late 20th and early 21st centuries, foreign powers usually did not have sovereign authority over the territories to which they sought to transfer institutions but had to use indirect methods such as foreign assistance, technical advice, and conditionality in lending for structural adjustment and other purposes. There continued to be instances of direct rule by international actors, however, under postconflict conditions in places such as Haiti, Somalia, Bosnia, Kosovo, Timor-Leste, Afghanistan, and Iraq (see Chesterman 2004). Over the years, the international donor community has been increasingly concerned with improving the governance and institutional performance of developing countries, to the point where a substantial proportion of lending by multilateral institutions such as the World Bank and the Inter-American Development Bank are linked to public sector reform (World Bank 1997, 2000, 2002).

It is difficult to assess the overall impact of these external interventions designed to strengthen institutions and governance. In certain regions of the world such as Latin America, there has been a clear improvement in public sector performance, particularly in the area of macroeconomic policy management (Lora 2007). On the other hand, there has been much less progress in strengthening judicial systems, fighting corruption, or improving the performance of social sector institutions in education and health. In either case, it is not clear the extent to which existing institutional reform has been the product of external advice, help, and pressure, or internally driven reform processes. The World Bank's program to improve financial management in Highly Indebted Poor Countries has yielded very ambiguous results (Levy and Kpundeh, 2004). In Timor-Leste, the United Nations Transitional Authority for East Timor undertook the direct rule of a new nation between 1999 and 2002; while this was initially regarded as a big success for international state-building, Timor-Leste's army and police collapsed in internal fighting in 2006. The American experience in trying to create liberal democracies in Afghanistan and Iraq has been, to say the least, disappointing.

Theorizing Governance Recent efforts to improve governance have been conceptualized under a principal-agent framework. Governments are understood to be hierarchies in which principals (in a democracy, the sovereign people) direct agents to perform certain activities. The agents, however, have their own interests, which are not always aligned with the interests of the principals. Improving governance is therefore understood to be a matter of aligning agent incentives with those of their principals, largely by creating systems of monitoring and accountability.

Public sector services can be characterized along two dimensions: transaction volume and specificity. *Transaction volume* refers to the number of decisions or other outputs that a particular public sector agency has to make; they can range from small, in the case of a central bank or finance ministry, to large, in the case of a judicial system or public education system. *Specificity* refers to the degree to which the quality of the output of a public sector agency can be externally monitored. Macroeconomic policy institutions such as central banks and finance ministries have much lower transaction volume and higher specificity than institutions providing public education or legal services; their performance can therefore be much more easily monitored and brought under a principal-agent framework. This explains why most improvement in institutional performance in recent years has come in low-transaction-volume, high-specificity parts of the public sector.

This framework indicates why legal systems protecting property rights are particularly hard to transfer. Legal systems involve high transaction volumes, and their output is very difficult to measure. Property rights can be and often are selectively enforced, leading to rent-distribution systems with highly variable effects on economic growth (Khan and Jomo 2000).

Why Institutions Are Difficult to Transfer More broadly, there are four reasons why institutions are generically difficult to transfer across national boundaries. The first is that there are often large problems of fit between desired institutions and the nature of the underlying society. The models for well-functioning states in the minds of Western donors are often idealized versions of their own political institutions, which in turn are based on some vision of a Weberian rational-bureaucratic state. These embed certain clear value choices and moral perspectives: that exchange should be impersonal, that obligations to the society as a whole should trump narrower communal attachments, that hiring and advancement should not be based on kinship but on merit, and so on. These values do not come naturally to any human society and emerged in the West and in parts of East Asia only after a prolonged historical process. It is therefore not surprising that there is a poor fit in virtually all developing countries between the existing normative order and social structure and the kinds of institutions that donors prefer. Many donors believe that the burden falls on the developing country to adjust to this idealized model. The adjustment, however, must be mutual. There are no "optimal" forms of institutions; among developed liberal democracies, there is a wide variance in the ways institutions are implemented that make them "fit" their societies better.

The second obstacle to institutional reform concerns the problem of transmission mechanisms and ownership. The objectives of service delivery and capacity-building are often at odds; because public sector services are weak or nonexistent, donors are often tempted to provide them directly, which then weakens the capacity of the reforming country's government to provide them over the long term. Most successful state-building projects, such as those of the East Asian fast developers, have been driven by domestic elites; the latter may have gotten help in the form of resources or technical assistance from outside allies or donors, but themselves created demand for reform. In the absence of such internal demand, donors are often tempted to stimulate it artificially, either through conditionality in lending to mechanisms like the European Union's accession criteria. America's Millennium Challenge Account seeks to provide similar incentives for governance reform. Alternatively, donors can seek to promote independent civil society and independent media, which, it is hoped, will unlock a latent demand for change by putting pressure on corrupt or incompetent governments. Although breakthroughs such as Ukraine's Orange Revolution occasionally occur, externally stimulated demand for reform is seldom sufficient to produce decisive results.

The third obstacle is that state-building is at base a political process and not a technical one, one that involves access to power and resources and is therefore highly contested. Most dysfunctional public bureaucracies can trace their poor performance directly to the intervention of politicians who want to use the administrative machinery for their own purposes or prevent it from interfering in their activities. This, of course, presents a major obstacle for external donors, whose influence on local politics is either prohibited by statute, as in the case of the World Bank, or else is limited by past historical colonial relationships. Administrative reform pursued as a technical assistance project can get only so far if political will is lacking, and donors often do not have the patience to wait for the emergence of the right political conditions.

The fourth obstacle has to do with the need for nation-building in addition to state-building. It is common for those involved in postconflict reconstruction to concentrate on improving the capacity of public sector institutions and to shy away from attempts to help formulate or strengthen national identity, common culture, or shared values within the client country's society. Yet the latter is critical for the success of the former in the long run. If bureaucrats in a public agency, for example, do not identify the public good with that of the nation as a whole, but rather see their purpose as helping one particular ethnic or kin group advance relative to others, then that agency's purposes will be corrupted from the start. Outsiders usually have limited means of fostering national identity. Although it has been done in the past (for example, by the British in India), building a national identity is a very slow process and does not suit the timetables of most donors.

Future Directions The difficulty of transferring institutions has led to suggestions that institutions need to be, in effect, outsourced. Krasner (2004) has suggested the need for a system of "shared sovereignty" in which certain state functions are performed by international organizations or other external actors. Other writers have suggested that it is often well-meaning interventions on the part of the international community that create state weakness in the first place, and that states may be better off being left alone to generate institutions endogenously (Weinstein 2005). It is clear, however, that the realities of globalization mean that institutional development in many parts of the world will be inescapably linked to external actors, ideas, resources, and influences. To an increasing degree, it is impossible to separate the exogenous and endogenous, internal and external, sources of growth and decay of institutions.

See also aid, international; development

FURTHER READING

Acemoglu, Daron, James A. Robinson, and Simon Johnson. 2001. "The Colonial Origins of Comparative Development: An Empirical Investigation." *American Economic Review* 91 (5): 1369–401. Widely cited article attributes institutional transfer to disease burdens, which determine the likelihood of Europeans settling in a particular colony.

Chesterman, Simon. 2004. *You the People: The United Nations, Transitional Administration, and State-Building*. Oxford: Oxford University Press. A comprehensive study of post–Cold War, postconflict interventions by the UN.

De Soto, Hernando. 1989. *The Other Path: The Invisible Revolution in the Third World*. New York: Harper and Row. A classic account of informality in developing countries as a consequence of weak formal institutions.

Easterly, William R., and Ross Levine. 2002. *Tropics, Germs, and Crops: How Endowments Influence Economic Development*. NBER Working Paper No. 9106. Cambridge, MA: National Bureau of Economic Research. Analysis confirms the importance of institutions relative to factor endowments and geography.

Engerman, Stanley L., and Kenneth L. Sokoloff. 2002. "Factor Endowments, Inequality, and Paths of Development among New World Economies." *Economia* 3 (1): 41–101. Authors suggest that factor endowments determined the nature of institutions and inequality when comparing Latin and North America.

Fukuyama, Francis. 2004. *State-Building: Governance and World Order in the 21st Century.* Ithaca, NY: Cornell University Press. A general account of the role of states in development and of the limits to our knowledge about institutional transfer.

Khan, Mushtaq H., and Kwame Sundaram Jomo, eds. 2000. *Rents, Rent-Seeking, and Economic Development: Theory and Evidence in Asia.* Cambridge: Cambridge University Press. Shows that rent-seeking is not uniformly harmful to growth and suggest a typology of rent-seeking regimes.

Knack, Stephen, and Philip Keefer. 1995. "Institutions and Economic Performance: Cross-Country Tests Using Alternative Measures." *Economics and Politics* 7: 207–27. An early econometric study linking institutions to growth.

Krasner, Stephen D. 2004. "Sharing Sovereignty: New Institutions for Collapsed and Failing States." *International Security* 29 (2): 85–120. Suggests that, given the difficulty of institutional transfer, permanent shared sovereignty with international actors may be the only possible way of providing good governance for failed states.

Levy, Brian, and Sahr Kpundeh, eds. 2004. *Building State Capacity in Africa: New Approaches, Emerging Lessons.* Washington, DC: World Bank. Surveys the success of the World Bank's public sector reform efforts in sub-Saharan Africa.

Lora, Eduardo, ed. 2007. *The State of State Reform in Latin America.* Stanford, CA: Stanford University Press/IDB. This collection of studies of institutional reform in Latin America since the debt crisis shows the glass half-full, with importance governance gains in some areas and stagnation or regress in others.

North, Douglass C. 1990. *Institutions, Institutional Change, and Economic Performance.* New York: Cambridge University Press. Provides the classic framework for understanding institutions in terms of transaction costs.

Sachs, Jeffrey. 2005. *The End of Poverty: Economic Possibilities for Our Time.* New York: Penguin Press. Sachs returns to the development policies of the 1950s with his call for an injection of massive donor resources to overcome the "poverty trap" in which he argues much of Africa is stuck.

Weinstein, Jeremy. 2005. *Autonomous Recovery.* Washington: Center for Global Development. A passionate but not always persuasive plea for greater resources as a means of spurring development.

Woo, Jung-En. 1991. *Race to the Swift: State and Finance in Korean Industrialization.* New York: Columbia University Press. Indicates the importance of Japanese colonial institutions to South Korea's postwar development.

World Bank. 1997. *The State in a Changing World.* Oxford: Oxford University Press. This report marked an important shift away from the Washington consensus in the Bank's internal thinking, giving new emphasis to the importance of the state for development.

———. 2000. *Reforming Public Institutions and Strengthening Governance.* Washington, DC: World Bank. This World Development Report marked an important turning point in the World Bank's thinking about the centrality of institutions and governance to development.

———. 2002. *Building Institutions for Markets: World Development Report 2002.* Washington, DC: Oxford University Press. A follow-up to the 1997 World Development Report that provides further conceptual and empirical grounding for the Bank's focus on institutional reform.

FRANCIS FUKUYAMA

■ international investment agreements

Investment provisions in bilateral investment treaties and reciprocal preferential trade agreements (PTAs) are intended to promote investment flows by granting investors greater predictability of the policies regulating foreign investment. These agreements typically provide for transparency, national treatment, nondiscrimination among foreign investors, and guarantees against expropriation. Some agreements may include disciplines preventing trade-related investment measures (TRIMS), such as local content requirements and local hiring requirements. Finally, nearly all provide some sort of dispute settlement provisions.

The Rise of Bilateral Investment Treaties (BITs)
BITs are the primary vehicle for international cooperation on the regulation of investment flows.

They customarily provide a definition of investment coverage, include rules of origin to determine the nationality of investors, and specify the treatment of inward investment and investors, either once established and/or preestablishment. Most BITs do not deal with market access restrictions per se—such as restrictions on sectoral entry or equity ownership limitations—although some do impose disciplines on performance requirements and similar TRIMs. They generally guarantee most favored nation (MFN) and national treatment (banning discrimination among investors from signatory countries and guaranteeing treatment of foreign investors on the same footing as domestic investors, respectively). Often the treatment that is guaranteed foreign investors is actually better than that accorded to domestic investors, for example, in terms of access to foreign exchange or ability to transfer capital outside of the country, or in terms of investor protection/rights.

A major function of BITs is to provide investor protections such as against expropriation, stipulating that there be due process, transparency and compensation for any expropriation of foreign investments. They also provide for a dispute resolution mechanism to enforce these provisions. Dispute settlement provisions vary, but usually include arbitration procedures, often based in recent BITs on international standards, such those of the World Bank Group's International Center for Settlement of Investment Disputes (ICSID) or the UN Commission on International Trade Law. BITs involving the United States generally allow private investors to bring cases against host-country governments, thereby removing any foreign policy–driven uncertainty regarding the willingness of their home country governments to defend their rights.

BITs have proliferated sharply since the 1980s. The total number of BITs in force has risen from 355 in 1990 to 1,891 by the end of 2005; another 604 had been signed but not yet entered into force (UNCTAD 2006a). The pace of new annual signings decreased—from more than 200 in the mid-1990s to 70 in 2005—as the pool of countries willing to enter into agreements began to reach full coverage. Although the majority of agreements are North-South arrangements, recent signings feature agreements among developing countries. South-South agreements now constitute 29 percent of the total. The top 10 signatories of BITs included seven from Europe (Germany, France, the United Kingdom, Italy, Belgium, the Netherlands, and Switzerland). China, Egypt, and Romania round out the top 10.

BITs now cover a substantial share of foreign direct investment (FDI) flows from members of the Organisation for Economic Co-operation and Development (OECD) to developing countries. In 1990, roughly 9 percent of investment flows were covered (though data in the early years are somewhat understated). By 2004, 43 percent of investment was covered.

Preferential Trade Agreements (PTAs) PTAs, like BITs, have multiplied in the years since 1990. The United Nations Conference on Trade and Development (UNCTAD) reports that 232 PTAs were in force at the end of 2005, 86 of which were purely South-South arrangements. Many of these agreements, particularly the North-South agreements, now cover investment. PTAs involving the United States and the European Union (EU) have been important drivers. By 2006, the United States had in force free trade agreements with investment provisions involving 14 countries, including Mexico, Chile, and Singapore, with three signed and before the U.S. Congress, and three more under negotiation. The EU engagement in PTAs is even more extensive, with more than 100 PTAs as of 2003, and investment is more frequently covered. Thus, for example, investment policies are being discussed as part of the Economic Partnership Agreement negotiations with African, Caribbean, and Pacific countries and the recent agreements with southern Mediterranean countries.

U.S. Free Trade Agreements (FTAs) Recent U.S. FTAs include preestablishment rights of market access. These provisions imply opening services markets to competition from foreign suppliers—or locking in prior autonomous liberalization—except in those sectors excluded (through a negative list). This therefore may expand on the coverage of commitments in the General Agreement on Trade in Services (GATS), where a positive list is used and greatly enhances the transparency of prevailing policies. Since most of the countries with which the United States has concluded bilateral PTAs are already open in most sectors, the agreements lock in prevailing openness and generally effect changes in only a few still-restricted activities. Common provisions range from inclusion of insurance, financial advisory services, and selected telecommunications services to arguably relatively inconsequential changes to already open regimes, such as the commitment by Singapore to cease cross-subsidies in express mail delivery or the commitment of Chile in insurance services and a few other sectors. Moreover, notable for their absence is the exclusion of labor services, except provisional visas for professionals associated with investing firms.

All U.S. FTAs provide for national and MFN treatment. For many of the initial FTA countries, these had long been included in national legislation and/or have been incorporated into bilateral investment treaties on a postestablishment basis.

The U.S. FTAs have subsumed preexisting BITs and provided new measures covering investment. Agreements, especially those signed after the North American Free Trade Agreement (NAFTA), include broad definitions of investment, including not only FDI but also portfolio flows, private debt and even sovereign debt issues as well as intellectual property. Such broad definitions of investment policies can expose countries to dispute settlement across a wide range of assets.

The inclusion of intellectual property rights in the definition of assets covered by the investment provisions creates a potential liability for signatory governments. Not only are the intellectual property rights far more extensive under the recent PTAs than under the WTO's Agreement on Trade-Related Aspects of Intellectual Property Rights (TRIPS) (see Fink and Reichenmiller 2005), the dispute settlement provisions are more powerful. For example, if a government decides to issue a compulsory license to control drug prices and the patent owner disputes this action under the terms of the U.S. PTA, the patent holder can take the claim to commercial arbitration under the PTA's investment provisions. This instrument is considerably more powerful for intellectual property rights enforcement than the state-to-state provisions under the TRIPS Agreement (see World Bank 2003).

Another area of disciplines concerns trade-related investment measures (TRIMs)—government policies that require foreign companies to export in a certain portion of their sales or balance trade, using local inputs to achieve value-added objectives. All of the bilateral U.S. PTAs ban TRIMs. The U.S. bilateral agreements have in effect established a "WTO TRIMs Plus" set of obligations that include outright bans on certain performance requirements, including management restrictions and export, minimum domestic content, domestic sourcing, trade balancing, and technology transfer requirements. Government procurement, environmental standards, and requirements for local research and development are generally not covered.

A key feature of U.S. agreements is the use of negative lists excluding sectors or industries from coverage. This feature implies that all other sectors not mentioned—including new economic activities—are included; this is distinct from the positive list approach typically found in EU agreements and most South-South agreements. Ratchet provisions, also a feature of U.S. agreements, bind liberalizing policies enacted subsequent to the agreement's entrance into force, thus locking the policy framework progressively in ever greater openness and certainty.

Finally, with the exception of the Australian FTA, all the U.S. agreements contain an investor-state dispute resolution provision that permits investors to take foreign governments to dispute resolution for violation of the treaty's national treatment, nondiscrimination, or expropriation provisions, among others.

European Union Agreements Because investment is the competence of the EU member states, not the European Commission, EU PTAs have treated investment only generally or indirectly. The earliest (and least comprehensive) are the Euro-Mediterranean Partnership agreements (starting in 1995) and the South African agreement (1999), which contained virtually no investment provisions. Thus the market access provisions were general, directed mainly at services, and contain only the promise of potential liberalization after discussions to transpire some 5 years after the entry into force of the agreement. In the EU-Mexico PTA, several general provisions were included, many ratifying GATS arrangements, as well as specific liberalization commitments in the financial sector. The EU-Chile agreement goes further by additionally locking in some liberalization of telecommunications and maritime services.

The EU agreements with Mexico and Chile, though more comprehensive than earlier agreements, do not have the same strength of disciplines as the U.S. agreements. The trade provisions use a positive list and implicitly exclude new products. The treatment of investment and capital flows in both agreements were not extensive. For example, the EU-Mexico agreement simply states that the existing restrictions on investment will be progressively eliminated and no new restrictions adopted, without specifying particular sectors or setting a timeline for liberalization. The language in the EU-Chile agreement is even more general, calling for "free movement of capital relating to direct investments made in accordance with the laws of the host country." Both agreements allow for use of safeguards in the event of monetary or exchange rate difficulties, and although the time limit is set at 6 months for Mexico and 12 months for Chile, allow for continuation of the safeguard after the time limit through its formal reintroduction.

The treatment of dispute settlement involves state-to-state mechanisms rather than the investor-state provisions in U.S. agreements that allow private companies to initiate arbitration cases against governments. The EU provisions pertaining to investment are subsumed in the general dispute settlement provisions for all matters in the PTA. State-to-state dispute settlement is first attempted through consultations with a Joint Committee (Association Committee in the case of Chile and Mediterranean countries) within 30 days of a party's request. If this step of "dispute avoidance" proves unsuccessful, in the case of Chile, the concerned party can forward its request to an arbitration panel comprising representatives of both parties. The arbitration panel's decisions are binding, and the panel can also rule on the conformity of any measures undertaken as a result of its decision with the original ruling. Both agreements provide extensive detail on the process of appointing members to the arbitration panel, timelines for the panel's ruling, and compliance with the panel's decisions. Still, companies in member states that have their own BITs with recipient countries can activate investor state arbitration through BIT mechanisms.

Multilateral Initiatives Since 1948 when the Havana Charter was created, governments in high-income countries have sought to weave investment provisions into international trade law. While selected investment issues were addressed with the creation of the UN Center on Transnationals and the OECD Guidelines for Multinationals, it was not until the OECD launched the Multilateral Agreement on Investment in 1995 that a full-scale effort was resumed. This effort eventually foundered in the face of resistance from labor and environmental groups as well as developing countries that were largely excluded; when France withdrew from the negotiations in 1998 over the failure to protect its media and cultural interests, the negotiations collapsed.

With the launching of the Doha Development Agenda in the Ministerial Meeting of the WTO in November 2001, it seemed that investment would once again be taken up as part of the negotiating mandate for the so-called Singapore issues. Discussions in the 20 subsequent months before the next Ministerial meeting in Cancun, Mexico, in 2003, focused on the definition of investment to be covered, whether to adopt positive or negative lists, and the type of dispute resolution to be adopted. In each of these areas, the contentious negotiations tended to gravitate toward outcomes favoring the lowest common denominator: narrowly focused definitions of investment, positive lists with abundant room for exclusions, and state-to-state dispute resolution.

However, progress in the Doha Round was painfully slow in the run-up to the Cancun meeting, and disagreement on the Singapore issues was only one symptom. The inclusion of investment in the negotiations encountered vehement opposition from a coalition of developing countries, including most notably India and Malaysia. Negotiations were stymied over other major issues in agriculture and nonagricultural products, and many developing countries considered the heated discussions on the Singapore issues a distraction and of little value to their development.

Finally, in an ill-fated effort to move the discussions off dead center, the EU, the principal *demandeur* of Singapore issues, at the last minute offered to abandon investment and competition—and even cease future WTO activity in the Working Group. The Cancun Ministerial nonetheless broke down in acrimony. Only later when India offered to accept one of the four Singapore issues, trade facilitation, did this later become the accepted position in subsequent negotiations. Investment was officially dead as an issue for negotiation in the WTO's Doha Round.

Effects on Investment A main objective of a BIT is to increase the flow of investment to signatory countries. Does the signing of bilateral investment treaties in fact increase the flow of FDI? Hallward-Driemeier (2003), in one of the first systematic statistical analyses, considered bilateral flows from OECD members to 31 developing countries over two decades. Her analysis found that, controlling for a time trend and country-specific effects, BITs had virtually no independent effect in increasing the share of FDI to a signatory country from a home country. Countries signing a BIT were no more likely to receive additional FDI than countries without such a pact. Even comparing flows in the three years after a BIT was signed to the three years prior, there was no significant increase in FDI. Rose-Ackerman and Tobin (2005) analyzed the flows to 63 countries with data averaged over a five-year period and found that only with countries at very low levels of risk was there any increase of investment from the signatory home country; in a detailed analysis of U.S. FDI behavior,

they failed to find any statistically significant effects on U.S. FDI to 54 countries, irrespective of political risk.

In contrast to these findings, Neumayer and Spess (2005), using a larger sample over a longer period and considering simply the number of BITs signed, found robust and positive effects of the total number of BITs on total inflows of FDI. This finding relies heavily on the notion that signing a BIT signals to all would-be investors that the environment is more welcoming. In this model, the signal is more important than the specific investor protections. These contradictory findings at minimum suggest that the jury is still out and that it cannot be accepted axiomatically that BITs increase investment flows.

Assessing the evidence of investment provisions in PTAs is more difficult. The reason is that it is difficult to distinguish the effects on investment flows of creating a larger, single market from the effects of investor protections and other investment provisions in the trade agreement. Empirical studies generally consider the combined effects of PTAs—trade and investment provisions together.

Available evidence suggests mild positive effects on overall investment. The Global Economic Prospects 2005 (World Bank 2004) examined the effects of PTA membership and other variables on FDI inflows for a panel of 152 countries during the 1980–2002 period. The study found that PTAs that result in larger markets do attract greater FDI. The interaction of signing a PTA and expanded market size associated with the integrated markets is significant and positively related to FDI. On average, a 10 percent increase in market size associated with a PTA produces an increase in FDI of 5 percent.

One example is NAFTA, which is a comprehensive arrangement that includes significant investor protections in combination with broad-based tariff reductions and border liberalizations. Chapter 11 of the NAFTA agreement allows investors to sue the government in the event of regulatory or other actions that might diminish the value of a foreign investment. In their study, Lederman, Maloney, and Serven (2003) find that, in addition to positive forces in the global economy that propelled investment into Mexico and other emerging markets after 1994, the trade opening and NAFTA accession also played a role in Mexico's FDI rise.

Neither this study nor others attempt to distinguish the role of enhanced investor protections from access to the Mexican market and its other resources in increasing the flow of FDI. It may be that simply liberalizing the investment law in 1993 and making it easier to take advantage of productivity-adjusted wage differentials in the NAFTA countries was sufficient to explain the difference. However, it is possible that investor protections in chapter 11 played an important independent role because Mexico's legal framework was seen as less reliable than other investment destinations. In an analysis of shareholder rights, creditor rights, efficiency of judiciary, rule of law, and absence of corruption, Mexico scores below the Latin American average in four of five measures (as cited in Lederman, Maloney, and Serven 2003). To the extent that chapter 11 provided investors with additional comfort over and above the existing investment climate, its protections would have offset these disadvantages. In any case, Lederman et al. (2003) conclude that Mexico's entry into NAFTA led to an increase in annual FDI by around 40 percent.

Dispute Settlement: Rising Case Load and Rising Awards The costs of resolving investor disputes can be large. The number of cases brought under the various bilateral investment treaties and PTAs has risen dramatically. Though the absence of reporting data from all the dispute tribunals prevents full analysis, the International Center for Settlement of Investment Disputes (ICSID) at the World Bank reports a steady increase in the number of cases from an annual average of 1.5 cases in 1972–95 to 29 in 2003–4, after which a tapering off is evident. However, UNCTAD has established a database that includes other sources, and its main report (UNCTAD 2005) and subsequent update (UNCTAD 2006b) point to a continued upward trend through 2005. Some 48 known cases were brought in 2005 (UNCTAD 2006b).

In fact, the dispute settlement process is cloaked in opaqueness. The ICSID registry contains only minimal information about the dispute—it is not known whether the dispute arises from a BIT provision, a FTA provision, or some other state contract. Information often becomes available only when one of the parties to an arbitration makes it public. Many of the disputes outside of the ICSID tribunal are never made public, and even less is known about their resolution.

United States FTAs do provide for somewhat greater transparency. In NAFTA, for example, as of July 2004, there were 31 cases brought under chapter 11 (including 14 against Mexico, 9 against Canada, and 8 against the United States). Six cases have been decided in favor of the investor, but the amount awarded has been small compared to initial (undoubtedly inflated) claims. Tribunal awards have totaled $35 million compared to claims of $1.0 billion.

At least 61 governments—47 from the developing world (including transition countries)—have faced investment treaty arbitration. Forty-two cases were lodged against the Argentine government after its devaluation of the peso in 2001. Causes have varied from changes in tax policy perceived as adverse by investors to expropriations following conflict or coups, irregularities in bidding processes, and others (Peterson 2003a, 2003b).

Awards can be hefty. In February 2005, the Slovak Republic agreed to comply with an ICSID arbitral award of $830 million to CSOB, a Czech bank. This award surpassed that of a tribunal in Stockholm, which required the government of the Czech Republic to pay one company, Central European Media (CME), $350 million for violation of a BIT that deprived CME of a stake in an English-language TV station in Prague. This amount was ten times higher than previously known awards under arbitration cases and about equal to the entire public sector deficit of the Czech Republic (Peterson 2003a, 2003b). But the biggest case has been filed against the Russian Federation, involving a claim for $28 billion for the alleged expropriation of Group Menatep's majority shareholding in the Yukos oil firm under the 1994 Energy Charter Treaty (as yet unratified). In one of a series of decisions that have gone against the government of Argentina, in February 2007 Siemens was awarded $217 million for violation of a Germany-Argentina bilateral investment treaty (Peterson 2007). To these awards must be added legal fees and tribunal costs. Governments may have to pay costs that can range from $1 million to $2 million (UNCTAD 2005).

Flaws in the System of Property Rights Enforcement Theodore Moran (2006) discusses weaknesses in the dispute settlement procedures through the lens of prominent NAFTA cases. Perhaps the most detailed case study of investment dispute resolution and its consequences is the Wells and Ahmed (2007) study of Indonesia in the wake of the 1998 East Asia crisis. In an illuminating history of the collapse of private power contractual arrangements and subsequent dispute resolution, Wells and Ahmed conclude that the arbitration process "served the host countries poorly" and that companies found the promised protections were "largely illusory." Wells and Ahmed point to five weaknesses:

1. The system of contracts and enforcement is overly rigid, failing to take into account changed circumstances, excessively large claims, the role of corruption, and reasonable expectations from public policy.
2. The system produces inconsistent outcomes, as "tribunal shopping" has led to wildly different outcomes based on differing standards of evaluation using the same contracts.
3. The investor-state arbitration system is inherently asymmetric, according investors a superior position in the resolution process, in relation to both governments (that cannot initiate a case against an underperforming investor) and to domestic investors (who cannot avail themselves of the system).
4. The system creates a "moral hazard" that effectively discourages companies, based on rigidly interpreted rights, from seeking resolution through renegotiating contractual arrangements.
5. The system, by focusing only on awarding damages, foregoes the opportunity to encourage mutually beneficial contractual restructuring, policy changes, or negotiated settlements.

Many of these conclusions also emerge from the study of Cosbey, Mann, Peterson, and Von Molke (2004) who examine investment agreements from a cross-country perspective. They underscore the lack of transparency, potential conflicts of interests in the selection of arbitrators, inconsistency across multiple tribunals reviewing the same case, and lack of accountability of the system. Moran (2006) detects a lessening of salience of treaty-driven investor protections as experience tends to caution investors against overrelying on these instruments and moderate expectations of developing countries about higher investment flows.

In conclusion, international investment agreements are on the rise, even though their ability to promote investment remains unclear. Several questions merit additional exploration: What recourse do investors have legally if a government refuses to pay claims awarded against it, and does recourse provide sufficient incentive for full payment? Because the costs of enforcing payment of an award are usually high, governments could negotiate down the final settlement. What has been the experience of investors after being awarded large claims; have they collected full amounts, and if not, what was the negotiating process that led to final settlement?

Further, how can the arbitration process be made more transparent, fairer, and more open? Is there a synergy between investor protections and free trade provisions that would encourage FDI? Do countries with negative list provisions in their BITs and FTAs attract more investment than countries with positive list provisions?

If the objective is to increase the inflows of FDI, countries should begin with improvements in the domestic investment climate—sound macroeconomic policies, stable property rights for all investors, and sound regulatory policies—and treat investment treaty provisions as a complement rather than a substitute for an attractive policy framework.

See also domestic content requirements; foreign direct investment and international technology transfer; foreign direct investment and tax revenues; foreign equity restrictions; free trade area; trade costs and foreign direct investment; trade-related investment measures (TRIMs)

FURTHER READING

Cosbey, Aaron, Howard Mann, Luke Peterson, and Konrad Von Moltke. 2004. *Investment and Sustainable Development: A Guide to the Uses and Potential of International Investment Agreements.* Ottawa: International Institute for Sustainable Development. A comprehensive guide to international agreement provisions.

Fink, Carsten, and Patrick Reichenmiller. 2005. "Tightening TRIPS: Intellectual Property Provisions of U.S. Free Trade Agreements." In *Trade, Doha, and Development: A Window into the Issues*, edited by Richard Newfarmer. Washington, DC: World Bank, 187–97. One of the first detailed analyses of IPR provisions in U.S. FTAs and their impact on access to medicine.

Hallward-Driemeier, Mary. 2003. "Do Bilateral Investment Treaties Attract FDI? Only a Bit . . . and They Could Bite." World Bank Policy Research Paper No. 3121. Washington, DC: World Bank. A sophisticated econometric study of the effects of BITs on investment flows.

Lederman, Daniel, William F. Maloney, and Luis Serven. 2003. *Lessons from NAFTA for Latin America and Caribbean.* Washington, DC: World Bank. The most detailed study of NAFTA to date.

Moran, Theodore. 2006. "Toward a Development-Friendly International Regulatory Framework for Foreign Direct Investment." (September). Washington, DC: mimeo. A thoughtful discussion of ways to improve development outcomes through multilateral regulation.

Neumayer, Eric, and Laura Spess. 2005 "Do Bilateral Investment Treaties Increase Foreign Direct Investment to Developing Countries?" *World Development* 33 (10): 1567–85. Another serious study of BITs and investment flows to developing countries.

Peterson, Luke. 2003a. "Research Note: Emerging Bilateral Investment Treaty Arbitration and Sustainable Development." IISD Invest New Bulletin (April). Winnipeg, Canada: International Institute for Sustainable Development. Renamed the Investment Treaty News, this electronic newsletter is an invaluable source of current information on investment disputes and related developments.

———. 2003b. "Czech Republic Hit with Massive Compensation Bill in Investment Treaty Dispute." IISD Invest New Bulletin (March 21). Winnipeg, Canada: International Institute for Sustainable Development.

———. 2007. "Argentina Liable for $217 Million in Investment Treaty Arbitration with Siemens." *Investment Treaty News* (February 19). Available at http://www.iisd.org. Winnipeg, Canada: International Institute for Sustainable Development.

Rose-Ackerman, Susan, and Jennifer Tobin. 2005. "Foreign Direct Investment and the Business Environment in Developing Countries: The Impact of Bilateral Investment Treaties." Yale Law and Economics Research Paper 293 (May). New Haven: Yale University. A useful analysis of BITs and investment.

United Nations Conference on Trade and Development (UNCTAD). 1998. *Bilateral Investment Treaties in the Mid-1990s.* New York: United Nations. UNCTAD is the leading data source for information on FDI around the world.

———. 2005. "Investor-State Disputes Arising from Investment Treats: A Review." Geneva: UNCTAD.

———. 2006a. "Entry into Force of Bilateral Investment Treaties (BITs)." IIA Monitor No. 3. Geneva: UNCTAD.

———. 2006b. "Latest Developments in Investor-State Dispute Settlement." IIA Monitor No. 4. Geneva: UNCTAD.

Wells, Louis, and Ahmed, Rafiq. 2007. *Making Foreign Investment Safe: Property Rights and National Sovereignty.* New York: Oxford University Press. One of the most in-depth political-economic studies of investment disputes and their causes, resolutions, and weaknesses.

World Bank. 2003. *Global Economic Prospects 2004: Investing to Unlock Global Opportunities.* Washington, DC: World Bank. Examines investment policy from a development perspective, with a chapter on investment in WTO negotiations.

———. 2004. *Global Economic Prospects 2005: Trade, Regionalism, and Development.* Washington, DC: World Bank. Provides a comparative analysis of investment provisions in different settings from U.S. and EU agreements.

RICHARD NEWFARMER

■ International Labor Organization

The International Labor Organization (ILO) was created in the wake of World War I and the communist takeover of Russia with the narrow goal of improving working conditions around the world. The underlying objectives, however, were to avoid political instability by addressing issues of social justice and concerns that global competition could undermine countries' efforts to improve working conditions at home. The first wave of globalization had already crashed on the shoals of World War I by the time the ILO had come into being. But a century later, a new wave of globalization triggered similar concerns and the ILO once again found itself at the center of debates over how to address economic insecurity and inequality.

The ILO is the only League of Nations institution to survive World War II and is also the only international organization that is not purely intergovernmental in its governance structure. Union and employer group representatives are part of each country's delegation and have the same right to vote as government representatives at policymaking meetings. As of 2006, the ILO had adopted 187 conventions determining international standards for various aspects of work and employment. Some of the standards dealt with fundamental rights of workers, but most are narrow and technical, on issues of importance only to labor, management, or regulators in specific sectors, for instance, shipping or communications.

In 1998, the ILO approved a "Declaration on Fundamental Principles and Rights at Work," which provided a consensus definition of four core labor standards that became the centerpiece of the global standards movement. In the face of accelerating globalization, the ILO has also focused more attention on employment, adjustment, and migration issues. In 2002, it established a World Commission on the Social Dimensions of Globalization to explore ways to make economic globalization more inclusive and to spread its benefits more broadly.

The Organization of the ILO The ILO is a tripartite organization with 179 member states and 716 voting delegates, with each member having two government representatives and one each representing employers and workers. In theory, worker and employer delegates are not bound by their government's position and vote independently. Delegates gather annually at the International Labor Conference, where new conventions may be adopted, implementation of existing conventions is reviewed, and the budget is approved. The Governing Body, except for ten permanent members, is elected by the conference and is the executive body of the organization, responsible for developing policy, electing the director-general, and overseeing the organization's work program.

The International Labor Office, headed by the director-general, is the secretariat of the organization with headquarters in Geneva and branch offices around the world. The office provides advisory services and technical assistance, for example on how to create or reform laws for social protection, and carries out research projects, such as studying the implications of the end of the Multifiber Arrangement for workers in clothing factories around the world. The activities of the office are organized around the theme of "decent work" and four strategic objectives: rights at work, employment, social protection, and social dialogue.

The ILO's Tools In addition to standards-setting, the ILO has three main tools for improving working conditions. It supervises compliance with global labor conventions and publicizes violations of standards to shame countries into improving. It gives technical assistance to labor ministries and other agencies, unions, and employer groups to address employment-related issues and to improve the implementation of labor standards. And it can punish countries that do not comply with their commitments, though complaints have rarely led to formal enforcement measures.

Supervising and Publicizing Country Performance
The ILO has extensive mechanisms for supervising the application of conventions, including routine reporting by countries on implementation of conventions they have ratified, why they have not ratified others, and what they are doing to achieve the goals of those conventions. These reports are reviewed by independent experts who identify areas both of progress and of special concern, which may be taken up by the Conference Committee on the Application of Standards at the annual conference.

The most important innovation in ILO monitoring came with the 1998 Declaration on Fundamental Rights and Principles at Work, which defined four core labor standards:

- freedom of association and the right to organize and bargain collectively;
- freedom from forced labor;
- the eventual abolition of child labor;
- nondiscrimination in employment.

The follow-up mechanism for implementing the declaration requires member countries that have not ratified one or more of the eight conventions associated with these principles to report annually on what they are doing to promote the conventions and encourages employer and worker groups to comment on the national submissions. In addition, the conference requires the director-general to prepare a global report summarizing how each core standard is being implemented around the world and identifying key obstacles to compliance.

Technical Assistance Ministries of Labor and other organizations seeking to raise standards and improve the operation of labor markets are often weak bureaucracies with inadequate resources and limited support from political leaders. In such situations, even modest ILO technical assistance can be helpful. The ILO also conducts extensive research and outreach on issues related to employment and underemployment in developing countries, as well as the obstacles to standards compliance posed by extensive employment in the informal sector in many countries.

For decades ILO technical assistance programs received only modest funding from wealthier member states and the agency had a limited presence in developing countries. In the 1990s, however, many countries, including the United States, responded to demands that the world community do more to improve labor standards by increasing their funding for ILO programs. As a result, technical cooperation spending increased from an average of just over $90 million per year in 1998–2000 to nearly $140 million in 2004. Virtually all of the increase went to programs to eliminate child labor, which accounted for nearly 40 percent of total technical assistance in 2004.

Enforcement of Conventions and Standards In addition to routine reporting and review, the ILO has two ad hoc mechanisms for promoting compliance with labor standards, though critics charge that the organization is toothless. Article 24 of the ILO Constitution allows any worker or employer organization in the world to file a complaint alleging that a member government is not complying with a convention it has ratified or that a country has violated freedom of association (regardless of whether it ratified the relevant conventions). If such complaints are not resolved through informal consultation, the Governing Body can refer them to the Committee on Freedom of Association or appoint an ad hoc committee to analyze the situation, ask the government to respond, and make recommendations on what the government can do to comply. If the problem remains unresolved, official ILO delegates can file an article 26 complaint.

The ILO Governing Body will again try to resolve the problem informally through consultations. But if that leads nowhere, it can appoint a Commission of Inquiry to formally investigate the charges and recommend how to correct the problem. The target of the complaint can appeal the commission's finding to the International Court of Justice. If the commission's findings are upheld and a satisfactory resolution is still not forthcoming, article 33 of the ILO

Constitution provides that "the Governing Body may recommend that the Conference take such action as it may deem wise and expedient to secure compliance therewith."

Between 1919 and 1960, there was only one article 26 complaint. From 1961 to 2000, there was an average of six complaints per decade. In its history, the ILO has appointed only nine Commissions of Inquiry, usually regarding alleged violations of one of the four fundamental rights. The ILO did not take the next step of invoking article 33 until 2000, when the conference approved a resolution calling on member states "to review their relationship with the Government of Myanmar (Burma) and to take appropriate measures to ensure that Myanmar 'cannot take advantage of such relations to perpetuate or extend the system of forced or compulsory labour.'" Raising questions about the ILO's effectiveness in difficult situations, however, the annual conference asked the Governing Body to consider what additional steps might be taken if the government in Myanmar remained uncooperative.

In sum, the ILO aims to improve living conditions for people around the world by increasing employment opportunities, making work safer and more productive, and in recent years, ensuring that workers share in the benefits of globalization. It does this by promoting social dialogue and basic rights that allow workers to bargain over wages and working conditions; by promulgating, monitoring, and enforcing other standards; and by providing technical assistance to employers associations, unions, and governments in pursuit of these objectives. The ILO also conducts research on a variety of employment-related issues and is the major source for what data exists on labor markets.

See also child labor; labor standards; trade and wages

FURTHER READING

Charnovitz, Steven. 2000. "The International Labor Organization in Its Second Century." In *Max Planck Yearbook of United Nations Law*, edited by Jochen A. Fruwein and Rudige Wolfram. New York: Kluwer, 147–84. Analyzes the challenges and opportunities facing the ILO in a world with a more globalized economy and greater involvement by developing countries.

International Labor Organization. http://www.ilo.org. The ILO's Web site provides an immense amount of information about the organization's history and current operations.

Sengenberger, Werner, and Duncan Campbell. 1994. *International Labor Standards and Economic Interdependence: Essays in Commemoration of the 7th Anniversary of the International Labor Organization and the 50th Anniversary of the Declaration of Philadelphia*. Geneva: International Institute for Labor Studies. Covers the history and economics of international labor standards, as well as issues such as new challenges from the latest wave of globalization and whether or which standards should be universal.

World Commission on the Social Dimensions of Globalization. 2004. *A Fair Globalization: Creating Opportunities for All*. Geneva: International Labor Organization. Report of an independent commission chaired by the presidents of Finland and Tanzania and including representatives from governments, nongovernmental organizations, business, and labor.

KIMBERLY ANN ELLIOTT

■ international liquidity

International liquidity refers to the availability of internationally accepted means of settling international debts relative to the demand or potential demand for such financial assets. The availability or supply of international liquidity depends on the stock of total reserve assets owned by world central banks or national monetary authorities, as well as the ability of these institutions to borrow from the International Monetary Fund (IMF), the Eurocurrency market, and other financial institutions. The adequacy of international liquidity also depends on the demand for, or the expectation of, having to make such payments.

International reserve assets comprise reserve currencies, Special Drawing Rights (SDRs), and gold owned by nations' central banks or monetary authorities, as well member nations' reserve position in the IMF. Reserve currencies are foreign currencies held by central banks or monetary authorities that can be used (i.e., are accepted) for the settlement of intergovernmental claims. Reserve currencies represent almost 90 percent of total international reserve assets and the U.S. dollar accounts for about 65 percent of the total stock of reserve currencies. The second most important reserve currency is the euro. Other reserve currencies are the Japanese yen, the British pound, and the Swiss franc.

Special Drawing Rights (SDRs) are accounting entries on the books of the IMF introduced in 1967 to supplement international reserves. SDRs are used only among central banks to settle balance-of-payments deficits or surpluses; they cannot be used in private commercial dealings. At the 1967 IMF meeting it was agreed to create SDRs in the amount of $9.5 billion to be distributed to member nations according to their quotas in the IMF in three installments in January 1970, 1971, and 1972. Further allocations of SDRs made in the 1979–81 period brought their total to about $19 billion. The value of one SDR was originally set equal to one U.S. dollar, but rose above $1 as a result of the devaluations of the dollar in 1971 and 1973.

Starting in 1974, the value of SDRs was tied to a basket of currencies.

Gold was the international reserve asset par excellence during the gold standard period (1870–1914). Under the Bretton Woods system of fixed exchange rates (1947–71), gold was one of several types of international reserve asset held by national central banks or monetary authorities and the United States used gold as backing for the dollar reserves held by foreigners. In 1971, the United States suspended the dollar convertibility into gold at the fixed price of $35 per ounce. The price of gold then increased on the world market, but monetary gold (the amount held by nations' central banks or monetary authorities) continued to be valued at $35 per ounce in official transactions. Today, gold has lost a great deal of its importance as an international reserve asset and the IMF is moving toward demonetizing it, so that in the future gold would be used only for commercial purposes.

Member countries' reserve position in the IMF also constitutes a part of international reserves. This is equal to the amount of international reserves (originally, gold and reserve currencies but now only reserve currencies) that nations pay into the fund (based on their quota into the fund) on becoming

Table 1
International reserves, 1950–2005 (billions of SDRs, at year-end)

International reserve asset	1950	1960	1970	1980	1990	2000	2005
Foreign exchange	13.3	18.5	45.1	292.6	611.3	1,490.2	2,918.2
SDRs	—	—	3.1	11.8	20.4	18.5	20.1
Reserve position in the fund	1.7	3.6	7.7	16.8	23.7	47.4	28.6
Total reserves minus gold	15.0	22.1	56.2	321.3	655.4	1,556.1	2,966.8
Gold at SDR 35/ounce	32.2	37.9	37.0	33.5	32.9	33.3	30.9
Total with gold at SDR 35/ounce	48.2	60.0	93.2	354.7	688.3	1,589.4	2,997.7
Gold at SDR market price	33.0	38.6	39.6	455.4	253.1	200.6	316.6
Total with gold at market price in SDR	48.0	60.7	95.8	776.6	908.3	1,756.7	3,283.4
U.S. dollar per SDR	1.0000	1.000	1.000	1.2754	1.4227	1.3029	1.4293

Source: IMF, *International Financial Statistics Yearbook,* various issues.

members, and which nations can automatically borrow from the fund without any restrictions or questions asked.

The amount of the various international reserve assets available to nations from 1950 to 2005 (at ten-year intervals) is given in table 1, with and without the inclusion of gold reserves, and with gold at the official price of SDR 35/ounce and at market price. Note that the amounts of the various international reserve assets are given in SDRs by the IMF, but their dollar value can be obtained by multiplying them by the dollar value per SDR shown in the last row of the table. For example, the foreign exchange reserves of SDR 2.9185 trillion at the end of 2005 was equal to $4.171 trillion (SDR 2,918.2 billion times the dollar value of the SDR of $1.4293/SDR in 2005).

The adequacy of international liquidity depends not only on the supply or availability of liquidity but also on the demand for liquidity. Under the Bretton Woods system, nations needed international reserves to pay for temporary balance-of-payments deficits, without the need to restrict imports directly or indirectly through slower domestic growth. During this period, most of the increase in world liquidity resulted from the increase in official holdings of foreign exchange reserves, mostly dollars, to finance U.S. balance-of-payments deficits. The problem was that the more U.S. deficits persisted and the more dollars accumulated in foreign hands, the less willing foreigners were to hold additional dollars and the less confidence they had in the dollar (i.e., that the dollar would retain its international value and that the United States would be able to honor its commitment to redeem dollars in gold at the fixed price of gold of $35 per ounce, in the face of dwindling U.S. gold reserves). Indeed, it was precisely to avoid this confidence problem that the IMF decided to create SDRs in 1967. But this was not enough to prevent the collapse of the Bretton Woods system in 1971, when some central banks demanded conversion of some of their dollar reserves into gold, thus triggering the collapse of the system.

After the collapse of the Bretton Woods system, most developed nations and many developing nations moved to a system of managed exchange rate flexibility, which persists to this day. Under such a system, a nation with an actual or potential balance of payments deficit would experience a depreciation of its currency, which would correct the deficit by stimulating the nation's exports and discouraging its imports. Since the adjustment takes time, however, nations continue to need international reserves or liquidity. Nations also use international reserves or liquidity to intervene in foreign exchange markets to smooth out excessive exchange rate volatility or when attempting to influence the underlying value of the exchange rate of their currencies. Central banks could also increase their interest rate to attract international capital flows to cover balance of payments deficits or borrow additional reserves from the IMF or in the Eurocurrency market at a charge. In the case of currency crises (such as those that afflicted several emerging markets economies from 1994 to 2002), liquidity could be mobilized on an international scale under IMF leadership.

See also balance of payments; Bretton Woods system; currency crisis; dominant currency; Eurocurrencies; foreign exchange intervention; gold standard, international; international financial architecture; International Monetary Fund (IMF); international reserves; money supply; reserve currency; special drawing rights; vehicle currency

FURTHER READING

Bank of International Settlements. *Annual Report*. Basel: BIS. A report on the world's financial and banking situation.

De Vries, M. G. 1986. *The IMF in a Changing World*. Washington, DC: IMF. An authoritative discussion of the operation of the International Monetary Fund from its creation after World War II until the early 1980s.

International Monetary Fund. Annual. *International Financial Statistics Yearbook*. Washington, DC: IMF. The most complete and comparable financial data of member nations of the International Monetary Fund.

Mundell, Robert A. 2000. "A Reconsideration of the Twentieth Century." *American Economic Review* (June): 327–40. A review and interpretation of the operation of the international monetary system during the past century by a Nobel Prize winner in economics.

Salvatore, Dominick. 2007. *International Economics*. 9th ed. Hoboken, NJ: Wiley, chapter 21. An examination and evaluation of the operation of the international monetary system from the time of the gold standard to the present and a discussion of its possible reforms in the future.

Triffin, Robert. 1961. *Gold and the Dollar Crisis*. New Haven, CT: Yale University Press. A classic of the early postwar trouble of the dollar resulting from the "dollar overhang," or the excessive supply of dollars in the hands of foreign monetary authorities.

Willett, Thomas D. 1980. *International Liquidity Issues*. Washington, DC: American Enterprise Institute. A discussion of the adequacy of international liquidity required for the smooth operation of the international monetary system.

DOMINICK SALVATORE

■ International Monetary Fund (IMF)

The International Monetary Fund (IMF) is an intergovernmental organization that seeks to advance global financial stability. The IMF's responsibilities, as set out in its Articles of Agreement, include promoting international monetary cooperation and exchange stability, facilitating the expansion and growth of international trade, and making its resources available to members experiencing balance of payments difficulties. There are 185 member nations, and the headquarters is in Washington, DC.

The IMF was established in 1944 at the Bretton Woods Conference in New Hampshire. The representatives of 44 nations also created the International Bank for Reconstruction and Development (World Bank) for the purpose of postwar reconstruction; its mandate was later expanded to encompass economic development. The chief architects of the new international monetary system were Harry Dexter White of the U.S. Department of the Treasury and the noted British economist John Maynard Keynes. They sought to design a system that would prevent repetition of the chaos of the interwar period, when countries abandoned the gold standard and depreciated the values of their currencies in attempts to use exports to bolster their economies.

In the Bretton Woods system, central banks maintained fixed rates for their currencies in relation to the U.S. dollar. They held their foreign currency reserves in the form of dollars, which they could exchange for gold from the United States. The IMF served as a monitor of the system to ensure that governments fulfilled their obligations. The IMF also provided credit to members with balance of payments deficits in order to provide time for their governments to implement policies to restore equilibrium.

The Bretton Woods system collapsed in the early 1970s, in part because foreign central banks feared the inflationary consequences of the flow of dollars from the United States. However, the IMF acquired new roles by dealing with the debt crisis of the 1980s and then the emergence of the transition economies at the end of that decade. In the 1990s it coped with international financial crises, such as those that occurred in 1994 in Mexico and in East Asia in 1997, while promoting growth in its poorest members.

Governance The IMF is under the jurisdiction of its Board of Governors, which includes one member and one alternative member appointed by each country, and meets once a year. The Board of Governors delegates the responsibility for supervising the daily operations of the IMF to the Board of Directors. A country's position and voting power on the Board of Directors is based on the size of its quota. A country's quota is determined by its economic size and the value of its international transactions. The United States currently has the largest quota share, 17.09 percent, while Palau has the smallest relative quota, .001 percent. Since major decisions require a special majority of 85 percent of the votes cast, the United States has an effective veto.

There are 24 executive directors representing the IMF's members. The five countries with the largest quotas appoint executive directors to represent their interests on the board, while smaller members form constituencies and elect a joint director. The members with the largest quotas and their own directors are the United States, Japan, Germany, France, and the United Kingdom; Saudi Arabia, a major creditor to the fund, China, and Russia form single member constituencies and also name their own directors.

The Board of Governors conducts quota reviews at regular intervals, usually every five years. The Twelfth General Review took place in 2003, without any change in the quotas, and the Thirteenth General Review was scheduled to be completed by 2008. In the period between the 2003 and 2008 reviews, many members believed that the relative allocation of quotas was skewed in favor of some European nations at the expense of Asian economies and contended that there should be a reallocation of quota shares.

A country's quota also determines the amount of money it contributes to the IMF, called its subscription, and the limits on its access to financing. When it joins the IMF, a member makes a payment equal to its quota; one quarter of this subscription must consist of widely accepted currencies, such as the U.S. dollar or the euro. Increases in quotas require increases in the subscriptions paid in by the member nations. The quota payments provide the IMF the financial resources for its lending operations. In 2006 the IMF had $175 billion available for loans over the next one-year period.

The executive directors appoint a managing director to administer the fund's activities. The managing directors have always been Europeans, and Dominique Strauss-Kahn of France became the IMF's tenth managing director in 2007. There are three deputy directors to assist the managing director, and approximately 2,700 staff members, of whom about two-thirds are economists. The IMF has five area departments (African, Asia and Pacific, European, Middle East and Central Asia, and Western Hemisphere), eight functional departments (Finance, Fiscal Affairs, IMF Institute, Legal, Monetary and Capital Markets, Policy Development and Review, Research, and Statistics), and several information and support services departments. There is also an Independent Evaluation Office, which reports to the Executive Board.

Special Drawing Rights Special Drawing Rights (SDRs) are a unit of account used by the IMF. In the 1960s, central bankers outside the United States became concerned about the use of U.S. dollars as international reserves. The IMF's Board of Governors amended the original Articles of Agreement in 1969 to allow the introduction of the SDR by the IMF as a supplementary reserve asset. The first general distribution of SDRs was made in 1970–72. However, the need for new reserves diminished with the collapse of the Bretton Woods system and the development of private capital markets. The IMF continues to use SDRs as a monetary measurement. The value of the SDR is based on the foreign exchange value of the dollar, the euro, the yen and the British pound, and is posted on the fund's Web site (www.imf.org) daily.

Surveillance The IMF engages in surveillance activities to monitor and guide the economic policies of its members. The fund conducts bilateral surveillance of its individual members, as authorized under Article IV of the Articles of Agreement. A group of its economists, known as a staff mission, travel to a member's capital to consult with government officials about the member's exchange rate and monetary and fiscal policies. In recent years the talks have broadened to include the financial sector and assessments of vulnerability to capital flows, as well as structural issues such as fiscal reforms.

The IMF's economists submit a report of their findings to the fund's Executive Board, which uses it as the focus of its discussion of the country. Approximately nine out of ten of the IMF's members allow summaries of the staff's and board's views to be made public in the form of Public Information Notices, which are available at the IMF's Web site. Many countries also allow publication of the staff's report.

The IMF engages in multilateral surveillance to assess regional conditions and the world economy. The results of this work are published in the IMF's *World Economic Outlook* and its *Global Financial Stability Report*, each of which appears twice a year. The IMF has initiated a process of multilateral consultations with members in areas where there is a need for collective action, such as resolving global payments imbalances. However, the IMF can only operate through persuasion in these circumstances because it has no power over sovereign governments.

Technical Assistance The IMF provides technical assistance to its members, particularly lower-income members, on macroeconomic policies, financial sector regulation, and the collection and maintenance of databases. This assistance is financed by the IMF itself and the contributions of members as well as multilateral donors. The IMF integrates technical assistance with its surveillance and lending activities whenever possible. The IMF makes its assistance available through different mechanisms. It may send a team of economists to a country for a short-term project, or a resident advisor for a longer period. It also offers courses and training programs at the IMF Institute at its Washington, DC, headquarters and its six regional technical assistance centers and seven regional training institutes and programs in Africa, Asia, the Caribbean, Europe, the Pacific Islands, and South America.

Lending The IMF offers credit to countries with balance of payments imbalances; the institutional arrangements targeted for special circumstances are known as "facilities." The most commonly used mechanism is the Stand-By Arrangement (SBA), which is designed to assist countries with short-term problems, and usually lasts for 12 to 18 months. The Extended Fund Facility (EFF) was established to assist countries with longer-term problems and operates for up to three years. The Supplemental Reserve Facility (SRF) was introduced in 1997 to provide large amounts of funds to countries which experience sudden capital outflows, and these programs operate for two to three years. The Compensatory Financing Facility provides credit to countries subject to a shortfall in their export earnings or an increase in the cost of cereal imports. The fund also provides emergency assistance in special circumstances, such as natural disasters. The amount of money that a country can borrow from the fund —its access limit—depends on the type of program and the size of the country's quota. However, the IMF's lending can exceed this limit if a SRF is activated. All of these loans carry a market-based rate of charge, and large loans carry a surcharge.

The IMF also makes credit available to its poorest members through special facilities. The Poverty Reduction and Growth Facility (PRGF) is the successor to the Enhanced Structural Adjustment Facility (ESAF), which in turn followed the Structural Adjustment Facility (SAF). The new name was chosen to emphasize the twin goals of poverty reduction and growth.

A government that seeks external funding consults with the IMF about its needs and then signs a Letter of Intent (LOI), which is presented to the Executive Board for approval. A country can borrow up to 25 percent of its quota on liberal terms; larger amounts require activation of a lending arrangement. The LOI specifies the amount of available credit and also the policy conditions that the borrowing government agrees to implement. Once the LOI is signed, the IMF releases the credit in phased installments, which are tied to the adoption of the policies enumerated in the LOI. This practice is known as conditionality.

These conditions traditionally dealt with monetary and fiscal policies and a country's exchange rate. However, as upper-income countries turned to the private international capital markets in the 1980s, developing economies and subsequently the transition countries became the IMF's borrowers. The scope of conditionality expanded to include policies that were designed to improve the efficiency of these economies and promote growth. Structural policies included the liberalization of foreign trade, the restructuring of the financial sector, and privatization of state enterprises. Many of these conditions were consistent with the set of market-oriented policies that became known as the Washington consensus. By the 1990s, structural conditions appeared in virtually all of the IMF's programs.

The use of structural conditions, however, was widely criticized. The effectiveness of these conditions in promoting growth was questioned by critics, who pointed to counterexamples of successful development. China and India, for example, opened up their economies, but their governments played a role in the allocation of resources among firms and sectors. In addition, the record of implementation of structural conditions was mixed, in part because of domestic opposition.

The IMF reviewed its conditionality practices in 2002 and issued new guidelines. The Executive Board announced that the focus of structural conditionality in the future would be streamlined and limited to achieving the macroeconomic goals of the program. Moreover, the IMF acknowledged that programs were successful only when the borrowing government was committed to the process of reform—a concept known as country ownership. Ownership required the full participation of the government in developing the program with a regard for the country's circumstances.

Criticisms The IMF has been the subject of criticisms from both wings of the political spectrum. As noted above, structural conditionality was often viewed as inappropriate and misguided. Some critics charged that it had unduly harsh impacts on the poor because of cutbacks in government spending on social policies. A number of nongovernmental organizations (NGOs) have protested the fund's use of conditions, and the IMF's Annual Meetings have been the subject of picketing and demonstrations.

The fund's macroeconomic conditionality was also criticized in the wake of the 1997–98 East Asian crisis, when Thailand, Indonesia, and Korea turned to the IMF for assistance. The IMF initially called for contractionary fiscal and monetary policies, consistent with its traditional view of a crisis as the consequence of expansionary domestic policies. However, these crises were driven by capital outflows that in some cases were prompted by contagion from neighboring countries, and the countries were already undergoing contraction as domestic private expenditures collapsed. The increases in interest rates recommended by the IMF for the purpose of supporting exchange rates also deepened the decline in output. The IMF subsequently revised these programs to allow fiscal deficits, but defended its call for higher interest rates as necessary to arrest further depreciations and inflation.

The IMF has also been charged with indirectly contributing to the emergence of these crises through its lending, an example of the phenomenon of moral hazard. Critics assert that foreign lenders have been willing to make risky loans because they believed that the IMF would provide financial support in the event of a crisis. Some of these critics have called for the abolition of the IMF, which they claim no longer serves the purpose for which it was created.

However, many observers believe that in a world of global capital flows and recurring financial crises, there is a need for an organization to deal with breakdowns in international monetary flows. Many of these collapses require collective action to resolve, and an institution like the IMF has the capability to coordinate the private and official responses.

However, in recent years the number of new lending arrangements has fallen sharply. Part of this decline is due to economic growth in developing countries and increased holdings of foreign exchange reserves by central banks. But many of the emerging markets can now obtain credit in the private capital markets and therefore do not borrow from the IMF except in crisis conditions. The IMF needs to redefine its role in a world of global financial markets if it wants to retain its relevancy.

See also asymmetric information; bail-ins; bailouts; balance sheet approach/effects; Bretton Woods system; capital flows to developing countries; currency crisis; financial crisis; global imbalances; gold standard, international; hot money and sudden stops; international financial architecture; International Monetary Fund conditionality; International Monetary Fund surveillance; lender of last resort; special drawing rights; Washington consensus; World Bank

FURTHER READING

Blustein, Paul. 2001. *The Chastening: Inside the Crisis that Rocked the Global Financial System and Humbled the IMF*. New York: Public Affairs.

———. 2005. *And the Money Kept Rolling in (and Out): Wall Street, the IMF, and the Bankrupting of Argentina*. New York: Public Affairs. An engaging account by a *Washington Post* reporter of the global financial crises of the 1990s and the subsequent one in Argentina and the IMF's responses.

Boughton, James M. 2001. *Silent Revolution: The International Monetary Fund, 1979–1989*. Washington, DC: IMF. A history of the IMF from the IMF's own historian.

International Monetary Fund, Independent Evaluation Office. 2003. *IMF and Recent Capital Account Crises: Indonesia, Korea, Brazil.* Washington, DC: IMF.

———. 2004. *Report on the Evaluation of the Role of the IMF in Argentina, 1991–2001.* Washington, DC: IMF. Thorough analyses of the fund's involvement in some of the major crises by the IMF's own Independent Evaluation Office.

James, Harold. 1996. *International Monetary Cooperation since Bretton Woods.* Washington, DC: IMF and Oxford University Press. A history of the IMF.

Stiglitz, Joseph E. 2002. *Globalization and its Discontents.* New York: W. W. Norton. A far-ranging examination and critique of the IMF's policies.

Woods, Ngaire. 2006. *The Globalizers: The IMF, the World Bank, and Their Borrowers.* Ithaca, NY: Cornell University Press. An analysis of the relations of the IMF and World Bank with their member governments and their programs in Mexico, Russia, and Africa

JOSEPH P. JOYCE

■ International Monetary Fund conditionality

The International Monetary Fund (IMF) lends to its member nations with balance of payments problems in order to promote international financial stability. The government of a country that borrows from the IMF agrees to implement economic policies to rectify the situation, and the IMF disburses the credit as these policies are implemented. This monitoring mechanism is known as conditionality. The IMF uses conditionality to ensure that the borrowing country is resolving its problems and that the IMF's financial resources will be available to other members. The nature of conditionality has evolved over time in response to changes in the role of the IMF in the international economy and with its members.

Lending Procedures A country can borrow an amount equal to 25 percent of its quota with the IMF on liberal terms; larger amounts require the establishment of a policy program. The IMF uses a number of administrative programs to make credit available to its members. The most commonly used are the Stand-By Arrangement (SBA), which is designed to assist countries with short-term (1 to 2 years) problems, and the Extended Fund Facility (EFF) for countries with longer-term (typically 3 years) problems. Both programs carry a market-related interest rate. Between 1953 and 2007, there were 835 SBAs approved and 76 EFFs.

The IMF also lends to its poorest members at a below-market rate through the Poverty Reduction and Growth Facility (PRGF), which is the successor to the Structural Adjustment Facility (SAF) and Enhanced Structural Adjustment Facility (ESAF). The interest rate on a PRGF loan is 0.5 percent, and the lending typically takes place over a 3-year period. There are approximately 75 members of the IMF are eligible for the PRGF. There were 199 SAF/ESAF/PRGFs approved between 1953 and 2007.

After consultation with the IMF, a government that seeks credit signs a Letter of Intent, which specifies the amount of credit to be made available and the policy conditions that the government agrees to implement. A country applying for a PRGF must submit a Poverty Reduction Strategy Paper, which describes the steps that its government will undertake to foster growth and reduce poverty. Once the arrangement is approved by the IMF's Executive Board, the IMF releases the credit in phased installments, which are tied to the adoption of the enumerated policies.

The IMF monitors compliance with the policy conditions through a variety of institutional mechanisms. Prior actions are prerequisites that a country undertakes before the program actually begins. Performance criteria are specific conditions that a country must meet before it receives a disbursement of credit. Quantitative performance criteria include macroeconomic policy targets, such as monetary aggregates and fiscal balances. Structural performance criteria deal with an economy's efficient use of its resources and include measures such as deregulation. There may also be structural benchmarks that provide additional information about a country's program implementation.

The IMF will suspend a program if its conditions are not met. Waivers can be granted, however, when implementation has been delayed due to circumstances outside a government's control, such as lower than expected tax revenues or insufficient external financing. The IMF's Executive Board can perform a program review in situations where the original program requires revision due to new developments.

Analytical Tools The IMF draws on analytical frameworks in formulating the policies it recommends to borrowing countries. Among these is financial programming, which was developed at the IMF in the 1950s. This model links balance of payments deficits under fixed exchange rates to domestic monetary policy. It is based on two behavioral equations (the demand for money and import demand), two identities (the base money supply and the balance of payments), and an equilibrium condition (money market equilibrium). Private capital flows were considered to be fixed, as they often were in the Bretton Woods era. Financial programming is based on data that are usually available to policymakers, and the model's simplicity was an asset in the postwar era when data limitations were more common.

In the model, a rise in a central bank's holdings of domestic credit leads to an increase in national income and consequently imports. The immediate result is a current account deficit and a loss of reserves. In the long run, the initial change in domestic credit is completely offset by the change in foreign reserves. The solution to a balance of payments deficit lies in curbing the growth of domestic credit. This adjustment in monetary policy can be linked to the government's fiscal position, since in many developing countries a fiscal deficit is financed by the central bank.

The other model developed at the IMF is the absorption model, which relates the state of the current account to domestic expenditures and output. In this model, the current account reflects the difference between domestic output and absorption, which is the domestic demand for goods and services. A surplus is recorded when national output is higher than absorption, and a deficit in the opposite situation. Contractionary spending policies are required to lower or eliminate the deficit.

The policies in IMF-supported programs have been based on these models. Fund programs usually call for a tightening of monetary and fiscal policies in order to reduce total expenditures, and the IMF's performance criteria often include limits on domestic credit expansion and government expenditures and increases in tax revenues. In addition, the IMF in some cases has recommended a depreciation of the exchange rate in order to switch expenditures to domestically produced goods and stimulate exports.

There have been a number of criticisms of these models. The demand for money is often not stable and predictable, and changes in velocity affect the transmission of monetary changes within the economy. Moreover, the liberalization of the capital account and the increase in private international capital flows have introduced new sources of volatility into the financial sector.

The IMF's macroeconomic policy conditionality came under sharp criticism during the 1997–98 East Asian financial crisis. The cause of the crisis was a rapid outflow of capital, not expansionary government policies. Critics claimed, however, that the IMF misjudged the nature of the crisis and promoted contractionary policies at a time when output in the crisis countries was already falling. As the crisis progressed, the IMF realized that the emerging fiscal deficits reflected the crisis-induced declines in output and relaxed its call for fiscal consolidation. The IMF defended the use of higher interest rates, however, as necessary to prevent further depreciation of the exchange rates and an outbreak of inflation.

The IMF developed new tools in response to the emergence of capital account crises, such as those that occurred in East Asia and in Mexico in 1994–95. The balance sheet approach specifies the assets and liabilities of the different sectors of the economy, including the financial liabilities that are denominated in a foreign currency. These represent a source of vulnerability if foreign creditors lose confidence in domestic borrowers' ability to fulfill their obligations and decide to withdraw their funds. Economists at the IMF have also sought to develop indicators of impending currency crises that would serve as early warning systems and give the IMF and the country at risk time to prevent the crisis.

Structural Conditionality During the 1980s, the IMF's lending focused on developing economies drawn into the debt crisis. In the following decade, the transition economies that emerged after the dissolution of the Soviet Union also became fund borrowers. The governments of these countries were concerned about economic growth as well as external stability and sought to enact policies that would accelerate growth. In response, the IMF and its sister institution the World Bank devised structural adjustment policies to improve the efficiency of an economy and promote growth. These policies originally were included in the IMF's concessionary lending programs for the poorest members, but over time appeared in the SBAs and EFFs as well.

Structural adjustment policies can include fiscal reform, the privatization of government-owned enterprises, and the reorganization of the financial sector. These measures are intended to replace government allocation of resources with those of the market. Some of these reforms appeared in the set of market-oriented policies known as the Washington consensus, which encapsulated the state of thinking among many policymakers and advisors in the late 1980s and early 1990s regarding the steps needed to advance growth in developing countries.

Over time the scope and number of conditions rose. The specification of conditions became more detailed because implementation of structural policies is more difficult to assess than the traditional macroeconomic conditions. The IMF (2001b) reported that more slippage took place in the implementation of structural conditions than occurred with conditions in the traditional area of macroeconomic policies.

Structural conditionality became a focus of criticism. First, many of these policy areas were outside the IMF's expertise in macroeconomics. Second, there was limited evidence connecting many of the structural conditions to increased growth. Countries that had established strong records of growth in the past, such as Taiwan and Korea, had allowed do-

mestic firms to develop before opening up their economies. Third, in many cases there was limited domestic political support for structural conditions, which were viewed as an infringement of national sovereignty.

The criticisms of structural conditionality peaked after the East Asian crisis. Goldstein (2003) reported that the number of structural conditions totaled about 140 in the case of Indonesia, 90 in Korea, and 70 in Thailand. In the case of Indonesia, many of these conditions dealt with issues that had only tangential relevance to the goal of balance of payments equilibrium. Moreover, critics charged that the IMF itself had indirectly precipitated the crisis through its earlier promotion of financial liberalization.

The IMF undertook a review of its conditionality practices in response to the criticisms and issued new guidelines in 2002, which were reviewed in 2005. These guidelines emphasize the need for national ownership of the policies contained in a lending program. The IMF has subsequently sought to deepen government involvement in the formulation of programs. The Poverty Reduction Strategy Papers for the PRGF programs, for example, are prepared by governments in consultation with civil society and other participants. The new guidelines also called for the streamlining of conditions to those areas that were seen as essential to reestablishing a sustainable balance of payments.

Compliance and Recurring Usage Other aspects of IMF conditionality that have received scrutiny and discussion are the implementation and the recurring use of the IMF's resources. In some cases governments do not implement all the conditions contained in their Letter of Intent, and in response the IMF suspends its disbursement of funds. Countries with interrupted programs do not establish strong records of economic performance. Empirical analyses of these situations reveal that domestic political economy factors, such as a lack of cohesion within a government, can impede the progress of a program.

Governments that do not complete one program may adopt another. A study by the IMF's Independent Evaluation Office (2002) found that when prolonged usage is defined as the adoption of

IMF programs for 7 or more years in a 10-year period, then 44 countries were prolonged users between 1971 and 2000. The report also found that prolonged usage expanded consistently since the 1970s, and the authors attributed this development in part to the expansion of the goals of the IMF's lending programs. Studies of frequent usage find that these recurring borrowers do not achieve a stage of economic performance in which they can dispense with the IMF's assistance. Incomplete implementation and frequent usage detract from the effectiveness of fund programs and may delay the establishment of national policies and institutions to resolve continuing deficits.

See also balance sheet approach/effects; Bretton Woods system; capital flows to developing countries; currency crisis; early warning systems; expenditure changing and expenditure switching; financial crisis; financial liberalization; hot money and sudden stops; International Monetary Fund (IMF); International Monetary Fund surveillance; money supply; Washington consensus

FURTHER READING

Bird, Graham, Mumtaz Hussain, and Joseph P. Joyce. 2004. "Many Happy Returns? Recidivism and the IMF." *Journal of International Money and Finance* 23 (2): 231–51. A study of recurring lending arrangements.

Corden, W. Max. 2001. "The World Financial Crisis: Are the IMF Prescriptions Right?" In *The Political Economy of International Financial Crisis*, edited by Shale Horowitz and Uk Heo. Lanham, MD: Rowman and Littlefield, 4–61. A comprehensive review of the features and impact of fund conditionality.

Drazen, Allan. 2002. "Conditionality and Ownership in IMF Lending: A Political Economy Approach." *IMF Staff Papers* 49 (Special Issue): 36–67. An analysis of the roles of conditionality and ownership within IMF programs.

Easterly, William. 2005, "What Did Structural Adjustment Adjust? The Association of Policies and Growth with Repeated IMF and World Bank Adjustment Loans." *Journal of Development Economics* 76 (1): 1–22. An empirical study of recurring lending arrangements.

Ghosh, Atish, Charis Christofides, Jun Kim, Laura Papi, Uma Ramakrishnan, Alun Thomas, and Juan Zaluendo. 2005. *The Design of IMF-Supported Programs.* IMF Occasional Paper No. 241. Washington, DC: IMF. A review of the objectives and development of IMF programs from 1995 to 2000.

Goldstein, Morris. 2003. "IMF Structural Programs." In *Economic and Financial Crises in Emerging Market Economies*, edited by Martin Feldstein. Chicago: University of Chicago, 363–437. A comprehensive review of the features and impact of Fund conditionality.

International Monetary Fund. 1987. *Theoretical Aspects of the Design of Fund-Supported Adjustment Programs.* Washington, DC: IMF. The IMF's explanation of the analytical frameworks underlying conditionality.

———. 2001a. *Conditionality in Fund-Supported Programs—Policy Issues.* Washington, DC: IMF. A review of the objectives and history of conditionality.

———. 2001b. *Structural Conditionality in Fund-Supported Programs.* Washington, DC: IMF. An assessment of the record of structural conditionality.

———, Independent Evaluation Office. 2002. *Evaluation of Prolonged Use of IMF Resources.* Washington, DC: IMF. A study of recurring lending arrangements.

Joyce, Joseph P. 2006. "Promises Made, Promises Broken: A Model of IMF Program Implementation." *Economics and Politics* 18 (3): 339–65. An examination of the implementation of program conditions.

Khan, Mohsin S., and Sunil Sharma. 2003. "IMF Conditionality and Country Ownership of Adjustment Programs." *World Bank Research Observer* 18 (2): 227–48. An analysis of the roles of conditionality and ownership within IMF programs.

JOSEPH P. JOYCE

■ International Monetary Fund surveillance

Surveillance, as practiced by the International Monetary Fund (IMF), is the process of overseeing the functioning of the international monetary system and certain economic and financial policies of IMF member states. The legal mandate for this activity is Article IV of the IMF Articles of Agreement, which was rewritten after the 1973 collapse of the Bretton Woods system, when exchange rates were no longer anchored by gold, and currency values of most of the major industrial countries floated. Section 1 of the new Article IV (adopted in 1978) requires "each member . . . to collaborate with the Fund and other members to assure orderly exchange arrangements and to promote a stable system of exchange rates." Section 3 requires the IMF to "oversee the international monetary system in order to ensure its effective operation, and [to] oversee the compliance of each member with its obligations under Section 1 of this Article." To that end, the fund is required to exercise "firm surveillance" over member countries' exchange rate policies, and those members are required to consult with the fund on their policies.

Practice The two main methods of surveillance are periodic (usually annual) consultations between the fund and each member and the preparation by the fund of periodic reports on global economic and financial conditions. The first method—the Article IV consultation—is known as bilateral surveillance, and the second as multilateral surveillance. Since 2006, the second form has been expanded to include multilateral consultations, in which the IMF convenes discussions involving several members and covering issues of mutual interest and systemic consequence.

An Article IV consultation is primarily a confidential discussion between the fund and the country's monetary authorities (the finance ministry and the central bank). Increasingly in recent years, these consultations have also provided a means for the IMF to convey its views to the general public and to financial markets. Each consultation begins with a visit to the country by a team of IMF staff, referred to as a staff mission. The mission meets with officials in the finance ministry, the central bank, other official agencies as needed, and usually with representatives of the business community, labor, and civil society. At the conclusion of these talks, the mission chief presents a preliminary report to the government setting out the fund staff's assessment of economic and financial conditions in the country and its advice on exchange rate and related policies. With the government's permission, he or she may also hold a press conference to make the mission's findings known more widely.

After returning to the IMF headquarters in Washington, DC, the mission prepares a more detailed report, which the IMF Executive Board discusses. The board chairman then issues a summary of the discussion that sets out the fund's policy advice in final form. With the government's consent, the fund may then issue a public information notice (PIN) based on the summing up. Each PIN is published on the IMF's Web site, often together with the staff report.

The core of multilateral surveillance is the *World Economic Outlook* (WEO) exercise, which is normally conducted semiannually. The staff prepares a set of studies on world and regional economic developments, including forecasts and medium-term scenarios under specified assumptions and detailed analyses of key policy issues. The WEO reports have been published since 1980 and have become the flagship publication of the IMF. The other major component of multilateral surveillance is the preparation of the semiannual *Global Financial Stability Report*, which includes an analysis of developments in financial markets, incorporating both official and private capital flows.

Limitations Although the IMF considers surveillance to be its core activity and responsibility, critics argue that bilateral surveillance is an ineffective way to influence and discipline countries' policies. In broad terms, the success of surveillance depends on the quality of the fund's analysis and policy advice, the effectiveness of the dialogue and the communication of the fund's views to the authorities and to the public, and the willingness of members to accept the fund's advice. Although specific criticisms can always be leveled at specific aspects of the dialogue and the conclusions regarding a country's economic and financial policies, the central difficulty in bilateral surveillance is in persuading the authorities to act on the basis of advice from the IMF. In many cases, governments may have shorter-term domestic objectives or domestic political constraints that conflict with the longer-term and more international objectives promoted by the IMF. In other cases, there may be genuine differences of economic philosophy between the fund and the authorities.

The voluntary nature of the response to IMF surveillance contrasts with the position of countries that borrow from the IMF. For the latter, because the fund's lending is generally conditional on the borrower's adherence to an agreed program of policy improvements, a country that needs the fund's financial support faces practical constraints in its choice of policies. Advanced economies with ready access to private capital markets and developing countries that have accumulated foreign exchange reserves by running external payments surpluses are thus freer to accept or reject policy advice from the IMF than are countries with more limited financial means. These differences, of course, reflect disparities in the world economic order, not an institutional weakness in surveillance.

History When the IMF began operations in 1946, it conducted consultations only with countries that availed themselves of the temporary provisions of Article XIV of the Articles of Agreement. Under the terms of that article, these countries were still imposing exchange restrictions on foreign trade and other current account flows, and were obligated to consult with the IMF on their plans to eliminate those restrictions when practicable. At the beginning, most members maintained such restrictions, and the number fell only gradually. By 1960, only 10 of the fund's 68 members had accepted the obligations of Article VIII prohibiting further recourse to current-account restrictions. In 1961, however, the number of Article VIII countries more than doubled, in response to the restoration of current account currency convertibility across much of Europe. Thus the need for Article XIV consultations began to fall.

In that same year, 1961, the United States—the IMF's largest member country and the first to accept the obligations of Article VIII in 1946—agreed voluntarily to hold annual consultations with the fund "as a means of exchanging views on monetary and financial developments." From that point on, an increasing number of countries volunteered to hold these "Article VIII" consultations. None of this activity was yet called "surveillance," but it did lay the groundwork for the more formal and obligatory system of consultations that would come later.

IMF surveillance, in the sense that the term is used today, began with the collapse of talks by a committee of the IMF's governing board in 1974. For two years, this Committee of Twenty tried to devise a new system of stable exchange rates to replace the Bretton Woods par-value system that had been abandoned in 1973 after the United States terminated the gold convertibility of the dollar. When it finally became clear that the United States and some other major countries were not prepared to peg their exchange rates again, the committee fell back on the subtle distinction of promoting a "stable system of exchange rates" rather than a "system of stable exchange rates."

In order to achieve stability while exchange rates were floating, the Committee of Twenty reasoned that the IMF could play a key role by overseeing the international financial system and the macroeconomic policies that underpinned it. The fund's charter was then amended in 1978 to let countries choose their own exchange arrangements—pegged to another currency or a basket of currencies, freely floating, or managed more or less flexibly—subject to a requirement to consult regularly with the IMF on how they were implementing their policies. As noted above, the IMF was given a mandate to exercise "firm surveillance" over the conduct of members' exchange rate policies and to oversee the functioning of the system. Hence, modern surveillance was born.

A tug-of-war quickly emerged between the desirability of focusing on key issues and problem cases, on the one hand, and trying to be comprehensive and even-handed with all member countries, on the other. If the IMF conducted annual consultations with all members covering all policies and conditions with significant effects on exchange rates and international payments balances, staff resources would be stretched thin and the process would become routine. If it was more selective, it risked missing some brewing problems and violating the requirement that the fund treat all of its members in an even-handed manner. In either case, surveillance would fall into disrepute and again become ineffective. Attempts were made to hold ad hoc special consultations with countries that were suspected of manipulating their exchange rates for competitive advantage, but resistance to such procedures proved to be strong. Regularly scheduled bilateral consultations continued to be the primary means of communicating the fund's advice to members.

In two respects, the effectiveness of surveillance was enhanced during the 1990s. First, the Interim Committee (the successor to the Committee of Twenty) agreed in general terms on standards for the conduct of macroeconomic policies, most notably through the declaration of the Partnership for Sustainable Global Growth in 1996. Those standards, which the IMF managing director dubbed the "Eleven Commandments," enabled the fund to give more pointed advice to countries whose policies appeared to be out of line. Second, the fund adopted new procedures to open up the dialogue to wider participation and to allow the publication of staff reports and PINs. This new transparency facilitated public scrutiny and international comparisons of countries' policies and made it more difficult for governments to ignore the fund's recommendations.

By the late 1990s, two other problems with the effectiveness of surveillance had become clear. First, the quality and timeliness of financial data published (or even provided privately to the fund) by monetary authorities were not uniformly high. In a few cases, countries that had been particularly reluctant to reveal the state of their official reserve position were hit by severe financial crises. In response, the IMF embarked on a major effort to encourage members to improve financial reporting, including the establishment of standards for data dissemination and a system for disseminating data electronically to the public. Second, the fund's traditional emphasis on dialogue with members' monetary authorities occasionally left it with insufficient information about developments in financial markets. This problem was particularly acute in so-called emerging market countries, where bank loans and other private capital flows were major sources of external financing. After a wave of financial crises hit emerging market countries in the late 1990s, the IMF responded by greatly expanding its contacts with and analysis of capital markets and strengthening its capacity to assess countries' vulnerability to crises.

In 2006, when the world economy was growing rapidly but was at risk because of large and growing imbalances among the large economies, it again appeared that the tools of IMF surveillance needed to be further strengthened. That led to the inauguration of multilateral consultations, the first of which was aimed at enhancing the dialogue among the countries with the largest surpluses and deficits and seeking a commonly acceptable solution.

See also balance of payments; Bretton Woods system; currency crisis; exchange rate regimes; global imbalances; gold standard, international; international financial architecture; International Monetary Fund (IMF); International Monetary Fund conditionality; international policy coordination; twin deficits

FURTHER READING

The following sources provide histories of the evolution and operations of the IMF:

Boughton, James M. 2001. *Silent Revolution: The International Monetary Fund 1979–1989*. Washington, DC: International Monetary Fund.

de Vries, Margaret Garritsen. 1976. *The International Monetary Fund 1966–1971: The System under Stress*. 2 vols. Washington, DC: International Monetary Fund.

———. 1985. *The International Monetary Fund 1972–78: Cooperation on Trial*. 3 vols. Washington, DC: International Monetary Fund.

Horsefield, J. Keith. 1969. *The International Monetary Fund, 1945–1965*. 3 vols. Washington, DC: International Monetary Fund.

International Monetary Fund. Available at http://www.imf.org. The best source for up-to-date information on IMF surveillance.

For specific analyses of surveillance, the following sources are useful:

International Monetary Fund, Independent Evaluation Office. 2006. *Multilateral Surveillance*. Washington, DC: International Monetary Fund.

James, Harold. 1995. "The Historical Development of the Principle of Surveillance." *IMF Staff Papers* 42 (December): 762–91.

———. 1996. *International Monetary Cooperation since Bretton Woods*. Washington, DC: International Monetary Fund and Oxford University Press. A one-volume history of the IMF's role in the financial system, including the context in which surveillance has been practiced.

Pauly, Louis. 1997. *Who Elected the Bankers? Surveillance and Control in the World Economy*. Ithaca, NY: Cornell University Press.

JAMES M. BOUGHTON

■ international policy coordination

The coordination of economic policies among countries is a means to promote economic and financial stability and a way to orchestrate growth, particularly in periods of depression, without the costs of additional inflation. At first it was viewed in terms of coordinating monetary policies to reduce the tendency for interest rates to rise and fluctuate as countries attempted to emerge from recession (the Bonn Summit, 1978), or to eliminate the need for competitive devaluations as economies attempted to expand in a world of increasing trade flows and capital links (European Monetary System, 1979). Later, as inflation performance came into line with the targets set for it, the focus shifted to fiscal coordination (the Plaza Agreement, 1985), joint exchange rate targeting (Louvre Accord, 1987), and to institutional coordination within an economy or group of economies. In the early 21st century, policy coordination is mostly implicit: often discussed, but seldom in the form of explicit rules or agreements. What survives is the staff work behind the annual Group of Eight (G8) summits of the world's largest economies.

Rationale for Coordination The rationale for coordinating the policies of interdependent, but politically sovereign, policymakers is usually efficiency. Formal game theory models show that policy bargains can always be found that will leave some countries better off without others being worse off in terms of their own policy objectives. By cooperating to improve the performance of domestic policy targets and to account properly for the consequences of the spillover effects of their own policies on others, each country may achieve its own objectives, relative to what could be obtained by adopting the alternative strategy of determining its policies independently. This argument is well established in theory and has been demonstrated formally in a range of analytic and empirical models (Hamada 1976; Canzoneri and Gray 1985; Hughes Hallett 1986).

It is sometimes useful to think in terms of absolute and relative coordination. Absolute coordination focuses on the overall stance of policy to ensure that countries do not, in pursuing their own interests, adopt policies that are too tight or too loose for the world as a whole. This has to do with efficiency, or comparative advantage in getting better outcomes for all. Relative coordination, meanwhile, is concerned with adverse spillovers, redistribution, and the relative positions of countries. It therefore tends to focus on exchange rates, trade imbalances, or fiscal imbalances. Policymakers usually appear to be more interested in relative coordination (for example, the current trade imbalances), but turn to issues of absolute coordination in periods of widespread recession or inflation. Given that, the academic literature has been concerned with the following issues:

1. How large are the gains from policy coordination in practice, and how will they be distributed among participating economies?

2. What are the key determinants of the size and distribution of the payoffs?

3. Are the policies of a coordinated policy bargain stable? The problem is that once a country is persuaded to adopt policies different from those that are optimal in a noncooperative context, the other countries have an incentive to reoptimize once again on the basis that their partners are now committed to particular policy paths.

4. What are the obstacles to coordination? There may be political and institutional

reasons why it is more difficult to secure an agreement on certain policy variables, but easier on others.

5. To what extent are coordinated policies sensitive to errors, or to disagreements among policymakers about the assumed policy responses in the economy or what the appropriate policy priorities might be?

Levels of Policy Cooperation and Coordination
The potential benefits and costs of policy coordination will depend on the degree of cooperation among policymakers. There is a natural hierarchy here:

Information exchanges. Countries freely exchange information about their targets, priorities, information sets, and how they think those targets would respond to domestic or foreign policy changes. But given that information, national policymakers would continue to make decisions in a decentralized, autonomous way. By pooling their information, countries could make gains by eliminating incomplete or faulty information over objectives, expectations, and assumed policy responses.

Crisis management. Coordination would respond to episodes of particular difficulty in the international economy, involving policy changes that are particular to that episode. It might involve ad hoc policy adjustments for difficult periods, when imbalances and current policies have interacted to yield a crisis.

Avoiding conflicts over shared targets. Shared targets arise where countries actually target the same variable (for example, a mutual exchange rate), or where they target variables that are linked by an identity that cannot be relaxed via policy (for example, the "n − 1 problem" in a set of current accounts, which will be discussed later). In this case, coordination could generate gains by means of agreements that prevent countries from setting incompatible targets for the same variable, or by preventing countries from attempting competitive policy changes that cannot all be achieved simultaneously.

Intermediate targeting. A limited degree of coordination may be achieved when countries jointly control the variables that form the main monetary, fiscal, or financial links between their economies. In that case, the linked variables are treated as intermediate targets, being instrumental in obtaining better results for the other targets but without significance in themselves. Intermediate targets may or may not be shared targets, although the scope for fruitless competition over shared targets makes them the most obvious candidates.

Partial coordination. Countries cooperate in achieving certain targets but may aim at other targets uncooperatively or according to some preassigned (national) rules. It is often suggested that countries should coordinate their monetary policy, leaving fiscal policy (which is hard to manipulate in the short term) for domestic targets—as happens in the European Monetary Union. Fiscal policy needs to be sustainable, however, so a minimal degree of fiscal coordination may be required to permit effective monetary coordination.

Full coordination. Countries adopt a certain bargain across all targets and fiscal, monetary, or exchange rate instruments. They would aim to maximize the gains over the noncooperative policy settings, subject to an acceptable distribution of those gains among participants or countries.

The Gains from Coordination Studies designed to evaluate the gains from policy coordination empirically have found the benefits to be valuable but small. The gains for industrial countries from cooperating are generally thought to be in the range of 0.5–1.5 percent of gross national product (GNP) to each country, over the best available noncooperative outcomes (Oudiz and Sachs 1984; Hughes Hallett 1986). Nevertheless, these gains turn out to increase significantly with the size and persistence of external shocks and the reputations (for consistency) of the governments concerned (Currie, Levine, and Vidalis 1987). It can be debated whether one-half of 1 percent of GNP is only a "small" gain. It would represent a significant amount of extra productive capacity if fully invested. But it is not large compared to annual growth rates. Moreover, if the expected gains are small relative to the imprecision with which policies can be implemented, those gains may be hard to realize in practice. Consequently, the robustness of these gains is particularly important.

Far less attention has been given to the likely distribution of the gains among countries. Empirical studies generally find that the gains from cooperation are asymmetric, and it is usually very difficult to find ways of improving the lot of the countries that benefit least from coordination (Hughes Hallett, Holtham, and Hutson 1989). These are important results because they suggest that, whatever the overall gains, (1) it will be hard to secure *and maintain* a coordination agreement in the face of significant uncertainties, and (2) if those who make the gains and those who shoulder the burden of adjustment are different sets of people, then securing any agreement will be politically difficult.

Cooperation through Information Exchanges
The gains from coordination relative to noncoordination may well be smaller than those of efficient noncooperative policies relative to strategies that ignore predictable policy changes abroad or elsewhere in the system. Thus coordination in the sense of *information exchanges,* rather than a negotiated solution across all variables, may supply the major part of the improvements. If this is so, an important function of international policy discussions or policy meetings is going to be the exchange of information among policymakers concerning their policies, their aims, and the state of their economies. The implication is that much of the value of policy coordination may in fact lie in tying the national policymakers into a regime in which it is far more difficult for them to make poorly designed or misguided policy choices—either through misplaced self-interest or through ignorance—rather than in introducing qualitatively different policies.

Coordination Substitutes: Avoiding Conflicts over Shared or Linked Targets None of the original studies of policy coordination considered exchange rates to be a target of policy. Yet the policy debate has often been concerned with exchange rate management, with the aim of either stabilizing exchange rates or of making controlled realignments. When exchange rates are included among the targets during policy selection, they can either be included in the associated objective function evaluations (in which case exchange rate stability becomes a target

in its own right) or excluded from those evaluations (in which case exchange rates are just an intermediate target, instrumental in securing improvements elsewhere, but of no interest in itself). In the former case, the gains from coordination appear larger than before, at about 3–6 percent of GNP as estimated across seven multicountry models. If exchange rates are treated merely as intermediate targets, the gains are significantly smaller and much as in the earlier literature cited above (Holtham and Hughes Hallett 1987).

The point here is that an exchange rate is a shared variable whose domestic impact is the same whether exchange rate changes originate at home or abroad. By contrast, most other variables exert impacts that are significantly smaller internationally than domestically. The need to limit exchange rate spillovers is therefore greater in problems with shared targets than in those with other linkage variables.

Second, success with shared targets, whether treated as intermediate or not, requires a measure of coordination in how they are controlled and also some consensus about the target path that they should pursue. If this is missing, countries will inevitably waste policy power pushing against one another in a vain attempt to achieve the impossible. This holds in particular for the n − 1 problem. In that case, there is one fewer independent exchange rate (or current account) than the number of independent policymakers so that not all n target values can be reached at once. At least one must be missed, or be allowed to float free. On the other hand, it is not true that any agreed target path is better than none. Jointly specifying exchange rate target paths independently of any other objectives is frequently more damaging than moderate disagreement about what that target path should be. Hence the problem appears to be one of choosing an appropriate set of target paths, not one of securing precise agreement on the policies to support some path.

In addition, not only may intermediate targets serve to promote relative coordination between economies, they may also be conducive to absolute coordination. This is an important part of the rationale for joint monetary targeting or for a system of exchange rate targets. Nevertheless there are important qualifications to this argument. The gains to exchange rate targeting may be small, hard to achieve, or badly distributed across countries. It is not just that some countries do better than others. Some may actually lose compared with the no-targeting case. Moreover, the target paths have to be very carefully chosen to achieve any of these gains (Hughes Hallett 1992). This suggests that the losses attributable to attempts to manipulate monetary policies (or exchange rates) within a given regime are generally small but may become significant in particular episodes when countries have uniform objectives or attach great weight to one objective. At other times, the potential gains to eliminating competitive policymaking are easily outweighed by the losses resulting from the attempt to achieve an extra, and possibly inappropriate, exchange rate target.

In short, since any targeting regime implies an additional constraint, the sacrifice in the other targets, which this extra constraint implies, must be less than the efficiency gains from a more effective design of the policies or a more appropriate allocation of interventions between national policy instruments and policy institutions.

The Dangers of Coordination Because the gains may not be large, obstacles to coordination may easily create losses that overwhelm those potential gains. Policymakers may decide not to cooperate if they think that other countries will not stick to their part of the bargain, or if they think that there are potential information errors or other shocks that would invalidate their calculations, or if they think that they may have misestimated the priorities of other players, or if there is a serious possibility that policymakers are uncertain or differ in their views of how the economy works (Holtham and Hughes Hallett 1992).

Sustainability Will policymakers stick to their part of the bargain? Or will policymakers cheat by redesigning their future policies once they have maneuvered the other participants into taking certain actions? The first question involves breaking a bargain, with one party finding it advantageous to deviate from what was previously agreed once the other participants have established their policies. In that case governments try to cheat on one another. The second is the usual time-inconsistency problem in which governments cheat on the private sector over time. The latter does not involve a bargain as such but represents an internal inconsistency in one of the policy sequences. A standard example is discussed by the economist Rogoff (1985), who points out that policy coordination may actually be welfare-decreasing if the coordination process eases the constraints imposed on governments engaging in inflationary expansions. The reason is that, in reality, there is more than one set of actors per economy (the government, the central bank, and a private sector whose forward-looking expectations affect the exchange rate and, hence, policy success) so that coordination among governments may represent a coalition against the private sector or central bank, rather than full coordination. Although the example is specific, it is a general point that coordination without credibility may be counterproductive. Nevertheless, coordinated policies will prove robust against cheating if the losses the first country (or actor) would suffer under retaliation (or preemptive cheating) by its opponent are larger than the gains that the same country (or actor) could make by unopposed cheating.

Policy Errors Shocks to the system can affect the incentive to coordinate. But those shocks have to be both large and persistent (Canzoneri and Minford 1986). By contrast, coordination may reduce policy errors because decision-makers try to share the risks rather than offload them onto their rivals. Performance indicators are generally aggregations of national targets that are affected in different and mutually conflicting ways by external shocks, while coordinated policies follow by aggregating those national indicators into some global performance index. Coordinated policies will, therefore, normally be *more* robust than noncooperative policies, which lack that extra aggregation and hence that extra ability to cancel out errors.

Interinstitutional and Rule-Based Coordination Another form of policy coordination is rule-based coordination. In this case benefits arise from the credibility associated with committing to a set of rules that are well designed and capable of being monitored easily. Rule-based coordination has the advantage that it may be used to avoid the inefficiencies of short-term policymaking, or where there are temptations to manipulate or opportunistically free ride on the expectations of others. One example is the "fiscal leadership" model in which fiscal policymakers are made to decide their policies first, with an eye to their long-run commitment to public services and the stability of public finances, under the threat that an independently run monetary policy that follows can take away any short-term or special interest gains that the fiscal leaders may be tempted to create for themselves (Hughes Hallett and Weymark 2007).

In fact, leadership under suitable conditions (that the players' reaction functions form an acute angle so that their policies could be aligned) will always induce a degree of coordination and the gains will increase the more the policymakers differ in terms of goals and priorities. A simple way to implement this idea is to give fiscal policymakers a debt target. Being a stock, not a flow, such a rule would induce the leadership we require automatically. More generally, this option opens up the whole area of interinstitutional coordination. The early studies ignored that issue, but more recent work has focused on the interactions among institutions (Foreman-Peck et al. 2007; Pappa 2004). Policy coordination is often more important in this context because the effects go through the domestic markets as well as through the international or foreign markets. Interinstitutional coordination is therefore likely to have a greater effect than intercountry coordination.

Explicit rules incorporating an automatic degree of coordination may also act as an important discipline on the actions of governments in the international arena. Although democratic governments should, and do, have appreciable freedom of action, the public choice literature emphasizes that pressure groups and special interests may exert undue influence on government policy, leading to inefficient outcomes for the economy as a whole. There may be scope for constraining government action to

more efficient outcomes on the basis that "what benefits others benefits everyone." Such rules may be internal, as in the separation of fiscal and monetary powers in some countries, or externally imposed as in exchange rate targeting or common inflation policies.

Going Forward Academic research has produced an extensive literature on policy coordination. Much of the work has been theoretical and based on simplified models. As these have abstracted from some of the difficulties of which policymakers are most aware, the literature may have a flavor of unreality to practitioners. Moreover, much of the impetus to cooperation has come from experience, not from explicit demonstrations of the benefits. Bringing theory to bear on current concerns is therefore unfinished business. But there is little sign as yet that our understanding of policy coordination needs to be revised (Canzoneri et al. 2005).

See also Bonn Summit; contagion; discipline; euro; European Monetary Union; exchange rate regimes; foreign exchange intervention; Louvre Accord; Maastricht Treaty; monetary policy rules; Plaza Accord; Smithsonian Agreement; spillovers; time inconsistency problem

FURTHER READING

Bryant, Ralph C. 1995. "International Coordination of National Stabilization Policies." Brookings Institution, Washington, DC. A background framework.

Canzoneri, Matthew, Robert Cumby, and Behzad Diba. 2005. "The Need for International Policy Coordination: What's Old, What's New, and What's Yet to Come." *Journal of International Economics* 66: 363–84. Summarizes the results we have so far with different theoretical models.

Canzoneri, Matthew, and JoAnna Gray. 1985. "Monetary Policy Games and the Consequences of Noncooperative Behavior." *International Economic Review* 26: 547–64. An early demonstration of the disadvantages of uncoordinated policies.

Cazoneri, Matthew, and Patrick Minford. 1986. "When Coordination Matters: An Empirical Analysis." *Applied Economics* 20: 1137–54. The gains from coordination depend on the size, incidence, and duration of shocks.

Currie, David, Paul Levine, and Nic Vidalis. 1987. "Cooperative and Noncooperative Rules for Monetary and Fiscal Policy in an Empirical Two Bloc Model." In *Global Macroeconomics: Policy Conflict and Cooperation*, edited by Ralph Bryant and Richard Portes. London: Macmillan, 73–122. The importance of commitment.

Feldstein, Martin. 1988. "Thinking about International Economic Cooperation." *Journal of Economic Perspectives* 2: 3–13. How coordination could make matters worse.

Foreman-Peck, James, Andrew Hughes Hallett, and Yue Ma. 2007. "Trade Wars and the Great Slump." *European Review of Economic History* 11: 73–98. The failure of internal versus international coordination as a cause of the Great Depression of the 1930s.

Hamada, Koichi. 1976. "A Strategic Analysis of Monetary Interdependence." *Journal of Political Economy* 83: 677–700. This paper introduces the importance of international monetary coordination from a theoretical perspective.

Holtham, Gerald, and Andrew Hughes Hallett. 1987. "International Policy Cooperation and Model Uncertainty." In *Global Macroeconomics: Policy Conflict and Cooperation*, edited by Ralph Bryant and Richard Portes. London: Macmillan, 128–77. Uncertainty about the correct model may destroy the gains from coordination.

———. 1992. "International Policy Coordination When Policy Makers Do Not Agree on the True Model." *American Economic Review* 82: 1043–51. The form of policy bargain matters when there is uncertainty about how the economy works or about the transmission of policy effects.

Hughes Hallett, Andrew. 1986. "International Policy Design and the Sustainability of Policy Bargains." *Journal of Economic Dynamics and Control* 10: 467–94. The sensitivity of the gains from coordination to different types of policy bargains and cheating.

———. 1992. "Target Zones and International Policy Coordination: The Contrast between the Necessary and Sufficient Conditions for Success." *European Economic Review* 36: 893–914. Exchange rate stabilization as a partial substitute for formal policy coordination.

Hughes Hallett, Andrew, Gerald Holtham, and Gary Hutson. 1989. "Exchange Rate Targeting as a Surrogate for International Policy Coordination." In *Blueprints for Exchange Rate Management*, edited by Barry Eichengreen, Marcus Miller, and Richard Portes. New York: Academic Press, 239–78. The distribution of the gains, especially among simplified forms of coordination.

Hughes Hallett, Andrew, and Diana Weymark. 2007. "Government Leadership and Central Bank Design." *Canadian Journal of Economics* 40: 607–27. Fiscal-monetary interactions can be used to promote greater internal coordination under the appropriate institutional structures.

Oudiz, Gilles, and Jeffrey Sachs. 1984. "Macroeconomic Coordination among Industrial Economies." *Brookings Papers on Economic Activity* 1: 1–64. The original calculation of the gains from coordination.

Pappa, Eva. 2004. "Do the ECB and the Fed Really Need to Cooperate? Optimal Monetary Policy in a Two-Country World." *Journal of Monetary Economics* 51: 753–79. A modern example of monetary coordination.

Rogoff, Kenneth. 1985. "Can International Monetary Policy Coordination Be Counterproductive?" *Journal of International Economics* 18: 199–217. Coordination among a subset or coalition of policymakers can be counterproductive for the whole.

ANDREW HUGHES HALLETT

■ international reserves

International reserves are the liquid external assets (foreign currency, foreign currency bonds, and gold) under the control of the central bank. Under the Bretton Woods system, adequate reserves were measured by months of imports: the prevailing rule of thumb considered four months of imports to be reasonable coverage. This perspective fitted well in a world with limited financial integration, in which trade openness reflected a country's vulnerability to external shocks (Fischer 2001). In the absence of reserves, balance of payment deficits would have to be corrected through a reduction in aggregate expenditures, imposing macroeconomic adjustment costs, manifested in sharp contractions of investment and consumption, thereby inducing recessionary pressures. As greater trade openness increased the exposure to trade shocks, minimizing adjustment costs required higher reserve holdings. An intriguing development since the 1960s has been that, despite the proliferation of greater exchange rate flexibility, international reserves/gross domestic product (GDP) ratios have increased substantially. Reserve holdings have trended upward; at the end of 1999, reserves were about 6 percent of global GDP, 3.5 times what they were at the end of 1960 and 50 percent higher than in 1990. Practically all the increase in reserves/GDP holding has been by developing countries, mostly concentrated in East Asia (Flood and Marion 2002).

International Reserves as a Buffer Stock The earlier literature focused on using international reserves as a buffer stock, part of the management of an adjustable-peg or managed-floating exchange-rate regime. Accordingly, optimal reserves balance the macroeconomic adjustment costs incurred in the absence of reserves with the opportunity cost of holding reserves (Frenkel and Jovanovic 1981). The buffer stock model predicts that average reserves depend negatively on adjustment costs, the opportunity cost of reserves, and exchange rate flexibility and positively on GDP and reserve volatility, driven frequently by the underlying volatility of international trade. Overall, the literature of the 1980s supported these predictions (see Flood and Marion 2002).

Post-1998 trends in hoarding reserves, especially the large increase in hoarding international reserves in East Asia, stirred lively debate among economists and financial observers. Although useful, the buffer stock model has a limited capacity to account for the recent development in hoarding international reserves—the greater flexibility of the exchange rates exhibited after 1990 should work in the direction of reducing reserve hoarding, in contrast to the trends reported earlier. As an indication of excess hoarding, some observers noted that developing countries frequently borrow at much higher interest rates than what they earn on reserves.

International Reserves and Self-Insurance The recent literature provided several interpretations for these puzzles, focusing on the observation that the deeper financial integration of developing countries has increased exposure to volatile short-term inflows of capital (dubbed "hot money"), subject to frequent sudden stops and reversals (see Calvo 1998; Edwards 2004). Looking at the 1980s and 1990s, the magnitude and speed of the reversal of capital flows throughout the 1997–98 East Asian financial crisis surprised most observers (Aizenman and Marion 2003). Most viewed East Asian countries as less vulnerable to the perils associated with hot money than Latin American countries. After all, East Asian countries were more open to international trade, had sounder fiscal policies, and showed much stronger growth performance. In retrospect, the 1997–98 crisis exposed hidden vulnerabilities of East Asian countries, forcing the market to update the probability of sudden stops affecting all countries.

These observations suggest that hoarding international reserves can be viewed as a precautionary adjustment, reflecting the desire for self-insurance against exposure to future sudden stops. Self-insurance has several interpretations. The first focuses on precautionary hoarding of international reserves needed to stabilize fiscal expenditure in developing countries (see Aizenman and Marion 2004). Specifically, a country characterized by volatile output, inelastic demand for fiscal outlays, high tax collection costs, and sovereign risk may want to accumulate both international reserves and external debt (sovereign risk is the added risk, such as default of sovereign governments on debts, and nationalization, assumed by investors with funds invested in foreign counties). External debt allows the country to smooth consumption when output is volatile. International reserves that are beyond the reach of creditors would allow such a country to smooth consumption in the event that adverse shocks trigger a default on foreign debt.

Another version of self-insurance and precautionary demand for international reserves views international reserves as output stabilizers (Ben-Bassat and Gottlieb 1992; Aizenman and Lee 2007). Accordingly, international reserves can reduce the probability of an output drop induced by a sudden stop and/or the depth of the output collapse when the sudden stop materializes. This argument is in line with the Guidotti-Greenspan rule of thumb of the 1990s—countries should hold liquid reserves equal to their foreign liabilities coming due within a year. This rule reflects the shifting focus from reserve adequacy measured in terms of trade flows of goods to flows of assets.

Back of the envelope estimation suggests that the expected benefits of following a Guidotti-Greenspan rule is about 1 percent of gross domestic product (GDP). This would be the case if a country holding reserves equal to its short-term debt reduces the annual probability of experiencing a sharp reversal in capital flows by 10 percent on average (in line with Rodrik and Velasco 1999, see Rodrik 2006) and if the output cost of a financial crisis is about 10 percent of GDP, as found by Hutchison and Noy (2006). Similar results have been obtained using more elaborated models (see Garcia and Soto 2004; Jeanne and Ranciere 2005). These authors concluded that self-insurance against sudden stops plays an important role in accounting for recent hoarding of international reserves.

While the Guidotti-Greenspan-IMF rule focused on the ratio of reserves to short-term debt, Kim et al. (2005) looked at a more flexible rule, based on the behavior of different types of capital flows during currency crises. Application to selected Asian countries leads them to conclude that the countries affected by the East Asian crisis held excessive reserves by 2003—the affected countries have already built up more than adequate reserve levels to handle a repeat of the actual capital outflows that occurred during the 1997–98 crises scaled up to 2003 values. One may note, however, that the rapidly changing structure of the developing countries' financial integration implies that future possible crises would not resemble the previous ones. For example, Korea, one of the countries affected by the 1997–98 crisis, lifted restrictions on foreign equity ownership in the aftermath of the crisis. In response, foreigners' shareholding as a percentage of the total market capitalization has risen from 12 percent in 1997 to 40 percent by 2003. Arguably, the sizable accumulation of reserves by Korea during that period may reflect the wish to cover short-term external debt plus some portion of foreigners' shareholdings, in the desire to reduce possible real exchange rate repercussion of future reversals of capital flows.

International Reserves: Precaution versus Mercantilism The Korean policy suggests another angle associated with international reserves—the possibility that international reserves management may lower real exchange rate volatility, which in turn may allow a smoother output and potentially higher growth rate. To put this topic in broader context, note that the literature of the 1990s identified large adverse effects of exogenous volatility on the GDP and economic growth in developing countries. An important channel that may explain such negative levels and growth effects of volatility are capital market imperfection and low levels of financial development (Aghion et al. 2006).

The views linking the large increase in hoarding reserves to growing exposure to sudden stops associated with financial integration face a well-known contender in a modern incarnation of mercantilism (Dooley et al. 2003). According to this interpretation, reserves accumulation is a by-product of promoting exports, which is needed to create better jobs, thereby absorbing abundant labor in traditional sectors. Though intellectually intriguing, this interpretation remains debatable—the history of Japan and Korea suggests the near absence of mercantilist hoarding of international reserves during the phase of fast growth, and the prevalence of export promotion by preferential financing in targeted sectors. Foundering economic growth led to the onset of large hoarding of reserves both in Japan and Korea, probably due to both mercantilist motives and self-insurance to deal with growing fragility of the banking system. These perspectives suggest that the massive hoarding of reserves by China is a hybrid of the mercantilist and self-insurance motives (Aizenman and Lee 2006). Yet mercantilist hoarding by one country may induce competitive hoarding by other countries to preempt any competitive advantage gained by the first country, a reaction that would dissipate most competitiveness gains. This view is supported by the interdependence of the demand for international reserves among ten East Asian countries (Cheung and Qian 2006).

Overall, greater exposures of developing countries to sudden stops and reversals of hot money, growing trade openness, and the desire to improve competitiveness and to reduce real exchange rate volatility go a long way toward accounting for the observed increase in the rapid and massive stockpiling of international reserves by developing markets.

See also Bretton Woods system; currency crisis; dollar standard; dominant currency; exchange rate regimes; exchange rate volatility; financial crisis; foreign exchange intervention; global imbalances; gold standard, international; hot money and sudden stops; international liquidity; mercantilism; real exchange rate; reserve currency; sterilization; vehicle currency

FURTHER READING

Aghion, Philippe, Philippe Bacchetta, Romain Ranciere, and Kenneth Rogoff. 2006. "Exchange Rate Volatility and Productivity Growth: The Role of Financial Development." NBER Working paper No. 12117. Cambridge, MA: National Bureau of Economic Research. Evidence that real exchange rate volatility is associated with lower productivity growth.

Aizenman, Joshua, and Jaewoo Lee. 2006 "Financial versus Monetary Mercantilism—Long-run View of Large International Reserves Hoarding." NBER Working Paper No. 12718. Cambridge, MA: National Bureau of Economic Research. A key instrument of the East Asian development strategy has been subsidizing the cost of capital; hoarding international reserves tend to occur in the aftermath of floundering growth; defines and explains competitive hoarding.

———. 2007. "International Reserves: Precautionary versus Mercantilist Views, Theory and Evidence." *Open Economies Review* 18 (2): 191–214. Evidence and a model of the relative importance of the precautionary and mercantilist views of international reserves.

Aizenman, Joshua, and Nancy P. Marion. 2003. "The High Demand for International Reserves in the Far East: What's Going On?" *Journal of the Japanese and International Economies* 17 (3): 370–400. Explains the higher demand for reserves using the precautionary demand and downside risk aversion motives.

———. 2004. "International Reserves Holdings with Sovereign Risk and Costly Tax Collection." *Economic Journal* 114 (July): 569–91. Models precautionary use of reserves by developing countries and the negative impact of political instability on international reserves.

Ben-Bassat, Avraham, and Daniel Gottlieb. 1992. "Optimal International Reserves and Sovereign Risk." *Journal of International Economics* 33: 345–62. Explains and estimates the importance of sovereign risk and the cost of default as a major determinant of the demand for international reserves.

Calvo, Guillermo. 1998. "Capital Flows and Capital-market Crises: The Simple Economics of Sudden Stops." *Journal of Applied Economics* 1 (1): 35–54. Explains mechanisms through which a sudden stop in international credit flows may bring about financial and balance of payments crises and examines factors triggering sudden stops.

Cheung, Yin-Wong, and Xing Wang Qian. 2006. "Hoarding of International Reserves: Mrs. Machlup's Wardrobe and the Joneses." Manuscript. Santa Cruz: University of California at Santa Cruz. Shows the interdependence of the demand for international reserves among 10 East Asian countries.

Dooley, P. Michael, David Folkerts-Landau, and Peter Garber. 2003. "An Essay on the Revived Bretton Woods System." NBER Working Paper No. 9971. Cambridge, MA: National Bureau of Economic Research. The use of fixed exchange rate in Asia has reestablished the United States as the center country in the modified Bretton Woods system; links it to an export-led growth supported by undervalued exchange rates strategy of East Asia.

Edwards, S. 2004. "Thirty Years of Current Account Imbalances, Current Account Reversals, and Sudden Stops." *IMF Staff Papers* 51 (special issue): 1–49. Major reversals in current account deficits have been associated to sudden stops of capital inflows; the probability of a reversal depends on external debt/GDP, international reserves/GDP, and debt services. More open countries suffer less in a reversal.

Fischer, Stanley. 2001. "Opening Remarks." IMF/World Bank International Reserves: Policy Issues Forum. Washington, DC. Overview of the changing patterns of hoarding international reserves.

Flood, Robert, and Nancy P. Marion. 2002. "Holding International Reserves in an Era of High Capital Mobility." In *Brookings Trade Forum 2001*, edited by S. Collins and D. Rodrik. Washington, DC: Brookings Institution Press. Buffer-stock reserve models work about as well in the modern floating-rate period as they did during the Bretton Woods regime. During both periods models' fundamentals explain only about 15 percent of reserves volatility.

Frenkel, Jacob, and Boyan Jovanovic. 1981. "Optimal International Reserves: A Stochastic Framework." *Economic Journal* 91 (362): 507–14. Adjustment cost model of the demand for international reserves, highlighting the role of uncertainty.

Garcia, Pablo, and Claudio Soto. 2004. "Large Holdings of International Reserves: Are They Worth It?" Central Bank of Chile Working Papers No. 299 (December). Santiago: CBC. Estimate crisis probabilities and apply it to evaluate the optimal stock of reserves, concluding that observed stocks of reserves for most of the cases are consistent with an optimal self-insurance policy.

Hutchison, M. Michael, and Ilan Noy. 2006. "Sudden Stops and the Mexican Wave: Currency Crises, Capital Flow Reversals, and Output Loss in Emerging Markets." *Journal of Development Economics* 79 (1): 225–48. Sudden-stop crises have a large negative, but short-lived, impact on output growth over and above that found with currency crises. The cumulative output loss of a sudden stop is around 13–15 percent over a 3-year period.

Jeanne, Olivier, and Romain Ranciere. 2005. "The Optimal Level of International Reserves for Emerging Market Economies: Formulas and Applications." Washington, DC: IMF Research Department. An insurance model of international reserves in the presence of sudden stop can explain reserves of the order of magnitude observed in many emerging market countries, but not the recent buildup of reserves in Asia.

Kim, Jung Sik, Jie Li, Ramkishen Rajan, Ozan Sula, and Thomas D. Willett. 2005. "Reserve Adequacy in Asia Revisited: New Benchmarks Based on the Size and Composition of Capital Flows." In *Claremont-KIEP Conference on Monetary and Exchange Rate Arrangements in East Asia*. Korean Institute of International Economic Policy, Seoul. Presents new benchmarks for judging reserve adequacy and concludes that the reserve levels in East Asia are more than that needed to finance capital outflows of the severity of the 1997–98 Asian crises.

Rodrik, Dani. 2006. "The Social Cost of Foreign Exchange Reserves." *International Economic Journal* 20 (3): 253–66. Cost-benefit analysis of hoarding international reserves using the self-insurance motive. Explaining why developing countries have not tried harder to reduce short-term foreign liabilities instead of hoarding reserves remains a puzzle.

Rodrik, Dani, and Andres Velasco. 1999. "Short-Term Capital Flows." NBER Working Paper No. 7364. Cambridge, MA: National Bureau of Economic Research. A model of self-fulfilling crises; estimation shows that greater short-term debt/reserves ratio is a robust predictor of financial crises and is associated with more severe crises when capital flows reverse.

JOSHUA AIZENMAN

■ **international risk sharing**

See capital mobility

■ **intrafirm trade**

Intrafirm trade is international trade that occurs between different affiliates of the same multinational firm. In the United States, intrafirm trade accounted for approximately 35 percent of all international trade in 2004, and it has been a large fraction of international trade in the United States for decades. In the 2002 *Economic Outlook* of the Organisation for Economic Co-operation and Development there is some evidence of increases in intrafirm trade in other countries.

Data on intrafirm trade are difficult to find consistently across countries. The U.S. data come from the Bureau of Economic Analysis, which undertakes annual surveys of U.S. multinational firms and their affiliates abroad as well as foreign-based multinational firms and their affiliated firms in the United States.

The large magnitude of intrafirm trade has been emphasized by many scholars of foreign direct investment (FDI). Furthermore, many scholars have discussed the increasing importance of vertical specialization in international trade. Vertical specialization includes the segmentation of production across national boundaries, whereby different stages of the production process are done in different countries, in line with their natural comparative advantage. Yi (2003) argues that vertical specialization can help explain the growth in world trade. Still, it is important to distinguish trade in intermediate inputs from intrafirm trade, as the former need not occur within the firm.

Understanding the nature of intrafirm trade therefore requires understanding the motives behind FDI more generally, or the rationale for organizing cross-border economic activity within the firm. Theoretical models of multinational activity emphasize several possible motives for internalizing activity within the firm. For example, there may be a need to control the quality of the product, accompanied by difficulties in the formation of contracts at arm's length to ensure the reputation of the firm. Also, proprietary firm-specific knowledge can make it difficult to appropriate the gains from production via licensing, as it is difficult to charge the appropriate fee for the knowledge without revealing the knowledge itself, thus lowering the incentive to pay for it. There is evidence in favor of such motivations. For example, the literature has consistently shown a correlation between the propensity to exchange goods within the firm and the research and development intensity of production; see Borga and Zeile (2004) for an overview of findings in this area.

An additional motive for internalization is tax avoidance. Gordon and Hines (2002) undertake a comprehensive survey of international taxation and find little evidence for viewing multinational firms as financial intermediaries, facilitating the movement of capital to higher return locations. Instead, they find more support for models of multinational firms as facilitators of tax avoidance or owners of firm-specific intangible capital.

Countries tax multinational firms in a variety of ways. Some countries exempt the foreign earnings of their resident firms from taxation; these are referred to as territorial systems. Multinational firms based in such countries have an unambiguous incentive to shift income to low-tax locations. Other countries (such as the United States) tax the worldwide income of their resident firms, but they still generally allow deferral of taxation on income earned in low-tax countries until that income is repatriated. These are referred to as credit systems. Deferral, as well as other methods of lowering the residual tax due, provides multinational firms in credit system countries with a substantial incentive to shift profits to low-tax countries.

Intrafirm trade may facilitate international tax avoidance by multinational firms in several ways. By altering the prices of transactions that occur within the firm, firms can effectively shift income from high-tax locations to low-tax locations. For example, given these tax incentives, multinational firms have an incentive to overprice intrafirm trade flows originating in low-tax countries and underprice intrafirm trade flows originating in high-tax countries. Evidence that firms follow such strategies is provided in Clausing (2003), which examines intrafirm trade prices directly. Data on intrafirm trade prices are uncommon, but most of the literature in this area provides consistent, if indirect, empirical support for the importance of tax-motivated transfer pricing. Hines (1999) reviews this body of literature.

In addition to tax distortions on the pricing of intrafirm transactions, there is evidence (e.g., Clausing 2006 and references within) that firms undertake greater quantities of intrafirm trade with low-tax countries. This finding may indicate that low-tax locations are attractive places to undertake FDI, and thus intrafirm trade is also encouraged as it is complementary to multinational activity. This finding may also indicate that greater quantities of intrafirm trade are undertaken in order to facilitate tax avoidance; these two motives are difficult to distinguish given data constraints.

Aside from the tax influences on intrafirm trade, the behavior of intrafirm trade more generally has also received attention in the literature. Some scholars have argued that intrafirm trade by multinational enterprises may be more responsive to changes in economic conditions than international trade between unaffiliated entities. Feinberg and Keane (2006, 2007) consider the relationship between changes in technology, tariff reductions, the restructuring of multinational firm production, and the growth of world trade and intrafirm trade. They find that the growth in Canadian-U.S. intrafirm trade is due in large part to technical change and in particular improvements in logistics management and "just-in-time" production systems. Tariff reductions play a relatively minor role in intrafirm trade, although they are important in explaining arm's-length trade by multinational firms. So the reasons for growth in intrafirm trade appear to differ from the reasons for the growth in arm's-length trade by multinational firms.

International trade by multinational firms is a majority of all trade for the United States, and it is likely to be of similar importance for many other countries. While some of this trade occurs at arm's length among unaffiliated firms, an important part of the international trade of multinational firms is intrafirm trade. Intrafirm trade, or trade between different affiliates of the same multinational firm, may differ from conventional trade in important ways. Foremost, it is influenced by international tax incentives, but it also may respond differently to other key economic variables.

See also foreign direct investment (FDI); multinational enterprises

FURTHER READING

Borga, Maria, and William J. Zeile. 2004. "International Fragmentation of Production and the International Trade of U.S. Multinational Companies." Bureau of Economic Analysis Working Paper No. 2004-02. Washington, DC: BEA. Discussion of intrafirm trade.

Clausing, Kimberly A. 2006. "International Tax Avoidance and U.S. International Trade." *National Tax Journal* 59 (2): 269–87. Provides evidence regarding tax incentives and intrafirm trade.

———. 2003. "Tax-Motivated Transfer Pricing and U.S. Intrafirm Trade Prices." *Journal of Public Economics* 87 (9–10): 2207–23. Provides evidence regarding tax-motivated transfer pricing and intrafirm trade prices.

Feinberg, Susan E., and Michael P. Keane. 2006. "Accounting for the Growth of MNC-Based Trade Using a Structural Model of U.S. MNCs." *American Economic Review* 96 (5): 1515–58. Evidence that growth in U.S.–Canadian intrafirm trade was due to technical change, not tariff reductions.

———. 2007. "Advances in Logistics and the Growth of Intrafirm Trade: The Case of Canadian Affiliates of U.S. Multinationals, 1984–1995." *Journal of Industrial Economics* 55 (4): 571–632. Shows that improved logistics, including "just-in-time" production, explains much of growth in intrafirm trade.

Gordon, Roger H., and James R. Hines Jr. 2002. "International Taxation." In *Handbook of Public Economics*, vol. 4, edited by Alan Auerbach and Martin Feldstein. North Holland, 1935–95. Overview of international taxation.

Hines, James R. Jr. 1999. "Lessons from Behavioral Responses to International Taxation." *National Tax Journal* 52 (2): 305–22. Overview of international taxation literature, with an emphasis on empirical work.

Yi, Kei-Mu. 2003. "Can Vertical Specialization Explain the Growth of World Trade?" *Journal of Political Economy* 111 (1): 52–102. Examines the contribution of vertical specialization to the growth of world trade.

KIMBERLY A. CLAUSING

■ intraindustry trade

Intraindustry trade arises if a country simultaneously imports *and* exports similar types of goods or services. Similarity is identified here by the goods or services being classified in the same sector. Suppose, for the sake of argument, that we focus on the sector "cars." Intraindustry trade then occurs, for example, if Germany exports cars to France and simultaneously imports cars from Italy. On the one hand this raises the question why Germany is (at least partially) exporting cars in exchange for importing cars instead of focusing exclusively on so-called *inter*industry trade, namely exporting cars in exchange for importing different types of goods (such as food or airplanes). On the other hand, this raises the question why different goods are lumped together in the same sector, as the exported Volkswagen Golfs differ from the imported Ferraris. We address these two basic questions in what follows.

Although in hindsight various antecedents can be traced, the phenomenon of intraindustry trade as such first received attention in the 1960s in studies by Pieter Verdoorn and Bela Balassa on the increased trade flows among European countries. Herbert Grubel and Peter Lloyd (1975) provided the definitive empirical study on the importance of intraindustry trade and how to measure it. Solid theoretical foundations for explaining intraindustry trade came later (in the 1980s and 1990s) with the new trade literature, to a large extent based on a monopolistic competition framework.

Types of Intraindustry Trade It is customary to distinguish between two different types of intraindustry trade, each warranting a different type of explanation, namely:

Horizontal intraindustry trade. This refers to the simultaneous exports and imports of goods classified in the same sector and at the *same stage of processing*. This is likely based on product differentiation, for example, South Korea's simultaneous import and export of mobile telephones in the final processing stage. As these mobile phones are produced using similar technology and provide similar functions they are classified in the same sector. Nonetheless, the exported Samsung telephones differ in appearance and product characteristics slightly from the imported Nokia telephones, catering to the desires of different types of consumers.

Vertical intraindustry trade. This refers to the simultaneous exports and imports of goods classified in the same sector but at *different stages of processing*. This is likely based on the increasing ability to organize fragmentation of the production process into different stages, each performed at different locations by taking advantage of the local conditions. China,

for example, imports technology-intensive computer components and uses its abundant, low-wage labor force to assemble these components in the labor-intensive final production stage, before the components (as part of a finished computer) are exported again to Europe or the United States.

Measuring Intraindustry Trade: The Grubel-Lloyd Index The most often used method for determining the extent of intraindustry trade was proposed by Grubel and Lloyd (1975). This measure, now known as the Grubel-Lloyd index, is simple to calculate and intuitively appealing. Once a country's export and import value for a particular sector and period are known, it is calculated as:

$$GL_{sector\ i} = 1 - \left(\frac{|export_{sector\ i} - import_{sector\ i}|}{export_{sector\ i} + import_{sector\ i}} \right). \quad (1)$$

If the country only imports or only exports goods or services within the same sector, such that there is no intraindustry trade, the second term on the right-hand side of equation (1) is equal to one, such that the whole expression reduces to zero. Similarly, if the export value is exactly equal to the import value ($export_{sector\ i} = import_{sector\ i}$), the second term on the right-hand side of equation (1) is equal to zero, such that the whole expression reduces to one. The Grubel-Lloyd index therefore varies between zero (indicating pure *inter*industry trade) and one (indicating pure *intra*industry trade).

Data Aggregation As already indicated, to some extent intraindustry trade can be considered a classification problem as different types of goods and services are lumped together in the same sector. In practice, international trade flows are classified in various ways. Using the SITC (standard international trade classification) we can distinguish ten different broad sectors (the so-called one-digit level). Each of these one-digit sectors can, in principle, be subdivided into ten more detailed two-digit sectors. Each of the two-digit sectors can in turn, in principle, be subdivided into ten even more detailed three-digit sectors, and so forth. Sector 6 at the one-digit level, for example, consists of "manufactured goods." One of the subsectors at the two-digit level is sector 61 "leather manufactures" while another is sector 63 "cork/wood manufactures." Analyzing intraindustry trade at the very broad one-digit level therefore classifies trade of leather manufactures in exchange for cork/wood manufactures as intraindustry trade, which seems unwarranted. Looking at the more detailed two-digit level this problem partially disappears and a smaller extent of trade is therefore classified as intraindustry trade. A further reduction occurs if we look at even more detailed levels of aggregation. The three-digit level, for example, distinguishes between cork manufacturers (sector 633) and different types of wood manufacturers (sectors 634 and 635) separately.

Table 1 illustrates the data aggregation problem for China for three different levels of aggregation (consisting of 10, 67, and 237 different sectors) by reporting a trade-weighted average Grubel-Lloyd index for a selection of years. We report the one-digit level only for the sake of argument as it is generally considered too crude a classification in practice. Three things are clear from the table. First, as we distinguish between more sectors a smaller fraction of trade is classified as intraindustry trade, for example reducing it from 58 percent to 49 percent to 42 percent of total trade in China in 2005. Second, even though intraindustry trade reduces as we identify more sectors, it does not disappear. It is, for example,

still 42 percent of total trade at the three-digit level in China in 2005. This is a general characteristic of current trade flows as intraindustry trade exists for very detailed sector classifications. Third, and most important, intraindustry trade seems to become more important over time, for example increasing at the three-digit level in China from 20 percent in 1980 to 42 percent in 2005. We now turn to this issue.

Empirical Characteristics of Intraindustry Trade
There are structural differences across sectors regarding the extent of intraindustry trade. To demonstrate this, we use the factor-intensity classification of the International Trade Center, a joint agency of the United Nations Conference on Trade and Development and the World Trade Organization, which distinguishes between five broad factor-intensity categories at the three-digit level, namely (within parentheses the number of the sector belonging to the particular category):

Primary products (83): e.g. meat, dairy, cereals, fruit, coffee, minerals, and oil.
Natural-resource-intensive products (21): e.g. leather, wood, pig iron, and copper.
Unskilled-labor-intensive products (26): e.g. textiles, clothing, ships, and footwear.
Human-capital-intensive products (43): e.g. perfumes, cosmetics, cars, and watches.
Technology-intensive products (62): e.g. chemicals, electronics, tools, and aircraft.

Table 2 depicts the extent of intraindustry trade for these different types of sectors in China for selected years. It shows that the level of intraindustry trade is particularly low for unskilled-labor-intensive sectors, particularly high for technology-intensive sectors, and intermediate for the other types of sectors. As countries such as China successfully develop, the composition of their trade flows tends to move away from primary products, initially toward unskilled-labor-intensive products and subsequently toward technology- and human-capital-intensive products. Associated with these changes there is an ultimate increase in the extent of intraindustry trade.

Table 1

Intraindustry trade and aggregation: China, selected years (trade-weighted average Grubel-Lloyd index, different levels of aggregation)

	3-digit 237 sectors	2-digit 67 sectors	1-digit 10 sectors
1980	0.20	0.30	0.63
1985	0.20	0.29	0.44
1990	0.36	0.45	0.60
1995	0.38	0.48	0.67
2000	0.39	0.48	0.57
2005	0.42	0.49	0.58

Source: Author's calculations based on United Nations (2006) COMTRADE data from World Integrated Trade Solution (WITS), Geneva.

Table 2
Intraindustry trade and composition of trade flows: China, selected years
(trade-weighted average Grubel-Lloyd index [3-digit level] and percent of total trade)

	Type of products				
	Primary products	Natural-resource intensive	Unskilled-labor intensive	Technology intensive	Human-capital intensive
Weighted average Grubel-Lloyd summary statistics for product type, 1980–2005					
average	0.27	0.38	0.16	0.56	0.36
st dev[a]	0.11	0.07	0.04	0.04	0.08
Share of product type in total trade (percent)					
1980	51.4	3.4	27.8	8.1	9.2
1985	49.5	2.0	33.7	7.1	7.7
1990	19.4	2.9	46.5	15.6	15.5
1995	10.1	4.0	45.4	24.9	15.6
2000	7.5	3.2	39.2	35.5	14.6
2005	4.6	3.3	28.9	47.7	15.5

Source: Author's calculations based on United Nations (2006) COMTRADE data from World Integrated Trade Solution (WITS), Geneva.
[a] st dev = standard deviation.

In a study summarizing the growing importance of intraindustry trade, the Organisation for Economic Co-operation and Development (OECD 2002) lists the following empirical characteristics: Intraindustry trade

- has risen significantly since the 1980s in most (OECD) countries
- is particularly high for sophisticated manufactured products (chemicals, machinery, transportation equipment, electrical equipment, and electronics; both based on product differentiation and fragmentation)
- is particularly high for very open countries ("supertrading" economies, where both imports and exports account for more than half of GDP)
- is connected to foreign direct investment inflows, particularly in Eastern European "transition" economies
- is related to preferential trade agreements, for example, the sharp increase in intraindustry trade in Mexico after the North American Free Trade Agreement
- is to a large extent based on intrafirm trade, either based on product variety or on fragmentation (intrafirm trade accounts, for example, for one-third of exports in Japan and the United States).

See also economies of scale; fragmentation; Heckscher-Ohlin model; intrafirm trade; monopolistic competition; New Trade Theory; vertical versus horizontal foreign direct investment

FURTHER READING

Grubel, Herbert G., and Peter Lloyd. 1975. *Intraindustry Trade: The Theory and Measurement of International Trade in Differentiated Products*. London: Macmillan. Most influential study on measuring and understanding intraindustry trade.

Helpman, Elhanan, and Paul Krugman. 1987. *Market Structure and Foreign Trade: Increasing Returns, Imperfect Competition, and the International Economy*. Boston:

MIT Press. Overview of the main theories explaining intraindustry trade by two prominent contributors.

Organisation for Economic Co-operation and Development (OECD). 2002. "Intraindustry and Intrafirm Trade and the Internationalisation of Production." *Economic Outlook*, no. 71, chap. 6: 159–70. A recent discussion of the growing importance and characteristics of intraindustry trade.

United Nations (UN). 2006. COMTRADE data from World Integrated Trade Solution (WITS). Geneva. Available at https://unp.un.org/comtrade.aspx. A large trade data set from over 200 reporting countries or areas, covering 45 years of data and more than 5,000 different products.

CHARLES VAN MARREWIJK

■ J-curve effect

The J-curve effect describes the time lag with which a currency depreciation or devaluation leads to an improvement in the trade balance. Although the trade balance may improve in the long run, it may worsen initially so that it follows the pattern of a *J* tilted to the right. The origin of the J-curve is usually attributed to economist Stephen Magee's (1973) attempt to find an explanation for the short-run behavior of the U.S. trade balance in the early 1970s. In 1971 a balance of trade surplus turned into a deficit, and although the U.S. dollar was devalued, the trade balance continued to deteriorate.

The theoretical basis of the J-curve effect is the elasticities approach to the balance of payments. According to this theory a currency devaluation or depreciation is expected to improve the trade balance by changing the relative prices of domestic and foreign goods. By making foreign goods more expensive in the home country and the home country's goods cheaper abroad, demand for imports will be low and foreigners will buy more of the home country's exports. Provided that the responses of importers and exporters to the price changes are strong enough, the Marshall-Lerner condition will be fulfilled and the trade balance will improve.

Importance of the J-Curve The J-curve effect is important because it has implications for the effectiveness of policies designed to improve the balance of payments. During the 1997 financial crisis in Asia, for example, the International Monetary Fund encouraged currency depreciation as part of a package of policies to stabilize the balance of payments of countries hardest hit by the crisis. If the J-curve effect is important then it will take a longer period of time before the balance of payments improves than if the adjustment to the currency depreciation had been instantaneous.

The J-curve phenomenon has also been invoked to explain the persistence of the U.S. trade deficit following the fall in the U.S. dollar from its peak in 1985. Even after two years of a falling dollar, the trade deficit failed to show a marked improvement. According to this perspective, while the U.S. trade balance was expected to improve in the longer term, the substantial lags in the adjustment of both prices and quantities to exchange rate changes contributed to the sluggish response of the U.S. deficit to the U.S. dollar depreciation.

Causes of the J-Curve The causes of the J-curve effect are generally traced to a currency contract effect and/or weak short-run responses to changes in the relative prices of exports and imports following a depreciation or devaluation of the home country's currency. The currency contract effect arises when import and export orders reflect decisions made in advance of the devaluation at the old exchange rate. Therefore, immediately after a devaluation there may be a period when contracts signed prior to the exchange rate change become due. The J-curve can then occur if the home country's exports are invoiced in the home currency but its imports are invoiced in the foreign currency: during the currency contract period the value of exports in the home country's currency is unaffected by the devaluation, but import values measured in home currency will rise, thus worsening the trade balance. Only in the longer run when new contracts are signed will the value of home imports fall and home exports rise sufficiently to improve the trade balance.

Even in the absence of a currency contract period, a J-curve can occur if responses to the changes in import and export prices are weak, so that quantities traded do not change much in the short run. This would imply a failure of the Marshall-Lerner condition over this period. If the demand for imports is unresponsive, the total import bill could rise until the home country's buyers find suitable substitutes, while the demand for exports may be insensitive if foreign buyers do not increase their demand for the home country's goods in the short run even though their prices have fallen in the foreign country's currency.

Estimating the J-Curve Although economists have done a substantial amount of empirical work on the J-curve, the results seem to depend on the particular country and the period selected for investigation. What is clear is that the short-run response of the trade balance to a devaluation or depreciation of the currency does not follow a uniform pattern. One reason for this is that other factors may be involved. For example, the rapid improvement in the Mexican trade balance with the United States following the sharp depreciation of the peso against the dollar in December 1994 is often cited as a successful balance of payments adjustment with the absence of any obvious J-curve complications. But the massive size of the devaluation and the financial crisis that accompanied it may have persuaded exporters and importers that the devaluation was permanent and therefore speeded up their adjustment. In addition, an improvement in the trade balance may have resulted from a fall in spending on imports as government spending was cut, and prior trade liberalization may have made import and export volumes more sensitive to relative price changes.

A second factor is that the response to the exchange rate change may vary according to the level of sectoral aggregation. Countries with a high proportion of natural resources, such as crude petroleum and agricultural products, in their exports and/or imports may find their trade balance is less sensitive to exchange rate changes than countries that predominantly trade manufactured goods. A further problem is the need to look beneath the aggregate trade balance to see what is happening at the bilateral level. The trade balance may be improving in the short run with respect to one trading partner but simultaneously deteriorating with respect to another.

See also balance of payments; currency crisis; effective exchange rate; exchange rate pass-through; financial crisis; Marshall-Lerner condition; real exchange rate; vehicle currency

FURTHER READING

Bahmani-Oskooee, Mohsen, and A. Ratha. 2004. "The J-Curve: A Literature Review." *Applied Economics* 36: 1377–98. Provides a recent review of the vast empirical literature on the J-curve effect.

Krugman, P. 1989. "The J-Curve, the Fire Sale, and the Hard Landing." *American Economic Review* 79: 31–35. An interesting attempt to unravel the reasons for the sluggish improvement in the U.S. trade balance following the sharp fall in the U.S. dollar in 1985.

Magee, Stephen. 1973. "Currency Contracts, Pass-Through, and Devaluation." *Brookings Papers on Economic Activity* 1: 303–25. The pioneering work on the J-curve effect.

PETER WILSON

■ **joint ventures**

A joint venture is a mechanism for combining complementary assets owned by separate firms. These assets can be tangible, such as machinery and equipment, or intangible, such as technological know-how, production or marketing skills, brand names, and market-specific information. In an equity joint venture the partner firms transfer all or part of their assets to a legally independent entity and share the profits from the venture. Contractual arrangements that do not involve shared equity control are sometimes referred to as nonequity joint ventures; examples include licensing and management contracts, as well as supply and distribution agreements. Shared ownership and contractual arrangements are also frequently grouped together under the term *alliances*. This entry focuses on equity joint ventures, specifically international joint ventures involving partners from different countries.

From a world economy perspective there are at least two reasons for examining international joint ventures. First, international joint ventures represent a form of foreign direct investment (FDI). Multinational enterprises often have to decide whether to wholly own a foreign affiliate or to share equity control with a local partner. This decision is a key element of the foreign investment strategy. Second, the ownership structure of a foreign investment project affects host-country welfare. A direct effect comes from the sharing of profits between the multinational and the local firm. Indirect effects arise because ownership influences investors' incentives to commit resources to the project, such as capital and technology. Some host countries impose local ownership requirements that limit the equity stake foreign investors can take in local companies. This raises the question of what the economic effects of such requirements are.

Probably the most comprehensive data on international joint ventures come from the U.S. Department of Commerce benchmark surveys. Although they are not representative for the world as a whole, these data still offer information on long-run trends in international joint venture activity for one of the most important source countries of FDI. According to Desai, Foley, and Hines (2004), who have examined these data, about 80 percent of all U.S. affiliates abroad in 1997 were wholly owned, with the remaining 20 percent equally divided between minority- and majority-owned affiliates. The ownership share is positively correlated with host-country gross national product (GNP). In the richest quartile of host countries, partially owned affiliates accounted for only 15.5 percent, whereas in the poorest quartile they made up more than half of all U.S. foreign affiliates. The data exhibit considerable variation in ownership shares across industries and over time. Since the mid-1980s there has been a downward trend in minority-owned and an upward trend in majority- and wholly owned affiliates, partly due to changes in U.S. tax laws.

Profit-Maximizing Joint Ventures Consider a multinational firm contemplating a foreign investment project that requires a combination of its own assets and those of a local firm in the host country. What is the appropriate ownership structure of the project? The extensive literature on this issue starts from the premise that the ownership structure is a response to the presence of market failures (or high transaction costs) in asset markets. This can best be understood by assuming—counterfactually—that there are no such failures. This is the case, if (1) all assets and other inputs to and outputs from the project are observable and verifiable by third parties, such as courts; (2) it is possible to write contracts specifying the provision of each input, and the distribution of output and profits under all possible contingencies; and (3) these contracts can be enforced at no cost. Under these ideal conditions, the ownership structure is indeterminate, since the firms can simply use contracts to coordinate the use of their assets.

Such ideal conditions are unlikely to prevail in practice. Suppose, for example, that the project requires a combination of the multinational's production technology and the local firm's marketing know-how. It may be very difficult to specify what these assets entail, to assess how valuable each asset will be for the project, and hence to write a contract on what each party has to contribute and how profits are to be shared. Even if the two parties both knew how important the technology and the marketing know-how were, it would be next to impossible for a third party to verify this and hence to determine whether both parties have fulfilled their contractual obligations. It may also be impossible through contractual means to prevent spillovers of the technology to the local firm, which could then use it for its own purposes. Specifying appropriate management contracts to ensure that profits from the project are maximized may be difficult, especially if monitoring costs are high. In short, contracts will generally be insufficient to prevent opportunistic behavior. Retaining (partial) ownership of assets, and hence

715

residual rights of control over them, may then be preferable because it ensures that a firm will obtain at least some return from the project and hence have an incentive to contribute assets to the project and provide effort in running it.

Shared ownership of an investment project is only a second-best solution. First, it may be impossible to guarantee each party the full return from the use of its assets. Hence there may be too little provision of assets or insufficient investment in tailoring the assets to the project. Second, joint ventures require significant management resources due to the need to coordinate decisions between the partners. Why then would one of the partners, say the multinational, not simply acquire the other and assume whole ownership of the project? One obvious advantage of shared ownership is that it requires less capital than a complete takeover. Moreover, the multinational may be interested in only some of the assets of the local firm. If these are hard to disentangle from the local firm's other assets, a joint venture may be the better option. Incomplete information about the value of the local firm's assets provides another reason for shared ownership, since letting the local firm choose how much ownership to retain may reveal information to the multinational.

Empirically it is difficult to distinguish between different explanations for shared ownership, since the information on which firms base their decisions is often confidential. In addition, the ownership decision may be made simultaneously with other decisions concerning the firm's operations. Desai, Foley, and Hines (2004) therefore use changes in U.S. tax laws affecting ownership and the liberalization of local ownership requirements to identify possible interactions between these decisions. They find a complementary relationship between the ownership share of the multinational and the amount of intrafirm trade between the affiliate and the parent company. Firms that trade more internally are more likely to have whole or majority ownership, whereas affiliates selling more of their output or buying more of their inputs locally are more likely to be organized as joint ventures. Possible reasons for this are that

whole ownership reduces the cost of coordinating intrafirm transactions and makes it easier to set internal transfer prices to avoid taxes.

Host-Country Policy Local ownership requirements are most frequently imposed by developing and transition countries, although some high-income countries also put limits on foreign ownership in certain sectors. Possible economic rationales for requiring local equity participation in low-income countries are that they might facilitate spillovers of technology and management know-how to local firms and might secure a share of the project's earnings for the host country when the fiscal system is too inefficient to do this directly through taxes. Some authors argue that multinationals, too, may have an interest to take on a local partner to smooth relations with the host-country government and reduce the risk of expropriation.

See also foreign direct investment (FDI); mergers and acquisitions

FURTHER READING

Asiedu, Elizabeth, and Hadi S. Esfahani. 2001. "Ownership Structure in Foreign Direct Investment Projects." *Review of Economics and Statistics* 83 (4): 647–62. Shows that foreign equity shares rise with the importance of foreign investor assets and decline with the contribution of local assets toward the surplus generated by the project.

Caves, Richard E. 2007. *Multinational Enterprise and Economic Analysis*. 3d ed. Cambridge: Cambridge University Press. A classic examination of the economics of foreign direct investment.

Desai, Mihir A., C. Fritz Foley, and James R. Hines. 2004. "The Costs of Shared Ownership: Evidence from International Joint Ventures." *Journal of Financial Economics* 73 (2): 323–74. Finds that whole ownership is most common when firms coordinate production activities across locations, transfer technology, and implement global tax planning. Observes that much of decline in use of joint ventures can be attributed to increased importance on intrafirm transactions.

Müller, Thomas, and Monika Schnitzer. 2006. "Technology Transfer and Spillovers in International Joint Ventures." *Journal of International Economics* 68 (2):

456–68. Shows why, on account of host country policies, a multinational might enter a joint venture even when spillovers result. Finds that joint venture may not benefit the host country, despite spillovers.

Nakamura, M., and J. Xie. 1998. "Nonverifiability, Non-contractibility, and Ownership Determination Models in Foreign Direct Investment, with an Application to Foreign Operations in Japan." *International Journal of Industrial Organization* 16 (5): 571–99. Finds support for theory that ownership share depends on the importance of the firm's intangible assets and its bargaining power relative to local partners, using data on foreign manufacturing operations in Japan.

Raff, Horst, Michael Ryan, and Frank Stähler, 2007. "Whole versus Shared Ownership of Foreign Affiliates." Kiel Economics Working Paper 2007-18. Available at http://opus.zbw-kiel.de/volltexte/2007/5684/pdf/EWP-2007-18.pdf. Shows how partial ownership can be used as a screening device to elicit private information from a local firm. Application to Japanese firm-level data.

HORST RAFF

■ knowledge-capital model
of the multinational enterprise

The knowledge-capital model of the multinational enterprise (KC model hereafter) incorporates the theories of horizontal and vertical foreign direct investment (FDI) into a model of the New Trade Theory (see Markusen 2002). The KC model is then used to explore how the location decision of potential multinational firms, their production decisions, the international trade structure (and volume), factor prices, and welfare depend on relative and absolute country size, relative factor endowments, trade barriers, and investment costs.

The term *knowledge-capital model* is derived from the assumption that multinational firms have an ownership advantage compared with other firms due to some knowledge asset, such as patents, blueprints, procedures, brand names, trademarks, or reputation. Knowledge capital has three properties. First, its usage in plants is cheap to separate geographically from its creation in headquarters (fragmentation). Second, knowledge-capital creation is skilled labor intensive (skilled labor intensity). Third, once produced in the headquarters, it can be used in multiple plants within the firm (joint input). The KC model regards FDI as a flow of knowledge in the form of managerial and engineering services, financial services, reputation, and trademarks across borders.

From the central features of knowledge capital derive several location advantages that countries must have to attract FDI. Since the headquarter activity is skilled labor intensive while production is relatively unskilled labor intensive, factor costs are minimized by locating headquarters in relatively skilled-labor-abundant countries and plants in unskilled-labor-abundant countries, motivating vertical FDI. However, separation of production from the headquarters will require trade of goods across borders to serve the home market. To avoid trade costs, producing locally in several locations (horizontal FDI) may be worthwhile. Since there are plant-level fixed costs in addition to firm-level fixed costs, host country markets need to be sufficiently large because otherwise the profits from saving trade costs would not cover the additional plant-fixed costs of local production compared with exporting. If a foreign market is small, it may be optimal for the firm to abstain from production abroad and export from home instead.

Due to knowledge capital, firms favor corporate control of foreign operations over outsourcing. With international outsourcing, the knowledge capital may dissipate faster to competitors (internalization advantage).

Model Description In the standard KC model, there are two countries, two factors of production (skilled and unskilled labor), and two homogeneous goods. Countries differ in their factor endowments. Production of one good is perfectly competitive and subject to constant returns to scale (competitive sector). FDI can occur only in the second sector, which operates at increasing returns to scale, using a three-stage production process (increasing-returns sector). In the first stage, a firm must undertake some headquarter services such as R&D, management, accounting or marketing activities, and firm-level fixed costs accrue. In the second stage, plant-level fixed costs are incurred. In the final stage, firms compete in an oligopolistic goods market, choosing simultaneously supply (Cournot competition). Markets are segmented and part of the export value is wasted (iceberg trade costs) when shipping goods of the increasing-returns sector across borders.

Assuming headquarter activities are more skilled labor intensive relative to integrated plant and final production in the increasing-returns sector, which, in turn, is more skilled labor intensive than production in the competitive sector, three firm types can emerge:

- *Horizontal* FDI firms have their headquarter activities tied to the home plant and duplicate the domestic production plant in the host country. These firms sell their entire production locally.
- *Vertical* FDI firms locate skilled-labor-intensive headquarter services in the skilled-labor-abundant home country and relatively unskilled-labor-intensive production activity in the unskilled-labor-abundant host country. Foreign affiliates of the vertical type export (part of) their production to the home country.
- *National* firms solely produce in the home country and serve foreign markets by exports.

Firm Location, Foreign Affiliate Production, and International Trade The model is too complex to be solved analytically and must be explored numerically. A standard display of such numerical analysis uses three-dimensional diagrams based on the Edgeworth box (see figure 1). Given a fixed world endowment in both production factors, the bottom of the box depicts the two countries' shares in the world endowments' skilled and unskilled labor, S and U, respectively. At the left corner is the origin of the first country denoted i where its share both in skilled and unskilled labor is zero. Conversely, the origin of the other country j is at the right corner.

First consider the effects of varying the relative size of the two countries. Along the diagonal connecting the two origins the relative factor endowments are

identical in both countries. Beginning along this diagonal with the i country very small in terms of endowments, the prevalent firm types are vertical FDI firms with headquarters in i and national firms with headquarters in j. National firms of country j benefit from their large home market, saving more on foregone plant-fixed costs by exporting than losing from variable trade costs, because their foreign market is small. Vertical FDI from country i benefits also from the large market of country j, minimizing trade costs. At this stage country i firms are multinational, but they are few. There are simply not enough endowments in skilled labor to support many headquarters. Hence aggregate sales of affiliates from country i are small. Affiliate sales start rising with a proportional increase in country i's world endowment shares of skilled and unskilled labor. Horizontal FDI firms with headquarters in i enter, as the home market size grows sufficiently for operating profits to cover the fixed cost.

At still larger relative size of country i, the national firms of country j begin to turn into horizontal firms. Since j-firms then gain competitiveness on the i-market by saving trade cost, they push some i-horizontal firms out of the market, which causes a dip in aggregate affiliate sales until only horizontal firms are left.

Increasing country i's relative size further, there is a continuous rise in affiliate sales, because the larger endowments of i support continuously more headquarters of horizontal FDI firms and correspondingly more foreign affiliates. A peak in country i's affiliate sales are attained when it is slightly larger than country j.

At still a further increase in country i's relative size, its aggregate affiliate sales tend toward zero rapidly, because the foreign market size shrinks and country i's horizontal FDI firms are gradually replaced by national firms without affiliates.

Along the ray connecting the origins, the larger country exports the increasing returns and imports the competitive good because of its comparative advantage in the increasing-returns sector.

Next, the relative endowment shares are varied, keeping income of both countries and the world

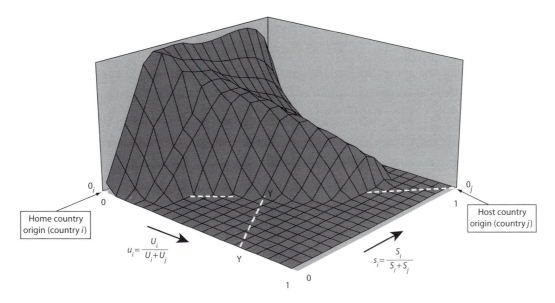

Figure 1
Simulated affiliate sales based on the KC model from Markusen (2002)

endowment equal, which is approximately true for endowment combinations along the line denoted YY in figure 1. Affiliate sales of firms with headquarters in country i have an inverse U-shape along this line.

When countries are identical and trade costs sufficiently high or world endowments sufficiently large, then horizontal FDI firms prevail, and there are equally many in each country. As country i's skilled-endowment share rises relative to country j's, production plants remain equally spread. More and more headquarters relocate to country i, however, since headquarters are skilled labor intensive, absorbing the excessive skilled-labor supply there.

The peak in aggregate affiliate sales of firms with headquarters in country i occurs when the i country is moderately skilled labor abundant. Then country i is residence to a maximum number of headquarters from horizontal-FDI firms while the number of j-country horizontal-FDI firms has shrunk to zero.

Further increasing relative skilled labor abundance of country i, horizontal firms begin to switch gradually into national firms, and country i begins to export the increasing returns good in exchange for the competitive good. Since all world headquarters are already located in country i and still dispropor-

tionately much skilled labor is left in country i, the second most intensive activity—production of the increasing returns good—is located there, too. But this makes up national firms that do not have foreign affiliate sales. The more horizontal firms are replaced by national firms, the less aggregate affiliate sales country i firms will have.

When almost all skilled labor of the world is concentrated in country i, horizontal firms vanish and vertical FDI firms emerge next to the national firms—all with headquarters in country i. Vertical FDI firms of country i have only headquarter activities there, which absorbs the largest possible amount of skilled relative to unskilled labor.

Overall, the peak of affiliate sales due to vertical FDI occurs when the home country is small and relatively skilled labor abundant. A peak of horizontal affiliate sales occurs when both countries are similar in size and relative factor endowments. National firms are prevalent when the home country is large and skilled labor abundant.

FDI Liberalization, Factor Prices, and Welfare

How does the factor income distribution and countries' welfare change if FDI is inhibited initially, and then free to exist? Such FDI liberalization increases the skilled-wage premium (the ratio of the wage paid to skilled labor relative to that paid to unskilled labor) of the skilled-labor-abundant country, because the specialization in headquarters either of the horizontal or vertical type shifts labor demand toward skilled labor. If relative factor endowments are equal across the two countries, the skilled-wage premium will rise nevertheless whenever horizontal FDI emerges (at sufficiently similar country sizes), because horizontal FDI incurs fixed costs for two plants rather than one, and fixed costs will be intensive in skilled labor. The relative skilled-wage premium even rises in the unskilled-labor-abundant country when the relative abundance is very strong and relative country size similar. The reason is that production plants of more-skilled-labor-intensive vertical FDI from the other country begin to replace firms of the unskilled-labor-intensive competitive sector, shifting relative labor demand toward skilled labor.

Instead, when a country is very small and unskilled labor abundant or very large and skilled labor abundant, FDI is unattractive, and neither firm types nor relative factor prices change. Only a large unskilled-labor-abundant country will experience a fall in the skilled-wage premium, as national firms are replaced by affiliates of foreign vertical FDI firms, substituting skilled-labor-intensive headquarters for less-skilled-labor-intensive production activities.

Turning to welfare, countries that lose from investment liberalization are primarily large, or somewhat smaller, and very skilled labor abundant. The welfare loss arises from relocating production of the increasing-returns good to the foreign country while agglomerating the headquarter activities at home. In this case the increasing-returns good needs to be imported at trade costs and the competition on the domestic market between local producers and importers is less fierce, increasing the profit margins. Both the trade costs and the increase in the profit margin contribute to the rise in the relative price of the increasing-returns good, which decreases consumer rent and welfare.

A welfare gain for both countries arises, for example, if both countries are similar in size and relative skill endowments. Both countries gain then from the savings of trade costs and lower product prices through horizontal FDI, which must overcompensate for the additional fixed costs. Otherwise firms would not choose horizontal FDI.

Empirical Evidence The empirical evidence on the KC model is mixed. Pooling inward and outward FDI data for the United States, Carr, Markusen, and Maskus (2001) provide strong support for the KC model, finding that affiliate sales increase in the total income of the host and home countries, in skill differences, and in similarities of country size. In addition, they find that home countries, which are simultaneously skilled labor abundant and small, have higher affiliate sales.

However, Markusen and Maskus (2001) find a negative relation between affiliate sales and skilled labor abundance in the home country when investigating outward U.S. FDI only. Moreover, Markusen and Maskus (2002) cannot prove the KC model favors a horizontal model where vertical FDI is ruled out by assumption. Blonigen, Davies, and Head (2003) first reestimate the U.S. data separately on observations with negative and positive skill differences, and then apply the absolute values of differences in skill endowments and size in pooled regressions. Finding that increasing skill differences—whether positive or negative—decrease affiliate sales, they conclude this pattern consistent only with horizontal FDI and not with vertical FDI, hence rejecting the KC model. Markusen and Maskus (2003) in their reply call this finding inconsistent with any model.

Recently, some evidence in favor of vertical FDI in the KC model has been provided, however. Braconier, Norbäck, and Urban (2005) collect data on affiliate sales from home countries that are small and skilled labor abundant and add them to the U.S. data to have more observations where vertical FDI is expected. Moreover, they define the relative skill variable not as absolute but as relative distance, which puts more weight on large differences. Then they obtain in their estimates the typical surface of the KC model.

Extension Two stylized facts are not accounted for by the standard model. Bilateral affiliate sales are positively correlated with FDI stocks, and there are both more bilateral affiliate sales and exports the more similar countries are in size. These two stylized facts are explained by Bergstrand and Egger (2007), assuming that plant (headquarter) fixed costs consist of physical capital from the home country (skilled labor) and that there are three instead of two countries.

Suppose there were only horizontal firms when countries are symmetric in endowments, then demand for physical capital would be at a maximum, raising the rental rate of capital and fixed cost. Since national firms have one plant less, they save on fixed costs at the expense of larger trade cost. Hence a mix of national and horizontal firms will emerge such that both types are equally well off. Bergstrand and Egger show further that the addition of a third country helps explain that both affiliate and export sales rise as two countries become more similar.

In sum, the KC model provides a rich description of the types of activities undertaken by multinational enterprises, including vertical and horizontal FDI. The degree of empirical support for the KC model is undergoing debate, with an extension to include a third country currently showing the most promise.

See also factor endowments and foreign direct investment; fixed costs and foreign direct investment; footloose production; foreign direct investment (FDI); location theory; market access; market size and foreign direct investment; outsourcing/offshoring; proximity-concentration hypothesis; trade costs and foreign direct investment; vertical versus horizontal foreign direct investment

FURTHER READING

Bergstrand, Jeffrey H., and Peter Egger. 2007. "A Knowledge-and-Physical-Capital Model of International Trade Flows, Foreign Direct Investment, and Multinational Enterprises." *Journal of International Economics* 73 (2): 278–308. Important extension of KC model to three countries.

Blonigen, Bruce, Ron Davies, and Keith Head. 2003. "Estimating the Knowledge-Capital Model of the Multinational Enterprise: Comment." *American Economic Review* 93 (3): 980–94. Comment on the first estimation of the KC model.

Braconier, Henrik, Pehr-Johan Norbäck, and Dieter Urban. 2005. "Reconciling the Evidence on the Knowledge-Capital Model." *Review of International Economics* 13 (4): 770–86. Empirical evidence in favor of the KC model.

Carr, David, James R. Markusen, and Keith E. Maskus. 2001. "Estimating the Knowledge-Capital Model of the Multinational Enterprise." *American Economic Review* 91 (3): 693–708. First estimation of the KC model.

Markusen, James R. 2002. *Multinational Firms and the Theory of International Trade*. Cambridge, MA: The MIT Press. Seminal publication including many of Markusen's models of FDI.

Markusen, James R., and Keith E. Maskus. 2001. "Multinational Firms: Reconciling Theory and Evidence." In *Topics in Empirical International Economics: A Festschrift in Honor of Robert E. Lipsey*, edited by Magnus Blomstrom and Linda Goldberg. Chicago: Chicago University Press, 71–95. Extension to the first estimation of the KC model.

———. 2002. "Discriminating among Alternative Theories of the Multinational Enterprise." *Review of International Economics* 10 (4): 694–707. Mixed evidence on the KC model when discriminating it against the horizontal or vertical FDI model.

———. 2003. "Estimating the Knowledge-Capital Model of the Multinational Enterprise: Reply." *American Economic Review* 93 (3): 995–1001. Enlightening explanations on how to estimate the KC model and how to discriminate it against alternatives.

DIETER M. URBAN

■ **Kyoto Protocol**
See multilateral environmental agreements

■ labor standards

Cross-country variations in labor market practices and protections can have implications for the pattern and terms of trade. Weak labor protections that augment the supply of unskilled labor, such as forced labor and child labor, can increase the supply of unskilled-labor-intensive exports on world markets, thereby depressing wages of unskilled workers world-wide. Inhumane labor practices may also generate negative reactions from consumers and investors globally. The external effect of one country's labor practices on its trade partners provides a basis for international coordination of labor market regulations. Internationally coordinated labor practices are commonly referred to as *international labor standards*.

Proponents of international coordination of labor standards emphasize the consequences that trade with low-wage countries will have for workers in industrialized countries. In the absence of international coordination, there may be a *race to the bottom* in labor protections. Opponents of coordination argue that international labor standards are a form of protectionism.

International coordination of labor market regulations was first advanced by Switzerland in 1881. A subsequent series of international conferences over the following 32 years produced agreements prohibiting international trade in white phosphorous matches and limits on night work for women.

Currently, labor standards in international trade agreements are limited. Article XX(e) of the World Trade Organization (WTO) Charter permits members to refuse imports of goods produced with prison labor. Broader labor standards have been incorporated into regional trading agreements such as the North American Free Trade Agreement. Further coordination of labor standards within the General Agreement on Tariffs and Trade (GATT), and subsequently the WTO, was proposed by the European Parliament in 1983 and 1994, by the U.S. government in 1986, and at every WTO Ministerial between 1996 and 2001. The Singapore Ministerial Declaration (December 1996), however, while acknowledging the importance of international labor standards, identified the International Labor Organization (ILO) as the competent body to establish and monitor labor standards.

Labor standards commonly fall into two broad groups. *Process*, or *core*, labor standards regulate the basic function of labor markets and are considered by many to be basic human rights. Core labor standards, as identified by the ILO, are (1) rights to free association and collective bargaining, (2) prohibition against forced labor, (3) abolition of exploitative child labor, and (4) elimination of discrimination in employment. *Outcome* standards place limitations on aspects of the labor contract such as hours worked and wages.

Labor Standards and International Trade Negotiations The link between domestic labor regulations and the international terms of trade has implications for international trade negotiations. A labor-scarce country that makes tariff concessions granting market access to a labor-abundant trade partner in a round of international trade negotiations can in effect offset those concessions by easing costly domestic labor standards that adversely affect import-competing producers. The *ex post* reduction in domestic labor protections is referred to as a *race to the bottom*.

In the absence of a mechanism to restrict *ex post* changes in domestic regulations, the labor-scarce country cannot guarantee the promised market access. For this reason, efficient bargaining requires that tariffs and domestic policy be negotiated simultaneously.

More generally, a country's domestic labor practices generate an external effect on its trade partners through the terms of trade. Labor-using standards, such as a prohibition against prison labor, reduce the supply of labor relative to capital on world markets. As a consequence, the price of labor-intensive goods rises and the price of capital-intensive goods falls on the world market. Thus, labor protections improve the terms of trade for a labor-abundant country but worsen the terms of trade for a labor-scarce country. The existence of such an external effect creates an incentive for labor-abundant countries to overregulate their labor markets (from a global efficiency perspective) while labor-scarce countries have an incentive to underregulate their labor markets.

Existing provisions of the GATT have been proposed to coordinate labor practices internationally; these include anti-dumping measures (Article VI), the prohibition against export subsidies (Article XVI), the opt-out provision (Article XXXV), the Trade Policy Review Mechanism, and the Nullification and Impairment clause (Article XXIII). Of these, only Article XXIII has been found to provide a legal basis for regulating domestic policies within the WTO. Negotiations within the WTO are understood to provide each country with a certain level of access to its trade partners' markets. Any acts by the importer that nullify or impair the expected access can form the basis of a complaint and trigger renegotiation of the tariff agreement. In the context of the labor standards debate, a labor-scarce importer that relaxes its labor protections in an attempt to limit the import exposure created by its tariff reductions would then be required to make additional tariff reductions as compensation to a labor-abundant

exporter. The exercise of the Nullification and Impairment clause thus internalizes the external effect of domestic labor standards policies.

Use of Article XXIII has not been pursued in the WTO for the purpose of coordinating labor practices. Rather, two other options were advocated in the 1990s to manage the interrelationship between border controls and domestic policies. Some delegates sought to extend the General Exceptions provisions of Article XX to include a range of labor practices (beyond prison labor). A social clause was also proposed that would harmonize labor standards among members of the WTO. Members were unable to agree, however, on a common set of universal standards that would be enforced within the WTO. At the conclusion of the 1996 Singapore ministerial, the task of establishing and monitoring labor standards was delegated to the ILO, and WTO members committed themselves to cooperate with the ILO on these issues.

The ILO was created in 1919 as part of the League of Nations and became part of the United Nations after 1946. The ILO promulgates conventions and recommendations concerning labor practices that member governments may or may not choose to ratify. Compliance is voluntary but the ILO provides technical assistance on improving labor practice.

Enforcement and Issue Linkage Given the lack of enforcement power within the ILO, it has been recommended that some enforcement power from the WTO be transferred to the ILO. Under linkage, a WTO member, adversely affected by noncompliance with ratified ILO Conventions by its trade partner, could make a complaint under Article XXIII that its expected market access has been nullified or impaired. Some compensation in the form of other tariff concessions could then be required.

Critics of this approach contend that simultaneous negotiations of trade and labor issues will produce stricter labor standards but less trade liberalization than would be otherwise forthcoming from two separate agreements. Issue linkage may also increase enforcement power, however. The impact of coordination depends on how countries calculate the payoffs from cooperation on the two issues. If a failure to reach a cooperative agreement on one issue increases the value of cooperation on the other issue, these two coordination objectives are *substitutes*. In this case, countries will find it easier to sustain cooperation on either issue if negotiations on both issues are linked in a single agreement. A country considering defection on labor practices, for example, will see cooperation collapse on labor and trade if cooperation is linked in a single agreement. The consequent increase in the cost of defection achieved by linking issues will strengthen the capacity of countries to negotiate self-enforcing agreements on both trade and labor.

Market Mechanisms Market-based mechanisms have also been proposed for improving labor practices. Product labels characterizing conditions of work in the production process offer consumers an opportunity to pay a premium for goods produced under humane working conditions. Market efficiency will be achieved with a credible product label if consumers have a *private* distaste for poor working conditions.

By contrast, if the external effect of working conditions on consumers is a *public* good, product labels may not correct the market failure. In the case of child labor, firms seeking a *child labor–free* label will be required to discharge underage employees. If child employment in the export sector is the first-best option for the child, termination of employment will force the child to the second-best choice. Child welfare will only improve if (1) product labeling is sufficiently pervasive that it raises the wages of adult labor above the level at which families withdraw children from the labor force, or (2) some portion of the premium paid by consumers is diverted to a fund used to provide welfare services to former child workers.

Corporate codes of conduct relating to the general conditions of work for adult employees have greater potential to improve working conditions. First, codes may simply require factories to employ more humane, though more costly, means of production in order to satisfy the demands of consumers and stockholders. Second, compliance officers may impart knowledge concerning labor management practices that are both more humane and more efficient. For example, factory managers may not fully appreciate the role harsh treatment and low wages play in increasing manpower turnover and retaining investment in skill trainings. Production inefficiencies such as poor line organization may have the effect of increasing overtime, thereby reducing productivity and wages. Third, corporate compliance officers that enforce codes requiring free association and collective bargaining may also inhibit monopsonistic employment practices, such as exploiting the lack of market experience of young female employees.

At the end of 2007, labor standards in the world economy are limited to voluntary initiatives and regional trading arrangements. Individual countries establish their own labor protections within the confines of a set of global ethical and domestic political considerations. Concern with the impact of trade on labor ebbed during the early part of the 21st century. Continuing integration of global labor markets may increase the pressure to implement labor protections, however.

See also child labor; comparative advantage; General Agreement on Tariffs and Trade (GATT); International Labor Organization; terms of trade; trade and wages; World Trade Organization

FURTHER READING

Basu, Kaushik, Henrik Horn, Lisa Roman, and Judith Shapiro, eds. *International Labor Standards*. Malden, MA: Blackwell, 2003. Four papers covering the theory and history of labor standards, an application to child labor, and a discussion of the role of labor standards in international organizations.

Brown, Drusilla K. 2001. "Labor Standards: Where Do They Belong on the International Trade Agenda?" *Journal of Economic Perspectives* 15 (3): 89–112. A concise discussion of the basic issues relating to labor standards and trade policy.

DRUSILLA K. BROWN

■ Latin American debt crisis

The Latin American debt crisis officially began in August 1982 with Mexico's announcement that it could no longer meet its interest payment obligations. External debt in Latin America had quadrupled from a 1975 level of $75 billion to more than $315 billion by 1983, which was about 50 percent of gross domestic product for that region. Variable interest rate loans meant that debt service (interest payments and the repayment of principle) grew even faster, rising to $66 billion by 1982 from $12 billion in 1975 (Gruppen 1986). The crisis was set in motion in the early 1970s when private bank lending to Latin America began to expand rapidly, eventually overtaking international development bank lending as the primary source of external funding for many rapidly growing Latin American countries.

This excessive private lending has roots in the oil price dynamics of the early 1970s. In 1973, the Organization of the Petroleum Exporting Countries (OPEC) cut production for the first time, resulting in a fourfold increase in the price of oil worldwide. This phenomenon, combined with the fact that oil bills were paid almost exclusively in dollars, resulted in large inflows of dollars into oil-producing countries. For the most part, oil-rich OPEC countries lacked an industrial manufacturing infrastructure that could absorb significant new domestic investment in the short term. The only choice for OPEC countries was to deposit dollars in what was by then a relatively well-established Eurodollar market. This consisted mostly of U.S. and Japanese banks with branches in Europe that accepted dollar deposits. These massive deposits quickly became known as petrodollars. The stage was set for a massive lending spree from private banks to newly industrializing countries, especially in Latin America. Most scholars agree that there was significant overlending during the period from 1973 to 1982. The important question is why.

From Boom to Bust On the supply side of the loanable funds market, the answer is relatively clear. Eurodollar deposits dramatically increased banks' desire to lend. Banks saw in oil-exporting less-developed countries (LDCs) an opportunity for big profits. Given that traditional business-sector demand for loans in developed countries (DCs) had all but dried up due to the supply shock–induced recession (a sudden inward shift in the aggregate supply curve caused by the dramatic increase in oil-related manufacturing costs), the Latin American loan market served as an attractive alternative. Moreover, authoritarian governments were standing at the ready to accept and guarantee repayment of private bank loans. This was a bonus for banks, which worked on the principle that sovereign loans (that is, loans to governments) carried very little risk of default compared with private sector loans.

On the demand side of the loanable funds market, Latin American countries exhibited considerable eagerness to borrow. One reason for this eagerness stemmed from the exigencies of state-led growth. By the late 1960s, Latin American newly industrialized economies (NIEs) faced the end of what scholars have referred to as "the easy phase" of import-substituting industrialization (ISI). The import-substituting strategy was first employed by most Latin American countries in the 1930s in an effort to break dependence on primary exports by producing previously imported consumer goods for the domestic market. By the late 1960s, continued growth under the ISI model meant producing more capital intensive consumer goods. This meant that if state-led growth was going to continue at comparable rates, new investments in heavy manufactured goods (i.e., cars and other consumer durables) would have to take place (Krueger 1993). Moreover, the majority of Latin American NIEs were governed by bureaucratic authoritarian regimes whose legitimacy hinged on the continued ability to deliver rapid industrial growth.

Some scholars have argued that Asian countries were better equipped to deal with the external shocks of the 1970s because they had already begun to shift their policies from import substitution to an export-oriented economy (Sachs 1985). In Latin American countries, the choice to deepen ISI rather than abandon it for an export-led approach was reinforced by the fact that the 1973 oil crisis caused severe recession in most developed countries, thus drying up the potential export market for Latin American NIEs. One consequence of the push toward heavy manufactured products in Latin America was that non-oil exporters became desperate for funds to cover increasing production costs and growing balance of payments deficits.

Certainly, these countries could have turned to their traditional source of balance of payments financing, the International Monetary Fund (IMF), but the fact that they could borrow from private banks allowed them to avoid IMF conditionality, which had always been a point of political discontent (Bird 1996). But even the oil-exporting LDCs in Latin America, Mexico and Venezuela in particular, saw the availability of private bank credit as an opportunity for industrialization backed by state leadership.

The most obvious incentive for Latin America to borrow during the 1970s grew out of financial market conditions. Inflation had skyrocketed after the 1973 oil price hikes while nominal interest rates had leveled off and even fallen in some cases due to the credit glut. Together these phenomena resulted in extremely low and even negative real interest rates. For a time, banks were paying Latin American governments to take their money (Sampson 1981). Ultimately, the buildup of excessive debt in the 1970s grew out of a coincidence of political and economic interests among Latin American NIEs and private banks.

The stage had been set for a major crisis when another oil crisis hit in 1979. This time oil prices did not rise by nearly as much as they had in 1973. The effects of 1973 had been stagflation: severe recession coupled with accelerating inflation. This time, the crisis led to deepened recession but very little inflation. Part of the reason was that the Federal Reserve Board, under Paul Volcker's conservative monetary leadership, opted to raise interest rates to fight inflation despite continuing recessionary conditions. As a result, real interest rates on existing variable rate loans began to rise rapidly. For non-oil-producing LDCs, the combination of high oil prices, recession, and skyrocketing loan commitments spelled disaster. But even Mexico, the model debtor, had come to discover that its oil fields were much less extensive than originally predicted, while it still faced all of the aforementioned challenges. Meanwhile, lenders became increasingly hesitant to make new loans as the credit glut conditions of the early 1970s had largely disappeared. Not surprisingly, although it seemed to take the major players by surprise, Mexico announced in August 1982 that it could not meet even its interest payments on its massive debt obligations, thus triggering the debt crisis.

Crisis Resolution and Reform In response to the crisis, the Baker Plan (named for then U.S. treasury secretary James Baker who proposed the plan) focused on rescheduling payments and arranged a $12 billion rescue package funded primarily by the United States and the IMF to Mexico. The Mexico loans were part of a larger $29 billion proposal for the Latin American and several other debtor nations (Bogdanowicz-Bindert 1986). The plan did not get banks to resume lending, although banks did eventually discount, forgive, and/or reschedule existing debt. Ultimately, the crisis underscored a problem of debt dynamics rather than sheer mass. In other words, the Latin American debt crisis points to a breakdown in the cycle of lending and repaying. The amount of debt buildup in the 1970s was by no means unique historically, but the breakdown or interruption of the financial system cycle of lending and repaying was unprecedented (Fishlow 1985). In a panicked response to Mexico's announcement that it could not pay, banks immediately stopped lending to all developing countries, which triggered a massive and unprecedented debt crisis because even relatively sound borrowers could not make payments on existing loans without access to new lines of credit. This dynamic problem of debt buildup and repayment problems has led to considerable debate on the merits of debt relief and debt forgiveness. The Debt Laffer Curve suggests there is a critical debt stock beyond which both the lenders and borrowers lose. That is, as the external debt stock rises, the indebted country will try to produce less (discouragement effect) or intentionally default on the existing debt (sabotage) so the foreign lenders will receive less than full repayment. If the debt stock is already above this level, as it certainly was in 1982, it may be in the interest of the lenders to forgive some of the debt.

In the end, the lasting story behind the Latin American debt crisis revolves around its consequences for Latin American countries and particularly the most vulnerable segments of the population. Between 1982 and 1984, the net transfer of capital from Latin America to developed countries' banks approached $75 billion, an amount equal to one-quarter of all Latin American exports for the same period. Growth rates and living standards declined in the region for virtually the entire decade of the 1980s, a decade now commonly referred to as "the lost decade" in Latin America.

The Latin American debt crisis had long-lasting political, economic, and social repercussions. Ultimately, the debt crisis led to an abandonment of import substitution industrialization policies and a move toward trade and financial liberalization. Proponents of neoliberalism thus see the debt crisis as a difficult but necessary lesson for policymakers and their constituents about the inefficiency of state interventionist policies. Opponents of neoliberalism view the debt crisis as a tragedy that put Latin American countries in the unenviable position of having to choose between adopting neoliberal policy reform and remaining cut off from global financial markets. Regardless of which view one takes, there is little dispute that the Latin American debt crisis triggered an era of neoliberal reform.

See also bail-ins; banking crisis; capital flows to developing countries; currency crisis; Eurocurrencies; Federal Reserve Board; financial crisis; financial liberalization; International Monetary Fund (IMF); peso problem; petrodollars, recycling of; sovereign risk; Washington consensus

FURTHER READING

Auerbach, Nancy Neiman. 2007. "The Meanings of Neoliberalism." In *Neoliberalism: National and Regional Experiments with Global Ideas*, edited by R. Roy, A. Denzau, and D. North. New York: Routledge, 26–50. Identifies the Latin American debt crisis as the impetus that not only leads to the neoliberal era in Latin America but gives Latin American neoliberalism some of its unique characteristics.

Bird, G. 1996. " The International Monetary Fund and Developing Countries: A Review of the Evidence and Policy Options." *International Organization* 50 (3): 477–511. Using a political economy framework, ana-lyzes the part played by the IMF as a balance of payments financing and economic adjustment organization.

Bogdanowicz-Bindert, C. A. 1986. " The Debt Crisis: The Baker Plan Revisited." *Journal of Interamerican Studies and World Affairs* 28 (3): 33–45. Describes the immediate and ongoing effects of the Baker Plan on debt crisis countries.

Fishlow, Albert. 1985. "Lessons from the Past." In *The Politics of International Debt*, edited by Miles Kahler. Ithaca, NY: Cornell University Press, 37–93. Argues that the major difference between the Latin American debt crisis and other historical instances where countries were so heavily indebted that they threatened default is that private lenders stopped lending cold-turkey and created a dynamic crisis where the lack of new lending made it impossible to pay off existing loans.

Gruppen, N. 1986. *The Debt Crisis in Latin America*. Stockholm: Institute of Latin American Studies. Detailed overview of the financial picture leading up to and precipitating the Latin American debt crisis.

Krueger, A. O. 1993. " Virtuous and Vicious Circles in Economic Development." *The American Economic Review* 83 (2) (Papers and Proceedings of the 105th Annual Meeting of the American Economic Association): 351–55. Focuses on the political-economic interactions surrounding externally versus internally oriented trade policies. It suggests that Pareto-optimal policies cannot be identified absent consideration of political responses.

Sachs, Jeffrey. 1985. "External Debt and Macroeconomic Performance in Latin America and East Asia." *Brookings Papers on Economic Activity* 2: 523–64. Provides an excellent overview of the macroeconomic effects of heavy debt burdens in Latin America.

Sampson, A. 1981. *The Money Lenders*. New York: Penguin. Paints a vivid picture of the lending market in the 1970s when private banks literally begged Latin American finance ministers to take the money off their hands.

Wellons, P. A. 1985. " International Debt: The Behavior of Banks in a Politicized Environment." *International Organization* 39 (3): 441–71. One of the few scholarly pieces that focuses on explaining bank behavior within a political context leading up to the debt crisis.

NANCY NEIMAN AUERBACH

■ **law of one price**

See purchasing power parity

■ **learning by doing**

See infant industry argument

■ **lender of last resort**

The classical role of a lender of last resort (LOLR) is to provide solvent participants of the financial system with liquidity in times of crisis. In practice, however, the LOLR function of central banks has been used to help banks in distress. Rules with respect to the LOLR are often ambiguous. In the European Monetary Union (EMU) in particular, the European Central Bank (ECB) as well as national central banks are assigned LOLR responsibility. On the international level, the International Monetary Fund (IMF) is sometimes viewed as a LOLR for governments.

The Financial System Safety Net Banks have a special role in the financial system as the main providers of liquidity. Behind the commercial banks, a central bank uses monetary policy instruments to control the availability of liquidity in an economy. In some countries central banks are responsible for financial supervision, and banking supervision in particular, as well as monetary policy. In other countries, a financial supervisory authority is responsible for the "safety and soundness" of individual banks, while the central bank retains responsibility for the payments system.

As a result of the important role of banks in the payments system and the risk of runs on banks, most countries have developed a "safety net" for banks, in particular. The safety net includes a LOLR function along with deposit insurance, capital requirements, regulation, and supervision. These aspects of the safety net should jointly protect the banking system while providing banks with the appropriate rules and incentives to allocate credit efficiently.

Two Views of the LOLR The classical formulation of the LOLR function goes back to Henry Thornton in 1802 and Walter Bagehot in 1848, and the term goes back even further to Sir Francis Barings, who referred to the Bank of England as the "dernier resort" providing liquidity to banks in times of crisis. Bagehot's classical formulation as interpreted by Humphrey (1989) and Gaspar (2006) includes the following characteristics:

1. The LOLR has the objective of protecting the integrity of the financial system rather than individual institutions;
2. The LOLR supports the central bank's monetary policy objectives;
3. Insolvent institutions should be allowed to fail;
4. LOLR assistance should be provided to solvent, illiquid institutions;
5. LOLR lending should be granted at penalty rates;
6. LOLR lending should be granted only against good collateral; and
7. Conditions for LOLR lending should be announced and well understood before a crisis event.

Although these characteristics lack specificity with respect to, for example, rate setting, acceptable collateral, and operational definitions of liquidity and solvency, they quite clearly identify the LOLR function as an aspect of monetary policy in times of potential or actual liquidity problems in the economy. Thus, in this classical view, the LOLR stands ready to lend to any entity offering collateral and willing to pay the penalty rate. An example of this LOLR function in practice occurred on September 11, 2001. After the terrorist attacks on New York and Washington, the Federal Reserve in the United States pronounced its readiness to supply liquidity "to support the economic and financial system," and the European Central Bank (ECB) also stood ready to "support the normal functioning of the markets" (see Gaspar 2006).

The more common interpretation of the LOLR, as well as the most commonly practiced role, is that the central bank supplies emergency liquidity assistance to specific financial institutions. In this case, the LOLR function becomes part of the crisis management framework for specific institutions in distress.

The requirement that LOLR lending should be reserved for solvent banks facing liquidity problems remains valid under this interpretation. The rationale for this LOLR function is the common view that contagion of one bank's problem to other solvent banks can occur as a result of the problems of evaluating the risk level of individual banks. Thus LOLR activities become oriented toward specific banks.

The difficulty of distinguishing between liquidity and solvency problems in a banking crisis often leads central banks to provide assistance to insolvent banks. Thereby, the LOLR function of central banks can become the source of moral hazard in banking; if emergency assistance can be expected, bank managers' incentives to extend risky loans increase. Furthermore, emergency assistance to insolvent banks causes delays in closing the banks. Thereby, the final costs of a bank failure for creditors and taxpayers may increase.

When a central bank provides liquidity assistance it faces a trade-off between reducing the risk of contagion and reducing the moral hazard problem caused by expectations of aid to insolvent banks.

The EMU System For international banks working within the jurisdictions of several central banks it can be important whether the home or the host country central bank serves as the LOLR. In the EMU, responsibility for monetary policy, which includes the LOLR function, lies clearly with the ECB.

The assignment of responsibility with respect to emergency liquidity assistance for an international bank is less clear. On the face of it, one expects that emergency liquidity would be provided by the central bank in the country where the bank is incorporated. Subsidiaries are often strongly integrated with the parent, however, and therefore indirectly beneficiaries of home country assistance. Assistance to a bank in crisis can arise suddenly and conflicts of interest with respect to burden-sharing are likely. Furthermore, emergency assistance by a LOLR is only one form of assistance to a bank in distress. Thus there is a need to coordinate activities of the central bank, financial supervisors, and fiscal authorities.

In the EU and, therefore, in the EMU, responsibility for financial stability, bank supervision, and crisis management is decentralized to the national level. Thus, LOLR responsibility in the form of emergency liquidity assistance rests with the individual countries, while the classical LOLR function as a provider of liquidity to the financial system as a whole is the responsibility of the ECB.

The ambiguity in the EMU arises because emergency liquidity assistance by a national central bank has monetary implications. Monetary policy can be conducted only by the ECB, however. As pointed out by the European Shadow Financial Services Regulatory Committee (1998)—a committee of independent experts analyzing and publicly commenting on regulatory issues—"any operation that is undertaken on the national level has EMU-wide monetary repercussions. For example, an interest rate subsidy to a local problem bank may in the end be paid for by other banks in the EMU and their customers." The committee recommended that procedures for emergency liquidity assistance should be established within the EU to resolve this ambiguity.

According to some commentators a degree of "constructive ambiguity" is desirable in crisis management on the grounds that it can reduce the moral hazard problem discussed earlier. Indeed, ambiguity is what EU law provides with respect to the division of LOLR responsibility between the ECB and national central banks in the Euro system. It may take a first pan-European crisis to bring some clarity to the division of LOLR responsibilities within the EU.

The IMF as International Lender of Last Resort The International Monetary Fund's (IMF's) role in helping Mexico during the Tequila crisis in 1995 has been widely blamed for contributing to the Asian crisis in 1997 by causing expectations among lenders that loans to sovereign countries are safe. The IMF does not protect banks directly but through its assistance to countries like Mexico in balance of payments crises or when the threat of crisis is substantial, it may provide indirect protection for banks that have lent to the government in a crisis country.

The proper role of the IMF in sovereign crises has been the subject of debate after the Mexican and

Asian crises. Prominent economists like Meltzer (1998) have suggested that the IMF should limit its role in crises to serve as a LOLR in the classical sense. In other words, the IMF should provide loans to bridge a crisis only in the case of pure liquidity crisis. In such a crisis a country's fundamental ability to repay loans is not impaired. Instead, the crisis could arise because a country has run out of foreign exchange reserves, and liquidity is not forthcoming in international financial markets as a result of a lack of information about a country's prospects. In this situation, based on its superior access to information about countries' prospects, the IMF could step in.

Focusing the IMF's role in country crises as an LOLR when there are liquidity crises could require financial resources beyond the capability of the IMF. Many observers argue, however, that the IMF's involvement, even on a small scale, will increase the willingness of private lenders to extend loans to countries in crisis, since the IMF is considered particularly well informed about economic conditions in member countries.

See also asymmetric information; banking crisis; currency crisis; deposit insurance; European Central Bank; European Monetary Union; Federal Reserve Board; international financial architecture; international liquidity; International Monetary Fund (IMF); International Monetary Fund conditionality; international reserves; money supply

FURTHER READING

Eichengreen, Barry. 2004. *Capital Flows and Crises*. Cambridge, MA: MIT Press. Provides analyses of the origin of sovereign crises and the appropriate response of international financial institutions.

European Shadow Financial Regulatory Committee. 1998. "EMU, the ECB, and Financial Supervision." Statement No. 2 (October 1). Downloadable at http://www.ceps.be. Addresses the role of the ECB in financial supervision and crisis resolution.

Gaspar, Vitor. 2006. "Bagehot and Coase Meet the Single European Market." Conference Paper, Federal Reserve Bank of Chicago (October 6). Argues that the European Central Bank is suitable as the Lender of Last Resort in the classical sense.

Goodhart, Charles A. E. 1995. *The Central Bank and the Financial System*. Cambridge, MA: MIT Press. Provides a comprehensive analytical treatment of the different roles of the central bank in the economy

Goodhart, Charles A. E., and Haizhou Huang. 2005. "The Lender of Last Resort." *Journal of Banking and Finance* 29: 1059–82. Models the trade-off between costs in terms of risk-taking incentives and benefits of reduced contagion.

Humphrey, Thomas M. 1989. "Lender of Last Resort: The Concept in History." *Federal Reserve Bank of Richmond Economic Review* 75 (March/April): 8–16. Reviews the history of the lender of last resort function of central banks and provides an economic analysis of its historical development.

Lastra, Rosa M. 1999. "Lenders of Last Resort: An International Perspective." *The International Comparative Law Quarterly* 48: 340–65. Discusses alternative views, as well as benefits and costs, of the lender of last resort and compares its role in Europe, the United States, and Asia.

———. 2006. *Legal Foundations of International Monetary Stability*. Oxford: Oxford University Press. Provides a legal perspective on central banking, including responsibility and contents of the lender of last resort function on the national, the EU, and the international level.

Meltzer, Alan. 1998. "The Asian Problem of the IMF." Testimony prepared for the Joint Economic Committee, U.S. Congress (24 February), Washington, DC. Presents a critique of the IMF's activities in the Asian crisis.

CLAS WIHLBORG

■ linkages, backward and forward

Linkages are input-output relationships between firms or industrial sectors in the same economy. A firm purchasing inputs from a local supplier is an example of a backward linkage, while a firm selling intermediate inputs to another firm creates a forward linkage. The importance of such linkages with the local economy for economic development has long been recognized in the economics literature. For example, Marshall (1920) argues that input-output relationships between firms are one of the advantages of localized industry, since "subsidiary trades grow up in the neighborhood, supplying [the firm] with implements and material, organizing its traffic, and in many ways conducing to the economy of its material" (271).

In an early view, Hirschman (1958) discusses the importance of linkages between sectors in an economy in the context of his strategy of unbalanced growth for developing countries. At the heart of this strategy is the suggestion that developing countries should aim at generating imbalances in demand and supply in order to achieve continuing growth. An important part of the unbalanced growth strategy is the potential to develop linkages between sectors in which a leading sector, through linkages with a follower sector, may foster the development of the latter industry.

The issue of local linkages has regained importance in the last decades of the 20th century due to the increasing globalization of the world economy, where many inputs and outputs can be internationally traded, and therefore, inputs can easily be sourced locally or abroad. Given the increasing significance of foreign direct investment and multinational companies in many developed and developing countries alike, a particular focus of interest has been on interfirm linkages between foreign multinationals and indigenous firms, which to some extent echo the role of linkages in Hirschman's earlier work.

Whereas in Hirschman's concept of unbalanced growth "leading sectors" (which have the highest potential for linkages creation) induce growth in other sectors, the more recent view on multinationals largely sees these as "leading firms" inducing growth in local enterprises. Hence one can think of the former concept as intersectoral linkages, while the latter are interfirm linkages. Essentially, the interfirm linkage is at the heart of the Hirschman-style intersectoral linkage, since a sector is composed of a number of firms. The concept of interfirm linkages is a much wider and richer concept, however, and the intersectoral linkage leading to economic development is only one of many effects of interfirm linkages.

Intersectoral Linkages Hirschman's (1958) theory of unbalanced growth suggests that development policy should focus on promoting the growth of "leading sectors," which would result in growth being transferred from these key sectors to the followers. The way of linking key sectors and induced sectors is the development of backward and forward linkages between these sectors. In his words: "The input-provision, derived demand, or *backward linkage effects* . . . will induce attempts to supply through domestic production the inputs needed in that activity," and "the output-utilization or *forward linkage effects* . . . will induce attempts to utilize outputs as inputs in some new activities" (100).

Clearly, Hirschman has linkages between different sectors in mind when he defines these concepts. Also, linkages are seen as a causal (ex ante) concept, that is, linkages from the leading sector A to the following sector B allow sector B to develop; in effect, sector B would not have come into existence without the linkage from sector A. This point indicates the importance of intersectoral linkages and the benefit of these linkages for the development of other sectors and for the economy as a whole.

Intersectoral linkages are generally measured using input-output (I-O) tables, that is, tables of all inputs and outputs of an economy's industries, including intermediate transactions, primary inputs, and sales to final users. As a crude measure, backward linkages can be estimated as the proportion of an industry's output that are purchases from other industries, while forward linkages are the proportion of an industry's total output that is not directed to final demand but rather is an input used by other industries. Based on this idea several more refined indexes based on input-output tables have been suggested in the literature to measure linkages (e.g., Yotopoulos and Nugent 1976; Lall 1980).

These ratios measure only the degree of interdependence of different sectors, to what degree a sector uses inputs from other sectors, and not necessarily the true, induced, linkage effects, however. Although the true linkage is a causal concept, that a sector develops strictly as a result of a linkage to a leading sector only, one could also find sectors with high ratios that are not due to linkage effects but are only due to sectoral interdependence. In this case, the sector did not develop as a result of linkages to another sector but rather *in tandem* with it.

Interfirm Linkages In the more recent literature the focus on local linkages has shifted away from being concerned with sectors to individual firms. Hence, research has attempted to determine what the implications of such linkages between firms are for the development of the local economy. Another focus is the measurement of linkages, in order to determine whether individual firms create backward linkages specifically through the purchase of inputs in the local market or whether they create forward linkages through selling output as intermediate inputs to other local firms.

One reason for the interest in interfirm linkages is the increasing globalization of production and the importance of multinational companies and foreign direct investment for host countries. A crucial question is whether foreign multinationals create linkages with the host economy or whether they operate in so-called enclave sectors with no links to the domestic economy that surrounds them. This issue is important in a world economy where many inputs and outputs can be internationally traded. In such a context it seems important to establish whether firms create backward or forward linkages with the local economy or whether they import and export most or all of their inputs and output. Of course, the answer to this question may change over time, as multinationals may initially source inputs from suppliers in their home country but over time develop relationships with local suppliers.

Furthermore, backward interfirm linkages become important when analyzing local content requirements in international trade agreements. Regional trade blocks, such as the European Union or the parties to the North American Free Trade Agreement, frequently impose minimum requirements of domestic inputs that foreign firms must use in their production. An analysis of backward interfirm linkages shows the extent of local buying and may indicate whether or not local content requirements are met by foreign multinationals in the host economy.

In a world with imperfect competition and economies of scale, interfirm linkages between mul-

tinationals and domestic firms can have positive effects on firms through the emergence of externalities. This issue has attracted considerable attention in the economics literature, and various positive effects of interfirm linkages have been identified. Most directly, interfirm linkages can have effects on the creation of secondary (or indirect) employment generated in supplier firms. If firms are linked through seller-supplier linkages, sellers will have a role to play for employment in the supplier firms.

Theoretical models and empirical research furthermore show some more indirect effects of linkages between multinationals and domestic firms. For example, linkages may encourage the establishment and growth of local companies in the same or different sectors in the host country (Markusen and Venables 1999). Backward linkages, created through the purchase of intermediate goods by final good–producing multinationals, can reduce costs for local intermediate good suppliers by increasing the scale of their production. These reduced costs imply, in turn, that final good producers have to incur fewer costs for intermediate products, which is the forward linkage. In such a setting, if multinationals increase demand for intermediate products through backward linkages, indigenous intermediate good suppliers, in turn, can establish forward linkages with indigenous final good producers. Thus backward linkages by multinationals can foster the development of both indigenous suppliers (through expanding their output) and indigenous final good production (through lowering their costs for intermediate inputs).

Related models also discuss the possibility that firms that are linked through production inputs may tend to agglomerate geographically (Krugman and Venables 1995). The existence of input-output linkages and imperfect competition creates positive externalities that benefit the agglomeration of industries in particular regions. These agglomerations can occur both within narrowly defined industrial sectors only or across all industries.

The importance of interfirm linkages has also been emphasized in the literature on technology transfers from multinationals to indigenous firms (Javorcik 2004; Moran 2001). The main argument is that in the case where firms are interlinked, local firms can improve their productivity as a result of forward or backward linkages with multinationals affiliates. For example, local firms supplying inputs to multinationals may be able to improve the quality of their output as multinationals set high quality standards for them and, as case study evidence for developing countries shows, may even instruct them in the use of advanced production technology.

Measuring interfirm linkages is, at least in theory, straightforward, as it involves determining the amount of inputs purchased from local suppliers, or output sold as intermediate inputs to domestic customer firms (e.g., Görg and Ruane 2000). A number of issues arise, however. First, these absolute values need to be expressed relative to some firm characteristic in order to be comparable across firms. For forward linkages it is generally expressed as locally sold output relative to total output, while backward linkages are usually calculated by dividing local inputs by either total inputs or total output. The simple ratio of local inputs to total outputs could be misleading as an indicator of backward linkages, however. A firm with a low ratio of local inputs to output could source all of its inputs in the local economy, since total inputs are not considered in this expression. This possibility could, for example, be a particular problem in industries that have a high content of value added but only a relatively low input content, such as, for example, software development or software production.

For forward linkages, the main difficulty is to determine what amount of output is directed to other firms as an intermediate input (i.e., the linkage) as opposed to output sold directly on the market to final consumers.

Policy Implications The purpose of measuring intersectoral linkages in the spirit of Hirschman (1958) is to determine key sectors in the economy, those sectors in which resources should be concentrated to achieve the highest growth. The interfirm linkage concept analyzes the extent of integration of firms, particularly affiliates of foreign multinationals into the host economy.

Although the empirical estimation of backward and forward linkages using the interfirm approach can be seen as an approximate indicator of the degree of a firm's integration into the host economy, this measurement in itself provides only limited information, giving no consideration to the effectiveness of these linkages. For a complete analysis more relevant to policy, there would need to be an examination of their effects, for example, on the development of local firms, indirect employment generated in domestic firms, the emergence of agglomerations, or the transfer of technology to linked local firms. This issue forms an important research agenda for academics and policymakers.

See also appropriate technology and foreign direct investment; footloose production; foreign direct investment and labor markets; foreign direct investment under monopolistic competition; foreign direct investment under oligopoly; location theory; multinational enterprises; technology spillovers

FURTHER READING

Görg, Holger, and Frances Ruane. 2000. "An Analysis of Backward Linkages in the Irish Electronics Sector." *Economic and Social Review* 31: 215–35. An empirical analysis of linkages in domestic firms and multinationals using firm-level data for Ireland.

Hirschman, Albert O. 1958. *The Strategy of Economic Development*. New Haven: Yale University Press. An early contribution setting out the benefits of intersectoral linkages for economic development.

Javorcik, Beata Smarzynska. 2004. "Does Foreign Direct Investment Increase the Productivity of Domestic Firms? In Search of Spillovers through Backward Linkages." *American Economic Review* 94: 605–27. An empirical analysis of the importance of linkages between multinationals and domestic firms for technology transfer.

Krugman, Paul R., and Anthony J. Venables. 1995. "Globalization and the Inequality of Nations." *Quarterly Journal of Economics* 110: 857–80. A theoretical model showing the importance of linkages for agglomeration of production.

Lall, Sanjaya. 1980. "Vertical Inter-Firm Linkages in LDCs: An Empirical Study." *Oxford Bulletin of Economics and Statistics* 42: 203–26. An early empirical analysis of linkages by multinational companies in developing countries.

Markusen, James R., and Anthony J. Venables. 1999. "Foreign Direct Investment as a Catalyst for Industrial Development." *European Economic Review* 43: 335–56. Theoretical model highlighting the importance of linkages between multinationals and domestic firms for development of local industry.

Marshall, Alfred. 1920. *Principles of Economics*. 8th ed. London: Macmillan. Discusses, among other things, the potential benefits of input-output linkages between firms for development.

Moran, Theodore H. 2001. *Parental Supervision: The New Paradigm for Foreign Direct Investment and Development*. Washington, DC: Institute for International Economics. Presents many case studies on backward linkages between multinationals and domestic suppliers.

Yotopoulos, Pan A., and Jeffrey B. Nugent. 1976. "In Defence of a Test of the Linkage Hypothesis." *Quarterly Journal of Economics* 90: 334–43. Early contribution to the measurement of intersectoral linkages using input-output tables. There are other papers on this topic in the same issue of the journal.

HOLGER GÖRG

■ liquidity trap, the

The liquidity trap refers to a state in which the nominal interest rate is close or equal to zero and the monetary authority is unable to stimulate the economy with monetary policy. In such a situation, because the opportunity cost of holding money is zero, even if the monetary authority increases money supply to stimulate the economy, people hoard money. Consequently, excess funds may not be converted into new investment. A liquidity trap is usually caused by, and in turn perpetuates, deflation. When deflation is persistent and combined with an extremely low nominal interest rate, it creates a vicious cycle of output stagnation and further expectations of deflation that lead to a higher real interest rate. Two prominent examples of liquidity traps in history are the Great Depression in the United States during the 1930s and the long economic slump in Japan during the late 1990s.

Conventional Monetary Policy Ineffectiveness

An economy's monetary authority typically tries to manipulate money supply through open market operations that affect the monetary base—for example, buying or selling government bonds. As long as banks are legally required to maintain a certain level of reserves, either as vault cash or on deposit with the central bank, a one-unit change in the monetary base leads to more than one-unit change in money supply—the ratio between the two is referred as the money multiplier and is usually greater than one. The reason for this relationship is that banks do not have any incentives to hold reserves, which typically do not earn interest, beyond the legal requirement, and therefore they lend out any excess reserves. Nonbank firms and individuals behave in parallel with the banks' behavior; they have no incentive to hold excess money or funds above transaction needs, so they invest it in interest-earning financial assets such as bonds and bank deposits. Thus excess money or funds go back to the hands of banks, leading to rounds of lending known as money creation. However, the important assumption for such behavior is that the nominal interest rate is positive, or not extremely low. In other words, money creation arises as long as the opportunity cost of holding money is greater than zero.

When the nominal interest rate is very close or equal to zero, the opportunity cost of holding money becomes zero, and economic agents—banks, firms, or individuals—tend to hoard money even if they have more money than they need for transaction purposes. More important, traditional monetary policy becomes ineffective in stimulating the economy because the money creation process does not function as theory predicts. Even when the monetary authority increases the monetary base, money supply becomes unresponsive or even falls. In such a situation, because the nominal interest rate cannot be negative, there is nothing the monetary authority can do.

When an economy falls in a liquidity trap and stays in recession for some time, deflation can result. If deflation becomes severe and persistent, people effectively expect negative inflation going forward. Accordingly, the real interest rate (which is defined as nominal interest rate minus expected inflation) will be expected to rise. This in turn harms private investment through increased real cost of borrowing and thereby widens the output gap. Thus the economy falls into a vicious cycle. A persistent recession causes deflation, which raises real interest rates and lowers output even further, while monetary policy is ineffective.

In the case of the Great Depression in the United States, between 1929 and 1933, the average inflation rate was –6.7 percent. It was not until 1943 that the price level went back to that of 1929. In the case of the more recent Japanese slump, deflation started in 1995 and continued till 2005, although the degree of deflation was not as severe. Indeed, during the deflationary period, the average inflation rate was –0.2 percent.

Such a spiral deflationary situation is highly likely to involve failures in the financial system. Financial failure can intensify a liquidity trap because unexpected deflation increases the real value of the debt. Borrowers' ability to repay their debt, which is already weakened by the overall slump in consumption and investment, declines and banks' portfolios become burdened with nonperforming loans—loans that are not repaid. Both the Great Depression and the Japanese 1990s slump involved banking failures. In such circumstances, banks often try to reduce the amount of new loans and terminate existing loans—credit contraction called credit crunch—in order to improve their capital conditions, which are worsened by writing off nonperforming loans. A credit crunch can feed the vicious cycle by making less capital available to potential borrowers, and therefore contracting investment and output. An increase in the amount of nonperforming loans in the overall economy can result in banks with good capital conditions becoming more even more cautious in their extensions of credit. Furthermore, in an economy with a fragile financial system, a liquidity trap can occur when the nominal interest rate does not reach zero because holding nonmoney financial assets may involve the risk of losing the assets and once the risk is incorporated, an extremely low level of the nominal interest rate would be essentially the same as zero.

Overcoming a Liquidity Trap Because conventional monetary policy becomes ineffective in a liquidity trap, other policy measures are suggested as a remedy to get the economy out of the trap. The monetarist view suggests quantitative easing as a solution to the liquidity trap. Quantitative easing usually means that the central bank sets up a goal of high rates of increase in the monetary base or money supply and provides liquidity in the economy so as to achieve the goal. It has been argued, for instance, that the Great Depression was caused and aggravated by the misguided policies of the Federal Reserve Board, that is, monetary contraction subsequent to the stock market crash in 1927 (Friedman and Schwartz 1963). According to this viewpoint, unconventional money easing—or money gift, in Friedman's words—would be the appropriate policy measure. Between 1933 and 1941, the U.S. monetary stock increased by 140 percent, mainly through expansion in the monetary base. More recently, after lowering the policy target rate to zero in February 1999, the Bank of Japan implemented quantitative easing policy and set a goal for the reserves available to commercial banks from March 2001 through March 2006.

The monetarists also suggest other unconventional market operations that include the direct purchasing by the monetary authority of other financial assets such as corporate papers and long-term foreign and domestic bonds. They argue that purchasing merely short-term assets in open market operations does not function as a remedy to a liquidity trap. The idea is that because long-term bonds and securities are still assumed to be imperfectly substitutable to short-term assets even in a liquidity trap situation, the former can be purchased in open market operations to drive the long-term interest rate down.

In the Keynesian view, expansionary fiscal policy is the conventional measure to overcome a liquidity trap; the government can implement deficit spending policy to jumpstart the demand. A typical example of expansionary fiscal policy is the implementation of the New Deal policy by President Franklin Roosevelt in 1933. This policy included public works programs for the unemployed, including the Tennessee Valley Authority project. In the case of the Japanese liquidity trap, the Japanese government spent about ¥100 trillion (equivalent to 20 percent of GDP in 2005) for a series of public works programs over the course of a decade.

See also Bank of Japan; banking crisis; debt deflation; Federal Reserve Board; money supply; Mundell-Fleming model; quantity theory of money; seigniorage

FURTHER READING

Blanchard, Olivier. 2006. *Macroeconomics.* 4th ed. New York: Pearson/Prentice Hall. One of the chapters of this book presents a basic IS-LM framework to explain the mechanism of a liquidity trap and analyzes the U.S. Great Depression and the Japanese 1990s recession.

Friedman, Milton, and Anna J. Schwartz. 1963. *A Monetary History of the United States.* Princeton, NJ: Princeton University Press. This book is a seminal work in which the authors examine the development of the U.S. economy in the post–Civil War era. The biggest contribution of this book is their monetarist views on the cause of the U.S. Great Depression; they argue that the Federal Reserve Board is responsible for worsening the Great Depression by implementing monetary contraction immediately after the stock market crash in New York.

Krugman, Paul. 1998. "It's Baaack: Japan's Slump and the Return of the Liquidity Trap." *Brookings Papers on Economic Activity* 2: 137–87.

———. 2000. "Thinking about the Liquidity Trap." *Journal of the Japanese and International Economies* 14 (4) (December): 221–37. In these two papers, Krugman presents his Keynesian views on the Japanese recession of the 1990s and policy solutions to it. The author emphasizes the importance of creating expected inflation to get the economy out of the liquidity trap situation and doubts the effectiveness of any monetarist policies such as quantitative easing.

Svensson, Lars E.O. 2001. "The Zero Bound in an Open Economy: A Foolproof Way of Escaping from a Liquidity Trap." *Monetary and Economic Studies* 19 (S-1): 277–312. The author agrees with Krugman in that creating expected inflation will help the Japanese economy out of a liquidity trap. However, he clearly differs
from Krugman's view in that he proposes a fixed exchange rate policy to create expected inflation until the liquidity trap situation disappears.

HIRO ITO

■ location theory

Location theory addresses the important questions of who produces what goods or services in which locations, and why. As many government policies involve attempts to shift production, one must first examine the basis for the initial location decisions in order to understand the impact of altering incentives.

Nearly 200 years ago, the primary concern of early location theorists, most notably Johann-Heinrich von Thünen (1783–1850), was the optimal location of cities and farms, balancing both land costs and transport costs. In von Thünen's model, concentric rings of agricultural activity develop around a city. The production of perishable goods and/or goods needing to get to market quickly locate in the rings closer to the city, and other activities such as ranching locate in outer rings. Since von Thünen, many other scholars have proposed more complex location models, incorporating the production of industrial and agricultural goods and services.

Many of the questions addressed in location theory are highly relevant to international economics. For example, trade theory explains patterns of international production and trade. Similarly, much of the research on foreign direct investment (FDI) looks at where multinational firms locate various activities. Policy applications of location theory have examined ways in which different countries, states, and regions can actively compete to be production locations for both trade and FDI. Before turning to the applications of location theory in international economics, it is important to review the basic elements of location theory.

Standard Assumptions Most theories of economic location start with these main assumptions:

1. The production process for particular goods is uniform, independent of locations.

Producing corn requires a certain amount of a particular quality of land, farm machinery, chemicals, climate, etc. Therefore, some locations are more suitable for producing corn than others. Factors of production cannot be substituted for one another. For example, superior farm machines cannot substitute for scarce land to grow corn in a big city.

2. The demand for products is separated from the production, or supply, of the products. Corn producers want to put the money they earn from farming into banks in cities. Bankers in cities want to consume agricultural goods. Therefore, transportation costs affect where goods are produced. If both Iowa and Nebraska have the same amount of corn-producing factors of production, but most of the demand for corn is in New York City, other things being equal, Iowa's shorter distance to New York makes Iowa the better location for producing corn.

3. Factors of production are immobile. Inhabitants of New York City cannot import Iowa's cheap land to grow corn locally, and Iowans cannot import New York's bankers. While some factors (capital, migrant workers) are in fact mobile, land and most natural resources are not.

Theories based on these assumptions generate the clear prediction that, to minimize production and transportation costs, certain locations will specialize in the production of particular goods and services and "export" these goods to other locations.

Trade Theory There is considerable overlap between location theory and trade theory. Krugman (1993) compares and contrasts location theory and trade theory. Differences aside, the theories are ultimately quite similar in the questions they address and the assumptions they make. Neither trade theory nor location theory is inherently international. Optimal production locations could be within one country, such as Iowa and New York City in the example already given.

Neither location theory nor trade theory identifies the specific countries or regions in which production of particular goods will be located. Trade theory speaks to characteristics of production locations, such as relative endowments of factors of production required to produce particular goods, or comparative advantage in producing one good relative to another. Location theory speaks to the optimal location of production given the cost of factors of production and transportation costs to consumers. In order to determine specifically which countries or regions will specialize in producing which goods, researchers have tested these theories using data on the production characteristics of particular goods, the factor endowments of countries, and transportation costs. In *Sources of International Comparative Advantage*, Leamer (1984) tests the precise relationships specified in neoclassical trade theory and predicts the specific countries in which production for export should be located. The evidence is, at best, an imperfect fit with the predictions of both location theory and neoclassical trade theory.

Location of FDI Location theory is frequently applied by researchers wanting to understand factors that influence where multinational firms (MNCs) choose to locate their foreign operations. Typically lacking data on the production costs of individual MNCs or data on an MNC's costs in countries where the firm does not operate, researchers tend to study features of the different locations that should make them more or less attractive, such as a country's corporate tax rate. These features include factors related to a country's policy, economy, and technology environments, and strategic considerations for individual MNCs. These are discussed in detail below.

Host-Country Policies The policy environment of a country has an important impact on its attractiveness. Policies such as corporate tax rates affect the costs of an MNC. Hence disproportionate amounts of FDI (relative to gross domestic product, GDP) occur in low-tax countries such as Ireland and tax havens such as the Cayman Islands. Conversely, some countries put restrictions on FDI such as not allowing wholly owned subsidiaries, requiring technology transfer, limiting the repatriation of profits, and mandating a certain proportion of added value be produced in the local market. Other things being equal, countries with more restrictive policies toward FDI tend to be less attractive FDI locations. Despite a global trend of liberalization of policies toward FDI (OECD 2006), restrictions continue in some form in almost every country.

Other features of a country's policy environment also affect its attractiveness. Labor market institutions such as the degree of unionization affect FDI flows. Similarly, the protection of property rights and intellectual property, strong institutions for contract enforcement and capital market governance, environmental regulation, and trade policy may also affect MNCs' FDI location choices (Javorcik and Spatareanu 2005).

Recently, researchers have studied various types of political risk as influences on MNCs' FDI location decisions. MNCs make location decisions based on expected future profits, and greater risk creates greater uncertainty with regard to future income streams. Thus, other things being equal, risk reduces FDI inflows. Countries that are politically risky in the sense of having a history of expropriating FDI, weak institutions, endemic corruption, autocratic governments, periodic coups d'état, or ethnic tension tend to receive negligible FDI flows (or far less than would otherwise be expected). Many of the poorest countries in the world, for example, Haiti, Honduras, and much of sub-Saharan Africa, are beset with political risk and receive very little FDI. To a greater or lesser extent, some of the aforementioned risks are present in many countries, some of which, for example, China and Nigeria, are recipients of large FDI inflows, as other things are not equal. Nigeria is one of the most oil-rich countries in the world, and China has the largest population in the world and a rapidly growing economy. These factors offset some of the risk MNCs encounter in China and Nigeria. However, if these countries were less risky, they likely would enjoy even larger inflows of FDI.

Economic Environment Features of a country's economic environment are also important determinants of FDI location. Capital, and human and natural resource endowments such as labor in China and oil in Nigeria, continue to be significant influ-

ences on FDI location choices. The importance of neoclassical factors of production (e.g., land, labor, capital, raw materials) to MNCs' FDI location choices is consistent with the predictions of location theory.

Factors of production can be intrinsic or created. The Silicon Valley area receives large inflows of FDI due in part to the quality of its human capital. The geographically concentrated pool of specialized human capital arose, in part, from the presence of leading-edge domestic companies and the entry of foreign companies. Hence, specialized labor in Silicon Valley can be viewed as a created and dynamic factor of production: created in the sense that high-tech workers developed their knowledge through their experience working at different Silicon Valley firms, dynamic in the sense that the entry of more firms into the area expanded the skill set and enlarged the pool of specialized labor.

The size of a country's economy is another important economic influence on FDI location decisions. Market size can be viewed as an indirect measure of transportation costs, since it reflects the ability of a firm to reach many consumers at a relatively low cost. The attractiveness of large countries is particularly true when an economy is both large in terms of absolute size (GDP) and wealthy in terms of GDP per capita. Brainard (1997) finds that proximity to customers is an important factor in an MNC's FDI location choices.

Finally, like political risk discussed above, economic risk is also an important influence on FDI location decisions. Countries that have experienced very high rates of inflation or currency exchange rate shocks may have difficulty attracting FDI. Similarly, other things being equal, highly indebted countries and countries with periodic fiscal crises are typically not recipients of large FDI inflows.

Technology and Agglomeration Economies Studies of the effects of spillovers, external economies, or agglomeration economies on FDI location choices date back to Alfred Marshall (1920). Agglomeration economies are benefits that accrue to firms that locate in geographically concentrated areas or "clusters" such as Silicon Valley.

Several types of benefits can arise when firms collocate. First, a geographically concentrated cluster of activity in a particular sector creates a specialized pool of skilled labor that can lower a firm's search and training costs. Second, due to labor mobility and social networks, firms can potentially gain some knowledge about the proprietary technology and processes of their competitors. At the same time, of course, firms also risk losing some of their own proprietary knowledge in this context. Third, specialized suppliers often locate near clusters, again, lowering firms' costs and giving firms more choice in make-or-buy decisions. Fourth, when clusters exist, firms and states often make significant investments in infrastructure development such as building roads, upgrading airports, and improving local universities. These features of industrial clusters create an environment where firms can potentially reap benefits larger than their direct costs.

The existence of spillovers and their influence on the location decisions of MNCs has been a controversial topic that has received considerable attention from academic researchers. Since spillovers are nearly impossible to measure, their very existence is controversial. Firms in the same sectors often do tend to locate in clusters. Some researchers take this empirical fact as prima facie evidence for the existence of agglomeration economies. However, Head, Ries, and Swenson (1995) point out that clusters could exist for many reasons that have nothing to do with spillovers. Firms might collocate for economic reasons such as the local presence of factors of production or strategic reasons such as the ability to better monitor competitors. Local governments wanting to attract high-quality jobs might offer subsidies to firms in particular industries. Thus the fact that firms do cluster is not, in itself, evidence of spillovers.

Another controversy in the literature on agglomeration economies is the question of what, if any, effect they have on the production cost of firms and hence firms' decisions to collocate. If knowledge spillovers exist, why would a leading-edge firm risk locating close to competitors that could free-ride on its investments in proprietary technology? Similarly, clusters often do eventually result in crowding. After

experiencing rapid growth, the Silicon Valley area became such a high-cost location for land and labor that many firms wanting to move there were ultimately priced out of the market. Crowding should eventually increase the production costs of all firms, including early entrants into the cluster.

Spillovers of knowledge have a less straightforward effect on firms' costs in the sense that some firms might gain and others might lose. By focusing on micro mechanisms such as buyer-supplier relationships between firms, recent research allows us to better understand which firms would benefit from knowledge spillovers. Since firms do tend to collocate, and since proprietary technology is so important to firms, further research in this area will help us better understand the complex links between spillovers, production costs, and FDI location decisions.

Firm Strategy Strategic factors that influence the location choices of MNCs include the need to locate near important clients or customers, to locate close to key rivals in order to monitor their actions, or to deter the entry of key rivals. For example, service firms such as advertising agencies often locate their foreign operations near important clients.

This literature uncovers some fundamental motives underlying firms' FDI location decisions. First, and perhaps most important, although FDI flows are often discussed in the aggregate by economists and policymakers, it is important to remember that these aggregate flows represent the sum of a great many decisions made by individual MNCs. Since firms are so different from one another, clearly, their own state variables will be very important in determining where they choose to locate. Second, the heterogeneity of firms implies that all the aforementioned characteristics of locations will not be equally attractive to all firms. Advertising agencies probably will not care about the presence of natural resources such as coal, and even manufacturing firms might not care about labor or natural resources if they are trying to decide where to locate a research and development (R&D) laboratory.

Thus, in focusing on micro mechanisms underlying FDI location choices, recent research on firm strategy has considerable potential to shed light on which location characteristics will be valued by what type of MNC. Moreover, by looking at different kinds of location decisions such as the location of manufacturing plants and the location of R&D, this research should contribute valuable insight into the conditions under which some location characteristics may be more or less important. The recent availability of large new data sets on multinational firms such as the data from the U.S. Department of Commerce, Bureau of Economic Analysis, should help advance research in this area.

Empirical Research on FDI Location Empirical studies of FDI location have typically used one of two general research designs. First, using aggregate data on FDI flows into different countries, researchers have studied the correlation between aggregate FDI flows and many of the location characteristics discussed earlier. The problem with this type of research design is that FDI locations are chosen by individual firms, and aggregate data do not give us much insight into the micro mechanisms underlying firms' choices.

The second type of research design uses micro data on multinational firms to examine decisions to enter particular markets. Entries are generally observed as discreet data points. For example, an MNC that has operations in Canada and the United Kingdom in 1989, and then has operations in Canada, the United Kingdom, and France in 1990, has "entered" France. Although entry data give us much more insight into decisions at the firm level, there are two problems with using this type of research design in studies of FDI location. First, with only a few exceptions, publicly available data on MNCs that contain reliable information on entries often do not contain information on the size of the entry or the purpose of the entry (e.g., production facility, R&D lab, distribution operation, etc.). Second, and perhaps more important, most location decisions made by MNCs are incremental. MNCs might choose, for example, to reduce the scope of their existing operations in Canada and double the scale of their existing facilities in India. If the researcher only observes countries in which the MNC has operations, no location change would be noted. In this example,

however, there has been a fundamental shift in the locations in which the MNC operates. In the day-to-day operations of MNCs, the decision to enter a new market is made relatively infrequently. In contrast, MNCs with established subsidiaries in many different markets frequently make decisions about how much to reinvest in their existing foreign operations.

A consequence of the widespread use of entry studies in research on FDI location is that we know very little about how the location characteristics that are correlated with MNCs' entry decisions affect decisions about growing or shrinking existing operations at the margin (see Feinberg and Keane 2001). From a policy standpoint, most countries are at least as concerned about retaining, growing, and upgrading existing FDI as they are concerned about luring new FDI. Therefore, additional research on MNCs' incremental FDI location choices could contribute significantly to FDI policy.

New Location Theory: Random Chance and Time Recently, researchers applying location theory to international trade and FDI have begun to incorporate important new theoretical developments such as the role of chance and dynamics. Random chance plays a critical role in determining real-world patterns of production. For example, Krugman (1991) traces the location of the carpet industry in Dalton, Georgia, to Catherine Evans, who in 1895, by chance, made a tufted bedspread as a wedding gift. The bedspread was regarded as so beautiful that neighbors began demanding tufted items. From that beginning, with the addition of modern technology, the carpet industry grew and became concentrated in Dalton. A general theory of location or trade could not account for the chance events that give rise to global production locations such as carpets in Dalton. Rational planning, rather than historical accident, would be more consistent with the predictions of location or trade theory. The Dalton, Georgia, carpet industry example shows how chance events combine with dynamic factors such as new or increased demand, technological and infrastructure development, and the entry of new firms to create permanent global production locations. Chance and dynamics are both present in the Dalton example because the bedspread maker could have been born anywhere.

In contrast, agglomeration economies often do not arise by chance, but they do have a dynamic component. For example, the San Francisco Bay area location of the Silicon Valley tech cluster is much less surprising and random than the Dalton, Georgia, carpet location. The Bay area is home to several of the top research universities in the world and numerous government research laboratories. The state of California has a large and thriving defense industry. Thus both demand and supply conditions favored the creation of the Silicon Valley technology cluster.

A final new contribution to the literature on location theory, FDI, and trade is the literature on hysteresis, or path dependence. Hysteresis occurs when temporary economic shocks such as exchange rate volatility result in permanent transformations in global patterns of production and trade. For example, many Japanese auto and auto parts manufacturers that exported cars to the United States endured considerable economic hardship in the 1980s when the U.S. dollar began to decline. Since there was no certainty as to when the dollar would stop falling, many firms eventually decided to relocate production from Japan to North America. Thus the global pattern of production and trade was permanently changed as a result of transitory exchange rate shocks (see Baldwin and Krugman 1989).

The idea that temporary changes in the economic environment can cause permanent changes in global production patterns potentially gives significant discretion to policymakers to use short-term policies such as subsidies and tax breaks to attract global production. However, as we discuss below, when the use of such policies is widespread both within countries and internationally, bargaining power tends to shift from states to firms, and billions of dollars in dead-weight economic loss arise every year from competition to redistribute global production.

Policy Applications In a policy context, researchers have studied the following question: What can policymakers to do to enhance the attractiveness of their locations and thus increase the likelihood of

multinational firms will decide to choose the particular location? Much of the work in this area evolved from two important areas of research.

First, New Trade Theory (see Krugman 1994) introduced economies of scale into theories of international trade. In the extreme, some industries such as airplane manufacture and semiconductor fabrication are so costly to set up that the world might support only a very small number of firms. In such a case, a country could "win" a two-country game in which both countries decide whether to subsidize its own firm so that firm is able to lower its cost and take the entire world market for producing a particular good (see Brander and Spencer 1985). This type of policy is often referred to as "strategic trade policy." Despite there being no empirical evidence for the existence of industries with such extreme production structures that support only a single global firm (suitable subsidy targets), many billions of dollars are wasted every year by countries and states in subsidy games designed to "win" a larger share of global production. Knowing countries and states are willing to offer payments to lure and keep production gives firms an incentive to threaten to move. In many cases, these threats lead to bidding wars that reduce firms' costs at the expense of countries and states.

Second, Porter's *Competitive Advantage of Nations* (1998) directly considered a positive role for governments in making locations more attractive. Unlike proponents of strategic trade policy, Porter advocated broader types of policy actions to enhance the attractiveness of a location. These actions include increased spending on education and R&D, government spending on infrastructure, institutional development, and the like. This goal of these policies would be to create Silicon Valley–like clusters by improving the quality of domestic factors of production such as labor and capital. Since high-quality factors of production can be deployed across many different sectors, there is much less waste involved in policies that improve factor quality than in policies that merely seek to redistribute the location of existing economic activity.

Location theory addresses the important questions of who produces what goods or services in which locations, and why. Ideas from location theory have been widely used in international economics, in particular, to predict which countries will specialize in the production of certain goods for export, and which countries MNCs will choose as production locations. In early location models, factors of production were given rather than created, and technologies for producing particular goods were unalterable. Clearly, modern applications of location theory to trade, FDI, and international economic policy have considerably expanded the scope of these location models. However, fundamental insights from the earliest theories of location such as the importance of factors of production, trade, and transportation costs remain powerful explanations for the location of global production today.

See also foreign direct investment: the OLI framework; New Economic Geography

FURTHER READING

Baldwin, Richard, and Paul Krugman. 1989. "Persistent Trade Effects of Large Exchange Rate Shocks." *Quarterly Journal of Economics* 104 (4): 635–54. Examines the issue of hysteresis and trade: the notion that permanent changes in the location of production and trade can result from transitory economic shocks.

Brainard, S. Lael. 1997. "An Empirical Assessment of the Proximity-Concentration Trade-off between Multinational Sales and Trade." *American Economic Review* 87 (4): 520–44. Finds evidence that proximity to consumers is an important consideration for the location decisions of multinational firms.

Brander, James A., and Barbara J. Spencer. 1985. "Export Subsidies and International Market Share Rivalry." *Journal of International Economics* 18 (1-2): 83–100. One of many fundamental papers that Brander and Spencer have done relating to strategic trade theory; provides a theoretical background for policy-related papers on strategic trade theory.

Feinberg, Susan, and Michael Keane. 2001. "U.S.-Canada Trade Liberalization and MNC Production Location." *The Review of Economics and Statistics* 83 (1): 118–32. In this and several other papers, Feinberg and Keane examine incremental location decisions of multinational firms, as opposed to entry decisions.

Head, Keith, John Ries, and Deborah Swenson. 1995. "Agglomeration Benefits and Location Choice: Evidence from Japanese Manufacturing Investments in the United States." *Journal of International Economics* 38 (3–4): 223–47. Examines whether clustering is caused by spillovers or other unobservable country and industry characteristics such as factor endowments.

Isard, Walter, and Merton J. Peck. 1954. "Location Theory and International and Interregional Trade Theory." *Quarterly Journal of Economics* 68 (1): 97–114. A fundamental paper on location theory.

Javorcik, Beata Smarzynska, and Mariana Spatareanu. 2005. "Do Foreign Investors Care about Labor Market Regulations?" CEPR Discussion Paper No. 4839. London: Centre for Economic Policy Research. This article, and other research by Javorcik, examines many different features of countries' economic and policy environments and their relation to the location of FDI.

Krugman, Paul R. 1991. *Geography and Trade.* Cambridge, MA: MIT Press. A nontechnical overview of the linkages between international trade and location theories.

———. 1993. "On the Relationship between Trade Theory and Location Theory." *Review of International Economics* 1 (2): 110–22. Compares and contrasts location theory and trade theory, finding that despite some differences, the theories are asking similar questions and making similar assumptions.

———. 1994. *Rethinking International Trade.* Cambridge, MA: MIT Press. An introduction to New Trade Theory, the intersection of industrial organization economics and neoclassical trade.

Leamer, Edward E. 1984. *Sources of International Comparative Advantage: Theory and Evidence.* Cambridge, MA: MIT Press. An in-depth and extensive examination of how to test the predictions of neoclassical trade theory. Uses a structural estimation to test the predictions of trade theory using an extensive cross-country data set containing detailed information on factor endowments, production, and trade.

Marshall, Alfred. 1920. *Principles of Economics.* London: Macmillan.

OECD. 2006. *International Investment Perspectives.* Paris: OECD. Source of information on the worldwide trend toward liberalization of FDI policies.

Porter, Michael E. 1998. *The Competitive Advantage of Nations.* New York: Free Press. Combines industrial organization, international trade, and economic geography to investigate why some countries are systematically more competitive at producing particular goods and services.

SUSAN FEINBERG

■ Louvre Accord

The Louvre Accord is an agreement reached in Paris on February 22, 1987, among the Group of Six countries (the United States, Canada, Japan, Germany, France, and the United Kingdom) to stabilize the value of the dollar. Since the Plaza Accord in September 1985, the nominal dollar exchange rate against other major currencies had fallen more than 25 percent. The goal of the Louvre Accord was to arrest the decline of the dollar and to stabilize it around the prevailing levels.

Although the U.S. dollar began falling in 1985, the U.S. current account deficit in 1986 and 1987 remained large. United States treasury secretary James Baker sought to correct the imbalances by encouraging trading partners to stimulate their economies and therefore to purchase more U.S. exports (Frankel 1994). If trading partners did not want to grow more quickly, he would allow the dollar to fall more, which would stimulate U.S. net exports while reducing the net exports of America's trading partners. Baker secured an agreement during the Tokyo Summit of May 1986 to use macroeconomic indicators such as gross domestic product (GDP) growth and inflation to guide Group of Seven policy discussions. This indicator approach was intended to prompt the Japanese and Europeans to stimulate their economies in order to reduce U.S. current account deficits.

Although the Japanese and Europeans viewed this approach as an intrusion into their domestic policy arena, the Japanese, in particular, were willing to accept it in order to obtain relief from the strong yen (*endaka*). The yen had appreciated from almost 240 to the dollar before the Plaza Accord to 155 to the dollar a year later. Profit margins of Japanese exporting firms had fallen drastically, and Japanese officials did not want the yen to appreciate further.

U.S. policymakers were also concerned about the dollar depreciating further. The U.S. current account deficit had reached 3.5 percent of GDP and was financed heavily by foreign capital flows. United States officials were concerned that expectations of further depreciations could make dollar assets less attractive to foreign investors and force U.S. interest rates to increase. Such a destabilizing shift in portfolio preferences was sometimes referred to as the "hard landing" scenario (see Marris 1985; Frankel 1994).

Components of the Louvre Accord The Louvre Accord, as negotiated a few months later, stipulated:

1. The United States would reduce its budget deficit from 3.9 percent of GDP in fiscal year 1987 to 2.3 percent in fiscal year 1988.
2. Japan would cut its policy interest rate (discount rate) by 0.5 percent and enact a fiscal stimulus package.
3. France and Germany would cut taxes.
4. All countries would fight pressure from interest groups to enact tariffs and other impediments to free trade (Meyer et al. 2002).

The participants agreed in the accompanying statement to keep exchange rates within ranges broadly consistent with economic fundamentals (Funabashi 1989). The closing rates from February 20, 1987, were to be used as midpoints. Appreciations or depreciations of the dollar by 5 percent or more would trigger obligatory consultation on policy responses, appreciations or depreciations of 2.5 percent could lead to voluntary mutual intervention, and appreciations or depreciations between 2.5 and 5 percent would lead to progressively stronger interventions.

Despite heavy intervention by the United States and Japan, the dollar fell another 10 percent against the yen over the next two months. James Baker and Paul Volcker, then the chairman of the Federal Reserve, became increasingly concerned about a hard landing. In April 1987 Baker expressed the most alarm he ever had about the fall of the dollar. Volcker warned Congress of the incipient dangers and emphasized the need to cut the budget deficit (Funabashi 1989).

Germany and Japan While the United States made slow progress in reducing its budget deficit, Baker lobbied hard for Japan and Germany to stimulate their economies. Japan proposed an urgent stimulus package. German officials demurred, however, claiming that their economy had already reached its potential output level. The German central bank (the Bundesbank) even raised the discount rate in September 1987. The unwillingness of Germany to stimulate its economy led to open conflict between Baker and German finance minister Gerhard Stoltenberg (see James 1996). On September 27, 1987, Baker said that surplus countries would have to pay more attention to their macroeconomic indicators, meaning that they would have to stimulate their economies more to help the United States reduce its current account deficit. On October 18, 1987, he again called on Stoltenberg to undertake stimulative policies and threatened to let the dollar depreciate further if Germany did not. When the market opened the next day, the Dow Jones industrial average fell 23 percent.

James (1996) notes that, before the confrontation between the United States and Germany, the Bank of Japan had been contemplating raising the discount rate to slow down a developing bubble. After watching the conflict unfold, however, Japan went along with U.S. demands to pursue expansionary policies. In the face of this pressure from the United States, monetary policy in Japan was perhaps too expansionary (Bernanke and Gertler 1999). In 1989 and 1990 the Bank of Japan finally raised interest rates to prick the well-developed asset price bubble. Share prices then fell 90 percent between 1989 and 1992 and remained stagnant thereafter. The bursting of the bubble was disastrous for Japan because of its bank-based financial system. Falling asset prices eroded bank capital and restricted banks' ability to extend credit (Okina and Shiratsuka 2003). This in turn contributed to the "lost decade" of the 1990s, a period during which the Japanese economy remained stagnant.

Following these events, disillusionment with international policy coordination grew. Many came to view coordination efforts as thinly disguised attempts by the United States to get other countries to rescue it from the effects of its own unwise domestic policies (McCallum 1996). Even mild forms of macroeconomic policy coordination became difficult for developed economies to achieve.

See also balance of payments; Bonn Summit; Federal Reserve Board; international policy coordination; Plaza Accord; Smithsonian Agreement

FURTHER READING

Bernanke, Ben, and Mark Gertler. 1999. "Monetary Policy and Asset Price Volatility." In *New Challenges for Monetary Policy*. Kansas City: Federal Reserve Bank of Kansas City, 77–128. A discussion of the relationship between monetary policy and asset price bubbles.

Frankel, Jeffrey. 1994. "The Making of Exchange Rate Policy in the 1980s." In *American Economic Policy in the 1980s*, edited by Martin Feldstein. Chicago: University of Chicago Press. A readable and insightful history of exchange rate policy in the 1980s.

Funabashi, Yoichi. 1989. *Managing the Dollar: From the Plaza to the Louvre*. Washington, DC: Institute for International Economics. Provides a thorough, behind-the-scenes account of how the G5 countries were able to agree on the Plaza Accord.

James, Harold. 1996. *International Monetary Cooperation since Bretton Woods*. Oxford: Oxford University Press. A scholarly account of international monetary affairs from 1945 until the early 1990s.

Marris, Stephen. 1985. *Deficits and the Dollar. The World Economy at Risk*. Washington, DC: Institute for International Economics. Argues that America's deficits in the 1980s were unsustainable.

McCallum, Bennett. 1996. *International Monetary Economics*. Oxford: Oxford University Press. Covers international monetary issues.

Meyer, Laurence, Brian Doyle, Joseph Gagnon, and Dale Henderson. 2002. "International Coordination of Macroeconomic Policies: Still Alive in the New Millennium?" International Finance Discussion Paper 723. Washington DC: Federal Reserve Board. Surveys models of policy coordination.

Okina, Kunio, and Shigenori Shiratsuka. 2003. "Japan's Experience with Asset Price Bubbles: Is It a Case for Inflation Targeting?" In *Asset Price Bubbles: The Implications for Monetary, Regulatory, and International Policies*, edited by William Hunter, George Kaufman, and Michael Pomerleano. Cambridge, MA: MIT Press. Examines the relationship between Japan's asset price bubble and monetary policy.

WILLEM THORBECKE

■ Maastricht Treaty

Maastricht is the city in the Netherlands where heads of government reached agreement on a document that would give birth to the European Union. The treaty represents a landmark in the process of European integration as it would define the rules of the game under which member states would eventually gain membership into the single currency area. Originally, the European Union (EU) consisted of 12 member states when the treaty first came into force in November 1993. Later, there would be further enlargements, the most recent occurring in 2004 when 10 new member states were admitted. In 2007, 2 more member states (Bulgaria and Romania) were admitted, bringing the total EU membership to 27 countries that would eventually subscribe to the treaty.

Because it was designed to deal with existing member states, not ones that would join in future, the original Maastricht Treaty could not cope with enlargement. Consequently, the Maastricht Treaty was followed by the Treaty of Amsterdam in 1997 and the Treaty of Nice in 2001. The most important change to the original Maastricht Treaty dealt with voting rules for policy approval: the Maastricht Treaty required unanimous approval of policy changes at the EU level, whereas succeeding treaties allowed for majority approval. The system in place in 2007 essentially assigned a weight to each country's influence in the EU roughly based on population size. Although some decisions require unanimity (e.g., foreign policy questions), others would henceforth require a qualified majority, that is, a vote that reflects the relative importance of some EU members based on their population (e.g., measures affecting the operations of the internal European market). Even when a qualified majority is used to make a decision, the number of votes must exceed a threshold (more than 50 percent of votes) before any decision can be adopted.

The grand objective behind the Maastricht Treaty was to put in place institutions and policies that would advance the ideal of a unified Europe. Although the centerpiece of the treaty concerned the rules intended to foster economic and monetary union, it also included social and legal provisions to harmonize existing laws and regulations among the member states and to develop common foreign and security policies. Some governments objected to particular provisions. The United Kingdom, for example, found the Social Chapter, a legal provision that dealt with policies concerning wage setting and health and safety regulations, unacceptable and opted out of the relevant provisions. Denmark rejected the treaty after putting it to a vote in a referendum. Eventually, the United Kingdom and Denmark received an opt-out agreement that would give them the option to join the monetary union in the future.

Maastricht Convergence Criteria The road map to monetary union was first laid out in the Delors Report of 1989, named after the former French politician who is also a former president of the European Commission. Critical to achieving monetary union were the so-called convergence criteria. The goal was a simple one in principle, namely to ensure that the members of the area that would form a monetary union would have comparable macroeconomic environments. This would, first, facilitate the introduction of an unalterable fixed exchange rate, to be followed by the introduction of a common currency. The original report called for European Monetary Union (EMU) by 1999. At the end of 1995, leaders of the EU announced plans for a single currency that would be called the euro.

The road to the single currency proceeded in three stages. The first stage, which began in January 1990, was intended to liberalize the movement of capital. The second stage began in January 1994 when member states began to enact economic policies that would lead to a form of convergence as defined in the treaty. It is perhaps the so-called convergence requirements that have received the most attention among policymakers and academics over the years. These continue to form the core of the treaty. The member states that joined the enlarged EU in 2004 are also required to adhere to the convergence requirements in order to adopt the euro. Unlike Denmark or the United Kingdom, however, all new members of the EU eventually must adopt the euro.

The convergence criteria consist of five elements:

1. Inflation rates up to a maximum of 1.5 percentage points above the average of the three lowest national inflation rates.
2. Interest rates up to a maximum of 2 percentage points above the average of the three lowest national long-term interest rates.
3. Budget deficits up to a maximum of 3 percent of gross domestic product (GDP).
4. An accumulated public or government debt of up to 60 percent of GDP; and
5. Maintenance of stable exchange rates for at least two years.

Although the convergence principles seem clear, they are not unambiguous. Over the years countries have haggled over the exact definition of stability in the exchange rate and what could or could not be included in the deficit calculations. Disputes over the precise interpretation of the deficit principle eventually led to a separate agreement known as the Stability and Growth Pact, which laid down a series of fiscal rules that themselves are subject to continuing debate. Similar concerns arose with respect to the

debt to GDP ratio principle. The treaty suggests that if the 60 percent threshold is not met, the ratio should show signs of diminishing sufficiently in the future and, consequently, approach the reference value of 60 percent at a "satisfactory pace." The wiggle room in the convergence criteria allowed Belgium, Italy, and Greece to join the euro area. It is, therefore, clear that the inflation convergence requirement is first among equals in the list of Maastricht convergence principles.

The third stage began in January 1999 with the establishment of a European Central Bank and culminated in the introduction of the single currency in January 2002.

See also common currency; euro; European Central Bank; European Monetary Union; European Union; optimum currency area (OCA) theory

FURTHER READING

De Grauwe, Paul. 2005. *The Economics of Monetary Union.* 6th rev. ed. Oxford: Oxford University Press. Covers the history and the case for or against monetary integration as well as the economics of monetary unions more generally.

European Union. *Treaty of Maastricht on European Union.* Downloadable at http://europa.eu/scadplus/treaties/maastricht_en.htm. The text, written in legal language, of the actual Maastricht Treaty.

Fratianni, Michele. 1992. "The Maastricht Way to EMU." Princeton Essays in International Finance No. 187. Princeton, NJ: Princeton University. Describes the essential events and issues surrounding the decision to adopt convergence requirements in the Maastricht Treaty.

PIERRE L. SIKLOS

■ market access

Acquiring market access is one of the main motives that drive multinational firms to invest abroad. To serve foreign markets, firms are often faced with two choices: exports versus foreign direct investment (FDI). In the presence of large trade costs (e.g., tariff and transportation costs), firms are less inclined to export to the foreign market. Instead, they are more likely to supply foreign consumers through local production. This incentive to avoid trade costs by producing inside a foreign market is also referred to as the tariff-jumping motive. As a result, multinational firms duplicate their production in the foreign countries and expand horizontally. The FDI arising from this consideration has been defined by the researchers as the horizontal type of FDI. This horizontal type of FDI is distinguished from vertical FDI, in which a firm shifts production to a low-cost location and serves all markets from there.

The Proximity-Concentration Trade-off The theoretical literature on horizontal FDI is led by the seminal work of Markusen (1984), one of the first authors to show from an international trade perspective that multinationals may arise endogenously in equilibrium. A key ingredient of the models in this literature is the interaction of trade costs and plant-level scale economies. While multinational firms are able to avoid trade costs by operating local production plants in foreign countries, they must pay a plant-level fixed cost for each additional plant. In contrast to the trade costs that prompt firms to produce the same goods and services in multiple countries, the plant-level scale economy encourages firms to concentrate their production in one location. Hence, as predicted in these studies, multinational activity is more likely to arise in industries that require a relatively small plant-level fixed cost and in countries that impose large trade costs on imported goods. Moreover, multinational activity should be concentrated among countries that are similar in both market size and factor endowment.

These predictions have been formally examined in several important empirical studies, including Brainard (1997); Carr, Markusen, and Maskus (2001); and Yeaple (2003) among others. These papers formally examine the extent to which the decision by multinationals to invest overseas is affected by their motive of maximizing proximity to consumers and the trade-off in plant-level scale economy.

Multinational firms' market access motive is broadly confirmed. Based on mainly the U.S. inward or outward FDI data, these studies show that multinationals'

affiliate sales increase with both the tariff rate the foreign country imposes on the parent country and the transportation cost between the two. When the plant-level fixed cost, measured by the average size of a plant in terms of production workers, is larger, however, the affiliate sales decrease. Furthermore, Carr, Markusen, and Maskus (2001) find that the smaller the difference between two countries in market size (i.e., GDP) and factor endowment (i.e., capital labor ratio), the greater the FDI flow between the two. These results strongly suggest the existence of horizontal FDI that is motivated by market access.

Market Potential A more recent study by Head and Mayer (2004) further extends the notion of market access. They introduce the importance of market potential in multinationals' location choice and point out that, while the ability to access a foreign market at little cost motivates firms to locate production in that country, the ability to access other markets from that country also matters. In other words, the definition of "market" in the market access motive should not be limited to the market of the host country; it should include all the markets that can be more easily accessed by the host-country plant.

To test this idea, Head and Mayer (2004) construct a measure of market potential for each potential host country. This measure represents the demand of all markets weighted by the trade costs required to export to these markets from the host. Countries with better access to other markets due to, for example, geographic proximity have greater market potential. Using a sample of Japanese multinational firms, Head and Mayer (2004) offer important evidence that regions with a larger market potential indeed attract more multinationals.

The Impact of Regional Economic Integration Given the role of market access in foreign direct investment, any change in market accessibility is expected to have an impact on multinationals' activities. In particular, regional economic integration, by reducing the trade barriers between participating countries (and keeping barriers against the rest of the world intact) will likely alter the location decision of multinational firms in the integrated region.

First, a decline in trade costs between home and host countries raises the profit associated with exporting. Multinationals' market access motive may hence be weakened and even dominated by their incentive to concentrate production geographically and achieve economies of scale. As a result, FDI could be replaced by exports. For example, a great concern in Canada during the formation of the Canada-U.S. Free Trade Agreement was that U.S. multinational affiliates located in Canada would leave Canada and serve the Canadian market through exports originating in the United States. This expectation is, however, inconsistent with the evidence. The study by Feinberg and Keane (2001) offers direct empirical insights to this issue. They show that reductions in the Canadian tariff against the United States have little impact on the U.S. multinational firms' affiliate sales in Canada and, moreover, reductions in the U.S. tariff against Canada increase the U.S. multinationals' export sales from Canada to their home countries. These findings suggest that regional economic integration does not necessarily lower multinationals' incentive to invest abroad; it may in fact increase multinationals' incentive to produce in the integrated foreign country and export back to home.

Second, regional economic integration that improves the market access among member countries could also affect the location decision of outsider firms. As the benefit of improved market access is exclusive to firms located within the integrated region, outsider firms have an increased incentive to produce in a member country and supply the rest of the region through exports. The underlying logic is closely related to the notion of market potential in Head and Mayer (2004): regional economic integration increases members' market potential and thus their ability to attract multinationals. This intuitive prediction is derived and empirically examined by Ekholm, Forslid, and Markusen (2007), who emphasize multinationals' exports to third countries. As demonstrated in this study, after the formation of a preferential trading bloc both insider and outsider firms tend to adopt an export-platform FDI strategy, in which they increase their investments in some members of the bloc and supply the other member countries through exports.

In sum, market access, or more generally market potential including the ability to better access other markets, is an important motivation for firms to engage in FDI and establish production facilities abroad. Regional economic integration, by lowering internal trade barriers, can make a region more attractive to multinational firms and lead to an expansion in export-platform FDI into the region.

See also foreign direct investment: the OLI framework

FURTHER READING

Brainard, S. Lael. 1997. "An Empirical Assessment of Proximity-Concentration Trade-off between Multinational Sales and Trade." *American Economic Review* 87 (4): 520–44. Examines the role of a trade-off between achieving proximity to customers and achieving scale economies in multinationals' investment activities abroad and finds that overseas production by multinationals increases when transport costs and trade barriers are higher and when investment barriers and plant-level scale economies are lower.

Carr, David, James Markusen, and Keith Maskus. 2001. "Estimating the Knowledge-Capital Model of the Multinational Enterprise." *American Economic Review* 91 (3): 691–708. Offers a direct test of the predictions generated in a knowledge-capital model, estimates the volume of foreign affiliate production as a function of host- and home-country characteristics, and finds evidence of both horizontal and vertical types of foreign direct investment.

Ekholm, Karolina, Rikard Forslid, and James Markusen. 2007. "Export-Platform Foreign Direct Investment." *Journal of European Economic Association* 5 (4): 776–95. Examines theoretically and empirically the determinants of export-platform FDI, in particular the effect of a free-trade area between a high-income and a low-income country on firms' location decision, and shows that this free-trade area can lead both the insider- and outsider-country firms to adopt an export-platform FDI strategy.

Feinberg, Susan, and Michael Keane. 2001. "U.S.-Canada Trade Liberalization and MNC Production Location." *Review of Economics and Statistics* 83 (1): 118–32. Examines how the bilateral trade flows of U.S. multinational corporations and their Canadian affiliates responded to U.S.-Canadian tariff reductions and finds that the bilateral trade liberalization motivated U.S. multinationals to integrate their North American production and increase their exports from Canadian affiliates to the United States.

Head, Keith, and Thierry Mayer. 2004. "Market Potential and the Location of Japanese Investment in the European Union." *Review of Economics and Statistics* 86 (4): 959–72. Examines the effect of market potential on Japanese multinational firms' location decision and finds that not only the size of the domestic market but also the size of export markets matter significantly in multinationals' location choice.

Markusen, James. 1984. "Multinationals, Multiplant Economics, and the Gains from Trade." *Journal of International Economics* 16 (3–4): 205–26. Develops a general equilibrium model of a multinational firm in which the productivity of a joint input is independent of the number of plants operated by a firm and finds that the existence of multinational firms increases technical efficiency as it eliminates the duplication of the joint input among independent national firms.

Yeaple, Stephen. 2003. "The Role of Skill Endowments in the Structure of U.S. Outward Foreign Direct Investment." *Review of Economics and Statistics* 85 (3): 726–34. Investigates empirically the industry and country determinants of U.S. outward foreign direct investment and finds evidence of both market access and comparative advantage motives in U.S. multinationals' investment activities.

MAGGIE XIAOYANG CHEN

■ market efficiency

See interest parity conditions; forward premium puzzle

■ market size and foreign direct investment

Market size is an important factor in determining bilateral activities of multinational firms, regardless of whether these activities are measured as foreign affiliate sales, affiliates' employment, or foreign direct investment (FDI). FDI reflects the objective of establishing a lasting interest by a resident enterprise in one economy in an enterprise that is resident in another economy. Discussions often focus on the market size of the host country, although the size of neighboring countries and other countries more easily reached from the host country also play a role. Market size refers mainly to the size of markets for goods and services. Although market size of the host country is widely considered, the size of the home country is also important for bilateral FDI. Larger and more advanced countries are home to more multinational firms. The pool of knowledge necessary to generate the specific advantages that enable firms to survive in a foreign environment increases along with a country's size and level of development.

Empirical Evidence and the Gravity Equation Most FDI flows toward large markets. Since the 1980s, the United States has received the largest inflows and holds the largest FDI stocks. Among the developing countries, China has gained the dominant position. The size effect of the host country has been the object of empirical studies since the early 1960s. The market size hypothesis states that FDI flows are positively related to the host country's market size. Various studies have found that market size and market growth affect FDI flows positively.

Gravity equations explain activities between two countries by the size of the source and the destination country and the distance between the two. Originally developed to explain international trade, the gravity equation successfully explains aggregated activities of multinational firms such as foreign affiliate sales or FDI as well. Using bilateral data at the country or sector level, about 60 percent of the variation in multinational firms' activities are explained by these three variables. The effect of the size variables (mostly gross domestic product or population) is found to be robust and positive (Brainard 1997; Buch et al. 2005). Moreover, the relationship is robust over different time periods and against changes in the analyzed sample. In particular, no systematic differences are found with respect to the size variables in studies explaining FDI in developing countries relative to FDI in members of the Organisation for Economic Co-operation and Development (OECD).

Market size as a determinant of FDI has received increasing attention because the expansion of FDI activities after 1985 has predominantly been among OECD countries. The bulk of the FDI flows involves the same countries as home and as host countries even within narrowly defined industries. Thus factor cost differentials could not have been the source of this increase in FDI activities. The motive behind the increased FDI activities has not been found in lower production cost but in improved market access for products. Thus the new theoretical explanation for the emergence of multinational firms placed goods market access and therefore market size in the center of the analysis.

FDI for Market Access According to this line of the literature, named proximity-concentration theory, or theory of the horizontal firm, the choice of a particular mode of market access drives the internationalization of firms. Firms invest abroad to serve the foreign market by production abroad instead of exporting there. Producing abroad saves distance costs and improves market access. Distance costs comprise all costs that come with segmented markets, including transportation costs, tariffs, quotas, information costs, and registration costs.

At a given level of distance costs, a firm is more likely to decide in favor of production abroad the larger its sales are in the foreign country, because distance costs savings through production abroad are per-unit savings. Sales of the firm in the foreign country in turn depend on the foreign country's market size. Thus a firm is likely to realize larger savings the larger the foreign country's market. The additional costs associated with producing in the foreign country, in contrast, are fixed costs, that is, costs independent of sales. These fixed costs can be huge, so it does not pay to replace exports by production abroad if per-unit distance cost saving are not large enough. Hence a larger country attracts more foreign multinational firms, because market size increases the per-unit cost saving but leaves the fixed costs unaffected.

While market access is important, it is certainly not the only factor determining the decision of a firm to go abroad. Factor costs are also important (Braconier, Norback, and Urban 2005). The high explanatory power of market size in the gravity equation does not necessarily mean that goods market access is the most important motive of engagement in FDI. The size of host country's *factor* markets can also affect FDI positively. A large pool of well-trained labor with specific skills drives FDI in areas such as finance or software development to London and Bangalore, respectively. The large supply of cheap labor attracts FDI in manufacturing to China.

Factor market potential also stands behind the positive effect of the *home* country's size on FDI. The relevant factor here is knowledge capital, as Markusen (1995) calls it. Knowledge capital can be proprietary product or process know-how, efficient organizational structures, a brand name, or reputation. Knowledge capital enables firms to generate the firm-specific advantage that is necessary to produce successfully in a foreign environment. Knowledge capital increases with the stage of development and with population, since knowledge is embodied in people. Hence knowledge capital, that is, the ability to generate the firm-specific advantages, rises with the market size of the home country.

Policies to Attract FDI Given that market size is such an important determinant of FDI, restrictions on market access have been used to attract FDI. That has mainly been done by excluding or obstructing other channels to supply the market, mainly trade. FDI carried out to circumvent trade barriers has been named tariff-jumping FDI. Such tariff-jumping FDI has been found to be important for Japanese FDI to the United States and to Europe (Barrel and Pain 1999). Tariff jumping has also been a motive for FDI in Latin American countries, particularly Brazil, during their period of import substitution.

Although restricting trade is an option to attract FDI, particularly for large countries, the opposite strategy has proven more successful. By regional integration, that is, through the reduction of trade barriers, countries in the European Union (EU) and in East Asia have successfully enlarged their markets in order to attract FDI. Regional integration has increased the market potential of individual countries tremendously. Ireland, for example, is chosen as host country by many multinational firms from outside the EU that aim at supplying goods and services in the whole EU. In addition to the increase of FDI from outside, regional economic integration has increased FDI within the region. That can be observed in the EU, as well as in the North American Free Trade Area (NAFTA) and in East Asia. Reducing internal barriers to trade alters location decisions within the regions. Firms can exploit cost differences within the region, which motivates increased FDI from within the region.

In sum, there is strong empirical support for the importance of market size as a determinant of multinational activity. This has spurred theoretical research that has found market access to be a strong motive for FDI. The market access motive has received support by intensified FDI flows following market size growth through establishing regional integration areas such as the EU and NAFTA.

See also factor endowments and foreign direct investment; gravity models; location theory

FURTHER READING

Barba Navaretti, Giorgio, and Anthony J. Venables, eds. 2005. *Multinational Firms in the World Economy.* Princeton, NJ: Princeton University Press. A comprehensive overview of today's stand of economic research on multinational firms.

Barrel, Ray, and Nigel Pain. 1999. "Trade Restraint and Japanese Direct Investment Flows." *European Economic Review* 43 (1): 29–45. An empirical examination of the effect of trade protection measures on FDI.

Braconier, Henrik, Pehr-Johan Norback, and Dieter Urban. 2005. "Multinational Enterprise and Wage Costs: Vertical FDI Revisited." *Journal of International Economics* 67: 446–70. An important empirical analysis of determinants of FDI based on a data set that includes many developing countries and almost all OECD countries.

Brainard, S. Lael. 1997. "An Empirical Assessment of the Proximity-Concentration Trade-off between Multinational Sales and Trade." *American Economic Review* 87

(4): 520–44. The first empirical assessment of the proximity-concentration theory.

Buch, Claudia M., Jörn Kleinert, Alexander Lipponer, and Farid Toubal. 2005. "Determinants and Effects of Foreign Direct Investment: Evidence from German Firm Level Data." *Economic Policy* 20 (41): 51–110. An early study of microlevel evidence on multinational firms.

Markusen, James R. 1995. "The Boundaries of Multinational Enterprises and the Theory of International Trade." *Journal of Economic Perspectives* 9 (2): 169–89. The first formulation of a theory of the multinational firm that includes horizontal and vertical firms based on the idea of knowledge capital as a defining element.

———. 2002. *Multinational Firms and the Theory of International Trade.* Cambridge, MA: MIT Press. A comprehensive summary of microeconomic general equilibrium theory on multinational firms.

JÖRN KLEINERT

■ Marshall-Lerner condition

The Marshall-Lerner condition establishes the circumstances in which a country's trade balance, or current account balance of payments, would improve as a result of a currency devaluation or depreciation. It was named after the economists Alfred Marshall and Abba Lerner, who are thought to have first discovered it. The theoretical basis of the Marshall-Lerner condition is the "imperfect substitutes model," which is a workhorse model of international trade that assumes that neither imports nor exports are perfect substitutes for domestic goods. It is also closely linked to the so-called elasticities approach to the balance of payments and the J-curve effect, since the answer depends on how responsive (or "elastic") imports and exports are to changes in their relative prices.

The Marshall-Lerner condition is the specific condition under which a real currency depreciation, interpreted as a fall in the relative price of exports in terms of imports, will improve the current account. More specifically, if the current account balance is initially zero—neither a deficit nor a surplus—the

Marshall-Lerner condition requires that the sum of the absolute values (ignoring signs) of the price elasticity of export demand, which measures the response of exports to the fall in the relative price of exports, and the price elasticity of import demand (the numerical response of import demand to the rise in the relative price of imports) exceed one. The export and import demand elasticities will be "elastic" if a 10 percent change in their prices brought about by the fall in the currency leads to a change of more than 10 percent in the quantities demanded. Moreover, the greater the amount by which the sum of these elasticities exceeds one the greater the improvement in the current account. On the other hand, a currency appreciation or revaluation will worsen the current account.

Intuitively, the reasoning is that when foreign goods become more expensive in the home country, fewer imports will be demanded—and when the home country's goods become cheaper abroad, foreigners will buy more of its exports. Thus, provided the responses of buyers of imports and exports to the price changes are strong enough, the Marshall-Lerner condition will be satisfied. Export values will rise and import values will fall so the net effect will be an improvement in the current account.

Note that this is the simplified version of the Marshall-Lerner condition, which focuses on the responses of demand for exports and imports and assumes that responses on the supply side, measured by the elasticities of import and export supply, are both set to infinity. This implies that the home country is small in terms of its influence on international prices, meaning that it can buy all the imports it wishes at a given international price and is willing to sell to foreign countries as much as they want at a fixed price. The outcome is more complex if this assumption is relaxed and/or the current account is not initially zero. In addition, the predicted outcome for the current account is conditional on holding everything else constant, such as the effects of the fall in the value of the currency on incomes in both the home country and abroad.

Importance of the Marshall-Lerner Condition
The Marshall-Lerner condition is important because it enables policymakers to predict the effects of changes in the exchange rate on the balance of payments (equivalent to the current account if capital flows are ignored). This is especially relevant to developing countries that find it difficult to sell their goods abroad because their currencies are "overvalued," or overpriced, or that wish to devalue their currencies in an attempt to reduce their current account deficits. In 1994, for example, a number of countries belonging to the African Financial Community franc zone, an arrangement under which several former French colonies fix their currencies to the French franc, devalued simultaneously by 50 percent to improve their balance of payments. But the condition is also of interest to developed countries, including the debate over the sustainability of the large U.S. current account deficit and the extent to which this can be reduced by a depreciation of the U.S. dollar.

The Marshall-Lerner condition also has important implications for the stability of the foreign exchange market. A foreign exchange market is stable if a disturbance that upsets the balance between the supply and demand for foreign exchange is corrected automatically through adjustment of the exchange rate. If, however, market movements in the exchange rate result in a movement further away from a supply and demand equilibrium, then the foreign exchange market is unstable. Although it is possible to establish conditions for the stability of the foreign exchange market based on the supply and demand curves for foreign exchange, these cannot be measured empirically. It turns out, however, that if the Marshall-Lerner condition is fulfilled, the foreign exchange market will also be stable, so all one has to do is to measure the price elasticities of demand for exports and imports.

Empirical Studies Not surprisingly, there has been a substantial amount of empirical work testing the Marshall-Lerner condition both for one country's trade with the rest of the world and for trade flows between two countries. Early work following Marshall's (1923) original publication tended to support the condition giving rise to the expression *elasticity optimism* but later studies in the 1940s and after World War II were more "pessimistic" and suggested that the sum of the demand elasticities might be below or close to one. In the 1990s and early 21st century many of the earlier methodological and measurement problems associated with the testing of the Marshall-Lerner condition have been addressed and a consensus picture has emerged.

Relative prices do seem to play a significant role in determining exports and imports so the Marshall-Lerner condition is likely to be satisfied for most countries, but there are some important qualifications. First, although studies measuring export and import demand elasticities for samples of countries are generally supportive of the condition, other studies looking at individual countries over a long period of time have found little evidence of a systematic relationship between the trade balance and the relative prices of exports and imports. One also has to distinguish carefully between developed and developing countries and countries that have a high proportion of natural resources, including crude petroleum, and services in their exports and imports, since these structural differences in their economies may result in differences in their responses to export and import price changes. Third, it is crucial to allow for the fact that export and import demand may adjust only slowly over time to changes in relative prices. In particular, elasticities measured over a six-month period following the currency depreciation may be substantially less than one and may give rise to the "J-curve effect." Even short-run elasticities based on a one-year delay could still be quite low. Only when a longer period has elapsed can one be confident that the responses are large enough to satisfy the Marshall-Lerner condition.

Finally, one has to be careful to allow for episodes in history that may make the measured elasticities unreliable or unrepresentative of normal behavior, such as following the reunification of Germany in 1989, or the establishment of the North American Free Trade Agreement among Canada, Mexico, and the United States in 1994.

See also balance of payments; fear of floating; foreign exchange intervention; international reserves; J-curve effect; North American Free Trade Agreement (NAFTA); real exchange rate

FURTHER READING

Hooper, P., K. Johnson, and J. Marquez. 2000. "Trade Elasticities for the G-7 Countries." *Princeton Studies in International Economics* 87 (August): 1–29. An influential empirical study that is supportive of the Marshall-Lerner condition and looks at the evidence for the so-called Group of Seven advanced industrialized countries.

Lerner, A. 1944. *The Economics of Control*. London: Macmillan. Provides the origins of the Marshall-Lerner condition.

Marshall, A. 1923. *Money, Credit, and Commerce*. London: Macmillan. Provides the origins of the Marshall-Lerner condition.

Reinhart, C. 1995. "Devaluation, Relative Prices, and International Trade." *International Monetary Fund Staff Papers* 42 (2): 290–312. An influential empirical study that is supportive of the Marshall-Lerner condition and focuses on the adjustment of developing countries facing large imbalances in their balance of payments.

Rose, A. 1991. "The Role of Exchange Rates in a Popular Model of International Trade." *Journal of International Economics* 30: 301–16. Provides an explanation of the relationship between the Marshall-Lerner condition, the imperfect substitutes model, and the elasticities approach and an example of the empirical literature.

PETER WILSON

■ **mercantilism**

A school of economic thought developed in 16th- and 17th-century England, mercantilism argued that a country's primary economic objective should be the achievement of a trade surplus with the associated inflow of gold. The central idea was that trade was a zero-sum game and that a country could amass gold through a balance-of-trade surplus only at the expense of another country. Mercantilism is therefore a form of economic nationalism, with foreign trade used to enhance the wealth and power of one country at the expense of others.

Mercantilism is not a unified body of thought; however, Thomas Mun's *England's Treasure by Foreign Trade*, published in 1664, is typical of mercantilist writings. The policy implications of the mercantilist position included the limitation of imports and the promotion of exports. Mercantilism formed the basis for the organization of Britain's trade with its colonies, with the colonies restricted to supplying the raw materials for Britain's emerging manufacturing sector. The colonies were prohibited from competing with these so-called enumerated goods, and the entire colonial trading system was organized to promote the economic strength of the mother country and produce a trade surplus. The popularity of mercantilist thinking has been attributed to the realities of 16th- and 17th-century statecraft, in which the ability to fight foreign wars depended on having the gold resources to finance such adventures; in this case, gold accumulation through export surpluses did contribute to national power.

Adam Smith and Mercantilism The protectionist implications of mercantilism led Adam Smith to identify mercantilism as one of the erroneous systems of political economy that he sought to displace with his *An Inquiry into the Nature and Causes of the Wealth of Nations* (1776). For Smith, the mercantilists were guilty of a simple confusion about the nature of wealth, believing that it consisted of gold rather than the human and physical stock of capital. Smith believed free trade was the appropriate policy. David Hume's essay "Of the Balance of Trade" (1752) demonstrated that the objective of a balance-of-trade surplus was self-defeating, as the specie-flow mechanism would lead to domestic price level changes, which would bring the trade balance back into equilibrium. In arguing this, Hume developed an early version of the quantity theory of money. By the mid-18th century, therefore, mercantilism had been discredited and was entirely eclipsed by the theory of comparative advantage and the associated benefits of free trade developed by David Ricardo in *Principles of Political Economy and Taxation* (1821). Britain abandoned mercantilism and its associated trade restrictions in the 1840s.

Mercantilism was gradually replaced by free trade and comparative advantage as the new economic orthodoxy at the theoretical level, although one of the mercantilists' central policies—protectionism—continued to have its adherents, especially in Germany and the United States, the late industrializers of the 19th century. Both Friedrich List and Alexander Hamilton, influential German and American thinkers, respectively, advocated protectionist policies to spur their countries' industrialization. Even where free trade had become the orthodoxy, such as in Britain, protectionist policies returned in the face of the economic disaster of the 1930s. Even John Maynard Keynes, in *The General Theory of Employment, Interest, and Money* (1936), included the mercantilists among his predecessors in believing that an increase in the money supply could increase domestic production. Keynes argued that there was an "element of scientific proof in mercantilist doctrine" (335).

Neomercantilism In the post-1945 period, the successful late, late industrializers of East Asia, especially Japan, South Korea, and Taiwan—and in the 1990s and early 21st century, China—have been described as "neomercantilist." These economies ran trade surpluses during much of their post-1950 rapid growth periods, based on import restrictions, the promotion of exports, and an exchange rate pegged to the U.S. dollar (at artificially low levels, according to some). The trade surpluses enabled the East Asian economies to achieve rapid economic growth over a long period without being subject to a balance of payments constraint—a constraint that affected many other developing countries' growth prospects, especially in Latin America. The prefix *neo* in *neomercantilism* therefore referred to the new period in which countries pursued trade surpluses as well as the economic, as opposed to military, definition of "national power." The term is usually used in a normative way to indicate that East Asian countries, and occasionally others, have been following nationalist policies at the expense of other countries.

See also balance of payments; beggar-thy-neighbor policies; Bretton Woods system; comparative advantage;

gold standard, international; international reserves; money supply; quantity theory of money

FURTHER READING

Hecksher, Eli. 1955. *Mercantilism*. 2 vols. London: Allen and Unwin. A classic text on mercantilist writings by one of the pioneers of modern trade theory.

Keynes, John Maynard.1936. *The General Theory of Employment, Interest, and Money*. London: Macmillan.

Nester, William. 1990. "The Development of Japan, Taiwan, and South Korea: Ends and Means, Free Trade, Dependency, or Neomercantilism?" *Journal of Developing Societies* 6: 203–18. Examines whether the East Asian countries can be accurately described as pursuing "neomercantilist" policies.

Viner, Jacob. 1937. *Studies in the Theory of International Trade*. New York: Harper and Brothers. A historical examination of theories of international trade that includes a critique of mercantilist thinking.

PAUL BOWLES

■ Mercosur

Traditional rivals in the southern cone of Latin America, Argentina and Brazil first explored economic collaboration in the early 1980s. For the first time in centuries, the moment was right. Both countries underwent political transitions in the mid-1980s from military rule to civilian regimes—Argentina in 1983 and Brazil in 1985. The reestablishment of democratic governments provided an opportunity to seek policies that would consolidate the democratic process and limit the sphere of influence of the armed forces. In November 1985, newly elected democratic presidents met to inaugurate a new bridge at Iguaçu Falls on the border between the two nations. They agreed to create a binational commission to study the possibilities of increased economic cooperation and integration. In 1986, the Argentine-Brazilian Program for Integration and Cooperation was announced. In 1986, the two presidents signed the Act of Brazil-Argentine Friendship in Brasília. It was also announced that the two countries would pursue a policy of peaceful nuclear development.

In July 1990, the heads of state of Argentina and Brazil signed the Act of Buenos Aires. The document called for the creation of a common market by 1995, instead of by the earlier announced date of 1999. The Treaty of Asunción, signed in March 1991, brought Paraguay and Uruguay into the common market process and marked the creation of a "Common Market of the South," or Mercosur. This new organization's principal goal was to have a free trade area in place among all four countries and a common external tariff (CET) created by 1995. At the time of this writing, the deadline had been extended to 2010. The Protocol of Ouro Preto came into effect in December 1995 and established a new institutional framework for Mercosur. In addition to the Administrative Secretariat located in Montevideo, Uruguay, and the Common Market Council and Common Market Group, set up in 1991, it was decided to add a Joint Parliamentary Commission, a Trade Commission, and a Socio-Economic Advisory Forum. A new date of 2006 was established for the creation of a full common market. As the institutional structure evolved, Chile (1996), Bolivia (1997), Peru (2003), Colombia (2004) and Ecuador (2004) were added as Associate Members (Associate Members enjoy tariff reductions but are not subject to the CET system). In December 2004, Mercosur signed a cooperation agreement with the Andean Community trade bloc, and they published a joint letter of intention for a future negotiation toward integrating all of South America. A year later, President Alvaro Uribe of Colombia signed a law that ratified a Free Trade Agreement with Mercosur. In June 2006, Mercosur expanded further and incorporated Venezuela as a full member.

Tariffs among the four Mercosur member countries were gradually eliminated in the 1990s, and the common market was essentially completed by 1995 with the reduction of 85 percent of tariffs and nontariff trade barriers. Trade expanded rapidly among the Mercosur countries, especially between the two largest countries. According to the IMF's *Trade Statistics Yearbook*, Argentina's exports to Brazil climbed from $3.6 billion to $5.3 billion between 1995 and 1996, and Brazil's exports to Argentina grew from $4.0 billion to $5.2 billion in the same period.

In retrospect, the late 1990s were the high point of southern cone integration. A maxi-devaluation of the Brazilian currency in January 1999 was the first shock to disturb Mercosur's consolidation. Argentina experienced an institutional crisis in 2001–2 that led to the resignation of President Fernando de la Rua, the collapse of the convertibility plan that had linked the peso to the dollar (one to one), and a massive default on the country's outstanding debt. As a result of the crisis in Argentina, Uruguay's economy stalled and growth rates plummeted and only revived a few years later.

There was little activity in Mercosur in the years following the Argentine-Uruguayan crises. Chile decided that its development goals were best served by negotiating bilateral trade agreements and did so successfully with the United States and China. In an effort to reinvigorate the organization, the heads of state convened the 30th presidential summit, held in Córdoba, Argentina, in July 2006. The formal agenda included discussions of pending trade agreements with external allies, a common customs code, the appointment of members to the Administrative Labor Court, and the establishment of a consistent Mercosur negotiating position for the all-but-collapsed World Trade Organization Doha Round.

Many observers believe that the Córdoba meeting marked the end of Mercosur as it was conceived in 1991. By the end of the two-day meeting, Mercosur appeared to be more of a political organization than a trade facilitating mechanism. The summit addressed the growing importance of political and social integration in addition to strengthening the common market. There were two dramatic aspects to the meeting: the addition of Venezuela as a full member and the attendance of President Fidel Castro of Cuba. The addition of President Hugo Chávez spoke to the increasingly political nature and societal orientation of Mercosur. His public calls to destroy neoliberalism and fight for social justice revealed his ambitions to expand Mercosur's political scope. The noncommittal responses from the other members, however, suggested internal divisions within Mercosur itself. Nevertheless, for the first time in the history of the common market, the five full members organized a social summit, bringing together civil society leaders who met in a parallel summit to spell out the social needs and goals of the organization.

In a surprise decision, member states addressed the issue of a pending trade agreement between Cuba and Mercosur that would dictate the reduction of tariffs on a number of goods traded between the two entities. Although nominally for economic purposes, the trade agreement emphasized a growing political solidarity that could be interpreted as less than friendly to the United States.

The increasing political nature of Mercosur had been made clear during the Fourth Summit of the Americas in November 2005, held in Mar del Plata, Argentina. At that meeting, the 34 member states of the Organization of American States failed to reach consensus to move ahead with negotiations to conclude the Free Trade Area of the Americas (FTAA). Although 29 states voted to continue the dialogue, with the strong backing of the U.S. delegation led by President George W. Bush, the five dissenting votes cast by the then four full members of Mercosur and by Venezuela were sufficient to destroy the already foundering process.

Although the increasingly political nature of the common market is notable, there are other developments that threaten the future development and consolidation of Mercosur. Paraguay and Uruguay believe that they benefit the least from its current structure. And the reality is that Brazil and Argentina, with more developed and sophisticated industrial agricultural sectors, have benefited disproportionately when compared with the two smaller states.

A 2006 conflict between Argentina and Uruguay highlights the inherent conflict between the two large states and the two smaller partners. Uruguay successfully concluded negotiations to have Spanish and Finnish companies construct two paper mills along the Uruguay River, which forms a natural border between the two states. The mills, estimated at a cost of $1.6 billion, would represent the largest foreign investment in Uruguay's history. Argentina objected strenuously to the project, arguing that the mills would destroy the river's environment and threaten the fishing and tourism industries. The issue was taken to the International Court of Justice in The Hague; the tribunal's decision favored Uruguay but the government of President Nestor Kirchner in Argentina continued its opposition. As of 2007, it was thought that the principal motivation of the Kirchner government was internal politics—there were to be national elections in Argentina in 2007, and this nationalist stance plays well with the voters on the Argentine side of the river.

As of 2007, there were other pending disagreements between the two smaller states and Argentina and Brazil. There was talk in both Paraguay and Uruguay of leaving Mercosur and negotiating trade agreements directly with the United States. Under current rules, Mercosur does not allow bilateral trade agreements outside of the common market. Whether either or both countries would decide to proceed was an important pending issue for the future of the organization.

The institutionalization of Mercosur has been difficult and little had been achieved by late 2007. In this regard, structures were broad but not very deep. The heads of state made all major decisions in periodic summits. The technical staff in Montevideo was small and marginal. The reluctance to give up national sovereignty plagued the organization—it was impossible to develop dispute resolution mechanisms, for example, unless member states were willing to cede decision-making authority to supranational tribunals.

There was a growing impression that Mercosur is most valuable to its members as a political counterweight to the United States. That raises doubts about the future. The group dashed the hopes of the United States for a revival of FTAA talks in Mar del Plata. Efforts by the United States to revive the Doha Round discussions met strong resistance from the Mercosur countries, acting within the broader structure of the Group of Twenty (G20), created in 2003

in Cancún, Mexico, as a means of protesting agricultural protection in the European Union and the United States.

Like that of other regional trade movements such as the stalled FTAA, Mercosur's viability has been called into question, and the organization will need to prove it can provide benefits for all member countries to stay intact. As member countries grow disillusioned and increasingly court bilateral trade agreements, Mercosur's unity, influence, and economic potential have diminished. Thus the original goals of Mercosur set forth in the early 1990s have not been achieved, and the organization has taken a polemical turn that deemphasizes integration and gives preference to regional and hemispheric politics.

See also Andean Community; common market; customs unions; Doha Round; Free Trade Area of the Americas (FTAA); regionalism; World Trade Organization

FURTHER READING

Aladi Web site: http://www.aladi.org. Statistics and databases of trade information for Mercosur member and other Latin American countries.

Baer, Werner, Tiago Cavalcanti, and Peri Silva. 2002. "Economic Integration without Policy Coordination: The Case of Mercosur." *Emerging Markets Review* 3 (3): 269–91. Analyzes the evolution of Mercosur and how the lack of coordination of macroeconomic and exchange rate policies has hampered the realization of regional trade benefits.

Carranza, Mario E. 2003. "Can Mercosur Survive? Domestic and International Constraints on Mercosur." *Latin American Politics and Society* 45 (2): 67–103. Examines the impact of domestic politics in Argentina and Brazil, and of the relationship between the two countries, on the ability of Mercosur to weather various crises.

Jelin, Elizabeth. 2001. "Cultural Movements and Social Actors in the New Regional Scenarios: The Case of Mercosur." *International Political Science Review* 22 (1): 85–98. Studies how Mercosur's top-down regional integration policies affect societal and cultural actors, movements, and transformations.

Malamud, Andrés. 2005. "Mercosur Turns 15: Between Rising Rhetoric and Declining Achievement." *Cambridge*

Review of International Affairs 18 (3): 421–36. Provides a retrospective on Mercosur's record of achievements and weaknesses and critically considers prospects for strengthening and enlarging the organization.

Mercosur Web site: http://www.mercosur.int/. Comprehensive archive of official treaties, declarations, and publications of Mercosur, in addition to information about the institutional structure.

RIORDAN ROETT

■ mergers and acquisitions

A merger is the amalgamation of two or more firms into a single firm. This is typically accomplished when one firm acquires the assets of the other firm(s). Such transactions are referred to as mergers and acquisitions (M&As). There are three types: *horizontal* mergers involving firms in the same industry, *vertical* mergers between firms at different stages of the production chain, and *conglomerate* mergers between firms in unrelated industries.

M&As may not involve a complete takeover of another firm's assets. Rather, an investor may acquire a majority or even only a minority stake. This raises the question of what the appropriate ownership structure of the newly created entity should be. Partial ownership entails the sharing of control rights and implies different levels of commitment by the parties involved. There is no clear dividing line between M&As and other forms of organization that allow firms to share assets and coordinate their interests, such as joint ventures.

It is interesting to examine M&As from an international perspective for at least three reasons. First, cross-border M&As have fueled the growth in international production for more than a decade. Since the 1990s, most foreign direct investment (FDI) has been carried out through the acquisition of foreign firms' assets rather than the creation of new firms (the latter also known as greenfield investment). Second, there is evidence that economic integration affects M&A activity by increasing the incentives to undertake cross-border M&As and by forcing industries to restructure. This restructuring is often accomplished through M&As. Third, both cross-border mergers and mergers between domestic firms engaged in international trade pose challenges for competition policy. Such mergers affect several countries and hence are subject to review by different national competition authorities. These authorities may come to conflicting conclusions, especially if some countries bear more of the costs while others receive more of the benefits of the merger. A prominent example of such conflicts is the merger between two American companies, General Electric and Honeywell, which was approved by U.S. authorities but was ultimately blocked by the European Commission.

Cross-border M&As account for a significant and growing share of total M&A activity. They make up around 25 percent of worldwide M&As. Between 1996 and 2005, the annual average value of cross-border M&As worldwide was U.S. $533 billion, or about 70 percent of annual world FDI flows (UNCTAD 2006). Cross-border M&As, like all M&A activity, tend to occur in waves. In 2000, for example, cross-border M&As peaked at $1.14 trillion. Most cross-border M&As involve developed-country firms. FDI in developing countries is still dominated by greenfield investment. Horizontal mergers account for roughly 70 percent of all cross-border mergers, vertical mergers for around 10 percent. Mergers are much more common in the service sector than in manufacturing (UNCTAD 2000).

Horizontal mergers have attracted the most attention both from scholars and from governmental authorities concerned with competition. The study of these mergers typically involves an analysis of the following two aspects. First, horizontal mergers tend to be anticompetitive. They raise industry concentration and therefore potentially lead to higher prices for consumers or, in the case of intermediate goods, for downstream industries. Another consequence of increased industry concentration is that competitors may benefit even more from the merger than the merging firms themselves. Specifically, as prices rise following the merger, competitors will be tempted to increase their output, thus gaining market share at the expense of the merging firms.

Second, a merger may allow firms to realize synergies and thus become more efficient. Firms will merge provided that these synergies are sufficiently big to offset the competitive disadvantage outlined in the previous paragraph. If the efficiency gains from the merger are large, prices for consumers may even fall as a result of the merger. But even if they do not, a competition authority may approve a horizontal merger provided that the efficiency gains in production are larger than the losses suffered by consumers due to higher prices. How competition authorities should weigh consumer well-being and economic efficiency in their decisions is an issue that has generated some debate.

The preceding analysis did not distinguish between domestic and cross-border M&As, simply because it applies to both. Still, it is important to point out some of the distinguishing features of cross-border mergers. The main motive for horizontal cross-border M&As is to establish a market presence abroad. They are therefore an alternative to greenfield FDI or exporting. Compared with these alternative choices, cross-border M&As tend to raise industry concentration, thereby potentially hurting consumers and benefiting local competitors. They also offer additional efficiency advantages, however. These include the avoidance of set up costs and of the fixed costs of operating a production facility arising in the case of greenfield FDI, and the avoidance of transportation costs and trade barriers associated with exporting.

Economic integration affects M&A activity in at least two ways. First, it puts pressure on firms to restructure. Specifically, less efficient firms in an industry are forced by import competition to contract or close, whereas improved access to export markets offers more efficient firms an opportunity to expand. An empirically important way in which this restructuring is accomplished is through M&As, whereby efficient firms acquire the assets they need to expand from less efficient firms (Breinlich 2006). Second, trade liberalization raises the incentive to undertake cross-border mergers. A simple example illustrates the point. Suppose there are two countries, A and B, each with one firm. When trade barriers are high, there is no incentive for the firms to merge, since each already has a monopoly in its market. As trade barriers fall, competition between the firms increases, giving them an incentive to merge in order to reduce competition.

Except in the European Union, where large cross-border mergers and mergers involving domestic firms with a significant market share in other EU member countries are reviewed by the European Commission, competition policy generally remains the responsibility of national authorities. This may cause problems exactly for the reasons that have led the EU to implement a unionwide competition policy. A simple example helps illustrate them. Consider an industry in which two locally owned firms in country A export all their output to country B, and suppose there are no local competitors in B. A horizontal merger between the two firms allows them to monopolize the market in B. This hurts consumers in B, but raises profits for the firms in A. Synergies involving the elimination of fixed production costs have no effect on prices and hence only boost profits. Provided that competition authorities are guided by considerations of national social welfare, the competition authority in A would approve the merger and the one in B would prohibit it. This raises the possibility that a merger would be blocked even if the efficiency gains accruing to the firms in A outweigh the losses suffered by consumers in B so that a merger would raise the overall welfare of the two countries.

The case of the GE/Honeywell merger mentioned earlier is much more complicated than the case illustrated by this simple example. In particular, it has not only a horizontal dimension (both companies produce jet engines for regional aircraft), but also a significant vertical dimension. Specifically, Honeywell is a leading supplier of an intermediate good, namely engine starters, to GE and its two main competitors in the market for large jet engines. A merger between GE and Honeywell may thus have allowed them to cut off supplies to these two competitors, thereby monopolizing the engine market.

Vertical mergers are best viewed as an alternative to vertical contractual arrangements—also known as vertical restraints—between firms and their suppliers and/or distributors. An analysis of vertical mergers—as in the case of horizontal mergers—involves weighing efficiency-enhancing against competition-reducing effects.

See also corporate governance; foreign direct investment (FDI); joint ventures

FURTHER READING

Breinlich, Holger. 2006. "Trade Liberalization and Industrial Restructuring through Mergers and Acquisitions." CEP Discussion Paper No. 0717. London: Center for Economic Performance. Available at http://cep.lse.ac.uk/pubs/download/dp0717.pdf. Shows that the Canada–United States Free Trade Agreement led to a significant increase in M&A activity, which transferred substantial resources from less productive to more productive firms.

Horn, Henrik, and Lars Persson. 2001. "The Equilibrium Ownership of an International Oligopoly." *Journal of International Economics* 53 (2): 307–33. Examines how the ownership pattern depends on features of trade and production costs. Shows that private and social incentives for M&A are aligned for strong synergies, but may differ when the synergies are weak.

Motta, Massimo. 2004. *Competition Policy*. Cambridge: Cambridge University Press. Through case studies compares merger policy in the United States and the European Union.

Neven, Damien J., and Lars-Hendrik Röller, eds. 2005. Special Issue on Merger Control in International Markets. *International Journal of Industrial Organization* 23 (9–10): 665–848. A collection of articles on merger control.

Raff, Horst, Michael Ryan, and Frank Stähler. 2006. "Firm Productivity and the Foreign-Market Entry Decision." Kiel Economics Working Paper 2008-02. Available at http://www.wiso.uni-kiel.de/Ordnung+Wettbewerbspolitik/ewp/EWP-2008-02.pdf. Empirical analysis of different investment options (greenfield FDI, M&A, joint ventures) using Japanese firm-level data.

United Nations Conference on Trade and Development (UNCTAD). Various years. *World Investment Report.* New York: United Nations. Annual overview of trends in FDI, including cross-border M&As. Detailed report on cross-border M&As in 2000.

HORST RAFF

■ **migration, international**

International migration involves the movement of people, on either a temporary or permanent basis, among the countries of the world economy. Throughout human history these changes of residence have helped to alleviate human suffering, enhance technological progress, and promote cultural exchange. As of 2006 approximately 200 million people, or 3 percent of the world's population, lived outside their country of birth. Although by historical standards this percentage is low, international migration has doubled since 1980. Migration continues to be a key dimension of globalization, albeit one that has complex determinants and outcomes.

As a field of inquiry, international migration has received less attention from social scientists than many other aspects of the world economy. Nonetheless, it is one with a relatively long intellectual history that originally goes back to Ravenstein (1889), with modern contributions going back to Lee (1966). Theoretical and empirical research into international migration underwent a significant renaissance beginning in the 1990s, and multilateral financial institutions gave increased amounts of attention to the subject (e.g., World Bank 2006). A grounded understanding of migration requires an investigation of its recent history, types of migration, the migration decision itself, impacts of migration on both source and destination countries, and current policy debates.

Recent History The modern era of globalization began in the late 19th century. A central component of this was the "Age of Mass Migration" described by Hatton and Williamson (1998). Between 1850 and 1914, approximately 55 million Europeans migrated, most of them unskilled males who settled in the United States. As Manning (2005) emphasizes, however, the Age of Mass Migration was not just European in nature, with 50 million Chinese and 30 million Indians also migrating (not all voluntarily), primarily to serve as unskilled laborers in British colonies in Africa and the Pacific.

The transatlantic mass migration increased the New World labor force by a third and reduced that of the European economies by an eighth. As a result, the wage gap between North America and the leading European countries narrowed, and flows of migrations from traditional sources slowed. Yet as Western Europe was reaching the end of this migration cycle, other less-developed countries in Eastern Europe were just getting started, giving rise to new sources of migration. The new migration proved to be politically controversial, however, and in 1917 the United States introduced a literacy test for new migrants. This, as well as the outbreak of World War I and its accompanying restrictions on movements of people, effectively brought an end to this era of migration.

Starting in 1917 and continuing throughout the 1920s, isolationist policies characterized much of the Western world. The onset of the Great Depression and the outbreak of World War II only reinforced this trend. International migration declined dramatically. In the aftermath of World War II, however, resurgent nationalism and the spread of communism sent millions of refugees across the European continent. In Western Europe, once a major source of migrants, rapid economic growth in the late 1940s and 1950s led to a shortage of low-wage labor. Initially, the demand was met by migrants from southern European countries, but such sources quickly proved insufficient. By the 1960s, countries across Western Europe were admitting millions of guest workers from Turkey and North Africa. Although the 1973 oil crisis and the ensuing high unemployment brought an abrupt end to these programs, the oil-exporting countries in the Middle East later replicated and expanded the guest-worker model, thereby ensuring that flows of low-skilled migrants remained a significant component of world migration.

In the mid-1960s, Australia, Canada, and the United States overhauled their immigration policies, allowing for a much greater volume of flows and opening the door to migration from countries in Asia, Africa, and Latin America. Together with the precipitous decline in the cost of intercontinental transportation and communication, these reforms have led to steady growth in both the volume and diversity of migrant flows. Yet, as international migration became subject to expanded legal provisions, increasing numbers of migrants opted to forgo legalities altogether. Consequently, undocumented migrants posed increasing challenges for destination countries.

Since the late 1980s, migration flows have continued to grow rapidly. Although Western Europe is an increasingly popular destination for migrants, the United States accepts more immigrants than any other country in the world. The Gulf countries of the Middle East have also emerged as a major destination for migrants, particularly for low-skilled workers from South and Southeast Asia. As of 2006, Mexico and the Philippines were significant sources of low-skilled labor, the latter having 10 percent of its population in foreign countries. China and India predominate as sources of high-skilled migrants.

Types of Migration Migrants leave their home countries and are admitted into destination countries for a wide variety of reasons, and distinct administrative channels have evolved to facilitate these flows. Following are some of the major channels, both legal and unregulated, that define the current international migration system.

Permanent high-skilled migration. Over recent decades, Australia, New Zealand, Canada, and the United States have selectively granted permanent residence to a limited number of high-skilled foreigners who are likely to offer these countries positive economic benefits. Whereas Australia, Canada, and New Zealand operate a "points" system to rate the desirability of potential immigrants, the United States primarily relies on nominations of potential immigrants by local companies that wish to hire them. Among source countries, India and China lead the way, although some high-income countries such as South Korea and the United Kingdom also supply significant numbers of this kind of migrants. Several Western European countries have recently adopted similar programs to citizenship in order to entice high-skilled migrants.

Temporary high-skilled migration. In many developed countries, programs that grant permanent residence to foreigners who do not have ties to the destination country can be politically controversial. In such cases, governments may seek to fill occupational shortages through the recruitment of high-skilled migrants on a temporary basis. Historically, these flows have been concentrated in education and health-related services. During the 1990s, however, booms in information and communications technology (ICT) led to a shortage of related skills in many high-income countries, resulting in a jump in flows of technology professionals, mostly from India. In the early years of the 21st century, even nontraditional immigration destination countries, such as China and the Czech Republic, began to grant temporary work visas to high-skilled foreigners.

Temporary low-skilled migration. Despite the fast growth of temporary high-skilled migration, these flows are dwarfed by temporary low-skilled migration, in which countries admit migrant workers to provide low-cost services on a strictly temporary basis. Countries typically implement these programs when rapid economic growth has improved the wages and work conditions of the local workforce and left them correspondingly unwilling to work at low-wage jobs. One of the best-known programs of this kind was the West German *Gastarbeiter* program of the 1960s and 1970s in which West Germany recruited large numbers of Turkish and North African guest workers. These programs were rolled back in the low-growth, high-inflation period of the 1970s, but low-skilled migration programs have since grown significantly in the Middle East. In 2006, approximately 10 million temporary low-skilled migrants were employed in the Saudi Arabia, Kuwait, and the UAE. India and Pakistan are major sources of manual laborers and construction workers, with domestics, nurses, and other service workers coming primarily from Sri Lanka, the Philippines, and Thailand. The

rights of temporary low-skilled migrants, however, are often not well defined or protected.

Family migration. Family migration is among the largest official channels of migration and represents a disproportionate share of flows from low- and middle-income countries to high-income countries. This mode of migration enables foreign spouses of citizens, children born abroad, and even foreign-born parents and siblings of citizens to gain permanent residency in the country of the respective relative. Although almost all countries in the world permit some form of family migration, countries differ significantly in their definitions of which types of relatives are eligible to migrate, and which are not. Over recent years, many high-income countries have tightened restrictions on family migration in order to limit the volume of politically controversial inflows of migrants from low-income countries.

Coethnic and national priority migration. A number of programs provide permanent residency to foreigners on the basis of their ethnic background, religious affiliation, or national origin. In many European countries, coethnic migration functions through the liberal application of the *jus sanguinis* citizenship tradition, whereby citizenship rights can be inherited through long lines of ancestry. Israel's Law of Return is one of the most controversial instruments of coethnic and national priority migration as it provides a path to permanent residency to all those who practice Judaism, irrespective of any other criteria. The United States operates dedicated paths to permanent residency for migrants from Cuba and a number of other countries, while also operating a "diversity visa" lottery of the United States, purportedly to diversify immigration flows, but which in fact was originally proposed by lawmakers as a means to provide a new channel for Irish migration to the United States.

Asylum seekers. The 1951 Geneva Convention protects persons with a "well founded fear of persecution [by state agents] for reasons of race, religion, nationality, membership of a particular social group, or political opinion" from return to their country of origin. Asylum seekers commonly invoke the 1951 convention in seeking permission to remain permanently in a destination country. In order to assess asylum claims, major recipient countries have established elaborate administrative legal procedures, including access to counsel and the right to appeal initial decisions. As a result, individual claims can sometimes take years to resolve. In some destination countries, asylum seekers qualify for social services. In others, they are granted only the right to work. In yet others, they remain in detention until a final decision on their application is reached.

Refugees. Groups of people who have fled to neighboring countries due to war, famine, environmental collapse, or political strife are considered refugees. Refugees are often hosted in makeshift camps set up by international humanitarian agencies along the border of the affected country with the expectation that they will return to their country of origin at the conclusion of the disturbance. Where this is not possible, the United Nations High Commissioner for Refugees (UNHCR) might seek to resettle refugees in a third country or help them to settle in the country of refuge.

Undocumented migration. Reliable data on the number of people involved in undocumented migration are limited and estimates vary widely. There is evidence, however, that flows increased markedly in the 1990s and the early years of the 21st century, particularly to Europe, where the implementation of the free movement of labor within the European Union has increased the potential rewards for illegal migrants who reach a member country. Major flows also exist between Mexico and the United States and among countries in West Africa, Southern Africa, and Southeast Asia. Flows of undocumented migrants include those who move voluntarily and those who are trafficked against their will.

Visa-free migration. Visa-free migration exists (with some exceptions) within the European Union, as well as between New Zealand and Australia. This channel grants citizens the right to work for an unlimited time in any of the countries that are party to the agreement.

The Migration Decision The economic, social, and psychological consequences of migration to the individual are profound, and it can be very difficult for anyone to predict with any certainty whether migration will actually improve their life. The inherent unpredictability of migration tends to discourage people from leaving their home countries, even when doing so would increase their expected income. Those who do choose to migrate are often unusual in their willingness to tolerate risk. The predominance of young males in migration flows reflects this reality.

Migration is an expensive endeavor in terms of both the direct costs involved and the opportunity costs of leaving a livelihood in the home country. These costs prevent a large number of people from migrating even if they wish to do so. This, in conjunction with the unwillingness of those earning high incomes to migrate, gives rise to the so-called migration hump. That is, those with the highest inclination to migrate come from middle-income countries, where wages are high enough to provide the base level of wealth necessary to finance migration, but also low enough to generate significant financial incentives for migrating to high-income countries. Thus as incomes in middle-income countries increase, migration rates tend to decline. On the other hand, when incomes rise in low-income countries, migration rates tend to increase. Such was the case during the Age of Mass Migration, with significant increases in emigration rates following industrial revolutions by four or more decades.

Another important factor that can either spur or restrict migration is the presence of familial or trusted contacts in the destination country. If a large number of people from their community have migrated, potential migrants have easy access to information on the experiences of other migrants and relatively high confidence that their migration experience will conform to what they are told. Immigrant communities can also provide essential services to new arrivals, such as accommodation and employment, thereby lowering the cost and risk of resettlement.

In some cases, neither financial resources nor information networks in destination countries allow migrants to fully assess their prospects. Some high-skilled migrants, for example, fail to secure a job that utilizes their skills. This causes what analysts refer to as brain waste.

Impacts on Source Countries High-skilled migrants are commonly trained at substantial costs to the taxpayers of source countries through public education systems. Their departure thus has profound effects in the form of what is known as *brain drain*. Source countries can also lose tax revenues that migrants would have generated. More important, many of the skills sent from less-developed to more-developed countries are already scarce in source countries. In the case of medical services, for which more-developed countries have a strong desire and less-developed countries an urgent need, brain drain can potentially imperil the quality of medical care. In many southern African countries, high emigration rates for health care professionals have existed alongside unprecedented medical crises brought on by the HIV/AIDS pandemic. In Malawi, for example, it is estimated that approximately half of the country's nursing staff has been lost to migration. Meanwhile, the rate at which Malawian women die during pregnancy and childbirth doubled during the 1990s to one of the highest levels in the world.

The emigration of skilled workers does not always create problems for source countries. In some cases, emigration alerts outside investors to a large or relatively underused skill base of the source country. The success of skilled Indian migrants in the United States, for instance, possibly helped to spur the large inflow of ICT-related foreign direct investment (FDI) to India seen over recent years. Thus, when the conditions are right, skilled migrants are able to generate networks of investment, trade, and technology transfer that increase the productivity and demand for skills in the home country while extending the global technology frontier and lowering the cost of products used by billions of people worldwide.

Another potentially compensating benefit of the brain drain is that it tends to increase the demand for skills in the source country by raising the rate of return to education. Some researchers have suggested that, even accounting for the emigration of skilled individuals, the increase in demand for education gener-

ated by the brain drain may actually *increase* the number of skilled workers in the population. This is known as a brain gain. Although brain gain outcomes are possible, they depend on large responses in the supply of education and training. They are not, therefore, a *general* outcome of high-skilled migration.

The most easily quantifiable benefit of emigration to source countries is the flow of money, or *remittances*, sent by migrant workers to their home countries. Recent estimates suggest that the total remittance flow to developing countries exceeds U.S. $200 billion. In a number of countries, remittance inflows are larger than inflows of FDI and can compose up to 10 percent of national incomes. Such flows can make a significant difference for families living in poverty in source countries, which is a common reason for communities to allow and sometimes even encourage their family members to seek work abroad.

Under the auspices of the World Trade Organization (WTO), the liberalization of services trade has occurred in a number of sectors, such as finance and telecommunications, of interest to developed countries. The WTO's General Agreement on Trade in Services recognizes the *temporary movement of natural persons* as a way to export certain labor-intensive services such as housekeeping and construction. Given the natural comparative advantage of developing countries in such labor-intensive services, this channel could be of great importance to their trade and development prospects. The WTO protocol on the temporary movement of natural persons, however, is largely limited to the exchange of corporate personnel and is not designed to enhance the delivery of labor-intensive services.

Impacts on Destination Countries The world's most productive economies often depend on and benefit greatly from the presence of migrant workers. Currently, the world's richest countries continue to import labor at high rates. For example, in Southeast Asia's richest country, Singapore, migrants make up around one-quarter of the workforce. In Europe, those countries with the highest number of migrant workers, such as Switzerland and Luxembourg, are also the wealthiest. In Dubai, currently among the world's fastest expanding areas of economic activity, as of 2006 there were nine times as many migrant workers as resident nationals.

Across all regions of the world, the correlation between levels of economic growth and immigration is clear, not only because migrants wish to move to where they can earn the highest wages, but also because immigration is often much less politically controversial when an economy is growing quickly and unemployment is low, thereby easing the liberalization of migration restrictions.

Critics of immigration are usually concerned with its impact on social fabric, national culture, environment, social welfare programs, or the wages of low-skilled workers. Correspondingly, advocates of increased immigration have turned their attention to the potential role further inflows could play in ensuring the sustainability of pension systems in the face of aging populations.

A common claim against migration is that migrants, particularly those who are low-skilled or undocumented, consume far more in public services than they contribute in tax revenue to destination countries. However, many studies paint a different picture. Research in Europe, for instance, indicates that immigrants (even undocumented immigrants) contribute more in taxes and pension funds than they consume in benefits or other public services. Interestingly, some commentators have argued that increased migration will actually be critical to the survival of social security systems in high-income countries over the coming decades. For instance, as the proportion of retirees in the population increases, many social security systems will need to find sources of tax revenues in order to fund pension payouts. Migrants are one potential source through which tax revenues might be increased.

The contention that migrants "take the jobs" or reduce the wages of native workers is probably the most common argument advanced against migration. Economic theory suggests that increasing the size of the labor force will lower the wage level, all other things being equal. Yet when a region receives an influx of immigrant labor, native workers may choose to move to other regions, thereby masking any changes in the aggregate wage. Firms may also decide to move into a region experiencing such an influx, causing local wages to increase. Accordingly, it has been very difficult for studies to accurately assess the impact of migration on unemployment or wage levels and fierce academic debates continue to rage on the topic.

Unlike statistically testable hypotheses regarding the effect of migration on public finances or low-skill wages, claims that immigrants alter culture or threaten national cohesion are difficult to assess. Fears that migrants threaten the cultural or social order remain among the most instrumental sources of resistance to migrant inflows. Yet the historical record shows that many of the perceived cultural idiosyncrasies of migrants fail to outlive the first generation, while others, such as music, cuisine, and sport, are co-opted by the native culture due to their popularity among natives.

Policy Priorities Migration has always been and will continue to be a central feature of the world economy. It does, however, involve a number of important policy issues that have not yet been resolved: increased multilateral coordination of migration flows, prevention of human rights abuses, care of refugee populations, facilitation of the temporary movement of natural persons in services trade, the harnessing of remittance flows for poverty-reducing investments, management of brain drain, and reduction of brain waste. These priorities compose a large and important policy agenda for better harnessing this important socioeconomic process for development purposes in the modern world economy.

See also brain drain; brain gain; brain waste; European Union; General Agreement on Trade in Services (GATS); information and communications technology; migration governance; remittances; temporary movement of natural persons

FURTHER READING

Adams, Richard H. Jr., and John Page. 2005. "Do International Migration and Remittances Reduce Poverty in Developing Countries?" *World Development*

33 (10): 1645–69. An empirical examination of the influence of migration and remittances on poverty levels in a relatively large sample of developing countries.

Borjas, George J. 1994. "The Economics of Immigration." *Journal of Economic Literature* 32 (4): 1667–1717. An often-cited, early review of the research on international migration.

Chiquiar, Daniel, and Gordon H. Hanson. 2005. "International Migration, Self-Selection, and the Distribution of Wages: Evidence from Mexico and the United States." *Journal of Political Economy* 113 (2): 239–81. An empirical examination of the role of skill in international migration decisions.

Global Commission on International Migration. 2005. *Migration in an Interconnected World: New Directions for Action.* Geneva. A thorough overview of international migration trends and policies that summarizes the work of a commission of notable international policymakers.

Hatton, Timothy J., and Jeffrey G. Williamson. 1998. *The Age of Mass Migration: Causes and Economic Impact.* Oxford: Oxford University Press. A central, historical reference on the history of international migration.

Lee, Everett S. 1966. "A Theory of Migration." *Demography* 3 (1): 47–57. An early theoretical analysis that elucidates some basic features of migration.

Manning, Patrick. 2005. *Migration in World History.* London: Routledge. A comprehensive, historical account of migration going back to the movements of the earliest humans.

Mora, Jorge, and J. Edward Taylor. 2006. "Determinants of Migration, Destination, and Sector Choice: Disentangling Individual, Household, and Community Effects." In *International Migration, Remittances and the Brain Drain*, edited by Çaglar Özden and Maurice Schiff. Washington, DC: World Bank and Palgrave Macmillan, 21–51. An important empirical exploration of the variables that help to explain the migration decision.

Nyberg-Sorensen, Ninna, Nicholas Van Hear, and Poul Enberg-Pedersen. 2002. *The Migration-Development Nexus: Evidence and Policy Options.* Geneva: International Organization for Migration. A thorough review of the role of migration in development with a helpful set of references for researchers.

Ottaviano, Gianmarco I. P., and Giovanni Peri. 2005. "Rethinking the Gains from Immigration: Theory and Evidence from the U.S." NBER Working Paper 11162. Cambridge, MA: National Bureau of Economic Research. A sophisticated empirical examination of the way that immigrant and native-born workers substitute for one another in U.S. labor markets.

Ravenstein, Ernest George. 1889. "The Laws of Migration." *Journal of the Royal Statistical Society* 52 (2): 241–305. One of the earliest systematic inquiries into the phenomenon of migration.

World Bank. 2006. *Global Economic Prospects 2006: Economic Implications of Remittances and Migration.* Washington, DC. An important look at migration from a development perspective that provides a number of policy recommendations.

ANDREW L. BEATH, IAN GOLDIN, AND KENNETH A. REINERT

■ migration governance

People migrate from one nation state to another, and *governance of international migration* refers to the national and international laws and norms regulating such movements. Even though international migration by definition involves two nation states, and the people moving between them, most migration occurs under the national laws of receiving states, although these national laws may be shaped by international norms.

The best example of international governance of migration applies to refugees, about 5 percent of the world's 200 million migrants. The 1951 Geneva Convention relating to the Status of Refugees and its 1967 Protocol define a refugee as a person who, "owing to well-founded fear of being persecuted for reasons of race, religion, nationality, membership of a particular social group or political opinion, is outside the country of his nationality and is unable or, owing to such fear, is unwilling to avail himself of the protection of that country." The 138 signatories to the Convention and Protocol pledge not to return or "refoul" persons who satisfy this definition to their countries of origin.

Geneva Convention countries sometimes resettle persons recognized by the UN High Commissioner for Refugees (UNHCR), as when the United States resettled Vietnamese who fled to Thailand and other Southeast Asian countries in the late 1970s. Other countries that do not resettle refugees often participate in burden sharing, providing funds to support refugees who have taken refuge in poor countries, such as Afghanis in Pakistan, and supporting repatriation when their countries of origin become safe.

Countries also establish systems to screen foreigners who arrive and apply for asylum, with those who need protection being allowed to stay. Countries differ in how they implement the Geneva refugee convention, with traditional immigration receiving countries such as the United States and Canada resettling more refugees, while European countries such as Britain and France deal with asylum seekers. National laws determine exactly what assistance refugees and asylum applicants receive. European countries often provide housing and other assistance to both refugees and applicants for asylum, while the United States relies on private organizations such as churches to integrate refugees and care for asylum applicants.

Governance and Migration The 1995 report of the Commission on Global Governance defined governance as "the sum of the many ways individuals and institutions, public and private, manage their common affairs . . . a continuing process through which conflicting or diverse interests may be accommodated and cooperative action taken." Governance of international issues is agreed to by nation-states that see advantages in creating rules and norms, and institutions to ensure that they are followed. For example, the World Trade Organization (WTO) establishes rules for international trade in goods and services, establishing mechanisms to resolve trade disputes, and the International Labor Organization (ILO) promotes policies that protect workers. Nation-states may delegate a part of their national sovereignty to international institutions such as the WTO and ILO, agreeing to incorporate the agreements or conventions they establish into national laws governing trade and worker rights.

International organizations such as WTO and ILO set rules for the behavior of nation-states, while organizations such as the International Organization for Migration (IOM) provide services to states. IOM began as an intergovernmental organization that moved refugees and displaced persons to new homes at the end of World War II. It has evolved into an organization of 118 countries that aims to improve migration management by providing services as well as advice to governments. IOM acts as secretary for a variety of ad hoc efforts to improve migration management, including the Berne Initiative that led to the International Agenda for Migration Management, a "non-binding reference system and policy framework."

The stock of international migrants doubled between 1985 and 2005 to almost 200 million; migrants are persons outside their country of citizenship a year or more, regardless of their legal status and reason for being abroad. International migration is likely to continue increasing because of demographic and economic inequalities among countries as well as revolutions in communication and transportation that make it easier to learn about opportunities abroad and travel over national borders to take advantage of them. Winning international agreement on a system to manage migration is difficult, however, because sovereignty includes the right to determine who enters and stays in a country. With no consensus on whether migration is good or bad for sending and receiving countries, there is no legal and institutional framework for dealing with migration cooperatively on a global scale except for UNHCR and the protection of refugees.

Developing a global policy framework is difficult because policy contradictions at the national level are mirrored at the international level. This occurs in other areas with global frameworks, as when national governments promote freer trade at the WTO but protect their farmers with subsidies and import barriers, making it hard for a WTO that operates by achieving consensus among its nation-state members to lower farm trade barriers. Similarly, if industrial countries want to encourage the best and brightest from developing countries to work and settle, they may retard economic development and accelerate unwanted migration of less-skilled workers, so that global discussions of such migration can quickly devolve into arguments over compensation for the brain drain.

Top Down, Bottom Up Most international organizations operate in a top-down fashion, seeking to establish norms that protect migrants in nation-states that ratify conventions and protocols approved by the organization's members. International human rights conventions give individuals the right to leave their country, but there is no comparable right to enter or stay in another country. The ILO approved major conventions in 1949 and 1975 to protect migrant workers, and the United Nations General Assembly approved a more expansive migrant convention in 1990. Finally, the UN approved two protocols in 1998 aimed at curbing smuggling and trafficking in persons over national borders.

The ILO's Convention 97 (1949) established the fundamental principle of equality of treatment for migrant workers, meaning that migrants should be treated as other workers in the countries in which they work. The ILO called for migrant workers to move across national borders under the terms of bilateral agreements and to have labor rights ranging from the right to organize unions to the right to work-related benefits. ILO Convention 143 (1975) emphasized the steps governments should take to minimize illegal migration and to promote the integration of settled migrants.

Both of these controversial provisions, ILO migrant conventions have fewer-than-average ratifications, 42 for Convention 97 and 18 for Convention 143 as of 2005. The reluctance of countries to ratify ILO migrant conventions is often attributed to provisions in the conventions that conflict with national legislation. For example, migrant workers in the United States have the same union rights as U.S. workers, but if unauthorized migrants are unlawfully fired because of their union activities, they are not entitled to pay for the time they did not work. The U.S. Supreme Court held in Hoffman Plastics (2002) that requiring back pay for unauthorized migrants would "encourage the successful evasion of apprehension by immigration authorities, condone prior violations of the immigration laws, and encourage future violations." In effect, the court ruled that an unauthorized worker's violation of immigration laws was more serious than an employer's violation of labor laws.

On December 18, 1990, the UN General Assembly approved the International Convention on the Protection of the Rights of All Migrant Workers and Members of Their Families. This 8-part, 93-article convention went into force in July 2003 to "contribute to the harmonization of the attitudes of States through the acceptance of basic principles concerning the treatment of migrant workers and members of their families." The UN Convention has been ratified by 35 major emigration sending countries, in part because it goes beyond the protections of ILO Conventions to cover all migrants, authorized and unauthorized.

The major employment-related protections of the UN Convention are in part III, particularly articles 25–27, which prescribe equality in wages and working conditions for authorized and unauthorized migrant and national workers, assert that migrants should be allowed to join unions, and call for migrant workers to receive benefits under social security systems to which they contribute, or to receive refunds of their social security contributions on departure. Authorized migrants should have additional rights set out in part IV, including the right to information about jobs abroad before they arrive as well as a list of "equal treatments," including freedom of movement within the host country, freedom to form unions and participate in the political life of the host country, and equal access to employment services, public housing, and educational institutions.

The United Nations has a High Commissioner for Human Rights that examines compliance with seven "core human rights treaties" that implement the Universal Declaration of Human Rights (1948). These include the International Convention on the Elimination of All Forms of Racial Discrimination (1965); the International Covenant on Civil and Political Rights (1966); the International Covenant on Economic, Social, and Cultural Rights (1966);

the Convention on the Elimination of all Forms of Discrimination against Women (1979); the Convention against Torture and Other Cruel, Inhuman, or Degrading Treatment or Punishment (1984); the Convention on the Rights of the Child (1989); and the International Convention on the Protection of the Rights of All Migrant Workers and Members of Their Families (1990).

Other international instruments and declarations also call for equal treatment for migrants. The Vienna Declaration and Programme of Action on Human Rights (1993) and the Cairo Programme of Action of the International Conference on Population and Development (1994) affirmed the importance of promoting and protecting the human rights of migrant workers and their families, and the Beijing Platform of Action of the Fourth World Conference on Women (1995) paid special attention to the rights of women migrants and urged that migrants be protected from violence and exploitation. The World Conference on Racism, Racial Discrimination, Xenophobia, and Related Intolerance in 2001 issued the Durban Declaration and Program of Action, calling on countries to allow migrants to unite their families and to make active efforts to reduce discrimination against migrant workers. The UN General Assembly in 2000 adopted the Convention against Transnational Organized Crime, which has two additional protocols: the Protocol to Prevent, Suppress, and Punish Trafficking in Persons, especially Women and Children, and the Protocol against the Smuggling of Migrants by Land, Sea, and Air.

The UN in 2006 held a high-level dialogue on migration and development, endorsing a new "moving forum" to discuss best practices to maximize the development impacts of migration, remittances, and migrants' returning or staying abroad but forging new trade and investment links to their countries of origin. The forum is an alternative to proposals for a new "World Migration Organization" analogue to the WTO, advocated by some as a way to improve the governance of international migration.

Most migration is governed unilaterally by receiving countries, which decide whether they are destinations for immigrants, guest workers, and other types of foreigners and establish rules governing entries and stays. Since most migration occurs between neighboring countries, however, there are many bilateral and regional agreements dealing with migration. The world's largest bilateral migration flow involves an average 200,000 Mexican immigrants, millions of nonimmigrant visitors and guest workers, and the settlement of perhaps 400,000 unauthorized Mexicans each year in the United States. There are regular consultations between Mexican and U.S. immigration officials, and former Mexican president Vicente Fox (2000–2006) made improving the status of Mexicans in the United States his top foreign policy priority.

The Regional Migration Conference, or the Puebla Process, an initiative launched by the Mexican government in the city of Puebla in 1996 in response to voter approval of Proposition 187 in California in 1994, includes 11 countries that meet at least once a year to discuss migration issues: Canada, the United States, Mexico, and Central American countries plus the Dominican Republic. The discussions cover changes in national migration policies, the link between migration and development, migrant trafficking, cooperation for the return of extraregional migrants, and the human rights of migrants.

Puebla Process consultations are credited with paving the way for the United States to legalize the status of many Central Americans who fled to the United States during civil wars in the 1980s, and to grant temporary protected status to Central Americans in the United States when Hurricane Mitch carved a path of destruction in 1998 and after El Salvador had severe earthquakes in 2001, and with encouraging cooperation to improve safety at the Mexican-U.S. and Mexican-Guatemalan borders. There are many other regional migration forums, including those between the European Union and North African countries, among African countries, and among the Andean countries of South America. These forums discuss economic issues such as remittances and development as well as migration management issues such as traffickers and criminals (International Organization for Migration 2005b).

Whither Migration Governance About two-thirds of the world's migrants are in the high-income countries that have one-sixth of the world's people but five-sixths of the world's economic output. Even though there are almost as many migrant workers from developing countries in other developing countries (about 30 million in 2005) as there are developing country migrants in industrial countries (31 million), most unresolved governance issues involve developing and industrial countries. For example, one major issue is conditionality, or whether industrial countries that provide aid or open doors for guest workers can require sending countries to cooperate to accept the return of apprehended nationals.

Many observers believe that bringing governments together to talk about migration is the first step toward improved governance. Major concrete outcomes of regional organizations aimed at improving migration governance include making it more difficult for unauthorized foreigners to apply for asylum in more than one country. Both the United States and Europe have persuaded neighboring southern countries to prevent the transit of migrants headed for their borders (pushing the borders out), sometimes with financial assistance, as when the United States helps Mexico to prevent the transit of third-country nationals headed for the United States.

Most migration occurs within regions, and regional organizations that discuss migration issues can be more informal and flexible than global organizations that fix rules and enforcement mechanisms. Most regional organizations include sending and receiving countries but do not develop binding rules. It is generally far easier to achieve consensus in a closed-door meeting on regional migration issues than to negotiate global rules in forums in which national interests may vary widely.

The role of migration governance in the modern world economy is to establish rules governing the movement of workers over borders for temporary periods of employment. The fundamental principle in international conventions protecting migrants is equality, treating migrant workers as local workers. The gap between this equality goal and migrant realities is often large.

See also brain drain; brain waste; International Labor Organization; migration, international; remittances; temporary movement of natural persons

FURTHER READING

Gibney, Matthew, and Randall Hansen, eds. 2005. *Immigration and Asylum: From 1900 to the Present.* Santa Barbara, CA: ABC-CLIO. Downloadable from http://www.abc-clio.com/products/overview.aspx?productid=108786. Covers the major types of migration and migrants, with extensive references to international, regional, and national migratory movements.

International Organization for Migration. 2005a. "Costs and Benefits of International Migration." Downloadable from http://www.iom.ch/jahia/Jahia/cache/bypass/pid/8?entryId=932. A reference that provides perspectives on a major migration issue on a biennial basis.

———. 2005b. "Interstate Cooperation and Migration." Downloadable from http://www.iom.ch/jahia/Jahia/cache/bypass/pid/8?entryId=932. Includes contributions from governments and academics discussing the challenges and opportunities of cooperating to improve migration management.

Martin, Philip, Manolo Abella, and Christiane Kuptsch. 2006. *Managing Labor Migration in the Twenty-First Century.* New Haven, CT: Yale University Press. Overview of labor migration issues that includes a global survey of stocks and flows and issues in various regions and countries, closer examination of migration at the top and bottom of the job ladder, and a comparison of migration and other flows, including foreign direct investment and aid.

Martin, Philip, Susan Martin, and Patrick Weil. 2006. *Managing Migration: The Promise of Cooperation.* Lanham, MD: Lexington Books. Provides an overview of migration management issues and discussions of specific migration corridors, including Mexico-United States, Morocco-Spain, and Albania-Italy.

Migration News. Quarterly. Downloadable from http://migration.ucdavis.edu/ Comprehensive analysis of ongoing migration developments in the Americas, Europe, Asia, and other regions of the world.

PHILIP MARTIN

■ Millennium Development Goals

The Millennium Development Goals (MDGs) were introduced in the Millennium Declaration, which was signed by 189 states and adopted by the General Assembly of the United Nations during the United Nation's Millennium Summit on September 6–8, 2000. The 8 MDGs and 18 targets formulate a comprehensive set of development objectives to be attained by 2015. Additionally, the United Nations observes 48 indicators to measure progress toward the MDGs. As the MDGs have been endorsed by a large number of UN member governments and international organizations, they also provide a framework of accountability for the outcomes of international development efforts.

Specifically, the Millennium Declaration establishes the following goals and targets:

Goal 1: Eradicate extreme poverty and hunger.

Target 1: Halve, between 1990 and 2015, the proportion of people whose income is less than $1 a day.

Target 2: Halve, between 1990 and 2015, the proportion of people who suffer from hunger.

Goal 2: Achieve universal primary education.

Target 3: Ensure that by 2015, children everywhere, boys and girls alike, will be able to complete a full course of primary schooling.

Goal 3: Promote gender equality and empower women.

Target 4: Eliminate gender disparity in primary and secondary education, preferably by 2005, and at all levels of education no later than 2015.

Goal 4: Reduce child mortality.

Target 5: Reduce by two-thirds, between 1990 and 2015, the mortality rate among children younger than five.

Goal 5: Improve maternal health.

Target 6: Reduce by three-quarters, between 1990 and 2015, the maternal mortality rate.

Goal 6: Combat HIV/AIDS, malaria, and other diseases.

Target 7: Have halted by 2015 and begun to reverse the spread of HIV/AIDS.

Target 8: Have halted by 2015 and begun to reverse the incidence of malaria and other major diseases.

Goal 7: Ensure environmental sustainability.

Target 9: Integrate the principles of sustainable development into country policies and programs and reverse the loss of environmental resources.

Target 10: Halve by 2015 the proportion of people without sustainable access to safe drinking water and basic sanitation.

Target 11: Have achieved a significant improvement by 2020 in the lives of at least 100 million slum dwellers.

Goal 8: Develop a global partnership for development.

Target 12: Develop further an open, rule-based, predictable, nondiscriminatory trading and financial system (including a commitment to good governance, development, and poverty reduction, nationally and internationally).

Target 13: Address the special needs of the least-developed countries (including tariff- and quota-free access for exports of the least-developed countries; enhanced debt relief for heavily indebted poor countries and cancellation of official bilateral debt; and more generous official development assistance for countries committed to reducing poverty).

Target 14: Address the special needs of land-locked countries and small island developing states.

Target 15: Deal comprehensively with the debt problems of developing countries through national and international measures to make debt sustainable in the long term.

Target 16: In cooperation with developing countries, develop and implement strategies for decent and productive work for youth.

Target 17: In cooperation with pharmaceutical companies, provide affordable access to essential drugs in developing countries.

Target 18: In cooperation with the private sector, make available the benefits of new technologies, especially information and communication.

The United Nations measures progress toward these goals and targets using 48 Millennium Development Indicators, such as the proportion of people living on less than U.S. $1 per day, the net enrollment rate in primary education, the ratio of literate women to men (ages 15 to 24), the mortality rate of children younger than five, HIV prevalence among women ages 15 to 24, the proportion of land area covered by forest, and the level of official development assistance.

As of mid-2007, progress toward achieving the MDGs was uneven. For example, the World Bank's *Global Monitoring Report 2006* observed that the share of people in developing countries living on less than U.S.$1 per day was expected to fall to 10.2 percent by 2015, from 27.9 percent in 1990. Most of this progress was accounted for by large declines in poverty rates in Asia, while poverty rates in sub-Saharan Africa had improved only modestly since 1990, from 44.6 percent in 1990 to 44.0 percent in 2002, and under 2007 projections were expected to fall to 38 percent by 2015, far above the target of 22.3 percent.

By specifying quantitative targets for development outcomes, the MDGs also provide a framework for holding development agencies, international organizations, and recipient countries accountable for the outcomes of development assistance. For example, they lend themselves to analyses of whether aid commitments are consistent with or fall short of the goal of attaining the MDGs. (The *Global Monitoring Report 2006* suggests that, in most cases, aid commitments fall short of the goal.)

The commitment to attaining the MDGs has contributed to (or at least coincided with) an increase in official development assistance, which has risen from an average of U.S. $59 billion annually (1996–2000) to U.S. $106 billion in 2005 for Organisation for Economic Co-operation and Development (OECD) donor/creditor countries, partly reflecting an increase in debt relief and the emerging international response to HIV/AIDS. Although the 2006 data on external aid showed no further increase in external aid (excluding debt relief) for OECD countries, aid specifically to sub-Saharan Africa was expected to increase, in line with commitments made at the G8 Summit in Gleneagles in 2005, and some "new" donor countries, most notably China, had increased their aid commitments.

Have the MDGs been effective? Although it is too early (as this is written in 2007) to answer this question, recent experience provides some pointers. Overall aid has increased during the period the MDGs relate to, although these increased efforts fall short of what would be required to meet the MDGs. Nevertheless, the MDG targets provide a measure of accountability for aid outcomes, and therefore reinforce or sustain the momentum toward increased development aid.

See also aid, international; United Nations Conference on Trade and Development

FURTHER READING

Most of the information relating to the Millennium Development Goals is available online, including through Web sites that provide regular data updates. The most important ones are the United Nations Millennium Assembly Web site (http://www.un.org/millennium/), the United Nations Millennium Goals Web site (http://www.un.org/millenniumgoals/), the United Nations Millennium Development Indicators Web site (http://mdgs.un.org/), and the World Bank's MDG Web site (http://ddp-ext.worldbank.org/ext/GMIS/home.do?siteId=2).

MARKUS HAACKER

■ monetary conditions index

A monetary conditions index (MCI) is a simple device that combines movements in different financial variables, notably the interest rate and the exchange rate, into a single number. It serves as an easy-to-understand reference or information variable to financial markets and the general public at a point in time relative to some point in the past. In addition, a MCI can function as a short-term operating target in the conduct of monetary policy in small open economies.

The Bank of Canada pioneered the construction of a MCI in the early 1990s. The original MCI consisted of a weighted average of the real short-term interest rate and the real exchange rate, the respective nominal rate adjusted for inflation and the price of domestic relative to foreign goods. In practice, however, the MCI has been stated in terms of the nominal short-term interest rate and the nominal exchange rate, two of the most readily observable financial variables in the economy.

The basic idea behind the MCI is that in an open economy, both the real interest rate and the real exchange rate help determine aggregate demand. They can be combined to produce a simple gauge that measures the influence of both variables on aggregate demand. This indicator captures changes in the stance of monetary policy and the associated effects on the exchange rate. In addition, it records changes in the exchange rate that are not accompanied by changes in the interest rate, such as terms of trade shocks or loss of confidence. Finally, it registers movements of the interest rate and exchange rate in opposite directions in situations where, for instance, an announced policy change lacks credibility.

Explaining the MCI In its simplest form an aggregate demand relation can be modeled as follows:

$$y_t = -a_1 r_t - a_2 e_t + v_t \qquad a_1, a_2 > 0$$

where

y_t = aggregate demand,

r_t = real interest rate,

e_t = real exchange rate (rise implies that domestic currency is appreciating, all other things being equal), and

v_t = other factors that influence aggregate demand.

The size of a_1 and a_2 reflect the relative effect of the real interest rate and exchange rate channel on aggregate demand. Both parameters are important ingredients in the construction of the MCI:

$$MCI_t = (r_t - r_0) + \frac{a_2}{a_1}(e_t - e_0) + 100$$

The MCI at time t is a weighted sum of the change in the real rate of interest and the change in the real exchange rate relative to the base period. The interest rate is measured in percentage points while the exchange rate appears in index form with 100 being its value in the base period. The selection of the base period is arbitrary. The weight on the real exchange rate is typically less than or equal to one.

According to the above specification, a one-point rise in the real interest rate at time t is associated with a one-point rise in the MCI. If the relative weight on the real exchange rate is one half, then a two-point rise in the real exchange rate also leads to a one-point increase in the MCI. It is important to keep in mind that the absolute level of the MCI is meaningless. Changes in the MCI reflect changing monetary conditions between two points in time. An increase (decrease) in the index indicates that monetary conditions have tightened (eased).

MCI in Practice MCIs figured prominently in monetary policy deliberations at the Bank of Canada and the Reserve Bank of New Zealand in the 1990s. The rationale for constructing these indexes was grounded in the assumption that a central bank can wield considerable control over monetary conditions and that in a small open economy changes in monetary conditions are reflected mainly by changes in the interest rate and the exchange rate, which in turn affect aggregate demand. The level of aggregate demand is the most important factor in determining the rate of inflation. With price stability being an important, if not the overriding, goal of monetary policy, it was incumbent on the central bank to establish desirable monetary conditions that are consistent with price stability. In practice, the central bank prepared a path for the monetary conditions index that was compatible with inflation forecasts. In the interval between inflation forecasts, the bank monitored the actual MCI to see if it diverged from its desired path or range. In the event that marked differences appeared, the central bank would adjust the interest rate to correct the course of the actual MCI. If evidence emerged for a change in expected inflation, the central bank adjusted the path of the MCI to be compatible with the inflation objective. Given the close attention both central banks paid to the MCI in the day-to-day operation of monetary policy, it seems clear that the MCI served as a short-term operating target.

For other central banks, MCIs have figured less prominently as indicator variables next to the term spread or monetary and credit aggregates. The International Monetary Fund and the Organisation for Economic Co-operation and Development, as well as commercial banks, have also published monetary conditions indexes for various countries. These MCIs serve primarily as information variables: the banks use the actual MCI to assess current monetary conditions and their likely effect on inflation and real economic activity.

Beginning with the new millennium, the prominence of MCIs has waned considerably. Central banks, international organizations, and commercial banks still calculated and monitored MCIs as of 2007, but they played a minor role in monetary policy deliberations. The virtual demise of the MCI is due to several factors, some of which are related to its construction and underlying view of the transmission mechanism. Interpreting observed changes in the index can also be problematic as they depend on one's view of how the economy works.

Role of Exchange Rate An important issue in the construction of a MCI pertains to the determination of the relative weight on the real exchange rate. The two parameters a_1 and a_2 that make up the relative weight are not observable and must therefore be estimated. Whichever relative weight appears in the MCI depends on the specification of the model chosen to estimate aggregate demand. Empirical studies have shown that the range (statistical confidence intervals) for the empirical estimates of the key parameters is excessively wide and often includes zero

as a possible estimate. Other issues pertain to the selection of interest rates and exchange rates: real versus nominal, short-term versus long(er)-term interest rates, trade-weighted versus bilateral exchange rates.

The usefulness of a MCI is also hampered by its rather narrow view of the monetary transmission mechanism. In essence, the conception of the original MCI rests on the assumption that the real exchange rate affects aggregate demand and that aggregate demand in turn affects the rate of inflation. Direct effects of the real exchange rate on the rate of inflation through import prices are thus ruled out. Yet in an open economy this direct exchange rate channel plays an important role in determining overall inflation.

The literature explaining the design and use of an MCI warns against mechanically adjusting the interest rate in the wake of a weaker or stronger exchange rate. Careful analysis of the circumstances that gave rise to the change in the exchange rate is warranted before a central bank contemplates a change in the policy instrument. Shocks that originate in the real sector of the economy and lead to changes in the real exchange rate call for a change in monetary conditions, whereas lack of credibility in the conduct of monetary policy or portfolio shocks, that is, shocks in financial sector of the economy, that lead to a weakening of the real exchange rate are to be countered by increases in the interest rate so as to leave monetary conditions unchanged.

It is conceivable that different constellations of the interest rate and the exchange rate could yield the same level of the MCI. In such a situation monetary conditions are the same and the policymaker may be tempted to choose a particular mix of the interest rate and the exchange rate. Yet the outcome for real economic activity and the rate of inflation will most certainly depend on the particular mix chosen, especially if time lags play an important role in the transmission process of monetary policy.

MCIs were still being published around the world as of 2007, because they provide a simple gauge of monetary conditions in an economy. Although MCIs are of some use to financial markets and the general public as an information variable, they play only a minor role in the implementation of monetary policy at central banks.

See also capital mobility; exchange rate regimes; inflation targeting; interest parity conditions; monetary policy rules; money supply; Mundell-Fleming model; real exchange rate; Swan diagram

FURTHER READING

Deutsche Bundesbank. 1999. "Taylor Interest Rate and Monetary Conditions Index." *Monthly Report* (April): 47–63. A critical assessment of the usefulness of MCIs in the conduct of monetary policy.

Freedman, Charles. 1995. "The Role of Monetary Conditions and the Monetary Conditions Index in the Conduct of Policy." *Bank of Canada Review* (autumn): 53–59. An early contribution by a central banker that explains the rationale for constructing MCIs.

Guender, Alfred V. 2005. "On Optimal Monetary Policy Rules and the Construction of MCIs in the Open Economy." *Open Economies Review* 16: 189–207. This theoretical essay shows that standard MCIs are misspecified if a real exchange rate channel exists in the Phillips curve.

Reserve Bank of New Zealand, Economics Department. 1996. "Summary Indicators of Monetary Conditions." *Reserve Bank (of New Zealand) Bulletin* 59 (3): 223–28. Offers the Reserve Bank of New Zealand's perspective on the usefulness of MCIs.

Stevens, Glenn. 1998. "Pitfalls in the Use of Monetary Conditions Indexes." *Reserve Bank (of Australia) Bulletin* (August): 34–43. A cogent summary of the reasons why central banks should exercise caution in basing the conduct of monetary policy on MCIs.

ALFRED V. GUENDER

■ **monetary integration**

See common currency

■ **monetary policy rules**

Monetary policy rules (MPRs) are one of many mechanical processes that guide the implementation of monetary policy. Other processes include a currency board, an exchange rate crawl, or a money growth rate rule. This discussion will be limited to the type of MPR made famous by the Taylor rule (Taylor 1993).

A monetary policy *rule* is an alternative to a *discretionary* policy framework. There are many reasons why rules might possibly be seen as a better option by economists and policymakers. First, rules are more transparent than discretion and, as such, easier to understand and use as the basis for decisions. This, in turn, assists with establishing and maintaining a credible central bank and monetary policy regime. Second, rules are able to convey greater information about the future direction of policy. Third, outcomes under a rules-based policy tend to be better than those from discretionary policy.

Constructing a Monetary Policy Rule An MPR is an algebraic representation of a policy rule that stipulates how an instrument of monetary policy will react to key economic variables and therefore achieve a specific policy objective. There are three main components to the MPR. The first is the policy instrument. This is the variable that the policymaker adjusts to affect its monetary policy. In the Taylor rule, the MPR is a short-term interest rate.

In the subsequent literature on MPRs, economists have investigated the use of other possible instruments of policy. These include the exchange rate, a combination of the interest rate and the exchange rate (a monetary conditions index, or MCI), and even a monetary aggregate such as the monetary base, or M2. Whichever one is used, the instrument is essential for two reasons: it represents the policy lever and therefore must be subject to the policymaker's control, and it must be able to influence economic activity to the extent that it satisfies the policy objectives.

The second component of an MPR is the set of variables to which the policy instrument responds. These variables convey information about the stance of monetary policy and signal how the instrument ought to react so that the policy targets are met. In the basic Taylor rule, the variables to be included are the deviation of inflation from a preannounced target and the deviation of output from a long-run value designed to represent full employment. Under this specification, the Taylor rule essentially implies that the inflation and output deviations contain sufficient information about the stance of monetary policy to adequately drive interest rate movements.

Although not explicitly stated in the rule, the third component of an MPR is the policy regime that it is supposed to represent. The monetary policy regime most commonly pursued with MPRs is inflation targeting. As such, the boundaries of the MPR reflect how the instrument should react to the right-hand-side variables in a manner that achieves the stated policy.

But how does one link the policy objective to the MPR? The answer is through a statement of central bank objectives—usually depicted by a central bank loss function. The loss function is an algebraic representation of the policymaker's objectives and will typically detail the variables that the central bank is interested in targeting. If there are multiple objectives, the weight that the central bank attributes to each objective becomes important. The minimization of the loss function subject to the constraints imposed by a macroeconomic model will yield an MPR.

The MPR emerging from this minimization exercise is known as an *optimal* MPR—one that is derived from an explicit policy objective. The Taylor rule itself is an example of a *simple* MPR, one where the rule is specified without reference to explicit objectives. In this instance, the variables captured by the MPR reflect the policy objectives. For example, if the simple MPR contains expressions for output and inflation deviations, then it is assumed that these are the objectives of policy regardless of the model used to depict the macroeconomy. Under an optimal rule, the variables that appear on the right-hand side may not actually be policy objectives—they may simply be variables that appear as part of the model used for optimization. Herein lies the difference between simple and optimal MPRs. Optimal MPRs are highly dependent on the model used to derive the rule but are explicitly reflective of the actual policy preferences of the central bank. Simple MPRs are imposed on a macroeconomic model and, as such, do not explicitly reflect central bank policy preferences, but are likely to be robust across many model specifications.

Exchange Rate and Monetary Policy Rules The role the exchange rate ought to play in the adoption of an MPR is a common subject of debate. There are two broad discussions in this area. The first relates to whether the instrument of monetary policy should react—in a significant way—to the exchange rate when setting policy. The second is whether the exchange rate ought to be used as an instrument, or coinstrument, of policy (see Cavoli and Rajan 2007).

The literature on inflation targeting using MPRs makes it clear that the exchange rate should have no part in the implementation of policy and, if using simple MPRs, should not appear at all in the MPR. The reason for this is that a policy trade-off between the exchange rate and domestic objectives may occur—it may be difficult to address both objectives with a single policy instrument. This may well appear to be an appropriate strategy for large, relatively closed economies such as the United States, but the debate is more complicated for open, developing economies. The simple reason for this is that the exchange rate may contain information (about global events or capital flows) that is important in the operation of a MPR that is not contained in other variables (such as output and inflation). This is so even if the exchange rate is not itself an objective of monetary policy. Hence, under these conditions, there is a strong argument for the inclusion of the exchange rate in the rule—it helps provide all the necessary information for the attainment of domestic policy.

Once the decision is made to include the exchange rate in the rule, how might one manage the possibility that the exchange rate and inflation may suggest opposing instrument changes? One possibility is to use a partial adjustment. Under this process, the MPR instrument will react to both current and lagged exchange rates. Then, if there is a shock that requires a strong reaction to the current exchange rate but is an inappropriate reaction for inflation, then that reaction can be partially offset next period.

The second issue relates to the possibility of using the exchange rate as an instrument of policy. There are two lines of research here. The first examines a policy rule called a monetary conditions index (MCI). The MCI is an MPR in which the policy instrument is a linear combination of the interest rate and the exchange rate. They are effectively coinstruments of policy. The main premise behind the MCI is that both interest rates and exchange rates indicate monetary conditions and that, for example, a tightening of these conditions can be brought about by an interest rate rise, an increase in the foreign currency value of the domestic currency, or both. As such, it is possible that the variables can move in opposite directions so that monetary conditions are not affected. Therefore, it is the imperative of the policymaker that if a change in one of the variables leads to changes in monetary conditions, the other must be moved to maintain the present policy position and offset monetary changes.

The way that the MCI is typically captured in an MPR is by both the exchange rate and the interest rate appearing on the left side of the rule (see Ball 1999). The economist Laurence Ball (2001), however, believes that this situation is broadly equivalent to an MPR where the interest rate is the main instrument and the exchange rate appears on the right-hand side. Under this version of an MPR, the implicit assumption is that the interest rate is the main instrument of policy and is able to be competently controlled by the policymaker. The exchange rate still offers the policymaker information about the relative tightness of policy and can still guide movements in the instrument and therefore the direction of policy.

The second way that the exchange rate can be used is as a policy instrument in its own right. There is a line of research (particularly in relation to Singapore) where variables such as the nominal bilateral or nominal effective exchange rate (NEER) appear on the left side of an MPR as the sole policy instrument. Underlining this rule is the ability to control the nominal exchange rate (in the conventional manner through foreign reserves). This rule works in precisely the same way as the Taylor-type specification using the nominal interest rate—the right-hand side of the rule would contain expressions for the inflation gap, output gap, possibly lagged exchange rate term, and any other variable deemed to possess information sufficiently important to guide the exchange rate toward the policy objective (Cavoli and Rajan 2006). The overall policy objectives need not be any different from the Taylor-type MPRs; the rule simply reflects the opinion of the policymaker that the exchange rate does a better job at reaching the policy target.

See also exchange rate regimes; inflation targeting; monetary conditions index; money supply; quantity theory of money; time inconsistency problem

FURTHER READING

Ball, L. 1999. "Policy Rules for Open Economies." In *Monetary Policy Rules*, edited by M. Taylor. Chicago: University of Chicago Press, 144–54. Excellent exposition on the construction of open economy MPRs and MCIs.

———. 2001. "Policy Rules and External Shocks." NBER Working Paper 7910. Cambridge, MA: National Bureau of Economic Research. Provides a discussion on open economy MPRs.

Cavoli, T., and R. S. Rajan. 2006. "Managing in the Middle: Characterizing Singapore's Exchange Rate Policy." *Asian Economic Journal* 21 (3): 321–42. Contains an MPR for Singapore where the exchange rate (NEER) is the policy instrument.

———. 2007. "Inflation Targeting Arrangements in Asia: Exploring the Role of the Exchange Rate." Briefing Notes in Economics No. 74 (September–October). Presents simple analytics in the construction of closed versus open economy rules and the role of the exchange rate.

Cecchetti, S. 2000. "Making Monetary Policy: Objectives and Rules." *Oxford Review of Economic Policy* 16: 4. Excellent paper on the formulation of closed economy MPRs.

Taylor, J. B. 1993. "Discretion versus Policy Rules in Practice." *Carnegie-Rochester Conference Series on Public Policy* 39: 195–214. Seminal paper on the Taylor rule.

———. 2001. "The Role of the Exchange Rate in Monetary Policy Rules." *American Economic Review Papers and*

Proceedings 91: 263–67. Looks at the policy implications of open economy MPRs.

TONY CAVOLI

■ monetary versus fiscal dominance

The terms *monetary dominant* and *fiscal dominant* refer to a central bank's ability to pursue goals of its own choice. Under a monetary dominant regime, the central bank is free to pursue its main goal: stable prices. By contrast, under a fiscal dominant regime, the central bank is not free to fight inflation, since it must print money to fill a fiscal financing gap, now or in the future.

The distinction between monetary and fiscal dominance is of great practical importance for policymakers. For example, central banks have adopted inflation targeting programs in increasing numbers. Inflation targeting, or any other independent monetary regime, is not viable if there are other competing demands on the central bank, such as financing the government's fiscal deficit (when expenditures exceed revenues). In the face of such competing demands, the central bank can limit inflation only in the short run and only with interest rates that are high enough to keep government debt attractive to investors. Upward pressure on interest rates can also be exacerbated if a country suffers capital outflows or adverse shocks to risks as perceived by potential investors in the country.

Economists disagree, however, about how to implement the notions of fiscal or monetary dominance. All agree that markets must be convinced that the central bank is indeed free from other demands. The disagreement lies in exactly how "tight" or "disciplined" fiscal policy must be, currently or prospectively, in order to convey that message. How large must the primary (noninterest) surplus be in order to ensure that the central bank can restrain inflation without excessively high interest rates? The case of Brazil in 2002–3 helps illustrate this point. At that time, Brazil's fledgling inflation targeting program faltered. Even while interest rates were kept high,

the central bank failed to meet its inflation target. Fiscal policy was not overtly "undisciplined." Rather, the government attempted to stabilize its debt when it raised the primary surplus to more than 3 percent of gross domestic product (GDP). Nonetheless, adverse shocks threatened to raise public debt further still, against policy intentions. Fears that the central bank would be forced to buy this extra debt by printing money—fiscal dominance—thus jeopardized the inflation targeting program (Blanchard 2005).

Explaining Dominance The economists Sargent and Wallace (1981) envisaged a standoff between a central bank and a fiscal authority. They asked what might happen if the central bank signals an unwillingness to satisfy a long-run financing gap. They conclude that, in some cases, even while money is tight and interest rates are high *today*, inflation might still rise *today*.

Their starting point was the government's *intertemporal* budget constraint:

$$B_t/P_t = PV(ps) \qquad (1)$$

where B_t is the nominal value of government claims today (time t), P_t is today's price level, and $PV(ps)$ is the present value of real primary (noninterest) surpluses from today forward. Note that B_t/P_t is real government debt: nominal government debt deflated by the price level. Equation (1) is often called the government's "intertemporal solvency," or "present value," condition. This condition says that, barring default (either explicitly or through a surprise inflation), today's real debt B_t/P_t must be paid for either now or in the future with primary surpluses (ps); the present value of all current and future primary surpluses must be enough to pay off the debt.

Under a monetary dominant regime the fiscal authority meets condition (1) by adjusting the primary surplus (i.e., fiscal balance net of interest payments on existing debt, that is, raising revenues and/or reducing expenditures). If there is an adverse fiscal shock in some period—an unanticipated increase in expenditures or fall in tax revenues—the fiscal authority should respond by raising taxes or cutting expenditures at some future date. Such an adjustment must offset the initial shock in present value terms. In this sense, primary surpluses are said to be *endogenous*. Since such a policy environment is typically featured in discussions of the Ricardian equivalence hypothesis named after the economist David Ricardo (see Barro 1974), a monetary dominant regime is also called a Ricardian one.

By contrast, under a fiscal dominant (or non-Ricardian) regime, primary surpluses are set exogenously. Even if a shock occurs, the fiscal authority will not adjust its policies. Instead, market participants immediately recognize that the present value of primary surpluses $PV(ps)$ has fallen and is now insufficient to amortize the real value of outstanding debt B_t/P_t. Instead, as equation (1) implies, the real debt B_t/P_t must also fall.

How does this happen? The government might simply announce that it will default on a portion of its debt (or impose a capital levy). A default need not be explicit, however. When market participants themselves recognize that their bonds will not be fully backed by future surpluses, they attempt to reduce their bond holdings. Although any single individual can sell his or her bonds, the market as a whole (in a closed economy) cannot. Instead, when all market participants attempt to sell their debt in exchange for goods, the price of goods will rise just enough to maintain the equality in (1). Sargent and Wallace show how, in such an environment, the inflation rate might rise today, even while money remains tight (see Sargent and Wallace 1981).

The Role of Money and the Fiscal Rule In traditional models, people first exchange their bonds for money and then for goods. In a fiscal dominant regime, money, which is passively supplied by the central bank, bridges the fiscal financing gap. Then, when all agents attempt to purchase goods with their newly printed money, prices rise. Money's role is not essential, however. The economist Woodford (2000) has discussed a case in which paper money is replaced entirely by electronic accounts. According to Woodford, although money itself is not required to pin down the price level, a Ricardian, or monetary dominant, regime is.

Concretely, under such a regime, the primary surplus would be determined according to a rule like:

$$(ps/y)_t = \kappa + \alpha * (b/y)_{t-1} \qquad (2)$$

where ps is the real primary surplus, $b = B/P$ is real debt, and y is real GDP. Such a rule may be tacit; it need not be legally stipulated. Note that, if $\alpha = 0$, for any value of κ, fiscal policy is non-Ricardian. In some countries, $\kappa < 0$; this suggests that the government is giving a rebate to current taxpayers (potentially at the expense of future taxpayers). It can be shown that, for (1) to hold ex ante, primary surpluses and debt must rise together ($\alpha > 0$), but not necessarily on a one-to-one basis ($\alpha < 1$). More precisely, to ensure that (1) holds, α must exceed zero—even if only by a small amount.

A rule like (2), in which κ typically equals zero, often appears in the computable general equilibrium real business cycle models that emerged in the 1990s, which are increasingly used by central banks in many countries to guide policy decisions (including inflation targeting programs). Such a rule pins down the price level in the model.

The condition $\alpha > 0$ (κ unrestricted) is a very weak one. For example, if

$$0 < \alpha < [(\rho - \gamma)/(1 + \gamma)] - [\kappa/(b/y)_{t-1}],$$

where $\rho \equiv$ long-run interest rate, $\gamma \equiv$ long-run GDP growth, the debt ratio b/y grows over time. To be sure, the solvency condition (1) is satisfied, but only because primary surpluses ps/y themselves also grow over time—passing an ever larger fiscal burden to future taxpayers. A more stringent policy would be one in which the authority attempts to stabilize the debt ratio b/y, specifically $\kappa = 0$ and $\alpha = (\rho - \gamma)/(1 + \gamma)$. This means that the primary surplus is large enough to cover interest payments, minus an adjustment for growth:

$$(ps/y) = [(\rho - \gamma)/(1 + \gamma)]^* (b/y).$$

Such a policy appeals to intergenerational equity: both debt b/y and the primary surplus ps/y stay constant over time. In this way, current and future taxpayers face similar burdens.

Current Practical Approaches for Policymakers In practice, what does it take to reassure market participants that the central bank will not face pressures to finance deficits? Is it enough that the government has kept itself solvent in the past (i.e., $\alpha > 0$)? Not necessarily. Unless primary surpluses are expected to equal or exceed $[(\rho - \gamma)/(1 + \gamma)]^*(b/y)$, the debt ratio b/y will grow. Such a policy is *unsustainable*: as b/y rises, so too must the primary surplus *ps/y*. Markets recognize that future fiscal adjustments may be *politically* difficult for the government to achieve.

Even under a debt-stabilizing policy, where primary surpluses equal, on average $(ps/y) = [(\rho - \gamma)/(1 + \gamma)] * (b/y)$, markets may not be convinced that the central bank is free to stabilize prices. This is especially true in developing countries, where external shocks affect debt ratios through their impacts on interest rates, exchange rates, and GDP growth. Often, adverse shocks are not immediately offset by favorable ones. In this case, under a debt-stabilizing rule $(ps/y) = [(\rho - \gamma)/(1 + \gamma)]^*(b/y)$ there is a 50 percent chance that the debt ratio will rise.

This also implies a 50 percent chance that another fiscal adjustment will be needed. Markets may find this probability too high. Governments may wish to reduce that probability. To do so, their primary surpluses must on average *exceed* their debt-stabilizing value. For example, the primary surplus might also be linked to the *volatility* of the fiscal burden (*vol*):

$$(ps/y) = [(\rho - \gamma)/(1 + \gamma)]^*(b/y) + \omega^*(vol),$$

where $\omega > 0$ reflects policymaker preferences. Thus a policy of $\omega^* (vol) > 0$ may be justified as a preemptive cushion that reduces the probability of future adjustments. But, in addition, if $\omega^* (vol) > 0$, public debt will *fall*.

Hence, more recent views have emphasized that, in order to guard against fiscal dominance, governments should aim to *reduce* public debt—not just stabilize it. While all governments face a trade-off between costly primary surpluses and the cushion they provide, each will choose a precautionary cushion according to its own circumstances.

In this vein, gauging fiscal dominance (or market perceptions thereof) may require more than simply estimating an equation like (2). For example, some authors have recently developed Monte Carlo tech-

niques (i.e., simulation exercises) that yield estimates of the *probability* that the debt will rise to a certain level during a certain time horizon. And, with an eye toward policy, several papers (see, for example, Tanner and Samake 2008) suggest a method to calculate the primary surplus required to obtain a desired probability. Because such techniques clearly present the trade-off between higher primary surpluses and more security, they should lead to better and more informed policy.

See also debt deflation; discipline; inflation targeting; monetary policy rules; money supply; quantity theory of money; seigniorage; time inconsistency problem

FURTHER READING

Barro, Robert J. 1974. "Are Government Bonds Net Wealth." *Journal of Political Economy* 82 (6) (November–December): 1095–1117. A seminal article that spawned a lively debate regarding the Ricardian Equivalence Hypothesis.

———. 1979. "On the Determination of the Public Debt, Part 1." *Journal of Political Economy* 87 (5) (October): 940–71. A seminal article that introduced the notion of fiscal objective functions and "tax smoothing." The article began a series of papers about how to spread the deadweight losses of taxation over time.

Blanchard, Olivier J. 2005. "Fiscal Dominance and Inflation Targeting: Lessons from Brazil." In *Inflation Targeting, Debt, and the Brazilian Experience, 1999 to 2003*, edited by C. Favero and F. Giavazzi. Cambridge, MA: MIT Press, 49–80. A discussion of Brazil's policy dilemmas in recent years.

Celasun, Oya, Xavier Debrun, and Jonathan Ostry. 2006. "Primary Surplus Behavior and Risks to Fiscal Sustainability in Emerging Market Countries: A 'Fan-Chart' Approach." IMF Working Paper No. 06/67. Washington, DC: International Monetary Fund. An examination of debt sustainability under uncertainty in emerging markets.

Garcia, Marcio, and Roberto Rigobon. 2005. "A Risk Management Approach to Emerging Market's Sovereign Debt Sustainability with an Application to Brazilian Data." In *Inflation Targeting, Debt, and the Brazilian Experience, 1999 to 2003*, edited by C. Favero and F. Giavazzi. Cambridge, MA: MIT Press, 163–88. This article presents a "fan chart" approach to examining public debt.

International Monetary Fund. 2003. "Public Debt in Emerging Markets: Is It Too High?" *World Economic Outlook* (September): 113–52. Available at http://www .imf.org/external/pubs/ft/weo/2003/02/pdf/chapter3 .pdf. A survey of fiscal policy issues in emerging markets.

Sargent, Thomas, and Neil Wallace. 1981. "Some Unpleasant Monetarist Arithmetic." *Federal Reserve Bank of Minneapolis Quarterly Review* 5 (fall): 15–41. A seminal article that examines the strategic interactions between fiscal and monetary authorities. The piece discusses how inflation could rise even if money was tight if the government budget was not in intertemporal balance.

Tanner, Evan, and Alberto Ramos. 2003. "Fiscal Sustainability and Monetary versus Fiscal Dominance: Evidence from Brazil, 1991–2000." *Applied Economics* 35 (7) (May): 859–73. Features an estimated fiscal reaction function for Brazil.

Tanner, Evan, and Issouf Samake. 2008. "Probabilistic Sustainability of Public Debt: A Vector Autoregression Approach for Brazil, Mexico, and Turkey." *IMF Staff Papers* 55 (1) (February): 149–82. Presents an *objective function* for fiscal policy under uncertainty, corresponding debt sustainability simulations for emerging markets, and a clear menu of options for policymakers.

Woodford, Michael. 2000. "Monetary Policy in a World without Money." *International Finance* 3 (2) (July): 229–60. Presents a model of price level determination in which the money stock does not play a crucial role.

EVAN TANNER

■ money laundering

Money laundering involves the transformation of the proceeds of crime into riches, which can then be enjoyed while disguising their illegal origins. It generally includes three steps: the introduction of the criminal proceeds into the financial system; hiding the proceeds through a variety of transactions and financial vehicles; and investing the laundered proceeds in financial and related assets. These operations often involve international transactions as a means of "layering," or obscuring, the source of the funds. National governments and the international community have worked for many years to combat money laundering, but these efforts were redoubled—and expanded to include terrorist financing—after the terrorist attacks of September 11, 2001, on the United States.

Measurement of the global volume of money laundering is extremely difficult given that the intrinsic nature of the transactions is intended to disguise the source of funds. Several indirect measurements of the volume of money laundering have been derived, using, for example, estimates of activity in the underground economy and the income generated from criminal activity. The range of these estimates is very broad, from less than one-half to several percent of gross domestic product.

Combating terrorist financing has become an integral part of the international efforts on anti–money laundering. Terrorist financing can be defined as the processing of property from any source (perhaps a legitimate one) to finance terrorist activity that has been or will be committed. This activity is thought to use many of the techniques of money laundering and many of the possible countermeasures are similar. Furthermore, several terrorist organizations are known to finance their activities out of the proceeds of crime. Nonetheless, terrorist financing differs from money laundering in several ways that affect public policy. It may be much more difficult to detect terrorist financing than money laundering, since it is mainly directed at future activity: it is possible that the only offense that has been committed when the financing takes place is conspiracy to commit a terrorist act. Also, the amounts of money needed to finance terrorism are widely believed to be relatively small. The September 11 terrorist attack was believed to have required less than $1 million in financing. This compares with the typical volumes of money being laundered by, say, large drug trafficking operations, which in total might approach several hundred billion dollars a year.

International efforts to combat money laundering (and terrorist financing) reflect both a law enforcement strategy to "follow the dirty money" and a concern to protect the global financial system from abuse by criminal elements. When an institution is used unwittingly by criminal elements or terrorists, it risks damage to its reputation. Once the integrity of an institution or financial center is brought into question, its long-term viability is put at risk, with potentially serious economic consequences. If the staff of a financial institution collude with criminal elements to launder funds or channel financing to terrorists, the damage can be much greater. The most serious dangers arise when important financial institutions are controlled by criminals, since these circumstances can compromise the integrity and operations of the whole financial system by corrupting the allocation of resources, misallocating investment, and lowering economic growth.

Combating Money Laundering Money laundering is intrinsically global. If one country or jurisdiction sharpens its focus to prevent money laundering and combat the financing of terrorism (AML/CFT), money-laundering activity will quickly shift to a less-regulated environment. Hence the efforts to combat money laundering and terrorist financing have also been global, centered on the development of international codes and standards that all jurisdictions are expected to follow.

A prerequisite for an effective anti-money-laundering regime is to have in place an adequate general legal framework. Such legislation needs to define and criminalize money laundering and terrorist financing with suitably graduated penalties. It has to cover a wide set of "predicate crimes"—that is, the criminal activity that gives rise to the cash or other valuables to be laundered—and define the scope of the AML/CFT regime. Commercial banks are generally obligated to be especially vigilant given their role in the payment system. However, as criminals will exploit loopholes, wide sectoral coverage is needed.

The typical measures that financial institutions have to apply include checks on the identity and legitimacy of their clients—the "know-your-customer" requirements. Major shareholders and senior managers in financial institutions demonstrate that they are "fit and proper" to hold these positions of control and oversight. Financial institutions must

establish systems of identifying and reporting unusual or suspicious transactions. The financial institutions themselves need to train their staff adequately to spot activities that raise a suspicion of money laundering and to have clear processes in place to report back to the authorities. The reporting of unusual transactions and "know-your-customer" rules need to be supported by adequate record keeping. When the authorities, for example, investigate a suspicious transaction, a financial institution must be able to help establish an audit trail.

Typically, financial sector regulators are responsible for supervising the AML/CFT procedures of financial institutions and for checking that their managers and owners meet the "fit and proper" test. Much of this supervision is not separable from other aspects of prudential supervision. For example, a bank supervisor will have to review a commercial bank's internal control procedures to prevent internal fraud or imprudent behavior and, at the same time, can check on whether the bank has in place the means to limit vulnerability to money laundering.

Many countries have also set up specialized agencies called financial intelligence units (FIUs). These agencies investigate, analyze, and pass on to the competent authorities financial and related information concerning suspected proceeds of crime. A key component of an FIU's work is to collaborate with like agencies in other countries in sharing information on suspicious transactions.

A number of organizations are involved in the international efforts on AML/CFT. This includes the Financial Action Task Force (FATF), which sets the global AML/CFT standards; a number of FATF-style regional bodies, such as the Caribbean Financial Action Task Force, which have focused on the development of sound AML/CFT regimes within their regions; as well as the International Monetary Fund, the World Bank, and the United Nations. Together, these bodies provide a network for the global assessment of jurisdictions' compliance with the AML/CFT standards. These assessments identify potential weaknesses in the AML/CFT regimes and develop plans of corrective action. Several of these bodies support the global AML/CFT efforts through training and technical assistance and through their typologies of money laundering and terrorist financing.

One of the key challenges for any anti-money-laundering regime is that criminal elements are very adept at finding ways to avoid the controls. In an effort to fill possible loopholes in the anti-money-laundering regimes, in 2003 the FATF expanded the AML/CFT standards that countries should comply with to cover a range of new sectors outside of regulated financial institutions, and tightened requirements on existing sectors. The revised standard is comprehensive and demanding, and a number of jurisdictions, especially but not limited to low-income countries, have had difficulty meeting its rigorous requirements. The application of the standard illustrates an ongoing anti-money-laundering issue: how to balance the costs on consumers and industry of tightened regulation with the benefits, when the volume of money laundering has proved difficult to measure.

See also international financial centers; International Monetary Fund (IMF); offshore financial centers

FURTHER READING

Reuter, Peter, and Edwin M. Truman, 2004. *Chasing Dirty Money*. Washington, DC: Institute of International Finance. Provides a comprehensive survey of anti-money-laundering issues, including a review of effectiveness of the regimes.

R. BARRY JOHNSTON

■ money supply

Money has been used by civilized societies for millennia, but in its modern macroeconomic context it is identified with "the money supply." Almost all economies have moved beyond commodity money to paper money; however in economies with reliable banks, most money takes the form of bank deposits. To the extent that they are transferable by check, bank deposits satisfy the official definition of money as "a generally acceptable means of payment."

Economists define a country's money supply along a spectrum ranging from high to low liquidity: the ease with which an asset can be used as a generally acceptable means of payment, or at least converted into a means of payment. Various monies can range along a spectrum from coin and paper currency ("cash"), called M0; to M1, which is M0 plus checkable bank deposits; to M2, which is M1 plus savings and other similar short-term but noncheckable deposits; to M3, which includes longer-term deposits; and so on. The precise definitions vary from country to country.

What matters from a macroeconomic point of view is, first, how controllable is the money supply, and second, how much and how quickly it affects output, interest rates, exchange rates, and the overall price level. Governments wish to control their own money supplies in the short run to stimulate output in the face of unemployment, and in the long run to control inflation.

Controllability of Money Supply Controllability of the money supply has long been a matter of debate, but economists generally agree that any central bank with a monopoly on issuance of its domestic currency can control its country's money supply as long as it is not committed to buy and sell foreign currencies at a fixed exchange rate. On the other hand, a central bank that is committed to a fixed exchange rate will be forced to sell or buy unlimited quantities of domestic currency in exchange for foreign currency and will be forced to contract or expand its money supply in the process. The phrase *impossible trinity* refers to the fact that monetary control, fixed exchange rates, and unrestricted international currency flows cannot coexist.

However, controllability is subject to a second constraint. The link between central banks' "instruments" of control and the money supply itself is neither tight nor predictable. One way of conceptualizing this link is via the monetary base, or what is sometimes called "high-powered money": the sum of a country's cash (coin plus paper money, both in circulation and inside banks, or "vault cash") and, more sizably, its central bank's deposits in domestic commercial banks.

Central banks conventionally control money supplies by depositing or withdrawing their deposits with commercial banks, sometimes in exchange for purchases or sales of government bonds on the open market, and sometimes by other means. Commercial banks then use these "central bank reserves" (defined as central bank deposits plus vault cash) to leverage the creation of deposits—that is, money. They do this by purchasing interest-bearing securities (typically government bonds) and by writing loans, in return for which they issue deposits to sellers of the securities or recipients of the loans. Commercial banks need these reserves at minimum for check-clearing purposes, but also for prudential purposes, against unforeseen cash drains. The central bank often also requires that commercial banks hold a minimum ratio of reserves to deposits.

The problems with trying to control the money supply via the monetary base are threefold. First, the public's desired ratio of cash to deposits is variable and partially unpredictable. When commercial bank deposits expand via an injection of central bank reserves into the banking system, the public will choose to withdraw a fraction of their new bank deposits as cash. This depletes the banks' vault cash and thus their reserves. For prudential and perhaps also regulatory reasons, banks will be forced to reduce their rate of deposit expansion. Hence central banks try to anticipate such cash withdrawals by injecting reserves ex ante, and they also try to reverse unanticipated cash withdrawals by injecting reserves ex post.

Second, the commercial banks' desired ratio of reserves to deposits is also variable and partially unpredictable. Even if, as in many countries, they are required to hold a minimum ratio, they will likely hold some "excess reserves" to guard against unwanted cash withdrawals. How much they choose to hold depends on their opportunity costs: notably, on the yields they earn on alternative assets, such as government treasury bills.

Third, the extent to which banks, after receiving new reserves, choose to expand "demand" or "time" deposits is also variable and unpredictable. Demand deposits (i.e., those on which checks can be written) require more reserves for prudential reasons than do time deposits (i.e., noncheckable) because the likelihood of withdrawals for cash is greater.

In short, the ratio of a country's money supply to its monetary base is variable and partially unpredictable because the public's desired cash-to-deposits ratio, the banks' desired reserves-to-deposits ratio, and the banks' desired mix between demand and time deposits are all unpredictable. Hence the central banks' control of the money supply via the monetary base is imperfect. Of course much of the response of the money supply to the monetary base *is* predictable: it generally rises with income (because the cash-to-deposits ratio falls with income), and it also rises with interest rates (because the excess reserves ratio falls and the time-to-demand-deposits ratio rises). This means that not only is the central banks' job of controlling the money supply made more simple, it also means that money supplies expand and contract endogenously with upswings and downswings in the business cycle, lessening the need for exogenous control by the central bank.

Macroeconomic Implications of Money Supply Growth The second major macroeconomic issue surrounding money supplies is their impact on interest rates, exchange rates, output, and the overall price level. In theory, and subject to many simplifying assumptions, when a country's money supply increases, short-term interest rates will fall in the short run, the exchange rate (in terms of units of domestic currency needed to buy one unit of foreign currency) will rise in the short run, output will rise but perhaps not permanently, and in the long run, overall prices will also rise. The rationale for these effects is that the economy's demand for money depends in the short run negatively on interest rates and in the long run positively on output and overall prices. In the short run, interest rates will fall in order to raise money demand to the new level of money supply, and as a result, the price of foreign currency will rise. In the long run, nominal income—which is the product of output and the price level—will rise. Other things being equal, the increase in nominal income will cease when money demand has increased sufficiently to match the initial rise in money supply. Interest rates and exchange rates will return to their previous levels.

This simple scenario becomes more complex once we consider the dynamics of interest rate and price adjustments between the short run and the long run. In the medium run, the fall in interest rates as well as the increased availability of money for spending will cause macroeconomic demand to increase. This will induce more output—that is, more production of goods and services. The rise in the exchange rate will also increase foreign demand for the country's exports, which will induce a further increase in output. Whether this output increase is temporary or permanent will depend on whether inputs—so-called "factors of production" like labor and capital—are already fully employed. If workers are unemployed and factories are operating at less than full capacity, output can increase permanently. Otherwise, the effect of an increased money supply in the long run is simply to raise prices.

More realistically, we should consider increases in the rate of growth of the money supply, rather than simply its level. In the short run, until factors of production are fully employed, increasing monetary growth increases the rate of increase of output. In the long run, increasing monetary growth increases the rate of increase of prices—that is, it increases the inflation rate—rather than the level of prices per se. Long-run interest rates, which rise with expected inflation, will also rise.

Money Supply in an Open Economy The causes and effects of increased monetary growth are radically modified once we open an economy to inflows and outflows of capital from abroad. If the exchange rate is fixed and foreign currency can readily flow into and out of the country, interest rates will not fall except in the very short run. This is simply a manifestation of the "impossible trinity" mentioned earlier. Any attempt by a central bank to increase monetary growth will result in a small and short-lived decrease in short-run interest rates that will cause foreign currency to flow out until the increase in monetary growth is reversed. Since the central bank is committed to a fixed exchange rate, it will sell enough foreign currency to accommodate the outflow, and in the process it will buy domestic currency,

thereby taking it out of circulation. Interest rates (risk adjusted) will remain unchanged, at "world" levels.

Finally, it is important to understand the effects of the money supply on the exchange rate if it is *not* fixed by the central bank. Briefly, if and when an economy's factors of production are fully employed, a permanent increase in monetary growth will, in the long run, increase the nominal domestic-currency value of foreign currency but leave the "real" value unchanged. A permanent increase in monetary growth is accompanied by a permanent increase in inflation. The country will gradually price itself out of export markets unless it offers an increase in domestic currency per unit of foreign currency equal to the increase in its inflation rate minus any increase in its trading partners' inflation rates. This leaves the "real" exchange rate unchanged.

In short, the rate of growth of a country's money supply is the crucial determinant of its long-run inflation rate. It is also a determinant of short-run interest rates, short-run exchange rates, and short-run rates of output growth. Whether central banks can or should attempt to control short-run interest rates, exchange rates, and output growth by manipulating money supplies is a matter of both theoretical and policy controversy. Indeed, the controversy is moot for central banks that are committed to fixing their exchange rates, since in a world with globalized capital flows they simply have little or no control over their own money supplies.

See also European Central Bank; exchange rate regimes; Federal Reserve Board; impossible trinity; inflation targeting; monetary policy rules; real exchange rate; seigniorage

FURTHER READING

Friedman, Milton. 1968. "The Role of Monetary Policy." *American Economic Review* 58: 1–17. The seminal theoretical statement of relationships between money and real income in the short run, and nominal income and the price level in the long run. The theory linked the short run to the long run via expectations, paving the way for the "rational expectations" revolution that changed macroeconomics forever in the early 1970s.

Friedman, Milton, and Anna Schwartz. 1960. *A Monetary History of the United States: 1867–1960*. Princeton, NJ: Princeton University Press. This meticulous and now-classic study demonstrates convincingly the relationships between the money supply, nominal and real income, and the price level for the United States and, by implication, for other countries.

Mishkin, Frederic S. 2004. *The Economics of Money, Banking, and Financial Markets*. 7th ed. Boston: Addison Wesley, chap. 3. One of the best textbook treatments of the institutional arrangements surrounding the creation and control of money in a modern, free-market economy.

JAMES W. DEAN

■ monopolistic competition

Most products in the world, even standard commodities such as oil and wheat, are naturally differentiated because nature is not uniform. But such generic differentiation is quite different from the economic heterogeneity that arises from a deliberate investment in a location, patent, plant, process, or personnel. One must think of the firm as purchasing the differentiation with some sort of investment of fixed resources. This gives rise to monopolistic competition, because other firms can produce a similar or even identical variety at a different location with a high degree of substitution for the original variety. This means that there is free entry but also some degree of monopoly power for each firm. The prototypical example of a differentiated product in international trade is the automobile. Indeed, one can think of the auto industry as monopolistically competitive, with free entry by conglomerate firms such as Toyota, General Motors, Nissan, Mercedes-Benz, and Ford into various segments of the motor vehicle market, such as sport utility vehicles and sport cars. Since an aggregation of customers in every country demands all or most of the varieties offered on the world stage, intraindustry international trade

is the major consequence. In most advanced countries, intraindustry trade constitutes more than 50 percent of exports and imports.

Models of Monopolistic Competition The theory of monopolistic competition was developed independently in the 1930s by Robinson (1933) and Chamberlin (1933). This model is strictly partial equilibrium and involves free entry with firms producing output levels that are short of the optimum scale, with the higher costs of production viewed as the cost of variety. To apply the model to international trade, theorists have been quite explicit about tastes, costs, and resources. The most realistic model, offered by Lancaster (1979), assumes heterogeneous consumers with each choosing a preferred variety. This approach, however, is complex because it involves the distance of each consumer's favored variety from the next best variety to that consumer. Consequently, the most popular approach has been to assume a representative consumer who buys some of each variety offered by an industry. This follows the pioneering paper by Dixit and Stiglitz (1977). Dixit and Norman (1980) and Krugman (1979, 1981) applied the Dixit-Stiglitz model to international trade in a way that has now become standard.

In a world of perfect competition, there are gains from trade because a country can import things that would otherwise be produced at home at a higher cost. The gains from trade under monopolistic competition need not be from comparative advantage, but rather from achieving greater variety and/or lower costs for those differentiated goods. With differentiated products and free entry, the larger market from international trade allows each country to exploit economies of scale for some selected products but at the same time give consumers even greater variety from other countries.

The basic idea of the model of monopolistic competition is simple: abstract completely from comparative advantage and make the simplest assumptions regarding preferences and costs. Thus it is assumed that all products are produced by labor alone, as in the Ricardian trade model, but each variety has exactly the same production function. Thus consider the set of products to belong to an industry in which all the varieties are close substitutes. This can easily be captured by a constant-elasticity-of-substitution utility function, $u = \left(\Sigma c_i^a\right)^{1/\alpha}$. With this utility function for each consumer, each variety, regardless of how many, faces the same demand at the same price. As in standard trade models, there is full employment and adjustment costs are ignored in the interests of focusing on the long run. Finally, to capture the features of monopolistic competition, products are always produced under economies of scale and there is free entry and exit of firms. Under these conditions, each firm will be identified with a unique product. Two or more firms could not produce a unique variety unless the average cost curves were U-shaped, which is ruled out by assumption.

Understanding monopolistic competition involves two concepts: economies of scale caused by the fixed costs of setting up a new variety of a particular product, and the elasticity of substitution between the varieties of a certain generic product. The elasticity of substitution between X and Y is simply the percentage increase in the relative demand for good X, defined as X/Y, caused by a 1 percent change in the relative price of good Y, defined by the price ratio p_y/p_x. The higher the elasticity of substitution between two products, the higher the numerical value of elasticity of demand for each of the products. Generally speaking, such a numerical elasticity of demand for good X will be somewhat smaller than the elasticity of substitution, because when the price of good X falls, causing a greater quantity of good X to be demanded, people will buy less of good Y, which increases the elasticity of substitution over the elasticity of demand (because X/Y increases more than X). The more varieties of a single product that exist, of course, the closer the elasticity of demand for any variety will be to its elasticity of substitution with other varieties.

The economics of monopolistic competition is straightforward. Consumers have a love for variety that is reflected in the elasticity of substitution. The higher the elasticity of substitution, the *smaller* the love for variety. With an infinite elasticity of substi-

tution, consumers would be indifferent between the two products: essentially no love for variety. The greater the love for variety, the smaller the elasticity of substitution and, therefore, the smaller the elasticity of demand. But the smaller the elasticity of demand, when firms have control over the price, the higher the markup over marginal cost. Thus the love for variety translates into greater potential profits for introducing a new variety. But this comes into conflict with the fixed cost of introducing the new variety, or the economy of scale. The formula is thus simple: smaller elasticity of demand (greater love for variety) and small fixed costs translate into more varieties of product. Note that the love for variety gives rise to a profit incentive for more variety.

This is where international trade or the size of market comes into play. The larger the market, which is what international trade represents, the less important are fixed costs or economies of scale as an impediment to more varieties of product. Thus international trade results in more varieties being produced, but also more of each variety. When trade opens, the producers of existing varieties find their profits increasing, thus giving an incentive for new firms with different varieties to enter. Consumers are better off because they have more varieties to choose from at lower prices.

Following Dixit and Stiglitz (1977) and Krugman (1979, 1981), the model can be described by just three equations if we assume that all varieties face the same demand and costs: a profit-maximizing equation that is the same for each variety, marginal revenue (MR) equal to marginal cost (MC); a free entry equation, the same price (p) equal to same average costs (AC) for each variety; and a full employment equation, the supply of labor (L) equal to demand, which is simply the number of varieties multiplied by the same labor demand of each variety. Labor is the numéraire, so the wage rate is unity. Let $F =$ fixed costs in terms of the amount of labor required to produce any particular variety, and $c =$ marginal costs in terms of how much labor is required to produce another unit of any variety, which we assume to be constant. If $x =$ the output of each firm, the $AC = F/x + c$. Each firm will charge a price p that is a markup k over marginal costs. The equilibrium price, p, the output of each firm x, and the number of varieties, n, are then determined by:

$$p = kc \qquad (1)$$

$$p = F/x + c \qquad (2)$$

$$L = n(F + cx) \qquad (3)$$

The markup in equation (1) decreases if there are more varieties. The second equation (2) represents free entry. The last equation (3) is for full employment of the labor resources devoted to the industry. Even though there are three equations, we can represent the model by a diagram with only two variables, the price of each variety and the number of varieties. This is because the last two equations can be used to eliminate x, and to write

$$p = c[(n/L - nF) + 1] \qquad (4)$$

as a substitute for (2) and (3). This equation shows free entry as well as the average cost of production as an increasing function of the number of varieties.

Equations (1) and (4) are shown in figure 1. The curve PP is the price equation (1), which shows that the price of each variety falls as more varieties are produced because individual firms face more competition from substitutes and must lower their prices to maximize profits. The cost equation (4) is CC (ignore the C*C* and C°C° for the moment). It is upward sloping because an increase in the number of varieties, for any labor supply, must reduce the output of each product. But with economies of scale, average costs must then rise so that the free entry price must rise. The equilibrium, a, is the autarky solution for the country in question.

The model is intuitively straightforward. What happens if there is an *increase* in L? This will initially shift all demand curves for the existing n varieties proportionately to the right, without affecting the elasticity of demand at the initial price. Now new firms enter because profits are positive, and this forces all firms to lower p until all profits are again eliminated. Each firm moves down its AC curve and more of each variety is produced, both the old ones and the new ones. With a lower price and more varieties, per capita well-being must increase.

This tells us what happens with international trade. Suppose there are two countries, Home and Foreign. Assume Home and Foreign are identical in all respects but the labor force L, where the foreign L* exceeds home L. In figure 1, PP is the same; but with Foreign being larger than Home, C*C* for the foreign country must lie to the right of CC for the home country since a larger number of varieties is compatible with the same costs. This is clear from equation 4. With free trade and zero costs of transferring goods, the world economy works like one large economy. The cost curve for the world economy is C°C°, which lies to the right of the foreign C*C*. We can see in figure 1 but also by general reasoning that the free trade level of output for each firm will exceed

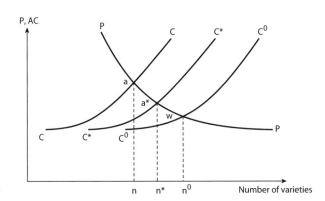

Figure 1
A model of monopolistic competition

the autarkic levels simply because the price of the variety is smaller. But each country will produce a smaller number of varieties because with the same labor force, the only way full employment can be maintained with a larger output of each variety is to reduce the number of varieties produced compared with the number of varieties produced under autarky. Note that with free entry and exit which varieties are produced by which country cannot be determined. To the extent that comparative advantage is not involved, the pattern of trade is indeterminate. When economies of scale are involved, who exports what can be determined by the accident of history.

Now it should be clear that the smaller of the two countries will gain the most from international trade. This is because the price will fall more in that country and the number of varieties will increase. This is clear from the vertical axis of figure 1 and the comparison of the free trade solution at point w with the autarky solution at point a. This is a much stronger theorem in the model of monopolistic competition than in the analogous Ricardian theorem (Ruffin 1988). In the Ricardian model, the result depends on there being only two countries. With more than two countries, the Ricardian result can vanish because the smallest country could have a comparative advantage in between the comparative advantages of the larger countries. But this will never be the case in the present model.

Clearly, this model gives us an explanation of intraindustry trade because in each country all varieties are consumed. All trade is intraindustry in this model because there are no comparative advantages for any industry. Krugman (1981) and Dixit and Norman (1980) show that we can combine intraindustry trade with comparative advantage in a simple way by assuming two such monopolistically competitive industries, but with immobile specific labor assigned to each. Countries can now be defined as having different relative quantities of specific labor, say L_1 and L_2. This allows us to examine the interaction between comparative advantage and intraindustry trade.

Since the price of every variety in this simplified case is the same, we can measure the total output of the industry i as simply the labor supply devoted to that industry divided by the price of the product, p_i, *because if labor is the numéraire, the price of the variety is the amount of labor used in a unit of the product. Thus:*

$$Q_i = L_i / p_i \qquad (5)$$

Since in free trade $p_i = p_i^*$, it follows from equation 1 that

$$Q_i / Q_i^* = L_i / L_i^* \qquad (6)$$

In other words, the relative size of an industry across countries exactly reflects the relative amounts of industry resources across countries. Now if $L_1 / L_1^* > L_2 / L_2^*$, the home country will on net export commodities in industry 1 and import commodities in industry 2. It should be clear that the greater the difference in factor endowments between countries, the larger the volume of interindustry trade and the smaller the volume of the intraindustry trade.

Thus this simple model can explain why a country such as Japan or Australia would have a much smaller amount of intraindustry trade than the United States or any of the European countries. Japan has a much smaller relative endowment of land and Australia a much larger relative endowment of land than the rest of the world, leading to more interindustry trade because Japan must import more raw materials and Australia must export more primary products.

Intraindustry trade enhances the gains from trade through better exploitation of economies of scale rather than through comparative advantage as trade leads countries to concentrate on a limited number of varieties within any particular industry. This leads to an expansion of world output because of the saving of fixed costs.

As Adam Smith himself observed, specialization within industrial categories may also stimulate innovation more than specialization in primary products such as wheat, oil, and copper. A manufactured good often suggests its own shortcomings or new varieties to the human imagination. Producing a greater variety and number of goods increases our general knowledge about technology, and greater knowledge implies smaller costs of knowledge accumulation. This has led to the theory of endogenous growth, which augments the model of monopolistic competition with a dynamic structure in which consumers maximize over an infinite horizon and firms innovate to make a profit in such a way that there is still a free entry equilibrium. In this free entry equilibrium, arbitrage profits cannot be made by selling the firm and investing the proceeds. Endogenous growth occurs because every new variety lowers the cost of future new varieties (Grossman and Helpman 1991; Ruffin 1994).

The role of monopolistic competition in international trade is to show how intraindustry trade can arise even in the absence of comparative advantage, and to demonstrate how the gains from trade result from both lower prices and more variety. The model also provides a framework for studying innovation and growth in the world economy.

See also comparative advantage; foreign direct investment under monopolistic competition; gains from trade; New Trade Theory

FURTHER READING

Chamberlin, Edward H. 1933. *The Theory of Monopolistic Competition*. Cambridge, MA: Harvard University Press. A detailed study of both cost and demand conditions in both monopolistic competition and oligopoly.

Dixit, Avinash K., and Victor D. Norman. 1980. *Theory of International Trade*. Cambridge: Cambridge University Press. Applies the theory of monopolistic competition to international trade.

Dixit, Avinash K., and Joseph Stiglitz. 1977. "Monopolistic Competition and Optimum Product Diversity." *American Economic Review* 67 (3): 297–308. This paper rescued the theory of monopolistic competition from irrelevance.

Grossman, Gene M., and Elhanan Helpman. 1991. *Innovation and Growth in the World Economy*. Cambridge, MA: MIT Press. Applies various models of monopolistic competition to the problem of explaining some patterns of economic growth in a global economy.

Helpman, Elhanan, and Paul Krugman. 1985. *Foreign Trade and Market Structure*. Cambridge, MA: MIT Press. Considers the impact of oligopoly and monopolistic competition on the volume and gains from trade.

Krugman, Paul R. 1979. "Increasing Returns, Monopolistic Competition, and International Trade." *Journal of International Economics* 9 (4): 469–79. Presents a simple version of the Dixit-Stiglitz model of monopolistic competition.

———. 1981. "Intraindustry Specialization and the Gains from Trade." *Journal of Political Economy* 89 (5): 253–66. Applies monopolistic competition to the explanation of intraindustry trade.

Lancaster, Kelvin. 1979. *Variety, Equity, and Efficiency: Product Variety in an Industrial Society*. New York: Columbia University Press, 1979. Applies an innovative theory of product differentiation to the theory of monopolistic competition.

Robinson, Joan. 1933. *The Economics of Imperfect Competition*. London: Macmillan. Presents all of the geometric tools necessary to explain monopoly, monopolistic competition, and price discrimination.

Ruffin, Roy J. 1988. "The Missing Link: The Ricardian Approach to the Factor Endowments Theory of Trade." *American Economic Review* 78 (4): 759–72. Shows how the Ricardian theory of international trade can be used to simplify the Heckscher-Ohlin theory and the gains from trade.

———. 1994. "Endogenous Growth and International Trade." *Review of International Economics* 2 (1): 27–39. Summarizes the Grossman-Helpman model of innovation and growth in the world economy.

ROY J. RUFFIN

■ **moral hazard**
See asymmetric information; bail-ins; bailouts

■ **most favored nation**
See nondiscrimination

■ **movement of natural persons**
See temporary movement of natural persons

■ multilateral environmental agreements

Since 1933, hundreds of agreements have been negotiated among sovereign nations to protect natural resources and the environment. The United Nations Environment Program (UNEP) (2004) identifies the first multilateral environmental agreement (MEA), dating to 1933, as the Convention Relative to the Preservation of Fauna and Flora in Their Natural State. From 1940 until 1960, UNEP lists an additional 23, including the International Convention for the Regulation of Whaling (1946), the International Convention for the Protection of Birds (1950), the International Plant Protection Convention (1951), and the Antarctic Treaty (1959).

Since 1960, hundreds more have proliferated. Among the most well-known are the Convention on International Trade in Endangered Species of Wild Fauna and Flora (CITES 1973), the UN Convention on the Law of the Sea (1982), the International Tropical Timber Agreement (1983, amended 1994), the Montreal Protocol on Substances That Deplete the Ozone Layer (1987, 1990, 1992, 1997), the Rio Convention on Biological Diversity (1992), the Kyoto Protocol to the UN Framework Convention on Climate Change (1997), the Basel Protocol on Liability and Compensation for Damage Resulting from Transboundary Movements of Hazardous Substances and Their Disposal (1999), and the Cartagena Protocol on Biosafety to the Convention on Biological Diversity (2000).

Even this small sample of MEAs presents a legal, jurisdictional, and monitoring thicket. Many different international institutions and groups are empowered with implementation and oversight of these agreements, including more than a dozen agencies in addition to UNEP in the UN alone. Apart from the problem of the internal coherence of the many MEAs, throughout the 1990s these agreements were often at odds with other international obligations forbidding restrictions on the free flow of goods and services in international trade, setting up the "trade and environment" debate (Runge 1994, 2001). The World Trade Organization (WTO) and its predecessor, the General Agreement on Tariffs and Trade (GATT), were criticized for undermining environmental obligations under MEAs, as several celebrated cases brought attention to the potential for conflict.

Perhaps the most famous were the pair of "Tuna-Dolphin" disputes in the 1990s, in which environmentalists argued that the GATT articles had been used to overturn a U.S. embargo on tuna harvested by Mexico and other countries using nets that also killed dolphins as by-catch. In imposing the embargo, the United States argued that such fishing methods violated the U.S. Marine Mammal Protection Act (MMPA). The U.S. embargo was overturned by a GATT panel decision in 1994, which concluded that it violated GATT prohibitions on quantitative restrictions to trade and that the MMPA did not qualify for exemptions granted under GATT Article XX(g) "relating to the conservation of exhaustible natural resources."

This infuriated parts of the environmental community, which saw GATT and later the WTO poised to strike down many trade sanctions designed to protect natural resources authorized under both domestic legislation and MEAs.

In 1994, partly in response to this furor, the WTO established a Committee on Trade and Environment (CTE) to respond to these questions. However, as Esty noted, the CTE "has failed to make any policy recommendations of consequence" (Esty 2003). Furthermore, the balance between MEAs and the WTO has been a continuing source of anxiety in environmental circles. In general, analysts have concluded that MEAs lack the coherence, reach, and financial backing of the WTO, leaving them vulnerable to challenge when they attempt to use trade barriers, sanctions, or embargoes as mechanisms of compliance: "Judged in terms of size and teeth," one analyst wrote, "we might regard the WTO as a large tiger and MEAs as a ragged collection of small cats" (Eckersley 2004, 24). This comment is qualified by the observation that there are hundreds of such cats, the herding of which is increasingly difficult.

First, can the tension between MEAs and the WTO be dealt with under existing institutional arrangements? Second, what alternative arrangements might remedy these tensions and provide greater clarity and coherence to the large number of MEAs? Third, how might these alternatives be approached and successfully implemented in the years ahead?

MEAs and the WTO: Which Way Out? The asymmetrical relationship between the WTO and the multifoliate pattern of MEAs arises from both the structure and content of each set of norms. The structure of the WTO that emerged in the Uruguay Round after nearly 50 years operating under the GATT articles was first developed in the 1947 Havana Charter. In many ways, in 1995 the WTO achieved a vision of an International Trade Organization conceived after World War II as one of three international economic foundations (including the World Bank and International Monetary Fund) to buttress the global economy and resist a return to the beggar-thy-neighbor trade policies of the interwar years. Then, as now, such institutions induced anxiety among those who saw an international trade authority as a threat to national and even intranational sovereignty. In the 1990s, this anxiety extended to national and subnational environmental protection. Whereas the current structure of WTO rules is considered relatively "hard" law in dispute resolution, MEAs are much "softer." And although the contents of MEAs are often tested for consistency with trade rules, trade rules are seldom challenged as inconsistent with MEAs. The result is to discourage the development and implementation of new and existing MEAs and to reinforce their subservience to the trade regime.

There is doubt, given this asymmetry (which many in the trade community consider appropriate), whether a more balanced relationship can be achieved under existing institutions. A number of institutional "fixes" have been proposed. One is to amend GATT Article XX, pertaining to exhaustible natural resources and other exceptions to the rules of nondiscrimination, to better account for MEAs (Nissen 1997). Some precedent for this is reflected in exceptions (article 104) to the North American Free Trade Agreement (NAFTA) for three specific MEAs: CITES, the Montreal Protocol, and the Basel Convention. A less incremental but more direct approach would be to create a new WTO agreement dedicated specifically to MEAs (Brack and Grey 2003, 36). This could define the general scope of MEAs, the possible use of specific trade measures to enforce or implement their environmental objectives, and criteria for making more nonspecific measures consistent with Article XX. A third proposal, advanced by Switzerland in a submission to the CTE in 2000, would create a clear division of responsibility between the WTO and MEAs, defining their respective trade versus environmental competency. The WTO's responsibility would extend to questions of trade discrimination and disguised protection, while the MEAs' responsibility would be determining environmental objectives and "choosing the means, instruments, mechanisms and measures necessary to achieve these objectives" (CTE 2000, 2). Such an agreement would reduce the asymmetry between trade and environmental measures by asserting the absence of hierarchy and the importance of mutual support and deference.

There is, however, considerable mutual suspicion and derision between the trade and environmental communities resulting from the trade/environment battles of the last two decades. This has led a number of authors to propose the less incremental and more sweeping creation of a World Environment Organization (WEO) (see also Biermann 2000; Esty 2000; Runge 2001).

The WEO Alternative In the early 1990s, transnational environmental policy challenges led to calls for a World Environmental Organization (WEO). By 2000, support extended from the French prime minister Lionel Jospin and president Jacques Chirac to the former WTO director general Renato Ruggiero, the *Economist* magazine, and others. The argument for a WEO arose primarily from those who felt that the WTO system was ill-equipped to respond when trade questions intersected with environmental issues, including MEAs. Apart from trade/environment conflicts, however, the anarchy of the MEA arrangement also suggested a need for better-coordinated multilateral responses to transnational environmental issues even if trade was largely unaffected. In other words, whether or not the WTO could be "greened," international environmental challenges clearly required their own multilateral responses, and these responses required greater coherence and consistency. Just as the GATT/WTO system had evolved out of growing *commercial* interdependence following World War II and had helped to foster a set of rules by which the trade game should be played, so *ecological* interconnections created the need for a more unified set of global environmental rules. The parallelism of trading rules and environmental rules arose from the fact that interdependent states could not cope with commercial *or* environmental challenges solely through unilateral or ad hoc solutions. Moreover, the coexistence of multilateral trade and environmental rules gave rise to the questions of priority and consistency noted earlier.

A prototype for such an overarching institution arose from the environmental side agreement to NAFTA. In late 1993, NAFTA was ratified by the U.S. Congress, together with provisions that would create the North American Commission for Environmental Cooperation (CEC), headquartered in Montreal. By late 2007, the CEC had survived more than a decade of service, although it remained underfunded and often unsupported by the governments of Canada, Mexico, and the United States. Despite its small size, the CEC's mandate extended beyond the trade effects of NAFTA on the environment to include an array of transborder ecological issues. It also provided for a dispute settlement mechanism for environmental questions. From a legal perspective, the CEC derived from an executive agreement, which "steers clear of the normative realm and concerns itself with things institutional, primarily because it is the product of an intergovernmental process between entities that each want to set their own standards" (Johnson and Beaulieu 1996).

The basic design of a WEO modeled on the CEC would be the creation of a Secretariat and a Multilateral Commission on Environment. The Secretariat would be the formal, ministerial-level body of government representatives, meeting periodically to affirm certain policies. The commission would be a policy-oriented group of environmental experts drawn from nongovernmental organizations (NGOs), academia, business, and government. Although the representatives to the WEO Secretariat would, like WTO representatives, be government officials, expert environmental and business involvement, similar to the International Labor Organization (ILO), could occur via the commission. The commission would thus be composed of a standing group of environmental experts and government and business representatives from all member counties. Its meetings would be open to the public and would allow worldwide access to the data and analysis underlying its work. The primary focus of this work would be to propose ways to harmonize national environmental standards and MEAs, while carefully considering the technical issues and problems of this process. This task would resemble in some respects the technical harmonization of food and safety requirements under the Food and Agriculture Organization–affiliated Codex Alimentarius. The process would allow for public comments from any group, governmental or nongovernmental, opening the WEO to full public participation and review.

The Years Ahead The CTE's limited terms of reference clearly suggest that the WTO does not care to bring order to MEAs, except insofar as they impinge on trade rules. This substantial institutional gap can be filled by a WEO dedicated to transnational environmental challenges that may or may not have direct linkages to trade, but which have given rise to the crazy-quilt of MEAs.

Until such an overarching structure is articulated, two fundamental questions will challenge MEAs, individually and collectively. First, if MEAs involve explicit trade measures or sanctions, they will be subject to continuing challenges under the WTO. Second, the hundreds of existing MEAs, and those that may be negotiated in the coming decades, cannot be adequately managed without linking them to an overarching set of norms. In the short to intermediate term, waivers to WTO rules have been proposed for some MEAs, renewable over regular time intervals. The presumption that trade ministers should vet each MEA, however, would seem to place them in regular and recurring judgment of environmental policy measures, a position which they evidently prefer to avoid.

Over the longer term, there appears to be a clear need for the overarching role of a WEO Secretariat to coordinate disparate environmental efforts and MEAs and function as a go-between and buffer relating MEAs or other environmental policies to the WTO system. MEAs (and national environmental programs) designed to minimize trade-distorting effects and advance market-based environmental initiatives such as trading schemes could contribute to this institutional oversight. When obvious conflicts between MEAs and WTO rules arose, a WEO could help to prepare sound arguments in favor of an Article XX exception, based on the necessity of trade measures in an MEA, a waiver if deemed appropriate, or some other GATT-legal "window" allowing an exception for the environmental measure.

An even more significant function might be the consolidation of claims made under myriad environmental agreements into a unified dispute settlement process, in which NGOs and other interested parties could participate. Precisely because an independent entity such as WEO is lacking, a greater temptation exists to use trade measures to enforce environmental obligations. Trade interests may condemn the use of such measures for environmental goals, but in the absence of effective multilateral environmental rules and an overarching entity such as the WEO, environmentalists may claim that they have no recourse. Although it is naïve to imagine that these two realms of policy can be entirely disjoint, the creation of a WEO would assist in separating many issues that do not need to be in conflict. The weaker the perceived ability of environmental groups to influence international policies, however, the greater their incentive to use "linkage" destructively: to threaten the trading system in order to gain environmental concessions.

See also Basel Convention; Convention on Biological Diversity; Convention on International Trade in Endangered Species (CITES); General Agreement on Tariffs and Trade (GATT); Global Environment Facility; trade and the environment; World Trade Organization

FURTHER READING

Biermann, Frank. 2000. "The Case for a World Environmental Organization." *Environment* 42 (9): 23–31. An accessible article laying out the reasons a WEO should be created.

Brack, Duncan, and Kevin Gray. 2003. "Multilateral Environmental Agreements and the WTO." London: The Royal Institute of International Affairs. Sustainable Development Program Report (September). A somewhat technical assessment of the trade issues surrounding MEAs.

Committee on Trade and Environment (CTE). 2000. "The Relationship between the Provisions of the Multilateral Trading System and Multilateral Environmental Agreements (MEAs)." Submission by Switzerland (June 8) (WT/CTE/W/139). A trade negotiator's note on trade and MEAs.

Eckersley, Robyn. 2004. "The Big Chill: The WTO and Multilateral Environmental Agreements." *Global Environmental Politics* 4 (2): 24–50. A political scientist's analysis of MEAs and conflicts with trade rules.

Esty, Daniel C. 2000. "The Value of Creating a Global Environmental Organization." *Environment Matters* (annual review). Washington, DC: World Bank. A former trade negotiator argues for a world environmental body.

———. 2003. "Introduction: Achieving Harmony in Trade and Environment." In *GETSView* (online journal) 2 (2). Downloadable from http://www.GETS.org/pages/harmony/. An introduction to a collection of papers on trade-environment interactions.

Johnson, Pierre Marc, and André Beaulieu. 1996. *The Environment and NAFTA: Understanding and Implementing the New Continental Law.* Washington, DC: Island Press. The most complete analysis of the environmental side agreement to NAFTA in print.

Nissen, J. L. 1997. "Achieving a Balance between Trade and the Environment: The Need to Amend the WTO/GATT to Include Multilateral Environmental Agreements." *Law and Policy in International Business* 28 (3): 901–28. A legal analysis of the WTO/MEA relationships.

Runge, C. Ford (with François Ortalo-Magné and Philip Van de Kamp). 1994. *Freer Trade, Protected Environment: Balancing Trade Liberalization and Environmental*

Interests. New York: Council on Foreign Relations Press. A monograph resulting from the Council on Foreign Relations study group on trade and environment.

———. 2001. "A Global Environment Organization (GEO) and the World Trading System." *Journal of World Trade* 35 (4): 399–426. The author's arguments in favor of and against a global environment organization.

United Nations Environment Program (UNEP). 2004. "Chronological List of Environmental Agreements." Division of Policy Development and Law. A comprehensive listing of all MEAs to 2004.

C. FORD RUNGE

■ multilateral trade negotiations

Broadly defined, a multilateral trade negotiation is any trade negotiation occurring between more than two countries. However, since the advent of the General Agreement on Tariffs and Trade (GATT) in 1947, the term has come to refer specifically to the periodic negotiating "rounds" (meetings) conducted under the auspices of the GATT and successor, the World Trade Organization (WTO). There have been nine such rounds since 1947, with the most recent—the Doha Round—not yet completed as of 2007. The purpose of these rounds is to reduce barriers to international trade and establish or modify rules of conduct for trade policy. What distinguishes them as multilateral is that participation is open to all member countries and the results generally apply to all members on a nondiscriminatory basis. As each successive round builds on the results of the one before, the GATT/WTO system evolves, as both the product of multilateral trade negotiations and the framework in which the negotiations are conducted.

Basic Concepts and Terminology Throughout history, countries have sought to obtain access to foreign markets for the goods and services they export, while protecting their own domestic markets from foreign competition. This behavior is reflected in the terminology of trade negotiations. If a country lowers one of its tariffs or otherwise opens its market to imports from another country, it is said to have granted a "concession" to that country. Trade negotiators view receiving a concession as beneficial and granting a concession as costly, though the magnitude of the benefits and costs may vary from sector to sector. The mutual exchange of concessions of roughly equal value is known as "reciprocity."

Both economic theory and ample empirical evidence have shown that, in general, concessions produce welfare benefits to the affected exporting countries that outweigh whatever welfare costs are experienced by the importing country granting the concession, provided the concessions are nondiscriminatory, that is, provided the concession is granted to all exporters. This suggests that if all countries exchange concessions on a reciprocal and nondiscriminatory basis, then all stand to benefit. This insight is at the heart of multilateral trade negotiations. Indeed, the stated purpose of the GATT is to raise incomes, employment, and growth "by entering into reciprocal and mutually advantageous arrangements directed to the substantial reduction of tariffs and other barriers to trade and to the elimination of discriminatory treatment in international commerce" (Preamble of the General Agreement on Tariffs and Trade, 1947).

Pre-GATT Trade Negotiations Prior to the GATT, countries negotiated trade agreements on a bilateral basis. Two countries interested in expanding trade with each other would meet and negotiate reductions in trade barriers, usually tariffs, on a more or less reciprocal basis. Early trade agreements negotiated in this way were relatively few in number, short in duration, and usually discriminatory (i.e., concessions applied only bilaterally). This changed substantially in the mid-19th century, however. A surge in global trade, fueled by the industrial revolution and technological improvements in transportation and communications, coincided with changes in the political and intellectual landscape in favor of freer trade. Many countries responded by opening their markets, both unilaterally and through bilateral agreements.

The most important bilateral agreement of the period was the Cobden-Chevalier treaty of 1860 between the United Kingdom and France, which cut tariffs between two of the largest trading nations of the time. It also included the most-favored-nation (MFN) clause, under which both countries committed to giving each other the best treatment they offered to any other country. This had the effect of guaranteeing that neither country would discriminate against the other in any subsequent agreements they might negotiate with other countries. A wave of bilateral MFN agreements followed, as countries rushed to avoid being the victims of discrimination, so that by 1870, almost all major traders were involved in a web of nondiscriminatory bilateral agreements.

The successful bilateral trade regime of the 19th century was suspended during World War I and suffered a series of setbacks until the end of the World War II. The most notable setback was a global trade war touched off by the U.S. Smoot-Hawley Tariff Act of 1930. Four years later the United States attempted to reverse the slide toward protectionism with the passage of the Reciprocal Trade Agreements Act (RTAA), which gave the president wide latitude to negotiate bilateral reciprocal trade agreements on an MFN basis. Although this effort to revive the bilateral system was cut short by World War II, many of the concepts, rules, and procedures of the RTAA were subsequently incorporated into the GATT after the war.

Negotiations in the GATT Era In 1946, the United Nations, responding to a proposal from the United States, established a preparatory committee to draft a charter for an International Trade Organization (ITO). The ITO was meant be a multilateral trade organization with open membership, founded on the principles of reciprocity and nondiscrimination, to serve as the trade counterpart to the organizations set up by the Bretton Woods conference of 1944—the International Monetary Fund and the World Bank. At its first meeting in London, the preparatory committee established procedures for conducting multilateral trade negotiations, which were put to use at a meeting held in Geneva in 1947 involving 23 countries: Australia, Belgium, Brazil, Burma, Canada, Ceylon, Chile, the Republic of China, Cuba, the Czechoslovak Republic, France, India, Lebanon, Luxembourg, Netherlands, New Zealand, Norway, Pakistan, Southern Rhodesia, Syria, South Africa, the United Kingdom, and the United States. The countries exchanged concessions in the form of tariff "bindings"—maximum limits on tariff levels—covering thousands of manufactured products. They also agreed that all signatories should grant one another MFN status, and they drafted a set of general rules on the use of other trade-related policies, such as subsidies and quantitative restrictions, to ensure that countries did not circumvent their tariff obligations. The concessions and rules together constituted the General Agreement on Tariffs and Trade (GATT), and the Geneva meeting became known as the first GATT round. The GATT was supposed to be incorporated into the ITO Charter. Although the charter was finally completed in Havana in 1948, it was never ratified, however. Thus, the GATT emerged as the basis of the multilateral trading system.

Subsequent rounds of multilateral trade negotiations were held in Annecy, France (1949), Torquay, United Kingdom (1950), and Geneva (1956). After this, rounds were given names: the Dillon Round (1960–61) was named after the U.S. undersecretary of state C. Douglas Dillon, the Kennedy Round (1963–67) after the U.S. president, and the Tokyo (1973–79) and Uruguay (1986–94) Rounds after the places where they were launched. The Doha Development Round, so named because issues of developing countries were supposed to be high on the agenda, was launched in Doha, Qatar, in 2001. A summary of these rounds is found in table 1.

Subjects and Modalities At the beginning of each round, the participating countries convene to decide on the subjects to be negotiated and the "modalities"—the rules and procedures—for conducting the negotiations. In the first five GATT rounds, the primary subjects were tariff concessions on manufactured products and the accession of new members. New members are required to negotiate tariff concessions and other terms with existing members prior to their entry. In the Kennedy Round, the scope of the negotiations was broadened to include concessions on nontariff barriers to trade in manufactures. The Tokyo Round continued this

Table 1
GATT/WTO rounds, 1947–2007

Name of round or meeting	Period	Number of parties	Subjects and modalities	Results
Geneva	1947	23	Tariffs: item-by-item request-offer negotiations	Concessions covering 15,000 tariff lines
Annecy	1949	33	Tariffs: item-by-item request-offer negotiations	5,000 tariff concessions; 9 accessions
Torquay	1950	34	Tariffs: item-by-item request-offer negotiations	8,700 tariff concessions; 4 accessions
Geneva	1956	22	Tariffs: item-by-item request-offer negotiations	Modest reductions
Dillon Round	1960–61	45	Tariffs: item-by-item request-offer negotiations.	4,400 tariff concessions.
Kennedy Round	1963–67	48	Tariffs: formula approach (linear cut) and item-by-item negotiations. Nontariff measures: anti-dumping, customs valuation	Average tariffs reduced by 35%; 33,000 tariff lines bound; agreements on customs valuation and anti-dumping
Tokyo Round	1973–79	99	Tariffs: formula approach with exceptions. Nontariff measures: anti-dumping, customs valuation, subsidies and countervail, government procurement, import licensing, product standards safeguards, special and differential treatment of developing countries	Average tariffs reduced by one-third to 6 percent for OECD manufactures; voluntary codes of conduct agreed for all nontariff issues except safeguards
Uruguay Round	1986–94	117	Tariffs: formula approach and item-by-item request-offer negotiations. Nontariff measures: all Tokyo issues, plus services, intellectual property, preshipment inspection, rules of origin, trade-related investment measures, dispute settlement, transparency and surveillance of trade policies	Average tariffs again reduced by one third; agriculture and textiles and clothing subjected to rules; creation of WTO; new agreements on services and TRIPs; majority of Tokyo Round codes extended to all WTO members
Doha Round	2001–	150	Tariffs: formula approach and item-by-item request-offer negotiations. Nontariff measures: trade facilitation, rules, services, environment	

Source: World Trade Organization, *World Trade Report 2007.*

trend and added voluntary codes of conduct on various trade-related policies. The Uruguay Round expanded into the areas of agriculture, services, intellectual property, and trade-related investment measures.

Elaborate modalities have been developed for the negotiation of concessions on market access. The first five rounds used the procedure known as the item-by-item, request-and-offer method. Under this method, each participating country simultaneously submits a "request list" to each of its trading partners. A request list is a list of concessions (products and tariff cuts) that the country requests from its trading partners. Each trading partner responds with an offer list, a list of concessions that the country is willing to make. Each participating country has full flexibility on granting concessions on individual products and is free to refrain from concessions on any item. Moreover, countries may request concessions only on products for which they are among the largest suppliers to the countries from which the concessions are asked. This is known as the "principal supplier" rule. The reason for this rule is that all concessions in GATT negotiations must be made on an MFN basis, which means that they must be extended to all GATT members. If a small supplier were to request a concession, then to grant that concession would imply that most of the benefit, in terms of improved market access, would accrue to countries (the large suppliers) that did not request the concession and therefore would be unlikely to "pay" for it with reciprocal concessions. Countries that receive concessions via MFN without paying for them are free riders. The principal supplier rule is a method for containing the free-rider problem.

The Kennedy Round brought two significant changes in modalities. First, it was agreed that negotiations would center on across-the-board linear tariff cuts. Countries were expected to cut tariffs on all manufactured products by an equal percentage (50 percent was the agreed number) but could submit lists of exceptions. These lists are referred to as "negative lists" (lists of tariffs *not* to be reduced, or reduced by less than 50 percent), as opposed to the "positive lists" (list of tariffs to be reduced) in the item-by-item approach. The second change was the adoption of special and differential treatment for developing countries. In particular, it was decided that less-developed countries should not be expected to reciprocate tariff reductions made by developed countries. These changes in modalities reflected a growing concern about the unwieldiness of the item-by-item approach as the number of GATT members grew. They also reflected concern among developing countries that trade liberalization would interfere with their development policies and that negotiations based on the principal-supplier rule had put them at a disadvantage.

The Tokyo Round operated with a similar procedure as the Kennedy Round, except that instead of a linear tariff cut, countries used a more complicated formula designed to achieve larger reductions on tariffs that were initially high. This became known as the "formula" approach. The Uruguay Round involved a mixture of the formula approach and the item-by-item approach. Some countries, led by the European Union, used the formula approach with negative lists, while the United States and other countries used the item-by-item approach, submitting positive lists.

Negotiations are normally carried out by representatives from each individual country. However, in some cases, countries join coalitions and negotiate as a group. The most common form of this is the customs union. A customs union is a group of countries with free trade among them and a common external tariff. Examples include the European Union, the South American customs union Mercosur, and many others. Typically they send a single representative to negotiate changes in the common external tariff. Other coalitions will typically form around a common interest in a specific topic. For example, agricultural exporters have created coalitions to make common offers on agricultural tariffs and subsidies. Small countries often create coalitions to gain greater weight in negotiations.

Results Of the first five GATT Rounds, the first was by far the most productive in terms of tariff concessions. It involved on the order of 45,000 concessions on 15,000 tariff lines, covering about

$10 billion worth of trade. Such extensive tariff reductions were not repeated until the Kennedy Round, at which point the GATT had more than twice the number of members. The lack of productivity of the negotiations during the intervening rounds, however, does not mean that trade liberalization was halted. In fact, tariff cuts agreed to by Europe and Japan in 1947 were rendered largely ineffective by quantitative restrictions and exchange controls in those countries, until the late 1950s. As these measures were eliminated on a unilateral basis in the late 1950s and early 1960s, the international trade of these countries soared.

The linear approach to tariff reductions used in the Kennedy Round proved effective, though tariffs were ultimately reduced by an average of only 35 percent, instead of the 50 percent target, and many countries opted out of the linear reduction entirely. This round also produced agreements on customs valuation and anti-dumping. The Tokyo Round achieved similar tariff reductions and added voluntary codes of conduct on subsidies, technical barriers to trade, import licensing, government procurement, customs valuation, anti-dumping, meat and dairy products, and civil aircraft. The Uruguay Round cut tariffs again by a third, created a new organization, the WTO, with a revised organizational structure, and strengthened the dispute settlement system.

The creation of the WTO did not fundamentally change the nature of multilateral trade negotiations; however, it did create additional opportunities for countries to discuss trade policy on an ongoing basis. An important innovation is the Ministerial Conference, which meets every two years. This conference is attended by the top trade representative of each country and is intended to provide direction and political impetus for moving trade negotiations forward. The Doha Development Round was launched at the Doha Ministerial Conference in 2001.

It is fair to conclude that multilateral trade negotiations have played, and continue to play, a key role in shaping the modern world trading system. They have established the general rules and terms that now govern the trade of more than 150 countries and have brought about dramatic, if uneven, reductions in tariffs and nontariff barriers since 1947. Whether they will continue to work as the primary mechanism for trade liberalization in the future is unknown. Increases in membership and greater complexity of the issues under negotiation have made recent multilateral negotiations slow and difficult. Preferential trade agreements, such as customs unions and free trade areas, negotiated bilaterally or among small groups of countries, have been on the rise since the mid-1990s. They offer greater speed and focus than negotiations involving the whole WTO. Whatever the ultimate effect of preferential arrangements, however, multilateral trade negotiations will continue to be important, because they are the only option for addressing trade issues of global consequence.

See also agricultural trade negotiations; General Agreement on Tariffs and Trade (GATT); multilateralism; nondiscrimination; tariff-cutting formulas; World Trade Organization

FURTHER READING

Bagwell, Kyle, and Robert W. Staiger. 2002. *The Economics of the World Trading System*. Cambridge, MA: MIT Press. Suitable for advanced students of economics, this book provides a theoretical framework for understanding the economics of trade negotiations, agreements, and WTO rules.

Hoda, Anwarul. 2001. *Tariff Negotiations and Renegotiations under the GATT and the WTO: Procedures and Practices*. Cambridge: Cambridge University Press. An excellent source for the details, large and small, of multilateral trade negotiations.

Hoekman, Bernard, and Michel Kostecki. 2001. *The Political Economy of the World Trading System*. 2d ed. New York: Oxford University Press. Offers a broad introduction to the WTO, along with an accessible treatment of the economics and politics of multilateral trading system.

Jackson, John H. 1997. *The World Trading System: Law and Policy of International Economic Relations*. Cambridge, MA: MIT Press. A classic, this book gives a broad and insightful introduction to the history and institutions of the GATT/WTO, organized by policy type.

World Trade Organization (WTO). 2007. *World Trade Report 2007: Sixty Years of the Multilateral Trading System, Achievements and Challenges.* Geneva: WTO. Written by a team of WTO experts, this book offers thorough treatment of the history of the GATT and WTO.

RODNEY LUDEMA

■ multilateralism

With a membership of more than 150 nations in the World Trade Organization (WTO) and a broad mandate covering trade in goods and services, the multilateral trade system has come a long way since its inception in the early postwar years as the General Agreement on Tariffs and Trade (GATT)—a provisional treaty that was signed by merely 23 founding member countries (contracting parties).

Under the GATT, member countries agreed to adhere to specific rules and principles relating to goods trade and to participate in periodic rounds of multilateral trade negotiations to lower trade barriers. The Uruguay Round of multilateral trade negotiations (1986–94) created the WTO—subsuming the GATT under it and adding two new agreements for the WTO to oversee: the General Agreements on Trade in Services and the Agreement on Trade-Related Aspects of Intellectual Property Rights. Although the WTO is a complex and multifaceted institution, its core purposes are to serve as a forum in which countries reach *agreement* on rules governing their trade policies and on reductions in their trade barriers and to *enforce* these agreements.

It may seem surprising that the theoretical literature on international trade relations does not unconditionally prescribe a multilateral institution to mediate trade relations among nations. Specifically, it is well known that in perfectly competitive contexts, a "small" country maximizes its national welfare by *unilaterally* choosing free trade. This benchmark setting offers no reasons for trade negotiations between countries. When a country is "large" enough to influence prices in international markets, however,

a rationale for trade negotiations emerges. Although the exercise of market power by a large country through the imposition of trade restrictions leads to an improvement in its terms of trade (the relative price of its exportables to its importables) and welfare, global welfare declines. Large countries may therefore find themselves in a "prisoner's dilemma": individually rational behavior leads them to impose trade barriers on one another, even though they would all be better off (relative to this outcome with mutual barriers) by lowering their trade barriers instead (Johnson 1953–54; Bagwell and Staiger 1999). Clearly, negotiations may help to move these countries to the superior outcome with lower trade barriers. It may be noted that domestic political factors may prevent even a "small" country from achieving free trade. Here, too, international negotiations involving reciprocal trade liberalization by partner countries may induce countries jointly to liberalize trade by suitably altering the factors influencing domestic politics and decision making.

The WTO system provides mechanisms in the form of explicit and implicit rules, norms, and principles to increase the incentives for agreements to be reached and for agreements to be enforced. Primary among these are *reciprocity* and *nondiscrimination*. Although *reciprocity* has not been formally defined in the WTO, in practice it calls for a balance of "concessions" to be made by the parties to an agreement. Since the initial trade barriers may be suboptimal to begin with, lowering them may improve welfare, and thus this need not be regarded as a "concession" in the first instance. Nondiscrimination, formally explicated in the GATT (Article I), requires that no member country be discriminated against—specifically that imported goods need to be treated equally regardless of country of origin.

In the multilateral system, reciprocity and nondiscrimination alter the incentives for agreement to be reached and for agreements to be enforced. Where trade barriers come about due to countries' exercise of market power, unilateral liberalization may reduce welfare by worsening the liberalizing country's terms of trade. Reciprocal trade liberalization, on the other hand, will allow countries to maintain their terms of trade while achieving enhanced production and consumption efficiency. When tariffs are determined by domestic political factors, such as the political strength of the import-competing sector, reciprocal liberalization, by improving outcomes for domestic exportable sectors, enhances the prospects for trade liberalization. Note that nondiscrimination can add significant leverage to reciprocity. By ensuring that one country's liberalization extends to all partners, nondiscrimination creates a wider set of reciprocal liberalization obligations. This, in turn, again due to nondiscrimination, creates an even wider set of reciprocal liberalization obligations. Nondiscrimination coupled with reciprocity may thereby create a virtuous circle of liberalization. On the other hand, some argue that nondiscrimination creates "free-rider" problems within the system, since countries not engaging in liberalization of their own nevertheless benefit from the liberalization of others. In practice, however, the scope for free riding is minimized by exercising selectivity and exclusion of goods chosen for liberalization (that is, a country may liberalize trade only in those specific goods that are relevant to a reciprocating partner country and exclude those goods that may be of value to other nonliberalizing countries).

Enforcement of WTO agreements is achieved through a well-specified dispute settlement mechanism that involves a series of steps progressing through consultation between members, adjudication by WTO panels, and adoption by its dispute settlement body. Thus transgressions of WTO agreements require that the affected parties be offered compensation by the transgressor or that they be allowed reciprocally to withdraw "equivalent concessions" (compensation may be preferred, as raising trade barriers in retaliation may be costly for the retaliating country as well).

Nondiscrimination implies that more than one country will be affected by transgression of WTO agreements—the withdrawal of equivalent concessions by all of these affected parties increases the costs of violating WTO agreements. Multilateral punishments may also be valuable in sustaining the system and "leveling the playing field" when there are trans-

gressions of WTO agreements on a bilateral basis (discussed later) and when countries are asymmetric in their economic power or vulnerability (Maggi 1999). Thus reciprocity and nondiscrimination acting together play an important role in the enforcement of agreements as well.

WTO agreements provide a number of provisions that allow for temporary, and sometimes even permanent, suspension of previously undertaken obligations. To protect industries against a sudden surge of imports, the GATT permits countries to take "safeguard" actions that are temporary, nondiscriminatory, and transparent (Article XIX). The GATT also allows for anti-dumping duties to be imposed on imports that are being sold at prices lower than costs or lower than prices in the exporter's home market (Article VI). Countervailing duties may be imposed on imports from suppliers who have been "unfairly" subsidized by their governments (Article VI). In contrast to "safeguard" actions, which must, at least in principle, be applied on a nondiscriminatory basis, anti-dumping and countervailing duties are generally country specific. The multilateral retaliation that supports enforcement of agreements in the multilateral trade system is clearly weakened in these cases.

In a significant derogation of the GATT's non-discrimination principle, member countries are permitted to enter into preferential trade agreements (PTAs) in the form of *free trade areas* and *customs unions* (Article XXIV). Although PTAs are subject to the requirement that trade restrictions imposed by the members of the preferential agreement on nonmember countries will not be more restrictive than before the preferential agreement and a further restriction that the member countries eliminate barriers to "substantially" all trade among themselves, violations of these restrictions abound—with the WTO showing limited enforcement ability.

PTAs have rapidly proliferated in recent years, as have uses of nontraditional (and bilaterally implemented) forms of protection such as anti-dumping and countervailing duties. Reining in these significant challenges to multilateralism will require the multilateral trade system to strengthen its enforcement mechanisms and to revitalize interest in its nondiscriminatory liberalization mechanisms.

See also Doha Round; General Agreement on Tariffs and Trade (GATT); multilateral environmental agreements; multilateral trade negotiations; nondiscrimination; regionalism; Uruguay Round; World Trade Organization

FURTHER READING

Bagwell, K., and R. Staiger. 1999. "An Economic Theory of GATT." *American Economic Review* 89 (1): 215–48. A theoretical rationalization of the principles of reciprocity and nondiscrimination in the international trade system.

Hoekman, B. 1993. "Multilateral Trade Negotiations and the Coordination of Commercial Policies." In *The Multilateral Trading System: Analysis and Options for Change*, edited by R. Stern. University of Michigan Press, Ann Arbor, 29–62. A comprehensive discussion of the rationale for multilateralism and the relevant characteristics of the GATT/WTO system.

Johnson, H. G. 1953–54. "Optimum Tariffs and Retaliation." *Review of Economic Studies* 1 (2): 142–53. A seminal theoretical analysis of self-interested behavior of countries in setting trade policy and inefficiency of the resulting policy outcomes.

Maggi, G. 1999. "The Role of Multilateral Institutions in International Trade Cooperation." *American Economic Review* 89 (1): 190–214. A theoretical analysis of the role of multilateral enforcement in sustaining trade cooperation.

PRAVIN KRISHNA

■ multinational enterprises

The multinational enterprise (MNE), also referred to as the multinational corporation, the international corporation, the global firm, or the transnational corporation, is a multiplant firm that controls and coordinates operations in at least two countries (Caves 2007). Although there is a tendency to associate the control and coordination of an MNE's international operations with majority-owned foreign affiliates (undertaken through foreign direct investment, or FDI), both control and coordination may be achieved through a minority ownership and in some cases through nonequity means.

Historically, FDI and MNE activity have been synonymous. International and national agencies that maintain and collect data on MNE activity generally define the MNE as a firm that *owns* and controls value-adding operations in more than one country (Dunning 1993). Although FDI is one of the main modes by which MNEs engage in cross-border value-adding activities, the MNE may also control and engage in value-adding activities through nonequity means, such as through cooperative agreements and outsourcing, sometimes without de jure ownership of the productive assets but de facto controlling the operations of the nonlegally affiliated operation. Therefore, the use of the term *MNE* as a synonym for FDI is increasingly inaccurate (Wilkins 2001).

The MNE has traditionally also been regarded as having a distinct "home country" where its headquarters are located and which acts as the command center, providing primary strategic direction for its affiliates in various "host countries," as well as providing the primary or core assets on which the affiliates base their operations. Indeed, the home country establishment is referred to as the "parent firm," implying that the home country is at the top of a hierarchy of affiliates or subsidiaries. Furthermore, residents of the home country are assumed to own (and therefore control) the international operations of the MNE. Although most MNEs are still organized along these lines, there are a growing number of firms in which ownership and control are spread across several countries, as well as several cases where an MNE may locate its headquarters in a country other than its home country. Furthermore, a number of MNEs have multiple headquarters located in different countries, with strategic control distributed along geographic, product, or functional lines.

The nature, structure, and organization of the MNE has changed considerably since it has become an object of specialist study, and this change has been exacerbated by development associated with the globalization of products, markets, and services, as well as political and economic developments associated with shifting political hegemonies and economic liberalization (Narula 2003). Thus a more accurate and current definition of an MNE is: a firm that engages in international business activities, has affiliates in more than one country, and whose operations and activities in different locations are actively coordinated by one or more headquarters organizations. Emphasis is placed on the presence of interdependencies between the various economic units in different locations, and their active coordination and control across borders, and not on the ownership structure (Narula 2003).

Significance of MNEs United Nations Conference on Trade and Development (UNCTAD) data indicate that in 2004 there were an estimated 77,135 MNEs worldwide, with 773,019 affiliates of various types (UNCTAD 2006). Although MNEs are often regarded as large, global firms, the majority of MNEs are small and medium-sized enterprises, with relatively small international operations, often concentrated in their home region.

Despite the importance given to MNEs, they do not account for a dominant or even a major share of the world's economic activity. In terms of employment, the world's largest nonfinancial MNEs employed 14.9 million people in 2004. This number represented only 6 percent of total global employment. Despite the relatively small role of MNEs on an aggregate level, the situation differs substantially across countries. MNEs account for less than 5 percent of the total employment in countries such as Japan and Indonesia, but this figure rises to well over 40 percent in countries such as Malaysia, Argentina, and Ireland. The significance of MNEs in terms of sales, value added, and ownership of assets is of similar magnitude. In the United States, value added, exports, imports, and research and development (R&D) by foreign MNEs in 2002 as a percentage of total activity by all private businesses were 5.7, 19.8, 27.9, and 14.4 percent, respectively.

Two characteristics of the operations of MNEs stand out. First, larger MNEs have been found to be concentrated in the more "dynamic" sectors of the economy. Thus even though they play a relatively small role in most economies in terms of the level of total employment, MNEs often play a disproportionately large role in two different types of industrial sectors. They tend to be most active in dynamic sectors typified by high growth rates and the use of new and emerging technologies (e.g., electronics, communication equipment, and industrial machinery), and also in mature sectors where economies of scale, branding, and advertising determine market share (e.g., petroleum products, chemicals, automobiles, food and beverages, and consumer goods). In mature sectors, while the technology underlying these industries may be diffused and codified, capital limitations and marketing capabilities can cause just a few MNEs to maintain a large share of the global market.

A majority of MNE activity is associated with firms from developed countries. As data on value adding and ownership are not readily available in a comparable form for all MNEs, most analyses rely on outward FDI data as a proxy for MNE activity. Approximately 87 percent of all outward FDI stock in 2004 was associated with MNEs whose ultimate beneficiary owner was based in the developed countries. Of the U.S. $1.4 trillion of outward FDI from developing countries, a vast majority—some 90 percent—is associated with 20 emerging market and transition economies and about 100 MNEs. These trends reflect the strong positive correlation between the level of economic development and the growth of firms from these economies with the technological and organizational capabilities to compete globally with the more established MNEs in world markets (UNCTAD 2006).

History of the MNE The MNE as a cross-border-coordinating, organizational entity (as it is known today) is a relatively new phenomenon that arose toward the end of the 19th century. During the 18th century, the large trading houses (state owned or state sanctioned) engaged primarily as traders, moving natural resources from the developing world to Europe and manufactures in the other direction. Although there were considerable foreign investments abroad, these were mainly associated with long-term capital flows—the financing of debts, bonds, and other financial instruments—required to support large-scale private and public projects in the colonies. Firms were *international*, but not *multinational*. International business and economic activity was *extensive* in the sense that the value of goods and capital exchanged was considerable and involved numerous countries and actors. But it was not *intensive*, in that activities were largely not integrated across borders, with the possible exception of the large trading companies and other state-sanctioned de facto monopolies (Held et al. 1999). In addition, where private investments by individuals occurred, these were freestanding companies—companies established by investors of a foreign nationality who were located in the host country, but not part of any firm located in the investor's home country. They were not strictly domestic firms, since their capital (and entrepreneurial basis) came from abroad, but they did not represent a direct investment since the foreign-located firm was not a subsidiary of another firm in another country. Jones (1996) notes that such investments were often associated with colonial interests. Indeed, even by 1914, the number of freestanding companies far outnumbered true MNE subsidiaries by a large order of magnitude. Both types of MNEs were predominantly in services and natural resource extraction. Most activities were *trade-supportive* in nature and involved little interdependence.

The first MNEs did not blossom until well into the 20th century, as the concept of large firms did not make its debut until late in the 19th century. The importance of size arose for several reasons, some technological. First, the large firm emerged about the time of the second industrial revolution, which featured innovations associated with mass-production techniques. These innovations particularly benefited more capital-intensive industries that were characterized by economies of scale and scope, such as refineries (both for sugar and petroleum), animal and vegetable oils, chemicals, iron, copper and aluminum (both primary processing and products), and packaging and processing of food products; by standardized machinery; and by the development of large-scale enterprises. Second, developments in transportation and communication made efficiently coordinating far-flung activities much more feasible.

Third, the brief period of free trade that had flourished in the 19th century was replaced after about 1880 by high trade barriers. FDI continued to be dominated by MNEs from the major European colonial powers—Netherlands, the United Kingdom, and France—and the United States, which was by this time firmly established as the technological and economic hegemon. These four countries accounted for about 87 percent of FDI stock in 1938 (Jones 1996).

Motives for MNE Investment There are four main motives for investment: to seek natural resources, to seek new markets, to restructure existing foreign production through rationalization, and to seek strategically related created assets. The first three represent motives that are primarily *asset-exploiting* in nature: the investing company's primary purpose is to generate economic rent through the use of its existing firm-specific assets. The last is a case of *asset-augmenting activity*, whereby the firm wishes to acquire additional assets that protect or augment its existing created assets in some way.

Typology of MNE Subsidiaries The literature on subsidiary development has greatly expanded over the last 20 years, evaluating the dynamics behind the evolution of subsidiary roles, beginning with the seminal work of Bartlett and Ghoshal (e.g., 1989). The strategic management literature on the role, dispersion, and development of subsidiaries is now well developed (see e.g., Pearce 1989; Birkinshaw and Hood 1998).

The nature of the activities undertaken by a subsidiary and its potential level of embeddedness in the host economy vary according to the level of competence of the subsidiary and the scope of its activities. The typology of subsidiaries can be analyzed according to these two scales. A typical value chain can be viewed from a "level of competence" perspective consisting of "strategic" and "operational" elements. Activities such as sales and manufacturing are operational in nature, while R&D centers and headquarters functions are strategic in nature. In general, strategic elements tend to be located close to locations regarded as important to the MNE. There is a close link between the influence of the subsidiary and the strategic importance of its local environment. Strategic elements perform a critical role in a network of units, adding value through contributing their own expertise as well as by coordinating the flow of knowledge within the network. Second, there is considerable variation between subsidiaries in the scope of their activities, with certain subsidiaries performing single and specialized activities, and others performing a larger variety and of greater value.

Truncated miniature replicas. As their name implies, truncated miniature replicas are essentially a duplication of the parent firm, although not with the same scale of production and not all components of value adding activity. Typically, they do not undertake basic research but may modify and adapt products originally developed by the parent. Although truncated miniature replicas vary in the extent to which they are truncated, they tend to have a low or medium level of competence. Truncated miniature replicas tend to have an extensive market scope, in the sense that they have a large product range, but supply a limited and isolated market. Truncated miniature replicas tend to have a considerable autonomy in their activities, although the parent company exerts overall strategic control. This means, for instance, that the parent decides new additions to the product range. They are nationally responsive and, apart from a few advantages derived from being part of a MNE network such as lower cost of capital and technology, they are similar to other indigenous firms. Their primary motive is market-seeking and most often associated with import-substituting programs. The parent-affiliate relationship is weakly developed.

Rationalized affiliates. Rationalized affiliates are much more closely integrated into the MNE network. Their operations are motivated by efficiency seeking, aimed at optimizing costs over multiple locations. There is a strategic interdependence between the MNE network and the affiliate. Two types of rationalized affiliates can be distinguished: the rationalized production subsidiary and the world product mandate subsidiary. World product mandate subsidiaries maintain global or regional control over a particular product line or functional area and are designated

centers of excellence. That is, strategic activities such as R&D and headquarters functions are included in the affiliate's responsibilities and it exerts control over other affiliates in the same region or worldwide. A rationalized production subsidiary is part of the MNE's global strategy and is engaged in the production of a particular value-adding aspect based on specific competitive advantages of the subsidiary relative to other subsidiaries. Its products are often intermediate goods, or products, or services complementary to other rationalized production subsidiaries.

Single-activity affiliates. Single-activity affiliates are a cross between truncated miniature replica and rationalized production subsidiary. On the one hand, they represent an extreme version of a truncated miniature replica, in that they undertake a single aspect of value-adding activity. On the other hand, such affiliates may in fact be part of a company's rationalized strategy: the comparative advantage of the location is best suited for such activities. These affiliates are not involved in decision making or strategic planning. Such affiliates typically tend to be engaged at the extremes of the value-adding chain. The first type is *trading affiliates*, engaged in trading activities, and, in the limit, in marketing and after-sales service. The second subcategory is *resource-extractive affiliates*, at the other end of the value chain, engaged in acquiring (primarily through extractive activity) scarce or otherwise valuable crude resources, and exporting these raw materials for use in other locations, whether by another affiliate or by an unrelated firm.

There is considerable variation between industrial sectors, individual MNEs, as well as host and home country factors. For instance, in the food and beverages sectors, subsidiaries are organized primarily as truncated miniature replicas. MNEs with greater international exposure and dependence on foreign markets are more inclined toward rationalized production subsidiaries or world product mandates. Subsidiary roles evolve over time, due both to internal, MNE-specific factors and to changing non-firm exogenous developments, including liberalization of markets and regional integration.

The changing external environment inevitably induces some changes in subsidiary roles. Once an MNE rationalizes the number of subsidiaries or reorganizes the activities across borders, the remaining and/or new units will likely experience changes in scope and areas of responsibility. Increases in scope can typically be found when the number of subsidiaries is rationalized or local conditions encourage localization of activities (Birkinshaw 1996). Similarly, the scope may be narrowed to focus on specific activities and build expertise within the selected area. Hence changes in scope are often related to both organizational and spatial considerations.

MNEs and Economic Development One of the key features of policy liberalization since the 1980s has been the desire to attract FDI as a means to acquire or improve technological capabilities through MNE activity. The role of the MNE as an additional source of capital and technology is one of the key features of this openness. The failure of protected industries in developing and developed countries to become competitive in global markets has highlighted the limitations of the arm's-length technology transfer approach. Hence, in recent years, both governments and supranational organizations have increasingly come to focus on the role MNEs and FDI can play in development. This has been accompanied by a lifting of many types of regulations that previously limited the role of FDI and MNEs.

MNEs have played and are likely to continue to play an important role in the structural upgrading of countries. However, the extent and pattern of these benefits is strongly dependent on the form of economic and social development desired by the host countries and on the policies of host governments in pursuing these goals. Although not the only means available, MNE spillovers are regarded as one of the most practical and efficient means by which industrial development and upgrading can be promoted (Narula and Dunning 2000).

While the *potential* for MNE-related spillovers is clear, as are the opportunities for industrial upgrading therefrom, it is increasingly acknowledged that the nature, level, and extent of the benefits vary considerably. Even where MNEs do seek to transfer knowledge, they prefer to use technologies that are suited (first and foremost) to their own needs and the purposes for which they have made the investment. MNEs tailor their investment decisions to the existing market needs and the relative quality of location advantages, especially skills and capabilities that the domestic economy has a comparative advantage in (Lall and Narula 2004).

Once the decision to enter a given market through FDI is taken, the kinds of activity and the level of competence of the subsidiary are also codetermined by the nature of the location advantages of the host location. While MNE internal factors such as their internationalization strategy, the role of the new location in their global portfolio of subsidiaries, and the motivation of their investment are pivotal in the structure of their investment, they are dependent on the location-specific resources available for that purpose.

The relative importance of the main motives of MNE investment partly reflects the stage of economic development (Dunning and Narula 1996). Least-developed countries tend to have mainly resource-seeking MNEs and countries at the catching-up stage mostly market-seeking MNEs. Efficiency-seeking investments, with the most stringent capability needs, will tend to focus on the more industrialized developing economies (though three or four decades ago they went to countries with relatively low capabilities, e.g., the electronics industry in Southeast Asia in the 1970s).

Not all affiliates offer the same spillovers to host economies. A sales office, for instance, may have a high turnover and employ many people, but its technological spillovers will be limited relative to a manufacturing facility. Likewise, resource-seeking activities like mining tend to be capital intensive and provide fewer spillovers than market-seeking manufacturing FDI. During import substitution, most MNEs set up truncated miniature replicas of their facilities at home. The extent of truncation, however, varied by host country. The most important determinants of truncation—and thus the scope of activities and competence of the subsidiary—were market size and local industrial capabilities (Dunning and Narula 2004). Countries with small markets and weak local industries had the most truncated subsidiaries, often only single-activity subsidiaries (sales and marketing or natural resource extraction). Larger countries with domestic technological capacity (such as Brazil and India) had the least truncated subsidiaries, often with R&D departments.

With liberalization, MNE strategies on affiliate competence and scope have changed in four ways (Dunning and Narula 2004). First, there has been investment in *new affiliates.* Second, there has been *sequential investment* in upgrading existing subsidiaries. Third, there has been some *downgrading of subsidiaries*, whereby MNEs have divested in response to location advantages elsewhere or reduced the level of competence and scope of subsidiaries. Fourth, there has been some *redistribution of ownership* as the result of privatization or acquisitions of local private firms. In many, but certainly not all, cases this also led to a downgrading of activities.

MNEs are taking advantage of liberalization to concentrate production capacity in a few locations, exploiting scale and agglomeration economies, favorable location, and strong capabilities. Some miniature replicas have been downgraded to sales and marketing affiliates, with fewer opportunities for spillovers. Countries that receive FDI with the highest potential for capability development are those with strong domestic absorptive capacities.

MNEs transfer technology to local firms in four ways: backward linkages, labor turnover, horizontal linkages, and international technology spillovers. Studies of backward linkages have identified various determinants, including those internal to MNEs and those associated with host economies. The ability of the host economy to benefit from MNE linkages has been found to depend crucially on the relative technological capabilities of recipient and transmitter: the greater the distance between them, the lower the intensity of linkages.

Again, MNE motives and strategies matter. Market-oriented affiliates generally purchase more locally than export-oriented firms because of lower quality requirements and technical specifications.

MNEs create more linkages when they use intermediate goods intensively, communication costs between parent and affiliate are high, and the home and host markets are relatively similar in terms of intermediate goods. Affiliates established by mergers and acquisitions are likely to have stronger links with domestic suppliers than those established by greenfield investment—which is a subsidiary that has been established from scratch, as opposed to the acquisition of an existing facility—since the former may find established linkages that they are likely to retain if the linkages are efficient. Linkages vary significantly by industry. In the primary sector, the scope for vertical linkages is often limited, due to the use of continuous production processes and the capital intensity of operations. In manufacturing, the potential for vertical linkages is broader, depending on the extent of intermediate inputs to total production and the type of production processes.

Furthermore, the individual MNE's choice of mode of entry—whether to create a wholly owned subsidiary or engage in a joint venture or minority ownership—plays a significant role in the extent that spillovers and externalities accrue to host locations and firms. For instance, MNEs may be more likely to transfer sophisticated technologies and management techniques to wholly owned subsidiaries than to partially owned affiliates.

MNEs and unrestrained flows of inward FDI may well lead to an increase in productivity and exports, but they do not necessarily result in increased competitiveness of the domestic sector or increased industrial capacity, which ultimately determines economic growth in the long run. FDI *per se* does not provide growth opportunities unless a domestic industrial sector exists that has the necessary technological capacity to profit from the externalities from MNE activity. To put it simply, FDI is not a sine qua non for development (Lall and Narula 2004).

Political Economy, International Regulation, and MNE The role of foreign capital and foreign capitalists—as MNE activity was referred to in the literature prior to the 1950s—has historically been seen with some suspicion, due in part to the association of MNEs with imperialism, consequential dependent development, and political and economic intervention by the home countries of MNEs on their behalf. MNE activity has often been inhibited as a result of protectionism, technonationalism, and the support of domestic industry against the possible negative effects of MNEs on domestically owned firms.

Economic liberalization—whether voluntary, imposed as a condition for lending by international institutions, or as a precondition for membership of a regional integration program—has led to a sea change in the policies of many countries. However, although policies may have changed, the underlying attitudes have not. The politics of state-MNE relationships have remained strongly associated with national interests, domestic interest groups, and the importance of protecting the state as a political and economic sovereignty. Supranational agreements such as the North American Free Trade Agreement and the agreements that formed the European Union and the World Trade Organization have reinforced, accelerated, and created standardized regulation for economic activity, acting as a virtuous circle with regard to economic integration that had been occurring as a matter of course.

See also foreign direct investment (FDI); globalization

FURTHER READING

Bartlett, Christopher, and Sumantra Ghoshal. 1989. *Managing Across Borders: The Transnational Solution.* Cambridge, MA: Harvard Business School Press. A strategic management approach to how MNEs are best organized and run.

Birkinshaw, Julian. 1996. "How Multinational Subsidiary Mandates Are Gained and Lost." *Journal of International Business Studies* 27 (3): 467–95. Explains how the different subsidiaries can have different roles.

Birkinshaw, Julian, and Neil Hood. 1998. "Multinational Subsidiary Evolution: Capability and Charter Change in Foreign-Owned Subsidiary Companies." *Academy of Management Review* 23 (4): 773–95. Paper that examines how subsidiary mandates evolve over time.

Caves, Richard. 2007. *Multinational Enterprises and Economic Analysis.* Cambridge: Cambridge University Press. An authoritative text that takes a primarily economics view.

Dunning, John. 1993. *Multinational Enterprises and the Global Economy.* Wokingham, UK: Addison Wesley. A classic reference that covers the subject from economics, management, and international business perspectives.

Dunning, John, and Rajneesh Narula. 1996. *Foreign Direct Investment and Governments.* London: Routledge. A study of how MNE activity, economic structure, and economic development are interrelated.

———. 2004. *Multinationals and Industrial Competitiveness: A New Agenda.* Cheltenham, UK: Edward Elgar. Collection of essays that examines current issues in international business.

Held, David, Anthony McGrew, David Goldblatt, and Jonathan Perraton. 1999. *Global Transformations: Politics, Economics, and Culture.* Cambridge: Polity Press. An authoritative study of globalization, linking the political, sociological, and economics perspectives.

Jones, Geoffrey. 1996. *The Evolution of International Business.* Routledge: London. A text that takes a business history approach to MNEs.

Lall, Sanjaya, and Rajneesh Narula. 2004. "FDI and its Role in Economic Development: Do We Need a New Agenda?" *European Journal of Development Research* 16 (3): 447–64. Covers the main issues of FDI and development in a post-WTO world.

Narula, Rajneesh. 2003. *Globalization and Technology.* Cambridge: Polity Press. Analysis of the interdependencies between economic globalization, innovation, technology, and industrial policy.

Narula, Rajneesh, and John Dunning. 2000. "Industrial Development, Globalization, and Multinational Enterprises: New Realities for Developing Countries." *Oxford Development Studies* 28 (2): 141–67. Looks at the effect of MNEs in industrial development.

Pearce, Robert. 1989. *The Internationalization of Research and Development by Multinational Enterprises.* Macmillan: London. How MNEs have internationalized their R&D activities.

UNCTAD. 2006. *World Investment Report 2006.* Geneva: United Nations. Part of an annual series of reports by UNCTAD with relevant statistical and anecdotal data on MNE activity.

Wilkins, Mira. 2001. "The History of the Multinational Enterprise." In *The Oxford Handbook of International Business*, edited by Alan Rugman and Thomas Brewer. Oxford: Oxford University Press, 3–35. A historical overview of the evolution of the MNE.

RAJNEESH NARULA

■ multiple currencies

When multiple currencies circulate in a country or region, it is possible to pay for most goods and services there with more than one currency. This entry focuses on government-issued currencies. The entry on *currency competition* discusses the interaction of government-issued money with privately issued monies.

Historically, it has been common for multiple currencies to circulate in a given area. In medieval Europe, for example, and in the United States before the Civil War, coins from many countries circulated side by side. More recently, multiple currencies have circulated in developing countries, notably in South America and Asia, and in some areas of developed countries. In certain parts of England, for instance, most goods and services can be purchased with euros and pounds sterling.

In developed countries, multiple currencies circulate mainly for convenience, to attract or accommodate the business of merchants or tourists. In developing countries in which multiple currencies circulate today, the purpose may be different. The possibility of using dollars or euros protects people in these countries from the cost of inflation of their domestic currencies and provides a way to discipline their monetary authorities.

Benefits of Multiple Currencies Central banks today issue fiat money, or money that is intrinsically worthless and is not backed by an asset or a commodity at the central bank. Fiat money has value because people anticipate that others will agree to exchange goods and services for the money. It is generally well understood that issuance of fiat money suffers from a time inconsistency problem, in which the government chooses to change its policy from that promised earlier, often after other actors have made decisions or investments based on the previously announced policy. The monetary authority, or the government that controls it, has an incentive to issue too much money because the cost of producing an extra unit of money is lower than the value of the money.

Businesses and consumers can choose to trade in another currency, one that they expect will retain its value. This gives them some protection from the inflation tax, a term that refers to the erosion of purchasing power. For this reason, one would expect multiple currencies to circulate in countries that have suffered from high inflation. Further, one would expect that the foreign currency that circulates is issued by a central bank with a reputation for maintaining the value of its currency.

Over the last 20 years, the Federal Reserve's record of keeping inflation low in the United States has been much better than that of a number of developing countries. Moreover, the institutional setting in which the Federal Reserve operates suggests that the U.S. dollar is unlikely to suffer from high inflation in the future. This is also true of other currencies, such as the euro. Hence, it is not surprising that the dollar or the euro often circulate in other countries.

The circulation of multiple currencies can also help discipline a monetary authority because it reduces the incentives to set high inflation. The easier it is for businesses and consumers to trade with another currency, the more constrained the monetary authority is. In some extreme cases, the local currency can disappear entirely and be replaced by a foreign currency. Because multiple currencies can serve to discipline a monetary authority, they can also be used as a commitment device in a country where institutions make it difficult for the monetary authority to commit to low inflation. This means that the impetus for multiple currencies may come from a government, rather than consumers and businesses. In such a case, the government aims to signal that it wants the monetary authority to refrain from implementing high inflation.

Costs of Multiple Currencies Although multiple currencies have benefits, they also have a number of costs. An important cost is the loss of flexibility in the conduct of monetary policy. It is generally believed that central banks can help smooth the fluctuations affecting an economy with the judicious use of monetary policy. In a recession, an expansionary monetary policy can stimulate the economy; in an expansion, a tight monetary policy can prevent the economy from growing too fast.

Multiple currencies reduce the central bank's ability to stimulate the economy with an expansionary policy that increases the rate of growth of the money supply. Moreover, monetary policy is less effective since it affects only a fraction of the economic activity. The central bank is unable to stabilize the local economy as well as it could if multiple currencies did not circulate. The consequence is volatility that hurts businesses and consumers.

Of course, the constraint imposed on monetary policy by multiple currencies is partly by design. The benefits of multiple currencies arise because the monetary authority has a tendency to choose a monetary policy that is too loose. There is a trade-off between reducing the incentives of the monetary authority to choose high inflation and giving it flexibility to stimulate the economy. Multiple currencies can be socially desirable if the costs of high inflation are higher than the benefits of stabilization policy. This is likely to be the case when the monetary authority finds it especially difficult to implement low inflation.

The use of multiple currencies also reduces flexibility in other areas, such as the ability of the central bank to implement lender-of-last-resort policies. In cases of financial crises, the central bank can sometime enhance the stability of the financial system by temporarily providing a large amount of liquidity. The effectiveness of this kind of policy is likely to decline in the presence of multiple currencies. This is especially true if the financial system relies heavily on the foreign currency. For example, a lender-of-last-resort policy to prevent bank runs is less effective if a large fraction of deposits at banks are denominated in dollars. An additional cost of multiple currencies is the inconvenience experienced by businesses and consumers when they have to deal with several currencies, such as keeping track of inventories for each currency.

Need to Weigh the Costs and Benefits Multiple currencies protect consumers from the inflation tax if their monetary authority is unable to keep inflation low. They impose discipline on the monetary authority and can be used as a commitment device to signal an intention to keep inflation low. Multiple currencies also reduce the ability of a country's monetary authority to smooth fluctuations, however, and can reduce the effectiveness of lender-of-last-resort policies. Because of these costs, multiple currencies are likely to circulate only in countries with a history of high and/or volatile inflation rates.

See also banking crisis; currency competition; currency substitution and dollarization; discipline; dollar standard; dominant currency; Federal Reserve Board; financial crisis; lender of last resort; reserve currency; seigniorage; time inconsistency problem; vehicle currency

FURTHER READING

Martin, Antoine. 2006. "Endogenous Multiple Currencies." *Journal of Money, Credit, and Banking* 38: 247–64. Formalizes many of the arguments described in this entry and provides a number of references.

ANTOINE MARTIN

■ Mundell-Fleming model

The Mundell-Fleming model, named for J. Marcus Fleming (1911–76) and Robert A. Mundell (born 1932), in its most familiar form is the "internationalized IS-LM model," a diagrammatic representation of the way in which a small, open economy responds to shocks that take the form of internal policy initiatives. The innovation in this approach is that the exchange rate regime is a crucial determinant of the policies' effects on economic variables, and specifically on the level of gross domestic product (GDP) generated by the country under analysis. In two particular cases, contrary to expectations, these initiatives do not have an impact on output in the small, open economy in the perfect capital mobility setting. This is true both for monetary policy under fixed exchange rates and for fiscal policy under flexible exchange rates. For these situations the model shows that the initiatives are ineffective for influencing the level of output and employment.

The clear implication is that policymakers should be aware of the impotence of these initiatives and not rely on them in a fruitless attempt to stabilize the economy. Canada was faulted in the late 1950s for depending on expanded government expenditures to end a stubborn recession. Fleming's ineffectiveness result demonstrates that the impact of Canada's fiscal policy was vitiated because the Bank of Canada allowed the price of its dollar to be determined in the financial markets, rather than fixing it at a given value. The clumsy conduct of monetary policy by the Bank of Canada at the time was particularly unfortunate because this flexible exchange rate regime enhanced the potency of that policy. Although these observations were articulated by Fleming and Mundell a few years after these events, the intuitive feeling at the time was that something was amiss at the Bank of Canada, and dissatisfaction with its policies lay behind the impeachment of its governor in 1961.

The Hallmarks of the Mundell-Fleming Model
The Mundell-Fleming model is based on a small group of papers, including Fleming (1962) and Mundell (1963). Others, such as Mundell (1960, 1961, and 1962), at times have been incorporated into the rubric, but doing so risks jeopardizing the key insights derived from the central papers. Some of Mundell's papers (e.g., Mundell 1960) present models designed to generate comparative static results that are independent of the nature of the exchange-rate regime in effect. Others (e.g., Mundell 1961) find comparative static results that contradict the ineffectiveness conclusions of the central papers. A key reason for this is that many of these papers assume that monetary policy can be gauged in terms of the level of interest rates rather than the quantity of money outstanding. Still others (e.g., Mundell 1962) are phrased entirely in dynamic terms rather than in the comparative statics one finds in the central papers.

Readers of these central papers face daunting challenges, as the mathematics presented is either elliptical (Mundell) or complicated (Fleming). But what is distinctive about these papers is that they employ a definition of monetary policy that maintains its coherence when capital mobility becomes perfect, and that they deal consistently with the flexible exchange rate case.

Diagrammatic Representation The Mundell-Fleming model is portrayed in figure 1. On the axes are two variables central to macroeconomic performance: on the horizontal axis, Y measures domestic output (GDP) produced in the small, open economy; on the vertical axis, r is the level of domestic interest rates. Two of the loci are familiar from Hicks's (1937) classic article: XX, representing equilibrium in the domestic goods market; and LL, representing equilibrium in the domestic assets market.

The XX locus is negatively sloped because some expenditures are sensitive to interest rates. With a higher interest rate, such expenditures are reduced, and other things being equal, this causes output to decrease. One of the variables held constant in drawing this curve is the value of the exchange rate. Defining the exchange rate as the domestic-currency price of one unit of foreign currency, we note that a rise in the exchange rate's value tends to raise the price

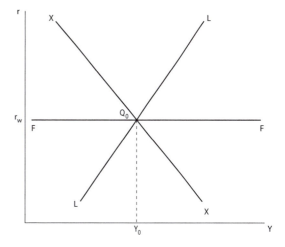

Figure 1
The Mundell-Fleming model

of foreign goods relative to domestic goods. The resulting lower relative price for domestic goods increases demand for them and, according to the Keynesian view of supply, output responds to this rise in demand at constant prices. With such a change, the XX locus would shift to the right. We proceed with the assumptions that the quantity of money in this small economy does not have a direct impact on the goods market equilibrium condition, and that the domestic-currency price level has a value which is given.

The LL locus is positively sloped, being drawn for a given quantity of money and given values of domestic-currency prices. Everywhere along this locus the quantity of money demanded is constant, consistent with its given supply, so that for these points there is equilibrium in the domestic financial assets market. The reason is that an increase in interest rates causes the quantity of money demanded to be lower, since now bonds, an alternative form in which to hold funds, provide a higher yield. If this is matched by an increase in output, then the resulting higher volume of transactions necessitates an increase in the quantity of money held. In the right proportions, these two influences on money demand exactly offset each other and demand is back at its original (equilibrium) value. An increase in the money supply will cause a rightward shift in the LL curve.

The argument concerning the LL locus, for the simple case in which domestic-currency prices are taken to be constant, can be represented algebraically as follows:

$$M = l(r) \cdot Y \qquad (1)$$

This specification is consistent with the one in Fleming, in that it assumes a unitary income elasticity of demand for money, where l is the inverse of velocity. If l depends negatively on the interest rate, then a rise in r must be matched by a rise in Y in order to keep the product of the two factors on the right-hand side of this equation constant. This is necessary in order to maintain equality to the given value of the money supply, M, in this equation. This specification employs the assumption of the standard model that demand for money is independent of the exchange rate.

As noted, these two curves are identical to those in Hicks (1937). Hicks's model is the basis for the simplified presentations of conventional macroeconomic theorizing, so little further discussion is needed here, except to note that the XX locus is relevant for equilibrium in the domestic goods market alone. No separate analysis needs to be carried out for the market for imports, since this small economy is able to obtain all the foreign-produced goods it demands.

The final curve, FF, was added by Mundell to represent equilibrium in the foreign exchange market. In the perfect capital mobility case shown, this locus is horizontal: if domestic bonds are perfect substitutes for foreign bonds, then their rates of return must be equated. No matter what the level of domestic output, the yield on domestic bonds must equal the yield available from holding foreign financial instruments, denoted by r_w.

The economy is assumed to start in equilibrium at point Q_0, where there is clearing (so that supply and demand are equated) of all the markets analyzed here.

Policy Shocks This diagram can be used to derive the effects of monetary policy (changes in the quantity of money, causing the LL locus in figure 1 to shift) and fiscal policy (changes in the level of expenditures by government, which shift the goods-market clearing condition, XX in figure 1, independent of displacements caused by exchange rate changes) under fixed and flexible exchange rates. These are the central applications of the Mundell-Fleming model. The difference between these two exchange rate regimes is that under fixed exchange rates the value of the exchange rate is given, and the central bank, in pegging the exchange rate at a particular value, uses changes in the quantity of money to maintain this value. That is, for this regime the money supply becomes a variable that responds to shocks, while the value of the exchange rate does not change. In contrast, for flexible exchange rates the quantity of domestic money outstanding is treated as a given, and the value of the exchange rate moves reactively in order to reequilibrate the system.

The effects of expansionary monetary and fiscal policy actions can be stated easily when the exchange rate is flexible: in that case fiscal policy has no impact on output, whereas monetary policy has the effect to which we are accustomed. These conclusions derive directly from equation (1).

If the money supply is held constant in the face of an increase in government expenditures, then the level of output does not change. With such a shock, M is fixed, and the value of l, as well, is constant, because the perfect capital mobility assumption views the interest rate as unchanging. If both M and l are given, then Y cannot change, as equation (1) shows. This is the famous "crowding out" or "ineffectiveness" result Fleming derived, which Mundell repeats.

In contrast, changes in the money supply, due to monetary policy initiatives, cause output to change in proportion to those changes. This conclusion is an unusual but straightforward implication of the Fleming specification of money demand. Once again the derivation depends on the assumption of perfect capital mobility, which causes the value of l to be given because it is a function of only the interest rate, whose value is set by world market conditions.

These results are portrayed in figure 2. An increase in government expenditure shifts the XX locus to the right by a multiple of the amount of increase. With its original position shown as XX, this shift generates a new position for this locus shown by X'X', drawn as a

dotted line to emphasize that this is the new displaced position of that curve.

If the exchange rate is fixed by the central bank, then it must provide the larger quantity of money that is required at an unchanged interest rate. As this happens, the LL locus shifts to the right; this process continues until the locus attains the position shown as L'L'. The new equilibrium is at point Q_1 where output and the money supply have increased (with output now having a value shown by Y_1 whereas its previous value was Y_0), and the values of both the interest rate and the exchange rate are unchanged.

In contrast, the same increase in government expenditures will have no effect on output and employment if the central bank is pursuing a flexible exchange rate regime. For this case, the money supply is held constant, and the value of the exchange rate must change in order to clear the various markets. Since money demand does not depend on the value of the exchange rate, its changing value does not alter the position of LL, which continues to run through point Q_0. Instead, it is the XX locus that shifts back to its original position, as the value of the exchange rate falls, in order to reequilibrate all of these markets. Since the equilibrium under this exchange rate regime does not move, it is clear that any increased government expenditures come at the expense of exports and imports. There is complete crowding out of such expenditures, so the composition of expenditures on domestic output changes, but its total quantity does not.

This idea—that with high capital mobility, fiscal policy has a more limited impact on output under flexible exchange rates than its does under fixed—is usually associated with Rhomberg (1964), who did the original empirical work on the Canadian experiment with flexible exchange rates in the 1950s. He appears to have inspired Fleming's interest in this topic, as the Canadian experience seemed to suggest that flexible exchange rates vitiated fiscal policy. Mundell, as well, credits Rhomberg's work in this area.

The argument is reversed for monetary policy. In this case the increase in the money supply is the given impulse that moves the money market equilibrium locus to position L'L'. Does this locus maintain this position, setting up an equilibrium level of output

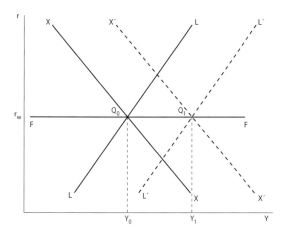

Figure 2

The Mundell-Fleming model: Changes in government expenditures and money supply

equal to Y_1, or does its revert to its original position, so that output remains at Y_0? The answer depends again on the exchange rate regime.

For fixed exchange rates, the quantity of money in the domestic economy is used to peg the value of the exchange rate. If that value is not changed, then there is no reason why the equilibrium quantity of money should change either. This means that the quantity of money quickly reverts to its former value (or perhaps does not move at all). The end result is that output is not affected by monetary policy in the fixed exchange rate case.

The quantity of money is a responding variable under a fixed exchange rate regime. So there is the logical problem that the quantity of money cannot legitimately be changed in an arbitrary fashion. As McCallum (1996) noted, one should describe this Hume impotency conclusion as demonstrating not the ineffectiveness of monetary policy, but rather its unavailability.

For flexible exchange rates, there is no commitment to keeping the value of the exchange rate at a particular peg. As a result, the decision to increase the quantity of money causes the money market locus to move to the dotted position shown, $L'L'$. In that case the value of the exchange rate must rise to clear the various markets. As domestic currency depreciates against foreign denominations, the goods market locus shifts over to the dotted position, $X'X'$. Output in this case increases to Y_1 showing that monetary policy is effective in influencing the level of domestic economy activity in the small country case.

Coining of the Expression The central articles in the Mundell-Fleming canon were written in the early 1960s. The expression *Mundell-Fleming model* was introduced, at the earliest, five years later. Soon after the term became part of the everyday vocabulary of researchers in international finance, but it was only after 1975 that the expression was used in print. Although many economists have used the alphabetical ordering of the names in the expression (Kenen 1985; Boughton 2003), and some have referred to it as just the "Fleming model" (Cooper 1976), *Mundell-Fleming model* came into common use by economists in the later 1970s and 1980s. During this

period even significant extensions of the basic framework were still identified as being part of the Mundell-Fleming model (Marston 1985; Frenkel and Razin 1987).

The economists Maurice Obstfeld and Kenneth Rogoff (1996), in their monumental graduate textbook in international finance, refer to the Mundell-Fleming-Dornbusch model, and they do not use the conventional name. In the 1990s, Obstfeld and Rogoff developed the New Open Economy Macroeconomics (NOEM) model, which has the potential of supplanting the standard model as the basic benchmark formulation of the ideas and mechanisms of international financial analysis.

See also capital mobility; exchange rate regimes; impossible trinity; New Open Economy Macroeconomics; quantity theory of money; Swan diagram

FURTHER READING

Boughton, James. 2003. "On the Origins of the Fleming-Mundell Model." *IMF Staff Papers* 50 (1) (April): 1–9. Analyzes the writing of Fleming's 1962 contribution to the Mundell-Fleming model and concludes that Fleming's work was substantially independent of Mundell's.

Cooper, Richard N. 1976. "Monetary Theory and Policy in an Open Economy." *Scandinavian Journal of Economics* 78 (2) (June): 146–63. Provides an analysis of financial policies in the open economy and calls the conventional framework at the time "the Fleming model."

Fleming, J. Marcus. 1962. "Domestic Financial Policies under Fixed and under Floating Exchange Rates." *IMF Staff Papers* 9 (4) (November): 369–79. Considered to be the classic contribution by Fleming, this paper reports both verbally and mathematically the ineffectiveness result for fiscal policy, and the proportionality result for monetary policy for the flexible exchange rate, perfect capital mobility case.

Frenkel, Jacob A., and Assaf Razin. 1987. "The Mundell-Fleming Model a Quarter Century Later." *IMF Staff Papers* 34 (4) (December): 567–620. Characterized by the authors as a survey piece, this paper presents a complicated two-country model of the world economy in the perfect capital mobility setting. Since the analysis specifies the asset markets in a portfolio-balance manner, the connection between this framework and what is usually termed the Mundell-Fleming model is unclear.

Hicks, John. 1937. "Mr. Keynes and the 'Classics': A Suggested Interpretation." *Econometrica* 5 (2) (April): 147–59. The diagram included in this article has been the basis for most textbook presentations of closed economy macroeconomic theory right up to the present. The longevity of this framework has surprised both its proponents and its many critics.

Kenen, Peter B. 1985. "Macroeconomic Theory and Policy: How the Closed Economy Was Opened." In *Handbook of International Economics*, vol. 2, edited by Ronald W. Jones and Peter B. Kenen. North-Holland, Amsterdam, 626–77, chapter 13. A survey piece that covers the traditional way of thinking about the development of the open-economy macroeconomic model, using a number of distinct models and different modes of analysis.

Marston, Richard C. 1985. "Stabilization Policies in Open Economies." In *Handbook of International Economics*, vol. 2, edited by Ronald W. Jones and Peter B. Kenen. North-Holland, Amsterdam, 859–916, chapter 17. Presents a portfolio-balance analysis of the effects of standard macroeconomic shocks. The author uses a complex model and the stock specification of the asset markets. He describes his framework as a "modified Mundell-Fleming model."

McCallum, Bennett T. 1996. *International Monetary Economics*. New York: Oxford University Press. A standard presentation of open-economy macroeconomic topics. The author concludes that Mundell's 1962 and 1963 papers are his central contributions to the Mundell-Fleming model.

Mundell, Robert A. 1960. "The Monetary Dynamics of International Adjustment under Fixed and Flexible Exchange Rates." *Quarterly Journal of Economics* 74 (2) (May): 227–57. Includes a model specifically designed so that the comparative static responses of the values of real variables are independent of the nature of the exchange rate regime. Despite its title, this article includes neither the money supply nor the exchange rate in the central mathematical model, which one finds in its extensive appendix.

———. 1961. "Flexible Exchange Rates and Employment Policy." *Canadian Journal of Economics and Political Science* 27 (4) (November): 509–17. Although the fixed exchange rate case is not treated explicitly in this presentation, its conclusions appear to conflict with those published in the famous paper two years later. In particular, monetary policy seems to have potency under fixed exchange rates, and fiscal policy is reported as being effective under flexible exchange rates.

———. 1962. "The Appropriate Use of Monetary and Fiscal Policy for Internal and External Stability." *IMF Staff Papers* 9 (1) (March): 70–77. Presents in a dynamic form an argument found at the end of another Mundell article, which deals with the appropriate response to a situation of internal and external imbalance. This article has been the basis for the author's thinking about the "policy mix" and supply-side economics.

———. 1963. "Capital Mobility and Stabilization Policy under Fixed and Flexible Exchange Rates." *Canadian Journal of Economics and Political Science* 29 (4) (November): 475–85. Mundell's most frequently cited paper. Reports results like those in Fleming (1962), especially for the flexible exchange rate, perfect capital mobility case. Juxtaposes the Fleming and Hume ineffectiveness results and presents the famous "internationalized IS-LM" diagram.

Obstfeld, Maurice, and Kenneth Rogoff. 1996. *Foundations of International Macroeconomics*. Cambridge, MA: MIT Press. A monumental textbook presenting the state of the subject at the time of publication. The analysis focuses on current account dynamics for its real coverage, and on the flexible exchange rate case in its monetary topics. It has an extensive treatment of the Dornbusch "overshooting" framework, which the authors call the "Mundell-Fleming-Dornbusch model"

Rhomberg, Rudolph R. 1964. "A Model of the Canadian Economy under Fixed and Fluctuating Exchange Rates." *Journal of Political Economy* 72 (1) (February): 1–31. Finds that government expenditures are likely to lead to an appreciation of domestic currency in the intermediate run. This argument may have inspired Fleming to write down his model so as to explain how the effects of fiscal policy were vitiated in Canada in the late 1950s.

RUSSELL S. BOYER

■ **national treatment**
See nondiscrimination

■ **neoliberalism**
See dependency theory

■ **New Economic Geography**

Abundance of natural resources, proximity to natural means of communication, and climatic conditions vary from place to place. These variations, however, provide only a partial explanation of the pronounced differences in development that exist even between areas that have fairly similar characteristics. Other forces inherent to the functioning of economic interactions are able to cause uneven development even across otherwise identical places.

While geographers have proposed a rich list of such forces, since the mid-1990s the work of regional scientists and urban economists called "New Economic Geography" (NEG) has gained momentum in mainstream economics. What distinguishes NEG from other approaches is its focus on the localized market rather than nonmarket interactions within a "general equilibrium" framework that emphasizes the determination of good and factor (capital, labor and land) prices as well as the importance of economywide budget constraints.

Location Decision The cornerstone of NEG is the location decision of the firm. This is a nontrivial practical problem provided that the shipment of goods and factors across space as well as the fragmentation of production affect the firm's total costs due to the presence of trade obstacles and plant-level scale economies, respectively. It is also a well-defined theoretical problem provided that the firm has some market power, because plant-level scale economies are incompatible with a perfectly competitive equilibrium. Increasing returns to scale at the plant level and costly transportation generate an economic trade-off between the proximity to dispersed customers and suppliers on the one hand, and the concentration of production in a few large plants on the other. Proximity reduces transportation costs but requires the firm to fragment production across many small plants. Concentration allows the firm to exploit scale economies but increases its transportation costs. Accordingly, the firm will prefer to run several small dispersed plants when returns to scale are weak and transportation costs are large. It will prefer to concentrate production in a few large plants when returns to scale are strong and transportation costs are small. Other things being equal, transportation costs and scale economies also imply that the firm will be attracted to markets with large local demand. This is sometimes called the home market effect, whereby firms tend to solve the trade-off between proximity and concentration by locating in the larger market and serving the smaller one from there rather than vice versa. The more significant the home market effect, the lower the transportation costs and the stronger the scale economies.

The location decision of the firm is made more complex by the presence of competitors because its geographical position with respect to them affects the market power that necessarily stems from plant-level economies of scale. Generally speaking, firms have market power when they do not take market prices as given, as perfectly competitive firms would, and therefore trade quantity against price in making their profit-maximizing decisions. This price-making behavior is the essence of imperfectly competitive market structures that arise when competitors are a small group (oligopoly) or when they are a large group offering differentiated products (monopolistic competition). Although NEG models focus mainly on the latter, in both cases location turns out to be a crucial decision variable for profit maximization because it allows firms to increase market power and thus profits by carefully choosing their production sites.

In terms of social welfare, the presence of market power implies that prices, on which households and firms base their consumption, production, and location decisions, do not fully reflect the corresponding social values. Thus market interactions generate "side effects" for which no quid pro quo is paid. Side effects that are associated with market transactions are called "pecuniary externalities" and imply that the location decision of the firm does not fully take into account its effects on customers, suppliers, and competitors. Approaches other than NEG prefer to focus instead on "technological externalities." These are independent of any market interaction; they materialize through sheer physical proximity. Because they are the outcome of nonmarket interactions, by definition no quid pro quo is paid for them. As an example, consider an industry ("upstream") that supplies intermediates to another industry ("downstream"). A positive pecuniary externality for the downstream industry is the fall in intermediate input prices due to the increase in upstream competition triggered by the entry of a new technologically advanced supplier; a positive technological externality is the increase in productivity that other upstream suppliers may experience through informal knowledge transmission (spillover) generated by their proximity to their new technologically advanced rival. Although both concepts

have their own merits, the logical advantage of pecuniary externalities lies in the possibility of relating their emergence to a set of well-defined microeconomic parameters. So far this has proven to be quite difficult in models based on technological externalities because these remain mostly black boxes. Models with pecuniary or technological externalities do, however, share similar welfare implications: the free-market economic landscape is inherently inefficient and appropriate public intervention is generally needed.

Cumulative Causation No matter whether through market or nonmarket interactions, the attractiveness to a firm of alternative production sites depends on where other firms locate. This may activate a mechanism of cumulative causation among firms' location decisions through which firms' interactions may alter the economic landscape implied by natural resources, natural means of communication, and climatic conditions.

To understand how cumulative causation might work, let us go back to the previous example of upstream and downstream industries. For simplicity, consider a stylized economy made of two initially identical locations, A and B. Both host similar production chains in which there are three vertically linked activities: intermediate production, final production, and consumption. For simplicity, assume that final production uses only intermediate inputs, intermediate production employs only labor, and workers are the only source of final demand and are geographically immobile. If for any reason a new firm starts producing intermediates in A, it will increase local labor demand and intermediate supply. Due to excess demand and supply, respectively, local wages will go up while local intermediate prices will fall. This is bad news for the other local intermediate producers (market crowding effect due to competitor proximity). It is good news, however, for local final suppliers since they experience falling production costs and higher demand by richer workers. As new final producers are induced to enter the market in A, the expansion of final production will feed back into stronger intermediate demand so that intermediate suppliers will benefit (market expansion effect due to customer proximity). Clearly, when the latter effect dominates the former, both final and intermediate firms will end up being agglomerated in A. Through these processes, cumulative causation among firms' location decisions can generate persistent differences even among places that are initially identical.

Both labor mobility and capital accumulation tend to reinforce the market expansion effect through the additional income they generate. Intermediate entry expands labor demand and final production, which itself feeds back into stronger demand and hence increased production of intermediates. If labor is geographically mobile, the associated rise in wages in location A attracts workers from B. As these migrate, demand in the final market increases, generating a second cycle of cumulative causation between firms' and workers' location decisions. Analogously, the expansion of intermediate and final markets increases firm profitability, thus fostering investment in capital accumulation and innovation. The additional income generates a third cycle of cumulative causation.

As a parallel and opposite cycle of income and expenditures contraction arises in location B, even small and transitory location-specific shocks can give rise to large, permanent geographical imbalances. Thus there is a priori great flexibility on where particular activities locate. Once the agglomeration process has started, however, spatial differences take shape and become quite rigid, a process known as putty clay geography.

Trade Liberalization Although cumulative causation is present in many models of regional development with localized externalities, the crucial contribution of NEG is that its microeconomic foundations allow the evolution of the spatial landscape to be related to measurable microeconomic parameters. A first example is the prediction that agglomeration is more likely to take place in sectors where increasing returns are more intense and product differentiation is more pronounced. The reason is that in those sectors the market crowding effect is weaker as more intense returns to scale reduce the number of active competitors and more product differentiation reinforces market power. A second

example highlights what is arguably the most celebrated insight of NEG models: the impact of freer trade on the economic landscape.

NEG argues that the level of trade barriers affects the balance among market expansion and market crowding. Consider a situation in which some factors such as land are immobile and ubiquitous. Assume also that the incomes they generate are spent locally. With extremely high trade barriers, firms will be dispersed as scattered customers can be reached only through local production. As trade barriers fall, however, it becomes economically viable to serve scattered customers remotely. This unleashes cumulative causation so that regional imbalances may arise endogenously through the location decisions of firms and mobile factors. As trade barriers keep on falling, however, firms' geographical positions gradually become immaterial in terms of product market interactions. Eventually what is left is only the dispersion force due to the higher prices of immobile factors in the crowded place. As agglomeration unfolds in the process of moving toward low-level trade barriers, trade liberalization has a nonlinear effect on the spatial concentration of economic activities by promoting agglomeration at early stages and dispersion afterward.

Multilocation Economies The results surveyed so far are typically derived in stylized economies in which there are only two locations. A more realistic description of the geographical space entails investigating the behavior of multilocation economies. Considering more than two locations does not affect the agglomeration effect of more intense scale economies and stronger market power. It also does not affect the nonlinear impact of trade barriers on the spatial concentration of economic activities as agglomeration is still likelier for intermediate obstacles to trade. Nonetheless, with more than two locations, relative market sizes are not enough anymore to determine where firms cluster. The relative positions of locations within the network of trading relations are also crucial: locations that have better accessibility will be more likely to attract firms.

In two-location models the home market effect implies that an expansion of expenditures in a certain location causes a more than proportionate increase in local supply thanks to the influx of new firms. This effect, which is at the source of cumulative causation, does not generally survive scrutiny in multilocation economies. The reason is that, even in the presence of only a third location C, if this is large and well connected to both A and B, an increase in A's expenditure share may well map into a less than proportionate increase in its output share as location C drains away some firms. In more extreme cases, an increase in the expenditure share of a location may even lead to a decrease in its output share. This would be the case, for instance, if location C were a transport hub or gate. A hub is a location with better accessibility to all other locations; a gate is a location through which most goods flow in and out of a country. Positive demand shocks to any other location could result in supply expanding in the hub or in the gate and contracting elsewhere. Hence, agglomeration is more likely to take place in the presence of and close to hubs and gates. By analogy, preferential trade liberalization attracts firms to liberalizing countries while repelling them from other countries. The reason is that liberalizing countries improve their accessibility and become better export bases: they gain better access to one another's markets while maintaining the same ease of access to other countries' markets.

In contrast to the home-market effect, other insights of two-location models survive scrutiny for multilocation economies. First, if a location has a sufficiently large share of the economy's expenditures, a single cluster will emerge and will be hosted by that location (dominant market effect). Second, starting with prohibitive trade barriers, freer trade initially leads to a more uneven spatial distribution of firms (magnification effect).

Finally, having more than two locations allows one to model complex economies in which countries are themselves divided in regions. In this more complex scenario, one has to distinguish between international and interregional trade barriers while also keeping in mind that labor mobility is negligible at the international level but much greater at the

regional level. The result is that agglomeration within countries is shaped mainly by interregional trade impediments while agglomeration between countries is shaped mainly by international trade barriers. This result has been derived both with and without interregional migration as well as with and without input-output linkages.

To summmarize, by relating the emergence and the strength of localized externalities to a set of well-defined microeconomic parameters, NEG allows one to understand the effects of international trade, migration, and capital flows on the geographical patterns of economic development in the world economy.

See also capital accumulation in open economies; fragmentation; linkages, backward and forward; location theory; monopolistic competition; New Trade Theory; oligopoly; technology spillovers

FURTHER READING

Baldwin, Richard, Rikard Forslid, Philippe Martin, Gianmarco Ottaviano, and Frederic Robert-Nicoud. 2003. *Economic Geography and Public Policy*. Princeton, NJ: Princeton University Press. A thorough analysis of a wide range of NEG models and a systematic investigation of how they affect our thinking about welfare and public policy issues.

Brakman, Steven, Harry Garretsen, and Charles van Marrewijk. 2001. *An Introduction to Geographical Economics*. Cambridge: Cambridge University Press. A simplified presentation of NEG models for advanced undergraduate and first-year graduate students.

Fujita, Masahisa, Paul Krugman, and Anthony Venables. 1999. *The Spatial Economy: Cities, Regions, and International Trade*. Cambridge, MA: MIT Press. The first book and still the main reference on NEG.

Fujita, Masahisa, and Jacques-François Thisse. 2002. *Economics of Agglomeration: Cities, Industrial Location, and Regional Growth*. Cambridge: Cambridge University Press. A rigorous synthesis of spatial economics from traditional location theory to models of systems of cities, from microfounded urban structure to NEG.

Henderson, Vernon, and Jacques-François Thisse, eds. 2004. *Handbook of Regional and Urban Economics*.

Vol. 4. Amsterdam: Elsevier. A presentation of the most important recent developments in spatial economics in terms of both theory and empirics.

GIANMARCO I. P. OTTAVIANO

■ New Open Economy Macroeconomics

The New Open Economy Macroeconomics (NOEM), also referred to as new Keynesian open economy models, is a class of models that addresses open economy issues in a framework with dynamically optimizing agents with nominal rigidities (prices or wages that change slowly in response to shocks) and market imperfections (firms or households with some ability to set their own prices or wages). The NOEM model has become a "workhorse" framework for studying a variety of questions in international macroeconomics. These questions include whether international policy coordination could increase the welfare of households by improving economic outcomes, the welfare implications of simple monetary policy rules in an open economy, and how exchange rate behavior is affected by how firms set prices. As NOEM is more a framework than a particular model and one that economists use as the basis of current investigations, the assumptions of the model are still evolving. What follows is a short description of the original NOEM model written by the economists Maurice Obstfeld and Kenneth Rogoff (see Obstfeld and Rogoff 1996, 2000; Obstfeld 2001), some of its key results, and then several extensions of the model.

The Baseline NOEM Model Assume that in two symmetric countries, home and foreign, each household produces a differentiated good. Households produce goods using only their own labor but require increasing amounts of labor to produce additional goods (i.e., the production function exhibits decreasing returns to scale). Each product is distinct and is produced only by a particular household, such that each household has some market power—in other words, some scope to choose the price at which it sells its good. Knowing what the demand for its good will

be at every price, each household chooses the price of its good in its own currency (called "producer-currency pricing," PCP), and during the following period the good's price will be fixed. Admittedly, this last assumption is somewhat ad hoc, but it is meant to capture the empirical fact that prices for most goods are not updated continuously, perhaps because there are some costs associated with changing prices. Since the price is set above the household's marginal cost, in the short run it is in the household's interest to supply more goods at the fixed price in response to small fluctuations. Both the law of one price (each foreign good costs its price set in the foreign currency converted to home currency by the nominal exchange rate) and purchasing power parity (which in one form says that the foreign bundle of goods costs the same as the home bundle of goods when converted into the home currency) hold. Note that this setup is equivalent to a profit-maximizing firm setting prices and wages paid to households, and the households supplying their labor to the firm as demanded.

Home and foreign households' utility depends on their consumption and work: they are made happier the more they consume and less happy the more they have to work. In particular, households would like to consume some of each of the goods produced in both the home and foreign economies. Households face budget constraints, however. Their income—from selling their products, accumulation or decumulation of assets (which include both money and internationally traded bonds), and transfers from the government—must equal their spending on consumption and the taxes they pay. This budget constraint must be satisfied across time, so home households could borrow from foreign households to purchase goods during a particular period but would have to pay foreign households back with interest. Each household chooses how much to produce in order to maximize its lifetime utility subject to its budget constraint.

This model will have some of the same effects found in the Mundell-Fleming model. For example, monetary policy, in the form of an unexpected increase in the money supply in the home country, will lead to households in the home country increasing their demand for all consumption goods both home and foreign. It also will lead to a depreciation of the exchange rate, which temporarily raises domestic income relative to foreign income, and results in a current account surplus for the home country. This current account surplus increases the home country's net domestic claims on foreigners. All of these effects are largely permanent. Households in the home country will increase not only how much they consume today but also how much they consume in all future periods, because they will use some of their current income increase to acquire more assets. Although the real interest rate may move to offset some of this effect, changes to relative consumption demand will be permanent because domestic and foreign households face the same real interest rate.

Contrast with Earlier Models This baseline NOEM model is different in several key ways from both the Mundell-Fleming model and the intertemporal approach to the current account that preceded it. Unlike the intertemporal approach to the current account (earlier multiperiod optimizing models of the open economy), the NOEM model includes nominal rigidities and market imperfections. These features allow the NOEM model to look at the short-run effects of policy decisions, including any effects of monetary policy. Unlike the Mundell-Fleming model, this NOEM model is a dynamic general equilibrium model: it has explicit microfoundations (all agents are given objective functions to determine their behavior) and it has intertemporal choice (agents are making choices taking into account future periods). These differences allow the models to look at the *dynamic* effects of policies or shocks (as opposed to solely comparative *statics*), in particular on the current account and budget deficits. In addition, the NOEM model can evaluate different policies based on explicit welfare criteria that are consistent with the structure of the model.

For example, unlike later versions of the Mundell-Fleming model, in reaction to the home central bank loosening monetary policy this version of the NOEM model has no exchange rate overshooting,

where the exchange rate moves by a greater amount immediately than it will in the long run. This result is of interest to international economists because they would like to explain why exchange rates seem to move more than can be explained by changes in other macroeconomic variables or in ways contrary to what their models would suggest. For the reasons described earlier, home consumption relative to foreign consumption will immediately move to its new level, as will the relative money supplies in the two countries, and therefore the exchange rate.

Moreover, in the Mundell-Fleming model, the unexpected easing of home-country monetary policy raises output in the home country and lowers it in the foreign country, as the depreciation of the exchange rate makes home goods cheaper for foreigners. The depreciation is therefore said to have a beggar-thy-neighbor effect. In contrast, in the original version of the NOEM model, home and foreign households benefit equally from the easing of monetary policy in the home country. Both gain because households in each country have some monopoly power over their output and produce less individually than they would if society as a whole would choose their output for them. Monetary policy increases the utility of all households because it causes the expansion of output, and because both home and foreign households are equally affected by the market distortion. The point, however, is not so much the differences in results—extensions to the original model can restore some of the conclusions from earlier models—but rather the ability to look at dynamics and welfare conclusions.

Extensions of the Original NOEM Model Although the quantity of published research makes it difficult to discuss all of the extensions, some extensions of the original model have changed its basic results sharply. For example, the exchange rate will "overshoot" in response to a monetary policy shock if the two countries are no longer symmetric. If households in each country have "home bias"—that is, prefer their own country's goods more than the other's goods—or if some of the goods that each produces are not traded (such as most houses and some services), then the real exchange rate (the exchange rate adjusted for differences in each country's inflation) will move in response to shifts in wealth between the two countries and differences in the real interest rate in the home and foreign nations. Because the tastes of the two households are no longer identical, purchasing power parity will no longer hold.

Extensions to the model can also change its welfare implications. Differences in the symmetry of home and foreign households can result in shocks, such as the home monetary policy shock, having a larger effect on the welfare of one country. With nontraded goods or home bias, households in the home country will gain more when domestic output increases. The degree to which households would be willing to substitute between goods (also called the elasticity of substitution), in other words, consume alternative goods, either another home good or a foreign good, can affect how they benefit from (or are harmed by) shocks. Therefore, if households are more willing to substitute for goods from the other country than they are for goods from the same country, then the unexpected home monetary policy expansion will benefit the home country more than the foreign one. If the difference between the two elasticities of substitution is large enough, then the welfare of the foreign country will be reduced—a different version of the beggar-thy-neighbor effect from earlier models. If instead households are more willing to substitute for a good from the same country than for a good from the other country, perhaps because each country specializes in a certain type of goods, the foreign country will gain more: the home country has to work more but cannot consume as much because of the strong adverse movement in the cost of its imports relative to its exports, its terms of trade. The policy may even have a "beggar-thyself" effect if the difference in elasticities is large enough.

One extension that has been particularly discussed in the literature is whether agents use PCP or price their goods in the currency of the other country, referred to as "local-currency pricing" (LCP). Assuming LCP is attractive because it helps the model explain several things we observe in the real world: the nominal and real exchange rate will be perfectly correlated in the short run; changes in exchange rates will have little or no short-term pass-through to

consumer prices; and because the exchange rate has to move more to affect the relative import price, the nominal exchange rate will be more volatile. Assuming LCP, however, means that, contrary to empirical evidence, a country's terms of trade will improve when its exchange rate depreciates (Obstfeld 2001). Several papers try to have agents optimally choose which currency to price in; this choice can depend on how easily people in both countries can share risk, how variable the exchange rate is, and the size of a firm's market share in the other country.

Neither PCP nor LCP makes the distinction between consumer prices and wholesale or intermediate prices, and as a result neither can capture both the relatively low pass-through of exchange rate movements to consumer prices and the larger pass-through to wholesale import prices. A number of authors explore this distinction by extending the model to include marketing and a distribution network—goods require transportation and retail services, which are two nontraded goods, in order to be sold to households—or to have nontraded goods produced by combining imported and domestically produced intermediate goods. Moreover, including a distribution sector in the model can help explain the behavior of the real exchange rate relative to movements in other macroeconomic variables, such as consumption.

In our description of the original NOEM model, all agents had perfect foresight and shocks were completely unexpected; in other words, they thought they knew everything that was going to happen in the model, and that anything could change came as a complete surprise to them. A number of researchers have extended NOEM models to a stochastic framework in which agents know that unexpected events will hit the economy and may even know the distribution of these shocks, but they do not know in any given period what the shock will be. In a stochastic model, where some prices or wages are set in advance of shocks, uncertainty or the volatility of variables can affect the means of variables in the economy, because households do not like risk. So risk can affect things such as welfare, the exchange rate, terms of trade, consumption, and how prices are set.

For example, since workers like to consume more but dislike working, if households are able to consume a large amount at the same time they are required to work more, they may wish to have higher wages to reduce the amount of work they have to do.

To take the example of monetary policy again, with floating exchange rates, more variable monetary policy (with no other shocks) can lead to a more variable nominal exchange rate and higher preset wages. These changes can increase the volatility of household consumption and move production in the economy farther away from the optimal level, and as a result lower welfare in the economy. One question that has particularly interested international economists is whether exchange rate volatility reduced the flow of goods, services, and assets traded in the world. The economists Philippe Bacchetta and Eric van Wincoop (2000) show that nominal exchange rate volatility does not necessarily have a negative effect on trade flows, although it probably has a negative effect on capital flows. Despite this theoretical work that shows a link between exchange rate uncertainty and both prices and real macroeconomic variables, however, earlier empirical results are mixed.

Researchers have also used the NOEM framework, with its explicit specification of a welfare criterion, to evaluate a variety of simple monetary policy rules and to solve for "optimal" monetary policy rules in an open economy. Whether a monetary policy rule, an equation for the central bank's policy instrument, includes some form of the exchange rate depends in part on the degree of pass-through from exchange rate to consumer prices. When firms price their goods only in their own currency, the home country's monetary policy may affect only the home country's producer currency prices since there is complete pass-through from exchange rate movements; foreign producer prices denominated in foreign currency will not change. In this case, the central bank should attempt to stabilize only domestic prices. With incomplete pass-though firms may charge higher export prices to compensate them for exchange rate risk. Because the central bank can affect the variability of the exchange rate and therefore possibly lower the risk premium charged on imports, it should no longer target the domestic price level only. Because policy decisions in one country can have implications for welfare in other countries, economists have also looked at whether policy coordination among policymakers in different countries yields welfare benefits.

In addition to the extensions outlined here, researchers have tried to address a variety of other questions, including currency crises, the short-run sustainability of the current account, the persistence of changes in the exchange rate, and the implications of agents not being able to completely share risk across markets. Policymakers use these models as well. For example, in recent years central banks in a number of countries as well as international organizations have built empirically relevant NOEM models to forecast the economy and to analyze alternative scenarios.

See also balance of payments; beggar-thy-neighbor policies; currency crisis; exchange rate pass-through; exchange rate regimes; exchange rate volatility; home country bias; international policy coordination; international reserves; monetary policy rules; Mundell-Fleming model; nontraded goods; purchasing power parity; real exchange rate

FURTHER READING

Bacchetta, Philippe, and Eric van Wincoop. 2000. "Does Exchange-Rate Stability Increase Trade and Welfare?" *American Economic Review* 90 (December): 1093–1109. One of the earliest papers with a stochastic version of the NOEM framework.

Bowman, David, and Brian Doyle. 2003. "New-Keynesian, Open-Economy Models and their Implications for Monetary Policy." In *Price Adjustment and Monetary Policy*. Ottawa: Bank of Canada, 247–93. A longer and more in-depth survey piece on NOEM models and extensions to them with a particular emphasis on issues related to monetary policy.

Corsetti, Giancarlo, Luca Dedola, and Sylvain Leduc. 2005. "DSGE Models of High Exchange-Rate Volatility and Low Pass-Through." CEPR Discussion Paper 5377 (December). London: Center for Economic Policy Research. Available at http://www.cepr.org/Pubs/new-dps/

dplist.asp?dpno=5377. Incorporates a distribution sector in the NOEM framework and tries to explain empirical observations about exchange rate behavior.

Corsetti, Giancarlo, and Paolo Pesenti. 2005. "The Simple Geometry of Transmission and Stabilization in Closed and Open Economies." NBER Working Paper 11341. Cambridge, MA: National Bureau of Economic Research. Available at http://www.nber.org/papers/w11341/pdf. Provides an excellent and relatively accessible discussion of optimal monetary policy, as well as an overview of the NOEM model and pass-through.

Devereux, Michael, Charles Engel, and Peter Storgaard. 2004. "Endogenous Exchange Rate Pass-Through When Nominal Prices Are Set in Advance." *Journal of International Economics* 63: 263–91. A recent example of trying to model firms' choice over which currency to price their exports.

Erceg, Christopher, Luca Guerrieri, and Christopher Gust. 2006. "SIGMA: A New Open Economy Model for Policy Analysis." *International Journal of Central Banking* 4 (March): 1–50. Available at http://www.ijcb.org/journal/ijcb06q1a1.htm. Outlines one of many open economy models being used for policy analysis at international organizations and central banks around the world.

Obstfeld, Maurice. 2001. "International Macroeconomics: Beyond the Mundell-Fleming Model." *IMF Staff Papers* 47 (Special Issue): 1–39. Puts the New Open Economy Macroeconomics approach in the context of the history of international macroeconomics from the classical paradigm of the late 19th century and early 20th century through today.

Obstfeld, Maurice, and Kenneth Rogoff. 1996. *Foundations of International Macroeconomics*. Cambridge: MIT Press. Chapter 10 provides a textbook introduction to the earliest version of the NOEM model, as well as chapters on the Mundell-Fleming and intertemporal approaches.

———. 2000. "New Directions for Stochastic Open Economy Models." *Journal of International Economics* 50 (February): 117–53. Outlines a benchmark stochastic version of standard model.

Svensson, Lars, and S. van Wijnbergen. 1989. "Excess Capacity, Monopolistic Competition, and International Transmission of Monetary Disturbances." *Economic Journal* 99 (September): 785–805. The most-cited immediate precursor to the original Obstfeld and Rogoff NOEM paper.

BRIAN DOYLE

■ New Trade Theory

New Trade Theory is the descriptive term for theories that assume imperfect competition and increasing returns to scale (internal scale economies at the firm level) in order to explain international trade. In contrast, traditional trade theories, such as the Ricardian or the Heckscher-Ohlin model, assume perfect competition and constant returns to scale, and attribute the emergence of international trade to cross-country opportunity cost differences (i.e., comparative cost advantage) caused by either differences in production technology (Ricardian model) or factor endowments (Heckscher-Ohlin model).

Reasons for Developing New Trade Theory

The New Trade Theory originated in the late 1970s and early 1980s when advances in the industrial organization literature were incorporated into trade theory. It was developed to explain four major stylized facts (Helpman and Krugman 1985):

> Fact 1: *The increase in the trade to income ratio, and the high and increasing percentage of trade taking place between industrialized nations, even though these countries are seemingly becoming more similar.*

Traditional models predict that trade benefits increase the more different trading partners are. This is puzzling because, in reality, trade is much more prevalent between quite similar countries, in particular between industrialized nations. For example, in 2005, the United States exported (imported) $186.4 ($308.8) billion worth of goods and services to (from) the European Union. In the same period, the U.S. export (import) value to (from) Africa was only $15.5 ($65.2) billion (Census FT900 Report).

> Fact 2: *The high percentage of intraindustry trade, particularly between industrialized nations.*

Traditional trade theories cannot explain the existence of intraindustry trade. In the Ricardian and the

Heckscher-Ohlin models, only interindustry trade takes place. That is, if one country exports cars to another country, it does not import cars from the same country. In contrast, trade statistics for industrialized nations consistently reveal intraindustry trade to account for well above 50 percent of total trade. Although part of this may just be an aggregation problem, that is, different products are aggregated into one industry so that actual interindustry trade appears as intraindustry trade, it is clearly not the whole story.

Fact 3: *Intrafirm transactions and foreign direct investment by multinational firms.*

In the constant returns–perfect competition world of the traditional theories, it is essentially impossible to talk about the scope of activities carried out within firms because there is no true concept of "a firm," the number and size of firms being indeterminate.

Fact 4: *Trade liberalization and the associated increase in factor productivity in spite of only limited resource reallocation.*

According to the traditional theories, trade liberalization results in substantial factor reallocation, most notably in the Ricardian model, where one industry closes down completely and all resources concentrate in the industry for which a country has a comparative advantage. The effect is qualitatively similar in the Heckscher-Ohlin framework, except that specialization is incomplete. In reality, however, trade liberalization seems to cause rather limited resource reallocation.

Some, usually nonacademic, literature claims that the raison d'être of the New Trade Theory is to provide arguments against free trade. Although there is research showing that active trade policy may improve welfare under imperfect competition, these findings are usually too assumption-dependent to warrant a recommendation for a widespread deviation from free trade.

Models in the New Trade Theory can be distinguished by the type of imperfect competition. The first approach uses the monopolistic competition model with differentiated goods, typically as proposed by Dixit and Stiglitz (1977). Research in this area began with seminal articles by Krugman (1979,

1980, 1981). The second approach, starting with Brander (1981) and Brander and Krugman (1983), uses an oligopolistic setup.

Explaining Intraindustry Trade The basic model (Krugman 1979) assumes that consumers value variety, but it is also possible to set up the model so that each consumer has a preferred variety that differs across consumers (Helpman and Krugman 1985). Each variety is produced by a single firm using labor. The cost function of the firm consists of fixed and variable costs; marginal cost is constant, and average cost is decreasing (internal economies of scale). The consumers' utility function is such that the price elasticity of demand for any variety is finite and exceeds one, so that the profit-maximizing price exceeds marginal cost by a positive markup. The number of firms is limited by the zero profit condition.

When the domestic country opens up to trade with an otherwise similar economy, foreign consumers create additional demand for domestic varieties. In equilibrium, individual consumption per variety and the price-wage ratio both fall. The trade-induced increase in demand allows firms to move down their average cost curve and increase production. At the same time, the full employment condition still holds. Hence, since firm-level production increases, the number of domestic firms goes down. Yet the number of varieties, domestic plus foreign, available to domestic consumers increases.

Gains from trade arise for two reasons. First, trade allows firms to better exploit economies of scale; as a result, the domestic real wage rises. Second, domestic consumers have access to a larger number of varieties.

To analyze the impact of transportation costs and home market effects, consider two differentiated industries A and B and two groups of consumers in countries 1 and 2 (Krugman 1980). The first group consumes only products from industry A and the second group only products from industry B. Type A consumers have a higher population share in country 1 and type B consumers in country 2, while country population levels are the same. Due to positive transportation costs, the consumption ratio of foreign to domestic goods is below one in both countries. In this case, each country will produce relatively more of the product for which it has the larger home market. If countries' tastes are sufficiently dissimilar (i.e., if the population shares of A-consumers in 1 and B-consumers in 2 are high), specialization will be complete: industry A will be located only in country 1 and industry B only in country 2. The model thus explains how a bigger home market can give an industry a comparative advantage.

To investigate the determinants of intraindustry trade shares, consider two differentiated-goods industries and two sector-specific inputs (Krugman 1981). To keep things simple, let the two countries have equal population size, but country 1 has a share z < 50 percent of industry B–specific labor and country 2 has a share z of industry A–specific labor. Whereas the trade volume is constant and does not depend on z, the share of intraindustry trade becomes maximal as z approaches 50 percent. This model can thus explain why we see more intraindustry trade between countries that are more similar in terms of factor endowments.

Intraindustry trade also arises in a model with one domestic and one foreign market and two firms, domestic and foreign, who produce a homogeneous good and compete Cournot style (i.e., each firm treats the output level of its competitor as fixed) in both markets (Brander 1981). The markets are segmented, and shipping goods from one country to the other is costly. In this case, as long as the per unit transportation cost does not exceed the monopoly price markup over marginal cost, both firms will sell goods in both markets, so intraindustry trade arises.

Topics in New Trade Theory Traditional trade theory shows that small countries (those that cannot influence world market prices) typically have nothing to gain from pursuing an active trade policy. This seems at odds with the empirical observation that trade intervention is widespread across countries and industries. Although both monopolistic competition and oligopoly models can provide additional reasons for active trade policy (see Helpman and Krugman 1989; Rivera-Batiz and Oliva 2003), the literature on what is known as strategic trade policy has focused more on oligopoly. Using active trade policy, the domestic government can alter the strategic position of domestic firms against foreign competitors and help them capture additional rents. Oligopoly models can also be used to explain why a government may prefer tariffs over quotas or other nontariff barriers and vice versa; in contrast, tariffs and quotas are usually equivalent in the perfect competition model. Although imperfect competition can be used to show why active trade policy may make sense, this does not imply that free trade should be abandoned. In the absence of correct information about market structure and cost, governments can easily lower welfare by using active trade policy. Recent research, using asymmetric information models, has investigated whether governments can induce firms to reveal this information.

Models of imperfect competition can also be employed to explain multinational corporations, outsourcing, and the exporting decision of firms. Summarizing Dunning (1988), multinational corporations arise due to three reasons (OLI theory):

1. *Ownership advantage*: Knowledge capital (headquarter services) can be used at the same time by different production facilities.
2. *Location advantage*: Having a subsidiary in a foreign market makes sense when the market is large and trade costs are high (for horizontal firms) or when trade costs are low and factor prices differ substantially across countries (for vertical firms).
3. *Internalization advantage*: Transfer of knowledge-based assets in order to have other firms produce inputs for one's own firm is risky.

This last point leads to the question of firm organization; namely, when would firm A want to build a subsidiary instead of outsourcing production to another firm B? The answer depends on transaction costs. Letting firm B produce the required input may be more efficient in terms of production costs, but problems may arise because of input specificity and the related holdup problem. Suppose the input that firm B manufactures can be used only by firm A. Assuming incomplete contracts, firm A can then force firm *B* to sell below production value (holdup problem). Foreseeing this, firm *B* may be tempted to produce an input that is not well suited for *A* but can be more easily sold to other firms. Grossman and Helpman (2002) and Antras (2003), among others, have integrated the transaction cost approach into a monopolistic competition trade model to investigate when outsourcing will occur.

In reality, only a small fraction of firms actually export. The question of which firms will export can be addressed in a monopolistic competition model, where different firms have different variable costs and face per unit transportation costs and fixed costs of exporting (Melitz 2003). In this framework, it can be shown that when a country opens up to trade, less productive firms will exit the market and only a more productive subset of the remaining firms will decide to export.

New Growth Theory (Grossman and Helpman 1991) and New Economic Geography (Fujita, Krugman, and Venables 1999) are closely related to the New Trade Theory since they also heavily rely on the Dixit-Stiglitz model of monopolistic competition and emphasize the importance of trade. These theories are usually not considered part of the New Trade Theory, however, and are thus not discussed here any further.

The New Trade Theory, based on the concepts of imperfect competition and increasing returns to scale, complements traditional trade theories and has contributed substantially to a better understanding of the world economy and its patterns of trade.

See also comparative advantage; economies of scale; foreign direct investment (FDI); foreign direct investment: the OLI framework; gains from trade; Heckscher-Ohlin model; intraindustry trade; monopolistic competition; New Economic Geography; oligopoly; Ricardian model

FURTHER READING

Antras, Pol. 2003. "Firms, Contracts, and Trade Structure." *Quarterly Journal of Economics* 118 (4): 1375–1418. Integrates incomplete-contracting model of firm boundaries into monopolistic competition trade model.

Brander, James A. 1981. "Intraindustry Trade in Identical Commodities." *Journal of International Economics* 11 (1): 1–14. Shows how intraindustry trade in homogeneous goods can arise in segmented oligopoly markets.

Brander, James A., and Paul R. Krugman. 1983. "A 'Reciprocal Dumping Model' of International Trade." *Journal of International Economics* 15 (3–4): 313–21. Discusses price discrimination and reciprocal dumping in segmented oligopoly markets.

Dixit, Avinash K., and Joseph E. Stiglitz. 1977. "Monopolistic Competition and Optimum Product Diversity." *American Economic Review* 67 (3): 297–308. Develops model of monopolistic competition and differentiated goods.

Dunning, John H. 1988. *Explaining International Production.* London: Unwin Hyman. Lays out the eclectic paradigm, also known as OLI theory, for explaining multinational enterprises.

Fujita, Masahisa, Paul Krugman, and Anthony J. Venables. 1999. *The Spatial Economy.* Cambridge, MA: MIT Press. A book-length treatment of the New Economic Geography, which analyzes the causes for spatial economic agglomeration in a general equilibrium framework.

Grossman, Gene M., and Elhanan Helpman. 1991. *Innovation and Growth in the Global Economy.* Cambridge, MA: MIT Press. A book-length treatment of the New Growth Theory, which considers intentional technological innovation as the driving force behind economic growth.

———. 2002. "Integration versus Outsourcing in Industry Equilibrium." *Quarterly Journal of Economics* 117 (1): 85–120. Discusses firms' integration versus outsourcing choice in transaction cost setting.

Helpman, Elhanan, and Paul R. Krugman. 1985. *Market Structure and Foreign Trade.* Cambridge, MA: MIT Press. Combines Heckscher-Ohlin model with monopolistic competition and differentiated goods model and discusses the impact on trade volume and gains from trade.

———. 1989. *Trade Policy and Market Structure.* Cambridge, MA: MIT Press. Discusses impact of imperfect competition on optimal trade policy.

Krugman, Paul R. 1979. "Increasing Returns, Monopolistic Competition, and International Trade." *Journal of In-

ternational Economics 9 (4): 469–79. Shows gains from trade in monopolistic competition model.

———. 1980. "Scale Economies, Product Differentiation, and the Pattern of Trade." *American Economic Review* 70 (5): 950–59. Introduces transportation costs and home market effects into monopolistic competition model.

———. 1981. "Intraindustry Specialization and the Gains from Trade." *Journal of Political Economy* 89 (5): 959–73. Discusses determinants of intra- vs. interindustry trade in monopolistic competition model.

Markusen, James R. 2002. *Multinational Firms and the Theory of International Trade*. Cambridge, MA: MIT Press. A book-length treatment of the theory of multinational firms under oligopoly and monopolistic competition.

Melitz, Marc J. 2003. "The Impact of Trade on Intra-Industry Reallocations and Aggregate Industry Productivity." *Econometrica* 71 (6): 1695–1725. Provides a model of firms' exporting choice in a monopolistic competition framework.

Rivera-Batiz, Luis A., and Maria-Angels Oliva. 2003. *International Trade*. Oxford: Oxford University Press. A comprehensive textbook on international trade with large part devoted to new literature, in particular on trade policy.

XENIA MATSCHKE

■ **nominal anchor**

See discipline

■ **nondiscrimination**

The nondiscrimination obligation commits World Trade Organization (WTO) members to avoid discriminating among products solely on the basis of their national origin. This obligation is manifested in two basic provisions in the WTO. The most-favored-nation (MFN) clause essentially requires that equal treatment be afforded to all imported goods, irrespective of their origin, as long as they are "like"; the basic incarnation of MFN is found in Article I of the General Agreement on Tariffs and Trade (GATT). The other nondiscrimination principle is the national *treatment* (NT) *obligation, w*hich appears in its original form as Article III in the GATT. It requires WTO members to treat imported goods no less favorably than domestically produced "like" products. By virtue of the MFN obligation, a WTO member cannot treat goods originating in a non-WTO member better than a like good originating in a WTO member. The MFN obligation applies not only to trade instruments (tariffs), but also, by virtue of Article I.1 GATT, to all *domestic* measures that affect trade. NT, on the other hand, covers domestic instruments only. Both MFN and NT are relevant irrespective of whether tariff commitments have been entered on a particular good. Thus, with respect to tariffs, for example, MFN is relevant both for the tariff levels that members agree not to exceed—the "bound rates"—and for the tariff levels that are actually applied (which may be lower).

The MFN principle has a long history. For instance, Hudec (1988) reports that the medieval city of Mantua (Italy) obtained from the Holy Roman emperor the promise that it would always benefit from any privilege granted by the emperor to "whatsoever other town." According to Jackson (1997, 158), the term *MFN* appears for the first time at the end of the 17th century. During the 19th century, the provision appeared in a number of treaties across European states. For instance, the Cobden-Chevalier Treaty of 1860, liberalizing trade between Great Britain and France, included an MFN clause guaranteeing that a signatory would not be treated worse than any other state with which the other signatory had, or would assume, trade relations. Such schemes, however, did not amount to a worldwide nondiscriminatory trade; if at all, nondiscriminatory trade existed between a subset of all states, those that had entered into a similar contractual arrangement espousing the MFN clause.

Nondiscrimination provisions appear in the WTO Agreement in all three Annex 1 Agreements, that is, in the General Agreement on Tariffs and Trade (GATT), in the General Agreement on Trade in Services (GATS), and in the Agreement on Trade-Related Aspects of Intellectual Property Rights (TRIPs). The GATS and the TRIPs contain MFN and NT provisions that are essentially identical to those in GATT, as described above. However, the GATS NT provision (Article XVII) covers only domestic instruments with respect to sectors that a WTO member has decided to liberalize, and to the extent that no liberalization commitment has been entered, it is of no relevance. We will focus on the MFN and NT obligations in the GATT context. There are also NT-like provisions in some of the other agreements constituting the WTO Agreement. For instance, the "consistency" requirement embedded in Article 5.5 of the Agreement on the Application of Sanitary and Phytosanitary Measures (SPS) has a strong flavor of NT by requiring that WTO members treat comparable risks associated with imported and domestic products in similar fashion.

WTO adjudicating bodies have understood MFN and NT to ban both de jure and de facto discrimination. The former concept covers cases where a discriminatory treatment is afforded by virtue of the origin of the product; the latter refers to cases where treatment that is nondiscriminatory on its face effectively confers an advantage to the domestic good. While the de jure cases are easy to delineate, this is not the case with de facto violations, where case law has developed in a rather erratic manner.

Nondiscrimination and Negative Integration
The inclusion of the nondiscrimination obligations is largely the direct result of the decision to construct the GATT as a negative integration contract: policies are defined unilaterally and, to the extent that there are international spillovers, they will be internalized by virtue of the nondiscrimination obligation. This means that a WTO member can in practice adopt any regulation (rational or irrational) to the extent that it does not discriminate. The agreements on Technical Barriers to Trade (TBT) and Sanitary and Phytosanitary measures (SPS) do request a certain degree of rationality from regulatory interventions, but without negating the nondiscrimination disci-

pline. For example, a WTO member has (at least in principle) to base its SPS regulations on scientific evidence. Regulation not based on scientific evidence (when such evidence is available) is SPS-inconsistent, even if nondiscriminatory.

A widespread view among policymakers, lawyers, and many economists is that there are a number of strong economic rationales for nondiscrimination. For instance, it seems to be commonly believed (in particular among noneconomists) that nonuniform tariff structures give rise to inefficient production and consumption patterns in a static sense. Other arguments in favor of nondiscrimination hold that it eases tariff negotiations, or may prevent the formation of preferential trading agreements that are formed to exploit market power in world markets. However, a general theoretical prima facie case for nondiscrimination is not as easily advanced as might be thought. Indeed, Johnson (1976, 18) goes as far as arguing that "the principle of non-discrimination has no basis whatsoever in the theoretical argument for the benefits of a liberal international trade order in general, or in any rational economic theory of the bargaining process in particular."

Nondiscrimination in the Form of Most-Favored-Nation Treatment The MFN obligation, as interpreted in case law, consists of the following elements:

1. with respect to, in principle, all measures that affect trade either de jure or de facto, any advantage granted to goods originating anywhere in the world;
2. must be extended to the like products;
3. originating in any WTO member;
4. immediately and unconditionally.

It emerges from the case law that two products sharing the same tariff classification will be deemed *like*. There is no WTO agreement on rules of origin, and, consequently, every WTO member can unilaterally define its own policy in this respect and apply it in a nondiscriminatory manner. *Immediately* means that the importing WTO member has to grant an advantage with no passage of time. *Unconditionally* means that it cannot impose conditions that it has not imposed to another beneficiary. The standard of review applied by WTO adjudicating bodies in MFN cases is quite favorable to the complainant: there is no need to demonstrate intent to discriminate, and there is no need to demonstrate the resulting trade effects either.

There are two important exceptions to MFN: preferential trade agreements (PTAs), and special and differential treatment for products originating in developing countries that, by virtue of their origin, are granted in donors' markets better treatment than like products originating in developed countries.

A number of factors contribute to make an economic analysis of MFN complicated. First, in a world where free trade maximizes global welfare, there is of course no scope for tariffs at all, discriminatory or not. Any meaningful analysis of the desirability of MFN must therefore include a reason why there are tariffs at all. Consequently, it will involve comparisons of distorted equilibria, with associated second-best problems. Also, a study of MFN must involve at least three countries, with the plethora of different possible trade patterns and analytical difficulties this typically incurs.

Yet another difficulty in analyzing MFN is the fact that there is no general well-defined uniform structure with which to compare the nondiscriminatory tariff structure. This is problematic since it is a priori clear that the arbitrary choice concerning this level will have a profound effect on the outcome: if the uniform level is the same as the lowest discriminatory tariff, the uniform structure will most likely be preferred, while an equally nondiscriminatory structure, but set at the level of the highest discriminatory tariff, will most likely be worse from a welfare point of view. In neither case can the outcome be said to be related to discrimination, however. More generally, we lack a meaningful measure of the *degree* to which a structure fulfills MFN; it is not possible to simply "turn up" the degree of non-MFN and observe the outcome.

Despite these inherent complexities, several strands of economic theory can shed light on the impact of an MFN clause. Both the literature on optimal taxation and the industrial organization (IO) literature on price discrimination suggest reasons why discrimination may be socially desirable. For instance, if the raison

d'être for tariffs is to raise government revenue, tariffs (like taxes in general) should be levied so as to minimize the resulting distortions, and this will often call for nonuniform structures.

Economic analyses of MFN can be divided into two categories. The first comprises models in which governments set tariffs unilaterally. In a typical setup, firms decide on investment, the level of which is influenced by firms' perceptions of tariff treatment, and thus on whether MFN has to be respected or not. A basic mechanism here is that MFN hinders ex post opportunistic taxation of economic rents and may thereby increase the ex ante private incentives for the creation of such rents. This mechanism lies behind several observations. For instance, by affecting the strategic interaction between firms and governments, an MFN clause may have a positive welfare impact even if the government would choose to set nondiscriminatory tariffs in its absence; and a government that, absent an MFN clause, would choose to discriminate may gain from being prevented from discriminating.

A second and more recent strand of literature is concerned with the role of MFN for multilateral trade liberalization, and in particular tariff negotiations. One fundamental role of trade agreements is to prevent negative externalities from nationally pursued trade policies. These international externalities may work through a number of different routes. For instance, they may take the form of changes in terms-of-trade, or through domestic prices affecting import demand. Bagwell and Staiger (2002) suggest that a central role of MFN is to channel these externalities through the terms of trade. This is important, since tariff negotiations can directly address terms-of-trade externalities, but are less effective to address other forms of externalities. Bagwell and Staiger also show how MFN may work in concert with other characteristic features of the GATT/WTO system, such as reciprocity, to make multilateral trade agreements immune to Article XXVIII GATT renegotiations.

The complexity of multicountry tariff negotiations is reflected in the wide variety of intuitively plausible but often contradictory arguments that have been advanced in the informal academic literature and in policy discussions. For example, MFN is said to promote tariff liberalization by making trade agreements more credible; the increased cost of giving concessions makes it less attractive for a party to undermine an agreement by subsequently offering better terms of market access to a third country ("concession diversion"). MFN also makes it attractive for outsiders to enter into an existing agreement, since they get access to a package of low tariffs. And since entrants have to grant MFN, insiders get access to many foreign markets through the incentives for entry. On the other hand, MFN is also claimed to reduce the incentives to liberalize. It increases the costs of giving concessions, since the latter have to be given to all countries with which a country has MFN agreements; MFN makes large countries unwilling to make concessions to small countries, since in return for "peanuts" large countries have to extend their concessions to a large volume of trade; MFN reduces the benefit from a given concession since it has to be shared with other countries; MFN promotes free riding, since countries may opt to wait for agreements between other countries to spill over via MFN, rather than contribute with concessions themselves, and MFN also prevents countries from punishing free riding; or MFN prevents subsets of countries from going further in liberalization than what is desired by the rest of the world. A number of studies examine the validity of these types of claims. We will here just mention two of these.

The role of MFN to prevent concession diversion is at focus in Ethier (2004), who takes a very long-run perspective on its impact. Governments are assumed to initially form reciprocal bilateral agreements. To be meaningful, these must include MFN to avoid concession diversion. As more and more bilateral agreements are formed, the incentives to participate in further agreements gradually diminish, since each agreement has through the partner's MFN commitment to be shared by more and more other countries, and more and more market access has to be given away through a country's own MFN commitments. A process of liberalization through bilateral agreements will therefore eventually come to a halt. It will become necessary to internalize the external effects of any further agreements by making the agreements multilateral. Hence, MFN causes multilateralism, not the other way around. This study can also be seen as an illustration of the more general point that bilateral negotiations conducted under MFN generally are associated with externalities, since the outcome of such negotiations affect parties who are not present in the negotiations.

MFN may potentially cause free riding in at least two ways. One is that a country rejects an offer in order to let other countries reach agreements that it can benefit from without having to make concessions itself. This would be inefficient either because there would be delays in achieving an agreement, or because the agreement would feature higher tariffs compared to some other (undefined) situation. This possibility has as far as we know not found any support in the literature so far. For instance, Ludema (1991), which is one of the few studies that employ a noncooperative sequential bargaining model to study the impact of MFN on multilateral bargaining, shows how negotiators may find it optimal to devise equilibrium offers such that free riding does not occur, despite there being incentives and possibilities to free-ride.

As mentioned, in this entry we do not for the most part cover the literature on PTAs, since it tends not to focus on MFN as such. Nevertheless, some recent work on PTAs is of direct relevance to the issues at stake here. In particular, the literature has highlighted the interplay between the domestic political system and the formation of PTAs, as exemplified by the studies by Grossman and Helpman (1995), Levy (1997), and Krishna (1998), all of which suggest that MFN may have desirable welfare consequences by constraining the domestic political process.

Finally, there are some intuitively important aspects of MFN that have not been formally scrutinized, as far as we know. For instance, as noted already by Viner (1931), the administration of discriminatory tariffs is costly because of the need to keep track of product origin, and MFN thus significantly simplifies customs procedures. Another aspect that we believe is of considerable importance is the fact that MFN reduces the cost and complexity of negotiations by reducing the number of possible bids and outcomes. Finally, under MFN countries may have incentives to use narrow product classifications in order to avoid having to extend concessions granted on an MFN basis. There should thus be reasons for countries to try to manipulate customs classification schemes.

To conclude, the implications of MFN for multiparty tariff negotiations are inherently complex. A large number of partial effects have been suggested, but the economic theory literature has only examined a few of these. It does support some of the claims concerning beneficial effects of MFN, but provides a far too scattered picture to serve as a basis for any more general claim concerning the desirability of MFN.

Finally, it is sometimes argued that MFN is today of limited practical importance, given the low average tariffs of developed countries on imports of industrial products. However, current tariffs are the result of a system built on MFN, and there is no guarantee a priori that the same levels could be supported in its absence. Also, there are important sectors such as agriculture, textiles, and services where barriers are still high and where MFN (or its absence) might clearly be important. Furthermore, as discussed above, the MFN principle does not apply only to tariff negotiations in the rounds, but also to many other facets of the WTO.

Nondiscrimination in the Form of National Treatment Article III GATT divides domestic policy interventions into fiscal (Article III.2) and nonfiscal (Article III.4) measures. With respect to fiscal measures, any tax differential across two "like" products will violate the NT discipline, whereas the tax differential across two "directly competitive or substitutable" (DCS) products must operate "so as to afford protection to domestic production," in order to be in violation of NT. Case law so far has held that large tax differentials across DCS products suffice for this requisite to be fulfilled. Two products are in a DCS relationship if they are considered by consumers to be interchangeable. A demonstration of interchangeability can be based on either econometric or noneconometric indicators. Two products are like if they are DCS *and* also share the same tariff

classification, to the extent that it is detailed enough. Turning to nonfiscal measures, a measure roughly speaking violates NT if it affords to an imported good less favorable treatment than that afforded to a domestic like product. The term *like* has here been interpreted in a manner that roughly corresponds to the DCS notion for fiscal measures.

Two domestic instruments are by virtue of Article III.8 GATT excluded from the coverage of NT: production subsidies and government procurement. But the GATT does not contain a list of domestic instruments that have to observe the NT discipline. WTO adjudicating bodies have adopted an all-encompassing attitude in this respect and have never so far refused the application of Article III GATT on the grounds that a particular measure does not come under its coverage. There is indirect legislative support for this approach: Article III.2 GATT stipulates that imported products shall not be subject "directly or indirectly" to higher taxation or levies than those imposed "directly or indirectly" to like domestic products. Hence fiscal measures that only indirectly hit products are covered by the NT discipline as well. Likewise, the term *affecting* in Article III.1, which includes nonfiscal as well as fiscal measures, is in the same broad vein; finally, the Interpretative Note to Article III states that measures enforced at the border should still be considered domestic, if they are designed to regulate both domestic and imported goods.

Case law has established that violations of the NT discipline can be justified through recourse to one or more of the public order grounds reflected in Article XX GATT. The intellectual merits of constructing Article XX as an exception to Article III are highly doubtful however, since both provisions contain a nondiscrimination clause. There is no doubt, though, that NT can lawfully be disrespected on national security grounds (Article XXI GATT).

Turning to the rationale for NT, the most striking feature of the economic literature is the near-complete nonexistence of studies of NT. The question of what role NT plays in trade agreement is part of the larger question of why trade agreements typically treat internal measures very differently from border measures. Border measures are largely explicitly regulated; tariff levels are bound, import and export quotas as well as export subsidies are prohibited, and so forth. Internal measures, on the other hand, are left to be unilaterally determined by the contracting parties. Intuitively, the reason for this asymmetry seems to stem from a combination of two facts. First, a trade agreement is typically in place for a long period of time because of the costs of negotiating it, even if only binding border measures. Second, during the life span of the agreement various nonprotectionist regulatory needs are likely to arise. The agreement must therefore leave sufficient flexibility for the contracting parties to use domestic instruments for nonprotectionist reasons. It would be extremely costly to condition the agreement on all possible developments; on the other hand, it cannot leave internal instruments completely unregulated, since this would enable countries to use internal measures to undo whatever restrictions are agreed on regarding border measures. NT is the first line of defense against such behavior. That is, NT can be understood as an attempt to remedy problems caused by incompleteness of the agreement.

In order to save on contracting costs, an NT provision is likely to impose a less than perfectly flexible discipline on domestic measures. The question therefore arises as to whether the restriction increases welfare. Horn (2006) shows how an extreme version of an NT provision—a dictum never to tax foreign products higher than domestic products— may improve the contracting parties' welfare even if it would be desirable to tax foreign products higher from an efficiency point of view. Basically, the NT restriction makes internal instruments blunter tools for protectionism: domestic instruments can be used against foreign products, but they also have to hit domestic like products to the same extent. As a result, taxes will be used less to protect, and countries may go further in their tariff liberalization, creating overall gains from the imposition of the NT provision. Such a strict NT restriction will not completely eradicate the problem caused by incomplete contracting, however.

A fundamental weakness of the whole incomplete contract trade agreement literature is the fact that the structure of the incompleteness—what is contracted and what is not—is simply assumed. In practice, parties to an agreement can choose not only tariff levels, say, but also whether or not to include an NT provision. A natural question, therefore, is when, if at all, an NT provision is likely to be part of an optimal agreement. Horn, Maggi, and Staiger (2006) employ a model with explicit contracting costs to endogenously determine the incomplete structure of a trade agreement. It is shown how a strict NT-like provision of the above-mentioned type may be an optimal component of a trade agreement, by combining limited contracting costs with a degree of discipline on countries' use of domestic taxes for beggar-thy-neighbor purposes.

Overall, the analysis of the implication, and even more the optimal design, of NT has only just begun. This is an unfortunate state of affairs, considering the importance of NT and NT-like provisions in the WTO Agreement and in high-profile WTO trade disputes. Without NT (or a provision with a similar type of effect), agreements on border measures could be rendered entirely meaningless by opportunistic domestic policies; to take the simplest case, a domestic tax on imported products could perfectly replace a tariff that is bound through a trade agreement. Nonfiscal measures can be used in a similar nondiscriminatory fashion. It is thus not by chance that NT-like provisions appear in several of the main agreements regulating trade in goods, and also in regulation of trade in services and intellectual property in the WTO.

See also General Agreement on Tariffs and Trade (GATT); multilateralism; regionalism; World Trade Organization

FURTHER READING

Bagwell, Kyle, and Robert W. Staiger. 2002. *The Economics of the World Trading System.* Cambridge, MA: MIT Press. These authors have examined MFN in a series of writings, and this book summarizes some of this work.

Caplin, Andrew, and K. Krishna. 1988. "Tariffs and the Most-Favored-Nation Clause: A Game Theoretic Approach." *Seoul Journal of Economics* 1: 267–89. One of the first formal economic analyses of MFN.

Ethier, Wilfred J. 2004. "Political Externalities, Non-discrimination, and a Multilateral World." *Review of International Economics* 12 (3): 303–20. Discusses the role of MFN in the evolution of multilateralism.

Grossman, Gene, and Elhanan Helpman. 1995. "The Politics of Free Trade Agreements." *American Economic Review* 85 (September): 667–90. Highlights implications of MFN for the domestic political process.

Horn, Henrik. 2006. "National Treatment in Trade Agreements." *American Economic Review* 96 (1): 394–404. A formal economic analysis of implications of NT.

Horn, Henrik, Giovanni Maggi, and Robert W. Staiger. 2006. "Trade Agreements as Endogenously Incomplete Contracts." NBER Working Paper No. 12-745. Cambridge, MA: National Bureau of Economic Research. Shows how NT can arise as an optimal part of a trade agreement in the presence of contracting costs.

Horn, Henrik, and Petros C. Mavroidis. 2001. "Legal and Economic Aspects of MFN." *European Journal of Political Economy* 17 (2): 233–79. Summarizes core legal aspects of MFN and surveys the economic literature on the topic.

———. 2004. "Still Hazy after All These Years: The Interpretation of National Treatment in the GATT/WTO Case-Law on Tax Discrimination." *European Journal of International Law* 15 (1): 39–69. Discusses the WTO dispute settlement case law on NT as it applies to taxation.

Hudec, Robert E. 1988. "Tiger, Tiger in the House: A Critical Evaluation of the Case against Discriminatory Trade Measures." In *The New GATT Round of Multilateral Trade Negotiations: Legal and Economic Problems*, edited by Ernst-Ulrich Petersmann and Meinhard Hilf. Deventer, Holland: Kluwer, 165ff. An early and notable legal view of discriminatory trade measures.

———. 1998. "GATT/WTO Constraints on National Regulation: Requiem for an 'Aims and Effect' Test." *International Lawyer* 32 (3): 619–45. Provides a sophisticated legal argument in favor of introducing an intent test in Article III.

Jackson, John H. 1997. *The World Trading System: Law and Policy of International Economic Relations*. Cambridge: Cambridge University Press. A comprehensive analysis of the WTO.

Johnson, Harry. 1976. "Trade Negotiations and the New International Monetary System." In *Commercial Policy Issues*, edited by G. Curzon and V. Curzon. Leiden: A. W. Sijthoff. An early economic analysis of trade negotiations.

Krishna, Pravin. 1998. "Regionalism and Multilateralism: A Political Economy Approach." *Quarterly Journal of Economics* 113 (1): 227–52. Highlights implications of MFN for the domestic political process.

Levy, Philip. 1997. "A Political-Economic Analysis of Free Trade Agreements." *American Economic Review* 87 (4): 506–19. Highlights implications of MFN for the domestic political process.

Ludema, Rodney. 1991. "International Trade Bargaining and the Most-Favored-Nation Clause." *Economics and Politics* 3 (1): 1–20. Uses noncooperative bargaining theory to highlight the implications of MFN.

Schwarz, Warren, and Alan O. Sykes. 1998. "The Positive Economics of the Most-Favored Nation Obligation and Is Exceptions in the WTO/GATT System." In *Economic Dimensions in International Law*, edited by J. Bhandari and A. Sykes. Cambridge: Cambridge University Press, 43–75. A survey of the MFN literature, with particular emphasis on political economy aspects.

Staiger, Robert W. 1995. "International Rules and Institutions for Trade Policy." In *Handbook of International Economics*, vol. 3, edited by G. Grossman and K. Rogoff. Amsterdam: North Holland, 1495–1551. A survey of the economic literature on trade agreements.

Viner, Jacob. 1924. "The Most-Favored-Nation Clause in American Commercial Treaties." *Journal of Political Economy* 32 (February). Reprinted in J. Viner. 1951. *International Economics*. Glencoe, IL: Free Press. Several of these arguments were made by Viner (1924, 1931). A very early discussion of economic and political implications of MFN.

———. 1931. "The Most-Favored-Nation Clause." Index VI (January). Stockholm: Svenska Handelsbanken. Reprinted in J. Viner. 1951. *International Economics*. Glencoe, IL: Free Press. See previous entry.

HENRIK HORN AND PETROS C. MAVROIDIS

■ nongovernmental organizations (NGOs)

Nongovernmental organizations (NGOs) have been described as "private, not-for-profit organizations that aim to serve particular societal interests by focusing advocacy and/or operational efforts on social, political and economic goals, including equity, education, health, environmental protection and human rights" (Teegen, Doh, and Vachani 2004, 466). NGOs are an important and influential set of institutional actors within the broad context of the world economy. They have emerged as critical organizations in shaping governmental economic policy and practice, influencing global economic institutions and structures, and affecting corporate and business activities. NGOs have grown in number, power, and influence since the 1980s. They have contributed to a range of international economic debates and issues, and NGO activism has been responsible for major changes in global economic policy, law, and regulation.

According to Lindenberg (1999), fiscal crises, ideological shifts, and privatization have all led to a decline in the scope and capacity of the state. In response, a growing global not-for-profit sector has emerged that, in part, has begun to fill the humanitarian vacuum left by the corporate sector and the nation-state. Teegen, Doh, and Vachani (2004) argue that international NGOs constitute another face of globalization and that large, multinational NGOs have emerged, in part, to serve as counterpoints to concerns about the growing power and influence of multinational enterprises (MNEs) and international organizations such as the International Monetary Fund, the World Bank, and the World Trade Organization.

Civil Society Associations *Civil society*, also referred to as the *third sector* or the *nonprofit sector*, is used broadly to refer to all aspects of society that extend beyond the realm of the public sector and the traditional private sector. Although the term *NGO* is relatively recent, associations among like-minded individuals have been part of ancient and modern history.

When individuals or groups within civil society work together to advance a broad common set of interests, and these interests become a significant force in shaping the direction of society, social movements emerge as the outcomes of this process. Social movements are broad societal initiatives organized around a particular issue, trend, or priority. Modern examples related to economic issues include the environmental movement and the movement to improve working conditions in developing countries. When civil society groups band together to form organized relationships, the emergent entities are often referred to as NGOs.

NGO is a broad term that somewhat loosely refers to all organizations that are neither official parts of government (at any level) nor private, for-profit enterprises. Among NGOs, however, there are many different types, characteristics, and purposes.

Definitions and Classifications Scholars of political economy sometimes separate "club" and "social purpose" NGOs. Club NGOs are membership associations designed primarily to provide a benefit to their members, generally because of pooling interests. Examples of club NGOs are unions, business associations, and church groups.

In most of the contemporary literature the focus is on social purpose NGOs. Social purpose NGOs are engaged in a range of activities that have direct bearing on the world economy, including lobbying global economic institutions such as the WTO to more fully consider the environmental, labor, and developmental impacts of their activities; working with industries and companies to develop codes of conduct governing their activities; providing on-the-ground programs in the areas of health, nutrition, and poverty alleviation; and otherwise supporting institutional developments that promote social welfare.

Teegen, Doh, and Vachani (2004) further differentiate among various functions of NGOs. Advocacy NGOs work on behalf of others who lack the voice or access to promote their interests. They engage in lobbying, serve as representatives and advisory experts to decision makers, conduct research, hold conferences, stage citizen tribunals, monitor and expose actions (and inactions) of others, disseminate information to key constituencies, set and define agendas, develop and promote codes of conduct, and organize boycotts or investor actions. In these ways, advocacy NGOs give voice and provide access to institutions to promote social gain or mitigate negative spillovers from other economic activity.

Operational (or programmatic or service-oriented) NGOs provide critical goods and services to clients with unmet needs. NGOs have long stepped in to provide critical social safety nets, where politically challenged, indebted, or corrupt states are unable or unwilling to provide for unmet needs, and where global problems defy neat nation-state responsibilities. Examples of such operational activities include relief efforts provided by the Red Cross or Red Crescent, natural resources monitoring by the World Wide Fund for Nature, and the distribution of medicinal drugs by Doctors without Borders. Although some NGOs focus primarily on advocacy or operational service delivery, many others pursue both sets of activities simultaneously, or evolve from one to the other. For example, Oxfam, the global development and poverty relief organization, advocates for changes in public policy that would provide greater support to its efforts while also contributing directly to health, education, and food security in the developing countries in which it operates. Brown and Moore (2001) add another category: capacity-building NGOs, which are large global organizations that use their expertise and financial resources to build the capability of smaller, local NGOs.

The Role of NGOs in the United States and the World Economy NGOs have assumed a significant and influential role in modern societies. The modern era of NGO activism can be traced to 1984, when a range of NGOs, including church and community groups, human rights organizations, and other anti-apartheid activists, built strong networks and pressed American cities and states to divest their public pension funds of companies doing business in South Africa. A U.S. statute banned new U.S. investment in South Africa, export sales to its police and military, and new bank loans, except to support trade. The combination of domestic unrest, international governmental pressures, and capital flight posed a direct,

sustained, and ultimately successful challenge to the white minority rule, resulting in the collapse of apartheid.

NGOs have also pushed to have greater access to trade policy and international governmental agreements and processes, systems that have historically been limited to governments acting as agents of their domestic constituencies. NGOs have expressed a great deal of interest in the trade policy dispute settlement mechanism under the General Agreement on Tariffs and Trade (GATT) and its successor agreement, the World Trade Organization (WTO), as well as in the practices and reform of the International Monetary Fund and the World Bank.

NGOs have also been active in collective efforts to develop, implement, and enforce industrywide standards, codes of conduct, and agreements. Examples of intergovernmental agreements shaped and influenced by NGOs include the WTO and the North American Free Trade Agreement, the United Nations' Global Compact on Business Responsibility, the International Labor Organization's Declaration of Principles Concerning Multinational Enterprises and Social Policy, and the Organisation for Economic Co-operation and Development's guidelines for multinational enterprises (MNEs). Examples of international codes sponsored directly by NGOs include the Social Accountability International SA8000 standard; Rugmark, a standard that certifies rugs and carpets as meeting basic standards for labor and human rights; and the Forest Stewardship Council standard that certifies lumber as consistent with sustainable practices.

According to a 1995 World Bank report, since the mid-1970s, the NGO sector in both developed and developing countries has experienced exponential growth. In terms of international development, more than 15 percent of total overseas development aid is channeled through NGOs. Indeed, a report published by the United Nations and the NGO SustainAbility notes that the global nonprofit sector, with its more than $1 trillion turnover, could rank as the world's eighth largest economy. Teegen, Doh, and Vachani (2004) argue that the emergence of civil society in general, and the activism of civic NGOs in particular, have broad implications for the role, scope, and definition of corporations in the global economy, and therefore for international management as a research field. Doh and Teegen (2003) point out that the emergence of NGOs, in some cases, has supplanted the role of host governments in the historic business-government bargaining relationship such that NGOs yield significant power over MNEs' right to operate in developing countries.

Another vehicle used by NGOs to advance their agenda is shareholder activism. NGOs may buy shares of corporations and use ownership to promote proxies and other resolutions to effect change. They often use their status to urge institutional shareholders, such as public employee pension and retirement funds, to pursue changes in corporate governance and conduct. They also work with and through socially responsible investment funds, serving as advisors and experts on ethical and social responsibility screens used to determine the composition of such funds and by drawing attention to shortcomings in the mechanisms used by such funds to choose and retain specific stocks within their portfolios.

Challenges to NGOs NGOs face challenges, including the wide diversity of the principals they serve and the constant demands for resources. Variations in national context can also challenge NGOs, as was evidenced by a 2005 Russian law that would appear to limit their ability to mobilize.

In addition, NGOs are facing criticism and pressures over the perception that they are often less accountable for their actions than their government and business counterparts. Specifically, the corporate governance scandals in the United States and around the world have resulted in increasing attention to the role of boards, interlocking board directorates, and overlapping board memberships among corporations and NGOs. The American Enterprise Institute, in cooperation with the Federalist Society for Law and Public Policy Studies, has launched a program initiative called NGO Watch, whose mission is to highlight issues of transparency and accountability in the operations of NGOs and international organizations.

Finally, some argue that, like the MNEs and international organizations they seek to influence, international NGOs are primarily financed and supported by individuals and organizations in wealthy countries and are not as attuned to the interests and needs of the developing world (Lindenberg and Dobel 1999). As a result, many international and local NGOs have developed collaborative relationships that seek to bridge this aspect of the North-South divide.

See also aid, international; anti-globalization; World Bank; World Trade Organization

FURTHER READING

Brown, David L., and Mark H. Moore. 2001. "Accountability, Strategy, and International Nongovernmental Organizations." *Nonprofit and Voluntary Sector Quarterly* 30 (3): 569–87. Discusses and reviews the challenges facing international NGOs, especially as they are called on to fill roles traditionally occupied by governments.

Doh, Jonathan P., and Terrence R. Guay. 2004. "Globalization and Corporate Social Responsibility: How Nongovernmental Organizations Influence Labor and Environmental Codes of Conduct." *Management International Review* 44 (3): 7–30. Discusses the role of NGOs in developing codes of conduct regulating industry.

———. 2006. "Corporate Social Responsibility, Public Policy, and NGO Activism in Europe and the United States: An Institutional-Stakeholder Perspective." *Journal of Management Studies* 43: 47–73. Compares and contrasts NGO activism in Europe and North America.

Doh, Jonathan P., and Hildy Teegen, eds. 2003. *Globalization and NGOs: Transforming Business, Government, and Society.* Westport, CT: Praeger. Comprehensive edited volume with contributions from scholars and practitioners.

Guay, Terrence R., Jonathan P. Doh, and G. Sinclair. 2004. "Nongovernmental Organizations, Shareholder Activism, and Socially Responsible Investments: Ethical, Strategic, and Governance Implications." *Journal of Business Ethics* 52: 125–39. Discusses the role of NGOs in corporate social responsibility, especially socially responsible investment.

Lindenberg, Mark. 1999. "Declining State Capacity, Voluntarism, and the Globalization of the Not-for-Profit Sector." *Nonprofit and Voluntary Sector Quarterly* 28: 147–67.

Lindenberg, Mark, and Patrick J. Dobel. 1999. "The Challenges of Globalization for Northern International Relief and Development NGOs." *Nonprofit and Voluntary Sector Quarterly* 28: 4–24.

Teegen, Hildy, Jonathan P. Doh, and Sushil Vachani. 2004. "The Importance of Nongovernmental Organizations (NGOs) in Global Governance and Value Creation: An International Business Research Agenda." *Journal of International Business Studies* 35: 463–83. Provides a broad review of the role of NGOs in global business affairs.

United Nations. 2006. "UNIC and Nongovernmental Organizations (NGOs)." Downloadable from http://www.un.org.pk/unic/ngo.htm. Reviews the ways in which the UN interacts with NGOs.

World Bank. 1995. *Working with NGOs.* Washington, DC: The World Bank. Provides a guide to World Bank divisions and affiliates on how to work with NGOs.

JONATHAN P. DOH

■ nontariff measures

Nontariff measures (NTMs) are policies, rules, regulations, and practices *other than tariffs* that distort international trade flows. Tariffs are taxes imposed on imported goods as they cross borders and clear customs. Any other measures that, intentionally or unintentionally, distort international trade flows are considered nontariff measures. Most NTMs are nontariff trade *barriers* (NTBs) that reduce trade flows. Import quotas, countervailing or anti-dumping duties, and import surcharges are NTBs specifically designed to restrict international trade. Other government regulations, such as sanitary requirements or product safety standards, are directed at protecting public health and safety, but become NTBs if they also restrict imports. Not all NTMs restrict trade. *Export subsidies,* for example, distort trade flows, but increase rather than decrease international trade.

The most important of the vast array of potential NTMs can be categorized as (1) taxlike measures, (2) cost-increasing measures, (3) quantitative trade measures, or (4) government procurement policies.

Taxlike Nontariff Trade Measures Tariffs usually apply to imports from all sources and usually remain in effect at the same rates for many years. Some taxlike NTMs apply only in special circumstances to imports from selected countries and/or are only temporary.

Anti-dumping duties are additional import taxes imposed in response to the "dumping" of products by foreign firms. Dumping occurs when an exporter sells abroad at a price below the price charged for the same product in the home market, or sells abroad at a price below its average cost of production. Importing countries levy anti-dumping duties only on imports of the product from the country of the firm found to be dumping. The anti-dumping duty is set at a rate equal to the "dumping margin," which is the difference between the price the firm charges in the home market and in the importing country, or the difference between the exporter's average cost of production and the price charged in the importing country. Anti-dumping duties are imposed in addition to the standard tariff on the product.

Countervailing duties are extra import taxes imposed on goods receiving subsidies from the exporting country's government. The size of the countervailing duty normally equals the size of the subsidy. Countervailing duties also are imposed in addition to the regular tariff.

Temporary import surcharges are extra import taxes imposed in "emergency" circumstances, often in response to a sudden increase in a country's balance of payments deficit. For example, the United States imposed a temporary 10 percent import surcharge during the second half of 1971 following several years of growing balance of payments deficits.

Variable levies are taxes on imports that vary in size depending on the price of the imported product in a particular shipment. For example, the European Community's system of variable levies on agricultural imports imposed an import tax just large enough to eliminate any difference between the internal support price and the price of the imported shipment. The variable levies ensured that agricultural goods could not enter the EC at prices lower than domestic support prices.

Cost-Increasing Nontariff Trade Barriers Some NTBs do not directly tax goods, but discourage imports by increasing either the exporter's cost of production or the cost of clearing customs and complying with import regulations.

Prior import deposits are requirements that importers submit deposits to the importing country's Central Bank equal to a percentage of the value of the shipment. These deposits usually are denominated in the importing country's currency, pay no interest, and are held for about 6 months. For example, Uruguay at one point required importers of certain products to submit prior import deposits of up to 1200 percent of the value of the shipment that were held for 6 months at no interest when the inflation rate was about 50 percent per year. Prior import deposits can create delays and impose extra costs on importers.

Product standards, technical regulations, labeling requirements, and sanitary and phytosanitary requirements make imported goods more expensive by increasing an exporter's cost of production to comply with the standard, or by imposing costs on importers due to shipment delays or inspection or certification requirements. For products subject to economies of scale in production, altering a product to comply with widely differing product standards across countries can preclude cost-reducing long production runs. Importers may also have to turn over a significant portion of a shipment for testing. Technical standards such as the European Union's (EU's) import ban on beef that has been fed growth hormones and the French ban on imports of products containing asbestos completely prohibit trade in those products.

Customs procedures that are costly, cause lengthy delays, or create uncertainty for importers discourage trade. International traders complain that inspection and customs clearance procedures in many countries are time consuming and costly. Importers may hesitate to import if they are uncertain as to how goods will be classified and thus what tariff rate will apply.

Reference prices or minimum import prices are official prices used to value import shipments to calculate the amount of duty owed. The usual basis for valuation is the amount the importer pays the exporter, including insurance and freight charges. Reference prices increase the amount of duty paid by an importer by using arbitrary (and higher) prices to value shipments. The United States for many years valued imports of benzenoid chemicals, rubber-soled footwear, woolen knit gloves, and clams at the (higher) internal "American selling price" instead of the actual cost of the shipments.

Quantitative Measures In contrast to tariffs, taxlike NTMs, or other measures that discourage imports by making them more expensive, quantitative trade restrictions directly or indirectly restrict the *quantity* of a product that can be imported or exported.

An *import quota* sets a maximum permissible volume or value of a product that can enter a country during a particular time period. The import quota limit is normally declared before the beginning of the time period. The overall quota limit is often subdivided by country of origin. Import quotas can be administered on a "first-come, first-served basis" by allowing imports until the quota ceiling is reached and then closing the border to further imports. However, governments normally distribute licenses or permits to import among importing firms. The distribution is most often determined by the amounts imported in a base year. *Export quotas* are maximum limits on the amount of a product that can be exported during a particular period of time.

Embargos are total prohibitions on trade of a particular good or trade with a particular trading partner. Most countries prohibit trade in products originating from endangered species or trade in weapons or radioactive materials. Embargos on trade with particular trading partners are usually for political reasons, such as the U.S. embargo on trade with Cuba or the United Nations embargo on trade with South Africa during the period of apartheid.

A *voluntary export restraint* (VER) is an export quota on shipments of a product to a particular importing country that is "voluntarily" applied by the exporting country, usually as the result of negotiations with the importing country. Negotiating VERs with exporting countries was a way governments could protect troubled domestic industries when they could not unilaterally increase trade barriers without violating existing international trade agreements. Exporting country governments often agreed to restrict exports to avoid even more severe unilateral import restrictions by the importing country. Major VERs included European and Japanese limits on steel exports to the United States, Japanese VERs on automobile exports to the United States and European countries, and the complicated web of VERs on textile and apparel products under the Multifiber Arrangement (MFA).

Import licensing requirements are regulations that prohibit importation of designated products without a license issued by a government agency. The agency in charge may base the number of import licenses approved on foreign exchange availability and the state of the overall balance of payments. But the authorities granting import licenses often have a high degree of discretion as to which products can be imported and which importers receive licenses. *Export licensing requirements* are the equivalent restrictions on the export side.

Foreign exchange controls are regulations requiring that exporters turn over any foreign exchange (foreign currency) earnings to the Central Bank in exchange for domestic currency. The Central Bank then allocates the foreign exchange among importers. Importers cannot import without access to foreign exchange to pay for the goods, so foreign exchange allocation decisions limit import and also determine which goods can be imported.

A tariff quota, or *tariff rate quota*, is a hybrid form of trade restriction that allows imports at a "within-quota" tariff rate up to a maximum quantity (the "quota" part of the tariff quota). Additional imports "over-quota" are allowed but are subject to a higher tariff rate. If imports fall short of the quota limit, then the impact of a tariff quota is similar to that of a tariff at the "within-quota" rate. If imports enter "over-quota," then the impact of the tariff quota is similar to that of a tariff at the "over-quota" rate. But if the over-quota tariff rate is so high that no imports enter in excess of the quota limit, then the tariff quota acts like an import quota. The United States, Canada, and the EU apply tariff quotas to some agricultural imports.

Local (or "domestic") content requirements indirectly limit imports of components by mandating that goods sold on the domestic market must contain a minimum percentage of local value added or a minimum percentage of components sourced from local producers. Mexico, Brazil, Argentina, Uruguay, Peru, and the Philippines have at one time required minimum local content in motor vehicle or household appliance industries. *Mixing regulations* or *quantity-linking schemes* require importers to purchase a minimum amount of domestic product before they are permitted to import that product from abroad. An example would be the requirement in Mali that sugar importers purchase one ton of sugar from the domestic sugar refinery for each ton of sugar that they import. Unless the country in question is granted a special exemption, these measures are now prohibited for World Trade Organization members under the Agreement on Trade-Related Investment Measures.

Import/export balancing requirements, sometimes called *compensatory export requirements*, force firms to export to earn foreign exchange equal to a specified percentage of the value of the goods they import. These regulations often apply to motor vehicle assembly. Firms must export motor vehicles or parts to earn foreign exchange to pay for a given percentage of their imported components.

Government Procurement Practices In most countries, regardless of the stage of development, government is the single largest purchaser of goods and services. Purchases of goods and services by governments represent a large potential market for foreign suppliers. Government procurement practices include the method of soliciting bids, requirements placed on bidders, and the method of selecting winning bids and awarding contracts. Discrimination against foreign suppliers could take the form of allocating contracts exclusively to domestic firms, not allowing foreign bidders to participate in procurement solicitations, not providing adequate information to potential foreign bidders, or establishing preference margins for domestic firms. In the United States, for example, the Buy American Act of 1933 required government agencies to purchase only products produced domestically, unless the cost would be "unreasonable." The interpretation of "unreasonable" gave domestic firms a preference margin as high as 50 percent.

Comparison of Tariffs and NTMs Tariffs increase the prices of imported goods and shift demand toward domestically produced substitutes. Consumers bear the burden of higher prices of both imported and domestic goods. Domestic producers benefit because they sell a greater quantity at a higher price. Tariffs also provide revenue to the government. Tariffs generally result in net losses to the importing country overall because the loss to consumers from higher prices exceeds the gains to domestic producers and the government.

NTBs also increase the prices of imported goods and domestic substitutes. The taxlike NTMs provide the government with revenue, but cost-increasing NTMs raise prices to consumers without transferring revenue to the government. Quotas provide windfall profits to whoever is able to trade the good under quota. Depending on how the quotas are administered, the windfall gains may be captured by exporters, which would increase the net loss to the importing country from restricted trade.

In general, NTMs are less transparent, more discriminatory, and more discretionary than tariffs. Tariffs are said to be *transparent* because the amount by which a tariff increases the price of an imported good is clear. A 20 percent tariff increases the cost of a shipment to the importer by 20 percent. The extra cost imposed by customs procedures, inspections, and compliance with standards is far more difficult to quantify. Quantitative trade restrictions also are less transparent than tariffs because the price-increasing

effect of an announced quota ceiling expressed in tons or square yards is not immediately apparent. With tariffs it is also clear that the government receives the tariff revenue. Quantitative restrictions generally provide no government revenue, but create profits for the limited number of traders who are able to import within the quota.

The welfare impact of NTMs such as product safety standards, sanitary requirements, and labeling requirements is particularly difficult to assess. These measures generate social benefits (such as improved health, safety, or improved information for consumers) that can outweigh the costs. To the extent that these measures reduce consumer uncertainty about the quality of imported goods, they may increase, rather than decrease, international trade.

NTMs also provide more scope for *discrimination* against particular exporting countries. Tariffs normally apply at the same rate to products from most exporting countries. Import quotas, however, are often subdivided among exporting countries. VERs are more often negotiated with countries that are viewed as source of increased imports, or countries over which the importing country has more political leverage. Inspections to assure compliance with sanitary or product standards can be applied more frequently or more stringently to products from particular sources.

NTMs are often more *discretionary* than tariffs. Tariffs apply to all shipments at a preestablished rate. Import licensing, foreign exchange control systems, or import quotas give government authorities much more discretion to control what can be imported, when it can be imported, from which exporting countries, and by which importers.

NTMs in International Trade Agreements and Negotiations Two important fundamental principles of the General Agreement on Tariffs and Trade (GATT) and its successor, the World Trade Organization (WTO), are the use of tariffs as the primary form of trade barrier, and nondiscriminatory treatment of imports from all parties to the agreement. Successive rounds of trade negotiations between 1947 and 1994 under the auspices of the GATT made remarkable progress in lowering tariff rates on trade in manufactured goods. Following the principle of nondiscrimination, the lowered tariff rates applied to imports from all exporting countries that were parties to the GATT.

As tariff rates fell, the trade-restricting effect of NTBs became increasingly apparent. Lower tariff rates made preexisting NTMs more evident. But lower tariffs also prompted import-competing industries to seek additional protection through antidumping and countervailing duties, VERs, and technical barriers to trade. The perceived proliferation of NTMs prompted governments to try to negotiate limitations on their spread and rules on their application.

The first negotiated agreement on NTMs was the Anti-dumping Code that emerged from the Kennedy Round (1963–67). Subsequent rounds of trade negotiations put increased emphasis on negotiations to reduce the trade-distorting effect of NTMs. The Tokyo Round (1973–79) resulted in the negotiation of ancillary codes on import licensing procedures, technical barriers to trade, customs valuation, subsidies and countervailing duties, and government procurement. The Uruguay Round (1986–94) further strengthened the rules governing the use of NTMs by specifically prohibiting VERs, replacing agricultural NTMs (such as U.S. import quotas and the EU variable levies) with tariffs or tariff rate quotas, and incorporating agreements on anti-dumping duties, subsidies and countervailing duties, and sanitary and phytosanitary measures into the main WTO agreements. An agreement was also reached in the Uruguay Round to totally phase out the Multifiber Arrangement, arguably the worst of all nontariff measures, by 2005. Despite these changes, however, NTMs still play an important role in the world trading system, and understanding their impacts is an ongoing area of study for trade policy analysts and researchers.

See also anti-dumping; countervailing duties; government procurement; political economy of trade policy; quotas; tariff rate quotas; tariffs; technical barriers to trade; trade facilitation; trade-related investment measures (TRIMs)

FURTHER READING

Baldwin, Robert E. 1970. *Nontariff Distortions of International Trade.* Washington, DC: The Brookings Institution. An early and thorough survey of the different types of nontariff trade barriers.

Corden, W. M. 1971. *The Theory of Protection.* Oxford: Oxford University Press. Contains analyses of mixing regulations (quantity linking schemes), content protection, and an extensive analysis of quotas.

Deardorff, Alan V., and Robert Stern. 1998. *Measurement of Nontariff Barriers.* Ann Arbor: University of Michigan Press. Describes the difficulties involved in measuring the impact of various types of NTMs and cites previous studies. Also includes an appendix with a somewhat different method of categorizing NTMs.

Finger, J. Michael, ed. 1993. *Antidumping: How It Works and Who Gets Hurt.* Ann Arbor: University of Michigan Press. A collection of essays on the origins of anti-dumping actions and case studies of anti-dumping actions. Also includes enforcement experience in Australia, Canada, the United States, and the European Community.

Hillman, Jimmye S. 1978. *Nontariff Agricultural Trade Barriers.* Lincoln: University of Nebraska Press. A early survey of NTBs in agriculture with case studies.

Laird, Sam, and Alexander Yeats. 1990. *Quantitative Methods for Trade Barrier Analysis.* New York: New York University Press. Analyzes the economic impact of selected NTMs, discusses the methods of estimating their impact, summarizes previous studies by country and product, and includes a glossary of NTMs.

Maskus, Keith E., and John S. Wilson, eds. 2001. *Quantifying the Impact of Technical Barriers to Trade: Can It Be Done?* Ann Arbor: University of Michigan Press. Includes chapters that model the impact of technical barriers to trade and review attempts to quantify their impact.

Vousden, Neil. 1990. *The Economics of Trade Protection.* Cambridge: Cambridge University Press. Compares tariffs and quotas and contains analyses of VERs, local content schemes, variable levies, and export subsidies, with descriptions and explanations.

WENDY TAKACS

■ nontraded goods

Even in today's increasingly integrated world a host of goods and services—health care and housing, for example—are not traded across national borders, either because they simply cannot be traded or because barriers to trade are too high. Sometimes political barriers also may prevent trading of some goods, such as strategic military equipment. These commodities, traded exclusively at home (domestically), are broadly labeled as nontraded goods.

Nontraded goods must have their markets cleared locally, and in this respect, differ fundamentally from traded goods for which local excess demand or supplies can be accommodated in the world markets. Although recent trends in globalization, characterized by sharp declines in transportation and communication costs, tend to convert nontraded goods into traded goods, nontraded goods and services continue to represent the large majority of world consumption.

Goods that are traded internationally can be transported or provided in another country at some cost. In principle, therefore, the providers of such goods in different countries compete with one another. In contrast, nontraded goods have to be provided locally and do not involve competition among international providers. The classic textbook example of a nontraded good is a haircut (albeit a service). Though substantial differences may exist in the prices of haircuts across countries, trade does not develop by shipping haircuts from low-price to high-price countries. The cost of transporting either the barber or the customer to take advantage of the low price would far outweigh the price differential. As such, a barber in the United States need not be excited to learn that an appreciation of the pound has made haircuts in the United Kingdom relatively costlier.

The importance of nontraded goods in a trading world was discovered by Ohlin (1929) in his criticism of Keynes's (1929) views on the German transfer problem and has subsequently been illuminated by many prominent economists. Keynes and Ohlin agreed that a transfer would inevitably result in a reallocation of resources between the traded and nontraded sectors. Keynes had argued, however, that

the presence of a nontraded good would shift resources away from the nontraded sector into the exporting sector to exacerbate the donor's terms of trade deterioration as a result of a transfer. Ohlin, in contrast, saw no reason for a movement in the terms of trade and expected only opposing changes in the prices of traded goods relative to those of nontraded goods for the donor and recipient.

Prices of nontraded goods are determined exclusively by local conditions that affect demand and supply, whereas prices of traded goods are determined by conditions around the globe. As such, the distinction between traded and nontraded goods becomes even more important for relatively small trading countries: a small country, through policy changes, can affect prices of nontraded goods but it cannot affect prices of traded goods.

Theories of Trade and Nontraded Goods Are the results of the models of international trade sensitive to the presence of nontraded goods? Jones (1974) presented an elegant model, in which he assumed away the possibility of import-competing production and local consumption of exports, providing a clear view of the way in which the market for nontraded goods is linked to that for traded goods. Komiya (1967) was the first to generalize the standard Heckscher-Ohlin (H-O) model for international trade to incorporate a third, nontraded good. The presence of a nontraded good removes the production indeterminacy of a two-factor, three-commodity (two traded and one nontraded) H-O model. The factor price equalization (FPE) theorem and Rybczynski theorem on the effect of a change in factor endowments on the output levels hold in the new three-commodity model. A country's trade bias (pro or anti) depends on the elasticity (or inelasticity) of the demand for the nontraded good as well as the relative factor intensities of all three commodities. Technological progress in the traded sector does not necessarily result in an increase in its output. Technological progress in the nontraded sector, however, raises the output of the nontraded goods sector if inferior goods are ruled out.

Ethier (1972) analyzed the effects of integrating nontraded goods on each of the four basic results of the H-O model: the FPE theorem, the Rybczynski theorem, the Stolper-Samuelson theorem, and the proposition that a change in the terms of trade will cause an increase in the output of the good whose relative price has risen and a decrease in the output of the other when there are fixed-factor endowments. It can also be shown that the Rybczynski theorem for net output movements stays unaffected by interindustry flows in the two-factor, two-commodity Heckscher-Ohlin model for gross and net output movements in the presence of traded and nontraded intermediate inputs. If the nontraded commodity is a pure intermediate commodity, the Rybczynski theorem still holds with some modifications for gross and net output movements.

In a two-factor, three-commodity model where the third commodity is a nontraded good, the Rybczynski theorem holds for output movements if there is no inferiority in consumption. This is true with some modifications for gross and net output movements when interindustry flows exist. A sufficient condition for this generalized version of the Rybczynski theorem, applicable to a two-factor, three-good economy where one of the goods is nontraded and indecomposable interindustry flows exist, is that the net output change of the nontraded good is bounded by the factor changes.

Following Rivera-Batiz (1982), Komiya's results on the effect of technological changes and changes in factor endowments in the presence of nontraded goods do hold, in a framework where the number of factors and the number of goods are equal, if and only if the sum of the own price elasticities of demand for traded and nontraded goods is equal to unity. Otherwise, a Hicks-neutral technological change in the nontraded goods sector will reduce the price of nontraded goods proportionally less (more) in absolute value than the technological change when the aggregate elasticity is greater (smaller) than unity. Factor prices measured in terms of the traded goods will in general not be fixed, and factor prices measured in terms of the nontraded goods will not change proportionally to the same extent as the change in the price of the nontraded goods, as long as the aggregate elasticity is different from one. The

exact effect on the factor prices will depend in the magnitude of the aggregate elasticity and on the factor-intensity of the nontraded goods' production relative to the traded goods' production. Also, factor prices and the price of nontraded goods are affected by changes in factor endowments in this framework. If the endowment of any factor increases, the price of nontraded goods will decrease if the nontraded goods production is relatively intensive in the expanding factor. Income distribution will turn against the expanding factor. In the context of the specific-factors model, in which an extreme asymmetry in factor mobility is assumed, Clague (1985) showed that increases in the endowment of a specific factor increases the real reward of the mobile factor when nontraded goods exist.

Adding nontraded goods to a conventional factor proportions model, according to Deardorff and Courant (1990), will reduce the likelihood of FPE. Specifically, in the presence of nontraded goods, the reduction in the likelihood of FPE is equal to the fraction of income spent on nontraded goods. For given prices, the set of factor endowment combinations that are consistent with producing the same set of goods and having the same factor prices will shrink, reducing the chance that a country's factor endowments lie in the set, and therefore the likelihood of FPE is reduced. A generalization of the Stolper-Samuelson theorem to include the role of the nontraded goods sector in explaining the effects of price changes in traded goods on relative and absolute wages, provided by Beladi and Batra (2004), reveals that if the import and nontraded sectors are reduced, then freer trade can harm skilled and unskilled labor while improving capital.

Some of the standard conclusions about international trade are disrupted when market imperfection is present in the nontraded goods sector. The fact that some commodities are not traded internationally may itself suggest the presence of product market imperfections. Prohibitive tariffs, for instance, are a source of nontraded goods that may confer market power. In the presence of a monopolized nontraded good, the Rybczynski theorem remains intact as long as the price elasticity of demand for nontraded goods depends only on relative prices. Following Cassing (1977), however, the Stolper-Samuelson theorem is modified in an important way depending on the degree of monopoly and the specific taste patterns of the factors. An increase in the relative price of a traded good will raise the nominal reward for the factor used intensively in that sector but will lower the price elasticity of demand in the nontraded sector which, in turn, will raise the price of the nontraded good relative to the gaining factor whose nominal reward improved. The real reward of the factor, used intensively in the traded sector experiencing a price increase, can fall for sufficiently high propensity of nontraded goods consumption by that factor. Within the same framework, Hazari and Kaur (1995) show that when a nontraded good is produced by a monopoly, a tourism boom can lead to a decrease in the domestic residents' welfare because of drastic movements in the terms of trade.

Policy Relevance of Nontraded Goods The existence of nontraded goods has nontrivial implications for a country's domestic or international policies. An expansionary fiscal policy in nontraded goods and an expansionary monetary policy in international bonds can have offsetting effects on a country's reserves. When the production possibility set is strictly convex (i.e., there are no economies of scale), if the highest tariff rate is reduced to the level of the next highest, welfare improves under certain conditions: specifically, no inferior goods can exist in the economy, the commodity with the highest tariff rate must be substitutable, and the nontraded goods must be substitutable. When multiple commodities share the highest tariff rate, and the highest tariff rate is reduced to the level of the next highest rate, the level of utility increases under substitutability. When all tariff rates move proportionally to a given rate (uniform tariff change), utility increases. Tariffs and production subsidies can reduce the price of nontraded goods. A consumption subsidy may be the optimal policy decision in a model with nontraded goods and production externalities.

When there exists a high intertemporal elasticity of substitution in consumption, contrary to the case with traded goods only, a temporary fiscal expansion (in the form of government spending) on nontraded goods causes real interest rates to move in different directions in each country. More specifically, a fiscal expansion of nontraded goods with a low elasticity of substitution will decrease the domestic interest rate relative to world real interest rates, deteriorating the expansionary country's current account. With a high substitution elasticity, however, the expansion increases domestic real interest rates relative to foreign real interest rates while improving the domestic country's current account. In the presence of a generalized cash-in-advance constraint, when a monetary distortion of the nontraded good is present, a tariff may not be dominated by a consumption tax.

In a two-sector economy, if one of the sectors is characterized by monopolistic competition, a tariff leads to an improvement in welfare if the differentiated good is nontraded but leads to a deterioration of welfare if the homogeneous good is nontraded. Decreases in import prices or tariffs will increase the price of nontraded goods when cross-substitution effects are dominated by the income effect. In a setting of differentiated traded goods, welfare decreases as a result of the tariff causing a demand shift away from the differentiated goods market toward the market for the nontraded homogeneous good. Devereux (1988) offers an insightful discussion on these issues.

Welfare Analysis and Nontraded Goods The relevance of nontraded goods for welfare analyses, including but not limited to the "transfer paradox" (i.e., the possibility that a transfer may reduce the recipient's welfare even when markets function perfectly), has added interest in the topic. Early attempts at identifying a distinct role of nontraded goods in welfare convincingly argued that the effects of neutral technical progress on output and welfare are sensitive to the inclusion of nontraded goods. The welfare of the host country can be shown to unambiguously improve with foreign investment in nontraded goods. The gains-from-trade proposition applies to a monopolistic competition framework that extends to include nontraded goods when differentiated nontraded goods are present as well as traded goods.

Technical progress in manufacturing increases the price of nontraded goods and improves national welfare, and deterioration in the terms of trade increases the price of the nontraded goods and improves national welfare, if the gain of the induced employment effects exceeds the direct loss of the terms-of-trade decline. Those who own traded goods suffer welfare deterioration while owners of nontraded goods experience welfare improvement following a temporary devaluation.

It is important to realize that international trade grows not only as countries trade (on the intensive margin) more of the goods they had already been trading but also when countries begin trading goods (on the extensive margin) they had previously not been trading (nontraded goods). As such, it is hardly surprising that nontraded goods continue to draw our attention even in today's increasingly globalized world.

See also gains from trade; Heckscher-Ohlin model; real exchange rate; tariffs; terms of trade

FURTHER READING

Beladi, Hamid, and Ravi Batra. 2004. "Traded and Non-Traded Goods and Real Wages." *Review of Development Economics* 8 (1): 1–14. Generalizes the Stolper-Samuelson theorem to include the role of nontraded goods.

Cassing, Jim. 1977. "International Trade in the Presence of Pure Monopoly in the Non-Traded Goods Sector." *Economic Journal* 87 (347): 523–32. Provides one of the most insightful analyses of the role of the nontraded sector with market power.

Clague, Christopher K. 1985. "A Model of Real National Price Levels." *Southern Economic Journal* 51 (4): 998–1017. Analyses the real return to the mobile factor in the presence of nontraded goods.

Deardorff, Alan V., and Paul N. Courant. 1990. "On the Likelihood of Factor Price Equalization with Non-Traded Goods." *International Economic Review* 31 (3): 589–96. Provides implications of nontraded goods for factor price equalization.

Devereux, Michael. 1988. "Non-traded Goods and the International Transmission of Fiscal Policy." *Canadian Journal of Economics* 21 (2): 265–78. Contains an insightful analysis of differentiated good market and nontraded goods.

Ethier, Wilfred. 1972. "Nontraded Goods and the Heckscher-Ohlin Model." *International Economic Review* 13 (1): 132–47. Contains some of the most effective arguments raising concerns regarding the implications of a model of nontraded good with an equal number of goods and factors.

Hazari, Bharat R., and Charanjit Kaur. 1995. "Tourism and Welfare in the Presence of Pure Monopoly in the Nontraded Goods Sector." *International Review of Economics and Finance* 4 (1995): 171–77. Explores tourism booms under a monopolized nontraded sector.

Jones, Ronald W. 1974. "Trade with Non-traded Goods: The Anatomy of Inter-connected Markets." *Economica* 41 (162): 121–38. Offers one of the most elegant formulations of the link between traded and nontraded goods.

Keynes, John M. 1929. "The German Transfer Problem." *Economic Journal* 39 (153): 1–7. Contains one of the earliest assessments of the importance of nontraded goods.

Komiya, Ryutaro. 1967. "Non-Traded Goods and the Pure Theory of International Trade." *International Economic Review* 8 (2): 132–52. Provides one of the most general treatments of a trade model with nontraded goods.

Ohlin, Bertil. 1929. "The Reparation Problem: A Discussion. I. Transfer Difficulties, Real and Imagined." *Economic Journal* 39 (154): 172–78. Shaped one the most compelling criticisms of Keynes' assessment of the significance of nontraded goods in a trading world.

Rivera-Batiz, Francisco L. 1982. "Non-traded Goods and the Pure Theory of International Trade with Equal Numbers of Goods and Factors." *International Economic Review* 23 (2): 401–9. Contains an analysis of the effects of changes in factor endowments on the factor prices in the presence of nontraded goods.

HAMID BELADI AND AVIK CHAKRABARTI

■ North American Free Trade Agreement (NAFTA)

The United States, Canada, and Mexico are signatories to the North American Free Trade Agreement (NAFTA). In 2006, the pact covered a combined economy of more than $14 trillion and a population of about 435 million people. In large measure, NAFTA represents the agglomeration of Mexico into the existing Canada–United States Free Trade Agreement (FTA) that was signed in January 1988 and became effective a year later. Mexico initially sought a bilateral FTA with the United States; the two countries announced their intent to pursue an FTA in June 1990, which evolved into NAFTA when Canada joined the process several months later. Negotiations began in May 1991 and concluded in August 1992; U.S. president George H. W. Bush, Mexican president Carlos Salinas, and Canadian prime minister Brian Mulroney signed the agreement in December 1992.

Prior to its ratification, however, the incoming U.S. president, William J. Clinton, demanded additional commitments regarding labor, the environment, and import safeguards. Subsequent negotiations during the first eight months of 1993 produced three side agreements to NAFTA: the North American Agreement on Labor Cooperation (NAALC); the North American Agreement on Environmental Cooperation (NAAEC); and the Understanding between the Parties to the NAFTA Concerning Chapter 8—Emergency Action (that is, against import surges). In addition, the United States and Mexico signed the Border Environmental Cooperation Agreement, which, inter alia, created the North American Development Bank with the aim of funding environmental projects on both sides of the border. Together, these "side accords" supplemented NAFTA provisions and helped Clinton secure congressional approval of the pact in November 1993 by a vote of 234 to 200 in the House and 61 to 38 in the Senate. NAFTA entered into force on January 1, 1994.

Why NAFTA? NAFTA arose because Mexico needed and asked for free trade with the United States. Given the legacy of the debt crisis of 1982, low domestic savings, and an overvalued peso, Mexico needed to import technology and capital to propel economic growth. By ensuring open access to the U.S. market and making it harder to reverse Mexican reforms implemented since the *apertura* (opening)

of the 1980s, Mexico expected NAFTA to complement continuing domestic reforms and create new trade and investment opportunities within the Mexican economy. In fact, the mere announcement of NAFTA talks elicited significant new commitments of foreign direct investment in Mexico in anticipation of the new trade regime with the United States.

For the United States, NAFTA served both economic and political objectives. NAFTA created new opportunities to increase trade and investment with its southern neighbor; U.S. officials also touted—though greatly exaggeratedly—the employment implications of the trade pact. At the same time, they saw the initiative as a way to support the growth of political pluralism and democracy in Mexico, and as part of the long-term response to chronic immigration problems.

Overall, NAFTA has had only a glancing effect on these nontrade issues. NAFTA's first decade coincided with profound changes in Mexico's political regime and the end of 70 years of one-party rule. Mexico's political reform has been a uniquely Mexican achievement, however. NAFTA deserves little credit, except to the extent that increased U.S. interest in Mexico made the 2000 election in Mexico harder to rig. On immigration, NAFTA has not met expectations. Migration from Mexico, both legal and illegal, increased over NAFTA's first decade. Demographers initially forecast increased flows of Mexican migration to the United States, followed by declines in the medium and long run as Mexican economic prospects brightened. But these estimates had to be recalibrated in light of the peso crisis, enduring poverty in states south of Mexico City, persistent rural-urban migration, and the impact of Chinese competition on Mexican industry.

What Is NAFTA? NAFTA was the first free trade agreement involving developed and developing countries that established a comprehensive set of obligations on trade and investment in goods and services. Its detailed chapters cover subjects such as customs procedures, technical standards, sanitary and phytosanitary measures, government procurement, intellectual property rights, investment and competition policy, and sectors such as agriculture, energy, and cross-border services trade in telecommunications and financial services.

With a few notable exceptions, the pact removes barriers to trade and investment in goods and services among the three economies. It does not create a customs union; each member maintains an independent trade regime governing its transactions with nonmember countries. On agriculture, a sector often excluded from disciplines in trade accords, NAFTA comprises three bilateral pacts (U.S.-Mexico, U.S.-Canada, and Canada-Mexico). The U.S.-Mexico accord comes closer to free trade in farm goods than any other extant trade agreement and provides more pervasive liberalization of trade barriers than the U.S.-Canada pact, which contains important exceptions to the free trade regime originally included in the Canada-U.S. FTA that were carried over into NAFTA.

In addition, NAFTA incorporates six dispute settlement processes to manage and expedite the resolution of disputes among the three countries. The six processes cover chapter 11 (investment), chapter 14 (financial services), chapter 19 (anti-dumping and countervailing duties), chapter 20 (functioning of the agreement), the NAALC (labor), and the NAAEC (environment). Chapter 19 cases have been by far the most numerous; chapter 11 provisions involving investor-state disputes have been the most controversial, contrary to initial expectations. When these investor rights were first conferred, the chapter 11 provisions were hailed as a better forum than national courts for resolving investment disputes. In practice, however, the rules (e.g., the ban on indirect expropriation under article 1110 and the minimum standards under article 1105) have fostered litigation by business firms against a broader range of government activity than originally envisaged. Environmental groups, in particular, have raised concerns about the impact of chapter 11 tribunals on state and local environmental standards.

By contrast, NAFTA's institutional structure is skeletal. The signatories did not want to create a new bureaucracy; the governance structure of the pact is minimalist and its budget insufficient to achieve even its modest mandate. The pact is governed by a Free Trade Commission composed of the three trade ministers that oversee the operation of the agreement. In addition, there are more than 30 working groups that provide advice to the commission on specific issues (e.g., rules of origin), a small NAFTA Secretariat to administer the dispute settlement procedures and other work of the commission and working groups, and separate advisory bodies for the labor and environment accords.

Although the pact is comprehensive compared with other trade agreements, it has important limitations. First, NAFTA omits important rights and obligations on subsidies, energy trade, and investment, and the use of anti-dumping and countervailing duties. The pact also maintains restrictions on U.S.-Canadian agricultural trade excluded from their bilateral FTA. In addition, its side pacts on labor and the environment are primarily consultative arrangements and not backed by meaningful arbitration mechanisms or financial resources.

Second, NAFTA was not designed to cure the manifold ills of North American societies, including high levels of illegal immigration, slow progress on environmental problems, growing income disparities (particularly within Mexico), weak growth in real wages, and trafficking in illegal drugs. Some of these problems are correlates of economic integration and higher incomes; all of them require policy responses that range well beyond the competence of trade officials.

The NAFTA Experience to Date In commercial terms, NAFTA has met the stated objectives of its signatories but failed to justify either the inflated promises of its political supporters or the harsh defamations of its critics. Over its first decade, intra-NAFTA trade soared, building on the extensive network of cross-border investments already linking, in particular, the auto and electronics industries of North America. Merchandise trade among the three countries rose almost threefold and was valued at more than $800 billion in 2006; exports to and imports from Canada and Mexico accounted for 30 percent of total U.S. trade. Direct investment by the

United States in Mexico grew robustly but still represented only a small fraction of total investment in American plant and equipment by U.S. firms. The stock of U.S. holdings in Mexico was valued at more than $71 billion at year-end 2005, up from $17 billion in 1994. Canada-Mexico trade and investment also grew rapidly from a low base.

Net employment rose sharply in all three countries during NAFTA's first decade, aided by the positive add-on effects of strong U.S. economic growth. Millions of jobs were created in each country and a sizable but smaller number of jobs were lost each year. On balance, employment rose by 15 million in the United States, 3 million in Canada, and 8 million in Mexico. To be sure, employment in Mexican maquiladoras fell sharply from peak levels in 2000, but those losses resulted primarily from the U.S. economic downturn in 2001–2, changes in Mexican tax policy, and the impact of a strong peso on industrial competitiveness. In the United States, NAFTA-related job losses represented a small fraction of displaced workers—whether one counts the official tally of the NAFTA–Trade Adjustment Assistance program (about 60,000 per year) or the higher numbers cited by NAFTA critics.

Similarly, NAFTA's impact on wages got swamped by other factors in the massive U.S. economy. Claims that NAFTA has contributed to the suppression of U.S. wages are supported only by anecdotal evidence, not serious statistical analysis. There has been no material difference in wage rates between states and industries with a large volume of U.S. imports from Mexico and those with a small volume. By far the most important channel by which Mexico influences U.S. wages is immigration—and this is a function of geography, not trade. In Mexico, real wages did take a big hit in 1995 due to the peso crisis and subsequent deep recession, but rebounded sharply in the decade following 1997.

From day one, NAFTA results were skewed by the political tumult in Mexico caused by a populist revolt in Chiapas, assassinations that marred the 1994 Mexican presidential election campaign, and the peso crisis that erupted in December 1994. NAFTA

obligations helped Mexico weather the financial storm of late 1994–95 in two ways: by channeling the Mexican response toward orthodox fiscal and monetary policies instead of trade protection and subsidies, and by encouraging U.S. financial support for its troubled neighbor. The Mexican economy rebounded quickly and resumed robust growth in the second half of 1996.

Since then, Mexican economic growth has been solid but not spectacular and (as of late 2007) not good enough to redress decades of economic problems. Tight fiscal and monetary policies brought the macroeconomy quickly back into balance, but constrained growth well below levels needed to solve the problems of Mexican society. Investments in physical infrastructure, human capital, and social services have been inadequate. As a result, the Mexican government has not been able to allocate the growth dividend across a broad spectrum of society, and Mexican firms and workers have not been able to take full advantage of the opportunities created by NAFTA. Moreover the growth has been highly skewed among regions within Mexico, exacerbating income disparities between the northern and southern states.

In the United States, NAFTA has had a more profound impact on trade *politics* than on trade itself. The rancorous ratification debate in the U.S. Congress in 1993 galvanized an emerging anti-globalization movement that demanded "No More NAFTAs" and a substantial restructuring of the international economic order. Recurring claims by NAFTA critics that the pact has displaced large numbers of U.S. jobs and investment have proven unfounded, however.

Nonetheless NAFTA became a lightning rod for concerns about the adverse effects of globalization on American workers and industries. The traditional protrade coalition in Congress fractured. Democrats abandoned support for new trade initiatives in response to their labor constituents and in retaliation for the highly contentious and partisan debate in the Republican-led Congress over tax policy and social issues. "Fast-track" trade negotiating authority lapsed in 1994 and major new trade initiatives were deferred until August 2002, when the Congress narrowly restored the trade mandate under the re-branded title of "Trade Promotion Authority" (TPA). Even with TPA, however, U.S. officials struggled to secure passage of NAFTA's phonetic cousin: the U.S.–Central American–Dominican Republic FTA, or CAFTA-DR, passed the House of Representatives by a narrow 2-vote margin in the summer of 2005 (contrasted with a 34-vote margin for NAFTA itself in 1993).

In sum, NAFTA has had a positive effect on economic growth in all three countries, but challenges remain. Even though each country, on balance, has profited from the regional trade deal, the aggregate gains mask adjustment problems besetting members of each society. The solution to such problems for each signatory may be in domestic policies that allow its workers, farmers, and firms to take advantage of the opportunities created by NAFTA and that retrain, retool, and provide income support for those adversely affected by the new competition.

See also Central American Common Market (CACM); Central American–Dominican Republic Free Trade Area (CAFTA-DR); customs unions; free trade area; Free Trade Area of the Americas (FTAA); regionalism

FURTHER READING

Hufbauer, Gary Clyde, and Jeffrey J. Schott. 2005. *NAFTA Revisited: Achievements and Challenges.* Washington, DC: Institute for International Economics. A comprehensive overview of NAFTA's first decade with detailed analyses of key sectors (autos, agriculture, energy) and issues (labor, environment, dispute settlement, migration) covered by the trade pact.

Martin, Philip L. 1993. *Trade and Migration: NAFTA and Agriculture.* Washington, DC: Institute for International Economics. Analyzes the "migration hump" likely to occur in response to Mexican farm reforms and NAFTA, which could increase migration flows to the United States in the short run.

Pastor, Robert A. 2001. *Toward a North American Community.* Washington, DC: Institute for International Economics. Assesses NAFTA's pros and cons and proposes initiatives to deepen economic integration among the three countries.

Weintraub, Sidney, ed. 2004. *NAFTA's Impact on North America: The First Decade.* Washington, DC: Center for Strategic and International Studies. Edited volume on the economics and politics of U.S.-Mexican relations during NAFTA's first decade.

World Bank. 2003. *Lessons from NAFTA for Latin America and the Caribbean Countries: A Summary of Research Findings.* Washington, DC: World Bank. In-depth analysis of the impact of Mexican reforms pursuant to NAFTA on economic growth, the distribution of income, and poverty in Mexico.

JEFFREY J. SCHOTT

■ North-South trade

North-South trade refers to trade between rich (or developed) countries—the North—and poor (or developing) ones—the South. The essence of North-South trade is that the two regions differ, and the variety of assumptions about the cause—for instance, differences in capital per head or technology—goes a long way toward explaining the variety of conclusions that are drawn about it. In addition, researchers vary as to (1) whether they consider North-South trade to mean trade that reflects only the differences between regions per se, or trade stimulated by reductions in trade barriers (natural or policy), (2) whether they permit other changes (e.g., in capital flows or technology), and (3) what they are seeking to explain—for example, divergence between regions or within them (income distribution).

This entry presents a few data on North-South trade, discusses a number of models that predict divergence between North and South, and explores the hypothesis that North-South trade explains widening income inequalities.

The Data Traditionally North-South trade was conceived of as the trade of Northern manufactures for Southern primary goods, which bears a close relationship to analyses of the terms of trade under the so-called Prebisch-Singer hypothesis. This view of North-South commodity trade once had some empirical validity, but it is now severely dated.

Defining the North as the members of the Organisation for Economic Co-operation and Development as of 1990 less Turkey, and the South as all other countries, North-South trade accounted for 38.4 percent of world trade in 1962 and 38.6 percent in 2005 (provisionally), with an (oil-induced) high of 42.6 percent in 1981 and a low of 30.9 percent in 1988. One big change, however, was that whereas in 1962 the North exported twice as much to the South as it imported, the South had a trade surplus with the North over the period 1999–2005. Since 1962 the South's share of world exports to all destinations has increased from 18.1 to 40.7 percent. The story in manufacturing is similar, with a huge growth in Southern capacity and share of world trade—see figure 1, which shows Southern exports growing from less than 5 percent of the world total to 37.5 percent. Within Southern exports to the North, the transformation from primary to secondary sector exports is striking (see figure 2). From a share of 10.7

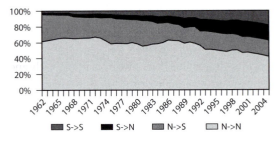

Figure 1

Shares of world manufacturing trade. Source: World Bank, World Integrated Trade System (WITS).

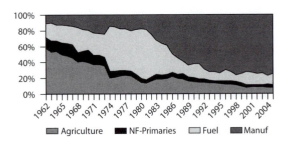

Figure 2

Shares in Southern exports to North. Source: World Bank, World Integrated Trade System (WITS).

percent in 1962, manufactures now account for about 75 percent of exports to the North.

North-South Trade Models The mainstream neoclassical model of international trade—the Heckscher-Ohlin model—does not adequately explain the long-run differences in income and/or growth that are of interest in the North-South literature. It assumes identical technologies and, in the absence of complete specialization, it predicts equal factor prices in the North and South. Although assuming economywide Hicks-neutral technical differences could explain differences in average income within the Heckscher-Ohlin framework, this begs the question of why they exist. (Hicks-neutral technical differences between countries arise when the productivities of every factor production differs by the same proportion between them.) Similarly, a simple Ricardian model, in which the only difference between countries lies in the different efficiencies of labor—the only factor—in the various sectors, is thrown back on such a deus ex machina to explain North-South differences.

In order to explain unequal and possibly diverging incomes between North and South, researchers have had to delve into more fundamental characteristics. Marxian economists adopt the theory of "unequal exchange," whereas mainstream economists using, say, a Ricardian approach, take comparative advantage as given and locate North-South differences in, for example, the elasticities of demand for their products, their market structures, or their labor markets. The first two, frequently associated with Raúl Prebisch and Hans Singer, can explain the declining terms of trade of Southern countries and their inability to grow out of poverty. An early model of the labor-market style (Findlay 1980) had a "manufacturing" North with full employment and an "agricultural" South with fixed wages and surplus labor (as in Arthur Lewis's model of development). Growth arose spontaneously in the former and was transmitted to the latter via the demand for imports. With a fixed real wage and given technology, the critical variable in equilibrating the world economy was the terms of trade which, given unitary income elasticities of demand for both products, adjusted to produce equal growth in the North and South even though the North had a higher income level. Increased Southern productivity depressed the terms of trade rather than boosted growth. Subsequent theoretical developments that allowed capital to move internationally or equalized profit rates in some other way produced divergence (unequal growth) even with unitary demand elasticities.

Nicholas Kaldor located the asymmetry in economies of scale of manufacturing, so that a country that had more manufacturing initially would achieve higher growth rates and be "Northern." Among several formalizations of this idea, Krugman's (1981) is the most elegant. Economies of scale in industry raise profits and accumulation in the North and eventually erode the South's industrial sector. The process stops only when one or both of the regions becomes completely specialized in production. It is likely that the South benefits from the earlier stages of this process and possible that it does so relative to autarky (i.e., no trade at all) even at the final point. And if capital is mobile between North and South as well as goods, such gains are probably more likely.

Kaldor thought of economies of scale in rather physical terms and hence as internal to the firm, but they are probably better thought of as external, residing, for example, in the thickness of labor or intermediate markets, backward or forward linkages, or spillovers of knowledge. This highlights the similarity of these models with those of economic geography. Knowledge spillovers could in fact operate throughout the economy, being related to, say, average levels of human capital, but provided that goods have different human capital intensities, trade and specialization would give the model the same feel as above. In such models human capital (skilled workers) may well have incentives to migrate from South to North.

Related to knowledge is innovation—the ability to develop new products or varieties. If this skill differs between North and South this too can generate unevenness. Again Krugman (1979) offers an elegant model. Only the North can innovate but eventually the ability to produce any good becomes

worldwide as in Vernon's product cycle theory. Providing that it keeps innovating the North will employ at least some of its factors on "new" products and thus will export "new" goods in return for "old." It will earn higher incomes than the South via its quasi-monopoly in these products even though it has only equal productivity with the South in established (old) products. This implies that a reduction in the rate of innovation or an increase in the speed of imitation in the South could actually reduce real wages in the North. This introduces potential North-South conflict, a feature that some consider a necessary component of North-South trade models, although in the basic version of Krugman's model Northern innovation is always good for the South absolutely. If, however, capital were mobile, Southern workers could lose from increased innovation as capital flowed from South to North.

The simple innovation model has spawned many offspring. It has been located in richer models of production by combining it with factor abundance–driven trade. Krugman's horizontal product differentiation (each new product is of the same quality as each old one) has been replaced by vertical differentiation whereby innovation creates better varieties. Innovation and imitation have been made costly and endogenized. And policies have been introduced: Northern trade restrictions typically slow down innovations at everyone's expense, except (possibly) Northern workers', and restrictions on Southern imitation (fierce intellectual property rights regimes) hurt the South and, quite possibly, the North as well.

The North-South trade literature has been mostly theoretical; it has been tested only informally against alleged stylized facts. In particular, there is no convincing empirical evidence that North-South trade has held the South back—not least because it is so difficult to formulate a plausible counterfactual without such trade. There is, however, a vigorous debate about whether trade in general enhances Southern growth, income, or development. Early positive results from cross-country exercises were largely demolished by Rodriguez and Rodrik (2001). Even these authors admit, however, that there is no general presumption that openness harms average incomes, and more careful research is starting to rehabilitate the positive view. Case studies also suggest that openness is commonly a key input to development.

A second component of empirical testing has plotted the effects of Northern research and development efforts on Southern productivity. It has suggested strong links via goods trade (perhaps via embodied technical progress), the importance of foreign direct investment, the need for local skills to ease adaptation, and the fact that knowledge apparently does not easily cross large skills gaps (e.g., Chad learns relatively little from the United States).

North-South Trade and Wages The second major stream of North-South trade research is shorter-run and empirical. It considers the effects of increasing global integration on North income inequalities over the last few decades. It stems from Wood (1994), which postulates a world of fairly free capital mobility and sector-neutral technology differences, and makes the critical difference between Northern and Southern countries their relative endowments of skilled and unskilled labor. Declining barriers to the South's exports of unskilled labor-intensive goods, particularly manufactures, were, he argued, a major explanatory factor in the widening differential between skilled and unskilled wages in the North. He showed that the unskilled labor embodied in a dollar's worth of Southern exports far exceeded that in a dollar's worth of Northern exports: the North was essentially importing labor. This drove down its price because countries produced different combinations of the many goods that existed, so that there was effectively specialization, and the factor price equalization theorem failed to apply.

No one denied the increasing skills wage gap and the weakness of unskilled wages and employment, but there were several challenges to Wood's explanation. Some argued that non-resource-based imports from developing countries were too small—perhaps 3–4 percent of Northern countries' GDP—to have such profound effects, especially given that the increase in labor supply embodied in net imports (i.e., imports less exports) was small. Others argued that in order to influence wages in the North,

Southern exports would also have to drive down the relative prices of unskilled-labor-intensive goods in the North, and this had not happened. In fact, however, this turned out to be only because technical progress was driving down the prices of electronic equipment, especially for information technology–related uses. Among "traditional" goods, the relative price decline was evident.

The principal counter was that technical progress had a strong skill bias. Two pieces of evidence suggested this: first, the ratio of unskilled to skilled workers fell in virtually every sector and every Northern country. Under a pure factor abundance theory it should have risen as unskilled labor became cheaper (the declining aggregate demand for unskilled labor arising from the switch in the production bundle away from unskilled-intensive goods). Second, the skills wage gap widened in the South as well as in the North, whereas the factor abundance approach predicted a narrowing.

In fact, however, each piece of evidence admits other explanations and so does not overturn Wood's conclusions. The definitions of sectors in empirical work are very broad and almost always include tasks with widely different skilled/unskilled labor ratios. Thus offshoring the unskilled-intensive activities within a sector would be consistent with both competition from Southern imports and falling relative unskilled labor use in the North. Several explanations have been advanced for the growing skills wage gap in the South. The most interesting, by Feenstra and Hanson (1997), starts by arraying activities or sectors by increasing unskilled labor intensity: the South does the low-ranked ones and the North the higher-ranked ones. If Southern costs fell, the North would outsource its least skill-intensive activity to the South, where it would become the most skilled activity. In *both* countries, the relative demand for skills would increase. The cost decline could be autonomous or, as in Feenstra and Hanson, driven by flows of capital from North to South, which in turn may be responding to declining trade barriers.

There is, finally, the question of what causes technical progress: even if it is skills biased, it may be induced by the need to withstand competition from cheaper labor in the South. This is certainly possible, but observe that except for very large changes over the longer run, the effect of technical progress on factor demands depends more on its sectoral composition than on which factor it tends to replace. If technical progress makes an unskilled-labor-intensive sector cheaper it will boost demand for it and hence for the bundle of factors it employs—that is, for an unskilled-intensive bundle. If North-South trade induces technical progress, the effects seem likely to be stronger in unskilled, not skilled, labor-intensive sectors.

In 2006, most economists accept that both autonomous skill-biased technical progress and North-South trade play significant roles in skills gap. Most accept that the latter effect is likely to get stronger in the future as trade and communications costs fall, allowing production processes to be even further divided. It is possible, however, that by making components cheaper, North-South trade sufficiently increases demand for products that require unskilled labor in the North (e.g., delivery services) that demand for Northern unskilled workers increases overall.

This literature does not deal directly with the effects of North-South trade on Southern development but is predicated on the South's strong expansion of production, as we have seen in Asia since 1960. Its consistency with rising skills wage gaps in the South is realistic and highlights one of the major challenges of future development—how to meet the (modest) income aspirations of the South's large less-skilled labor force.

See also North American Free Trade Agreement (NAFTA); primary products trade; terms of trade; trade and wages

FURTHER READING

Evans, D. 1989. "Alternative Perspectives on Trade and Development." In *Handbook of Development Economics*, vol. 2, edited by H. Chenery and T. N. Srinivasan. Amsterdam: North Holland, 1241–1304. Explores the relationship between North-South models and unequal exchange.

Feenstra, R., and G. Hanson. 1997. "Foreign Direct Investment and Relative Wages: Evidence from Mexico's Maquiladoras." *Journal of International Economics* 42 (3/4): 371–94. Introduces the model in which industries locating from North to South are the least skill intensive in the former and become the most skill intensive in the latter. The result is that the average skill intensity of industry rises in both places!

Findlay, R. 1980. "The Terms of Trade and Equilibrium Growth in the World Economy." *American Economic Review* 70: 291–99. Simple model where the terms of trade bear all the strain of adjustment as the South grows.

———. 1984. "Growth and Development in Trade Models." In *Handbook of International Economics*, vol. 1, *International Trade*, edited by R. W. Jones and P. E. Kenen, Amsterdam: North-Holland, 185–236. A useful survey of the early North-South modeling literature.

Haskel, J. E. 2000. "Trade and Labor Approaches to Wage Inequality." *Review of International Economics* 8 (3): 397–408. Debate on skills bias versus trade in explaining Northern income inequality.

Krugman, P. 1979. "A Model of Innovation, Technology Transfer, and the World Distribution of Income." *The Journal of Political Economy* 87 (2): 253–66. Higher Northern incomes arise from innovation, which is eventually imitated in the South.

———. 1981. "Trade, Accumulation, and Uneven Development." *Journal of Development Economics* 8 (2): 149–61. A two-country model with economies of scale and accumulation. An initial advantage in capital endowment confers permanent advantages on the North.

Rodriguez, F., and D. Rodrik. 2001. "Trade Policy and Economic Growth: A Skeptic's Guide to the Cross-national Evidence." *NBER Macroeconomics Annual 2000*. Cambridge, MA: MIT Press, 261–324. A strong critique of openness-growth regressions.

Wood, A. 1994. *North-South Trade, Employment, and Inequality: Changing Fortunes in a Skill-Driven World.* New York: Oxford University Press. A detailed account of how international trade can reduce unskilled wages in the North.

World Bank. World Integrated Trade System (WITS). Available at http://wits.worldbank.org/witsnet/StartUp/Wits_Information.aspx"

L. ALAN WINTERS

■ offshore financial centers

Offshore financial centers (OFCs), despite their name, are not necessarily islands—although many island jurisdictions have established OFCs—nor do they have a single universal definition. One definition of an OFC is a jurisdiction whose financial sector accounts for a significant—and disproportionate—share of its domestic economy. Another definition is a jurisdiction where a majority of financial transactions conducted by its institutions are done on behalf of clients who reside in other jurisdictions.

Some of the largest offshore centers in terms of business volume are Bermuda, the Bahamas, the Cayman Islands, Jersey, Guernsey, and the Isle of Man. International financial centers with characteristics similar to OFCs include Luxembourg, Ireland, Switzerland, Singapore, and Hong Kong.

Historically, OFC jurisdictions were associated with one or more of the following: low or zero taxation, moderate financial regulation and supervision, and secrecy or anonymity in financial dealings. Increasingly, the successful OFCs are associated with niche markets in which they have developed extensive professional expertise (for example, in reinsurance, trust business, and private banking) and have reputations for maintaining good supervisory and regulatory systems. Tax advantages continue to be a key driving force for the domicile of financial transactions in OFCs. Some jurisdictions consider the term *offshore financial center* pejorative because of its historical association with lax regulatory and anti-money-laundering regimes. A number of international financial centers have many of the characteristics of offshore centers concerning tax advantages, development of instruments to attract international financial business, and cross-border financial transactions that are significantly out of proportion with the size of their domestic economy.

Growth and Activities of OFCs The growth of OFCs can be traced to the restrictive regulatory regimes in many advanced countries in the 1960s and 1970s. These regimes restricted the flow of capital to and from other countries (excluding trade financing) or imposed restrictions on the interest rates banks could offer, or raised banks' funding costs in domestic markets (for example, through the imposition of high non-interest-bearing reserve requirements). These restrictions, which in many cases were intended to provide governments with more control over monetary policy or to protect the balance of payments, encouraged a shift of deposits and borrowing to less-regulated institutions, including banks in OFCs not subject to such restrictions. As large multinationals and financial institutions shifted financial activity "offshore," the "euromarket" was established. These activities began in the financial centers of Europe (mostly London) and soon spread to other offshore centers.

As with international financial centers, business conducted in OFCs covers a wide range of financial sectors such as banking, insurance, securities, and some nonfinancial activities such as shipping registries and company and trust service providers. Most OFCs specialize in specific types of financial services, however. Multinational corporations and high-net-worth persons are some of the most frequent users of OFCs.

Banking is the most prevalent business, and a significant volume of international banking transactions are conducted in OFCs. Most banks located in OFCs are branches or subsidiaries of international banks. Their main activity is collecting deposits from various markets and channeling them back to their parent institutions. Private banking is a major service offered to high-net-worth persons. Specialized services for such clients range from asset management to estate planning, foreign exchange trading, and pension arrangements.

Collective investment schemes (mutual funds and hedge funds) are also domiciled in OFCs, mainly for tax purposes. Related fund activities such as fund distribution, asset management, fund administration, custodian services, and back-office work are also conducted in these centers. Although a large number of hedge funds are domiciled and administered in OFCs, the management of the investment portfolios is normally conducted in the major financial centers such as London and New York.

Insurance business, including life, property, reinsurance (an insurance company that assumes all or part of a risk undertaken by another insurance company), and captive (a company owned by a noninsurance firm that provides insurance coverage to the owner), is also conducted in some OFCs. Innovative regulatory and legal environments have helped OFCs attract a large share of the world's captive and reinsurance market. For example, most of the new capital entering the reinsurance industry on the year following the catastrophic hurricane season of 2005 was placed in existing or start-up companies in OFCs. A large portion of the world's captive insurance companies is also domiciled in these centers.

A significant number of special purpose vehicles (SPVs)—that is, financial instruments that are tailored to meet the particular financing needs of financial and nonfinancial corporations—are registered in OFCs. Financial firms use SPVs for securitization, and nonfinancial corporations use them to lower the cost of raising capital. OFCs are attractive places to register SPVs because of the tax advantages they offer.

Asset protection, including the establishment of trusts, is another service offered by OFCs. Reasons for managing assets in OFCs include protection from weak domestic banks or currencies, additional legal protection from lawsuits in the home jurisdictions, and tax efficiency/avoidance.

Concerns about OFCs Some of the characteristics of OFCs raise concerns about potential risks to the international financial system. First, since the livelihood of OFCs depends on their ability to attract global financial business, competition among jurisdictions is strong. Such competition is beneficial when it contributes to innovation in financial instruments and products and lowers costs of financial services worldwide. It can also raise concerns, however, if the lower cost of financial services is achieved by lowering regulatory and supervision standards. Second, as OFCs provide financial services predominantly to nonresidents, the authorities in the transaction home countries are interested in the impact on their national economies of the operations in OFCs, especially when these operations are beyond the home country authorities' control. Third, anonymity and lack of transparency in OFCs, opaqueness of the operations of offshore corporations, and legal protections in some OFCs have created concerns. Historically, a lack of reliable data on activities in OFCs hampered analyses of the potential risk that OFCs pose to financial stability. SPVs domiciled in OFCs have been implicated in some of the large corporate frauds. Fourth, the anonymity of financial transactions makes OFCs attractive to money launderers. OFCs are a potential gateway for the proceeds of crime to gain access to and to be laundered through global financial markets. Money laundering is an international problem, and to be effective, international standards against money laundering and terrorist financing need to be applied worldwide, especially in large financial centers.

Concerns about the potential risk posed by OFCs resulted in OFCs being placed on "name and shame" lists by a number of international bodies in 2000, including the Financial Stability Forum (FSF), the

Financial Action Task Force on Money Laundering (FATF), and the Organisation for Economic Co-operation and Development (OECD). This posed significant reputation damage to OFCs. Also in 2000, the International Monetary Fund (IMF) was asked to intensify its oversight of OFCs in the context of its mandate to promote financial stability. The IMF's program has focused on (1) regular monitoring, (2) assessing OFCs' compliance with international supervisory and anti-money-laundering standards, (3) enhancing the transparency of activities in OFCs, and (4) strengthening international cooperation and information on supervisory and regulatory systems.

Because of the intensified international attention, many OFCs upgraded their supervisory and regulatory systems and improved the transparency in their operations. A number of smaller OFCs also decided to exit from part or all of their OFC activity after weighing the costs and benefits. Although a financial center can be a useful addition to an economy, a significant and costly investment in the supervisory and regulatory infrastructure is needed to provide the internationally accepted minimum supervisory system required to avoid reputation risk. At the same time, a number of new and aspiring OFCs are being established where the authorities have been willing and able to invest heavily in the necessary infrastructure.

See also capital mobility; hedge funds; international financial centers; International Monetary Fund (IMF); money laundering; trade in services

FURTHER READINGS

Darbar, Salim, et al. 2003. "Assessing Offshore Financial Centers—Filling a Gap in Global Surveillance." *Finance and Development* 40 (3) (September). Available at www.imf.org/external/pubs/ft/fandd/2003/09/pdf/darbar .pdf.

International Monetary Fund. http://www.imf.org/external/ np/mae/oshore/2000/eng/back.htm. IMF OFC Web site that reviews the issues raised by OFCs and the IMF's program to assess OFCs against international regulatory standards.

R. BARRY JOHNSTON

■ oil

See Organization of the Petroleum Exporting Countries (OPEC); petroleum

■ oligopoly

Oligopoly is a situation in which several firms compete over a given market, but there are so few firms that each one can earn a profit over and above what is earned in the more competitive industries. Barriers to entry in the form of information costs, economies of scale, franchises, and patents appear to be sufficient to keep out enough new competitors. Thus it is convenient here to think of oligopoly as imperfect competition without free entry, and monopolistic competition as imperfect competition with free entry.

Not surprisingly, international trade economists concerned with oligopoly have focused on the role of oligopoly profits. With monopolistic competition or perfect competition, there are no profits measured as the return over all opportunity costs. The existence of economic profits raises three large questions: How do those profits affect the pattern and volume of international trade? How do those profits affect who gains and who loses from international trade? And do those profits present policymakers with trade policy opportunities?

There are two approaches to studying oligopoly and trade: partial equilibrium and general equilibrium. The partial equilibrium approach concentrates on the world industry with no attempt to explain the division between exporters and import-competing firms or how oligopoly profits affect demand. This approach is most useful in studying questions involving trade policy. The general equilibrium approach seeks to examine how oligopoly profits affect the traditional trade questions of determining what is traded and the volume of trade, and identifying the winners and losers.

The Partial Equilibrium Approach In the first stage of development, the partial equilibrium approach dominated the literature with representative contributions by Dixit (1984), Brander and Spencer (1985), Eaton and Grossman (1986), and Brander and Krugman (1983). Global firms can sell in an integrated world market, segmented markets in each country (Dixit 1984; Brander and Krugman 1983), or in some outside country (Brander and Spencer 1985; Eaton and Grossman 1986). The market is integrated if arbitrage keeps prices at home tied to foreign prices. The market is segmented if there is no arbitrage to keep prices in different markets in line. With tariffs and quotas, imperfect markets are best considered segmented.

Probably the most interesting and yet most controversial contribution is the one by Brander and Spencer (1985), which shows that subsidizing the exports from a domestic firm can be beneficial to the economy by a strategic trade policy that transfers oligopoly profits from a foreign firm to the home firm in the same industry. This result was made intuitively clear by Eaton and Grossman (1986), who showed that by a different assumption regarding the behavior of firms it was optimal to tax rather than subsidize the export of the oligopoly. Why the difference? The explanation is extremely simple: if we assume the oligopolist is too conservative toward rivals, the government should subsidize its exports; if the oligopolist is too aggressive, the government should tax its exports. If the economist cannot distinguish between these two cases in practice, then our information does not allow a recommendation. The difference arises in the model as the difference between Cournot and Bertrand competition. Cournot is competition in quantities; Bertrand is competition in prices. Assume a firm in country A and one in country B compete in a third market with goods that are imperfect substitutes. In the case of Cournot competition, the firm assumes that the other firm will maintain its output; in truth, if it expands output, the other will contract its output. Had the firm known this, it would have expanded its output even more. In the case of Bertrand competition, the firm assumes the other firm will maintain its price; in truth, if it lowers the price, the other firm will lower its price. Had the firm known that, it would have lowered its price by a smaller amount. Thus the existence of oligopoly profits does not seem to have raised the likelihood of a beneficial trade policy over and above

traditional optimum tariff arguments. Even if strategic trade policies can be identified, they run into the same familiar problems: (1) governments correctly calculating optimizing tariffs or subsidies, (2) foreign retaliation can eliminate the benefits, (3) costly economic rent seeking by industries alerted to the policies, and (4) raising the cost of classifying goods for customs enforcement.

Brander (1981) and Brander and Krugman (1983) examine the role of price discrimination in international trade. In this case, it is assumed that there is an international oligopoly in which each country is a segmented market. Oligopolistic firms can raise profits by cutting prices in the market with a higher elasticity of demand. This implies that the standard theory of price discrimination can be applied, because now firms, regardless of their location, will sell in all markets at the prices prevailing in each segmented market. There now may be cross-hauling, or wasted transportation costs as even identical goods move in both directions (Brander and Krugman 1983). A felicitous mental picture would be two logging trucks going in opposite directions and carrying identical logs.

General Equilibrium and Oligopoly In the general equilibrium approach, it is important to explain the pattern of exports and imports as well as the costs and benefits of trade. The first problem to overcome is how to embed oligopoly in a general equilibrium model that was designed with perfect competition in mind. Some theorists have stressed the difficulties entailed by considering large firms, such as the possibilities of monopsony (or buyer power) in factor markets or considerations about what the large firm should maximize. Following the seminal paper by Lerner (1934) for the case of monopoly, Markusen (1981), Neary (2003), and Ruffin (2003a, 2003b) assume that it is more convenient to consider firms to be large in their industry but small in the economy. In this case, the firm can treat all factor prices and prices in other industries as fixed. Ruffin (2003a) shows that the firm's profit functions are then independent of the numéraire selected, so the problem of what the firm maximizes is avoided. In this case, clear and simple results can be reached.

Both Neary (2003) and Ruffin (2003a, 2003b) also employ the assumption that firms act as Cournot oligopolists; that is, they assume the outputs of their rivals are constant. Neary (2003) takes the assumption literally that firms are small in the economy by considering a continuum of firms, whereas Markusen (1981) and Ruffin (2003a, 2003b) simply consider a finite number of firms acting as if they are small in the economy.

The general equilibrium approach is most easily exhibited in a model in which Cournot oligopolies are selling in an integrated world market. Again, it is oligopoly profits that provide the key. How does oligopoly affect the costs and benefits of international trade? Consider two countries, Home and Foreign, that are the same size, with each having a comparative advantage in a good facing the same demand and costs. Since trade economists already know the impact of different factor intensities across industries, a Ricardian model (Neary 2003; Ruffin 2003a) with only one factor of production is often used. We shall call that factor "labor" but it could be a bundle of resources used in the same proportions in all industries. In this case, if we assume constant returns to scale, the production-possibility frontier for the economy is linear. With these assumptions we can assume that both countries have the same wages under perfect competition. Moreover, if we assume that under oligopoly all industries have the same degree of competition (same number of firms), it will also be true that both countries will have the same wages with or without trade. Thus if we take wages to be fixed per unit labor (as the unit of measure), we can take dollar costs as given for each country. Thus suppose, as in table 1, that it costs Home $4 to produce a bushel of apples and $6 to produce a bunch of bananas, and it costs Foreign $6 to produce apples and $4 to produce bananas. Note that it is best to take wages as the unit of measure rather than one of the commodities, because in imperfect competition firms are choosing commodity prices to maximize profits.

It will be useful to summarize the Cournot oligopoly model when the product is homogeneous. The key assumption is that firms conjecture that rivals will maintain their output, a conjecture that holds in the Cournot-Nash equilibrium. There is a Cournot-Nash equilibrium if no firm can make an additional profit by changing its strategy, given the strategies of all of the other firms. If $D(P)$ is the demand for the homogeneous product, $D'(P)$ the slope of the demand curve, x_i the output of the ith firm, and c_i the marginal cost of the ith firm, then the Cournot equilibrium is:

$$D'(P)(P - c_i) + x_i = 0 \qquad (1)$$

$$\Sigma x_i = D(P) \qquad (2)$$

If there are N firms, this is a system of $N + 1$ equations. The demand functions clearly must reflect all

Table 1

Gains to workers under competition and oligopoly

State	Country	Autarky		Free trade		Gains to workers
		apples	bananas	apples	bananas	
Perfect competition						
	Home	$4	$6	$4	$4	
	Foreign	$6	$4	$4	$4	17%
Tight oligopoly ($N = 2$)						
	Home	$8	$12	$6.67	$6.67	
	Foreign	$12	$8	$6.67	$6.67	31%
Loose oligopoly ($N = 3$)						
	Home	$6	$9	$6	$6	17%
	Foreign	$9	$6	$6	$6	

prices and incomes. Ruffin (2003b) describes the general equilibrium equations, taking account of the incomes of all factors of production and assuming all agents have identical, homothetic utility functions. Equations (1) and (2) replicate rivals holding output constant because when the ith firm adjusts its output, $D'(P)$ is the change in its demand by the resulting change in price. The interpretation of (1) is that if the firm adjusts output by $D'(P)$ by causing price to rise by a dollar, it loses the profit margin on those units but gains x_i on the resulting sales. But this becomes greatly simplified even in the case of nonidentical firms by adding the profit-maximizing equations (1) over the N firms and defining the price elasticity of demand as $\varepsilon = -D'(P)P/D$, resulting in:

$$P = \Sigma c_i/(N - 1/\varepsilon) \qquad (3)$$

For simplicity, suppose that $\varepsilon = 1$, which works for Cournot oligopoly for $2 \leq N$ (Ruffin 1971). Since oligopolists price according to elasticities of demand, this equation can be applied in general equilibrium without worrying about the impact of oligopoly profits on demand as long as we assume world symmetry so that costs can be taken to be independent. In a Ricardian trade model in which both countries have the same income and face the same demand for the good in which they have a comparative advantage, equation (3) works well because we merely have to add the costs of all the firms active in both countries and divide by 1 less than the number of firms in each world industry.

Consider first perfect competition in which prices must equal marginal costs. Table 1 shows both autarky and free trade. Thus in autarky, apples will be $4 and bananas $6 in Home, and the opposite in Foreign. Now if international trade is opened, in a competitive situation only Home would produce apples and only Foreign would produce bananas. Thus people of the world would pay only $4 for both apples and bananas. The gains from trade are simple to measure in this case, since equal amounts of money are spent on apples and bananas: The price of the importable falls by 33 percent, and the gain from trade for the economy as well as workers (the same in

this case) would be roughly one-half of 33 percent, or about 17 percent.

Under oligopoly both workers and oligopolists share in national income. There are two situations: a tight oligopoly in which the oligopoly profits protect high-cost producers from being driven out of business and a loose oligopoly in which oligopoly profits are insufficient for high-cost firms to survive the competition from low-cost rivals. For the moment assume the same degree of oligopoly in both industries, with only 2 or 3 firms in each country producing apples or bananas. With trade, each world industry has the potential of 4 or 6 firms. In the example, a tight oligopoly is when each country has only 2 firms producing apples and bananas, and a loose oligopoly prevails when each country has 3 firms producing both goods. Applying formula 3 to the autarkic state, as illustrated in table 1, we can see that under tight oligopoly Home will sell apples for $8 and bananas for $12. When trade is opened, apples will now be produced by 2 firms with costs of $4 and 2 firms with costs of $6, so according to formula 3 the price of apples (and bananas) will be $6.67 [= {2($4) + 2($6)}/3 = $20/3]. Economic logic tells us that the price must be less than $8, because there are more firms. For Home (and Foreign is symmetrical), the price of apples falls by 1.33/8, or 17 percent, and bananas by 5.33/12, or 44 percent, for a weighted average of 31 percent. Since we can hold worker wages the same (as the numéraire), workers must gain 31 percent from the opening of trade, a substantial improvement over the case of perfect competition. In this case, with equal degrees of competition between the two sectors, the gains from trade to the *economy* will be smaller than in the case of perfect competition because the inefficient banana industry in Home and apple industry in Foreign still operate. Accordingly, since workers gain more than under perfect competition, it follows that trade causes substantial losses to the oligopolists compared with autarky. *Nevertheless, the remaining oligopoly profits of the lower-cost firms serve to protect the higher-cost firms from competition, just as tariffs do.*

If we have looser oligopolies, the situation may be quite different. As shown in table 1 again, suppose that the number of firms in each industry prior to trade is 3. Then in Home, applying equation (3) once again shows that under autarky apples will sell for $6 and bananas for $9, with the opposite in Foreign. When trade opens, the Foreign apple industry and the Home banana industry will be unable to compete with their low-cost counterparts. Indeed, under Cournot, they will assume that any output will lower price below $6, so that the equilibrium price of each good will be $6. Notice that in this case we get a result similar to perfect competition: trade causes the shutdown of inefficient industries, and both oligopolists and workers gain precisely the same amount as under perfect competition.

The looser oligopoly drives higher-cost firms in the other country out of business simply because price is closer to their marginal costs. This is also a measure of the robustness of a country's comparative advantage. The more robust the comparative advantage, in the sense of the greater the difference in costs between the Home and Foreign countries, more oligopoly power is compatible with driving foreign rivals out of business. Had we assumed $4 costs for apples in Home and $8 costs for apples in Foreign, only two Home firms would have been sufficient to drive the high-cost firms out of business.

In the tight oligopoly case examined in table 1, both high-cost and low-cost firms share the market. With perfect competition or a loose oligopoly, the high-cost firms are driven out of business. In general, this means that oligopoly power can reduce the degree of specialization and so reduce the volume of international trade. This helps to explain one of the most interesting observations about world trade in the last 50 years, namely that it has increased at about twice the rate of world output. People have usually attributed this to reductions in communication costs, transportation costs, and trade barriers. But the deregulation of industry and the rise of domestic competition may be another cause.

The Gains from Trade We assumed in table 1 that there are equal degrees of oligopoly in both sectors of the economy. This implies that the gains from trade in the economy cannot exceed what would prevail under perfect competition, although workers can clearly gain more because of the procompetitive effects of trade on both export and import prices. But some authors have argued that with oligopoly the trade gains to the economy are greater than under perfect competition! As discussed in Ruffin (2003a, 2003b), this may arise when there are different degrees of competition between sectors. Markusen (1981) considers a two-sector model with perfect competition in one sector and monopoly in the other, and assumes that when international trade opens there is a two-firm Cournot oligopoly of Home and Foreign monopolists. He shows that even in the absence of actual trade, the potential for trade can improve welfare due to the procompetitive effects of the resulting two-firm world oligopoly. Markusen proves the result by making the strong assumption that under perfect competition there are no comparative advantages and, hence, no gains from trade. The existence of monopoly or oligopoly in part of the economy then improves the gains from trade because opening markets reduces those oligopoly powers. But there is no general rule that under oligopoly or monopoly the gains from trade are greater than under perfect competition, as pointed out by Ruffin (2003a). In fact, Ruffin (2003b) gives an example in which the country exporting the good produced by an oligopoly gains more from trade than under perfect competition, but the country importing that good gains less. The reason has to do with the unfavorable terms of trade effects related to exporting goods produced under competition compared with oligopoly.

Oligopoly also has important implications for the effect of trade on income distribution. Standard Heckscher-Ohlin trade theory predicts that abundant factors of production gain from trade while scarce factors lose from trade. The reason for this is that trade shifts resources from industries intensive in scarce factors to industries intensive in abundant factors. The imbalance of supply and demand requires the prices of abundant factors to rise, and those of scarce factors to fall. Thus a key characteristic of Heckscher-Ohlin theory is that the opening of international trade, or the expansion of trade from lower trade barriers, should cause a factor of production to lose in one country and gain in another country. The existence of oligopoly moderates this effect, and it is possible for oligopoly profits to rise everywhere or fall everywhere. In the case of loose oligopolies, trade can cause profits to soar because low-cost firms drive out high-cost firms and their gain in profits from the world market will offset the loss of profits from the high-cost firms. This can happen everywhere. With tight oligopolies, low-cost firms must compete with high-cost firms and their profits will fall everywhere.

The case of workers is quite different. It is possible to show that, abstracting from Stolper-Samuelson effects arising from different factor intensities, workers must always gain from international trade. This holds under quite general circumstances, regardless of differences in the degree of competition across the economy. The reason is that under all circumstances, prices must fall measured in terms of wage units. Examining equation (3) shows this. Unless the price elasticity of demand falls (an unlikely event in a larger market), an increase in the number of firms (both low- and high-cost) will cause the price of the product to fall for both export goods and import-competing goods. If there is the same number of firms, but the high-cost firms disappear compared with autarky, the prices of imported goods fall while the prices of exported goods remain the same: workers still gain. This, of course, ignores the adjustment costs that workers will suffer moving from high-cost to low-cost industries, as would be the case for perfect competition as well. So oligopoly raises no new issues here except for the possibility of long-term contracts that may be present in concentrated industries that may not be present in more competitive industries. The mobility of workers under oligopoly is an issue that can and should be studied.

The importance of oligopoly in international trade focuses on the role of profits. Trade policy that shifts profit from one country to the other faces informational problems and the possibility of retaliation. Generally speaking, oligopoly makes it more likely that trade will benefit nonprofit factors such as workers. Oligopoly can make trade gains to the economy smaller if oligopoly is widespread, but only if oligopoly is concentrated in the export sectors can trade be more beneficial to the economy.

See also comparative advantage; foreign direct investment under oligopoly; gains from trade; Heckscher-Ohlin model; monopolistic competition; New Trade Theory; Ricardian model

FURTHER READING

Brander, James A. 1981. "Intra-industry Trade in Identical Commodities." *Journal of International Economics* 11 (1): 1–14. Assumes segmented markets in each country so that oligopoly firms in separate countries sell in each market even if the commodity is homogeneous.

Brander, James A., and Paul Krugman. 1983. "A 'Reciprocal Dumping' Model of International Trade." *Journal of International Economics* 15 (3–4): 313–21. Price discrimination applied to international trade.

Brander, James A., and Barbara J. Spencer. 1985. "Export Subsidies and International Market Share Rivalry." *Journal of International Economics* 18 (1–2): 83–100. Shows an export subsidy to a home firm that competes with a foreign firm in a third market is optimal for the case of Cournot competition.

Dixit, Avinash K. 1984. "International Trade Policy for Oligopolistic Industries." *Economic Journal* 94 (1): 1–16. A survey of partial equilibrium models.

Eaton, Jonathan, and Gene M. Grossman. 1986. "Optimal Trade and Industrial Policy under Oligopoly." *Quarterly Journal of Economics* 101 (2): 383–406. Shows an export duty on a home firm that competes with a foreign firm in a third market is optimal for the case of Bertrand competition.

Krugman, Paul R. 1979. "Increasing Returns, Monopolistic Competition, and International Trade." *Journal of International Economics* 9 (4): 469–79. A simplification of the Dixit-Stiglitz model.

Lerner, Abba. 1934. "The Concept of Monopoly and the Measurement of Monopoly Power." *Review of Economic Studies* 1 (3): 157–75. Explains the economic inefficiency of monopoly in a general equilibrium context.

Markusen, James R. 1981. "Trade and Gains from Trade with Imperfect Competition." *Journal of International Economics* 11 (4): 531–51. The existence of monopoly can increase the gains from trade under some circumstances.

McGahan, Anita M., and Michael E. Porter. 1999. "The Persistence of Shocks to Profitability." *Review of Economics and Statistics* 81 (1): 143–53. Shows that industry characteristics determine the persistence of oligopoly profits.

Neary, J. P. 2003. "The Road Less Traveled: Oligopoly and Competition Policy in General Equilibrium." In *Economics for an Imperfect World: Essays in Honour of Joseph Stiglitz*, edited by R. Arnott, B. Greenwald, R. Kanpur, and B. Nalebuff. Cambridge, MA: MIT Press, 485–500. Surveys various approaches to oligopoly in general equilibrium and introduces an approach based on Cournot oligopoly with a continuum of firms.

Ruffin, Roy J. 1971. "Cournot Oligopoly and Competitive Behavior." *Review of Economic Studies* 38 (4): 493–502. Clarifies the relationship between oligopoly, perfect competition, and the number of firms.

———. 2003a. "Oligopoly and Trade: What, How, and For Whom?" *Journal of International Economics* 60 (2): 315–35. Shows trade gains under oligopoly can be larger or smaller than under perfect competition in a Ricardo-Cournot setting.

———. 2003b. "International Trade under Oligopoly Conditions." *Review of International Economics* 11 (4): 577–87. Gives some simple examples of oligopoly and trade as well as describing the general equations of an oligopolistic world economy.

ROY J. RUFFIN

■ optimum currency area (OCA) theory

Optimum currency area (OCA) theory originates from two seminal articles in the early 1960s by the economists Mundell (1961) and McKinnon (1963). These articles drew on contemporary debates about fixed versus flexible exchange rates, treating a common currency as the extreme case of a fixed exchange rate. At the time, under the Bretton Woods system of fixed exchange rates, the choice of exchange rate was seen as a theoretical rather than practical issue, and applicability of the OCA analysis to the choice of currency domain was limited by the almost universal one country–one currency rule (Pomfret 2005). The shift to generalized floating of the major currencies, however, and the move to European Monetary Union (EMU), which began in the early 1970s, generated practical interest in currency areas that has continued to grow.

Despite the huge subsequent literature and increased practical applicability, the theory of currency areas has remained centered on the Mundell-McKinnon approach of identifying the area within which the macroeconomic flexibility gains from having an independent currency are significant. This article focuses on OCA theory and the empirical evidence, while the complementary article on common currency analyzes actual experience with shared currencies.

Variants of OCA Theory In OCA theory the key issue is the extent to which macroeconomic policy can be effective in an open economy. An external shock, such as a recession induced by a drop in export demand, can be countered by cutting interest rates to stimulate investment. An economy with capital mobility and a fixed exchange rate does not have monetary policy independence, however, because the cut in interest rates will lead to capital outflows and an unsustainable balance of payments deficit. Mundell (1961) identified the point at which currency independence becomes worthwhile as the point at which factors cease to be mobile. The boundary of the OCA is set by breaks in factor mobility, that is, points at which the movement of labor or capital becomes more difficult.

The openness of an economy also can determine the effectiveness of exchange rate changes as a macroeconomic policy instrument. In very open economies, currency devaluation is ineffective because prices and wages immediately increase to remove any competitive advantage. Openness undermines the money illusion (or failure to distinguish nominal from real price changes) that permits the exchange rate to be an effective policy instrument. Larger economies have lower ratios of trade to gross domestic product (GDP), and currency devaluation can have a positive impact on output. Thus very open economies are suboptimal currency areas, but for a larger and less open economy the effectiveness of the exchange rate as a policy tool increases;

at some point the currency area becomes optimal (McKinnon 1963).

In the decades following the original contributions of Mundell and McKinnon, subsequent writers lengthened the list of criteria that might be relevant to an assessment of the optimality of a currency area. Recent contributions have argued that the trade-off may be mediated by history and by geography (Alesina and Barro 2002). With multiple criteria a unique ranking of suitability for currency union is unlikely to exist and the theory becomes difficult to test, but the essential structure of OCA theory has remained remarkably robust since 1961.

OCA theory characterizes the choice of currency area as a cost-benefit analysis trading off microeconomic efficiency against macroeconomic flexibility (Krugman 1993). Microeconomic efficiency would be maximized with a global currency. Thus, subglobal OCAs imply the existence of distortions, such as nonclearing labor markets that lead to involuntary unemployment, whose negative effects can be reduced by macroeconomic policy. Another benefit of a larger currency area is that disturbances are likely to be offsetting, so that exchange rate changes are smaller, with less feedback on domestic prices. The greater price stability is usually ascribed to random shocks being offsetting, but other mechanisms include reduction in the impact of outliers in the consumer price index, or CPI (i.e., goods with a particularly large weight in a region's consumption bundle), and reduction in the ratio of trade (or rather transactions denominated in potentially volatile foreign currencies) to GDP.

The cost-benefit perspective suggests an equal role for microeconomic and macroeconomic analysis, but the currency area literature has been dominated by macroeconomists, in part because the micro benefits of reduced transactions costs from a common currency are simple to visualize but difficult to measure. Although the benefit from a common currency (or fixed exchange rate) in terms of lower transactions costs has long been accepted as the overwhelming argument for mini states (such as Luxembourg or Brunei) not to have independent currencies, the argument becomes less potent as the

currency area becomes large enough to have well-functioning foreign exchange (including forward) markets. Thus the increasing efficiency of financial markets becomes an argument for OCAs becoming smaller because it reduces the benefits via reduced transactions costs of a common currency. This may explain why it is feasible to have a small currency domain, as in countries such as Iceland or New Zealand, without incurring huge costs, but whether the trade-off between macropolicy flexibility and transactions costs is optimal for these small states is another question, and one which is impossible to answer without a good understanding of the nature and size of the transactions costs associated with independent currencies. Before the beginning of the 21st century little research had been done on the transactions cost benefits of a common currency, but this has changed since the controversial article by the economist Andrew Rose was published in 2000.

Testing OCA Theory The OCA literature has dominated the theoretical explanation of currency areas for almost a half century. There have, however, been few systematic tests of OCA theory and little positive support for OCA theory as a useful way of explaining the composition of existing currency areas or of predicting changes in currency domains. One empirical challenge was the rarity of changes in currency areas during the 1970s and 1980s. In the early 1990s it was argued that the stability of actual currency arrangements may be explained by switching costs (Dowd and Greenaway 1993), but the many changes in currency arrangements in Eastern Europe in the 1990s and the introduction of the euro in Western Europe suggest that the mechanics of changing currency arrangements are neither difficult nor especially costly.

With multiple OCA criteria, the theory becomes difficult to test: a small open economy has the biggest potential gain from joining a larger currency area in order to reduce transactions costs, but it may also be most vulnerable to external shocks and hence has the most to lose from giving up the exchange rate as a macropolicy instrument. The economists Kreinin and Heller (1974) synthesized the various criteria into the single question of whether a country could better deal with external imbalance through devaluation or through adjustment of domestic demand. Their conclusion was that Italy, Sweden, and Switzerland were the three Organisation for Economic Co-operation and Development countries most likely to abandon their national currencies. Thirty years later only one of the three had done so, while ten of the "less likely" countries had abandoned their national currencies.

If currency areas become "optimal" ex post, then OCA theory may be untestable. A common currency might promote closer trade links and more synchronized cycles, both of which are OCA criteria; closer trade ties increase the benefit from a common currency, and synchronized cycles reduce the cost of giving up independent currencies. This is not a theoretical result but a hypothesis to be tested empirically because more bilateral trade could promote interindustry specialization and less synchronized cycles. Using various measures of bilateral trade intensity and cycle synchronization for 21 developed economies, Frankel and Rose (1998) find a robust relationship between the two variables, which they interpret as evidence that as a common currency promotes bilateral trade it also increases cycle synchronization. Thus actual currency areas fit OCA criteria better than potential currency unions, and the OCA criteria are endogenous.

The impact of currency union on bilateral trade flows has been the subject of a burgeoning literature initiated by the economist Rose (2000). Using a gravity model, Rose found that currency union has a large effect on bilateral trade, which he interpreted as evidence that a common currency substantially reduces transactions costs. Although it is plausible that a common currency reduces transactions costs and stimulates trade, the magnitude of the common currency effect is hotly debated. In Rose's study the countries in currency unions are not from a random draw; several authors have shown that currency union members are smaller and more open than their natural comparators and that history (usually in the form of colonial background) matters.

The debate has been conducted with analysis of currency area changes over time. Analyzing time-series data for correlations between changing currency union status and bilateral trade flows, Glick and Rose (2002) estimated that dissolution of a currency union halves bilateral trade. Currency union breakup is, however, usually associated with other events that disrupt trade; out of some 60 cases of post-1947 currency union dissolutions in the Glick-Rose data set, more than two-thirds broke up within a decade of the end of a colonial relationship, and the end of the ruble zone, which is not in the data set, would increase the percentage still further. In tranquil currency union changes, notably Ireland's secession from its currency union with the United Kingdom in 1979 and subsequent participation in the process leading to the euro, the impact on bilateral trade is unclear. The weaker the link between currency union and bilateral trade, the less convincing is the claim that OCA criteria become self-fulfilling ex post.

In practice, irrespective of whether the criteria may become endogenous, most of the literature on currency domains treats OCA theory as having predictive capability. Yet, the general track record of OCA theory in explaining the monetary history of the post-1945 international economic order has been miserable. Despite the increasing openness of national economies and increasing capital mobility, both unambiguous pressures for larger currency areas according to OCA theory, the number of currencies has increased substantially and the geographical size of currency domains has shrunk correspondingly. The sole significant exception is the introduction of the euro, but in Europe and the former Soviet Union as a whole there were more currencies in 2002 than a decade earlier. Globally, over the last half century, the exogenous increase in the number of countries drove the number and size of currency areas, and the OCA criteria were irrelevant to explaining this pattern. In sum, although OCA theory has dominated the analysis of currency domains, the empirical support for the theory is weak.

See also Bretton Woods system; capital mobility; common currency; dollar standard; dominant currency; euro; European Monetary Union; exchange rate regimes; impossible trinity; multiple currencies

FURTHER READING

Alesina, Alberto, and Robert J. Barro. 2002. "Currency Unions." *Quarterly Journal of Economics* (May): 409–36. A recent restatement of OCA theory.

De Grauwe, Paul. 2000. *The Economics of Monetary Union.* 4th rev. ed. Oxford: Oxford University Press. The best textbook treatment of monetary union.

Dowd, Kevin, and David Greenaway. 1993. "Currency Competition, Network Externalities, and Switching Costs: Towards an Alternative View of Optimum Currency Areas." *Economic Journal* 103: 1180–89. An influential explanation of the costs of changing currency arrangements, although to some extent countered by the relative lack of technical problems associated with the introduction of new currencies in the former Soviet Union and the introduction of the euro.

Frankel, Jeffrey, and Andrew Rose. 1998. "The Endogeneity of the Optimum Currency Area Criteria." *Economic Journal* 108 (July): 1009–25. An attempt to introduce systematic cross-country evidence into the debate about OCA criteria.

Glick, Reuven, and Andrew Rose. 2002. "Does a Currency Union Affect Trade? The Time-Series Evidence." *European Economic Review* 46 (June): 1125–51. A follow-up to Rose's 2002 paper, which used cross-country data.

Kreinin, Mordechai, and H. Robert Heller. 1974. "Adjustment Costs, Optimal Currency Areas, and International Reserves." In *International Trade and Finance: Essays in Honour of Jan Tinbergen,* edited by Willy Sellekaerts. London: Macmillan, 127–40. A pioneering attempt to introduce empirical evidence into the debate over the OCA criteria, although limited to European countries.

Krugman, Paul. 1993. "What Do We Need to Know about the International Monetary System?" *Essays in International Economics No. 190.* International Economics Section. Princeton, NJ: Princeton University (July). An important reminder not to neglect transactions costs and to remember the microeconomic benefits from a well-functioning international monetary system (and a common currency).

McKinnon, Ronald. 1963. "Optimum Currency Areas." *American Economic Review* 53: 717–25. One of the two articles initiating OCA theory.

Mundell, Robert. 1961. "Theory of Optimum Currency Areas." *American Economic Review* 51: 657–65. The original OCA theory.

Pomfret, Richard. 2005. "Currency Areas in Theory and Practice." *Economic Record* 81 (253): 166–76. A recent review of the evidence on OCA theory.

Rose, Andrew. 2000. "One Money, One Market: The Effect of Common Currencies on Trade." *Economic Policy* 30 (April): 9–45. An innovative and controversial cross-country study of the impact of a common currency on bilateral trade flows, and implicitly on transactions costs.

Tower, Edward, and Thomas Willett. 1976. "The Theory of Optimum Currency Areas and Exchange-Rate Flexibility." *Princeton Special Papers in International Economics, No. 11.* International Finance Section. Princeton, NJ: Princeton University (May). A classic survey of OCA theory.

RICHARD POMFRET

■ Organisation for Economic Co-operation and Development (OECD)

The Organisation for Economic Co-operation and Development (OECD) is an international organization located in Paris. It was founded in 1960 as the successor to the Organisation for European Economic Co-operation (OEEC), which was established in 1947 to administer American and Canadian aid under the Marshall Plan for reconstruction of Europe after World War II. OECD members are governments of nation-states that meet the criteria of pluralistic democracy and free market economies. The founding members were Austria, Belgium, Canada, Denmark, France, Germany (Federal Republic), Greece, Iceland, Ireland, Italy, Luxembourg, Netherlands, Norway, Portugal, Spain, Sweden, Switzerland, Turkey, the United Kingdom, and the United States. Since then 10 more countries have joined: Australia (1971), Czech Republic (1995), Finland (1969), Hungary (1996), Japan (1964), Korea (1996), Mexico (1994), New Zealand (1973), Poland (1996), and Slovak Republic (2000). The OECD aims to enlarge its membership and to find the means to integrate nonmember governments into its organization. The secretary-general Angel Gurria said he envisioned the OECD as the "secretariat of the process of globalization."

The basic document of OECD is the Convention of December 1960. It states that the organization shall promote policies (1) to achieve the highest sustainable economic growth and employment and a rising standard of living while maintaining financial stability, (2) to contribute to sound economic expansion, and (3) to expand world trade on a multilateral, nondiscriminatory basis.

Members are obliged to promote the efficient use of their economic, scientific, and technological resources; to pursue policies designed to achieve economic growth without thereby endangering the economies of other countries; to pursue efforts to reduce or abolish obstacles to the international movement of goods, services, payments, and capital; and to contribute to the economic development of member and nonmember countries by appropriate means. In addition, members must furnish the OECD with the information necessary for its tasks, consult together on a continuing basis, cooperate closely, and take coordinated action where appropriate.

The OECD may make decisions that are binding on all members. In addition, it may make recommendations to members and enter into agreements with member and nonmember states. Binding decisions and recommendations have to be made by mutual agreement. Abstention from voting does not invalidate the decision or recommendation, which is applicable to the other members but not to the abstaining member. This consensus method is the standard decision procedure of international organizations.

The OECD is entitled to diplomatic privileges and immunities, as are officials and member country representatives. The OECD is exempt from paying taxes related to its operating revenues and expenses.

Organization, Output, and Analytical Perspectives The supreme body of OECD is the Council, which is composed of all members and one representative of the European Union (EU) commission. It is a permanent intergovernmental conference that meets in sessions of ministers or permanent representatives. Representatives of the members meet in committees to discuss and review policies in various fields. There are about 200 committees, working groups, and experts groups. Each year some 40,000 senior officials from national administrations attend OECD committee meetings, where they request or review work of the secretariat or respond to requests by the secretariat. The OECD budget is financed by the member states. Their contributions are proportional to the size of their economies, with a floor of 0.1 percent and a cap of about 25 percent of total contributions. In 2006, the contributions of the United States, Japan, and Germany made up respectively 25, 17.5, and 9.4 percent of total contributions, while Iceland, Luxembourg, and the Slovak Republic each paid less than 0.25 percent of all contributions. Contributions make up about 80 percent of all operating revenues, which amounted to about U.S. $500 million per annum in 2005.

The secretary-general heads the secretariat. The Council elects him or her for a term of five years. He must neither seek nor receive instructions from any national government. The OECD has had five secretary-generals since its establishment: Thorkil Kristensen of Denmark (1961–69), Emil van Lennep of the Netherlands (1969–84), Jean-Claude Paye from France (1984–96), Donald Johnston of Canada (1996–2006), and Angel Gurria of Mexico (2006–). Each secretary-general has had academic training in economics or law, a career in public service as a member of government or senior civil servant, and a political leaning toward economic liberalism.

The OECD has a staff of about 2,000, including about 700 economists, lawyers, and other professionals. The secretariat is structured by departments or directorates, working in parallel to the committees they serve.

Unlike the World Bank or the International Monetary Fund, the OECD does not dispense money to national governments. Instead, it uses its resources for gathering and analyzing data, as well as for publications and conferences. Major products of OECD are statistical data of great quality, analyses of such data, the development of standards on matters such as corporate governance, and policy reviews. Among the most prominent of these reviews are the economic surveys. An economic survey is published every 1.5 to 2 years for each OECD member and for some large nonmember countries. The surveys analyze national economic policy, discuss policy options, and make recommendations.

The making of an economic survey reflects the political processes and structures within the OECD. The economics department, probably the most important of the 12 departments of the secretariat, organizes the procedure that leads to an economic survey. Within the economics department the Country Studies Branch, with its 15 country desks, is responsible for preparing the review of economic policy in close discussion with senior servants from the country under review. The draft of the economic survey is then submitted to the Economic and Development Review Committee (EDRC), composed of representatives of member countries. Two countries are responsible for the examination. They ask critical questions addressed to the delegation of the country under review. After the interaction of national civil servants, country desks, and examining countries, and after examination in front of the EDRC, the draft is revised and the members of the committee may comment on it. Discussion continues until the committee of representatives of 30 national governments makes a unanimous decision about the publication of the review.

As this example shows, continuous discussion, peer review, and consensual decision making are at the heart of this process, which requires representatives of national governments with very different political leanings to agree on analyses and recommendations for the economic policy of member countries.

The analytical perspectives of OECD have changed over time. When the organization started out it was concerned with core economic variables and had many intellectual affinities to Keynesian thinking. Beginning in the late 1970s it took a more monetarist outlook, and since the 1990s the OECD has broadened its former economic focus to include social and education policies and their different national configurations.

OECD and National Economic and Social Policy One of the major tools that the OECD uses to affect national economic and social policies is its data sets and reports produced by the secretariat in Paris. These reports point to shortcomings in national policy and describe alternative policies that are effective in other countries. The organization also diffuses ideas about good economic governance within an epistemic community of economists, lawyers, and social scientists from the OECD Secretariat and from national governments.

Finally, although the OECD issues standards, recommendations, and decisions, it does not employ sanctions if member countries ignore or violate these norms. "Naming and shaming" of such countries sometimes is taken up by national mass media and politicians. Analyses of the impact of the economic surveys have shown, however, that this is a rare event, especially for large countries. The OECD method of pressure by discussion, peer review, consensual decision taking, and naming and shaming has become a model for other organizations such as the EU, which adopted the OECD method as its "Open Method of Coordination" (OMC) as an alternative to less efficient and more problematic hierarchical methods of political steering. The EU applied OMC for the first time in 1997 and officially endorsed it as an EU method in 2000.

See also aid, international

FURTHER READING

Armingeon, Klaus, and Michelle Beyeler, eds. 2004. *The OECD and European Welfare States.* Cheltenham, UK: Edward Elgar. This volume contains 13 comparable country studies of the OECD's impacts on national welfare policy. An additional chapter describes the internal processes within the OECD, and a further comparative chapter draws conclusions based on the data of the country analyses.

Deacon, Bob. 2007. *Global Social Policy and Governance.* Los Angeles: Sage Publications. This book describes institutions of global social policies such as the World Bank, the United Nations, the International Monetary

Fund, and international nonstate actors. One section deals with the OECD.

Pagani, Fabrizio. 2002. *Peer Review: A Tool for Cooperation and Change. An Analysis of an OECD Working Method.* Paris: OECD. This paper describes the peer review process, which is the standard working method of the OECD when it evaluates countries and policies.

Sullivan, Scott. 2002. *From War to Wealth: 50 Years of Innovation.* Paris: OECD. This book is an official "birthday book" on the occasion of the OECD's 50th anniversary.

KLAUS ARMINGEON

■ Organization of the Petroleum Exporting Countries (OPEC)

The Organization of the Petroleum Exporting Countries (OPEC) is an international cartel of oil-producing states that has attempted, with varied success, to manipulate world oil prices. OPEC was founded in 1960 by Iran, Iraq, Kuwait, Saudi Arabia, and Venezuela, a group of major oil-producing countries that wished to coordinate national petroleum policies and forge a more united front in dealings with the multinational oil companies that were licensed to produce and export petroleum from their lands. Within the next dozen years, eight additional members (Algeria, Ecuador, Gabon, Indonesia, Libya, Nigeria, Qatar, and the United Arab Emirates) joined in, which brought the total membership of OPEC to 13 by 1973. At that time, the combined membership of OPEC accounted for more than half of worldwide crude oil production. Two small producers (Gabon and Ecuador) withdrew during the 1990s and Angola joined in 2007, bringing OPEC membership to its current level of 12 countries.

As with any cartel, OPEC's ability to hold the price of oil above the competitive level is dependent on barriers to entry, which in this case hinge on OPEC's dominant ownership and control of low-cost oil reserves. By accident of nature, some 75 percent of the world's proved reserves of crude oil are located in OPEC nations. Proved reserves constitute that portion of the ultimate resource base that has already been discovered and is commercially producible. Additional reserves can and will be developed through exploration, discovery, and development of new fields, but this process has become increasingly difficult and expensive—even more so outside the OPEC nations than within. Thus, while production of crude oil from non-OPEC sources does expand in response to the higher prices that result when cartel members restrict output, the scope for this is limited and will remain so. Moreover, OPEC's coordinated efforts to manipulate the price of oil are protected from antitrust enforcement and legal intervention by the sovereign rights of its members.

Economists have debated and tested various theories about how OPEC actually goes about exerting its influence on the market, whether through the independent initiatives of individual members, actions and strategies undertaken by semiautonomous coalitions working within the larger organization, or concerted plans embraced and executed by the organization as a whole. Some researchers might question whether OPEC has ever managed to operate successfully in the manner of a classic cartel. Whatever one's opinions on those matters, OPEC members have restricted production in ways that are unrelated to the inherent scarcity of crude oil. Although OPEC's proved oil reserves rose steadily between 1973 and 1985, production was cut by nearly half during that 12-year interval, falling from 31 million barrels per day (mbpd) in 1973 to an all-time low of 16 mbpd in 1985. As of late 2007, OPEC continued to hold production below the 1973 level, although the proved oil reserves of OPEC members had doubled in volume since then and total worldwide consumption of crude oil had grown by roughly 50 percent.

Evolution of OPEC The history and development of OPEC can be viewed in three phases. During the first phase (1960–70), OPEC's primary objective was to win for its members a larger *share* of the oil profits that private companies generated within their territory. The stated goal of increasing government take from 50 percent to 80 percent of total profits was pursued largely through the imposition of tax and administrative reforms by individual OPEC members, including the introduction of fictional "tax reference prices" that boosted the tax base, and therefore government take, without altering the stated tax rate and without much impact on the market price of oil. During this phase, there was no direct attempt by OPEC to raise the overall level of world oil prices, and perhaps there was not even the realization that such a feat would be possible. In those early years, OPEC was concerned with winning for itself a bigger share of the pie, rather than growing the size of the pie.

The second phase (1970–82) saw greater reliance on collective deliberations and coordinated actions designed to reverse a long period of decline in world oil prices (and therefore tax revenues) that had set in after World War II. These efforts began with a series of dictated agreements (the so-called Teheran-Tripoli agreements of 1970–71) by which the OPEC members unilaterally raised posted tax reference prices by 21 percent. The members also announced that further increases could and would be imposed as they saw fit under the doctrine of "changing circumstances," one of which was the declining exchange value of the dollar, the currency in which oil prices were denominated. Indeed, it was during a special OPEC conference convened to review these matters that the October 1973 Arab-Israeli war broke out, which prompted the Arab members of OPEC to declare an embargo on sales to Israel's allies (the United States and the Netherlands). Although the embargo did not have much effect on actual deliveries of oil to those countries, and was soon rescinded, this bold move panicked the markets and fueled a speculative demand for oil inventories, which ultimately drove prices in the spot market to unprecedented levels and taught OPEC ministers something about the value of their oil.

By 1974, the "official" OPEC price had reached $11.25 per barrel, a startling increase from the $2.18 price level that had been established just two years before. By 1975, the posted price was no longer merely a fictional "tax reference" price used by OPEC members to compute their share of company profits. Indeed, the multinational companies were mostly removed from the equation by a wave of nationalizations that began in earnest in 1974, after which OPEC members sold their oil outright to whichever customers were willing to pay the official price. The posted price was successively increased during the 1970s by collective agreement of the OPEC ministers, but the real price of oil actually declined as the decade progressed since the posted price failed to keep pace with accelerating inflation.

Such was the state of affairs at the onset of the Iranian Revolution, when the expulsion of foreign oil field service firms and a series of labor strikes in 1978 and 1979 disrupted Iranian output. Disruptions spread to Iraq in 1980 with the outbreak of the Iran-Iraq war. Again the market panicked, and again the OPEC members were taught something about the value of their oil. By October 1981, the posted price of OPEC oil reached $34 per barrel (which in real terms still represents the all-time high).

A sharp downturn in the oil market led to the third (and current) phase in OPEC's evolution. Already by 1982, individual OPEC members were offering customers large discounts below the "official" OPEC price in order to maintain or even increase their share of what had become a dwindling market. Sluggish OPEC sales and falling prices were the product of reduced consumption and rising non-OPEC oil supplies, both spurred by the price shocks of the 1970s. To deal with the growing surplus of oil in the marketplace, OPEC adopted in March 1983 a formal system of production allocations that imposed—for the first time—individual ceilings on the output of each member. During this third phase of OPEC's development, OPEC members met at regular intervals (and sometimes more frequently on an emergency basis) to review market conditions and adjust members' quotas as needed to support or "defend" the market price within a desired range. This phase of OPEC's history is the one that most resembles the textbook example of a cartel, at least outwardly.

OPEC's Future Prospects When judging OPEC's past success or contemplating its future course of action, several things must be kept in mind. Foremost is the fact that any system of output restraint is vulnerable to the classic free-rider problem.

OPEC as a whole may benefit from reducing total output, but each member has an incentive to produce beyond its assigned quota. From the individual member's point of view, marginal revenue from incremental sales exceeds the marginal cost of extraction, which creates the temptation to cheat. Cartel membership is most beneficial to a producer when other members are doing the hard work. But if they will not, who will? Without a system to detect and punish cheating, the cartel is hampered by a prisoner's dilemma in which the dominant strategy for most, if not all, members is to ignore their assigned production quotas.

In fact, OPEC lacks an effective means to monitor, detect, and punish members who exceed their quotas. A monthly chart of OPEC's combined crude oil production level relative to the agreed ceiling indicates the scope and persistence of this problem (see figure 1). Compliance has been sporadic. Since the inception of the quota system, total OPEC production of crude oil has exceeded the ceiling by 4 percent on average, but on numerous occasions the excess has run to 15 percent or more. For the most part, compliance has been achieved only during episodes (like 2005–6) when the production ceiling itself pushed the limits of each member's available production capacity.

A second factor that confounds OPEC's attempt to manage the market price is the lack of timely and accurate information about changes in the level of demand for oil and the availability of non-OPEC oil supplies. Several forecasts of demand and supply are available at any given time (including those prepared by the U.S. Energy Information Administration, the International Energy Agency, and by the OPEC Secretariat itself), but the precision of these forecasts is low and surprises are frequent. For example, none anticipated the surge in Asian demand that triggered the sudden tightening of oil markets in 2005. OPEC's forecasting problem is compounded by the fact that several years may elapse, due to rigidities in both supply and demand, before the full impact of a price change can be observed—so if a mistake is made, it may go undetected for several years and then take several years more to rectify.

Even if perfect information about future market conditions were available, there is no assurance that the interests of individual OPEC members could be easily aligned around a single "correct" price or production target. OPEC has very limited means by which to redistribute earnings among members. Therefore, any given set of quotas determines not only the overall profit of OPEC, but also the individual revenues that accrue to each member.

If the members were more homogeneous demographically and economically, the problem of misaligned interests would be less severe. As things happen, however, large volumes of low-cost reserves are concentrated in certain countries with small populations and relatively high incomes (e.g., Kuwait, Saudi Arabia, and the United Arab Emirates), while smaller volumes of higher-cost reserves are found in populous and relatively poor countries (e.g., Nigeria, Indonesia, and Venezuela). Table 1 sets forth some of the more salient differences among the members of OPEC. The potential for conflicting interests involves not only the question of which members "deserve" larger quotas, but what is the preferred market price level for OPEC oil.

What price would the respective members of the cartel like to see? Members with low-cost, long-lived reserves will take a long view of the future and may be reluctant to push prices too high given the fear of induced technological innovations that would usher

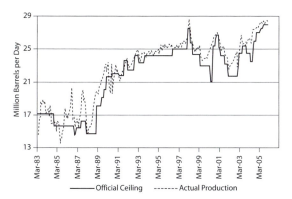

Figure 1

OPEC production compliance (monthly data). *Source:* ceilings, OPEC annual statistical bulletins; actuals, U.S. Energy Information Administration.

Table 1

Differences among OPEC members

Member	since	GDP ($ per capita)	Value of oil exports ($ per capita)	Proved oil reserves (bbl per capita)	Crude oil production (bbl per capita)	Reserves to production ratio (years)
Algeria	1969	3,113	999	373	15	25
Indonesia	1962	1,290	42	20	2	11
Iran*	1960	2,863	704	1,986	22	91
Iraq*	1960	1,063	812	3,989	24	165
Kuwait*	1960	27,028	15,429	36,775	340	108
Libya	1962	6,618	4,839	7,084	106	67
Nigeria	1971	752	355	275	7	42
Qatar	1961	45,937	22,614	18,455	339	54
Saudi Arabia*	1960	12,931	6,876	11,029	143	77
UAE	1967	29,367	11,044	21,733	193	113
Venezuela*	1960	5,240	1,796	2,990	43	70
OPEC average		2,649	941	1,660	21	81

Source: OPEC Annual Statistical Bulletin, 2005
Note: Angola joined OPEC in 2007; data for that country are not included here.
*Founding member of OPEC

in new forms of energy (or energy conservation) that eventually may compete against OPEC. Members holding fewer reserves and shorter horizons are less vulnerable to this type of risk and therefore perhaps less averse to high prices. Internal divisions between "price hawks" and "price doves" have been observed previously and will likely surface within OPEC again.

A final factor that looms large in the future of OPEC is the role to be played by serendipitous events and geopolitical tensions. A large portion of OPEC's apparent historical impact on the price of oil has come about not as the result of deliberate plans crafted by a purposeful cartel, but as the by-product of clashing national agendas that encompass far more than the petroleum sector. Since the early 1970s, most of the idle capacity held by OPEC members has been involuntary—taken out of production due to military conflict. Much of the hard work that any cartel has to do—commanding the determination and discipline to restrict output—has in OPEC's

case been provided fortuitously. For that reason, the ultimate strength and cohesion of OPEC had perhaps not yet been tested by the end of 2007.

The value of crude oil produced and sold on the world market exceeds $1 billion each day. Even a relatively small impact on the unit price of oil represents an enormous transfer of wealth between consumers and producers. Moreover, the disruptive impact of sudden price "shocks" and heightened volatility threatens the goal of sustained and steady global economic growth. As consumers, investors, and government officials continue to wrestle with these problems, it is no exaggeration to say that OPEC has left an indelible imprint on the world economy through its impact on the price of oil.

See also Gulf Cooperation Council; petroleum; primary products trade

FURTHER READING
Adelman, M. A. 1995. *The Genie Out of the Bottle: World Oil since 1970*. Cambridge, MA: MIT Press. A compre-

hensive study of the world oil market and OPEC's central role within it.

————. 2002. "World Oil Production and Prices: 1947–2000." *Quarterly Review of Economics and Finance* 42 (2): 169–91. A briefer and more recent examination of OPEC and its antecedents.

Amuzegar, Jahangir. 1999. *Managing the Oil Wealth: OPEC's Windfalls and Pitfalls.* London: I. B. Taurus. Insightful commentary on the financial challenges that confront oil-dependent economies.

Claes, Dag Harald. 2001. *The Politics of Oil-Producer Co-operation.* Boulder, CO: Westview Press. A look at the basis for economic cooperation among oil producers from a political science perspective.

Crémer, Jacques, and Djavad Salehi-Isfahani. 1991. *Models of the Oil Market.* Chur, Switzerland: Harwood Academic. Quantitative modeling of OPEC behavior.

Jones, Donald W., Paul Leiby, and Inja K. Paik. 2004. "Oil Price Shocks and the Macroeconomy: What Has Been Learned Since 1996." *Energy Journal* 25 (2): 1–32. A survey that also reveals much about what had been learned prior to 1996.

Parra, Francisco. 2004. *Oil Politics: A History of Modern Petroleum.* London: I. B. Taurus. A fascinating insider's guide to OPEC policies and politics.

Smith, James L. 2005. "Inscrutable OPEC? Behavioral Tests of the Cartel Hypothesis." *Energy Journal* 26 (1): 51–82. An interpretation of OPEC production patterns in terms of competitive versus collusive behavior.

JAMES L. SMITH

■ original sin

The term *original sin*, obviously an allusion to Christian theology, was coined by economists Barry Eichengreen and Ricardo Hausmann to refer to the inability of a particular country (most notably, emerging-market economies) to borrow funds in international capital markets in its own currency. The inability to borrow in domestic currency units necessarily forces the country in question to raise external funds using a foreign convertible currency instead, such as the U.S. dollar, the British pound, the euro, or the Japanese yen. Countries that choose to borrow external funds in this fashion expose themselves to a currency mismatch problem in their balance sheets, as their liabilities are denominated in foreign currency units, while their assets are denominated in domestic currency units. If there were no exchange rate movement over time, there would be no balance sheet valuation effects. If the domestic currency were to depreciate or be devalued, however, the country in question would experience a reduction in the market value of its assets, with little or no change in the value of its liabilities. As a result, the likelihood of insolvency and default increases. The risk of currency mismatch affects all sectors exposed to the problem: governments, banks, and even corporations.

Economic Impact of Original Sin There is a large and growing theoretical and empirical literature that analyzes the effect of original sin on macroeconomic performance. To be sure, standard models of the open economy do not directly address the issue of original sin. In these models, access to external debt (whether foreign-currency or domestic-currency denominated) is seen as beneficial, as this facilitates the country's ability to smooth out fluctuations in aggregate demand. A country that lacks the ability to borrow funds from the rest of the world is presumably worse off than it would otherwise be as it must depend solely on its own savings for financing consumption and investment expenditures. If domestic savings is insufficient for funding consumption and investment, access to external capital markets can help to finance the gap, thereby helping to maintain macroeconomic stability and growth. More recent models, however, show that when a large portion of the external debt is foreign-currency denominated, the likelihood of experiencing a balance of payments crisis may increase (e.g., Jeanne and Zettelmeyer 2005). Macroeconomic stability can therefore be seriously compromised when a country is exposed to original sin. In addition, monetary and fiscal policy tools can also be adversely affected by original sin. In particular, original sin could make monetary policy more complex, causing it to lose some of its effectiveness in influencing output (Cespedes, Chang, and Velasco 2005; Rajan 2006).

Empirically, many researchers find that original sin actually amplifies macroeconomic volatility. In particular, the higher the level of original sin, the more likely is the country to suffer from instability in output and capital flows. Many researchers see original sin as at least partly responsible for many banking crises in recent decades (Kaminsky and Reinhart 1999). The reasoning behind this belief is that the banking sector in many emerging market economies is often exposed to currency fluctuations: deposits are often denominated in a foreign, convertible currency (in order to attract funds that would otherwise go abroad), while bank assets are primarily loans denominated in domestic currency. When the currency depreciates or is devalued, the market value of bank loans declines; the value of liabilities, on the other hand, remains roughly unchanged, thereby compromising the solvency of the banking sector. The effect of such an event on the rest of the economy can be quite devastating as banks, in an effort to increase liquidity, contract their lending, thereby creating a "credit crunch" that amplifies an economic downturn. Indeed, many researchers argue that original sin is largely responsible for some of the most devastating financial crises in recent history, such as the Asian financial crisis of 1997–98.

Reasons behind Original Sin Given that original sin appears to cause a significant amount of macroeconomic problems, it is natural to ask why countries borrow in foreign currency units. The literature mentions several reasons, including (1) weak economic credibility, (2) weak financial institutions, and (3) structural impediments to domestic currency debt issuance. First, emerging market economies typically lack a strong track record of economic performance. For example, emerging market economies tend to have long-lasting inflation problems. Because of lack of monetary credibility, foreign investors may be reluctant to lend to such countries in domestic currency units, demanding instead that countries issue foreign-currency denominated debt (Jeanne 2005). Second, it is likely that foreign investors are uneasy about holding the debt of countries with weak institutions, such as a poor track record on the enforcement of contracts, and poorly

enforced property rights. Facing this constraint, countries may choose to issue debt denominated in foreign currency units as a way to signal to potential investors that they are committed to keep their end of the obligation (Reinhart, Rogoff, and Savastano 2003). Third, the international financial architecture simply does not allow many countries to issue debt in domestic currency units. In particular, some researchers have noted that countries that borrow in international markets using their own currency tend to have large economies and deep financial systems (Flandreau and Sussman 2005). If so, this would imply that issues related to economies of scale, network externalities, or liquidity allow only a handful of currencies to be effectively used in international financial contracts.

See also balance sheet approach/effects; banking crisis; conflicted virtue; convertibility; currency crisis; currency substitution and dollarization; dollar standard; dominant currency; financial crisis; reserve currency

FURTHER READING

Calvo, G., and C. Reinhart. 2002. "Fear of Floating." *Quarterly Journal of Economics* 117: 379–408. Investigates whether countries that claim to have a floating exchange rate actually allow their currencies to fluctuate. They find that, for the most part, countries do not. They argue that the "fear of floating" appears to be epidemic.

Cespedes, L. F., R. Chang, and A. Velasco. 2005. "Must Original Sin Cause Macroeconomic Damnation?" In *Other People's Money: Debt Denomination and Financial Instability in Emerging Market Economies*, edited by B. Eichengreen and R. Hausmann. Chicago: University of Chicago Press, 48–67. Presents a theoretical model showing that original sin can undermine the effectiveness of fiscal and monetary policy tools, thereby compromising a country's ability to stabilize output.

Eichengreen, B., and R. Hausmann. 1999. "Exchange Rates and Financial Fragility." NBER Working Paper No. 7418. Cambridge, MA: National Bureau of Economic Research. Introduces for the first time the term *original sin* as one of the avenues through which exchange rate volatility can induce financial fragility.

———. 2005. "Introduction: Debt Denomination and Financial Instability in Emerging Market Economies."

In *Other People's Money: Debt Denomination and Financial Instability in Emerging Market Economies*, edited by B. Eichengreen and R. Hausmann. Chicago: University of Chicago Press, 3–12. Offers an excellent exposition on the issues pertaining to original sin. The introductory chapter summarizes the main contributions of the papers included in the book.

Eichengreen, B., R. Hausmann, and U. Panizza. 2005. "The Pain of Original Sin." In *Other People's Money: Debt Denomination and Financial Instability in Emerging Market Economies*, edited by B. Eichengreen and R. Hausmann. Chicago: University of Chicago Press, 13–47. Presents empirical evidence showing that financial and macroeconomic instability in emerging market economies tends to increase with original sin problems.

Flandreau, M., and N. Sussman. 2005. "Old Sins: Exchange Clauses and European Foreign Lending in the Nineteenth Century." In *Other People's Money: Debt Denomination and Financial Instability in Emerging Market Economies*, edited by B. Eichengreen and R. Hausmann. Chicago: University of Chicago Press, 154–89. Argues that the main cause of original sin is not the lack of credibility and discipline of governments, as others have argued, but rather it is the result of historical path dependence and market liquidity.

Jeanne, O. 2005. "Why Do Emerging Economies Borrow in Foreign Currency?" In *Other People's Money: Debt Denomination and Financial Instability in Emerging Market Economies*, edited by B. Eichengreen and R. Hausmann. Chicago: University of Chicago Press, 190–217. Explores the causes of original sin and argues that original sin in private debt markets is mainly the result of monetary policy.

Jeanne, O., and J. Zettelmeyer. 2005. "Original Sin, Balance-Sheet Crises, and the Roles of International Lending." In *Other People's Money: Debt Denomination and Financial Instability in Emerging Market Economies*, edited by B. Eichengreen and R. Hausmann. Chicago: University of Chicago Press, 95–121. Explores two classes of models and finds that in both of them crises can be self-fulfilling prophesies. The paper also investigates the role of international lending in ameliorating the effect of financial crises stemming from original sin problems.

Kaminsky, G., and C. Reinhart. 1999. "The Twin Crises: The Causes of Banking and Balance-of-Payments Problems." *American Economic Review* 89 (3): 473–500. Investigates the links between banking crises and currency crises. Its main finding is that banking problems typically precede currency crises, and once a currency crisis is triggered, it amplifies banking problems, culminating in a banking crisis.

Rajan, R. S. 2006. "Managing New Style Currency Crisis: The Swan Diagram Approach Revisited." *Journal of International Development* 18: 1–24. Presents a model useful for understanding how countries can manage economic disruptions stemming from crises driven by original sin problems.

Reinhart, C., K. Rogoff, and M. Savastano. 2003. "Debt Intolerance." *Brookings Papers on Economic Activity* 1: 1–74. Quantifies a country's vulnerability to a debt crisis as it accumulates external debt. Its main finding is that having experienced debt problems in the past makes a country more susceptible to external debt crises in the future.

CARLOS D. RAMIREZ

■ outsourcing/offshoring

The terms *foreign outsourcing* or *offshoring* apply when the components of a good or service are produced in several countries. The term *offshoring* often refers to a company moving some of its operations overseas, but retaining ownership of those operations. Intel, for example, produces microchips in China and Costa Rica using subsidiaries that it owns, so these production activities have moved offshore. In contrast, *outsourcing* refers to moving activities outside of a firm (which could be to another firm in the same country, as with *domestic* outsourcing, or to another firm in another country, as with *foreign* outsourcing). Mattel, for example, arranges for the production of the Barbie doll in several different countries, so it is engaged in foreign outsourcing. Unlike Intel, however, Mattel does not actually own the firms in those countries. In this entry we will not be concerned with the distinction between foreign outsourcing or offshoring, and use either term to refer to shifting activities to another country.

While there are historical examples of companies doing some of their production in another country, outsourcing is generally thought to be a feature of the modern world economy made possible by improvements in international trade, transportation, and communication. Indeed, the earliest known use of the word *outsourcing* in a published source is from an American auto executive in the *Journal of the Royal Society of Arts*, 1979, who wrote: "We are so short of professional engineers in the motor industry that we are having to outsource design work to Germany" (Safire 2004). This example shows that outsourcing may involve the shifting of service activities (like design work) overseas, in addition to the shifting of production activities (like making the Barbie doll) overseas. In this entry we first concentrate on the shifting of *production activities* to other countries and then discuss *service outsourcing*.

Measures of Outsourcing There are several approaches that can be used to measure the amount of outsourcing. One approach is to look at "processing trade," which is defined by customs offices as the import of intermediate inputs for processing and subsequent reexport of the final product. This activity has grown enormously in China, for which Hong Kong often serves as an intermediary. For example, between 1988 and 1998, processing exports grew from $12.4 billion to $97.2 billion, or from about one-third to over one-half of total Chinese exports (Feenstra and Hanson 2004). This outward processing serves newly industrialized countries in Asia, but also developed countries such as the United States, Japan, and countries in Europe. Between the industrialized countries, too, there has been an increase in processing trade. Görg (2000) reports on the increase in U.S. processing trade with the European Union between 1988 and 1994. He finds that U.S. processing imports into these countries (as a share of their total U.S. imports) increased slightly from 17.7 percent to 19.8 percent, but this same ratio increased more significantly from 13.7 percent to 23.7 percent for U.S. exports into the "periphery" countries of Greece, Ireland, Portugal and Spain.

Another way to measure foreign outsourcing is by the amount of imported intermediate inputs, which can be estimated by using the purchases of each type of input and multiplying it by the economywide import share for that input. Adding overall inputs used within each industry, we obtain estimated imported inputs, which can then be expressed relative to total intermediate input purchases. Feenstra and Hanson (1999) perform this calculation for U.S. manufacturing industries and find that imported inputs increased from 6.5 percent of total intermediate purchases in 1972 to 8.5 percent in 1979, and 11.6 percent in 1990. Campa and Goldberg (1997) make the same calculation for Canada, Japan, the United Kingdom, and the United States. The United States shows a doubling of the share of imported inputs between 1975 and 1995 for all manufacturing, from 4.1 percent to 8.2 percent, though it is still at a low level compared with other countries. Canada shows an increase in the share of intermediate inputs from 15.9 percent to 20.2 percent from 1974 to 1993, and the United Kingdom shows an especially large increase in this share, rising from 13.4 percent to 21.6 percent over the same years. The exception is Japan, where the share of imported inputs in manufacturing fell. With that single exception, the increased use of imported inputs was a characteristic feature of many industrial countries during the 1980s and 1990s.

Effect of Outsourcing on Wages: Evidence from the 1980s Much of the academic and policy interest in outsourcing is due to its potential effect on wages and employment. During the 1980s there was a surprising movement in wages and employment in the United States and other countries. During that decade, the real wage of less-skilled workers (with high-school education or less) fell in the United States, whereas the real wages of the more highly skilled workers (college graduates) rose. Therefore, the ratio of the skilled wage divided by the unskilled wage—or the relative wage of skilled/unskilled workers—rose. At the same time, the relative employment of skilled/unskilled workers also went up, especially in manufacturing. That pattern is surprising because normally when the relative wage of skilled/unskilled workers rises, we expect that companies will hire fewer skilled employees (since they are more expensive); instead, the opposite happened and companies hired relatively more skilled workers. The only explanation for this pattern is that the relative *demand* for skilled workers must have increased, especially in the manufacturing sector. What factors can explain this increase in the relative demand for skilled workers?

Two factors that can explain the increase in relative demand for skilled workers are: (1) the increased use of computers and other high-technology equipment, and thus an increase in the skilled workers needed to operate them; and (2) outsourcing. To understand how outsourcing will increase the relative demand for skilled labor, we use the "value chain" of a firm, which includes all the activities involved in the production of a good or service, from research and development (R&D) to assembly to marketing and after-sales service. For the purpose of modeling outsourcing, rather than arranging activities in the order they are actually performed, we instead arrange them in increasing ratio of skilled/unskilled labor used in each activity, as shown in figure 1.

Assembly uses the least amount of skilled labor relative to unskilled labor in figure 1, followed by component production, then marketing and sales, and finally R&D. A firm that is outsourcing to another country with lower relative wages for unskilled labor will want to send those activities using the most unskilled labor. So in figure 1, activities to the left of the line AA will be sent offshore to the foreign country, while activities to the right of the line AA will be performed at home.

Now suppose that the home firm wishes to offshore more activities. The reason for this could be a trade agreement with the foreign country, leading to

reduced tariffs; or improvement in the infrastructure in the foreign country, leading to reduced costs there; or an increase in costs at home. When deciding what extra activities to offshore, the firm will look to those activities that were just on the borderline of being outsourced before, that is, those activities just to the right of the line AA, which used to be profitably performed at home but now are shifted abroad. The borderline between the activities performed at home and abroad therefore shifts from the line AA to the line BB.

What is the impact of this increase in outsourcing on the relative demand for skilled labor at home and abroad? Notice that the activities no longer performed at home (i.e., those in between AA and BB) are *less* skill-intensive than the activities still done there (those to the right of BB). This means that the range of activities now done at home is more skilled-labor intensive, on average, than the set of activities formerly done at home. For this reason, the relative demand for skilled labor at home increases, as occurred in the United States during the 1980s. That increase in demand will also increase the relative wage for skilled labor.

What about in the foreign country? The activities that are newly sent offshore (those in between AA and BB) are *more* skill-intensive than the activities that were initially outsourced to the foreign country (those to the left of AA). That means that the range of activities now done abroad is more skilled-labor intensive, on average, than the set of activities formerly done there. For this reason, the relative demand for skilled labor in the foreign country also increases. With this increase in the relative demand for skilled labor, the relative wage of skilled labor also increases in the foreign country. That outcome occurred in Mexico, for example, during the 1980s, as well as in Hong Kong.

Outsourcing versus Technological Change By shifting activities from one country to the other, outsourcing can increase the relative demand for skilled labor in *both* countries, as has actually occurred in a number of industrial and developing countries. However, the same result can occur from skill-biased technological change, such as the

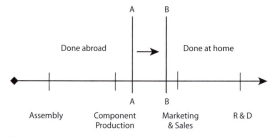

Figure 1

Outsourcing on the value chain

increased use of computers, which can increase the relative demand for skilled labor across countries. Given that outsourcing and skill-biased technological change both predict an increase in the relative wage of skilled labor, it becomes an empirical issue as to which is more important.

A study for the United States (Feenstra and Hanson 1999) seeks to explain the increase in the share of total wage payments going to nonproduction (skilled) versus production (unskilled) labor in U.S. manufacturing industries over the period 1979–90 and analyzes the increase in the relative wage of nonproduction labor over the same period. The study considers two possible explanations for the change in wages: outsourcing and the use of high-tech equipment such as computers. High-technology equipment can itself be measured in two ways: either as a fraction of the total capital equipment installed in each industry or as a fraction of new investment in capital that is devoted to computers and other high-tech devices.

Using the first measure of high-tech equipment (i.e., fraction of the capital stock), 20–23 percent of the increase in the share of wage payments going to nonproduction workers was explained by outsourcing, and 8–12 percent of the increase was explained by the growing use of high-tech capital. Thus, using the first measure of high-tech equipment, it appears that outsourcing was more important than high-tech capital in explaining the change in relative demand for skilled workers. The story is different, however, when the second measure of high-tech equipment (i.e., fraction of new investment) is used. In that case, outsourcing explains only 13 percent of the increase in the nonproduction share of wages, whereas high-tech investment explains 37 percent of that increase. So we see from these results that both outsourcing and high-tech equipment are important explanations for the increase in the relative wage of skilled labor in the United States, but which one is more important depends on how we measure the high-tech equipment.

Moving on to the increase in the relative wage of nonproduction workers, using the first measure of high-tech equipment (fraction of the capital stock),

21–27 percent of the increase in the relative wage of nonproduction workers was explained by outsourcing, and 29–32 percent of the increase was explained by the growing use of high-tech capital. Using the other measure of high-tech equipment (fraction of new investment), the large spending on high-tech equipment in new investment can explain *nearly all* (99 percent) of the increase in the relative wage for nonproduction workers, leaving little room for outsourcing to play much of a role (it explains only 12 percent of the increase in the relative wage). These results are lopsided enough that we might be skeptical of using new investment to measure high-tech equipment and therefore prefer the results using the capital stocks. Summing up, both outsourcing and high-tech equipment are important explanations for the increase in the relative wage of nonproduction/production labor in U.S. manufacturing, but the relative contributions of the two measures are very sensitive to how we measure the high-tech equipment.

Trade Costs and Outsourcing across Firms The effects of outsourcing described in figure 1 can be thought of as occurring along the value chain of a firm. One natural way to examine these changes is by examining the impact of falling trade costs on manufacturing establishments with different characteristics. It is likely that as firms move production activities offshore, they will outsource the least skilled activities (as depicted in figure 1), or close the plants focusing on these activities.

Bernard, Jensen, and Schott (2006) examine the implications of falling trade costs on U.S. manufacturers, and specifically examine the channels by which trade affects the distribution of economic activity. They find when trade costs in an industry fall, plants are more likely to close. They also find that low productivity, nonexporting plants are more likely to die. This is one channel by which outsourcing can affect the distribution of economic activity. Falling trade costs tend to reduce the amount of economic activity at the low end of the productivity distribution. Because low-productivity plants also tend to be production-worker intensive, this change is likely to reduce the relative demand for unskilled workers.

Bernard, Jensen, and Schott (2006) also find that relatively high-productivity nonexporters in industries with falling trade costs are more likely to start exporting. The magnitude of the effect of falling trade costs on becoming an exporter is substantial. Because higher-productivity plants are more skilled-worker intensive, as these plants expand they will increase the relative demand for skilled workers. They also find that existing exporters increase their shipments abroad as trade costs fall. Because exporters have relatively high-productivity plants, the expansion of the high end of the productivity distribution will tend to raise aggregate productivity (even if no plants changes its productivity). Because exporters are skill- and capital-intensive, this will also tend to increase relative demand for these factor inputs. Finally, these authors find that plants in industries with falling trade costs have faster productivity growth, possibly due to increased outsourcing.

It should be noted that the productivity increase associated with outsourcing means that the real wage of workers (even the less-skilled workers) need not fall due to outsourcing. That result is shown in the model of Feenstra and Hanson (1996), from which figure 1 is drawn. The same result occurs more strongly in the recent model of Grossman and Rossi-Hansberg (2006), where the real wage of less-skilled worker are guaranteed to rise due to the productivity-enhancing effect of outsourcing.

Regional Variation in Wage Inequality in the United States The increase in wage inequality due to outsourcing has not been uniform across the United States. Bernard and Jensen (2000) find that the changing composition of employment in regional economies is strongly correlated with changes in wage inequality in the United States. Somewhat surprisingly, they find that while many regions in the United States experienced increasing wage inequality, some regions experienced *decreasing* wage inequality over the 1970–90 period.

Figure 2 shows the variation across states in changes in residual wage inequality for 1970–80 (upper map) and 1980–90 (lower map). States with large increases in wage inequality are in the traditional "Rust Belt," and states with decreases in wage

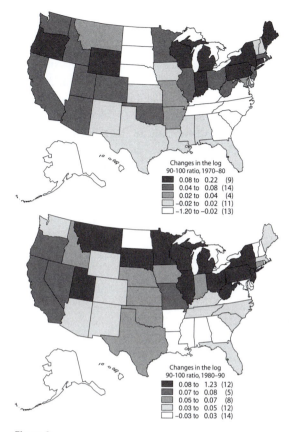

Figure 2

Changes in inequality by state. Source: Bernard and Jensen (2000).

inequality are in the Southeast. Bernard and Jensen find that decreases (increases) in the share of manufacturing sector employment in the durable goods sector is strongly correlated with increasing (decreasing) wage inequality.

One specific example of how these heterogeneous responses to trade pressures can affect regions differentially is the case of Appalachian manufacturing. Appalachian manufacturing is concentrated in low-wage, labor-intensive industries, and Appalachian manufacturers within those industries tend to be lower wage and lower productivity than plants in those industries elsewhere in the United States. This combination of industrial mix and plant production technology leaves the region particularly susceptible to import competition from low-wage countries. For example, low-wage competition shows a more pronounced effect on Appalachian plants in terms of employment growth and plant failure than elsewhere in the United States. Plants in the Appalachian region have higher shutdown probabilities and lower employment growth when facing low-wage imports than do firms in the rest of the United States.

Service Outsourcing in Manufacturing: Evidence from the 1990s The patterns of wages and employment in U.S. manufacturing changed in the 1990s, with rising relative wages and employment for skilled workers. The relative wage of nonproduction/production labor in U.S. manufacturing continued to increase from 1989 to 2000, but in addition, the relative employment of production workers *decreased*. A likely explanation for this new pattern of wage and employment is that it reflects service outsourcing from U.S. manufacturing. To the extent that the back-office jobs being outsourced from manufacturing use the lower-paid nonproduction workers, then the offshoring of those jobs could very well *raise the average* wage among nonproduction workers, while lowering their employment. So that pattern would be consistent with what has actually occurred in U.S. manufacturing. In the rest of our entry, then, we focus on service outsourcing.

Examples of service outsourcing from the manufacturing sector include the offshoring of services such as communication, finance, insurance, computer, and information services. Amiti and Wei (2006) report that in the United States, the amount of imported service inputs is small but growing. Measured as a share of total inputs purchased, imported services were 0.2 percent in 1992 (i.e., two-tenths of one percent of total inputs), and grew to 0.3 percent in 2000 (i.e., three-tenths of one percent). The fact that imported services are small does not necessarily prevent them from being important for productivity and employment.

In terms of the impact of service outsourcing and high-technology equipment on manufacturing productivity measured by value added per worker, over the eight years 1992–2000, Amiti and Wei find service outsourcing can explain about 11 percent of the total increase in productivity. Despite the small amount of service imports, they find it explains a significant portion of productivity growth. It may be some of that productivity growth is actually due to domestic outsourcing of service activities, which is confounded in the data with foreign outsourcing of services. The contribution of service outsourcing can be compared to the offshoring of material inputs, which explains a further 5 percent of the total increase in productivity. Adding together these contributions, we see that these two factors explain about 16 percent of the increase in value added per worker, or as much as one-sixth of productivity growth. Since productivity rose by about 4 percent per year in manufacturing, these results show that outsourcing of services together with material inputs during the 1990s can explain two-thirds of a percentage point in productivity growth per year, which is economically important.

Offshoring's Impact on the Service Sector In the previous section we examined the impact of service outsourcing on the manufacturing sector. In this section we consider the potential impact of offshoring on the service sector. While work on trade in services is quite recent and hampered by less detailed information than trade in goods, Jensen and Kletzer (2006) provide evidence on the potential impact that trade in services will have. They use the geographic concentration of service activities within the United States to identify industries and occupations that appear traded across regions within the United States and classify these activities as tradable. They find that a significant share of total employment is in tradable service activities: in fact, more employment is in tradable professional and business services than in manufacturing. They also find that workers in tradable service activities are different than workers in nontradable activities, even in the same sector. Workers in tradable services have more education and significantly higher earnings (after controlling for observable differences). They examine recent trends in employment growth and find little evidence that tradable services have lower employment growth than no-tradable services, though they do find some evidence of higher displacement rates in tradable service activities.

These results suggest that the potential scope for tradable services is large enough to have a significant impact on the U.S. economy. It seems likely that increasing trade in services will have a similar effect as the increased trade in goods. Trade in services is likely to increase productivity through a number of channels, including closure of low-productivity service producers, entry into exporting of relatively high-productivity service providers, and expansion of service firms that already export. Similar to manufacturers, service exporters likely have superior operating characteristics and use a different skill mix than nonexporters. We expect increased trade in services will affect the relative demand for skilled and unskilled labor, though it may affect a different portion of the skill distribution than we witnessed in the manufacturing sector in the 1980s and 1990s.

See also fragmentation; internalization theory; trade and wages

FURTHER READING

Amiti, Mary, and Shang-Jin Wei. 2006. "Service Offshoring and Productivity: Evidence from the United States." NBER Working Paper No. 11926. Cambridge, MA: National Bureau of Economic Research. Estimates the impact of service outsourcing from the manufacturing sector on wages and productivity in the United States.

Bernard, Andrew B., and J. Bradford Jensen. 2000. "Understanding Increasing and Decreasing Wage Inequality." In *The Impact of International Trade on Wages*, edited by Robert Feenstra. Chicago: University of Chicago Press, 227–61. Examines the regional variation in wage inequality in the United States.

Bernard, Andrew B., J. Bradford Jensen, and Peter K. Schott. 2006. "Trade Costs, Firms, and Productivity." *Journal of Monetary Economics* 53 (5): 917–37. Examines the impact of falling trade costs on firm entry, exit, and productivity.

Campa, Jose, and Linda Goldberg. 1997. "The Evolving External Orientation of Manufacturing Industries: Evidence from Four Countries." NBER Working Paper No. 5919. Cambridge, MA: National Bureau of Economic Research; *Economic Policy Review,* The Federal Reserve Bank of New York (July). Presents evidence on the amount of outsourcing for four industrial countries: Canada, Japan, the United Kingdom, and the United States.

Feenstra, Robert C., and Gordon H. Hanson. 1996. "Foreign Investment, Outsourcing, and Relative Wages." In *The Political Economy of Trade Policy: Papers in Honor of Jagdish Bhagwati,* edited by R. C. Feenstra, G. M. Grossman, and D. A. Irwin. Cambridge, MA: MIT Press, 89–127. Presents a model of outsourcing and some preliminary empirical results.

———. 1999. "The Impact of Outsourcing and High-Technology Capital on Wages: Estimates for the U.S., 1979–1990." *Quarterly Journal of Economics* 114 (3) (August): 907–40. Estimates the impact of outsourcing and computer use on wages in U.S. manufacturing.

———. 2004. "Intermediaries in Entrepôt Trade: Hong Kong Re-Exports of Chinese Goods." *Journal of Economics and Management Strategy* 13 (1) (spring): 3–35. Discusses Chinese processing trade and intermediation by Hong Kong.

Görg, Holger. 2000. "Fragmentation and Trade: U.S. Inward Processing Trade in the EU." *Weltwirtschaftliches Archiv (Review of World Economics)*: 136: 403–22. Discusses processing trade between the United States and Europe.

Grossman, Gene, and Esteban Rossi-Hansberg. 2006. "Trading Tasks: A Simple Model of Outsourcing." NBER Working Paper No. 12721. Cambridge, MA: National Bureau of Economic Research. A theoretical exposition of outsourcing in a two-sector model.

Jensen, J. Bradford, and Lori Kletzer. 2006. "Tradable Services: Understanding the Scope and Impact of Services Offshoring." In *Offshoring White-Collar Work–Issues and Implications*, edited by Lael Brainard and Susan M. Collins (Washington, DC: Brookings Institute Trade Forum 2005), 75–134. Examines outsourcing from the service sector of the United States.

Safire, William. 2004. "On Language." *New York Times Magazine* (March 21), 30. Discusses the earliest known use of the word *outsourcing* in a published source.

ROBERT C. FEENSTRA AND J. BRADFORD JENSEN

■ parallel imports

Parallel imports (also known as gray products) are products imported into a country without the authorization of the intellectual property right owner. They arise when international price differences exceed the costs of transporting the products across borders. No precise data exist on parallel imports, but their volume is considered to be large (up to a market share of 20 percent in some countries and for some products), especially for products such as musical recordings, cosmetics, fragrances, soft drinks, clothing, confectionery, automobiles, motorcycles, consumer electronics, and pharmaceuticals (Maskus 2000).

The international system of intellectual property rights allows each country to establish its own legal regime concerning parallel trade. It is based on the concept of exhaustion of property rights (known as "first-sale" doctrine in the United States), whereby countries choose the geographical area (national, regional, international) within which the owners of intellectual property rights lose (and thus "exhaust") their rights on products after first sales. Most countries have a regime of *national* exhaustion of intellectual property rights allowing the owner of that right to exclude legally parallel imports through trademark, copyright, and/or patent laws. For instance, the United States has national exhaustion on the three property rights fields, but authorized dealers mainly use trademark and copyright laws to block parallel trade (Gallini and Hollis 1999). The other extreme is an *international* exhaustion regime, which makes parallel imports legal. This is the case in Japan (with restrictions) and Australia and New Zealand (for most copyrighted and trademarks goods). A *regional* exhaustion regime, as in the European Union (EU), represents an intermediate case, since it makes parallel imports legal when they originate from EU members but illegal when they originate from non-EU members.

The main economic policy question about parallel imports is whether a property right owner should be entitled to international exclusive distribution territories. The fact that different regimes have been adopted indicates the existence of conflicting views about the motives and economic effects of parallel imports. In a nutshell, views range from banning parallel trade because intellectual property owners should have the right to control the international distribution of their products, to unregulated parallel trade because restrictions are nontariff barriers to trade that are inconsistent with World Trade Organization principles.

Price discrimination is generally considered the primary motive behind a manufacturer's support of a parallel import ban. Income differences, for instance, are typically more important across countries than within them, and they imply different demand elasticities across countries. This provides a strong incentive to manufacturers with market power to set country-specific prices. Because of arbitrage, this strategy would not be sustainable with parallel imports. Allowing international price discrimination (i.e., banning parallel imports) does not imply that international welfare decreases (Malueg and Schwartz 1994). A necessary condition for global welfare to be higher under international price discrimination is that overall output be greater under discrimination than without it. This is a poor consolation for the high-price country but not for the low-price country, especially if the latter country is not served under a regime allowing parallel imports. This may well arise when income differences are large enough, a case that is relevant in the ongoing dispute about the availability of some critical pharmaceutical products in developing countries. In short, price discrimination does not provide a strong guide about policy prescription concerning parallel trade.

A second important motive behind manufacturers' attitude toward parallel trade is linked to vertical control over intermediaries selling these products to consumers. In particular, banning parallel trade and having exclusive intermediaries may help facilitating collusion among manufacturers or among dealers. It may also provide incentives to these exclusive intermediaries to undertake specific investments in activities such as advertising or after-sales services. If parallel imports were allowed, free riding would take place and, with it, very little incentive to invest in such activities. In other words, whenever exclusive territories are useful to motivate dealers, there are good reasons to ban parallel imports as well. Still, manufacturers who deal with intermediaries may have a strong incentive to let dealers engage in parallel trade. This is particularly the case in markets where production and shipments must take place before demand is really known and for products whose sale value drops at the end of the demand period (Raff and Schmitt 2007). If parallel trade was banned in such markets (for instance, confectionary), intermediaries could be stuck with worthless inventories when the demand in their market turns out to be low. Fearing this possibility, intermediaries would naturally place smaller orders to manufacturers than they would if they were free to resell unsold inventories in high-demand markets. Thus, when seasonality and uncertainty are important market demand features, manufacturers' profits may well be significantly higher when parallel trade is allowed than when it is not.

A third set of motives for banning parallel trade has to do with its dynamic impacts on markets. For instance, banning parallel trade may prevent confusion among consumers when the products have different specifications (whether due to different tastes across locations, safety standards, or packaging). More significantly, parallel imports may reduce manufacturers' incentives to engage in research and development or product innovation. This argument is often made in relation to the pharmaceutical industry (see Li and Maskus 2006).

These possibilities show that parallel trade can have nontrivial implications for the competitive environment of manufacturers and intermediaries. Clearly, a policy about parallel imports, whether at the national or at the international level, can rarely be reduced to a trade policy recommendation but must typically also include strong competition policy considerations.

Empirical evidence shows that the threat of parallel imports does decrease retail prices. In itself, these price effects are not enough to justify a free regime concerning parallel trade. Since a worldwide ban on parallel trade cannot be recommended either, a policy about parallel imports can be designed only on a case-by-case basis, depending on the characteristics of each country or region.

See also access to medicines; Agreement on Trade-Related Aspects of Intellectual Property Rights (TRIPS); World Trade Organization

FURTHER READING

Gallini, Nancy, and Aidan Hollis. 1999. "A Contractual Approach to the Gray Market." *International Review of Law and Economics* 19 (1): 1–21. A very useful law and economics discussion of the U.S. intellectual property laws with respect to parallel trade.

Li, Changying, and Keith Maskus. 2006. "The Impact of Parallel Imports on Investments in Cost-Reducing Research and Development." *Journal of International Economics* 68: 443–55. Develops a theoretical model about the links between innovations and parallel trade.

Malueg, David, and Marius Schwartz. 1994. "Parallel Imports, Demand Dispersion, and International Price Discrimination." *Journal of International Economics* 37

(3–4): 167–95. The seminal theoretical paper on price discrimination and parallel trade.

Maskus, Keith. 2000. "Parallel Imports." *World Economy* 23 (9): 269–84. A nontechnical survey of the policy issues concerning parallel trade.

Raff, Horst, and Nicolas Schmitt. 2007. "Why Parallel Imports May Raise Producers' Profits." *Journal of International Economics* 71 (2): 434–47. Develops a simple model explaining the circumstances under which allowing parallel imports is beneficial to manufacturers.

NICOLAS SCHMITT

■ partial equilibrium models

Partial equilibrium models are used to analyze trade issues in a single market or, alternatively, in a few closely related markets. They are adaptations of standard supply and demand analysis to the specific features of trade policies. Partial equilibrium models are used in cases where linkages to other sectors of the economy are negligible enough to be ignored. They have the advantage of being relatively easy to construct and lend themselves to transparent application in policy analysis. They are extensively used in the analysis of anti-dumping and countervailing duties, as well as to assess the probable effects of many types of trade policy changes in narrowly defined sectors.

A decision not to use partial equilibrium modeling (or the more involved approach of applied general equilibrium modeling) usually results in the deployment of some sort of trend analysis, which focuses on whether the direction and timing of changes in one set of economic variables are coincident with another set of economic variables. Trend analysis is sometimes implemented in the form of an interpolation based on trend lines before and after a critical event, such as a change in trade policy. Trend analysis has two problems, however. First, the causative links between the two sets of variables are never made explicit, and the relative contribution of one factor to a given set of events is therefore difficult to assess. Second, while the number of necessary parameter estimates is minimal, this is simply a consequence of the implicit assumptions embedded in

the approach. Partial equilibrium analysis is a superior approach in almost all circumstances.

To construct a partial equilibrium trade policy model, the analyst first needs to determine whether the imported and domestic competing goods are perfect or imperfect substitutes and then needs to determine whether the country is "small" with reference to the rest of the world (in which case the import supply curve is horizontal or perfectly elastic) or "large" with reference to the rest of the world (in which case the import supply curve is upward sloping or less than perfectly elastic). These fundamental choices, which ideally should reflect the empirical reality of the situation being modeled, determine the appropriate modeling framework. If imports and domestic competing goods are best modeled as imperfect substitutes (following Armington 1969), the transmission of shocks from the market for the imported good to the market for domestic goods relies on the cross-price elasticity of demand or, alternatively, the elasticity of substitution. This measure affects the extent to which changes in the price of an imported good affect demand for the domestic competing good. Partial equilibrium models, whether perfect or imperfect substitutes, are typically implemented using spreadsheet software, examples of which are included in Francois and Hall (1997) and Roningen (1997).

A Perfect Substitutes Model We will first consider a perfect substitutes model with "second-best" effects in the "small" country case. This model proceeds as indicated in the supply and demand diagram of figure 1. The supply curve S represents the behavior of domestic firms, and the demand curve D represents the behavior of domestic households. Imports are available from the world market at a constant price P^w. It is the constant nature of this price that puts us in the "small" country case. The domestic government has imposed a specific tariff on imports of amount T_1. At the resulting domestic price of $P^w + T_1$, imports are of an amount equal to Z_1. The policy change we are to consider here is an increase in this tariff of up to level T_2.

The supply and demand curves in figure 1 are linear, that is, they can be expressed in the form of

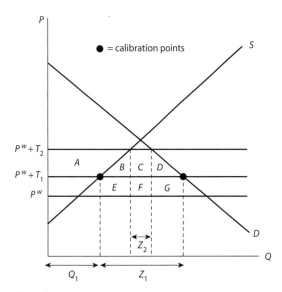

Figure 1

A small-country, perfect-substitutes model

$Q = a + bP$. However, it is also common to use a constant elasticity functional form, in which case the curves are expressed as $\ln Q = c + d \ln P$, where "ln" denotes the natural logarithm. In the former case, the price elasticities of demand and supply vary along the curves, while in the latter case, they are constant and equal to d.

The increase in the tariff level raises the domestic price to $P^w + T_2$ and reduces imports to Z_2. Consumer surplus (a measure of household welfare) falls by area $A + B + C + D$, and producer surplus (a measure of firm welfare) increases by area A. The government gains tariff revenue due to the increase of the tariff of area C but also loses tariff revenue due to the reduction in imports of areas E and G. Area F is collected as tariff revenue both before and after the increase in the tariff. The net result of all these changes is that welfare as conventionally measured declines by $B + D + E + G$. Note also that the increase in domestic output from Q_1 along the supply curve can be easily translated into an increase in employment using a fixed employment-output ratio and that this change is often of key political interest.

Calibrating this simple model involves the same three elements that are used in more complex models: functional forms, initial values, and elasticities. In the present context, the functional forms are those of the supply and demand curves (either linear or constant elasticity) and the elasticities are those related to these functions. The elasticities are estimated prior to applying the model. With regard to initial values, the calibration can be made easier by defining the initial domestic price ($P^w + T_1$) to be unity. Then the sum of the border value of the initial imports plus the initial tariff revenue gives the quantity Z_1, and the value of domestic output give the quantity Q_1. Q_1 determines the calibration point along the supply curve, and $Q_1 + Z_1$ determines the calibration point along the demand curve. This way of defining units is typical of applied trade policy models.

Imperfect Substitutes Model We next consider an imperfect substitutes model in the "large" country case, allowing for terms of trade effects. This model is presented in figure 2. The important difference between figures 1 and 2 is that, in the imperfect substitutes framework of the latter, there are now *two* closely related markets, one for the imported good Z and another for the domestic competing good D. The demand curves in these two markets are related through the cross-price elasticity of demand (or alternatively the elasticity of substitution) between the two goods. The initial equilibrium in the absence of a tariff results in the two prices P_{Z1} and P_{D1}. The imposition of a specific tariff T on imports of good Z causes the supply curve of this good to shift upward by the amount of the tariff, raising the domestic price of the imported good along the demand curve. The increase in the price of good Z affects the demand for good D, shifting the curve out as households substitute toward the domestic good. This increases the domestic price of good D and in turn causes a substitution toward good Z and a shift out of the demand curve for imports. These two substitution effects are simultaneous, and the resulting, new prices are P_{Z2} and P_{D2}.

We next consider the welfare effects of the tariff in this imperfect substitutes framework. In the market for the domestic good, there is an increase in producer surplus along the supply curve equal to trapezoid H (extending from the vertical price axis all the

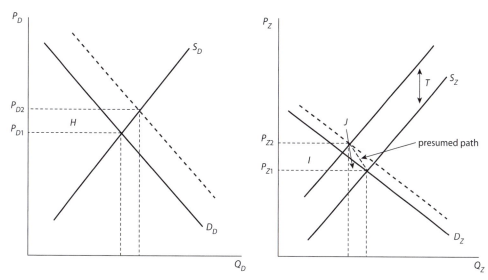

Figure 2
A large-country, imperfect-substitutes model

way to the supply curve). This entire area, however, comes as a cost to the consumers, with the producer gain and the consumer loss exactly offsetting each other. In the market of the imported good, there are no domestic producers to account for. However, the estimation of the consumer welfare effect is troubled by the fact that both the supply curve and the demand curve in the market for good Z have shifted. The standard approach to this, introduced by analysts such as Morkre and Tarr (1980), is to measure the change in consumer surplus along the presumed path between the initial and final equilibria points. The resulting consumer surplus loss is the trapezoid $I+J$. Rectangle I represents an increase in tariff revenue, so the net welfare effect in figure 2 is just triangle J.

One important aspect of figure 2 is that, discounting for the effect of the shift of the demand curve, the rise in the domestic price of the imported good is less than the tariff. This is because there is a movement in world quantity supplied down S_Z and a resulting decline in the border price of the imported good. This terms-of-trade effect of the tariff is missing in figure 1. The terms-of-trade effect has the property of reducing the height of the net welfare triangle J and is present unless the import supply

curve S_Z is horizontal or infinitely elastic, putting us back into a "small" country case.

As in the perfect substitutes model, the increase in domestic output along S_D can be easily translated into an increase in employment using a fixed employment-output ratio, and calibration to the initial equilibria points can be made easier by defining the initial domestic prices of the imported and domestic goods to be unity.

Partial equilibrium modeling of trade policy changes will continue to be an important analytical tool for situations where the linkages of the trade policy change to the broader economy under consideration are weak. Despite some complications in the imperfect substitutes case, the models are relatively easy to implement in spreadsheet form and are widely used by trade policy analysts.

See also applied general equilibrium models; gravity models; quotas; tariffs

FURTHER READING

Anderson, Kym. 1992. "The Standard Welfare Economics of Policies Affecting Trade and the Environment." In *The Greening of World Trade Issues*, edited by Kym Anderson and Richard Blackhurst. Ann Arbor, Michigan:

University of Michigan Press, 25–48. A noted application of partial equilibrium modeling to the issue of trade and the environment.

Armington, Paul. 1969. "A Theory of Demand for Products Distinguished by Place of Production." *IMF Staff Papers* 16 (3): 159–76. The key contribution on product differentiation by country of origin used in partial equilibrium trade policy modeling.

Baldwin, Robert E., and Tracy Murray. 1977. "MFN Tariff Reductions and Developing Country Trade under the GSP." *Economic Journal* 87 (345): 30–46. An early application of partial equilibrium trade policy modeling applied to the General System of Preferences using the imperfect substitutes model.

Francois, Joseph F., and H. Keith Hall. 1997. "Partial Equilibrium Modeling." In *Applied Methods for Trade Policy Analysis: A Handbook*, edited by Joseph F. Francois and Kenneth A. Reinert. Cambridge: Cambridge University Press, 122–55. A more advanced introduction to partial equilibrium trade policy modeling.

Morkre, Morris E., and David G. Tarr. 1980. *Effects of Restrictions on United States Imports: Five Case Studies and Theory.* Washington, DC: United States Federal Trade Commission. An early application of the imperfect substitutes model to U.S. trade policy.

Reinert, Kenneth A., and David W. Roland-Holst. 1992. "Armington Elasticities for United States Manufacturing Sectors." *Journal of Policy Modeling* 4 (2): 631–39. The first estimation of elasticities of substitution between imported and domestic competing goods.

Roningen, Vernon O. 1997. "Multimarket, Multiregion Partial Equilibrium Modeling." In *Applied Methods for Trade Policy Analysis: A Handbook*, edited by Joseph F. Francois and Kenneth A. Reinert. Cambridge: Cambridge University Press, 231–99. An introduction to the extension of partial equilibrium trade policy modeling to multiple markets and multiple regions.

Rouslang, Donald J., and John W. Suomela. 1988. "Calculating the Welfare Costs of Import Restrictions in the Imperfect Substitutes Model." *Applied Economics* 20 (5): 691–700. An often cited study using the imperfect substitutes version of the partial equilibrium model.

KENNETH A. REINERT AND JOSEPH F. FRANCOIS

■ **patents**
See Agreement on Trade-Related Aspects of Intellectual Property Rights (TRIPS); intellectual property rights

■ **peso problem**
The term *peso problem* generically refers to situations in which the possibility of a significant change in the distribution of future shocks to the economy influences the expectations of economic agents. The interaction of expectations and shifts in the distribution of economic shocks can lead to behavior in the prices of assets such as stocks and foreign exchange that is not in accord with the predictions of standard economic theory.

The precise origin of the term is uncertain, but is often attributed to comments made by Milton Friedman regarding the Mexican peso in the early 1970s. At that time, the Mexican peso traded at a fixed rate against the U.S. dollar while the interest rate on Mexican bank deposits exceeded that on comparable U.S. deposits. The existence of such an opportunity to earn a profit with little or no risk might appear to present a problem for rational-agent-based models of financial markets. Such an interest differential would fail to be arbitraged away, however, if investors thought that the peso would be devalued in the future. Indeed, in August 1976, the peso was allowed to float against the dollar and subsequently declined in value.

Peso Problems and Forecasts The peso problem is intimately related to economic forecasting. Good forecasts of future events have two important properties: they are unbiased, meaning that forecast errors are zero on average, and forecast errors are themselves unpredictable. Forecasting models are typically constructed and tested with historical data that are assumed to accurately represent the statistical distribution of the variables under consideration. When the statistical distribution is invariant over time, historical data can be used to assess the likelihood of future outcomes and generate forecasts with good properties. If the distribution of outcomes is shifting over time, however, then forecasts that are conditioned on historical data may be biased or have predictable forecast errors because the historical data may not give an accurate representation of the changing statistical distribution.

Peso problems may occur when an economy faces this sort of instability. The use of historical data to predict the future becomes more difficult if the likelihood of future outcomes differs significantly from what was observed in the past. For example, wars and severe political turmoil are extremely hard to predict and may lead to significant changes in the economic environment. If economic agents believe there is a large enough possibility that such infrequent events might occur, there can be a significant impact on forecasts and forecast errors. To an outside observer, it may then appear that forecasters are making persistent errors, even though forecasters are using best practices in conditioning on such infrequent and hard-to-predict events.

Technically, peso problems can be interpreted as a failure of the methodology of rational expectations econometrics (Evans 1996). Rational expectations econometrics requires that the actual, or objective, distribution of economic variables be equal to the distribution expected by economic agents when they make decisions. The expected distribution may put weight on events that subsequently fail to be realized, and so may not be accurately represented in the ex post distribution. Under such circumstances, the predictions of rational expectations models may appear to be at variance with the data.

The Forward Premium Puzzle The forward premium puzzle is an asset-pricing anomaly that has lent itself to a peso problem interpretation. The foreign exchange market allows individuals to purchase forward contracts on currencies. A forward contract is an agreement to buy or sell a currency on a future date for a specified price called the forward rate. Consequently, the forward rate embodies investors' beliefs about the future value of the spot rate, which is the price at which a currency can be bought or sold for immediate delivery. The forward rate would thus seem to be a good predictor of the future spot rate on the date that the forward contract matures. A large amount of evidence indicates that the forward rate is not an unbiased predictor of the future spot rate, however. Under a peso problem interpretation, the bias, which is a tendency for the forward rate to stay above or below the spot rate for extended periods of time, could be due to investors' perceptions that there is a chance that the exchange rate will change substantially. If so, and until the exchange rate actually does shift, the forward rate will remain persistently above or below the spot exchange rate. Such a peso problem explanation of the forward premium puzzle has some validity in the data (Evans and Lewis 1995).

Stock Market Returns and Peso Problems Historically, the U.S. stock market has performed well relative to the stock markets of other industrialized nations. The historical, real return on U.S. equities is about 4.7 percent compared with a median return of about 1.5 percent for a sample of 39 countries (see Jorion and Goetzmann 1999). Peso problems offer one potential explanation for the large relative return. Investors must be rewarded for taking risks. Risk-averse stock market investors will demand a high return on equities in normal times to compensate them for the risk of extreme losses in bad times. But for the United States, extreme bad outcomes have largely bypassed the stock market. For example, unlike the stock markets of France, Russia, Germany, and Japan, the operation of the U.S. stock market was not interrupted for significant stretches of time by war. Nonetheless, stock market investors presumably attached some positive probability to a severe market disruption and factored that in to the returns they require to make their investments worthwhile. Since such a U.S. market disruption has not occurred, actual historical returns on equities have not reflected it. Thus the large realized U.S. equity return may be tied to investors' assessment of the possibility of extreme outcomes that never actually materialized for the U.S. economy.

Models Peso problems clearly present a difficulty for estimating and evaluating economic models. Good models require that events are realized often enough in historical data samples that researchers can accurately determine their probabilities of occurrence. In the context of peso problems, this requires that infrequent events be observed often enough in the data for scholars to accurately assess the likelihood of repeated occurrence. One methodology that has been applied with some success to cases in which the distribution of outcomes shifts over time is the Markov regime-switching model (see Hamilton 1989). This model assumes that the economy can be in one of several distinct regimes and that regime switches are stochastic. That is, they change in a random fashion over time. If regime switches are observed to occur often enough in the historical data, researchers can estimate the probability of being in a particular regime and incorporate that information into the structure of economic models. This framework has had some success in modeling expectations of a possible future change in the economic environment that can in turn have implications for the behavior of asset prices.

See also capital mobility; exchange rate forecasting; foreign exchange intervention; forward premium puzzle; interest parity conditions; sovereign risk

FURTHER READING

Evans, Martin D. D. 1996. "Peso Problems: Their Theoretical and Empirical Implications." In *Statistical Methods in Finance*, edited by G. S. Maddala and C. R. Rao. Amsterdam: Elsevier, 613–46.

Evans, Martin D. D., and Karen Lewis. 1995. "Do Long-Term Swings in the Dollar Affect Estimates of the Risk Premia?" *Review of Financial Studies* 8: 709–42. Both this and the preceding work by Evans study the ways in which peso problems can affect inference about foreign exchange risk premiums.

Hamilton, James D. 1989. "A New Approach to the Economic Analysis of Nonstationary Time Series and the Business Cycle." *Econometrica* 57: 357–84. Develops a methodology for incorporating Markov regime switching into models of economic time series. The technique has since been used in many papers that formally analyze peso problems.

Jorion, Philippe, and William Goetzmann. 1999. "Global Stock Markets in the Twentieth Century." *Journal of Finance* 54: 953–80. Collects data on equity returns for 39 markets going back to the 1920s and shows that U.S. equities had the highest returns of all countries over 1921 to 1996.

Sill, Keith. 2000. "Understanding Asset Values: Stock Prices, Exchange Rates, and the 'Peso Problem.'" *Federal Reserve Bank of Philadelphia Business Review* (September/October): 3–13. An introduction to how peso problems can affect the relationship between economic models and data.

KEITH SILL

■ petrodollars, recycling of

Recycling of petrodollars refers to what becomes of revenues earned by oil-exporting countries, particularly after major oil price shocks. Countries may spend some portion on foreign goods and services, but typically the increases in oil revenues following price shocks have been so large that oil exporters have been unable to absorb these petrodollars into their domestic economies either through consumption or through investment. Instead, petrodollars usually get recycled in the form of foreign asset savings held abroad. Such foreign assets may range from deposits held in foreign banks to bonds and private equity.

The most significant oil price shock followed the 1973 oil embargo imposed on the United States by the Organization of the Petroleum Exporting Countries (OPEC), but petrodollar recycling was one result of a steady increase in oil prices from 2002 to 2005. Oil prices reached an average $53 per barrel in 2005, more than twice their level just three years before. As a result, for a significant group of oil-exporting countries, oil export revenue rose from $262 billion in 2002 to an estimated $614 billion in 2005. These revenues in turn were invested in foreign assets, making oil exporters important counterparts to the United States in the ownership of foreign savings. In 2005 their current account surplus represented nearly 40 percent of the U.S. current account deficit.

What has the impact been and what is the impact likely to be of petrodollar recycling on global financial imbalances? If energy exporters spend their oil revenue, part of the petrodollar inflows would flow out again to pay for imports of goods and services, boosting the economies of the industrialized oil-importing countries from which the petrodollars originated. This process would serve as a counter-vailing force to the oil price shock, rebalancing some portion of global imbalances. If, on the other hand, oil exporters save their revenue, this would exacerbate global imbalances by draining resources away from investment or consumption in the oil-importing world, in turn reducing growth and employment. To the extent that oil-exporting countries deposit their petrodollars in U.S. banks, however, this would mitigate the dampening effect. This is precisely what happened in the aftermath of 1973. But as we shall see, the real legacy of petrodollar recycling in the 1970s was not global financial imbalance but a third-world debt crisis.

Oil Shock of 1973 The oil shock of 1973–74 scaled up the size of postwar global economic imbalances by an order of magnitude and gave rise to widespread fears of a depression similar to the Great Depression of the 1930s. This episode gives important insights into issues of collective action problems, the resilience of international financial markets, and the uses and limitations of exchange rate adjustments.

The shock was generated by the large rise in oil prices following the oil embargo imposed against the United States in retaliation for its support of Israel in the Yom Kippur War of 1973. Because of the low price sensitivity of the demand for oil over the short and medium terms, this resulted in a significant increase in revenues for the oil-exporting countries. Combined with limitations on the speed with which the oil-exporting countries could increase their expenditures on imports (limitations of the capacities of their ports was a major initial bottleneck) and the fact that oil bills were paid primarily in dollars, this resulted in massive inflows of dollar reserves to oil-exporting countries, particularly in the Middle East.

The economies of the oil-importing countries were subject to three sets of pressures. Consumer prices rose while purchasing power drained away. For many oil-importing economies, the resulting stagflationary effects—rising inflation combined with reduced growth and employment—were on the order of several percentage points of gross domestic product. On top of this, large current account deficits could cause severe balance of payments problems.

It soon became clear that in the aggregate there would not be a balance of payments problem corresponding to the huge current account imbalances. Had the world still been on a gold standard the situation would indeed have been dire since these imbalances would have drained gold out of the oil-importing countries, forcing monetary contraction and magnifying the initial recessionary effects of the oil price increases. Indeed, under the rules of the gold standard, the oil shock would have generated a new Great Depression.

Gold convertibility no longer existed, however, so the oil-exporting countries had to hold non-interest-bearing foreign currencies or, more reasonably, invest the surplus back into oil-importing countries through banks that accepted dollar deposits, primarily in Europe. Thus, in the aggregate, the oil surpluses created a financing glut instead of a financing shortage. In effect, the oil exporters recycled the funds by making very large deposits, which swelled the supply of loanable funds, forcing banks to offer extremely low-interest loans to any reasonable taker.

This in turn caused serious problems. Oil-importing countries with strong financial markets, such as the United Kingdom and the United States, began to run overall payment surpluses as the oil-related investment inflows exceeded their increased oil payments. As a result, there was an urgent need for secondary recycling of the petrodollars (as these surplus investment funds were called) more in line with the patterns of current account deficits.

Some of this alignment was accomplished by foreign aid from the oil exporters and some from a special recycling facility set up by the International Monetary Fund (IMF) in cooperation with oil-exporting nations. The oil exporters placed funds directly with the IMF that the IMF, in turn, then re-lent to oil-importing countries. The bulk of recycling took place through the international banking and financial sectors, however: a substantial amount of the funds placed in the major financial centers (including the Eurodollar market) were re-lent mostly to newly industrializing countries (NICs) in Latin America and Asia.

Global Savings Glut Because of the sudden deposit glut, banks were eager to re-lend funds. The demand for loans within advanced industrial countries had slowed considerably due to recessionary conditions following the oil crisis. Banks saw the opportunity for big profits in loans to oil-exporting NICs, however, as oil prices had nearly quadrupled, making these countries appear to be good risks. Moreover, banks were attracted to the Latin American market, where authoritarian governments were standing ready to accept and guarantee repayment of private bank loans. Banks operated on the principle that sovereign loans carried very little risk of default compared with private sector loans. This was assumed true even for the oil-importing NICs, which also benefited from large loan packages.

Of course, Latin American countries exhibited considerable eagerness to borrow. Having reached the end of what scholars have referred to as "the easy phase" of import-substituting industrialization, Latin American NICs required new infusions of capital to maintain high growth rates. This process of borrowing to maintain high growth rates became known as debt-led growth. Moreover, the majority of Latin American NICs were governed by bureaucratic authoritarian regimes whose legitimacy hinged on their ability to continue delivering rapid industrial growth. To these regimes, the ability to borrow from private banks and thus bypass IMF conditionality was simply a bonus. But perhaps Latin American NICs' greatest incentive to borrow grew out of financial market conditions. Inflation had skyrocketed after the 1973 oil price hikes while nominal interest rates had leveled off and even fallen in some cases due to the credit glut. Together these phenomena resulted in extremely low and even negative real interest rates. Quite literally, for a time, banks were paying Latin American governments to take their money.

Another concern with respect to global financial imbalances after the oil shock was that instead of borrowing to finance their current account deficits,

countries would want to adjust their payments imbalances. But in the aggregate this was not possible in the short and medium term. Devaluations by all oil-importing countries would in effect raise the real price of oil, and because of the short-term inelasticity of demand for oil such actions would increase rather than reduce the aggregate current account imbalances.

For individual countries, however, devaluation would work by increasing their exports to, and reducing their imports from, other oil-importing countries. This process could work only if it were not practiced by too many other countries. This collective action problem was quite similar to the one countries faced during the Great Depression. Any one country could stimulate its domestic economy by increasing exports and reducing imports, but if all countries followed this strategy, the result would worsen the economic situation for everyone. In the 1930s, the combination of understanding of this problem and willingness to cooperate internationally was insufficient to avoid economic catastrophe.

Avoiding Beggar-Thy-Neighbor Policies Another Great Depression, therefore, was a realistic concern in the 1970s. Fortunately both the economic understanding of government officials and willingness to pay some attention to the international repercussions of national actions had developed sufficiently so that with valiant efforts from international organizations such as the IMF and the Organisation for Economic Co-operation and Development a repeat of the widespread beggar-thy-neighbor problems of the 1930s was avoided. Of course, cooperation was far from complete and many countries were criticized for not taking what was considered by others to be their fair share of the collective oil deficits (numerous calculations of "fair shares" were undertaken by various economists and organizations), but overall the initial handling of the oil shock was much better than could have been realistically hoped for.

Indeed, the international pressure to avoid overadjustments in the form of reduced spending and economic contraction following the oil shocks was so successful that over the medium term many developing countries did not adjust enough, continuing to rely for too long on heavy amounts of borrowing. This, in turn, was one of the major contributing factors to the Latin American debt crisis of the 1980s. Nevertheless, the overall success in avoiding a repeat of the economic catastrophes of the 1930s was a major tribute to the growth of international cooperation and set the basis for dealing with several subsequent major run-ups in oil prices.

See also balance of payments; beggar-thy-neighbor policies; convertibility; Eurocurrencies; expenditure changing and expenditure switching; global imbalances; gold standard, international; International Monetary Fund (IMF); International Monetary Fund conditionality; international reserves; Latin American debt crisis; petroleum; twin deficits

FURTHER READING

Nsouli, Saleh. 2006. "Petrodollar Recycling and Global Imbalances." Presented at the CESifo's International Spring Conference. Berlin: Center for Economic Studies, Information and Forschung Institute (March 23–24). Downloadable from http://www.imf.org/external/np/speeches/2006/032306a.html. A useful analysis of petrodollar recycling in the new millennium.

Willett, Thomas D. 1995. "The Oil Transfer Problem and International Economic Stability." Princeton Essays in International Finance No. 113 (December). Princeton, NJ: Princeton University. Provides a more detailed treatment of the 1973 oil shock and its international financial repercussions.

**THOMAS D. WILLETT AND
NANCY NEIMAN AUERBACH**

■ petroleum

The world petroleum sector includes the exploration, extraction, and transportation of crude oil, and the refining of crude oil into finished products. Participants in the world petroleum sector include fully integrated oil companies, national oil companies, independent oil and gas producers, refiners and marketers, pipeline operators, and others. The fully integrated companies explore for and produce oil and gas around the world, own pipelines and tankers to transport oil and gas, process the crude oil into refined products, and sell finished products through a global network of wholesale and retail outlets. Typical fully integrated companies are often international oil companies (IOC) such as Exxon Mobil Corporation, BP, Chevron Texaco, ConocoPhillips, and Royal Dutch/Shell. In contrast to IOCs, national oil companies are owned by national governments and are typically found in major oil-producing nations. Independent oil and gas producers only explore and/or produce crude oil and natural gas. Independent refiners purchase crude oil and process it into finished products. These companies may also own wholesale and retail marketing outlets or sell their products to marketing companies. Independent marketers purchase refined products, usually gasoline, and sell them at retail outlets. Pipeline companies transport crude oil, refined products, natural gas and natural gas liquids using networks of pipes and pumping or compressor stations.

Oil and natural gas provide nearly 60 percent of the world's primary energy and will remain indispensible in meeting the projected growth in energy demand during the early decades of the 21st century. The rapidly growing world economy will require large increases in oil, which will come from a variety of sources, including existing production capacities, development of existing reserves, new discoveries, and development of nonconventional liquids. Yet there is uncertainty about the industry's ability to overcome the multiple increasing risks of meeting the growing demand for oil. Such risks include gaining access to promising resources, making investment in infrastructure, and determining how much oil is recoverable.

Oil Demand Between 1960 and 1972, world consumption of oil increased by one and one-half times, about 7 percent on average per year. In turn, the world's industries, including transportation and commerce, and individual households became increasingly dependent on oil. In the years immediately following the Arab oil embargo in 1973 and the subsequent shock in 1979, world demand for oil greatly diminished. From 1980 to 2000, the annual growth in world oil demand averaged 0.9 percent.

The average growth in world oil demand for the future is expected to be much greater than in the past. Between 2000 and 2030, oil demand is projected to increase at an annual rate of from 1 percent to 1.9 percent. World demand for oil is expected to grow from about 76 million barrels per day in 2000 to between 98 and 138 million barrels per day in 2030. On a global basis, the transportation sector accounts for 68 percent of the total projected increase in oil consumption between 2004 and 2030, followed by the industrial sector, which accounts for another 27 percent of the increased consumption (Energy Information Administration, *International Energy Outlook, 2007*).

The largest increases in oil consumption from 2004 to 2030 are projected to be 7 million barrels per day in North America and 15 million barrels per day in Asian countries that do not belong to the Organisation for Economic Co-operation and Development (OECD). It is projected that non-OECD countries' oil consumption will continue to grow, driven by strong economic and industrial growth and rapidly expanding transportation use. It is further estimated that the fastest growth in oil consumption will occur in non-OECD Asia, averaging 2.7 percent per year from 2004 to 2030. Non-OECD Asia accounts for 43 percent of the overall increase in world liquids consumption (Energy Information Administration, *International Energy Outlook 2007*).

Prices Historically, world oil prices were low and stable in the 1950s and 1960s, driven by new discoveries in the Middle East, the North Sea, Alaska, and Nigeria. Cheap oil thus contributed to strong worldwide economic growth, which in turn stimulated greater consumption. With the first oil shock in 1973, prices increased fourfold, and in 1979, prices increased by another threefold. Prices thereafter declined haltingly and gradually until 1986 and then collapsed until late 1992. From 1992 to the beginning of 2007, oil prices increased fivefold.

Future projections of world oil prices, in constant 2006 dollars, have been projected by the U.S. Energy Information Administration (EIA) to decline from $68 per barrel in 2006 to $49 per barrel in 2014, then rise to $59 per barrel in 2030 ($95 per barrel on a nominal, noninflation-adjusted basis). The EIA low- and high-price cases suggest great uncertainties in the reference case projections, however. In the low-price case, world oil prices are projected to be $36 per barrel in 2030 ($58 per barrel on a nominal basis), while in the high-price case, oil prices are estimated to be $100 per barrel in 2030 ($157 per barrel on a nominal basis).

Production Oil production is projected to increase by 35 million barrels per day in 2030 over 2004 levels. To meet the demand for oil, production is expected to increase in both the Organization of the Petroleum Exporting Countries (OPEC) and non-OPEC producers, with most (65 percent) of the total increase coming from OPEC countries.

It is generally acknowledged that OPEC members with large reserves and relatively low costs for expanding production capacity can accommodate sizable increases in the world's petroleum consumption. Geopolitical issues in a number of the OPEC countries, including Iraq, Iran, Venezuela, and Nigeria, lead to great uncertainty in making projections of future production levels. Projections of Iraq's future oil production are well below its prewar production.

Reserves and Resources As of January 1, 2007, "proved" world oil reserves were estimated at 1,208 billion barrels. Proved reserves are estimates of the amount of oil recoverable from known reservoirs under current economic and operating conditions. Proved reserves reflect only a fraction of the oil that a reservoir may hold. "Recoverable" oil includes proved reserves and undiscovered oil that is economically extractable.

Reserves are concentrated in the Middle East and North Africa (MENA), together accounting for 62 percent of the world total. Saudi Arabia, with the largest reserves of any country, holds about a fifth of the world's total reserves. Of the twenty countries with the largest reserves, seven are in the MENA region. Iranian oil reserves have increased by 46.6 billion barrels, or 52 percent, since 2000. Kazakhstan has had the third-largest increase, 24.6 billion barrels, since 2000. Among the top 20 reserve holders in

2007, 11 are OPEC member countries that, together, account for 65 percent of the world's total reserves.

The United States Geological Survey (USGS) mean estimate of ultimately recoverable global conventional oil plus natural gas liquids (NGL) was 3.345 trillion barrels at the beginning of 1996. The estimates range from 2.5 to 4.4 trillion barrels, expressed in statistical terms, where 2.5 trillion barrels represents a 95 percent probability that the quantity size will exceed the estimate, and 4.4 trillion barrels indicates a 5 percent probability that the quantity will exceed the estimate. By comparison, IOCs project an average of 3.5 trillion barrels. The IOC most-likely estimates for ultimately recoverable global conventional oil range from 2.8 to 4.0 trillion barrels.

The uncertainty of ultimate recoverable oil and NGL has led to a continuing debate about the prospect of a future oil production peak and eventual decline. The timing of a peak and subsequent decline is subject to interpretation because of a number of variables, such as lack of transparent reporting of producing fields, conflicting estimates of recoverable oil, the increased costs of producing oil from conventional and nonconventional sources, and the timing and scale of development of alternative fuels.

Oil Companies State-owned, or national, oil companies control most of the global proved oil reserves. As of 2005, the global proved oil reserves were 1.148 trillion barrels, with national oil companies (NOCs) in control of 77 percent of the total (886 billion barrels) and allowing no private equity ownership. According to an 2005 annual survey published by *Petroleum Intelligence Weekly*, 12 of the top 20 oil companies are traditional (100 percent state-owned) national oil companies (NOCs) or hybrid, partly state-owned NOCs. *Petroleum Intelligence Weekly*'s ranking shows that Saudi Aramco, Iran's NIOC, Iraq's INOC, Kuwait's KPC, Venezuela's PDVSA, United Arab Emirates' Adnoc, Libya's NOC, and Nigeria's NNPC hold the largest reserves in the world.

National oil companies' objectives often differ greatly from those of the privately owned international oil companies. The NOC objectives go beyond maximizing returns on investments, and often include redistribution of wealth in society, foreign policy objectives, energy security, wealth creation, and economic development. The NOCs' noncommercial objectives tend to interfere with decisions regarding investments in oil production expansion. However, not all NOCs have the same interests. In more mature NOCs, such as Statoil (Norway) and Petronas (Malaysia), the focus is on returns on investment, and the companies exhibit more familiar corporate behavior. At the opposite extreme, the business practices of PDVSA (Venezuela) and NNPC (Nigeria) are heavily influenced by domestic policies. These firms are focused squarely on increasing the revenues to the government. Saudi Arabia has used its oil reserves in its foreign policy strategy, given its role as the world's oil swing producer. In its role as having the largest spare crude oil production capacity in the world, Saudi Arabia has the ability to replace the exports of any small- or medium-sized oil-producing country with days or weeks.

Investment The International Energy Agency estimates that over the period of 2005–2030 $4.3 trillion in new investments will be needed in the global oil sector to meet rising world demand for oil. The largest investment projections are in the Middle East and developing Asia, where most of the upstream (exploration and production) and downstream (refineries, pipelines, tankers) investments will be needed. The upstream sector accounts for the bulk of this investment requirement, with required investments averaging $125 billion per year. Almost three-quarters of the upstream investments will be required to maintain existing production capacity in the face of declining capacity of existing oil wells as reserves are depleted. Downstream investment requirements are projected to be about $700 billion from 2005 to 2030. This projection includes the addition of new refineries to meet the rising demand and additional investments on existing refineries.

There is no guarantee that the projected levels of investment will actually occur, as several barriers exist to upstream and downstream investments. First, most privately owned IOCs have large cash reserves and are able to borrow at reasonable rates from capital markets when necessary for new projects. Because of restrictions on access to oil reserves in many resource-rich countries, however, many IOCs may not be able to invest in upstream development. A large portion of oil reserves are found in countries where there are restrictions on foreign investment. Kuwait, Mexico, and Saudi Arabia, for example, remain totally closed to upstream oil investment by foreign companies. Other major oil-producing countries, such as Venezuela, Russia, Iran, Algeria, and Qatar, have effectively restricted foreign investment as well. Second, even in those cases where IOCs are willing to invest, other barriers such as licensing and fiscal terms, or the investment climate, may discourage them from doing so. Stability of the political regime, war or civil conflict, or other geopolitical tensions act to dissuade inward investment in the development of countries' resources.

See also Organization of the Petroleum Exporting Countries (OPEC); petrodollars, recycling of

FURTHER READING

Baker Institute for Public Policy. 2007. "The Changing Role of National Oil Companies in International Energy Markets." March. Houston, TX: Baker Institute. Provides a review of the strategies, objectives, and performance of national oil companies.

BP Statistical Review of World Energy. 2007. http://www.bp.com/liveassets/bp_internet/globalbp/globalbp_uk_english/reports_and_publications/statistical_energy_review_2007/STAGING/local_assets/downloads/pdf/statistical_review_of_world_energy_full_report_2007.pdf. June. Authoritative source of data related to demand and production of oil and natural gas by region and country.

Energy Information Administration. 2007. *International Energy Outlook 2007*. Washington, DC: EIA. Provides an assessment of the outlook for international energy markets through 2030.

International Energy Agency. 2006. *World Energy Outlook 2006*. Paris: OECD/IEA. Provides an assessment of the outlook for international energy markets and additional insights into the most critical energy issues.

National Petroleum Council. 2007. *Hard Truths—Facing the Hard Truths about Energy*. Washington, DC: NPC.

Evaluates the ability of global oil and natural gas supply to keep pace with growing world demand.

Simmons, Matthew R. 2005. *Twilight in the Desert—The Coming Saudi Oil Shock and the World Economy*. New York: Wiley. Analyzes Saudi Arabia's oil exploration and production industry and whether it will be able to continue in a swing producer role in the coming decades.

Yergin, Daniel. 1991. *The Prize—The Epic Quest for Oil, Money, and Power*. New York: Simon and Schuster. Tells the history of oil and how it has shaped the politics and the global economy.

MICHAEL R. CURTIS

■ pharmaceuticals

The pharmaceutical industry provides an important part of fundamental health care to the citizens of any given nation. Besides its social value, the industry is also important in economic terms—its innovative capabilities contribute significantly to the knowledge and skills-based economy of advanced industrialized nations. Since the 1970s, the pharmaceutical industry has experienced considerable structural change. Government regulation continues to play a significant role in the industry, as does the drug discovery process and the cost of bringing a new drug to market.

Government Regulation The majority of new drugs are developed within the United States, the European Union (EU), and Japan, where the agencies responsible for their approval are the Food and Drug Administration; the European Medicines Agency (EMEA); and the Ministry of Health, Labor, and Welfare, respectively. Within the EU, marketing authorizations can be granted by either the EMEA or individual member states. If the product is derived from biotechnology, a firm must use the centralized system of the EMEA. Otherwise, if the firm chooses the national route, the procedure of mutual recognition, in which a product that has been judged safe for sale in one member state will be sold in all other member states, is adopted.

Although government regulation has increased to ensure the efficacy and safety of new drugs, important steps have also been taken toward increased international harmonization. The EU, for example, developed a single market for pharmaceuticals, culminating in the formation of the EMEA. In addition, the International Conference on Harmonization (ICH) was set up in 1990 to bring together regulatory authorities and drug developers from the EU, the United States, and Japan to attempt to eliminate duplicative requirements for drug development and approval. Since its inception, ICH has achieved the harmonization of technical guidelines and, more recently, of the format and content of registration applications.

Variations in pharmaceutical pricing, however, remain extreme due to the many differences in national health care systems. In Japan and the EU member states, the government is the main purchaser, and indeed, parallel trade (estimated at 4.2 billion euros in 2005) is allowed under the single-market rules. Thus third parties exploit price differences by buying pharmaceuticals in markets where low prices are enforced and selling them to governments and other purchasers in markets where higher prices have been agreed. In the United States, although the government is not the main purchaser, the rapid expansion of health care maintenance organizations has led to a concentration of purchasing power.

The only major national markets in which firms are free to set the price of new drugs are the United States, the United Kingdom, and Germany (since 2005), but soaring health care costs in advanced industrialized nations have led to tougher price competition. Governments and other purchasers have reduced reimbursement rates, increased the use of "limited lists" (which define drugs that may be prescribed and/or reimbursed for different diseases), and placed pressure on prescribers to substitute generics for branded drugs wherever possible. For example, the generic market grew by 13 percent in the eight largest national markets in 2005, compared to around 5 percent for "branded" pharmaceuticals, and generic prescription volume was greater than branded volume for the first time ever in the United States.

Drug Discovery Process At the end of World War II, the pharmaceutical industry experienced a radical shift from very little new drug development toward a research-oriented environment in which firms essentially screened thousands of chemical compounds for efficacy against a given disease (so-called random screening). Serendipity mattered: the mechanisms of how drugs worked were not well understood, and firms correspondingly maintained huge libraries of chemical compounds. As basic biomedical knowledge increased in the 1970s, a second technological shift occurred: "rational drug design" was adopted, which involved more precise models of how particular diseases function and the design of molecules that target particular cells or cause particular biological interactions. Since the 1980s, biologics (derived from biotechnologies) constitute the third shift and provide a crucial arena for the development of new drugs in the 21st century. Approximately 20 percent of new drugs launched on the world market are biotechnology derived, and biologic sales were $52.7 billion in 2005. The United States was the single most important national market in 2005 in terms of research and development (R&D) expenditure (78 percent) and turnover (76 percent), with approximately 140,000 employees as compared with Europe's 33,000.

Over time, the average cost of developing a new drug has increased substantially. The cost was estimated at $897 million in 2003, compared with $500 million in the 1990s and $231 million in 1987. This compares with the first ever estimate of the average cost of developing a new biologic, which was estimated to be $1.2 billion in 2006, reflecting both the cost of time and the drugs that fail (Tufts Center for the Study of Drug Development). This increased cost is primarily due to the increasing focus on chronic rather than acute illnesses as populations age (i.e., targeted diseases such as Alzheimer's are more "complex," and the cost of R&D varies across therapeutic groups), tougher governmental regulations that have lengthened development times and increased the number of clinical trials, and finally, the need to convince prescribers that the new drug has significant benefits as compared with rival pharmaceuticals on the market.

Table 1
Top 20 global market shares and R&D expenditure

	2005				1998		1992	
	Sales ($bn)	Market share (%)	R&D ($bn)	Top-selling drugs ($bn)	Market share (%)	R&D ($bn)	Market share (%)	R&D ($bn)
Pfizer (US)	44.3	7.4	7.4	Lipitor: 12.2 Norvasc: 4.7 Zoloft: 3.3	3.9	2.3	2.0	0.8
GlaxoSmithKline (UK)	34.0	5.6	5.7	Advair: 5.5 Avandia: 2.1 Lamictal: 1.5	4.2	1.9	3.8	1.0
Sanofi Aventis (Fr)	33.9	5.6	5.0	Lovenox: 2.7 Plavix: 2.5 Taxotere: 1.9	2.5	1.4	2.6	0.8
Novartis (Ch)	25.0	4.2	4.4	Diovan: 3.7 Gleevec: 2.2 Zometa: 1.2	4.2	1.8	2.2	0.8
Astra-Zeneca (UK)	24.0	4.0	3.4	Nexium: 4.6 Seroquel: 2.8 Seloken: 1.7	2.8	1.3	1.4	0.4
Johnson & Johnson (US)	22.3	3.7	4.4	Risperdal: 3.6 Eprex: 3.3 Remicade: 2.5	3.6	1.8	1.9	0.9
Merck (US)	22.0	3.7	3.8	Zocor: 4.4 Fosamax: 3.2 Cozaar: 3.0	4.2	1.8	3.6	1.1
Roche (Ch)[a]	21.9	3.6	4.0	Rituxan: 3.4 Epogin: 1.8 Herceptin: 1.7	3.0	1.9	2.1	1.1
Wyeth (US)	15.3	2.5	2.6	Effexor: 2.5 Protonix: 1.7 Prevnar: 1.5	3.1	1.5	2.0	0.6
Bristol-Myers Squibb (US)	15.3	2.5	2.5	Plavix: 3.8 Pravachol: 2.3 Avapro: 1.0	3.9	1.6	2.8	1.1
Eli Lilly (US)	14.7	2.4	3.0	Zyprexa: 4.2 Gemzar: 1.3 Humalog: 1.2	2.9	1.7	2.0	0.9
Abbott (US)	13.7	2.3	1.8	Humira: 1.4 Depakote: 1.0	2.5	1.2	1.8	0.8
Amgen (US)	12.0	2.0	2.3	Neupogen: 3.5 Aranesp: 3.3 Enbrel: 2.6	X	X	X	X
Boehringer-Ingelheim (Ger)	11.4	1.9	1.7	Spiriva: 1.2 Mobic: 1.1	1.4	0.9	1.3	0.4
Takeda (Jap)	9.0	1.7	1.5	Prevacid: 3.4 Actos: 2.2 Blopress: 1.7	1.6	0.6	1.5	0.5

Table 1

(continued)

	2005				1998		1992	
	Sales ($bn)	Market share (%)	R&D ($bn)	Top-selling drugs ($bn)	Market share (%)	R&D ($bn)	Market share (%)	R&D ($bn)
Astellas (Jap)[b]	7.5	1.2	1.2	Prograf: 1.2 Harnal: 1.2	X	X	X	X
Schering-Plough (US)	7.6	1.3	1.9	Remicade: 0.9	2.5	1.0	1.5	0.5
Novo Nordisk (Den)	5.6	0.9	0.8	Antidiabetics: 4.0	X	X	X	X
Bayer (Ger)	5.0	0.8	1.2	Kogenate: 0.8	2.1	1.1	1.8	0.9
Schering (Ger)	4.8	0.8	1.2	Betaferon: 1.1	X	X	X	X
Total Sales ($bn)		602.0	66.3		302.0	40.0	229.9	26.0
TOP 5 SHARE		26.8	40.6		20.4	24.3	15.0	20.8
TOP 10 SHARE		41.6	65.9		35.9	44.7	25.4	38.0

Source: Firms' Annual Reports, *Pharmaceutical Executive* (May 2006).

Note: Where merger/acquisition has occurred, the market shares in 1998 and 1992 represent the larger of the two previously separate entries. Thus, for GlaxoSmithKline, the 1998 and 1992 market share data represent Glaxo's only.

[a] The data for Roche include Genentech's sales (as they own a majority holding). Genentech's sales in 2005 = $5.5 billion, with $1.3 billion on R&D.

[b] Astellas was incorporated on April 1, 2005, through the merger of Yamanouchi (Jap) and Fujisawa (Jap).

X: outside the Top Twenty

On average, it takes 12 years from a scientific discovery to bring the drug to market. The shorter effective patent life (reflecting the longer development period, which leaves a shorter period for sales of the pharmaceutical before it goes off patent), the increased ability by rival firms to use rational drug design to produce close substitutes, and the increase in generic competition due to changes in regulations have all eroded the length of market protection once enjoyed by the pioneer developer of a pharmaceutical. As the competitive environment has moved from the national to the global level, firms currently attempt to launch a new drug in as many major national markets as possible, as well as design various (incrementally innovative) formulations of the drug, license promising new compounds, and advertise directly to consumers where government regulations allow.

Industry Structure The pharmaceutical industry is best characterized as a global oligopoly in which large multinational firms dominate. Moreover within these firms, "blockbusters" (defined as drugs that generate more than $1 billion in worldwide sales annually) dominate the product range, as shown in table 1. A good descriptive measure of success is the proportion of leading global medicines that national firms (in terms of the location of company headquarters) account for. In 2004, Germany owned 0 of the top 75 (as measured by worldwide sales), France owned 5, Japan owned 5, Switzerland owned 8, the United Kingdom owned 17, and the United States owned 40.

Total global pharmaceutical sales in 2005 were $602 billion, with the United States accounting for 44 percent, the EU for 30 percent, and Japan for 11 percent. Table 2 highlights the substantial increase in merger and acquisition activity in the 1990s, where a significant proportion was cross-border activity. Table 1 also gives the market shares of the 20 leading firms in the period 1992–2005, showing that the ranking of the leading companies changed significantly even in this rather short time period. Note also the relatively high increase in industry concentration. In 1992, the top five firms accounted for 12.9 percent of the global market. By 1998 this had increased to

Table 2
Merger and acquisition activity in the pharmaceutical industry

1989	SmithKline Beckman (US) and Beecham (UK)
	Bristol-Myers (US) and Squibb (US)
	Dow (Merrell) (US) and Marion (US)
	American Home Products (AHP) (US) and AH Robins (US)
1990	Rhône-Poulenc (Fr) and Rorer (US)
	Roche (US) and Genentech (US:60%)
1993	Synergen (US) and Amgen (US)
	Hoechst (Ger) and Copley (US)
1994	Ciba Geigy (Ch) and Chiron (US: 50%)
	AHP (US) and American Cyanamid (US)
	Roche (Ch) and Syntex (US)
	SmithKline Beecham (UK) and Sterling Health (US) (resold the OTC part to Bayer [Ger])
1995	Glaxo (UK) and Wellcome (UK); Glaxo (UK) and Affymax (NL)
	Hoechst (Ger) and Marion Merrell Dow (US)
	Pharmacia (Swed) and Upjohn (US)
	Rhône-Poulenc Rorer (Fr) and Fisons (UK)
	BASF (Ger) and Boots (UK)
1996	Ciba-Geigy (Ch) and Sandoz (Ch)
1997	Roche (Ch) and Boehringer Mannheim (Ger)
1998	Astra (Sweden) and Zeneca (UK)
	Rhône-Poulenc Rorer (Fr) and Hoechst Marion Roussel (Ger)
	Sanofi (Fr) and Synthélabo (Fr)
1999	Monsanto (US) and Pharmacia & Upjohn (US/Sweden)
2000	G. D. Searle (US) and Pharmacia & Upjohn (US/Sweden)
	Pfizer (US) and Warner-Lambert (US)
	Glaxo Wellcome (UK) and SmithKline Beecham (UK)
	Abbott Laboratories (US) and BASF Knoll (Ger)
2001	Bristol-Myers Squibb (US) and DuPont Pharmaceuticals (US)
2003	Pfizer (US) and Pharmacia-Upjohn (US/Sweden)
2004	Aventis (Fr) and Sanofi (Fr)
2006	Bayer (Ger) and Schering (Ger)

20.4 percent and to 26.8 percent by the end of 2005. The leading firms also rapidly increased their proportion of industry R&D: in 2005, for example, although the 10 top firms accounted for only 41.6 percent of the market by sales, they accounted for 65.9 percent of total R&D expenditure. Moreover it must be noted that an increasing proportion of firm-level R&D was spent in the United States, at the expense of Europe and Japan. In 1990, the respective R&D expenditures were $6.8 billion, $9.9 billion, and $3.6 billion, compared with $29.6 billion, $26.3 billion and $8.4 billion, respectively, by 2004.

Outlook Health care costs have increased steadily in advanced industrialized nations, due mainly to aging populations. In turn, this has led to the increased substitution of drugs for more expensive alternatives such as surgery and hospitalization. Moreover rapidly rising health care costs have led to more intense pressure on how pharmaceuticals are priced. National governments have tried various containment measures, such as allowing increased competition from generics. In addition, R&D costs have risen due to the increasing costs of clinical trials and other regulatory hurdles, as well as the focus on chronic rather than acute diseases and the movement toward new drug discovery through biotechnology. In response, the industry experienced unprecedented mergers and acquisitions during the 1990s.

Overall the pharmaceutical industry plays a vital role in the modern world economy. Health care is one of the major issues when thinking about what welfare means in the 21st century. The industry is an enormous generator of innovation, investment, and high-skilled employment. Given the high cost of innovation, notwithstanding the significant public funding in basic medical research, however, there remains a relative lack of research into rare (genetic) diseases that afflict the few and diseases that primarily affect developing countries. Other major issues for the industry include the protection of intellectual property and the improvement of access to medicines in developing countries.

See also access to medicines; foreign direct investment under oligopoly; health and globalization; mergers and acquisitions; multinational enterprises

FURTHER READING

Association of the British Pharmaceutical Industry. 2006. *Pharmaceutical Industry Competitiveness Taskforce: Competitive and Performance Indicators 2005.* Available at http://www.abpi.org.uk. Trade association that provides industry statistics and important information and articles, primarily on the UK pharmaceutical industry.

Busfield, J. 2003. "Globalization and the Pharmaceutical Industry Revisited." *International Journal of Health Services* 33 (3): 581–605. A survey of the trends in the pharmaceutical industry at the beginning of the 21st century.

European Federation of Pharmaceutical Industries and Associations. 2006. *The Pharmaceutical Industry in Figures.* Available at http://www.efpia.org. Brussels. Represents the research-based pharmaceutical industry in Europe; provides information/articles and statistics.

Gambardella, A., L. Orsenigo, and F. Pammolli. 2000. *Global Competitiveness in Pharmaceuticals: A European Perspective.* Brussels: European Commission Enterprise and Industry Directorate-General. An empirical investigation into the determinants of firm performance in the pharmaceutical industry.

German Association of Research-Based Pharmaceutical Companies. Industry statistics and other information available at http://www.vfa.de/en/articles/index_en .html. Trade association that provides industry statistics and important information and articles, primarily on the German pharmaceutical industry.

Helms, R. B., ed. 1996. *Competitive Strategies in the Pharmaceutical Industry.* Washington, DC: The American Enterprise Institute Press. Notable authors consider pharmaceutical pricing, forces affecting global competition, and the risks of and returns to pharmaceutical research and development.

Matraves, C. 1999. "Market Structure, R&D, and Advertising in the Pharmaceutical Industry." *Journal of Industrial Economics* 47 (2): 169–94. An empirical investigation of the relationship between sunk costs and market structure.

Pharmaceutical Executive. Industry statistics and other information available at http://www.pharmexec.com/ pharmexec/. Industry publication that covers key trends and issues, as well as providing industry data.

PhRMA. Industry statistics and other information available at http://www.phrma.org/. Trade association that provides industry statistics and important information and articles, primarily on the U.S. pharmaceutical industry.

U.S. Congressional Budget Office. 2006. *Research and Development in the Pharmaceutical Industry.* Washington, DC: CBO. An overview of pharmaceutical R&D expenditure and new drug output.

CATHERINE MATRAVES

■ **Plaza Accord**

The Plaza Accord was an agreement reached on September 22, 1985, at the Plaza Hotel in New York, among the G5 countries (the United States, Japan, Germany, France, and the United Kingdom) to push down the value of the dollar in order to reduce large U.S. trade deficits. On the day that the Plaza Accord was announced, the trade-weighted or effective value of the dollar fell 4 percent. The dollar fell 17 percent against the Japanese yen and 15 percent against the German mark between September 1985 and the end of the year.

Background In the 1970s, the United States had frequently sought to push down the value of the dollar to reduce its trade deficit. In 1976 and 1977 expansionary monetary and fiscal policies, together with attempts by Treasury secretary Michael Blumenthal to "talk down" the dollar, caused the exchange rate to depreciate (Frankel 1994). The fall of the dollar, aggravated by inflationary pressures, subsequently led to consternation among policymakers.

In October 1979 Fed chairman Paul Volcker initiated a change in monetary policy operating procedures designed to fight inflation and strengthen the dollar. The new strategy allowed interest rates to reach very high levels if necessary in order to defeat inflation. Over the next two years the overnight interbank interest rate (the federal funds rate) increased 800 basis points and the 10-year Treasury bond rate increased 600 basis points. Long-term real interest rate differentials between the United States and its trading partners increased 4 percentage points between September 1979 and the end of 1982, contributing to an appreciation of more than 21 percent in the Federal Reserve's real trade-weighted value of the dollar.

Although the Volcker disinflation succeeded by the end of 1982 in breaking the back of inflation, interest rates in the United States remained stubbornly high. The real interest rate differential between the United States and its trading partners increased another 100 basis points in 1983–84 as compared with 1981–82. The real exchange rate also appreciated another 20 percent over this period (Frankel 1994). The most likely explanation for the continued increase in U.S. interest rates and the dollar over this period was the large increase in the U.S. structural budget deficit.

The dollar continued appreciating between June 1984 and February 1985 even though real interest rate differentials, trade imbalances, and other fundamental factors were moving against the dollar

(Boughton 2001). Many argued that the appreciation at this time was due to a speculative bubble. The Reagan administration, however, maintained a position of benign neglect toward the exchange rate. The strong dollar made U.S. exports, measured in foreign currencies, more expensive and U.S. imports measured in dollars cheaper. It thus led to a burgeoning trade deficit. Between 1980 and 1985, the trade deficit increased by $87 billion, reaching $112 billion in 1984. The automobile, steel, textile, agriculture, and capital goods sectors were particularly hard hit. Firms responded to these pressures by seeking tariffs and other protectionist restrictions on free trade. In 1985, for example, more than 300 trade bills were introduced in Congress; of these, 99 were directly and seriously protectionist and 77 were potentially so (Destler 1986).

Coordinated Action to Correct the Global Imbalances These protectionist pressures jolted the Reagan administration and foreign leaders into action. They saw the world trading system that had been carefully built up over 40 years in danger of collapsing. Foreign leaders were also concerned because the strong dollar was raising import prices and generating inflationary pressures.

In January 1985, the incoming treasury secretary James Baker suggested that the Reagan administration should reconsider its policy of benign neglect toward the exchange rate. In February 1985, the G5 countries engaged in coordinated interventions in foreign exchange markets to lower the value of the dollar. The dollar began falling in February 1985 and fell 15 percent against the German mark and 10 percent against the Japanese yen before the signing of the Plaza Accord in September of that year. It is unclear whether these currency realignments were due to market forces correcting the overvaluation of the dollar (Feldstein 1988) or to foreign exchange intervention by G5 countries in February (Frankel 1994; Funabashi 1989).

The actual agreement sought to correct trade imbalances not only through exchange rate changes but also through expenditure-reducing policies in the United States and expenditure-increasing policies in the other countries. The agreement stipulated:

1. The U.S. would reduce its budget deficit by more than 1 percent of gross domestic product (GDP) in fiscal year 1986 and reduce it further in the future;

2. Japan would liberalize financial markets to ease up on consumer credit and would take into account the yen exchange rate when conducting monetary policy;

3. Germany would cut taxes;

4. All the countries would cooperate closely in foreign exchange markets to encourage further depreciation of the dollar; and

5. All trading partners would resist protectionist pressures (Meyer et al. 2002).

The U.S. current account balance improved over the next several years and returned to balance in 1991. Although several factors, including a recession in the United States, were responsible for this improvement, the orderly exchange rate adjustments following the Plaza Accord were important factors as well. In the first decade of the 21st century, as U.S. trade deficits as a percentage of GDP have reached levels twice as large as the imbalances of the 1980s, there have been calls for a new Plaza Accord (see, e.g., Cline 2005). Since the United States is running trade deficits with many countries, a new agreement to reduce the value of the dollar would probably involve many more countries than the five that took part in the original accord.

See also balance of payments; Bonn Summit; effective exchange rate; expenditure changing and expenditure switching; Federal Reserve Board; foreign exchange intervention; global imbalances; international policy coordination; Louvre Accord; mercantilism; real exchange rate; twin deficits

FURTHER READING

Bergsten, Fred, Olivier Davanne, and Pierre Jacquet. 1999. "The Case for Joint Management of Exchange Rate Flexibility." Institute for International Economics Working Paper 99-9. Washington, DC: Institute for International Economics. Argues that there is a need for more economic policy coordination among G7 countries.

Boughton, James. 2001. *Silent Revolution: The International Monetary Fund, 1979– 1989*. Washington, DC: International Monetary Fund. A history of the IMF between 1979 and 1989 by its own official historian.

Cline, William. 2005. "The Case for a New Plaza Agreement." Institute for International Economics Policy Brief 05-4. Washington, DC: Institute for International Economics. Argues that a new Plaza Agreement is needed to help correct global imbalances in the 21st century.

Destler, I. M. 1986. *American Trade Politics: System under Stress*. Washington, DC: Institute for International Economics. A useful history of trade policy in the 1980s.

Feldstein, Martin. 1988. "Distinguished Lecture on Economics in Government: Thinking about International Economic Coordination." *Journal of Economic Perspectives* 2: 3–13. A negative assessment of international economic coordination by an influential economist.

Frankel, Jeffrey. 1994. "The Making of Exchange Rate Policy in the 1980s." In *American Economic Policy in the 1980s*, edited by Martin Feldstein. Chicago: University of Chicago Press, 293–341. A readable and insightful history of exchange rate policy in the 1980s.

Funabashi, Yoichi. 1989. *Managing the Dollar: From the Plaza to the Louvre*. Washington, DC: Institute for International Economics. Provides a thorough, behind-the-scenes account of how the G5 countries were able to agree on the Plaza Accord.

Meyer, Laurence, Brian Doyle, Joseph Gagnon, and Dale Henderson. 2002. "International Coordination of Macroeconomic Policies: Still Alive in the New Millennium?" International Finance Discussion Paper 723. Washington DC: Federal Reserve Board. A review of the theory of international macroeconomic policy coordination combined with a summary of recent experience in this area.

WILLEM THORBECKE

■ political economy of policy reform

Policy reforms create winners and losers. Hence, implementation of policy reforms requires attention to political economy. Even when reforms are efficient in the aggregate, the absence of compensation means that reforms create losers who may oppose reforms. Thus many reforms that may be efficient will not be implemented. Even reforms that will benefit a broad swath of society are often delayed for long periods of time. The political economy of policy reform studies the implementation of reforms and why they are often delayed.

The political economy of reform can be viewed as an issue of how to get reforms enacted, and then how to keep them from being reversed. The first problem involves relaxing ex ante political constraints. The latter problem is to relax the ex post political constraints (Roland 2002).

An important aspect of implementation is the design of reforms. How reforms are designed may affect both the likelihood of implementation and the sustainability of reforms. The major distinction in this area is between "big bang" and gradual reforms. Big bang reforms are attempts at comprehensive reforms, the idea being that unless a slate of reforms is undertaken simultaneously the policy will be unaffected. Gradual reform focuses on sequencing and the benefits of trial and error in policymaking. The argument is that reform on too broad a front is too difficult to implement. Getting the sequence of reforms right can build momentum for reform; thus the argument is also one of political acceptability. This controversy has been most discussed in the literature on economic transition, though it has more general application. Often Russia is taken (incorrectly) to be an example of big bang reforms and China is taken as the premier example of gradual reforms.

To fix ideas, consider a policy of tariff liberalization in a small economy. Implementation of the reform will raise national income. But it will cause losses among factors in the import-competing sector while leading to gains in those sectors that consume the imports and in the export sector. Assuming the gains exceed the losses the potential for compensation could lead to a Pareto-improvement and thus no problem with implementing the policy. But as compensation is problematic, the potential losers may oppose the policy or at least cause significant delay. This is the problem that is the focus of the political economy of policy reform.

Implementing Reforms Fernandez and Rodrik (1991) developed a model of status quo bias in re-

form that has become classic in the literature. The idea is that when individuals are uncertain over the benefits of reform potentially beneficial programs may not be implemented. Even if everyone knows that in the aggregate the policy will be beneficial (i.e., there is no aggregate uncertainty), if individuals are uncertain over their own situations a status quo bias may still arise. Individual specific uncertainty implies that agents do not know whether or not they will win from reforms. Even if they know that a majority will benefit they may vote against reforms if they believe that they may be losers.

One may suspect that compensation packages may be useful in alleviating this problem, but there is a credibility problem at work. Ex post a majority of voters benefit; hence the losers have little power to enforce a promise for compensation. And with a majority in favor, there will be little chance to reverse the reform. Hence, potential losers know that a promise of compensation is not credible, and this may cause them to oppose reforms. Moreover in practice, it is very difficult to identify who the losers are. This demonstrates that the potential losers have a strong incentive to prevent implementation—their bargaining power drops dramatically after the policy is passed.

The Fernandez-Rodrik model explains why reform may not be implemented, but reforms do take place. To explain why suboptimal policies are reversed requires a dynamic analysis. Alesina and Drazen (1991) developed a model in which interest groups differ over the net benefits of reform. They consider a reform that has public good aspects—a fiscal reform, for example. The problem is that there is a distributional conflict over who wins most from the reform. Each group prefers that the other group pay a higher share of the costs. Delay in reform is modeled as a war of attrition. Reform occurs when one of the groups realizes that it has more to lose from delay than from reform. When one side capitulates, the reform occurs. This also implies that reform will take place sooner the greater the crisis, since this makes delay more problematic. The problem of reform is then to overcome distributional concerns to create consensus over reform.

While the Fernandez-Rodrik model emphasizes winners and losers (and is applicable to reforms that need not have public good aspects) the Alesina-Drazen model emphasizes the need to form consensus for reform to eventually occur. What is common to both, however, is the emphasis on heterogeneity and the conflict of interests that this implies. The models are essentially complementary.

Another mechanism that may lead to blockage of beneficial reforms reflects the influence of special interest groups. Grossman and Helpman (1994) analyzed how such interest can have influence on political decision making (through monetary contributions or information transmission) and used their model to explain the structure of trade protection. Politicians care about social welfare and campaign contributions that can be used to get votes in future elections. They show how even if politicians care about social welfare, the campaign contributions that can be raised by running on a platform of trade protection, for instance, may cause them to place greater weight on workers and capital owners in some sectors of the economy than on others (Grossman and Helpman 1994).

Big Bang versus Gradualism An important debate in the literature on policy reform concerns the *dimensionality* of reform: Shall reform be piecemeal or comprehensive? In the literature on economic transition, the debate has centered on two dimensions: speed and comprehensiveness. The form this debate has taken is often characterized as shock therapy (or big bang) versus gradualism. Related is the issue of whether there is a single blueprint—sometimes called the Washington consensus—that suits all reforming countries. It is important to note that this debate often conflates two dimensions of reform: timing and scope. This is perhaps inevitable, as big bang reforms typically push for rapid, comprehensive reform. But it must be noted that gradual reforms can be comprehensive as well, but over time.

Big bang reform packages are obviously comprehensive in intent. It is crucial to emphasize, however, that gradual reform is not at all the same thing as partial reform. The primary debate is over pace and sequencing. In the case of emerging market reforms,

the debate centers on whether financial institutions and the rule of law must be implemented before capital markets are liberalized. This argument has been made most forcefully by McKinnon (1993), for example. The broader issue is whether markets can operate before the institutions that support them are established, or whether broad-brush market reform creates an environment where the institutions will develop.

Especially in the transition context, the goal is eliminating the command principle and moving to a private property–based market economy. Hence, *eventually* the same steps must be taken. The question is how many steps to take at once and whether they must be taken in a precise order or not. For example, do you need to establish institutions of a private property economy before privatization, or will privatization create the *demand* for private property institutions? There is little debate over the importance of institutions for the success of the market economy, but there is still debate over how to induce their development.

The competing principles are easy to understand. The need for a big bang seems almost implied by the lessons from partial reform (e.g., Murphy, Shleifer, and Vishny 1992). Partial reforms—for example, enterprise autonomy without price liberalization—lead to supply diversion and inferior outcomes. If reforms are complementary, then partial implementation may lead to outcomes inferior to the status quo. When reforms are complementary, implementation of the whole package may be necessary for the reforms to succeed. Moreover partial reforms in this context create rents for insiders who then may oppose further reforms. And if there is a window of opportunity for reform, it may be advantageous to implement a far-reaching reform before the window is shut.

For example, in the case of transition there is a question of how much of the infrastructure of a market economy is needed for markets to be effective. Privatization cannot work without price liberalization, and neither policy can work without stabilization and the elimination of the soft budget constraint. If the command system is not dismantled the private sector will not be able to compete. The big bang view thus argues for reform on a broad front so that complementarities across reforms can be utilized.

The case for a big bang approach often builds on the argument that it takes some time for people to realize whether they are going to win or lose from reform, and to form a powerful opposition against reform if they expect to lose, so by moving quickly, the politician prevents emergence of opposition powerful enough to actually stop or reverse reforms. This is often referred to as the "window of opportunity." It was a prime consideration of reformers in Poland and the architects of privatization in Russia.

A related argument for the big bang stems from the problem of state capture (Hellman 1998; Sonin 2008). Suppose that a complete set of reforms must be implemented and that reforms imply short-term costs. Then *if* the reform package gets stuck partway, voters may fear they will reap only costs and no benefits and hence they will oppose reforms all together. This may happen when the reform process is likely to be captured by winners from partial reform. Hence when the political environment is such that this may occur, big bang policies may be the only way to implement reforms. Forward-looking agents that would be willing to bear the short-term costs if they were sure to reap the long-run benefits may withdraw their support for reform if the realization of the long-run benefits becomes uncertain because of the risk of getting stuck in a partial reform equilibrium.

Another potential argument for the big bang approach (noted by Olofsgård 2003) can be derived from the recent literature on self-control problems. The idea is that voters may not have the self-control to stick with a schedule of partial reforms. The urge for immediate gratification may induce voters to delay reforms or to support the nonreformer in order to avoid the short-term cost of reforms. This may occur even though voters' lifetime expected utility as calculated *in the very beginning of the reform process* is higher with continuation of reform. The big bang approach may thus serve as a commitment device in this case, because it restricts the choice set of the voters if reform reversal is unlikely or very costly.

The alternative view—dubbed the "evolutionary-institutional view" by Roland (2002)—is motivated,

first of all, by the recognition that one cannot do all at once. There are limited skills and limited amounts of time available to policymakers. This alternative conception—gradualism—sees the trial-and-error method as a virtue. Gradualists often accuse proponents of the big bang approach of hubris. McMillan (2004, 35), for example, argues: "Reform is hard to do because we cannot predict its effects. The big bang approach presumes we know where we are going and we know how to get there. But we don't." This argument, also put forward by Easterly (2006) and Rodrik (2008), emphasizes humility and a menu of approaches rather than a unique program applicable in all countries.

This argument is extended to the issue of complementarities in reform. Although the necessity for implementing a package of reforms would seem to argue against gradualism, McMillan (2004, 36) argues to the contrary: "The systemic interactions are hard to predict. We know little about how the pieces of the market system fit together. Some interactions may be complex and indirect, and so we may not even be able to anticipate their existence. Others are straightforward . . . but we have little data on their magnitude."

Opponents of big bang reforms point out that if they are designed incorrectly they can lead to a lock-in of bad reforms. Sonin (2003) argues that mass privatization in Russia created a lock-in of power among early winners. These oligarchs could afford their own property rights protection and thus were opposed to the development of the rule of law, government reform, tax reform, and other policies that would threaten their own incumbent position. Indeed this argument has been made in a more general way by Rajan and Zingales (2004), who argue that the biggest threat to capitalist economies often comes from incumbents. It is not clear, however, to what extent this is an argument against big bang so much as against bad sequencing of reform. It is certainly the case that bad reform will lead to bad effects.

The classic example pointed to by proponents of gradualism is the dual track system in China. This system liberalized at the margins: enterprises were required to continue fulfilling the central plan but could use the market to sell above-plan-level production. Li (1999) provides an interesting analysis contrasting the big bang and dual track reforms with special emphasis on the Chinese experience. The success of Chinese reforms is frequently attributed to the dual track. This makes it all the more ironic that the dual track closely resembles Soviet partial reforms—the "law of state enterprises" of 1987— which performed so poorly. This suggests that the success of reforms may be attributable to the specific conditions of the case rather than to general principles. What worked in China did not work in the Soviet case, most likely because state authority remained strong in China but was deteriorating rapidly when these reforms were implemented in the Soviet Union.

To some extent, gradualism may require that political control, à la China, remains. This seems to be the lesson of the comparison of Gorbachev's reforms regarding the Law on State Enterprises with the dual track system in China. Both allowed enterprises to use markets to allocate above-plan-levels of production. In China the system has been a success, as enterprises continued to produce for the plan, although significant corruption occurred as well. In the Soviet Union, on the other hand, plan fulfillment fell dramatically as supplies were diverted to take advantage of higher market prices, and as a result, planners increased targets continually. The lack of enforcement power of the government made it hard to utilize this mechanism in the Soviet Union. Without such control it may be difficult to control the pace of transition. And democracy may work against more gradual mechanisms. This suggests that often the difference between the relative successes of the two approaches may be due to a third, independent, factor: the nature of the political equilibrium in a reforming country.

A related argument in favor of gradualism stems from the notion of an incubation period. In the late Soviet period there was the idea of the "500-days" plan. This was a blueprint for reform, written by leading reformers and accepted by Yeltsin that was eventually rejected by Gorbachev. The essence of the plan was to move in a steady way to a market economy. Enterprises would be broken up before being privatized to reduce monopoly power. Apartments would be privatized before price liberalization to soak up the monetary overhang. The key idea was to prepare the system for the transformation.

The opposite view is that crisis prevents an incubation period. This is certainly true in the Polish case and also in the Russian case. The problem is that the urge to undertake radical reform did not take hold until a crisis emerged, at which point there was no time left for incubation. This argument is less important in the case of Czechoslovakia and Hungary, where in fact some incubation did take place. These considerations point to the fact that the amount of hemorrhage in the fiscal budget may be a critical factor in deciding the outcome of reform.

Sequencing is also important for the continuation of reform. If early reforms lead to an improved situation for the median voter, this may create support for future reforms. The success of agricultural reform in China is often seen as creating a favorable environment for reforms of industry. This suggests that starting with a reform that increases the welfare of a majority runs a smaller risk of reversal. In contrast, incorrect sequencing (starting transition with the more painful reforms) undermines popular support and may unnecessarily lead to reform reversal. The case for gradualism thus crucially hinges on correct reform sequencing (Dewatripont and Roland 1995, 1209).

One way to cope with the status quo bias is to provide compensation. This need may also argue for partial reform as it reduces the fiscal cost of compensation. For example, unemployment is very likely to increase during transition. To avoid opposition to a reform by the unemployed, the government needs to provide unemployment benefits. In these conditions, Dewatripont and Roland (1995) point out that a slower, feasible speed of transition may be preferable because the pressure on the fiscal sector is lessened. Of course fiscal costs are not the only costs that should be considered, but imperfect reforms that are actually implemented may be preferable to perfect reforms that cannot be implemented.

The importance of political constraints may thus alter the balance between big bang and gradual reforms.

Reversal Costs A big bang strategy involves high reversal costs, which are often considered to be an advantage ex post since they reduce the reversibility of enacted reforms, which is a constant concern for reformers. Thus Anatoly Chubais, the architect of Russian privatization, spoke of the irreversibility of mass privatization as one of its most important benefits. If reforms are irreversible, then a concerted effort can achieve a permanent impact on performance. The problem with this view, however, is that it ignores the ex ante problem. If reversal costs are high, then it may be harder to implement reforms in the first place. After all, if reversal costs are high and reforms have unexpected consequences, any learning cannot be acted on. Hence if there is significant uncertainty about the consequences of reform—that is, if there is significant probability of learning—then high reversal costs make it harder to enact reforms in the first place. From the ex ante point of view, however, high reversal costs in the case of a negative aggregate outcome may make a big bang approach politically unfeasible. Gradualism makes reforms easier to start because it gives an additional option of early reversal at a lower cost after some learning has taken place (Dewatripont and Roland 1995).

If partial reform is less costly to reverse than full reform, gradual reforms may be more politically acceptable than full reforms because they provide an option of early reversal (Dewatripont and Roland 1995). If after partial reform is implemented, a continuation of reform toward full reform seems unattractive to a majority because the signals given by partial reform about the future are not promising enough, then it is always possible to come back to the status quo. On the other hand, if the signals given by early reform are promising enough, then the reforms can continue with greater support. Gradualism thus lowers the cost of experimenting with reform and makes a move away from the status quo more acceptable to a majority.

Note that this argument for partial reform is intimately connected with learning. If reforms are complementary, then one may learn from partial reform. Suppose that one can decompose a reform package into two parts. A gradual reform would implement one part first—price liberalization in agriculture before industry, for example. One may then learn about the consequences of the package from experiencing the first part. Informativeness is the key necessary condition for gradualism to dominate the big bang strategy in the sense that learning about the first reform tells whether to try the second reform or not, depending on the realization of the state after the first reform is implemented. If there is no complementarity, there is nothing to learn and hence you might as well do all at once.

Costs and Benefits of Gradual Reform We can summarize this discussion by considering the costs and benefits of gradual reform. The most important cost is simply the delay in improved performance. If some important reforms are only implemented later, then the full benefits of reform are delayed. An equally important cost may be that delayed reforms continue the hemorrhaging that is taking place. This is especially true when reforms are undertaken in economies suffering crisis. When the IMF is called to provide support for an economy it is already in an economic crisis. Similarly, in the case of transition economies, the status quo may not be feasible. The economy is in crisis and gradual reform may not be possible. A third important cost of gradual reform is that it may dissipate the credibility of reformers, given that partial reform was a frequent failed policy in planned economies.

The benefits of gradual reform are also straightforward. Most important, perhaps, is that if it is carried out successfully, momentum for further reforms can be built. Building constituencies that support reform may enhance the sustainability of reform. Gradual reforms also allow for learning and may be easier to implement when reversal costs are high. They allow for experimentation. Finally, gradual reforms may involve a lower level of transfers, and hence, a more feasible fiscal burden.

On balance, the choice between big bang and gradual reforms may come down to the extent of current crisis and the strength of the state. If there is significant political legitimacy or control, gradual reforms may be feasible. If reforms are taking place in a period of extraordinary politics, however, big bang reforms may be the only choice.

Empirical Evidence Given the experiences of emerging and transition economies what has been the experience of big bang versus gradualism? The question is not easy to answer, though advocates of each approach have plenty of cases to point to. The experience of Russia and China are often contrasted and used to illustrate the relative success of big bang and gradual reform policies, respectively. The problem, however, is that policies are not implemented in isolation. The success of policies will depend on external circumstances. Russian reforms took place during a period of very low oil prices. When the economy deteriorated, it was natural to blame reforms. But this may miss the essential point. For an economy that is the second largest exporter of oil and whose economy is heavily resource-dependent, this fact accounts for economic performance far more than any reform packages.

A related problem is that the choices between the two programs are not chosen randomly. The choice is endogenous, and the political equilibrium in the country is often decisive. In more stable societies gradual reform may be chosen, but if the society has a stable political system even big bang reforms may be successful. In contrast, most economies in crisis choose big bang approaches, and performance is frequently less than stellar. But there is a reason these economies were in crisis, and it is not clear that a gradual program would succeed in these countries.

Another fundamental problem with empirical work focusing on this question is how to identify whether a country chose a big bang or gradual approach. Often, this judgment is made ex post via expert surveys. The identification is thus influenced by how successful reform was thought to be. But this just ensures that one's prior assumptions are confirmed. If a country announces a big bang reform but is only partially successful at implementing the various parts of the program, should this country be classified as big bang or gradual? This is a knotty problem that has plagued this literature and is a major reason for a lack of consensus about outcomes.

See also evolution of development thinking; international institutional transfer; political economy of trade policy; structural adjustment; transition economies; Washington consensus

FURTHER READING

Alesina, Alberto, and Allan Drazen. 1991. "Why Are Stabilizations Delayed?" *American Economic Review* 81 (5): 1170–88. Discusses why stabilization packages are typically implemented only after long delays.

Dewatripont, Mathias, and Gerard Roland. 1995. "The Design of Reform Packages under Uncertainty." *American Economic Review* 85 (5): 1207–23. Examines how uncertainty affects the design of reform packages.

Easterly, William. 2006. *The White Man's Burden: Why the West's Efforts to Aid the Rest Have Done So Much Ill and So Little Good.* New York: Penguin Press, 2006. An account of why foreign aid is ineffective, focusing on the lack of accountability.

Fernandez, Raquel, and Dani Rodrik. 1991. "Resistance to Reform: Status Quo Bias in the Presence of Individual-Specific Uncertainty." *American Economic Review* 81 (5): 1146–55. Demonstrates how the presence of uncertainty regarding the distribution of gains and losses from reform can prevent efficiency-enhancing reforms from taking place.

Hellman, Joel. 1998. "Winners Take All: The Politics of Partial Reform in Postcommunist Transitions." *World Politics* 50 (2): 202–34. Argues that the process of economic reform in transition is threatened less by the losers than by the net winners.

Grossman, Gene M., and Elhanan Helpman. 1994. "Protection for Sale." *American Economic Review* 84 (4) (September): 833–50. Develops a model where special-interest groups make political contributions in order to influence an incumbent government's choice of trade policy.

Li, Wei. 1999. "A Tale of Two Reforms." *Rand Journal of Economics* 30 (1): 120–36. Identifies conditions under which a big bang reform reduces output initially while a Chinese-style reform increases output.

McKinnon, Ronald. 1993. *The Order of Economic Liberalization: Financial Control in the Transition to a Market*

Economy. 2d ed. Baltimore: Johns Hopkins Press. Outlines the appropriate sequencing of liberalizing government policies in domestic finance and foreign trade for securing open markets.

McMillan, John. 2004. "Avoid Hubris and Other Lessons for Reformers." *Finance and Development* 41 (3): 34–37. Argues for a gradual reform process and against big bang reforms.

Murphy, Kevin M., Andrei Shleifer, and Robert W. Vishny. 1992. "The Transition to a Market Economy: Pitfalls of Partial Reform." *Quarterly Journal of Economics* 107 (3) (August): 889–906. Demonstrates how partial reforms in a planned economy can cause performance to deteriorate via diversion of inputs.

Olofsgård, Anders. 2003. "The Political Economy of Reform: Institutional Change as a Tool for Political Credibility." Mimeo. World Bank. December 4. Argues that institutional change is a critical step for reformers to obtain credibility.

Rajan, Raghuram G., and Luigi Zingales. 2004. *Saving Capitalism from the Capitalists.* Princeton, NJ: Princeton University Press. Asserts that capitalism's biggest threat is that insiders continually try to eliminate competition and that financial markets are the best means to preserve open markets.

Rodrik, Dani. 2008. *One Economics, Many Recipes: Globalization, Institutions, and Economic Growth.* Princeton, NJ: Princeton University Press. Argues that globalization reduces poverty only when countries tailor policies to their own specific constraints.

Roland, Gerard. 2002. "The Political Economy of Transition." *Journal of Economic Perspectives* 16 (1): 29–50. Argues that the experience of transition economies demonstrates the superiority of the evolutionary-institutional approach.

Sonin, Konstantin. 2003. "Why the Rich May Favor Poor Protection of Property Right." *Journal of Comparative Economics* 31 (5): 715–31. Shows that in unequal societies the rich may benefit from shaping economic institutions in their favor, in particular by weakening public property rights enforcement.

———. 2008. "State Capture in Transition: Corruption." In *New Palgrave Dictionary of Economics.* London: Palgrave. Analyzes how during transition the fear of the *Leviathan* state has been transformed into the reality of
the captured state, where powerful large interests control the playing field.

BARRY W. ICKES

■ political economy of trade policy

After the provision of internal order and external security (and bound up with both as a source of revenue), the regulation of international trade is one of the oldest known activities undertaken by states. Thus it is not surprising that we have records of analytical comment on commercial policy from the earliest writings on economics and political economy. Most of this early writing is "political economy" in the sense of practical policy advice, but this is not unrelated to the term's more modern meaning as positive accounts of policy choice. Policy advice is given under an implicit model of government (sometimes called the Weberian model after Max Weber) that the government is willing and able to act on advice intended to improve aggregate social welfare. Given its focus on explaining welfare-worsening policy, contemporary political economy research generally rejects this model (even when, as in the case of very low levels of protection, it would seem to be a more accurate model than the obvious alternatives). Instead, we take the obvious fact that trade policy deviates from virtually any straightforward model of welfare maximization as a warrant to consider alternative accounts of policy determination. The great majority of this work begins with an attempt to link policy preferences of the relevant agents to their material self-interests, defined in terms of the primitives (axiomatic assumptions) of some underlying model of the economy, and then seeks to map these policy preferences into policy outcomes via some (usually extremely spare) model of policy determination.

Early Steps in the Political-Economy Analysis of Trade Policy The most immediate predecessors of modern research on the political economy of trade policy are three works by political scientists that still repay close study and that contain most of the themes that still motivate contemporary research:

Schattschneider's *Politics, Pressure, and the Tariff* (1935); Bauer, Pool, and Dexter's *American Business and Public Policy* (1963); and Lowi's "American Business, Public Policy, Case Studies, and Political Theory" (1964). The first of these treats trade policy (in this case the Hawley-Smoot tariff) as the outcome of an asymmetric lobbying process in which protection seekers dominate and certain sectors are more effective than others. Bauer, Pool and Dexter saw their work as a rejection of Schattschneider's. Looking at omnibus trade legislation in the period 1953–62, they found (among other things) members of Congress to be relatively free from lobbying constraint and saw lobbying primarily as information transmission. Lowi's brilliant review and reconciliation argued that a fundamental institutional change had resulted in a redefinition of trade policy such that the politics had changed between the periods studied in these two classic works. Although the great bulk of contemporary research on the political economy of trade is rooted in the asymmetric group theoretic tradition presented in Lowi, a growing body of work emphasizes institutional features and, while not much applied to trade policy, the dominant strand of research on lobbying in political science now emphasizes informational issues.

The first wave of research by economists on the political economy of trade protection was actually less concerned with developing a coherent and, at least in principle, testable positive theory than with finding a way to increase the costs of protection. In the first paper of this sort, Tullock (1967) argued that the standard welfare analyses (focused on what economists call "deadweight loss" or "welfare triangles") were sizable underestimates of the actual welfare costs of protection (and monopolies). Specifically, potentially productive resources were spent seeking the rents implied by the presence of the tariff. Accounting for these would permit us to count the rent rectangle, as well as the deadweight loss triangles, as costs. The empirical application of this logic by Krueger (1974) to the case of Turkey, in which rent seeking clearly added to the costs of protection, moved political economy analysis to the center of trade policy analysis, at least in developing countries.

This approach reached its most sophisticated form in the work of Bhagwati and his coauthors on directly unproductive profit-seeking activities (e.g., Bhagwati and Srinivasan 1980). As applied to pathological situations (e.g., Turkey) this approach makes a lot of sense, but as a general extension of the normative analysis of trade policy, it is deeply problematic: adding the economic costs of political action to the costs of protection without a systematic normative analysis of political action makes little sense. After all, in a nonpathological situation, lobbying or directly unproductive political activities are just other terms for citizens approaching their government. The ability of citizens to do this is an essential component of the democratic political process, something most of us would consider highly positive.

The other precursor to current work grows out of Olson's *Logic of Collective Action* (1965) and the closely related earlier work by political scientists on the foundations of group theoretic models of political action. Olson's key insight, relative to much of the earlier research on the political activity of groups in the determination of policy outcomes (called "pluralist theory" by political scientists), was that the decision to invest real resources (e.g., time and effort, as well as money) in group membership was a rational decision, constrained by the expected impact of those resources on the goals of the group. Because groups, especially political groups, seek goals that benefit all members, regardless of their level of investment, the decision to invest has the form of a decision to provide a public good (i.e., it has a prisoners' dilemma structure). In addition, asymmetries in group effort can be expected to emerge based on group size. That is, large groups will find it hard to provide the optimal level of the public good, while small groups with concentrated benefits from political action will find it relatively easier to organize. Thus small groups expecting concentrated benefits can be expected to be more politically successful than large groups with diffuse benefits.

In the case of trade policy, the most common form of this argument is that producers of an import-competing good will expect concentrated benefits (not only supporting higher factor returns, but protecting jobs and immobile capital from unemployment) and will find it in their interest to organize to support protection, while a large number of consumers, each of whom bears only a small additional cost as a result of the protection, will not find it in their interest to organize. Thus we will observe protection even if it is welfare-reducing in aggregate. Although this may well explain why we do not observe much in the way of consumer activity on trade policy, it does not explain why large retail intermediaries (e.g., Wal-Mart) or industrial users of intermediate goods are not more active on trade, or why what little consumer activism we do observe tends to support protection (e.g., Public Citizen, a U.S. consumer rights organization founded by Ralph Nader).

A sizable empirical literature developed to account for tariff structure in terms of a number of more or less ad hoc variables in a linear regression framework. Sign patterns in these variables were suggested in terms of a number of loose explanatory frameworks. This work increasingly focused on variables seen to be associated with effective group formation and then used loosely construed models linked to early Chicago school political economy as an interpretive framework. Overall this work provides quite strong evidence that political-economic factors must be part of any coherent account of systematic patterns in the tariff structure.

Political Preference and Minimally Institutional Political Economy The core of virtually all political economy models developed by economists is a formal derivation of preferences over policy from primitives of the underlying model of the economy. More formally, endogenous policy models build some form of explicit political structure into some form of neoclassical general equilibrium model. That is, the underlying economy is made up of households, characterized by preferences over final goods and portfolios of productive factors, and firms, which transform factors of production into final goods. We can denote a neoclassical economy with the set: $E = \{Z, F, R\}$, where Z is a matrix allocating factors of production among households, F a vector of technologies, and R a vector of household prefer-

ences over final commodities. To this economy we attach a vector of possible interventions (t) and a political mechanism (M) yielding a political economy: $\Pi = \{Z, F, R; t, M\}$. The easiest part of the analysis of a system like Π involves the derivation of citizen preferences over policy. For a given household, $h(R_h \in R, z_h \in Z)$, for a fixed E, we simply ask how any relevant state of the policy variable (t) affects household welfare. By answering this question for every feasible state of the policy variable, we trace out household political preferences over that policy.

It is now well known that the most general version of this model (usually called the Arrow-Debreu-McKenzie model) does not yield comparative static results of the sort necessary for this exercise. As a result, most work in this area builds on either a Heckscher-Ohlin-Samuelson (HOS) model (i.e., a model in which all factors are fully mobile between sectors) or a Ricardo-Viner model (i.e., a model in which every sector is characterized by a specific-factor and a single mobile factor is used by all sectors). The former yields conflict based on factor ownership (i.e., class conflict), while the latter yields conflict based on industry attachment. Recently, a specialized form of the latter has been widely used, in which n-1 sectors are characterized by a specific factors structure and the nth sector (the *numeraire* sector) is a freely traded Ricardian good (Grossman and Helpman 1994). This is usually combined with quasilinear preferences to produce an economy in which virtually all general equilibrium linkages have been severed. This makes for an extremely tractable, if somewhat implausible, framework for political economy modeling of contemporary trade policy. If we think of the HOS model (and its dimensional generalizations) as a model of the long run and the Ricardo-Viner model as representing a relatively short run, it is probably clearest to treat their use in political economy models as reflecting the period of political calculation. That is, if political agents make their calculations over a relatively short time period, the most appropriate model would be some form of specific-factors model; while, if the time horizon of political calculation is long, the HOS model is more appropriate.

The evidence is somewhat mixed, but the bulk of it would seem to suggest that, for most agents, the time horizon of political calculation is relatively short. The most compelling evidence comes from actual political activity. Starting with Magee's (1978) classic study of testimony on trade legislation, most work has found strong evidence of sector-based political activity. This is consistent with studies of capital and labor mobility that suggest relative immobility over politically plausible time horizons (i.e., two to six years in the United States). Research on policy preferences revealed by public opinion polls is generally interpreted as more consistent with factor-based calculation, but the implications of these results for either factor mobility or the time horizon of political calculation are currently a matter of considerable dispute.

Just as knowing preferences over final goods is not sufficient for a theory of market equilibrium, knowledge of political preferences is not sufficient to determine political-economic equilibrium. In principle, a model of political action must be combined with a model of policy determination to determine a full political-economic equilibrium. Here there are many possibilities. One convenient way of distinguishing among the basic models is in terms of what is assumed about the activity permitted of demanders of policy and suppliers of policy. If we consider that each type of agent (demander and supplier) may be active or passive, we get the simple typology shown in table 1.

The simplest approach is to assume that policy is determined by a referendum on the tariff. Under the

Table 1
Political-economic equilibrium

	Groups are	
	Passive	*Active*
The state is		
Passive	Referendum	"t" formation function
Active	Political response function	Menu auction

assumption that voting is costless (and the assumption that preferences are single-peaked over a one-dimensional *t*), this approach simply determines the policy outcome at the most preferred point of the median voter. No resources are used up in the political process, there are no gains from misrepresentation of preferences, so once citizen policy preferences have been determined, the step to final policy determination is straightforward (Mayer 1984). The virtue of this approach is its simplicity, but it has at least two major drawbacks as a framework for empirical work: there have been almost no actual referenda on trade policy, and at the level for which general equilibrium analysis is appropriate, trade policy is inherently multidimensional. As a public issue, trade policy usually is discussed in terms of the overall level of protection offered in the country as a whole (not in terms of tariffs on specific line items in a tariff schedule). Seen in this way, there have been times and places in which "The Tariff" was sufficiently important to public partisan competition that a given election could be seen as a referendum on the tariff (e.g., the Canadian election of 1911 and the British elections of 1906 and 1914).

An extension of this approach implicitly assumes that representatives are elected to represent their constituencies *on trade policy*, so that their votes on trade policy can be treated as determined by the material interests of their constituents. However, as Bauer, Pool, and Dexter argued, and as implied by theoretical work on voting in high dimensional issue spaces, given the dimensionality and complexity of the issue environment in which representatives operate, they will generally be free to vote on virtually any issue as they prefer. Thus, especially for issues such as trade, which are not major reelection issues, inference based on this constraint seems less than well grounded. Given that, at least until recently, trade policy has not been a major public issue, some form of lobbying model would seem to be a more solid basis for framing the analysis of the political economy of trade policy.

The simplest approach is to follow Peltzman (1976) in doing away with the attempt to model demanders and focusing on the behavior of suppliers who face an untheorized (but completely plausible) function of implicit group demands and a concern with the general welfare consequences of their actions. Hillman (1982) develops a model of this sort applied to trade policy. The *political response function* reflects the trade-off facing a politician who seeks to favor one group (say, producers) at the expense of another (consumers). While Hillman motivates his analysis by loose reference to lobbying in the context of an election constraint, neither the lobbying nor electoral competition are explicitly modeled. The general pattern of signs could emerge from a variety of institutional environments. Thus it seems sensible to characterize this approach as "active state/passive groups." The essentially ad hoc form of the political support function makes for a natural match with the ad hoc empirical analysis referred to in the previous section.

Where the political support function approach abstracts from the political activity of groups, lobbying models, with a passive register state, introduce an explicit analysis of costs of political action and rational strategic behavior by groups, but abstract from active decision making by the state. Findlay and Wellisz (1982) develop a model of this sort for the case of trade policy. The core institutional assumptions of this model are: (1) effective political demand is represented by the lobbying activity of entrepreneurial political action committees (PACs); (2) political activity involves no fixed costs, and there are no collective action problems in the organization of group activity; and (3) the state is a passive register of effective citizen demand. That is, politically active sectors hire labor to engage in lobbying, and the state is represented by a *tariff-formation function*: $t = \tau(\boldsymbol{L})$ where $\boldsymbol{L} = \{L_1, \ldots, L_n\}$ is a vector of quantities of labor hired for lobbying. The outcome is determined as the Nash equilibrium in lobbying, where PACs take into account the direct cost of lobbying (i.e., wL_i), the indirect costs (i.e., the effect on the market wage of withdrawing labor from production for use in lobbying), and the return on lobbying via $\tau(\boldsymbol{L})$.

A major advance in the formal theory of lobbying was made by Grossman and Helpman (1994), who developed a model in which the state and economic agents are politically active, thus rendering both the political support function and the tariff-formation function approaches essentially irrelevant. Grossman and Helpman's essential insight was that the relationship between lobby groups and the state could be effectively modeled as one of common agency (with politically organized sectors as the principals and the state as the common agent) and that the menu auction model of common agency was a tractable framework for developing a broader model of political-economic equilibrium than had previously been presented. Each active PAC offers the state a menu associating a payment with every possible tariff *schedule* and the state then chooses a tariff schedule that maximizes its welfare. Unlike the passive register state, the Grossman-Helpman state is explicitly concerned with overall welfare as well as bribes. Specifically, their state's objective function is a linear combination of bribes and aggregate welfare:

$$G = \sum_{i \in I} C_i(\mathbf{p}) + aW(\mathbf{p})$$

where the C_i are the bribes ("contributions"), W is the aggregate welfare, both conditional on the state's choice of $\mathbf{p}$ (the price vector—determined via the small country assumption by the tariff), and a is the weight the government attaches to aggregate welfare. Note how this structure embeds both the Weberian state and the passive register state as special cases.

Given the menu auction structure as a characterization of politics, and the claim that truthful equilibria are focal among the continuum of equilibria that generally result, and the Grossman-Helpman economy characterized by quasilinear preferences, n-1 sectors characterized by a specific factors structure, and a freely traded Ricardian numeraire sector, Grossman and Helpman show (proposition 2) that equilibrium trade taxes and subsidies must satisfy a *modified Ramsey rule*:

$$\frac{t_i^\circ}{1 + t_i^\circ} = \frac{I_i - \alpha_L}{a + \alpha_L} \left(\frac{z_i^\circ}{e_i^\circ} \right),$$

where I_i is an indicator variable that takes a value of 1 if the sector is organized and 0 otherwise, α_L is the fraction of the total population that is organized by some lobby, z_i° is the ratio of domestic output to imports, and e_i° is the elasticity of import demand. This form has been widely taken to be a framework for structural estimation. Overall, there seems to be considerable econometric support for lobbying as a key determinant of the cross-section pattern of protection.

For all the success of the basic models reviewed in this section, primarily in providing a general account of deviations from welfare optimal policies in terms of political pressure and in providing a specific account of the cross-section pattern of protection, it is hard to escape the conclusion that, more than other branches of research on political economy (in particular, local public finance and macroeconomic policy), the gap between the models and their object (either as formal empirics or as a framework for understanding) is large. The next section considers several avenues of current research that seek to extend the scope of research on the political economy of protection, but we conclude this section with one problem fundamental to lobbying models: exogeneity of group organization.

All of the research on lobbying we have considered to this point treats group organization as exogenous: there is no formal analysis of groups at all in the political response function literature; tariff-formation function and menu auction models treat active groups as fully organized and completely efficient in extracting resources to pursue political goals (the menu auction models explicitly treat organization as primitive—reflected in I_i in the modified Ramsey rule). This was a sensible strategy in the early development of lobbying models, but before they can be treated seriously as frameworks for empirical analysis, group formation needs to be systematically integrated into the analysis. The few attempts that have been made to construct such an analysis build, sensibly, on Olson's (1965) theory of collective action. Two approaches seem to have been pursued, both of which treat lobbying as an example of voluntary provision of a collective good. The approach that matches the lobbying models most directly focuses on the decision to join under the assumption that agents joining a PAC will be taxed optimally by the PAC organizer (Mitra 1999). While this is a good match to the theory of lobbying, it is a poor match to the empirical reality in which groups seem not to be either perfectly organized or perfectly unorganized, but rather to be more-or-less well organized. The alternative is to assume that all groups are potentially active and consider contributions from zero to some maximal (or optimal) level. While there is no shortage of work that considers contributions to a single lobby (treated as a public good), there is very little work that considers those contributions in a strategic context. The problem with this latter approach is that "groups" are not really organized but simply exist as a function of a common pattern of individual contributions. One of the early fundamental criticisms of Olson's work was the lack of attention to political entrepreneurship in the formation of groups, and it seems like an explicit introduction of political entrepreneurs might be a route to linking these two approaches.

Frontiers of Research on the Political Economy of Protection The essentially context-free theoretical environment of the models we have considered to this point is a feature, not a detriment. As with virtually all good modeling programs, the endogenous policy approach to political economy modeling achieves its cutting power by abstracting from details that interfere with the main line of the story—in this case, the contest of material self-interest projected from the economy to the political system. Models serve a number of purposes:

1. *Cautionary tales*: most people think X, but in my model X does not occur;
2. *"Just So" stories*: here is a fact, and I can construct a model rationalizing that fact;
3. *Loose frameworks for thinking about issues*; and
4. *Generators of structural frameworks for econometric analysis.*

The Tullock-Krueger-Bhagwati work discussed earlier was essentially of the first sort (protection is more costly than you might think as a result of rent-seeking costs); most of the work discussed after that is of the second and third sort (it is plausible to think about "bad policy" as the outcome of a political process and the empirical work is loosely consistent with those accounts). Grossman and Helpman's modified Ramsey rule has been treated as a structural form, but the results of that work do little more than underwrite the use of the model for purposes 2 and 3. Making these models more operationally relevant means introducing more of the relevant context into the models. Current work focuses on both political and economic context.

In terms of political context, one approach that is receiving attention is the attempt to explicitly model the link between contributions, elections, and policy outcomes (rather than burying the link in a political response function or the government's objective function). The focus on the role of partisan competition opens the door to both theoretical and empirical work of a comparative nature, as well as cross-sectional work on the foundations of partisan support. This work is interesting, but given that protection is now rarely set by legislatures, it seems unlikely that this line of work will be much help in extending the applicability of current models. By contrast, the sizable body of work that builds on detailed knowledge of the GATT/WTO-legal administered protection mechanisms has already begun to provide a rich body of theoretical and empirical work consistent with the more general models discussed above (see Blonigen and Prusa 2003; and Nelson 2006 for surveys).

An alternative direction of generalization abstracts from the assumption that markets are complete and perfect. One of the standard results of time-series work on the correlates of protection is that demand for protection, and protectionist outcomes, are positively related to unemployment. This is loosely consistent with public opinion data suggesting that support for protection increases if questions are "framed" in terms of unemployment. This suggests that modeling the economy, on which the political economy is based, as characterized by equilibrium involuntary unemployment, could make a major contribution to our understanding of the political economy of trade policy. Recent work by Bradford (2006) and Matschke and Sherlund (2006) make a start in this direction, but there is room for much more. Similarly, standard models assume that political preferences are strictly self-regarding. Experimental results and public opinion data suggest, however, that political preferences are more complex. In particular, it seems clear that widely held notions of fairness strongly affect expressed preferences over trade policy. To the extent that public politics constrain trade policy, it would seem to be important to try to incorporate such considerations in our models.

Thinking about "Good" Trade Policy Virtually all of the work we have considered to this point has attempted to account for "bad" (i.e., welfare-reducing) trade policy. Given that the single most important fact of trade policy in the era since World War II is the historically striking trend toward greater trade liberalism and, by the mid-1980s, the truly extraordinary low level of overall protection (aside from agriculture) in the world's major trading nations, this focus seems a bit peculiar. If we believe, as surely we must, that political economy forces help explain the structure of protection, it seems equally clear that political economy forces must help explain this liberality. These forces need not be the same and, in fact, are unlikely to be the same. Thus the gains from new work on the domestic political economy of liberalization would seem to be sizable. One approach to this question might be to study the link between liberalization and protection. Whereas in the era of tariff politics, liberalization and protection were simply directions in a relatively unidimensional scale, in an era in which omnibus trade legislation endorses the power to liberalize at the same time it changes the terms of administered protection, it is not only difficult to say whether a piece of such legislation is protectionist or liberalizing, it seems likely that the two are related. Nevertheless, the extant models have brought us some distance in understanding the political economy of trade policy.

See also Heckscher-Ohlin model; nontariff measures; quotas; specific-factors model; tariffs

FURTHER READING

Anderson, Kym, and Robert Baldwin. 1987. "The Political Market for Protection in Industrial Countries." In *Protection, Cooperation, Integration, and Development*, edited by Ali M. El-Agraa. New York: Macmillan, 20–36. An excellent survey of empirical work on the political economy of trade policy.

Bauer, Raymond, Ithiel de Sola Pool, and Lewis Anthony Dexter. 1963. *American Business and Public Policy: The Politics of Foreign Trade*. Chicago: Aldine. A classic work on the political economy of trade policy that emphasizes, among many other things, the independence of legislators in the determination of trade policy using a framework that captures information transfer and communication.

Bhagwati, Jagdish, and T. N. Srinivasan. 1980. "Revenue Seeking: A Generalization of the Theory of Tariffs." *Journal of Political Economy* 88 (6):1069–87. Systematized and extended to the case of general equilibrium the argument that resource using political competition increases the costs of protection.

Blonigen, Bruce, and Thomas Prusa. 2003. "Antidumping." In *Handbook of International Trade*, edited by E. Kwan Choi and James Harrigan. Oxford: Blackwell, 251–84. A survey of contingent protection.

Bradford, Scott. 2006. "Protection and Unemployment." *Journal of International Economics* 69 (2): 257–71. Incorporates both labor market search and unions into a political economy model with equilibrium unemployment.

Dixit, Avinash, Gene Grossman, and Elhanan Helpman. 1997. "Common Agency and Coordination: General Theory and Application to Tax Policy." *Journal of Political Economy* 105 (4):752–69. A particularly clear exposition of the Grossman-Helpman model.

Findlay, Ronald, and Stanislaw Wellisz. 1982. "Endogenous Tariffs, the Political Economy of Trade Restrictions, and Welfare." In *Import Competition and Response*, edited by Jagdish Bhagwati. Chicago: University of Chicago Press, 223–34. Standard reference on the "tariff-formation function" model of lobbying on the tariff. Make sure to read the comment by Leslie Young that follows the main paper.

Gawande, Kishore, and Pravin Krishna. 2003. "The Political Economy of Trade Policy: Empirical Approaches." In *Handbook of International Trade*, edited by Kwan Choi and James Harrigan. Oxford: Blackwell, 213–50. An excellent survey of empirical work on the political economy of trade policy.

Grossman, Gene, and Elhanan Helpman. 1994. "Protection for Sale." *American Economic Review* 94 (4): 833–50. By making both the state and groups active participants, this important paper embeds lobbying models that treat the state as passive and political response function models that make groups passive. This is probably the currently most widely used framework for theoretical and empirical research on trade.

Helpman, Elhanan. 1997. "Politics and Trade Policy." In *Advances in Economics and Econometrics: Theory and Applications*, vol. 1, edited by David Kreps and Kenneth Wallis. Cambridge: Cambridge University Press, 19–45. A survey of the political economy of trade policy with a theoretical focus.

Hillman, Arye L. 1982. "Declining Industries and Political Support Protectionist Motives." *American Economic Review* 72 (5): 1180–87. Standard reference on the political response function model of tariff formation.

Hiscox, Michael. 2001. *International Trade and Political Conflict: Commerce, Coalitions, and Mobility*. Princeton, NJ: Princeton University Press. A particularly thorough theoretical and empirical analysis of the link between factor mobility and the determination of equilibrium protection.

Krueger, Anne O. 1974. "The Political Economy of Rent-Seeking Society." *American Economic Review* 64 (3): 291–303. Drawing on Tullock's analysis of rent seeking, this important paper develops an empirical analysis of the costs of protection including rent-seeking costs.

Lowi, Theodore. 1964. "American Business, Public Policy, Case Studies, and Political Theory." *World Politics* 16 (4): 676–715. A classic work on the political economy of trade policy that might be the highest impact book review ever written. Lowi mediates the apparent conflict between Schattschneider and Bauer/Pool/Dexter by arguing that changes in the institutional definition of trade policy induced changes in the structure of politics.

Magee, Stephen. 1978. "Three Simple Tests of the Stolper-Samuelson Theorem." In *Issues in International Economics*, edited by Peter Oppenheimer. Stocksfield, UK: Oriel Press, 138–53. This widely cited paper sought to test whether factors are intersectorally mobile (consistent with the Heckscher-Ohlin model) or sectorally fixed (consistent with the Cairnes-Haberler model and, more loosely, the Ricardo-Viner model of fixed factors with a single mobile factor) by examining the lobbying positions of factor and labor on a trade bill. Magee found that capital and labor tend to lobby together by sector.

Magee, Stephen, William Brock, and Leslie Young. 1989. *Black Hole Tariffs and Endogenous Policy Theory*. Cambridge: Cambridge University Press. Magee, Brock, and Young developed one of the first systematic lines of research on the political economy of trade policy. They sought to integrate lobbying and electoral politics. This book collects and extends this important early body of research.

Matschke, Xenia, and Shane Sherlund. 2006. "Do Labor Issues Matter in the Determination of U.S. Trade Policy." *American Economic Review* 96 (1): 405–21. Matschke and Sherlund argue theoretically and empirically that ignoring labor market structure in Grossman-Helpman empirics leads to faulty inference.

Mayer, Wolfgang. 1984. "Endogenous Tariff Formation." *American Economic Review* 74 (5): 970–85. In addition to a very clear explanation of the derivation of preferences over policy from primitives of the economy, this paper lays out the referendum model with great clarity.

Mitra, Devashish. 1999. "Endogenous Lobby Formation and Endogenous Protection: A Long-Run Model of Trade Policy Determination." *American Economic Review* 89 (5):1116–34. Develops a model in which the decision of whether or not to join a group is endogenized. This analysis is then integrated into the Grossman-Helpman model.

Nelson, Douglas. 2006. "The Political Economy of Antidumping: A Survey." *European Journal of Political Economy* 22 (3): 554–90. A survey of contingent protection.

Olson, Mancur. 1965. *The Logic of Collective Action*. Boston: Harvard University Press. Classic treatment of group formation by rational agents when the goal of the group is to provide a public good.

Peltzman, Sam. 1976. "Toward a More General Theory of Regulation." *Journal of Law and Economics* 19 (2): 211–40. Original model of the political response function as a basis for political-economic analysis.

Rodrik, Dani. 1995. "Political Economy of Trade Policy." In *Handbook of International Economics*, vol. 3, edited by G. Grossman and K. Rogoff. Amsterdam: North-Holland, 1457–94. An often-referenced survey of the political economy of trade policy with a theoretical focus.

Schattschneider, Edward Elmer. 1935. *Politics, Pressure, and the Tariff*. Englewood Cliffs, NJ: Prentice Hall. A classic work on the political economy of trade policy that emphasizes the role of groups in lobbying for protection.

Tullock, Gordon. 1967. "The Welfare Costs of Tariffs, Monopolies, and Theft." *Western Economic Journal* 5 (3): 224–32. Classic paper arguing that resources used in the pursuit of a political goal must be counted in the cost of that policy.

DOUGLAS NELSON

■ pollution haven hypothesis

A pollution haven is a country or region that attracts pollution-intensive industry because its environmental policy is less stringent than that of its trading partners. A key issue in the debate over the effects of trade on the environment is whether globalization leads to the emergence of pollution havens: that is, does trade and investment liberalization cause pollution-intensive production to relocate from (mostly high-income) countries with stringent environmental policy to (mostly low-income) countries with weak or loosely enforced environmental regulations? The pollution haven hypothesis posits that the answer is yes.

If this hypothesis is correct, there is reason for concern about the effects of trade on global environmental quality. If production shifts from a region with stringent environmental policy to one with weak policy, the average pollution intensity of global production rises, increasing global environmental degradation. Moreover the shift in the incidence of environmental harm from rich to poor countries could increase human suffering, both because poorer countries are less able to afford to respond to the health effects of environmental damage and because poor countries are much more reliant on natural capital (which is vulnerable to environmental damage) to sustain their income. Finally, an exodus of pollution-intensive production from rich to poor countries could lead to a political backlash against stringent environmental policy. This possibility is sometimes referred to as a "race to the bottom"—governments may weaken or fail to enforce environmental policies due to fear of job loss as firms threaten to leave for countries with weaker policy.

Discussions of the pollution haven hypothesis often confuse two different questions. One question is whether tightening environmental policy in a country (holding all else constant, including the trade regime) reduces net exports and/or net inward foreign direct investment in pollution-intensive industries. This question is simply whether environmental policy is one of the many factors that affect international competitiveness in pollution-intensive industries. I will refer to this as the *competitiveness hypothesis*.

A second question is whether changing the trade regime by liberalizing trade or investment leads to a systematic reallocation of pollution-intensive production from countries with stringent environmental policy to countries with weak environmental policy. For this to be true, something much stronger than the competitiveness hypothesis must be satisfied: the effect of environmental policy on competitiveness has to be strong enough to be the key determinant of the overall pattern of trade and investment. I will refer to this as the *pollution haven hypothesis*.

Some authors distinguish between the two questions by defining a pollution haven *effect* to exist if the competitiveness hypothesis is satisfied. The stronger pollution haven *hypothesis* then requires both that a pollution haven effect exists and that it be strong enough to determine the direction of trade and investment flows.

Competitiveness and the Pollution Haven Effect: Theory The prediction that tighter environmental policy will reduce competitiveness is quite robust and requires only one key assumption—that more stringent environmental policy raises production costs. The most prominent alternative hypothesis is the Porter hypothesis. Porter and van der Linde (1995) argued that more stringent environmental

policy may actually increase productivity, for example by stimulating innovation. However most standard economic models predict that placing increased constraints on firms (such as via tighter environmental policy) will raise costs and hence reduce competitiveness.

Competitiveness and the Pollution Haven Effect: Empirical Evidence Testing the competitiveness hypothesis has been very challenging (see Copeland and Taylor 2004; and Copeland and Gulati 2006 for more detailed reviews). The most significant difficulty has been a lack of good data on the stringency of environmental policy. Pollution taxes are rarely used by governments, and other forms of environmental policy are difficult to quantify. A number of researchers have used county-level compliance with the Clean Air Act as a proxy for the stringency of environmental policy in the United States. The idea here is that states are required to have a plan to improve air quality in counties not in compliance with the act; consequently, noncompliance is taken to be a measure of relatively stringent environmental policy. Measures of abatement costs at the firm level have also been used; however, they are not available for very many countries, they are based on survey data, and they are problematic because they are endogenous: if the pollution haven hypothesis is correct, the most polluting firms will have been driven away by tight pollution regulation, which would lead to lower measured average abatement costs in jurisdictions with stringent environmental policy (Keller and Levinson 2002).

A second set of difficulties arises from unobserved heterogeneity across jurisdictions. Trade and investment are affected by many factors, and if some of these factors are correlated with the stringency of pollution policy, but not controlled for, then results will be affected by omitted variable bias. Recent work has used panel data techniques to deal with this type of issue; however the availability of such data is limited.

Endogeneity problems have also been a challenge. Pollution policy may respond directly to trade flows and investment and to variables correlated with trade and investment. As an example, suppose that the competitiveness hypothesis is true but countries facing significant import pressure in pollution-intensive industries respond to trade liberalization by weakening environmental policy to help protect local firms from foreign competition. Then we could find that high imports are correlated with weak environmental policy, which is opposite to what the competitiveness hypothesis predicts. This type of problem has been dealt with by using techniques such as instrumental variables.

Early work testing the competitiveness hypothesis mainly used cross-sectional data to investigate how cross-industry differences in abatement costs affected trade or investment flows (for a survey, see Jaffe et al. 1995). Most of this work found that environmental policy had little or no effect. In some cases the estimated sign was opposite to what the competitiveness hypothesis predicted—more stringent environmental policy was correlated with increased net exports. Some interpreted this finding as support for the Porter hypothesis; however, recent work has emphasized the role of omitted variable bias in affecting the results obtained from cross-sectional studies.

More recent work using panel data, mostly from the United States, has found support for the competitiveness hypothesis. A number of researchers have found that pollution regulations arising from the Clean Air Act had a significant effect on the location of new plants in pollution-intensive industries. Becker and Henderson (2000) found that new plant births in polluting industries in counties not in compliance with the Clean Air Act (and therefore subject to more stringent environmental policy) were 26–45 percent below levels in counties that were in compliance. There is also evidence that environmental policy affects trade flows. Levinson (1999) found that (all else being equal) high taxes on the disposal and processing of hazardous waste deter shipments of such waste from other states. Levinson and Taylor (2008) found that U.S. net imports are higher in industries with high abatement costs (once they accounted for the endogeneity of pollution policy using instrumental variables). This finding is consistent with the competitiveness hypothesis. The

results on foreign direct investment have been mixed. Keller and Levinson (2002) used a panel of U.S. state level data and found that states with relatively more stringent environmental policy (measured with an index of abatement costs per unit output) were less likely to attract foreign direct investment. So far, however, there is little evidence on whether the stringency of environmental policy affects the decisions of foreign firms to locate in developing countries.

Overall, a growing body of evidence supports the competitiveness hypothesis. Almost all of this work is based on U.S. data, however. More work, especially with data from developing countries, is still needed.

It is important to note that evidence that more stringent environmental policy reduces competitiveness in polluting industries does not imply that such policy is welfare decreasing. Weak environmental policy is an implicit subsidy for pollution-intensive production. Increased efficiency (and improvements in environmental quality) requires removal of this implicit subsidy, and this change will result in a shift from pollution-intensive production toward other cleaner production.

Pollution Haven Hypothesis: Theory The first pollution haven model was developed by Pethig (1976). He considered two countries that are completely identical except that one (North) has a higher pollution tax than the other (South). North's high pollution tax gives it a comparative advantage in the clean good. When trade is liberalized, trade shifts pollution-intensive production to the low-regulation country (South).

Copeland and Taylor (1994) showed how pollution havens could develop in poor countries even if all governments were free to choose whatever pollution policy best suited their countries. In the Copeland and Taylor model, countries are completely identical except in income levels. Northern countries are richer than Southern countries. The key assumption is that environmental quality is a normal good—as income increases, consumers demand higher environmental quality. If government policy is responsive to consumer demand, then the model predicts that richer countries will have more stringent environmental policy than poorer countries. Consequently, poor countries will have a comparative advantage in pollution-intensive production. When trade is liberalized, North exports clean goods, and South exports pollution-intensive goods: poor countries will become pollution havens.

This result is only part of the story. In reality, there are many reasons for trade, and the actual pattern of trade depends on the interaction among all such motives. Antweiler, Copeland, and Taylor (2001) developed a pollution haven model suitable for empirical testing by allowing for more than one motive for trade. In this model, countries differ in capital abundance as well as in income levels. Suppose that pollution-intensive industry is also capital intensive and that North is capital abundant. North's capital abundance tends to give it a comparative advantage in the pollution-intensive industry, but its stringent pollution policy tends to give it a comparative advantage in the clean industry. If the effects of North's capital abundance on the trade pattern are more important than the cost-increasing effect of its stricter environmental policy, then North will have a comparative advantage in the pollution-intensive good and trade liberalization will shift pollution-intensive production from the low-income South to the high-income North. In short, theory predicts that pollution policy is but one of many factors that affect trade. Whether or not trade liberalization leads to pollution havens depends on whether the effects of differences in environmental policy on production costs are more or less important than all of the other motives for trade.

Pollution Haven Hypothesis: Empirical Evidence Surprisingly, there is relatively little work that directly tests the pollution haven hypothesis. Several studies have found that the share of pollution-intensive goods in exports from developing countries has risen over time and the share of pollution-intensive goods in exports from members of the Organisation for Economic Co-operation and Development (OECD) has fallen over time. These trends are also consistent, however, with economic growth and capital accumulation in developing countries and are not a full test of the pollution haven hypothesis.

Ederington, Levinson, and Minier (2004) looked at the pollution content of U.S. exports and imports during the period 1972–94 and found that U.S. imports from non–OECD countries have become less pollution intensive over time relative to U.S. exports. This finding is opposite to what the pollution haven hypothesis predicts. Antweiler et al. (2001) estimate the effects of increased openness to trade on sulfur dioxide pollution, controlling for scale and other factors. They found that, all else equal, increased openness tended to increase SO_2 pollution in rich countries and reduce it in poor countries. Again this is opposite to what the pollution haven hypothesis predicts. Both Ederington et al. and Antweiler et al. argue that the evidence suggests that other factors (such as capital abundance or agglomeration) are more important than environmental policy in explaining trade flows.

In summary, there is a growing body of evidence that more stringent environmental policy does reduce a country's competitiveness in pollution-intensive industry, but there is little or no evidence to support the strong version of the pollution haven hypothesis: other factors are more important (on average) for affecting trade patterns. These are, however, the results of studies that look at broad patterns. There will be cases where poor countries have a comparative advantage in polluting industry for reasons unconnected with environmental policy (such as in polluting industries intensive in the use of unskilled labor). In cases such as this, weak pollution policy will reinforce the preexisting comparative advantage and increase the tendency for such industry to locate in a poor country.

Consumption-Generated Pollution Much analysis of the pollution haven hypothesis has focused on production-generated pollution. However, much pollution is generated by consumption (such as home heating, automobile transportation, and sewage). The effects of environmental policy on competitiveness are very different when regulations target consumption-generated pollution. For example, stringent automobile emission standards are applied to all automobiles sold within a country, regardless of whether they are produced locally or imported. Consequently, tighter emission standards need not reduce domestic competitiveness. In fact, if it is easier for domestic producers than foreign producers to comply with stringent emission standards, then tighter environmental policy aimed at consumption-generated pollution may favor domestic producers over foreign producers. Hence the scope for trade-induced pollution haven effects is reduced when environmental policy affects consumption-generated pollution.

Natural Capital and Pollution Havens The effects of environmental policy on natural capital can be critically important for trade patterns. Consider the example of fisheries (where the fish stock is natural capital). Conservation requires that harvest rates be held below open access levels to ensure that the fish stock is sustainable. Hence in the short run, a country with weak conservation policy may harvest fish at a much greater rate than countries with good conservation policy. This can lead to a result analogous to pollution havens—trade liberalization would increase pressure on fish stocks in countries with weak conservation policy and exacerbate resource depletion in those countries.

However, it is possible for trade to have the opposite effect, especially in cases where resources are severely depleted. If a country has severely depleted its fish stock, then its potential supply of fish will be low. On the other hand, countries with relatively stringent conservation policies will have a much larger fish stock and hence a greater sustainable supply of fish. Hence when trade is liberalized, it is quite possible that countries with good conservation policies will be net exporters of fish and countries with poor conservation policies will be net importers of fish (Brander and Taylor 1997). Again, this is opposite to what the pollution haven hypothesis would predict.

See also location theory; trade and the environment

FURTHER READING

Antweiler, W., B. R. Copeland, and M. S. Taylor. 2001. "Is Free Trade Good for the Environment?" *American Economic Review* 91 (4): 877–90. An empirical study assessing the effect of trade on sulfur dioxide pollution.

Becker, R., and V. Henderson. 2000. "Effects of Air Quality Regulations on Polluting Industries." *Journal of Political Economy* 108 (2): 379–421. An influential study that investigates the effect of the Clean Air Act on industrial location.

Brander J. A., and M. S. Taylor. 1997. "International Trade between Consumer and Conservationist Countries." *Resource and Energy Economics* 19 (4): 267–98. A theoretical paper that shows how natural capital depletion affects trade flows.

Copeland, B. R., and S. Gulati. 2006. "Trade and the Environment in Developing Economies." In *Economic Development and Environmental Sustainability: New Policy Options*, edited by R. Lopez and M. A. Toman. Oxford University Press, 178–216. A nontechnical review of the literature on trade and the environment.

Copeland, B. R., and M.S. Taylor. 1994. "North-South Trade and the Environment." *Quarterly Journal of Economics* 109 (3): 755–87. The first model of endogenous pollution havens.

———. 2004. "Trade, Growth, and the Environment." *Journal of Economic Literature* 42 (1): 7–71. A more technical review of the literature on both the competitiveness hypothesis and the pollution haven hypothesis.

Ederington, W. J., A. Levinson, and J. Minier. 2004. "Trade Liberalization and Pollution Havens." *Advances in Economic Analysis and Policy* 4 (2): Article 6. One of the few studies to explicitly test the pollution haven hypothesis.

Fullerton, D., ed. 2006. *The Economics of Pollution Havens.* Cheltenham, UK: Edward Elgar. An excellent collection of original research papers examining the pollution haven hypothesis.

Jaffe, A., S. Peterson, P. Portney, and R. Stavins. 1995. "Environmental Regulation and the Competitiveness of U.S. Manufacturing: What Does the Evidence Tell Us?" *The Journal of Economic Literature* 33 (1): 132–63. An influential review of the literature on the competitiveness hypothesis, but it came out before the recent work using panel data and confronting endogeneity problems.

Keller, W., and A. Levinson. 2002. "Pollution Abatement Costs and Foreign Direct Investment Inflows to U.S. States." *Review of Economics and Statistics* 84 (4): 691–

703. Uses panel data to assess the effects of environmental policy on inward foreign direct investment.

Levinson, A. 1999. "State Taxes and Interstate Hazardous Waste Shipments." *American Economic Review* 89 (3): 666–77. A test of the competitiveness hypothesis using a panel of U.S. data on hazardous waste flows.

Levinson A., and M. S. Taylor. 2008. "Trade and the Environment: Unmasking the Pollution Haven Effect." *International Economic Review* 49 (1): 223–54. A test of the competitiveness hypothesis using a panel of U.S. trade data.

Pethig, R. 1976. "Pollution, Welfare, and Environmental Policy in the Theory of Comparative Advantage." *Journal of Environmental Economics and Management* 2 (3): 160–69. The first pollution haven model.

Porter, Michael E., and Claas van de Linde. 1995. "Toward a New Conception of the Environment-Competitiveness Relationship." *Journal of Economic Perspectives* 9 (4): 97–118. Hypothesizes that environmental policy can increase competitiveness.

BRIAN R. COPELAND

■ poverty, global

The most commonly used definition of poverty is a lack of income; more specifically, having an income below an amount (the poverty line) deemed necessary for a minimum acceptable level of material well-being. Income is just a means to an end, however. There are more direct measures of the quality of life, such as health, education, and possibly freedom of expression. Poverty estimates also regularly make reference to mortality rates, schooling, and literacy.

Poverty may be defined and measured in either a relative sense (deprivation compared to societal norms) or an absolute sense (deprivation compared to being able to afford "objective" basic needs of food, clothing, and shelter). Discussions of global poverty have settled on an absolute definition of poverty, implicitly relegating concerns about income distribution to secondary importance. Doing so has deflected attention from redistribution and the role it can play in poverty reduction. Since the World Bank's 1990 *World Development Report*, "a dollar a day" has become the standard international poverty line—a level based on an average of the poverty line being used in 10 developing countries at the time, although more recent estimates also use two dollars a day, which is a more relevant poverty line for middle-income countries such as those in Latin America.

Poverty estimates using the dollar-a-day line are made using "purchasing power parity," meaning they allow for differences in purchasing power as many items cost less in developing countries than in developed ones. The most commonly reported measure is the poverty headcount (the percentage of the population below the poverty line), but the same data can be used to calculate the poverty gap, which is a summary measure of the average distance of the poor below the poverty line, and the poverty severity index, which gives greater weight to the poorest. The poverty measures used in health and education are also absolute; that is, they do not base well-being on a comparison of the same indicators for the better off at either the national or international level.

Patterns of Poverty Estimates of dollar-a-day poverty are calculated only for the developing world. The proportion of absolutely poor in developed countries by this measure is nil or negligible. Figure 1 shows the evolution of dollar-a-day poverty since the early 1980s. The most striking trend is the dramatic fall in poverty in East Asia, powered largely by reductions in the number of poor in the world's most populous country, China, but assisted by more recent declines in neighboring Vietnam. There has been a slower, but still marked, decline in the poverty headcount in South Asia, including in the world's second largest country, India. By the mid-1990s the rate of decline was sufficient for the absolute number of poor people in South Asia to start falling. Asia thus makes up the vast bulk of poverty reduction in the closing decades of the last century. During the 1990s global poverty fell from 27.9 percent in 1990 to 21.1 percent in 2001, but excluding China these figures were 26.1 and 22.2 percent, respectively. That is, more than half the decrease in poverty came from China alone. Indeed sub-Saharan Africa, which has suffered economic hardship since the 1970s, saw a rise in income poverty, with close to half the people

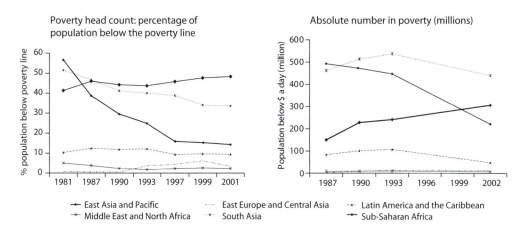

Figure 1

Dollar-a-day poverty by region, 1983–2002. Source: World Bank Poverty Monitoring Web site, http://web.worldbank.org/WBSITE/EXTERNAL/TOPICS/EXTPOVERTY/EXTPAME/0,,contentMDK: 20188187~pagePK:210058~piPK:210062~theSitePK:384263,00.html.

on the subcontinent now living on less than a dollar a day. Africa's poor performance lies behind the low overall decrease in the number of poor from 1.20 billion in 1987 to 1.03 billion in 2002. Africa's share in this total rose from 12 percent to 30 percent over this period (whereas Asia's fell from 80 percent to 64 percent). The final trend of note is the resurgence of poverty in the formerly centrally planned economies following the collapse of the communist governments, though there has been some remission since the beginning of the 21st century.

The Africanization of poverty is also evident when considering other poverty measures. Health is commonly measured by infant mortality (the number of children who die before their first birthday per 1,000 live births) and child mortality (deaths between first and fifth birthdays per 1,000 children); these two indicators are combined to make under-five mortality. The United Nations Population Division reports population data, including mortality, from 1950, with projections to 2050, though only those to 2010 are shown here. The positive news is that mortality rates have been falling across the world (figure 2), although some African countries experienced a reversal in the 1990s as a result of HIV/AIDS and worsening health systems after three decades of economic decline. At the extreme, life expectancy in

Botswana has fallen by 29 years since 1990, from 64 to just 34 years. In Africa as a whole the decline in mortality rates has been insufficient to keep up with population growth, so the number of deaths has continued to increase. A turnaround is expected, but another expectation is that the situation in Africa will improve less than that elsewhere, so the continent will account for close to two-thirds of the world's under-five deaths in the coming decades.

Progress in education has gone in stops and starts. During the colonial period there was little formal education for most of the population in much of the developing world other than that provided by mission schools. Newly independent governments undertook substantial expansions of the education sector at all levels, though enrollments remained well below half of all children, especially in rural areas. Since 2002 there has been a renewed emphasis on raising primary education levels with the international Fast Track Initiative. Many countries, notably in Africa, have pushed for higher enrollments, scrapping school fees at the primary level, resulting in rapid increases in student numbers, although across the subcontinent as whole about 30 percent of children do not attend school, and many of those who do learn little. In Asia also large strides have been made in moving toward full enrollment in recent years so

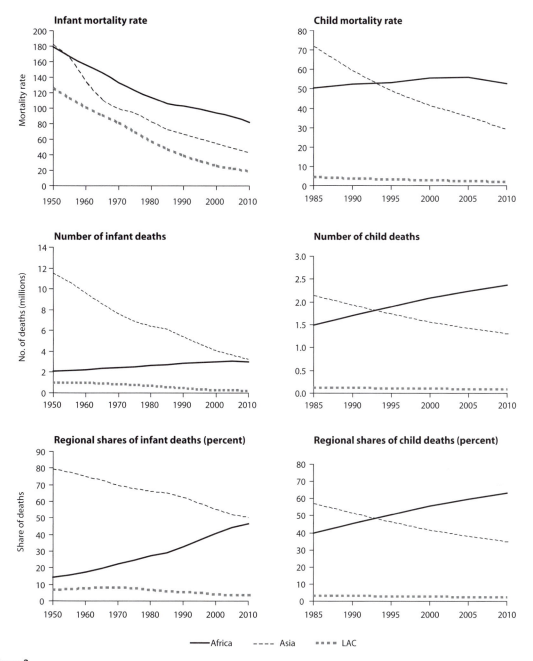

Figure 2

Trends in infant and child mortality. Source: UN Population Division database, http://esa.un.org/unpp/.

that primary enrollments exceeded 90 percent as of 2007, and the focus has shifted to secondary education with international agencies financing stipend schemes for girls in rural areas.

These aggregates hide systematic patterns in poverty at the national level. Poverty is nearly always higher in rural areas than urban ones: at least 80 percent of Africa's poor live in rural areas, where income opportunities are fewer and service provision lower. There are usually disadvantaged regions where poverty is higher: for example, infant and child mortality rates may be twice the national average. In Bangladesh, for instance, neonatal mortality (death in the first month) is 32 per 1,000 live births in Barisal Division, but 63 per 1,000 in the more conservative Sylhet Division, where tradition prevents women from seeking medical assistance even in the case of birth complications. These variations may reflect ethnic or racial biases and are not confined to developing countries: African Americans have a higher rate of under-five mortality than do white South Africans (indeed, the United States as a whole has a higher under-five mortality rate than does Cuba).

Gender also plays an important role in poverty. Girls are less likely than boys to be in school, and women continue to earn less than men for their labor. In rural India a woman's daily agricultural wage is typically half that of a man's. Female-headed households are typically poorer than those that are male-headed, although this is not the case when there is an absent male sending remittances back to the household. And families in most of Asia prefer sons to the extent that female infants are often neglected, with food and health care given preferentially to male children.

Globalization of Poverty The globalization of poverty is the view that we are today affected by the poverty of those in other nations in ways we were not in the past. In the words of the former German premier Willy Brandt, who led the team responsible for the 1980 report *North-South*, "Ignoring the problems of the South is like a person on a sinking ship saying 'I'm all right, my end's not sinking.'" Brandt's view was one of global Keynesianism: growth in the

developing world will power growth at home through increased demand for our exports, whereas decline overseas will cause eventual decline at home. Other aspects of global poverty are also thought to spill over to affect the West in ways that did not happen before, such as disease and the increased flow of refugees fleeing from conflict or disasters.

These views overstate the extent to which global interdependence is a new phenomenon. One-quarter of the Irish population emigrated to the United States during the potato famine of the 1840s, and a similar percentage of the Scottish population did so as a result of Highland clearances in the same century (landlords turning land cultivated by smallholding tenants over to sheep grazing). Earlier settlers brought with them illnesses that wiped out a large part of the indigenous population. Centuries earlier the Black Death spread from Asia to Europe, killing up to two-thirds of the European population.

Strategies to Tackle Global Poverty Two broad approaches may be identified in the dominant discourses on development. Official agencies emphasize the role that growth can play and believe that growth is best brought about through liberalization of markets. Others, including most nongovernmental organizations, place greater emphasis on the need for development aid.

According to the first view, the best support the West can give to reduce poverty is to encourage developing countries to deepen their engagement with the global economy and to open up to private sector capital flows. But critics point to the apparent hypocrisy of developed countries, which continue to practice protective policies, notably subsidies to agriculture, that are harmful to the welfare of developing countries. For example, U.S. subsidies to domestic cotton producers reduce the prices received by farmers growing cotton in countries such as Brazil and Zambia. Furthermore, although there can be benefits from capital inflows, short-term speculative flows can be destabilizing, as shown by the East Asian crisis of the late 1990s. Others point out that an increased global flow of labor, rather than capital, would probably do most to reduce poverty but is restricted by the developed countries. On balance, however, one can say that many developing countries engaged in excessive degrees of state intervention following independence and that dismantling these controls has freed up resources to be used more productively in growth. But this argument does not support the view that full liberalization of all markets is the most conducive means to sustained growth and certainly not the fastest route to poverty reduction.

Aid's impact on poverty has been muted since poverty reduction has not always been the explicit focus of foreign aid. This is partly because donor countries also use aid to pursue their own political and commercial objectives. But it is also because aid has focused on other issues, such as the development of infrastructure in the 1950s and 1960s and on restoring economic growth, albeit with mixed success, in the 1980s. There was a clearer poverty focus in the 1970s, under the banner of Basic Needs, and it reemerged more strongly in the 1990s. Reviews of aid's poverty impact provide a mixed picture—there are undoubted success stories of aid improving the lives of poor people, but a lot of aid at best leaves them unaffected and at worst harms them. Efforts to ensure that aid indeed benefits the poor are being made but can run into political opposition in both developed and developing countries.

The latest stage in efforts to focus aid on poverty are the Millennium Development Goals (MDGS), formerly the International Development Targets. These are a set of targets based on various UN resolutions, such as the halving of income poverty by 2015, a two-thirds reduction in infant and child mortality by the same date, and the already missed target of equality in girls' education by 2005. Aid donors have responded to this increased poverty focus by concentrating aid on poorer countries and reorientating it toward basic services, such as providing money for rural health clinics rather than urban hospitals and the stipend schemes for girls to attend secondary school in Asia mentioned earlier.

In most low-income countries aid is given in the context of Poverty Reduction Strategy Papers (PRSP), which are a formal requirement for countries receiving debt relief from the Highly Indebted Poor Country Initiative. Central to these strategies,

promoted by the World Bank and the International Monetary Fund, is the notion that economic growth is the key to poverty reduction and that growth is best brought about by liberalized markets: hence critics argue that PRSPs are just "business as usual." A contrary view of development comes from the United Nations Development Program (UNDP) through its *Human Development Reports*, which argues that there is a larger role of government through direct investments in social infrastructure, which can bring about reductions in poverty faster than is possible by growth alone.

Future Poverty Trends Analysis of likely future trends shows a continuation of the patterns discussed here, most notably the continuing Africanization of poverty as poverty levels fall in Asia but with at best slow progress in Africa. The MDG for a halving of income poverty will be met in most of Asia, but not in Africa or in the former communist countries of Eastern Europe; poverty in these regions began to rise after the MDG base year of 1990 and is unlikely to meet its former low levels by 2015, let alone fall to half the 1990 levels.

These forecasts assume "business as usual." But it is likely that things will be worse than that on account of both manmade and natural disasters. Poor countries and poor people are least able to withstand these shocks; households do not have insurance and the country is less able to afford reconstruction—as shown comparing the amounts spent on reconstruction after Hurricane Katrina in 2005 and after the far worse Indian Ocean tsunami in 2004. Conflict destroys livelihoods, disrupts education, allows the reemergence of disease, and can set growth back by years. Civil wars and regional conflicts continue to have these adverse effects around the world. A larger shock from a global conflict is not an impossibility, which would render all projections meaningless.

See also development; evolution of development thinking; global income inequality; International Monetary Fund (IMF); World Bank

FURTHER READING

Black, Richard, and Howard White, eds. 2004. *Targeting Development: Critical Perspectives on the Millennium*

Development Goals. London: Routledge. Critiques each of the MDGs and what governments in both the developed and developing world can do to achieve them.

UNDP. Annual. *Human Development Report.* New York: UNDP. Focuses on a different development-related issue each year and updates various development and poverty measures, such as the Human Poverty Index.

World Bank. Annual. *Global Monitoring Report.* Washington, DC: World Bank. Covers MDG-related indicators, with summary overview and a different thematic focus each year.

HOWARD WHITE

■ **preferential trade area**
See free trade area

■ **pricing to market**
See exchange rate pass-through

■ **primary products trade**
Primary products are unprocessed raw materials. They include agricultural, forestry, fishing, and mining products, including minerals and fuels. Unlike the processing of these raw materials into manufactured goods, the ability to produce primary products is limited by natural endowments: some regions have the deposits of oil or minerals, the soil and climate, or the natural fisheries that make it possible to obtain these products, while other regions do not. As a consequence, human beings have engaged in primary product trade from time immemorial. Today, primary products account for around 25 percent of global merchandise trade. The ability to exchange agricultural and fisheries products has enriched diets, while access to forestry and mining products has enhanced the consumption possibilities of communities located far from the sources of these products.

Despite the advantages of primary product trade to consumers, it has been the subject of intense criticism. Do the countries producing these products gain equivalent benefits? Does concentrating a country's resources in the production of primary products enhance the welfare of its citizens? Does it provide a sound basis for a country's long-term growth and development? These questions are of more than academic concern for developing countries, many of whose exports are heavily concentrated in primary products. Indeed, today primary products account for only 19 percent of the merchandise exports of high-income countries, but 36 percent of the exports of middle-income countries and 50 percent of the exports of low-income countries. For many developing regions, this figure is even higher: 69 percent in sub-Saharan Africa and fully 80 percent in the Middle East and North Africa.

Classical and Neoclassical Trade Theory Classical economists were the first to systematically address whether primary exports were good for welfare, which they answered in the affirmative. Based on differences in techniques of production, the Ricardian trade model showed that there were potential gains for each country engaging in comparative advantage trade. In such trade, each country specializes in those products it can produce at lower relative labor cost than other countries. The Heckscher-Ohlin trade model of the 1920s assumed countries could choose from the same array of technologies to produce any product, but they still faced differences in their factor endowments and therefore in relative factor prices. These differences resulted in different choices of technology and in different relative product costs. If each country chose to specialize in the products in which it had a lower opportunity cost, global production would be carried out by the most efficient producers, and global output would increase. Trade would allow consumers in all countries to increase their consumption beyond the limits imposed by their own capabilities.

Prebisch-Singer Critique The Heckscher-Ohlin model and its variants, generally referred to as the neoclassical trade model, showed that every country gains from comparative advantage trade, no matter what specific product a country exports. This conclusion was based, however, on the assumption that markets are perfectly competitive and that relative prices therefore reflect relative costs. The first serious critique of the neoclassical model came in the 1930s and 1940s, from the economists Raúl Prebisch and Hans Singer, who challenged this fundamental assumption. They argued that the benefits for primary exporters were limited. Primary exporters faced both fluctuating prices for their products and declining terms of trade, resulting in volatile and diminishing gains over time.

The most commonly cited elements of their critique have to do with the elasticities involved. First, price inelastic demand for agricultural products combines with frequent weather- or pest-induced shifts in supply to create considerable volatility in agricultural prices. Second, income inelastic demand for many primary products, especially agricultural products (Engel's Law), combined with considerably higher income elasticities for manufactures, contributes to declining relative prices or commodity terms of trade for many primary exporting countries. In addition, the development of synthetic substitutes can contribute to sharp declines in primary product prices. Synthetic dyes, chemical fertilizers, and synthetic fibers, for example, have caused collapses in the markets for natural dyes, for organic and mineral fertilizers, and for natural fibers, while plastics have affected the markets for a broad range of forestry and mineral products. Critics of primary export specialization point to numerous episodes of economic collapse in primary-exporting countries resulting from these developments.

In addition, Prebisch and Singer first advanced the argument that markets were not perfectly competitive and that international market prices might in fact not reflect relative costs of production. Although the production of many primary products could be said to occur under competitive conditions, producers faced a limited number of buyers (oligopsony or monopsony) when they sold their raw materials. These buyers had the market power to drive producer prices below their competitive level. On the other hand, manufactured goods purchased by developing countries tended to be produced in oligopolistic markets, where suppliers had the market power to

potentially raise prices above competitive levels. Put together, these market characteristics suggested that primary-exporting developing countries got paid too little for their exports, while paying too much for their imports. A corollary is that technological progress would be encouraged in the industrial countries but discouraged in the primary exporting developing countries. More recent trade models have included elements of noncompetitive markets, especially increasing returns to scale, which capture these aspects of international pricing that disadvantage primary exporters (e.g., Greenaway 1991).

The experience of the Latin American region in the century following independence in the 1820s provided Prebisch with clear evidence of the volatility of primary product export earnings, as countries experienced related boom-and-bust cycles with alarming frequency. More recently, commodity crises have affected producers of coffee, cocoa, tin, and cotton, to name but a few. Prebisch also found evidence for his arguments in the data collected by the United Nations, which showed a steady decline in the prices of primary products compared with manufactures in international markets from 1876 to 1938. More recent studies have found similar declines over the 20th century for non-oil-exporting developing countries.

This original empirical evidence was critiqued, however, because it did not take account of changes in the costs of production. Productivity gains in primary production could have accounted for the relative decline in primary product prices. Given the difficulty of calculating the "double-factoral" terms of trade that take account of productivity changes, the debate over the empirical evidence continues today.

Agricultural Subsidies and Developed-Country Trade Barriers What is not subject to debate is the effect that agricultural subsidies have had on global prices for many products. For decades, the advanced industrial countries have provided large subsidies to their agricultural producers, especially producers of grains, dairy, cotton, and tobacco. These subsidies have given developed-country agricultural products a price advantage that has lowered global prices of these products and undercut less subsidized producers in developing countries (Oxfam 2002). The decline in international prices for these products has also been encouraged by persistent protectionist policies in the industrial countries, as well as by efforts to encourage increased production of agricultural exports in developing countries under structural adjustment programs. Developing country protests regarding these pricing issues led to the breakdown of the World Trade Organization's Doha Round of negotiations.

Distribution of Gains from Trade Another element of the critique of primary product exports is the question of the distribution of any gains within the producing country. The Stolper-Samuelson extension of the neoclassical model predicts that trade will raise the price of the factor utilized intensively in the exported product. Many observers assumed that for developing countries this factor would be labor, since capital was scarce, and that as a result international trade would benefit the poor through increased wages. Primary products exports increase the demand for natural resources much more than for labor, however, so most of the benefits of such trade accrue to landowners, often an already wealthy elite. It is no surprise, then, to find that the century of primary export specialization and trade in Latin America, from the 1820s to the 1920s, created a region with the most unequal income distribution in the world, a legacy that persists to this day. The increasing concentration of natural resource ownership over this period ensured that most of the benefits from primary export trade went to a small land-owning elite. In more recent times, many developing countries have found that much of the wealth from exploitation of natural resources has accrued to foreign investors.

If there are overall gains from trade, it is possible to distribute the gains broadly, although whether this occurs in practice depends on the social and political institutions that influence access to natural resources. One approach is to maintain public ownership of key natural resources and to use the revenues for public expenditures that provide widespread benefits to the population. Unfortunately, this is not always the way these revenues are actually used. Another approach is to allow private development of natural resources but tax resource owners in order to spread the benefits

of trade. These efforts have met with mixed success due to the ability of foreign investors to influence political outcomes. In Guatemala, for example, the United Fruit Company, a large landowner and the country's main banana exporter, was able to avoid all but minimal taxes for more than 50 years.

Dynamic Trade Benefits Beyond these issues regarding the static gains from trade, perhaps of even greater significance for the developing countries is the effect of primary product specialization and trade on the long-term growth of the economy: the "dynamic" trade effect. Proponents of comparative advantage trade argue that it can serve as an "engine of growth" for the overall economy. This will occur through expanded factor endowments and spillovers or linkages.

Expanded factor endowments will occur if the export sector is able to attract foreign investment and the capital, skilled labor, and technological know-how that it can bring into the country. Human capital may expand as a result of the "learning-by-doing" effect. These effects will increase productivity and incomes in the export industries, creating profits that can be reinvested into continued productivity gains and expansion of the sector.

At the same time, spillovers and linkages may develop to other productive activities in the economy. The income from primary exports increases consumer demand and may finance investment in new industries. Backward linkages may develop to domestic suppliers of inputs for the export industry, as demand for those inputs grows and allows suppliers to produce at efficient levels. Forward linkages may develop to the processing, transportation, storage, and marketing of the export products, with spillovers to services for other domestic products. Infrastructure constructed to facilitate the production and trade of the export products may also serve other productive sectors. Exports can therefore serve as a growth pole, stimulating other economic activities in an ever-expanding process of economic diversification.

Limited Dynamic Benefits for Primary Product Exporters While advocates of comparative advantage trade predict that dynamic benefits will accrue to any country, regardless of the specific products they export, critics argue that the extent of these benefits can be limited for countries whose comparative advantage lies in primary products. Indeed, some have gone so far as to posit a "resource curse" effect, whereby abundant natural resources reduce a country's growth rate.

There are numerous theories as to why this may be the case. Factor endowments will not expand if declining terms of trade reduce profitability of primary exports. The same negative impact on investment can occur if extraction of nonrenewable resources raises production costs or if renewable resources are overtaxed, so that the country's comparative advantage gradually declines.

Even if investment in the primary sector continues to be robust, critics argue that spillovers and linkages are unlikely to develop, for many reasons. Some arguments focus on the employment and income effects of resource wealth. Rural wealth and employment may raise industrial real wages and therefore reduce incentives to invest in manufacturing. At the same time, primary products may generate fewer learning effects than manufactures, so that the country's labor force skills remain underdeveloped.

On the other hand, some primary products may be land- and capital-intensive, generating limited employment and therefore limited consumption multiplier effects. This is most likely with mining activities, but can also occur with large-scale, mechanized agricultural production. While these activities can create considerable wealth for investors and landowners, this wealth may not remain in the developing country, especially in the case of multinational investment. Profits, dividends, royalties, and the earnings of skilled expatriate employees may be remitted rather than entering into domestic financial institutions.

One reason for this capital flight may be the continued low profitability of manufacturing investment in the country, as spillovers fail to materialize. Economies of scale in manufacturing, especially in the case of technologically complex production processes, can make it difficult for developing countries to produce on a profitable scale. This can limit backward linkages to capital and intermediate goods, forward linkages to processing, or consumption linkages to consumer durables, especially for smaller countries. These cost disadvantages can be compounded by the limited technological capabilities of the labor force and the underdeveloped state of the country's institutions and infrastructure. While there may be spillovers from infrastructure developed to support primary production, these extractive activities are often geographically isolated from main population centers, their infrastructure therefore conferring few external benefits.

Geographic isolation is not the only reason why centers of primary production may become "enclaves." The very success of primary exports can, paradoxically, have this effect, in a process that has been dubbed the "Dutch disease." A booming export sector can act as a black hole, pulling resources into itself and thereby raising production costs for domestic manufacturers, while the inflow of foreign currency causes the prices of competing manufactured imports to fall. Rather than creating positive spillovers, the booming export sector creates negative externalities for other tradables sectors. Resource windfalls have also been found to have a negative effect on overall savings and investment and to stimulate rent-seeking behavior.

There is evidence to support the contention that primary exporters do not gain dynamic trade benefits. Sachs and Warner (2001), for example, found that countries with a higher percentage of natural resource–based exports in 1970 grew more slowly from 1970 to 1990. There are, nevertheless, exceptions to this general rule, as proponents of the "staples theory" argue (Lewis 1989). Malaysia and Thailand, for example, are resource-rich countries that have experienced exceptionally high growth rates since the 1970s (Reinhardt 2000). Recent literature suggests that the impact of resource abundance on growth is not immutable but rather depends on institutions, educational and industrial policy, and the nature of the learning process (Mehlum, Moene, and Torvik 2006). On the other hand, there is evidence that these variables are themselves influenced by natural resource abundance, being indirect channels through which resource wealth inhibits economic growth (Papyrakis and Gerlagh 2004).

While the debate over primary exports continues, trade liberalization in the past several decades has increased the importance of this issue for many developing countries, who find their short-term welfare and long-term prospects tied to the fortunes of their primary products. Although commodity price booms such as those of recent years have created windfall gains for many developing countries, they still face the difficult task of turning those primary export gains into a sound basis for growth and development.

See also North-South trade; terms of trade; trade and economic development, international

FURTHER READING

Atkinson, Giles, and Kirk Hamilton. 2003. "Savings, Growth and the Resource Curse Hypothesis." *World Development* 31 (11): 1793–1807. Shows link between resource wealth and low rates of savings and growth.

Auty, Richard. 1994. "Industrial Policy Reform in Six Large Newly Industrializing Countries: The Resource Curse Thesis." *World Development* 22 (1): 11–26. Case studies that demonstrate the "resource curse" argument.

Dodaro, Santo. 1991. "Comparative Advantage, Trade, and Growth: Export-Led Growth Revisited." *World Development* 19 (9): 1153–65. Demonstrates importance of industrial exports to growth.

Greenaway, David. 1991. "New Trade Theories and Developing Countries." In *Current Issues in Development Economics*, edited by V. N. Balasubramanyam and Sanjaya Lall. New York: St. Martin's Press, 156–70. Reviews literature incorporating noncompetitive models.

Lewis, S. R. 1989. "Primary Exporting Countries." In *Handbook of Development Economics*, vol. 2, edited by Hollis Chenery and T. N. Srinivasan. Amsterdam: North-Holland Press, 1541–99. Detailed review of primary trade theory and country examples showing how developing countries can benefit from it.

Mehlum, Halvor, Karl Moene, and Ragnar Torvik. 2006. "Institutions and the Resource Curse." *Economic Journal* 116 (508): 1–20. Suggests that the resource curse is a matter of policy rather than necessity.

Oxfam. 2002. *Rigged Rules and Double Standards: Trade, Globalization, and the Fight against Poverty*. London: Oxfam International. Estimates costs to developing countries of developed country agricultural subsidies and tariffs on primary imports.

Papyrakis, Elissaios, and Reyer Gerlagh. 2004. "The Resource Curse Hypothesis and Its Transmission Channels," *Journal of Comparative Economics* 24 (1): 181–93. Empirical study demonstrating the mechanisms by which resource wealth can slow growth.

———. 2006. "Resource Windfalls, Investment, and Long-term Income." *Resources Policy* 31 (2): 117–28. Shows how primary export windfalls can lower investment and long-run growth.

Prebisch, Raúl. 1950. *The Economic Development of Latin America and Its Principal Problems*. Lake Success, NY: United Nations. Prebisch's classic paper outlining his theory of primary product trade.

Reinhardt, Nola. 2000. "Back to Basics in Malaysia and Thailand: The Role of Resource-Based Exports in Their Export-Led Growth." *World Development* 28 (1): 57–77. Shows how some countries have benefited from primary product trade.

Sachs, Jeffrey, and Andrew Warner. 1995. "Natural Resource Abundance and Economic Growth," NBER Working Paper No. 5398. Cambridge, MA: National Bureau of Economic Research. Reviews the arguments and evidence against primary product trade.

———. 2001. "The Curse of Natural Resources." *European Economic Review* 45 (4–6): 827–38. Empirical study showing the negative relationship between primary product exports and developing country growth.

Singer, Hans. 1950. "The Distribution of Trade between Investing and Borrowing Countries." *American Economic Review* 40 (2): 473–85. Singer's classic paper critiquing developing country primary product trade.

NOLA REINHARDT

■ private sector involvement

See bail-ins

■ protectionism

See nontariff measures; tariffs

■ proximity-concentration hypothesis

The proximity-concentration hypothesis or trade-off is a way to explain why firms undertake horizontal foreign direct investment (FDI), in which firms produce the same product at plants in multiple countries. Firms do so when the benefits of avoiding high trade costs outweigh the costs incurred when producing in multiple markets. Firms are more likely to undertake horizontal FDI as transport costs and trade barriers become higher and as investment barriers and scale economies at the plant level become lower.

Horizontal FDI models are motivated by a large and increasing share of FDI, especially two-way FDI, which takes place between economies with similar factor proportions. Models of vertical FDI (in which different parts of the production process are done in different countries), by contrast, suggest that FDI should arise between economies with different factor proportions (and in only one direction). The proximity-concentration hypothesis also draws from the literature on ownership, location, and internalization advantages as drivers of FDI (mostly ownership and location advantages).

Understanding why multinationals often establish multiple plants in various countries is important because it highlights factors that affect these decisions and informs businesses and policymakers on appropriate policy measures that could influence such investments.

Theoretical Framework A firm has several modes of servicing an overseas market: exports, FDI, or licensing. In deciding on its overseas expansion strategy, a firm faces trade-offs between proximity and concentration advantages. Proximity advantages could arise from savings on transportation, tariff, and warehousing costs, superior customer services, better understanding of the local market conditions, and access to specialized inputs. The concentration advantage arises from any scale economies at the firm or plant level. Economies of scale at the firm level are associated with activities such as research and development, marketing, advertising, and management services, while economies of scale at the plant level result in lower per unit cost as the scale of production increases. Brainard (1997) states, "The proximity-concentration hypothesis predicts that firms should expand horizontally across borders whenever the advantages of access to the destination market outweigh the advantages from production scale economies."

Among the many models of horizontal FDI, Markusen (1984) pioneered one in which multiplant economies are a driver for multinational investment. Multiplant economies are the result of a joint input that can be shared across multiple production facilities and whose productivity is not affected by the number of facilities at which it is used. In this scenario, multinational production avoids costly duplication of the joint input that would arise with independent national firms.

Brainard (1993) coined the term *proximity-concentration trade-off/hypothesis*. She uses a model in which firms chose between exports and FDI based on scale economies at the firm and plant level, and transportation costs that increase with distance. Absent factor price differences, firms compare the additional variable cost of exporting with the additional fixed cost of setting up a plant overseas. This model has three possible equilibria: a multinational equilibrium where all firms are multinationals with plants in both countries; a trade equilibrium where all firms are national with a single plant and export to foreign countries; and a mixed equilibrium where multinational and national firms coexist.

With a two-stage production structure, two-way horizontal intraindustry FDI completely crowds out trade in goods even without differences in factor proportions, as long as proximity advantages are strong relative to concentration advantages. For intermediate ranges of transportation costs and scale economies at the firm level relative to plant-level scale economies, there is a mixed equilibrium in which national and multinational firms coexist in this sector: there is two-way trade in final goods and two-way FDI. For a fixed number of firms, the proportion of firms that export is greater the larger the plant-level fixed costs and the smaller the transportation and other trade costs and the size of each market.

If concentration advantages dominate in upstream activities (activities that take place at the initial stages of production, e.g., production of intermediate inputs) and proximity advantages dominate downstream activities (activities that take place after the final stage of production through the consumption stage, e.g., transportation, distribution, and marketing activities), the incorporation of a third stage of production, such as sales, results in two-way intrafirm, intraindustry trade in intermediate goods replacing trade in final goods; here multinational activity is complementary to trade in goods. When both factor proportions differences and proximity-concentration trade-off are combined, firms decide whether to export or undertake overseas production based on the relative strength of these considerations.

In the knowledge capital model (see Markusen 1997; Markusen and Maskus 2001; Carr et al. 2001) both horizontal and vertical multinationals can arise depending on country characteristics such as size, size differences, relative differences in endowments, trade costs, and investment costs. Horizontal multinational firms are associated with similarities between countries in both size and relative factor endowments. The model suggests that affiliate production and trade tend to be substitutes for similar countries and complements for countries with substantially different relative factor endowments.

An extension of the horizontal model introduces intraindustry firm heterogeneity in the proximity-concentration framework to examine the trade-off between exporting and FDI (Helpman et al. 2003). Exporting involves lower sunk costs but higher per-unit costs relative to FDI. Every industry has heterogeneous firms that differ in productivity. Firms with higher productivity are more profitable in all three activities: production for the domestic market, exports, and FDI.

The least productive firms are not profitable and exit the market. Low-productivity firms serve only the domestic market as they expect to incur losses from exports or FDI. We then have a range of higher productivity firms that can serve both domestic and foreign markets. The less productive among these expect to be profitable through exporting, but anticipate losses from FDI. Hence they undertake exports but not FDI. The most productive firms, on the other hand, chose FDI over exports as they expect greater operating profits from FDI than from exporting. Thus, while proximity-concentration variables determine the level of firm productivity needed to make international expansion attractive, the intraindustry distribution of firm productivity plays an important role in explaining the composition of trade and the firm's choice between exports and FDI.

Empirical Validation In empirical tests of the proximity-concentration hypothesis, we expect to find the share of affiliate sales in total foreign sales to be positively related to distance/trade costs, local market size, and firm-level economies of scale, and negatively related to plant-level economies of scale. Several papers provide some empirical support for this hypothesis. Using industry-level data from U.S. multinationals, Brainard (1997) finds that the proximity-concentration hypothesis is fairly robust in explaining the share of total sales accounted for by exports as compared with affiliate sales. The share of affiliate sales increases as income similarities between trading partners, transportation costs, foreign trade barriers, and firm-level scale economies increase, and decreases as foreign investment barriers, foreign taxes, and scale economies at the plant level increase.

Ekholm's (1998) analysis, using Swedish firm-level multinational data, finds some support for the proximity-concentration hypothesis: concentration advantage negatively affects the likelihood of affiliate production, while an increase in transportation costs/ geographic distance increases the share of affiliate sales in total foreign sales. Carr et al. (2001) find results consistent with Brainard (1997): outward investment increases with the sum of the economic sizes of the source and host countries, their similarity in size, the relative skilled-labor abundance of the parent nation, and the interaction between size and relative endowment differences. Using firm-level U.S. multinational data, Helpman et al. (2004) find firms substitute FDI for exports where transportation/tariff costs are high and plant-level returns to scale are relatively weak. When firm-level heterogeneity is introduced, however, greater firm-level heterogeneity in productivity leads to significantly more subsidiary sales relative to exports and the size of this effect is the same order of magnitude as that of trade frictions/costs.

Policy Implications The proximity-concentration hypothesis provides explanations for FDI between countries with very similar factor proportions, cross-border multiplant configurations, intraindustry trade, and complementarities between trade and investment. Several policy implications arise from proximity-concentration models. Local governments can undertake policy initiatives such as tariffs, subsidies, or taxes to influence the type of multinational activity undertaken in their country. Brainard (1993) suggests that the relative structure of tariffs on intermediate and final goods influences firms' decision regarding what to produce at home and what to produce overseas. Where there are relatively large proximity advantages and scale economies at the firm level, restrictions on investments may have more damaging welfare effects than restrictions on trade.

The proximity-concentration hypothesis suggests some factors that influence whether a firm decides to establish plants in both countries or to serve the foreign market by exports. There is broad empirical support for the theory that firms do indeed weigh the benefits of proximity against the costs of forgoing the economies of scale that would be enjoyed by concentrating production.

See also foreign direct investment: the OLI framework

FURTHER READING

Brainard, S. Lael. 1993. "A Simple Theory of Multinational Corporations and Trade with a Trade-off between Proximity and Concentration." NBER Working Paper No. 4269 (February). Cambridge, MA: National Bureau of Economic Research. The first paper to introduce the term *proximity-concentration trade-off*.

———. 1997. "An Empirical Assessment of the Proximity-Concentration Trade-off between Multinational Sales and Trade." *American Economic Review* 87 (4): 520–44. An empirical examination of the proximity concentration hypothesis.

Carr, David, James Markusen, and Keith Maskus. 2001. "Estimating the Knowledge-Capital Model of the Multinational Enterprise." *American Economic Review* 91 (3): 693–708. Empirical test of the predictions of the knowledge capital model on the relationship between foreign affiliate sales and country characteristics.

Ekholm, Karolina. 1998. "Proximity Advantage, Scale Economies, and the Location of Production." In *The Geography of the Multinational Firm*, edited by Pontus Braunerhjelm and Karolina Ekholm. Amsterdam: Kluwer Academic Press, 59–76. An empirical paper that examines among other things the proximity concentration trade-off.

Helpman, Elhanan, Marc J. Melitz, and Stephen R. Yeaple. 2003. "Export versus FDI." NBER Working Paper No. 9439 (January). Cambridge, MA: National Bureau of Economic Research.

———. 2004. "Export versus FDI with Heterogeneous Firms." *American Economic Review* 94 (1): 300–16. Both papers by Helpman et al. introduce intraindustry firm heterogeneity in the proximity-concentration framework and examines the trade-off between exporting and FDI.

Markusen, James R. 1984. "Multinationals, Multiplant Economies, and Gains from Trade." *Journal of International Economics* 16 (3-4): 205–26. One of the early papers explaining horizontal FDI in the presence of multiplant economies.

———. 1997. "Trade versus Investment Liberalization." NBER Working Paper No. 6231 (October). Cambridge, MA: National Bureau of Economic Research. Uses the knowledge capital framework to examine the relationship between trade and investment liberalization.

Markusen, James R., and Keith E. Maskus. 2001. "General Equilibrium Approaches to the Multinational Firm: A Review of Theory and Evidence." NBER Working Paper No. 8334 (June). Cambridge, MA: National Bureau of Economic Research. A useful review of the literature on multinational firms.

USHA NAIR-REICHERT

■ purchasing power parity

The notion of purchasing power parity (PPP) has a long intellectual history and can be traced to the 16th-century writings of scholars from the University of Salamanca in Spain. The modern definition of PPP, usually credited to Gustav Cassel (1918), is quite intuitive: when measured in the same unit, the monies of different countries should have the same purchasing power and command the same basket of goods. Otherwise, international arbitrage should bring about adjustments in prices, exchange rates, or both, which will ultimately restore parity. Another way to interpret the parity condition is that the exchange rate between two currencies should equal the ratio of the countries' price levels.

Despite its simplicity, the parity condition is the subject of many empirical studies, driven mainly by its significant implications for the global economy. For instance, PPP is a major building block of most models in international economics. The relevance of these models and their policy implications thus depends critically on the validity of PPP. Another application of PPP is the comparison of national income levels. Some economists believe that a meaningful comparison of income across countries should be based on, instead of market exchange rates, PPP exchange rates that control for price differentials of same goods across countries.

The use of PPP goes beyond academic interest, however. In the context of the global economy, exchange rate misalignment is a main source of imbalances in trade and capital accounts. These imbalances, if left unchecked, can create intense stresses for both individual economies and the global system. The PPP condition describes the relationship between exchange rates and national price levels and is commonly used as a benchmark for evaluating exchange rate misalignment.

The absolute and the relative PPP conditions are the two commonly discussed versions of PPP. The absolute PPP is given by

$$s = p - p*$$

where s is the exchange rate expressed as the domestic price of the foreign currency, p is the domestic price index, and p* is the corresponding foreign price index. All the variables are in logs. The relative version is given by

$$s = c + p - p*$$

where c is constant.

Under the absolute PPP, movements in the relative price, $p - p*$, and in the exchange rate offset each other to maintain the parity. On the other hand, the relative PPP is a less stringent condition and requires only that the proportion of exchange rate variations is the same as the proportion of variations in the relative price.

Law of One Price and PPP The law of one price (LOP) states that prices of identical goods from different locations are the same after adjusting for exchange rates. International arbitrage is the main argument behind the LOP. The difference between LOP and PPP is that the former concept refers to the actual price level of a good while the latter refers to an index of prices for different goods. LOP is a main building block of PPP. For instance, it can be shown that the PPP condition can be derived when only one good satisfies LOP (Niehans 1984). The requirement of only one good, instead of all the goods, satisfying LOP is an interesting result and it implies a high likelihood that PPP holds.

Most studies that evaluate the LOP condition find that, in general, the condition does not hold and deviations from the LOP vary substantially across product types. These studies, however, usually employ price subindexes, such as the price of chemical products. Thus they are examining the relative rather than the absolute LOP. Studies that use actual individual prices are far less common. The documented price convergence in the European car market during the integration process is one of the few pieces of evidence that are in favor of LOP (Goldberg and Verboven 2005). Overall, while one is hard pressed to find favorable evidence among the empirical studies, a casual look at, say, the global precious metal market suggests that the presence of one good satisfying the LOP may not be an extremely stringent condition.

Basics of Evaluating PPP Arguably, the PPP is the most intensely examined parity condition in international economics. Constrained by data limitations, empirical studies usually examine the validity of relative instead of absolute PPP. Specifically, price indexes do not allow an easy comparison of absolute price levels across countries.

The choice of price indexes is an issue in evaluating PPP. The common choice is between consumer price and producer (wholesale) price indexes. Some researchers use the former index as a proxy for the price index of nontradable goods and the latter one as a proxy for tradable goods. In general, the use of producer price index yields stronger evidence in favor of PPP than the use of consumer price index does. Other candidates include price indexes of imports and exports, the GDP deflator, and components of the GDP deflator.

The sample period used in PPP studies ranges from the post-1973 floating period to historical samples that cover 100 years or more. There is a trade-off between short and long samples. An advantage of long historical samples is that they are better suited for studying long-term trends and thus for evaluating the long-run PPP. A drawback, however, is that these samples cover periods of different exchange regime arrangements and significant economic changes that may complicate the analysis. Compared with long historical samples, the post-1973 period may not have enough observations to reveal reversion to the PPP. Nonetheless, results from the post-1973 period are derived from a more homogenous setting and are likely to be more relevant for current policy considerations.

Real Exchange Rate Persistence The persistence of real exchange rates is commonly used to infer the validity of PPP. If PPP holds continuously, the real exchange rate is constant. It is not difficult to verify that the instantaneous PPP does not hold since a constant real exchange rate is typically not observed in reality. This is why most empirical exercises focus on long-run PPP. Under the long-run PPP regime, deviations from parity are possible but short-lived. Over time, the relative price and the exchange rate adjust to restore the parity condition and the corresponding real exchange converges to its equilibrium value. Thus an operational interpretation of long-run PPP is that real exchange rates are mean-reverting,

and the test for the validity of PPP can be translated to a test for mean-reverting behavior of real exchange rates.

The mean-reverting behavior of real exchange rates and, hence the PPP condition, is commonly assessed using unit root test procedures. Indeed, the evolution of these empirical studies closely tracks the development of unit root test procedures. In the 1980s, the introduction of the Dickey-Fuller test revolutionized the assessment of economic data persistence in general and real exchange rate persistence in particular. Since then, a flurry of studies have used various versions of unit root tests, including the original augment Dickey-Fuller (ADF) tests, improved versions of ADF tests, Bayesian unit root tests, the fractional integration test, panel data unit root tests, and procedures allowing for alternative adjustment mechanisms to evaluate real exchange rate persistence.

Traditionally, real exchange rate persistence is evaluated in a linear time-series framework. If the real exchange rate follows a nonlinear path, then the use of a linear model can overstate its degree of persistence. A few nonlinear models, including models with structural breaks, fractional integration models, Markov switching models, and threshold autoregressive models, have been applied to real exchange rate data. In general, allowance for nonlinear dynamics enhances the ability to reveal the reversion to the PPP and lowers the empirical estimate of real exchange rate persistence (Michael, Nobay, and Peel 1997).

On balance, the empirical evidence suggests that PPP tends to hold in the long run but not in the short run. Complementing academic empirical findings, foreign exchange dealers, who jointly determine exchange rates in the global market, also indicate that PPP provides a good gauge of exchange rate movements only in the long run (Cheung and Chinn 2001).

Of particular importance is the survivorship bias in PPP analysis (Froot and Rogoff 1995). This bias refers to the common practice of investigating long historical data from developed countries. The practice mainly reflects data availability rather than research interest. One implication of the bias is that results from developed countries may overstate the empirical support for PPP. A related issue is whether developed and developing countries have similar real exchange rate behavior. Cheung and Lai (2000a) conduct a large-scale analysis and find substantial cross-country heterogeneity in the persistence of deviations from parity, and it is more likely, rather than less likely, to find parity reversion for developing countries than developed countries.

A perplexing and well-known empirical regularity is that real exchange rates display both a high level of persistence and an intense amount of short-term volatility (Rogoff 1996). If one attributes large short-term volatility to some dominating nominal shocks, then the observed persistence is too high to be explained by price stickiness. This phenomenon is labeled a "PPP puzzle." Several attempts have been made to explain the puzzle. One study shows that, when sampling uncertainty is taken into consideration, the estimated persistence parameter gives only a very imprecise measure of the true persistence (Cheung and Lai 2000b). Thus the observed persistence puzzle may not be a well-defined puzzle. Subsequent studies also point out that the estimated level of persistence can be reduced to a "nonpuzzling" level when, say, nonlinearity adjustment mechanisms are considered.

Economic Factors So far the discussion has mainly drawn from studies based on the time-series (à la intertemporal) properties of exchange rate and price data. What economic factors affect the behavior of the real exchange rate, which is a measure of PPP deviations?

The Balassa-Samuelson effect is perhaps the most discussed economic force shaping real exchange rate behavior. The hypothesis is related to the observation that, when measured in the same unit, price levels in high-income countries are higher than those in low-income countries. The price differential is due to the difference in productivities in the tradables and nontradables sectors. The Balassa-Samuelson effect is a supply-side factor. A demand-side factor is government spending. It is perceived that nontradables account for a large fraction of government spending. Thus government spending tends to have a positive impact on a country's real exchange rate.

Other economic factors that affect real exchange rates include net foreign asset position, distribution sector, and market structure. Since the turn of the 21st century, the net foreign asset position has been introduced to a real exchange rate equation via portfolio-balance channels (Lane and Milesi-Ferretti 2002). The role of net foreign asset position is related to the effect of current/trade account balances articulated in the 1980s and 1990s. The effect of net foreign asset position is verified in a number of empirical studies. It is noted, however, that the construction of data on national net foreign assets involves approximations and these data are all in U.S. dollars.

The prices faced by consumers are affected by distribution costs. The productivity and efficiency of the distribution sector will have an impact on the price structure and, thus, on real exchange rate behavior. Intuitively, the distribution activity occurs within a locale and is likely to be a "nontradable" service. In the Balassa-Samuelson effect parlance, improved distribution sector productivity should be associated with a depreciation of the real exchange rate. Nonetheless, the extant empirical evidence points in a different direction—a result that may be driven by tradable components in the distribution sector (MacDonald and Ricci 2005). One caveat is the paucity of data on productivities of distribution sectors.

The implication of market structure for the adjustment of relative prices to exchange rate movements was recognized in the 1980s. A model with, say, a markup pricing strategy that is a function of the degree of monopolistic power offers an easy illustration of the market structure effect on real exchange rate behavior. Indeed, the market structure has implications for both the persistence and volatility of real exchange rates. As always, the availability of proper data is a challenge for the empirical valuation of the market structure effect. Since the turn of the 21st century, some positive evidence of market structure effects has been reported using sectoral data (Cheung, Chinn, and Fujii 2001).

Inter- and Intracountry Analysis Usually, both LOP and PPP are stated with the implicit assumption that prices in different countries are being compared. There is no reason, however, that the two parity conditions should not apply to prices of the same goods within a country. Indeed, the study of relative price behavior within a country avoids a few problems that plague the cross-country analysis.

For instance, the procedures for compiling price data and constructing indexes can differ across countries. Within a country, however, price data are likely to be collected and recorded in one unified system. Thus data compatibility should not be a significant issue in comparing the prices of same goods across cities and regions within a country.

There are a few other reasons why results based on intracountry data are easier to interpret than those from intercountry data. First, intracountry relative prices are subject to similar fiscal and monetary policies, whereas intercountry relative prices are subject to possibly different policies. Second, the trade barriers within a country are usually less severe than those across countries. Third, the intracountry relative prices are literally linked via an exchange rate that is credibly fixed at the one-to-one level and, thus, are free from uncertain exchange rate variability. Indeed, Engel and Rogers (1996) have shown that there is an enormous increase in relative price variability across national borders. These factors imply that intracountry relative prices of identical goods are more likely to meet the parity condition.

Given these considerations, it is perhaps not too surprising to find that intracountry data, compared with intercountry data, display a faster convergence rate and are more likely to satisfy the parity condition. The result is supported by studies using either individual goods prices or price indexes.

See also Balassa-Samuelson effect; equilibrium exchange rate; exchange rate forecasting; exchange rate volatility; interest parity conditions; nontraded goods; real exchange rate

FURTHER READING

Cassel, Gustav. 1918. "Abnormal Deviations in International Exchanges." *Economic Journal* 28: 413–15. Brings the PPP to its current context.

Cheung, Yin-Wong, and Menzie Chinn. 2001. "Currency Traders and Exchange Rate Dynamics: A Survey of the U.S. Market." *Journal of International Money and Finance* 20: 439–71. One of a series of articles using survey responses to examine issues in exchange-rate economics including PPP.

Cheung, Yin-Wong, Menzie Chinn, and Eiji Fujii. 2001. "Market Structure and the Persistence of Sectoral Real Exchange Rates." *International Journal of Finance and Economics* 6: 95–114. Explicitly documents the effects of market structure on real exchange rate behavior.

Cheung, Yin-Wong, and Kon S. Lai. 2000a. "On Cross-Country Differences in the Persistence of Real Exchange Rates." *Journal of International Economics* 50: 375–97. Reports different country groups display different mean-reverting real exchange rate dynamics and different persistence patterns.

———. 2000b. "On the Purchasing Power Parity Puzzle." *Journal of International Economics* 52: 321–30. Shows that the PPP puzzle may not be well founded because data only give a very imprecise estimate of real exchange rate persistence.

Cheung, Yin-Wong, Kon S. Lai, and Michael Bergman. 2004. "Dissecting the PPP Puzzle: The Unconventional Roles of Nominal Exchange Rate and Price Adjustments." *Journal of International Economics* 64: 135–50. Reports the perplexing result that, compared with relative prices, exchange rates display a slower speed of adjustment toward equilibrium.

Chinn, Menzie D. 2000. "The Usual Suspects? Productivity and Demand Shocks and Asia-Pacific Real Exchange Rates." *Review of International Economics* 8: 20–43. Documents the presence of the Balassa-Samuelson effect in a group of Asia-Pacific economies.

Engel, Charles, and John H. Rogers. 1996. "How Wide Is the Border?" *American Economic Review* 86: 1112–25. The first paper that quantifies the effect of a national border on real exchange rate volatility.

Froot, Kenneth A., and Kenneth Rogoff. 1995. "Perspectives on PPP and Long-Run Real Exchange Rates." In *Handbook of International Economics*, edited by Kenneth

Rogoff and Gene Grossman. Amsterdam: North Holland, 1647–88. An often-cited survey article with a lot of references.

Goldberg, Pinelopi K., and Frank Verboven. 2005. "Market Integration and Convergence to the Law of One Price: Evidence from the European Car Market." *Journal of International Economics* 65: 49–73. Presents evidence in favor of LOP.

Lane, Philip, and Gian Maria Milesi-Ferretti. 2002. "External Wealth, the Trade Balance, and the Real Exchange Rate." *European Economic Review* 46: 1049–71. Connects real exchange rate behavior to net foreign asset positions.

MacDonald, Ronald, and Luca Antonio Ricci. 2005. "The Real Exchange Rate and the Balassa Samuelson Effect: The Role of the Distribution Sector." *Pacific Economic Review* 10: 29–48. Develops a theoretical model and provides empirical evidence of the link between the distribution sector and real exchange rate dynamics.

Michael, Panos, A. Robert Nobay, and David A. Peel. 1997. "Transaction Costs and Nonlinear Adjustment in Real Exchange Rates: An Empirical Investigation." *Journal of Political Economy* 105: 862–79. Appealing to the effect of transaction costs, the study uses nonlinear models to describe real exchange rate behavior.

Niehans, Jurg. 1984. *International Monetary Economics.* Baltimore, MD: Johns Hopkins University Press. Presents a model that gives the PPP condition with the assumption of one product satisfies the LOP condition.

Officer, Lawrence H. 1982. *Purchasing Power Parity and Exchange Rates: Theory, Evidence, and Relevance.* Greenwich, CT: JIA Press. An extensive review of the early literature on PPP.

Rogoff, Kenneth. 1996. "The Purchasing Power Parity Puzzle." *Journal of Economic Literature* 34: 647–68. An often-cited survey article with a lot of references.

Sarno, Lucio, and Mark P. Taylor. 2002. "Purchasing Power Parity and the Real Exchange Rate." *IMF Staff Papers* 49: 65–105. Covers some recent developments in the empirical PPP literature.

YIN-WONG CHEUNG

■ quantity theory of money

The classical equation of exchange as it is applied today equates the money supply multiplied by the velocity of circulation (the number of times the average currency unit changes hands in a given year) with the economy's gross domestic product (the quantity of output produced multiplied by the price level). Although the American economist Irving Fisher originally included transactions of previously produced goods and assets as part of the output measure, only newly produced goods are included in present-day calculations of gross domestic product. If the velocity of circulation and output are both constant, there is a one-to-one relationship between a change in the money supply and a change in prices. This yields a "quantity theory of money" under which a doubling of the money supply must be accompanied by a doubling of the price level (or, when the rate of money supply growth doubles, the rate of inflation also doubles). The Nobel Prize–winning economist Milton Friedman (1956) restated this quantity theory of money by modifying the assumption of constant velocity, allowing velocity to adjust in response to changes in expected inflation and the returns available on other assets such as bonds and equities.

The tendency for velocity to rise as expected inflation rises reflects people's incentive to unload a depreciating currency before its purchasing power erodes. This reinforces the effects of faster money supply growth on inflation because, at the same time that more money is being printed, people want to hold even less of it than they did before the inflationary process began. There is, in fact, an exact inverse relationship between the proportion of income held as money and the velocity of circulation with, say, a halving of average money holdings requiring that the currency circulate at double the old rate in order to buy the same goods as before. In the extreme case of "hyperinflation" (broadly defined as inflation exceeding 50 percent per month), money holdings plunge and the inflation rate significantly outstrips the rate of money supply growth. Conversely, under deflation, velocity is likely to fall: people hold onto their money longer as they recognize that the same funds will buy more goods and services over time if prices continue to decline. Thus money demand rises as money supply falls, again exaggerating the effects of the money supply change on the aggregate price level.

The demand for money is also influenced by the economy's output level. If output rises, money demand should rise too, as increased production generates more income and spending power. This would put downward pressure on prices. Just as sustained inflation is possible only when the rate of money growth rises above the rate of growth of output (and money demand), so too does sustained deflation occur under conditions of insufficient money growth. According to the monetarist school, which emphasizes the importance of the money supply as a long-run determinant of prices and gross domestic product, stable prices could be achieved by simply tying the rate of money supply growth to the long-run rate of growth of output. This would keep money demand and money supply in balance so long as velocity is stable.

Critics, such as those of the Keynesian school, which views the effects of monetary policy as unreliable and uncertain in practice, argue that such a policy rule would have undesirable consequences because velocity historically has been subject to fluctuations that require offsetting movements in the money supply. On the other hand, Friedman (1960) argued that velocity has been unstable only because policy has been unstable and that adoption of a constant growth rate rule for the money supply would keep inflation expectations, along with velocity, steady.

Friedman's restatement of the quantity theory of money tempers the classical prediction that money supply increases exert one-to-one effects on prices even in the short run. Under the restatement, velocity is allowed to adjust to a new level if the inflation environment changes. However, once real money holdings have adjusted to their new lower equilibrium level following a rise in inflation, the rise in velocity should end with a one-to-one relationship between money growth and inflation. Such a pattern is typically observed over extended periods. Moreover Friedman's (1992) famous proposition that inflation is always and everywhere a monetary phenomenon receives support from the fact that it is hard, if not impossible, to find any episodes of significant inflation that have not been accompanied by accelerating rates of monetary expansion. The importance of this link is further illustrated by the fact that, while a one-third money supply reduction in the eastern Confederate States in April 1864 dramatically reduced inflation there, inflation continued to run rampant in the western portion where the monetary cutback was postponed.

Criticisms of Quantity Theory Critics of the quantity theory approach have questioned not only the stability of velocity and money demand but also the determination of the money supply itself. That is, a link between money and prices does not necessarily prove that money supply movements are driving price movements. The economists Sargent and Wallace (1973) argue that such "reverse" causation could arise when a government is dependent on the revenue earned by inflating away the value of its outstanding money issues. Here, higher inflation produces faster rates of monetary expansion, and not the other way around. As higher expected inflation leads individuals to reduce their real money balances, this reduces individuals' exposure to the inflation tax and reduces the government's revenue from inflation. To keep inflation tax revenue at its old level, the government must accelerate the rate of monetary expansion so as to increase the inflation tax rate and offset the decline in the inflation tax base as real money balances fall. This novel, albeit controversial, perspective could not apply in the more usual situation where governments are able to finance their expenditures through conventional taxes and bond issues.

The quantity theory's predictions have also been questioned by adherents of "backing theory." Under this view, it is the quality rather than the quantity of money that matters. Whereas unbacked paper money may well be as inflationary as the standard quantity theory assumes, this need not be true of money that is credibly backed by future taxes or other provisions for their future retirement from circulation. Pioneering analysis of the American colonies prior to the Revolutionary War by Smith (1985) suggests that even large money issues might be willingly held rather than spent—implying a fall in the velocity of circulation and an absence of the inflationary pressures predicted by the quantity theory—provided that they were properly backed. The case of Maryland stands out because that colony undertook to accumulate funds set aside for future purchases of pounds sterling that would retire the colony's paper money at a predetermined rate of exchange. Data limitations make it hard to conclusively determine the practical extent to which backing reduced the inflationary effects of the Maryland currency issues and those of other colonies, but recent work suggests that Pennsylvania enjoyed the long-run constancy of velocity, and proportional relationship between money and prices, implied by the quantity theory (Grubb 2005).

Excess Monetary Creation Whatever predictive power the quantity theory approach may have over the long term, even its strongest adherents would accept that short-run dynamics and adjustments militate against a one-for-one relation between money and prices in the short run. Excess money creation will eventually lead to inflation, but extra liquidity may well initially push down interest rates and encourage greater output and employment. Until these beneficial effects are reversed, the extra money issue may "buy" at least the illusion of greater prosperity. This, in turn, may produce a temptation to inflate. While the continued ratcheting up of the money supply will eventually lead to hyperinflation, such an extreme outcome usually occurs only when a government finds itself unable to obtain funding from any source other than the printing press. Such episodes, while unfortunate, have nevertheless provided economists with ample opportunity to observe not only the inflationary consequences of such rampant excess money growth but also the surge in the velocity of circulation as individuals become progressively less willing to hold the depreciating currency.

See also debt deflation; Federal Reserve Board; money supply; purchasing power parity; seigniorage; time inconsistency problem

FURTHER READING

Burdekin, Richard C. K., and Marc D. Weidenmier. 2001. "Inflation Is Always and Everywhere a Monetary Phenomenon: Richmond vs. Houston in 1864." *American Economic Review* 91 (5): 1621–30. Illustrates how divergent inflation performance in the eastern and western Confederacy was linked to a reform measure that reduced the money supply in the eastern Confederacy while initially leaving the money supply unchanged in the west.

Fisher, Irving. 1922. *The Purchasing Power of Money: Its Determination and Relation to Credit, Interest, and Crises.* New York: Macmillan. Fisher's original exposition of the equation of exchange and quantity theory of money.

Friedman, Milton, ed. 1956. *Studies in the Quantity Theory of Money.* Chicago: University of Chicago Press. Includes Friedman's own restatement of the quantity theory and Phillip Cagan's pioneering analysis of money demand under hyperinflation.

———. 1960. *A Program for Monetary Stability.* New York: Fordham University Press. Lays out Friedman's case for a constant growth rate rule for monetary policy.

———. 1992. *Money Mischief: Episodes in Monetary Policy.* New York: Harcourt Brace Jovanovich. Highly accessible general analysis of the causes and consequences of monetary expansion, both past and present, can be found in chapters 2 and 8.

Grubb, Farley. 2005. "Two Theories of Money Reconciled: The Colonial Puzzle Revisited with New Evidence." NBER Working Paper No.11784. Washington, DC: National Bureau of Economic Research. Available at http://www.nber.org/papers/w11784. Revisits the applicability of the quantity theory of money to the American colonial experience and finds Pennsylvania data to be consistent with the quantity theory's predictions.

Sargent, Thomas J., and Neil Wallace. 1973. "Rational Expectations and the Dynamics of Hyperinflation." *International Economic Review* 14 (2): 328–50. Points to the potential dependence of money supply movements on price movements when a government must support its operations through the inflation tax.

Smith, Bruce D. 1985. "Some Colonial Evidence on Two Theories of Money: Maryland and the Carolinas." *Journal of Political Economy* 93 (6): 1178–1211. Suggests that even large money supply increases need not be inflationary if the money is backed by future tax revenue or other provisions for the retirement of the currency.

RICHARD C. K. BURDEKIN

■ quotas

Quotas in international trade are government-imposed maximum amounts of a product that can be imported into or exported from a country during a specific period of time (usually a year). The maximum can be a quantitative limit specifying the maximum tons or units or square yards that can be traded, or it can be a maximum in value terms, denominated in either domestic or foreign currency. A *global* import quota sets a single maximum amount

quotas

that can be imported, regardless of the country of origin. Import quotas are frequently subdivided among exporting countries, specifying a maximum amount that can be imported from each trading partner.

Use of Quotas Governments have used import and export quotas to achieve a number of different policy objectives. Governments often used import quotas to protect domestic producers from import competition or to encourage domestic production. An example would be the import quotas on petroleum in the United States from 1959 to 1973, intended to promote domestic exploration for oil and oil production to enhance national security. The United States relied on import quotas to prevent lower-priced imports from undermining price supports for domestic agricultural products, or from increasing the cost of the support program. Countries with fixed exchange rates and escalating balance of payments deficits often resorted to import quotas to limit payments for imports and prevent large losses in international reserves. In a balance of payments "crisis," governments often chose quotas because of the certainty that a quota ceiling would limit imports.

Governments sometimes impose export quotas to ensure sufficient supplies of a product for domestic consumption or processing. Romania, for example, used export quotas on logs, lumber, and plywood to ensure a supply of inputs for domestic furniture producers. Another objective is to keep domestic prices of sensitive goods below world market prices. The United States, for example, imposed export quotas on logs in the mid-1970s in an attempt to prevent increases in the price of lumber from driving up the cost of homebuilding. For countries that are major suppliers of an export commodity, export quotas reduce supply to the world market and keep world market prices high. An example would be the Organization of the Petroleum Exporting Countries' (OPEC's) export quotas on petroleum. Voluntary export restraints (VERs) are export quotas that were imposed by an exporting country on shipments of a good to a particular importing country *at the request of the importing country.* They allowed importing countries to protect struggling industries without

violating international trading agreements by imposing their own import restrictions.

Administration of Import and Export Quotas Governments have used many different rules or mechanisms to determine which international traders effectively receive the right to import or export under quota systems.

"First come, first served." One method of administering a quota restriction is to simply allow traders to import or export the restricted product starting at the beginning of the quota period until the quota ceiling is reached and then close the border to additional trade for the rest of the time period. This method can cause a chaotic situation as traders "stampede to the border" at the beginning of the quota period. Countries that attempted to administer quotas under a first-come, first-served rule in the 1930s found that quota limits were often exceeded because information flows to the authorities were too slow to close the border quickly enough to prevent the quota from being overshipped. Governments began to allocate the rights to import under quota to firms or individuals according to sets of rules or allocation mechanisms.

Allocation by "traditional trade shares." This method allocates shares of the quota among traders on the basis of their trade volumes during a specified base period. A firm that had imported 10 percent of total imports during the historical base period would be allocated 10 percent of the total amount allowed in under the quota restriction. This method excludes traders who did not happen to be trading in the base period, so governments often reserve a small portion of the quota for "new" or "nontraditional" importers or exporters. The United States Department of Agriculture allocated import quotas for cheese to importing firms on the basis of historical trade shares.

Allocation in proportion to domestic production. During the period in which the United States used import quotas to restrict petroleum imports, import licenses were allocated to domestic refineries in proportion to refinery output (Bohi and Russell 1978). McCulloch and Johnson (1973) discuss the efficiency properties of this allocation rule in the face of a set of different noneconomic objectives. They point out

950

that a proportionally distributed quota tends to produce an additional subsidy to production and a reduced tax on consumption relative to a tariff or standard quota.

Allocation by political decision. In some instances quota allocation is determined on the basis of politics. The U.S. Congress decided the distribution of sugar import quota allocations among sugar exporting countries and the secretary of agriculture sent "certificates of eligibility" to bring sugar into the United States to the governments of the exporting countries. Cuba, which had been the major exporter of sugar to the United States, lost its sugar quota allocation due to disapproval of Fidel Castro's government.

Quota auctions. Australia and New Zealand were two of the very few countries that auctioned quotas to the highest bidders. Auctions provide a market-oriented method of allocating quotas and also raise revenue for the government (Bergsten, Elliott, Schott, and Takacs 1987).

Economic Impact of Import Quotas An import quota is "binding" if the quantity that would be imported without the quota restriction exceeds the quota ceiling. A binding import quota reduces the supply of the product on the domestic market of the importing country and drives up its price. Domestic producers benefit from the quota restriction because the higher price encourages them to produce a larger quantity, which they sell at the higher price. Domestic buyers of the product are worse off because they pay a higher price and buy a smaller amount.

The increase in price of the restricted good in the internal market creates a gap or wedge between the higher internal price and the price of the good on the world market. Traders who can import under the quota system earn a windfall profit, called a "quota rent," because they can buy the product at the going world market price, import, and resell at the higher internal price. The choice of the allocation method for quotas is thus important because it determines who can import and thus who receives the windfall gains from the quota rents.

Import quotas also create net losses in total welfare for the country that imposes them because of resource misallocation and efficiency losses in both production and consumption. On the production side, the quota encourages expansion of domestic production of the restricted good, but the extra production takes place at a higher cost than the price of the good on the world market. The cost of the domestic resources used up to expand domestic production exceeds what it would cost to buy the imported goods that they replace. On the consumption side, buyers lose welfare because they pay a higher price and cut back their purchases of the restricted good in response to the artificially high price. Quotas often cause additional inefficiencies because an overall quota limit on imports of a general product category is often subdivided into smaller quotas for particular varieties of the product, and often further subdivided to specify the country of origin of the imports. For example, the U.S. import quotas on cheese were subdivided into subquotas on different types of cheese (Swiss, provolone, parmesan, cheddar, etc.) and those subquotas were further subdivided to impose upper limits on imports from each exporting country. Thus the quota system arbitrarily determined the distribution of cheese imports by type and source, without regard to cost or consumer preferences (Anderson 1988).

Economic Impact of Export Quotas A binding export quota constrains the amount of a good that can leave the country, forcing more of it onto the domestic market. The larger supply on the domestic market reduces the internal market price. Domestic producers of the restricted good lose because they produce a smaller quantity that sells at a lower price. Domestic buyers or users gain because they obtain the good at a lower price and buy more of it.

Export quotas cause distortions on the production and consumption sides that create overall welfare losses for the economy as a whole. On the production side, artificially constrained exports preclude domestic firms (and thus the economy as a whole) from capturing the gains from selling in the world market at a price above production cost. On the consumption side, the decrease in price encourages domestic buyers to expand purchases, but the extra units they buy could have been sold in the world market at a price higher than the value to domestic users.

Export quotas also generate quota rents because the decrease in the domestic price of the restricted good due to the export quota creates a wedge between domestic and world market price, so whoever can export the good receives a windfall gain equal to the difference between the world market and domestic price. VERs also involve quota rents because the restriction in supply will push up the price of the restricted good in the domestic market of the importing country. Exporters who receive quota allocations to ship to the importing country are likely to receive the quota rents. De Melo and Tarr (1992) calculated very large losses to the United States due to the transfer of quota rents to exporting countries under VER agreements on textiles and apparel, automobiles, and steel.

Comparison of Quotas to Tariffs Quotas influence international trade flows by directly limiting the quantity of a product that can be imported or exported. An import tariff, in contrast, reduces imports through the price mechanism by making imported goods more expensive. A major question in the analysis of international trade barriers is the equivalence of quotas and tariffs (Bhagwati 1968). The question is, "Under what conditions will an import tariff and an import quota that result in the same amount of imports have exactly the same economic impact?" If market conditions remain unchanged, and the product markets are perfectly competitive, an import quota and a tariff that result in the same import quantity will also result in the same domestic price, quantity produced, and quantity consumed. The literature on the equivalence of tariffs and quotas has identified a number of ways in which the impacts of tariffs and quotas differ, however (for detailed explanations see Vousden 1990).

Government revenue. The government collects revenue from an import tariff or an export tax, but import or export quotas generate quota rents, which do not directly go to the government. Governments could in principle attempt to capture what would be quota rents by auctioning quota licenses, but quota auctions are rare (Bergsten, Elliott, Schott, and Takacs 1987). Quota rents may be captured by the nationals of the country imposing the quota: for example, if import licenses are allocated only to domestic firms importing the good. But if import licenses or permits are given to exporters (as in the case of the U.S. sugar import quotas or under VERs), the quota rents are very likely to be captured by nationals of the exporting country and thus represent an additional loss to the importing country, in addition to the welfare losses from production and consumption distortions. The possibility that quota rents may be lost to the quota-imposing country is one reason to favor tariffs over quotas as a policy instrument to reduce imports or protect a domestic industry.

Noncompetitive market structure. If the domestic industry producing the good in the importing country is not perfectly competitive, the economic impact of a quota and a tariff can differ. If only one domestic firm produces an imported good, that domestic monopoly faces quite different demand conditions for its product under a tariff than under a quota. If the monopoly firm is protected by a tariff, it can sell its product at a price above the world market price, but it cannot control the price at which it can sell. If it attempts to raise its price above the world price plus tariff, buyers can simply buy from foreign suppliers and pay the tariff. The monopoly has no ability to control the domestic price with a tariff. It has no "market power." But if the monopoly is instead protected by an import quota set to allow in the same quantity of imports as the tariff, the firm will raise its selling price because buyers no longer have the option of importing more from abroad than is allowed by the quota. An import quota gives a domestic monopoly "market power" that it would not have under the tariff, which it will exploit by reducing output and charging a higher price. This extra distortion that arises from a quota when domestic industries are highly concentrated is another reason to favor tariffs over quotas.

Changes in market conditions. A tariff and a quota also lead to different outcomes if market conditions change after the tariff or the quota is imposed. The difference arises because a tariff allows imports to increase if market conditions change, whereas a quota does not. Assume a small country that is too small to influence world prices by the amount that it imports. If a binding quota restricts imports to the quota ceiling and domestic demand for the product subsequently increases, imports cannot increase to satisfy the extra demand, so the domestic price of the product will rise and domestic production will increase. In contrast, if a tariff had restricted imports to the same initial level (resulting in the same initial domestic price, production, and consumption) an increase in domestic demand simply would increase the quantity imported, without any increase in the price, which would remain equal to the world market price plus the tariff.

A tariff and an import quota also lead to different outcomes if international market conditions change. If the world market price of an imported good falls, but domestic demand and supply conditions remain unchanged, the import quota prevents imports from increasing even though their price is falling. The external price decline will not be transmitted into the domestic economy. If a tariff had been used to control imports, falling world prices would make imports less expensive, and the quantity of imports would increase. The world market price decline would be transmitted into the domestic economy. This difference between tariffs and quotas is the main reason governments used quotas to control imports of products subject to domestic price supports.

Upgrading of product quality. If a product category contains varieties of different qualities that sell at different prices, the composition of imports will differ under a tariff regime and a quota regime. Import quotas result in "upgrading," or a shift toward imports of higher-quality, higher-priced varieties, rather than lower-quality, lower-priced varieties. The quota creates a wedge, or price gap, between the domestic price and the world price of the imported products. The given price gap represents a larger percentage price increase for lower-priced goods than for higher-priced goods, so lower-priced goods become more expensive relative to higher-price goods and there is a tendency for buyers to substitute higher-quality goods for lower-quality goods.

Directly unproductive activities. The quota rents earned by those individuals or firms who receive the rights to import under quota provide a powerful incentive to engage in activities to influence quota allocation decisions. Thus quota regimes encourage individuals to spend time and use up real resources in their attempt to influence quota allocation decisions in their favor (Krueger 1974). Tariff revenue accrues directly to the government, so a tariff regime does not promote similar unproductive activities.

Quotas have long been a feature of global trade policies. While the role of quotas has diminished somewhat with recent progress in liberalizing trade in the textile, clothing, and agricultural sectors under the auspices of the World Trade Organization, the analysis of quotas remains an important area in theoretical and applied trade policy research. As such, it informs a preference in the trade policy community for tariffs as a more appropriate trade policy intervention.

See also nontariff measures; tariff rate quotas; tariffs

FURTHER READING

Anderson, James E. 1988. *The Relative Inefficiency of Quotas.* Cambridge, MA: MIT Press. Examines the inefficiencies caused by quotas, including estimates of the cost of U.S. cheese quotas and analysis of quotas under imperfect competition and uncertainty.

Bergsten, C. Fred, Kimberley A. Elliott, Jeffrey Schott, and Wendy E. Takacs. 1987. *Auction Quotas and U.S. Trade Policy.* Washington, DC: Institute for International Economics, 1987. A discussion of auctioning import quotas, with a description of the experience of Australia and New Zealand with their quota auctions.

Bhagwati, Jagdish. 1968. "More on the Equivalence of Tariffs and Quotas." *American Economic Review* 58 (1): 142–46. An analysis of the conditions under which tariffs and quotas have an equivalent economic impact.

Bohi, Douglas R., and Milton Russell. 1978. *Limiting Oil Imports: An Economic History and Analysis.* Baltimore: Johns Hopkins University Press. A presentation of the details of the history and administration of the U.S. petroleum import quota system, with an economic analysis.

Corden, W. M. 1971. *The Theory of Protection.* Oxford: Oxford University Press. An accessible discussion of trade policy instruments that contains an extensive analysis of quotas.

de Melo, Jaime, and David Tarr. 1992. *A General Equilibrium Analysis of U.S. Foreign Trade Policy.* Cambridge, MA: MIT Press. An explanation of general equilibrium modeling with estimates of the impact of voluntary export restraints on shipments of textiles and clothing, automobiles, and steel to the United States under a variety of assumptions.

Hamilton, Carl. 1988. "ASEAN Systems for Allocation of Export Licenses under VERs." In *The Political Economy of Manufacturing Protection: Experiences of ASEAN and Australia,* edited by Christopher Findlay and Ross Garnaut. London: Allen and Unwin, 235–47. Reviews alternative methods governments used to decide on the allocation of export quotas among firms.

Krueger, Anne O. 1974. "The Political Economy of the Rent-Seeking Society." *American Economic Review* 64 (3): 291–303. The original analysis of directly unproductive activities associated with quota regimes.

McCulloch, Rachel, and Harry G. Johnson. 1973. "A Note on Proportionally Distributed Quotas." *American Economic Review* 63 (4): 726–32. An analysis of the economic impact of quota allocation to domestic producers in proportion to their production levels.

Vousden, Neil. 1990. *The Economics of Trade Protection* Cambridge, MA: Cambridge University Press. Contains extensive and detailed analyses of the economic impact of quotas, including losses to consumers, transfers to producers and recipients of quota rents, and the efficiency losses from distortions in production and consumption. Also discusses the effects of quotas in the presence of retaliation by trading partners, the rent-seeking costs of tariffs and quotas, product upgrading when quotas are imposed on differentiated products, and a discussion of the comparison of quotas with tariffs when the protected sector is a monopoly.

WENDY TAKACS

■ **real exchange rate**

The real exchange rate, a linchpin of international economics, tells us about the overall costs in one country compared with another. Defined as the cost of a bundle of goods in one country relative to the cost of the same bundle of goods in another country, it is conventionally written as the nominal exchange rate adjusted for international differences in prices levels:

$$Real\ Exchange\ Rate \equiv$$

$$Nominal\ Exchange\ Rate \times \frac{Domestic\ Prices}{Foreign\ Prices},$$

where the nominal exchange rate is specified here in terms of foreign currency units per unit of domestic currency.

From this expression, one sees that if the nominal exchange rate fluctuates widely while the price indexes are relatively stable, then the real exchange rate will move with the nominal exchange rate. This indeed has been the pattern under floating exchange rates: real exchange rates have been nearly as volatile as nominal exchange rates have been. Moreover changes in the real exchange rate seem to persist for a very long time. Explaining the behavior of real exchange rates therefore requires both an understanding of why nominal exchange rates are so volatile under floating exchange rate arrangements and an understanding of what keeps prices from fluctuating proportionately.

Theoretical Approaches Most theoretical approaches to understanding real exchange rates focus on the price of goods. These explanations generally fall into two categories. The first category emphasizes the importance of international borders, particularly those aspects of borders that prevent the law of one price from holding internationally. The second category emphasizes what goes on within countries, especially what happens to the relative prices of traded and nontraded goods within an individual country. International failures in the law of one price and international differences in relative prices within countries are related, but they each capture different ideas of what is important in determining real exchange rates.

Across international borders, the law of one price fails for many goods, and its failure is particularly notable for final goods. Its failure can occur most obviously because of transportation costs and official trade barriers, but it also can occur because of noncompetitive market structures, in which prices resist change. In many new open economy macroeconomic models, firms have monopoly power and prices are set as a markup over marginal cost. In these models, the law of one price can fail, at least in the short term. Failures of the law of one price represent impediments to the adjustment of the real exchange rate.

Looking within countries, explanations of real exchange rate behavior emphasize distinctions between different sectors of the economy, such as the traded and nontraded sectors, or the intermediate and final sectors. These explanations tend to rely either on differential changes in productivity across the sectors or on changes in the relative demands across the sectors. All such changes affect the relative prices and the composition of what is produced and consumed in each country. Such changes, in turn, affect the real exchange rate via the price indicators that we see in its definition. The most prominent of these explanations is the Balassa-Samuelson effect.

The other explanations of real exchange rate behavior are primarily shorter-term explanations. Changes in preferences across an economy's traded and nontraded sectors—whether due to changes in consumption or government expenditures—will affect relative prices for as long as it takes for the factors of production to move across the sectors within a country. (Some of the new open economy models fit into this category as well.) In the short run, the supply of nontraded goods is inelastic, and the demand for nontraded goods matters. So changes in the consumption of nontraded goods will affect relative prices, and real exchange rates will change.

Empirical Challenges Despite much work, little is known about the empirical determinants of real exchange rates. A large number of econometric studies have attempted to determine whether the exchange rate converges over time to an equilibrium value—that is, whether it is stationary. The focus on this particular issue arises in large part because it is equivalent to knowing whether relative purchasing power holds, in which case nominal exchange rate changes and inflation differences eventually offset each other. The persistence of real exchange rate changes, however, means that tests even of this fairly clear-cut hypothesis lack statistical power, even with long time series or with panel data.

Econometric work that attempts more broadly to discern the real exchange rate's most important determinants and thereby to distinguish among competing theories has had only limited success. The real exchange rate's volatility and persistence are not matched by observations of its theoretical fundamentals, and it is difficult to generate endogenous persistence in real exchange rate models without introducing other counterfactual implications.

Thus empirical studies have been able to tell us only a few things. First, real exchange rates tend to move with nominal exchange rates, and their behavior correspondingly depends on prevailing nominal exchange rate arrangements. Second, real exchange rates are volatile. Finally, their changes are persistent.

Even this last conclusion is subject to the criticism that it may be an artifact of poor measurement.

Measuring the Real Exchange Rate Empirical work on real exchange rates involves many judgments about how to construct real exchange rate measures. Most important, appropriate price indicators and suitable aggregation methods must be selected. Typically, price indexes, such as the consumer price index or the producer price index, are used. Just as those indexes show price changes rather than price levels, real exchange rates so constructed will gauge real exchange rate changes, rather than their levels. These measures tell us what the real appreciation or depreciation has been relative to some point in time, but they do not provide the real exchange rate's actual value. Calculation of the real exchange rate's level requires information about price levels, information that is not always readily available. Such distinctions between *indexes* and *levels* can be important in debates about exchange rate policies and trade policies. For example, an index can tell how much the value of the Chinese currency has changed since the Asian financial crisis in 1997–98, but only a measure of the real exchange rate's level can tell us if it is weak or strong relative to another currency or relative to a theoretical value.

One also faces the question of what categories of prices to use. Consumer prices are used most often. Producer and wholesale price indexes, and even export price indexes, are sometimes chosen over the consumer price index because they better represent the notion of export competitiveness, which often is of particular interest. As the set of prices narrows increasingly toward including only actually traded goods, however, it also becomes increasingly like a measure of the terms of trade—the relative price of imports and exports—and less a measure of the real exchange rate.

Finally, since currency values so often diverge, real exchange rate measures can be sensitive to the set of countries included and to their weights. A country's real exchange rate often is measured bilaterally, that is, against only one other country. A broader—multilateral—measure can differ markedly from a bilateral one, however. For example, a country that pegs its nominal exchange rate against that of a single trading partner is likely to have a relatively stable bilateral real exchange rate against that country. Against other countries, however, its real exchange rate could be very unstable, either rising or falling. A multilateral or effective real exchange rate will capture those broader movements.

Whether one is interested in questions about the fundamental determinants of the real exchange rate or has questions about the experience or policies of a single country, all of the measurement choices affect the measures and thereby shape the conclusions.

See also Balassa-Samuelson effect; currency crisis; effective exchange rate; equilibrium exchange rate; exchange rate regimes; exchange rate volatility; New Open Economy Macroeconomics; purchasing power parity

FURTHER READING

Cheung, Yin-Wong, Menzie Chinn, and Antonio Garcia. 2005. "Empirical Exchange Rate Models of the 1990s: Are Any Fit to Survive?" *Journal of International Money and Finance* 24:7, 1150–75. Updates Meese and Rogoff (1983) and finds models to have limited and uneven empirical success.

Froot, Kenneth, and Kenneth Rogoff. 1995. "Perspectives on PPP and Long-Run Real Exchange Rates." In *Handbook of International Economics*, vol. 3, edited by Gene Grossman and Kenneth Rogoff. Amsterdam: Elsevier Science, 1647–88. Reviews empirical studies of real exchange rates, emphasizing tests of stationary and the Balassa-Samuelson effect.

Meese, Richard, and Kenneth Rogoff. 1983. "Empirical Exchange Rate Models of the Seventies: Do They Fit Out of Sample?" *Journal of International Economics* 14: 3–24. The classic real exchange rate horserace, in which a random walk beats all.

Obstfeld, Maurice, and Kenneth Rogoff. 1995. "Exchange Rate Dynamics Redux." *Journal of Political Economy* 103: 624–60. A pioneering piece in new open macroeconomics: combines dynamic optimization with imperfect competition and nominal rigidities in a single theoretical approach to modeling exchange rates and current accounts.

HELEN POPPER

■ **regional currency areas**

See common currency; optimum currency area (OCA) theory

■ **regional development banks**

Regional development banks (RDBs) play a critical role in the international financial architecture. They provide development finance to their poorer member countries on highly concessional terms, mobilizing between U.S. $15 billion and $20 billion a year, compared with about U.S. $20 billion for the World Bank. By comparison, foreign direct investment flows represent more than U.S. $300 billion per year, albeit concentrated in a few emerging markets.

RDBs are central components of the constellation of the 20 or so multilateral development banks that emerged after World War II: the World Bank; five RDBs, four dealing with transition and developing countries (the African Development Bank, the Asian Development Bank, the European Bank for Reconstruction and Development, and the Inter-American Development Bank) and one, the European Investment Bank, dealing mainly with members of the European Union, although the level of its operations in developing countries is significant at around U.S. $3 billion a year; and 13 subregional development banks of varying size, such as the Council of Europe Development Bank, the Caribbean Development Bank, and the West African Development Bank.

Lending for Development The RDBs' mandate has evolved over time, as has the rationale for development finance. They are multilateral organizations mobilizing development finance to their member countries to promote growth, encourage development, and reduce poverty. They act as financial intermediaries, leveraging resources from international capital markets that they lend-on at advantageous conditions to their members, which often have limited and volatile access to those markets. Each of them has built up a corpus of economic and technical expertise, and in 2004, their combined outstanding loans were more than U.S. $1 trillion, of which U.S.

$128 billion was for the RDBs operating in transitional and developing countries (compared with U.S. $225 billion for the World Bank).

Two general characteristics distinguish RDBs from private financial institutions and bilateral donors: their multilateral shareholding structure and preferred creditor status, and a subsidized capital base and access to other subsidies. Their financing model is similar to that of the World Bank, with which there is a certain degree of competition. They are perceived as generally less efficient and more politicized, imposing less stringent conditions than the World Bank. Their comparative advantage resides in their regional constituency, governance structures, and closeness to their members, as well as the low interest rates they charge their borrowing members.

Features The financing model of RDBs consists of three main features: a financial leverage mechanism, a preferred creditor status, and a soft-lending window. RDBs borrow on international capital markets, backed by a capital structure with a low paid-in amount (direct cash contributions representing between 4 and 20 percent of subscribed capital, or issued share capital). They are thus able to borrow in international capital markets at lower rates than their borrowing members could individually, and the RDBs pass on to their members the low interest rates they pay. Their preferred creditor status is anchored in the support of their shareholding governments, reflected in capital contributions and pledges to soft-lending windows providing loans with extended grace periods, longer amortization and lower interest rates than conventional bank loans, and the incentives for borrowing countries to service their debt in order to secure continued access to concessional sources of development finance. Their membership typically includes regional borrowing members, as well as regional and nonregional nonborrowing countries.

Members contribute to the authorized capital, partly paid-in but mainly in the form of callable capital should an RDB become unable to meet its obligations to bondholders. Each member's financial contribution is a function of its relative affluence and determines its voting rights as a shareholder. Nonborrowing members contribute grant resources to their soft-lending windows, which they replenish every three to five years, allowing them to lend-on at highly concessional rates and on a very long-term basis to poorer members.

Functions RDBs provide nonconcessional loans and concessional credits, as well as nonrepayable grants, technical assistance, and policy advice. They also generate and disseminate knowledge, through advisory and analytical work, which shapes public policies and informs policy reform. Typically, they have four main lending instruments: a window providing nonconcessional loans to its wealthier members, financed with ordinary capital and with a repayment period typically of 15–30 years; a soft-lending window established as a separate development fund providing long-term concessional credits to poorer members with low creditworthiness, essentially in Africa and Asia, with a large grant element and a repayment period of up to 40–50 years; a private sector lending window operating on a commercial basis and providing a mix of financing instruments (loans, equity finance, risk management, intermediary finance); and a guarantee window promoting foreign direct investment.

Instruments RDBs provide two main types of sovereign loans or credits. Policy-based loans (also called adjustment or programmatic loans) provide general budget support against a program of reform and are linked to disbursement conditions, at times earmarked to specific sectors such as health, education, or social protection. Investment loans are designed to support specific development projects in sectors such as water, sanitation, infrastructure, or energy utilities. The banks increasingly support subnational governments and large municipalities, sometimes without sovereign guarantee from the central government. They are also prompted to increase their support to the private sector in better-off regions, especially small and medium enterprises, directly or through commercial banks (lines of credit).

Stepping Up to the Future The RDBs, like most multilateral development banks, are confronted with multifaceted challenges from a changing environment and the evolving financing needs of their members, especially middle-income countries. The rapid development of international capital markets and recent financial crises have prompted many reassessments of the role of multilateral finance, including by the G7 since 2001. Key challenges evolve around the RDBs' corporate mandate, comparative advantage, and lending strategies.

Corporate Mandate Many attempts are being made to redefine the banks' mission, as part of a gradual rethinking of the purpose and effectiveness of multilateral lending. RDBs are to focus more narrowly on reducing poverty and inequality and address a broader set of development challenges, including governance and anticorruption strategies. They are pressed by their richer shareholders to deliver results, and by civil society to show greater corporate social responsibility in their sovereign loans and equity investments in sensitive sectors such as extractive industries. They are under external pressure to increase transparency and accountability in their internal governance and modus operandi and are often criticized for operating as foreign policy extensions of powerful shareholders, especially the United States.

Strategic Selectivity RDBs are pressed to act more strategically and selectively, concentrating in those countries with sound institutions and good governance where aid has been found to be more effective. Calls for more selective engagement are part of the broader debate on the balance between grants and loans, lending instruments and pricing policies. Shifting to grant aid, it is argued, would help avoid the reaccumulation of unsustainable levels of debt. A

Table 1
Basic facts about regional development banks, 2005

	World Bank	Inter-American Development Bank	African Development Bank	Asian Development Bank	European Bank for Reconstruction and Development[b]
Year established	1945	1959	1964	1966	1990
Membership	184	46	77	63	62
Soft-window	IDA	FSO	AfDF	AsDF, NTF	
Private sector window	IFC	IIC, MIF			
Credit rating	AAA	AAA	AAA/AA+ (2003)	AAA	AAA
Subscribed capital (2004, U.S.$bn)	178	101	32	32	32
Of which paid-in	*11.5*	*4.34*	*3.24*	*2.32*	*6.4*
Total loan portfolio[a] (disbursements 2005, U.S.$bn)	225.3	55.0	33.8	24.5	45.5
Lending volume (gross disbursements 2005, U.S.$bn)	18.7	5.3	1.8	4.7	2.8
Net lending (net disbursements 2005, U.S.$bn)	2.2	−0.2	0.7	−0.4	0.3
Total voting rights for nonconcessional window for (%):					
Borrowing countries (2006)	38.2	50.4	56.5	40.5	11.7
Nonborrowing countries (2006)	61.8	49.6	43.5	59.5	88.3

Sources: Annual reports of the World Bank and RDBs.
[a] Measured as total loans outstanding and excluding private sector affiliates.
[b] Exchange rate used for EBRD: €1 = U.S.$1.28.

major debt relief initiative for highly indebted poor countries was launched in 1996 (enhanced in 1999), amounting to about U.S. $100 billion in nominal terms. In 2005, the Multilateral Debt Relief Initiative agreed to cancel the eligible debt of 22 poor countries, in particular in Africa, owed to the concessional lending arms of the African Development Bank and Inter-American Development Bank (as well as the World Bank and the International Monetary Fund).

In addition to pressuring the RDBs for greater reliance on grants in low-income countries with limited fiscal capacity, observers often question the banks' relevance and effectiveness in middle-income countries, partly as a result of developing countries' increased access to capital markets. In 2000, the U.S. Congress's Meltzer Commission recommended that the RDBs essentially end nonconcessional lending to middle-income countries and that their assistance to low-income countries be mainly in the form of grants. The commission also suggested that RDBs should assume most of the lending to their respective regions, except for Africa. Nevertheless, the emerging markets crises of the late 1990s showed that middle-income countries' access to private capital remains volatile and precarious.

Changing Context In a changing environment, the RDBs' importance as a source of development finance is declining, overtaken by private sector flows and remittances. Moreover grant financing from bilateral donors is set to increase sharply. New actors, especially China, are emerging as alternative sources of development finance, with fewer strings attached. In addition, the RDBs' loan portfolios are maturing, resulting in transfers out of developing countries as repayments and prepayments are made. In 2005, for example, net lending was nil, if not negative, reflecting patterns of "defensive lending," whereby new loans are made to ensure that past loans are repaid (see table 1).

Repositioning Efforts The RDBs are thus seeking to reposition themselves along different directions, through a more selective approach in middle-income countries, a sharper poverty focus in lower-income countries, and greater synergies with the private fi-

nancial sector. They are concentrating on good performers with sound economic policies in order to improve portfolio performance, tackling global public goods, and restricting their balance of payment support, especially emergency lending in crisis situations. Borrowers see competition among the multilateral development banks as providing them with greater choice and therefore improving loan quality, but specialization and cooperation between the World Bank and regional and subregional development banks are areas for further improvement.

See also aid, international; World Bank

FURTHER READING

Bergsten, Fred. 2000. *Reforming the Multilateral Development Banks.* Washington, DC: U.S. Senate. Testimony before the Subcommittee on International Trade and Finance Committee on Banking, Housing, and Urban Affairs, 8 June.

Bezanson, Keith, Francisco Sagasti, Silvia Charpentier, and Ricardo Gottschalk. 2000. *A Foresight and Policy Study of the Multilateral Development Banks.* Stockholm, Sweden: Ministry of Foreign Affairs. The report looks at the current pressures on the MDBs to reform their governance and retarget their operations in terms of their triple function of mobilizing financial resources; building institutional capacity and brokering knowledge; and finally, providing regional and global public goods.

Culpeper, Roy. 1997. *Titans or Behemoths? The Multilateral Development Banks.* London: Intermediate Technology. This final volume in the five title series on the MDBs examines the effectiveness of the MDBs and studies the overarching role of the World Bank. Arguing for a process of reform of the global governance system rather than its reinvention under a new framework, Culpeper urges the MDBs to build on their efforts to improve transparency and accountability.

Gurría, José Angel, and Paul Volcker. 2002. *The Role of Multilateral Development Banks in Emerging Market Economies.* Washington, DC: CEIP. This report from a commission cochaired by former Mexican finance minister José Angel Gurria and former U.S. Federal Reserve chairman Paul Volcker, assesses the activities of the MDBs in emerging market economies and recommends changes on long-standing MDB approaches toward these countries.

International Financial Institutions Advisory Commission. 2000. *Report of the International Financial Institutions Advisory Commission.* Washington, DC: U.S. Congress. The International Financial Institution Advisory Commission, also known as the Meltzer Commission—named for its chair, professor Allan Meltzer—was established by the U.S. Congress in November 1998 "to recommend future US policy toward several multilateral institutions: the IMF, the World Bank group, the regional development banks." The commission's influential majority report proposed changes to the operations of the IMF and especially to those of development banks such as the World Bank, which the majority recommended should withdraw from lending to so-called middle income countries.

Rodrik, Dani. 1995. "Why Is There Multilateral Lending?" NBER Working Paper No. 5160. Cambridge, MA: National Bureau of Economic Research. Reviews the rational for multilateral lending to developing countries.

CARLOS SANTISO AND EMILE-ROBERT PERRIN

■ regionalism

Enshrined in Article I of the World Trade Organization's (WTO's) General Agreement on Trade and Tariffs (GATT) is the key principle of the multilateral trade system—the principle of nondiscrimination—which prevents member countries from discriminating against imports based on the country of origin. In an important exception to this central prescript, however, the GATT (Article XXIV) permits WTO members to enter into preferential trade agreements (PTAs), provided these preferences are complete. In so doing, it sanctions the formation of free trade areas (FTAs), whose members are obligated to eliminate internal import barriers, and customs unions (CUs), whose members additionally agree on a common external tariff against imports from nonmembers. In addition, the Enabling Clause allows tariff preferences to be granted to developing countries (in accordance with the Generalized System of Preferences) and permits preferential trade agreements among developing countries in goods trade. Among the more prominent existing PTAs are the North American Free Trade Agreement (NAFTA), the European Economic Community (EEC), and the European Free Trade Association (EFTA), all formed under Article XXIV, and Mercosur (the CU encompassing Argentina, Brazil, Paraguay, and Uruguay) and the ASEAN (the Association of Southeast Asian Nations) Free Trade Area (AFTA), both formed under the Enabling Clause. Other forms of integration, such as the formation of a common market, involve the further elimination of barriers to factor mobility, as in the Common Market for Eastern and Southern Africa (COMESA) and the use of a single currency to form a common currency area (as in the European Union). Since preferential integration has often (but not always) involved geographically proximate countries, the term *regionalism* has been used to describe such regional groupings and sometimes to describe the broader phenomenon of preferential integration itself.

Economic Analysis Motivated by ongoing discussions concerning optimal trade arrangements in the postwar period, especially over the possibility of a European customs union, Viner (1950, 41–50) developed a seminal analysis of the economics of preferential trade. Viner's analysis disputes the presumption that cutting tariffs necessarily improves welfare. On the one hand, because of discriminatory liberalization, there will be commodities that a member country may "newly import from the other but which it formerly did not import at all because the price of the protected domestic good was lower than the price of any foreign source plus the duty." Viner calls this shift from a high to a lower cost point "trade creation" and associates it with welfare improvement for the importing country. He also argues that, on the other hand, "there may be other commodities, which one of the members will now newly import from the other," whereas before the PTA it "imported them from a third country, because that was the cheapest possible source of supply even after the payment of duty." He calls this shift in imports from a low-cost third country to a higher-cost member country "trade diversion," associating it with an increase in the cost of imports and, thus, welfare losses for the importing country.

The demonstration that preferential trade liberalization may be welfare decreasing stimulated a substantial theoretical literature on the "static" welfare effects of PTAs. Post-Vinerian analysis of the welfare effects of preferential trade developed examples of both welfare-improving trade diversion and welfare-decreasing trade creation in general equilibrium contexts broader than those considered by Viner (see Panagariya 2000 for a comprehensive discussion). The intuitive appeal of the concepts of trade creation and trade diversion and supporting empirical findings, however, have ensured their continued use in the economic analysis of preferential trade agreements, especially in policy analysis.

It has sometimes been argued that countries entering into preferential arrangements with geographically proximate countries are likely to do better than in agreements with distant countries, because the former are more likely than the latter to be trade creating. The theoretical literature has provided a number of examples, however, in which, between two otherwise identical potential partners, a country achieves a superior outcome by granting trade preferences to the distant partner (see Panagariya 2000). Moreover empirical analysis of this question has not found any support for the hypothesis that regional trading partners should be considered "natural" partners in the context of preferential trade (see Krishna 2005).

The generally ambiguous welfare results provided by the theoretical literature raised an important question relating to the *design* of necessarily welfare-improving PTAs. A classic result by Kemp and Wan (1976) provided a welfare-improving solution for the case of CUs. Starting from a situation with an arbitrary structure of trade barriers, if two or more countries freeze their net external trade with the rest of the world through a set of common external tariffs and eliminate the barriers to internal trade (which implies the formation of a CU), the welfare of the union as a whole necessarily improves and that of the rest of the world does not fall. A Pareto-improving

CU is thus achieved. Panagariya and Krishna (2002) have provided a corresponding construction of necessarily welfare-improving FTAs where, in analogy with Kemp and Wan, external trade is frozen for each FTA member country. Common to these analyses of welfare-improving preferential trade blocs is the elimination of trade diversion—achieved in each case by freezing external trade. To ensure this outcome, the trade barriers imposed on nonmembers must generally be less restrictive than before. Since existing GATT rules require only that external barriers not be raised, some trade diversion is likely in practice.

Recent analysis in the literature has focused on issues concerning the effects of preferential agreements on the multilateral trade system. Will PTA membership encourage governments to expand their agreements to include new countries or will there instead be political-economy incentives to keep new countries out? (Or, as Bhagwati 1993 has phrased it, will trade blocs serve as "building blocs" or "stumbling blocs" in the path to multilateral free trade?) Does the answer depend on the (trade-creating or trade-diverting) nature of the PTAs involved?

Modeling the endogenous determination of trade policy while emphasizing the role of powerful domestic interests in influencing policy, it has been argued that PTAs that divert trade are more likely to win internal political support. This is so because the political costs of liberalization are alleviated when gains to domestic firms of member countries come largely at the expense of outsiders. It follows that such PTAs will lower the incentives for any subsequent multilateral liberalization due to the fact that producers in trade-diverting PTAs may oppose multilateral reform since this would take away the gains from benefits of preferential access that they enjoyed in the PTA that diverted trade to them. Indeed, the incentives for further multilateral liberalization may be completely eliminated. The literature has obtained similar results when trade policy is determined by majority voting. If bilateral agreements occur between similar countries, so that there are gains from trade but no major income distributional shifts, bilateral agreements could render multilateral liberalization infeasible, as the latter may involve income

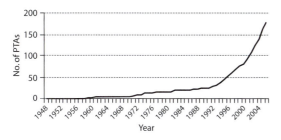

Figure 1
PTAs in force by date of entry into force. Source: World Trade Organization.

distributional changes that worsen the lot of the median voter. These analyses demonstrate the possibility that preferences in trade may have a negative impact on multilateral liberalization incentives for member countries. On the other hand, nonmember countries may see their incentives for multilateral liberalization increased. Thus, it has been argued that PTA expansion could have a "domino" effect—increasing the size of a bloc increases the incentive for others to join it (as they then gain preferential access to increasingly large markets). Assuming open membership rules (i.e., insiders do not oppose the entry of new members who abide by the same rules as the members), it has been shown that the successive expansion of a PTA could then lead to multilateral free trade, but this desired outcome is not achieved under alternative membership rules (see Krishna 2005 for a survey discussion).

A half century of research has significantly advanced our understanding of the implications of trade discrimination even if the frequently equivocal theoretical and empirical results have established among economists and policymakers an ambivalent attitude toward preferential trade agreements. Concerns regarding the fragmentation of the world trade system, however, have grown with the rapid proliferation of preferential trade in recent years (see figure 1). Several hundred PTAs were in existence in 2007 (with many countries belonging to multiple PTAs), and several more were in process. With this inexorable erosion of nondiscriminatory disciplines within the trade system, research on preferential trade is

certain to remain central to the field of international trade policy for many years to come.

See also common currency; common market; customs unions; free trade area; multilateralism; nondiscrimination

FURTHER READING

Bhagwati, J. 1993. "Regionalism and Multilateralism: An Overview." In *New Dimensions in Regional Integration*, edited by Jaime de Melo and Arvind Panagariya. Cambridge: Cambridge University Press, 22–46. An insightful historical and analytical survey of preferential trade and its interaction with the multilateral trade system.

Kemp, M., and H. Wan. 1976. "An Elementary Proposition Concerning the Formation of Customs Unions." *Journal of International Economics* 6 (1): 95–97. A seminal contribution describing the design of necessarily welfare-improving customs unions.

Krishna, P. 2005. *Trade Blocs: Economics and Politics.* Cambridge: Cambridge University Press. A discussion of recent developments in the economic, political, and quantitative analyses of preferential trade agreements.

Panagariya, A. 2000. "Preferential Trade Liberalization: The Traditional Theory and New Developments." *Journal of Economic Literature* 38 (2): 287–331. A comprehensive survey of the theoretical literature on preferential trade agreements.

Panagariya, A., and P. Krishna. 2002. "On the Existence of Necessarily-Welfare-Improving Free Trade Areas." *Journal of International Economics* 57 (2): 353–67. A theoretical contribution describing the design of welfare-improving free trade areas.

Viner, J. 1950. *The Customs Unions Issue.* New York: Carnegie Endowment for International Peace. A seminal contribution characterizing the economic consequences of preferential trade.

PRAVIN KRISHNA

■ remittances

International remittances, the sums of money and goods that immigrants send home, have recently captured the attention of bankers, economists, and policymakers. Previously, little effort was expended

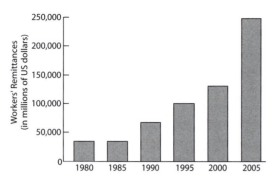

Figure 1

World receipts of workers' remittances. Source: World Bank, World Development Indicators.

to measure and analyze these flows because they were thought to be small in magnitude and of little significance for most countries. Evidence to the contrary has motivated policymakers and others to pay closer attention to the measurement, determinants, and impact of remittances.

Trends and Geography Using a broad definition of international remittances—workers' remittances and compensation of employees—we find that these flows increased from U.S. $37 billion in 1980 to U.S. $249 billion in 2005 (World Bank Indicators). This almost sevenfold increase (see figure 1) exceeds the growth of many macroeconomic variables, including world trade. Although some of the growth in remittances is simply due to better tracking and reporting of these flows at the aggregate level, microeconomic surveys also indicate that there has been brisk growth in the flows of resources from immigrants to their families. It is likely that this growth will persist as an important by-product of world migration.

Figure 2 reports on the worldwide distribution of remittance receipts, revealing that 50 percent of total receipts flow to Latin American, East Asia, and the Pacific regions. South Asia, the Middle East, and North Africa account for about another quarter of flows, while 14 percent flows to Europe and Central Asia. Sub-Saharan Africa, the region most in need of resource inflows, has the smallest share—only 4 percent.

Data Sources Individuals interested in obtaining yearly country-level data on international remittances can consult *The Balance of Payments Statistics Yearbook*, a publication of the International Monetary Fund (IMF). Since these data originate from reports submitted by member nations, more detailed information on remittances can sometimes be obtained directly from reporting agencies of individual countries. For example, Mexico provides monthly data on remittances on its Web site (www.banxico .org.mx). These are disaggregated by transmission method—whether the receipts arrived by money order, check, electronic transfer, or cash. In contrast, understanding how remittances affect household behavior (e.g., schooling, labor force participation) requires obtaining microeconomic data that report on both the household receipt of remittances and household characteristics. Many national income and expenditure surveys, a handful of censuses, and some specialized migration surveys provide this information.

Definition and Measurement of International Remittances At the time of this writing, the term *remittances* is used to refer to one or a combination of three separate concepts: workers' remittances, compensation of employees, and migrants' transfers. The first of these, workers' remittances, are current transfers by nonresidents to resident households, for example, the sums of money that a Dominican national with *U.S. residency* sends to her family in the Dominican Republic each month. In contrast, if the Dominican had been hired to work in the United States for five months only, her earnings net of travel expenses would be classified as compensation of employees. The main distinction in this latter case is her classification as a *Dominican resident* due to the temporary (less than one year) nature of her stay in the United States. The third category, migrants' transfers, are the changes in asset designations that take place when an individual changes residency. Take the case of an individual moving from the United States to Thailand. His U.S. saving account changes from being owned by a *U.S. resident* to being owned by a *Thai resident* and would be recorded under migrants' transfers. In practice there is considerable confusion and practical difficulties regard-

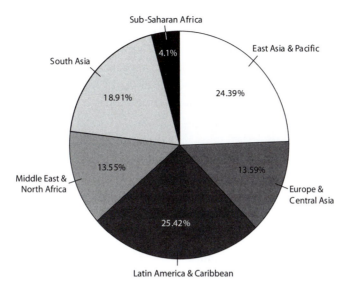

Figure 2

Share of world remittance receipts. Source: World Bank, World Development Indicators.

ing the three designations of remittances. Efforts to change and simplify the reporting and categorization of these international money flows were under discussion as of 2005 (see International Monetary Fund 2005).

Aside from these definitional difficulties, the researcher is likely to be challenged by the noncomparability of data across countries and over time. Although annual data on remittances are derived from standardized reports submitted to the IMF, countries still use different methodologies to collect the data. Some countries measure remittances by aggregating reports of inflows by the banking system and by money transfer firms such as Western Union. Different country-specific reporting requirements and thresholds make for variations in the scope of these reports, however. In other cases, central banks estimate flows using household surveys. Reliability, in these cases, rests with the ability of the survey instruments to capture all flows. Furthermore some surveys ask only about monetary remittances while others collect information on both monetary and in-kind transfers.

Nonuniformity of series across time can cause additional problems. There are variations in the abilities of statistical agencies to track different methods of transmission. It may be relatively easy for central banks to account for transfers made through officially regulated channels (e.g., banks and money transfer firms). Informal transfers—those that are hand carried, mailed as cash, or transmitted through hawalas—are harder to track (a participant in the hawala system provides a sum to a hawaladar who, in turn, directs a counterpart in another country to pay out that same sum of money to the intended recipient). Variations in policies and regulations can affect the choice of transmission method of immigrants remitting money home, which, in turn, affects the officially reported flows but not the actual flow of money across borders. For example, in 2002 a number of large banks chose to recognize the Mexican *matricula consular* (identification card issued by Mexican consulates to Mexicans residing outside of Mexico) as a valid form of identification, thereby facilitating the opening of bank accounts by many unbanked Mexican immigrants in the United States. An observed surge in *recorded* remittances following the policy change was likely due to shifting from harder to track informal transmission methods to more easily measured formal bank channels.

Determinants of Remittances To appreciate the impact of remittances it is helpful to understand why migrants remit. What motivates remittances? Do remitters respond to economic variables in both the host and home communities? Do incentives to remit change with policy? If we can describe their determinants, we can better predict and influence remittances.

Various motives for remitting have been put forth and tested (Rapoport and Docquier 2006). The motive most commonly cited is altruism—to facilitate higher levels of consumption by the family left in the home country. In fact, the prospect of earning higher wages abroad and sharing those with family back home is thought to be at the heart of much migration. But migration may also be motivated by a desire to accumulate assets, to purchase housing, land, or capital goods, to begin or expand a business in the origin community, or to cover for risky ventures away from home.

Many find it useful to think of migration and remittances as an overall strategy to permit the family to gain from the geographic dispersion of its members (Lucas and Stark 1985). Rosenzweig and Stark (1989) provide a good example of this, demonstrating how marriage with migration takes place to diversify income streams. Total household income remains more stable in these geographically dispersed households as members suffering from income shortfalls are compensated with income transfers by those in preferable situations, lowering consumption variance for all.

Isolating the determinants of remittances is helpful for predicting how remittances may respond to policy and to changing economic conditions. If migration and remittances take place to diversify income, remittance flows may rise and fall with economic shocks. If migration takes place to take advantage of higher earnings to purchase large-ticket items, remittances may subside once the purchase is made. If remittances are purely altruistic in nature, we can expect to observe that they flow and ebb with crisis situations in the home community. If remittances are undertaken to invest in the community of origin, local economic conditions and exchange rate policy are apt to have impacts on the volume and timing of flows.

Impacts of Remittances While many argue that remittances are beneficial, raising living standards, others emphasize negative effects of remittance inflows. This has led to confusion regarding appropriate policy. Should remittances be supported and encouraged or should we impede and slow growth in these money transfers? As with many phenomena, the issue is complex with both viewpoints earning currency.

Macroeconomic impacts: In an often-cited report, Ratha (2003) lauds remittances as more stable and reliable than foreign direct investment or foreign aid and thus an important source for financing development. Chami, Fullenkamp, and Jahjah (2005) take issue with this view, finding remittances to be negatively correlated with economic growth, compensatory in nature, and sent to families during hard times. As such they do not view remittances as a source of funding for investment and growth. Fajnzylber and López (2007) find that remittances contribute to surprisingly modest economic growth, while Adams and Page (2005) credit remittances with reducing both the rate and depth of poverty in developing countries.

The scorecard on remittances becomes even more difficult to interpret when we consider that remittances have uneven, time-sensitive, and redistributive effects. For example, given that international migration is costly, the benefits from remittances often bypass the poorest, who lack the means to finance migration. But this is found to change over time because as migration networks become more widespread, individuals lower in the income distribution obtain the means to migrate and in turn benefit from remittances too (McKenzie 2005).

Additional redistributive impacts may result when remittance spending patterns cause the relative prices of nontraded goods to increase, causing real exchange rate appreciation. This places the export sector in a less competitive position and results in an additional set of gainers and losers. If national policy is set on fueling economic development via export growth, changing real exchange rates due to remittances may thwart those efforts.

Microeconomic impacts: Understanding the microeconomic impacts of remittance inflows might help settle some of the controversy regarding their macroeconomic impacts. Are remittances all "squandered away" on consumption and thus have no chance to contribute toward longer-term economic growth? Or are these flows invested, increasing the physical and human capital stock? Surveys that simply ask senders what the transfers are intended for have sometimes been consulted to determine the share invested and the share consumed. But while senders claim to transfer money for specific purposes, it lies with the recipient to actually allocate the inflows.

Many researchers use microeconomic-level surveys that link remittances with household characteristics. Using such, Cox Edwards and Ureta (2003) found that remittances positively affect the level of schooling in children. Others, however, have found only very modest increases in schooling levels due to remittances. Differences in research outcomes are likely due to difficulties in separating the "migration effect" from the "remittance effect." Remittances are often a by-product of migration by a household member. Although remittances may loosen liquidity constraints, facilitating school attendance, the absence of a family member may force children to assume the role of an absent member in home or market work, reducing time available for school.

What is the impact of remittances on work behavior? Do remittances promote dependency by inducing individuals who would otherwise work to refrain from supplying their labor? Amuedo-Dorantes and Pozo (2006) find that women remittance recipients in Mexico appear to work fewer hours, perhaps because the additional income allows the women to tend to children instead. Men also appear to change their behavior but not in terms of hours of work. They appear to move away from formal sector work and toward informal sector work—much of which is self-employment. Perhaps

remittances facilitate self-employment by providing resources to acquire the necessary capital stock or a "backup fund" to permit the recipient to engage in riskier entrepreneurial ventures. Evidence that remittances are used for the acquisition of physical capital is furthered by Woodruff and Zenteno (2007), who find that attachments to migration networks in Mexico are associated with increases in investments in microenterprises.

Since migrants are complex individuals facing a variety of choices, circumstances, and constraints, it stands to reason that there are many different motives for remitting. Differing motives will result in varying impacts of remittances. In many cases the impacts will benefit recipients, but in other circumstances they might not. Nevertheless, remittances will likely continue to grow and take on greater importance. Continued research to further our understanding of remittances will permit the tailoring of policy to better unlock their potential to do good for recipient households and nations.

See also balance of payments; brain drain; brain gain; brain waste; migration governance; migration, international; real exchange rate

FURTHER READING

Adams, Richard H. Jr., and John Page. 2005. "Do International Migration and Remittances Reduce Poverty in Developing Countries?" *World Development* 33 (10): 1645–69. A large study covering the impact of remittances on poverty rates.

Amuedo-Dorantes, Catalina, and Susan Pozo. 2006. "Migration, Remittances, and Male and Female Employment Patterns." *American Economic Review Papers and Proceedings* 96 (2): 222–26. Covers labor supply impacts of remittances.

Chami, Ralph, Connel Fullenkamp, and Sanir Jahjah. 2005. "Are Immigrant Remittance Flows a Source of Capital for Development?" *IMP Staff Papers* 52 (1): 55–81. Challenges the notion that remittances are stable funding for development.

Cox Edwards, Alejandra, and Manuelita Ureta. 2003. "International Migration, Remittances, and Schooling: Evidence from El Salvador." *Journal of Development*

Economics 72 (2): 429–61. Addresses remittances' impacts on schooling,

Fajnzylber, Pablo, and J. Humberto López. 2007. *Close to Home: The Development Impact of Remittances in Latin America*, Washington, DC: World Bank. An extensive treatment of remittance flows to Latin America.

International Monetary Fund. 2005. *Remittances and Statistics*. Downloadable from http://www.imf.org/external/np/sta/bop/remitt.htm. Papers and presentations produced for a joint World Bank/IMF meeting to discuss the measurement of remittances.

Lucas, Robert E. B., and Oded Stark. 1985. "Motivations to Remit: Evidence from Botswana." *The Journal of Political Economy* 93 (5): 901–18. Pioneering study of the economics of remittances.

McKenzie, David J. 2005. "Beyond Remittances: The Effects of Migration on Mexican Households." In *International Migration, Remittances, and the Brain Drain*, edited by Çaglar Özden and Maurice Schiff. Washington, DC: World Bank, 123–47. Highlights the distinct impacts of migration and remittances on household behavior in Mexico.

Rapoport, Hillel, and Frederic Docquier. 2006. "The Economics of Migrants' Remittances." In *Handbook of the Economics of Giving, Altruism, and Reciprocity,* vol. 2, edited by Serge Christophe Kolm and Jean Mercier Ythier. Amsterdam: North Holland, 1135–98. An advanced treatment of the determinants of remittances and their impacts on economic growth.

Ratha, Dilip. 2003. "Workers' Remittances: An Important and Stable Source of External Development Finance." *Global Development Finance: Striving for Stability in Development Finance*. Washington, DC: World Bank, 157–75. An often-cited article on remittances in the context of financial flows for development.

Rosenzweig, Mark R., and Oded Stark. 1989. "Consumption Smoothing, Migration, and Marriage: Evidence from Rural India." *Journal of Political Economy* 97 (4): 905–24. A classic article on the interplay of remittances and migration.

Woodruff, Christopher, and Rene Zenteno. 2007. "Migration Networks and Microenterprises in Mexico." *Journal of Development Economics* 82 (2): 509–28. An excellent treatment of migration, remittances, and small business development in Mexico.

World Bank. Monthly. World Bank Indicators online. Accessed May 2007. Available at http://web.worldbank .org/WBSITE/EXTERNAL/DATASTATISTICS.

SUSAN POZO

■ **rent seeking**

See political economy of trade policy

■ **research and development intensity**

See foreign direct investment (FDI)

■ **reserve currency**

A reserve currency is a foreign currency held by central banks or monetary authorities for the purpose of exchange intervention (to influence the exchange rate of the national currency) and the settlement of intergovernmental claims (debts). A reserve currency is also used in the pricing of goods, services, and assets entering international trade and finance. A reserve-currency status allows the nation issuing the currency to pay a somewhat lower price for imports (because it need not incur the small cost of exchanging its currency for another to pay for its imports), borrow at marginally lower rates, and earn seigniorage (the difference between the minimal cost of printing money and its face value).

The U.S. dollar is by far the largest vehicle currency in the world today. The euro (the currency of the European Monetary Union, or EMU) has increasingly been used as a vehicle currency since its creation in 1999. To be a vehicle currency, a national currency must (1) be stable in value; (2) belong to a nation that occupies a central, or at least a very important, position in world production, trade, and finance; and (3) be fully convertible into other currencies and freely tradable in a viable foreign exchange market.

Table 1 shows that the share of national currencies in official holdings of foreign exchange reserves in the form of U.S. dollars rose from 62.1 percent in 1996 to 71.0 percent in 1999, declined to 65.8 percent in 2004, then rose to 66.5 percent in 2005. The Japanese yen was 6.7 percent of the total in 1966 but declined to 3.6 percent in 2005; the British pound was 2.7 percent in 1996 and rose to 3.7 percent in 2005; the Swiss franc's share was very small (0.3 percent) both in 1996 and in 2005 (0.1 percent). The euro accounted for 17.9 percent of official holdings of foreign currency reserves in 1999 (the year of its

Table 1

Share of national currencies in official holdings of foreign exchange reserves at year-end

	1996	1998	1999	2000	2001	2002	2003	2004	2005
U.S. dollar	62.1	69.4	71.0	71.0	71.4	67.0	65.9	65.8	66.5
Japanese yen	6.7	6.2	6.4	6.1	5.1	4.4	3.9	3.8	3.6
Pound sterling	2.7	2.7	2.9	2.8	2.7	2.8	2.8	3.4	3.7
Swiss franc	0.3	0.3	0.2	0.3	0.3	0.4	0.2	0.2	0.1
Euro	—	—	17.9	18.4	19.3	23.9	25.3	25.0	24.4
Deutsche mark	14.7	13.8	—	—	—	—	—	—	—
French franc	1.8	1.6	—	—	—	—	—	—	—
Nether. guilder	0.2	0.3	—	—	—	—	—	—	—
ECUs	7.1	1.2	—	—	—	—	—	—	—
Other currencies	4.4	4.5	1.6	1.4	1.2	1.5	1.9	1.8	1.7
Total	100.0	100.0	100.0	100.0	100.0	100.0	100.0	100.0	100.0

Table 2

Currency composition of official holdings of foreign exchange reserves at year-end (in million $)

	1996	1998	1999	2000	2001	2002	2003	2004	2005
U.S. dollar	760.1	888.7	977.4	1,077.6	1,117.7	1,202.2	1,465.9	1,737.2	1,869.9
Japanese yen	82.3	80.0	87.8	93.3	79.4	78.4	87.8	101.5	100.7
Pound sterling	32.9	34.1	39.8	41.8	42.4	50.5	61.6	89.2	105.3
Swiss franc	3.7	4.2	3.2	4.1	4.4	7.3	4.9	4.3	4.0
Euro	—	—	246.9	279.5	301.9	428.1	562.4	660.0	685.4
Deutsche mark	179.9	176.9	—	—	—	—	—	—	—
French franc	22.5	20.8	—	—	—	—	—	—	—
Nether. guilder	2.9	3.5	—	—	—	—	—	—	—
ECUs	86.6	15.3	—	—	—	—	—	—	—
Total of Above	1,170.9	1,223.5	1,355.1	1,496.3	1,545.8	1,766.5	2,182.6	2,592.2	2,765.3
Other currencies	53.2	57.4	21.6	22.2	19.5	27.0	42.8	48.0	44.9
Overall total[a]	1,566.2	1,643.8	1,783.7	1,942.6	2,053.0	2,409.1	3,029.2	3,749.4	3,171.9

Source: IMF, *Annual Report* (2006).

[a] Includes foreign exchange reserves whose currency composition could not be determined.

creation) and rose to 25.3 percent in 2003; it was 24.4 percent in 2005. This was less than the EMU's share of world output and trade but much larger than the sum of the share of the deutsche mark, French franc, Netherlands guilder, and ECU foreign currency reserves that it replaced. The ECU (the European Currency Unit) was introduced in March 1979 by the European Monetary System (EMS), a forerunner of the EMU. On December 31, 1998, ECUs were unwound into gold and dollars. Table 2 gives the dollar amount of the various foreign exchange reserves from 1996 to 2005.

Before World War I, gold was the only international reserve held by nations and the British pound was the only important international currency. Under the Bretton Woods system, which operated from 1947 until 1971, the value of the U.S. dollar was fixed in terms of gold and the international value of other currencies were then fixed in terms of dollars. The fact that U.S. dollars held by foreign central banks were redeemable in gold made the dollar "as good as gold." In time, a few other currencies joined the dollar as international currency reserves. Thus the Bretton Woods system was a gold-exchange standard, with both dollars and international currency reserves held as official reserves by nations' central banks and monetary authorities.

After World War II, the dollar replaced the British pound as the most important international reserve currency, to reflect the much greater importance of the United States than the United Kingdom in world output, trade, and finance, and also because the dollar better satisfied the other conditions for serving as an international reserve currency. The British pound, however, remained a significant international reserve currency after World War II because of tradition (recognition) and inertia, but its importance declined sharply after the mid-1970s when the pricing of petroleum and other primary commodities switched from British pounds to U.S. dollars.

In August 1971, the dollar was devalued (the dollar price of gold increased) and its convertibility into gold was abolished, thus ushering the world into a pure paper (essentially a de facto dollar) standard.

Early in the 21st century, foreign exchange reserves constitute the bulk of international reserve assets, with the dollar by far the largest and the euro second largest. Although gold remains an important international reserve asset, its relative importance has greatly diminished. Other official reserve assets are nations' net IMF positions (the amount that a nation could borrow without questions asked by the International Monetary Fund, or IMF) and special drawing rights, or SDRs.

In the present managed exchange rate system, the importance of international reserves ought to be less than under the previous fixed exchange rate system because a nation facing a balance of payments deficit can allow its currency to depreciate, thus correcting its deficit without the need to continuously finance it with international reserves—unless more drastic forms of adjustment become necessary, such as a devaluation of the currency or import restrictions.

See also balance of payments; Bretton Woods system; convertibility; dollar standard; dominant currency; euro; exchange rate regimes; foreign exchange intervention; gold standard, international; International Monetary Fund (IMF); international reserves; money supply; reserve currency; seigniorage; special drawing rights; sterilization; vehicle currency

FURTHER READING

Bank for International Settlements. *Annual Report*. Basel: BIS, 2006. Report on the world's financial and banking situation, including the use of reserve currencies.

International Monetary Fund. *Annual Report*. Washington, DC: IMF, 2006. An analysis of the world's economic and financial situation, it includes a discussion of the relative use of various vehicle currencies.

Mundell, Robert A. 2000. "A Reconsideration of the Twentieth Century." *American Economic Review* (June): 327–40. A review and interpretation of the operation of the international monetary system during the past century by a Nobel Prize recipient in economics.

Salvatore, Dominick. 2007. *International Economics*. 9th ed. Hoboken, NJ: Wiley, chapter 21. An overview of the functioning of the international monetary system and the use of reserve currencies.

Taiwan, Government of. http://investintaiwan.nat.gov.tw/en/env/stats/foreign_exchange.html. Data on the foreign exchange reserves held by each country.

Widdershins. "Reserve Currency." Available at http://mg.blogs.com/reserve. A discussion of the role of a reserve currency in international finance.

DOMINICK SALVATORE

■ revealed comparative advantage

Revealed comparative advantage (RCA) is an empirical measure of the extent to which a given country specializes in the export of a particular product or range of products, compared with a reference set of countries. It is usually computed from trade data.

International trade theory starts from the premise that production specialization across different countries, followed by exports of the goods specialized in and imports of goods specialized in by other countries, leads to overall welfare gains for all economies. The pattern of specialization is called "comparative advantage," which is the result of relative advantage in access to materials, energy, or technological skills that are crucial for the efficient production of the exported good. Other countries would establish relative advantages in other goods that they export. The patterns of exports and imports would then derive from this relative or comparative advantage in production.

Trade theory begins by predicting patterns of trade from the existence of relative or comparative differences in natural resource endowments or capability acquired from production experience or technological change. The RCA approach starts from the other end of the production-trade chain, that is, the empirically observed patterns of export and import specialization revealed by the trade data. The explanation of the pattern of specialization is treated as a secondary matter to be inferred from the observed data on trade. Thus if the proportion of wine in France's exports is higher than the ratio of wine to all exports in the Organisation for Economic Co-operation and Development (OECD) group as a whole, France is said to have revealed comparative advantage in the export of wine relative to the OECD reference set. Note that this does not imply that France would have RCA with respect to some other set of countries.

Origin and Mathematical Formulation The index most commonly used to measure RCA is the Balassa index (BI), which was developed and popularized by Bela Balassa (1965, 1989), though the concept of a specialization index was first proposed by Liesner (1958). If we wish to examine whether country i has manifest advantage in the export of product line j (at some level of product aggregation) over a set of reference countries represented by the symbol w, we construct the following simple Balassa index:

$$BI_{ij} = \text{share of } j \text{ in country } i\text{'s exports/} \atop \text{share of } j \text{ in set } w\text{'s exports} \qquad (1)$$

If BI_{ij} is greater than 1.0, then country i would have RCA in product line j with respect to reference set w, since a proportionately greater share of its exports consist of j. If BI_{ij} is less than 1.0, the country is said to have revealed comparative disadvantage in good j. If we wish to be precise, we would have to specify the set w in the index as well, say as BI_{ijw}, since the index depends on the particular set of countries chosen. Exports are measured as total export values to the rest of the world expressed in a particular year's currency units. Clearly this index is very simple to compute from the actual trade data for any level of aggregation of export lines and is intuitively meaningful.

The index can also be extended from a single country i to a set k within a larger reference set w. For example, if we wish to compute the RCA of advanced industrial countries (AIC) in the export of capital goods, we would need to first aggregate all capital goods exported by all AICs and compute the share of these in total exports. This ratio would then have to be divided by the share of aggregated capital goods in total world exports. The index can be similarly modified to track the relative strength of any given trading region with respect to any particular characteristic of exports, provided that it can be quantified, measured, and aggregated across a range of product lines.

In formal terms the Balassa, or revealed comparative advantage, index is often defined as follows for exporting region i, export line j and reference region w, where X_{mn} stands for export value of good n from region m and t stands for all exports from the particular region. The reference set w is often taken as the whole world:

$$RCA_{ij} = (X_{ij}/X_{it})/(X_{wj}/X_{wt})$$
$$= (X_{ij}/X_{wj})/(X_{it}/X_{wt}) \qquad (2)$$

Practical Issues Since its initial formulation, RCA indexes have been widely used to track specialization with regard to participation in the international economy. Starting from specialization in particular goods or ranges of goods, RCAs have been calculated for goods intensive in capital or labor, intermediate products, energy, a wide range of agro-based exports, and exports that use particular technologies. It is often the "first cut" analytical tool in export competitiveness studies carried out by academics and international consultants.

RCAs are even worked out for the generation of patentable innovations (Laursen 1998). The RCA concept has turned out to be a very flexible tool of analysis and the original formula has been modified in a wide variety of ways, a few of which are outlined in the next section. It is also clear that the formulation can be adapted easily for import specialization as well and there are indexes that use both export and import data.

RCAs must be used with some care. They are useful to identify sectors that are strong and have the potential to be built up further. But the index cannot be used to infer competitive strength vis-à-vis another country in the same reference set. A large country with a more diverse range of exports will have a smaller RCA than a small nation that concentrates on a much smaller set of exports but has comparable competitive strength. Nor do relative values of different products for the same country say much about the relative importance of these products for the economy. For example, tobacco has the highest Balassa index for the United States over a long time span, but this is hardly its most important export product (Marrewijk 2002).

RCA measures are also affected by trade barriers or subsidies since these could distort exports or raise production costs by raising the price of imported inputs. Reexports and a high degree of intraindustry trade also pose special problems, which can be handled by the use of alternative measures (Laursen 1998; Utkulu and Seyman 2004).

Extensions One problem with the basic Balassa index is that it is not symmetrically distributed around the neutral value 1.0, ranging from 0 to 1 for comparative disadvantage and indefinitely upward from 1.0 for comparative advantage products. This problem is easily corrected by taking natural logarithms of the ratios with the index defined as follows:

$$RCA_{ij} = \ln(X_{ij}/X_{it}) - \ln(X_{wj}/X_{wt}) \qquad (3)$$

The revised index is now symmetric around 0. This form is particularly useful for econometric studies. An alternative transformation, which yields RCA values between -1 and $+1$ around 0, is given in Laursen (1998), but it is probably less useful than the log form for econometric work.

Vollrath (1991) proposed the following alternative index of trade specialization, which brings imports into the calculation:

$$RCA_{v1} = RXA - RMA \qquad (4)$$

Where $RXA = (X_{ij}/X_{it})/(X_{wj}/X_{wt})$, the original export specialization index, and $RMA = (M_{ij}/M_{it})/(M_{wj}/M_{wt})$, which is a similar import specialization index.

An alternative formulation of the Vollrath index takes the following form:

$$RCA_{v2} = \ln RXA - \ln RMA \qquad (5)$$

The Michaely index MI (see Laursen 1998) for country i and product j is defined as the difference between the share of sector j in total exports minus the share of sector j in total imports. There is no reference set of countries, so the index ranges from -1 to $+1$ and is 0 if import shares are perfectly balanced with export shares:

$$MI_{ij} = X_{ij}/X_{it} - M_{ij}/M_{it} \qquad (6)$$

A particularly useful measure of normalized revealed comparative advantage (NRCA), proposed by Yu et al. (2008), is defined in equation 7, where w

refers to the entire world and t to total exports. This index can be interpreted as the deviation of the normalized value of country i exports of product line j with respect to total world exports (the first term) from its expected comparative advantage neutral value (the second term).

$$NRCA_{ij} = X_{ij}/X_{wt} - X_{wj} \cdot X_{it}/X_{wt}^2 \qquad (7)$$

The equivalent form of equation 8 shows an alternative deviation kernel (term one) normalized by the relative weight of country i exports in world exports (term two).

$$NRCA_{ij} = [X_{ij}/X_{it} - X_{wj}/X_{wt}]\{X_{it}/X_{wt}\} \qquad (8)$$

This index has some useful properties: it is symmetrical about zero and displays additive consistency across product lines and country groupings. It just needs to be scaled up by an arbitrary factor to facilitate numerical comparisons, since both terms in equation 7 yield very small values; but this is no problem since RCA is a relative measure in any case. Furthermore the sum of NRCA across all commodities for any one country is zero as is the sum of NRCA across all countries for any one commodity.

Overall the RCA concept has proved to be an enduring and easily computable measure that can be used to track patterns of trade and production specialization. It has been used to study the performance of individual countries or groups of countries with respect to a larger set or even to comprehensively compare countries with one another, as in Batra and Khan (2005), which compares the evolution of India and China. RCA is therefore a very useful and powerful tool of trade analysis, used by academics and economic consultants to study evolving patterns in the world economy.

See also comparative advantage; intraindustry trade

FURTHER READING

Balassa, Bela. 1965. "Trade Liberalization and 'Revealed' Comparative Advantage." *Manchester School of Economic and Social Studies* 33 (2): 92–123. The first published use of the Balassa index to measure RCA.

———. 1989. "'Revealed' Comparative Advantage Revisited." In *Comparative Advantage, Trade Policy, and Economic Development*, edited by Bela Balassa. New York: New York University Press, 63–79. In this paper, Balassa further develops RCA measures in trade analysis.

Batra, Amita, and Zeba Khan. 2005. "Revealed Comparative Advantage: An Analysis for India and China." Working Paper No. 168. New Delhi: Indian Council for Research on International Economic Relations. Downloadable from http://www.icrier.org. Illustrates the value of the RCA concept to track evolving patterns of export and production specialization in India and China.

Laursen, Keld. 1998. "Revealed Comparative Advantage and the Alternatives as Measures of International Specialization." DRUID Working Paper 98-30. Copenhagen. An exposition of various RCA measures that are compared for many countries.

Liesner, H. H. 1958. "The European Common Market and British Industry." *Economic Journal* 68 (270): 302–16. The first use of the relative share concept to measure specialization in trade.

Marrewijk, Charles Van. 2002. *International Trade and the World Economy*. Oxford: Oxford University Press, 36–40. Presents a simple introduction to the Balassa index along with practical applications.

Utkulu, Utku, and Dilek Seyman. 2004. "Revealed Comparative Advantage and Competitiveness: Evidence for Turkey vis-à-vis the EU-15." European Trade Study Group, 6th Annual Conference (ETSG 2004). Nottingham, UK. Employs alternative RCA indexes to examine Turkey's exports to the European Union and discusses the merits of various indexes.

Vollrath, T. L. 1991. "A Theoretical Evaluation of Alternative Trade Intensity Measures of Revealed Comparative Advantage." *Weltwirtschaftliches Archiv* 127 (2): 265–80. A theoretical assessment of the various RCA measures in use.

Yu R., J. N. Cai, and P. S. Leung. 2008. "The Normalized Revealed Comparative Advantage Index." *Annals of Regional Science*. Available online at http://www.springerlink.com/content/qx7j588366801n05/fulltext.pdf.

G. CHRIS RODRIGO

◼ Ricardian model

The Ricardian model is the simplest and most basic general equilibrium model of international trade that we have. It is usually featured in an early chapter of any textbook on international economics. Historically, it is the earliest model of trade to have appeared in the writings of classical economists, at least among models that are still considered useful today.

It is indeed still useful. In spite of being superseded over the years by models with much more complexity (more factors of production, increasing returns to scale, imperfect competition), the Ricardian model often provides the platform for the introduction of today's new ideas. Dornbusch, Fischer, and Samuelson (1977) examined a continuum of goods first in a Ricardian model. Eaton and Kortum (2002) incorporated an ingenious and elegant treatment of geography into a Ricardian model. Melitz (2003) started a small revolution in trade theory by modeling heterogeneous firms within what was essentially a Ricardian model.

The Ricardian model itself, as a new idea, came many years after Ricardo. According to Ruffin (2002), in 1816 David Ricardo introduced only a portion of the model that now bears his name, focusing primarily on the amounts of labor used to produce traded goods and, from that, the concept of comparative advantage. The first appearance of the Ricardian model, according to Ruffin again, was in Mill (1844).

The Simple Ricardian Model The simple Ricardian model depicts a world of two countries, A and B, each using a single factor of production, labor L, to produce two goods, X and Y. Technologies display constant returns to scale, meaning that a fixed amount of labor, a_g^c is needed to produce a unit of output of each good, $g = X,Y$, in each country, $c = A,B$, regardless of how much is produced in total. All markets are perfectly competitive, so that goods are priced at cost in countries that produce them, $p_g^c = w^c a_g^c$, where w^c is the competitive wage in country c. Labor is available in fixed supply in each country, L^c; it is immobile between countries but perfectly mobile within each. The Ricardian model typically leaves demands for goods much less fully specified than supplies, though a modern formulation may specify for each country a utility function, $U^c = U^c(C_x^c, C_y^c)$, which the representative consumer maximizes subject to a budget constraint. Utility functions may, or may not, be assumed in addition to be identical across countries, or to possess other regularity properties, although most properties of the model's solution do not require any of these assumptions.

The most basic use of the model compares the equilibriums in autarky (that is, complete self-sufficiency without trade) with those of free and frictionless trade. In autarky, since both goods must be produced in each country, prices are given immediately by the costs stated above, and further analysis is needed only if one wants to know quantities produced and consumed. If so, the linear technology implies a linear production possibility frontier (PPF) that also serves as the budget line for consumers in autarky. The autarky equilibrium is as shown in figure 1, where ~ indicates autarky and Q represents production.

Comparison of the two countries in autarky depends primarily on their relative costs of producing the two goods, which in this model defines their comparative advantage. For concreteness, assume that country A has comparative advantage in good X: $a_X^A/a_Y^A < a_X^B/a_Y^B$, so that $\tilde{p}_X^A/\tilde{p}_Y^A < \tilde{p}_X^B/\tilde{p}_Y^B$. Without further assumptions about preferences, little more can be said about autarky, but with addi-

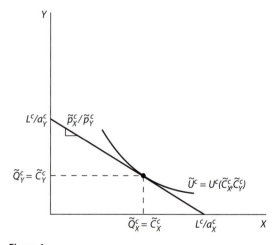

Figure 1
Ricardian model equilibrium in autarky

tional assumptions about preferences, one can infer that $\tilde{Q}_X^A/\tilde{Q}_Y^A > \tilde{Q}_X^B/\tilde{Q}_Y^B$.

With free and frictionless trade, prices must be the same in both countries. Two kinds of equilibrium are possible, depending on the supplies and demands for goods in the two countries. One kind of equilibrium has world relative prices, denoted here by ˘, strictly between the relative prices of the two countries in autarky: $\tilde{p}_X^A/\tilde{p}_Y^A < \breve{p}_X/\breve{p}_Y < \tilde{p}_X^B/\tilde{p}_Y^B$. In that case, each country must specialize in producing only the good for which its relative cost is lower than the world relative price, thus the good in which it has comparative advantage. Each must necessarily export that good.

With such complete specialization, outputs of the goods are determined by labor endowments and productivities, so equality of world supply and demand must be achieved from the demand side. That is, world prices are determined such that the two countries' demands sum to the quantity produced in one of them. These demands derive from the expanded budget constraints of each country's consumers, reflecting the value at world prices of the single good that the country produces. Consumers can now, unless they wish to consume only that single good, consume more of both goods than they did in autarky. Whether they choose to do so depends on the extent to which they substitute toward the cheaper good now imported from abroad, but in any case they reach a higher indifference curve and are better off. All of this is shown in figure 2. For this to be an equilibrium, the quantity of each good exported by one country must equal the quantity imported by the other, so the heavy arrows showing net trade in each panel of the figure must be equal and opposite.

Such an equilibrium with specialization will arise only if the two countries' capacities to produce their respective comparative-advantage goods correspond sufficiently closely to world demands for the goods. If this is not the case—if one country's labor endowment is too low and/or its labor requirement for producing its comparative-advantage good is too high for it to satisfy world demand—then while that country will specialize, the other country (call it the larger one, although that is not strictly necessary) will not. Instead of world relative prices settling between the two autarky levels as described earlier, prices will exactly equal the autarky prices of the larger country, and that country will produce both goods. At those prices, producers in the larger country will be indifferent among all output combinations on the PPF,

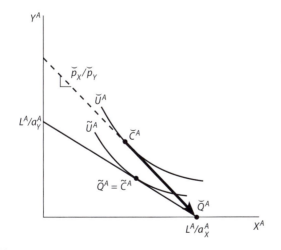

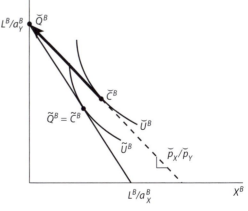

Figure 2

Free trade equilibrium with complete specialization

and output in the large country will be determined instead by the need to fill whatever demand is not satisfied by the smaller country.

Such an equilibrium is shown in figure 3, where in comparison to figure 2 country B's labor endowment has been made smaller and both countries' preference for good Y has been increased. As a result, country B is too small to meet world demand for good Y, even at country A's autarky prices. Therefore the free trade equilibrium has country A consuming where it did in autarky, while its production, $\breve{Q}^A$, moves down along its PPF so that, again, its trade vector can be equal and opposite to that of country B. Note that, in this trading equilibrium, the larger country neither gains nor loses from trade.

The following are some of the implications of this simple model, some of which have been illustrated above, while others can be derived rather simply:

Effects of trade:

- Each country exports the good in which it has comparative advantage, as defined by having a lower relative autarky price than the other country.
- Trade causes each country to expand its production of the good it exports, with labor being reallocated to it from the import-competing industry.

- Trade causes the relative price of a country's export good to rise, except in the case of a "large" country, defined here as one whose trading partner is too small to meet its demand for imports.
- Consumption and welfare are unchanged by trade in a large country; in any country that is not large, consumers buy more of one or both goods and welfare increases.
- Because all income accrues to labor, which earns the same wage in both industries due to mobility, conclusions about welfare or utility apply equally well to the real wage.

Effects of changes in trading equilibriums (assuming a bit more about preferences):

- An increase in the labor endowment of a country, holding other labor, technology, and tastes constant, hurts the growing country and benefits the other.
- A fall in the labor required by a country to produce its export good, holding other technology, endowments, and tastes constant, benefits the other country but may either benefit or harm ("immiserize") the growing country.
- A rise in the labor required by a country to produce its import good has no effect if it does not produce that good; if it does pro-

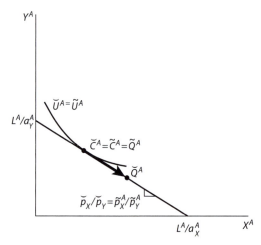

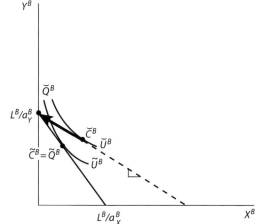

Figure 3
Free trade equilibrium with country A incompletely specialized

duce it (like country A in figure 3), the world price of that good rises, that country is harmed, and the other country gains.

- A change in preferences, in either country, in favor of one of the goods has no effect on prices or production if one of the countries is incompletely specialized. If both are specialized, however, then the relative price of that good rises, improving the terms of trade of the country that exports it.

Extensions of the Simple Ricardian Model Before considering several extensions of the simple model described here, it is reasonable to ask what extensions would *not* be acceptable, in that they would lead to a model that would no longer be "Ricardian," as trade economists understand the term. Ricardo himself might disagree, were he alive, but the essential features of a Ricardian model seem to be two: that production uses only homogeneous labor as a primary input and that comparative advantage arises from differences across goods and countries in the technology for producing goods from that labor. Both of these requirements distinguish a Ricardian model from the other principal model of trade theory, the Heckscher-Ohlin or factor-proportions model. With primary factors other than labor (including different kinds of labor based on skill and/or industry of location), a model takes on features that differ in essential ways from the Ricardian model. On the other hand, with only homogeneous labor as a factor of production, if technologies do not differ across countries then there is no scope for comparative advantage–based trade.

More Goods and/or Countries Therefore, keeping the number of factors at one, the most obvious things to extend in the simple model are to add to the numbers of goods and/or countries. This is relatively easily done, as long as one does not try to do both.

With two countries and many goods, the goods can be ranked in a chain of comparative advantage based on the ratios of their unit labor requirements in the two countries. That is, if one numbers N goods such that $a_1^A/a_1^B < a_2^A/a_2^B < \cdots < a_N^A/a_N^B$, then country A has comparative advantage in the low end of this ranking while country B has it in the high end.

Further one can show that under free trade, each country will specialize in and export goods in its respective end of the chain, with at most one good (and perhaps no good) being produced in common by both countries. The division between A's exports and B's exports depends on country sizes, technologies, and tastes, much as in the choice between figures 2 and 3. For example, the larger the labor endowment and/or efficiency of country A compared with B, the further up the chain will A produce and export.

Similarly, with two goods and many countries, the countries can be ranked in a chain of comparative advantage based on the ratios of their unit labor requirements for producing the two goods. That is, if one numbers M countries such that $a_X^1/a_Y^1 < a_X^2/a_Y^2 < \cdots < a_X^M/a_Y^M$, those countries in the low end of this ranking will specialize in and export good X to those in the high end, which export good Y. Again there will be at most one country (and perhaps no country) that produces both goods. And the division between X-exporters and Y-exporters depends on country sizes, technologies, and tastes.

Unfortunately, extending to more than two of both goods and countries is not so simple or intuitive. Jones (1961) seems to have done about as well as one can, showing that an efficient assignment of countries to goods will minimize the product of their unit labor requirements. This certainly suggests the importance of comparative advantage, in the form of low relative unit labor requirements, which is perhaps all that one should hope for from a many-good, many-country Ricardian model (though see Eaton and Kortum's solution to this problem, which we discuss later).

A Continuum of Goods A less obvious, but much more useful, extension of the Ricardian model was provided by Dornbusch, Fischer, and Samuelson (1977)—hereinafter DFS—who took the number of goods to infinity, in the form of a continuum. Indexing goods by the continuous variable j on the interval [0,1], they specified technologies for each of two countries as $a^c(j)$ representing the amount of labor required in country c to produce one unit of good j. The ratio of these in the two countries of the model, ordered monotonically in a function $A(j)$, then plays the same role as the chain of relative labor requirements mentioned earlier for the many goods case. But with a continuum of goods, the good at the dividing line between a country's exports and its imports is of negligible importance for labor markets, since it employs a negligible amount of labor, and this removes the need to consider whether a good is produced in both countries. Such a good now always exists, as the dividing line between one country's exports and its imports, but it is of negligible importance for employment.

This simplicity is helpful in itself, but the more important advantage of the continuum model is that it facilitates the analysis of the range of goods that a country will export and import, something that the two-good model could not usefully address. One finds, for example, that an expansion of the labor endowment of one country relative to the other will cause it to expand its exports, not just by exporting more of what it already exported (though that happens too), but by exporting goods that it previously imported.

The model in its simplest form is depicted in figure 4, which is taken directly from DFS's figure 1. The downward sloping function $A(j)$ is the ratio of the two countries' unit labor requirements, ordered so that country A's comparative advantage declines with rising j. Letting $\omega = w^A/w^B$, for any given value of this relative wage, free and frictionless trade will lead to country A producing and exporting all goods with $A > \omega$ and importing goods with $A < \omega$. To determine the equilibrium value of ω one needs assumptions about demand, which are reflected in the upward sloping curve $B(j; L^B/L^A)$. Assuming that preferences are identical and that constant shares of expenditure are spent on each good, this curve measures the relative wage at which demands for each country's range of goods produced would equal their supplies (or, equivalently, the relative wage at which values of a country's exports and imports will be equal). This requires simply that the ratio of expenditures on the two sets of goods equals the ratio of the incomes of those who produce them. As the definition of this market-clearing relative wage shown in figure 4 indicates, it depends positively on $\vartheta(j)$, the

fraction of income spent on the goods produced by country A, which in turn rises with the fraction of goods that A produces. It also depends positively on the relative size (labor force) of country B, since the larger that is, for a given division of goods between the two countries, the higher must be the relative wage in A to keep the expenditure ratio constant.

Figure 4 immediately yields the result mentioned earlier, that as a country's labor force rises relative to the other country (shifting the B curve up or down), its share of goods produced increases as well, while its relative wage falls. Likewise, if a country becomes more productive in producing all goods (its $a^i(j)$ shifts down, shifting the A curve up or down), it also produces more goods but its relative wage increases. Other exercises are possible with the simple model, and DFS extend the model in a variety of directions to illuminate many issues that could not be readily addressed in models with a finite number of goods.

Most notably, they incorporate transportation costs, giving rise to a third endogenous range of goods, in addition to those exported by countries A and B: nontraded goods, whose costs differ too little between countries to overcome the barrier of transportation costs. This is particularly useful, since it

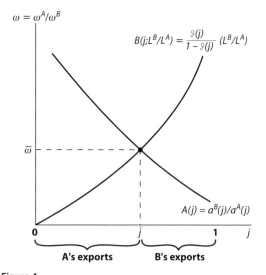

Figure 4

Ricardian model with a continuum of goods

implies that as a country's relative productive capacity rises, some of the goods it previously imported become nontraded, while it begins to export some of the goods that were previously nontraded.

Multiple Countries with Random Technologies A limitation of the DFS model is that it applies to a world of only two countries, and because of its reliance on ratios of values in those countries it is not readily extended to more, although some (e.g., Wilson 1980) have had some success. A breakthrough was provided by Eaton and Kortum (2002), however, who extended the DFS model to an arbitrary number of countries by assuming that, in effect, the labor productivities of each good and country are determined randomly. Specifically, they let labor productivity, $z^i(j) = 1/a^i(j)$, be determined by a random draw from a probability distribution, such that each country has some probability, regardless of its overall technical ability and its wage, of having a lower cost than any other country. This probability, then, translates into the fraction of the continuum of goods that the country is able to produce and export under free and frictionless trade. More important, by including transportation costs for each pair of countries, each country has a fraction of goods that it will be able to produce even without necessarily having the lowest costs, since they only need to cost less than goods from other countries inclusive of transportation cost. Furthermore if transportation costs are low enough that a country imports anything, then it will also export some fraction of goods, since if necessary the wage will fall until some fraction of goods can be exported to one or more countries for delivered prices below those countries' domestic prices. This formulation therefore extends the Ricardian model not only to multiple countries but to a context that can account for bilateral trade.

The Eaton-Kortum model generates equations for prices and trade shares that provide the basis for empirical estimation as well as being susceptible to solution and comparative static analysis by numerical methods. The model provides an elegant and parsimonious theoretical justification for the gravity model of bilateral trade flows while illustrating the interaction between the forces of comparative advantage that give rise to trade and the geographical resistance to those forces in the form of transportation and other costs of trade that limit trade and direct it over particular geographical routes.

The Role of the Ricardian Model in Understanding the World Economy The Ricardian model was introduced long ago to explain one of the most basic concepts of economics, comparative advantage, but it continues to be useful as a framework for understanding how countries interact in trade. Countries continue to differ in their abilities to produce goods and services, and the extent of these differences varies across products. This is not the only reason for international trade, but it is surely the most basic. Modern extensions of the Ricardian model are essential for understanding this trade and anticipating its effects.

See also absolute advantage; comparative advantage; gravity models; Heckscher-Ohlin model; New Trade Theory; specific-factors model

FURTHER READING

Collins, Susan M. 1985. "Technical Progress in a Three-Country Ricardian Model with a Continuum of Goods." *Journal of International Economics* 19 (1–2): 171–79. Shows in a Ricardian model that technical progress in one country can hurt another whose exports are close substitutes for the first.

Deardorff, Alan V. 2001. "Fragmentation in Simple Trade Models." *North American Journal of Economics and Finance* 12 (2): 121–37. Examines the splitting of production processes across countries in a Ricardian model.

Dornbusch, Rudiger, Stanley Fischer, and Paul A. Samuelson. 1977. "Comparative Advantage, Trade, and Payments in a Ricardian Model with a Continuum of Goods." *American Economic Review* 67 (5): 823–39. The seminal paper extending the Ricardian model to an infinite number of goods, with additional extensions to include transport costs, tariffs, money, and exchange rates.

Eaton, Jonathan, and Samuel Kortum. 2002. "Technology, Geography, and Trade." *Econometrica* 70 (5): 1741–79. Uses randomized technologies to extend the Ricardian model to multiple countries and a continuum of goods;

rich with both theoretical implications and empirical applications.

Hicks, John R. 1953. "An Inaugural Lecture." *Oxford Economic Papers* 5 (2): 117–35. Includes a classic treatment of the effects of technological progress in a Ricardian model.

Jones, Ronald W. 1961. "Comparative Advantage and the Theory of Tariffs: A Multi-Country, Multi-Commodity Model." *Review of Economic Studies* 28 (3): 161–75. Extends the predictions of comparative advantage to a model with multiple (but finite numbers of) goods and countries.

Melitz, Marc J. 2003. "The Impact of Trade on Intra-industry Reallocations and Aggregate Industry Productivity." *Econometrica* 71 (6): 1695–25. Seminal paper modeling heterogeneous firms in a one-factor trade model.

Mill, John Stuart. 1844. "Of the Laws of Interchange between Nations; and the Distribution of the Gains of Commerce among the Countries of the Commercial World." *Essays on Some Unsettled Questions of Political Economy.* London: John W. Parker. Classic treatment of international trade that includes the first full specification of the Ricardian model.

Ruffin, Roy J. 2002. "David Ricardo's Discovery of Comparative Advantage." *History of Political Economy* 34 (4): 727–48. Documents the process by which David Ricardo discovered the idea of comparative advantage, including his thinking that anticipated much of modern trade theory.

Stern, Robert M. 1962. "British and American Productivity and Comparative Costs in International Trade." *Oxford Economic Papers* 14 (3): 275–96. A classic empirical test of the Ricardian model.

Wilson, Charles A. 1980. "On the General Structure of Ricardian Models with a Continuum of Goods." *Econometrica* 48 (7): 1675–1702. Extends the Dornbusch-Fischer-Samuelson model to multiple countries.

ALAN V. DEARDORFF

■ rules of origin

Rules of origin (ROOs) specify the conditions under which a good is deemed to originate from a country and hence is eligible for preferential treatment. Such treatment could involve zero or preferential tariffs in a free (or preferential) trade area (FTA), or the right to export under a country-specific quota as under the old Multifiber Arrangement regime in textiles and clothing. Since there are zero (or preferential) tariffs on goods imported from member countries of an FTA, but tariffs on nonmembers differ across countries, the opportunities for arbitrage are obvious: imports into the area as a whole should take the path of least resistance, that is, enter through the country with the lowest tariffs on them and flow freely from there into other FTA member markets. As a result the lowest-tariff country would gain tariff revenue at the cost of other members. This suggests that countries would compete to set the lowest tariffs in order to attract such trade flows (see Richardson 1995). This seems to have actually happened in the United States after the colonies obtained independence from the British but before they fully integrated and set a common tariff (see McGillivray and Green 2001; Viner 1950). ROOs are seen as limiting such arbitrage possibilities.

Defining ROOs There are four common criteria for defining rules of origin.

1. Domestic content: content can be defined in terms of value added or in physical terms.

2. Change in tariff heading (CTH): a product must change its tariff heading (i.e., where it is classified in the tariff code) in a specified way within the FTA or customs union (CU) to obtain origin and hence be eligible for the preferential treatment reserved for the country.

3. Specified process: this outlines the processes that must be performed within the FTA or CU to obtain origin. Restrictiveness depends entirely on the steps prescribed and the nature of the production technology. The difference between this and the CTH criterion is only that the latter is based on some commonly used descriptions such as the tariff code, whereas the specified process definition is defined in terms of production processes specific to each industry.

4. Substantial transformation: this is more loosely defined. In the United States the term *substantial transformation* has come to mean the determination of origin based on common law, reasoning from case to case. This process results in a commodity-specific ROO that falls into one of the first three categories.

Origin requirements can be made more restrictive by requiring more than one criterion to be met. Exceptions can also be used to make the origin requirement more restrictive. For example, under the North American Free Trade Agreement (NAFTA), transformation from any other chapter (two-digit classification level) of the harmonized system to tomato catsup, chapter 21, confers origin *except* transformation from tomato paste, which falls in chapter 20!

Effects of ROOs Although it is tempting to think of ROOs as necessary bureaucratic nuisances, they are often far more. First, ROOs raise the costs of exports when they force a firm to use a particular process or input to obtain origin. This cost increase can significantly erode the benefits supposedly offered to developing country exports through special trade preferences. For example, Mattoo et al. (2002) argue that the value of concessions by the United States under the African Growth and Opportunity Act are cut in half by stringent ROOs. In addition, ROOs are often quite expensive to document, as detailed records need to be kept and certification procedures may need to be followed. As a result, even if a product satisfies origin, an importer may prefer to pay the tariff rather than bother with the documentation needed. Herin (1986) shows that the cost of proving origin seems to have led more than a quarter of European Free Trade Area (EFTA) exports to pay the tariff despite the possibility of not having to do so. These costs are a pure waste of resources and work to reduce aggregate income and welfare.

Second, ROOs are, in themselves, a form of hidden protectionism: they provide an incentive for regional producers to buy intermediate goods from regional sources, even if their prices are higher than those of the identical import from outside the FTA,

in order to make their product originate in the FTA and qualify for preferential treatment. This, in effect, protects FTA suppliers. As a result, trade patterns and investment flows needed to sustain them can be profoundly affected by a FTA. Consider a producer of shirts in Bangladesh. If he uses imported fabric the shirt would not meet the ROOs under the EBA (everything but arms) initiative and be eligible for zero tariffs in the European Union (EU). Only when cloth made from Bangladeshi yarn (the so-called yarn forward rule) is used is origin granted. Otherwise, the most-favored-nation tariff (of about 12 percent to 15 percent) is applied. As a result, the shirt maker is better off using more expensive Bangladeshi cloth, so long as the Bangladeshi cloth does not raise his costs by more than the amount he saves by avoiding the tariff. In this manner, the ROOs act as a hidden subsidy for domestic cloth and a tax on imported cloth; small wonder that Bangladeshi textile producers support such ROOs, while apparel exporters oppose them (Demidova, Kee, and Krishna 2006).

Third, as ROOs are negotiated industry by industry during the negotiations for the agreement, they are both hard to change ex post and allow enormous scope for well-organized industries to essentially insulate themselves from the effects of the FTA by devising suitable ROOs. The fact that ROOs are negotiated in such an industry-specific manner may be exactly why FTAs are so popular; however, they allow organized interest groups to evade the FTA by setting strict ROOs, thereby removing their opposition to the FTA. Grossman and Helpman (1995), for example, argue that being able to exclude certain sectors (what appropriately constructed ROOs will do) can make an FTA viable.

That ROOs may be protectionist does not prove that they are. Work by Estevadeordal (2000) suggests, however, that ROOs are being used to prevent trade deflection, as the sectors that have large differences in tariffs between the partners are the ones where ROOs are strongest. The work of Anson et al. (2005) on NAFTA also suggests that ROOs negate the effects of tariff reductions due to an FTA. They show that while the severity of ROOs reduced

Mexican exports, tariff preferences raised them, and the net effect was close to zero.

As ROOs are extremely opaque and arcane, they are easily overlooked, and given that there is much potential for abuse, the cost of overlooking them may be substantial.

See also customs unions; free trade area; regionalism

FURTHER READING

Anson, José, Olivier Cadot, Antoni Estevadeordal, Jaime de Melo, Akiko Suwa-Eisenmann, and Bolormaa Tumurchudur. 2005. "Rules of Origin in North-South Preferential Trading Arrangements with an Application to NAFTA." *Review of International Economics* 13 (3): 501–17. An early paper showing how ROOs limit the market access NAFTA seems to give.

Demidova, Svetlana, Hiau Looi Kee, and Kala Krishna. 2006. "Do Trade Policy Differences Induce Sorting? Theory and Evidence from Bangladeshi Apparel Exporters." NBER Working Paper No.12725. Cambridge, MA: National Bureau of Economic Research. An early paper that shows how in a heterogeneous firms setting, differences in effective preferences given to less-developed countries by developed ones results in firms sorting themselves across markets.

Estevadeordal, Antoni. 2000. "Negotiating Preferential Market Access: The Case of the North American Free Trade Agreement." *Journal of World Trade* 34: 141–200. An early empirical approach that constructs an index of the restrictiveness of ROOs and relates it to preference margins and other variables.

Grossman, Gene, and Elhanan Helpman. 1995. "The Politics of Free Trade Agreements." *American Economic Review* 85 (4): 667–90. A classic paper that develops the use of the menu auction framework to understand the political economy behind the formation of FTAs.

Herin, Jan. 1986. "Rules of Origin and Differences between Tariff Levels in EFTA and in the EC." EFTA Occasional Paper No. 13. Geneva: European Free Trade Association. Provides evidence in support of significant documentation costs in FTAs.

Krishna, Kala, and Anne Krueger. 1995. "Implementing Free Trade Areas: Rules of Origin and Hidden Protection." In *New Directions in Trade Theory*, edited by Alan Deardorff, James Levinsohn, and Robert Stern. Ann Arbor: University of Michigan Press, 149–87. Shows how ROOs affect trade and investment flows in a simple analytical model.

Krueger, Anne O. 1999. "Free Trade Agreements as Protectionist Devices: Rules of Origin." In *Trade, Theory, and Econometrics: Essays in Honor of John Chipman. Routledge Studies in the Modern World Economy*, edited by James R. Melvin, James C. Moore, and Raymond Riezman. London: Routledge, 91–102. An early paper showing how ROOs act as hidden protection.

Mattoo, Aaditya, Devesh Roy, and Arvind Subramaniam. 2002. "The Africa Growth and Opportunity Act and Its Rules of Origin: Generosity Undermined?" *World Economy* 26 (6): 829–51. A good example showing how preferences may not be doing much for developing countries.

McGillivray, Fiona, and Matt Green. 2001. "Trading in a Free Trade Area with No Rules of Origin: The U.S. Under the Articles of Confederation." Mimeo. New Haven, CT: Yale University. This provides a neat historical example of an FTA without ROOs.

Richardson, Martin. 1995. "Tariff Revenue Competition in a Free Trade Area." *European Economic Review* 39: 1429–37. A simple model showing how tariffs might be competed down to get revenue in FTAs.

Viner, J. 1950. "The Customs Union Issue." New York: Carnegie Endowment for International Peace. A classic work on customs unions.

KALA KRISHNA

■ Rybczynski theorem

See Heckscher-Ohlin model

■ safeguards

The term *safeguards* refers to trade intervention by national governments to address the injurious effects of import surges on import-competing industries. Trade intervention for this purpose has been subject to discipline under the General Agreement on Tariffs and Trade (GATT) since its inception in 1947 pursuant to GATT Article XIX. During the Uruguay Round of GATT negotiations, which culminated in the creation of the World Trade Organization (WTO) in 1994, discipline over safeguard measures was expanded and deepened through a new WTO Agreement on Safeguards. In addition, Article X of the General Agreement on Trade in Services authorizes negotiations over the possibility of safeguards in service sectors, but those negotiations have not yet resulted in any agreement. Consequently, safeguards are confined to goods sectors.

The Legal Foundation for Safeguards and Its Evolution in the WTO GATT Article XIX(1) provides:

> If, as a result of unforeseen developments and of the effect of the obligations incurred by a contracting party under this Agreement, including tariff concessions, any product is being imported into the territory of that contracting party in such increased quantities and under such conditions as to cause or threaten serious injury to domestic producers in that territory of like or directly competitive products, the contracting party shall be free, in respect of such product, and to the extent and for such time as may be necessary to prevent or remedy such injury, to suspend the obligation in whole or in part or to withdraw or modify the concession.

Article XIX thereby establishes four prerequisites for the use of safeguards. First, imports of the good(s) in question must have increased. Second, the increase must be a result of "unforeseen developments" and the "effect of the obligations incurred" under GATT. Third, the import-competing domestic industry must be suffering "serious injury" or a threat of such injury. Finally, a causal linkage must exist between the import surge (or the underlying developments that precipitated it) and the present or threatened injury.

Paragraphs two and three of Article XIX further provide that a party invoking its right to suspend or modify concessions must negotiate with adversely affected parties over the possibility of compensatory trade concessions. If these negotiations are unsuccessful, safeguards may be imposed nonetheless, but adversely affected trading partners then have the right to suspend "substantially equivalent concessions" in response. Thus the original structure of Article XIX permitted the use of safeguards but only at a price— the GATT bargain was to be rebalanced either through an offer of trade compensation (the preferred outcome) or through a retaliatory withdrawal of substantially equivalent concessions.

Over the years, formal reliance on Article XIX within the GATT system diminished. Safeguard measures were largely replaced by what came to be known as "gray area" measures, such as voluntary restraint agreements and orderly marketing agreements. These agreements were typically negotiated on a bilateral basis with major suppliers.

The proliferation of gray area measures was viewed as a serious problem by many observers. Gray area measures were not time-limited in the manner contemplated by Article XIX(1) and were employed regardless of whether the prerequisites for safeguards under Article XIX were met. In addition, gray area measures were often discriminatory in their impact, as less significant or less competitive suppliers were often exempted. A constituency thus developed for reform, which culminated in the Agreement on Safeguards in the Uruguay Round.

A key achievement of this agreement was a prohibition on gray area measures in Article XIII, coupled with a requirement for the phase out of existing gray area measures. In addition, to make reliance on formal safeguards more attractive, Article VIII(3) eliminated the rebalancing requirement (compensation or retaliation) for the first three years of any safeguard measure imposed in compliance with the agreement following an absolute increase in imports (as distinguished from a mere increase in their market share).

Other significant features of the agreement include a general prohibition on discriminatory safeguard measures, along with numerous transparency and procedural requirements applicable to any decision by national authorities to employ safeguards. The agreement limits the duration of safeguards to a maximum of eight years and provides that members proposing to employ them for more than four years must demonstrate anew that the prerequisites for safeguard measures are satisfied. It also requires progressive liberalization of safeguards over the course of their application.

The Agreement on Safeguards appears to have achieved its central objective. Preexisting gray area measures have been abolished, and WTO members have not sought to introduce new gray area measures. Likewise, formal reliance on GATT Article XIX is now far more common than in the waning years of GATT.

Safeguards have been a frequent target of litigation in the WTO system, however, and in every case to date that has reached the point of a formal ruling, the challenged measure has been ruled illegal. In some instances, national governments using safeguards have ignored obvious requirements under the law, but the litigation has also revealed some fundamental problems with the treaty text and with the ability of WTO members to implement it faithfully. The most difficult issues arise in connection with the requirement that import surges be attributed to "unforeseen developments" and with the requirement of a causal linkage between import surges and serious injury or threatened injury. We consider these issues further after reviewing the state of economic thinking about the proper role of safeguards in the international trading system.

The Economic Function of Safeguards The standard economic case for free trade counsels against the use of safeguards. They create the deadweight costs of protection while delaying the redeployment of resources in declining industries to more productive uses. Only if safeguard measures were routinely coupled with compensatory trade concessions would there be any basis for hope that their direct welfare effects are reasonably benign, but compensation has been the exception rather than the rule in practice.

Why, then, do nations employ safeguards, and why does the WTO/GATT system permit them? The answers to these questions are not entirely clear, although they have sparked a considerable amount of political and academic commentary.

Perhaps the most often invoked arguments for safeguard measures are those recited in U.S. national legislation. Section 201 of the U.S. Trade Act of 1974 indicates that safeguards may have one of two objectives—to restore the competitiveness of a declining industry or to facilitate its orderly contraction. Both of these possible justifications are problematic.

The notion that safeguards can be used to "restore competitiveness" presupposes that governments can accurately identify, and will choose to protect, only those industries that can become competitive again. But politically organized industries may seek and obtain trade protection irrespective of the impact that it is likely to have on long-term competitiveness because of the short-term profits that it brings. Moreover even if governments were able to identify appropriate candidates for assistance and would properly exclude poor candidates, protection is not necessarily the best way to provide such assistance. Direct loans or subsidies to the troubled industry are in theory superior to protection. Finally, and most important, government intervention to restore competitiveness is simply unnecessary in countries with reasonable access to private capital markets. Private lenders will finance efforts to become "competitive" as long as the returns from such investments justify the apparent risk. Their unwillingness to do so is a strong signal that the investment is not justified, and there will often be little basis for governments to second guess the judgment of the capital markets.

The suggestion that safeguards can facilitate "orderly contraction" is also suspect. Beyond question, safeguards can slow the rate of industrial contraction in response to import competition, or end contraction altogether. But such delay is ordinarily an economic vice, not a virtue. Absent some market failure, resources will move to alternative uses at an appropriate pace without safeguards. To be sure, market failures are possible, and an important possibility in this regard is downward wage stickiness, perhaps due to unionization or to subsidies to the unemployed. But trade protection is likely to be an inferior policy instrument for addressing an unemployment problem that results from wage stickiness. Direct intervention in the labor market, through employment or retraining subsidies, targets the wage stickiness problem without introducing the costs of protection. Moreover safeguards are temporary and may thus do little more than postpone the unemployment problem to a future period.

For these reasons, modern economic commentary emphasizes alternative explanations for the existence of safeguards in the WTO/GATT system, generally grounded in political economy considerations. These accounts fall into roughly three categories. The first is the notion that safeguards afford a domestic political "safety valve" for protectionist pressures, deflecting them into an administrative process that ultimately affords less protection than would be put in place by the legislature absent the safety valve (see Lawrence and Litan 1986). Whatever the merits of the safety valve hypothesis as a justification for an administrative route to protection in a domestic political system such as that of the United States, however, it affords a questionable basis for safeguards in the WTO system. If the putative policy goal is to create obstacles to domestic interest groups seeking new or renewed protection, inescapable international commitments to eschew trade protection would seem helpful, which would themselves allow legislatures to "deflect" protectionist pressures by insisting that their hands were tied.

A second political economy account of safeguards is that of Bagwell and Staiger (1990, 2002), who argue that the function of a safeguard mechanism in the WTO/GATT system is to legalize behavior that might otherwise count as "cheating" and cause the system to unravel. A temptation to "cheat" arises in their framework because nations are "large" and can use tariffs to improve their terms of trade. The desire to cheat on tariff commitments increases in the face of import surges because cheating then yields more tariff revenue. If cheating occurs, Bagwell and Staiger assume that nations will revert to their preferred tariff policies in the absence of cooperation. To avert this prospect, it may be in the interest of the parties to a trade agreement to permit temporary deviation from tariff commitments in response to temporary import surges.

Although Bagwell and Staiger's account of safeguards is clever and rigorous, it has some difficulty explaining the structure of safeguard rules in practice. Among other things, nothing in their theory makes the condition of the import-competing industry relevant to the use of safeguard measures—any import surge suffices for the temptation to "cheat" to arise. Yet, the requirement of "serious injury" or threat thereof to an import-competing industry is central to the prerequisites for safeguards under WTO law. In addition, it is not clear that safeguards are needed to address the problem of "cheating" in a system with a well-functioning dispute resolution system and calibrated retaliation such as that of the WTO.

A third political economy account of safeguards, first suggested by Dam (1970) and elaborated by Sykes (1991, 2006), posits that safeguards reduce the political risk of trade concessions under conditions of uncertainty. The analysis builds on Hillman (1982) and Baldwin (1982), which explain why declining industries will invest more resources than other industries (ceteris paribus) in lobbying for protection. Because it may be difficult for trade negotiators to predict the trade impact of concessions on their constituent industries, they may discover ex post that an import-competing industry is more harmed by concessions than expected and is clamoring loudly for relief. Temporary protection for that industry while its sunk capital depreciates may ameliorate heavy domestic pressures for protection. Because trade negotiators know that they can deviate from the bargain under these circumstances, they may be more willing to grant concessions ex ante. The welfare effects of safeguards then depend on whether safeguards do more to facilitate additional trade concessions ex ante or to allow renewed protection ex post.

Legal Issues If safeguards have any useful role to play in the trading system, their ability to play that role going forward is in some jeopardy. As noted, every safeguard measure that has been challenged to date since the inception of the WTO, and that has reached the stage of a formal ruling, has been found to be illegal. The problem is not simply a matter of WTO members failing to comply with clear obligations. Rather, the treaty text as interpreted by the WTO Appellate Body contains some confusing and illogical requirements that members have great difficulty interpreting (see Sykes 2006).

GATT Article XIX requires a linkage between the import surge and "unforeseen developments." This obligation raises two challenging issues—what "counts" as an "unforeseen development," and how do members demonstrate a linkage between it and the import surge? The difficulties here have led to findings of illegality in several cases. It remains unclear how members are to determine what is "fore-seen" and whether every "unforeseen" shock that leads to a rise in imports is a permissible predicate for safeguards (consider an unforeseen domestic supply shock, for example, that precipitates an import surge). Further, once an appropriate unforeseen development has been identified, the task remains to show how that development has affected import volumes. To do so convincingly may require elaborate econometric modeling, an exercise that is difficult to undertake given the time and data limitations in safeguards cases.

Article XIX also requires a causal linkage between increased imports and injury. The interpretation of this requirement has proven problematic, among other reasons, because import quantities are endogenous. It is thus difficult to treat import quantities as a causal variable at all. Moreover the Agreement on Safeguards requires national authorities to ensure that injury attributable to "other factors" is not erroneously "attributed" to imports. The task of defining the "other factors" has proceeded quite incoherently, even to the point of deeming an underlying cause of increased imports to be an "other factor." It then becomes impossible to distinguish the causal effect of "imports" from the causal effect of "other factors." It remains unclear how members can undertake the requisite nonattribution analysis in a fashion that will withstand legal scrutiny.

The future role of safeguards in the WTO system is thus in some doubt. An obvious concern is that if nations cannot employ safeguards legally, they will drift back toward the extralegal measures that motivated the Agreement on Safeguards during the Uruguay Round, and the key achievements of that agreement may be undermined. As of 2007, the larger trading entities such as the United States and the European Union—whose safeguards are almost certain to be subject to legal challenge—have simply stopped using them. The long-term systemic effects of this state of affairs remain to be seen.

See also General Agreement on Tariffs and Trade (GATT); nontariff measures; political economy of trade policy; Uruguay Round; World Trade Organization

FURTHER READING

Bagwell, Kyle, and Robert W. Staiger. 1990. "A Theory of Managed Trade." *American Economic Review* 80 (4): 779–95. Looks at safeguards as an aid to sustained cooperation in trade agreements.

———. 2002. *The Economics of the World Trading System.* Cambridge, MA: MIT Press. Develops terms-of-trade model of trade agreements and applies them to various topics, including safeguards.

Baldwin, Robert E. 1982. "The Political Economy of Protectionism." In *Import Competition and Response*, edited by Jagdish N. Bhagwati. Chicago: University of Chicago Press, 263–94. Discusses the pressures for protection from troubled industries.

Dam, Kenneth. 1970. *The GATT: Law and International Economic Organization.* Chicago: University of Chicago Press. Classic reference on economic structure of GATT.

Hillman, Arye L. 1982. "Declining Industries and Political Support Protectionist Motives." *American Economic Review* 72 (5): 1180–87. Discusses the pressures for protection from troubled industries.

Lawrence, Robert Z., and Robert E. Litan. 1986. *Saving Free Trade.* Washington, DC: Brookings Institution. Develops safety valve theory of safeguards.

Sykes, Alan O. 1991. "Protectionism as a 'Safeguard': A Positive Analysis of the GATT 'Escape Clause' with Normative Speculations." *University of Chicago Law Review* 58 (1): 255–305. Looks at safeguards as a response to political uncertainty and a device for facilitating trade concessions.

———. 2006. *The WTO Agreement on Safeguards: A Commentary.* Oxford: Oxford University Press. A comprehensive review of law and economics safeguards in the WTO system.

ALAN O. SYKES

■ sanctions

International economic sanctions are often favored by nation-states and by international organizations as a means of projecting power or influencing another government's behavior without resorting to military conflict. The utility of sanctions as an instrument of foreign policy is attested to by their growing popularity since the end of the Cold War. Economic sanctions include trade sanctions, which restrict imports from or exports to a target country; investment sanctions, which include restrictions on capital flows to the target and, in some cases, mandatory disinvestment; and more narrowly targeted so-called smart sanctions, such as asset freezes and travel bans on individual members of the target nation's ruling elite.

A common argument against sanctions is that they are ineffective tools of foreign policy because of the relative ease with which target countries can find alternative markets and suppliers. In a study of 116 sanctions episodes imposed since 1914, for example, Hufbauer, Schott, and Elliott (1990) concluded that only 34 percent were successful in achieving their political objectives. Even this estimate may be optimistic, however, especially if success is interpreted to mean that sanctions were the *primary* factor contributing to the desired outcome (Pape 1997). An alternative view is that sanctions are necessarily successful as long as they impose costs on the target's behavior or enhance the sanctioner's international reputation. Galtung (1967) was one of the first to point out that sanctions are often imposed not primarily for instrumental purposes—that is, to induce the target to comply with the sanctioner's demands—but instead for expressive or demonstrative purposes. Thus one reason for sanctions' inefficacy is that they may not be designed to be effective in the first place: economic sanctions that are costly to a target are also costly to the sanctioner and are therefore likely to be avoided in favor of less costly, sometimes merely symbolic, measures.

Economic and Political Effects of Sanctions
Both the sanctioning nation(s) and the target nation are, in general, made worse off by a trade embargo. The degree to which trade sanctions reduce welfare in these nations depends on the sanctions' terms-of-trade effects, which are larger in the case of multilateral than unilateral sanctions. Moreover any price distortions caused by sanctions inevitably create opportunities for nonsanctioning third parties to capture rents by continuing to trade with the target. Under multilateral sanctions, much sanctions-busting activity is likely to involve traders in the target

nation itself, thereby channeling some of the rents into the very country that is supposed to be punished (Kaempfer and Lowenberg 2007). Sanctions rents might even, perversely, enrich the target country's own rulers if they are able to participate in sanctions-busting trade. Empirical studies have confirmed that multilateral sanctions, despite, and indeed because of, their greater terms-of-trade effects, are typically less successful than unilateral sanctions.

Financial and capital sanctions, too, can have unintended consequences. In the case of disinvestment, the physical plant and capacity previously owned by foreigners is purchased by domestic capital owners at reduced prices, which increases their rate of return. The resulting windfall gain to domestic capital owners potentially increases the tax base available to the government to finance its objectionable policy (Kaempfer and Lowenberg 2007). Of course, in the long run, a decrease in the inflow of new capital and technology from abroad is likely to limit the target's growth potential.

Even if sanctions impose substantial economic damage on a target nation, there is no guarantee that the target will reform its behavior in conformity with the sanctioner's demands. In his classic study, Galtung (1967) noted that sanctions are often followed by increased levels of political integration in the target country, the so-called rally-around-the-flag effect, which has since captured the attention of many observers.

Sanctions have distributional effects. For example, an embargo on exports to a target country benefits domestic producers of importables in the target country at the expense of consumers. There are similar distributional effects within the sanctioning country. It follows that interest group politics in both countries are important in explaining the political origins and outcomes of sanctions. Thus the level of sanctions imposed by a sanctioning country depends on the relative political influences of prosanctions and antisanctions groups within that nation's domestic polity. In the target state, sanctions that are successful in bringing about a change in policy in the desired direction will generally do so by diminishing the political influence of the regime's supporters

relative to that of its opponents (Kaempfer and Lowenberg 2007). There is considerable consensus on the utility of smart sanctions that pinpoint those groups most responsible for the objectionable policy while minimizing "collateral damage" to innocent citizens (Cortright and Lopez 2002).

Game-theoretic work on sanctions demonstrates that, given perfect information, sanctions would never be implemented: if a threatened sanction were sufficiently effective, the target would comply immediately, obviating the need to impose the sanction, while if the sanction were ineffective, the sanctioner would not threaten it in the first place (Eaton and Engers 1992). Thus the sanctions that are most likely to succeed will often do so as threats, without having to be imposed at all. It has also been shown that the success of sanctions depends on conflict expectations: target states that anticipate future conflict with a sanctioner are relatively unlikely to comply with the sanctioner's demands, although these are precisely the countries that are most likely to be sanctioned (Drezner 1998).

Empirical Findings on Sanctions Many studies have attempted to identify the correlates of sanctions success. The most common findings are that the success of sanctions is positively correlated with political instability and economic weakness in the target country and with close, cordial ties between sanctioner and target prior to sanctions. Some scholars also find a significant positive relationship between the cost of the sanctions to the target, measured as a percentage of the target's gross national product, and the success of the sanctions.

Most of the empirical literature uses the data compiled by Hufbauer, Schott, and Elliott (1990), which include only those sanctions that were actually applied, despite the fact that successful sanctions often end at the threat stage. Consequently empirical studies of actually implemented sanctions are likely to be biased against sanctions success. Such selection bias is part of a broader problem, namely, that the factors determining whether sanctions are used are intrinsically linked to the factors determining their success. Recent empirical work therefore uses simultaneous equations techniques to estimate models of jointly determined policy choice and sanctions outcome.

Another focus of empirical inquiry is the role of political regime type in determining sanctions usage and success. The interest of sanctions scholars in regime type stems from the literature on the democratic peace, which is the theory that democracies typically do not go to war against other democracies. Lektzian and Souva (2003) investigate whether there is an analogous "economic peace" among democracies. They find that, although democracies impose sanctions more often than other regime types, democracies are indeed less likely to sanction other democracies than they are to sanction nondemocracies. However, others have found evidence that sanctions are more successful when imposed against democracies than nondemocracies, suggesting that democracies make more attractive targets (Nooruddin 2002).

See also nontariff measures; terms of trade

FURTHER READING

Cortright, David, and George A. Lopez, eds. 2002. *Smart Sanctions: Targeting Economic Statecraft*. Lanham, MD: Rowman and Littlefield. Contains several illustrative case studies of smart sanctions.

Drezner, Daniel W. 1998. "Conflict Expectations and the Paradox of Economic Coercion." *International Studies Quarterly* 42 (4): 709–31. Emphasizes the importance of future conflict expectations in determining sanctions initiation and compliance.

Eaton, Jonathan, and Maxim Engers. 1992. "Sanctions." *Journal of Political Economy* 100 (5): 899–928. One of the first and most often cited game-theoretic treatments of sanctions.

Galtung, Johan. 1967. "On the Effects of International Economic Sanctions: With Examples from the Case of Rhodesia." *World Politics* 19 (3): 378–416. The earliest classic in the international relations literature on sanctions, considered a seminal work and widely cited.

Hufbauer, Gary Clyde, Jeffrey J. Schott, and Kimberly Ann Elliott. 1990. *Economic Sanctions Reconsidered: History and Current Policy*. 2d ed. Washington, DC: Institute for International Economics. The main source of data for empirical work on sanctions.

Kaempfer, William H., and Anton D. Lowenberg. 2007. "The Political Economy of Economic Sanctions." In *Handbook of Defense Economics*, vol. 2, *Defense in a Globalized World*, edited by Todd Sandler and Keith Hartley. Amsterdam: Elsevier North-Holland, 867–911. Provides a wide-ranging survey of the sanctions literature and an exposition of the interest group model originally developed by Kaempfer and Lowenberg in a September 1988 *American Economic Review* article.

Lektzian, David, and Mark Souva. 2003. "The Economic Peace between Democracies: Economic Sanctions and Domestic Institutions." *Journal of Peace Research* 40 (6): 641–60. The first attempt to extend the democratic peace literature to sanctions.

Nooruddin, Irfan. 2002. "Modeling Selection Bias in Studies of Sanctions Efficacy." *International Interactions* 28 (1): 59–75. A good example of recent empirical work that addresses the problem of selection bias in sanctions data.

Pape, Robert A. 1997. "Why Economic Sanctions Do Not Work." *International Security* 22 (2): 90–136. An influential critique of sanctions as a policy instrument.

**WILLIAM H. KAEMPFER
AND ANTON D. LOWENBERG**

■ sanitary and phytosanitary measures

Since the 1990s, attention to agricultural trade policy has widened to include issues related to technical barriers to trade, particularly sanitary and phytosanitary (SPS) measures that regulate movement of products across international borders. SPS measures protect plant, animal, and human health from hazards such as pests, diseases, contaminants, and toxins that might be found in imported agricultural and forestry products. Unlike most nontariff measures, they are potentially welfare increasing because they may correct market failures stemming from externalities that arise from importing goods that may be accompanied by these hazards. But like other regulations, they arise from an equilibrium process of policy determination. The observed levels of intervention emerge from the interaction of the demands for measures by various domestic interest groups (including producers, processing industries, and consumers) and the supply of these barriers by policymakers. That regulatory processes can be captured by interest groups with a vested interest in a particular regulatory outcome is well recognized in the economic theory of regulation, and cases involving the promulgation of SPS measures are no exception. Since the 1990s, objective economic analysis and international trade rules have provided the basis for reform of some SPS regulations that lowered net social welfare by restricting imports that posed negligible risks.

Measurement of Economic Effects Although traditional trade barriers have been extensively studied, informing policy trade-offs and negotiating priorities in the Uruguay and Doha trade rounds, far less is known about the impacts of SPS measures on trade. The analytical complexity and scant data available for quantifying the economic effects of SPS measures pose significant challenges for analysts. Conceptual difficulties stem from the heterogeneous nature of SPS measures, the fact that multiple measures are aimed at a particular product, and that measures are difficult to aggregate.

Data scarcity is perhaps an even more significant challenge. No registry for SPS measures comparable to tariff schedules exists at either national or international levels. The UN Conference on Trade and Development is leading an effort to update its Trade Analysis and Information Systems database, an international inventory of nontariff barriers, to fill this data gap. At present, however, direct measures of the economic effects of SPS and other technical regulations are limited to the evidence from business surveys. Surveys by the Organisation for Economic Cooperation and Development and the World Bank indicate that these regulations can significantly increase costs or limit market access for exporters of selected products in developing and developed countries alike.

Indirect methods of measuring the effects of SPS measures on trade are important because of the paucity of direct measures. These methods rely on comparison of prices or are inferred from trade quantities in the context of a well-specified model of trade flows. Many studies in the literature have used partial equilibrium simulation models or gravity models to estimate the costs of specific measures, including Australia's ban on banana imports, the European Union's (EU's) ban on growth hormones in beef production, Japan's restrictive fire blight measures for apple imports, and the EU's aflatoxin standards for dried nuts and fruits. A smaller number of case studies have integrated risk and economic assessment in the analysis of SPS measures under alternative risk scenarios to inform specific policy changes—for example, the gradual lifting of the United States' long-standing ban on imports of Mexican avocados. These studies have made important contributions to the development of methodology and policy formulation, but their results are not easily generalizable to other products or sectors in other countries.

More recently, a few econometric studies have examined the effects of SPS and other nontariff measures on food trade at a more aggregate level, finding that their effects are larger than tariff effects for product categories, including fruits and vegetables as well as meats. This emerging body of literature, which is still in its early stages and fraught with measurement, endogeneity, and other econometric difficulties, reinforces the perception that SPS barriers have a substantial influence on agricultural trade.

International Trade Rules Although it has been difficult to assess the aggregate effects of SPS regulations on trade in agricultural goods, or to evaluate their relative importance in the world trading system, there has long been broad recognition that these measures can significantly impede trade. Disciplines on SPS measures and other technical regulations were included in the original General Agreement on Tariffs and Trade (GATT) adopted by the Contracting Parties in 1947. The GATT treaty recognized the need to subject domestic regulations to international scrutiny so that the strategic application of these measures would not subvert the commercial opportunities created by other trade policy reforms.

The original GATT rules for SPS and other technical measures were expanded in the Tokyo

Round (1973–79) of multilateral trade negotiations and again during the Uruguay Round (1986–93) when a separate agreement for SPS measures was established. The challenge before the negotiators of the World Trade Organization (WTO) Agreement on the Application of Sanitary and Phytosanitary Measures (the SPS Agreement) was to create a set of rules that would strike the proper balance between allowing health and environmental protection while disallowing mercantilist regulatory protectionism. In broad terms, the SPS Agreement recognizes the right of each WTO member to adopt measures that achieve its "appropriate level of protection" but requires such measures to be based on a scientific assessment of the risks and to be applied only to the extent necessary to achieve the country's public health or environmental goals. As a benchmark, the SPS Agreement recognizes the international standards promulgated by the *Codex Alimentarius*, the International Organization of Epizootics, or the International Plant Protection Convention to be " safe harbor" standards. Members adopting these standards are " rebuttably presumed" to be in compliance with the agreement.

The compliance of countries with the SPS Agreement is reinforced by the WTO's formal dispute settlement procedures. Only a few conflicts over SPS measures have led to the establishment of dispute panels, but these few cases have played a critical role in establishing how trade rules place bounds on national sovereignty in this policy area. Of 30 requests for formal consultations on SPS measures from 1995 to 2006, 11 have advanced to dispute settlement proceedings. Landmark SPS disputes included the EU ban on hormone-treated beef and the EU's regulations for approval and marketing of biotech products.

The EU's defense of its hormone ban rested on its claims that existing international standards for hormone use in beef cattle did not meet its public health goals, and that the ban represented a precautionary approach to managing uncertain risks. In their rulings, the WTO affirmed the right of WTO members to establish a level of consumer protection that was higher than international health standards. The ban was nonetheless judged to be in violation of the SPS Agreement because it was not backed by a scientific risk assessment. The WTO likewise ruled against the EU and some individual member states in the more recent biotech case because risk assessments did not support the disputed measures. These results remove a degree of national political sovereignty for regulations in cases in which evidence has not been marshaled to demonstrate any risk from trade. But the limits to what the WTO can achieve in this policy area is seen in the fact that the formal rulings have triggered additional scientific assessments rather than meaningful policy changes leading to increased trade in these two long-running disputes.

Prospects for Regulatory Reform of SPS Measures Although current international trade rules curb the protectionist abuse of SPS measures, they still allow countries to adopt measures for which global or even national costs outweigh their national benefits. Economic analysis that examines the benefits (reduced risks) and costs (reduced trade) of SPS regulations is important for regulatory reform efforts that seek to identify the most efficient policy instruments to manage SPS risks. Failure to work through the challenges of data and methodology will create the potential for anecdote and allegation to play a larger role in SPS policy formulation, which would likely result in increased costs to consumers and increased tensions between trading partners.

See also gravity models; nontariff measures; partial equilibrium models; technical barriers to trade; World Trade Organization dispute settlement

FURTHER READING

Beghin, J. C., and J. C. Bureau. 2002. "Quantitative Policy Analysis of Sanitary, Phytosanitary, and Technical Barriers to Trade." *Economie Internationale* 87: 107–30. A concise description and evaluation of the various methods available for measuring the effects of SPS and other technical measures on trade and welfare.

Josling, T., D. Roberts, and D. Orden. 2004. *Food Regulation and Trade: Toward a Safe and Open Global System*. Washington, DC: Institute for International Economics. A roadmap of SPS and other technical measures in international food markets, including definitions and classification, explanation of economic rationales and effects, and authoritative description and analysis of the institutions that govern the intersection of regulation and trade.

Maskus, Keith E., and John S. Wilson. 2001. *Quantifying the Impact of Technical Barriers to Trade: Can It Be Done?* Ann Arbor: University of Michigan Press. An often-cited early survey of methods for empirical analysis of SPS and other regulations on trade.

DONNA ROBERTS

■ **savings glut**

See global imbalances; twin deficits

■ **seigniorage**

Seigniorage is profit from money creation, a way for governments to generate revenue without levying conventional taxes. In the days of commodity money, seigniorage revenue was the difference between the face value of the minted coins and the actual market value of the precious metal they contained. When this markup was insufficient for the government's revenue needs, the authorities might substitute less valuable base metal for some of the precious metal that was supposed to be in the coins. Such a practice has a long history, dating back at least to Roman times. Although this allowed the government to issue more coins without acquiring more precious metal, the coins quickly depreciated as agents became aware of their less valuable content. The continued partial precious metal backing still placed some limit on the possible issuance.

With the demise of the gold standard in the early 1930s, almost all nations abandoned commodity-backing for their currencies and adopted a fiat money standard under which the paper issued is backed by nothing more than faith and confidence in the issuer. Under this system, the cost of issuance declines close to zero and there is no longer any limit on the quantity of money that can be issued. Under a fiat

money system, seigniorage revenue is given by the product of the inflation rate and the inflation tax base. This inflation tax base reflects the purchasing power of the public's money holdings and is the level of *real* money balances (nominal money holdings divided by the price level). Undertaking more rapid monetary expansion causes the inflation rate to rise, but the revenue effects are partially offset as individuals attempt to quickly spend the extra money before it depreciates further. If people spend money faster than it is being printed, the rate of price increase comes to exceed the rate of money issuance.

Hyperinflation A government that is unable to fund its expenditures through conventional taxes or bond sales may become dependent on seigniorage revenues to maintain its existence. Attempts to raise seigniorage revenues are, however, not only inflationary but eventually self-defeating. Under circumstances where the decline in real money balances becomes proportionately larger than the rise in the inflation rate, the inflationary policy actually backfires and lowers seigniorage revenue. The economist Phillip Cagan's classic analysis of hyperinflations, with inflation rates exceeding 50 percent per month, suggested instances where the process had, in fact, been pushed beyond the revenue-maximizing point. It is possible that lags in the adjustment of inflation expectations may actually have allowed continued seigniorage gains, however, and subsequent analysis of the 1921–23 German hyperinflation points to seigniorage levels rising year by year (see Cukierman 1988).

Whatever success the German government may have attained in raising seigniorage revenues, such surging, and highly volatile, inflation rates interfere with the price mechanism and cloud production and employment decisions. Meanwhile attempts to economize on money balances require devoting more and more time to simply turning over the currency. By the end of the German hyperinflation, workers were being paid more than once a day because otherwise the value of the money would fall too much between the beginning and end of the shift! Other innovations, such as the indexation of bank deposits to inflation or establishing deposits denominated in a stable-value currency, require even faster rates of note issue to maintain seigniorage revenues, given that part of the money supply is now insulated from the inflation tax. This factor was particularly evident in the record-breaking post–World War II Hungarian hyperinflation. Negative effects on economic growth emerge well before such extreme circumstances, however. Recent work suggests that significant negative effects of inflation may emerge below the 10 percent level in both industrial and developing economies (Burdekin et al. 2004).

Certainly, even though conventional taxes impose their own distortions on the economy, few would argue that this justifies reliance on seigniorage as a deliberate policy choice. Dependence on seigniorage revenue seems, in practice, to be highly correlated with the degree of political instability. Vulnerability to this effect tends to be greatest in developing economies that are less democratic and/or more socially polarized (Aisen and Veiga 2005). High indebtedness is another common factor. In this respect, even a government that is initially able to fund its deficit through selling bonds to the public may eventually resort to inflation finance as the amount of debt approaches the saturation point. Thomas Sargent and Neil Wallace argue that such "unpleasant monetarist arithmetic" implies that, in the face of continued budget deficits, tighter monetary policy today simply implies more inflationary policy tomorrow once the limit on bond issuance is reached (see Sargent 1993). Furthermore the greater the outstanding stock of bonds, the greater the potential governmental gains from inflating away the real value of these obligations through inflation—which, in turn, likely limits the demand for such bonds unless inflation protection is built in.

The typical mechanism of inflation finance is for the government to sell bonds to the central bank, which then immediately "monetizes" the debt with new money emissions. This is therefore properly characterized as money finance rather than true bond finance and provides the government with new funds to spend only via excess money creation. Conversely selling bonds to the public, rather than the central

bank, is likely to be far less inflationary and has no direct effect on the money supply.

Making the central bank independent of the fiscal authority would seem to be a way of ending automatic government access to the printing press, and nations with independent central banks have historically tended to have lower inflation rates. But even in the United States, large deficits such as those incurred under the Reagan administration put considerable pressure on the central bank to at least partially monetize them insofar as very large bond issues push down bond prices and put upward pressure on interest rates. Moreover in a developing economy where the market for government bonds is much thinner, it is unrealistic to expect the central bank, nominally independent or not, to resist monetization pressures when no other financing options exist. Instituting central bank independence is probably better thought of as a way of discouraging future fiscal profligacy rather than something that alone can end an ongoing reliance on deficit monetization and seigniorage.

Reducing Reliance on Seigniorage Revenue A more drastic way of weaning a government away from reliance on seigniorage revenue is to dollarize the economy, following the example of countries like Panama (since 1904) and Ecuador (since 2000), which abandoned domestic currency issuance and adopted the U.S. dollar as their monetary standard. Another option is to maintain the domestic currency but link it to the U.S. dollar or another currency via a currency board arrangement, whereby the monetary authority commits to exchange local currency for the foreign currency on demand at a predetermined, fixed rate of exchange. Such a strategy still allows for some seigniorage revenue on interest-bearing dollar-denominated assets held to back the local currency. Although Hong Kong's currency board arrangement with the U.S. dollar has been maintained since 1983, Argentina's link with the U.S. dollar collapsed in 2001 in the midst of soaring unemployment and political unrest. The Argentinean case not only illustrates the potential dangers of tying the domestic currency to the dollar but also serves as a reminder that no such announced commitment is truly irrevocable. Another alternative is to enter into a currency union, such as the euro zone, that eliminates the scope for domestic inflation finance by dispensing with the national currency entirely yet allows participating nations to share in seigniorage revenue earned by the group as a whole.

See also commodity-price pegging; common currency; currency board arrangement (CBA); currency crisis; currency substitution and dollarization; dollar standard; euro; European Central Bank; Federal Reserve Board; gold standard, international; money supply; multiple currencies; quantity theory of money

FURTHER READING

Aisen, Ari, and Francisco José Veiga. 2005. "The Political Economy of Seigniorage." IMF Working Paper 05/175. Washington, DC: International Monetary Fund. Available at http://www.imf.org/external/pubs/ft/wp/2005/wp05175.pdf. Reviews factors influencing the extent to which governments rely on seigniorage revenue and presents evidence on the importance of political instability.

Banaian, King, J. Harold McClure, and Thomas D. Willett. 1994. "The Inflation Tax Is Likely to Be Inefficient at Any Level." *Kredit und Kapital* 27 (1): 30–42. Emphasizes that the costs of resorting to the inflation tax are significantly augmented by the increased uncertainty that typically accompanies higher levels of inflation.

Burdekin, Richard C. K., Arthur T. Denzau, Manfred W. Keil, Thitithep Sitthiyot, and Thomas D. Willett. 2004. "When Does Inflation Hurt Economic Growth? Different Nonlinearities for Different Economies." *Journal of Macroeconomics* 26 (3): 519–32. Examines the thresholds at which inflation may start to exert significant negative effects on growth in both industrialized and developing economies.

Cagan, Phillip. 1956. "The Monetary Dynamics of Hyperinflation." In *Studies in the Quantity Theory of Money*, edited by Milton Friedman. Chicago: University of Chicago Press, 25–117. Classic analysis of money demand and seigniorage using data from a number of post–World War I and post–World War II experiences. Cagan's work essentially gave birth to the study of hyperinflation as a burgeoning subfield in macroeconomics.

Cukierman, Alex. 1988. "Rapid Inflation—Deliberate Policy of Miscalculation?" *Carnegie-Rochester Conference Series on Public Policy* 29, edited by K. Brunner and B. McCallum (autumn 1988), 11–84. Reprinted in P. Siklos, ed. 1995. *Great Inflations of the 20th Century.* Aldershot, UK: Edward Elgar. Reexamines the seigniorage revenue raised during the post–World War I German hyperinflation and suggests that the inflation may have been more profitable to the government than the original Cagan analysis implied.

Gros, Daniel. 2004. "Profiting from the Euro? Seigniorage Gains from Euro Area Accession." *Journal of Common Market Studies* 42 (4): 795–813. Examines the distribution of the European Central Bank's seigniorage revenue and the prospective gains accruing to the new member states from Central and Eastern Europe.

Sargent, Thomas J. 1993. *Rational Expectations and Inflation.* 2d ed. New York: HarperCollins. Chapter 5 covers the "unpleasant monetarist arithmetic" when tight monetary policy is combined with continuing budget deficits, and chapters 2 and 6 assess the implications of the Reagan deficits and their possible rationale.

RICHARD C. K. BURDEKIN

■ **sequencing of financial sector reform**

Sequencing of financial sector reform is concerned with the ordering of reforms in the financial system and with designing a path for these reforms that will improve economic welfare. Economists generally acknowledge that liberalized or market-based financial systems enhance the mobilization and allocation of financial resources—and, therefore, economic growth and welfare—more than repressed financial systems in which allocation of financial resources is subject to administration. History has shown, however, that when a country moves from a repressed to a market-based system, it risks its financial and economic stability and can face an economic and financial crisis. Liberalization of certain financial transactions before the necessary financial infrastructure is in place can contribute to the incidence of these financial crises. The sequencing of the financial sector reforms is intended to ensure an orderly transition from repressed to market-based financial systems that avoids serious economic and financial crises.

Policy Issues Surrounding Sequencing The earliest literature on sequencing financial sector reform addressed the reform of financial systems as part of broader programs of economic reform that included, for example, trade liberalization and labor market reforms. The prevailing belief was that financial liberalization should occur late in the reform process since financial sector variables were seen as responding to relative prices and savings and investment decisions. Liberalizing financial systems before successful economic reforms that set the "correct" relative prices would lead to a less-efficient allocation of financial resources and could be destabilizing, as observed among some countries in Latin America during the 1970s.

A second strand of research addressed the speed of reform: whether it would be better to follow a gradualist approach or to have a rapid "big bang" program that reformed several sectors simultaneously. The arguments for "big bang" reform programs were motivated largely by political economy considerations, especially the need for a critical mass of reforms to break entrenched inertia and vested interests and to provide domestic and international credibility to the reform program. Financial sector reforms were seen as a key component of the "big bang" reform programs since they were often easier to implement than other components, such as labor market reform.

A third strand of the work on sequencing has focused on the design of the programs of financial sector reform. This strand identifies the major risks as well as benefits of the financial sector reform and seeks to mitigate these risks through the design of the financial liberalization. The emphasis is not on the speed of the reform but instead on putting in place a consistent set of polices that takes into account each country's unique circumstances.

A fourth related strand has focused on the liberalization of the capital account and, specifically, on the question of when countries should liberalize capital flows. This issue received additional attention following the Asian financial crisis of the mid-1990s, which was viewed as the result partly of a premature or an inappropriately sequenced liberalization of short-term capital flows.

Key Policy Insights As countries reform their financial systems, it is essential that they have instruments that allow them to exercise effective monetary control in a liberalized environment. The liberalization of financial systems is typically associated with significant initial expansions in monetary and credit aggregates and capital inflows. The expansions are largely the result of portfolio adjustments to the liberalized financial systems, but they can also have potentially destabilizing macroeconomic effects through increasing inflation or weakening of the balance of payments. Thus the authorities need to have flexible monetary instruments to manage these effects and avoid the buildup of potential fragility in the financial system that can result in financial crises. Typically, this has involved adopting techniques of indirect monetary control and following a consistent mix of monetary and exchange rate policies. For example, if countries seek to follow a restrictive interest rate policy to limit the credit expansions, they may need to adopt a flexible exchange rate regime.

Financial institutions typically need to be restructured early in the process of financial sector reform. Many of the financial crises that followed financial liberalizations can be traced to imprudent lending by weak banks. The bank restructuring programs include elements such as writing down the value of bad and doubtful debts and recapitalizing the banks to achieve a minimum level of capital at the beginning of the reform programs; reorganizing bank management and developing skills in risk assessment and management; introducing regulations of banks to limit large credit and currency risk exposures; and developing an effective system of prudential oversight. Experience has shown that banking failures can be costly to economies: they result in a loss of confidence in the currency and require significant government interventions to clean up bank balance sheets.

Implementation of the monetary and prudential elements of the reforms normally requires giving

shipping

some urgency to strengthening official institutions—
specifically, the central bank and the supervisory
authorities—in the early stages of the financial sector
reforms.

Reforms to develop longer-term capital markets
and nonbank financial intermediaries have tended to
occur at a later stage of financial sector reform. It
usually is easier to develop the markets in longer-term
instruments, the bond and securities markets, after
those in short-term instruments are in place. Reforms
of auditing and accounting, legal frameworks,
bankruptcy, and payments and settlement systems
generally should accompany these reforms. Derivative financial markets are normally the last to emerge
since they rely on well-functioning markets in the
underlying instruments on which the derivatives are
based.

Payments and transfers on current international
transactions have conventionally been liberalized
ahead of capital movements. The former are important elements in the growth of trade in goods and
services. The elimination of restrictions on current
international transactions has often depended on
foreign exchange market reforms.

A more controversial issue has been how to sequence the liberalization of capital movements with
the domestic financial-sector reforms. One of the
lessons of the Asian financial crises in the mid-1990s
is that capital account liberalization should be approached cautiously with special attention to avoiding reliance on short-term capital flows. These crises
were attributed in part to a premature opening of the
capital account to short-term capital inflows. These
flows were potentially destabilizing since, in the event
of a loss of confidence, they could be withdrawn
quickly, resulting in a balance of payments crisis. At
the same time, capital movements can be beneficial as
part of the financial-sector reform program. For example, allowing foreign direct investment (FDI) in
financial institutions can help in their restructuring
and in strengthening local technical and management skills. Notwithstanding the well-founded
concerns about an overreliance on short-term capital
movements, liberalization of certain short-term
capital transactions is a key element in developing

efficient foreign exchange and domestic money
markets. Hence capital account liberalization involves various complex elements, making it difficult
to generalize on the optimal approaches.

Although it is neither desirable nor possible to
have a one-size-fits-all approach to sequencing, some
important technical and policy lessons have emerged
on how to sequence reform measures to avoid major
pitfalls. A key lesson is that at the beginning of the
reform program, the authorities need to develop
monetary instruments to maintain macroeconomic
control. They will also probably need to restructure
or recapitalize their commercial banks to avoid a
major failure that could disrupt the domestic financial system and lead to a loss of international confidence. Finally they should approach the liberalization of short-term capital movements cautiously to
avoid an overreliance on this source of capital.

See also banking crisis; capital controls; capital mobility;
currency crisis; exchange rate regimes; financial crisis; financial liberalization; financial repression; hot money and
sudden stops; impossible trinity

FURTHER READING
Harwood, Alison, and Bruce L. R. Smith, eds. 1997. *Se-
quencing? Financial Strategies for Developing Countries.*
Washington, DC: Brookings Institution Press.
Johnston, R. Barry, and V. Sundararajan, eds. 1999. *Se-
quencing Financial Sector Reforms: Country Experience
and Issues.* Washington, DC: International Monetary
Fund.

R. BARRY JOHNSTON

■ **services**
See trade in services

■ **shipping**
Shipping, the movement of people and commodities
by ship, has long been the dominant form of transportation for the movement of bulk commodities,
especially over long distances. Many of the major

996

cities in the world have grown because of their seaports or access to good inland navigation. Physically, some 90 percent of world trade (nearly 7 billion tons) is carried by the international shipping industry, although because of the nature of the goods moved, the proportion is considerably less in terms of value. Shipping also is a growth industry, with the amount of seaborne trade in terms of tonne-miles (the amount carried, measured in metric tonnes, multiplied by the distance moved) rising from less than 6,000 in 1965 to nearly 30,000 in 2005.

As of 2006 there were about 50,000 mercantile vessels in the world, totaling some 650 million gross tons, engaged in international trade, and many more providing domestic coastal and ferry services. The merchant fleet consisted mainly of general cargo vessels (38 percent of the ships), oil tankers (25 percent), and dry bulk carriers (14 percent). It is, however, the container fleet that has expanded most rapidly, not only in relative numbers but also in size—the average capacity rising from 1,944 twenty-foot equivalent units (TEUs) in 2002 to 2,108 in 2004. It is also a newer fleet: the average age of the overall merchant fleet is 12.5 years, but only 9.2 years for container ships. Passenger ships accounted for about 7 percent of the fleet. The majority of vessels register in developed countries (27 percent) or in the major open-registry ("flag-of-convenience") countries that allow foreign ships to register under their flag and offer attractive financial and other incentives to shipping companies to do so (Panama, Liberia, and the Bahamas, which register a total of 250 million gross tons). More than 97 percent of the world's merchant fleet was registered in just 35 countries.

The world's shipbuilding industry delivered 2,129 new ships, amounting to a record 70.5 million tons of new shipping capacity, in 2005, up from 49.4 million tons in 2004. This increased global net capacity by 7.2 percent. The major shipbuilding nations include South Korea, Japan, China, Germany, and Russia, with China taking an increasingly important role. Structurally, the shipbuilding industry tends to be more fragmented in Europe than in Asia where it is concentrated in a limited number of countries.

Although, because of technological advances, shipping is becoming more capital intensive and crews levels are getting smaller for any given size vessel, its overall size and growth rate means that it remains a major employer of labor. There are 466,000 officers and 721,000 sailors serving merchant ships that trade internationally with Organisation of Economic Co-operation and Development (OECD) countries. East Asia provides the majority of merchant ships' officers and developing countries the majority of sailors. Indirectly, the shipping industry creates much greater employment than these numbers indicate because ships need labor for their building, maintenance, chandelling (fitting out vessels), and vittling (supplying food for vessels).

Although there has been volatility over time, the costs of shipping have never been cheap and have varied considerably across markets. The cost of international freight transportation, for example, was 5.8 percent of the import value for developed countries in 2002 but ranged from 8.8 percent for developing nations overall to 12.4 percent for African countries. Although estimates of the income earned from international shipping are imprecise, the approximate figure is about $380 billion annually.

Structure of the Shipping Industry The shipping industry is segmented in a number of ways. The largest part of the industry involves the movement of cargo, with more limited transportation of people by ferries and cruise ships. A small number of passenger liners still provide scheduled services on oceanic routes, but this type of traffic has largely transferred to air transportation. The cargo part of the industry is divided into coastal activities and deep-sea shipping. The former serves point-to-point short-haul routes and acts as a distributor for large consolidating ports that collect and dispatch larger ships on deep-sea routes. Coastal shipping serves a key function in many countries where, for economic or geographical reasons, land transportation is of poor quality. For example, more than 70 percent of maritime activity in China is cabotage (coastal water transportation) traffic and accounts for nearly 55 percent of the total domestic ton-miles transported in the country.

Sliced another way, shipping offers regular, scheduled services ("liner services") and irregular sailings ("tramp shipping"). Liner services cater to customers who have partial shiploads—often involving container shipments—and who need to incorporate their cargo into a predetermined supply chain. Modern, just-in-time production demands reliability as well as speed in maritime logistics. To improve service, liner operations generally involve some form of cooperation between shipping companies to ensure regular sailings offering common-carrier services at frequent intervals. Traditionally, since the 1870s, when steam power made for reliable schedules with published rates, "conferences" have offered this service, although these have become refined into more integrated "consortia" and "alliances" that, for example, involve operating agreements allowing liners to share space on one another's ships. Containerization has provided scope for this interoperability by which ships from any line can carry standard containers. Although these agreements among shipping companies offer benefits in terms of coordinated, more stable rates and more frequent service, they also raise concerns about the concentration of market power that they may foster. Since the early 1990s, partly because of the wider use of long-term leases, greater competition for high-value cargo from air transportation, and tighter regulatory controls, but also because consolidation of liner operations has taken place, the number of conference type arrangements has declined.

Tramp shipping companies are often as large as their liner counterparts but are usually hired to carry entire shiploads of cargo, especially dry bulk or liquids. They often operate specialized vessels. In many cases these markets may involve the long-term leasing of vessels to a single customer, especially if they are for specific cargoes over a single route. The market for tramp shipping is highly competitive both for spot hires and for long-term leases. Rates tend to be highly volatile, reflecting the prevailing demand in the markets being served combined with the high degree of rigidity in short-term capacity. The rates are, at a macro level, highly correlated with international business cycles.

Economics of the Industry Shipping forms part of a more extensive supply chain. The industry directly interacts with ports, canals, and navigation systems and less directly with the operational surface modes (road, rail, and inland waterways) that service ports. This requires coordination of technology and of institutional structures if seamless service is to be provided to users, and so the industry has always been at the forefront of adopting up-to-date communications technology such as global positioning systems.

On the supply side, the technical peculiarities of the industry mean there are considerable economies of scale involved in the physical provision of individual ships. Simply put, a vessel 150 feet long, 20 feet high, and 20 feet wide has a capacity of 60,000 cubic feet and, assuming it is fully decked, has 12,800 square feet of steel plating. In contrast, a vessel 300 feet long, 40 feet high, and 40 feet wide has a carrying capacity of 480,000 cubic feet but requires only 51,200 square feet of plating. A doubling of dimensions increases capacity eightfold but the material needed to build the vessel rises only fourfold.

As engine technology and maritime engineering have allowed, the trend has been for larger cargo and passenger vessels—for example, super-post Panamax (50,000 to 79,999 deadweight tons [dwt]) and Capesize (more than 80,000 dwt) vessels used in the international movement of dry-bulk, ULCC (more than 300,000 dwt) crude oil tankers, and mega cruise liners. This challenges ports that do not have the depth or docking capabilities to handle such ships and water transit facilities, such as the Panama Canal, that do not have the width. Container traffic has grown considerably, especially in developing countries, and for this to be fully efficient ports also require specialized handling equipment that has to be upgraded as vessels get larger.

Institutionally shipping has always been seen as a risky activity, involving relatively large sums of capital and the commitment to tie up inventories for extended periods. Historically the sector expanded during the Classical Greek period only with the emergence of primitive insurance and later, in the Italian Renaissance, as more sophisticated banking developed. Today the insurance market at Lloyds of London and financial markets around the world provide the lubricant for a multibillion-dollar industry.

The aggregate demand for shipping services is strongly tied to the state of the international economy. The worldwide recession of the early 1980s led to marked downturns in demand, and growth slowed during the Asian financial crisis of the late 1990s. But there can be wide variations in specific geographical and commodity markets. The demand for oil tankers, for example, can vary considerably according to the price of crude. Economic expansion in India and China has spurred rapid growth in those particular markets, with accompanying high freight rates. There are also spatial imbalances in demand, with significant difference in the demand for outbound and inbound services. Many developing countries, for example, are major exporters of bulk ores but are recipients of high-value, less bulky manufacturers. Tankers usually return from refineries to oil-producing countries in ballast (that is, empty of cargo, carrying only ballast to provide stability and maneuverability). This situation often leads to ships serving an "interconnected" network rather than a simple back-and-forth, "connected" routing. The American slave trade of the 18th century, for example involved a triangular pattern of service, with vessels taking European manufactures to Africa, collecting slaves in Africa for transportation to America, and bringing raw materials from America such as cotton and sugar back to Europe. This type of complex network is more difficult for specialized fleets such as tankers.

International trade cycles, combined with the time it takes to build new capacity and the competitive nature of much of the industry, often mean that there is a mismatch between supply and demand. In particular, given the costs of mothballing vessels during downturns in the business cycle, there is a tendency for excess capacity to exist over the full cycle. Estimates by the United Nations suggest, for example, that globally there was a residual (excess) fleet capacity amounting to some 21.7 million dwt (2.6 percent of the world fleet) in 2002, falling to 10.3 million dwt (1.2 percent) in 2003.

Regulating Shipping Markets Institutionally, long-standing debates have focused on the appropriate economic regulation of shipping to ensure that overall logistics chains are not distorted and on the social regulation of shipping to ensure safety and security. The shipping industry is thus subject to a wide range of laws and agreements, but the size and diversity of the sector make analysis and subsequent policy formulation difficult. The International Maritime Organization, an arm of the United Nations, provides broad global oversight, although other agencies, such as the United Nations Conference on Trade and Development (UNCTAD), become involved in maritime affairs when shipping is seen as a tradable service in its own right. At the macroregional level, national groupings such as the European Union play a role in determining the structure of the industry within more limited spatial markets.

Many developing countries have felt disadvantaged because their trade has been carried on ships from wealthier nations. Seeking to safeguard the position of developing countries, UNCTAD initiated in 1974 a "40/40/20 rule" whereby the freight being moved is shared between ships from the developed countries (40 percent), the developing country (40 percent), and cross-traders from third states (up to 20 percent). Developing countries often do not have the maritime capacity to handle their share of traffic and, because far more tonnage leaves most primary goods–producing developing countries than is moved to them, efficiency drops.

Most nations allow free movement of shipping through their territorial waters and access to their ports, although there are limitations on the types of activity that may be pursued. Fishing and the extraction of minerals within territorial waters tends to be highly restricted. Many counties also limit maritime trade between their own ports (cabotage), even if international trade is allowed. The 1920 Merchant Marine (Jones) Act, for example, permits only U.S.-owned, -registered, and -built vessels, manned by citizen crews, to conduct cabotage between U.S. seaports.

Much of the economic regulation has focused on defining ownership and responsibilities for shipping and on ensuring that potential monopoly forces do not distort the market to the detriment of consignors or the public interest more broadly defined.

The growth of merchant shipping has always been vulnerable to attacks, and even in the early part of the 21st century there were more than 400 acts of piracy a year. Naval protection has thus often been seen as an important requisite of civilian shipping. Conversely merchant shipping has also been closely entwined with military operations, being a major part of many army and naval logistics operations. As a result, there are strong links between the merchant and military sides of shipping.

Despite the efforts of international bodies such as the World Trade Organization to remove tariffs and other institutional barriers to trade, the major factor that has facilitated the vast increase in the physical volume of goods trade has been technical improvements in the shipping sector. Without the advent of modern oil tankers, the energy required for production would not be available; without massive bulk carriers, food and raw materials could not be moved to places of production; and without the capabilities of container vessels, final products could not be moved to market. Shipping is the facilitator that allows the world economy to realize much of the division of labor so important for global economic growth.

See also air transportation; commodity chains; trade in services

FURTHER READING

International Ocean Institute and Dalhousie University Law School. Annual. *Ocean Year Book*. Chicago: University of Chicago Press. An annual publication initiated in 1978 that contains articles of current relevance to international shipping and related activities.

Maritime Policy and Management. Quarterly. London: Routledge. An international academic journal that contains peer-reviewed articles on the shipping and port industries.

United Nations. Annual. *Review of Maritime Transport, Report by the UNCTAD Secretariat*. New York: United Nations. Contains information and data on trends in international shipping together with a number of indepth assessments of particular markets or trades.

KENNETH BUTTON

■ **Singapore issues**
See competition policy; government procurement; trade facilitation

■ **Smithsonian Agreement**
The Smithsonian Agreement was the understanding by which the Organisation for Economic Co-operation and Development (OECD) economies agreed to suspend the Bretton Woods system of fixed exchange rates in December 1971. The Bretton Woods conference had established a system of fixed exchange rates in 1944, encompassing nearly all the currencies of the free world, in which each currency was pegged to within a band of ± 1 percent around a fixed parity against the U.S. dollar, and the dollar itself to a fixed price against gold. These systems had worked well and, with the exception of a few parity realignments in Europe in the 1960s, most countries had successfully kept to their parity values.

In the early 1960s, the United States still had a strong reserve position in which its gold holdings and foreign assets were larger than its liabilities to foreign institutions. But increasing balance of payment deficits later in the decade reduced those gold holdings, raised the United States' foreign liabilities, and weakened its reserve position. By the beginning of 1970, it was clear that the exchange rate regime was under threat when the U.S. balance of payments deficit sharply widened again and the (net) reserve position turned negative. In the first instance, these changes were the result of expansionary fiscal policies in Washington, driven mainly by President Lyndon Johnson's Great Society program and the expenditures of the Vietnam War. The result was a persistent tendency to large balance of payments deficits and a shortage of international liquidity, as the United States showed itself unwilling to restrain growth, employment, and the expansionary pressures that were starting to increase inflation as well as aggregate demand. The initial response by foreign governments was to buy dollars and sell their own currencies in an effort to support the Bretton Woods system—although some bought gold instead, which added to the American difficulties.

The United States meanwhile wanted to avoid devaluing the dollar (raising the dollar price of gold), not only to retain the support of the governments that had agreed to hold dollars but also, and more importantly, because such a move would achieve nothing if the other governments did not revalue against the dollar at the same time. However, as the American reserve position worsened and as inflation and unemployment began to increase, a change of policy leading to a general devaluation became inevitable. On August 15, 1971, President Richard Nixon temporarily froze wages and prices, imposed a 10 percent tariff on imports, and suspended dollar transactions in gold. This was designed to force a devaluation of the dollar on the existing system, while also cooling down the inflationary pressures within the U.S. economy.

The next step was to get the foreign governments to accept a revaluation of their own currencies against the dollar: a general realignment of the parities upward. The idea at this stage was not to create a regime of flexible exchange rates, but to force a general realignment in the parities before they were fixed again. The agreement that finally emerged after several months of hard bargaining at the Smithsonian Institution had to accommodate a 9 percent devaluation of the dollar versus gold and a continued suspension of gold transactions in order to force revaluations in the other currencies. Foreign governments also agreed to undertake a thorough review of the monetary system to achieve a suitable degree of flexibility and a significant liberalization of trade policies that would be acceptable to both sides.

The latter components of the agreement eventually led to the creation of the Committee of Twenty (of the leading OECD economies), which oversaw the attempt to design a system of "stable but adjustable" exchange rates, which was then used to legalize the float that followed under the International Monetary Fund's articles of agreement. The trade liberalization agreement, meanwhile, led to the Tokyo Round of trade negotiations in the later 1970s. The Smithsonian Agreement itself, however, proved to have been too little, too late, as the U.S. trade deficits and reserve position failed to respond. The U.S. economy continued to expand, other countries got into balance of payments difficulties too and floated, and dollars continued to flow into Germany and Japan. In 1973 the United States decided to devalue the dollar again, and one by one the other countries bowed to the inevitable and allowed their currencies to float beyond their new parities. The dramatic increase in energy prices that followed ensured that there was no going back to a regime of fixed parities, although the European Community did manage to create a system of stable but adjustable exchange rates among themselves six years later. In that sense, the Smithsonian Agreement did lead to the flexible exchange rates that we have today and to the European monetary system of 1979–99.

See also Bonn Summit; Bretton Woods system; European Monetary Union; exchange rate regimes; international liquidity; International Monetary Fund (IMF); international policy coordination; international reserves; Plaza Accord

FURTHER READING

Kenen, Peter. 1994. *The International Economy*. 3d ed. Cambridge: Cambridge University Press.

ANDREW HUGHES HALLET

■ smuggling

Smuggling is the surreptitious import or export of goods in violation of domestic or international law. Export smuggling is relatively rare and is mainly relegated to products involved in a multilateral boycott, such as a United Nations embargo on diamonds from African war zones, or state-subsidized products that consequently can be sold for higher prices abroad. Most commonly, smuggling involves the illegal import of banned goods or goods that face import quotas, significant tariffs, or other high taxes.

The preponderance of literature dealing with smuggling in the field of economics focuses on its impact on the welfare of the nation. In the mid-1970s, many believed that smuggling was beneficial, at least to a small country, because smugglers circumvented tariffs that undermined free markets. Consequently smuggled goods (or contraband) could be sold for lower prices and therefore enhanced welfare. Bhagwati and Hansen (1973) challenged this commonly held belief, arguing that the level of prices resulting from smuggling was not the only issue relating to national welfare. Smuggling could be welfare reducing when it undermined government policies of establishing tariffs to protect local industries. Subsequent writers also noted that smuggling could corrupt and demoralize a society as smugglers normally undermined law enforcement through bribery, intimidation, and even murder.

Recent Trends in Smuggling Prior to trade liberalization at the end of the 20th century, most developing countries placed significant tariffs on imports to protect local industries, raise taxes, and/or restrict local demand for scarce supplies of foreign exchange. Although these policies were designed to enhance national welfare, they in fact resulted in higher prices for many products sold in these countries as well as limited product choice. Such policies promoted the growth of widespread smuggling of consumer products into developing countries. Many smugglers proved adept at physically evading law enforcement agents or co-opting them through bribery. Smugglers also found a convenient distribution channel among the many unlicensed street vendors of the developing world's informal economy.

For many in the growing middle classes in these countries, smugglers were seen as benign if not heroic actors. By the mid-1990s, the impact of smuggled goods was substantial in many markets. Contraband in Poland was estimated to equal 20 percent of legally imported goods, and half the computers sold in Brazil were smuggled into the country. In one year alone, Chinese authorities confiscated nearly half a billion dollars in contraband. In developed countries, too, smuggling of certain products thrived. A study by Albers-Miller (1999) observed that consumers of smuggled cigarettes in the United Kingdom considered their actions to be a reasonable response to high cigarette prices.

Widespread trade liberalization in developing countries in the last quarter of the 20th century raised expectations that smuggling would disappear as import quotas were abandoned and tariff levels diminished. However, the relationship of trade liberalization to smuggling proved more complex than originally believed. Gillespie and McBride (1996) studied the impact of trade liberalization on smuggling in Mexico during the 1980s and 1990s. They concluded that 15 years into trade liberalization smuggling had diminished but remained significant.

One reason for the persistence of smuggling after trade liberalization was the continuation of certain cost advantages to smugglers over legitimate importers. Tariffs had been lowered by trade liberalization but still existed, allowing smugglers to profit from circumventing them. For example, in 2006 the Indonesian tire industry was threatened by a surge of smuggled tires from China despite the country's relatively low 15 percent tariff on tires. In addition to tariffs, smugglers could avoid other taxes that their legal counterparts had to pay. In postliberalization Mexico, smugglers who switched to legitimate importation faced paying income tax as well as a 15 percent value-added tax on the products they sold.

In addition, many smugglers protected their low-cost position by increasingly forgoing the smuggling of legitimate goods in order to smuggle stolen or counterfeit goods. Stolen automobiles became especially popular. Cars stolen in the United States were not only smuggled into Mexico but shipped as contraband to China. Counterfeits were another way smugglers lowered the cost of smuggled products by stealing the brand equity of the brand owner. The trend toward smuggling counterfeit goods was exacerbated by greater scrutiny by law enforcement regarding counterfeits crossing borders. Customs authorities of many countries improved their ability to identify and confiscate shipments of counterfeits, thus forcing counterfeiters to seek out smuggling channels.

The diversification of smugglers into other criminal activities signified another disturbing trend. Smuggling was becoming less a business of Robin Hoods who were arguably providing consumers with good products at good prices and more the domain of organized crime. Smuggling activities appeared to be consolidating in the 1990s with contraband gangs involved in moving large shipments of goods. Violence, long associated with organized crime, appeared among these gangs. In Colombia and the United States, smugglers played a new role in the black market peso exchange. After a crackdown on the money laundering of illicit drug profits through U.S. banks, Colombian drug dollars in the United States were used to purchase products that were subsequently smuggled into Colombia. There they were sold for the pesos necessary to support the cartels' production operations. In the late 1990s, Colombian officials estimated that as much as 45 percent of the imported consumer products sold in their country had arrived via the black market peso exchange.

In light of smuggling's failure to disappear with trade liberalization and its increased consolidation and violence, many governments began to attack the problem with more vigor. Penalties, aimed at both smugglers and government employees who accepted bribes from smugglers, were increased. China and Vietnam threatened participants with a newly enacted death penalty. In some countries, such as Mexico, customs authorities were overhauled. Nonetheless, smuggling often remains hard to eradicate due to its organized nature, government corruption, and a lack of resources for law enforcement.

Smuggling and Legitimate Economic Actors
The role in smuggling of legitimate economic actors remains obscure. Legitimate importers and distributors are put at a cost disadvantage when required to compete with contraband. This has led to conflict in the past. In the early 1990s, violent altercations occurred in Mexico City when store owners attempted to evict informal vendors selling contraband outside their stores. However, smugglers and legal distributors need not always constitute two mutually exclusive groups. Several researchers have proposed that smugglers could camouflage their smuggling with some legal imports and legal distributors could decrease their costs by including some contraband.

There are both benefits and disadvantages for producers of legitimate products that are smuggled. Smuggling works to their advantage when their products are barred from entering markets or when prohibitive taxation discourages purchase of those products. However, multinational corporations can suffer when smugglers undercut legitimate distributors, since legitimate distributors can provide greater oversight of product quality and deliver after-sales service. Relationships with strategic allies, such as licensees or joint venture partners in local markets, can be undermined when contraband enters a partner's market and diminishes legal sales.

The advantages and disadvantages of firms cooperating with smugglers are well illustrated by the case of the cigarette industry. In 1999, internal documents of the five largest tobacco companies were made public as part of a litigation settlement in the United States. These documents revealed a variety of ways in which cigarette producers cooperated with smugglers. These included sending cigarettes to known smugglers, destroying records related to smuggled cigarettes, discussions of how to disguise contraband shipments, setting up international financial accounts to camouflage contraband earnings, and buying air time on transnational media to provide advertising support for smuggled brands.

These revelations spurred a number of national and provincial governments to sue tobacco companies in U.S. courts. Besides seeking compensation for lost taxes and law enforcement costs related to the smuggling, some governments sought compensation for increased health costs due to greater cigarette consumption attributed to the lower price of contraband cigarettes. One suit brought by the European Union (EU) sought compensation of up to $1.7 billion a year. Another suit brought by Colombia charged Philip Morris employees with knowingly participating in the black market peso exchange, using cigarettes to help launder illicit drug money.

Despite the strong evidence of the public record, the plaintiffs were stymied by the U.S. Revenue Rule, which disallowed U.S. courts from assisting foreign governments in their collection of taxes. However, the EU won a ruling that allowed it to present its case anew as one involving money laundering. Subsequent to this decision, Philip Morris agreed to pay the EU more than $1 billion to settle the complaint.

Faced with increased public scrutiny, the multinational tobacco companies began to curtail supplies to distributors involved with smuggling. To the dismay of these multinational companies, smugglers who once helped them sell more of their branded cigarettes in high-tax countries quickly turned to smuggling counterfeit cigarettes instead. Practically overnight, smuggling ceased to be a major contributor to the profits of cigarette companies and became instead a substantial threat to their sales and brands.

Smuggling continues today to undermine public policy and challenge legitimate distribution channels. Trade liberalization has proven to be no panacea. For many governments, the increased association of smuggling with organized crime, counterfeiting, and money laundering only increases the urgency for its eradication.

See also illegal drugs trade; nontariff measures; political economy of trade policy; quotas; tariffs

FURTHER READING

Albers-Miller, Nancy D. 1999. "Consumer Misbehavior: Why People Buy Illicit Goods." *Journal of Consumer Marketing* 16 (3): 273–87. Examines why consumers buy contraband and how they justify their behavior.

Bhagwati, Jagdish, and Bent Hansen. 1973. "A Theoretical Analysis of Smuggling." *Quarterly Journal of Economics* 87 (2): 172–87. Presents one of the earliest and most influential discussions of the potential economic impacts of smuggling.

Gillespie, Kate. 2003. "Smuggling and the Global Firm." *Journal of International Management* 9 (3): 317–33. Explores and documents the role of multinational companies in smuggling.

Gillespie, Kate, and J. Brad McBride. 1996. "Smuggling in Emerging Markets: Global Implications." *Columbia Journal of World Business* 31 (4): 39–54. Traces the evolution of smuggling in the face of trade liberalization.

KATE GILLESPIE

■ social policy in open economies

Globalization and other forces are creating increased demand for social policies at the same time as they are restricting the ability of governments to supply such policies. Some observers see in this combination of increased demand and restricted supply a recipe for disaster in which globalization increasingly undermines the ability of governments to provide for the social well-being of their citizens. Both the theory and evidence available to date, however, suggest the glass is more half-full than half-empty: effective social policies remain alive and well in open economies, and the positive effects of the restrictions on governments' ability to provide social policy outweigh the negative effects.

The purpose of this entry is to outline the forces that increase the demand for social policies, the forces that restrict the ability of governments to supply such policies, and the conditions under which social policies can be provided. The concept of social policy as used here refers to the range of government policies that provide a social safety net, including employment standards involving factors such as minimum wages, hours of work, and terminations; health and safety regulations and programs, including workers' compensation, human rights and antidiscrimination legislation, and transfers such as unemployment insurance and welfare. Particular attention is paid to the United States and Canada, given the greater openness that has occurred in those countries after a number of recent free trade agreements.

Forces Increasing the Demand for Social Policy Initiatives The demand for social policy initiatives is increasing in part because of the interaction of three sets of interrelated forces: those affecting the demand side of the economy, especially the labor market; those affecting the supply side, especially related to demographics; and those affecting institutional changes.

On the demand side, labor markets are affected by a variety of interrelated forces: globalization and freer trade; technological change, the computer revolution, and the shift to a knowledge-based economy; industrial restructuring, especially from manufacturing to services; and deregulation and privatization. These pressures in turn give rise to a variety of manifestations, many of which increase the demand for social policy initiatives. Wage inequality has increased (Cline 1997; Rodrik 1997) as the lower end of the wage distribution has been adversely affected by various factors including import competition from low-wage countries, skill-biased technological change, outsourcing, and the supply influx from displaced workers who have lost their former blue-collar, male-dominated, often unionized jobs in manufacturing. Nonstandard, or "contingent," employment has increased in various forms (part-time, limited-term contracts, temporary-help agencies, self-employment, home work, and telecommuting). Many of these jobs have effectively shifted risk from employers to employees and created groups of vulnerable workers often without pensions or health care.

Numerous factors on the supply side are also increasing the demand for social policy initiatives. The population and labor force are aging and living longer, with the large baby-boom cohort entering the ages of retirement where disability and health care costs increase dramatically. The aging "gray panthers" are creating a voting constituency for social policies related to pensions, social security, and age discrimination—policies that often have to be financed by a smaller cohort of taxpayers in younger generations. Many are facing issues of elder care for their own ailing and longer-lived parents. The rise of the two-earner family means an increased demand for social policies in areas of institutional elder care and childcare as well as for "family friendly" policies in areas related to working time and parental leaves. The rise of single-parent families has increased the demand for state support as a surrogate parent. The growing diversity of the workforce is creating demands for policies in the areas of human rights, antidiscrimination, and reasonable accommodation for disabled persons.

At the same time as these demand- and supply-side forces are increasing the demand for social policy initiatives, various institutional changes are also working in the same direction. The decline of unionization is creating a vacuum in areas where unions once provided protection and a safety net for unionized workers. The declining real value of the minimum wage has left many lower-wage workers increasingly vulnerable (DiNardo, Fortin, and Lemieux 1996). The decline of employer-sponsored occupational pension plans has exposed workers to more insecurity with respect to their retirement income, and the shift from defined-benefit to defined-contribution pension plans has exposed them to more investment risk.

While these various forces have often increased the demand for social policy initiatives, in other ways they have also reduced that demand. The two-earner family with women increasingly participating in the labor force obviously provides greater income potential and insurance against the risk of income loss associated with one member being unemployed or underemployed or disabled. Nonstandard employment can provide the flexibility for families to provide childcare or eldercare. The ability of older workers to continue working (in part due to legislative bans on mandatory retirement) can provide the potential for retirement income. The application of human rights and antidiscrimination policies as well as employment standards can facilitate individuals' earning income and thereby reduce their reliance on social policies provided by governments.

Forces Inhibiting Governments from Supplying Social Policies Many of the same forces that are increasing the demand for social policies are also reducing the ability of governments to finance social policies. Specifically, under globalization, freer trade, and falling transportation and communication costs, companies are more able to relocate their plants and investment to low-cost jurisdictions and export their goods and services back into higher-cost jurisdictions. Regulatory costs, including those arising from social policies, can be an element of those cost considerations. Such costs can arise from various regulations: labor standards (e.g., such areas as minimum wages, hours of work and overtime, vacations, holidays and leave, terminations, severance pay, and unjust dismissal protection); collective bargaining regulations; antidiscrimination; reasonable accommodation requirements; workers' compensation; and health and safety regulations.

Because of the threat of the loss of business investment and the jobs associated with that investment, governments are under increasing pressure to compete in part by reducing their regulatory costs, including those arising from social policies. In essence, they are under more pressure to be "open for business." This is the case for governments across different countries as well as for local governments within countries.

Phrases used to describe this phenomenon generally have negative connotations: *social dumping, the rule of the market over the rule of law, harmonization to the lowest common denominator, regulatory meltdown, race to the bottom*, and *ruinous competition*.

Forces for Downward Harmonization to Occur
For such harmonization to occur and for it be to the lowest common denominator (i.e., to the jurisdiction with the least costly regulations and social policies) a number of conditions have to prevail (Gunderson 1998). First, the regulations and policies have to be enforced; otherwise there is no effective cost on employers. In many cases, initiatives that appear extremely costly "on the books" are simply not extensively enforced in practice. In this case, the intended benefit is also not realized.

Second, for the initiatives to be costly, the benefits to employers must be less than the costs. In many cases, employers themselves benefit from the initiatives, and this can offset at least part of the costs. Workers' compensation, for example, imposes a payroll tax on employers, but it also frees them from the threat of being sued by injured workers since workers gave up that right as the quid pro quo for essentially receiving "no-fault" coverage in the event of a workplace injury. Policies that require employers to give advance notice in the case of massive layoffs or plant closings can be costly, but they can also facilitate job searches that can benefit other employers.

Third, employers may shift much of the cost of work-related policies forward to customers or backward to workers. Shifting costs forward to customers is increasingly difficult in a world of global competition since customers can purchase from lower-cost sources that do not have such extensive regulatory costs. Shifting costs backward to labor, however, is possible since labor tends to be the immobile factor of production and hence cannot easily "escape" the cost shifting by moving to employers that do not shift their regulatory costs. Such cost shifting can occur in the form of lower compensating wages paid in return for the benefit workers receive from the policy. In other words, workers who receive those benefits effectively pay for them through receiving lower wages in return for the benefits. Evidence suggests, for example, that the majority of payroll taxes initially levied on employers for policies such as workers' compensation, pensions, and unemployment insurance are ultimately shifted back to workers in return for the expected benefits they receive (Kesselman 1996). In that vein, some of the populist views of imposing regulatory costs on large wealthy corporations are somewhat misguided in that the vast majority of those costs are shifted backward to workers in return for the benefits they receive from the regulations. There is no such thing as a "free lunch" in this area.

Fourth, for the harmonization to be downward, employers must respond to the cost increases by threatening to move their plants and investments to other, lower-cost jurisdictions. Although such a threat is now more credible, given the global conditions outlined previously, business investment and plant location decisions respond to a myriad of factors other than the cost of social programs. Furthermore, social programs can provide benefits to employers in forms such as infrastructure and political and social stability (Rodrik 1997).

Fifth, for downward harmonization to occur, governments must respond to the threat of capital mobility by reducing their costly social policy initiatives. Although there will be pressure in this direction, some governments (reflecting the preferences of their constituencies) may simply be willing to "pay the price" of their regulation. They may opt to be a "kinder and gentler society" and sustain their social safety net even if it costs them business investment and the associated jobs. They may hope to retain and attract what they regard as socially responsible business.

While these links must all be present for interjurisdictional competition for investment and the associated jobs to lead to downward harmonization to the lowest common denominator, the fact remains that the pressures are in the direction of such harmonization. That is, to a large degree each of the links is present: most policy initiatives are enforced; they impose net costs on employers; employers are not able to fully shift the costs; they have a credible threat to move to other jurisdictions that do not impose such costs; and governments do respond to the need to attract investment and jobs. As such, the pressures are in the *direction* of downward harmonization. The question is: How much? And are there countervailing pressures, often associated with openness and globalization, working against downward harmonization?

Forces for Upward Harmonization Although various forces foster downward harmonization, other forces, often associated with globalization and open economies, foster upward policy harmonization.

Consumer groups and nongovernmental organizations, often internationally organized and coordinated through the Internet, can put pressure on brand-name multinationals through various mechanisms including consumer boycotts, "Internet outings," and requiring a "social label" indicating the conditions under which the product was produced.

Multinationals themselves can foster upward harmonization by "exporting" the more advanced practices they follow in their home country and applying a more uniform set of their company practices across their different operations. Multinationals associated with brand names are especially sensitive to their public image and want to appear as good corporate citizens in the countries in which they operate. They often operate under voluntary corporate codes

of conduct and follow International Labor Organization/Organisation for Economic Co-operation and Development guidelines.

Open economies can also foster upward harmonization of social policies through the use of social clauses and side accords in trade agreements, such as the labor and environmental side accords under the North American Free Trade Agreement and the Social Charter of the European Union (EU). In such circumstances, countries that may not have enforced their labor standards are required to do so or even to raise them to the higher standards of trading partners, perhaps with the aid of funds such as the EU's Social Funds.

Social policies may also be harmonized upward through the emulation of best practices in the policy arena. To the extent that openness and globalization foster income convergence, the more rapid growth of the poorer countries may also enable them to afford more extensive social policies, again fostering upward harmonization. Empirical evidence supports the proposition that as income increases, the demand for social policies also increases (e.g., Fields 1995). Rodrik (1997) also emphasizes how social policies that assist those who are adversely affected by market-oriented policies such as free trade can foster efficiency by reducing public resistance to such market-oriented policies; equity and efficiency need not always conflict.

Forces for Sustained Divergence Various forces are also at work to sustain a divergence in social policies. Lower-income countries, for example, may be caught in a "low equilibrium" trap rather than converging upward. A divergence of social policies may therefore be sustained for an extended period of time, just as divergent growth rates may be sustained.

The conditions under which social policies are first established may exert a persistent influence on future policies. This is especially the case when bureaucracies and interest groups have a vested self-interest in sustaining the policies, and they become embedded in social structures and cultural norms within borders. Seymour Martin Lipset, for example, argued that the United States was initially influenced by the American Revolution, which fostered a path of individualism and distrust of government. Canada, in contrast, started off on a path of loyalty to Britain and less distrust of collective action through the state. Such different initial conditions and subsequent path dependence may help explain the more extensive social policies that prevail in Canada compared with the United States.

Sustained divergence can also be fostered by the heterogeneous demands of various groups with differences in their preferences or needs for social policies as well as in their willingness and ability to pay for such policies. In such circumstances, a Tiebout-type equilibrium may prevail where individuals and firms sort themselves into jurisdictions that offer the social expenditure–tax combination that meets their preferences. Just as openness and globalization can foster diversity in consumer options, they can foster diversity in choices of social policies.

Evidence: Harmonization or Sustained Divergence Clearly, theoretical reasoning suggests that globalization and openness along with other forces can foster harmonization in any direction: downward to the lowest common denominator, upward to a higher standard, or sustained divergence. As is commonly the case, theory covers all bases; hence the need for an appeal to the evidence.

The evidence, however, is not clear-cut. Gomez and Gunderson (2005) review the international evidence and particularly that of the United States and Canada. They conclude that increased openness has fostered a *tendency* toward harmonization of social policies and that harmonization has been *toward* the lower common denominator. Between the United States and Canada, for example, there has been recent downward harmonization toward the lower U.S. level in areas such as collective bargaining laws, minimum wages, unemployment insurance, equal pay laws, pension funding, and welfare and family benefits for working families. There has been sustained divergence in workers' compensation and health and safety, however, and some upward harmonization to the higher U.S. standards with respect to age discrimination. They also cite a wide range of studies, especially by political scientists (e.g., Garnett

1998), who tend to find more sustained divergence and emphasize that governments still maintain considerable degrees of freedom in setting their social policies in spite of greater openness and competitive pressures.

As indicated, Fields (1995 and other studies cited therein) have examined poor countries and indicated that as their incomes grow their demand for social policies also increases; that is, social policies are "normal goods" that are collectively desired and that can be afforded as income grows. In essence, the upward convergence of the income of poor countries toward that of wealthier countries also fosters an upward convergence in their social policies. It follows that prematurely imposing costly regulations on developing countries—for example, as a condition of a free trade agreement—can dampen the very growth process that would foster a natural upward convergence of social policies.

Countries of the EU did not experience a downward harmonization in their social policies as a result of the greater trade and capital and labor mobility after the formation of the union. This reflects the fact, however, that the EU Social Charter required the poorer countries such as Greece and Portugal to harmonize upward as a condition of entry into the EU. The EU also provided Social Funds to the poorer countries to facilitate their upward harmonization (Gomez and Gunderson 2005).

Even if there is a tendency toward downward harmonization, this should not automatically be regarded negatively. With greater openness, governments are simply under more pressure to pay attention to the cost consequences of their social policies; they face a "harder" rather than "softer" budget constraint. In such circumstances, social policies that are inefficient and involve mainly rent seeking (e.g., possibly procurement policies) are under the most pressure to dissipate since they do not foster the competitiveness that enables countries to ultimately afford their social policies. The competitive position of employers can be jeopardized by such policies, and their costs cannot be shifted back to workers since they do not have associated benefits for workers. In contrast, social policies that have positive feedback effects on efficiency and support a public infrastructure should survive—indeed thrive—under greater openness and competitive pressures since they foster competitiveness. The area of greatest concern, however, is whether governments can sustain pure equity-oriented social policies that do not have positive feedback effects on efficiency but protect the most vulnerable and disadvantaged groups in society. This is the main challenge to social policy under increased openness and competitiveness.

See also globalization; labor standards; trade and the environment

FURTHER READING

Cline, W. 1997. *Trade and Wage Inequality*. Washington, DC: Institute for International Economics. Discusses the theory and evidence behind how trade, globalization, skill-biased technological change, and other factors have led to growing wage inequality.

DiNardo, J., N. Fortin, and T. Lemieux. 1996. "Labor Market Institutions and the Distribution of Wages, 1973–92: A Semi-Parametric Approach." *Econometrica* 64: 1001–44. Discusses the role of changing labor market institutions such as declining unionization and declines in the real value of minimum wages in growing wage inequality.

Fields, G. 1995. *Trade and Labor Standards: A Review of the Issues*. Paris: OECD. Outlines the effect of labor standards on trade as well as how trade fosters growth in developing countries and how this in turn fosters higher labor standards.

Garnett, G. 1998. *Partisan Politics in a Global Economy*. Cambridge: Cambridge University Press. Provides a political science view of how governments have been able to maintain their role in the face of rising of global market pressures.

Gomez, Rafael, and Morley Gunderson. 2005. "Does Economic Integration Lead to Social Policy Convergence? An Analysis of North American Linkages and Social Policy." In *Social and Labor Market Aspects of North American Linkages*, edited by Rick Harris and Thomas Lemieux. Calgary: University of Calgary Press, 309–56. Discusses the empirical evidence on the harmonization of social policy, especially between Canada and the United States.

Gunderson, Morley. 1998. "Harmonization of Labor Policies under Trade Liberalization." *Relations Industrielles/Industrial Relations* 53 (1): 11–41. Outlines the pressures for the harmonization of labor laws and policies as well as the conditions under which there will be downward or upward harmonization.

Kesselman, J. 1996. "Payroll Taxes in the Finance of Social Security." *Canadian Public Policy* 22 (June): 162–79. Outlines the theory and evidence with respect to the cost shifting of payroll taxes used to fund social programs.

Rodrik, D. 1997. *Has Globalization Gone Too Far?* Washington, DC: Institute for International Economics. Emphasises the important role of the state in fostering labor and social standards that in turn reduces the resistance to globalization.

MORLEY GUNDERSON

■ **source country**

See multinational enterprises

■ **South-South trade**

South-South trade (SST) refers to trade between developing countries, which represent a limited share of the world economy in terms of supply capacity and markets. Trade between developing countries has been steadily limited despite the supposed gains associated with better matching of supply and demand characteristics and easier access due to less stringent standards, which should promote regional integration. Contrary to the common perception, however, in recent years SST has been a major contributor to the growth of world trade. Trade between developing countries accounted for 18 percent of world trade in 2005, an increase of 5 percentage points within five years. In contrast, the share of North-North shipments in world trade has been reduced by 5 percentage points over the same period.

China is the most prominent country in this regard. On the import side, China has become in 2005 the second largest market for exports from the South behind the United States, but ahead of Japan or

Germany. Moreover the pace of growth is impressive, with a 232 percent increase of Chinese imports from other developing countries within five years, excluding oil. Besides China, a series of developing countries contribute to SST by offering buoyant markets: essentially Asia (Hong Kong, Singapore, Korea, Taiwan, Malaysia, Thailand, India, etc.) and Mexico.

Still, a large number of developing countries have been missing this general trend, in particular the least-developed countries, and a key pattern of the recent increase is that it has been very unevenly distributed among countries in the South. The sectoral pattern of exports very much reproduces the general pattern of specialization of the developing countries. It does not come as a surprise, therefore, to see China importing natural resources from other developing countries.

Explanations of a deficit of South-South trade (SST) range from geography, institutions, and trade costs to the difficulty of pursuing regional integration in the South. The asymmetric nature of trade liberalization may have played a role too: preferences have been conceded by the North on a nonreciprocal basis, without requesting access to markets in the South. This approach has made it more appealing for the South to trade with the North than with the South (Bouët, Fontagné, and Jean 2006).

Vertical Division of Labor and Extensive Margin of Trade Two main determinants of the recent dynamism of SST must be stressed. First, the vertical specialization of countries (Hummels, Ishii, and Yi 2001) and the associated increasing fragmentation of the production processes translate into large flows of parts and components among developing economies. Vertical specialization accounts for roughly one-third of world trade growth. Such processing trade is well documented in the case of Asia. China, especially, is often used as an export platform, importing and assembling intermediate goods produced by affiliates of foreign firms located elsewhere in Asia.

Second, the diversification of numerous developing economies has led them to compete on a wide spectrum of products with industrialized countries. According to the distinction introduced by Melitz

(2003), the recent dynamism has been based on the extensive margin of developing countries' exports (that is, increasing the number of exported products or destination markets), rather than on the intensive one (exporting increasing values of the same products to the same markets).

Using detailed U.S. import data, Hummels and Klenow (2005) construct measures such that a country's share in world exports decomposes in an extensive export margin (the fraction of world exports occurring in the product-market categories where a country exports), times an intensive export margin (a country's share of world markets in the market-categories in which it exports). Though not specifically addressing SST, such a decomposition is very informative. The underlying question is: As a country develops and accumulates resources, how are these resources used? To increase the quantities exported of the existing set of goods? To improve the quality of these goods? Or to expand the set of goods or destination markets? The bottom line is that two-thirds of the growth pertains to the extensive margin, essentially due to a larger number of exported products: A simple count points to a 62 percent increase in their number when the economic size of the exporter doubles.

In 2005 China overtook France and the United States in terms of diversity of exports. Other highly diversified exporters include Korea, Taiwan, India, Turkey, Thailand, Brazil, Mexico, Malaysia, Singapore, Hong Kong, Indonesia, South Africa, United Arab Emirates, Argentina, and the Philippines. In contrast, Ethiopia has simply kept its number of products constant over the period 2000–2005, while Jamaica, Myanmar, El Salvador, Mali, and Côte d'Ivoire have recorded declines in the number of their exported products. Still, the question remains whether recorded SST flows remain too low, given the characteristics of these countries.

The Gravity Puzzle Using gravity equations to assess deviations between actual and predicted trade has been the most common approach to study SST. The augmented gravity equation explains the value of bilateral trade by the gross domestic products (GDPs) of exporter and importer, the distance between them, and a vector of control variables accounting for the level of trade resistance between them, such as the level of tariffs, whether they share a common language or a common border, and the existence of a free trade agreement (FTA). In the case of SST, the appealing feature of this approach is that the data involved are readily available.

This approach may be flawed, however, due to omitted variables and endogeneity problems, as examined in Baier and Bergstrand (2006). The latter type of problem is particularly penalizing, since it sheds doubt on the extensive literature addressing the trade impact of integration among developing economies. In a nutshell, are FTAs randomly formed, or are they formed among countries that share characteristics that make them good candidates for integration? If the latter, FTAs' impact on trade might well be overestimated.

Examining intra-WAEMU (West-Africa Economic and Monetary Union) trade, Coulibaly and Fontagné (2006) stress the combined role of economics and geography in the persistence of untapped trade potentials. Being poor and landlocked profoundly reduces trade: beyond distance, the worse combination for SST is accordingly to export from a landlocked country, through a transit country, with a limited share of paved roads.

Poor infrastructure is, however, only a partial explanation for the low level of SST, since it also affects domestic trade. Low levels of SST also result from tariffs, nontariff barriers (NTBs), preferences, and more generally all aspects that make it more difficult to trade with another country than with another region within the same country. Capturing such effects imposes a methodological shift: the right benchmark is domestic trade (the difference between domestic production and exports). A growing literature is using the trade and production database of the United Nations Industrial Development Organization and the World Bank to analyze sectoral trade and production data for a series of countries in the North and in the South. This makes it possible to use the so-called border effect methodology to assess whether something specific is hampering SST.

Controlling for supply capacity, demand, distance, tariffs, NTBs, and common colonial power, SST is much more deflected by the existence of borders than North-North trade or North-South trade are. Mayer and Zignago (2005) estimate that the impact on SST of the barriers (custom formalities and delays, differences in preferences or regulations, etc.) associated with the existence of a border is the equivalent of a 100 percent tax on imports, and this effect is in addition to that of any existing tariffs and NTBs.

In this context, do free trade areas offer a viable solution? Fontagné and Zignago (2007) address this issue in a study designed to control for systematic differences in trade across countries and productive sectors. The six most prominent preferential trade agreements (PTAs) according to their trade impact are the Central American Common Market, the Andean Community, the North American Free Trade Agreement, the European Union, Mercosur (the regional trade agreement among Brazil, Argentina, Paraguay, and Uruguay), and the Association of Southeast Asian Nations; other PTAs have a smaller impact on trade.

Another route to trade liberalization among developing countries proceeds from their active participation in the multilateral arena. Simulations conducted with computable general equilibrium models conclude that this is key to the "development part" of the ongoing multilateral round of negotiations (Francois, van Meijl, and van Tongeren 2005).

Recent literature reexamines the common view that trade promotes peace and finds that the impact of bilateral and multilateral trade is not the same. Considering military conflicts in the period between 1950 and 2000, the probability of a conflict is lower among countries trading more bilaterally, because of the larger trade losses incurred in case of conflict (Martin, Mayer, and Thoenig 2007). Hence regional agreements in the South, as opposed to the multilateral trade liberalization agreements, reinforce the bilateral dependence among developing countries and reduce the probability of occurrence of a conflict.

See also gravity models; Mercosur; North-South trade; trade and economic development, international

FURTHER READING

Anderson, James, and Eric van Wincoop. 2003. "Gravity with Gravitas: A Solution to the Border Puzzle." *American Economic Review* 93 (1): 170–92. The seminal paper regarding the right formulation of the augmented gravity equation.

Baier, Scott L., and Jeffrey Bergstrand. 2006. "Do Free Trade Agreements Actually Increase Members' International Trade?" *Journal of International Economics* 71 (1): 72–95. Correctly addresses endogeneity issues in assessing the trade impact of PTAS.

Bouët, Antoine, Lionel Fontagné, and Sébastien Jean. 2006. "Is Erosion of Preferences a Serious Concern?" In *Agricultural Trade Reform and the Doha Development Agenda*, edited by Kim Anderson and Will Martin. Washington, DC: Oxford University Press and The World Bank, 161–92. First exhaustive examination of the impact of conceded preferences, using detailed data.

Cheptea, Angela, Guillaume Gaulier, and Soledad Zignago. 2005. "World Trade Competitiveness: A Disaggregated View by Shift-Share Analysis." CEPII Working Paper 2005-23. World trade at a glance for some 5,000 products.

Coulibaly, Souleymane, and Lionel Fontagné. 2006. "South-South Trade: Geography Matters." *Journal of African Economies* 15 (2): 313–41. Derives and estimates a model highlighting the impact of geography and infrastructures on bilateral trade flows within the West African Economic and Monetary Union.

Feenstra, Robert C. 1998. "Integration of Trade and Disintegration of Production in the Global Economy." *Journal of Economic Perspectives* 12 (4): 31–50. How the value-added chain is decomposed internationally.

Fontagné, Lionel, and Soledad Zignago. 2007. "A Re-Evaluation of the Impact of Regional Agreements on Trade Patterns." *Économie internationale* 109: 31–51. Estimates the impact of regional agreements using a panel of 135 countries trading in 26 industries over the period 1976–2000.

Francois, Joseph, Hans van Meijl, and Frank van Tongeren. 2005. "Trade Liberalization in the Doha Development Round." *Economic Policy* 20 (42): 349–91. The round from a development perspective at a glance.

Hummels, David, Jun Ishii, and Kei-Mu Yi. 2001. "The Nature and Growth of Vertical Specialization in World Trade." *Journal of International Economics* 54 (1): 75–96. Quantifying the role of trade in intermediate goods in the observed world trade growth.

Hummels, David, and Peter J. Klenow. 2005. "The Variety and Quality of a Nation's Exports." *American Economic Review* 95 (3): 704–23. Do countries allocate their new resources to increase the quantity of exports of existing products or to enlarge the portfolio of their exported products?

Martin, Philippe, Thierry Mayer, and Mathias Thoenig. 2007. "Make Trade not War?" Mimeo. Paris School of Economics. Available at http://team.univ-paris1.fr/teamperso/martinp/war-april2007.pdf. New evidence explaining why globalization has not lived up to its promise of decreasing conflict.

Mayer, Thierry, and Soledad Zignago. 2005. "Market Access in Global and Regional Trade." CEPII Working Paper 2005-02. Border effects, the direction of trade flows, and the trade impact of PTAs.

Melitz, Marc J. 2003. "The Impact of Trade on Intra-Industry Reallocations and Aggregate Industry Productivity." *Econometrica* 71 (6): 1695–725. The seminal paper distinguishing between intensive and extensive margins of trade.

LIONEL FONTAGNÉ

■ sovereign risk

Sovereign risk refers to circumstances in which governments default on loan contracts with foreigners, seize foreign assets located within their borders, or otherwise prevent domestic holders of foreign capital from meeting obligations. Because there is no supranational authority that can enforce contracts across borders, when sovereigns choose not to honor contracts with foreign investors, those investors have little recourse to recoup their losses. Consequently relationships between foreign investors and sovereigns are dictated primarily by the sovereign's willingness to pay rather than its ability to pay.

Foreign governments could become better credit risks by waiving sovereign immunity. The legal doctrine of sovereign immunity can be interpreted as exempting the property of foreign governments from the jurisdiction of domestic courts. Historically, this doctrine has sometimes constrained the ability of creditors to sanction foreign governments that have defaulted. The doctrine has evolved over time to grant creditors some recourse against defaulting sovereigns, however.

History is replete with instances of sovereign default. During the 19th and 20th centuries, in many instances the repayments of loans to sovereigns were far from what was called for in contractual obligations. In the 1820s, for example, Latin America experienced a wave of defaults among its newly independent countries. Many Latin American countries defaulted again in the 1870s, as did Egypt and Turkey. In the 1930s, most sovereign debtors suspended interest payments in the wake of the global depression.

Sanctions and Reputation The risk that a sovereign will not honor its obligations with foreign investors is mitigated by two factors: the threat of sanction and the loss of reputation. Direct sanctions may involve significant costs for defaulting countries. For example, sanctions could take the form of intercepting payments that the sovereign might make to exporters or payments it might receive from importers. Potential exporters to the country might then be less willing to supply the debtor country, knowing that their compensation might be intercepted. Generally, however, the net gain to creditors from sanctions will be less than the cost to the debtor. In theoretical models of sovereign borrowing with sanctions, the optimal amount of borrowing is constrained by the sanction cost: the parties to the debt contract write an incentive-compatible contract that never calls on the sovereign to make a payment to foreign creditors in excess of the sanction cost. This incentive-compatibility constraint leads to less lending than would be the case in a world where no country ever defaulted. An implication of this line of theorizing is that stronger, credible sanctions would allow sovereigns to increase the amount of their borrowing.

Reputation considerations provide another motive for sovereigns to honor obligations with foreign investors. A sovereign might choose to repay in order to maintain continued access to international capital markets on favorable terms. This idea was articulated in work that showed formally the conditions under which countries repay debts in order to preserve a reputation for repayment (Eaton and Gersovitz 1981). Subsequent work questioned whether reputational considerations alone were enough to sustain international lending in the absence of effective sanctions (Bulow and Rogoff 1989). If defaulting countries are able to earn a market return on their savings abroad they could, in theory, borrow, invest the funds abroad, default on the loan, and use the proceeds of their investments abroad to finance domestic investment opportunities in perpetuity.

Reputation models of international lending were revived by Cole and Kehoe (1997), who countered that reputation alone may support international lending if reputational spillovers are important enough. They argue that sovereigns participate in many different relationships. If they renege in one of those relationships, the damage may have adverse consequences for other relationships. If the spillovers are large enough and last long enough, then reputation considerations alone cannot support international borrowing and lending, without resort to the threat of direct sanctions. In general, though, if countries with poor credit histories are able to borrow abroad without fear of their assets being confiscated, the threat of reputation loss becomes less of a factor in deterring default.

Causes and Consequences of Default Risk Several factors have been found to influence the likelihood of sovereign default. Historical data suggest that the risk premium on foreign debt (over the return on U.S. Treasury bonds or British consols) increases with the size of a country's trade deficit and budget deficit. In addition, internal political considerations play a role: those countries that respond to a crisis by raising taxes or cutting spending are less likely to default. Severe external shocks have been found to precipitate default (Diaz-Alejandro 1983). In addition, the debt-to-export ratio and deteriorating terms of trade appear to influence the likelihood of sovereign default. In general, a country's internal and external circumstances play a role in sovereign risk.

The tangible consequences of sovereign default have proven difficult to uncover. The economists Lindert and Morton (1989) examined data on the 10 leading debtor countries from 1850 to 1970 and found that, on average, foreign lending earned a higher return than domestic lending in the United States and the United Kingdom. Eichengreen and Portes (1989) examined data on bond issues in the 1920s and found that for bonds issued in London, foreign lending earned a higher return than on contemporaneous British consols. For loans originating in the United States, overseas lending earned a return only slightly lower than that on U.S. Treasury securities. Actual yields on foreign lending compensated British and U.S. investors for suspension of payments and write-downs of principal.

When countries default, have they been denied access to international capital markets? Here the evidence is somewhat mixed. Countries that did not default in the 1930s appear not have gained wider access to international capital in the 1930s, or following World War I. Indeed, default of some countries led to a shrinking of global capital flows to all, as the international capital market virtually shut down. A review of historical evidence suggests that there is little, if any, evidence to suggest that the volume of foreign funds a sovereign could borrow was adversely affected by a record of prior default (Eichengreen 1991).

Why do lenders keep lending to countries that have a history of default? Lenders are often uncertain about the characteristics of borrowers. Consequently, new information about borrowers can have a large impact on lending. In the case of countries, a credible change in policy regime may negate the influence of a history of default. If a country changes its regime to focus on economic stability and sound monetary and fiscal policies, history suggests that lenders will be willing to extend further credit.

See also asymmetric information; contagion; currency crisis; international financial architecture; Latin American debt crisis; original sin; peso problem; spillovers

FURTHER READING

Bulow, J., and K. Rogoff. 1989. "Sovereign Debt: Is to Forgive to Forget?" *American Economic Review* 79: 43–50. Shows how lending must be supported by direct sanctions available to creditors, and not by reputation for repayment.

Cole, H., and P. Kehoe. 1997. "Reviving Reputation Models of International Debt." *Federal Reserve Bank of Minneapolis Quarterly Review* 21: 21–30. If a country is involved in relationships with creditors that provide enduring benefits, reputation alone may be enough to support lending arrangements.

Diaz-Alejandro, C. 1983. "Stories of the 1930s for the 1980s." In *Financial Policies and the World Capital Market*, edited by Pedro Aspe Armella, Rudiger Dornbusch, and Maurice Obstfeld. Chicago: University of Chicago Press, 5–40.

Eaton, J., and M. Gersovitz. 1981. "Debt with Potential Repudiation: Theoretical and Empirical Analysis." *Review of Economic Studies* 48: 289–309. Analyzes borrowing in the absence of explicit penalties for nonpayment.

Eichengreen, B. 1991. "Historical Research on International Lending and Debt." *Journal of Economic Perspectives* 2: 149–69.

Eichengreen, B., and R. Portes. 1989. "After the Deluge: Default, Negotiation, and Readjustment during the Interwar Years." In *The International Debt Crisis in Historical Perspective*, edited by B. Eichengreen, and P. Lindert. Cambridge: MIT Press, 12–37.

Lindert, P., and P. Morton. 1989. "How Sovereign Debt Has Worked." In *Developing Country Debt and Economic Performance*, vol. 1, *The International Financial System*, edited by J. Sachs. Chicago: University of Chicago Press, 39–106. Historical analysis of the effect of sovereign default on interest rates.

Ozler, S. 1993. "Have Commercial Banks Ignored History?" *American Economic Review* 83: 608–20. Investigates how past defaults affected loan terms for developing countries during the 1970s. The paper finds evidence that lenders did take default history into account when issuing loans in the 1970s. Countries with a poor record of debt repayment faced higher commercial bank lending rates in the 1970s.

KEITH SILL

Many capital-exporting developing countries look for systematic ways of raising returns on their international currency reserves on a long-term basis by creating sovereign wealth funds (SWFs), which are designated pools of assets owned and managed by governments and predominantly deployed worldwide to attain higher returns.

Countries usually have their international reserves managed by their central banks and held in liquid assets in reserve currencies. Since the primary functions of international reserves are to finance payment imbalances and limit exchange rate volatility, the reserves must have a high degree of liquidity. Since assets typically have lower rates of return the more liquid they are, however, it can make sense for governments to invest in longer term, less liquid assets such as bonds and equities. Similarly there may be gains from diversification by investing in a broader range of countries than only those with major reserve currencies.

Perhaps the clearest rationale for the establishment of an SWF is to accumulate reserves in countries that are major exporters of nonrenewable resources such as oil and gas. Concern for future generations dictates that all current revenues from the sale of such commodities not be spent on current consumption. Nor, typically, could all of the remainder be spent productively on domestic investment. Usually a substantial proportion of these revenues accrue to governments from tax receipts or direct ownership. Thus governments accumulate reserves.

Oil-producing countries make up more than half of all SWF funds (i.e., commodity-based funds) in terms of assets under management. Kuwait's International Authority, funded by oil, was established in 1953 and is the oldest SWF. Another prime example is Norway's Global Pension Fund, funded by a portion of North Sea oil and gas. The United Arab Emirates' Abu Dhabi Investment Authority Fund, which was established in 1976, is the world's largest SWF currently, with U.S. $625 billion under management. Other oil exporters, Oman and Brunei, also created investment agencies to recycle their reserve holdings in the 1970s and 1980s, and Russia followed suit more recently, creating a Stabilization Fund in 2003 (Lyons 2007).

Among the better-known non-commodity-based SWFs in Asia are Singapore's Government Investment Corporation (GIC) and Temasek Holdings. Since some of the funding sources for the agencies also include pension contributions from Singapore residents, however, these entities are strictly speaking a combination of SWFs and sovereign provident funds. GIC, established in 1981, has around U.S. $215 billion under management and tends predominantly to make financial and real estate investments. Temasek, established in 1974, has around U.S. $100 billion under management and is a more active investor in international companies regionally and globally.

Although SWFs have been around since the 1950s, they have only recently attracted much public attention. SWFs have taken on increased prominence with their phenomenal growth in recent times (both in numbers as well as funds under management), especially with the creation of the China Investment Corporation (CIC) in 2007. The CIC, which is said to be modeled on Singapore's GIC in both concept and design, began operations when the Chinese government transferred U.S. $200 billion of its U.S. $1.3 trillion in reserves to the agency, making it the world's fifth largest SWF. The new fund's first major investment was a $3 billion investment in the U.S.-based Blackstone private equity group. SWFs took center stage at the October 2007 World Bank and the International Monetary Fund (IMF) annual meetings, and the G7 industrial countries have begun to pay greater attention to these entities.

Since many of the SWFs practice considerable secrecy, the total value of their assets is not known, but estimates put the figure at between $2 and $3 trillion, substantially larger than the global aggregate of all hedge funds. Estimates also project a rapid rate of growth, with figures of $10 trillion and more expected to be reached by early in the 2010s.

Another rationale for SWFs is to minimize the destabilizing effects of fluctuations in exports due to periods of more and less rapid growth in the world economy. Medium-term fluctuations are common for a wide range of agricultural as well as both renewable and nonrenewable raw materials, so economists have long recommended that governments should accumulate international reserves in good times and draw them down in bad. This has proven difficult to do in many developing countries because of political pressures to spend all increases in reserves. These tendencies can be partially countered through the establishment of SWFs. An example is Chile's Economic and Social Fund, established in 2006.

A third rationale for the creation of SWFs is to eliminate a continual surplus. When continuing disequilibrium in a country's balance of payments has led it to accumulate far more international reserves than it needs based on traditional criteria, and the country expects to continue to accumulate reserves (or at least, not have huge reductions), then it makes no sense to hold all of its reserves in low-yield liquid assets. The country could put its excess reserves into a new facility to earn higher returns, but if reserves are clearly excessive then it would most likely take actions to eliminate its continual balance of payments surplus. Only if the rate of return on domestic investment was quite low would it make sense for the government to continue to accumulate international financial assets, even if these were invested in less liquid, higher return securities. In a market-oriented economy without capital controls, private investment would tend to flow from lower- to higher-yield areas. Thus, if domestic investments were indeed lower yield, capital would flow out and eliminate the balance of payments surplus.

A prime example of such clearly excessive reserve accumulation is China since around 2000. China does have extensive capital controls that block this equilibrating flow of capital. The primary reason that the Chinese government has not taken sufficient adjustment actions to slow or reverse China's balance of payments surplus and accompanying reserves accumulation is that in the short run the needed adjustments would hurt some sectors of the economy, and the government is greatly concerned about the short-run political and social instability that such disruptions might generate. Thus, although adjust-

ment is in China's longer-run economic interest, in the government's calculation, this is outweighed by the likely short-run political costs. Numerous policy announcements have made clear that the government would be happier if the surplus were reduced, but its limited actions reveal the high priority given to avoiding short-run adjustment costs.

The limited adjustments taken by the Chinese government have also contributed to global economic imbalances and the risk they pose to global financial stability. Of course, China alone is not responsible for such global imbalances. From a global perspective, however, the creation of the SWF reduces the national economic cost of these continual reserve accumulations and hence reduces somewhat the pressures on China to do its part toward the needed mutual adjustments.

The greatest concerns about SWFs focus on a different type of issue, however: the fear of foreign government influence over the operation of key segments of domestic economies. As long as SWFs limit themselves to passive portfolio investments they do not pose major problems on this score. The problems come when they make direct investments of substantial stakes in sensitive industries. Such fears have been highlighted by the recent efforts of government-controlled enterprises in China and Dubai to purchase a U.S. oil company and port operator, respectively. Although in neither of these cases was an SWF involved (the bidders were state-owned companies), they have led to considerable speculation about what could occur. Concerns have also been raised that the large amounts of money controlled by some SWFs could generate disruptions in financial markets. These concerns and questions have been fuelled further by the purchase of fairly large stakes in major U.S. financial institutions by various SWFs. Although creating such disruptions would seldom, if ever, be in the interest of SWFs, this may not be sufficient to calm all fears. The likely greater danger is that this range of fear would stimulate protectionist backlashes that could hurt both the SWFs and potential investment recipient countries.

Certainly, some SWFs follow policies that are unlikely to generate conflicts. Norway, for example, provides considerable transparency and spreads its investments over a wide range of equities, taking only small stakes in any one. Many funds are currently quite opaque, however. Such considerations suggest that the development of an international code of conduct for SWFs could be in the mutual interests of both capital-exporting and capital-importing countries. The possibility of developing such codes has become a major topic of attention in many countries and international forums such as the G7 and the IMF (for instance, see Truman 2007).

See also capital controls; capital flows to developing countries; exchange rate volatility; fear of floating; foreign exchange intervention; global imbalances; hedge funds; International Monetary Fund (IMF); international reserves; reserve currency

FURTHER READING

Lyons, Gerard. 2007. "State Capitalism: The Rise of Sovereign Wealth Funds." Standard Chartered Bank (October 15). United Kingdom. Offers a detailed analysis of SWFs worldwide.

Truman, Edwin, M. 2007. "Sovereign Wealth Funds: The Need for Greater Transparency and Accountability." Policy Brief No. PB07-6 (August). Washington, DC: Peterson Institute. Offers an overview of SWFs, focusing on their lack of transparency, and presents a framework to help evaluate the extent of transparency and accountability of the SWFs.

THOMAS D. WILLETT
AND RAMKISHEN S. RAJAN

■ special and differential treatment

Special and differential treatment (SDT) refers to provisions in World Trade Organization (WTO) agreements under which developing countries or groups thereof receive more favorable treatment or undertake less onerous commitments than other members. Developing countries have long argued that their development status requires that they be subject to different and more favorable trade rules than other members. This principle was accepted in the General Agreement on Tariffs and Trade (GATT, Part IV) and later in the WTO agreements, which contain numerous provisions for SDT for developing countries, as well as additional provisions containing even more favorable treatment for the least-developed countries (LDCs), a group of 50 countries that meet certain development criteria defined by the United Nations.

The main conceptual premise that underlies SDT is that developing countries are intrinsically disadvantaged in their participation in international trade and multilateral agreements involving them, and developed countries must account for this weakness in specifying their rights and responsibilities. A related premise is that trade policies that maximize sustainable development in developing countries differ from those that do so in developed economies, and hence policy disciplines applying to developed economies should not apply to developing countries. The final premise is that it is in the interest of developed countries to assist developing countries in their fuller integration and participation in the international trading system.

The provisions introduced in the WTO agreements fall into two broad categories: positive actions by developed country members or international institutions and exceptions to the overall rules contained in the agreements. Developed countries have also agreed to take three kinds of actions to support developing countries' participation in international trade:

- Provide preferential access to their markets, such as through the Generalized System of Preferences (GSP), under which many developing country manufacturing exports enjoy duty-free entry into developed country markets.
- Provide technical and other assistance to permit them to meet their WTO obligations and otherwise enhance the benefits developing countries derive from international trade.
- Implement the overall agreements in ways that are beneficial or least damaging to the interests of developing countries and LDCs.

Developing countries and LDCs have accepted differential obligations under the WTO agreements, in that they are permitted to undertake policies that limit access to their markets or support domestic producers or exporters in ways not allowed to other members. Examples include GATT Article XVIII on government assistance and the general exemption from reciprocity in trade negotiations with developed countries to reduce or remove tariffs and other barriers to trade. Similar provisions for nonreciprocity are included in the General Agreement on Trade in Services (GATS, Article XIX:2), which states, "There shall be appropriate flexibility for individual developing countries members for opening fewer sectors, liberalizing fewer types of transactions, progressively extending market access in line with their development situation." Second, developing countries and LDCs get more time to meet obligations or commitments under the agreements (for example in Trade-Related Intellectual Property Rights—TRIPS).

Both the premises and the practice of SDT have proved controversial. Some have argued that the freedom provided to developing countries to protect their economies has harmed rather than promoted development and, similarly, that the lack of reciprocity in the mutual reduction of tariff barriers has contributed to the relatively high tariff barriers now facing developing countries in developed country markets. It is also argued that the GSP has provided significant benefits to only a few countries and has done little for the poorest and the LDCs.

Others have noted that most of the WTO commitments for SDT made by the developed countries have been vague and legally unenforceable. Many poorer developing countries have been pushed to participate in agreements such as TRIPS, sanitary and phytosanitary measures, technical barriers to trade, and customs valuation without taking into account their lack of capacity to implement their commitments and without ensuring the provision of adequate assistance. Moreover the transition periods envisaged under the WTO were unrealistic. The time limits for extensions had passed, and as of early 2008 there was little evidence that countries had made

sufficient progress in institution building to permit them to implement their obligations. Finally, there is the question of which countries should be receiving SDT. Many low-income and vulnerable economies face the same kind of developmental constraints as the LDCs, yet only the latter receive special consideration, probably because their total participation in world trade is so small as not to constitute a competitive threat to developed country producers. On the other hand, because the principle of self-selection is used in determining who is a developing country, large countries that are well integrated in the international trade such Brazil, China, or Singapore are in principle eligible for the same kind of SDT as small vulnerable economies such as Ghana or St. Lucia.

The Doha WTO Ministerial Declaration underlying the Doha Round of multilateral trade negotiations was replete with pronouncements about SDT. It stated that "provisions for special and differential treatment are an integral part of the WTO agreements," and it called for a review of SDT provisions with the objective of "strengthening them and making them more precise, effective and operational" (para. 44). As of early 2008, little progress had been made on these issues with the exception of a decision related to TRIPS and pharmaceuticals and a number of decisions related to LDCs. It was agreed that LDCs would not have to make any tariff reduction commitments as part of the multilateral negotiations. This was controversial as it raises the risk that LDCs will continue to maintain significant protective barriers that would undermine their development.

In TRIPS, developing countries can use compulsory licensing to reduce the cost of drugs for HIV/AIDS whose patents were held by developed country pharmaceutical companies. But this provision is of no use to countries that have no capacity to produce these drugs domestically. Under heavy public opinion pressure, the WTO agreed to an amendment permitting developing countries that do not have capacity to produce drugs needed to combat epidemics to import them from low-cost suppliers at low prices under carefully circumscribed circumstances. In a related action, negotiators also agreed to extend the transition period for the implementation of the TRIPS agreement for LDCs until 2013 and for pharmaceuticals until 2016. But the decision does not cover other low-income countries that face similar developmental constraints.

In parallel with the Doha Round negotiations, an effort was made to strengthen the international community's efforts to provide trade-related technical and other assistance. Agreement was reached for an enhanced Integrated Framework for Trade-Related Assistance to LDCs with a new independent secretariat housed in the WTO and the expectation of substantially increased aid resources. On the other hand, a WTO Task Force on Aid for Trade, which was supposed to address assistance needs of all developing countries, could only come up with general and vague recommendations.

Recent experience with SDT suggests an emerging consensus that SDT should be extended to many developing countries that do not have the institutional capacity to implement a number of WTO agreements—or for whom implementation of such agreements is not a development priority—and that many of these countries, especially the LDCs, are deserving of increased trade-related international assistance. Also, a number of proposals to strengthen monitoring of SDT needs and implementation, possibly in the context of WTO trade policy reviews, have received widespread support, though no specific agreement has been reached.

Controversies are likely to continue on specific developing country SDT proposals, however, especially those that affect basic WTO disciplines such as binding of all tariffs, commitments not to use non-tariff barriers to trade, or participation in the multilateral trade negotiations, as well as on which countries should receive SDT. Overall, the role of SDT in the world economy is going to continue to be small but important to a considerable number of poor developing countries, especially the LDCs.

See also access to medicines; Agreement on Trade-Related Aspects of Intellectual Property Rights (TRIPS); Doha Round; Trade Policy Review Mechanism; trade-related capacity building

FURTHER READING

Hoekman, Bernard, Constantine Michalopoulos, and Alan Winters. 2004. "Special and Differential Treatment of Developing Countries in the WTO." *World Economy* 27 (4): 481–506. A recent assessment of the economic merits of various approaches to SDT.

Hudec, Robert. 1987. *Developing Countries in the GATT Legal System.* Hampshire, UK: Gower. Basic reference to the legal provisions pertaining to SDT in the GATT, which were later incorporated in the WTO.

Michalopoulos, Constantine. 2001. *Developing Countries in the WTO.* Houndmills, Hampshire, UK: Palgrave. Contains a discussion of the merits of SDT in the context of trade theory and experience with developing country participation in the WTO.

World Trade Organization. 2000. "Implementation of Special and Differential Provisions in WTO Agreements and Decisions." WT/COMTD/W/77. Geneva: WTO. Basic reference that contains a listing of all the SDT provisions in WTO agreements prepared in advance of the Doha Round.

CONSTANTINE MICHALOPOULOS

■ special drawing rights

Special drawing rights (SDRs) are an internationally recognized unit of account and reserve assets issued by the International Monetary Fund (IMF) and allocated to IMF member countries in proportion to their quotas at the IMF. According to the IMF (2006a), the SDR is "a potential claim on the freely usable currencies of IMF members." SDRs can be exchanged for other currencies in two ways: first, through voluntary exchanges between members; and second, by an IMF directive, designating members with strong external positions to purchase these SDRs.

SDRs were initially created in 1969 to increase the availability of easily convertible reserve assets. Before 1969, reserve assets—those assets held by central banks to clear international transactions—were held mostly in U.S. dollars and gold. The economists Peter Clark and Jacques Polak (2004) note that, at the time, issuing SDRs was seen as a way of preventing official dollar holdings from undermining the stability of the system. Reserve accumulation was perceived as destabilizing since many central banks converted their dollar reserves into gold, thereby drawing down the limited U.S. gold stocks.

SDRs are also used as units of account by the IMF in all of its transactions. The IMF conditional loans are denominated in SDRs, while the interest rate on these loans is calculated on the basis of the SDR interest rate (in addition to an interest surcharge that varies with the different lending facilities).

Amended every five years, the value of an SDR unit is the sum of the values of the following as of January 2006: 0.632 U.S. dollars, 0.410 euros, 18.4 Japanese yen, and 0.0903 British pounds. As of February 1, 2007, 1.496137 U.S. dollars were worth one SDR unit. The SDR interest rate is calculated as the weighted average of interest rates on short-term instruments in the financial markets of the four currencies included in the SDR valuation basket; it is posted on the IMF Web site once a week. On the week of February 1, 2007, for example, the SDR interest rate was 4.20—the weighted average of the interest rates of a three-month U.S. Treasury bill, a three-month Europe rate, the Japanese government's 13-week financing bill, and a three-month UK Treasury bill.

Role of SDRs From their onset, SDRs could be held only by governments, central banks, and official bodies such as the IMF. The original SDR allocation of 9.3 billion SDRs was disbursed among the IMF members according to predetermined quotas over a two-year period (1970–72). An additional amount of 12.1 billion SDRs was allocated and distributed between 1979 and 1981. SDRs have not been allocated since. As a result of the reluctance among the IMF stakeholders to allocate new SDR issues, SDRs now amount to only about 1 percent of the international reserves held worldwide. SDRs clearly did not end up as the primary reserve asset in the global monetary system as envisioned in the IMF Article of Agreements (XXII). In addition, Clark and Polak (2004) suggest that the concerns of international liquidity (i.e., the worldwide lack of sufficient gold reserves) that led to the establishment of the SDR no longer apply.

Although the original rationale for the creation of SDRs is no longer relevant to the post–Bretton Woods system of flexible exchange rates, other reasons for their existence as reserve assets remain. Since capital accounts are now much more open than ever before (with the possible exception of 1880–1914), reserves are seen as a means to prevent fluctuations in the trade balance and domestic consumption that would be required in the face of fluctuations in capital flows. SDRs enable countries to diversify their reserve holdings, and more important for developing countries, the SDR can be held at a much lower cost than major currencies such as the U.S. dollar, the Japanese yen, the euro, or the British pound. This is especially true for the lowest-income countries, which are virtually cut off from the international financial markets and for whom the only means of obtaining reserves is running trade surpluses through reductions in imports.

Another possible future use for the SDR is as an alternative reserve asset that can be issued broadly in case of a dramatic U.S. dollar crash (Lissakers 2006). A dollar crash, a plausible event in light of the persistent U.S. balance of payment deficits, and the central role of the dollar as a reserve currency (roughly 70 percent of all foreign reserves are held in U.S. dollar–denominated assets), might create the conditions for a general flight from the dollar; this means that the question of constraints on international liquidity might reemerge.

See also balance of payments; Bretton Woods system; dollar standard; dominant currency; global imbalances; gold standard, international; hot money and sudden stops; international liquidity; International Monetary Fund (IMF); international reserves; reserve currency; Triffin dilemma; twin deficits; vehicle currency

FURTHER READING
Clark, Peter B., and Jacques J. Polak. 2004. "International Liquidity and the Role of the SDR in the International Monetary System." *IMF Staff Papers* 51 (1): 49–71. A

discussion of the 1969–70 introduction of SDR, written by senior IMF staffers at the time who argue for a reinvigoration of the SDR allocation program.

Goldstein, Henry N. 1969. "Gresham's Law and the Demand for NRUs and SDRs." *The Quarterly Journal of Economics* 83 (1): 163–66. A contemporary argument supporting the introduction of SDRs.

International Monetary Fund. 2006a. "A Factsheet—Special Drawing Rights (SDRs)." Downloadable from http://www.imf.org/external/np/exr/facts/sdr.htm (accessed August 15, 2006). Contains updated information about the current status and history of SDRs.

International Monetary Fund. 2006b. "SDR Valuation." Downloadable from http://www.imf.org/external/np/fin/rates/rms_sdrv.cfm (accessed August 17, 2006). Contains daily updates on the value of SDRs.

International Monetary Fund. 2006c. SDR Interest Rate Calculation. Downloadable from http://www.imf.org/external/np/fin/rates/sdr_ir.cfm (accessed August 17, 2006). Contains details on the current SDR interest rate.

Lissakers, Karin. 2006. "Is the SDR a Monetary Dodo? This Bird May Still Fly." In *Reforming the IMF for the 21st Century*, edited by Edwin M. Truman. Washington, DC: Institute for International Economics, Special Report #19. Written by a former U.S. executive director at the IMF, the paper advocates the allocation of SDRs in the case of a U.S. dollar crash. The book includes other useful discussions on various aspects of IMF reform proposals.

ILAN NOY

■ **special economic zones**

See South-South trade

■ **specific-factors model**

Most undergraduates in their first year in economics have been exposed to an important ingredient in the specific-factors model, a model in which each industry employs some factor used only in that particular industry. What happens to total output when more of a variable factor is added in a production process to a fixed quantity of this specific factor? The answer exemplifies the Law of Diminishing Returns, and this ingredient is basic in the general equilibrium context in which the specific-factors model is set. David Ricardo used this concept when referring to the differential rents that various qualities of land would receive, and Viner (1931) made use of it in his famous article in which he argued with Wong, his draftsman. Haberler (1936) in his classic text on international trade presents verbally some of the logic of what Samuelson (1971) later referred to as the Ricardo-Viner model. The formal exposition of the model in general equilibrium terms was carried out by Samuelson and by Jones (1971), both of whom emphasized the usefulness of the model in the theory of international trade, although the model itself is also applicable to closed economies.

The nature of the model is most easily discussed in the context in which only a pair of commodities is produced in competitive conditions, with each commodity making use of a factor employed only in that sector (i.e., a *specific* factor) as well as a factor of production (typically taken to be labor) that is used in both sectors (the *mobile* factor). In a competitive equilibrium, factor prices and input-output coefficients adjust to maintain full employment of all factors, and with constant returns to scale characterizing production processes, costs of production adjust to equal commodity prices if both commodities are produced. The process of solving the model formally for changes in factor prices and commodity outputs when commodity prices or factor endowments are altered is more simple than that found in the Heckscher-Ohlin model (the standard model used in trade theory since the Stolper-Samuelson article appeared in 1941) in that it is not necessary to solve more than one equation at a time. The key equation is the one that asserts full employment of the mobile factor. With techniques in each sector depending only on the wage rate relative to the commodity price in that sector (the important technological parameter being the elasticity of the demand curve for labor, exhibiting diminishing returns to labor as more is added to a given amount of the specific factor) and each output restricted by the given amount of the specific factor and the intensity of its use (which depends on the wage/price ratio), the change in the wage rate is seen to depend on commodity price changes and changes in factor endowments. These relationships are often portrayed in a "back-to-back" diagram, such as figure 1. A pair of (value of) marginal product schedules face each other, each assuming given values for the quantity of the specific factor available in that sector as well as that sector's commodity price. The intersection point, A, reveals both the equilibrium value of the wage rate and the quantity of labor assigned to each sector.

Details of the solution are found in many places, for example, in the supplement to chapter 5 of the Caves, Frankel, and Jones text (2007). The important results are (1) if either commodity price increases, the wage rate also increases, but by less than in proportion; (2) any increase in the labor endowment at constant commodity prices drives down the wage rate (to the benefit of both specific factors); and (3) any increase in the endowment of either specific factor lowers that factor's return, pushing up the nominal wage rate, and thus driving down the return to the other specific factor as well. The asymmetry

found in factor returns when the price of a single commodity increases reflects the asymmetry found in the mobility of the two factors: an increase in the price of the first commodity must lead to a matching increase in average cost. The return to labor is constrained by its use as well in the other sector, one that has not benefited by a price increase, while the return to the specific factor used only in the first sector is not constrained in this fashion. The consequence is that the wage rate cannot increase relatively as much as p_1, thus pushing up the return to the specific factor employed there by a magnified relative amount so that unit costs increase as much as price. With the nominal wage rate rising, the return to the specific factor in the second sector falls.

An important result in the field of political economy is immediately apparent, even in the two-commodity setting. Suppose the primary issue facing voters before an election is whether or not to impose a tariff on imports. The specific factor in the import-competing sector will be strongly in support of the tariff, while the other specific factor would be strongly opposed. This is not surprising. But what of the attitude of voters whose income is in the form of wages? Protection raises the nominal wage rate but also increases the cost of living. This may leave many voters with the desire to stay at home on election day (especially if the weather is inclement) since their real incomes do not depend that heavily on the outcome. (Ruffin and Jones 1977 argue that on balance labor will be mildly against protection in the specific-factors model.) This would help to explain relatively low voter turnout at election times in countries such as the United States. If, instead, the important issue before the voters concerns immigration, both specific factors stand to gain or lose together, and this may result in their joining forces in a political alliance.

The setting of the specific-factors model has two basic interpretations. On the one hand, the two specific factors may fundamentally be different—say, land and capital (e.g., in Jones 1971). On the other hand, they may represent, say, two kinds of capital that are specific in the short run but can become interchangeable with the passage of time (e.g., in Neary 1978). As Magee (1980) has argued, a

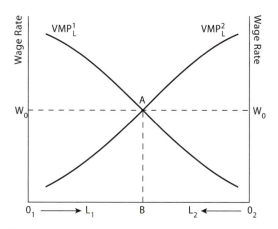

Figure 1

Wage rate determination

sector-specific type of capital might change its attitude toward protection in the long run. The Neary interpretation has become popular in explanations of how the specific-factors model may be linked to the standard Heckscher-Ohlin model, where both factors are intersectorally mobile. Such a link was given a different rationale in the model of Sanyal and Jones (1982), in which a country produces final commodities by using labor and *middle products,* that is, goods in process, raw materials, or intermediate goods that can be obtained on world markets. The country may export some of its own production of middle products in exchange for imports that are better suited to its own needs in producing final consumption goods. Thus middle products produced at home with labor and the country's own specific factors can be traded for middle products requiring, say, specific factors not available at home. In other words, final consumer goods are produced with two mobile factors: labor and traded middle products. (As the Canadian economist Doug Purvis once remarked, in this setting Heckscher-Ohlin does not explain trade, trade explains Heckscher-Ohlin.)

How does the specific-factors model match up with the Heckscher-Ohlin model? In the setting in which only two commodities are produced, differences between the specific-factors model and the Heckscher-Ohlin model are often emphasized in the theory of international trade, especially as regards the effects of free trade on a nation's factor returns. As Samuelson (1948) demonstrated, if endowment differences are relatively small between two countries sharing the same technology and facing the same traded goods prices, factor prices tend to be equalized by trade despite the fact that each factor has a purely national market. The specific-factors model does not share this property. With the number of factors (3) exceeding the number of produced commodities (2), any tendency for factor returns to become equalized with trade disappears. A related comparison concerns the effects of factors becoming mobile between countries. In the two-factor, two-commodity Heckscher-Ohlin model with countries sharing the same technology and endowments not too dissimi-

lar, a movement of factor(s) from one country to another can be absorbed by a change in the composition of outputs without requiring any change in factor prices. Not so in the specific-factors model with three factors and two commodities, because at given commodity prices changes in factor endowments exercise a direct effect on factor returns. This latter model is often more appreciated by labor economists, who may expect labor immigration to have a depressing effect on national wage rates.

The difference between these two models tends to be less apparent when a specific-factor model with *n* commodities (and *n+1* factors, only one of which is mobile) is compared with the so-called *strong* form of the *n*-factor, *n*-commodity Heckscher-Ohlin model in which the increase of any commodity price serves to raise the return to the factor used relatively intensively in that sector and to lower the returns to all other factors (e.g., see Kemp and Wegge 1969). Such a *magnification effect* of commodity prices on factor returns is shared by the specific-factors model—the return to one specific factor is raised, and to all others is lowered. Only the return to mobile labor is not so magnified. Indeed, suppose the mobile factor is not labor, but rather some intermediate good that is produced by all of the "specific" factors. This *produced mobile factor* model (Jones and Marjit 1991) becomes a Heckscher-Ohlin model that satisfies the strong conditions—one real winner and all others losers when a price changes—cited earlier.

The case can be made that the specific-factors model—with each sector having a unique specific factor but sharing mobile labor with all other sectors—is especially useful as a general equilibrium model of production because it does generalize so readily to higher dimensions and has highly appealing qualities: (1) If a single commodity price increases, the output of that commodity also rises, drawing resources (mobile labor) from *all* other sectors; (2) if the endowment of a specific factor increases (and commodity prices remain constant) not only is its return lowered, but the consequent increase in the wage rate pushes down the returns to *all* other specific factors. This latter result may yield a surprising consequence—the returns to some other specific factors may fall by a greater relative extent than does that of the factor whose endowment has increased.

Although the Heckscher-Ohlin model may not be especially useful in the many-factor case because extremely detailed structure must be imposed before explicit solutions can be obtained, it does have a distinct advantage in that the two-factor scenario is consistent with a world in which trade takes place in many commodities. There is no two-factor, many-commodity version of the specific-factor model. The theory of international trade emphasizes that trade encourages each country to specialize in a few activities in which it has the greatest comparative advantage, and the two-factor Heckscher-Ohlin model can well illustrate that *which* commodities a country produces depends both on world commodity prices and local factor endowments. This production choice becomes endogenous—it can vary as, say, the country grows and the capital/labor endowment ratio expands. Suppose, however, that a commodity that had been produced in the past now cannot earn as high a return on its capital as some new commodity on the trading scene. If this capital had become specific, that industry may nonetheless stay in business if its capital can earn anything exceeding scrap value. That is, the specific-factor model may prove useful in modeling why it is that some industries still produce even if they would not be viable if new capital had to be raised for production (Jones 2007).

Some disenchantment with general equilibrium models seems to be based on the widespread difficulty of obtaining comparative static results when an original equilibrium is disturbed by some change in prices or endowments. Detailed structure must be imposed on the model. Sufficient structure is a characteristic of specific-factor models, and further higher-dimensional results can be obtained by employing the following kind of *variation* on such models. Consider first the way in which a "bubble" diagram can be used to illustrate a three-factor, two-commodity specific factors model in figure 2(a). Each of the two X_i outputs is produced with specific factor K_i and mobile labor, L. Figure 2(b) adds another two sectors, with notations suggesting two

countries, with Y-type capitals, K_Y^* and K_Y, specific both to country and occupation. L^* and L are, respectively, foreign and home labor forces, each specific to the country but mobile between sectors, and K_X, assumed specifically used in the X industry, is now internationally mobile. This is a five-factor, four-commodity model, whose structure has specific factors used only for the "end" products and three types of mobile factors—labor in each country mobile between sectors but not internationally and X-type capital, mobile between countries but sector-specific. It is not difficult to analyze (see Jones 2000, chapter 3) because it can be treated in two stages. In the first, suppose that the allocation of X-type capital between home and foreign industries is kept the same so that figure 2(b) resembles two countries, each of the figure 2(a) type. In world markets suppose the prices of X-type goods increase by the same relative amount and that of Y-type goods stay the same. In each country separately standard specific-factor results are obtained: the return to X-type capital increases relatively more than does the price of X goods, the wage rate rises but by less than X's commodity price, and the return to Y-type capital falls. In the second stage, let X-type capital become mobile internationally. In which direction does it flow? Toward the home country if, and only if, in stage 1, the return to X-type capital at home increases by more than it does abroad.

Such a comparison depends largely, and indirectly, on how much the wage rate is stimulated in each country, and this comparison, in turn, is revealed by the solution for wage changes in the

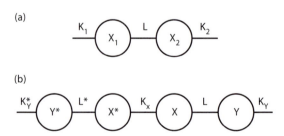

Figure 2
Bubble diagram of three-factor, two-commodity specific-factors model and five-factor, four-commodity specific-factors model

specific-factors model. The formal solution was not derived earlier, but it can be shown (e.g., in Caves, Frankel, and Jones 2007; Jones 2000, chapter 3) to depend on the product of three terms: s_X, i_X, and θ_X. s_X is the relationship between the elasticity of demand for labor (i.e., of the marginal product curve) in the X sector compared to the economy average. If X is "typical," this has value unity; i_X is equal to labor's distributive share in the X sector relative to its share in the economy and would be greater than unity if and only if X is relatively labor intensive. Finally, θ_X is the fraction of the country's income devoted to the production of X. If the X sector is fairly typical in terms of labor demand elasticity and labor intensity, everything depends on the relative size of the X industry. Suppose this is larger at home than abroad. If so, the wage rate will tend to increase more at home than abroad, and since both countries experience the same price rise for X, the return to capital will increase in both countries but tend to increase relatively more abroad. With a greater increase in the wage rate at home, fewer rents are available to attract capital to the home country.

This two-stage process illustrates how the variation in the specific-factors model that is exemplified for the four-commodity case in figure 2(b) leads to a modeling strategy that makes use of the specific-factor logic at the first stage and then completes the analysis by asking how rates of return to a mobile factor compare in two countries. Jones and Marjit (2003) explore a different interpretation of figure 2(b) in which the two labor forces shown there correspond to a single country's supply of skilled and unskilled labor. An interesting question might concern the consequences for the wage premium and wage levels of a training program that converts some unskilled labor into skilled labor.

The specific-factors model is a simple form of general equilibrium model in which an extreme asymmetry in factor mobility is assumed—one factor is mobile and the others are not. A model in which all factors have partial mobility would of course be more complex, even if attractive for modeling dynamic movements. The Heckscher-Ohlin model also has extreme assumptions—namely, that the two factors

(in the two-factor case) have the same degree of mobility instantaneously. As all theorists acknowledge, simplicity in model building is a strong virtue unless it rules out features of the setting that are of most concern. As illustrated earlier, departures from the specific-factors setting can often be better understood by making use of embedded features that do correspond to the specific-factor model even if other features are also involved. And, as Samuelson and others have often remarked, it is the general equilibrium model that captures much of the basic reasoning about diminishing returns in partial equilibrium settings.

See also comparative advantage; Heckscher-Ohlin model; migration, international; political economy of trade policy; trade and wages

FURTHER READING

Caves, Richard, Jeffrey Frankel, and Ronald W. Jones. 2007. *World Trade and Payments*. 10th ed. Cambridge, MA: Addison Wesley. A standard textbook used in undergraduate courses.

Haberler, Gottfried. 1936. *The Theory of International Trade*. London: Wm. Hodge. A classic prewar exposition of the theory of trade.

Jones, Ronald W. 1971. "A Three-Factor Model in Theory, Trade, and History." In *Trade, Balance of Payments, and Growth*, edited by Jagdish Bhagwati, Ronald Jones, Robert Mundell, and Jaroslav Vanek. Amsterdam: North-Holland, chapter 1. Along with Samuelson (1971) the pair of articles setting out the algebraic exposition of the specific-factor model.

———. 2000. *Globalization and the Theory of Input Trade*. Cambridge, MA: MIT Press. Discusses how international trade theory is altered when some inputs into production have international markets.

———. 2007. "Specific Factors and Heckscher-Ohlin: An Intertemporal Blend." *Singapore Economic Review* 52: 1–6. Points out how a blend of the two-factor, many-commodity version of Heckscher-Ohlin theory, combined with the $(n+1)$ by n dimensional specific-factors model, provides a simple model of competitive trade allowing both a heavy degree of specialization with trade and a variety of products produced by a given country.

Jones, Ronald W., and Sugata Marjit. 1991. "The Stolper-Samuelson Theorem, the Leamer Triangle, and the Produced Mobile Factor Structure." In *Trade, Policy, and International Adjustments*, edited by A. Takayama, M. Ohyama, and H. Ohta. San Diego: CA: Academic Press. An exposition of a simple *n*-factor, *n*-commodity model.

———. 2003. "Economic Development, Trade, and Wages." *German Economic Review* 4: 1–17. An adaptation of figure 2 to the question of the wage premium between skilled and unskilled workers.

Kemp, Murray, and Leon Wegge. 1969. "On the Relation between Commodity Prices and Factor Rewards." *International Economic Review* 9: 497–513: An extension of the Stolper-Samuelson theorem to three factors and three commodities.

Magee, Stephen. 1980. "Three Simple Tests of the Stolper-Samuelson Theorem." In *Issues in International Economics*, edited by P. Oppenheimer. London: Oriel Press, 138–53: An argument for the superiority of the specific-factors model in explaining supports for commercial policy.

Neary, J. Peter. 1978. "Short-Run Capital Specificity and the Pure Theory of International Trade." *Economic Journal* 88: 488–510. Shows how the passage of time can convert a specific-factors setting to the all-factors-mobile Heckscher-Ohlin setting.

Ricardo, David. 1817. *The Principles of Political Economy and Taxation*. Reprint, 1981. Cambridge: Cambridge University Press. Shows both the argument for comparative advantage and the analysis of rents in a specific-factor setting.

Ruffin, Roy, and Ronald W. Jones. 1977. "Protection and Real Wages: The Neo-Classical Ambiguity." *Journal of Economic Theory* 14: 337–48. Establishes a presumption that workers would prefer free trade to protection.

Samuelson, Paul A. 1948. "International Trade and the Equalisation of Factor Prices." *Economic Journal* 58: 163–84. The classical argument that factor prices could be equalized between trading countries with different factor endowments.

———. 1971. "Ohlin Was Right." *The Swedish Journal of Economics* 73: 365–84. An exposition of the algebra of the specific-factor setting.

Sanyal, Kalyan, and Ronald W. Jones. 1982. "The Theory of Trade in Middle Products." *American Economic Review* 72: 16–31. An analysis of trade that is in the "middle" of the production spectrum.

Stolper, Wolfgang, and Paul A. Samuelson. 1941. "Protection and Real Wages." *Review of Economic Studies* 9: 58–73. Shows how, in a Heckscher-Ohlin setting, a country would raise real wages if it imposes a tariff on labor-intensive imports.

Viner, Jacob. 1931. "Cost Curves and Supply Curves." *Zeitschrift für Nationalokonomie* 3: 23–46. Reprint, 1953. American Economic Association, *Readings in Price Theory*. London: Allen and Unwin. A discussion of a firm's short-run and long-run average cost curves, with a dispute over geometry.

RONALD W. JONES

∎ speculation

The economist John Maynard Keynes (1936) defined speculation as the purchase of securities at a price above their fundamental value with a view to sell them at yet a higher price in the subsequent trading periods. Ever since the economist Milton Friedman (1953) argued that such destabilizing speculation would be unprofitable and thus unsustainable in the long run, economists generally have discounted the possibility that speculation could cause asset prices to deviate from fundamental values, that is, prices warranted by the *true* earning potential of firms. The intuition behind Friedman's argument rested on a simple view of arbitrage. In a market that includes both smart traders who know the true values and those who make whimsical and misinformed trades, generally referred to as noise traders, the latter create riskless arbitrage opportunities from which smart traders could profit.

The rise of behavioral finance theory has made economists more receptive to studying the limitations of arbitrage in real-world markets. Informed traders with a "short" trading horizon who sell overvalued assets short can find that by the time they are supposed to close their position, the true value has increased, or the assets in question have become even more overpriced. Because the smart traders who have sold securities short could make losses in either situation, they limit the initial positions they take in an over- or undervalued asset, preventing the current price from smoothly adjusting to its true value as Friedman had envisioned. It might even be the case that it pays for smart traders to act like noise traders themselves in the short run, bidding prices further away from true values rather than helping to close the gap between the two (De Long et al. 1990; Griffin, Harris, and Topaloglu 2003). Thus an increasing number of economists now hold that *riskless* arbitrage is not always effective (Shleifer 2000).

This view is reminiscent of Keynes's (1936, chapter 12) famous beauty contest analogy, where speculators base their expectations of future asset prices not only on what they think the true value is, but, more important, on what they think the average opinion about the average opinion is. In other words, *noise* is at least as important as information about true values in causing asset price changes, rendering the resale price uncertain (Black 1986). This, in turn, implies that traders must not only form higher-order expectations (i.e., on what others think others think) but also decide how much weight to assign them relative to what they themselves think the true value is (Hirota and Sunder 2003).

If a trader observes that the price of an asset (or an asset group) which she thinks is already overvalued is still rising in price, she is led to surmise that either her opinion about the true value is wrong or that the price is rising on account of market sentiment (Abreu and Brunnermeier 2003). In either case, the information and opinion of others, as revealed in current price changes, are likely to gain in importance in how the trader forms his/her expectation about the future price. Such information becomes either a proxy for the higher-order expectations or a corrective on opinions about the true value, or some combination of both. Under these conditions whether speculation is stabilizing or not crucially depends on the relative weight traders assign to their higher-order expectations (i.e., what they think others think others think) relative to their own assessment of what the true value is. Though it appears to be long forgotten, this basic idea in its simplest form goes back to Kaldor (1939), where whether speculation is stabilizing or not de-

pends on the elasticity of future price expectations with respect to current price changes. In this early formulation, stability requires a less than unitary elasticity of expectations, where traders revise their expected future price proportionally less than the change in the current price.

In the modern literature, much more elaborate analyses of cases where agents make trades relying on information revealed by the past decisions of other traders rather than their own abound and are generally discussed under the heading of *herding* behavior. These generally model "momentum-investor" or "positive-feedback" strategies, where traders tend to buy assets whose price has been on the rise and sell those that have been falling in price. Short trading horizons, the sequential nature of trades, and information costs are the real-world market attributes that are emphasized in this body of work.

In contrast to standard models of asset pricing that implicitly assume long-term horizons, short-term trading horizons play an important role in persistent deviations of asset prices from true values (Dow and Gorton 1994). In these models, it is argued that the incentive structure that defines money managers' employment gives rise to agency problems (Allen and Gorton 1993), making it rational for speculators to have short trading horizons. In a world characterized by market imperfections and uncertainty, speculators who tie their resources to long-term investments would fail to exploit profitable investment opportunities that would unexpectedly arise (Shleifer and Vishny 1997).

Second, in real-world markets trading is sequential, which implies that traders observe and can learn from one another. Early action can enable traders to rationally exploit information revealed by the actions of other agents. Profit-maximizing traders can thus successfully focus on what other traders also know rather than trying to learn information others do not have. A narrow set of information can then become the primary focus of attention even when it has little bearing on fundamentals (Scharfstein and Stein 1990).

Finally, especially in international markets, gathering information requires large fixed costs which generate economies of scale for large investors. Thus the greater the cost of acquiring information, the higher is the incentive for uninformed small traders to imitate large investors (Calvo and Mendoza 2000). This also causes small investors to be much more aggressive, especially in their selling in markets where large investors have a significant presence (Corsetti et al. 2001), giving rise to increased volatility and likelihood of abrupt shifts in capital flows, leading to currency and financial crises.

See also contagion; currency crisis; exchange rate volatility; financial crisis; spillovers

FURTHER READING

Abreu, D., and M. Brunnermeier. 2003. "Bubbles and Crashes." *Econometrica* 71: 173–204. Shows that a bubble can exist despite the presence of rational arbitrageurs.

Allen, F., and G. Gorton. 1993. "Churning Bubbles." *Review of Economic Studies* 60: 813–36. Argues that agency problems caused by asymmetric information in financial markets cause financial assets to trade at prices different than fundamentals.

Black, F. 1986. "Noise." *Journal of Finance* 41 (July): 529–43. Argues that *noise* in financial markets plays a profound role in shaping our views of the world.

Calvo, G., and E. Mendoza. 2000. "Rational Contagion and the Globalization of Securities Markets." *Journal of International Economics* 51: 79–113. Argues that the large fixed costs of gathering information in foreign exchange markets incentivize small traders to imitate large investors.

Corsetti, G., A. Dasgupta, S. Morris, and H. S. Shin. 2001. "Does One Soros Make a Difference? A Theory of Currency Crises with Large and Small Traders." *Review of Economic Studies* 71: 87–113. Argues that the very existence of large investors in foreign exchange markets of emerging countries increases the vulnerability of these countries to speculative attacks.

De Long, J. B., A. Schleifer, L. Summers, and R. Waldmann. 1990. "Positive Feedback Investment Strategies and Destabilizing Rational Speculation." *Journal of Finance* 45 (2): 379–95. Shows that rational speculation might entail rational traders to act as noise traders, jumping on the bandwagon of an asset price bubble the latter might create.

Dow, J., and G. Gorton. 1994. "Arbitrage Chains." *Journal of Finance* 49: 819–49. Explores how and why limited trading horizons can give rise to inefficient asset prices.

Friedman, M. 1953. "The Case for Flexible Exchange Rates." *Essays in Positive Economics*. Chicago: Chicago University Press. In this famous paper, Friedman argued that speculation had to be stabilizing for it to be profitable.

Griffin, J., J. Harris, and S. Topaloglu. 2003. "The Dynamics of Institutional and Individual Trading." *Journal of Finance* 58 (6): 2285–2320. Summarizes the findings of studies that examine the relationship between institutional ownership and stock returns.

Hirota, S., and S. Sunder. 2003. "Price Bubbles sans Dividend Anchors: Evidence from Laboratory Stock Markets." Working Paper. Downloadable from http://www.som.yale.edu/faculty/Sunder/research.html. Tries to model higher-order expectations about what the average opinion expects what the average opinion expects and on and on.

Kaldor, N. 1939. "Speculation and Economic Stability." *Review of Economic Studies* 6 (3): 1–27. Specifies the conditions under which speculation can be stabilizing.

Kemp, M. C. 1963. "Speculation, Profitability, and Price Stability." *Review of Economics and Statistics* 45: 185–89. Provides an early criticism of Friedman's argument that profitable speculation must be stabilizing.

Keynes, J. M. 1936. *The General Theory of Employment, Interest, and Money*. Reprint, 1964. New York: Harcourt Brace Jovanovich. Keynes's major theoretical work where he lays out his theory of effective demand.

MacDonald, R. 2000. "Expectations Formation and Risk in Three Financial Markets." *Journal of Economic Surveys* 14 (1): 70–100. An overview of the empirical literature on expectations formation in financial markets.

Scharfstein, D., and J. Stein. 1990. "Herd Behavior and Investment." *American Economic Review* 80 (3): 465–89. Examining the conditions under which herd behavior occurs in financial markets, the paper shows why it can be rational for some traders to mimic other traders rather than relying on substantive private information.

Shleifer, A., and L. Summers. 1990. "The Noise Trader Approach to Finance." *Journal of Economic Perspectives* 4

(2): 19–33. Argues that riskless arbitrage is severely limited not only in relation to the prices of shares or bonds as a whole but also in relation to the prices of individual assets.

Shleifer, A., and R. Vishny. 1997. "The Limits of Arbitrage." *Journal of Finance* 52 (1): 35–55. Discusses how anomalies in financial markets can appear and why arbitrage would fail to eliminate them.

KORKUT A. ERTURK

■ spillovers

In international finance, spillovers are phenomena in which a change in asset price (or asset price volatility) in one country leads to a change in asset price (or asset price volatility) in another country. Interest in this topic resulted from the simultaneous declines in global equity markets during the 1987 stock market crash and the high comovement of asset returns in many countries during the financial crises in the late 1990s. This topic is crucial for our understanding of how information, often proxied by changes in asset price or volatility, in one market transmits to another market. In addition, the effect of foreign asset prices on domestic asset prices has implications for how we should value domestic assets and how we should allocate wealth across different countries.

Empirical Studies Most studies generally examine the spillover effect from three financial centers—the United States, the United Kingdom, and Japan—to other international financial markets, and, because of data availability, they focus mainly on equity markets. Existing studies use different sample periods, data frequencies, and econometric methods. The standard methods used to measure the spillover effect can be divided into two groups. The first group measures the spillover effect on changes in asset price (asset return). The second group measures the spillover effect on asset return volatility. This method examines the influence of foreign asset return volatility on domestic asset return volatility. Because the direction of the effect of foreign return on domestic return can vary over time, it is easier to measure the volatility spillover effect as changes in asset price

(independent of direction), which are always reflected in increases in asset return volatility; thus, the effect is always positive. The volatility spillover effect can give us only an indirect measure of asset price linkages, however.

These studies' general findings are: (1) return and volatility spillovers are present among major markets; (2) the majority of the spillover effect appears to originate from the United States to other foreign financial markets; (3) when volatility is high, the spillover effect in returns tends to be higher—returns are more correlated; and (4) the spillover effect on volatility is asymmetric, with the spillover effect from bad news (negative unexpected return) having larger effects than that from good news (positive unexpected return) (see Gagnon and Karolyi 2006).

Sources of Spillovers Spillovers have several possible sources. First, economic linkages between countries may lead to spillovers. A common shock to global economic fundamentals may lead to an observed spillover effect. For example, a surprise change in U.S. monetary policy stance may affect foreign asset prices simultaneously, which may generate the impression of a spillover effect. Alternatively, a change in an asset price in one country may affect another country's economic fundamentals. For example, a devaluation of one country's exchange rate may affect other countries' international trade, either directly or indirectly, which may in turn affect their asset prices. By and large, the empirical evidence supporting observable macroeconomic linkages as a primary source of spillovers is very weak.

Second, information asymmetry may lead to transmission of country-specific shocks from one country to another. This explanation was popularized following the stock market crash in 1987. This event not only caught market participants by surprise, but it was also hard to attribute the movements to economic fundamental linkages. The economists King and Wadhwani (1990) propose an information-based model in which price changes in one market depend on price changes in other markets and a domestic investor who observes a price change in a foreign market cannot distinguish between changes driven by economic fundamentals and those driven by foreign country–specific shocks (which should not have any influence on domestic asset prices). The implication of the model is that a price change attributable to foreign-specific shocks can lead to price changes in other countries, which in turn will increase volatility in foreign countries and increase the correlation between the two markets. The term for this channel of spillover with no economic fundamental link is *market contagion*.

Third, trading behavior may generate spillover effects. Following the high correlation among global financial markets during the financial crises in the late 1990s and the increase in global cross-border financial investments, global institutional investors have garnered attention as another source of spillover effects. Similar to the second source of spillovers, this source does not rely on economic fundamental linkages among countries. The spillover effect that occurs during financial crises is often referred to as *contagion*. Spillovers can occur because investors need to liquidate some of their assets when they lose money (Kyle and Xiong 2001) or face liquidity constraints (Yuan 2005), and they choose to sell assets in different countries simultaneously. Alternatively, spillovers may be the outcome of cross-market rebalancing (Kodres and Pritsker 2002). *Cross-market rebalancing* refers to investor behavior in which investors respond to changes in asset price in one country by optimally adjusting their asset holdings in other countries.

Although studies agree on the general empirical features of spillovers, their source is still a challenging research topic. Most studies find little evidence to support the role of economic linkages in explaining spillovers, and only a few studies find evidence to support the role of information asymmetry and trading behaviors in explaining spillovers. The lack of consensus on explanations for spillovers reflects the difficulty of measuring their source (e.g., information asymmetry or investors' trading behaviors). Future researchers will want to use new data and new econometric techniques to reexamine current explanations of spillovers before exploring new hypotheses.

See also asymmetric information; banking crisis; capital flows to developing countries; contagion; currency crisis; financial crisis; international liquidity

FURTHER READING

Gagnon, Louis, and G. Andrew Karolyi. 2006. "Price and Volatility Transmission across Borders." *Financial Markets, Institutions, and Instruments* 15 (3): 107–58. A review of the research on the dynamics of asset price and volatility spillovers across international financial markets.

King, Mervyn A., and Sushil Wadhwani. 1990. "Transmission of Volatility between Stock Markets." *Review of Financial Studies* 3 (1): 5–33. A classic, often-cited reference to the study of volatility spillovers.

Kodres, Laura E., and Matthew Pritsker. 2002. "A Rational Expectations Model of Financial Contagion." *Journal of Finance* 57 (2): 769–99. A theoretical model that demonstrates the role of investors' optimal trading strategies in generating return comovements among assets not sharing any common economic fundamentals.

Kyle, Albert S., and Wei Xiong. 2001. "Contagion as a Wealth Effect." *Journal of Finance* 56 (4): 1401–40. A theoretical model that demonstrates the role of investors' wealth constraints in generating return comovements among assets not sharing any common economic fundamentals.

Yuan, Kathy. 2005. "Asymmetric Price Movements and Borrowing Constraints: A Rational Expectations Equilibrium Model of Crises, Contagion, and Confusion." *Journal of Finance* 60 (1): 379–411. A theoretical model that demonstrates the role of investors' liquidity constraints in generating return comovements among assets not sharing any common economic fundamentals.

JON WONGSWAN

■ steel

Steel, one the most basic industrial commodities, has been the subject of numerous international trade disputes and policy interventions throughout the 20th and early 21st centuries. Because steel is a crucial part of many other manufactured products and of construction activity, policymakers often consider it to be a key sector for a nation's industrial development. Public support for steel industries has also responded to the recognition that jobs at steel plants usually offer higher-than-average wages, or what economists call "labor rents" (Scott and Blecker 1997). However, many economists consider the efforts of governments to protect or subsidize their national steel industries to be examples of inefficient, socially costly interventions that benefit small groups of workers and firms at the expense of consumers (see de Melo and Tarr 1993).

Technology, Costs, and the Location of Production Steel is a metal alloy of iron, carbon, and other minerals that has tremendous strength and ductility and is thus useful for a wide range of purposes from bridges and skyscrapers to motor vehicles and oil pipelines. Steel production developed during the industrial revolution of the 19th century in response to the discovery that pure iron was too brittle to be reliable for railroad tracks, steam engines, and other applications subject to stresses of heat and pressure. Steel is not a single product; the term encompasses a variety of specific types (for example, rust-resistant galvanized products and stainless steel for decorative uses).

Traditionally, basic steel production takes place in a two-step or "integrated" process. In the first step, iron ore is reduced to molten ("pig") iron in a blast furnace, using coke made from coal as fuel; in the second step, the molten iron is transformed into "crude" or "raw" steel in a steel-making furnace. After crude steel is produced, it is then subject to further casting, rolling, coating, and shaping operations to transform it into useful forms, such as sheets, girders, pipes, plates, tin-coated cans, and wire rods.

The progression from the Bessemer and Thomas steel furnaces of the 19th century to the open-hearth furnace and later the basic oxygen furnace in the 20th century is considered one of the classical examples of process-oriented technological change. In the second half of the 20th century, another important innovation was the electric arc furnace, which produces crude steel from "scrap" (recycled steel) in a one-step process with little or no iron ore and lower capital costs. By 2006, electric furnaces accounted for 57 percent of U.S. production and 32 percent of global production.

Originally, steel mills had to be located near sources of their principal raw materials, iron ore and coking coal, due to high transportation costs. However, advances in ocean shipping in the 20th century revolutionized the location of integrated steel production, allowing resource-poor countries such as Japan to produce steel efficiently using imported raw materials, provided that their steel mills were located near seaports. In addition, "minimills" that use the electric furnace technology can be located farther from resource deposits or seaports and closer to downstream users. These technological developments have led to greater geographical dispersion of steel production both internationally and regionally within nations.

It is often popular in the United States to blame losses of steel jobs on import competition. Although imports have adversely affected steel employment in some short-run situations, by far the main causes of decreased U.S. steel employment in the long run have been the dramatic increase in labor productivity in the industry and the slow growth of domestic steel demand (Grossman 1986). In 1955, the U.S. steel industry employed 707,000 people to make 77 million metric tons of shipments, while 50 years later in 2005 the industry needed only 122,000 employees to produce 95 million metric tons. Using a more refined measure that controls for product composition, the U.S. Bureau of Labor Statistics index of labor productivity in steel production shows a fourfold increase between 1950 and 2000.

Historically, steel industries generated large amounts of employment and were bastions of strong labor unions that won high wages and benefits for their members. The enormous shrinkage in U.S. steel employment in the late 20th century led to the problem of high "legacy costs" of pensions and benefits for retired steelworkers at some large U.S. steel corporations in the 1990s; the U.S. government addressed this problem by having the Pension Benefit Guarantee Corporation take over some of those obligations. However, labor costs of currently employed workers are now a relatively small portion of variable costs in the most modern steel mills—where production is so automated that a small number of skilled workers can operate the equipment using computerized controls—and many minimill firms are nonunion.

Steel production was originally concentrated in the technologically leading nations, led by Britain and followed by the United States, Germany, and other European nations, in the late 19th and early 20th centuries. As the technology matured during the 20th century, steel production spread to Japan, the Soviet Union, China, and the major developing nations (especially India, Brazil, South Korea, Turkey, Taiwan, and Mexico). As of 1965, the United States and Soviet Union were the two largest producers of crude steel, with 26 percent and 20 percent of total world output, respectively. By 2006, China had become the world's largest producer, accounting for 34 percent of global production; Japan and the United States ranked second and third at 9 percent and 8 percent, respectively.

The Role of Trade Policies Trade and industrial policies have long been key determinants of the location of steel production. In the late 19th and early 20th centuries, the United States, Germany, and other Western countries used tariffs to protect their "infant" steel industries, a policy that was followed later in the 20th century by Japan, India, Brazil, South Korea, and many others. Communist countries such as the former Soviet Union and the pre-reform People's Republic of China created steel industries based on state-owned enterprises managed through central planning. Steel was one of the most favored industries under "import substitution" policies in many developing nations between (roughly) the 1940s and 1970s and subsequently has been a frequent target of export-promotion efforts in many of these same nations.

Curiously, out of the five largest exporters of steel as of 2005, two countries had some of the most advanced steelmaking facilities in the world (Japan and Germany), while two others had some of the most technologically backward facilities (Russia and Ukraine, which were still using open-hearth furnaces for significant portions of their output); China, the third largest exporter, had a mix of older and newer steelmaking plants. As would be expected, Japan and Germany export relatively more specialty and high value-added steels, while Russia and Ukraine export mostly basic, commodity-grade products, and China is in the process of upgrading its exports.

Given that steelmaking technology is highly mobile and the main inputs (both raw materials and machinery) can be imported, some economists argue that there are no inherent (resource-based) "comparative advantages" in steel today and that competitive industries can be created in a wide range of countries. This view has been used (for example, by Howell et al. 1988) to justify government intervention to protect the U.S. industry against "unfair" competition from other countries that subsidize or protect their industries, or that gain artificial advantages through means such as undervalued currencies. Some East Asian countries have been accused of having "structural impediments" to steel trade because their vertically integrated industrial groups (*keiretsu* in Japan, *chaebol* in Korea) allegedly do not buy steel from outside companies. Other economists counter that steel exports are still explained by comparative advantage, because steel is exported by the countries that can make it relatively cheaper than other products, compared with other countries, regardless of the source of that relative cost advantage. In this latter view, efforts to protect domestic steel industries merely make steel more expensive for domestic consumers and downstream industries.

The nature of steel production has made the industry the subject of many international trade disputes. Steel production, especially in integrated mills, is capital intensive and has large economies of scale, which create a tendency toward the existence of excess capacity (except in times of strong demand). As a result, steel producers often have incentives to export as much as possible in order to bolster capacity utilization, which leads to accusations of "dumping" if the products are sold at lower prices in foreign markets. At the same time, import-competing steel producers also have incentives to maintain high rates of capacity utilization and are therefore likely to seek trade protection if they lose customers to imports.

When one adds in the popular view of steel as a "strategic" product for reasons of both economic development and national security, as well as union support for high-wage jobs, one has an industry in which policy intervention has generally been the norm rather than the exception.

Since World War II, multilateral trade liberalization under the General Agreement on Tariffs and Trade and subsequently the World Trade Organization (WTO) has greatly reduced or, for some products, completely eliminated the ordinary tariffs that formerly were used to protect national steel industries. Nevertheless many steel products continue to receive "administered" or "contingent" protection, mainly through the use of anti-dumping and countervailing duties.

The United States has adopted a variety of "trade remedies" for steel producers since imports achieved significant levels in the 1960s, including voluntary export restraints (VERs) in 1969–74, trigger prices (import price floors) in 1978–79, more VERs in 1982–91, and a safeguard tariff in 2002–3. In addition, many U.S. imports of particular steel products from specific countries have been subject to anti-dumping or countervailing duties, especially since the last VERs expired in 1992. Iron and steel mill products (excluding castings) accounted for 44 percent of all U.S. anti-dumping and countervailing duty orders in effect as of 2006. In spite of these trade barriers, however, the United States remained by far the largest net importer of steel as of 2005.

The United States is far from alone in its use of trade protection for its steel industry. The European Union (EU), Canada, and other industrialized countries have also imposed anti-dumping duties on specific steel imports, especially from newly industrializing countries and transition economies, and the latter groups of countries have begun to impose anti-dumping duties of their own.

An important change in recent decades is the increase in "vertical" trade in steel—that is, importing intermediate steel products to manufacture finished or semifinished products. For example, "slabs" of crude steel can be imported for flat-rolling into steel sheet, or steel sheet can be imported for the production of pipe and tube products. This change may alter the political economy of steel trade policy, since companies that rely heavily on such imports may not support protection of the intermediate products they import even though they may still seek protection for their own finished goods.

Changing Competitive Conditions In roughly the first six decades of the 20th century (and longer in some developing countries), the combination of large-scale economies, high transportation costs, and significant tariff barriers led to the creation of national steel industries that were relatively closed to international trade and dominated by small numbers of large firms. Steel companies were frequently cited as exemplars of firms that practiced collusion, price leadership, administered pricing, cartels, or other forms of oligopolistic behavior. Large oligopolistic steel firms in some countries were accused of being slow to adopt new technologies such as the oxygen furnace in the 1960s.

Since the 1960s, several of the structural changes referred to earlier have led to a more competitive market structure for most countries' steel industries (Barnett and Schorsch 1983; Blecker 1989). Mini-mills took advantage of lower unit costs to compete effectively with the older, integrated firms. Trade liberalization and reduced transportation costs, along with the diffusion of steelmaking technology to less-developed countries, led to increased international competition. As a result, basic steel products became "commodities" in the sense that their prices were determined by global supply and demand conditions, with little or no oligopoly power for even the largest national firms in most product lines (except where those firms enjoyed continued protection).

In Europe, the steel industry was at the center of efforts to promote regional integration in the post–World War II period. The European Coal and Steel Community (ECSC), founded in 1951, combined six major countries in an effort to rationalize their steel industries and make them more competitive while ameliorating the social costs of adjustment. The ECSC was an important forerunner of the European Economic Community and later the EU. As a result of these integration efforts, European steel firms began to consolidate on a multinational basis somewhat earlier than steel firms in other regions. However, joint ventures and foreign direct investment also increased in other areas of the world steel industry toward the end of the 20th century.

By the early 2000s, the steel industry was beginning to reconsolidate on a global scale. Through mergers and acquisitions, a number of large multinational corporations were formed with steel operations located across Europe, Asia, and the Americas. As of 2007, the world's largest steel company was ArcelorMittal, which had plants in 27 countries, employed 320,000 workers, and produced nearly 10 percent of total world steel output. Headquartered in London and Luxembourg, ArcelorMittal was formed by the merger of two former companies, both of which had grown through previous mergers and acquisitions, and one of which was founded by an Indian-born entrepreneur (Lakshmi Mittal).

In the late 1990s, the global steel market was afflicted by excess supply conditions, as a number of transition economies (led by China, Russia, and Ukraine) increased the world supply of steel at the same time as international demand conditions weakened due to financial crises in East Asia and elsewhere. This resulted in increased exports, falling prices, lower profits, and increased trade tensions. The U.S. safeguard tariffs of 2002–3 were a lagged response to this crisis, adopted after the recession of 2001 and the appreciation of the U.S. dollar further weakened the U.S. industry, and when a new president (George W. Bush) was more willing to support a safeguard remedy than his predecessor (Bill Clinton) (see Blecker 2008). Ultimately, these tariffs were ruled illegal by the WTO in 2003, partly because they were enacted so long after U.S. steel imports peaked in 1998. Liebman (2006) found that the safeguard tariffs, which covered only about one-third of U.S. steel imports, had little effect on domestic prices.

In a stunning reversal, global demand for steel began to outstrip global supply in 2004, leading to sharp price increases that restored industry profitability worldwide for the next few years. This reversal was due partly to an enormous increase in demand by China, where steel consumption nearly tripled between 2000 and 2006. However, steel producers around the world responded to the higher prices by building new capacity, and as a result the global industry is likely to experience more boom-bust cycles in the future.

In spite of its reputation as an "old" or "smokestack" industrial product, steel remains an important internationally traded commodity. World steel production grew by about 50 percent from 2000 to 2006, and almost 40 percent of global steel production is exported. Therefore, the global steel industry is likely to remain at the center of trade policy disputes for the foreseeable future.

See also anti-dumping; countervailing duties; European Union; export promotion; foreign direct investment and international technology transfer; import substitution industrialization; infant industry argument; joint ventures; mergers and acquisitions; political economy of trade policy; safeguards; shipping; technological progress in open economies; transition economies; World Trade Organization

FURTHER READING

Barnett, Donald F., and Louis Schorsch. 1983. *Steel: Upheaval in a Basic Industry.* Cambridge, MA: Ballinger. A comprehensive account of international and technological factors in the evolution of the U.S. and global steel industries.

Blecker, Robert A. 1989. "Markup Pricing, Import Competition, and the Decline of the American Steel Industry." *Journal of Post Keynesian Economics* 12 (1): 70–87. An econometric analysis of how import competition reduced oligopoly power in the U.S. steel industry.

———. 2008. "U.S. Steel Import Tariffs: The Politics of Global Markets." In *Contemporary Cases in U.S. Foreign Policy: From Terrorism to Trade*, edited by Ralph G. Carter. 3d ed. Washington, DC: Congressional Quarterly Press, 249–80. An examination of the political economy of the U.S. decision to impose safeguard tariffs in 2002–3.

Cockerill, Anthony, and Aubrey Silberston. 1974. *The Steel Industry: International Comparisons of Industrial Structure and Performance.* London: Cambridge University Press. A definitive study of scale economies and production costs.

de Melo, Jaime, and David Tarr. 1993. "Industrial Policy in the Presence of Wage Distortions: The Case of the U.S. Auto and Steel Industries." *International Economic Review* 34 (4): 833–51. A study of the welfare effects of steel protection using a computable general equilibrium model.

Grossman, Gene M. 1986. "Imports as a Cause of Injury: The Case of the U.S. Steel Industry." *Journal of International Economics* 20 (3/4): 201–23. An econometric study that pioneered the use of a reduced form model to estimate the causes of declining steel employment.

Howell, Thomas R., William A. Noellert, Jesse G. Kreier, and Alan Wm. Wolff. 1988. *Steel and the State: Government Intervention and the Steel Crisis.* Boulder, CO: Westview. A study of government efforts to promote national steel industries in numerous countries around the world.

International Iron and Steel Institute (IISI). 2007. *World Steel in Figures 2007.* Brussels: IISI. www.worldsteel.org. The standard statistical reference on the global steel industry (issued annually).

Liebman, Benjamin H. 2006. "Safeguards, China, and the Price of Steel." *Review of World Economics* 142 (2): 354–73. An econometric study of the effects of safeguard tariffs and other factors on steel prices in the early 2000s.

Scott, Robert E., and Robert A. Blecker. 1997. "Labour Rents, Adjustment Costs, and the Cost of U.S. Steel Restraints in the 1980s." *International Review of Applied Economics* 11 (3): 399–419. Estimates of the social costs and benefits of alternative U.S. steel trade policies.

ROBERT A. BLECKER

■ sterilization

Sterilization is the process by which monetary authorities ensure that foreign exchange interventions do not affect the domestic monetary base, which is one component of the overall money supply. Many governments try to influence the value of their currency on the foreign exchange market by selling or purchasing domestic currency in exchange for a foreign currency. If the monetary authority sells domestic currency that was not previously in circulation, the intervention will expand the domestic money base. Likewise, if the monetary authority purchases more of its domestic currency and takes the receipts out of circulation, the intervention will have a contractionary effect on the domestic money base.

Sterilized intervention operations involve domestic asset transactions that restore the monetary base to its original size. For example, a nonsterilized sale of foreign currency on the open market would result in a reduction in the central bank's net foreign assets (NFA) and a contraction of the domestic monetary base (MB). This operation can be sterilized, or neutralized, by an offsetting purchase of domestic currency that increases the central bank's net domestic assets (NDA) and returns the monetary base to its original level.

In theory the process of sterilization is quite straightforward, but in practice it may be difficult for the monetary authority to fully offset the effects of a change in net foreign assets. In countries with less-developed financial markets the ability to sterilize may be constrained by the size and depth of the domestic bond market. Additionally, monetary authorities may not be able to sterilize intervention operations in fixed exchange rate systems with some degree of capital mobility (Obstfeld 1982). For example, sales of domestic-currency assets will attract a capital inflow, forcing the authorities to buy more foreign assets in order to maintain the fixed value of the currency, thereby offsetting any attempt to sterilize the original open-market asset sale.

Costs of Sterilization Sterilization may also come at a fiscal cost. Governments attempting to lower or maintain the value of their domestic currency in the face of market pressure for a domestic currency appreciation will generally be purchasing relatively low-yield foreign assets while selling relatively high-yield domestic assets. The fiscal burden of sterilization will depend on the interest differential between the domestic and foreign assets. Further, the international accumulation that results from these sorts of sterilization operations will expose the government to foreign exchange risk. If the domestic currency eventually appreciates relative to the foreign currency denominations in a country's reserves, the country will experience a capital loss. On the other hand, governments attempting to prevent a depreciation of their domestic currency will generally be selling foreign assets and purchasing domestic assets. The constraint in this case will be the size of the country's foreign reserves.

The Efficacy of Sterilized Intervention Operations In most monetary and asset-pricing models of exchange rate determination, nonsterilized intervention will affect the exchange rate in proportion to the change in the relative supplies of domestic and foreign money, just as any other form of monetary policy does. The effectiveness of sterilized intervention operations in standard models depends on two additional assumptions: that domestic and foreign bonds are outside assets (i.e., the public considers these bonds as net wealth) and that they are imperfect substitutes (meaning that the currency denomination of the bonds matters to investors). Sterilized intervention can also influence the exchange rate in models where the government is assumed to have more information about relevant economic fundamentals (such as future money and income differentials) than the market and can credibly convey that information using intervention operations.

Governments generally finance their spending by raising taxes or borrowing by issuing bonds. If they issue bonds, the public has more money to spend. Further, if the public ignores the fact that taxes will need to be raised in the future to pay off the bonds, these bonds can be considered "outside assets" and are additions to net wealth. On the other hand, if the public recognizes that they (or future generations) will have to pay higher taxes in the future and therefore save the extra money in order to pay the future tax, bonds are "inside assets" and cannot be considered net wealth. The extra saving by the public would exactly offset the extra spending by the government, so overall demand would remain unchanged. This view of the implications of bond financing is termed Ricardian equivalence. Sterilized intervention operations in such a world are simply swaps in the currency composition of inside assets, and these should have no effect on the foreign exchange market equilibrium.

Even if it is granted that government bonds are outside assets, sterilized intervention will have no effect on the exchange rate if domestic and foreign bonds are perfect substitutes. If investors are completely indifferent between holding domestic and foreign bonds, then changes in their relative supply should have no effect. If bonds are not perfect substitutes, however, even if they are close substitutes, then changes in bond supplies matter, so changes in their relative supply can influence the exchange rate through the portfolio-balance channel.

In portfolio-balance models of exchange rate determination, investors diversify their holdings among domestic and foreign bonds as a function of both expected returns and the variance in returns. By changing their relative supply, sterilized intervention operations alter the risk characteristics of foreign and domestic bonds in the market portfolio, and thus alter the equilibrium exchange rate. For example, a sterilized sale of domestic-currency-denominated bonds may increase their relative riskiness because investors will be more vulnerable to unexpected changes in the value of the domestic currency. Investors will require a higher expected return on domestic bonds to hold willingly the larger outstanding stock, leading to a depreciation of the domestic currency.

Finally, even for those who hold either to the Ricardian equivalence or to the assumption that foreign and domestic bonds are perfect substitutes, sterilized intervention can have an effect on exchange rates if it provides the market relevant information that was previously not known or not fully incorporated in the current exchange rate. The information channel for sterilized intervention is controversial. It relies on the existence of an asymmetry between what is known by the government and what is known by market participants. In order for sterilized intervention operations to influence exchange rates via the information channel, the government must both have inside information and have the incentive to reveal the information truthfully by way of their operations in the foreign exchange market. Indeed, it has been suggested that sterilized intervention may be used by governments to " buy credibility" for their future policy intentions (Mussa 1981). If market participants believe the signals provided by sterilized intervention, they will influence exchange rates by betting with the operation.

The information channel for sterilized intervention need not exclusively serve to convey future policy intentions. For instance, intervention helps to convey information by the monetary authorities to the market in circumstances when such information might not be made directly available for security or other reasons (Friedman 1953). Intervention signals may also alter the market's expectations, especially when market participants are heterogeneous and there are signs of a bubble developing (Kenen 1987). As long as the information signaled through sterilized intervention policy is relevant and credible, it can potentially influence the exchange rate. If the information revealed involves the monetary authority's own future policy intentions, however, then sterilized intervention should not be considered an additional independent policy tool. The sterilized intervention operation may alter the timing or magnitude of the impact of monetary or fiscal policy on the exchange rate, but its effectiveness is not independent of those policies.

Empirical Evidence Is there empirical evidence that sterilized intervention operations affect exchange rates? In 1982 the Group of Seven (G7) economic summit at Versailles commissioned a comprehensive study of intervention policy in order to answer the question. The G7 working group report, completed in 1983, draws no explicit conclusions but suggests that the effects of sterilized interventions on the exchange rate were small and transitory at most over the period 1973–81 (Jurgensen 1983). Subsequent studies of G3 intervention policy suggest that more recent operations may have been more effective (Dominguez 1990, 2003, 2006; Dominguez and Frankel 1993a, 1993b; Sarno and Taylor 2001).

An indirect test of the efficacy of sterilized intervention involves examining whether the assumptions underlying the portfolio-balance channel are satisfied in the data. In particular, one such test examines whether foreign and domestic bonds are imperfect substitutes in investors' portfolios. If investors are indifferent between holding domestic assets and foreign assets, then once we take into account both the current and expected exchange rate, there should be no return differential (or risk premium) between the two. This hypothesis is commonly referred to in the literature as the uncovered interest parity condition. Most empirical tests of uncovered interest parity find that foreign and domestic bonds are not perfect substitutes.

The failure of uncovered interest parity is a necessary but not a sufficient condition for sterilized intervention to affect the exchange rate through the portfolio-balance channel. There must be a stable relationship between government debt supplies and the return differential between domestic and foreign bonds, and empirical studies have had mixed success relating the two. Studies that include government debt and other outside assets, which usually dwarf foreign exchange intervention in magnitude, in the definition of government debt supplies reject the hypothesis that the two are related. Empirical studies using daily (and intradaily) intervention data, which are able to focus exclusively on short-term changes in asset supplies through foreign exchange intervention, generally find evidence to support the hypothesis that sterilized intervention operations systematically influence return differentials (Dominguez 1990, 2003, 2006; Dominguez and Frankel 1993a, 1993b).

In order for the information channel to be operative, sterilized intervention operations must be observed by market participants. If only for this reason, it is puzzling that more governments do not disclose data on their intervention operations. Comparisons of actual intervention data with newswire reports of intervention suggest that G3 operations are generally reported in the financial media. Empirical tests that distinguish interventions that are reported (and therefore are capable of serving as signals) from those that remain secret generally find that it is mainly reported interventions that significantly influence exchange rates, providing indirect evidence for the signaling channel. The literature, however, has been less successful at finding a systematic link between reported interventions and future fundamentals (the information that is supposedly being conveyed by the government), making it difficult to find direct evidence for signaling (Sarno and Taylor 2001).

Theory suggests that sterilized intervention operations can potentially provide governments an additional policy tool with which to attain internal and external balance. Practice suggests that governments in both fixed and flexible exchange rate systems have frequently resorted to sterilized intervention policy. Empirical studies of the efficacy of these operations suggest that intervention in developed countries has often been successful, though whether sterilized intervention can serve as a fully independent policy tool remains controversial. The efficacy of sterilized intervention policies in developing countries has been less widely studied, in large part because governments have been reluctant to provide data on their operations. Developing countries are also not always able to fully sterilize their operations due to their illiquid domestic bond markets and the potentially high fiscal costs of foreign reserve accumulation.

See also asymmetric information; balance of payments; equilibrium exchange rate; exchange rate regimes; exchange rate volatility; foreign exchange intervention; interest parity conditions; international reserves; money supply; purchasing power parity; real exchange rate; twin deficits

FURTHER READING

Dominguez, Kathryn M. 1990. "Market Responses to Coordinated Central Bank Intervention." *Carnegie-Rochester Series on Public Policy* 32: 121–64. One of the first empirical studies of the efficacy of the intervention signaling channel.

———. 2003. "Foreign Exchange Intervention: Did it Work in the 1990s?" In *Dollar Overvaluation and the World Economy*, edited by Fred Bergsten and John Williamson. Special Report 15. Institute for International Economics. Washington, DC: IIE, 217–45. Updates the empirical work in Dominguez and Frankel (1993b) through 2002.

———. 2006. "When Do Central Bank Interventions Influence Intra-Daily and Longer-Term Exchange Rate Movements?" *Journal of International Money and Finance* 25: 1051–71. Examines both market micro-structure and longer-term effects of G3 intervention operations since 1989.

Dominguez, Kathryn M., and Jeffrey Frankel. 1993a. "Does Foreign Exchange Intervention Matter? The Portfolio Effect." *American Economic Review* 83, 1356–69. The first study to challenge the conventional wisdom exposed in the Jurgensen report that the portfolio-balance effect is economically unimportant.

———. 1993b. *Does Foreign Exchange Intervention Work?* Washington, DC: Institute for International Economics. A comprehensive survey of theory and experience regarding exchange-market intervention.

Friedman, Milton. 1953. "The Case for Flexible Exchange Rates." In *Essays in Positive Economics*, edited by Milton Friedman. Chicago: University of Chicago Press, 157–203. The classic reference for arguments on why flexible exchange rate regimes are better than fixed regimes.

Jurgensen, Philippe. 1983. "Report of the Working Group on Exchange Market Intervention [Jurgensen Report]." Washington, DC: U.S. Treasury Department. Suggests that the influence of intervention on exchange rates through the portfolio-balance channel is economically unimportant.

Kenen, Peter. 1987. "Exchange Rate Management: What Role for Intervention?" *American Economic Review* 77 (2): 194–99. Describes three ways (by brute force, by altering asset market equilibrium, or by altering expectations) that intervention operations can be used by governments to manage exchange rates.

Mussa, Michael. 1981. "The Role of Official Intervention." Group of Thirty Occasional Papers No. 6. New York: Group of Thirty. Provides one of the first informal expositions of the signaling hypothesis.

Obstfeld, Maurice. 1982. "Can We Sterilize? Theory and Evidence." *American Economic Review* 72 (2): 45–50. Reviews the empirical and theoretical scope of sterilization in the foreign exchange market.

Sarno, Lucio, and Mark P. Taylor. 2001. "Official Intervention in the Foreign Exchange Market: Is It Effective and, If So, How Does It Work?" *Journal of Economic Literature* 39: 839–68. An excellent survey of recent research on exchange rate intervention policy.

KATHRYN M. E. DOMINGUEZ

■ stock versus flow of foreign direct investment

See foreign direct investment (FDI)

■ Stolper-Samuelson theorem

See Heckscher-Ohlin model

■ strategic trade theory

See New Trade Theory

■ structural adjustment

Since the 1980s, the expression *structural adjustment* (SA) has been used to denote programs of policy reforms in developing countries undertaken with financial support from the World Bank. Structural adjustment programs (SAPs) would normally consist of two components: macroeconomic stabilization and microeconomic, supply-side reforms. The World Bank *Operational Manual* defines structural adjustment lending (SAL) as "non-project lending to support programs of policy and institutional change necessary to modify the structure of an economy so that it can maintain both its growth rate and the viability of its balance of payments in the medium term" (*Operational Manual*, Statement No. 3.58, Annex II, November 1982).

Through SAL the World Bank financed more than 650 reform programs. SAL represented about one-quarter of its total commitments from the mid-1980s to the late 1990s, when it increased to more than 50 percent as a response to the financial crises in East Asia and remained at about one-third thereafter. Sub-Saharan Africa accounts for 34 percent of adjustment operations and 16 percent of commitments. The Latin American and Caribbean region accounts for 24 percent of adjustment operations and, with 34 percent of lending commitments, is the largest recipient of SAL, followed by Europe and Central Asia with 24 percent; East Asia and the Pacific received 15 percent of SAL, South Asia 6 percent, and the Middle East and North Africa 5 per-

cent. SA shaped the strategy of the World Bank for nearly two decades and dominated policymaking in the developing world. During this period, almost all major programs of policy reforms were supported by SALs from the World Bank.

The bank started SAL in 1980 following serious balance of payments difficulties experienced in some of its member countries as a result of the second oil price shock in 1979. Many of these countries also had fiscal deficits and often high inflation, and the root of the external deficits was identified as excessive aggregate demand. In these circumstances, adjustment requires macroeconomic stabilization in order to reduce domestic demand to a level that is consistent with the level of external resources available to the country.

Since restrictive monetary and fiscal policies that cut demand (such as tax increases, spending cuts, and interest rate increases) also cause unemployment, they are normally accompanied by a currency devaluation that, by lowering the relative price of domestic goods with respect to foreign goods, leads to an increase in the foreign demand for domestic goods and an increase in the supply of exportable and import-substitute goods, and minimizes the employment costs of stabilization. Measures to restrain wages complement exchange rate policy to ensure that the competitive effect of nominal devaluation is not offset by wage inflation.

Macroeconomic stabilization alone may not give rise to faster growth in the future. In order to achieve this, a second type of adjustment is required, namely SA, which consists of microeconomic and institutional reforms designed to strengthen the supply response of the economy by letting the market determine the efficient allocation of resources. A central aspect of SA was market liberalization and deregulation along several dimensions, potentially including removal of price controls, deregulation of the domestic goods market, liberalization of the trade regime, deregulation of the domestic financial market, liberalization of the capital market—especially the removal of barriers to foreign direct investment—and deregulation of the labor market. A second component involved reform of public sector management, including fiscal reform, restructuring and privatization of state-owned enterprises, and restructuring of government spending. A final component consisted of reforms to create and strengthen institutions that would support stabilization and SA, such as institutions for banking supervision and the enforcement of property rights, an independent judiciary, and an independent central bank. Many economists believed that these microeconomic reforms would shift the economy to a sustainable path of higher economic growth.

The Rise of Structural Adjustment Lending
Several factors contributed to the establishment of SAL. One was the nature of the crisis that was affecting developing countries. Severe balance of payments deficits required faster and larger disbursements than were possible under the standard World Bank approach of project-based lending, in which disbursements are typically slow in the first two years. By contrast, SALs typically disburse within 18 months.

A second factor was the realization within the World Bank that project success was crucially dependent on the state of the broader economic environment. This implied, first, that the World Bank could no longer encourage the pursuit of economic growth without regard for macroeconomic stability, which thus became a priority over growth and was seen as the necessary foundation for sustainable growth. A second implication is that, as the development strategies of many developing countries were now being seen as highly distorted, the World Bank had to turn its attention to removing microeconomic distortions.

SA embodies the drastically new viewpoint that development is hampered not so much by capital shortage as by domestic economic policies that impede the operation of market forces. This new vision was influenced by neoliberal political economy theories that centered on the capture of the state by powerful pressure groups. The state came to be seen as the primary cause of the distortion of incentives, leading to misallocation of resources and economic failure. Free markets work well, and even where there are externalities and market failures, the state does not have the willingness or indeed the capacity to lead to a better outcome than the market would. This is a complete overturning of the view prevailing until the 1970s, according to which state intervention was necessary in order to correct distortions and facilitate structural transformation in developing countries, where free markets do not work well. In this older view, the state was a benevolent agent for development. By contrast, SA—through liberalization, deregulation, and privatization—aims to minimize state intervention in the economy and liberalize prices so that they can reach equilibrium levels.

Abandoning structuralist doctrines, which emphasize the existence of special characteristics in developing countries' economic and social structures and were the mainstream in development thinking in the 1960s and 1970s, the World Bank—through SA—presents a model for all countries to follow, irrespective of their development stage. Indeed SAPs have been characterized by a remarkable degree of uniformity.

With the outbreak of the debt crisis in the 1980s, the main objective of SAL was to prevent an international banking crisis by allowing debt restructuring and the continuation (or the resumption) of interest payments. The objective of poverty reduction—one of the bank's priorities since the late 1960s—was downgraded. Partly this was also a reflection of the negative assessment within the World Bank of the strategy pursued until then of attacking poverty directly. In addition, this critical assessment led to the view that the best way to reduce poverty is through the promotion of economic growth (the so-called trickle-down doctrine). Thus the policies of SA, which are designed to stimulate higher sustainable growth, may be justified in terms of greater equality and poverty reduction. For example, minimizing state intervention leads to higher growth and, through the trickle-down effect, to lower poverty. Moreover since poverty is particularly acute in rural areas, reducing state intervention—which typically favored industry over agriculture—lowers poverty and improves income distribution.

Empirical Assessment of the Effects of SAPs
The empirical literature in this area is extensive and

its findings are diverse, due to the variety of approaches used in the analyses and the methodological difficulties inherent in the evaluation of SAPs. Any short summary of the evaluation results is therefore inevitably partial. Generalizing and hence partly ignoring the diversity of individual countries' experiences, SAPs appear to have had their stronger positive effects on countries' external accounts (with increases in the rates of growth of exports and improvements in the balance of payments, though such positive results have also been found to be often temporary) rather than on the domestic economic performance (as typically investment fell and economic growth contracted or stagnated).

Indeed, growth in countries that have followed SA policies—especially in Latin America and Africa—was frequently lower than in the 1960s and 1970s, when these countries were following the highly distortionary policies that SA was meant to correct. Both in Latin America and Africa there have been instances when SA seemed to lead to economic success, but such cases were both isolated and short lived. Moreover the 1990s saw the countries that liberalized the domestic financial system and opened the capital account being hit by severe financial crises. The financial fragility of liberalized markets also seemed to make it possible for financial crises to propagate by contagion. In contrast to the experience of the countries that followed SA reforms, the countries that have managed to achieve sustained high growth are those that have significantly deviated from SA, for example by maintaining selective protection of infant industries, by maintaining controls on capital flows, or by liberalizing trade and capital movements at a slow pace.

SAPs also appear to have had negative effects on income equality and the general standards of living, as measured by health, education, and nutrition indicators. Cross-country analyses on poverty and income distribution do not provide a unified picture of worldwide trends (the different results are due to problems with the reliability and comparability of data, different country and time period samples used in the analyses, and different methodological approaches). There is evidence, however, of increases since the 1980s both in cross-country and within-country inequality as well as in poverty (once China is excluded from the sample). Such trends are attributed to many different factors but some of these factors are related to the adoption of SA policies, such as overly rapid trade and financial liberalizations, rapid and poorly designed privatization programs, and the erosion of labor institutions and of the state's redistributive role. A significant amount of empirical evidence also calls into question the effectiveness of the trickle-down mechanism: increases in average income do not appear to raise the income of the poor for prolonged periods.

What policy implications can be drawn from such empirical findings is a highly controversial matter for two related reasons: first, these findings may be the results of flawed evaluation methodologies, and second, the empirical results may be interpreted and explained in many different ways. Let us consider, for example, the findings concerning the effects of SAPs on economic growth. The expectation is that SAPs would result first in an economic contraction in the short run (as a result of the macroeconomic stabilization), which would then be followed by a recovery (led by the supply-side reforms) that shifts the economy onto a path of sustainable growth. It is clear therefore that SAPs cannot be criticized for causing a contraction, since this is inevitable if the cause of the crisis is an excess of demand over supply. Thus the relevant question to investigate is not whether SAPs caused a contraction but whether the contraction was deeper and/or lasted longer than necessary. Actual program effects should then be compared with what the economy could have done without an SAP (such a hypothetical outcome is called a counterfactual in the literature). Methodologically, the difficulty is that the counterfactual is not observable and can only be estimated.

The different evaluation methodologies can be seen as different approaches for the estimation of the counterfactual. Intuitively, such estimation is based on the economic situation in program countries during the period preceding the start of the SAP or on the economic situation in countries that did not enter a SAP. More sophisticated methodologies would account for the fact that program and nonprogram countries may be systematically different. For example, program countries are more likely to have been hit by a negative shock in the preprogram period and, consequently, there may be systematic differences in the policies pursued by the two groups of countries during the adjustment period. Alternately, program and nonprogram countries may differ in the extent of their relative policymakers' commitment to good policies. None of these different approaches is fully satisfactory as they all have important shortcomings. Moreover since in any selected sample period not all of the observed growth rates may be sustainable in the long run, ascertaining the true influence of policies on economic growth becomes very difficult. By implication, whatever empirical evidence is found cannot be clear-cut, because it is not possible to know whether it represents the true program effects or is the result of a wrong estimation of the counterfactual.

Inevitably, however, the effects of SAPs have raised concerns about poor economic performance, growing inequality, and increasing social problems, as a result of which the development agenda has been significantly broadened, with greater attention being given to the role of institutions and institutional reforms (particularly with respect to the quality of governance) and with poverty reduction becoming a top priority in World Bank operations. In short, in accordance with much of the empirical evidence, there is consensus—both within the World Bank and among its critics—that SAPs have produced disappointing results. This empirical fact has received different explanations. World Bank critics would argue that SA policies are fundamentally flawed and inappropriate to developing countries' circumstances. Others, including the World Bank, would instead point to the lack of government commitment to policy reform and the ineffectiveness of conditionality (i.e., the set of policy reforms that are required for loan disbursement) as policy leverage. The implication of this view is that policy reform programs can be made more effective by allocating financial resources more selectively to countries with good policies and good institutions.

The End of Structural Adjustment As a response to the perceived shortcomings of SAL, the World Bank formally announced its replacement with Development Policy Lending in August 2004. The latter sees reform ownership—which could be defined as the commitment by a recipient country to undertake reforms independently of the incentives provided by lenders—as essential for the success of reform programs. By implication, the promotion of ownership breaks with the idea, typical of the SA era, that there are universal policy prescriptions. Another major difference from SA concerns the characteristics of conditionality: under Development Policy Lending conditionality must be streamlined, so that the conditions focus only on the reforms that are regarded as essential for program success. In addition, conditionality is ex ante in that loan disbursement is made conditional on a country implementing key reforms, rather than promising to do so in the future, as was the case under SA. This new approach clearly implies much greater selectivity in the allocation of World Bank's financial resources. Criticisms center on the feasibility of the principle of selectivity (particularly its lack of credibility, since withholding finance from a country with weak policies and institutions would deteriorate that country's economic and social situation further) and the conflict between ownership and selectivity (since ownership must be more than the freedom to accept the bank's preferred policies).

See also aid, international; aid, international, and political economy; International Monetary Fund (IMF); International Monetary Fund conditionality; trade-related capacity building; Washington consensus

FURTHER READING

Corbo, Vittorio, and Stanley Fischer. 1995. "Structural Adjustment, Stabilization, and Policy Reform: Domestic and International Finance." In *Handbook of Development Economics*, vol. 3B, edited by Jere Behrman and T. N. Srinivasan. Amsterdam: North Holland, 2845–2924. Analytical frameworks supporting the policies of SAPs.

Cornia, Giovanni A., Richard Jolly, and Frances Stewart. 1987. *Adjustment with a Human Face: Protecting the*

Vulnerable and Promoting Growth. Oxford: Oxford University Press. Widely cited critical evaluation, focusing on the social impact of structural adjustment.

Fine, Ben, Costas Lapavitsas, and Jonathan Pincus, eds. 2001. *Neither Washington nor Post-Washington Consensus: Challenging Development Policy in the Twenty-First Century.* London: Routledge. Critical analyses of the neoliberal approach to policy reform.

Jayarajah, Carl, and William Branson. 1995. *Structural and Sectoral Adjustment: World Bank Experience, 1980–92.* Washington DC: World Bank. Large-scale World Bank evaluation.

Koeberle, Stefan, Harold Bedoya, Peter Silarszky, and Gero Verheyen, eds. 2005. *Conditionality Revisited: Concepts, Experiences, and Lessons.* Washington DC: World Bank. Review of the role of conditionality in aid and policy lending.

Mosley, Paul, Jane Harrigan, and John Toye. 1991. *Aid and Power: The World Bank and Policy-Based Lending.* London: Routledge. Widely cited critical evaluation, focusing on the relationship between the bank and adjustment lending recipients.

Paloni, Alberto, and Maurizio Zanardi, eds. 2006. *The IMF, World Bank, and Policy Reform.* London: Routledge. Looks at the changes in the intervention strategies of the international financial institutions.

Stiglitz, Joseph. 1998. "Towards a New Paradigm for Development: Strategies, Policies, and Processes." Prebisch Lecture at the United Nations Conference on Trade and Development, Geneva, October 19. Criticism of the Washington consensus and proposal of a "post-Washington consensus" by the then chief economist at the World Bank.

Williamson, John. 1990. "What Washington Means by Policy Reform." In *Latin American Adjustment: How Much Has Happened?,* edited by John Williamson. Washington, DC: Institute for International Economics, 5–20. Lays out the main points of the Washington consensus, an expression used to denote SA reforms.

World Bank. 1998. *Assessing Aid: What Works, What Doesn't, and Why?* New York: Oxford University Press. Final report on a multiyear research program on aid effectiveness.

ALBERTO PALONI

■ subsidiary

See multinational enterprises

■ subsidies and financial incentives to foreign direct investment

When considering the efforts of governments to attract foreign direct investment (FDI) through the use of subsidies and financial incentives, the game is not new, just the arena in which the game is played. In general, governments influence particular activities and pursue various objectives using instruments including taxes, public spending, regulations, subsidized credit, contingent liabilities, and others. In past decades, when the countries' economies were relatively closed and there was limited trade and scarce capital movements, the policy instruments were used mainly to influence the domestic allocation of resources. Especially in the 1950s and 1960s, governments, particularly those of developing countries, provided generous incentives to domestic enterprises to increase investment in the hope of stimulating higher economic growth.

In countries with federal structures of government, such as the United States, Brazil, Argentina, Canada, and some others, the subnational governments (states, provinces, regions) have often used their own policy instruments to attract economic activities to their area from the rest of the country. In some of these countries there has been intense competition among the states, often pursued through the use of tax incentives and other instruments to attract companies and investments to particular states. This competition has led to distortions in the allocation of resources and has generated a large literature on competition among the states (see, among others, Tanzi 1995, chapter 3; Kenyon and Kincaid 1991).

In today's globalizing world, countries have become more open to international trade flows and capital movements, and capital has become very mobile and highly sensitive to differences in rates of return earned from investing in different locations. Countries have recognized the possibility of attracting capital from the rest of the world through their policies. World capital has become a kind of common pool from which countries can extract a larger share of investment by pursuing particular policies. Given that most countries are a small part of the world economy, well-designed subsidies and financial incentives to FDI can, at least in theory, attract large amounts of resources relative to country size. These productive activities could create jobs for unemployed workers, or better jobs for underemployed ones, as well as faster growth for countries successful in attracting capital from the global pool. Malaysia, other countries from Southeast Asia, Ireland, and several transition economies from Eastern Europe have been particularly successful in attracting large amounts of FDI in part through the use of incentives directed to FDI. Other countries, including Latin American, African, and especially Caribbean countries have been much less successful in these attempts.

When a country that provides these incentives has many unemployed workers or many workers in unproductive activities that could find employment in more productive activities, the potential benefits for the country from the provision of incentives to FDI can be potentially high. Foreign capital could then be combined with domestic, previously unemployed or underemployed workers to generate new output. Furthermore FDI is often accompanied by new technologies and new managerial techniques that can be copied by domestic firms thus creating beneficial externalities and further growth. This inflow of new knowledge and technologies can, thus, create a theoretical justification for the provision of incentives (see Harrison and Aitken 1999). Even if the foreign enterprises did not pay taxes to the host country on their profits, the country might benefit because the workers would pay taxes on their wages and on their purchases and the domestic firms would become more productive. For these reasons, developing countries are understandably tempted to provide subsidies and financial incentives to FDI.

Types of Incentives There are several kinds of incentives that governments can give foreign investors to induce them to invest in their countries. First, they can provide incentives in kind, especially at the initial stage, to make a particular location more attractive than others to the investors. For example,

land or other real property can be made available free or at low cost and zoning restrictions can be relaxed to allow the foreign investors to build and operate industrial plants in particular areas. Alternatively countries can offer to build needed infrastructures, including roads, railroads, harbors, and so on. These incentives can be particularly valuable in attracting large industrial investments especially to areas that are still underdeveloped. The investments in infrastructures, although costly to the countries, can stimulate other domestic activities and thus create multiplier effects accompanying the foreign investments. In some cases the countries simply accelerate the building of infrastructures that would have been done at some later time.

Second, the foreign enterprises can be exempted from existing regulations, including labor regulations or environmental restrictions. Third, the countries could provide credit at subsidized rates, or facilitate borrowing from domestic sources. This approach would reduce the net capital inflow and the benefit from the foreign investment, however. Finally, the countries could provide incentives vis-à-vis the payment of taxes. These tax incentives are common and are the ones that attract most attention.

The tax incentives may be of various types. Their value to the foreign investors depends on several considerations but the most important is, probably, the level of effective tax rates to which they would be subjected in the absence of the tax incentives. This would depend on the way the taxes paid to the host country (the country where the investment is made) would be treated by the home country (the country of residence of the investor). If the tax incentive results in a reduction in tax payment to the host country but in a higher payment to the home country, the value of the incentive to the investor would be reduced or even eliminated.

The tax incentives can be divided into those against direct taxes and those against indirect taxes (see Zee, Stotsky, and Ley 2002). Among the incentives against direct taxes, the most important are (1) tax holidays against corporate income taxes (CIT); (2) reductions in CIT rates; (3) investment allowances; (4) investment tax credits; (5) accelerated depreciation; and (6) investment subsidies. Among the incentives against indirect taxes, the most important are tariff and value-added tax exemptions and incentives connected with export processing zones.

Tax holidays are especially common in developing countries, but much less so in advanced countries. They generally exempt foreign enterprises from the payment of CITs for a given number of years after the investment is made. Thus they are more attractive for those enterprises that expect quick and large profits. Tax holidays have some good and some less good features. Among the good features (for the enterprises) is the fact that during the period of the tax holiday the enterprises not only do not have to pay taxes but they do not need, generally, to comply with all the complexities of tax laws and regulations that can be quite burdensome and costly, especially when dealing with them for the first time in a foreign country. Thus the investors save in terms of both tax liability and tax compliance. Another good feature, from the point of view of the country, is that tax holidays tend to be neutral vis-à-vis the use of capital and labor. They do not distort the allocation of resources in this sense.

There are, however, some less good features of tax holidays. While tax holidays do not distort the choice between labor and capital, they do distort the choice between projects with short maturities and those with long maturities, favoring the former so that the profits earned by the enterprises can occur during the period when the tax holiday is in effect. Second, in practice, the tax holiday can often be extended (at times almost indefinitely) by making additional and often minor investments that allow the enterprise to claim an extension of the tax holiday. For example, in Jamaica and most Caribbean countries, enterprises that invest in hotels and that benefit from tax holidays can renew the tax holiday period by periodically adding a few hotel rooms. Another worrisome feature is that because the enterprises do not need to maintain accounting for tax purposes, there may not be any estimates of the revenue that the country loses due to the tax holidays. Thus it becomes difficult to make a cost-benefit evaluation of the incentives. Finally, in many cases, the enterprises would have made the investment even without the tax incentives, so that the country forgoes revenue needlessly.

While tax holidays exempt profits completely, *preferential CIT rates* tax their profits at lower rates than for ordinary enterprises. Thus they imply less revenue loss to the governments than tax holidays. They also require that the enterprises keep accounts so that the revenue forgone by the government due to the incentives can be estimated. The difference in tax rates between the enterprises that do not benefit from the incentives and those that do gives a measure of the revenue cost of the incentive under the assumption that the investment would have taken place even without the incentive.

Investment allowances allow the enterprise the immediate expensing of parts of the initial investment costs in addition to the normal allowable depreciation. *Investment tax credits* allow the deduction of parts of the investment costs from the CIT payment. In particular circumstances these two incentives tend to be the same. They are important for enterprises already in operation and that already have profits. *Investment subsidies* involve direct cash payments by the government to an enterprise for parts of an authorized investment. Thus they are a claim on the budgetary revenue of often cash-strapped governments. Finally, economists generally favor incentives given in the form of *accelerated depreciation*. These incentives have fewer disadvantages and lower budgetary costs than other incentives (see Tanzi and Zee 2000).

Indirect tax incentives can be costly to a country in terms of forgone revenue, because indirect taxes are often a large share of the country's gross domestic product (GDP). These incentives imply exonerations from import duties and from other indirect taxes, such as value-added taxes, excises, and other. These incentives lend themselves to abuses because the goods imported, or acquired duty free for the direct use of the enterprises, often find their way to other uses in the domestic market (for a discussion of the potential abuses of these tax incentives, see Zee et al. 2002).

Unfortunately, information on the use of incentives is limited, country specific, and often contained in confidential reports. Thus it is difficult, if not impossible, to assemble statistical information on the incentives just mentioned for groups of countries. As a consequence, the discussion that follows will not have the desirable backing of statistical information.

Before moving to the next section, it may be useful to mention a worrisome aspect of tax incentives. At times their features are specified precisely and in detail in the laws of the countries, so they have the backing of rule of law. At other times, they are given largely at the discretion of particular offices or officers. The latter may grant them to "essential" activities or "necessary" investments without a clear specification of what these terms mean. Often, the offices that make the decisions are not in the ministry of finance but in spending ministries (tourism, agriculture, industry, etc.) that are not responsible for the outcome of the public finances of the countries but represent sectoral interests. As a consequence, they tend to be generous—at times, too generous—with the public money.

Furthermore the discretion given to some bureaucrats in making decisions worth a lot of money to particular enterprises makes this an area particularly exposed to corruption. Foreign investors at times find poorly paid, easy to bribe civil servants to get decisions that to them are worth millions of dollars but that may not be particularly beneficial to the countries or decisions that the investors would have made in any case. For this reason, and apart from the intrinsic value of the incentives to a country, the rules that guide the granting of the incentives should be specified precisely in the legislation and should leave as little discretion as possible to civil servants and elected officials. Furthermore, they should be controlled at the highest level by the ministry of finance and possibly by some accountability office.

The Impact of Incentives on FDI Views about the merit of incentives and their impact on FDI diverge widely between those held by most economists who have studied the issues and those held by policymakers. Generally economists have concluded that incentives are often worthless or at least that they do not justify their costs. However, incentives remain popular with policymakers and, of course, with those who benefit from them, namely, the foreign investors. The latter often exert pressure to get the most generous incentives that the host country could provide.

Surveys of foreign investors that ask them the reasons why they have invested in a given country almost never list incentives at the top or near the top of the motivations for the choice of location. The responses mention reasons such as (1) the existence of domestic demand for the product or service produced; (2) the vicinity or the access to other markets; (3) the existence of valuable natural resources in the country; (4) the availability of cheap and skilled labor; (5) political stability, and so on. Incentives are generally mentioned way down the list. At the same time, attempts at removing the incentives often meet sharp reactions on the part of the investors and threats to move the activity to countries that offer incentives.

In a world of relatively homogeneous countries, the incentives provided by (only) one country would probably attract a lot of foreign investment to that country, especially in an open world in which companies can produce in one country and export what they produce to the rest of the world where import duties are lower than in the past. However, the world is far from homogeneous. There are great differences among countries in factors such as (1) inflation rates, (2) macroeconomic performance, (3) incidence of corruption, (4) stability and certainty of rule of law, (5) regulatory environments, (6) political stability, and (7) security. Often some of these factors overwhelm the advantages that incentives could provide to foreign investors in investing in specific countries. For this reason economists emphasize that the best incentives that countries can provide to investors are (1) a stable and good macroeconomic environment, (2) stable and clear regulations and rule of law, (3) tax rates that are competitive and tax systems that are not too complex, and (4) an environment that is relatively free of corruption.

An important element that often plays a major role in the willingness of countries' authorities to grant incentives for FDI is competition from other countries for FDI. This competition has been stimulated by what is at times called "incentive shopping" on the part of foreign investors. Consider a country, say Costa Rica, that is approached by an American company, say Intel, and is told that the company is considering a large investment in Central America but that the specific location has not yet been chosen. Suppose the investment would create many good jobs and would contribute significantly to the country's economy. The foreign company demands substantial incentives from Costa Rica with the implicit threat that a refusal will cause the company to invest in a neighboring country so that Costa Rica would lose the investment. This is the situation that often confronts policymakers; they face offers that they find difficult to refuse.

This shopping for the best incentive package at times places smaller and poorer countries at a disadvantage and forces them to make concessions that can significantly reduce or even eliminate the benefits that a country can derive from foreign investment. A solution to this problem of incentive shopping by foreign investors could only come in the form of agreements, on the part of all the countries from a particular region, not to give in to such pressures and to establish jointly agreed on rules that restrict what the countries grant in terms of incentives to foreign investors. However, no such agreements exist and the desire to attract foreign direct investment continues to be a strong motivation for providing often too generous terms. The fact that some countries have developed at fast rates with the help of FDI remains a strong reason for policymakers to continue to provide generous incentives.

The foregoing analysis points to two basic questions. The first is whether subsidies and financial incentives can succeed in attracting FDI (or more FDI) to a specific country. The second is whether total FDI to countries can change due to incentives. Different strands of economic literature have dealt with these two questions.

The answer to the first question is probably yes, provided that the pull exercised by the existence of the incentives is not neutralized by other factors. Ample evidence from many countries suggests that they have succeeded in attracting large FDIs through the use of generous and well-targeted incentives (see Tanzi and Shome 1992). Other conditions being equal, incentives can attract FDI to a specific country. However, the situation implicit in such a ceteris paribus assumption rarely holds in the real world so that the value of incentives to foreign investors can easily be wiped out by some of the other factors mentioned earlier. A country such as Haiti will not become as successful as Ireland or Malaysia in attracting FDI strictly by offering incentives to foreign investors. Also, for every "winner" of a competition for FDI, there may be many "losers" that tried to attract FDI using subsidies (or other incentives) but were beaten by the better offer.

The answer to the second question is more difficult and on this issue the literature is more ambiguous. Already in 1962 Kaldor (1965) was raising the question and was giving an agnostic answer. There is no literature that has addressed specifically and directly this question. However, there is a lot of literature that has dealt with the closely related, even though technically different, question of whether taxes have affected the location of firms and investment (see for example Devereux and Griffith, 2002). This literature has generally concluded that "taxation matters," and it is easy to predict that it will matter more with the passing of time. However, the various studies have focused exclusively on taxation and have ignored the effects of other policies that may have biased the elasticity of investment decisions with respect to changes in tax rates. Furthermore it is still not clear how large an effect taxes have on FDI. It should be added that this literature normally discusses the location of FDI within OECD countries rather than the flow of FDI to developing countries that was the main focus of Kaldor's paper. Thus we are unable to state with any certainty whether developing countries, as a group, have received more FDI due to the incentives that they have been providing.

The Costs of Incentives What are the costs of the incentives to the countries that give them, especially to developing countries? Against the potential benefits in terms of employment, transfer of technology, improved productivity, and higher exports, there are costs, some obvious and some less so.

A first cost is the erosion of the tax bases. Incentives can sharply reduce the bases for the corporate income tax, the value-added tax, and the import taxes. At the same time the inflow of FDI may require additional public spending for infrastructures and other costs. If the FDI leads to a significant increase in the country's rate of growth, other taxes may go up and may compensate for the incentives given. But this is not always the case.

A second cost, and one much related to the first, is that the erosion of the tax bases caused by the incentives often forces the countries to raise the statutory tax rates on the sectors and enterprises that do not benefit from the incentives, thus reducing the growth potential of those sectors.

A third cost is that incentives inevitably create distortions in the allocation of resources. These distortions may be desirable if the incentives compensate the enterprises that receive them for positive externalities that they bring to the countries. This is for example the case when FDI brings new technologies that can be used by domestic firms. But this is not always the case, so the distortions created by favoring some firms over others can be economically costly.

A fourth cost is the one mentioned earlier connected with corruption. Incentives often become a fertile field for corrupt acts. Many studies have shown that corruption is costly to countries in the impact that it has on economic growth and also on equity.

Finally, there are potential costs associated with the competition in the granting of incentives. When countries compete for limited FDI and do so by progressively increasing the attractiveness of the incentives that they are willing to give, there is inevitably a race to the bottom that may be costly to all. There is also the possibility of a "winner's curse" where a country overestimates the value of an investment, pays too much, and winds up worse off despite succeeding in attracting the FDI.

In conclusion, in particular circumstances, well-thought-out and limited subsidies and financial incentives to FDI may be beneficial to countries that give them. However, more often than not, the results are not as good as hoped.

See also foreign direct investment (FDI); location theory

FURTHER READING

Bernardi, Luigi, Angela Fraschini, and Parthasarathi Shome. 2006. *Tax Systems and Tax Reforms in South and East Asia*. London: Routledge. Provides up-to-date descriptions of the tax systems in Asian countries.

Billington, N. 1999. "The Location of Foreign Direct Investment: An Empirical Analysis." *Applied Economics* 31 (1): 65–76. A useful analysis of factors that have influenced the location of FDI.

Devereux, Michael P., and Rachel Griffith. 2002. "The Impact of Corporate Taxation on the Location of Capital: A Review." *Swedish Economic Policy Review* 9 (1): 79–102. A very good review of the impact of taxes on the location of investment.

Harrison, Ann E., and Brian Aitken. 1999. "Do Domestic Firms Benefit from Direct Foreign Investment: Evidence from Venezuela." *American Economic Review* 89 (3): 605–18. Discusses potential externalities associated with FDI.

Kaldor, Nicholas. 1965. "The Role of Taxation in Economic Development." In *Fiscal Policy for Economic Growth in Latin America* (Papers and Proceedings of a Conference held in Santiago, Chile, December 1962). Baltimore: The Johns Hopkins Press, 70–99. An early discussion by a major economist about the impact of taxes on economic decisions including capital flows.

Kenyon, Daphne A., and John Kincaid, eds. 1991. *Competition among States and Local Governments: Efficiency and Equity in American Federalism*. Washington, DC: Urban Institute Press. A review of tax competition among American states.

Organisation for Economic Co-operation and Development (OECD). 2000. *Recent Trends in Foreign Direct Investment*. Paris: OECD. A useful reference with a lot of factual information on FDI.

Shah, Anwar, ed. 1995. *Fiscal Incentives for Investment and Innovation*. New York: Oxford University Press. Contains several papers on the role of fiscal incentives.

Tanzi, Vito. 1995. *Taxation in an Integrating World*. Washington, DC: The Brookings Institution. An early book on the impact of globalization on tax systems.

Tanzi, Vito, and Parthasarathi Shome. 1992. "The Role of Taxation in the Development of East Asian Economies."

In *The Political Economy of Tax Reform,* edited by Takatoshi Ito and Anne Krueger. Chicago: The University of Chicago Press, 31–61. A detailed review of the role of tax incentives in the development of Southeast Asian countries.

Tanzi, Vito, and Howell H. Zee. 2000. "Tax Policy for Emerging Markets: Developing Countries." *National Tax Journal* 53 (2): 299–322. A review article on tax policy and tax incentives in developing countries.

Zee, Howell H., Janet G. Stotsky, and Eduardo Ley. 2002. "Tax Incentives for Business Investment: A Primer for Policy Makers in Developing Countries." *World Development* 30 (9): 1497–1516. A comprehensive article on the role and the cost of tax incentives for investment.

VITO TANZI

■ Swan diagram

The Swan diagram is an analytical tool that facilitates streamlined analysis of macroeconomic policy for a small open economy. Developed in the 1950s by Trevor Swan (see Swan 1960; Salter 1959) for Australia, the Swan diagram was used to model how to achieve the two objectives of internal and external balance with two kinds of policy instruments, one affecting aggregate demand, the other a relative price. More recently, however, the Swan diagram has been generalized to other times, countries, and different sets of instrument variables. It facilitates policy analysis and policymaking by showing the kind of disequilibrium in the macroeconomy and therefore the required policy response. Shocks can also be analyzed according to the kind of disequilibrium they create.

A country attains *internal balance* when the aggregate demand for domestic output equals the aggregate supply of domestic output at full employment of resources and prices are stable. *External balance* requires equilibrium in the balance of payments. The current account surplus or the net balance of trade is exports minus imports. It must be financed by sustainable capital flows. If imports exceed exports, capital inflows are required; otherwise capital can be exported. Adjustment normally requires a change in relative prices combined with changes in demand or expenditure.

A key conceptual distinction for a small country is that it must take international prices as given. If markets are competitive, exportable and importable traded goods can be combined into a single category because a perfectly elastic world demand for exports and a perfectly elastic world supply of imports make their prices independent of domestic variables. But this means that the terms of trade, or the ratio of export to import prices, cannot change to help the adjustment to full equilibrium or balance.

Analytics Because the terms of trade are independent of domestic actions, the key relative price becomes the real exchange rate, Z, defined as the ratio of traded to *nontraded goods* prices (E P^*_T/P_N). Traded goods prices, P^*_T, are determined in world markets. Nontraded goods do not enter world trade; internal costs and demand determine their prices (P_N). Z is, therefore, the ratio of external prices to domestic costs. The nominal exchange rate (E) is measured in units of domestic currency per unit of foreign currency so that a rise is a devaluation or depreciation of the currency.

Domestic aggregate demand, or *absorption*, is total real expenditure on home produced goods and on imports and is the sum of personal and government consumption and investment (A = C + I + G). It must equal domestic output plus exports minus imports or the current account surplus. Therefore output minus absorption gives the current account surplus.

Consider a simple framework where Z and A are the two variables influenced by two policy instruments—exchange rate policy, which changes E, and fiscal policy, which changes government expenditure, G. Fiscal policy directly affects absorption through government spending. If perfect capital mobility makes the domestic interest rate equal the international, and the nominal exchange rate is fixed, monetary policy has no freedom to change interest rates and affect domestic demand. If the nominal exchange rate, E, is fixed and world prices, P^*_T, are exogenous, the real exchange rate can change only with the nontradable goods price. E can, of course, be changed through a periodic devaluation; if the exchange rate is managed more continuous changes are possible, and monetary policy can also affect aggregate demand.

The Swan diagram (figure 1) has the real exchange rate on the vertical axis and real absorption on the horizontal axis. The schedule IB_f gives internal balance or the combinations of Z and A at which output demand equals full employment output. The schedule is downward sloping because a rise in demand raises output and so does a rise in foreign prices, relative to domestic prices. As domestic absorption rises, Z must appreciate to reduce foreign demand for exports, and therefore total demand, to the full employment output level. Values above the schedule generate inflation as a more depreciated exchange rate and higher absorption raise demand; those below the schedule generate unemployment/recession.

Schedule EB_0 gives external balance or the combinations of the two variables that yield an acceptable current account deficit. The EB schedule is upward sloping because the current account deficit worsens with A as imports rise, but a rise in Z improves it as exports rise and imports fall. As A rises Z must

depreciate to raise exports sufficiently to keep the current account deficit unchanged. The balance of payments is in surplus above the schedule since exports are higher and imports lower; it is in deficit below. The current account deficit is lower than capital inflows can safely finance above, and higher below, the EB schedule.

The point of full internal and external balance is F, where the two schedules intersect. These schedules divide the space into four zones of differing types of disequilibria. A combination of expenditure-changing and expenditure-switching policies is required to reach full balance F. The first changes the level of total demand in the economy. The second changes the direction of demand, shifting it between domestic output and imports and shifting domestic resources between traded and nontraded sectors. The latter is a necessary part of the adjustment process for a small open economy, where the real exchange rate can change only if the relative price of traded to nontraded goods changes. Switching effects are responsible for the slopes of the two schedules; otherwise they would be vertical. The shifting of resources on the production side occurs over a longer run com-

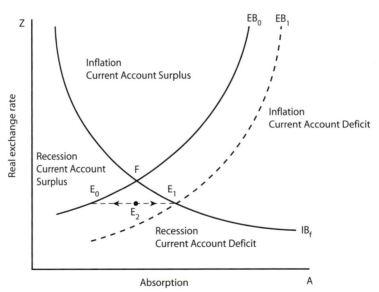

Figure 1
The Swan diagram

pared with the more immediate change in the direction of demand.

Domestic Costs and Wages If, as a simplification, labor is the only domestic resource, nontraded goods prices equal *unit labor costs*, or the nominal wage. Output supply depends on absorption and real wages and therefore on the real exchange rate. A rise in Z will make the production of export goods more profitable and labor will shift to this sector. In addition domestic demand will shift away from tradables, or the demand for imports will fall. But real wages themselves depend on the aggregate price level, which is a weighted average of the prices of traded and nontraded goods. Along EB, as Z rises, real wages must fall. If the price of the domestic good is closely linked to unit wage costs but wage earners spend on a weighted average of imported and nontraded goods, real wages must fall as imported goods become costlier than nontraded goods. Output is demand determined below the IB_f schedule and limited by available labor supply above it. Wage-price rigidities contribute to preventing labor market clearing.

Adjustment to Shocks Even if an economy is in full equilibrium a shock can place it in any one of the four quadrants where internal or external balance or both are missing. In analyzing adjustment to equilibrium it is useful to make a distinction between automatic forces of adjustment and policy responses. Prices of nontraded goods will rise with excess demand. This will reduce demand, but it will also appreciate Z, switch demand to tradables, and deteriorate the balance of payment. Over time labor will also shift to the production of nontradables, reducing the supply of exports and further deteriorating the balance of payments. Thus adjustment will be in the proper direction only in the top quadrant; in the quadrant to the right, the balance of payment will move further into deficit. Policy intervention, reducing government consumption of nontradables and depreciating the nominal exchange rate, would be required. A similar argument shows that deflation of prices and wages in the lower quadrants would be equilibrating for the balance of payment only in the bottom quadrant. In the quadrant to the left the surplus would tend to rise further, requiring policy intervention that revalues the nominal exchange rate or raises government expenditure.

Depending on the slopes and speeds of adjustment, it can be optimal to assign one policy instrument to achieving internal balance and the other to achieving external balance. This is called the *assignment problem*. Moreover, two instruments are required to reach two objectives. For example, consider the economy to be at E_2, with the nominal exchange rate and real wages fixed so that the only policy instrument is government spending. If the government increases spending to reach internal balance at E_1, it moves further away from external balance. If it decreases spending, it can reach external balance at E_0 as imports fall, but recession deepens as it moves further away from internal balance. Even if there is no conflict and one instrument is pushing toward satisfying both objectives, changing the second may be necessary to reach the equilibrium point.

When deflation is required for automatic market-based adjustment, policy intervention is all the more necessary because deflation can be a very slow and painful process. In most economies it is easier to raise prices and wages than to reduce them. A rise in nominal exchange rates achieves the required adjustment in relative prices with less pain. But this only works if there is nominal but not real wage rigidity. Real wages have to be flexible for real exchange rates or the terms of trade to change. Nominal devaluation can be an effective policy instrument only if there is some flexibility in real wages. Nominal rigidity and real flexibility is the normal assumption in Keynesian models.

Swan originally analyzed what he called the "dependent economy." In the modern literature this has transmuted to "the small open economy," which also takes world prices as given. In this form it lives on with the *microfoundations* of forward-looking consumers who maximize welfare over their lifetime (Gali and Monacelli 2005). Wages and prices that take time to adjust to changed circumstances play a vital role in these models; these delays allow demand to have persistent effects. Prices continue to be closely linked to unit labor costs through markups, validating Swan's other fundamental contribution of the importance of labor markets and domestic costs. The basic Swan diagram continues to be a useful simple approximation for policy analysis.

See also assignment problem; balance of payments; balance sheet approach/effects; currency crisis; exchange rate regimes; expenditure changing and expenditure switching; financial crisis; impossible trinity; Mundell-Fleming model; nontraded goods; real exchange rate

FURTHER READING

Corbo, Vittorio, and Stanley Fischer. 1995. "Structural Adjustment, Stabilisation, and Policy Reform: Domestic and International Finance." In *Handbook of Development Economics*, vol. 3, edited by Jere Behreman and T. N. Srinivasan. Amsterdam: North-Holland, chapter 44. An application of the Swan framework to stabilization and structural adjustment programs in the 1980s.

Corden, W. Max. 2002. *Too Sensational: On the Choice of Exchange Rate Regimes*. Cambridge MA: MIT Press. A readable and thorough application of the Swan framework to derive policy lessons from the East Asian crisis.

Dornbusch, Rudiger. 1980. "Home Goods and Traded Goods: The Dependent Economy Model." In *Open Economy Macroeconomics*. New York: Basic Books, chapter 6.

Frankel, Jeffrey. 2001. "Coping with Crises in Emerging Markets: Adjustment versus Financing." In *Key Issues in Reform of the International Monetary System*, edited by P. Kenen and A. Swoboda. International Monetary Fund: Washington, DC, 215–20. Works out interest rate and exchange rate options during a crisis with the Swan framework in the presence of balance sheet effects.

Gali, Jordi, and Tommaso Monacelli. 2005. "Monetary Policy and Exchange Rate Volatility in a Small Open Economy." *Review of Economic Studies* 72 (3): 707–34. A rigorous New Keynesian model and policy analysis for the small open economy.

Goyal, Ashima. 2005. "Asian Reserves and the Dollar: Is Gradual Adjustment Possible?" *Global Economy Journal* 5 (3): Article 3, Downloadable from http://www.bepress.com/gej/vol5/iss3/3. Implications of labor markets and wage behavior for adjustment.

Krugman, Paul. 1998. "Latin America's Swan Song." Mimeo. Downloadable from http://web.mit.edu/krugman/www/swansong.html. Working out Brazil's options with the Swan framework.

Rajan, Ramkishen S. 2006. "Managing New Style Currency Crises: The Swan Diagram Revisited." *Journal of International Development* 18: 1–24. Builds on Frankel (2001) and works out interest rate and exchange rate options during a crisis with the Swan framework in the presence of balance sheet effects.

Salter, Walter E. 1959. "Internal and External Balance: The Role of Price and Expenditure Effects." *Economic Record* 35 (August): 226–38.

Swan, Trevor W. 1960. "Economic Control in a Dependent Economy." *Economic Record* 36 (March): 51–66.

ASHIMA GOYAL

◼ target zones

See band, basket, and crawl (BBC); exchange rate regimes

◼ tariff-cutting formulas

A tariff-cutting formula is an approach to trade liberalization in which countries bargaining over mutual tariff reductions seek agreement on a general formula for cuts in one another's tariffs, rather than on particular cuts in individual tariffs. Tariff-cutting formulas have been an inherent part of multilateral trade negotiations.

Economists are generally agreed that tariffs and other trade barriers reduce global income, and reducing these barriers will raise world income and the incomes of most countries. For small countries, economic theory provides an even stronger result, that unilateral liberalization will raise national income in all but the most exceptional cases. Despite these important and well-known conclusions, trade barriers remain extremely prevalent. Reconciliation of this apparent paradox needs to take into account the problem of special interests. Within a country, there is scope for these interest groups to collude with policymakers in order to promote their joint interests at the expense of overall welfare—perhaps by the interest groups making campaign contributions to politicians (Grossman and Helpman 1994). However, this outcome is suboptimal, even for politicians, for two reasons. One is the fact that the same decisions taken in partner countries reduce the demand for exports and shrink the supply of imports, causing the country's terms of trade to deteriorate (Bagwell and Staiger 1999). Another is that policymakers alone are unable to commit to rejecting future appeals for protection, allowing interest groups to apply intense pressure for protection—perhaps by threatening plant closures—that create costs rather than benefits for politicians (Maggi and Rodríguez-Clare 2007).

International trade negotiations provide potential solutions to these problems. Negotiations with trading partners can potentially deal with these problems by reducing foreign barriers in line with domestic barriers and providing a mechanism for policymakers to commit to not raising protection in the future. The GATT (General Agreement on Tariffs and Trade) achieves the second of these outcomes by international agreements limiting tariffs on individual products to no more than an agreed, bound tariff rate. Regional trade arrangements typically involve similar international commitments.

Such negotiations typically need to involve a significant share of a country's total trade if there is to be sufficient balance of gains to tackle the more politically sensitive trade barriers. One approach is for countries simply to negotiate bilaterally and sequentially, but this proved unsatisfactory during the 19th century, since a seemingly generous offer to one partner can be undercut by a slightly better offer to the next negotiating partner. The GATT attempted to improve on this through a request-and-offer procedure, under which the best offer given to any negotiating partner was extended to all GATT members under the so-called most-favored-nation principle. By the 1960s, however, it was clear that this approach was yielding very little progress in terms of liberalization. The problem was that few bilateral trading relationships are intense enough that the gains in improved market access from an offer will offset the political costs involved in extending the offer to all GATT members when the number of participants becomes as large as the 74 participants involved in the GATT negotiations of the 1960s.

One solution, first adopted in the Kennedy Round (1963–67), was to negotiate a formula for cutting tariffs. In this situation, policymakers could potentially evaluate both the political costs of reducing their own tariffs and the political benefits from reducing tariffs in all of their trading partners. By agreeing on a proportional-cut formula during the Kennedy Round, participants in the GATT negotiations were able to achieve substantial cuts in protection—35 percent of initial tariffs as against an average of 2.5 percent in each of the previous four negotiations (Francois and Martin 2003). The next round, the Tokyo Round (1974–79), used a more sophisticated formula, the so-called Swiss formula, and achieved a 30 percent reduction in average tariffs. The Uruguay Round (1986–94) set broad tariff-reduction goals such as a 30 percent average-cut in agricultural tariffs, leaving the distribution of the cut across goods up to negotiations between trading partners, with a minimum cut of 15 percent for agricultural products. The Doha negotiations (2001–), the first GATT round conducted under the World Trade Organization (WTO), have been focused on what are known as "Swiss formulas" for nonagricultural tariffs and tiered formulas, under which tariffs are grouped into four bands, with higher cuts on higher tariffs, for agricultural products.

The two classic tariff-cutting formulas—the proportional cut and the Swiss formula—are both extremely simple, and the contrast between them shown in figure 1 is illuminating. Under the proportional cut, the new tariff, t_1, equals $(1 - \alpha)$ times the original rate, t_0, where α is the fraction by which tariffs are to be cut. The Swiss formula is:

$$t_1 = \frac{a \cdot t_0}{a + t_0} \qquad (1)$$

where a is a coefficient, or ceiling parameter, that no tariff will exceed after application of the formula. Figure 1 contrasts a proportional cut of 50 percent with a Swiss formula using a coefficient of 20 percent. Note that the proportional tariff-cutting rule results in a linear relationship between the original and final tariffs, while the Swiss formula is nonlinear. Note also that, for tariffs below the Swiss-formula coefficient of 20 in this case, the Swiss formula involves smaller cuts than the proportional cut of 50 percent. For tariffs above 20 percent, however, the Swiss formula involves larger cuts. These cuts become larger and larger as the initial tariff rises, in order that no postcut tariff will ever exceed the Swiss formula coefficient. This is evident from examination of equation (1), since $t_0/(a + t_0)$ comes closer and closer to 1 as the initial tariff rises toward infinity.

Progressivity A key difference between the approaches that have been used is the extent to which they are progressive in the sense of making the largest cuts in the highest tariffs. As is obvious from figure 1, the Swiss formula is sharply progressive. The proportional-cut approach cuts all tariffs by the same proportion, although this means larger absolute cuts in higher tariffs. The tiered-formula approach is somewhere in between, with higher cuts in higher tariffs. It is unlikely, however, that a tiered formula would be used to achieve such large cuts in very high tariffs as are implicit in the Swiss formula.

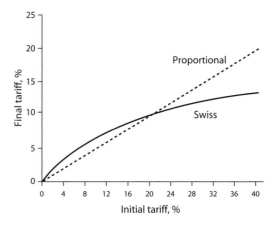

Figure 1

Proportional versus Swiss tariff-cutting formulas

The average-cut approach, by contrast, tends to focus the largest cuts on the lowest tariffs. It rewards equally a 50 percent cut in a 1 percent tariff and a 50 percent cut in a 1,000 percent tariff—potentially allowing a 50 percent average cut in this case to be achieved by a 100 percent cut in the 1 percent tariff and certainly encouraging policymakers to focus their largest cuts on the lowest tariffs. This approach can result in a seemingly impressive tariff cut, with an agreed average cut of, say, 50 percent, that yields completely insignificant tariff reductions when economies have large numbers of low tariffs. A simple move from focusing on the average cut in tariffs to the cut in the average tariff could avoid this presumably unintended outcome.

Although there are few general rules about which approaches to tariff cutting will bring about the greatest improvements in economic efficiency, there is a general presumption that lowering higher tariffs by the most will be desirable. This follows from the simple rule that the economic cost of protection rises with the square of the tariff, implying that cuts in high tariffs are worth generally much more than comparable percentage cuts in low tariffs. The best approach depends on the goal of the negotiation, however. As Anderson and Neary (2007) have pointed out, when expanding market access is the goal, it may be more useful to focus tariff reductions on goods that already have low tariffs, since these goods tend to have the largest initial trade volumes. They show that, for a given mean tariff, reducing the variability of tariffs around their mean raises economic welfare but actually reduces the market access gains resulting from application of a formula.

The actual choice between different formulas appears, in practice, to depend a great deal on the structure of countries' tariffs. In the Kennedy Round, for instance, the United States resisted application of a progressive tariff formula since it had more high tariffs than the European Community. In the Doha negotiations, the Swiss formula appears to be the most broadly accepted option for nonagricultural tariffs. From the viewpoint of developing countries, this is partly because the industrial countries have only a small number of high tariffs, but many of these

are on products such as textiles, clothing, and footwear that are of great interest to developing country exporters. Since developing countries themselves have tariffs that are much less widely dispersed than those of the industrial countries, they are likely to have to make smaller cuts in their own tariffs than would be the case with a proportional cut that brought about the same reduction in global tariffs. From the viewpoint of the industrial countries, the ceiling feature of the Swiss formula would put limits on the extent to which tariffs could rise in the future—in either developed or developing countries.

Flexibility A key difference between the different approaches used is the extent to which they impose disciplines on each tariff line. Line-by-line formulas such as the proportional cut or Swiss formula specify exactly what must be done with each tariff line. More flexible approaches, such as the average cut or an agreed cut in average tariffs, allow countries to choose what they do with individual tariffs subject to some overall constraint. Typically, when a line-by-line approach such as the Swiss formula is used, some flexibility is provided to allow for more lenient treatment for particular tariff lines. In the Kennedy and Tokyo Rounds, this was done by seeking as close as possible to full coverage, but ultimately allowing a substantial number of tariffs to be exempted from the formula treatment. In the Doha negotiations, constraints were being negotiated on the number of tariffs to be exempted from the full formula cut and the extent to which the cuts on these tariffs are allowed to deviate from the formula.

The ideal with such flexibilities is to provide the modest degree of flexibility needed to reach an otherwise unattainable agreement—a small hole in disciplines akin to that provided by the pressure valve on a boiler. The problem is that it is exceptionally difficult to know what represents such a modest degree of flexibility. What looks like a small hole, allowing dangerous pressures to escape, may turn out to be more like the small hole made in a balloon with a pin. Jean, Laborde, and Martin (2006) investigated the effect of allowing just between 1 and 5 percent of agricultural tariffs to be subjected to small tariff cuts instead of the full formula approach. They found that allowing smaller cuts in just 2 percent of tariff lines was enough to reduce the cut in the average tariff resulting from the formula by more than two-thirds. Providing a balance between allowing the flexibility needed to get an agreement and the disciplines needed to make it worthwhile seems to require discipline on both the number of tariff lines and the degree to which the products subject to flexibilities are cut.

Generalization and Simplicity Trade negotiations tend to be very complex, even if they begin with very simple formulas such as the proportional cut formula. The proportional cut and Swiss formulas are extremely simple, involving only one parameter value to choose in each case. Both of these can be slightly generalized. The proportional cut can, for instance, be converted into a linear formula by adding an intercept term, b (see Panagariya 2002):

$$t_1 = b + (1 - \alpha) \cdot t_0 \qquad (2)$$

This allows the marginal rate at which tariffs are cut to be higher than the average rate, perhaps to make the formula more progressive. One potential problem with this formula is that some initially low tariffs might actually be increased by a straightforward application of the formula.

The Swiss formula can be slightly generalized to allow for slightly smaller reductions in the highest tariffs balanced by slightly larger reductions in lower tariffs. Francois and Martin (2003) show that adding an additional flexibility parameter allows the shape of the formula to change in ways that could be useful in securing agreement. The resulting generalized Swiss formula is:

$$t_1 = \frac{a \cdot t_0}{a \cdot b + t_0} \qquad (3)$$

A much more common approach to generalization has been to seek to identify different parameters that can accommodate the needs of different negotiating parties. The tiered formula under consideration in the Doha negotiations on agriculture has done this by including four tariff bands each for developed and for developing countries, with different cuts in tariffs within each band. This has resulted in an unfortunate level of complexity, with a total of 14 different parameters to be chosen—a level of specificity that leaves many unsure of the impacts of different choices, particularly the impact on their export market opportunities.

One area in which even the simplest nonproportional formulas, such as the Swiss formula, are much more complex in practice than a proportional cut is in the presence of tariffs that are expressed in non-advalorem terms. Such tariffs, which include specific elements such as a tariff of $1 per kilo, are very common in industrial-country agricultural tariffs. These present no particular problem when using a proportional cut formula. Fifty percent of a tariff of $1 per kilo is clearly 50 cents per kilo. But all the nonproportional formulas require that tariffs be converted into ad valorem terms before they can be applied. Such conversions are, in practice, potentially quite complex and subject to manipulation since it is not always clear what import price should be used to make the conversion. In the Doha negotiations on agriculture, months of intense negotiations were required before a compromise was reached on the approach to be used to make this conversion.

Tariff formulas can provide a very useful approach for negotiating reciprocal tariff reductions, particularly when the number of participants in the negotiations is large. They can potentially allow negotiators to secure agreements that would not be attainable by bargaining over individual tariff reductions. Popular, simple formula approaches such as the proportional cut and the Swiss formula were central to the success of the GATT in reducing industrial-country protection between the 1960s and the 1990s. The formula approach is not a panacea, however. In practice, the apparent need for flexibility to deal with particularly sensitive industries and products can result in complex and difficult negotiations about flexibilities and exceptions, which require careful management if negotiations are not either to collapse or to yield agreements that achieve very little.

See also General Agreement on Tariffs and Trade (GATT); multilateral trade negotiations; tariffs; World Trade Organization

FURTHER READING

Anderson, James E., and J. Peter Neary. 2007. "Welfare versus Market Access: The Implications of Tariff Structure for Tariff Reform." *Journal of International Economics* 71 (1): 187–205. Shows and measures the trade-offs between tariff-cutting formulas that increase market access and those that improve economic efficiency.

Bagwell, Kyle, and Robert Staiger. 1999. "An Economic Theory of GATT." *American Economic Review* 89 (1): 215–48. Provides a model to explain the success of the GATT as a means of reducing the costs imposed on trading partners by terms-of-trade deterioration resulting from tariffs.

Baldwin, Robert E. 1986. "Toward More Efficient Procedures for Multilateral Tariff Negotiations." *Aussenwirtschaft* 41 (2–3): 379–94. Shows the potential advantages of formula approaches and the limitations on the request-and-offer approach to securing trade liberalization.

Francois, Joseph, and Will Martin. 2003. "Formula Approaches for Market Access Negotiations." *World Economy* 26 (1): 1–28. Surveys some of the key formula approaches that have been used in tariff negotiations and proposes a generalization of the Swiss formula approach.

Grossman, Gene, and Elhanan Helpman. 1994. "Protection for Sale." *American Economic Review* 84 (4): 833–50. This classic article seeks to explain the structure of protection when politicians choose trade policies taking into account both voter well-being and their ability to attract campaign contributions.

Jean, Sébastien, David Laborde, and Will Martin. 2006. "Consequences of Alternative Formulas for Agricultural Tariff Cuts." In *Agricultural Trade Reform and the Doha Development Agenda*, edited by Kym Anderson and Will Martin. Washington, DC: Palgrave Macmillan and the World Bank, 81–115. Examines the implications of tariff formulas under the Doha agricultural negotiations, taking into account the gaps between bound and applied tariffs and the presence of exceptions from the formula.

Maggi, Giovanni, and Andrès Rodríguez-Clare. 2007. "A Political-Economy Theory of Trade Agreements." *American Economic Review* 97 (4): 1374–1406. Integrates the terms-of-trade explanation for international trade negotiations with the special-interest model to provide a better understanding of the potential for trade reform through international trade negotiations.

Panagariya, Arvind. 2002. "Formula Approaches to Reciprocal Tariff Liberalization." In *Development, Trade and the WTO*, edited by Bernard Hoekman, Aaditya Mattoo, and Philip English. Washington DC: World Bank, 535–39. An accessible introduction to the use of a wide range of potential formula approaches for tariff negotiations.

WILL MARTIN

■ tariff escalation

Tariff escalation refers to a situation in which tariffs are low or nonexistent for raw materials but increase, or escalate, with the degree of processing. If the tariff on cocoa beans is zero, for example, the tariff on cocoa butter is 10 percent and the tariff on chocolate and chocolate products is 20 percent. In the late 1950s and early 1960s, policymakers in developed countries considered escalating tariff structures modern and rational. Some economists, however, found that escalation in importing countries could discourage exports of processed products and thereby limit the scope for processing in exporting countries (see Johnson 1965). Developing countries became increasingly concerned with this problem and made the reduction or elimination of escalation one of their main demands in multilateral trade negotiations.

Tariff escalation has been part of the tariff structures of advanced industrial countries, as well as of those of many developing countries, at least since the 1960s. The reduction and elimination of high tariffs, tariff peaks, and escalation figure prominently in multilateral negotiations such as the World Trade Organization's Doha Round (still ongoing as of late 2007).

Measuring Tariff Escalation Tariff escalation can be measured as the difference among the nominal tariffs of products at different stages of the processing chain. Tariff escalation exists if the nominal tariff on the output exceeds that on the input; tariff deescalation is present when the nominal tariff on the input exceeds that on the output. The practical difficulty when using this approach is to describe processing chains and/or to identify products at different levels of processing.

Two main methodologies are typically used. The first uses a categorization of all products (tariff items) in a given nomenclature according to their degree of processing: typically raw materials, semifinished products, and finished products. The second requires the identification of processing chains for specific commodities, such as cocoa, cotton, or tobacco (OECD 1999). These two simple methodologies have limitations. They do not measure the intensity of protection afforded the final product, and they cannot be used when the final product incorporates a variety of inputs.

The concept of effective rate of protection (ERP) was devised in the early days of the theory of tariff structure to measure the effects of tariff structures on the allocation of resources. The ERP is defined as the percentage increase in value added per unit in an economic activity attributable to the tariff structure relative to the free-trade situation. It quantifies the intensity of protection afforded to the final product and can be used where multiple inputs are involved.

Consider the following simple example of a producer of bicycle frames that requires only steel as an intermediate input. Suppose that the production of a frame worth 150 in free trade requires the use of steel worth 100 in free trade. Value added at free trade prices is thus 50. Now assume that the country where the producer operates provides nominal protection at a rate of 20 percent on frames and 10 percent on steel. Under this structure of protection the domestic price of frames becomes 180 while the cost of the steel required to produce the frame becomes 110. Value added in this case is 70, which is 40 percent higher than value added in free trade. This increase in value added permitted by the protection structure is known as the *effective rate of protection*.

As shown in this simple example, in the presence of tariff escalation, the ERP (40 percent) is larger than the nominal tariff on the output (20 percent). Its main advantage is to capture certain general equilibrium mechanisms while avoiding the infor-

mational requirements of full general equilibrium computations. In the early 1970s, the utility of the concept of effective protection was challenged by a number of authors. Eventually, economists recognized the descriptive value of the ERP concept in empirical studies of protection as well as its analytical value subject to some caveats.

Effects of Tariff Escalation In principle, tariff escalation would be expected to distort resource allocation in both the importing and the exporting countries. In the importing country, output should be skewed toward processed products while in the exporting country it should be skewed toward raw materials. Yeats (1984), however, argues that the tendency for tariffs to increase over stages of a processing chain is neither a necessary nor a sufficient condition to establish a bias against processed goods. There are two problems: first, the nature of tariff-induced trade biases has never been defined precisely; second, the changes in demand conditions over stages of a processing chain have never been considered. Yeats shows that because import demand elasticities consistently increase with the degree of processing, neutral tariffs (i.e., tariffs that do not change the shares of primary and processed goods in exports relative to free trade while maintaining the aggregate level of imports) would often be deescalating. In other words, a trade bias against processed goods may exist even when actual tariffs deescalate over a processing chain.

In the 1990s, concerns were raised that tariff escalation may be a source of environmental damage to exporting countries. The argument was that by shifting economic activity toward primary production and away from processing, escalation induced excessive extraction of natural resources with consequent degradation of the resource base. A literature review by Hecht (1997), however, suggested that tariff escalation was not a significant source of distortion in the economic system or of damage to the environment. First, tariff escalation decreased with the Uruguay Round of international trade negotiations (1986–94) and was further reduced by preferences. Second, there was evidence that processing activities would tend to cause more environmental harm in developing countries than in developed countries. Finally, the elimination of escalation would not boost income sufficiently in developing countries to significantly promote environmental protection.

Magnitude of Current Tariff Escalation In the last decade, a number of studies have assessed the incidence of tariff escalation in agricultural markets. These studies differ significantly in terms of methodology, country, and commodity coverage, as well as in the type of tariffs they consider. The studies generally point out the persistence of tariff escalation in the post–Uruguay Round tariff landscape, and they provide a number of more specific results.

The Uruguay Round reduced escalation of developed country–bound agricultural tariff rates. Even after full implementation of Uruguay Round tariff cuts, however, escalation persisted in developed countries in about half the agricultural product chains considered (Lindland 1997; UNCTAD 2003). USDA (2001) extends these results to developing countries. OECD (1999), which covers both agricultural and nonagricultural products as well as developed and developing countries, found that most processing chains in both members of the Organisation for Economic Co-operation and Development (OECD) and nonmembers are affected by escalation.

Applied tariffs also exhibit escalation. Elamin and Khaira (2004) show that for major developed importers, escalation prevails in 12 out of 16 of the agricultural product chains they consider. In developed countries, tariff escalation seems to be lower in the case of applied most-favored-nation tariffs than in the case of bound tariffs, while the opposite prevails in developing countries. When the nonreciprocal preferences that developed countries extend to developing countries are taken into account, escalation is clearly lower. In fact, the least-developed countries do not face any tariff escalation in markets where they are granted duty and quota-free access. It may be worth underlining, however, that nontariff barriers may also be escalating.

Since its effects on exporting countries were identified in the 1960s, escalation has been a concern for developing countries. Successive rounds of tariff negotiations have not gotten rid of it. How much the Doha Round of international trade negotiations will reduce escalation will largely depend on the degree of flexibility available to governments to protect specific products from formula cuts. In any case, for a reduction of escalation to have a substantial effect on the export structure of those countries that have not been able to diversify away from natural resources, most of which are least-developed countries, a number of other constraints on improved export performance will need to be released. Least-developed countries' poor export performance may be due in no small part to binding export supply response capacity constraints, which prevent fuller utilization of available market access opportunities.

See also commodity chains; effective protection; tariffs

FURTHER READING

Elamin, N., and H. Khaira. 2004. "Tariff Escalation in Agricultural Commodity Markets." *FAO Commodity Market Review 2003–4*, Rome: Food and Agriculture Organization of the United Nations, 101–20. A recent assessment of escalation in both bound and applied tariffs.

Hecht, J. E. 1997. "Impacts of Tariff Escalation on the Environment: Literature Review and Synthesis." *World Development* 25 (10): 1701–16. A review of the literature on the environmental effects of escalation.

Johnson, H. G. 1965. "The Theory of Tariff Structure with Special Reference to World Trade and Development." *Trade and Development*. Geneva: Institut des Hautes Etudes Internationales. One of the earliest analyses of the effect of escalation on exporting countries.

Lindland, J. 1997. "The Impact of the Uruguay Round on Tariff Escalation in Agricultural Products." FAO Commodities and Trade Division, ESCP No. 3. Rome: FAO. An assessment of tariff escalation in agricultural markets.

Organisation for Economic Co-operation and Development (OECD). 1999. *Post–Uruguay Round Tariff Regimes, Achievements and Outlook*. Paris: OECD. Includes an assessment of tariff escalation following the Uruguay Round in selected countries.

UN Conference on Trade and Development (UNCTAD). 2003. "Back to Basics: Market Access Issues in the Doha Agenda." UNCTAD / DITC / TAB / Misc. 9. Geneva: UNCTAD. An assessment of tariff escalation.

U.S. Department of Agriculture (USDA). 2001. "Profiles of Tariffs in Global Agricultural Markets." AER-796. Washington, DC: USDA. An assessment of post–Uruguay Round escalation that covers developing countries.

Yeats, A. J. 1984. "On the Analysis of Tariff Escalation." *Journal of Development Economics* 15: 77–88. An interesting discussion of the link between escalation and the existence of a bias against processed goods.

MARC BACCHETTA

■ tariff rate quotas

A tariff rate quota (TRQ) is unlike an ordinary quota because it does not set an absolute maximum level of imports. Instead, it sets a specified quantity of imports that can enter at a lower tariff (called an "in-quota tariff") than imports in excess of that limit. If the higher "over-quota tariff" is set so high that no imports occur above the limit, then the TRQ functions like an import quota. Historically the purpose of TRQs is to harmonize the common external tariff in a customs union or free trade area, implement tariff preferences for developing countries, or provide a special safeguard against import surges (Rom 1979). More than 1,425 TRQs were established in the Uruguay Round Agreement on Agriculture to facilitate the conversion of import bans and quotas into tariffs (WTO 2006). In some cases, these agricultural TRQs increased trade because countries were to provide "minimum access" (at least 5 percent of domestic consumption by 2001) and not restrict "current access" (quotas at historically established import levels). TRQs for agriculture are very important in members of the Organisation for Economic Co-operation and Development, protecting upward of 50 percent of the total value of domestic production (de Gorter and Kliauga 2006).

Article XIII of the General Agreement on Tariffs and Trade (GATT) 1994 governs the administration of quantitative restrictions including TRQs and can be interpreted as inherently contradictory because it advocates nondiscrimination yet allows "supplier tariff quotas" as opposed to global quotas open to all exporting countries (Skully 2001). The GATT advocates two criteria for proper administration: quota fill (where imports are to be determined by market conditions) and distribution of trade (trade patterns are to approach that without the restrictions). But importing countries have a GATT-consistent means of discrimination, because if agreement among all interested parties is "not reasonably practical," then quotas can be apportioned to exporting countries on a historical basis.

Disputes have resulted over the method by which country-specific export quotas are allocated. A classic example is the "Banana Dispute" (WTO 1997) where the method used by the European Union (EU) was deemed discriminatory because it did not reflect recent trade patterns. The WTO Appellate Body also ruled that the EU practiced discrimination in not requiring export licenses for all countries. The Banana Dispute also highlighted problems in allocating import licenses because the EU was found to be inconsistent across countries in terms of the period of validity of the license, the size of license, eligibility requirements for a license, reallocation of unused licenses, and the requirements for the use of the license. Some firms from Latin American countries faced complicated licensing procedures and had unnecessary burdens imposed on them. They were deemed to have been treated in a discriminatory and trade-distorting manner, so that the EU had to reform its banana quota licensing system.

Ideally quotas should be auctioned, but mostly other forms of administration along with additional regulations have been imposed. The issue of TRQ administration is one of two major issues; the other is how best to liberalize trade with TRQs.

Trade Liberalization Effects of Reducing Tariffs versus Expanding Quotas Three basic "regimes" can determine imports and domestic prices, corresponding to each of the three policy instruments comprising a TRQ: the in-quota tariff (t_1), the over-quota tariff (t_2), and the quota level itself. The in-quota tariff regime can result for two reasons: market conditions are such that underfill occurs (the quota is not binding) or the quota (and over-quota tariff) is disregarded, in which case either quota underfill or overfill can result. "Overfill" occurs when the government allows imports at the in-quota tariff to exceed the level of the quota. Imports paying the over-quota tariff (described later) are called "over-quota" and are not counted toward overfill.

Figure 1 shows the case of a small-country importer facing an import supply ES and an import demand curve ED such that the quota is not binding and underfill occurs. This shows that a quota fill rate of less than 100 percent does not necessarily imply inefficiency. But it could also be the case that the government allows the market to determine the equilibrium regardless of the quota level and so quota overfill could occur (not shown in figure 1), depending on market conditions and the levels of the quota and in-quota tariff. In either case, there are no quota rents. The domestic price Pd is equal to the world price inclusive of the in-quota tariff. Because the MFN over-quota tariff is the one under negotiation in the WTO, the difference between the over-quota and in-quota tariff represents "water" in the tariff, defined as that range over which a reduction in the over-quota tariff will have no impact on trade. An increase in the quota will have no impact initially with underfill due to market conditions and no impact at all if by government decree the quota is not a constraint.

The over-quota tariff determines the equilibrium in figure 2. One would normally expect the quota to be exactly filled, and imports beyond the quota to pay the over-quota tariff. But this particular case in figure

2 has quota underfill, which necessarily implies inefficiency in the administration of the quota licenses because some suppliers are forgoing quota rents in paying the higher tariff. Underfill in this case could be due to import quota licenses being allocated to higher-cost suppliers. Empirical research finds the situation depicted in figure 2 to be very common, but cases of exact fill and overfill also exist. Overfill can occur by government decree, when imports paying the lower tariff are extended beyond the quota while over-quota imports occur at the same time. In all cases, quota rents are positive, as are tariff revenues from both in-quota and over-quota imports. A reduction in over-quota tariffs will have an immediate trade liberalizing effect, while a quota expansion will have no initial impact because of over-quota imports and either quota underfill or overfill. Note that when a quota expansion does have an impact, there is a regime switch to the quota binding case (described next) but continued quota expansion will result in a switch to the in-quota tariff binding regime, in which case any further increases in the quota will have no trade liberalizing effects.

The case where the quota is binding initially is given in figure 3. The particular case shown has quota underfill, necessarily due to inefficient quota administration, but the cases of exact fill or quota overfill can occur as well. In all cases, there are positive quota rents and in-quota tariff revenues. A reduction in over-quota tariffs will have no immediate impact on trade because of water in the tariff due to

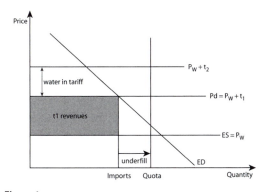

Figure 1
In-quota tariff with quota underfill

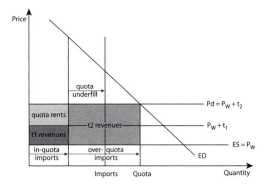

Figure 2
Over-quota tariff with over-quota imports and quota underfill

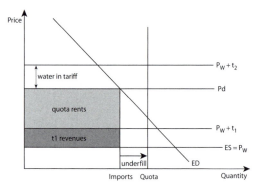

Figure 3
Quota binding with underfill

the binding quota. Expanding the quota will have an immediate impact only if there is exact quota fill initially; otherwise there will be no initial trade expansion with overfill and perhaps a less than one-to-one increase in trade with underfill, depending on the reason for the underfill.

The discussion shows that the efficacy of a tariff cut versus a quota expansion depends on a complex set of factors. The impact of tariff reductions depends on the level of water in the tariff, whereas that of quota expansion depends on the levels of over-quota imports, overfill or underfill, whether the in-quota tariff is initially binding, or how soon the in-quota tariff regime becomes binding with continued quota expansion.

TRQ Administration How the rights to quotas are distributed can affect the volume and distribution of trade, as well as the distribution of rents. With country-specific allocations, the exporting country may obtain the quota rents, depending on how the import licenses are awarded and the bargaining power between exporting and importing firms. The WTO (2006) identifies six principal methods of TRQ administration: applied tariffs; licenses on demand; first come, first served; historical imports; state trading enterprises (including producer groups); and auctions.

Applied tariffs refer to cases when the in-quota tariff determines imports and are usually used for less politically sensitive products. No licenses are allocated to importers—imports are not limited. There is

no inefficiency as a result except that due to the in-quota tariff itself.

With the *licenses-on-demand* method, firms request licenses and if the total licenses requested exceed the quota, then requests are reduced pro rata. Inefficiency is incurred because high-cost firms are allowed to operate closer to their optimal levels while low-cost firms are further from their desired levels. The ability to overbid exacerbates this inefficiency (Hranaiova, de Gorter, and Falk 2006).

Licenses allocated on the basis of *historical imports* also generate inefficiency if cost structures or demand change over time. Furthermore, firms may rent seek by importing at a loss at the over-quota tariff to increase their share of the licenses in the future.

The *first-come, first-served* basis hurries up imports and so causes inefficient allocation of imports over time. Because many agricultural products are perishable, rents are not dissipated with waiting in line. Instead domestic prices fall to world levels as exporters compete for the rent, which falls and so is appropriated by consumers. Domestic producers face the world price until the quota is filled, when the domestic price then spikes. The ability for firms to rent seek by storing the commodity or changing the seasonality of production will generate inefficiencies and reduce rent appropriation by consumers.

State trading enterprises (STEs) have direct control over imports; inefficiencies can result, depending on the STE's objectives and degree of control over imports and the domestic market. Some STEs in Asia tender licenses to the lowest-price bidder, resulting in low-quality imports (sometimes for animal feed) and so minimize the damage to producers for a given import quantity (Agricultural and Resource Economics Review 2000).

Because tariff quota administration is a rationing problem, economists favor a market-based system *auctioning* licenses to the highest bidder. Auctions account for the lowest level of agricultural trade under TRQs, however (de Gorter and Kliauga 2006).

Many additional regulations on import licenses can accompany each of these administration methods. The more onerous ones include domestic purchase requirements, time limits, limits per firm, and seasonal licenses. A restrictive *domestic purchase requirement* can cause underfill, whereas *time limits* and *limits per firm* can impose increased costs of importation. *Seasonal licenses* increase inefficiency, especially in agriculture, where different harvest seasons cannot be taken fully advantage of between countries in the northern and southern hemispheres.

The role of TRQs in the modern world economy is mostly limited to agriculture, where they are facilitating the transition from nontariff barriers to tariffs as the principal means of protection. As of 2007, several outstanding issues in the WTO trade negotiations remain unresolved, including how best to liberalize TRQs. Reducing over-quota tariffs is generally agreed to be the more trade-liberalizing approach, but many countries instead expand quotas. This would reduce the amount of preference erosion for developing countries who often receive the quota rents. But it also leaves open the possibility of continued inefficiency due to the many ways quotas are administered, often with restrictive additional regulations.

See also distortions to agricultural incentives; nontariff measures; tariffs; World Trade Organization

FURTHER READING

Agricultural and Resource Economics Review. 2000. "Special Issue: Issues in the Administration of Tariff-Rate Import Quotas in the Agreement on Agriculture in the WTO." ARER 20 (1): 54–124. A series of theoretical and empirical papers analyzing TRQs, with specific examples of country experiences.

de Gorter, Harry, and Erika Kliauga. 2006. "Reducing Tariffs versus Expanding Tariff Rate Quotas." In *Agricultural Trade Reform and the Doha Agenda*, edited by Kym Anderson and Will Martin. Washington, DC: World Bank and Palgrave Macmillan, 117–60. A comprehensive empirical analysis of TRQ liberalization in agriculture and the importance of alternative administration methods and additional regulations.

Hranaiova, Jana, Harry de Gorter, and James Falk. 2006. "The Economics of Administering Import Quotas with Licenses-on-Demand in Agriculture." *American Journal of Agricultural Economics* 88 (2): 3318–50. The only paper in the literature analyzing licenses on demand, the TRQ administration method that has affected by far the most trade.

Rom, Michael. 1979. *The Role of Tariff Quotas in Commercial Policy*. New York: Holmes and Meier. An often-cited, early analysis of the practice and theory of TRQs, including its history and treatment under the GATT.

Skully, David W. 2001. *Economics of Tariff-Rate Quota Administration*. U.S. Department of Agriculture, Economic Research Service, Technical Bulletin Number 1893 (April). Washington, DC: USDA. One of the earliest systematic analyses of the economics of alternative TRQ administration methods.

World Trade Organization (WTO). 1997. *European Communities-Regime for the Importation, Sale, and Distribution of Bananas*. Report of the Appellate Body (September 9). WT/DS27/AB/R. Geneva: WTO, Office of the Secretary General. A comprehensive account of the problems associated with the allocation of country specific quotas and import licensing schemes for EU banana imports, providing insightful details for researchers in understanding the variety of practical problems arising from the implementation of TRQs.

———. 2006. *Tariff Quota Administration Methods and Tariff Quota Fill*. Committee on Agriculture Background Paper TN/AG/S/22 (April 27). Geneva: WTO. A comprehensive compilation of quota fill rates by quota administration method and additional regulation for different countries and commodity groups.

HARRY DE GORTER

■ tariffs

Tariffs are taxes levied on imported or, less often, exported goods when they cross the border between one customs territory and another. The use of customs duties, a synonym for import tariffs, can be traced back to the Babylonian civilization (18th to 6th centuries BCE). In the 20th century, tariffs fluctuated considerably. Since the end of World War II, however, thanks to eight rounds of tariff negotiations under the General Agreement on Tariffs and Trade (GATT) and to a number of preferential tariff agreements, developed country tariffs have been on a downward trend from an average of 20–30 percent to between 3 and 7 percent. Developing country tariffs have also been substantially reduced, but only since the 1980s. Despite a substantial increase in the number of tariff lines, international comparability and overall transparency in the tariff area increased significantly with the adoption by all countries of a common nomenclature, the so-called Harmonized System (see Hoda 2001).

Because they are relatively easy to collect and seem to be paid by foreigners, tariffs have long been an instrument of choice for governments to collect revenue. In the late 20th and early 21st centuries, however, this role lost its importance among developed and most developing countries as governments became more interested in the effect of tariffs on the economy. Tariffs raise the price of imported products on the domestic market and reduce imported quantities. They yield revenue for governments and afford protection to domestic producers of the goods that compete with imports. A tariff imposed on some imported products will have two effects on the importing country: it will introduce welfare-reducing distortions of both production and consumption, and if the country that imposes it is large enough to affect foreign export prices, it will improve its terms of trade.

Types of Tariffs Tariffs are generally ad valorem, which means that they are expressed as a percentage of the value of imports, but they can also be *specific*, expressed as a number of monetary units per quantity unit (e.g., $5 per Kg). Other less common tariffs include *compound* tariffs, which have two components, one ad valorem and the other specific ($5 per Kg + 3 percent); *mixed* tariffs, which take the form either of a specific rate or of an ad valorem rate, whichever is the highest ($5 per Kg or 3 percent, w. i. t. h.); or *technical* tariffs, the level of which depends on the product's content of one or more specific input(s), such as sugar or alcohol. Non–ad valorem tariffs are most frequent in agriculture but they are also used by a small number of countries for certain nonagricultural products.

An important distinction that relates to tariff negotiations and trade agreements is between most-favored-nation and preferential tariff rates. A basic principle of the GATT and the World Trade Organization (WTO) is that governments should not set different tariff rates for different trading partners. This nondiscrimination principle takes the form of the most-favored-nation (MFN) clause, which dictates that a country must immediately extend any advantage, favor, privilege, or immunity granted to any product originating from or destined to any other country to the like product originating or destined to all other member countries. MFN tariffs apply to all trading partners with the exception of those that benefit from preferences. Multilateral rules allow exceptions to the MFN principle for regional trade agreements (GATT Article XXIV) and for nonreciprocal preferences granted to developing countries (1979 Enabling Clause). There are thus two different types of preferential tariffs: the nonreciprocal preferences granted by developed countries to developing countries, and the reciprocal preferences granted by participants in regional trade agreements to other participants.

From a legal perspective, a distinction is sometimes made between tariffs that are stipulated by laws, called statutory tariffs, and tariffs that are stipulated by conventions. The first category comprises, among others, the general rate that remains unchanged unless the situation substantially changes, temporary rates, preferential rates applicable to developing countries, and so on. Two types of duty rates are stipulated by conventions: conventional rates established in the WTO and preferential rates negotiated in regional trade agreements.

A second distinction that relates more specifically to the GATT/WTO is between bound and applied tariffs. When governments negotiate tariff reductions in the GATT/WTO, their commitments take the form of tariff bindings. MFN bound tariff levels, which are listed in a country's tariff schedule, indicate the upper limit at which the government is committed to set its MFN applied tariff. For a given tariff line, the MFN bound tariff must thus be higher than or equal to the MFN applied tariff, which is higher than the preferential tariff.

The concept of effective tariff or effective rate of protection serves to measure the encouragement provided to domestic production by tariffs on both inputs and outputs. Nominal tariffs do not measure this encouragement appropriately. If they are imposed on imports that compete with a country's outputs, tariffs provide a positive stimulus to domestic producers. If, however, tariffs are imposed on a country's imported inputs, domestic producers are worse off. To capture the net protective effect of a tariff structure, effective tariffs measure the stimulus to value added, in the production of a particular product provided by nominal tariffs. The effective rate of protection is defined as the difference expressed in percentage terms between a sector's value added at world market prices and its value added with tariffs imposed. If the nominal tariff on inputs and output is the same, the effective tariff is equal to the nominal tariff. If the nominal tariff on the output exceeds the nominal tariff on the input, the effective tariff is higher than the nominal tariff.

Economic Effects of Tariffs Starting from a situation of free trade, consider the effect of a specific tariff t introduced by country A on product X. In the absence of any tariff or other distortion, the domestic price of product X is equal to the world price. When tariff t is introduced, however, exporters renounce shipping product X to country A if the price in A does not exceed the world price by t. The price in A starts rising while, if A's market is large enough, world price starts decreasing until the wedge is equal to t. The rise in price in A encourages domestic supply and discourages domestic demand. The volume of trade decreases. If A's market is large enough, the price increase in A is less than the amount of the tariff t. The decrease in A's demand lowers the world price so that only part of the tariff is passed on to consumers in A. If A is small enough, however, the world price remains constant and the tariff is fully passed on to consumers.

Consumers in A lose from the tariff while producers gain and the government collects tariff revenue. If A is large enough and the world price decreases, foreign producers lose and foreign consumers gain. A simple cost-benefit analysis using the notions of producer and consumer surplus reveals that for a country without market power the best

policy is free trade. The cost of the tariff to consumers is only partly compensated by the gain to producers and the increase in government revenue. The tariff induces a net welfare loss (deadweight loss) that can be linked back to both a consumption distortion (consumers do not consume enough X) and a production distortion (producers produce too much X). For a country that is large enough for changes in its demand to affect world prices, however, free trade is not necessarily optimal. In the large market case, the loss resulting from the two distortions must be compared with a "terms-of-trade" gain resulting from the lower price paid by consumers for the imported product. Note that this gain corresponds to a loss in the exporting country, which adds up to a deadweight loss resulting from the distortions of both consumption and production.

Arguments in Favor of Tariffs The cost-benefit analysis of tariffs has shown that for small countries without influence on their terms of trade, free trade is optimal. For countries that are large enough to influence the price of their imports, however, a nonzero tariff can be preferable to free trade on efficiency grounds. As first demonstrated by Bickerdike (1906), an "optimum tariff" can be calculated that maximizes national welfare. This optimum tariff level is the one at which the marginal benefit from improved terms of trade is equal to the marginal cost from production and consumption distortions. The so-called terms-of-trade argument for a tariff raises a number of empirical and practical problems, however. First, the practical relevance of the terms-of-trade argument is a matter of controversy among international economists. Second, as explained in the previous section, the terms-of-trade gain comes at the expense of the exporting country. If a large country uses its market power to extract gains from its partners, it will most likely induce retaliation and trigger a trade war (Johnson 1954).

Another argument that may justify the use of tariffs is the presence of market failures. If, for instance, capital or labor markets do not function properly and slow down or prevent resource reallocation, if activities of potential interest for production and export diversification generate learning by doing spillovers, or if unemployment or under-employment is significant, the basic theoretical case for free trade does not hold. In the presence of market failures, the consumer and producer surplus concepts do not measure the costs and benefits of tariffs adequately. Consider the case where the production of some good or service generates productivity gains for the sector or even the whole economy and firms that produce the good cannot appropriate these benefits and thus do not take it into account in their production decisions. In such a case, firms will not produce the good despite the fact that it would be socially optimal to produce it. The spillovers could then be used as a justification for a temporary tariff that would stimulate production and thereby generate social benefits.

The market failure argument for protection has been criticized on two grounds. First, tariffs are not the first best response to most domestic market failures. In the spillover case, a production subsidy would also stimulate production, but unlike the tariff it would not distort consumption and would therefore be preferable. Second, the market failure argument in favor of tariffs has been criticized for practical and political reasons. For some economists, government failures cause more problems than market failures. Market failures are difficult to identify and appropriate policy responses difficult to design. Moreover special interests are likely to have more influence where governments pursue a more flexible trade policy.

Recent History By the end of World War I, high tariff levels, quantitative restrictions, and prohibitions combined with exchange controls dominated the trade policy scene. Countries that had become creditors to other nations, such as the United States, Argentina, Australia, Canada, and India, increased or kept tariffs very high by international standards. In the early 1920s, while various nontariff barriers introduced during the war were progressively lifted, tariffs were raised in compensation. In the late 1920s, a sharp fall in agricultural prices jeopardized attempts to negotiate tariff reductions. Germany, France, and Italy raised their agricultural tariffs and the U.S. Congress passed the protectionist Smoot-Hawley Tariff Act, which even before its implementation provoked widespread retaliation, contributing to a general increase in tariffs. The new trade restrictions aggravated the economic crisis and openly discriminatory trade relations evolved. In 1931, after almost one hundred years of a very liberal trade policy with minimal protection, the United Kingdom, still the largest importer, retreated via the Ottawa Agreement into a preferential trading system.

World War II severely affected the world trading system. A low level of trade went together with major trade imbalances. Trade policies were characterized by relatively high tariffs, the use of preferences by some countries, the extensive use of nontariff trade barriers by the European countries, and widespread government control of international transactions in order to manage scarce foreign exchange reserves of U.S. dollars. In 1947 the average tariff rate was between 20 and 30 percent (WTO 2007). The average U.S. tariff in 1947 was still considered to be among the highest in the major industrial countries despite a shift away from the extreme protectionist trade policies of the early 1930s. The average applied tariff rate among European countries ranged somewhere between 10 and 20 percent. A low-tariff country group (comprising Denmark, Norway, Sweden, and the Benelux countries—Belgium, the Netherlands, and Luxembourg) had tariffs somewhat below 10 percent while a high-tariff group (comprising France, Italy, Portugal, and the United Kingdom) had tariffs averaging close to 20 percent (Woytinski and Woytinski 1955). The situation in other regions of the world was relatively diverse, but available evidence suggests that independent countries had relatively high tariffs. Brazil, for instance, had shifted toward a strict form of industrial protectionism in the late 19th century to become one of the most highly protectionist countries in the world.

Since 1947, eight rounds of multilateral tariff negotiations under the GATT and the WTO contributed to a substantial reduction of industrial tariffs in developed countries. Tariffs on agricultural and textiles and clothing products, which did not follow the downward trend, stick out above the average. Until the 1980s, a majority of developing countries pursued import-substitution policies with relatively high tariffs. Starting in the 1980s, however, many if not most of them switched to more outward-oriented development strategies and started reducing their tariffs unilaterally, often in the context of structural adjustment programs.

At the same time, tariffs were also reduced on a discriminatory basis. In various regions of the world regional trade agreements were signed that resulted in the reciprocal elimination of tariffs on trade between a limited number of trading partners. Most developed countries also introduced nonreciprocal preferential tariff schemes aimed at encouraging imports from developing countries.

Priorities Because they have been brought down in most countries, tariffs are sometimes seen as history. In reality, however, they are still alive, and the evolution of the Doha Round of multilateral trade negotiations (ongoing as of late 2007) reflects how difficult it is for governments to agree to further cuts and bindings. There are a number of reasons for this. Tariff reductions tend to follow the path of least resistance, so the remaining duties can be expected to offer more resistance to liberalization efforts. It is not clear whether discriminatory tariff reductions facilitate or impede MFN reductions. More than anything else, however, skepticism regarding the benefits from tariff reductions in the public and in a number of governments has been growing. This may mean that the case for cutting and binding tariffs needs to be reassessed or simply that it needs to be made more convincingly.

See also effective protection; multilateral trade negotiations; nondiscrimination; tariff escalation; terms of trade; World Trade Organization

FURTHER READING

Bickerdike, C. F. 1906. "The Theory of Incipient Taxes." *Economic Journal* 16: 529–35. The earliest exposition of the terms-of-trade argument for a tariff.

Corden, W. M. 1974. *Trade Policy and Economic Welfare*. Oxford: Clarendon Press. A discussion of economic arguments in favor of and against protection.

Hoda, A. 2001. *Tariff Negotiations and Renegotiations under the GATT and the WTO*. Cambridge: Cambridge University Press. A discussion of procedures and practices in the implementation of the provisions relating to multilateral tariff negotiations and renegotiations.

Johnson, H. G. 1954. "Optimum Tariffs and Retaliation." *Review of Economic Studies* 21: 142–53. A demonstration of the fact that a country may gain by imposing a tariff even if other countries retaliate and a seminal contribution to the theory of trade agreements.

World Trade Organization (WTO). 2007. *World Trade Report*. Geneva: WTO. Chapter 2, "60 Years of International Trade Cooperation," includes a discussion of the history of tariff policies since World War I.

World Trade Organization, International Trade Center, and United Nations Conference on Trade and Development. 2007. *World Tariff Profiles 2006*. The most comprehensive source of aggregate tariff statistics.

Woytinski, W. S., and E. S. Woytinski. 1955. *World Commerce and Governments: Trends and Outlook*. New York: Twentieth Century Fund. Provides estimates of tariffs in the early 1950s.

MARC BACCHETTA

■ **tariffs and foreign direct investment**
See trade costs and foreign direct investment

■ **tax holidays (or waivers)**
See subsidies and financial incentives to foreign direct investment

■ **Taylor rule**
See monetary policy rules

■ **technical barriers to trade**
Standards and technical regulations exist to ensure consumer safety, environmental protection, national security, interoperability of electronic products, and many other goals. There is a wide variety of standards and technical regulations. These include guidelines for product certification, performance mandates,

testing procedures, conformity assessment rules, and labeling requirements, for example. The simple distinction between standards and mandatory technical regulations is that the latter refers to rules imposed by government, while standards are voluntary guidelines. Standards development may be encouraged by nongovernmental organizations, or required of a supplier to a manufacturer of a final good, for example.

From a producer's perspective, standards and technical regulations can overcome problems of fragmented markets and result in economies of scale. It is potentially more costly to produce for a market with many different incompatible products. This can deter firms from exporting to multiple markets with one product. Moreover, standards and regulations that promote compatibility or interoperability between products allow firms to supply goods at lower prices. From a consumer's perspective, efficient standards and regulations can make it easier to compare products to meet individual preferences and help to ensure that goods are safe or operate efficiently. Standards and mandatory regulations may also, however, act to restrict competition and act as a technical barrier to trade (Maskus, Otsuki, and Wilson 2005). This is particularly true when standards are nontransparent, imposed on a discriminatory basis, or not harmonized to international norms.

The majority of mandatory product regulations are set by national governments. Technical regulations may vary across countries given different views regarding optimal levels of safety, risk, levels of environmental protection, or national security, among other factors. Technical regulations that deviate from principles of reliance on international science, private sector–led development, or international norms can raise costs for producers seeking to enter export markets—and act as a technical barrier to trade. Technical regulations may discriminate against foreign suppliers, both in their design and implementation, and may be used to provide strategic trade advantages for domestic firms over foreign competitors. Technical regulations can also force firms to duplicate product testing and certification procedures required to test conformity to

standards—and therefore raise design and production costs. Regulations can also be crafted to exclude foreign entrants into a particular market in order to support domestic monopolies.

Firms in developing countries may be especially affected by these factors, given less efficient production facilities, or lack of access to testing and certification procedures or information on international standards. The overall findings from the World Bank Technical Barriers to Trade (TBT) survey conducted in 17 developing countries indicate that 70 percent of firms that export must comply with mandatory technical regulations. The majority of firms responding to the survey perceive technical regulations to be important for entering export markets (Otsuki and Wilson 2004).

There are general commitments under the World Trade Organization (WTO) Technical Barriers to Trade Agreement that address the use of technical regulations to block trade (WTO 2007). These provisions encourage use of international standards to meet regulatory goals, promote mutual recognition of tests and certification where possible among members, and codify the principles of nondiscrimination and national treatment in regard to technical regulations. The TBT Agreement also mandates that governments notify the WTO of any new draft technical regulation prior to final implementation.

There is an increasing number of empirical studies that examine standards and technical regulations and their impact on trade flows. Among others, Chen, Otsuki, and Wilson (2006) examine how meeting foreign standards affects firms' export performance, reflected in export propensity and market diversification. The study uses firm-level data from the World Bank Technical Barriers to Trade Survey. The results indicate that firms subject to mandatory testing procedures have an export share nearly nine percentage points lower than other firms. The existence of information inquiry difficulties in major export destinations is estimated to decrease exports by 18 percent of their total sales. Furthermore, long inspection times for products significantly reduce firms' export incentives.

The study also explores how standards and technical regulations vary across different types of firms and how market diversification might be affected. Results suggest that the export propensity of domestically owned firms is affected more by testing procedures relative to other firms and that the negative relationship between informational inquiry difficulty and export propensity is strongest for manufacturing firms. In terms of market diversification, the results imply that standards reduce the likelihood for exporters to enter multiple markets.

Questions of the utility of harmonization of national standards and technical regulations to international norms are also increasingly important in regard to the role of standards as technical barriers to trade. Czubala, Shepherd, and Wilson (2007) examine the impact of European Union (EU) standards on African textiles and clothing exports, a sector of particular development interest. Evidence suggests that EU standards not harmonized to de facto international standards reduce African exports of these products. EU standards that are harmonized to ISO standards are less trade restricting. Results suggest that efforts to promote African exports of manufactures may need to be complemented by measures to reduce the cost impact of product standards, including international harmonization. In addition, efforts to harmonize national standards with international norms, including through the World Trade Organization Technical Barriers to Trade Agreement, promise concrete benefits through trade expansion.

Technical barriers to trade represent one of the more important potential obstacles to the expansion of world trade. Nontariff barriers have fallen over the past decades, and traditional nontariff barriers such as quotas and other policy tools of protection have been reduced. Efforts to deregulate, basing technical regulations on international scientific risk profiles, and reliance on suppliers' declaration of conformity reinforced by postmarket surveillance systems, among other steps, can help reduce the scope for governments to protect domestic firms behind technical barriers. Strengthening the WTO disciplines in the TBT Agreement, including stronger provisions on notifications of new regulations by members and further encouragement of harmonization of standards to international norms, can also help.

See also nontariff measures; World Trade Organization

FURTHER READING

Chen, Maggie Xiaoyang, Tsunehiro Otsuki, and John S. Wilson. 2006. "Do Standards Matter for Export Success?" World Bank Policy Research Working Paper No. 3809. Washington, DC: World Bank. Examines the impact of standards and technical regulations on the propensity of firms to export.

Czubala, Witold, Ben Shepherd, and John S. Wilson. 2007. "Help or Hindrance? The Impact of Harmonized Standards on African Exports." World Bank Policy Research Working Paper No. 4400 Washington, DC: World Bank. Analysis in this paper draws on the first use of the World Bank EU standards database. It finds that, for African exporters, EU standards harmonized to International Standards Organization (ISO) standards in textiles and clothing are less trade restrictive than standards that are not.

Maskus, Keith, Tsunehiro Otsuki, and John S. Wilson. 2005. "The Cost of Complying with Foreign Product Standards for Firms in Developing Countries: An Econometric Study." World Bank Policy Research Paper No. 3590. Washington, DC: World Bank. Finds empirical evidence, based on the World Bank Technical Barriers to Trade database, that compliance with foreign product standards does involve costs to producers.

Maskus, Keith, and John S. Wilson. 2001. "A Review of Past Attempts and the New Policy Context." In *Quantifying the Impact of Technical Barriers to Trade: Can It Be Done?* Edited by Keith Maskus and John S. Wilson. Ann Arbor: University of Michigan Press, 1–7. Provides analysis of efforts to quantify the impact of standards and technical barriers on trade.

Otsuki, Tsunehiro, and John S. Wilson. 2004. "Standards and Technical Regulations and Firm's Ability to Export: New Evidence from World Bank Standards and Trade Survey." Mimeo. Washington, DC: World Bank. Provides a summary review of findings from the World Bank Technical Barriers to Trade database.

World Trade Organization (WTO). 2007. Technical Barriers to Trade: Technical Explanation. http://www.wto

.org/English/tratop_e/tbt_e/tbt_info_e.htm. Accessed June 2007. Provides an overview of rights and obligations of WTO members under the TBT Agreement.

JOHN S. WILSON

■ technological progress in open economies

Long-run economic growth is driven by technological progress, which in general takes two forms: product innovations and process innovations. The former refers to introduction of new or better quality products and the latter refers to implementation of resource-saving technologies. Diffusion of new products/technologies via imitation and direct technology transfer also promotes economic growth. This is especially valid for developing countries that are further away from the world technology frontier. The question of whether openness stimulates technological progress is important since openness is to a large extent determined by policy choices. Openness of an economy is measured by the degree of barriers to international trade, investment, and labor flows as well as by the volumes of these indicators.

Theory Openness can affect technological progress through a variety of channels. First, open economies can more easily acquire the state-of-the-art technologies available abroad via imports, foreign direct investment (FDI), and immigration. Second, exposure to international trade promotes competition among domestic firms. On the one hand, this can accelerate the pace of technological progress by motivating firms to escape competition via innovation. On the other hand, more intense competition can hurt profits, reduce the returns to research and thereby discourage innovation. Third, entrepreneurs in open economies have access to larger markets and thus enjoy larger returns on successful innovation. This raises the profitability of innovation and boosts growth. Fourth, open economies can avoid duplicating research conducted abroad and thus allocate their innovation resources more effectively. Fifth, under certain initial conditions, lowering trade barriers may reduce the relative price of skilled labor

and render research and development—which is a skilled-labor-intensive activity—less costly and thus stimulate growth. Finally, economies open to labor flows can experience higher growth by attracting human capital from abroad, which is known as brain gain. The opposite, brain drain, holds when human capital leaves the country. It should be noted that all of these mechanisms exert a short-run influence on economic growth but not necessarily a permanent influence on growth rates.

Case Studies Economists first investigated the linkages between growth and openness using case study techniques. These studies were conducted in the 1970s under the auspices of the World Bank, the Organisation for Economic Co-operation and Development, and the National Bureau of Economic Research (NBER). The basic methodology involved comparing the outcomes of import substitution (IS) strategies, as practiced in Argentina, Chile, Ghana, Mexico, Turkey, and other countries, with those of export promotion (EP) strategies, as implemented by Korea, Taiwan, Hong Kong, and Singapore. The premise of the IS policy was that developing countries need to protect their infant manufacturing industries by quotas and import tariffs in order to foster capital and technology accumulation. Proponents also suggested that by pursuing IS strategies developing countries would be able to avoid the adverse terms-of-trade effects associated with exporting raw materials. The premise of the EP policy was to provide market discipline to domestic firms by encouraging them to compete with foreign firms while keeping tariffs on imports at low levels. The case studies documented that pursuing EP strategies was a much more effective policy tool in fostering growth compared with IS strategies. These studies also underscored the need to complement trade liberalization with other fiscal, monetary, and structural changes such as stable government debt, market-determined exchange rates, and an improved education system.

Cross-Country Openness Growth Regressions Since the advent of broad international data sets in the early 1990s, economists have used cross-country growth regressions to investigate the openness-growth link. The basic statistical methodology involves running regressions to identify the impact of openness on economic growth while controlling for other factors that are known to affect growth such as initial income per capita, investment in physical and human capital, political stability indicators, and so on. These studies can be classified into two categories based on their choices of openness indicators.

Trade volumes regressions. The first group of these studies has used total trade share, import share, and export share in gross domestic product as openness measures. In general, these cross-country growth regressions have established a positive and statistically significant link between growth and trade volumes. They have been criticized on two accounts, however. First, statistically significant correlations do not necessarily imply a causality from trade to growth. Second, trade is an endogenously determined variable that responds to income per capita. To tackle these issues, economists have used geographic indicators—that is, variables that affect trade but are not influenced by policy and income—as instruments and have obtained predicted values for total trade flows. They then regressed income per capita on these predicted values in the presence of control variables. The instrumental variable (IV) estimates have shown that the empirical findings from the standard cross-country growth regressions continue to hold to a large extent. The robustness of these IV estimates, however, have also been challenged by economists who incorporated institutional quality and geographic indicators in the regressions.

Trade restrictions regressions. The second group of econometric studies has used tariffs and nontariff barriers as openness indicators. These studies offer mixed results on the relationship between openness and growth and are plagued with measurement problems and data availability issues. These problems led economists to construct trade restrictiveness indexes that combine tariff and nontariff barriers with other indicators that are known to adversely affect international trade and investment. The most popular among these is the Sachs and Warner (SW)

index, which combines information on tariff rates, quotas, political control of exports, exchange rate distortions, and market structure. Although many studies have found this index to have a positive correlation with economic growth, the index is too broad to interpret as a measure of trade or investment policy. Further, it was shown that when one uses specific trade-related subcomponents of the SW index—in particular tariff rates and nontariff barriers—the relationship between openness and economic growth becomes statistically insignificant.

As an alternative to cross-country studies, recent work has focused on within-country effects of trade liberalization. The methodology involved comparing the pre– and post–trade liberalization growth rates using econometric techniques. One study that determined the timing of trade liberalization based on the SW index calculates that on average countries that switch from being closed to being open experienced a large and statistically significant increase in their growth rates. Obviously, not all of the gain in growth can be attributed to opening up the economy, because in most cases trade liberalization is accompanied by other policy changes that may foster growth such as financial reform, privatization, and investment in infrastructure.

International Technology Diffusion via Imports and FDI Empirical studies have also examined the magnitude of technology diffusion via imports by accounting for the stock of knowledge embodied in imported products. These studies show that knowledge-intensive imported goods—in particular differentiated capital goods and high-technology imports—exert a large and significant influence on domestic productivity. This is consistent with endogenous growth theory, which predicts that openness increases access to new technologies and specialized high-quality intermediate inputs and thereby stimulates productivity growth.

Technology spillovers can also take place through FDI and multinational firm (MNF) activity. MNFs can bring new technologies that can be diffused to the local economy via labor training, labor turnover, and provision of high-quality intermediate products. Interactions between MNFs and domestic firms in the form of vertical production relationships can further contribute to technology diffusion. A number of industry- and plant-level studies have found that the presence of foreign-owned firms leads to technology spillovers, but the nature and magnitude of these spillovers may differ across countries. For instance, a study focusing on Venezuela finds that the intensity of foreign ownership adversely affects the productivity of domestic firms. Another study focusing on the United States reports that 11 percent of U.S. manufacturing productivity growth is accounted for by inward FDI to the United States. The number of industry- and plant-level studies has been quite limited so far, but recently there has been a call for such studies and more work appears to be on the horizon. In the meanwhile, cross-country growth regressions have found that the growth-promoting effects of FDI materialize only for countries that attain a threshold level of human capital and financial development.

Implications for Policy Even though substantial empirical evidence supports the view that trade promotes growth, most economists caution that it is not necessarily and exclusively policy-induced trade that serves as the magic bullet. Changes in national trade and investment policies bring forth a reallocation of resources within an economy. Growth-promoting effects of trade liberalization can be reaped fully only when complemented with appropriate fiscal, monetary, and structural policies that facilitate the allocation of resources to their most productive use. These include but are not limited to stable government budget positions, low inflation, market-determined exchange rates, an improved education system, a well-functioning legal system, and reduced corruption.

See also capital accumulation in open economies; economic development; foreign direct investment and international technology transfer; growth in open economies, Schumpeterian models; intellectual property rights; international income convergence

FURTHER READING

Baldwin, Robert E. 2003. "Openness and Growth: What Is the Empirical Relationship?" NBER Working Paper No. 9578. Cambridge, MA: National Bureau of Economic Research. Provides an overview on the theory and empirics of openness-growth relationship.

Frankel, Jeffrey A., and David Romer. 1999. "Does Trade Cause Growth?" *American Economic Review* 89 (3): 379–99. The first model to investigate the impact of trade on income per capita levels taking into account the endogeneity of trade.

Keller, Wolfgang. 2004. "International Technology Diffusion." *Journal of Economic Literature* 42 (3): 752–82. Provides an extensive survey of technology diffusion across borders through investment and trade.

Helpman, Elhanan. 2004. *The Mystery of Economic Growth*. Cambridge, MA: Belknap Press. Provides a summary of the evolution of growth theory with a chapter on the role of interdependence in affecting growth.

Rodriguez, Francisco, and Dani Rodrik. 2001. "Trade Policy and Economic Growth: A Skeptic's Guide to Cross-National Evidence." In *NBER Macroeconomics Annual 2000*, edited by Ben Bernanke and Kenneth Rogoff. Cambridge, MA: MIT Press, 261–325. Provides a critical evaluation of the cross-country studies on growth and trade.

Wacziarg, Romain, and Karen Welch. 2003. "Trade Liberalization and Growth: New Evidence." NBER Working Paper No. 10152. Cambridge, MA: National Bureau of Economic Research. Empirically investigates how trade liberalization changes the pattern of growth within a country.

M. FUAT SENER

■ technology licensing

Technology licensing occurs when an economic agent with a particular technology sells that technology to another economic agent without it. Depending on the characteristics of the licensed technology, technology licensing may either reduce the licensees' cost of production or increase the quality of the licensees' products.

The literature on technology licensing can be separated into two categories based on whether the licenser and the licensees compete in the product market. Whether the licenser and the licensees are from different countries may have also important implications.

Kamien (1992) surveys the work on patent licensing in cases where the licenser and the licensees are not competitors in the product market. This entry, in contrast, will concentrate mainly on cases where the licenser and the licensees compete in the product market.

Since licensing improves the licensees' technology, it affects the intensity of product market competition and the profits of the licenser and the licensees, thus changing the firms' product market strategies (such as output or pricing decisions), which may have important welfare implications.

Optimal Licensing Contract and Quality of the Technology Considering licensing between two final goods producers, Rockett (1990) derives optimal two-part tariff licensing contracts, which consist of an up-front fixed fee and a per-unit output royalty. Royalty-only licensing is the optimal contract if there is no threat of imitation from the licensee and the licensee's output is verifiable. If imitation is costless to the licensee, however, the optimal licensing contract involves only an up-front fixed fee. Combining a fixed fee and a royalty is optimal if the threat of imitation is credible and the cost of imitation is positive.

With regard to the quality of the licensed technology, where a lower marginal cost of production represents relatively better technology, the optimal decision of the licenser is not to license its best possible technology if the threat of imitation is credible and the cost of imitation is moderate.

Since output royalty softens competition in the product market, a licenser who competes in the product market with the licensee may find it optimal to charge a positive royalty rate even if the royalty rate distorts the licensee's output. If the products of the licenser and the licensee are horizontally differentiated (e.g., by different brand names or after-sales services of the firms), however, the incentive for fixed-fee licensing increases since product differentiation itself softens competition between the firms. Whether product differentiation increases the threat of imitation and the incentive for licensing a rela-

tively better technology is ambiguous. Product differentiation increases the incentive for imitation for a given royalty rate by increasing the gain from imitation, but product differentiation also reduces the royalty rate, thus reducing the incentive for imitation.

If the products are homogeneous, the optimal licensing contract may involve only an up-front fixed fee if the high cost of either technology licensing or technology adoption makes it possible to license the technology to only some competitors. Stealing market share from the nonlicensees makes fixed-fee licensing optimal.

The royalty rate does not have a competition-softening effect if the licenser and the licensee do not compete in the product market. As shown in Gallini and Wright (1990), however, there still may be a rationale for charging a positive royalty rate if the quality of the technology is proprietary information of the licenser, as the royalty rate helps to signal the quality of the technology. If there is licensing between competitors from different countries, the presence of trade costs provides a rationale for a combination of a fixed fee and a royalty.

In Rockett (1990), licensing intensifies competition in the product market and may induce the licenser not to license its best technology. Kabiraj and Marjit (1993) argue that even if the licenser and the licensee do not compete in the product market in the absence of licensing, a licenser may have an incentive not to license its best technology if the licenser and the licensee are from different countries. Government policy may prevent competition in the licensee's market; the licenser's having better technology than the licensee may prevent competition in the licenser's own market. If licensing the best technology would create competition in the licenser's market, the licenser may find it optimal not to license its best technology.

Licensing and Other Product Market Strategies While technology licensing allows a firm to increase its profit, other business strategies—such as mergers, joint ventures, and capacity commitments—also help firms to increase their profits.

Consider the impacts of product market competition on a bilateral licensing contract and a bilateral merger. If there are multiple technologically superior and technologically inferior firms, a licensing contract always dominates a merger in a Cournot oligopoly. If there are multiple technologically inferior firms and only one technologically superior firm, however, merger dominates licensing for a sufficiently large technological difference. Under merger, the merged firms lower their total outputs compared with no merger, which, in a Cournot oligopoly, induces the nonmerged firms to increase their outputs. Hence merger creates a positive externality on the nonmerged firms and reduces the benefit of merger. On the other hand, licensing increases output of the licensee by reducing its marginal cost of production. Hence in a Cournot oligopoly, licensing reduces output of the licenser and also steals market shares from the nonlicensed firms. Therefore, along with the benefit of cost efficiency of the licensee, stealing of market shares from the nonlicensed firms provides the incentive for licensing. The trade-off between the positive externality of merger on the nonmerged firms and stealing of market shares from the nonlicensed firms is responsible for these results. Roy et al. (1999) extend this line of research in open economies and show the relative profitability of licensing, joint venture, and cross-border merger.

In the case of international technology transfer, proprietary information about the quality of the foreign technology and imitation by the licensee are two common problems. Though strategic choice of the fixed fee and output royalty may help to resolve these problems, a joint venture between the licenser and the licensee may induce relatively better technology to be transferred compared with licensing.

If imitation under international technology transfer creates the threat of competition in the licenser's other product markets, a technologically superior firm may choose foreign direct investment (FDI) over licensing. Though FDI requires significant investment in the host country, it may help to protect the licenser's other markets by reducing imitation by host-country firms. Hence the patent policy of the host country may influence a foreign firm's incentive for licensing versus FDI, with FDI more likely to be observed under weak patent protection.

Instead of a cooperative strategy such as merger, a noncooperative strategy such as investment in capacity or incentive delegation to managers may also help to raise the profits of the firms. Using licensing with an up-front fixed fee, Mukherjee (2001) shows that capacity commitment and incentive delegation have significantly different effects on licensing. Whether both the licenser and the licensee or one of them has the opportunity to adopt these precommitment strategies also plays an important role.

Licensing and Innovation Differences in technologies, which create reasons for licensing, stem from innovation. The interaction between innovation and licensing is an important topic.

In a duopoly market structure, where the firms innovate and compete in the product market, Gallini and Winter (1985) consider licensing ex ante and ex post innovation. The trade-off between the replacement of inefficient production technology and the elimination of inefficient research expenditure shows that licensing encourages innovation if the firms' initial technologies are close in costs, but it reduces innovation if the costs are asymmetric.

Katz and Shapiro (1985) consider separately an innovator and producers who can be engaged in licensing and show that licensing between the producers reduces innovation if the licensee appropriates most of the gains from licensing. If the licensee appropriates a significant amount of gains from licensing, the incentive for getting property rights to the innovation is reduced, thus reducing the innovator's earnings and the incentive to innovate.

These two papers have important implications for innovation policies, but they are unable to show the effects of licensing on R&D organization. It is often found, however, that firms do cooperative R&D to reduce the cost of innovation, avoid duplication of research efforts, or both. Whether licensing increases the incentive for cooperative R&D depends on the motive for cooperative R&D and the nature of the product market competition.

Even if licensing does not affect innovation, it may affect the decision on technology adoption, which occurs after innovation. Given that a technology has a finite life span, Mukherjee and Pennings (2004) show that licensing (compared with no licensing) induces technology adoption earlier by eliminating imitation.

Glass and Saggi (2002) show the effects of licensing and FDI on innovation and growth in an open economy. There is a cost disadvantage under FDI, whereas licensing may require the firms to share the gains from licensing. If the mode of operation (i.e., licensing or FDI) of the foreign firm is fixed, a rise in the licensee's share of rents is detrimental for innovation and economic growth. A mode switch from licensing to FDI increases innovation and economic growth on average, however.

Welfare-Reducing Licensing The reason for encouraging technology licensing is its positive effect on welfare, since it replaces relatively inefficient technologies, thus eliminating production inefficiencies. Recent research shows, however, that one must be cautious in encouraging licensing. Since licensing makes the licenser and the licensee more symmetric, it helps to sustain collusion between the firms. This argument was first put forward by Eswaran (1994), who showed that cross-licensing of products between firms can be a collusive device.

Licensing of a superior process technology also helps to sustain tacit collusion between the licenser and the licensee by making them symmetric in terms of costs.

Fauli-Oller and Sandonis (2002) show that licensing may be welfare-reducing even in the absence of collusion. They show that if the firms compete on prices, licensing may reduce welfare by contracting output and thus raising product prices. If the firms compete on quantity and the licenser can commit its output before the licensee, the provision of output royalty in the licensing contract helps to reduce industry output and to raise the product price, and thus may reduce social welfare.

Another strand of literature shows that licensing may reduce welfare by affecting either an innovator's incentive to innovate or the firms' incentives for doing cooperative R&D.

In the presence of multiple licensees, if the technologically superior firm can choose a licensing contract contingent on the number of firms taking licenses, the licenser can earn the profit of a monopolist with the licenser's technology. Hence if the licenser can use a more complete contract in the sense that it does not need to follow a per-unit output royalty and can charge nonlinear royalties, it may reduce welfare by increasing market concentration.

Licensing to Create Competition A surprisingly common feature of most research on licensing is the assumption that input markets are perfectly competitive. Hence it is assumed that technology licensing, while affecting the licensees' marginal cost by making superior technology available to them, does not affect the licenser's marginal cost. It is often the case, however, that input markets are imperfectly competitive.

One such possibility arises when there are labor unions bargaining over wage rates. In this case, a monopolist final goods producer may license its technology to a potential competitor to create competition in the product market. While licensing increases competition in the product market, it may help to reduce the wage rate charged by the labor unions. Since a suitably designed royalty rate softens competition between the firms, the benefit of lowering the wage rate induces the monopolist final goods producer to create competition through licensing.

Even if there are no labor unions but a monopolist final goods producer is selling to a foreign country and is exposed to the host-country tariff policy, the monopolist may be better off creating competition through licensing. Whether the monopolist licenses the technology to another foreign firm (which also faces the tariff rate of the host country) or to a host-country firm may be a decision variable of the foreign monopolist.

Farrell and Gallini (1988) and Shepard (1987) show the rationale for licensing by a monopolist input supplier, which is a well-known phenomenon in the Ethernet market and the semiconductor industry. Licensing by the monopolist input supplier to a potential competitor creates competition in the input market and helps to reduce the input price, which in turn, increases profitability of the final goods producers. Hence higher competition in the input market due to licensing encourages entry in the final goods market, thus increasing the demand for inputs, and makes the monopolist input supplier better off compared with no licensing. Even if licensing in the input market does not affect the entry decision in the final goods market, it may increase the demand for inputs by raising the (expected) input quality, thus making the monopolist input supplier better off under licensing than no licensing. Higher competition in the input market due to licensing helps to commit to a lower input price or to a higher input quality, thus increasing the profit of the monopolist input supplier.

Future Research Significant effort has been devoted to several issues related to technology licensing; at least two areas deserve more attention, however. First, the literature has mainly focused on licensing of cost-reducing innovations, but firms often innovate to improve the quality of the product and/or to invent new products. Second, the licensing literature ignores licensing by several technologically superior firms. The presence of multiple licensers will affect market outcomes such as the terms of the licensing contracts, the quality of the licensed technology, and social welfare. Work by Saggi and Vettas (2002) that considers the equilibrium contracts when two upstream firms contract with multiple downstream firms may be reinterpreted as technology licensing by multiple technology producers to multiple final goods producers. However, this area requires further research.

See also foreign direct investment (FDI); foreign direct investment and international technology transfer; foreign direct investment under oligopoly; foreign market entry; intangible assets; intellectual property rights and foreign direct investment; internalization theory; intrafirm trade; joint ventures; outsourcing/offshoring; proximity-concentration hypothesis; technology spillovers

FURTHER READING

Eswaran, M. 1994. "Cross-Licensing of Competing Patents as a Facilitating Device." *Canadian Journal of Economics* 27 (3): 689–708. Shows that cross-licensing of products can facilitate tacit collusion.

Farrell, J., and N. T. Gallini. 1988. "Second-Sourcing as a Commitment: Monopoly Incentives to Attract Competition." *Quarterly Journal of Economics* 103 (4): 673–94. Shows optimality of technology licensing by a monopolist input supplier due to licensing.

Faulí-Oller, R., and J. Sandonis. 2002. "Welfare Reducing Licensing." *Games and Economic Behavior* 41 (2): 192–205. Examines welfare-reducing licensing under price competition.

Gallini, N. T., and R. A. Winter. 1985. "Licensing in the Theory of Innovation." *RAND Journal of Economics* 16 (2): 237–52. Looks at the effects of licensing on the incentive for innovation.

Gallini, N. T., and B. D. Wright. 1990. "Technology Transfer under Asymmetric Information." *RAND Journal of Economics* 21 (1): 147–60. Argues that optimal licensing contract involves both fixed fee and output royalty in presence of private information about the quality of technology.

Glass, A., and K. Saggi. 2002. "Licensing versus Direct Investment: Implications for Economic Growth." *Journal of International Economics* 56 (1): 131–53. Shows the effects of licensing and foreign direct investment on innovation and economic growth.

Kabiraj, T., and S. Marjit. 1993. "International Technology Transfer under Potential Threat of Entry—A Cournot-Nash Framework." *Journal of Development Economics* 42 (1): 75–88. Explores why, in an open economy, a licenser may not find it optimal to license its best technology.

Kamien, M. I. 1992. "Patent Licensing." In *Handbook of Game Theory with Economic Applications*, edited by R. J. Aumann and S. Hart, 331–54. Amsterdam: Elsevier Science B. V. (North-Holland). Surveys the works on licensing where the licenser and the licensees do not compete in the product market.

Katz, M. L., and C. Shapiro. 1985. "On the Licensing of Innovations." *RAND Journal of Economics* 16 (4): 504–20. Shows the effects of licensing on innovation when the innovator and the producers are different firms.

Mukherjee, A. 2001. "Technology Transfer with Commitment." *Economic Theory* 17 (2): 345–69. Shows the effects of capacity commitment and incentive delegation to managers on technology licensing.

Mukherjee, A., and E. Pennings. 2004. "Imitation, Patent Protection, and Welfare." *Oxford Economic Papers* 56 (4): 715–33. Examines the effects of licensing on technology adoption and welfare.

Rockett, K. 1990. "The Quality of Licensed Technology." *International Journal of Industrial Organization* 8 (4): 559–74. Looks at the effects of imitation on optimal licensing contract and the quality of the licensed technology.

Roy, P., T. Kabiraj, and A. Mukherjee. 1999. "Technology Transfer, Merger, and Joint Venture: A Comparative Analysis." *Journal of Economic Integration* 14 (3): 442–66. Shows the effects of cost asymmetry in an open economy.

Saggi, K., and N. Vettas. 2002. "On Intrabrand and Interbrand Competition: The Strategic Role of Fees and Royalties." *European Economic Review* 46 (1): 189–200. Characterizes equilibrium contracts with an up-front fixed fee and output royalty when the upstream firms contract with multiple downstream firms.

Shepard, A. 1987. "Licensing to Enhance the Demand for a New Product." *RAND Journal of Economics* 18 (3): 360–68. Shows the optimality of licensing by a monopolist input supplier due to the effect of licensing on the quality of input.

ARIJIT MUKHERJEE

■ technology spillovers

Technology spillovers are the beneficial effects of new technological knowledge on the productivity and innovative ability of other firms and countries. Technology is "nonrival": one's use of a technology does not limit its use by others, and the cost for an additional agent to use an existing technology is negligible compared with the cost of inventing it. Hence not all the benefits of technological knowledge are appropriated by the inventor; technological investments typically generate social returns that far outweigh private returns. Technology, once invented, can be used and diffused internationally with small added cost but substantial added benefit.

Technological research and innovation is mostly undertaken by firms and governments in the leading world economies that are also the world technological leaders. Then technology diffuses to the rest of the world through the main channels of trade, migration, foreign direct investment (FDI), and technological licensing (patents and copyrights).

International technology spillovers have received much attention in recent economic research from both theoretical and empirical perspectives. Theory identifies them as a key mechanism for the sustained growth of productivity and its diffusion across countries. From an empirical point of view, economists have studied how to measure technology spillovers and what channels are conducive to them. From a policy point of view, countries desiring greater technology spillovers use policies to promote trade and FDI and to promote better conditions for taking advantage of spillovers by absorbing them into domestic productivity gains.

Theory of Technology Spillovers Recent theories of economic growth and income differences across countries (see Eaton and Kortum 2002; and Klenow and Rodriguez-Clare 2005 for reviews) identify available technological and scientific knowledge as the most important determinants of productivity in a country. Scientific and technological innovation are the main engines of productivity growth in the rich countries (Europe, Japan, and North America). Their diffusion to industrializing countries, accompanied by investments in physical and human capital, is the main reason for the growth in productivity and income per capita of those economies. Yet some countries seem stuck far behind the technology frontier. The process of technological diffusion has a central position in the recent literature on development and growth. A better understanding of the nature of technology spillovers should help shed light on why some countries grow faster than others.

Due to its nonrival nature, technological knowledge can be used by producers other than the inventor to increase their productivity. Hence it generates two types of benefits called "spillovers."

1. First, new technological knowledge can be used in any country to produce more

efficiently or higher quality goods. This spillover increases the labor productivity of the country that adopts it.

2. Second, technological knowledge can be used in any country to produce new ideas or new applications in research and development (R&D). This increases R&D effectiveness in receiving countries.

Inventors usually appropriate at least part of the benefits from the first type of spillovers, either by producing goods with the new technology and exporting them to foreign markets (trade) or by setting up production that uses the new technology in other countries (FDI) or by licensing out the new technology and receiving royalty payments for it. International trade, FDI, and international patents and copyrights are therefore common channels for diffusing the benefits of technological innovations to consumers in other countries. At the same time those flows carry the knowledge related to the new technology embodied in goods, in machines, or in instructions. This new knowledge enables receiving countries to benefit from the second type of technological spillovers: other firms and producers may learn and improve their productivity as a consequence of exposure to better technology. The first type of technology spillovers are usually mediated by market mechanisms (trade, investments, and intellectual property rights) and are sometimes called technology diffusion. The second type of technology spillovers involve diffusion of knowledge to other firms of the receiving country via mobility of workers, learning, imitation, and subcontracting and are considered technology externalities.

In the light of these beneficial effects on productivity and growth, international technological spillovers (even more than international trade of goods and international movements of capital per se) have been identified as potentially the most beneficial aspect of globalization. The empirical research has consequently focused on measuring the intensity, quantifying the effects, and identifying the most relevant channels of these spillovers. At the same time researchers and policymakers have analyzed what are the characteristics that make a receiving country best positioned to receive the benefits from those spillovers.

Empirical Analysis of International Technology Spillovers Technology spillovers are not recorded in the data. The channels of their transmission (trade, FDI, patents) and their consequences (productivity benefits) can be recorded and measured, however. The recent empirical analysis has used a plurality of data and approaches to qualify and quantify the intensity and productive impact of those spillovers across countries.

Measuring Technology Spillovers Technological and scientific knowledge is an intangible asset not measurable directly. Economists have used measures of R&D resources (input) or measures of innovations such as patents or productivity (output) to approximate it. Aggregate studies have used country-level data, while microlevel studies have used firm-level data. Two general methods are used to identify spillovers. The first method considers the effects of R&D done in some countries (or firms) on the productivity of other countries (or firms) that are linked to the former via trade, FDI, or technological/geographical proximity. The basic features of this approach were first developed in a very influential paper by Coe and Helpman (1995) and will be described in the next section. The second approach considers directly the association between the presence/intensity of trade and FDI (channels of technology spillovers) and the productivity of the importing/receiving country or firms there. Both methods infer the existence of spillovers indirectly from the effects on productivity in firms of the receiving economy.

A third approach aimed at identifying more directly the linkages that reveal technology spillovers analyzes citations from a patent to previous patents, considering them as tangible signs of a knowledge spillover (Jaffe and Trajtenberg 2002). An existing idea recorded in a patent contributes to the development of a new idea (new patent), and the citation link reveals this spillover. This method isolates only spillovers of the second type described above (from R&D to R&D) and tends to emphasize the geographic localization of those technology spillovers. This method complements (but cannot substitute for) the other type of studies, as it only identifies the intensity and characteristics of technological spillovers but cannot quantify their impact on productivity.

Trade and Technology Spillovers A popular approach for analyzing the presence and the intensity of technology spillovers has been to analyze the association (correlation) between productivity in country j (or industry or firm) and the R&D activity in countries (industries or firms) other than j that are linked to j by potential channels of spillovers. The basic empirical procedure, presented in Coe and Helpman (1995), and expanded and updated since then, is to estimate some version of the following regression: $\text{Productivity}_j = \text{Function}(\mathbf{X}_j, \text{R\&D}_j, \text{R\&D}_{\text{spillovers}})$. The variable Productivity_j represents some measure of the productivity (usually total factor productivity or labor productivity) of country (industry, firm) j. The vector $\mathbf{X}_j$ is an array of country (industry, firm) characteristics relevant for its productivity. $\text{R\&D}_j$ is a measure of research and development activity performed in the country (industry, firm) j, and $\text{R\&D}_{\text{spillovers}} = \sum_{i \neq j} m_i (\text{R\&D})_i$ is a weighted sum of R&D activity in other countries. This term captures technology spillovers because the weights m_i are constructed to reflect the intensity of potential spillover channels between country (industry, firm) j, the receiver, and country (sector, firm) i, the sender. In the original work of Coe and Helpman (1995) m_i was measured as the share of imports from country j among trade partner of country i assuming that imports are the most relevant channel of technology spillovers. Subsequent research has experimented with different weights to capture other potential spillover channels. Some alternative measures of m_i have been the share of FDI from country j in total capital formation of country i, the share of imports of capital goods (rather than all goods), and the share of direct and indirect trade (i.e., trade through third-country mediation). More recently Keller (2002) has constructed the weights m_i based on geographical proximity between country j and i. This approach is based on the assumption that a whole array of potential spillover channels

(trade, FDI, migration, technological licensing, business travel, and others) are strongly enhanced by geographical proximity. A popular variation of the approach described above, mostly used on individual firm data, is to measure the effect of technological spillovers on production costs rather than productivity.

The limit of this type of approach is that the identification of externalities is based on correlations, and it is not easy to establish a real causation link. To address the limits of the reduced form approach, recent research by Eaton and Kortum (2002) has studied the relationship between R&D technology diffusion and domestic productivity in the context of general equilibrium models. In those models one can analyze and simulate the impact of increased research and trade liberalization on technology spillovers and productivity.

Overall the findings of this literature point to two rather robustly estimated regularities. First, the effect of R&D spillovers on productivity is consistently larger than zero and significantly positive for the average analyzed country (usually the data cover economies that are members of the Organisation for Economic Co-operation and Development, OECD). Second, while for the leading economies (G7 countries), the impact of domestic R&D on productivity is consistently larger than the spillover effects from other countries, for smaller and less advanced economies (other OECD countries) the impact of spillovers is larger than the impact of domestic R&D on productivity. These findings confirm that technological leaders tend to perform most of the R&D and innovation in the world and that spillovers from those technologies are a major source of productivity growth in other countries.

FDI and Technology Spillovers A second approach to identifying and quantifying international technology spillovers is based on the idea that FDI is an explicit activity set up to transfer technology across national borders (e.g., Markusen 2002). Hence FDI is a direct carrier of technology flows. The question is how much these flows benefit the productivity of the receiving economy and what are the features or policies of the receiving economy that enhance the positive effects of technology spillovers. Several theoretical models argue that multinational enterprises should generate technology spillovers to local firms through several channels, and many of them have been studied in detail using firm-level data. Imitation, learning, and acquisition of human capital through worker turnover are considered as the most important channels of spillovers. Competition, subcontracting, and supply of high-quality intermediate inputs are market-mediated mechanisms that make better inputs available to the local firms, stimulate more efficient technologies, and may also have positive productivity effects.

The typical empirical approach for identifying technological spillovers through FDI estimates the following model: Productivity$_{jk}$ = Function($\mathbf{X}_j$, FDI$_k$). The term (Productivity$_{jk}$) measures the productivity of firm j in sector k and the right-hand side of the expression implies that it is a function of a vector of firm characteristics $\mathbf{X}_j$ and of some measure (usually the share of employment or of sales) of the presence of multinational enterprises in sector k, (FDI$_k$). Usually these studies analyze firm-level data for one country at a time (hence no country subscript) and often they consider geographical proximity as a requisite for (or enhancer of) the technology spillovers: multinationals have larger productivity effects if they are located in the same region or area as the potential spillover-receiving firm j. Another relevant dimension of the spillovers is whether they benefit domestic firms "horizontally" (namely, those in the same industry) or "vertically" (those that supply inputs to or buy inputs from the multinational enterprise).

Using cross-section and panel data from several different industrialized and industrializing countries, many researchers have estimated technology spillovers through FDI using the method described above. Interestingly, the evidence in favor of positive effects of technology spillovers on productivity of domestic firms is scant, especially when considering developing countries. Blomström and Kokko (1998) and more recently Görg and Greenway (2004) review dozens of such studies and conclude robust evidence of positive effects of FDI spillovers is found mainly for industrialized countries. For developing countries results are much less clear. A typical example of those studies is the influential article by Aitken and Harrison (1999), which, in analyzing evidence from FDI in Venezuela, does not find any positive effect on productivity of local firms. In fact, the study finds some negative effects on domestic firms and attributes them to increased competition from FDI and crowding out of domestic firms.

Absorptive Capacity These findings have prompted research on the role of the receiving firm or country in determining the impact of technology spillovers. While the potential for technology spillovers is intrinsic to FDI activity, the actual impact on productivity of domestic firms depends on the absorptive capacity of those firms. Human capital and investment in R&D by the receiving country (firm) are important prerequisites to generating positive effects of technology spillovers on productivity. Insufficient human capital in local firms could be the explanation for the lack of spillovers from FDI in developing countries. Using firm-level data, several articles (e.g., Glass and Saggi 1998) confirm that firms using low-skilled workers and backward technology are unable to benefit from FDI technology spillovers.

Policy Considerations FDI is seen by governments of several industrializing countries as highly beneficial to the domestic economy. Technology spillovers are only one of its effects, as FDI also increases employment opportunities, consumption, and government income. Nonetheless technological spillovers generate probably the most important and lasting effects in the long run as they channel technological transfer and induce productivity growth. In the light of the empirical findings, policies promoting higher education and skill-formation of workers and R&D investment of domestic firms are needed complements to policies that attract FDI, if a country is to maximize the absorption of technological spillovers. At the same time some policies such as R&D requirements, technology transfer requirements, and local hiring targets for multinational enterprises can increase the intensity of technological activity and the benefits for the local economy.

Probably, however, a general framework of openness to international flows and free competition in trade, FDI, and technological licensing is the most important component for a country to attract technology spillovers and benefit from improved technologies as they become available to the global economy.

See also agglomeration and foreign direct investment; appropriate technology and foreign direct investment; foreign direct investment (FDI); foreign direct investment and international technology transfer; foreign direct investment and tax revenues; foreign direct investment under monopolistic competition; foreign direct investment under oligopoly; foreign market entry; intangible assets; intellectual property rights and foreign direct investment; internalization theory; joint ventures; linkages, backward and forward; location theory; proximity-concentration hypothesis; technology licensing

FURTHER READING

Aitken, Brian, and Ann Harrison. 1999. "Do Domestic Firms Benefit from Foreign Direct Investment? Evidence from Venezuela." *American Economic Review* 89 (3): 605–18. One of the most cited and influential articles on FDI spillovers in developing countries.

Blomström, Magnus, and Ari Kokko. 1998. "Multinational Corporations and Spillovers." *Journal of Economic Surveys* 12 (3): 247–77. An early comprehensive survey of the literature on FDI and technology spillovers.

Coe, David, and Elhanan Helpman. 1995. "International R&D Spillovers." *European Economic Review* 39 (5): 859–87. The initial and still one of the most influential articles on trade and technology spillovers.

Eaton, Jonathan, and Samuel Kortum. 2002. "Technology, Geography, and Trade." *Econometrica* 70 (5): 1741–79. A sophisticated theoretical and empirical analysis of technological diffusion and technology spillovers.

Glass, Amy, and Kamal Saggi. 1998. "International Technology Transfer and the Technology Gap." *Journal of Development Economics* 55 (2): 369–98. One of the most influential recent articles on the role of absorptive capacity in determining the impact of FDI spillovers.

Görg, Holger, and David Greenway. 2004. "Much Ado about Nothing? Do Domestic Firms Really Benefit from Foreign Direct Investment?" *World Bank Research Observer* 19 (2): 171–97. The most comprehensive recent review of the role of FDI in promoting technological spillovers.

Jaffe, Adam, and Manuel Trajtenberg. 2002. *Patents Citations and Innovations: A Window on the Knowledge Economy*. Cambridge, MA: MIT Press. The most comprehensive collection of research on the use of patent data and patent citations to measure technology spillovers.

Keller, Wolfgang. 2002. "Geographic Localization of International Technology Diffusion." *American Economic Review* 92 (1): 120–42. A very influential paper measuring the importance of geographical proximity for technological diffusion.

———. 2004. "International Technology Diffusion." *Journal of Economic Literature* 42 (3): 752–82. A comprehensive literature review on international technology diffusion.

Klenow, Peter, and Andres Rodriguez-Clare. 2005. "Externalities and Growth." In *The Handbook of Economic Growth*, edited by Aghion Philippe and Steven Durlauf. Amsterdam: Elsevier. An excellent review of the most relevant theoretical models of technological spillovers and economic growth.

Markusen, James. 2002. *Multinational Firms and the Theory of International Trade*. Cambridge, MA: MIT Press. An influential, mostly theoretical book on multinational firms and international trade

GIOVANNI PERI

■ temporary movement of natural persons

The phrase *temporary movement of natural persons* (TMNP) refers to one of several ways by which, according to the General Agreement on Trade in Services (GATS), international trade in services takes place when workers from one country travel abroad temporarily to supply particular services there.

The exact World Trade Organization (WTO) definition of TMNP can be found in Article I 2 (d) of the GATS, which refers to "the supply of a service, . . . by a service supplier of one Member, through the presence of natural persons of a Member in the territory of any other Member." This definition is further qualified in the GATS Annex on the Movement of Natural Persons Supplying Services under the Agreement, which states that GATS rules, negotiations, and commitments do not apply to persons seeking permanent citizenship, residence, or employment. TMNP in the strict WTO sense applies only to temporary migration of workers in service occupations and not to foreign workers employed temporarily in the manufacturing, mining, or agricultural sectors of another country. National immigration policy in most countries, however, covers temporary workers in different sectors of the economy. For example, U.S. visa rules on temporary foreign workers include an H2 visa category for temporary farm workers.

TMNP thus implies at least two things: first, the overseas travel by the worker has to be *temporary* in nature; second, it must have been undertaken in order to perform a *specific job or supply of a service*. Examples include senior managers posted abroad to manage operations of a multinational firm operating in the services sector of a foreign country; IT technicians traveling overseas to provide backup technical support for computer hardware or software; academic faculty traveling to foreign universities on short-term teaching assignments; nurses or teachers employed in foreign hospitals or educational institutions for a fixed tenure; seafarers working on contract in a foreign shipping line; household workers hired for a specific period as au pairs by families abroad; an accomplished doctor traveling to a foreign country to perform complicated surgery; cultural troupes performing overseas; and unskilled and semiskilled workers from one country employed on contract on construction sites in other countries.

Examples of TMNP that do not strictly fall within the GATS definition, but are perhaps as numerous and of equal economic significance include farm labor employed annually on agricultural lands and plantations overseas during peak seasons; foreign workers in major mining projects; and workers employed in labor-intensive manufacturing activities during, for example, an export boom in a foreign country. Several bilateral and some regional agreements cover such TMNP that takes place outside the services sector.

Temporary overseas travel that is *not* considered TMNP includes travel undertaken for tourism or for obtaining medical assistance or education. Such journeys, though recognized as contributing to international trade in services, are classified under a different category, namely "consumption abroad," in the GATS. The movement of refugees seeking temporary asylum in other countries is also excluded, as travel is not undertaken for a specified period or to perform a specific task.

Origins Temporary migration has been under discussion for a long time in various forums such as the International Organization for Migration and the International Labor Organization but only as a subset of migration in general. The WTO was the first international organization to focus exclusively on the temporary migration of workers. Furthermore, while other organizations use the conventional word *workers*, the WTO introduced the phrase *natural persons* instead, in order to distinguish people from juridical persons such as companies or organizations. This merely reflects a preference for legalistic terminology by the drafters of the GATS text, however; in practice, the terms are interchangeable.

The origins of the concept can be traced to the Uruguay Round trade negotiations (1986–94) of the General Agreement on Tariffs and Trade. During discussions to develop a framework for an agreement on international trade in services, it was recognized that one way in which services are delivered overseas is through the travel of workers. Although overseas travel to supply particular services was not a new phenomenon—traders, religious missionaries, and diplomats had been doing so for centuries—there had been a sharp rise in such travel during the preceding decades. Lower transportation costs, widening income differentials between countries, and global distribution of production chains facilitated by technological improvements in communications were some factors responsible for this trend. Aging workforces and income growth have also led to worker shortages in some countries, creating a demand for foreign workers. The emergence of significant numbers of temporary migrant workers worldwide by the 1980s appears to have contributed to the inclusion of TMNP as a negotiable trading activity during the Uruguay Round.

Leading TMNP Countries Reliable data on TMNP flows are not readily available. This is mainly because many countries do not keep records of persons going abroad for work. In host countries the statistics are complicated by the fact that many workers admitted temporarily get themselves converted into permanent workers.

Traditionally Mexico and the Philippines have been regarded as the world's leading source countries for TMNP. Because of the previously mentioned data limitations, some experts prefer to use workers' remittance figures as an indirect measure of TMNP, given that temporary workers tend to remit a significant part of their earnings to their home countries relative to permanent migrants. Measured in terms of the magnitude of remittances received in 2005, the top 10 countries sending temporary workers abroad were India, China, Mexico, the Philippines, France, Spain, Belgium, United Kingdom, Germany, and Egypt, in that order.

A similar indirect measure can be used for estimating the leading host countries for temporary migrant workers. This makes use of the data on wages and salaries earned by nonresident workers who have lived in the host country for less than a year. According to these data, in 2005 the United States was by far the leading host country for temporary foreign workers, followed by Saudi Arabia, Switzerland, Germany, Spain, the Russian Federation, Italy, Malaysia, the Netherlands, and France, in that order.

Significance for the World Economy The economic significance of TMNP for the world economy stems from the fact that the majority of temporary workers move from areas of low productivity to areas of higher productivity, thus bringing about global efficiency gains. Projections such as those made by Winters et al. (2003) also predict large economic gains for the world economy if TMNP is liberalized. Such studies also usually predict that the gains will be shared equally between sending and receiving countries. Despite this, both developed and developing countries have adopted a conservative policy approach with regard to the entry of foreign workers compared with other areas of international trade. WTO commitments on TMNP attached to the Third Protocol to the GATS are mostly confined to highly skilled labor and typically qualified by restrictions and exemptions. Part of the reason is the recognition that the labor market consequences of trade liberalization unravel differently for different sectors. For instance, the impact on the labor market of lower tariffs on industrial products occurs indirectly, and domestic workers lose jobs after a time lag. Liberalizing the entry of foreign workers, on the other hand, creates immediate and direct competition for domestic workers and is therefore much more challenging politically.

Experts have compiled lists of benefits and drawbacks of permanent migration for both source and host countries. The economic consequences of TMNP generally are the same as those of permanent migration, with a few important exceptions:

- There is no permanent brain drain caused by TMNP, although there is temporary loss of the migrant's contribution to home country output. It is argued that a returning migrant can bring back new ideas, technologies, and networks that would contribute to improved efficiency and productivity and partially compensate for the loss to national welfare caused by temporary absence.

- With TMNP, the option to post and rotate senior corporate personnel of choice abroad improves efficiency and control in the international operations of source country firms. This is especially helpful if qualified local personnel are not available in sufficient numbers in the host country.

- Unlike permanent migrants, temporary workers are less likely to put pressure on host-country public goods or infrastructure or undermine a foreign country's culture, customs, and values on account of the transitory nature of stay abroad.

- Remittances are likely to be higher from temporary migrants, so host countries are likely to experience a higher outflow of earnings under TMNP compared with permanent migration.

See also General Agreement on Trade in Services (GATS); migration, international

FURTHER READING

Bhatnagar, Pradip. 2004. "Liberalizing the Movement of Natural Persons—A Lost Decade?" *The World Economy* 27 (3): 459–72. Covers the various economic and noneconomic arguments for and against the liberalization of the temporary movement of natural persons.

Mattoo, Aaditya, and A. Carzaniga, eds. 2003. *Moving People to Deliver Services.* Washington, DC: World Bank and Oxford University Press. Compiles viewpoints of economists, regulators, negotiators, and private-sector stakeholders on the subject.

Nielson, Julia. 2003. "Labor Mobility in Regional Trade Agreements." In *Moving People to Deliver Services*, edited by Aaditya Mattoo and Antonia Carzaniga. Washington, DC: World Bank, 93–112. An excellent source of information on TMNP in different regional trading arrangements.

Winters, L.A., T. L. Walmsley, Z. K Wang, and R. Grynberg. 2003. "Liberalizing the Temporary Movement of Natural Persons: An Agenda for the Development Round." *The World Economy* 26 (8): 1137–61. One of the more recent in a series of endeavors to measure the global economic gains of liberalizing TMNP.

World Bank. 2007. *World Development Indicators.* A quick guide to leading source and host countries for TMNP using indirect data like remittances and wages and salaries earned by nonresidents. Released annually in CD-ROM format.

World Trade Organization. 1998. *Presence of Natural Persons (Mode 4). Background Note by the Secretariat (S/C/W/75).* Contains the main definitions, explanations, and a summary of GATS commitments made on the movement of natural persons in the GATS. Downloadable from http:/www.wto.org/english/tratop_e/serv_e/w75.doc

PRADIP BHATNAGAR

■ terms of trade

The current world economic situation is the legacy of the days of industrial revolution in the North and colonization of the major countries of the South. This divided the world economy into two regions: the industrially developed North and less-developed South. In the context of the North-South divide of the world economy, the long-term behavior of the terms of trade between the two regions has been a much discussed and much debated topic.

By terms of trade we usually mean commodity terms of trade, the term popularized by Jacob Viner. The commodity terms of trade of the South in relation to the North can be defined as the price (unit value index) of exports of the South to the North divided by the price (unit value index) of exports of the North to the South.

The commodity terms of trade is also known as net barter terms of trade, thanks to Frank William Taussig. He introduced another concept, the gross barter terms of trade. It is the ratio of the volume index of imports to the volume index of exports. It is not widely known or used in the literature.

G. S. Dorrence introduced the concept of the income terms of trade. It is an index of the value (= volume x unit value) of exports divided by the unit value of imports and it corresponds to the commodity terms of trade (= unit value of exports/unit value of imports) multiplied by the volume of exports. It measures the purchasing power of exports—the amount of imports that can be financed by total exports of a country or region.

If, instead of volume of exports, the commodity terms-of-trade index is multiplied by some index of factor productivity in the export sector, we get the single factorial terms of trade. To construct the double factorial terms of trade, the single factorial terms of trade is deflated by the index of factor productivity in the export sector of its trading partner. So, the double factorial terms of trade is the commodity terms of trade multiplied by the ratio of the indices of factor productivity in the export sectors of the trading partners. Usually labor productivity is considered for factorial terms-of-trade index calculation.

The single factorial terms-of-trade index has a simple intuitive implication: it indicates the amount of wheat (say) that can be imported by a country (say, Ghana) by employing one hour of labor in production of its export item, say, cocoa. An improvement in the index implies a rise in the country's labor productivity in the export sector valued in terms of its import goods. Among other possibilities, it may be due to a rise in the labor productivity in its export sector not fully counterbalanced by a (resulting) fall in its export prices relative to its import prices (that is to say, a fall in its commodity terms of trade)—trade has not wiped out the whole fruit of technical progress in its export sector. In the process, its trading partner can experience a rise in its single factorial terms of trade through an improvement in its commodity terms of trade.

There are many other cases where the single factorial terms of trade of two trading countries can rise or fall together, but a rise (fall) in the double factorial terms of trade of one country must imply a fall (rise) in the double factorial terms of trade of its trading partner. That is why the economists interested in relative gains from trade or unequal exchange focused on this concept of terms of trade.

Suppose the North and the South experience the same rate of technical progress and labor productivity improvement in their respective export sectors. One region (say South) experiences lower export prices in response to technical progress and cost reduction—wages do not rise in proportion to the rise in productivity because of (say) surplus labor and the consequent weak labor union. Suppose the other region (North) experiences rising wages and profit because of strong labor union and monopoly power of the producers and no fall in their export prices. Then double factorial terms of trade would move in favor of the North and against the South. This is what was highlighted by Prebisch (1950) and Singer (1950) in the context of trade between the industrially developed North and the less-developed South and gave birth to the well-known Prebisch-Singer hypothesis. They provided some evidence of a long-term decline in the commodity terms of trade of primary products and the primary-product export-

ing South since the last quarter of the 19th century and indicated a long-term decline in the double factorial terms of trade of the South vis-à-vis the North on the basis of the well-accepted fact that the industrial sector of the North experienced a higher rate of technical progress in those days.

This Prebisch-Singer hypothesis generated much controversy in the academic world both on empirical and theoretical grounds, and it was virtually discarded in mainstream economics. But there is now an increasing volume of literature in its support (see Sarkar 1986, 2001).

In the "mainstream" neoclassical, perfect competitive framework, each factor (including labor) is paid according to its productivity. So the single factorial terms of trade is the real wages measured in terms of import goods and the double factorial terms of trade is the wage ratio (measured in a common currency). In a simple classical political economy framework of the (North-South) world economy with free mobility of capital and labor, the North-South commodity terms of trade would be equal to the ratio of labor embodied in the production of export goods in the two regions (in accordance with the classical labor theory of value) and the double factorial terms of trade would be equal to one. This is the ideal situation—"equal exchange"—the Marxist economist Emmanuel (1969) had in mind. But in a world of nearly perfect mobility of capital and imperfect labor mobility, the commodity terms of trade is not in accordance with the labor theory of value. The double factorial terms of trade are equal to the wage ratio as in the neoclassical framework. Granted that Northern workers get higher wages (even after adjusting for their higher skill and productivity), the double factorial terms of trade of the South are less than one. That implies that one hour of Southern labor is exchanged for less than one unit of (comparable) Northern labor. This is a case of (static) "unequal exchange" at a point of time. If over time this North-South wage gap rises, the double factorial terms of trade would decline indicating increasing "unequal exchange." Thus there is a convergence between the Prebisch-Singer hypothesis and Emmanuel's dynamic "unequal exchange" idea.

Last there is another concept, employment-corrected double factorial terms of trade, introduced by Spraos (1983). It is based on the idea that if a country or region such as South has a large pool of unemployed labor force, a decline in its double factorial terms of trade is welcome if that is more than compensated by a rise in employment through the growth of trade and production. This index is calculated by multiplying the double factorial terms of trade of a country or region by the total employment in its traded sector (if both the countries or regions face this unemployment problem the multiplicative factor would be the employment ratio and the index would be turned into a ratio of export values!). On the assumption of near full employment in the North and a large-scale unemployment problem in the South, he calculated such indexes and found some evidence of decline in the terms of trade of the South from 1960 to 1977.

The concepts of terms of trade and a study of their behavior are useful in understanding whether the evolution of the world economy led to some kind of uneven development through the terms-of-trade movements against the interest of the less developed South, thereby hampering the process of catching up.

See also import substitution industrialization; North-South trade; primary products trade; trade and economic development, international

FURTHER READING

Emmanuel, Arghiri. 1969. *Unequal Exchange.* New York: Monthly Review Press (English translation, 1972). Develops the concept of unequal exchange on the basis of Marxian concepts and tools of analysis.

Prebisch, Raúl. 1950. *The Economic Development of Latin America and Its Principal Problems.* New York: United Nations. A critique of the Ricardian theory of comparative advantages and the international division of labor based on the comparative advantage pattern, this pamphlet also argues in favor of industrialization in the less-developed countries to avoid their terms-of-trade loss.

Sarkar, Prabirjit. 1986. "The Singer-Prebisch Hypothesis: A Statistical Evaluation." *Cambridge Journal of Economics* 10: 355–71. Questions the validity of the major statistical objections against the Prebisch-Singer hypothesis.

———. 2001. "The North-South Terms of Trade: A Reexamination." *Progress in Development Studies* 1 (4): 309–27. Surveys the literature concerning the terms-of-trade debate and discusses the theoretical issues.

Singer, Hans. 1950. "The Distribution of Gains between Investing and Borrowing Countries." *American Economic Review* 40: 473–85. Presented at the American Economic Association annual meeting (May 1949), this paper discounts the benefits of foreign investment and technical progress in the primary-product exporting sector of the less-developed countries because of the consequent terms-of-trade loss.

Spraos, John. 1983. *Inequalizing Trade?* London: Clarendon Press. Discusses different concepts of terms of trade, their welfare implications, and other issues between the North and the South.

PRABIRJIT SARKAR

■ textiles and clothing

The textiles and clothing supply chain consists of production of raw materials; spinning, weaving, or knitting; finishing; design; sewing; distribution; and marketing. The production of textiles was the first economic activity to be industrialized, starting in the United Kingdom around 1765 with the invention of the spinning jenny, a machine for spinning wool or cotton.

The clothing industry is unskilled and labor intensive. The technology is cheap and simple and did not change much over the 20th century. The fabric is first cut and then grouped, tied into bundles (preassembly), and sewn together. A worker receives a bundle of unfinished garments, performs her single task, and places the bundle in a buffer. It takes about 40 operations to complete a pair of pants, and about 100 operations for men's blazers. Improvements in technology have taken place in two areas: specialized machines for each task and better coordination of the tasks.

The textile and clothing sector also includes market segments where innovation, technology, and design are important for competitiveness. Examples are sophisticated textile materials for industrial and medical use, athletic sportswear and equipment, and up-market fashion clothing. In the United States about two-thirds of textiles production is for industrial use and household goods. Italy and, to a lesser extent, France are important producers and exporters of up-market fashion products, and the two combined accounted for about 10 percent of world clothing exports in 2005. In Italy, textiles and clothing as a share of total manufacturing value added declined from 12 percent of total manufacturing value added in 1980 to 10 percent in 2003.

Economies of scale in distribution favor large supplier countries that cover the entire supply chain, such as China, India, Mexico, and Turkey. Smaller producers tend to find niches where they establish a significant market position. Sri Lanka, for instance, is among the world's leading exporters of lingerie.

Although production technology has not fundamentally changed, distribution technology and the division of labor between manufacturers and retailers have changed substantially since the late 1970s. The shift of key functions from manufacturers to retailers started with the establishment of large discount retailers such as Wal-Mart in the United States. Using modern information technology to improve supply chain management and transforming the relationship between retailers and manufacturers, Wal-Mart pioneered a practice that has been coined "lean retailing."

Lean retailers insisted that suppliers take up information technologies in order to facilitate more efficient supply chain management. They typically require manufacturers to adopt their standards and make apparel shelf-ready, which includes price tags and other required labeling. This ensures quick replenishment of apparel, which in turn allows the retailer to offer a broad variety of clothing without holding much inventory. The attractiveness of such contracts for suppliers is first and foremost the scale of operation of the lean retailers, which provides a stable marketing outlet and often also low-cost fabric and other material inputs purchased in bulk by the retailer.

With the introduction of private labels or store brands, design has shifted from the manufacturer to retailers. Specialized clothing retailers such as H&M and The Gap led this development. Most retailers of cheap, mass-market apparel source private label/store brand items from manufacturers in low-cost countries. However, a much studied Spanish retailer (Zara, which is part of the Inditex Group) has combined lean retailing with vertical integration of design, manufacturing, and distribution. Zara is among the world's largest retailers with retail outlets in 68 countries in 2007. Its innovation is production in small batches, introducing new designs as frequently as twice a week. New designs are based on information from the retail outlets. According to the company's Web page, Zara largely manufactures in Spain, arguing that the benefits of being close to the market outweigh the higher cost of production in Spain compared with low-cost countries. The numerous studies of this retailer suggest that its business model may multiply.

As a labor-intensive industry, textiles and clothing have always been an important source of employment for unskilled workers, particularly women. Furthermore the sector typically clusters geographically, for instance in the Carolinas and Georgia in the United States and in the Emilia-Romagna district in Italy. Because the industry tends to cluster in regions where it constitutes an important source of employment, job losses, for example, due to trade liberalization, can have serious local labor market consequences. Trade in textiles and clothing has therefore always been politically sensitive, and the sector was governed by an international trade regime of import quotas from the early 1960s until 2005.

International Trade Regime The textiles and clothing sector has a long history of import protection. As new countries emerged as important exporters of textiles and clothing, demand for protection arose in the United States and other developed countries. Thus in the 1950s the United States entered into agreements on voluntary export constraints on cotton textiles and clothing with Japan, Hong Kong, India, and Pakistan. In 1962, a Long-Term Agreement Regarding International Trade in Cotton Textiles (LTA) was negotiated under the auspices of the General Agreement on Tariffs and

Trade (GATT). The LTA was extended to materials other than cotton in 1974 and became known as the Multifiber Agreement (MFA).

The MFA governed a trade regime in which the major importing countries negotiated import quotas bilaterally with exporting countries. It became part of the multilateral trading system in spite of breaking fundamental principles of the GATT, including the most-favored-nation (MFN) principle and the idea that trade restrictions should be in the form of tariffs, as tariffs are less trade distorting than quotas. The MFA was renegotiated four times, the last time in 1991, and it finally expired in 1994. At that point the European Union (EU), the United States, Canada, Norway, Austria, and Finland (Austria and Finland joined EU in 1995) applied quotas, almost exclusively on imports from developing countries.

While the most competitive textiles and clothing exporters such as China, India, Pakistan, Hong Kong, Taiwan, and South Korea faced binding quotas, several poorer developing countries had unfilled quotas and therefore attracted foreign investment from the quota-restricted countries. In addition, former colonies and other low-income countries obtained preferential access to the EU and the United States, including tariff and quota-free access in textiles and clothing. This further encouraged the establishment of export-oriented clothing production, often in export processing zones. Preferential access was typically conditioned on a minimum local content (intermediate input) requirement or complicated rules of origin.

Many low-income countries have a narrow industrial base and cannot easily source materials used in the manufacturing of apparel locally and fulfill the local content requirements. In such cases imports of material inputs from other low-income regional trading partners or preference-receiving countries were sometimes allowed. Finally, the United States and the EU had production-sharing programs in which the partner countries could import textiles or cut fabric and other inputs from the United States or EU and export ready-to-wear clothing back to them duty free or paying tariffs only on the value added in the exporting country. The relevant program in the United States was the 807/9802 production-sharing program (referring to chapter 9802 in the Harmonized Tariff Schedule of the United States relating to articles assembled abroad with components produced in the United States), while the EU had outward processing agreements with several countries, both as part of regional free trade agreements and as stand-alone agreements with a number of Asian countries.

The managed trade system—including the MFA, preferential access to major markets for small, low-income countries, and outward processing agreements—resulted in a highly distorted trade and production pattern. It has been estimated that the MFA regime cost the average U.S. household $105 per year, and the average EU household €270 per year around the year 2000. During the Uruguay Round of the GATT it was agreed to gradually phase out the MFA and subject the textiles and clothing sectors to the normal multilateral trade rules in the GATT. The MFA was replaced by a transitory regime known as the Agreement on Textiles and Clothing (ATC) in 1995. ATC envisaged the gradual phasing out of quotas over 10 years, ending January 1, 2005. Quotas were to be eliminated in four steps in 1995, 1998, 2002, and 2005, while the quotas remaining at each point in time were to be increased every year. In 2004 about 20 percent of U.S. imports came in under a binding quota.

While the ATC was followed to the letter, liberalization was largely back-loaded until 2005, as the nonbinding quotas were lifted first. When China became a member of the WTO in 2001, its considerable textiles and clothing sector became part of the liberalized multilateral trading system. Due to the size and competitiveness of China's manufacturing sector, many studies predicted that China and to a lesser extent India would dominate the post-quota world markets, to the detriment of preference-receiving developing countries and producers in the EU and the United States. Therefore safeguards were incorporated in China's Accession Agreement with the WTO.

When the remaining quotas were lifted on January 1, 2005, there was indeed a surge in imports to the

United States from China. Imports increased by more than 50 percent in value terms from 2004 to 2005, and China's market share increased from 20 to 28 percent in textiles and clothing. This surge triggered requests for safeguards, and the United States signed a Memorandum of Understanding with China in November 2005. The two countries agreed to set annual quantitative levels of imports in 22 categories of textiles and clothing for 2006, 2007, and 2008, in which import expansion volumes of 173–640 percent were allowed between 2004 and 2006 and thereafter by increases of 12.5–16 percent in 2007 and 15–17 percent in 2008.

Imports from China into the EU surged by almost 100 percent in value terms in the liberalized categories during the first three quarters of 2005 and the increase was even sharper in volume terms, as unit prices fell sharply. Imports from China largely replaced exports from other developing countries, while the total import value did not change much. This triggered a Memorandum of Understanding with China, and safeguards on 10 sensitive products were imposed, allowing imports to grow by between 10 and 12.5 percent for the years 2005, 2006, and 2007 in these products. It should also be noted that China has become one of the fastest-growing markets for EU textiles exports.

Both tariffs and quotas impose a wedge between world market prices and the domestic price in the importing country, allowing local high-cost producers to sell in the local market. Quotas have the additional effect that exporters shift to higher-value-added, higher-quality products within the quota in order to maximize income from the allocated quota. A sharp fall in unit prices both in the EU and the United States on imports from China in liberalized product categories during 2005 suggests that this effect may have been important, although elimination of quota rents and more competitive markets have also contributed to lower unit prices.

In spite of import protection, employment in the textiles and clothing sector has declined steadily over time in the United States and the EU. Furthermore the declining trend has continued, but apparently not accelerated, during the phaseout of import quotas under the ATC. In the United States, employment in the textiles sector fell from 701,000 in 1990 to 539,000 in 2001 and further to 390,000 in 2005. The clothing sector experienced an even sharper fall in employment, from 929,000 in 1990 to 426,000 in 2001 and further to 260,000 in 2005. The EU experienced a similarly falling long-term employment trend, from 2.6 million workers in 1995 to 2.2 million in 2001.

Even in the countries with an expanding textiles and clothing sector, employment has increased much less than output as increased international competition has led to the adoption of modern technology and sharp increases in labor productivity. The textile and clothing sectors employed 4.8 and 2.6 million people, respectively, in China in 2002, together about 16.5 percent of China's total manufacturing employment.

World Trade in Textiles and Clothing Textiles and clothing's share of world merchandise exports in value terms has fluctuated between 5 and 8 percent since the early 1960s and stood at 4.7 percent in 2005. The direction of trade has shifted substantially over the decades as textiles and clothing production tends to migrate to countries with relatively low labor costs. The first wave of migration came in the 1950s and 1960s from Europe and the United States to Japan. The second wave came in the 1970s and early 1980s from Japan to the rapidly industrializing countries in Asia: the Republic of Korea, Taiwan, and Hong Kong, which together accounted for about a third of world clothing exports at their peak. Finally there is an ongoing migration of production and trade from these middle-income Asian countries to China, India, Bangladesh, Vietnam, and other South Asian countries.

China has increased its world market share in clothing from 6 percent in the early 1980s to 26 percent in 2005, while India's world market share has fluctuated between 2 and 3 percent since the early 1980s. India's exports have been hampered by quotas and by domestic labor and product market regulation, but are likely to increase sharply in a quota-free trading regime, provided that domestic reforms take hold.

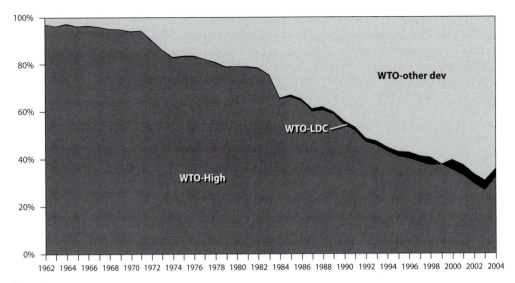

Figure 1

Exports of clothing by income group, shares of total. Source: Comtrade database (UNCTAD/World Bank).

The migration of clothing from high-income countries to developing countries is illustrated by figure 1, which depicts the shares of total WTO member countries' exports for high-income countries, least-developed (poor) countries, and other developing (middle-income) countries during the period 1962–2004. The countries that are currently classified as middle-income countries have increased their world market share from about 3 percent in 1962 to almost 70 percent in 2004. The countries currently classified as least-developed countries had a negligible world market share until the mid-1980s, but have since established themselves in the export markets. In 2005 the 10 largest exporters of clothing were China, the EU (extra-EU trade only), Turkey, India, Mexico, Bangladesh, Indonesia, the United States, Vietnam, and Romania. China alone accounted for 27 percent of total world exports, up from 4 percent in 1980 and 18 percent in 2000, while Hong Kong added another 10 percentage points in 2005 (with domestic exports plus reexports). The 10 largest exporters in textiles in 2005 were the EU (extra-EU trade only), China, the United States, South Korea, Taiwan, India, Pakistan, Turkey, Japan, and Indonesia.

The export success of some least-developed countries is largely based on preferential access to the quota-restricting countries. Some of these countries are not competitive under the normal market conditions that are emerging following the phasing out of quotas. Thus exports of textiles and clothing from ACP countries (African, Caribbean, and Pacific countries with preferential access to the EU market) to the EU fell by 17 percent in 2005.

With the increasing importance of design and rapid response to shifting consumer preferences and fashion trends, there has been a trend toward regionalization of the textiles and clothing trade. This development has been masked by the lifting of quotas where China and India were the most restricted countries. Mexico is the second largest exporter (after China) of clothing to the United States, however, while Turkey is the second (after China) and Romania the fourth (after India) largest exporter of textiles and clothing to the EU.

See also commodity chains; export promotion; fragmentation; quotas; safeguards

FURTHER READING

Abernathy, F. H., J. T. Dunlop, J. H. Hammond, and D. Weil. 1999. *Lean Retailing and the Transformation of*

Manufacturing—Lessons from the Textile and Apparel Industries. Oxford: Oxford University Press. Describes the textiles and clothing supply chain, focusing on the role of retailers, and documents how advances in communication technology have transformed the sector from being supply driven to becoming demand driven.

Eurostat. http://epp.eurostat.ec.europa.eu. Source of employment data for the EU.

Evans, C. L., and J. Harrigan. 2005. "Distance, Time, and Specialization: Lean Retailing in General Equilibrium." *American Economic Review* 95: 292–314. Provides empirical evidence that time is an important competitive factor in the clothing sector and finds that the sources of U.S. imports of "fast fashion" items have shifted to nearby countries.

Rivoli, P. 2005. *The Travels of a T-shirt in the Global Economy: An Economist Examines the Markets, Power, and Politics of World Trade.* Hoboken, NJ: John Wiley and Sons. Follows a T-shirt from the cotton fields in Texas to factories in China, sales in the United States, and resale on the secondhand clothing market in Dar es Salaam. At each leg of the journey, economic, policy, and social aspects are discussed.

UN Comtrade. http://comtrade.un.org/db/. Source of trade data.

UNIDO. http://www.unido.org/doc/3474. Source of employment data for countries other than the United States and the EU.

U.S. Bureau of Labor Statistics. http://www.bls.gov/ces/home.htm. Source of employment data for the United States.

World Trade Organization (WTO). 2001. "Comprehensive Report of the Textiles Monitoring Body to the Council of Trade in Goods on the Implementation of the Agreement on Textiles and Clothing during the Second Stage of the Integration Process." G/L/459 (July), 31. An official WTO report from the Textiles Monitoring Body assessing the implementation of the ATC, it provides comprehensive documentation of the implementation of the Agreement on Textiles and Clothing and its market access impact and can be downloaded from the WTO Web site.

HILDEGUNN KYVIK NORDÅS

■ time inconsistency problem

Suppose a government is responsible for setting a policy for several periods into the future. If the government chooses to change its policies from those promised at an earlier date, the policies are said to be *time inconsistent*. The modern interpretation of this issue relates to the time inconsistency of optimal policy rules (Kydland and Prescott 1977). Policymakers may announce in advance the policies they will follow to influence the expectations of private households. Once private decision-makers have acted on the basis of their expectations, however, a policymaker may be tempted to renege on an announcement, leading to suboptimal outcomes.

For example, consider the example of a central bank that is concerned about the inflation rate and the unemployment rate in an economy. The Phillips curve, which postulates an inverse relationship between inflation and unemployment, predicts that the trade-off between inflation and unemployment depends on expected inflation (Mankiw 2007). If policy setting in the central bank is guided by the Phillips curve, to reduce expected inflation the central bank might announce that low inflation is the main goal of its monetary policy. This is because a favorable trade-off between unemployment and inflation depends on the expected inflation rate being low. The announcement of a policy of low inflation is not credible, however. The central bank has an incentive to renege on its announcement and implement an expansionary monetary policy to further reduce the unemployment rate once firms and households have formed their expectations of inflation for the future, and set wages and prices accordingly. Private decision-makers understand the central bank's inherent incentive to shirk its announced policy and do not believe the central bank's announcement in the first place. The implication is that the economy ends up with a higher inflation rate without any lowering of the unemployment rate. Time inconsistency therefore leads to suboptimal outcomes.

Insights from the time inconsistency problem underlie the widely accepted contemporary view among economists that the best policies are the most predictable policies, or those that follow simple rules. This basic insight also relates to an earlier debate on rules versus discretion in macroeconomic policy (Friedman 1959). A rule specifies in advance the actions that policymakers will take or commit to. Commitment refers to the ability of a government to make binding choices. Economists have long recognized that unless a government can commit to a policy rule, it will in the future want to modify policies that are optimal from the standpoint of today. Further, without such binding policy commitments (i.e., policies aimed at tying the hands of the government), the private sector will fear that today's governments will make promises that its successors will refuse to honor.

Monetary Policies to Overcome Time Inconsistency Time inconsistency provides a rich explanation for a wide variety of issues, such as why capital accumulation in countries is low, or why countries choose to fix their exchange rate. In line with the earlier example, however, one of the most important applications of time inconsistent policies is the "inflation bias" inherent in monetary policy (Barro and Gordon 1983a, 1983b). *Inflation bias* refers to prolonged episodes of high inflation above what is socially desirable. An example is the "great inflation" of the 1970s in the United States. Time inconsistency hampers a government's efforts to keep inflation stable and leads to high and persistent inflation despite repeated promises to fight it. This affects the volatility of inflation, output, and interest rates, leading to a misallocation of resources.

Given the implications of time inconsistency, a large body of research has evolved since the 1980s on ways to overcome the time inconsistency problem in macroeconomic policy. For example, in the case of monetary policy, economists have suggested various types of monetary policy rules. Other solutions involve the delegation of monetary policy to an independent authority with well-defined objectives. This in turn has led to greater central bank independence. Central bank independence can help in situations where credible policy rules are not enforceable. In contrast to rules,

discretion implies the absence of commitment to a particular rule, leaving policymakers more flexible with their future actions.

Another solution to the time inconsistency problem involves reputation building. By acting consistently over a long period, a policymaker builds up a reputation that causes the private sector to believe its announcements. Once a reputation has been built, expectations of inflation become consistent with the announced low inflation policy. In some cases reputation can be imported. For instance, the monetary authority can peg its currency and import the monetary policy of another country with more credible institutions. This is often the primary motivation behind the adoption of hard pegs such as currency boards, dollarization, and common currencies.

Political Macroeconomics Since the early 1990s a line of research called political macroeconomics has evolved to explore the political determinants of macroeconomic policy (Drazen 2000; Persson and Tabellini 1994). This line of research recognizes that a policymaker's incentives and constraints originate in the political process. For example, within the context of fiscal policy, elected officials may be motivated by electoral reasons to enact time inconsistent expansionary policies that have long-term inflationary consequences. Alternatively, fiscal stabilizations—attempts to reduce a large fiscal deficit of a country—are likely to fail if the adjustments are achieved by higher taxes, as in Ireland's fiscal stabilization of 1982. The time inconsistency of this policy is that governments are unlikely to deliver on the promise of higher taxes, given the nature of the political business cycle. With respect to monetary policy, the economist Rogoff (1985) argues for the appointment of a conservative central banker who has greater inflation aversion than society as a whole to eliminate the inflation bias inherent in monetary policy. Welfare improves because the central bank trades some flexibility for some gain in credibility. Indeed, different views about rules and discretion—with the associated themes of commitment, credibility, and time inconsistency—are among the most pressing issues concerning the conduct of macroeconomic policy in a strategic setting.

See also common currency; currency board arrangement (CBA); currency substitution and dollarization; discipline; exchange rate regimes; inflation targeting; monetary policy rules; monetary versus fiscal dominance

FURTHER READING

Barro, R., and D. Gordon. 1983a. "Rules, Discretion, and Reputation in a Model of Monetary Policy." *Journal of Monetary Economics* 12: 101–21.

———. 1983b. "A Positive Theory of Monetary Policy in a Natural Rate Model." *Journal of Political Economy* 91: 589–610. These two articles show how an incentive toward time-inconsistent behavior in the Kydland-Prescott model can yield an inflationary bias in monetary policy. They also introduce a new solution to the time inconsistency problem: reputation building.

Drazen, A. 2000. *Political Economy in Macroeconomics.* Princeton, NJ: Princeton University Press. Represents the first full-scale effort to organize a large body of literature on political economy and macroeconomics. It has an extensive coverage and depth as well as critical assessment.

Friedman, M. 1959. *A Program for Monetary Stability.* New York: Fordham University Press. Contains a comprehensive discussion of an early debate between rules versus discretion in macroeconomic policy.

Kydland, F., and E. Prescott. 1977. "Rules Rather than Discretion: The Inconsistency of Optimal Plans." *Journal of Political Economy* 85: 473–91. The modern interpretation of time inconsistency of policy stems from this pathbreaking paper. It had a profound effect on the practice of policymaking.

Mankiw, G. 2007. *Macroeconomics.* 6th ed. New York: Worth. Contains economic and noneconomic examples on time inconsistency.

Persson, T., and G. Tabellini. 1994. *Monetary and Fiscal Policy.* Vol. 1. *Credibility.* Cambridge, MA: MIT Press. Contains a full treatment of political macroeconomics with a specific focus on policy issues.

Rogoff, K. 1985. "The Optimal Degree of Commitment to an Intermediate Monetary Target." *Quarterly Journal of Economics* 100: 1169–90. A pathbreaking paper in the time inconsistency literature on the importance of central bank independence.

CHETAN GHATE

■ Tinbergen principle/rule

See assignment problem

■ Tobin tax

Nobel Laureate economist James Tobin (1974, 1978) advanced a now well-known case for what has come to be known as the Tobin tax, namely, the imposition of a modest ad valorem tax (i.e., a percentage of value) on all spot transactions in foreign exchange. (Spot transactions are those that entail actual exchanges of currency at the existing market rates.) Tobin wrote that "the tax would apply to all purchases of financial instruments denominated in another currency. It would have to apply . . . to all payments in one currency for goods, services, and real assets sold by a resident of another currency area" (1978, 159). Tobin advanced the case for this tax on currency trading following the collapse of the Bretton Woods system of pegged exchange rates and attendant concerns about speculation, volatility, and misalignment in currency markets. Tobin also suggested that the tax could restore "some fraction of short-run [policy] autonomy"; however, he was careful to explain that "it will not, should not, permit governments to make domestic policies without reference to external consequences" (1978, 158).

The Tobin tax built on John Maynard Keynes's case for a securities transactions tax. Keynes (1936) proposed a substantial transfer tax on all transactions as a means to dampen the general tendency for speculation to dominate enterprise in liquid, competitive financial markets. Keynes (1980, chap. 36) also proposed taxation of foreign lending to contain speculative capital movements.

Several factors stimulated interest in the Tobin tax in the 1990s. These factors included the increase in currency speculation and volatility; the frequency of currency crises in developing countries; and the debate over the adequacy of the international financial architecture and the volume of international capital flows available to developing countries. This attention stood in sharp contrast to the silence that greeted Tobin's original presentation in the 1970s. The recent interest in the Tobin tax is located in a number of quarters—namely, academic economists identified with the Keynesian tradition, various United Nations agencies, governments in some countries that express support for the Tobin tax (namely, Canada, Belgium, and France), and nongovernmental organizations concerned with development finance and financial architecture. Tobin distanced himself from many of the nongovernmental organizations that advocated for the tax in the 1990s, however.

There is broad consensus that the tax must be levied at a low rate (Nissanke 2004 suggests 0.01 to 0.02 percent) in order to minimize the incentive to undertake tax evasion strategies (e.g., geographical or asset substitution) and to avoid other distortions of the foreign exchange market. Research has also focused on the issue of tax collection. In Tobin's original formulation, governments would levy and collect the tax nationally. But in view of the potential problems of tax competition among nations and the diversion of trading activity to "Tobin tax havens," many proponents focus on the need for a global tax agreement and the creation of a supranational authority to administer and collect the tax (Griffith-Jones 1996) and to allocate its revenues to projects that promote development (Kaul and Langmore 1996). Others, however, suggest that a Tobin tax could achieve some of its objectives absent global implementation (Baker 2001; Nissanke 2004).

Modifications to the Original Tobin Tax Concept In 1996 Tobin amended his original proposal to take account of the importance of new instruments of foreign exchange trading. In the amended version, Tobin (1996) argued that forward and swap transactions would be subject to taxation as well. (A for-

ward transaction is a contract in which parties agree to exchange currencies in the future at a price agreed on today. A swap combines spot and forward transactions.) Indeed, it is likely that if the tax is limited to spot transactions it would lead to a tax-saving reallocation of financial transactions from traditional spot transactions to derivative instruments. As such, in order to prevent tax avoidance via asset substitution or a changed product mix, it ought to be applied on all derivative products such as forwards, futures, options, and swaps.

Some proponents of the Tobin tax argue for modified versions of the proposal aimed at enhancing its ability to reduce currency market volatility. For instance, Crotty and Epstein (1996) argue for joint implementation of Tobin and securities transaction taxes. They argue that a securities transaction tax might reinforce the market-stabilizing function of a Tobin tax by increasing the cost of investor flight (since the sale of assets or borrowing must precede the flight of large sums of money from a country).

Spahn (1996) advances a case for a two-tiered Tobin tax. In this formulation, low transactions taxes on currency trading would be maintained during tranquil (or "normal") times. But a higher transaction tax would be activated whenever levels of market activity accelerated dramatically. Spahn argues that with knowledge of this variable tax structure, investors might be less likely ex ante to engage in activities that aggravate various types of financial risks. Moreover activation of a prohibitively high transaction tax (as a type of speed bump) might discourage some investors from liquidating their portfolios at precisely the time of greatest financial volatility.

The Debate over the Tobin Tax Most proponents of the Tobin tax argue that it has the potential to shift the balance of factors influencing the exchange rate away from short-term expectations toward long-term factors and to decrease exchange rate volatility caused by speculation in this market. Advocates maintain that speculation in currency markets would be dampened because the annualized cost of even a low tax could change trading behavior. Many proponents argue that the Tobin tax constitutes a progressive form of taxation, given its likely incidence (Baker 2001; Palley 2001). Following the East Asian financial crisis of 1997–98, a few advocates suggested that had a Tobin tax been in place it might have reduced the buildup risks that culminated in the crisis (Wade 1998).

Advocates of the Tobin tax are sanguine on the matter of revenue creation. For instance, Nissanke (2004) forecasts that a Tobin tax (even if not implemented by all countries at once) has the potential to raise between U.S. $17 billion and $35 billion in one year (using data for 2001). The taxes harvested would be allocated to various projects of developmental or global importance.

Critics of the Tobin tax, such as Dodd (2003), advance a number of arguments. Dodd argues that the tax is not politically feasible; that it is not feasible administratively or technically without imposing unreasonably high costs; that the issue of leakages through shifts to nontaxed assets and/or to Tobin tax havens is not considered seriously; that the tax would have perverse consequences insofar as it would reduce financial market stability and increase volatility in prices and capital flows; and that the proposed rate for the Tobin tax is actually quite large when one compares it with the transaction costs of trading in foreign exchange markets and most liquid securities and derivatives.

Critics have also taken issue with the claim that the Tobin tax could play any role in reducing the tendency toward financial crises in developing countries (Grabel 2003). This is because the Tobin tax is not designed to dampen speculation in all of the sectors of the economy that are prone to bubbles (e.g., real estate and construction). Even in those sectors that do fall under the authority of the tax, the presence of a tax is unlikely to undermine the attractiveness of activities and financing strategies that aggravate fragile financial environments. Implicit in this critique of the Tobin tax is the view that other strategies—ranging from prudential financial regulation, exchange controls, capital controls, capital management techniques, and taxation of other "global public ills" (such as pollution)—represent far better means than does the Tobin tax for reducing

financial volatility and currency misalignments, enhancing macroeconomic policy autonomy, and raising revenues for projects of global social importance.

See also Bretton Woods system; capital controls; capital flight; currency crisis; exchange rate volatility; financial crisis; global public goods; international financial architecture

FURTHER READING

Baker, Dean. 2001. "Why Do We Avoid Financial-Transactions Taxes?" *Challenge* 44 (3): 90–96. Focuses on the politics of the Tobin and other types of financial transactions taxes and argues that the primary obstacle to serious consideration of these measures is political, rather than technical or economic.

Crotty, J., and G. Epstein. 1996. "In Defence of Capital Controls." In *Are There Alternatives? Socialist Register 1996*, edited by Leo Panitch. London: Merlin Press, 118–49. Examines the economic and political arguments for various types of capital controls, including the Keynes and the Tobin tax.

Dodd, Randall. 2003. "Lessons for Tobin Tax Advocates: The Politics of Policy and the Economics of Market Micro-Structure." In *Debating the Tobin Tax*, edited by James Weaver, Randall Dodd, and Jamie Baker. Washington, DC: New Rules for Global Finance Coalition, 27–50. Presents a critical microeconomic and political analysis of the Tobin tax, takes issue with a great many of the arguments advanced by proponents, and focuses on the unanticipated negative economic and political consequences that would be associated with imposition of the tax.

Grabel, Ilene. 2003. "Averting Crisis: Assessing Measures to Manage Financial Integration in Emerging Economies." *Cambridge Journal of Economics* 27 (3): 317–36. Examines the ability of many policies (including the Tobin tax) to reduce financial instability in developing countries and concludes that the Tobin tax cannot reduce the most important types of financial risks confronting developing countries and, therefore, cannot reduce their vulnerability to crises.

Griffith-Jones, Stephany. 1996. "Institutional Arrangements for a Tax on International Currency Transactions." In *The Tobin Tax: Coping with Financial*

Volatility, edited by Mahbub ul Haq, Inge Kaul, and Isabelle Grunberg. New York: Oxford University Press, 143–61. Makes a case for the role of a supranational authority charged with administering and collecting Tobin tax revenues.

Kaul, Inge, and John Langmore. 1996. "Potential Uses of the Revenue from a Tobin Tax." In *The Tobin Tax: Coping with Financial Volatility*, edited by Mahbub ul Haq et al. New York: Oxford University Press, 255–72. Argues that Tobin tax revenues should be allocated to projects that promote economic development.

Keynes, John Maynard. 1936. *The General Theory of Employment, Interest, and Money*. London: Macmillan. Contains a brief discussion of the need to tax securities trading as a tool for reducing what Keynes saw as the tendency of speculation to dominate enterprise in liquid, competitive markets.

———. 1980. *The Collected Writings of John Maynard Keynes*. Vol. 6. *A Treatise on Money*. London: Macmillan. A brief passage in this volume contains the argument that foreign lending should be subject to taxation in order to reduce speculative capital movements.

Nissanke, Machiko. 2004. "Revenue Potential of the Tobin Tax for Development Finance." In *New Sources of Development Finance*, edited by A. B. Atkinson. New York: Oxford University Press, 58–90. Presents an estimate of the revenue-raising potential of the Tobin tax.

Palley, Thomas. 2001. "Destabilizing Speculation and the Case for an International Currency Transactions Tax." *Challenge* 44 (3): 70–89. Makes a case for the ability of the Tobin tax to reduce speculative pressures and presents a number of arguments from the public finance literature in support of the tax.

Spahn, Paul. 1996. "The Tobin Tax and Exchange Rate Stability." *Finance and Development* 33 (2) (June 24–27): 24–27. Advances an argument for a two-tiered Tobin tax.

Tobin, James. 1974. "Prospects for Macro-economic Policy." In *The New Economics One Decade Older*. Princeton, NJ: Princeton University Press.

———. 1978. "A Proposal for Monetary Reform." *Eastern Economics Journal* 4: 153–59. In the 1974 and 1978 papers, Tobin articulates the case for a tax on currency trading, which later became known as the Tobin tax.

———. 1996. "Prologue." In *The Tobin Tax: Coping with Financial Volatility*, edited by Mahbub ul Haq et al. New York: Oxford University Press, ix–xviii. In this short essay, Tobin updates his 1974 and 1978 arguments in light of changes in financial market structure.

Wade, Robert. 1998. "The Asian Debt-and-Development Crisis of 1997–?: Causes and Consequences." *World Development* 26 (8): 1535–53. Examines the causes of the East Asian financial crisis of 1997–98 and offers a brief counterfactual statement to the effect that a Tobin tax might have reduced some of the financial risks that contributed to the crisis.

ILENE GRABEL

■ trade and economic development, international

Since the study of economic development covers a wide array of topics, this entry looks at how international trade affects only certain very important aspects of development, particularly per capita real incomes and their growth rates, and the distribution of income. In studying the impact of trade on distribution-related aspects, the focus is first on poverty, then on the welfare of workers.

The Impact of Trade on Income Levels Theoretically trade is expected to have a positive impact on per capita real incomes through efficiency gains from specialization and exchange, as well as through the availability of larger varieties of goods. Trade has a further beneficial effect on resource allocation through the destruction of the monopoly power of inefficient domestic firms. Recent calculations using standard trade models for a small country show that the gains from moving from no trade to frictionless trade can result in substantial increases in real gross domestic product (GDP). Positive effects of trade on welfare (real incomes), however, may not be obtained in the presence of market distortions, externalities, or imperfections in institutions. Nevertheless, when direct policies to attack these distortions are in place, the positive effects of trade on welfare are restored (Bhagwati 1971).

At the macro level, Frankel and Romer (1999) find a positive effect of trade openness on income levels across countries. They address the issue of reverse causation through an instrumental-variables approach. Rodrik, Subramanian, and Trebbi (2004) use a simultaneous, structural-equations approach to study the effects of institutions, geography, and trade on per capita income levels. They find that "the quality of institutions trumps everything else." Trade and institutions have positive effects on each other, however, so trade affects incomes through institutions.

It is important to mention a few microlevel studies that look at a couple of channels mentioned above. Levinsohn (1993), Harrison (1994), and Krishna and Mitra (1998), using plant/firm-level data have found that the price-to-marginal-cost markup fell as a result of trade reforms in Turkey, Ivory Coast, and India, respectively. Thus the monopoly power of domestic firms (and therefore the deadweight losses associated with this monopoly power) went down. There is also some evidence on the variety channel. Using 8–10-digit–level data, Broda and Weinstein (2006) show that the gains from trade for the United States from greater varieties of goods through trade amounts to about 3 percent of GDP. These authors, in their more recent research, extend this empirical analysis and approach to investigating the growth effects of trade through an increase in varieties and find the gains to be even larger. The growth effects of trade will be discussed in detail in the next section.

In summary, the clear theoretical predictions of the positive effect of trade openness on real income or welfare have been supported by macro, cross-country studies. The microlevel studies have identified the main channels to be the market disciplining function of trade and its role in providing greater varieties of goods.

The Impact of Trade on Economic Growth The dynamic effects of trade are not straightforward to analyze and are sensitive to changes in assumptions. As a result, unlike the level effects of trade, there is disagreement on its growth effects.

In the beginning of the second half of the 20th century, the newly independent countries were concerned about possible adverse effects of trade on their growth, as their comparative advantage was in agricultural products. Furthermore they were concerned about adverse changes in the world relative prices of primary products. The early literature on trade and growth is motivated by such concerns.

According to Findlay (1984), the first implicit dynamic model of trade and growth is in David Ricardo's (1815) *Essay on the Influence of a Low Price of Corn upon the Profits of Stock*. This is explicitly and elegantly modeled by Findlay (1984) himself in a two-sector setup. While the profits in manufacturing are invested in increasing production and employment in the next period, land rents in agriculture are spent on consumption by "profligate landlords." Thus a country with a comparative advantage in manufacturing (agriculture) will experience an increase (decrease) in its growth rate on opening to trade.

Similar models of trade and growth were written to study how the North-South terms of trade move over time (Findlay 1984). Feeding stylized facts about relative productivity growth rates in the production of food, coffee, and steel into such models, the implication derived was that terms of trade for the South will deteriorate over time. Working with such models also showed that high growth in the presence of trade could result in a terms-of-trade loss, that is, the good that this rapidly growing country sells (exports) to the rest of the world becomes relatively cheaper while the good that this country buys (imports) from the rest of the world becomes relatively more expensive. When this terms-of-trade loss is large enough, there would be the possibility of a country's own growth reducing its real income. This possibility is called "immiserizing growth," analyzed in detail in Bhagwati (1958).

Another issue studied in the trade and growth literature was the impact of trade on growth through capital accumulation. In neoclassical models of trade and growth, there is either exogenous or no technological progress. Findlay (1984) presents such two-sector Solow- and Ramsey-type growth models to study the effects of trade. A country with a high savings rate has a high steady-state capital stock in autarky. Such a country will have a comparative advantage in the more capital-intensive of its two sectors. Opening to trade will result in (incomplete) specialization in the capital-intensive sector and will in turn lead to an increase in the rate of return on capital. Incentives to capital accumulation will therefore increase, and we will see an increase in the steady-state capital stock as a result of trade. Opening to trade also leads to transitional growth in this country. A country with a low savings rate has exactly the opposite experience. Importantly, in such multisectoral growth models, unlike a closed economy a small open (but diversified) economy does not experience diminishing returns to capital. With an increase in capital stock, production in a small open economy moves to more capital-intensive goods at a fixed world-price vector.

The issue of capital accumulation in an open economy has also been addressed by the "two-gap" models that emphasize the role of savings and foreign exchange in facilitating growth (Findlay 1984). Investment results in growth but it has to be financed by savings. Since this investment also requires the purchase of foreign capital goods, adequate foreign exchange should be available. That is why these models emphasize the need for aid and promotion of exports in generating growth.

In addition to these types of models, the early trade and growth literature also consisted of North-South models and the dual-economy models. While the former type focuses on the unequal relationship between the developed and the developing world, the latter looks at the asymmetry between regions within the same country. In North-South models, the developing world (the South) is structurally quite different from the developed world (the North)—not just in the model parameters but also with respect to the nature of factor markets and institutions. In dual-economy models, there is a modern urban sector and a primitive rural sector. In addition, there could be an unorganized subsector within the urban sector (see Findlay 1984).

While neoclassical growth theory assumed exogenous technological progress, in the endogenous growth theory, pioneered by Romer (1986), the rate of technological progress was determined within the model. Endogenous growth was a major breakthrough in growth research and attempted to explain the growth miracles of East Asia.

Grossman and Helpman (1991) developed a series of models using this new approach, where they clearly show that the growth effects of trade are very sensitive to the model structure assumed. While trade can increase productivity growth by avoiding duplication of effort in research and development (R&D), through the international exchange and transmission of technical knowledge and by allowing the pooling of knowledge across borders, it can reduce or increase productivity growth depending on whether a country is scarce or abundant in skilled labor (Grossman and Helpman 1991).

At the firm level, Rodrik (1992) shows that the market size of a domestic, import-competing firm may shrink as a result of reducing import protection (i.e., allowing more imports) and so will reduce the returns from and investment in R&D and in turn will reduce productivity growth. This is called the "market-size effect"; there is also what Devarajan and Rodrik (1991) call the "procompetitive effect" of trade liberalization, which results in the flattening of the demand for an import-competing good. The greater foreign competition increases the return to R&D and thus also R&D and growth.

At the macro level, the effects of trade barriers on growth and income have been studied empirically since the early 1990s. A variety of openness measures have been used to show positive effects of trade on growth. These studies have come in for heavy criticism by Rodriguez and Rodrik (2001), however, for problems with their openness measures and econometric analysis, as well as for the difficulty in establishing the direction of causality. One of the openness measures criticized by Rodriguez and Rodrik (2001) is the one used by Sachs and Warner (1995), which captures many aspects of the macroeconomic environment in addition to trade policy. However, the Sachs-Warner approach has recently been defended on the grounds that the other policy reforms captured in the measure accompany most major trade reforms and that we would like to know the value of the entire package of trade and accompanying reforms.

We next turn to the microlevel evidence. Harrison (1994) and Krishna and Mitra (1998) estimate a modified version of the traditional growth accounting equation to incorporate imperfect competition and nonconstant returns to scale. Using plant/firm-level data, they find evidence for an increase in productivity growth after trade reforms in the Ivory Coast and India, respectively. Pavcnik (2002), using a more sophisticated method to correct for simultaneity and selection problems, also finds evidence in support of productivity improvements in Chile after their trade reforms.

In summary, the trade and growth literature began by addressing interactions between trade and the asymmetries across developed and developing countries as well as those within developing countries. Subsequently the focus shifted to the interaction between capital accumulation and trade, in many cases analyzed in the presence of exogenous technical progress. This was followed by the trade and endogenous growth literature, motivated by the East Asian growth miracle. Across these three stages of the literature, the trade and growth models do not agree with each other on the predictions they make, as the results are highly sensitive to changes in assumptions. While most of the empirical literature has shown that trade has a positive effect on growth, the macro cross-country studies have come in for considerable criticism.

The Impact of Trade on Poverty While the literature on trade, incomes, and growth has implications for the trade-poverty linkage, there is also a small literature on the direct determinants of poverty rates (see comprehensive surveys by Goldberg and Pavcnik 2007; and Winters, McCulloch, and McKay 2004).

Dollar and Kraay (2002), using cross-country data, find that the growth rates of average incomes of people in the bottom quintile are roughly equal to the growth rates of overall per capita incomes, and the two are strongly correlated. Also policies known to be growth promoting, such as trade openness, macro-

economic stability, moderate government size, financial development, strong property rights, the rule of law, and the like, promote growth in the incomes of the poor as well. In subsequent work, the same authors infer from the data on the post-1980 "globalizing developing economies" that per capita income growth arising from expansion in trade in those countries has led to a sharp decrease in absolute poverty in the past 20 years.

Ravallion (2001) finds in his cross-country study that an increase in per capita income by 1 percent can reduce the proportion of people below the $1-a-day poverty line by about 2.5 percent on average. This varies across countries, depending on initial inequality.

Finally, a paper by Hasan, Quibria, and Kim (2003) argues, using cross-country evidence, that "policies and institutions that support economic freedom are critical for poverty reduction." Economic freedom indicators used by these authors include, among many components of freedom, the freedom to trade with foreigners.

Moving away from cross-country studies to within-country analysis, Topalova (2005) has examined the impact of trade liberalization on district-level poverty in India. She finds that "rural districts where industries more exposed to trade liberalization were concentrated experienced a slower progress in poverty reduction." She finds this effect not to be statistically significant in urban India. A recent study by Hasan, Mitra, and Ural (2007) uses data at the state and region levels for India and in no case do the authors find reductions in trade protection to have worsened poverty. Instead they find that states whose workers are on average more exposed to foreign competition tend to have lower rural, urban, and overall poverty rates (and poverty gaps), and this beneficial effect of greater trade openness is more pronounced in states that have more flexible labor market institutions. They also find that trade liberalization has led to poverty reduction to a greater degree in states more exposed to foreign competition by virtue of their sectoral composition.

Recent work by Guido Porto at the World Bank looks at the trade-poverty link in a more structural (model-based) way in a series of papers (e.g., 2006). Using this method, he decomposes the effects of trade into the consumption and income effects. Consumption effects take place through changes in goods prices, while income effects take place through changes in factor incomes. This methodology, developed by Porto, helps us understand how households in different income classes are affected by trade policies. Using this approach, Porto finds a beneficial impact of the South American regional trade agreement Mercosur on average and poor households in Argentina but not on rich households.

The literature on trade and poverty has evolved from cross-country studies to microlevel household studies. The state-of-the-art approach is fairly structural and can identify the various channels through which trade affects poverty. The literature, mainly but not entirely, provides evidence in support of the poverty-reducing effects of trade.

The Impact of Trade on Labor in Developing Countries There is, by now, a fairly rich micro-empirical literature on how labor is affected by trade policy in developing countries. Recent research draws attention to two opposing effects of trade for which there is some evidence: (1) an increase in wages (the Stolper-Samuelson effect in a labor-abundant country), everything else being equal, which reduces the amount of labor demanded, and (2) a reduction in the price-cost markup (due to more competition), which causes producers to increase their demand for labor. Also, there is evidence that imports can destroy or reduce monopoly rents that can be shared by employers and employees and thus lead to a reduction in the firm-specific wage rate and employment. Currie and Harrison (1997) argue that the employment reducing effects of trade reforms in import-competing firms may be partially or fully offset by positive effects brought about by attempts to reduce profit margins and to invest more resources into productivity enhancement to counter new competition. The mutually opposing forces end up offsetting each other as seen in their firm-level evidence from Morocco. It is important here to point out that many of the studies in the literature, including some of the studies described above, find little change in

the structure of employment across industries as a result of trade reforms, but there is evidence that sectors with larger tariff cuts experience larger declines in relative wages (see Goldberg and Pavcnik 2007).

Another important issue related to the trade-labor link is that of trade and wage inequality. Feenstra and Hanson (2003) summarize their research on this issue, published in a series of papers. Their analysis is based on a new type of trade, namely outsourcing through capital mobility. They assume that there is a final good that is produced using different types of intermediate goods, each of which in turn is produced using skilled and unskilled labor and physical capital. Different inputs have different skill intensities. Under free trade and no capital mobility, the Northern country produces inputs that are more skill intensive than those produced in the Southern country. Under a configuration in which the return to capital is lower in the Northern country than in the Southern country, allowing capital mobility leads to a flow of capital from the North to the South. There is a consequent shift in the production of the North's least skill-intensive intermediate inputs to the South (which still are more skill intensive than all the other inputs being produced in the South). Thus the relative demand for skills and consequently wage inequality go up in both countries. Feenstra and Hanson have found support for their theory using U.S. and Mexican data.

Let us next look at the pressure exerted by trade on labor markets through a new channel that has an impact on employment and wage risk and on the bargaining power of workers. This new linkage is the one between openness and the elasticity of labor demand emphasized by Rodrik (1997) and Slaughter (2001). The elasticity of labor demand here refers to the responsiveness of the quantity of labor demanded to its wage rate. Product-market elasticities (the responsiveness of quantity of final output demanded to the price of output) are likely to rise with trade liberalization. This is due to the availability of a greater variety of (imported) substitutes after opening up to trade, which makes it easier to move away from a good (or reduce its use) on a price increase. According to Hicks's well-known "fundamental law of factor demand," output-demand elasticities and factor-demand elasticities move in the same direction (see Slaughter 2001 for a more detailed discussion). Thus greater trade openness should lead to an increase in labor-demand elasticities. As Rodrik (1997) notes and as explained in Slaughter (2001) and Krishna, Mitra, and Chinoy (2001), bigger labor-demand elasticities shift the incidence of nonwage labor costs toward workers, lead to wider fluctuations in wages and employment due to fluctuations in labor demand, and reduce the bargaining power of workers. Slaughter (2001) was the first to perform an empirical investigation of this positive relationship between openness and labor-demand elasticities, but only for a developed country, namely the United States. He found mixed empirical support for this relationship using U.S. four-digit industry-level data. The first developing-country study in which this link has been investigated is Krishna, Mitra, and Chinoy (2001). Using a partial equilibrium, imperfectly competitive setup and plant-level data from the Turkish manufacturing sector, they find no linkage between greater trade openness and labor-demand elasticities. However, a recent paper by Hasan, Mitra, and Ramaswamy (2007), using state-level, industry-level data from a large developing country, namely India, finds a statistically significant effect in the predicted direction, the result being stronger in states with more flexible labor markets.

The literature on the link between trade and labor provides evidence that trade affects wages but does not affect industry-level employment due to the presence of various mutually offsetting channels. Trade has also been shown to have increased wage inequality. In addition, a new literature, with mixed evidence on the effects of trade on labor-demand elasticities has emerged.

Finally, there is some recent work on trade openness and child labor, which has not been covered in this entry (see Edmonds and Pavcnik, 2005).

The purpose of this entry is to examine the impact of trade on a few important aspects of development. Growth in incomes is an important component of development. However, if this growth takes place without any reduction in poverty, an important purpose of development is defeated. Therefore the impact of trade on incomes, growth, and poverty reduction has been discussed in this entry. Additionally, the trade-labor nexus has also been studied, as a large majority in developing countries does not possess any productive assets other than raw labor power.

See also child labor; export promotion; import substitution industrialization; North-South trade; terms of trade; trade and wages

FURTHER READING

Bhagwati, Jagdish N. 1958. "Immiserizing Growth: A Geometrical Note." *Review of Economic Studies* 25: 201–5. Geometrically demonstrates that the negative terms of trade effect (arising from growth) can dominate the direct effects of growth, leading to a welfare loss.

———. 1971. "The Generalized Theory of Distortions and Welfare." In *Trade, Balance of Payments and Growth*, edited by J. N. Bhagwati et al. North-Holland, Amsterdam, chapter 12. Looks at the effects of trade policy in the presence of market distortions and imperfections and argues that the positive effects of trade on welfare are restored in the presence of direct corrective policies.

Broda, Christian, and David E. Weinstein. 2006. "Globalization and the Gains from Variety." *Quarterly Journal of Economics* 121 (2): 541–85. Uses very disaggregate data to measure the impact of trade on welfare through the variety channel.

Currie, Janet, and Ann E. Harrison. 1997. "Sharing the Costs: The Impact of Trade Reform on Capital and Labor in Morocco." *Journal of Labor Economics* 15 (3): S44–71. Looks at some of the mutually offsetting effects of trade on firm-level employment.

Devarajan, Shantayanan, and Dani Rodrik. 1991. "Pro-Competitive Effects of Trade Reform: Results from a CGE Model of Cameroon." *European Economic Review* 35 (5): 1157–84. Analyzes the effect of import-competition on innovation through the flattening of the product demand curve.

Dollar, David, and Aart Kraay. 2002. "Growth Is Good for the Poor." *Journal of Economic Growth* 7 (3): 195–225. Shows empirically that growth reduces poverty.

Edmonds, Eric, and Nina Pavcnik. 2005. "Child Labor in the Global Economy." *Journal of Economic Perspectives* 18 (1): 199–220. Surveys literature on the impact of globalization on child labor.

Feenstra, Robert C., and Gordon H. Hanson. 2003. "Global Production and Inequality: A Survey of Trade and Wages." In *Handbook of International Trade*, edited by E. K. Choi and J. Harrigan. London: Blackwell, 146–85. Surveys how input trade can affect and has affected wage inequality.

Findlay, Ronald E. 1984. "Growth and Development in Trade Models." In *Handbook of International Economics*, vol. 1, edited by R. W. Jones and P. B. Kenen. Amsterdam: North-Holland, 185–236. Surveys the trade and growth literature prior to the emergence of endogenous growth theory.

Frankel, Jeffrey, and David Romer. 1999. "Does Trade Cause Growth?" *American Economic Review* 89 (3): 379–99. An empirical, cross-country study on trade and growth.

Goldberg, Pinelopi, and Nina Pavcnik. 2007. "Distributional Effects of Globalization in Developing Countries." *Journal of Economic Literature* 45 (1): 39–82. Survey article on the impact of globalization on the various aspects of inequality.

Grossman, Gene, and Elhanan Helpman. 1991. *Innovation and Growth in the Global Economy.* Cambridge, MA: MIT Press. Collection of their theoretical work on trade and endogenous growth.

Harrison, Ann E. 1994. "Productivity, Imperfect Competition, and Trade Reform: Theory and Evidence." *Journal of International Economics* 36 (1–2): 53–73. Empirical plant-level study of the impact of trade reform on productivity growth and market structure.

Hasan, Rana, Devashish Mitra, and K. V. Ramaswamy. 2007. "Trade Reforms, Labor Regulations, and Labor-Demand Elasticities: Empirical Evidence from India." *The Review of Economics and Statistics* 89 (3): 466–81. Empirical, state-level, industry-level study of the impact of trade liberalization on labor-demand elasticities in the presence of varying labor-market institutions.

Hasan, Rana, Devashish Mitra, and Beyza Ural. 2007. "Trade Liberalization, Labor-Market Institutions and Poverty Reduction: Evidence from Indian States." *India Policy Forum* 3: 71–122.

Hasan, Rana, M. G. Quibria, and Yangseon Kim. 2003. "Poverty and Economic Freedom: Evidence from Cross-Country Data." Economics Study Area Working Papers 60. Honolulu, Hawaii: East-West Center. An empirical analysis of how various components of economic freedom affect poverty.

Krishna, Pravin, and Devashish Mitra. 1998. "Trade Liberalization, Market Discipline, and Productivity Growth: New Evidence from India." *Journal of Development Economics* 56 (2): 447–62. Empirical firm-level study of the impact of trade reform on productivity growth and market structure, followed by some welfare analysis.

Krishna, Pravin, Devashish Mitra, and Sajjid Chinoy. 2001. "Trade Liberalization and Labor Demand Elasticities: Evidence from Turkey." *Journal of International Economics* 55 (2): 391–409. Empirical plant-level study of the impact of trade liberalization on labor demand.

Levinsohn, James. 1993. "Testing the Imports-as-Market-Discipline Hypothesis." *Journal of International Economics* 35 (1–2): 1–22. Empirical plant-level study of the impact of trade reform on market structure (the price-cost markups).

Pavcnik, Nina. 2002. "Trade Liberalization, Exit, and Productivity Improvements: Evidence from Chilean Plants." *Review of Economic Studies* 69 (1): 245–76. Empirical plant-level study of the impact of trade reform on productivity growth, using modern techniques to address various econometric issues.

Porto, Guido G. 2006. "Using Survey Data to Assess the Distributional Effects of Trade Policy." *Journal of International Economics* 70 (1): 140–60. Develops a method to estimate the general equilibrium distributional effects of trade policies using household survey data.

Ravallion, Martin. 2001. "Growth, Inequality and Poverty: Looking Beyond Averages." *World Development* 29 (11): 1803–15. Assesses the degree to which poor people share in growth.

Rodriguez, Francisco, and Dani Rodrik. 2001. "Trade Policy and Economic Growth: A Skeptic's Guide to the Cross-National Evidence." In *Macroeconomics Annual 2000*, edited by Ben Bernanke and Kenneth S. Rogoff. Cambridge, MA: MIT Press for NBER, 261–325. Economic and econometric critique of cross-country empirical work showing the positive effects of trade on growth.

Rodrik, Dani. 1992. "Closing the Productivity Gap: Does Trade Liberalization Really Help?" In *Trade Policy, Industrialization, and Development: New Perspectives*, edited by G. K. Helleiner. Oxford: Clarendon Press, 155–75. Analyzes how import competition affects growth by reducing the market size of domestic, import-competing firms.

———. 1997. *Has Globalization Gone Too Far?* Washington, DC: Institute for International Economics. A detailed analysis of the costs and benefits of international economic integration.

Rodrik, Dani, Arvind Subramanian, and Francesco Trebbi. 2004. "Institutions Rule: The Primacy of Institutions Over Geography and Integration in Economic Development." *Journal of Economic Growth* 9 (2): 131–65. Empirically investigates the interactions between trade, institutions, and geography and their effects on incomes.

Romer, Paul M. 1986. "Increasing Returns and Long-Run Growth." *Journal of Political Economy* 94 (5): 1002–37. Pathbreaking paper introducing and analyzing the concept of endogenous growth.

Sachs, Jeffrey D., and Andrew Warner. 1995. "Economic Reform and the Process of Global Integration." *Brookings Papers on Economic Activity*: 1–118. Studies the impact of economic reform on growth.

Slaughter, Matthew. 2001. "International Trade and Labor-Demand Elasticities." *Journal of International Economics* 54 (1): 27–56. Empirical investigation of the effects of trade on labor-demand elasticities using U.S. industry-level data.

Topalova, Petia. 2005. "Trade Liberalization, Poverty, and Inequality: Evidence from Indian Districts." In *Globalization and Poverty*, edited by Ann Harrison. Cambridge, MA: University of Chicago Press and National Bureau of Economic Research. Empirical, district-level study of the impact of trade liberalization on poverty in India.

Winters, L. Alan, Neil McCulloch, and Andrew McKay. 2004. "Trade Liberalization and Poverty: The Evidence So Far." *Journal of Economic Literature* 42 (1): 72–115. Surveys the empirical literature on trade and poverty.

DEVASHISH MITRA

■ trade and the environment

Trade, the exchange of goods and services across countries, is often viewed as an engine of economic growth. Benefits of liberalized trade include access to a larger variety of goods and services to consumers, easier access to foreign technologies, access to larger markets for producers, and increased efficiency in resource allocation. The impact of trade on the environment, however, is a contentious issue; air and water pollution, the degradation of natural habitats, loss of species, and global pollutants, particularly carbon dioxide emissions, are major concerns.

Recent Trends In the late 20th and early 21st centuries international trade has rapidly increased worldwide, while average tariffs and quantitative restrictions to trade (import and export quotas) have fallen steadily. Export growth has outpaced growth in gross domestic product (GDP) (World Bank 2006). With respect to the environment, there are persistent and widespread improvements in most *local* urban pollutants, mainly airborne pollutants (e.g., sulfur dioxide, nitrogen dioxide, carbon monoxide, air particles, and lead). An important exception is local ozone, a highly dangerous local pollutant that has increased over time in most cities, in part as a consequence of measures taken to reduce some other air pollutants. There are also less clear but perceptible trends to improve some indicators of water quality (United Nations 2006). In contrast, there is a clear worsening of the *global* pollutants (e.g., carbon dioxide) as well as of the rural or "green" environment (i.e., the natural forests and other important natural habitats). The latter phenomenon is causing a precipitous loss of species and has contributed to increased global warming through the emissions of carbon dioxide due to massive forest burning.

Thus while trade has rapidly expanded, the environmental trends show a sharp dichotomy: the local urban environment improves but the green or rural environments continuously deteriorate. One reason for this may be that local urban pollution is directly felt by large concentrations of population able to exert strong pressures on politicians to control it, while the rural environment affects directly a smaller fraction of the population which, due to its geographical dispersion, is less able to pressure governments. Rural environmental degradation and global pollution are less visible to the majority of the population than local urban pollution, which might explain the generally more lax response by governments to rural than urban environmental problems and to global rather than local pollutants.

Effects of Trade on the Environment The central issue is whether opening up to trade has magnified the trends described above or has instead mitigated some of them. The effects of trade on the environment can be broken down into scale, technique, composition, and growth effects (Antweiler, Copeland, and Taylor 2001; López, Galinato, and Islam 2007).

Scale effect. Most forms of pollution are a byproduct of a production process. Increased trade openness often implies an increase in economic activity. The scale effect, holding constant production techniques and the mix of goods produced, is likely to cause an increase in the level of local and global pollution and also faster degradation of natural resources. For example, expanding agricultural exports may increase agricultural activities, which may result in water pollution from extensive fertilizer use and deforestation from increased demand for agriculture. The scale effect may also include trade-related direct increases in pollution emissions through increase in air and road transportation. Empirical studies usually employ gross domestic product (GDP) per square kilometer as a proxy for the scale effect. López (1997), for example, found that in Ghana trade liberalization induced a faster rate of deforestation. Given the more lenient attitude of governments toward rural environmental degradation and global pollutants than to urban local pollution, the negative impact of the scale effect is likely to be worse for the green-global environment than for the urban environment.

Technique (wealth) effect. The technique effect refers to reductions in emission intensity per unit of output. If trade raises income, emission intensity may fall if environmental quality is a normal good. A normal good is one for which, as incomes rise, individuals would prefer more of it. Higher income may lead to stricter environmental regulation, under the assumption that country governments are responsive to the citizens' demands. A trade-induced rise in incomes would thus make higher environmental quality desirable. Empirical studies often use per capita GDP as a proxy for income. A more accurate measure is per capita household consumption expenditure, which is more directly related to permanent income or wealth than per capita GDP (López, Galinato, and Islam 2007). The technique effect of trade has been found to reduce certain pollutants, particularly air pollutants, but the effects on other environmental factors is less significant. The strength of the technique effect is weaker for the green and global environment than for the local urban environment because the citizens' demands for environmental quality are likely to be feebler in the rural areas and for global pollutants than for the control of local urban pollutants.

Composition effect. Trade may also alter the composition of the economy's output. If the economy's comparative advantages favor clean industries, increasing trade openness may switch from pollution-intensive "dirty" goods to less polluting, or "clean," goods and services. The general assumption is that production of dirty goods is more intensive in physical capital and natural resources while clean goods production is more intensive in human capital. Holding the scale of production and other factors constant, an economy that shifts its production toward physical capital–intensive goods will pollute more, and conversely, an economy that shifts its production away from physical capital–intensive goods will pollute less. Countries that have large endowments of natural resources are likely to relatively specialize in resource-intensive industries and thus increase the extraction of natural resources when they open to trade. In countries where property rights on resources are poorly defined or where environmental regulations are not properly enforced, increased trade is likely to result in more resource degradation and deforestation.

Even more seriously, lack of property rights on resources may lead countries to specialize in natural resource–intensive activities and hence to further environmental degradation even if they are not richly endowed in resources. That is, the institutional and regulatory failures may lead to false comparative advantages, in which case trade may reduce rather than raise income as is normally assumed (this is behind the *pollution haven hypothesis* as discussed later). In this perverse case the technique effect discussed earlier (which assumed that income increases with trade) would be reversed. Also, once again, the weight of the composition effect may be felt on the green-global environment because environmental control institutions and regulatory policies are less developed for the rural-global resources than for urban pollutants.

Growth rate effect. Trade openness may cause a number of dynamic forces that promote not only a once-and-for-all effect on the income level but also a faster pace of economic growth over time. For example, trade openness may cause an economy to adopt new technologies at a faster rate due to the fact that many new technologies are generated abroad. A faster pace of economic growth may cause lower environmental quality than a country growing at a slower rate (López, Galinato, and Islam 2007). The issue here is that environmental institutions and policies need time to be adapted. An economy growing at a fast rate will find it much more difficult to timely adapt their policies and institutions to properly respond to increasing pollution than an economy growing at a more moderate pace. This trade-induced growth rate effect may result in a decline in environmental quality.

The net effect. Empirical studies seem to corroborate the hypothesis that the positive-technique effect dominates the other effects for certain local urban pollutants resulting in trade being good for the urban environment (Copeland and Taylor 2003). However, the few empirical studies of the impact of trade on the rural environment, particularly the impact on wetlands and natural forests, suggest that the net effect of trade is negative (López 1997). This is consistent with the earlier conceptual discussion regarding the relative strength of the various partial effects on the urban and rural environments. The net effect of trade is also likely to be negative for global pollutants because the technique effect may be weak

for such pollutants as people care less for pollutants that do not affect them directly.

Pollution Haven Hypothesis According to this hypothesis the direction of trade between two countries may be dominated by differences in environmental regulatory strengths. Developed economies tend to have better environmental institutions and more efficient regulation than poorer countries. The pollution haven hypothesis states that rich countries may export their dirty industries to poorer countries due to the differences in regulation. Freer trade thus results in declining environmental quality in poorer economies and improving environmental quality in richer ones (Chichilnisky 1994). There are two main assumptions behind the pollution haven hypothesis: first, that pollution regulation differences are a key determinant of industry location, and second, that environment is a normal good and thus differences in regulation are due to income differences. A further implication of this hypothesis is that global environmental quality may deteriorate and the income of the poorer economies may fall. As polluting industries migrate to regions with less stringent pollution policy, overall global pollution will increase. The available empirical evidence generally rejects the pollution haven hypothesis, but this does not mean that environmental regulation plays no role in affecting trade (Copeland and Gulati 2006). The evidence simply says that environmental regulatory differences do not necessarily dominate the direction of trade as the pollution haven hypothesis suggests.

Factor Endowment Hypothesis The factor endowment hypothesis deviates from the pollution haven hypothesis by postulating that factor endowments, and not just differences in environmental regulations, are the main motivation for trade patterns. Economies engaging in trade will specialize in production where comparative advantage is exhibited. If the most developed countries are relatively abundant in factors (usually capital) used in pollution-intensive industries, then they may have a comparative advantage in dirty industries and thus will specialize in them. Consequently, dirty goods production may shift from developing to developed economies. Developed economies have better environmental regulation and institutions, and thus the consequence of trade would be an overall decline in pollution. Proponents of this hypothesis point to the fact that Europe and the United States have the most stringent pollution policies yet export manufactured goods that are highly pollution intensive. If developing countries have an abundance of the factor needed by pollution-intensive production, the predictions of the factor endowment hypothesis would be consistent with the pollution haven hypothesis. Furthermore, developed countries will lose their comparative advantage in dirty industries if stringency in pollution policy is increased. Thus there are two forces at play, pollution policy differences and factor endowments.

Trade Openness and the Environmental Kuznets Curve Part of the empirical environmental literature has been on the relationship between income and pollution, otherwise known as the Environmental Kuznets Curve (EKC) (Shafik and Bandyopadhyay 1992; Grossman and Krueger 1995). The EKC is an inverted U-shaped relationship: as income increases, pollution first increases until it reaches a turning point and then declines. The first empirical estimation of the EKC for air and water pollutants was carried out by Grossman and Krueger (1995). Estimation of the EKC has also been carried out for natural resources such as forests (López and Galinato 2005). There is much debate with regards to the empirical estimates, data accuracy, robustness, and theoretical underpinnings of the EKC (Harbaugh, Levinson, and Wilson 2000; Deacon and Norman 2007).

Trade plays an important role in some of the conceptual explanations of the EKC. The income effect theory identifies environmental policy response as the main reason for the EKC. As an economy grows, at first the benefits of increasing output are so large that they dominate the increased demands for environmental quality caused by a higher income and thus the scale effect dominates (the curve is upward sloping in this segment). Beyond a certain level of income, the marginal preference for more consumption declines and the preference for clean environment increases until the turning point occurs. Pollution declines as income increases beyond this point. What trade does is to enhance the process of economic growth and thus has an indirect effect on the EKC.

Another story focuses on the composition effect. In the early stages, countries grow through physical capital accumulation and expansion of industries intensive in physical capital, which are generally dirty; in the latter stages, a country grows through human capital and knowledge accumulation and thus cleaner industries emerge, yielding an EKC relationship. Trade liberalization may assist in the switch from dirty to clean industries by allowing the growing economy to increasingly specialize in clean industries. Without trade the assumptions required for an EKC process are much more stringent than with trade.

The Resource Curse Countries with larger endowments of natural resources apparently tend to grow less than resource-poor countries (Sachs and Warner 1999). There are several explanations for such a phenomenon (Barbier 2005). One of the most credible explanations is directly linked with trade, the so-called Dutch disease effect. As a natural resource–dependent economy booms, resources are allocated from other sectors to the natural resource sector. Furthermore, the currency of the economy appreciates, which renders other sectors in the economy uncompetitive in international markets. This results in further dependency on the natural resource sector. Hence the economy is more vulnerable to the price fluctuations inherent to primary commodities. Examples of the resource curse can be seen in oil-producing countries that are resource rich but are growing slowly.

The Role of Government Environmental quality is a public good; thus by definition the market will underprovide it. Although much emphasis has been placed on government efficiency and the provision of public goods such as environmental quality, there has been less emphasis placed on the efficiency of government subsidies. Governments that provide trade and other subsidies do so at the expense of underproviding public goods, given a fixed budget constraint. Public good investments by the government can complement private investments and alleviate market failures, thus resulting in economic growth (López and Miller 2007; López and Galinato 2007). Furthermore, government subsidies, including trade subsidies, would promote activities that would be more demanding for the environment as opposed to public good expenditures, which may compensate for credit market failures and promote human capital accumulation. A study by López, Galinato, and Islam (2007) finds that increasing the share of public goods in total government expenditures reduces SO_2, NO_2, and lead pollution.

Empirical and conceptual analyses suggest that trade has contributed to economic growth and has accelerated trends to ameliorate local air pollutants. This is particularly true of most local air pollutants affecting cities. Trade does not seem to mitigate the ever-increasing emission of global pollutants, particularly carbon dioxide. The few studies focused on the links between trade and the green environment suggest that increased trade appears to exacerbate the losses of natural forests and other natural habitats, thus aggravating the trends toward global climate change and loss of biodiversity.

See also Basel Convention; Convention on Biological Diversity; Convention on International Trade in Endangered Species (CITES); Global Environment Facility; multilateral environmental agreements; pollution haven hypothesis

FURTHER READING

Andreoni, James, and Arik Levinson. 2001. "The Simple Analytics of the Environmental Kuznets Curve." *Journal of Public Economics* 80 (2): 269–86. A theoretical and empirical analysis of the role of economies of scale of abatement technology on the Environmental Kuznets Curve.

Antweiler, Werner, Brian R. Copeland., and M. Scott Taylor. 2001. "Is Free Trade Good for the Environment?" *American Economic Review* 91 (4): 877–908. A rigorous theoretical and empirical examination of the relationship between trade and the environment.

Barbier, Edward B. 2005. *Natural Resources and Economic Development*. Cambridge: Cambridge University Press. A thorough review and exploration of the relationship between natural resources and development.

Chichilnisky, Graciela. 1994. "North-South Trade and the Global Environment." *American Economic Review* 84 (4): 851–74. An important theoretical paper on the relationship between trade and property rights.

Copeland, Brian, and Sumeet Gulati. 2006. "Trade and the Environment in Developing Countries." In *Economic Development and Environmental Sustainability*, edited by R. López and M. Toman. Oxford: Oxford University Press, 178–216. An exploration of the relationship among capital mobility, international trade, and environmental quality from a developing country perspective.

Copeland, Brian R., and M. Scott Taylor. 2003. *Trade and the Environment*. Princeton, NJ: Princeton University Press. A comprehensive theoretical and empirical exploration of several aspects of the relationship between trade and the environment.

Deacon, Robert T., and Catherine Norman. 2007. "Is the Environmental Kuznets Curve an Empirical Regularity?" In *Frontiers of Environmental and Natural Resource Economics*, edited by R. Halvorsen and D. Layton. UK: Edward Elgar. An empirical analysis of the robustness of the Environmental Kuznets Curve.

Grossman, Gene M., and Alan B. Krueger. 1995. "Economic Growth and the Environment." *Quarterly Journal of Economics* 112 (2): 353–78. One of the earliest examinations of the Environmental Kuznets Curve for a wide range of environmental indicators.

Harbaugh, William, Arik Levinson, and David Wilson. 2000. "Reexamining the Empirical Evidence for an Environmental Kuznets Curve." *Review of Economics and Statistics* 84 (3): 541–51. An empirical analysis update of the Environmental Kuznets Curve using revised data subject to various specification alterations.

López, Ramón. 1997. "Environmental Externalities in Traditional Agriculture and the Impact of Trade Liberalization: The Case of Ghana." *Journal of Development Economics* 53 (1): 17–39. A theoretical and empirical examination of the impact of trade policies on environmental resources in Ghana.

Lopez, Ramón. and Gregmar I. Galinato. 2005. "Deforestation and Forest-Induced Carbon Dioxide Emissions in Tropical Countries: How Do Governance and Trade Openness Affect the Forest-Income Relationship?" *Journal of Environment and Development* 14 (1): 73–100. Studies the implications of changes in land use induced by economic growth, economy-wide policies, and governance on deforestation and forest-induced atmospheric carbon dioxide emissions.

———. 2007. "Should Governments Stop Subsidies to Private Goods? Evidence from Rural Latin America." *Journal of Public Economics* 91 (5–6): 1071–94. An important analysis of the impact of government subsidies on per capita income, poverty, and environment in rural Latin America.

López, Ramón, Gregmar Galinato, and Asif Islam. 2007. "Government Expenditures and Air Pollution." University of Maryland at College Park Working Paper. An empirical analysis of the relationship between the share of government expenditures in public goods and air pollution.

López, Ramón, and Sebastian Miller. 2007. "The Structure of Public Expenditure: A Robust Predictor of Economic Development?" University of Maryland at College Park Working Paper. A thorough cross-country analysis of the impact of the share of government expenditures in public goods on economic growth.

Sachs, Jeffrey D., and Andrew W. Warner. 1999. "The Big Push, Natural Resource Booms and Growth." *Journal of Development Economics* 59 (1): 43–76. A theoretical and empirical examination of the relationship between natural resource booms and economic growth for Latin American countries.

Shafik, Nemat, and Sushenjit Bandyopadhyay. 1992. "Economic Growth and Environmental Quality: Time Series and Cross-Country Evidence." Policy Research Working Paper No. WPS 904. Washington, DC: World Bank. One of the earliest studies on the relationship between economic growth and environmental quality, later to be dubbed the Environmental Kuznets Curve.

United Nations. 2006. *Trends in Sustainable Development.* New York: UN Department of Economic and Social Affairs. An overview of global trends in sustainable development indicators.

World Bank. 2006. *Assessing World Bank Support for Trade, 1987–2004: An IEG Evaluation.* Washington, DC: World Bank. An evaluation of the World Bank's involvement and support for international trade.

RAMÓN LÓPEZ AND ASIF ISLAM

■ trade and wages

Beginning with Adam Smith and David Ricardo, economists have demonstrated the benefits of free trade in numerous ways, yet free trade has hardly become a universally accepted strategy. Even in cases where free trade maximizes a country's welfare (or generates a higher welfare than trade restriction), it is not necessarily a superior policy. Free trade creates both winners and losers in a trading nation. It is only through a compensation principle (by which the winners are forced to compensate the losers) that everyone can be made better off under free trade. In practice, however, such a compensation principle is seldom applied; more relevant, then, is how trade affects factor incomes or wages and thus the income distribution within a country. The study of trade and wages is important for two other reasons. First, as most of the poor belong to the working class, study of the effects of trade on wages helps us understand how trade alleviates poverty in the short term. Second, if free trade widens income inequality, it fuels interclass conflict. This makes it difficult for a democratic government to pursue free trade as a long-term development policy.

Theory The best-known result regarding the static effect of trade liberalization on wages is the Stolper-Samuelson (SS) theorem, or its more general version known as the price magnification effect (Jones 1965): In a two-commodity–two-factor (2x2) world, a decline in the (domestic) price of imports relative to that of the exports consequent on, say, trade liberalization leads to a more than proportionate fall in the rate of return to the factor used intensively in the import-competing sectors and a more than proportionate increase in the rate of return to the other factor used intensively in the export sectors. Thus one factor of production is unambiguously better off and the other unambiguously worse off in terms of their *real* returns.

Factor-intensity ranking of goods does not matter, however, in a two-commodity–three-factor setup of the specific-factor model, or in a 2x2 Heckscher-Ohlin (HO) model with sectorally immobile capital. The factor specific in the export sector gains unambiguously whereas the factor specific in the import-competing sector loses unambiguously in both absolute and real terms when trade is liberalized. The mobile factor, on the other hand, gains only when it spends a greater proportion of its income on the import-competing good than on the export good.

The impact of trade liberalization on income distribution is less clear in a many-good–many-factor scenario. If goods are ranked and indexed according to the descending order of magnitude of their price changes, the price magnification effect at most tells us that there exists one factor h that is unambiguously better off and one factor k that is unambiguously worse off (Samuelson 1953). But not much can be said about changes in the rate of return to other factors of production—in particular, whether they are rising or falling with trade liberalization. The natural enemy and natural friend propositions of Jones and Scheinkman (1977), however, provide us some direction in this regard. Commodity j is said to be a natural enemy (friend) of factor h if an increase in its price, all else being equal, lowers (raises more than proportionately) the rate of return to factor h. But whereas each factor has at least one natural enemy, there may not be any natural friend. The strongest resemblance of the 2x2 SS theorem can be found in Jones and Marjit (1985), which identifies for each factor a good as a natural friend and all others as natural enemies. It provides a natural sufficiency condition for the theorem in higher dimensions.

All these variants of the SS, or price magnification, effects, however, predict that opening up or multilateral liberalization of trade among nations leads to asymmetric wage movements. The wage-rental ratio should rise in the country exporting relatively labor-intensive commodities and should decline in its trading partner that exports relatively capital-intensive commodities. In a reinterpretation of capital as human capital, trade liberalization, therefore, should widen the wage gap between skilled and unskilled workers in one country and reduce it in the other. These asymmetric wage movements are due to the fact that starting from autarky the domestic prices move asymmetrically in trading nations to converge toward an intermediate equilibrium once trade opens up.

There are, however, two special cases where wages move in the same direction. First is the case of factor-intensity reversal with large difference in the factor-endowment ratios of the trading nations. Thus, for example, though the price of good X relative to that of good Y rises in one country and falls in another, since given the endowment patterns the same good X has different intensity ranking in the two countries, by the price magnification effect the wage-rental ratio (or the wage gap in a human capital reinterpretation) should move in the same direction in both the countries.

Second is the case of Metzler's paradox where deterioration of the terms of trade is so large after a tariff reduction by a home country as to raise, rather than lower, the tariff-inclusive domestic price, which can occur when the price elasticity of foreign import demand is smaller than home consumers' marginal propensity to consume the export good. With the foreign country keeping its (nonprohibitive) tariff rate unchanged, the domestic prices rise in both the countries and thereby produce symmetric wage movements.

Recent developments in theory, however, have provided us with three more *general* cases in which trade and investment liberalization can produce *symmetric* wage movements across the trading nations. In particular, as a response to the observed fact that relative wages of the unskilled have worsened all across the globe, such models bring in the trade pattern and structural characteristics of the developing world.

The first is the case of the generalized HO model with three goods but only two factors of production discussed in Marjit and Acharyya (2003) and Davis (1996). With different cones of diversification for North and South due to asymmetric endowment patterns, the middle good Y is ranked differently in two countries. Therefore, one can get symmetric movement in wages as effectively factor intensities differ. A large capital inflow from the capital-rich country to another (the host) country has the same effect, because such flows induce the host to specialize completely in the most capital-intensive good and relocate the global production of good Y entirely in the host country, thereby raising the demand for capital (relative to labor) everywhere. In a human capital reinterpretation, therefore, the skilled-unskilled wage gap should increase in both countries in such a generalized HO setting. At the same time the framework can be used to explain asymmetric wage movements following trade liberalization among the Southern countries (Davis 1996). Whereas symmetric changes in wage inequality in both North and South follow from the *local factor–intensity ranking*, the asymmetric effect across the Southern countries follows from *local factor abundance*.

The other two cases arise in the context of trade in intermediate products. Using a model with a continuum of stages of production, Feenstra and Hanson (1996) provide an interesting case in the context of the North American Free Trade Agreement and foreign investment. An inflow of U.S. capital into Mexico transfers some production activities from the United States to Mexico that are more skilled-labor-intensive in Mexico but less skilled-labor-intensive in the United States. Therefore relative demand for skilled labor increases in both countries, resulting in growing wage inequality across the border. Marjit and Acharyya (2006), on the other hand, present a more traditional production structure, with one homogeneous intermediate good being produced by skilled labor, which is then combined with skilled labor to produce the manufacturing good. This possibly captures the case of the computer industry. Some of the Southern countries such as India have emerged as phenomenal exporters of software-related products. But software sectors depend on hardware capabilities. If computers are imported from the North, a decline in the import tariff in the South must help the skilled labor in the software-processing industries in the South. But a lower tariff on hardware implies that items that are skilled-labor-intensive will be more profitable to produce in the North. This tends to increase wages for skilled labor across the globe. Marjit, Beladi, and Chakrabarti (2003), Jones and Marjit (2003), and Marjit and Kar (2005) present cases explaining how declining information costs, capital inflow, and unskilled labor outflow can lead to a rise in the relative wage of skilled labor in a developing economy.

Evidence: Developed Countries Since the late 1970s there has been a dramatic increase in the inequality of earnings based on education, experience, and occupation in the United States. The ratio of the average wage of a college graduate to that of a high school graduate rose by 15 percent. Leamer (2000) also observed a steady and persistent widening, since 1971, of the earnings gap in the manufacturing sector between college graduates and high-school dropouts. The 1994 share of salary of high-school dropouts compared with college graduates was only 15 percent of its 1971 level. For high-school graduates the situation improved during the first half of the 1970s, but after that deteriorated steadily. Similar increases in wage inequality during the 1980s and 1990s have been observed for Australia, Canada, Japan, and Europe. Between 1978 and 1988, the ratio of manual-labor to nonmanual-labor wages fell by 8.1 percent in Germany and by 3 percent in Italy whereas it actually increased in Belgium and Denmark. In the United Kingdom there was a substantial increase in the ratio of earnings of the highest to lowest percentiles.

Such a dramatic change in relative wages has triggered heated discussions and debates on the causes of these changes (Krugman 2000; Jones and Engerman 1996; Leamer 2000). Essentially, two sets of issues have become dominant in this debate: trade-related and technology-related. Though this debate is yet to be settled once and for all, to many researchers global competition has bifurcated American workers into two groups: the high-earning "symbolic analysts," whose talents are rewarded by globalization, and the mass of ordinary production workers, whose earnings are depressed by it. Similarly in the case of Europe, downward competitive pressures on working-condition standards as a result of freer trade with Eastern Europe and Asia have been conceived as the major cause of low wages. Moreover the accession of low-wage countries such as Spain, Portugal, and Greece into the European Union has worsened the scenario through relocation of firms to these countries. The relocation of the Hoover Corporation from France to Scotland in the year 1988, attracted by both lower wage costs and lower working-condition standards, is a glaring example. More recently, comparing merchandise trade with merchandise value added, Feenstra and Hanson (1996) have observed that, except for Australia, Japan, and the United Kingdom, all other industrial countries experienced substantial growth in trade in 1990 than in 1913.

Developing Country Experience There are quite a few systematic studies on the impact of liberal trade policies on internal distribution of wage and income in the developing world. Robbins (1995) demonstrated that while wage inequality decreased a bit in the East Asian nations, Latin America in general experienced a widening wage gap between the skilled and the unskilled after trade liberalization. Wood (1997) argued why such evidence was untenable in terms of traditional trade theoretic arguments. We have mentioned how subsequent theoretical research has used variants of standard trade models to justify double-sided wage gap outcome. A more detailed survey of the related empirical literature is available in Marjit and Acharyya (2003). Whether it is trade or technology that lies at the root of rising income inequality in the developing world is still very much an open question.

Trade and Skill Formation Globalization has meant a remarkable degree of economic integration, thanks to declining tariff walls and revolutionizing changes in information technology. There is a general tendency for the process to reward skills that tend to flourish through international trade and investment. Hence skill formation becomes the most fundamental driving force determining local as well as global patterns of income distribution. An enduring line of research will be whether trade promotes or inhibits acquisition of skills that are adaptable to changes in the global environment. Early attempts to model these are made in Marjit and Acharyya (2003) and Acemoglu (2003).

See also Heckscher-Ohlin model; International Labor Organization; labor standards; specific-factors model

FURTHER READING

Acemoglu, Daron. 2003. "Patterns of Skill Premia." *Review of Economic Studies* 70 (2): 231–51. Discusses skill acquisition and wage inequality in North and South.

Davis, Donald. 1996. "Trade Liberalization and Income Distribution." NBER Working Paper No. 5693. Cambridge, MA: National Bureau of Economic Research. A lucid theoretical illustration of asymmetric changes in the wage gap in the developing world.

Feenstra, Robert, and Gordon Hanson. 1996. "Foreign Investment, Outsourcing, and Relative Wages." In *Political Economy of Trade Policies: Essays in Honour of J. N. Bhagwati*, edited by Robert Feenstra, Gene Grossman, and Douglas Irwin. Cambridge, MA: MIT Press, 89–127. Establishes the two-way widening wage gap due to foreign investment in a Ricardian model with continuum of stages of production.

Jones, Ronald Winthrap. 1965. "The Structure of Simple General Equilibrium Models." *Journal of Political Economy* 73: 557–72. This pioneering and most-cited work provides the basic analytical structure and algebraic exposition of 2x2 general equilibrium trade models and their properties.

Jones, Ronald Winthrap, and Stanley Engerman. 1996. "Trade, Technology, and Wages: A Tale of Two Countries." *American Economic Review* 86: 35–40. Emphasizes the one-to-one correspondence between commodity and factor prices in an open economy that is often misunderstood by labor economists and summarizes the relevance of the technology and trade explanations in the wage gap debate.

Jones, Ronald Winthrap, and Sugata Marjit. 1985. "A Simple Production Model with Stolper-Samuelson Property." *International Economic Review* 26 (3): 565–67. Provides a sufficient condition and a related simple production structure for higher-dimensional proof of the Stolper-Samuelson theorem.

———. 2003. "Economic Development, Trade, and Wages." *German Economic Review* 4 (1): 1–17. Brings agriculture into the wage-inequality literature and shows that a price rise in agriculture may still widen the wage gap between the skilled and unskilled.

Jones, Ronald Winthrap, and Jose Scheinkman. 1977. "The Relevance of the Two-Sector Production Model in Trade Theory." *Journal of Political Economy* 85: 909–35. Extends the price magnification effect to n-commodity–n-factor cases and derives the natural enemy and natural friend propositions.

Krugman, Paul. 2000. "Technology, Trade, and Factor Prices." *Journal of International Economics* 50 (1): 51–71. Illustrates how one can isolate the extent of world price changes (and hence the extent of the rise in wage gap) that are caused by international trade per se in terms of the "but-for" question.

Leamer, Edward. 2000. "What's the Use of Factor Contents?" *Journal of International Economics* 50: 51–71. Brings out the limitation of the factor-content approach to trade in isolating the impact of international trade from that of technological change on the rising wage gap.

Marjit, Sugata, and Rajat Acharyya. 2003. *International Trade, Wage Inequality, and the Developing Economy: A General Equilibrium Approach.* Heidelberg: Physical Springer Verlag. Provides a brief documentation of the wage gap phenomenon, a brief survey on the trade versus technology debate, as well as analytical structures that can explain the rising wage gap in the North and the South alike caused by international trade.

———. 2006. "Trade Liberalization, Skill-linked Intermediate Production, and Two-Sided Wage Gap." *Journal of Policy Reform* 9 (3): 203–17. Provides an alternative theoretical explanation of the two-way wage gap caused by trade liberalization in a general equilibrium framework with trade in intermediate good.

Marjit, Sugata, Hamid Beladi, and Avik Chakrabarti. 2003. "Trade and Wage Inequality in Developing Countries." *Economic Inquiry* 42 (92): 295–303. Discusses the impact of fragmentation on wage inequality.

Marjit, Sugata, and Saibal Kar. 2005. "Emigration and Wage Inequality." *Economics Letters* 88 (1): 141–45. Shows that emigration of unskilled labor does not necessarily increase relative wage of the unskilled.

Robbins, Donald. 1995. "Trade, Trade Liberalization, and Inequality in Latin America and East Asia: Synthesis of Seven Country Studies." Mimeo, Harvard Institute of International Development. Studies the Latin American and East Asian experiences.

Samuelson, Paul. 1953. "Prices of Factors and Goods in General Equilibrium." *Review of Economic Studies* 21: 1–20. The foremost analysis that extended the Stolper-Samuelson and factor-price-equalization results to many-commodity–many-factor cases.

Wood, Adrian. 1997. "Openness and Wage Inequality in Developing Countries: The Latin American Challenges to East Asian Conventional Wisdom." *World Bank Research Observer* 11 (1): 33–57. Argues why the Latin American experience is untenable in terms of the traditional trade theoretic arguments.

Xu, Bin. 2003. "Trade Liberalization, Wage Inequality, and Endogenously Determined Nontraded Goods." *Journal of International Economics* 60 (2): 417–31. Explores the implication of nontraded production and the role of trade liberalization in widening of the wage gap.

SUGATA MARJIT
AND RAJAT ACHARYYA

■ trade costs and foreign direct investment

Foreign direct investment (FDI) takes place when a firm from one country sets up a plant or acquires a plant in another country. This entry explores the relationship between trade costs and various types of FDI, such as horizontal FDI, export-platform FDI, mergers and acquisitions, and vertical FDI. Trade costs refer to all costs incurred in getting a good from its production location to the final destination. They include transportation costs (both freight costs and time costs), policy barriers (tariffs and nontariff barriers), information costs, contract enforcement costs, costs associated with the use of different currencies, legal and regulatory costs, and local distribution costs (wholesale and retail). Mirroring the literature, this entry focuses on tariffs and transportation costs but also discusses the impact on FDI of information costs, contract enforcement costs, and costs associated with the use of different currencies.

Horizontal FDI Horizontal FDI refers to the case where a multinational firm produces and sells its product in a foreign market. The standard framework to study horizontal FDI is the ownership-location-internalization (OLI) framework of Dunning (1973). It suggests that a multinational firm wanting to sell goods in a foreign market faces a choice between exporting and FDI. The key trade-off involved in this choice is between the economies of scale in production and the trading costs of shipping goods to a foreign market, known as the proximity-concentration trade-off. While economies of scale in production favor exporting to the foreign market from the home production facility, a high trading cost of exporting to the foreign market favors FDI. The implication is that, for a given level of economies of scale, the higher the trading cost the greater the likelihood of FDI occurring. FDI in this framework acts as a substitute for trade, that is, increased FDI involves decreased exports. Brainard (1997) provides empirical support for this finding using data on U.S. multinationals: local production by the affiliates of U.S. multinationals relative to exports from the U.S. parent increases the higher the transport costs and trade barriers and the lower the plant level economies of scale.

Licensing versus Horizontal FDI While the proximity-concentration trade-off framework focuses on the choice between exports and FDI, in the OLI framework, once a multinational firm decides to produce the good locally rather than export it from its home production facility, it faces a choice between licensing the technology to a local firm and undertaking FDI. Since licensing involves arm's length transaction between two independent parties, contracting issues become important. The licensor and the licensee have different sets of information, which gives rise to the standard asymmetric information problem. For example, the licensee has a better idea about the local market conditions, while the licensor knows more about the technology. Neither party has an incentive to reveal its private information to the other party, and the acquisition of more information is costly for each party. In addition, the writing of a contract and its enforcement are costly as well. Therefore, the choice between licensing and FDI depends on these contracting costs. If these costs are high then there are internalization advantages, that is, a firm prefers to keep production internal by undertaking FDI rather than licensing its technology to a local firm. Therefore, while trade costs in the form of tariffs and transportation costs affect the location choice of production, costs arising due to informational asymmetry and contract enforcement determine the choice between production within the firm boundary (FDI) and licensing. All other things being equal, a reduction in the costs of information and contract enforcement would lead to more licensing and less FDI.

The proximity-concentration trade-off framework implies that a decrease in tariffs and transportation cost would reduce FDI, but this prediction is not borne out by the recent experience of European Union (EU) countries, where trade liberalization has been accompanied by increased FDI. One must consider other types of horizontal FDI (and other types of FDI) that could increase with trade liberalization.

Export-Platform FDI If two countries A and B preferentially liberalize trade with each other while keeping the trade barriers on the rest of the world intact, then the firms in a third country C will have an incentive to set up a plant in either country A or B and sell in both those markets from its single production facility. In this case, FDI by firms from country C into country A or B is not just meant for local sales but also serves as its export platform for sales to the other country. Ranjan (2006) shows that preferential trading agreements can create new investment as well as divert investment from nonmembers to members, thereby increasing FDI in the member countries. Ekholm, Forslid, and Markusen (2007) show that a free trade agreement between a high-cost and a low-cost country generates an incentive to an outside high-cost country to set up a plant in the low-cost country within the free trade area. Therefore, mutual trade liberalization within a group of countries can attract FDI into the group from outside countries.

Mergers and Acquisitions A multinational firm building a new plant in a foreign country is called a greenfield FDI, while if instead it acquires an existing plant, then it is classified under mergers and acquisitions (M&A). There is evidence from UNCTAD (2000) that a large amount of FDI is in the form of M&A rather than greenfield. M&As take place for both efficiency and strategic reasons. Efficiency gains come from the fact that a multinational firm may be able to produce at a lower cost by acquiring an existing firm rather than setting up a new plant. Strategic gains from acquiring an existing firm stem from the possibility that profits may increase due to a reduction in the number of firms in the market.

Focusing solely on strategic issues, Neary (2007) shows that a decrease in trade costs may increase the incentive for M&A. To see the intuition behind this result, suppose there are two countries, Home and Foreign, with oligopolistic market structures. In the case of free trade, only low-cost firms in each country survive. In the presence of high trade costs, relatively higher-cost domestic firms also survive because foreign firms have to bear the trade cost in addition to their production cost. A move from autarky to free trade would make many high-cost domestic firms in each country unviable, leading to M&A.

This result can be shown to hold for incremental trade liberalization as follows. Suppose a Foreign firm is contemplating acquiring a Home firm. Trade liberalization increases the Home firm's profits on its initial exports, which makes it a more expensive takeover target, thereby making cross-border M&As less likely. However, trade liberalization also increases the Foreign firm's profits from exporting and reduces both firms' profits in their home markets, both of which make cross-border M&As more likely. In the neighborhood of autarky, the first effect does not arise. Therefore starting from a high level of trade barriers, a small amount of trade liberalization raises the possibility of cross-border M&As.

Thus both export-platform FDI and M&A type FDI could potentially explain increased FDI in the EU countries concomitant with trade liberalization. However, there is another possible explanation: this result could also arise if FDI is of the vertical type.

Vertical FDI Vertical FDI refers to the case when a multinational firm breaks its production process into parts and carries out different parts in different countries. A standard modeling approach is to divide the production process into two stages: headquarters stage and production stage where the former is carried in the home country while the latter is carried in a foreign country. The motivation for fragmentation of production comes from differential factor intensity of different stages of production and differences in factor prices. In the presence of differences in factor prices, minimizing cost requires each stage of production be undertaken in the country where the cost of doing so is the lowest. With vertical FDI, the goods produced in a foreign country have to be sent back to the parent country and hence are subject to

the trading cost. Therefore there is a trade-off between a lower cost of production in a foreign country and a trading cost of shipping these goods back to the parent country. In this framework, higher trading costs in the form of tariffs and transportation cost would discourage FDI. Therefore while horizontal FDI is encouraged by high tariffs and transportation cost, vertical FDI is discouraged by it. Consequently EU trade liberalization could generate increased FDI of the vertical type.

Outsourcing versus Vertical FDI Even if it is cheaper to conduct a part of the production process in a foreign country because of lower costs of production, the question remains as to whether this activity should be done within the firm boundary (FDI) or at arm's length (outsourcing). Analogous to the choice between licensing and FDI for a horizontal multinational, a recent literature has emerged that focuses on the choice between outsourcing and FDI for a vertical multinational. The key determinant of this choice again is the cost due to informational asymmetry and contract enforcement. In general, a high contracting cost makes FDI more attractive compared with outsourcing (see Helpman 2006 for a recent survey of this literature). Therefore, while a reduction in tariffs and transportation cost increases vertical FDI, a decrease in contracting cost favors outsourcing over FDI.

Other Trade Costs and FDI In addition to the types of trade costs discussed earlier, there are several other trading costs that affect both horizontal and vertical FDI. A legal system protecting the property rights of foreign investors reduces the risk of expropriation and hence encourages foreign investment. A strong intellectual property rights regime on the other hand may reduce FDI and increase licensing or outsourcing by reducing opportunistic behavior in arm's length transaction.

Another type of trade cost that could affect FDI is the cost associated with exchange rate volatility. Since multinational firms repatriate their profits from their activities in the host countries to their home countries, exchange rate fluctuations affect their profits in their home currency. Theoretical work on the relationship between exchange rate volatility and FDI identifies offsetting effects. On the one hand, volatility increases the value of having production facilities in both the home country and the host country, allowing a multinational firm to shift production between the two plants depending on input costs. On the other hand, since FDI involves sunk costs to be incurred in the currency of the host country, greater volatility in exchange rate increases the option value of waiting for a multinational firm leading to reduced FDI. There is empirical evidence showing that exchange rate volatility reduces entry by multinational firms contemplating investment in the United States.

Policy Implications To the extent that FDI raises welfare in the host country, there would be scope for intervention to attract FDI. However, as discussed above, the relationship between trade costs and FDI is not straightforward. It depends on the type of trade cost and the type of FDI. While high tariffs and transportation cost may promote horizontal FDI of some types, they may discourage export-platform FDI and FDI through M&As. There is evidence of tariff-jumping FDI by Japanese firms in the automobile sector in the United States in the 1980s in response to a threat of higher tariffs. However, threatening a higher tariff to attract FDI is questionable strategy.

Tariffs and transportation cost usually reduce vertical FDI. If the good is assembled in the host country by a multinational subsidiary and sent back to the parent, then a higher tariff in the parent country will discourage this type of FDI. In this case, a higher tariff in the host country will also discourage FDI because usually some inputs are shipped from the parent country to the host country for assembly or further processing. If these inputs incur tariffs, then FDI would be discouraged. Therefore in the case of vertical FDI the policy implication would be for the host country to reduce tariffs to encourage FDI.

High contracting costs promote FDI at the expense of licensing in the horizontal case and at the expense of outsourcing in the vertical case. Therefore a reduction in the contracting cost is likely to reduce FDI and increase licensing and outsourcing. However, one should not jump to any policy conclusions here, because it is not clear whether FDI leads to greater welfare gains compared with licensing or outsourcing.

More important, the welfare implications of a policy of increasing trading cost to attract FDI is ambiguous even if FDI is welfare improving because an increase in trading cost has a direct negative effect on welfare that must be offset by the indirect positive effect arising from increased FDI.

In sum, the relationship between trade costs and FDI depends on the nature of FDI. Any view that trade costs always promote FDI is simplistic as it does not hold true for vertical FDI or even all types of horizontal FDI.

See also location theory; multinational enterprises

FURTHER READING

Anderson, James E., and Eric van Wincoop. 2004. "Trade Costs." *Journal of Economic Literature* 42 (3): 691–751. A survey on various types of trade costs and their importance for international trade.

Brainard, S. Lael. 1997. "An Empirical Assessment of the Proximity-Concentration Trade-off between Multinational Sales and Trade." *American Economic Review* 87 (4): 520–44. Empirical evidence on proximity concentration trade-off using data on U.S. multinationals.

Dunning, John H. 1973. "The Determinants of International Production." *Oxford Economic Papers* 25 (3): 289–336. Pioneering work outlining the ownership-location-internalization framework to study multinationals.

Ekholm, Karolina, Rikard Forslid, and James R. Markusen. 2007. "Export Platform Foreign Direct Investment." *Journal of the European Economic Association* 5 (4): 776–95. Builds a theoretical model of export platform FDI.

Helpman, Elhanan. 2006. "Trade, FDI, and the Organization of Firms." *Journal of Economic Literature* 44 (3): 589–630. A survey of the recent literature on trade and FDI focusing on the organizational features such as sourcing strategies of firms.

Markusen, James R. 2002. *Multinational Firms and the Theory of International Trade.* Cambridge, MA: MIT Press. Unified view of trade and FDI resulting from the interaction of scale economies, trade costs, factor endowments, and imperfect competition.

Neary, J. Peter. 2007. "Trade Costs and Foreign Direct Investment." Mimeo. Oxford: Oxford University.

Explains how trade liberalization could increase M&A and export platform FDI.

Ranjan, Priya. 2006. "Preferential Trade Agreements, Multinational Enterprises, and Welfare." *Canadian Journal of Economics* 39 (2): 493–515. Explains how preferential trading agreements affect FDI.

Russ, Katheryn N. 2007. "The Endogeneity of the Exchange Rate as a Determinant of FDI: A Model of Entry and Multinational Firms." *Journal of International Economics* 71 (2): 344–72. Studies the impact of exchange rate volatility on FDI.

UNCTAD. 2000. *World Investment Report: Cross-Border Mergers and Acquisitions and Development.* Geneva: United Nations. Provides data on M&As.

PRIYA RANJAN

■ trade facilitation

The expansion of world trade in the late 20th and early 21st centuries has been driven, in large part, by the changing nature of production and increased competition in international commerce. Another important factor has been the periodic rounds of successful multilateral trade negotiations. Talks at the World Trade Organization (WTO) have led to a considerable reduction in tariffs on goods crossing national borders. As the role of traditional trade barriers gradually vanishes, the focus of trade policy has shifted to lowering the remaining nontariff barriers to trade, including trade facilitation.

Trade facilitation involves a wide range of activities centered on lowering trade transaction costs for firms in global commerce. These costs include the price of moving freight from the factory to final destinations. Firms must manage border clearance procedures and pay trade services fees, among many other steps after goods and services are produced. As such, trade facilitation involves much more than trucking goods across national borders or shipping a package by sea transport.

Since trade facilitation can encompass a wide variety of measures, there is no single definition of the term. One might distinguish, however, between trade facilitation in a narrow or broad context.

Multilateral trade rules reflected in the three GATT articles V (freedom of transit), VIII (fees and formalities), and X (publication and administration of trade regulation) constitute a relatively narrow definition of trade facilitation. These articles call on WTO members to harmonize and simplify procedures related to the international exchange of goods and services.

Modern commerce involves a much broader scope of activities affecting trade facilitation not directly covered by WTO rules. This includes domestic policies, such as sanitary and phytosanitary standards, regulation of services, and use of information technology to lower trade costs. This wider definition takes into consideration the fact that "inside-the-border" issues such as the transparency of domestic regulations, institutional policies on foreign ownership of companies, and legal frameworks all affect a country's investment climate and transaction costs. In addition, the potential for efficiency savings due to electronic transmission of trade documentation and automation of customs operations suggest that global information technology infrastructure also drives trade facilitation.

The policy focus on these issues reflects the fact that trade can be a powerful engine for accelerating economic growth, job creation, and poverty reduction. Success in export markets for developed and developing country firms, therefore, is increasingly affected by the ability of countries to support an environment that promotes efficient and low-cost trade services and logistics.

Cross-Country Comparisons and Performance
There is an increasing body of empirical evidence about the impact of trade facilitation on export competitiveness and growth. Studies reviewed by the Organisation for Economic Co-operation and Development (OECD 2002) indicate that trade transactions costs can amount to as much as 15 percent of the value of traded goods globally. A subsequent OECD study (2003) found trade transactions costs to be higher on agricultural and food products, fish, and forest and wood products (since these products are subject to additional border procedures due to sanitary and phytosanitary requirements). These are

products for which many developing countries have an advantage. The same study also reported that small and medium-size enterprises suffer most from poor trade-related practices and poorer developing countries have a larger share of such enterprises. A number of other studies have illustrated the specifics of why trade facilitation matters and specific sources of trade costs. One study, for example, found that barriers to export performance in Africa are closely related to firm characteristics and policies that raise trade costs. This includes nontransparent customs laws and administration. Much less evidence, in comparison, was found that transportation infrastructure had a significant impact on export performance (Clarke 2005).

The World Bank's *Doing Business* report (2007) documents the wide range of reform needed in developing countries to lower trade costs. The report outlines procedural requirements for importing and exporting a standardized cargo of goods in 155 countries. While the total cost to import (in U.S. dollars per container) was $842 on average in high-income countries, it was $1,960 in low-income countries. Typical regulations in low-income countries required 13 documents from domestic regulatory agencies, as compared with 6 signatures in high-income, 9 in upper-middle-income, and 10 in lower-middle-income countries. On average it still costs almost two and a half times in expenses and requires more than twice as many documents and four times as many signatures to trade in a poor country as it does in rich countries.

The *Doing Business* report also provides concrete examples of efficiency savings made possible through trade facilitation reforms. Much of these relate to addressing regulatory reform and other steps that— in contrast to hard infrastructure—constitute the major part of why engaging in trade takes longer in developing countries. Progress in reducing costs, however, has been made. For example, Guatemala with the support of the Inter-American Development Bank changed to an electronic system for export authorization in 2000. Within four years the time for authorization of export documents dropped from one day to around three minutes. Tunisia has also introduced an automated system that provides a one-stop trade documentation-processing platform. Due to this innovation the processing time for trade documentation was reduced from 18 to 7 days, which probably has led to substantial productivity gains according to the United Nations Economic Commission for Africa.

The Gains to Trade from Cutting Costs and Red Tape What about the gains to trade with an ambitious reform agenda? There are important gains to lowering trade costs and facilitating trade with some variation across countries and sectors (Francois et al. 2005; OECD 2003). Several studies have focused on the impact of trade facilitation on the microlevel (e.g., Nomura Research Institute 2004; Keen 2003; OECD 2005). They observe that in some developing countries inefficient trade regulations, documents, and procedures are hindering firms' participation in export markets. The studies find large potential benefits from streamlining trade regulations and hence cutting the costs of exporting.

Analysis by the World Bank suggests that raising global capacity in trade facilitation (port efficiency, customs, regulatory transparency, and information technology used in trade transactions) halfway to the global average would increase world trade by $377 billion (Wilson et al. 2005). This is an increase of about 9.7 percent in global trade with the majority of the gains due to domestic reform and capacity building. About $107 billion of the total gain comes from the improvement in port efficiency and about $33 billion results from the improvement in customs environment. The gain from the improvement in regulatory environment is $83 billion. The largest gain ($154 billion) comes from an improvement in information technology infrastructure, which is increasingly applied all across the trade value and logistics chain. The important work ahead to lower trade costs, however, is outside the scope of trade policy and squarely centered within domestic reform agendas, including transportation, telecommunications, and other services that affect trade transactions costs. There is also a key role to be played by private sector–led policy reform.

Moving Ahead: Cutting Trade Costs Talks on revisions to the WTO rules on trade facilitation continued on the agenda in the Doha Development Agenda negotiations at the end of 2007. The outlines of a possible agreement included, among other provisions: (1) new obligations to promote electronic distribution and transmission of government trade regulations on imports and exports, (2) standardization of certain basic fees for imports, and (3) stronger rules to help ensure freedom of transit for goods crossing national borders. The WTO Secretariat tabulation of proposals from August 11, 2006, includes consideration of more ambitious changes to current obligations, such as establishment of a single window for exporters and importers at customs or accepting copies of documents for import and export in lieu of originals. Since 2002 there have also been talks about explicit ties between a package of technical assistance and development aid as part of any final agreement. Developing countries participated very actively in these negotiations and before the suspension of the Doha Round in late 2006 considerable progress had been achieved (World Bank 2006; Neufeld 2007).

Changes to the multilateral trade rules noted above can help in advancing transparent and predictable trading procedures for exporters. These rules have not been revised in more than 50 years, and crafting an achievable and focused next step in the Doha Agenda will be helpful to traders. This is especially true for small and medium-sized firms that lack resources and networks to overcome some of the more complex border rules now in place. Meeting trade facilitation goals in a broader and deeper context, however, will require action well outside and beyond the WTO framework. More effective delivery of development aid and technical assistance especially in projects to advance regulatory reform and support public agencies that promulgate and administer trade regulations is needed. A better understanding is required of conditions under which developing countries are ready to receive such assistance so that aid is effectively delivered.

The Agenda Ahead At the most basic level, better data, analysis, and indicators of performance are needed to inform discussions moving forward on how trade costs and facilitation measures affect global commerce. Progress in reaching development goals in trade can be made only with accurate data and analysis to drive policy choice and action. Taking advantage of the energy behind reaching the Millennium Development Goals (MDGs) and building on the data sets in the Global Monitoring Reports, which track progress in reaching poverty reduction goals, among other reports, makes significant sense. In sum, the data gathered to date illustrate the fact that the nontariff agenda in trade is increasingly important to economic development.

See also Doha Round; nontariff measures; sanitary and phytosanitary measures; technical barriers to trade; trade-related capacity building; World Trade Organization

FURTHER READING

Clarke, George. 2005. "Beyond Tariffs and Quotas: Why Don't African Manufacturers Export More?" World Bank Policy Research Working Paper No. 3617 (June). Washington, DC: World Bank. An empirical investigation of how weak customs regimes impede the export performance of manufacturing firms in African countries.

Francois, J., H. van Meijl, and F. van Tongeren. 2005. "Trade Liberalization in the Doha Development Round." CEPR Discussion Papers No. 4032. London: Center for Economic Policy Research. Provides estimates of possible welfare benefits from a successful completion of multilateral trade negotiations, including those on trade facilitation.

Keen, M. 2003. "The Future of Fiscal Frontiers and the Modernization of Customs Administration." In *Changing Customs: Challenges and Strategies for the Reform of Customs Administration*, edited by M. Keen. Washington, DC: IMF. Available online at http://www.imf .org/external/pubs/nft/2003/customs/. Outlines key reasons why modernization of customs administration is crucial and describes important aspects of customs reform.

McLinden, Gerard. 2006. "Trade Facilitation: Progress and Prospects for the Doha Negotiations." In *Trade, Doha, and Development: A Window into the Issues*, edited by

R. Newfarmer. Washington, DC: World Bank, 175–85. An examination of the progress in the WTO negotiations and the role of new WTO obligations to implement trade reforms in developing countries.

Neufeld, N. 2007. "WTO Negotiations on Trade Facilitation—Lessons for the Future? New Perspectives for and from the Developing World." In *Developing Countries and the WTO: Policy Approaches*, edited by G. Sampson and W. Bradnee Chambers. Tokyo: United Nations University Institute of Advanced Studies. A summary of recent multilateral trade negotiations on trade facilitation with a particular emphasis on the role of developing countries.

Nomura Research Institute. 2004. "Study on the Economic Effects Resulting from Reduction of Lead Time for Import Procedures." Customs and Tariff Bureau, Ministry of Finance of Japan, March 2004. An empirical review of how Japan was able to reduce the lead time of import procedures and the economic impact of these changes.

OECD. 2002. *Business Benefits of Trade Facilitation*. Paris: OECD (November). Provides an assessment of the business benefits of trade facilitation based on a survey of studies.

———. 2003. *Quantitative Assessment of the Benefits of Trade Facilitation*. Paris: OECD. A detailed empirical exploration of trade facilitation variables and their possible impact on trade.

———. 2005. "Trade Facilitation Reforms in the Service of Development: Country Case Studies." TD/TD/WP (2004)4/FINAL. Paris: OECD. Presents country studies (Mozambique, Angola, Pakistan, and Peru) of customs reform.

Wilson, John S. 2005. "Trade Facilitation and Economic Development." In The World Trade Brief. For the Fourth WTO Ministerial Conference, Hong Kong, 13–18 December. London: Agenda Publishing, 46–48. Provides a quick literature review on the topic, including important quantitative results.

Wilson, John S., Catherine L. Mann, and Tsunehiro Otsuki. 2005. "Assessing the Benefits of Trade Facilitation: A Global Perspective." *The World Economy* 28 (6): 841–71. An empirical investigation of the relationship between broad indicators of trade facilitation performance, trade flows, and benefits of reform.

World Bank. 2006. *Doing Business in 2007*. Washington, DC: World Bank. This database records regulatory and others costs of doing business in 175 economies. Accessible at http://www.doingbusiness.org/.

JOHN S. WILSON

■ trade in services

Since the conventional definition of trade—where a product crosses the frontier—would miss out on a whole range of international services transactions, it is now customary to take a broad view of services trade to include all modes of conducting international transactions. Services trade, according to this wide definition, is an increasingly important part of global commerce. Advances in information and telecommunication technologies have expanded the scope of services that can be traded across borders, from accounting to education. Many countries now allow foreign investment in newly privatized and competitive markets for services, such as telecommunications, transportation, and finance. More and more people are traveling abroad to consume tourism, education, and medical services, and to supply services ranging from construction to software development.

The Emerging Pattern of Trade Rigorous analysis of patterns of trade in services has been inhibited by the paucity of data. The only services trade statistics available on a global basis are the International Monetary Fund's balance of payments (BOP) statistics, which register transactions between residents and nonresidents. These statistics suggest that services have been among the fastest growing components of world trade, growing by more than 15 percent per year since 1980. The value of global services exports is now close to $3 trillion, representing more than one-fifth of aggregate world trade in goods and services. This value is certainly understated, because it does not include sales through an established presence, that is, via FDI and by individuals who stay longer than a year, both of which are treated as residents by the BOP statistics. Today more than half of annual world FDI flows are in services, and the value of sales abroad by foreign affiliates of U.S. service firms is estimated to be 3.5 times greater than their cross-border exports.

The United States and the European Union lead the world in a broad spectrum of services trade—telecommunications, transportation, finance, retail trade, and a range of business services. Together they account for more than 60 percent of world services exports. China and India jointly account for only 3 percent. But several developing countries are emerging as the most dynamic services exporters. Over the last decade, while the exports of the United States have grown at around 10 percent per year, the exports of countries such as India, China, and Brazil have grown at rates well above 15 percent per year. Some developing countries are even beginning to invest abroad to provide services—for example, Malaysia in environmental services, South Africa in telecommunications and retail, and India in software—but many more are supplying services via cross-border sales (e.g., data processing), tourism services for visiting foreign consumers, and the movement abroad of individual services providers (e.g., professional services or construction workers).

What Determines the Pattern of Services Trade? The two major explanations for trade between countries, comparative advantage and gains from specialization arising from increasing returns to scale or agglomeration effects, are equally relevant to services trade. Moreover both explanations apply not only to cross-border trade but also to other modes of trade, including commercial presence and the movement of people. Examples of trade based on comparative advantage include call centers in India that provide customer contact services for U.S. firms; nannies from the Philippines who move to Canada temporarily to provide child care services; and Europeans who travel to Peru for a week in the jungle as part of an ecotourism package. The trade in both child care and call center services is driven by differences in labor costs across countries; and the Amazon has unique attributes that are not available at home to the European tourists.

Although differences between countries are one of the major explanations for services trade, particularly

between countries with very different income levels, they cannot account for all trade. Much of the world's trade occurs between high-income countries, and much of the trade between similar countries is in similar services. For example, European banks operate in the United States and U.S. banks in Europe. Canadian engineers work on projects in the United States, and U.S. engineers work on projects in Canada. A labor market example helps explain how services trade can emerge between similar countries. Two students starting university are equally bright and talented. At this point their productive capacities may seem indistinguishable. However, suppose one chooses to study medicine and the other chooses to study engineering. If we revisit these same students 10 years later, they will have very different skills and they can trade with each other via the labor market, with the doctor selling medical services and the engineer selling engineering services. This example illustrates the genesis of a large part of trade today in services ranging from finance and communications to transport and education—all services where there are large economies of scale and consumers desire variety.

What Restricts Services Trade? In spite of recent liberalization, services trade still tends to be quite restricted. First, many types of services were publicly provided and a significant number continue to be produced by state-owned or regulated monopolies. The traditional rationale was the existence of natural monopoly in services such as telecommunications and transportation, and a social concern for equitable access in services such as health care and education. Second, entry and operation in a range of services, from financial to professional, are regulated on the grounds that it is particularly difficult for consumers to judge the quality of these "invisible" services before they are consumed.

In contrast to goods, relatively few services are subject to simple discriminatory taxes on trade. Instead barriers to trade in services arise from domestic regulations that often serve the dual purpose of responding to market failures (such as ensuring quality standards for medical practitioners) and protecting local suppliers from foreign competition. This means that identifying and measuring trade barriers in the service sector is very complex. It also means that simple rules for trade liberalization that have worked for goods trade (such as reducing all tariffs by 30 percent) are not available as an option for service trade liberalization. Instead service trade liberalization is organized around the notion of nondiscrimination and is often linked with domestic regulatory reform.

Even though tariffs are rare, quotas are pervasive. On cross-border trade, they are most evident in the transportation sectors. Foreign providers are either completely shut out of certain segments, such as cabotage (i.e., transport between locations within a country), or only provided limited access, as in international transportation. On commercial presence, quotas are imposed on the number of foreign suppliers who are allowed to enter sectors such as telecommunications and banking, or on the extent of foreign ownership in individual enterprises. Quotas are most stringent in the case of movement of service-providing personnel and affect trade not only in professional services but also in a variety of labor-intensive services.

What Are the Consequences of Liberalization?
Economic theory suggests that a country gains from the import of services, irrespective of the mode of transaction, if the terms at which international transactions take place are more favorable than those available on the domestic market. The limited empirical evidence suggests that liberalization of trade in services, accompanied by the reform of complementary policies, can produce substantial gains.

Removing barriers to trade in services in a particular sector is likely to lead to lower prices, improved quality, and greater variety. As in the case of trade in goods, restrictions on trade in services reduce welfare because they create a wedge between domestic and foreign prices, leading to a loss to consumers that is greater than the increase in producer surplus and government revenue. Furthermore, since many services are inputs into production, the inefficient supply of such services prevents the realization of significant gains in productivity for downstream firms. As countries reduce tariffs and other barriers to trade in goods, effective rates of protection for manufacturing industries may become negative if they continue to be confronted with input prices that are higher than they would be if services markets were competitive.

Several empirical studies provide evidence of gains (reviewed in Deardorff and Stern 2007). Estimates of benefits vary for individual countries depending on the initial levels of protection and the assumed reduction in barriers. Developed countries tend to gain more in absolute terms—which is not surprising given the relative size of their economies—but developing countries also see significant increases in their gross domestic product (GDP). One model predicts gains of between 1.6 percent of GDP (for India) to 4.2 percent of GDP (for Thailand) if tariff equivalents of protection were cut by one-third in all countries. The gains from liberalizing services are usually estimated to be substantially greater than those from liberalizing trade in goods, because current levels of protection are higher and because liberalization would also create spillover benefits from the required movement of capital and labor. Finally there is also some evidence—relatively strong for the financial sector and less strong but nevertheless statistically significant for the telecommunications sector—that openness in services significantly influences long-run growth performance.

These results are particularly striking because they are derived from models that do not fully allow for the temporary movement of individual service suppliers—potentially a major source of gain. Such movement offers arguably the neatest solution to the dilemma of how international migration is best managed, enabling the realization of gains from trade while averting social and political costs in host countries and brain drain from poor countries. Recent research finds that if members of the Organisation for Economic Co-operation and Development (OECD) were to allow temporary access to foreign services providers equal to just 3 percent of their labor force, the global gains would be more than $150 billion—more than the gains from the complete liberalization of all trade in goods (Winters et al. 2003). Both developed and developing countries would share in these gains, and they would be largest if both high-skilled mobility and low-skilled mobility were permitted.

How Is Liberalization Best Implemented? It would be wrong to infer that these gains can be realized by a mechanical opening up of services markets. A flawed reform program can undermine the benefits of liberalization.

For example, if privatization of state monopolies is conducted without concern to creating conditions of competition, the result may be merely transfers of monopoly rents to private owners (possibly foreigners). Similarly, if increased entry into financial sectors is not accompanied by adequate prudential supervision and full competition, the result may be insider lending and poor investment decisions. Also, if policies to ensure universal service are not put in place, liberalization need not improve access to essential services for the poor. Managing reforms of services markets therefore requires integrating trade opening with a careful combination of competition and regulation.

Sustaining openness may also require action to alleviate adjustment costs, even though the available evidence suggests that openness to services trade has not hurt overall employment. For example, in the United States, which in recent years has seen a significant growth in services outsourcing, private employment in services has actually expanded (in contrast to manufacturing) by more than a million jobs. The structure of employment has changed but more because of new technology than trade. Between 1999 and 2003, it is estimated that in the United States more than 70,000 computer programmers lost their jobs, whereas more than 115,000 higher-paid computer software engineers obtained jobs (Kirkegaard 2004). As in the case of goods trade, assisting dislocated workers is imperative if the gains from new trade opportunities and technological progress are to be widely shared. But this assistance is best provided through improved income support, retraining, and health insurance, rather than through restrictions on technology and trade.

To conclude, services trade continues to grow rapidly thanks to technological change and policy reform. Industrial countries dominate international transactions, but several developing countries are among the most dynamic participants. Trade has already produced significant benefits but the potential gains are even larger. There is a strong economic case for eliminating remaining barriers to trade, in particular the restrictions on foreign investment and temporary migration. But successful liberalization needs complementary policy action to improve the regulatory environment, to alleviate adjustment costs, and to ensure that the benefits of openness are widely shared.

See also comparative advantage; General Agreement on Trade in Services (GATS); World Trade Organization

FURTHER READING

Deardorff, Alan V., and Robert M. Stern. 2007. "Empirical Analysis of Barriers to International Services Transactions and the Consequences of Liberalization." In *Handbook of Services Trade*, edited by Aaditya Mattoo, Robert M. Stern, and Gianni Zanini. Oxford: Oxford University Press, 169–220. A review of attempts to quantify the magnitude and implications of trade barriers.

Hindley, Brian, and Alasdair Smith. 1984. "Comparative Advantage and Trade in Services." *World Economy* 7 (4): 369–90. A persuasive article arguing that the economics of services trade is not fundamentally different from the economics of goods trade.

Hoekman, Bernard. 2006. "Liberalizing Trade in Services: A Survey." World Bank Policy Research Working Paper No. 4030. Washington, DC: World Bank. An up-to-date review of the existing literature on services trade.

Kirkegaard, Jacob. 2004. "Outsourcing: Stains on the White Collar." Mimeo. Washington, DC: Institute for International Economics.

Mattoo, Aaditya, Robert M. Stern, and Gianni Zanini, eds. 2007. *Handbook of Services Trade*. Oxford: Oxford

University Press. A comprehensive volume that includes chapters on the economics of services trade, measuring services trade, and empirical analysis of barriers to trade as well as on specific sectors.

Winters, L. A., T. L. Walmsley, Z. K. Wang, and R. Grynberg. 2003. "Liberalizing Temporary Movement of Natural Persons: An Agenda for the Development Round." *World Economy* 26 (8): 1137–61. Estimates the potential gains from the OECD countries allowing increased immigration.

AADITYA MATTOO

■ Trade Policy Review Mechanism

The Trade Policy Review Mechanism (TPRM) involves periodic reviews of the trade and trade-related policies, practices, and measures of each member of the World Trade Organization (WTO). The reviews take place in the WTO's Trade Policy Review Body (TPRB), a senior body composed of representatives of all WTO members. The WTO's four largest trading entities (the United States, the European Community, China, and Japan) are reviewed every two years; the next sixteen are reviewed every four years; and other members are reviewed every six years, although a longer period may be allowed for least-developed countries. Each review is based on a report prepared by the member(s) under review and on a report drawn up by the WTO Secretariat, in its Trade Policies Review Division (TPRD), on its own responsibility. Both reports are published.

The TPRM's objective is to achieve greater transparency in, and understanding of, members' trade policies, practices, and measures. It permits the evaluation of trade and related policies and measures, including those that do not necessarily contravene, or indeed are not subject to, WTO obligations.

Transparency entails four key elements: (1) a description of the nature of policies and measures; (2) their rationale or objectives; (3) their costs (in terms of expenditures or taxes forgone); and (4) an economic evaluation of their effectiveness of policies and measures (relative to alternatives) in achieving their objectives. Accordingly, the TPRM enables the regular collective appreciation and economic evaluation of a full range of individual members' trade policies and practices, their consistency with the broad principles of nondiscrimination and predictability that underlie the WTO, and their impact on the functioning of the multilateral trading system.

By reviewing broad macroeconomic and structural policies, trade policy reviews (TPRs) attempt to place trade and trade-related policies in their broader policy setting, thereby assessing the coherence of these policies in achieving their objectives. In this regard, TPRs are being seen increasingly by many countries as a useful form of technical assistance.

The TPRM is not intended to serve as a basis for the enforcement of obligations under WTO agreements or for dispute-settlement purposes. Nor is it intended to impose new rules on members. Rather, one purpose is to contribute, essentially by moral suasion, to improved adherence by all members to disciplines and commitments agreed to under the WTO and thus to a smoother functioning of the multilateral trading system.

Trends and Lessons from Reviews Reviews conducted since the establishment of the TPRM have brought to light the benefits countries have obtained through their integration into the world trading system, while also highlighting the difficulties encountered by many (often developing) countries in this process. By and large, countries have become integrated in the world economy through unilateral measures and the multilateral trading system rather than through initiatives they have taken in regional agreements. Thus in numerous countries, developed and developing alike, unilateral liberalization of trade and investment policies, as well as deregulation programs, have taken place. Such reforms are often part of comprehensive integrated policy packages that include macroeconomic and other structural reform measures.

More generally, the reviews have shown that in most trade regimes tariffs have largely replaced quantitative restrictions and other nontariff measures as the main form of protection, although the process remains incomplete in some cases. Many tariff structures have been or are being rationalized and average tariffs have been reduced.

Although there have been reversals of trade liberalization in some countries (in the form of tariff increases, new surcharges on imports, or the reimposition of quantitative restrictions), in most cases these setbacks have been limited, rarely offsetting the earlier liberalization measures. The reviews have also shown that, in general, the experience in trade reform in less-developed countries has lagged behind that of developing countries.

Members that have undergone a review have repeatedly testified to the value of the experience for the development of their own trade policies. Past experience shows that through a review members engage in a process of self-examination in which they reflect both on their own policies and on their participation in the multilateral trading system and their engagement with the WTO. Many countries have started internal reviews of their trade policies on a yearly basis.

Inconsistencies identified in trade regimes have made members more aware of the necessity of having consistent trade policies, formulated and implemented at national levels, with the involvement of all the relevant departments. Thus in the process of reviews, members also increase their awareness of the economic role of customs tariffs, broadening their perception of tariffs as a fiscal policy instrument only. Many countries have also been led, in consequence of their reviews, to take steps to address some of the concerns likely to be expressed by other WTO members; as a result many, particularly less-developed, countries have improved compliance to their WTO commitments in areas such as notification. Throughout the process, members develop confidence in the TPRD professionals involved in their reviews and use them as de facto inquiry/focal points on WTO issues. More generally, the reviews help build knowledge in, and understanding of, the WTO. Also,

members that are in a process of trade policy reform have an opportunity to present the challenges, the process, and its results to a world audience. Discussions take place in the TPRD and with WTO economists that encourage trade policymaking to take directions foreseen in the WTO agreements and contribute to a member's greater integration into the multilateral trading system. In this context countries are provided with a framework for the formulation, implementation, and assessment of their trade policies and with an instrument to facilitate interministerial consultations for these purposes. The TPRM now also increasingly undertakes group reviews, for example of the Southern African Customs Union, the East African Community, and the Organization of East Caribbean States. This can foster regional integration that complements the WTO system.

Reviews also allow future technical-assistance priorities to be identified more clearly. In this respect, each Secretariat report for a review of a less-developed country now includes a section on capacity-building and technical-assistance needs; there is now also close cooperation with the WTO's Institute for Training and Technical Cooperation such that a needs assessment can be established and elaborated in the member's own report. The needs are invariably discussed during the review and have subsequently often been endorsed by the TPRB, thus forming the basis for a well-articulated future program of technical-assistance activities. In this context also, the process of reviewing less-developed countries now responds more systematically to technical-assistance needs. The review process for a less-developed country, and indeed for many developing countries, includes a two- to three-day seminar for its officials on the WTO and, in particular, the trade policy review exercise and the role of trade in economic policy.

Coverage of the TPRM Table 1 provides a list of WTO members reviewed in the period 1989–2007. In all, the TPRM conducted 248 reviews by the end of 2007. Increasing emphasis is given to less-developed countries, both because such members ask for reviews as an important element in their own

Table 1

Trade policy reviews: WTO members reviewed, 1989–2007

Europe/Middle East	Asia/Pacific	Africa	America
Austria[c]	Australia (5)	Angola[b]	Argentina (3)
Bahrain (2)	Bangladesh[b] (3)	Benin[b,h] (2)	Antigua and Barbuda[f] (2)
Bulgaria	Brunei Darussalam	Botswana[e] (2)	Barbados
Cyprus[c]	China	Burkina Faso[b,h] (2)	Belize
Czech Republic[c] (2)	Chinese Taipei	Burundi[b]	Bolivia (3)
European Communities (8)	Fiji	Cameroon[h] (3)	Brazil (4)
Finland[c]	Hong Kong, China (5)	Central African Republic[a,b]	Canada (8)
Hungary[c] (2)	India (4)	Chad[a,b]	Chile (3)
Iceland (3)	Indonesia (5)	Congo[a]	Colombia (3)
Israel (3)	Japan (8)	Côte d'Ivoire	Costa Rica (3)
Liechtenstein[d] (2)	Korea, Rep. of (4)	Djibouti[b]	Dominica[f] (2)
Norway (4)	Kyrgyz Republic	Egypt (3)	Dominican Republic (2)
Poland[c] (2)	Macau, China (3)	Gabon[h] (2)	Ecuador
Qatar	Malaysia (4)	Gambia[b]	El Salvador (2)
Romania (3)	Maldives[b]	Ghana (2)	Grenada[f] (2)
Slovak Republic[c] (2)	Mongolia	Guinea[b] (2)	Guatemala
Slovenia[c]	New Zealand (3)	Kenya[g] (3)	Guyana
Sweden[c] (2)	Pakistan (2)	Lesotho[b,e] (2)	Haiti[b]
Switzerland (4)	Papua New Guinea	Madagascar[b]	Honduras
Turkey (4)	Philippines (3)	Malawi[b]	Jamaica (2)
United Arab Emirates	Singapore (4)	Mali[b,h] (2)	Mexico (3)
	Solomon Islands[b]	Mauritania[b]	Nicaragua (2)
	Sri Lanka (2)	Mauritius (2)	Panama[a]
	Thailand (5)	Morocco (3)	Paraguay (2)
		Mozambique[b]	Peru (3)
		Namibia[e] (2)	St.Kitts and Nevis[f] (2)
		Niger[b,h]	St.Lucia[f] (2)
		Nigeria (3)	St.Vincent & Grenadines[f] (2)
		Rwanda[b]	Suriname
		Senegal[b,h] (2)	Trinidad and Tobago (2)
		Sierra Leone[b]	United States (8)
		South Africa[e] (3)	Uruguay (3)
		Swaziland[e] (2)	Venezuela (2)
		Tanzania[b,g] (2)	
		Togo[b] (2)	
		Tunisia (2)	
		Uganda[b,g] (3)	
		Zambia[b] (2)	
		Zimbabwe	
37 members (48 reviews)	24 members (69 reviews)	39 members (62 reviews)	33 members (69 reviews)

Notes:

( ) = Number of reviews completed where this is greater than one.

Reviews conducted at end-2007 = 248.

WTO members reviewed = 133 out of 151 members.

Least-developed WTO members reviewed = 27.

Share of world trade of WTO members reviewed (excluding significant double counting and intra-EC trade) = around 97%.

[a]First review in 2007.

[b]Least-developed member.

[c]Now included in European Communities (EC).

[d]Joint review with Switzerland (counted as two members, but one review for statistical purposes).

[e]Reviewed as member of the Southern African Customs Union (counted as five members, but one review).

[f]Reviewed as a member of the Organization of East Caribbean States (counted as six members, but one review).

[g]Reviewed as a member of the East African Community (counted as three members, but one review).

[h]Joint Review (two members, but one review for statistical purposes).

policymaking process and because the membership sees these reviews as essential to coming to a better understanding of the challenges that these members face and of how to respond to them.

WTO members have twice appraised the operation of the TPRM. In reports to WTO Ministerial Conferences they concluded that the mechanism, as the only multilateral, comprehensive evaluation of trade policies, functioned effectively, demonstrated a valuable public-good aspect, was a vehicle for members to reflect on their policies, served as an input into policy formulation, and highlighted general technical-assistance needs.

See also multilateralism; trade and economic development, international; trade-related capacity building; World Trade Organization

FURTHER READING

World Trade Organization. 1994. *The Results of the Uruguay Round of Trade Negotiations.* Annex 3. Geneva: WTO. Annex 3 provides the mandate of the TPRM.

———. 1995, 2005. *Rules of Procedure for Meetings of the Trade Policy Review Body.* WTO documents WT/TPR/6 and WT/TPR/&/Rev.1. Geneva: WTO. Sets out the procedures under which the TPRB conducts its work.

———. 1999, 2005. *Appraisal of the Operation of the Trade Policy Review Mechanism: Report to Ministers.* WTO documents WT/MIN(99)2 and WT/MIN(05)1. Geneva: WTO. Reaffirmed the importance that WTO members attach to the TPRM and found it to be functioning efficiently.

———. 2000–2006. *Trade Policy Review Mechanism: Report of the Trade Policy Review Body.* WTO documents WT/TPR/86, WT/TPR/101, WT/TPR/122, WT/TPR/140, WT/TPR/154, WT/TPR/173 and WT/TPR/192. Geneva: WTO. Provides details of the work of the TPRB in each of the years 2000 to 2006.

CLEMENS F. J. BOONEKAMP

■ trademarks

See Agreement on Trade-Related Aspects of Intellectual Property Rights (TRIPS); intellectual property rights

■ trade-related capacity building

Trade-related capacity building (TRCB) helps developing and transition economies to benefit from trade liberalization and a growing volume of trade opportunities. The underlying philosophy of this form of foreign aid is based on the conviction that trade positively affects economic development and provides domestic clients access to a greater variety of goods and services at lower prices. The aim of TRCB is to improve information flow, skills, relationships, institutional arrangements, and infrastructure, which affect a developing country's trade performance. This form of development aid enhances organizational and human capital through training, conducting research and consultancy projects, learning-by-doing, networking, and establishment of appropriate facilities. It aims at improving the beneficiary country's export performance (including widening its range of exports and selling in a greater number of markets), attracting foreign investment to create jobs and trade, and ensuring that the country benefits from the institutions of international trade, especially the World Trade Organization (WTO).

Depending on the area covered, two types of TRCB may be distinguished: (1) capacity building addressing trade policy issues and (2) capacity building in the area of trade promotion. The latter aims at improving the international business performance of the beneficiary country's firms and trade support institutions. The former—focused on trade policy and trade-related policy issues—develops know-how, networks, and institutions with the objective of optimizing the beneficiary country's policies and procedures, as well as implementation and control.

Capacity building aimed at business promotion may be seen as a value chain disaggregated into two types of strategically relevant activities: (1) primary activities, which are essentially marketing related, and (2) support activities, which provide the inputs needed for primary activities to occur. Primary activities relate to export market analysis, quality improvement of export products, transfer of technology and management skills, partner search, institution building in the area of trade and foreign direct investment support institutions, and improvements in the performance of trade infrastructure. The support activities comprise the maintenance of business data networks; organization of seminars, workshops, and corporate internships; publication of the relevant training material; execution of business consulting projects; organization of buyer-seller meetings, fairs, and expositions; and the like.

The nature and scope of TRCB have been evolving in response to the larger issue coverage of the trading system, increased participation of developing countries in the WTO and regional trade agreements, increased focus on market orientation and governance, and greater complexity of trade rules and procedures. Government administration in developing economies has been particularly affected by these developments. In addition there has been a clear tendency in the developing world toward a proactive involvement in trade negotiations and an increased role of advocacy in domestic and international decision making. In such an environment, it has been widely felt that the relevant institutions are weak and qualified personnel not easily available. Especially in least-developed countries (LDCs), the complex WTO procedures and requirements necessitated institutional capacities and budgetary resources that could not be provided, and TRCB was needed to reduce the transaction costs of integration into the global market. There was also a growing need for TRCB in trade promotion resulting from the desire to intensify the role of markets and the private sector, and a growing international orientation in development strategies. International rules are meaningless if they are not used, and the rules' real users—the business firms—need managerial capacities and support by trade-facilitation agencies, chambers of commerce, and business associations in order to compete in global markets.

Actors in the TRCB process include donors and beneficiaries, providers, policymakers, numerous government departments and specialized development agencies, the business community, nongovernmental organizations (NGOs), and academia. Considerable resources are donated to multilateral, regional, and bilateral TRCB activities. The budget of the TRCB projects of the U.S. Agency for International Development (USAID) alone—the leading supporter of TRCB—was close to US $700 million in fiscal year 2005, and it is estimated that more than US $2 billion per annum were spent on TRCB in the first years of this millennium. The other major donors include the European Union (EU) and the EU member states, such as the United Kingdom, Germany, and France, the Scandinavian countries, and Japan, Canada, and Australia. (A TRCB database established by the WTO jointly with the Organisation for Economic Co-operation and Development provides detailed information on TRCB projects.)

Most donors channel their support through governmental institutions (multilateral, regional, and national), NGOs, academia, or private firms. Among the beneficiaries are government departments and agencies, educational units, business associations, prioritized business firms, and other members of civil society. Among the leading providers of TRCB at the multilateral level are the World Bank and the International Monetary Fund (IMF), the WTO Secretariat, the United Nations Conference for Trade and Development (UNCTAD), the United Nations Development Program, the International Trade Center (ITC), and the World Intellectual Property Organization (WIPO). The WTO's assistance puts emphasis on trade policy rules, procedures, and rights and obligations of the WTO member states. The TRCB projects implemented by the World Bank, IMF, and UNCTAD emphasize the policy outcome and analysis of trade issues in the larger macroeconomic context. The ITC activities in TRCB are focused on issues of interest to the private sector, and WIPO concentrates on trade-related aspects of intellectual property. Regional governmental organizations conducting TRCB include the Organisation for Economic Co-operation and Development, the Asia Development Bank, the Secretariat of the Asia-Pacific Economic Cooperation (APEC) Forum, and so on.

At the national level many donor countries distinguish between the government departments in charge of formulating international development policies and the government-sponsored implementing organizations. The former comprise ministries such as the Department for International Development in the United Kingdom, the Federal Ministry for Economic Cooperation and Development (Bundesministerium für Wirtschaftliche Zusammenarbeit und Entwicklung) in Germany, the Ministry of Foreign Affairs in Japan, and the Department for International Cooperation and Development (Coopération internationale et développement) in France. Among the national providers, the leading agencies include USAID (an independent federal government agency that receives overall foreign policy guidance from the Secretary of State), the Canadian International Development Agency, Deutsche Gesellschaft für Technische Zusammenarbeit GmbH, the Japan International Cooperation Agency, Le Groupe de l'Agence française de développement in France, and the Australian Agency for International Development.

The nongovernmental or mixed government/private providers include a wide range of institutions such as the International Center for Trade and Sustainable Development (ICTSD), the Agency for International Trade Information and Cooperation, the North-South Institute, and the Center for Trade Policy and Law. An example of a nonprofit organization building trade law capacity in southern Africa is the Trade Law Centre for Southern Africa. The World Trade Institute, a joint venture between the University of Bern and the University of Neuchâtel in Switzerland, is a good example of another academic institution involved in TRCB with a special focus on international trade law. The role of such organizations is gaining importance with growing attention being paid to local ownership, efficiency, and diversity of TRCB services.

The lack of cooperation or coordination between the various providers is often quoted as one of the weaknesses of capacity building. Efforts for improvement included the launching of multiagency programs such as the Integrated Framework for Trade-Related Technical Assistance Programs to LDCs and the Joint Integrated Technical Assistance Program to selected LDCs and other African countries jointly conducted by ITC, UNCTAD, and

WTO. It is expected that important "aid for trade" provisions of the Doha Development Round (WTO) will further reinforce the TRCB activities.

The TRCB multilateral activities in the beginning of the 21st century were dominated by concerns such as (1) assistance in the WTO accession negotiations, (2) developing country compliance with the WTO rules and institution building to reap the benefits of WTO membership, (3) promotion of developing country service industries through appropriate reforms, (4) trade in agricultural products, (5) trade facilitation, (6) trade-related infrastructure development, (7) trade and environment, (8) modernization of the financial system, (9) improvements in labor standards, (10) competition policy, (11) procedures of trade policymaking and governance, and (12) assistance in dispute settlements or bilateral consultations on trade disputes.

See also aid, international; technical barriers to trade; trade and economic development, international; World Bank; World Trade Organization

FURTHER READING

Finger, J. Michael, and Philip Schuler. 1999. "Implementation of Uruguay Round Commitments: The Development Challenge." World Bank Policy Research Working Paper 2215. Washington, DC: World Bank. The paper discusses the post–Uruguay Round challenges of trade-related capacity building.

Kostecki, Michel. 2001. "Technical Assistance Services in Trade-Policy: A Contribution to the Discussion on Capacity-Building in the WTO." Geneva: International Center for Trade and Sustainable Development. Available at http://www.ictsd.org/pubs/respaper/TApaper 5-12-01.pdf. Comprehensive overview of trade-related capacity building, emphasizing the role of international organizations.

Organisation for Economic Co-operation and Development (OECD). 2001. "The DAC Guidelines: Strengthening Trade Capacity for Development." Paris: OECD. A document that helped to shape developments in trade-related capacity building.

Prowse, Susan. 2002. "The Role of International and National Agencies in Trade-Related Capacity Building." *World Economy* 25: 1235–61. Links trade-related capacity building to countries' trade and development strategies.

de Velde, Dirk Willem, Massimiliano Calì, Adrian Hewitt, and Sheila Page. 2006. "A Critical Assessment of the EU's Trade-Related Technical Assistance to Third Countries—Lessons from the Past, Policy Options for the Future." London: Overseas Development Institute. An outside assessment of trade-related capacity building efforts of the European Union.

World Bank, Independent Evaluation Group. 2006. "Assessing World Bank Support for Trade, 1987–2004." Washington, DC: World Bank. An outside assessment of trade-related capacity building efforts of the World Bank. Available at http://www.worldbank.org/ieg/trade.

World Trade Organization. 2005. "Strategic Review of WTO-provided TRTA Activities." Geneva: WTO. A critical assessment of technical assistance activities provided by the WTO Secretariat.

MICHEL KOSTECKI

■ trade-related intellectual property rights (TRIPS)

See Agreement on Trade Related Aspects of Intellectual Property Rights (TRIPS)

■ trade-related investment measures (TRIMs)

Governments adopt measures to attract foreign investment and to encourage the use of foreign investment in accordance with national priorities. Such measures that affect trade are known as *trade-related investment measures*. TRIMs designed to attract investment include fiscal incentives, tax rebates, and preferential terms on land and service. Common TRIMs designed to encourage investment in accordance with national priorities include local content requirements (requiring investors to use local inputs in production) and export performance requirements (requiring investors to export a certain proportion of their output). TRIMs also include trade-balancing requirements, foreign exchange balancing requirements, exchange restrictions, domestic sales requirements, manufacturing requirements, product mandating requirements, manufacturing limitations, technology transfer requirements, licensing requirements, remittance restrictions, local equity requirements, and employment restrictions.

The primary reason countries adopt TRIMs is to promote development. For example, some countries adopt TRIMs to foster domestic industries (through local content requirements), to expand exports (through export performance requirements), and to remedy deteriorating balance of payments (through foreign exchange balancing requirements). Countries also adopt TRIMs to address restrictive business practices and anticompetitive behavior of multinationals. One means is through technology transfer policies. For example, licensing requirements stipulate that foreign investors license technologies to host firms; and technology transfer requirements oblige foreign investors to transfer technologies on noncommercial terms or to conduct research and development locally.

The evolution of TRIMs as a policy tool coincides with changes in trade and investment. Since the late 1980s, foreign direct investment (FDI) has grown worldwide. According to the United Nations Conference on Trade and Development (UNCTAD), FDI increased from $203 billion in 1990 to $735 billion in 2001. Developing countries received $238 billion of this investment in 2001. Accordingly developed countries are the predominant sources and recipients of FDI. Further, FDI tends to be *horizontal* in that the output of foreign affiliates is sold in the foreign country. As FDI has grown, trade within companies has also grown. This trade (referred to as intrafirm trade) includes trade between subsidiaries located in different countries and between a subsidiary and its headquarters. According to the World Trade Organization (WTO), approximately one-third of the $6.1 trillion total of world trade in 1995 was intrafirm trade. Consequently since the 1980s an increasingly large share of trade is *related* to investment.

History of Agreements and Treaties Before 1995 few international frameworks provided disciplines for foreign investment. During the Uruguay

Round (1986–95) of the General Agreement on Tariffs and Trade (GATT), the United States proposed negotiations on policies that affect FDI. Weak support for these proposals, particularly among developing countries, resulted in negotiations on the narrower concept of trade-related investment measures.

At the conclusion of the Uruguay Round in 1995, members adopted the Agreement on Trade-Related Investment Measures (TRIMs Agreement) as one of four agreements of the WTO treaty. The agreement requires countries to phase out policies identified as inconsistent with GATT rules on national treatment and quantitative restrictions. TRIMs identified as inconsistent with national treatment rules include local content requirements and trade-balancing requirements. TRIMs identified as inconsistent with rules on quantitative restrictions include trade-balancing requirements constituting restrictions on imports, exchange restrictions resulting in restrictions on imports, and domestic sales requirements involving restrictions on exports.

On adoption in 1995, the TRIMs Agreement required member states to notify the WTO of existing TRIMs within 90 days. Members were then given a transition period to phase out the notified TRIMs (two years for developed countries, five years for developing countries, and seven years for least-developed countries). The agreement allows exceptions for developing and least-developed countries and permits the extension of the transition periods. For countries acceding to the WTO since 1995, obligations depend on their accession terms.

In addition to the TRIMs Agreement, other WTO agreements address specific aspects of TRIMs. These include the agreements on Trade-Related Aspects of Intellectual Property Rights, on Subsidies and Government Procurement, and the General Agreement on Trade in Services. However no comprehensive framework on TRIMs exists within the WTO to bridge these agreements.

Given its limited scope, the TRIMs Agreement was to be reviewed within five years to consider additional provisions. The 1996 WTO Ministerial Conference in Singapore initiated this process by calling for discussions in four areas (the "Singapore issues") including trade and investment, and by establishing working groups to facilitate analyses. The 2001 Ministerial Conference in Doha then produced the Doha Development Agenda (DDA), which mandated negotiations on new rules to begin after the 2003 Conference pursuant to a consensus on modes of negotiations. However the 2003 Ministerial Conference in Cancun ended without a consensus on several Singapore issues. In 2004 members dropped trade and investment from the DDA. Other efforts to create a multilateral agreement on investment include the Organisation for Economic Co-operation and Development's Multilateral Agreement on Investment. Negotiations on this agreement began in 1995, but subsequently stalled when participants were unable to reach a compromise.

The greatest challenge to creating a comprehensive framework is the divergent interests of countries. Those in favor of a new agreement on trade and investment (primarily developed countries) argue that the existing regime of bilateral and regional arrangements is confusing. They argue that a multilateral agreement would create a stable nondiscriminatory environment that would increase investment. Those against (primarily developing countries) argue that the existing regime provides adequate protections for multinationals and question whether a multilateral agreement would increase investment. Critics claim that a new multilateral agreement would add obligations while limiting countries' ability to align investment with development objectives.

See also domestic content requirements; foreign equity restrictions; international investment agreements

FURTHER READING

Balasubramanyam, V. N. 1991. "Putting TRIMs to Good Use." *World Development* 19 (9): 1215–24. Examines this relationship and argues that some (but not all) TRIMs promote development objectives.

Chao, Chi-Chur, and Eden S. H. Yu. 2000. "TRIMs, Environmental Taxes, and Foreign Investment." *Canadian Journal of Economics* 33 (3): 799–817. Considers the welfare effects of combinations of TRIMs and trade and environmental policies.

———. 2003. "Export Performance Requirements, Foreign Investment Quotas, and Welfare in a Small Dynamic Economy." *Journal of Development Economics* 72 (1): 387–400. Examine the welfare effects of specific TRIMs, including foreign-investment quotas and export-share requirements.

Correa, Carlos, and Nagesh Kumar. 2004. *Establishing International Rules for Foreign Investment: Trade-Related Investment Measures (TRIMS) and Developing Countries.* London: Zed Books. Considers the perspective of developing countries in a variety of initiatives to establish and reform international rules for foreign investment, including a new multilateral framework within the WTO.

Greenaway, David. 1992. "Trade Related Investment Measures and Development Strategy." *Kyklos* 45 (2): 139–59. Argues that TRIMs are second-best policies because they emerge as a consequence of preexisting distortions.

Greenaway, David, and Andre Sapir. 1992. "New Issues in the Uruguay Round: Services, TRIMs and TRIPs." *European Economic Review* 36 (2–3): 509–18. Discusses the motivation for including TRIMs in the Uruguay Round and whether international rules should be extended to embrace TRIMs.

PAMELA J. SMITH

■ **transaction costs**
See foreign market entry

■ **transfer pricing**

Transfer pricing decisions arise when one division of a firm sells goods or services to another autonomous division within the same firm. The firm's best interest is served when it selects a transfer price that maximizes total firm profits, which are generated by the aggregate efforts of the firm's separate divisions. Selecting the ideal transfer price, however, requires the firm to consider many facets and implications of its decision, including costs, incentives, and the details of the policy environment.

Firms often organize themselves as multidivision entities to reap the benefits of decentralized decision making. For example, in addition to the firm's headquarters, which coordinates the firm's activities and sets the rules for its subsidiaries, the firm might create separate divisions for parts production, assembly, research and development, advertising, and distribution. Thus transfer prices must be set when components from the parts division are provided to the assembly division, or when the final goods from the assembly division are supplied to the firm's distribution arm.

Hirshleifer's (1956) pioneering work on transfer pricing demonstrated that when there is no separate market for intermediate inputs, the transfer price should be set to the marginal cost of the producing division. In contrast, if there is a perfectly competitive market for intermediate inputs, the transfer price should be set at the market price for the intermediates. Aside from these simple cases, however, the optimal transfer price depends on a number of economic fundamentals, including the nature of competition in intermediate and final good markets, the structure of firm costs, and whether there is demand or technical dependence between separate divisions of the firm. As a result, firms not only must ask what the optimum transfer price is, but also, as noted by Holmstrom and Tirole (1991), need to determine whether it is best to organize the firm vertically, placing the coordination of all price decisions at the top.

When a firm locates its divisions in different jurisdictions—either different countries or different fiscal entities (states, provinces, or prefectures) within a country—differences in jurisdictional tax rates may influence transfer prices; firms have an incentive to maximize firm profits by strategically manipulating transfer prices as a means of locating profits in low-tax countries or locations. For example, consider a firm that produces inputs in a low-tax country that are used for assembly in a high-tax country. This firm can reduce its tax payments if it increases the declared value of the parts it sells to its assembly division in the high-tax country, because the price manipulation increases revenue and profits in the low-tax country while it increases costs and reduces profits in the high-tax assembly country. Similarly if the country tax environment is reversed such that the corporate tax rate is higher in the country where parts are produced and lower in the country where the firm does its assembly, the firm could reduce its tax burden by reducing the transfer price it declares on the parts it exports from the parts affiliate to the assembler in the low-tax country.

A full understanding of the incentives to manipulate transfer prices requires more information yet on the organization of the multinational and the firm's environment. For example, the simple case of transfer price manipulation suggests that a firm will reduce its current tax payment by the change in the declared value of its exports multiplied by the tax differential between the sending and receiving countries. Depending on the form of taxation in the firm's headquarters country, however, remaining taxes not paid in the current period may come due when income from a firm's overseas subsidiaries is repatriated to the firm's headquarters. Further, if the definition of taxable income differs across countries, the firm will have to evaluate the effect of its changed declaration on its worldwide tax payments. Finally, a firm's decision to engage in tax-driven transfer price manipulation may trigger other policy considerations. Along these lines, Horst (1971) describes how multinationals need to consider the effect of ad valorem tariffs, which provide a disincentive to increasing declared export prices and an incentive to underreporting of the export price. Further, when a horizontal multinational sets its transfer price, it may face further constraints on its choice of prices, since arbitrage conditions define the maximum degree of cross-country price differences that are sustainable.

Since tax authorities are aware that multinational firms may have strong financial incentives to manipulate their declared transfer prices to shift income from highly to more lightly taxed countries, most governments provide guidance on the setting of transfer prices for international transactions. For example, U.S. transfer price regulations instruct firms to use transfer prices for their internal transactions that are the same as the prices that would apply if the firm were conducting the sale at arm's length, as is the case when the firm sells the part or service to an unrelated party. Thus the ability of multinational firms to engage in tax-induced transfer price manipulation is limited when firms sell homogeneous goods or services. When firms do not have arm's length transactions to guide them in their choice of transfer prices, they are advised to use cost-plus or comparable profits as alternative methods for setting transfer prices. Although these guidelines prevent firms from declaring any arbitrary price, they nonetheless provide some latitude in price setting; the fact that many accounting firms have large divisions dedicated to transfer pricing attests to the complexity of these decisions, as well as the value associated with these choices.

Although transfer pricing decisions can occur in either a purely domestic or an international context, the nature of international investment makes transfer pricing a particularly salient issue. For example, due to international differences in comparative advantage, it often is attractive for firms to place their assembly facilities in low-wage, labor-abundant countries while they conduct more capital-intensive activities at home or in a capital-abundant country. Alternatively, in the case of horizontal investment, firms may decide to set up overseas production sites as a means of reducing variable transportation and tariff costs. In either case, firms that operate as multinationals are generally more productive than firms that are purely domestic, and it is the possession of intangible assets—designs, blueprints, trademarks, proprietary management systems—that enables firms that go multinational to expand across national borders successfully. As a result, the fact that intangible assets are generally present in and responsible for multinational firm activity implies that multinational firms will have more scope to manipulate transfer prices. At the same time, transfer pricing is not the only avenue for tax minimization, as multinational firms can reduce their worldwide payments through other means, such as their allocation of debt, timing of dividends, or—in the case of compensation for transferred intangible assets—use of royalty payments or licensing fees.

Finally, although there are many avenues for tax minimization by multinational firms, transfer price manipulation appears to be one that is actively pursued. Grubert and Mutti (1991) provide empirical evidence of this from U.S. multinational firms, showing that variation in the location of reported profits is consistent with income-shifting incentives and that real investment activity and firm exports of multinational firms are influenced by international differences in corporate taxation. Similarly, Swenson (2001) and Clausing (2003) find evidence in U.S. trade data that variation in trade prices is consistent with transfer pricing motives.

See also intangible assets; multinational enterprises

FURTHER READING

Clausing, Kimberly A. 2003. "Tax-motivated Transfer Pricing and U.S. Intrafirm Trade Prices." *Journal of Public Economics* 87 (9): 2207–23. Empirical evidence that transfer prices respond to incentives.

Grubert, Harry, and John Mutti. 1991. "Taxes, Tariffs, and Transfer Pricing in Multinational Corporate Decision Making." *Review of Economics and Statistics* 73 (2): 285–93. Documents that multinational firm decisions are consistent with tax-minimization incentives.

Hirshleifer, Jack. 1956. "On the Economics of Transfer Pricing." *The Journal of Business* 29 (3): 172–84. Pioneering paper examining optimal transfer price decisions for firms.

Holmstrom, Bengt, and Jean Tirole. 1991. "Transfer Pricing and Organizational Form." *Journal of Law, Economics, and Organization* 7 (2): 201–28. Places transfer pricing decision in its larger context, which includes organizational form.

Horst, Thomas. 1971. "The Theory of the Multinational Firm: Optimal Behavior under Different Tariff and Tax Rates." *Journal of Political Economy* 79 (5): 1059–72. Theoretical analysis of optimal transfer price setting by firms.

Rugman, A. M., and Lorraine Eden, eds. 1985. *Multinationals and Transfer Pricing*. New York: St. Martin's Press. Thorough reference on issues related to firm transfer pricing decisions.

Swenson, Deborah L. 2001. "Tax Reforms and Evidence of Transfer Pricing." *National Tax Journal* 54 (1): 7–25. Provides empirical evidence that reported transfer prices appear to reflect incentives based on tariffs and taxes.

DEBORAH L. SWENSON

■ transfer problem

International financial transfers take many forms. The classic example is war reparations, such as the payments by France after the 1870 Franco-German War and by Germany after World War I. The same general principles apply to other types of international transfer. These include foreign aid to developing countries, capital transfers from the richer to the poorer members of the European Union, and the remittances sent home by emigrants. Other pertinent cases include commodity producers that enjoy a windfall improvement in export prices (think of the impact of an increase in world oil prices on oil producers) and countries with net external liabilities that must make interest payments to foreign creditors.

The transfer problem relates to the impact of an international transfer on the structure of exchange rates and relative prices. To evaluate the full impact on the economies of the countries that pay and receive the transfer we need to assess the transfer problem.

There are circumstances under which an international transfer has no price impact. In the classic formulation of Keynes (1929a), "If £1 is taken from you and given to me and I choose to increase my consumption of precisely the same goods as those of which you are compelled to diminish yours, there is no Transfer Problem." It is implicit in this formulation, however, that the wealth transfer has no impact on supply capacities in either economy. This is open to question, since there is a natural tendency for an increase in wealth to be associated with a reduction in aggregate work effort. Accordingly, we may expect a decline in the level of production of the recipient economy relative to the level of production in the sender economy. To the extent that the two economies specialize in different goods, this shift in relative production levels may be expected to raise the prices of the goods produced by the recipient economy relative to the prices of the goods produced by the sending economy, even if consumption patterns are identical in both economies.

Moreover it is unrealistic to assume that households in both economies have the same consumption patterns. First, transportation costs means that domestically produced goods sell for lower prices to domestic consumers than to foreign consumers, which naturally tilts domestic spending patterns toward home-produced goods. For this reason, a transfer of wealth from the foreign country to the domestic country will be associated with an increase in the demand for home-produced goods and a decline in the demand for foreign-produced goods, leading to an increase in the relative price of home goods in terms of foreign goods. From the perspective of the home country, this implies an improvement in the terms of trade—the price obtained for exports improves relative to the price of imports.

Second, all countries produce a wide range of goods and services that are sold exclusively to domestic residents. A transfer of wealth from the foreign country to the home country means that demand for such nontraded goods rises at home and declines overseas. If the supply of such goods is somewhat inelastic, this will translate into an increase in the relative price of nontradables in the home country and a decline in the relative price of nontradables in the foreign country.

Third, there is considerable evidence that firms in some industries are able to set different prices in different markets, through segmentation strategies that make it difficult to arbitrage price gaps. An intuitive pattern is for firms to charge higher prices in wealthier markets. It follows that a transfer that enriches the home country relative to the foreign country may result in an increase in the prices of such goods at home relative to the foreign market. Each of these factors points to an increase in the domestic price level relative to the overseas price level—the recipient country experiences real exchange rate appreciation (equivalently, the sender country experiences real exchange rate depreciation).

The scale of the real exchange rate movements can be mitigated by several factors, however. For instance, international capital flows and the intersectoral mobility of labor between the traded and nontraded sectors may eliminate the impact of demand factors on the relative price of nontraded goods: if there is an increase in demand for nontraded goods, workers and entrepreneurs can switch from the export sector to the nontraded sector in order to meet the expansion in demand and capital can flow in from overseas to provide extra capacity. This supply response is more likely to apply over the medium term, with factors unlikely to move across sectors quickly or in response to purely temporary surges in demand. Similarly the supply response will be stronger for transfers that are signaled in advance, rather than unanticipated windfalls. Some factors (such as land) have limited supply elasticity, however, such that it remains likely that the level of demand influences the relative price of nontradables even over the long term.

In addition, an increase in demand for domestic tradables may in part be met by the entry of new firms that produce new varieties of goods—this is known as the "extensive" margin of adjustment. In this case, the expansion in demand has a smaller impact on the conventionally measured terms of trade, since the "extensive" margin of trade expands. This is most likely in advanced economies in which an active research and development sector fosters innovation.

Moreover, if countries have the ability to borrow and lend in international financial markets, the recipient may opt to save much of a temporary transfer by accumulating foreign assets. This strategy would allow the recipient to maintain a permanently higher level of consumption even after the expiration of the transfer, since the investment income on the accumulated assets would still be available. For this reason, countries such as Norway and Kuwait have opted to park much of their oil revenues in national investment funds, rather than enjoy a temporary boom in consumption that could not be sustained. A further advantage from this strategy is that it may help a recipient avoid the "Dutch Disease" syndrome whereby the increase in domestic wage costs that is precipitated by a surge in domestic demand leads to a contraction in the domestic export sector, which is costly if that sector has the greatest potential for delivering long-term productivity growth.

Unfortunately many developing countries have experienced problems in managing resource inflows (whether windfalls from surges in commodity prices or foreign aid receipts), such that there is a domestic demand surge and a sharp initial real appreciation. This is compounded by a propensity to increase external borrowing on the back of an increase in wealth, with the political pressures to increase spending exceeding the scale of the transfer. This "voracity effect" means that such countries experience macroeconomic instability, with the initial boom followed by a period of debt repayment, depressed consumption, and a decline in the real exchange rate (Tornell and Lane 1999).

Finally, we should note that the scale of the transfer problem may be expected to vary across economies of different sizes. In particular, the nontraded sector is relatively bigger in economies with larger populations and those that are more geographically isolated; larger economies may also have greater market power in international markets, such that their terms of trade respond more strongly to shifts in demand. For this reason, the empirical evidence shows that the transfer problem is much less important for small, open economies than for continental-sized economies (Lane and Milesi-Ferretti 2004). Even for small, open economies, however, the transfer problem remains central to the analysis of international resource flows.

See also capital mobility; nontraded goods; real exchange rate; terms of trade

FURTHER READING

Keynes, John Maynard. 1929a. "The German Transfer Problem." *Economic Journal* 39: 1–7. Keynes proposes that the payment of war reparations by Germany to France necessarily involves a reduction in the German price level relative to the French price level.

———. 1929b. "A Rejoinder." *Economic Journal* 39: 179–82. Keynes clarifies his argument, in response to the critique provided by Bertil Ohlin.

Lane, Philip R., and Gian Maria Milesi-Ferretti. 2004. "The Transfer Problem Revisited: Real Exchange Rates and Net Foreign Assets." *Review of Economics and Statistics* 86: 841–57. Provides empirical evidence in support of the transfer effect for a large group of countries.

Ohlin, Bertil. 1929. "Transfer Difficulties: Real and Imagined." *Economic Journal* 39: 172–78. Ohlin argues that

there are scenarios under which an international transfer need not affect relative price levels.

Tornell, Aaron, and Philip R. Lane. 1999. "The Voracity Effect." *American Economic Review* 89: 22–46. Analyzes the voracity effect, by which a divided society increases spending more than proportionally in response to a transfer.

PHILIP R. LANE

■ transition economies

Transition economies are those that are in the process of moving from central planning to markets. A centrally planned economy, sometimes also known as a command economy, is one where the means of production are publicly owned, the division of total product between investment and consumption is a centrally made political decision, and all economic activity is controlled in accordance with a central plan that assigns quantitative production goals and allots raw materials to enterprises. A market economy, on the other hand, is one where the means of production are mostly privately owned, the production and consumption of goods result from decentralized decisions made by individuals in pursuit of their own ends in light of prevailing prices, and prices adjust to equate supply and demand.

These definitions describe idealized types; in practice, most economies incorporate elements drawn from both, with the mixture determining whether they are closer to centrally planned or market economies. That said, an event of seminal significance in the late 20th century was the transition from plan to market in the countries of Eastern Europe and the former Soviet Union. An economic transition has also been underway in China and Vietnam. The former group of countries has, however, mostly seen transition as a broader concept, embodying a political transition from communism to multiparty democracy alongside the economic transition. This entry focuses on the economic transition in Eastern Europe and the Commonwealth of Independent States. Eastern Europe comprises Albania, Bosnia and Herzegovina, Bulgaria, Croatia, the Czech Republic, Estonia, Hungary, Latvia, Lithuania, Macedonia, Montenegro, Poland, Romania, Serbia, Slovakia, and Slovenia. The Commonwealth of Independent States (CIS) includes Armenia, Azerbaijan, Belarus, Georgia, Kazakhstan, the Kyrgyz Republic, Moldova, Russia, Tajikistan, Turkmenistan, Ukraine, and Uzbekistan.

An Analytical Framework The fall of the Berlin wall in 1989 heralded the demise of communism in Eastern Europe, whereas the exit from communism did not occur until 1991 in the former Soviet Union. A key first element signaling economic transition was the liberalization of most prices, so that households and firms henceforth faced international prices for tradable goods. However, large parts of the planned economy transacted at subsidized prices based on cheap energy and subsidized transport. Price liberalization, together with the disruption of the organizational arrangements governing production and trade under central planning, implied that many enterprises inherited by the transition countries were no longer viable. This found expression in what has come to be known as the "transition recession," during which gross domestic product (GDP) is estimated to have fallen by about 15 percent in Eastern Europe and by 40 percent in the CIS, reflecting in part the more distorted structure of the latter and, in the case of some of the poorer ex-Soviet republics, the cessation of budget transfers from Moscow. These numbers are not uncontroversial because the GDP data for the early years, by focusing on large enterprises where output had been declining and not adequately incorporating new businesses and an emerging informal sector, likely overestimate the severity of the transition recession. But this does not modify the qualitative thrust of the observations made here.

An important second element consisted of policy and institutional measures to elicit a supply response that would allow output to recover. These included (1) limiting state assistance (such as tax exemptions, fiscal and financial subsidies, budget and tax offsets, and directed credits) to enterprises, thereby promoting their restructuring or closure and making possible the transfer of assets and labor to viable enterprises; (2) preventing the theft of state assets, through either (a) privatization and an enforceable set of property rights in a private ownership economy, or (b) administrative methods in the few countries where centralized political structures had remained substantially intact; and (3) creating a business environment that did not discriminate among firms, whether old, restructured, or new, and comprised elements such as business licensing and registration, tax policy and administration, and a legal-cum-judicial system protective of property rights.

While restructuring and reallocation of resources in the enterprise sector constitutes the essence of the transition, implementation of this agenda required attention to two other sets of policies. Price liberalization implied that inflation, hitherto repressed in centrally planned economies through unavailability of consumer goods, and expressed in the form of forced monetary savings, had the potential to erupt into hyperinflation. This called for a third element in the set of policies, macroeconomic stabilization, to bring inflation under control.

Fourth, since restructuring and reallocation of resources involved the loss of workers' livelihood, social safety nets needed to be used—fiscal resources permitting—to finance retraining, early retirement, and cash assistance to bridge the period between job destruction and job creation and thus lower the political costs of the transition. This quartet of measures—(1) price liberalization; (2) creation of conditions for the growth of the private sector, including hard budget constraints on enterprises, a nondiscriminatory investment climate, and institutions to control managerial behavior; (3) macroeconomic stabilization; and (4) creation of social safety nets—made up the core of economic policy on managing the transition in Eastern Europe and the former Soviet Union from central planning to a market economy during the early years.

Initial Conditions or Policy Reforms? GDP in 2006 compared with 1990 was 50 percent higher in Eastern Europe and had nearly caught up with its 1990 level in the CIS. This was an increase of some three-quarters from the nadir of the transition recession in each subgroup of countries. An extensive debate surrounds the identification of the causes of the transition recession and the subsequent recovery from it. Cross-country statistical analysis suggests that initial conditions such as the degree of industrialization, trade dependence on other communist countries, repressed inflation, and black market exchange rates during the communist period were closely associated with lower growth during the early years of the transition. On the other hand, policy reforms, including elimination of central planning and mandated allocations through government orders, macroeconomic stabilization, trade liberalization, and competition, as well as a history of prior experience with market reforms and nationhood, were closely associated with subsequent growth performance, becoming stronger as the transition progressed.

The positive association between reforms and growth may seem surprising when the period of analysis includes recent years because the CIS, which has generally made less progress with reforms, has been growing particularly rapidly, more so than Eastern Europe since the Russian financial crisis of 1998. However, the positive impact of reforms on growth indeed continues to hold once two factors are controlled for: first, that the rapid growth in the CIS reflects in part catch-up from a deep recession, and second, that a surge in the price of oil has benefited the CIS oil exporters and other CIS countries through their trade linkages with those exporters (European Bank for Reconstruction and Development 2004).

Country Patterns of Transition The patterns emerging from cross-country statistical analysis need to be complemented by examining the experience of individual countries or subgroups of countries. The transition countries are highly diverse, with per capita incomes in 1991 ranging from an estimated $96 in Armenia to $6,368 in Slovenia. Although countries pursued different combinations of policies in the early years of transition, some broad generalizations are possible regarding the quartet of measures previously identified as key to managing the transition. Macroeconomic stabilization packages including,

among other things, tight monetary and credit policies, wage control policies, budget deficits financed from noninflationary sources, and suitable choice of exchange rate regimes, had been put in place in virtually all the transition countries by 1995. This helped bring down inflation, which had ranged from 26 percent in Hungary to a hyperinflationary 57,000 percent in Georgia prior to stabilization, to single digits in most countries by 1998 (Fischer and Sahay 2000).

Turning to enterprise sector reform, Estonia, Hungary, and Poland exemplify the imposition of hard budget constraints and the creation of an investment climate conducive to the entry of new firms in the early years of transition. This was less evident in those years in the Czech and Slovak republics and Lithuania, and it was only later that harder budget constraints were introduced, whereupon faster restructuring helped set these economies on the path followed by the earlier set of countries. In contrast, Bulgaria, Moldova, Romania, Russia, and Ukraine liberalized their economies but failed to impose hard budget constraints or contain the theft of assets either through law or administrative control. Russia and Ukraine encouraged new entry early in the transition, but the capture of the state by narrow vested business interests, comprising both old enterprises and well-connected early entrants, created a poor investment climate and discouraged further entry by potential competitors. Countries such as Belarus, Uzbekistan, and Turkmenistan, which retain strong elements of central planning, neither liberalized prices nor hardened budget constraints, but the survival of a highly centralized political structure allowed the apparatus of the command economy to be used to limit the extent of asset stripping by enterprise managers that had proved so damaging to growth elsewhere in the CIS.

Finally, adequate fiscal resources allowed countries in Central Europe to use social safety nets to cushion the impact of transition on displaced workers through retraining or early retirement. This option was not available to countries in the CIS due to a major loss of revenue from those state enterprises that were no longer profitable in a market economy.

The lack of a functioning social safety net implied that the deindustrialization that occurred in transition economies, which were typically overindustrialized compared with market economies at similar income levels, led to a movement of workers away from industry and into subsistence agriculture.

Institution Building The far-reaching nature of changes characteristic of the transition from a centrally planned to a market economy, particularly illustrated by the challenges of reforming the enterprise sector, implied that the countries of Eastern Europe and the former Soviet Union faced a formidable agenda of institutional reform. While this fact was recognized early, progress in creating the institutions of a market economy has lagged those reforms that could be accomplished by stroke-of-the-pen policy changes in all countries. As an example, this distinction is captured for the private and financial sectors by the European Bank for Reconstruction and Development's annual reports on transition. The EBRD defines "initial phase" reforms to include small-scale privatization, price liberalization, and trade and foreign exchange liberalization. "Second phase" reforms are defined to include large-scale privatization, governance and enterprise restructuring, competition policy, financial sector development, and infrastructure, the implementation of which calls for deep institutional reform. Initial phase reforms are virtually complete in the countries of Central Europe and the Baltic states that joined the European Union in 2004 and, to a lesser extent, in Bulgaria and Romania, which became European Union members in 2007. In contrast, second phase reforms lag virtually everywhere and especially in Eastern Europe outside the European Union and the CIS countries. In the context of economic integration, for example, most transition countries have generally liberal trade policy regimes. However, the countries where second phase reforms are lagging have not been able to attract the foreign direct investment that would enable deeper integration into global production and distribution chains and improve their longer-term prospects for economic growth. This is due to insufficient progress in developing institutions capable of implementing competition policy; effective regulatory supervision of services such as banking, telecommunications, and transport; as well as trade facilitation (World Bank 2005b).

Developing the Private Sector The share of the private sector in GDP, which is estimated to range from 25 percent in Belarus to 80 percent in Estonia, the Czech Republic, and Hungary, is often regarded as an important indicator of progress in transition. The private sector reflects both the results of privatization as well as entry and exit of privately owned firms that had never been owned by the state. Together with price liberalization and macroeconomic stabilization, privatization has been an important and widely discussed element in the transition from a command to a market economy. Privatization in the early years of transition was seen as a way of generating incentives for the new owners to use enterprise assets efficiently. This consideration was particularly important in the CIS countries, where weakening governments were unable to prevent asset stripping by enterprise managers, which had begun well before the exit from communism in the former Soviet Union. And, politically, privatization also helped ensure the irreversibility of the transition in its early years by creating a class of owners with a stake in the market economy.

While the privatization of small-scale enterprises was relatively uncontroversial, policymakers were faced with a difficult choice regarding the management of assets in medium- and large-scale enterprises. On the one hand, privatization in the absence of institutions of corporate governance could not guarantee that assets would not be stolen or that the rights of minority shareholders would be protected by the new owners. On the other hand, as noted, neither was the success of continued state ownership in an environment of weak government control assured. The problem of adequate monitoring of managerial behavior by shareholders could be overcome to some extent in cases where enterprises could be sold to concentrated private owners, that is, a few owners with larger stakes rather than many stakeholders with smaller stakes in the enterprise. However, the type of concentrated ownership mattered as well. Enterprises sold to strategic investors—equity capital investors that usually operate in the same or similar field and have a long-term interest in developing the company—particularly if they were foreign investors, performed much better than those controlled by holding companies or other financial institutions. The selection of strategic investors mattered too. Enterprises sold through transparent tenders or auctions generally attracted better owners, outperforming enterprises sold directly to politically connected parties, frequently at highly subsidized prices. Without such safeguards, concentrated ownership could not avoid the risk of expropriation of assets and income belonging to minority shareholders.

Many of the dilemmas surrounding medium- and large-scale privatization arose when the preferred method of privatization—direct sales through transparent tenders or auctions to strategic investors—was unavailable and a minimum of institutional capacity to prevent asset stripping by enterprise managers in the interim period was absent. Indeed the evidence suggests that privatization to concentrated outside owners has benefited restructuring whereas privatization to diffuse owners and to enterprise owners and managers has not (Djankov and Murrell 2002). Reforming laws and institutions to protect investors and monitor managerial behavior in countries with no market experience was rendered even more difficult when opposed by early winners from transition, who did so because such reforms would dissipate the rents accruing to them. In Russia, for example, powerful insiders frequently hampered enforcement efforts by the Securities and Exchange Commission. Hence in an environment of substantial capture of the state by narrow private interests, privatization did not create enough demand for the enforcement of property rights, contrary to early expectations. Indeed, while privatization has been found to be positively associated with a measure of public governance, namely, the state's capacity to provide key public goods in low-state-capture environments, the association turns out to be negative in high-state-capture environments (European Bank for Reconstruction and Development 1999).

The development of the private sector is also shaped by firm turnover—entry and exit—which has been substantial in the transition economies. The role of hard budget constraints on all enterprises and a business environment that does not discriminate between firms has been of particular importance in this regard. This is because the entry of new firms, which were able to occupy market niches that did not exist under central planning, as well as the exit of obsolete firms that were adapted to the command economy, contributed relatively more to productivity growth in transition economies compared with industrial and other developing countries. Furthermore, hard budget constraints and a nondiscriminatory business environment were mutually reinforcing. This is because hard budget constraints led to job destruction, which would have been politically difficult to withstand in the absence of job creation by new firms, which required, inter alia, a nondiscriminatory business environment. Early reformers such as Estonia and Hungary provide examples of job creation that was able to offset job destruction to a greater extent than in late reformers. Conversely the continued subsidization of unprofitable state-owned firms (soft budget constraints) could result in macroeconomic crises, as was the case in Bulgaria and Romania in the mid-1990s, resulting in a business environment that was not conducive to the development of new firms. Hence it is important that the share of the private sector in GDP as an indicator of progress in transition be complemented by an assessment of the extent to which the business environment provides incentives to privatized and new private firms to add value rather than engage in theft and rent seeking.

The Political Economy of Transition Why were most countries in Central Europe and the Baltic states able to implement more comprehensive reforms than those in the CIS? The answer depends, in part, on whether a government could credibly commit to a comprehensive reform program. This commitment would give potential winners such as owners of entrant firms and workers the confidence that they would eventually realize high enough returns to offset the initial adjustment costs incurred by them in exiting the state sector and entering the private sector. As reforms progressed, the expanding private sector created gains that were large enough to offset the losses of both (1) workers in a downsizing state sector and (2) early winners from partial reforms who had already established positions of advantage and whose gains would be competed away in the event of more comprehensive reform.

In former Soviet states such as Russia and Ukraine, the collapse of communism was rooted in a contest among competing elites rather than in any broad social movement. Governments, which had been captured by early winners from activities such as asset stripping and arbitrage between different sets of prices during price liberalization, lacked the credibility to build and sustain political support for a comprehensive reform program. This discouraged entry by competing groups that did not believe that the reform process would proceed far enough to deliver them a return net of adjustment costs. In much of Central Europe and the Baltic states, by contrast, political institutions emerged from round-table negotiations among broadly representative popular fronts in the aftermath of revolutions against communist rule. This, together with the pull of potential European accession that has been a powerful driver of political and economic institutional development, contributed to a wider social consensus on the main directions of reform and broad public support for comprehensive reform programs in the early stages of transition. These developments allowed those governments to be seen as credibly committed to such programs. As constituencies with a stake in reforms grew stronger, those groups that had gained an early advantage from liberalization and privatization were unable to convert those gains to erect barriers to competition and entry (World Bank 2002).

See also economic development; international income convergence; international institutional transfer; political economy of policy reform; Washington consensus

FURTHER READING

de Melo, Martha, Cevdet Denizer, and Alan Gelb. 1996. *From Plan to Market: Patterns of Transition.* Washington, DC: World Bank.

de Melo, Martha, Cevdet Denizer, Alan Gelb, and Stoyan Tenev. 1997. *Circumstance and Choice: The Role of Initial Conditions and Policies in Transition Economies.* Washington, DC: World Bank. The two papers by de Melo et al. introduced the Liberalization Index, a widely used measure of the extent of policy reform, and show that the extent of liberalization is an important determinant of economic growth during the transition.

Djankov, Simeon, and Peter Murrell. 2002. "Enterprise Restructuring in Transition: A Quantitative Survey." *Journal of Economic Literature* 40 (3): 739–92. Surveys the empirical literature analyzing the process of enterprise restructuring in transition economies.

European Bank for Reconstruction and Development. 1999. *Transition Report.* London: EBRD. Takes stock of the first ten years since the fall of the Berlin wall and examines the forces that moved transition forward as well as the constraints that held back progress.

———. 2004. *Transition Report.* London: EBRD. Reviews the relationship between reforms and growth in transition countries, including the role of factors such as the depth of the transition recession and rising oil prices.

Fischer, Stanley, and Ratna Sahay. 2000. *The Transition Economies after Ten Years.* IMF Working Paper No. 00/30. Washington, DC: IMF. Provides a summary of the macroeconomic performance of the transition economies.

World Bank. 1996. *World Development Report: From Plan to Market.* Washington, DC: World Bank. This report, written during the middle of the transition's first decade, assesses (1) how countries grappled with the initial dilemmas of transition and (2) how countries could best consolidate initial reforms to create institutions supportive of a market economy.

World Bank. 2002. *Transition: The First Ten Years—Analysis and Lessons from Eastern Europe and the Former Soviet Union.* Washington, DC: World Bank. Reviews the roles of policy, political economy, and external shocks in transition economy growth performance.

World Bank. 2005a. *Enhancing Job Opportunities: Eastern Europe and the Former Soviet Union.* Washington, DC: World Bank. Addresses why labor market outcomes have been disappointing during the transition and suggests policy interventions that can foster job creation and reduce unemployment.

World Bank. 2005b. *From Disintegration to Reintegration: Eastern Europe and the Former Soviet Union in International Trade.* Washington, DC: World Bank. Analyzes how Eastern Europe and the former Soviet Union have been reintegrated into international commerce since the disintegration of the Soviet trade bloc.

World Bank. 2008. *Unleashing Prosperity: Productivity Growth in Eastern Europe and the Former Soviet Union.* Washington, DC: World Bank. Examines the microfoundations of economic growth since 1998 and establishes that policy reforms that promote governance and microeconomic stability, market competition, infrastructure quality, financial deepening, labor market flexibility, and skill upgrading are important for achieving higher productivity growth.

PRADEEP K. MITRA

■ transnational corporations

See multinational enterprises

■ transport costs

See trade costs and foreign direct investment

■ transportation

See air transportation; shipping

■ Triffin dilemma

Little more than ten years after the creation of the Bretton Woods system, which was founded on the belief that the gold standard had contributed to the financial instability and widespread unemployment in the 1920s and 1930s, the Yale University economist Robert Triffin predicted in two separate articles in 1959–60 that internal contradictions would soon bring to an end the new international architecture constructed at Bretton Woods. Around ten years later his prediction, commonly called the Triffin dilemma, proved to be correct.

The major problem with the gold standard system was the failure of gold supplies to keep pace with the requirements of an expanding international trading system for adequate reserves and liquidity and its asymmetric adjustment mechanism that led to a predominance of restrictive domestic policies and a tendency toward global recession. Since limited gold reserves were used to meet international payments deficits, a country would eventually have to restrict domestic demand for foreign goods by reducing economic activity. On the other hand, there was no necessity for countries with payments surpluses who were receiving gold to contribute to adjustment by increasing their imports. Thus there was always a bias toward restrictive policies.

Despite many proposals to base the new system on an international unit of account or an international currency whose supply could by managed by a supranational bank to provide symmetric adjustment and support the needs of trade and global economic activity, the new system forged at the United Nations Monetary and Financial Conference held in 1944 at Bretton Woods, New Hampshire, was much less ambitious.

Under the Articles of Agreement of the International Monetary Fund (IMF), countries were given the choice of setting the par exchange value of their currencies for current account transactions in terms of gold or dollars. Since the United States held virtually all of the world's gold, it was the only country able to fix the par value of its currency in terms of gold. All other countries had no choice but to fix the par values of their currencies in terms of the dollar. This meant that these countries had to hold dollar reserves to ensure that market exchange rates did not diverge by more than 1.25 percent from par. The fixed exchange rate system was thus maintained by means of intervention in foreign exchange markets by all central banks, except the U.S. Federal Reserve, buying or selling dollars. The U.S. dollar was thus the sole intervention currency and effectively replaced gold in the Bretton Woods system.

Thus, the Bretton Woods system differed in one important respect from the gold standard. Instead of the supply being determined by mining and dis-hoarding, the supply of dollars to serve as international liquidity was determined by a deficit on the external trade and financial payments balance of the United States. In the immediate postwar period this balance was in substantial surplus, and most experts believed that the main problem with the new system would be dollar scarcity and a lack of international liquidity.

U.S. Dollar Overhang Unilateral transfers by the United States for political and military purposes, however, eventually led to current account deficits and an increasing stock of dollars held outside the United States. Triffin pointed out that while the successful operation of this new international financial system depended on an expansion of the U.S. current account deficit to keep international liquidity growing in step with rapidly expanding world trade, this would eventually create foreign claims on the United States that exceeded the gold supply. Once foreign claims on the United States exceeded the dollar value of the gold supply at the $35-an-ounce parity, the United States could no longer guarantee convertibility of the dollar into gold at the official parity. Fixed exchange rates required that foreign claims on the United States be kept below its holdings of gold reserves, while maintaining the growth in the supply of global liquidity to meet the needs of trade required just the opposite.

The survival of the dollar-based Bretton Woods fixed exchange rate system then depended on the willingness of foreigners to refrain from buying gold with their dollar reserves. Foreign holders of the dollar thus faced a dilemma: if they converted excess dollar balances into gold they risked devaluation and losses on their dollar holdings measured in their domestic currency on their balance sheets, but if they delayed and the dollar was devalued relative to gold they risked even larger losses.

Many countries argued that the United States could resolve the problem of excess dollar balances if it reduced domestic growth to create balance of payments surpluses, but this remedy would simply have reduced the growth of international liquidity

and created the risk of global recession. It was just such a case that John Maynard Keynes had warned against when he pointed out the necessity of avoiding asymmetric balance of payments adjustments. During the 1960s the United States introduced a series of ad hoc measures to manage the convertibility of the dollar into gold and to increase foreign demand for dollars, but the internal contradictions elucidated by Triffin were not eliminated.

There were three ways to resolve the problem:

1. create an international currency issued by a global central bank to replace the dollar at the center of the international system,
2. produce global deflation through an attempt to reduce the supply of dollars to the level of the remaining U.S. gold supply, or
3. allow the U.S. to default on its foreign debts through the elimination of the convertibility of the dollar, devaluation of the dollar, and the introduction of flexible exchange rates.

Triffin's prediction was proven correct when the last remedy was chosen in the early 1970s and fixed exchange rates were abandoned. Abandoning the dollar peg to gold did not completely resolve the problems Triffin raised, however, nor did it eliminate asymmetric adjustment. The current international financial system seems to exhibit a variant of the Triffin dilemma due to divergent policy objectives between developed and developing countries. The former tend to pursue policies to ensure exchange rate and asset price stability and allocative efficiency of financial markets at the cost of domestic growth performance below potential, that is, conditions of excess supply. On the other hand, developing countries are more interested in increasing their income and wealth levels via rapid growth.

Post–Bretton Woods: Flexible Exchange Rates One advantage of the shift to a floating exchange rate system after the collapse of the Bretton Woods system was to make diverse policy objectives compatible. The free global flow of capital in search of the most remuneration should maximize global growth. Developing countries in the post–Bretton Woods world, however, have high potential growth rates relative to developed countries and need to run balance of payments deficits to fill resource gaps by importing necessary goods. To pay for these imports, the developing country must borrow from foreign suppliers, which is financing with foreign capital inflows.

These flows are supported by the assumption that developing countries with high growth potential also have high relative real rates of return on investment and thus are ideal investment targets for developed countries with excess savings and few attractive domestic outlets for investment. Large differentials in relative growth rates as well as large resource gaps require large capital inflows and associated balance of payments deficits. The larger the deficit, the higher the likelihood of an exchange rate adjustment or depreciation, creating higher volatility in returns and greater risks to developed country investors. Thus the more successful the system is in allowing developing countries to achieve their potential growth rates, the less willing developed country investors are to finance these deficits.

Thus the Triffin dilemma of the 21st century implies that the more successful developing countries are in achieving their potential growth rates by borrowing in international capital markets to fill their resource gaps, the larger will be their foreign imbalances and the less likely they will be to retain the capital inflows required to support the growth rate. Just as large U.S. deficits increased the risk of holding dollars, larger developing country deficits increase the risk of holding assets denominated in their currencies.

Under the Bretton Woods system, countries held dollar balances because central banks had to support their Bretton Woods parity, and the dollar retained international value in excess of its gold backing. Since the Bretton Woods system ended, exchange rates in developing countries are held up by the force of capital flows themselves, which prior to crises exceed the funds needed to meet balance of payments shortfalls and produce a continuous upward pressure on the currency. Also, because of their higher po-

tential growth rates, the monetary policies in most developing countries produce interest rates that are higher than those abroad, providing an additional attraction for foreign investors. This produces a condition for foreign investors that is much like the catch-22 faced by central banks under Bretton Woods. As the balance of payments continues to deteriorate, the required risk-adjusted rate of return on investment increases—but withdrawing capital will inevitably produce exchange rate instability that erodes or eliminates the nominal excess returns expected to be earned in developing countries. Eventually the balance tips toward increased risk, and an exchange rate crisis requires an adjustment policy that generates a decline in income growth and employment.

Thus the same asymmetric adjustment that made deficit countries adjust their policies to those of surplus countries also forces developing countries to make their policies compatible with the policy objectives of the developed countries. Post–Bretton Woods, it is the reversal of international capital flows that produces the adjustment. A country that grows too rapidly and produces a large balance of payments deficit that threatens exchange rate stability, and thus its excess rate of return, finds that foreign capital flows out and a financial crisis forces adjustment.

New Triffin Dilemma After the 1997 Asian crisis, many developing countries shifted their policies toward current account surpluses and the accumulation of dollar reserves to protect themselves against capital outflows and the need to borrow from the IMF. As a result, the United States has accumulated large external account imbalances, so dollar holders face the same Triffin dilemma that occurred at the end of the Bretton Woods system. The Triffin dilemma thus seems to be of more general application than its author might have originally envisaged.

See also balance of payments; Bretton Woods system; convertibility; currency crisis; dollar standard; exchange rate regimes; financial crisis; global imbalances; gold standard, international; international liquidity; International Monetary Fund (IMF); International Monetary Fund conditionality; international reserves; money supply; twin deficits

FURTHER READING

International Monetary Arrangements: The Problem of Choice—Report on the Deliberations of an International Study Group of 32 Economists. 1964. Princeton, NJ: Princeton University International Finance Section. Proposals from an eminent group of international monetary experts on possible alternative international monetary arrangements.

Lary, Hal B. 1963. *Problems of the United States as World Trader and Banker.* New York: Columbia University Press for the National Bureau of Economic Research. Classic study outlining the conflicting role of the United States as a trading nation and as the provider of the global means of exchange.

Triffin, Robert. 1960. *Gold and the Dollar Crisis.* New Haven, CT: Yale University Press. Reprints of Triffin's original articles enunciating the dilemma.

———. 1966. *The World Money Maze: National Currencies in International Payments.* New Haven, CT: Yale University Press. Further extensions on the problems caused by an international monetary system based on national currencies.

JAN KREGEL

■ twin deficits

The *twin deficits hypothesis* refers to the belief that changes in fiscal policy that increase the budget deficit will also increase the current account deficit. The term gained popularity in the 1980s, when tax cuts that caused the U.S. budget deficit to increase by 3 percent of gross domestic product (GDP) between 1980 and 1985 were followed by trade deficits exceeding 3 percent of GDP in 1985 and 1986. The concept received renewed attention in the first decade of the 21st century, when a deterioration of the U.S. long-term or structural budget balance of 6 percent of GDP between 2000 and 2004 was accompanied by current account deficits of 5 percent of GDP in 2004 and 6.5 percent of GDP in 2005.

Accounting and Theoretical Relations In terms of accounting, the current account deficit and the budget deficit are related through the identity:

$$\text{Saving} + \text{Current Account Deficit}$$
$$= \text{Investment} + \text{Budget Deficit} \qquad (1)$$

The identity implies that an increase in the budget deficit that does not cause a change in private saving or investment will increase the current account deficit. Equation (1) can be rewritten as:

$$\text{Current Account Deficit}$$
$$= \text{Investment} - \text{National Saving} \qquad (2)$$

where national saving equals private saving minus the budget deficit (or private saving plus government saving). Written in this way, the identity highlights the fact that a country with insufficient domestic saving to finance its domestic investment must make up the shortfall by running a current account deficit (i.e., drawing on foreign saving).

To understand the relationship between budget deficits and current account deficits it is necessary to go beyond accounting identities to theoretical models. In the Mundell-Fleming model, a fiscal expansion increases aggregate demand and the domestic interest rate. This in turn generates a capital inflow that causes the currency to appreciate. The stronger currency then reduces net exports, returning aggregate demand and output to their original levels. Similar transmission mechanisms are operative in larger-scale general equilibrium macro models that build on equation (2) and the fact that income and exchange rate changes affect exports and imports (e.g., see Cline 2005).

An alternative theoretical perspective in which budget deficits do not affect current account deficits is the Ricardian equivalence model (Barro 1974). Under this theory, a reduction in taxes that raises the budget deficit will be followed by an increase in taxes in the future. Rational taxpayers will anticipate these future tax liabilities that will fall either on them or on their descendants and will increase savings by the amount of the tax cuts. Thus in equation (1), savings will increase by the same amount as the budget deficit. An increase in the budget deficit will thus have no effect on interest rates, exchange rates, investment, or net exports.

Choosing empirically between the Ricardian equivalence model and models where deficits matter has proven difficult. The simplest test may be to examine whether budget deficits raise interest rates. Since budget deficits vary countercyclically and interest rates vary cyclically, however, these tests are biased against finding a relationship between the variables. After many empirical studies of the Ricardian model, no clear consensus has emerged.

In spite of the difficulty with empirical testing, many have argued that the theoretical requirements for Ricardian equivalence to hold are too stringent (see, e.g., Haliassos and Tobin 1990). The model requires parents, children, grandchildren, great-grandchildren, and so on to be linked in an unbroken chain through the giving of intergenerational gifts. It requires capital markets to be perfect and agents to be able to borrow and lend on the same terms as the government. It requires taxes and transfers to be lump sum. Finally, it requires that tax cuts be followed by tax increases rather than by new debt issues to service the existing debt. Because these theoretical requirements seem too restrictive, many have argued that an increase in the budget deficit will not produce a dollar-for-dollar increase in private saving. In this case, an increase in the budget deficit will partly crowd out either net exports (the twin deficits hypothesis) or private investment.

The Mainstream Perspective on the Twin Deficits Proponents of the twin deficits hypothesis do not argue that budget deficits and current account deficits move in lockstep, but only that fiscal policy changes that increase the budget deficit can also increase the trade deficit. Many factors can attenuate the relationship between the two variables. For instance, a stock market boom can reduce savings, increase investment, and attract funds from abroad. These factors would all lead to a larger current account deficit. Greater tax revenues from the stock market boom, however, would move the budget toward surplus. Similarly a recession would reduce imports and improve the trade balance but reduce tax revenues and worsen the budget deficit.

The fact that the two deficits do not always move together is borne out by the data. The two deficits moved in the same direction in only ten years between 1980 and 2004 (Cline 2005). Formal econometric and calibration studies indicate that a $1 reduction in the budget deficit will reduce the current account deficit by between 20 and 40 cents (see Erceg, Guerrieri, and Gust 2005; Cline 2005; Chinn and Prasad 2003).

A major concern with the twin deficits is whether the borrowing associated with them will prove sustainable. The same framework can be used to think about the growth of government debt and the growth of external debt (Gramlich 2004). In both cases, the long-run value of the stock of debt relative to GDP n^* is given by:
$$n^* = d/(g - r) \qquad (3)$$
where d is the nominal primary budget deficit or current account deficit relative to GDP, g is the nominal growth rate of the economy, and r is the net nominal interest rate on the debt. Many authors have calculated that, given current trends, the stock of U.S. external debt could reach levels exceeding 100 percent of U.S. GDP.

An important question is whether foreign investors will at some point become unwilling to accumulate additional U.S. debt. This could lead to a hard landing for the dollar and the U.S. economy. The reluctance of foreigners to acquire additional U.S. assets could cause the dollar to fall, interest rates to rise, and stock prices to tumble. The adjustment could prove disorderly if the fall of the dollar led to a rush for the exits among investors holding dollar assets.

Arguments That the Twin Deficits Do Not Matter While many are concerned that the twin deficits will cause a hard landing for the U.S. economy, others are more sanguine. Arguments that the twin deficits do not matter point to valuation effects, the size of global capital markets, the impact of a global savings glut, and China's willingness to accumulate dollar assets.

Valuation effects refers to factors that offset the effect of large current account deficits on the value of the U.S. external debt. One such factor can be seen from equation (3). The interest rate r has been persistently negative (i.e., favorable to the United States), driving down the value of n*. The interest rate is negative because, up until now, investment income earned by U.S. residents from abroad has exceeded investment income paid by U.S. residents to the rest of the world. Since net international investment income has remained positive for the United States, some have in fact argued that the United States is a creditor and not a debtor in an economic sense (Cline 2005).

In a similar vein the economists Hausmann and Sturzenegger (2006) have argued that positive net income for the United States in every year from 1980 to 2005 implies that the economic value of U.S.-owned assets abroad exceeds the economic value of foreign-owned assets in the United States. They attribute the difference between the U.S. economic status as a creditor and the official data showing that the United States is a debtor to the presence of "dark matter." *Dark matter* refers to the value of know-how and brand recognition associated with U.S. foreign direct investment (FDI) abroad, the seigniorage gains the United States receives because people throughout the world are willing to hold U.S. dollars, and the "insurance premium" that the United States receives because investors are willing to hold U.S. Treasury securities at a lower rate of return than the United States can earn on foreign currency assets.

Others take issue with the argument that, because of dark matter, the United States is actually a net creditor. The data on net international investment income may be inaccurate because foreign firms underreport profits from U.S. operations to minimize tax liabilities. Further, U.S. assets from abroad are largely in the form of equities (including FDI), while U.S. external liabilities are largely in the form of fixed-income assets (including U.S. Treasury securities). Thus the average return received by U.S. investors exceeds the average return received by foreign investors because the United States is holding riskier and more profitable assets (Frankel 2006).

Some have argued that because global capital markets are large, the United States can continue borrowing massive amounts in the future without the

U.S. economy experiencing a hard landing (Cooper 2005). According to one calculation, the non-U.S. financial wealth equals about 700 percent of U.S. GDP (Cline 2005). Assuming that "home bias" in the rest of the world continues to decline, some have argued that foreign investors in the future may be willing to hold even the very large quantities of U.S. external debt implied by large U.S. current account deficits. Others suggest that country risk is better measured by a country's debt relative to its own exports or GDP rather than relative to the size of foreign portfolios (Frankel 2006). If measured by these criteria, U.S. external debt is on a trajectory in the first decade of the 21st century to reach precarious levels (see Obtsfeld and Rogoff 2005). Many argue that this growth in U.S. debt/GDP and U.S. debt/exports will multiply the risk of a hard landing.

The chairman of the Federal Reserve, Ben Bernanke (2005), has argued that the budget deficits of the George W. Bush administration were not an important cause of large trade deficits but instead that the external imbalances were driven by a global savings glut. Indeed many developing and developed countries have excesses of saving over investment that have flowed to the United States. These surplus funds have in turn reduced U.S. interest rates and pushed up U.S. housing prices. The resulting increase in household wealth has reduced U.S. private saving and led to large trade deficits. According to calculations by Cline (2005), a global savings glut can explain at most 35 percent of the U.S. current account deficit. The rest he attributes to U.S. fiscal policy and other factors.

Another argument against the significance of the twin deficits is that China and other developing countries running surpluses with the United States are willing to accumulate massive quantities of dollar assets. It has been suggested that this arrangement constitutes a new Bretton Woods system (see Dooley, Folkerts-Landau, and Garber 2004). China and East Asia are playing a role analogous to the role played by Europe in the 1960s. China has accumulated $1 trillion of reserves, predominantly in dollars, in order to maintain a competitive exchange rate and thus sustain the export-oriented thrust of its economy. This strategy will help China to provide jobs for hundreds of millions of underemployed rural workers and also facilitate the development of financial infrastructure and modern systems of corporate governance. If this thesis is accepted, the current system could well be sustained for a long time.

Others claim that this arrangement is not sustainable. For instance, China may either develop a workable system of finance and corporate governance or experience a financial crisis (Frankel 2006). Either way, the excess liquidity flowing from China to the United States will stop. In addition, foreign reserve accumulation can increase the money supply and exacerbate inflation. Sterilization policies to offset this effect may force commercial banks to hold more and more central bank bills, erode bank profitability, and interfere with the allocation of credit through the banking system. Further, continued accumulation of U.S. Treasury securities (external reserves) results in an increasingly inefficient allocation of resources since both private and social rates of return would be much higher for investments in the domestic economy (see Summers 2006). Thus many believe that foreign reserve accumulation by Chinese and other central banks will not prove sustainable.

There is thus a lively debate about the empirical relevance of the twin deficits hypothesis. More research is needed to clarify the relationships among budget deficits, current account deficits, and other variables.

See also balance of payments; Bretton Woods system; Federal Reserve Board; foreign exchange intervention; global imbalances; home country bias; international financial architecture; international reserves; mercantilism; Mundell-Fleming model; seigniorage; sterilization

FURTHER READING

Barro, Robert. 1974. "Are Government Bonds Net Wealth?" *Journal of Political Economy* 82: 1095–1117. Indicates that budget deficits do not affect current account deficits.

Bernanke, Ben. 2005. "The Global Saving Glut and the U.S. Current Account Deficit." Lecture presented to the Virginia Association of Economics, Richmond, VA, April 14, 2005. Downloadable at http://www

.federalreserve.gov/boarddocs/speeches/2005/default.htm. Argues that America's current account deficits in the 21st century are primarily due to excess saving abroad rather than U.S. budget deficits.

Chinn, Menzie, and Eswar Prasad. 2003. "Medium Term Determinants of Current Accounts in Industrial and Developing Countries: An Empirical Exploration." *Journal of International Economics* 59 (1): 47–76. Investigates the link between budget deficits and current account deficits.

Cline, William. 2005. *The United States as a Debtor Nation.* Washington, DC: Institute for International Economics. A comprehensive and extraordinarily useful reference on the subject.

Cooper, Richard. 2005. "Living with Global Imbalances: A Contrarian View." Institute for International Economics Policy Brief 05-3. Washington, DC: Institute for International Economics. Argues that, because global capital markets are large, the United States can continue borrowing massive amounts in the future without the U.S. economy experiencing a hard landing

Dooley, Michael P., David Folkerts-Landau, and Peter Garber. 2004. "The Revised Bretton Woods System." *International Journal of Finance and Economics* 9 (4): 307–13. Argues that China and East Asia will continue to accumulate dollar reserves for a long time.

Erceg, Christopher, Luca Guerrieri, and Christopher Gust. 2005. "Expansionary Fiscal Policy and the Trade Deficit." Federal Reserve International Finance Discussion Paper 2005-825. Washington, DC: Federal Reserve Board. Provides quantitative evidence of the link between budget deficits and current account deficits.

Frankel, Jeffrey. 2006. "Could the Twin Deficits Jeopardize U.S. Hegemony." *Journal of Policy Modeling* 28 (6): 653–63. An excellent defense of the position that the twin deficits matter.

Gramlich, Edward. 2004. "Budget and Trade Deficits: Linked, Both Worrisome in the Long Run, but Not Twins." Washington, DC: Federal Reserve Board. http://www.federalreserve.gov/boarddocs/speeches/2004/20040225/default.htm. A clear discussion of whether the borrowing associated with the twin deficits is sustainable.

Haliassos, Michael, and James Tobin. 1990. "The Macroeconomics of Government Finance." In *Handbook of*

Monetary Economics, edited by Benjamin Friedman and Frank Hahn. New York: Elsevier Science, 889–959. An excellent and comprehensive discussion of the macroeconomics of government borrowing.

Hausmann, Ricardo, and Federico Sturzenegger. 2006. "Global Imbalances or Bad Accounting?: The Missing Dark Matter in the Wealth of Nations." Kennedy School of Government Working Paper RWP 06-003. Cambridge, MA: Harvard University. Argues controversially that the United States is actually a creditor nation rather than a debtor nation.

Obtsfeld, Maurice, and Kenneth Rogoff. 2005. "The Unsustainable U.S. Current Account Position Revisited." In *G7 Current Account Imbalances: Sustainability and Adjustment*, edited by Richard Clarida. Chicago: University of Chicago Press, 339–66. Argues that the U.S. current account deficit is unsustainable and poses risks to the world economy.

Summers, Lawrence. 2006. "Reflections on Global Account Imbalances and Emerging Markets Reserve Accumulation." Speech presented at the Reserve Bank of India (March 24). Downloadable at http://www.president.harvard.edu/speeches/summers/2006/0324_rbi.html. Argues that central banks should hold external reserves in assets other than U.S. Treasury securities.

WILLEM THORBECKE

■ unions and foreign direct investment

Unionization has been falling over time, especially in the United States. In 2005, the unionization rate in Great Britain was 29 percent; Japan, 18.7 percent; Korea, 11.9 percent; and the United States, 12.5 percent. According to data for other years, the unionization rate in Australia was 24.7 percent (2000 data); Canada, 29.7 percent (2006 data), Germany, 26.6 percent (2002 data); Singapore, 21.5 percent (2004 data); and the Philippines, 26.0 percent (2002 data). Meanwhile foreign direct investment (FDI) has been growing rapidly. The United States, the largest recipient of FDI, has one of the lowest unionization rates. Is there a connection?

Theoretical Frameworks FDI can benefit or hurt labor, depending on factors such as its motivations, the structure of firms, the organization of labor-management negotiations, the preference of labor unions, and the location of workers. Firms can be horizontally or vertically related; labor-management bargaining can be firm specific, industrywide, or even nationally centralized; and unions may prefer wages more than employment, or vice versa.

Often the motivation for undertaking FDI is market access. With the classical *tariff-jumping FDI*, the motivation is to jump over existing import barriers such as tariffs, quotas, anti-dumping duties, and safeguard measures. By producing directly in the destination country, the multinational firm avoids import barriers that a national firm must face when exporting.

Related is the so-called *quid pro quo FDI*. The quid pro quo literature suggests that FDI may be induced by the threat of protection (possible protection in the future), and furthermore, that FDI may be used as an instrument to defuse a future protectionist threat. By investing directly in the host countries, foreign firms are creating jobs in the host country. As a consequence, domestic lobbying pressure against foreign imports decreases.

If FDI is undertaken for the purposes just mentioned, it benefits labor in both countries compared with the case of no FDI at all, because it raises output and employment, which in turn puts upward pressure on wages.

In unionized industries, multinationals may undertake FDI to reduce labor costs, to improve their relative bargaining position with the union, or to avoid employing union workers. Consequently, unions historically tend to view multinationals and FDI negatively, regardless of their sources or destinations.

When the motive is to reduce labor costs, FDI may benefit or hurt labor, depending on whether the multinational enterprise (MNE) is horizontally or vertically structured. A horizontal MNE produces identical goods in several countries, while a vertical MNE produces inputs in some countries and final goods in other countries. The theoretical literature suggests that horizontal MNE can hurt labor, because by moving production facilities across borders, firms shift the demand for labor, which drives down the negotiated union wage (see for instance Zhao 2001 and the references cited). Further, usually labor unions are assumed to maximize an objective function consisting of union employment and a union wage premium above the nonunion wage. If the labor unions are more interested in higher employment than in the wage premium, then horizontal FDI reduces union employment also. This result remains true regardless of whether labor-management bargaining is firm specific or industrywide. And if labor-management bargaining is firm specific and unionization is industrywide, the previously mentioned effects of FDI are substantially reduced, because union members can find work in other firms if bargaining breaks down. In this case, unions may welcome horizontal FDI also. In addition, under subsidiary bargaining in which the union negotiates with branches (not headquarters) of the MNE, union strikes affect only portions of the MNE earnings, while under headquarter bargaining in which the union negotiates with the MNE headquarters, the MNE's total earnings are affected. Thus the labor union prefers to bargain with the headquarters rather than with the subsidiary, even though the MNE may use transfer pricing to strategically influence the negotiated wages and employment by shifting profits across branches to gain a better position in negotiations.

Leahy and Montagna (2000) investigate the effects of different degrees of centralization in wage setting on the incentive of a MNE to locate in a host country, on the host country's welfare, and on the MNE's preference for centralized or decentralized bargaining. They find that if international product markets are interrelated, then centralized bargaining would help the MNE and hurt the host country. This arises because the more efficient MNE would try to raise the wage in the host country above the level host-country firms can afford (i.e., raising rivals' costs), thereby capturing a larger market share. Skaksen and Sorensen (2001) show that home workers may lose or gain depending on the substitutability of the multinational activities. If there is a high degree of substitutability (complementariness) between the activities in the home country and the host country, it is likely that the workers lose (gain) on FDI. Naylor and Santoni (2003) show that FDI is less likely, other things being equal, the greater the union bargaining power and the more substitutable the firms' products in the potential host country.

On the other hand, a vertical MNE can be good or bad for labor in the source country, depending on host-country wages and how much production is shifted overseas. Zhao and Okamura (2008) show that undertaking FDI in a lower-wage country has two effects: an output-expansion effect and a demand-shifting effect. The output-expansion effect stems from using cheaper labor in the host country, which reduces the MNE's overall average cost and enables higher output and employment. The demand-shifting effect is that FDI reduces labor demand in the source country but increases that in the host country. If the first effect dominates the second, then FDI benefits labor in the source country as well as in the host country. This case arises more often if the wage in the host country is not too much below that in the source country. Otherwise the second effect dominates the first and labor in the source country loses from FDI. One important conclusion is that if the wage in the host country is relatively high (nevertheless lower than in the source country), then FDI benefits the labor union and the MNE in the source country, as well as the host country itself.

Empirical Studies There are very few empirical studies concerning labor unions and FDI, and they use U.S. data and mostly confirm the theoretical predictions. Using U.S. Department of Commerce data published in 1992, Cooke (1997) examines the influence of several key industrial relations variables on U.S. outward FDI across nine industries and 19 members of the Organisation for Economic Co-operation and Development. He finds that FDI is negatively related to high levels of unionization, centralized bargaining structures, and industrial relations environments unfavorable to firms such as governmental restrictions on layoffs, but FDI is positively affected by high levels of worker education and policies requiring works councils. Using 1981–83 data on U.S. inward FDI, however, Coughlin, Terza, and Arromdee (1991) are surprised to find that higher unionization rates were associated with increased FDI.

Slaughter (2007) examines whether globalization has played a role in the falling private-sector unionization rate in the United States, with unions feeling pressured to reduce employment and/or compensation demands. He assembles a panel of U.S. manufacturing industries that matches union-coverage rates with measures of global engagement such as exports, imports, tariffs, transportation costs, and FDI. He finds a statistically and economically significant correlation between falling union coverage and greater numbers of inward FDI transactions. Because U.S. affiliates of foreign multinationals have higher unionization rates than U.S.-based firms do, this correlation may reflect pressure of international capital mobility on U.S.-based companies, consistent with research on how rising capital mobility raises labor-demand elasticities and alters bargaining power.

In sum, while the theories of unions and FDI are many, the empirical tests of these theories are few. More work is needed to establish the effects of FDI on unions, of unions on FDI, and of unions on how FDI affects host and source countries.

See also factor endowments and foreign direct investment; footloose production; foreign direct investment and labor markets; technology licensing; trade and wages

FURTHER READING

Cooke, William N. 1997. "The Influence of Industrial Relations Factors on U.S. Foreign Direct Investment Abroad." *Industrial and Labor Relations Review* 51 (1): 3–17. Finds FDI to be negatively related to unionization.

Coughlin, Cletis C., Joseph V. Terza, and Vachira Arromdee. 1991. "State Characteristics and the Location of Foreign Direct Investment within the United States." *Review of Economics and Statistics* 73 (4): 675–83. Finds unionization attracts FDI using U.S. data.

Leahy, Dermot, and Catia Montagna. 2000. "Unionization and Foreign Direct Investment: Challenging Conventional Wisdom?" *Economic Journal* 110 (462): C80–92. Shows that centralized bargaining helps the MNE but hurts the host country.

Naylor, Robin, and Michele Santoni. 2003. "Foreign Direct Investment and Wage Bargaining." *Journal of Interna-tional Trade and Economic Development* 12 (1): 1–18. Shows that FDI is less likely with greater union bargaining power or more substitutable products.

Skaksen, Mette Yde, and Jan Rose Sorensen. 2001. "Should Trade Unions Appreciate Foreign Direct Investment." *Journal of International Economics* 55 (2): 379–90. Shows that workers may lose or gain depending on the substitutability of multinational activities.

Slaughter, Matthew J. 2007. "Globalization and Declining Unionization in the United States." *Industrial Relations* 46 (2): 329–46. Finds significant correlation between falling union coverage and rising inward FDI.

Zhao, Laixun. 2001. "Unionization, Vertical Markets, and the Outsourcing of Multinationals." *Journal of International Economics* 55: 187–202. Analyzes horizontal and vertical MNE under unionization. References include many other contributions on union and FDI.

Zhao, Laixun, and Makoto Okamura. 2008. "Competing to Invest in the Foreign Market." Working Paper No. 217. Research Institute for Economics & Business, Kobe University. Presents cases of FDI benefiting the labor union, the MNE, as well as the host country.

LAIXUN ZHAO

■ United Nations Conference on Trade and Development

The United Nations Conference on Trade and Development (UNCTAD) was set up in 1964 as a forum for the negotiation of international trade policy issues that fell outside the scope of the General Agreement on Tariffs and Trade (GATT). In the 1990s, with the establishment of the World Trade Organization (WTO), it lost that function and has since become the UN body responsible for research, advocacy, and technical assistance on international trade issues.

The seeds of UNCTAD lie in the failure to establish an International Trade Organization (ITO) after World War II. Although negotiations for an ITO were concluded successfully in 1947–48, the United States subsequently failed to ratify the agreement and the ITO was stillborn. All that remained was an interim GATT, which covered the process for negotiating reduced tariffs on industrial goods traded across borders. This was of limited interest to developing countries that were then scarcely industrialized. Their major concern was the regulation of international trade in primary commodities, which had been provided for, to a limited extent, in the failed ITO agreement. During the 1950s, they pressed in the forum of the United Nations for new international machinery to address this and other issues of special interest to them.

Geopolitical circumstances proved favorable to their demands. As part of its Cold War tactics, the Soviet Union supported the developing countries' demand for a new international trade conference. The John F. Kennedy administration decided to abandon the U.S. government's public opposition to that proposal to prevent the issue from recruiting developing countries into the Soviet camp. As a result, the first UN Conference on Trade and Development was convened in Geneva from March to June 1964. The secretary-general was Raúl Prebisch, an Argentine economist who had previously been executive secretary of the UN Economic Commission for Latin America. The developing countries organized themselves into a caucus known as the Group of 77—even though its membership eventually exceeded 100.

Little was achieved initially, and the continued existence of the conference was at first in doubt, but eventually the United States agreed that it should reconvene. Thus UNCTAD is unlike most other international organizations. It is an international conference convened every four years in a different location and is serviced by a section of the UN Secretariat, based mainly in Geneva and numbering about 440 officials. Its governing organ, the Trade and Development Committee, meets regularly in Geneva between sessions of the conference to direct the Secretariat's programs.

Campaign for International Commodity Agreements The first several conferences were the site of negotiations on various trade issues that were not being negotiated in the GATT, but on which the UNCTAD Secretariat had produced a range of interventionist proposals. Most important, in 1974 UNCTAD emerged to international prominence as one of the forums for globally negotiating a New International Economic Order (NIEO). These negotiations centered on the Secretariat's proposal to extend the number of International Commodity Agreements (ICAs). The aim was to dampen the volatility of primary commodity prices, using a buffer stock mechanism, to be financed by a Common Fund that would also fund commodity diversification schemes.

This package of policies ultimately proved insufficiently attractive for the commodity-consuming countries, which did not really want a fund that they did not control and were more concerned about the security of oil supplies than security of supply of other primary commodities. The commodity-producing countries were also ultimately—for quite different reasons—ambivalent about it. Since many developing countries were highly dependent on just a few commodities, each was worried that a new Common Fund would weaken the control that they already exercised within existing ICAs over the commodities of special interest to them. In the end, no new ICAs emerged and the Common Fund that came into being was very much smaller than the $6 billion Fund first envisaged by Gamani Corea, UNCTAD's secretary-general from 1974 to 1980.

Post-NIEO Development UNCTAD has taken up a variety of other trade-related issues of special concern to developing countries. The transfer of technology was a concern that in the 1980s led to attempts to negotiate an international code of conduct on the subject. Projects of economic cooperation among developing countries were taken up as a theme in UNCTAD, as well as special issues affecting the least-developed countries. The results of this proliferation of activity following the NIEO failure were varied. It contributed to a loss of coherence and focus in the organization as a whole, as small units engaged on marginal and unrelated work multiplied. This fragmentation was aggravated by the UNCTAD Secretariat's growing practice of taking on technical assistance work as a subcontractor to other international public agencies. On the other side of the account, in some of these new niche activities, the UNCTAD Secretariat was able to develop special skills and deliver technical assistance that was valuable. By the 1990s, its sternest critics recognized its achievements in several important areas—the provision of information on statistics of international trade and of global data on private foreign investment—and specialized technical assistance in debt management systems.

UNCTAD has also maintained some high-quality publications that regularly analyze the world economic situation and its impact on trade, finance, and development. The annual *Trade and Development Report* series is preeminent in that respect. The UNCTAD Secretariat publishes several flagship reports, the others being the *World Investment Report* and *Least Developed Countries Report*.

Impact of the World Trade Organization The establishment in 1995 of the World Trade Organization (WTO) radically changed UNCTAD's position among the international trade institutions. In the presence of the WTO, it no longer made sense to have two international bodies for the negotiation of trade issues. The disempowerment of UNCTAD as a North-South negotiating forum started at UNCTAD VIII in Cartagena (1992) and was completed at UNCTAD IX at Midrand, South Africa (1996). After 1996, UNCTAD ceased to be a negotiating forum for world trade issues, and in line with this, it reduced the scale of its intergovernmental machinery and consolidated its divisional structure. It replaced 25 separate work programs and subprograms with 1 program consisting of 5 subprograms; it halved the number of intergovernmental bodies; it cut the number of meetings to one-third of what it had been in 1992; and it reduced the number of divisions in the secretariat from 9 to 5.

From 1996 on, its role has been ancillary to the WTO, providing a place to discuss trade and development issues, advocating for the views of developing countries, and offering advice and technical assistance to developing countries preparing for trade negotiations in the WTO. This reduction in function and size implied greater interagency cooperation

between UNCTAD and the WTO, building on previous GATT/UNCTAD cooperation, such as their joint International Trade Center to help developing countries to promote their exports.

The duration of each full session of UNCTAD has been shortened. The 11th session, held in July 2004 in Rio de Janeiro, lasted only a week and was used as a showcase for the organization and its remaining functions. As UNCTAD secretary-general from 1995 to 2005, Rubens Ricupero, himself a former trade negotiator for Brazil, was successful in adapting UNCTAD to this more modest role, and thereby gaining the goodwill of G8 governments. As of 2008, the current secretary-general is Panitchpakdi Supachai of Thailand, who was director-general of the WTO from 2002 to 2005.

No longer a forum for major global trade negotiations, UNCTAD is confined to carrying out international trade research, advocacy, and technical assistance functions and acting as a junior partner of the WTO.

See also trade and economic development, international; World Trade Organization

FURTHER READING

Corea, Gamani. 1992. *Taming Commodity Markets: The Integrated Program and the Common Fund in UNCTAD*. Manchester, UK: Manchester University Press. A history of the NIEO negotiation by a former UNCTAD secretary-general.

Griffin, Keith. 2003. "Economic Globalization and Institutions of Global Governance." *Development and Change* 34 (5): 789–808. Places UNCTAD within the spectrum of global governance institutions.

Henderson, David. 1998. "International Agencies and Cross-Border Liberalization." In *The WTO as an International Organization*, edited by Anne Krueger. Chicago: University of Chicago Press, 97–130. A critical and comparative evaluation of international bodies concerned with trade.

Toye, Richard. 2003. "Developing Multilateralism: The Havana Charter and the Fight for the International Trade Organization, 1947–48." *International History Review* 25 (June): 282–305. An account of the negotiations around the failed ITO and GATT.

Toye, John, and Richard Toye. 2004. *The UN and Global Political Economy.* Bloomington: Indiana University Press. A recent history of the role of economists within UNCTAD.

United Nations. 1985. *The History of UNCTAD: 1964–84.* Geneva: UNCTAD. An in-house 20-year history of UNCTAD.

———. 2004. *Beyond Conventional Wisdom in Development Policy: An Intellectual History of UNCTAD, 1964–2004.* Geneva: UNCTAD. An in-house 40-year intellectual history of UNCTAD.

JOHN TOYE

Uruguay Round

The Uruguay Round of multilateral trade negotiations (1986–94) was launched during a period when the world economy was experiencing slow growth. Stagflation—a mix of rising prices, weak output growth, and rising unemployment—was complemented by a debt crisis that affected a number of major developing countries. The need for developing countries to generate foreign exchange to service debt, the rapid growth of export capacity for labor-intensive manufactures such as textiles and clothing in East Asian economies (the "newly industrializing countries" or "East Asian tigers"), and rising trade imbalances gave rise to strong pressures to restrict imports in major countries of the Organisation for Economic Co-operation and Development (OECD).

Although large-scale protectionism was avoided during the late 1970s and early 1980s, extensive recourse was made to quantitative import restrictions, "voluntary" export restraint agreements (VERs), and anti-dumping actions. Trade restrictions formed part of an inappropriate policy response to structural adjustment pressures. Starting in the early 1980s, a number of contracting parties to the General Agreement on Tariffs and Trade (GATT) suggested that renewed efforts were needed to strengthen the trading system to address both rising protectionist pressures and to subject key areas of trade policy to multilateral disciplines. Of central importance was agriculture—largely exempted from GATT disciplines—and the Multifiber Arrangement (MFA), a complex system of bilateral trade restrictions that had been put in place to manage trade in textiles and clothing. In addition the United States argued for expanding the coverage of multilateral rules to new areas such as trade in services, intellectual property rights, and investment.

The Uruguay Round was the eighth round of trade negotiations under GATT auspices. It was very ambitious, spanning many more subjects than any of its predecessors or its successor, the Doha Round. Among the major achievements of the Uruguay Round were the creation of the World Trade Organization, new multilateral disciplines for trade in services and intellectual property, and the reintegration of agriculture into the trade regime. It also led to further liberalization of international trade in merchandise. In addition to an average 40 percent cut in tariff bindings, there was agreement to abolish quantitative restrictions on textiles and clothing trade over a 10-year period and, for the first time, to impose specific limits on agricultural export subsidies and trade-distorting production support. Few observers at the time had expected such an ambitious outcome to be feasible. At numerous points during the eight-year marathon the talks came close to failure. Their successful conclusion marks a high point for multilateral cooperation in the 20th century.

The process that led to the establishment of the negotiating agenda for the Uruguay Round took five years, starting with the preparation for a 1982 ministerial meeting on trade, during which the United States sought but failed to obtain agreement to launch a new round. This failure was not surprising as the previous round, the Tokyo Round, had only recently been concluded. The work program that was agreed at the 1982 ministerial laid the foundation for the Uruguay Round, however. Working groups were established to review, among other topics, the use of quantitative restrictions, agricultural trade policies, and trade in services. In March 1985 a study group established by Arthur Dunkel, Director-General of the GATT, and chaired by Fritz Leutwiler, the president of the Swiss central bank, who had been actively involved in efforts to address the ongoing debt crisis, issued the Leutwiler report. This provided support for the launch of new negotiations to tackle trade restrictions in agriculture and labor-intensive manufactures.

The 18 months after the publication of the Leutwiler report saw active efforts by proponents and opponents of a new round. The former spanned the OECD countries and many developing countries, especially in East Asia, that confronted trade restrictions in export markets. The latter comprised a number of developing countries, including India. By the time of the 1986 ministerial meeting in Punta del Este, Uruguay, the majority of the GATT contracting parties supported launch of a new round of negotiations. The main opponents—a group of ten developing countries (the G10, which included Argentina, Brazil, Cuba, Egypt, India, Nicaragua, Nigeria, Peru, Tanzania, and Yugoslavia)—sought to make new negotiations conditional on so-called standstill and rollback of existing trade restrictions imposed by OECD nations. They also rejected launching talks on services, trade-related aspects of intellectual property rights (IPRs), and trade-related investment measures (TRIMs).

The majority prevailed, adopting a compromise draft text proposed by Colombia and Switzerland. The major concession to the G10 was agreement that the services negotiations would proceed on a parallel track to talks on goods and that disagreements on IPRs and TRIMs would not be allowed to affect progress in other areas. Notwithstanding this procedural agreement, it was agreed that the negotiations were to be a "single undertaking."

The Negotiations: 1986–93 The talks spanned 14 areas related to trade in goods, plus services. The 14 subjects were tariffs, nontariff measures, tropical products, natural resource–based products, textiles and clothing, agriculture, GATT articles (rules), safeguards, the codes of conduct negotiated during the Tokyo Round, subsidies and countervailing measures, dispute settlement, trade-related aspects of IPRs, TRIMs, and "the functioning of the trading system." It was agreed that the talks were to be concluded by the end of 1990

and that there would be a midterm review meeting in the course of 1988.

The midterm review was held in Montreal in December 1988. Differences on agriculture dominated the meeting, but there was disagreement on other subjects as well, including liberalization of trade in textiles and clothing, how to deal with safeguard actions and VERs, and the scope of ambition regarding protection of intellectual property. Instead of an "early harvest" of agreements in a variety of areas, the meeting failed and the midterm review was suspended. The primary reason was the huge disparity in objectives on agriculture between the United States and the EU, with the former insisting that complete liberalization should be the long-term goal. Given that no compromise seemed possible, the main protagonists suggested that ministers sign off on interim agreements that had been reached in other areas and instruct negotiators to return to Geneva and continue efforts to negotiate on agriculture. This "solution" to the deadlock was rejected by a number of Latin American countries. For the first time in GATT negotiating history, developing countries made it clear to the EU and the United States that their differences would not define the outcome of a meeting. The result was a decision by ministers to suspend the Uruguay Round for four months—giving time to negotiators to come up with a substantive compromise on the outstanding issues, and making agreement on all other matters conditional on consensus regarding progress on agriculture. The Montreal meeting made clear that the EU had to make substantive commitments to liberalize trade in agriculture. Not doing so would mean the end of the Uruguay Round. The compromise that was hammered out in the subsequent months largely revolved around ideas proposed by the Cairns Group (see the next section).

During 1989–90 negotiations in all areas continued, the goal being to finalize negotiations at a December 1990 ministerial meeting. This meeting, held in Brussels, also ended in failure—reflecting substantive disagreements in a number of areas, but particularly in agriculture. The failure did not come as a surprise. The draft Final Act submitted to ministers had a huge amount of "square-bracketed" text, indicating alternative options or proposals on a subject, as well as "open questions." The unwillingness of the EU to make policy reform commitments on a commodity and instrument basis—a key demand of exporting countries—forced the round into overtime. The bottleneck was very similar to what would emerge in the Doha Round—strong resistance by the EU to suggestions that border protection be reduced and export subsidies constrained.

Talks continued through 1991, leading to a new draft Final Act in December 1991 encompassing some 30 negotiated agreements, including a proposed framework for market access commitments. Again it was agriculture that precluded agreement, with the EU and several in the Cairns Group rejecting the overall package. Although another two years of negotiations would be needed to conclude the deal, in the end the contours established by the 1991 draft final act—the so-called Dunkel text—defined what was ultimately agreed. What was missing were the specific market access commitments of the countries participating in the negotiations. This became the focal point for bargaining in 1992–93, which eventually led to a deal under the leadership of a new Director-General, Peter Sutherland, appointed in mid-1993.

In June 1993, the U.S. Congress granted an extension of fast-track authority to the U.S. Administration—under which Congress could not propose amendments to the outcome of negotiations—setting a December 15 deadline for talks to be concluded. This proved to be an effective focal point—the substantive negotiations were concluded on December 13, 1993. In Marrakesh, on April 15, 1994, ministers signed the Final Act establishing the World Trade Organization (WTO) and embodying the results of the Uruguay Round.

Key Issue Areas What follows briefly discusses a number of the main negotiating topics that figured in the final "grand bargain."

Tariffs In contrast to the previous two rounds (Kennedy and Tokyo), in the Uruguay Round negotiators did not use a formula approach to cut tariffs. Instead they reverted to an item-by-item, request-offer approach. This reflected the U.S. view that because average MFN tariffs were low, it made more sense to focus talks on specific sectors and on tariff peaks. Although a large number of countries would have preferred to use a formula approach, the United States prevailed. The result of the negotiations was to lower the average bound tariffs on manufactured products of industrial countries, weighted by the volume of trade in the products concerned, from 6.4 percent to 4.0 percent, a cut of some 40 percent. This compares with a weighted-average duty of about 25 percent before the creation of GATT (1947) and around 15 percent at the time of the Dillon Round (the early 1960s). Developing-country participation as measured by the scope of tariff bindings increased substantially during the Uruguay Round, with the percentage of bound lines increasing from 22 to 72 percent. In addition, all countries agreed to bind 100 percent of their agricultural tariff lines.

Agriculture The Punta del Este declaration broke new ground in making an explicit reference to liberalization, with all policies affecting agricultural trade to be discussed, including domestic and export subsidies. This contrasted with the Kennedy and Tokyo Round ministerial declarations, which emphasized the status of agriculture as a special (unique) sector and were oriented toward the negotiation of commodity-specific agreements. The Uruguay Round talks on agriculture were largely between the United States and a group of 14 other agricultural exporters that sought significant liberalization, and a set of countries that provided heavy protection for their farmers: the EU, other European countries (Switzerland, Norway, and Finland), Japan, and South Korea.

The coalition of 14 exporters was called the Cairns Group, after the Australian city that hosted the meeting at which it was established. Members included Argentina, Australia, Brazil, Canada, Chile, Colombia, Fiji, Hungary, Indonesia, Malaysia, New Zealand, the Philippines, Thailand, and Uruguay. It therefore had both high-income and developing country members, illustrating that on agriculture—in contrast to IPRs, safeguards, and textiles and clothing—the negotiations did not involve a North-

South split. The objective of the Cairns Group was to gradually attain free trade in agricultural commodities, eliminate production distortions, and ensure that binding undertakings to this effect were negotiated. The United States initially called for the complete liberalization of trade in agriculture, including the abolition of all export subsidies. The EU, in contrast, initially proposed that negotiations adopt the approach used in past GATT talks: focus on "emergency measures" for specific commodities such as cereals and sugar to reduce supply and seek to stabilize world agricultural markets. The differences between the United States and the EU were therefore very great: one proposing free trade, the other "managed trade." The Cairns Group was less extreme in pushing for liberalization than the United States, but took a position much closer to that of the United States than that of the EU and other protectionist countries.

Bridging the gap between the EU and the U.S.-Cairns positions proved extremely difficult, not only because of fundamental, substantive differences, but also because of the negotiating strategies that were pursued. Although it was clearly unacceptable to the EU, for the first two years the United States maintained its demand for the total elimination of trade-distorting support policies within 10 years. As already noted, the resulting standoff led to the breakdown of the Montreal midterm review of the round in December 1988. The April 1989 compromise was that the objective would be "substantial progressive reductions in agricultural support," to be implemented through specific commitments and/or agreement on a maximum "aggregate measure of support" (AMS).

At the December 1990 ministerial meeting in Brussels, the EU refused to accept the compromise text proposed by the chairman of the negotiating group—which would have averaged a cut of about 25 percent in protection levels. This had significant implications for EU farm policy, the reform of which was under active discussion at the time. The EU needed to settle its internal debates on agriculture first—in particular to placate the French, who opposed any significant move toward meeting U.S.-Cairns Group demands. Latin American members of

the Cairns Group played a major role in opposing any significant weakening of the chairman's proposed text. Argentina and Brazil refused to accept the proposed deal and were ready to scuttle the Uruguay Round over the issue.

An agreement between the EU and the United States was eventually reached—after much brinkmanship—with the so-called Blair House Accord in November 1992. Under the deal, EU policies to pay farmers to take land out of production would not be included in the definition of the Aggregate Measure of Support, nor would similar U.S. payments. The two players also agreed that the proposed 20 percent reduction in the AMS would be an average cut and not apply on a product-by-product basis and that the volume of exports benefiting from export subsidies would be cut by 21 percent.

Textiles and Clothing Liberalization of trade in textiles and clothing was a key demand of developing-country exporters, in particular those that were most restricted under the MFA. Negotiations were difficult. Major areas of disagreement concerned the modalities of phasing out the MFA, the implementation period, and the need for special safeguards. All these matters were eventually negotiated without the brinkmanship and breakdowns that characterized the agricultural negotiations. The deal stipulated that the MFA would be phased out over a 10-year period (1995–2004) in four stages. In 1995, quantitative restrictions affecting at least 16 percent of product lines were to be removed, in 1998 another 17 percent, in 2002 a further 18 percent, followed by the remaining 49 percent at the end of 2004. This did not imply the removal of all trade barriers: tariffs would continue to be imposed. As a result of the Uruguay Round, average tariffs were reduced to a trade-weighted average of 12.1 percent, down from 15 percent.

Services The move to consider rules for trade in services originated with the United States, which had a large services trade surplus. Early in the negotiations, many developing countries argued for a narrow definition of trade in services, excluding sales of services by foreign affiliates of multinational firms. These countries also emphasized the need for governments to remain unconstrained in their freedom to discriminate against foreign suppliers of services, including inward foreign direct investment (FDI). A consequence was outright rejection of any suggestion that the principle of national treatment apply to services. The EU disagreed with developing countries on how trade in services should be defined, arguing that all types of transactions required to achieve effective market access should be covered, including FDI. The EU agreed, however, that a multilateral agreement on trade in services should not necessarily involve far-reaching obligations of a generally binding nature. Specifically it proposed that national treatment be a specific commitment, to be negotiated on a sector-by-sector basis. As was the case in agriculture, the United States made the most far-reaching proposal, arguing that the nondiscrimination principle should apply to all countries as a binding, general obligation and that all measures limiting market access should be on the table.

Given the lukewarm interest of many developing countries in services negotiations, the EU position emerged as the compromise. In return for acceptance that trade in services be defined broadly to include FDI, national treatment would be sector specific and not a general commitment. In addition, commitments could be made on a limited number of specific policies deemed to restrict access to markets. Virtually all commitments made in the Uruguay Round were of a lock-in nature, that is, a promise not to become more restrictive than what was implied by actually prevailing policies for specific sectors.

In the closing days of the Uruguay Round it became clear that it would be difficult to come to closure on a number of services sectors, including financial services, basic telecommunications, maritime transportation, and one important mode of supply: movement of natural persons (service providers). (Air transportation was excluded from the negotiations altogether.) Rather than allow a situation to develop in which countries would withdraw previously negotiated commitments in these areas, it was agreed that talks on these services were to continue after the conclusion of the Uruguay Round. In addition, on a number of subjects where no agreement proved possible—subsidies, procurement, and safeguards—specific rules were left for future deliberations.

IPRs The negotiation on IPRs was one of the more difficult of the Uruguay Round, both politically and technically. The subject was new to the GATT. Moreover, in contrast to agriculture, it involved a North-South confrontation. Industrial countries, led by the United States, sought an ambitious and comprehensive agreement on standards of protection for IPRs, enforceable through the dispute settlement mechanism. The G10 and other developing countries sought to differentiate discussions on trade in counterfeit goods from IPRs more broadly defined, indicating a willingness to cooperate on the former but not the latter. A general concern was that greater protection of IPRs would strengthen the monopoly power of multinational companies and detrimentally affect poor populations by raising the price of medicines as well as other products.

The first two years of negotiations were dominated by disagreements over the mandate of the negotiating group. Areas of disagreement included standards of protection, use of unilateral sanctions, and the need for—and length of—transitional periods. One of the most difficult questions was whether it was acceptable for GATT contracting parties to draft substantive standards for IPRs. Some developing countries, led by India, argued that the trading system should not be in the business of setting or enforcing IPRs. This was a task for the World Intellectual Property Organization and national governments.

At the end of the day the outcome of negotiations was a far-reaching and comprehensive set of disciplines on IPRs. One reason why this was accepted by developing countries was that they obtained concessions in other areas that mattered more to them. Also important was that by agreeing to the inclusion of disciplines on IPRs, industrialized nations would no longer be able to impose unilateral sanctions on countries that they deemed to be violating IPRs. The United States in particular was an active user of such sanctions. Given a multilateral agreement on IPRs, multilateral dispute settlement procedures would apply. Finally, although the negotiations involved a confrontation between developing countries, led by India, and OECD nations, led by the United States, a number of developing countries felt that stricter IPR protection would be in their interest because it would encourage FDI, technology transfer, and innovation.

Safeguards and VERs Contingent protection was a key issue in the Uruguay Round. In the Tokyo Round, no agreement had proven possible on rules pertaining to safeguard actions—the reimposition of import barriers to protect domestic industries from serious injury caused by import competition. As noted previously, due to the global macroeconomic situation in the late 1970s and early 1980s, an increasing number of countries were imposing protectionist instruments, including in particular VERs. A major objective of developing country exporters—especially in East Asia—was to outlaw the use of these measures and to achieve stronger disciplines on the use of quantitative restrictions. In contrast to the Tokyo Round, these objectives were achieved, with not only agreement to abolish the Multifiber Arrangement that constrained trade in textiles and apparel, but also a new agreement on safeguards that banned VERs.

Other Subjects Space constraints preclude a discussion of the many other areas in which negotiations occurred. These resulted in many new disciplines on matters such as import licensing, customs valuation, product standards, nonagricultural subsidies, state-trading enterprises, TRIMs, transparency, and dispute settlement. The last subject was an important one. As a result of the round, significant changes were made to the way disputes are dealt with. Under the new WTO, countries would no longer be permitted to block adoption of dispute settlement findings by arbitration panels, instead being limited to appealing findings before a new Appellate Body whose rulings would be final.

Developing Countries Developing countries participated actively in the Uruguay Round negotiations and had a significant impact on the outcome. It became obvious that it was no longer appropriate to regard developing countries as a bloc (assuming this had ever been the case). Instead, countries pursued their self-interest and teamed up with high-income countries on a number of issues. The Cairns Group was just the most prominent example of a North-South coalition.

In contrast to the Kennedy and Tokyo Rounds, the Uruguay Round was a single undertaking: all agreements were to apply to all members. As a result, developing countries became subject to a large number of new obligations—some newly negotiated in the Uruguay Round, others originally negotiated during earlier rounds among industrialized nations. In recognition of the fact that the implementation burden associated with the round would fall heavily on developing countries, they were generally given longer transition periods.

The WTO The 1986 Punta del Este ministerial declaration made no mention of the possible creation of a new organization. A 1990 Canadian suggestion to establish a multilateral trade organization—supported by the EU—was therefore something of a surprise. The proposal was motivated by a desire to create a single institutional framework to encompass the modified GATT and the new agreements on services (the GATS) and intellectual property (TRIPS), as well as all other agreements and arrangements concluded under the auspices of the Uruguay Round. The United States initially opposed the idea of a new institutional framework, but eventually agreed to the creation of the World Trade Organization.

The Uruguay Round was a watershed event in the history of the trading system. In creating the WTO, it led to the realization of the original vision of those who had sought to create an international trade organization 50 years earlier but failed. It involved very active participation by developing countries and pragmatic cooperation between rich and poor nations on specific issues of mutual interest, and it illustrated that very politically sensitive policies could be subjected to multilateral disciplines. The "grand bargain" that was negotiated was a very complex one. Concerns that it was not sufficiently balanced became prominent in the years immediately following the conclusion of the round and were a major factor in the launch of the first round under WTO auspices, the Doha Round.

See also agricultural trade negotiations; Doha Round; General Agreement on Tariffs and Trade (GATT); General Agreement on Trade in Services (GATS); multilateral trade negotiations; World Trade Organization

FURTHER READING

Bhagwati, Jagdish, and Mathias Hirsch, eds. 1998. *The Uruguay Round and Beyond: Essays in Honor of Arthur Dunkel*. Ann Arbor: University of Michigan Press. A compilation of retrospectives by negotiators who participated in the round.

Croome, John. 1999. *Reshaping the World Trading System*. Leiden: Kluwer International. The best negotiating history of the round, discussing in depth the positions taken, compromises made, and the chronology of the negotiations.

Hoekman, Bernard, and Michel Kostecki. 2001. *The Political Economy of the World Trading System*. Oxford: Oxford University Press. Summarizes the law and economics of the Uruguay Round agreements, their genesis, and implementation.

Martin, Will, and L. Alan Winters, eds. 1996. *The Uruguay Round and the Developing Countries*. Cambridge: Cambridge University Press. Provides empirical assessments of the outcome of the negotiations.

Schott, Jeffrey, and Johanna Buurman. 1994. *The Uruguay Round: An Assessment*. Washington, DC: Institute for International Economics. Briefly summarizes and assesses all the results of the negotiations.

World Trade Organization. 2007. *World Trade Report 2007: Six Decades of Multilateral Trade Cooperation*. Geneva: WTO. An official review of the multilateral trading system that attempts to take a "long view" of the subject.

BERNARD HOEKMAN

■ vehicle currency

A vehicle currency is a reserve currency that central banks or monetary authorities use for the purpose of exchange intervention and the pricing of goods, services, and assets entering international trade and finance. A vehicle currency allows the nation issuing the currency to pay a somewhat lower price for imports, borrow at marginally lower rates, and earn seigniorage. The U.S. dollar is by far the most important vehicle currency in the world today. The euro (the currency of the European Monetary Union, or EMU) has also been used as an increasingly important vehicle currency since its creation in 1999.

A vehicle currency fulfills in the world economy the same basic functions that the currency performs in the economy of the nation. It serves as a unit of account (i.e., it is the primary invoicing currency for international commodity and asset trade), as a medium of international exchange (in that global foreign exchange transactions are overwhelmingly conducted in that currency), and as a store of value (i.e., it is the currency in which official reserve assets are primarily held by nations' central banks or monetary authorities). A national currency becomes a vehicle or international currency as a result of market forces that allow it to function as money for both private and official transactions in the world economy. The U.S. dollar serves as the vehicle currency par excellence in global foreign markets. More than 60 percent of the U.S. currency is actually held abroad.

During the 19th and early 20th centuries, the British pound sterling was the dominant vehicle currency. Since then, the international use of the U.S. dollar increased in step with the increase in the relative economic and political importance of the United States. After World War II, the dollar became the dominant vehicle currency. The reasons for the decline of the pound sterling and rise of the U.S. dollar as a vehicle currency after World War II were (1) the high rate of inflation in the United Kingdom and sharp fluctuation in the value of the pound compared with the low inflation in the United States and stability of the U.S. dollar during the late 1940s and early 1950s, (2) the existence of exchange controls in England in contrast to the relative openness of the U.S. financial market, and (3) the decline in the sterling area's share of world exports in comparison with the rise in the U.S. share. Today the pound sterling remains a vehicle currency, although to a much smaller extent than the U.S. dollar, because London remains a sophisticated international financial center. One indication of the changed international roles of the dollar and pound after World War II was the decision by the Organization of the Petroleum Exporting Countries (OPEC) in the mid-1970s to price petroleum in dollars instead of pounds.

Table 1 shows the relative importance of the dollar, the euro, and other major currencies in the world economy in 2004. The table shows that 44.1 percent of foreign exchange trading was in dollars, as compared with 18.6 percent in euros, 10.2 percent in Japanese yen, and smaller percentages in other currencies. The table also shows that 50.3 percent of international bank loans and 48.4 percent of

Table 1
Relative international importance of major currencies in 2004 (percent)

	Foreign exchange trading[a]	International bank loans[a]	International bond offering[a]	Trade invoicing[b]	Foreign exchange reserves[c]
U.S. dollar	44.1	50.3	48.4	52.0	65.9
Euro	18.6	51.0	44.3	24.8	24.9
Japanese yen	10.2	−7.6	1.2	4.7	3.9
Pound sterling	8.5	4.3	5.2	5.4	3.3
Swiss franc	3.1	0.4	−0.2	na	0.2
Other currencies	15.5	1.6	1.1	13.1	1.8

Sources:
[a]Bank of International Settlements, *Triennial Central Bank Survey* (Basle: BIS, March 2005) and BIS data set.
[b]P. Bekx, "The Implication of the Introduction of the Euro for Non-EU Countries," *Euro*, Paper No. 26, July 1998. Data are for 1995.
[c]*IMF, Annual Report* (Washington, DC: IMF, 2005).

international bond offerings were in dollars, and 52 percent of international trade invoicing was denominated in dollars. Also, 65.9 percent of foreign exchange reserves were held in U.S. dollars, as compared with much smaller percentages for the euro and other currencies.

Besides being the most important vehicle currency, the U.S. dollar is also used as the currency in a number of Latin American countries (Ecuador, El Salvador, Guatemala, and Panama), as well as in the Commonwealth of Puerto Rico and the U.S. Virgin Islands in the Caribbean, in a process called dollarization. Many developing countries also peg their currency to the U.S. dollar. Similarly, a number of small states use the euro as their national currency. Besides the 12 countries of the Eurozone, the euro also is the legal tender of Monaco, San Marino, Vatican City, Andorra, Montenegro, and Kosovo, as well as of the Eurozone overseas territories of French Guiana, Guadeloupe, Martinique, Mayotte, Reunion, and Saint Pierre et Miquelon. Slovenia adopted the euro on January 1, 2007. Cyprus, Estonia, Latvia, and Malta were scheduled to adopt the euro in 2008; Bulgaria, Slovakia, and Lithuania in 2009; the Czech Republic and Hungary in 2010; and Poland and Romania in 2011.

In recent years, the United States has faced unsustainably large trade deficits (exceeding 6.5 percent of gross domestic product—GDP—in 2005). Reducing U.S. trade deficits to sustainable levels (say, to 2 or 3 percent of GDP) may require, among other things, a large depreciation of the dollar. This could lead central banks or monetary authorities (particularly Asian ones, which are by far the largest foreign holders of dollar reserves) to reduce their holding of dollars and induce petroleum-exporting countries to switch to euros in the pricing of petroleum, and thus put at risk the vehicle-currency status of the dollar. Similar risks for the dollar arose at the time of the collapse of the Bretton Woods system in 1971, in the face of large U.S. trade deficits and the U.S. suspension of the dollar convertibility into gold. The dollar survived, however, and even increased its vehicle-currency status during the 1980s and 1990s because no other currency could assume that role. The situation is different today because of the existence of the euro as a possible alternative to the dollar. Although the vehicle-currency status of the dollar seems secure for now, the importance of the euro (and eventually of the Chinese yuan) is likely to grow at the expense of the dollar in the future (especially if Britain also adopts the euro), and these currencies could become as important vehicle currencies as the dollar if U.S. trade deficits remain excessive and the international value of the dollar falls significantly.

See also Bretton Woods system; convertibility; currency substitution and dollarization; dollar standard; dominant currency; euro; exchange rate regimes; foreign exchange intervention; global imbalances; gold standard, international; International Monetary Fund (IMF); international reserves; money supply; petrodollars, recycling of; reserve currency; seigniorage; special drawing rights; twin deficits

FURTHER READING

Bank of International Settlements (BIS). 2006. *Annual Report*. Basel: BIS. Report by the Bank for International Settlements on the world's financial and banking situation, including the use of vehicle currencies.

Cohen, B. J. 2000. *Life at the Top: International Currencies in the Twenty-First Century*. Princeton Essay in International Economics No. 221 (December). Princeton, NJ: Princeton University. An excellent discussion of the vehicle currencies during this century.

Golberg, Linda, and Cedric Tille. 2005. "Vehicle Currency Use in International Trade." Federal Reserve Bank of New York Staff Report No. 2000 (January). Estimates of the relative use of various vehicle currencies in international trade invoicing.

International Monetary Fund (IMF). 2006. *Annual Report*. Washington, DC: IMF. An analysis of the world's economic and financial situation by the International Monetary Fund; it includes a discussion of the relative use of various vehicle currencies.

Krugman, Paul. 1992. "The International Role of the Dollar." In *Currencies and Crises*, edited by Paul Krugman. Cambridge, MA: MIT Press, chapter 10. An analysis of the international role of the dollar before the creation of the euro.

Mundell, Robert A. 2000. "A Reconsideration of the Twentieth Century." *American Economic Review* 90 (June): 327–40. A review and interpretation of the operation of the international monetary system during the past century by a Nobel Prize recipient in economics.

"The Passing of the Buck?" 2004. *The Economist* (December 2), 78–82. A discussion of the possibility of the dollar losing its primary vehicle-currency role to the euro.

Salvatore, Dominick. 2004. "Euroization, Dollarization, and the International Monetary System." In *Monetary Unions and Hard Pegs*, edited by Volbert Alexander et al. New York: Oxford University Press, 27–40. Discusses the use of the euro and the dollar as vehicle currencies and their relationship to the operation of the present international monetary system.

Tavlas, George. 1998. "The International Use of Currencies: The U.S. Dollar and the Euro." *IMF Finance and Development* 35 (June): 46–49. Discusses trends in the international use of the dollar and assesses the possible impact of the euro in world financial markets.

DOMINICK SALVATORE

■ vertical versus horizontal foreign direct investment

Horizontal foreign direct investment (FDI), in which multiplant firms duplicate roughly the same activities in multiple countries, has been distinguished from vertical FDI, in which firms locate different stages of production in different countries. The bulk of FDI is horizontal rather than vertical. That developed countries are both the source and the host of most FDI suggests that market access is more important than reducing production costs as a motive for FDI.

Brainard (1993) reports that foreign affiliates owned by U.S. multinationals export only 13 percent of their overseas production back to the United States, so most production by U.S. multinationals appears to be motivated by the desire to serve markets abroad. Similarly, the U.S. affiliates of foreign multinationals export only 2 to 8 percent of their U.S. production back to their parents; 64 percent is sold in the U.S. market. The bulk of FDI is attracted to big markets, rather than to cheap labor (or other factors of production). The large volume of two-way FDI flows also seems to fit horizontal FDI models better than vertical ones.

Standard models of horizontal FDI revolve around the trade-off between plant-level fixed costs and trade costs (see Markusen 1984). When the potential host country is small, the potential savings in trade costs (which accrue per unit of exports to the country) are insufficient to offset the fixed costs of setting up a production facility there; hence, exports are chosen over FDI as the method for serving the market abroad. When a host country is large enough for the fixed costs of the plant to be offset by the trade costs saved, however, FDI is chosen over exports. Bigger market size of the host country, smaller plant-level fixed costs (smaller plant-level scale economies), and larger trade costs are more conducive to horizontal FDI. The *proximity-concentration hypothesis* refers to the common tenet that FDI occurs when the benefits of producing in a foreign market outweigh the loss of scale economies that could be reaped if produced in only one plant (in the firm's home country).

FDI may exist to avoid not only actual trade costs but feared trade costs as well. FDI, such as by Japanese firms into the European Union (EU) in electronics and into the Unites States in autos, may be motivated more by fear of impending trade barriers (anti-dumping duties or voluntary export restraints) than by any barriers in place at the time of the investments.

When the choice between FDI and exports involves a simple trade-off between trade costs and fixed costs, an interesting implication is that no firm should simultaneously engage in both FDI and exports. Even for the exact value of trade costs where the trade costs times the number of units exported equals the plant-level fixed costs, when the firm is exactly indifferent between FDI or exports, the firm will either pay the fixed costs to build the plant and serve the market exclusively through FDI, or not build the plant and serve the market only through exports.

Unlike horizontal FDI, with vertical FDI, firms engage in both FDI and exports. Whereas in horizontal FDI models, the two countries are often envisioned as being of similar size, in vertical FDI models, the home country is usually thought of as being much larger than the host country. Thus the horizontal FDI framework is more representative of a pair of developed countries, whereas the vertical FDI framework is like a developed source country and a developing host country. In horizontal FDI models, the question is how best to serve the host market (abroad), whereas in vertical FDI models, the question is typically how best to serve the domestic market.

Standard models of vertical FDI involve deciding where to locate production to minimize costs. Headquarters services are located in the home country; production of the good can be located with the headquarters in the home country or else separated from headquarters and located abroad. Production costs are assumed to be lower in the host country than at home. Hence the trade-off is between the lower costs of producing abroad and the need to pay trade costs to bring the goods back home. FDI occurs if the cost savings from producing abroad are greater than the trade costs incurred. Lower trade costs should encourage vertical FDI but discourage horizontal FDI. As trade costs fall, vertical FDI occurs for smaller differences in factor prices. In a simple setup where only one unit of labor is required to produce the good in either country, vertical FDI occurs if the wage difference across countries is greater than the trade costs. As vertical FDI is often called international *outsourcing/offshoring*, the production cost savings minus the trade costs can be called the gain from offshoring.

Anyone fearing that, as trade costs fall, all production will shift from rich countries such as the United States to poorer countries such as China or Mexico (where wages are lower) should bear in mind that the United States remains the largest recipient of FDI inflows. Also the comparison is not of wage levels alone, but efficiency wages—labor costs per unit of production. If wages elsewhere are one-tenth U.S. wages but workers are less than one-tenth as productive, labor there is not truly less expensive.

The *knowledge-capital model of the multinational enterprise* is an overarching model that includes both horizontal and vertical FDI as special cases. It has been used to test for evidence in support of horizontal versus vertical FDI. Most findings have been more supportive of horizontal FDI, but other research (such as Braconier, Norback, and Urban 2005) has emphasized that vertical FDI does indeed occur and is important to the host countries in which it occurs (sales by affiliates are large relative to GDP). Both horizontal and vertical FDI can occur in Markusen and Venables (2005)—the split between market-oriented and export platform activity depends mostly on trade costs, and factor endowments influence whether to specialize in components or assembly.

Given that the bulk of FDI is horizontal in nature, and that horizontal FDI is motivated by avoiding trade costs (tariff jumping), the trends in the 1990s were rather perplexing. Dramatic reductions in trade costs due to trade negotiations and technological change occurred together with substantial growth in FDI (outpacing the fast growth in world trade). Neary (2008) has put forth two potential explanations. He shows that cross-border mergers can be encouraged by reductions in trade costs. As mergers and acquisitions are quantitatively more important than greenfield investments (building from scratch), falling trade costs can be consistent with expansions in horizontal FDI. He also argues that horizontal FDI in trading blocks can be encouraged by trade liberalization within the trade block. When trade costs fall within the block, outside firms invest in one country as a means for serving the entire trade block. For example, a U.S. firm may produce in Ireland to serve all of Europe, or a German firm may produce in Canada to serve all of North America. These are examples of export-platform FDI, discussed below. Which explanation is most empirically relevant remains to be determined.

Export-Platform FDI Export-platform FDI is FDI motivated by a desire to export rather than to serve the local market. Vertical FDI is export-platform FDI where the exports are sent back to the home market. However, there is an increasing trend toward export-platform FDI where the exports are sent to third markets. The rise of trade blocks with low internal trade barriers but higher external barriers may contribute to this trend. Multinationals are establishing production subsidiaries within a trade block and using that plant to serve the entire block. To the degree that the host country is small relative to the overall size of the trade block, the vast bulk of production will be exported to other countries in the trade block.

Motta and Norman (1996) find that improved market access within a trade block leads to export-platform FDI in this manner. As an additional benefit, since FDI into the block becomes more attractive to outside firms, due to firms being better able to reach the majority of markets within the block through exports from one plant, the subsidies required to entice firms to locate in the block will be reduced. Instead of considering only the market size of a potential host country, firms now consider the broader, regional market that can be easily reached from the country. As trade blocks are often formed on a regional basis, avoiding artificial trade barriers (such as tariffs) and natural trade barriers (transportation costs) tend to go hand in hand.

Kumar (1998) emphasized the need to distinguish between export-platform FDI oriented toward the home market versus that oriented toward third countries. FDI for export back to the home market occurs to take advantage of cheaper factors of production elsewhere, and only trade costs between the home and host country matter. FDI for export to third countries, in contrast, is critically dependent on the ease of access to the third countries, and the trade costs back to the home market matter little.

Ekholm, Forslid, and Markusen (2007) further distinguish between three types of export-platform FDI. Home country export-platform FDI involves export back to the parent. Third-country export-platform FDI involves export to another large country (not home or host). With global export-platform FDI, the host plant exports to both the home country and the third country. When the home and the host countries form a free trade area, the outcome can be that the inside firm engages in home (or global) export-platform FDI, while the outsider firm opts for the third-country approach. Fitting this scenario, the North American affiliates of U.S. multinationals concentrate on exports back home, whereas affiliates in Europe concentrate on exports to third countries (see also Yeaple 2003). With the North American Free Trade Agreement, Mexico has seen increases in the share of production by affiliates of multinationals (both U.S. and from elsewhere) sent to the United States.

Using data for U.S. outbound FDI to members of the Organisation for Economic Co-operation and Development from 1980 to 2000, Blonigen et al. (2004) find evidence consistent with export-platform FDI in Europe. When measures of market potential (size of proximate third country markets) are included, they find a clear negative relationship between FDI into proximate countries. This pattern of substitution between industrialized countries in Europe provides strong evidence of export-platform FDI. Ireland is the EU economy most successful in attracting export-platform FDI.

The implications of export-platform FDI need further study. For example, when multinational enterprises (MNEs) use the host country as an export platform, local firms are often not competitors (unless also exporting) and thus the MNEs need not worry about restricting technology spillovers. As there is less risk of damaging local competitors, local governments may view export-platform FDI more favorably than FDI for the purpose of serving the local market. While there are potential employment gains from both, export-platform FDI does not generate the gains in consumer surplus that market-access motivated FDI would.

See also fixed costs and foreign direct investment; knowledge-capital model of the multinational enterprise; market size and foreign direct investment; outsourcing/offshoring; proximity-concentration hypothesis; trade costs and foreign direct investment

FURTHER READING

Blonigen, Bruce A., Ronald B. Davies, Glen R. Waddell, and Helen T. Naughton. 2004. "FDI in Space: Spatial Autoregressive Relationships in Foreign Direct Investment." NBER Working Paper No. 10939. Cambridge, MA: National Bureau of Economic Research. Available at http://www.nber.org/papers/w10939.pdf. Finds evidence consistent with export platform FDI in Europe.

Braconier, Henrik, Pehr-Johan Norback, and Dieter Urban. 2005. "Multinational Enterprises and Wage Costs: Vertical FDI Revisited." *Journal of International Economics* 67 (2): 446–70. Evidence in support of vertical FDI.

Brainard, S. Lael. 1993. "An Empirical Assessment of the Factor Proportions Explanation of Multinational Sales." NBER Working Paper No. 4583. Cambridge, MA: National Bureau of Economic Research. Available at http://nber15.nber.org/papers/w4583.pdf. Finds little support for factor proportion motivation for FDI.

Ekholm, Karolina, Rikard Forslid, and James R. Markusen. 2007. "Export-Platform Foreign Direct Investment." *Journal of the European Economic Association* 5 (4): 776–95. Examines conditions under which three different types of export platform FDI arise: back to MNE's home country, to a third country, or globally (to both).

Kumar, Nagesh. 1998. "Multinational Enterprises, Regional Economic Integration, and Export-Platform Production in the Host Countries: An Empirical Analysis for the U.S. and Japanese Corporations." *Weltwirtschaftliches Archiv/Review of World Economics* 134 (3): 450–83. Contrasts the determinants of production for export back to MNE's home market to those for export to third-country markets.

Markusen, James R. 1995. "The Boundaries of Multinational Enterprises and the Theory of International Trade." *Journal of Economic Perspectives* 9 (2): 169–89. Excellent review of empirical evidence on multinational firms.

————. 1984. "Multinationals, Multiplant Economies, and the Gains from Trade." *Journal of International Economics* 16 (3–4): 205–26. The original model of horizontal FDI.

Markusen, James R., and Anthony J. Venables. 2005. "A Multi-Country Approach to Factor-Proportions Trade and Trade Costs." NBER Working Papers No. 11051. Cambridge, MA: National Bureau of Economic Research. Available at http://www.nber.org/papers/w11051.pdf. Model where both horizontal and vertical FDI occur.

Motta, Massimo, and George Norman. 1996. "Does Economic Integration Cause Foreign Direct Investment?" *International Economic Review* 37 (4): 757–83. Three-country, three-firm model showing how improved market access within a region leads to export-platform FDI as outside firms invest in the region.

Neary, J. Peter. 2008. "Trade Costs and Foreign Direct Investment." In *Foreign Direct Investment and the Multinational Enterprise*, edited by Steven Brakman and Harry Garretsen. Cambridge, MA: MIT Press, 13–38. Provides two explanations for how falling trade costs can generate increased FDI, as seen in the data.

Yeaple, Stephen Ross. 2003. "The Complex Integration Strategies of Multinationals and Cross-Country Dependencies in the Structure of Foreign Direct Investment." *Journal of International Economics* 60 (2): 293–314. Describes how strategies of multinationals are richer than just horizontal or just vertical FDI.

AMY JOCELYN GLASS

■ **voluntary export restraints**

See quotas

■ **wages**

See trade and wages

■ **Washington consensus**

The term *Washington consensus* was coined by John Williamson (1990) to encapsulate the set of policy reforms advocated with a reasonable degree of consensus by international financial institutions, the U.S. government, the Federal Reserve Board, and the leading think tanks based in Washington. Those policies were deemed necessary to achieve growth, low inflation, a viable balance of payments, and equitable income distribution in the developing world at large, and especially in Latin America, which was still recovering from the debt crisis that erupted in 1982. The policies that defined the Washington consensus included (1) fiscal discipline, (2) increased public expenditure on social services and infrastructure, (3) tax reform to broaden tax bases and reduce marginal tax rates, (4) market-determined interest rates, (5) unified and competitive exchange rates, (6) import liberalization, (7) openness to foreign direct investment, (8) privatization, (9) deregulation, and (10) secure property rights.

As the term evolved in the 1990s, it became synonymous with the main policies promoted consensually by the International Monetary Fund (IMF), the World Bank, and the U.S. Treasury, with an emphasis on macroeconomic stability through sound fiscal and monetary policies, and a wider role for markets in relation to governments in the allocation

of resources through privatization, trade and capital account liberalization, and domestic market deregulation. The prescription to stabilize, privatize, and liberalize had gained traction among many policymakers in developing countries since the 1980s as import substitution and interventionist policies had led to bloated bureaucracies, grossly inefficient state-owned enterprises, unsustainable public indebtedness, inflation, and slow or even negative growth. The collapse of the Soviet bloc and the success of countries, such as Chile, that had already experimented with the new policies, contributed to their acceptance in the early 1990s. The limited role of government and the expanded role of markets have led some to refer to Washington consensus policies as "neoliberal" or based on "market fundamentalism," an expression that does not do justice to the scope and richness of the policies, especially those originally listed by Williamson (1990). This entry adopts the more recent and more widely used meaning of Washington consensus policies, in spite of its partial overlap with Williamson's list.

The Set of Policies For convenience, Washington consensus policies can be divided into macroeconomic and microeconomic, or structural, policies. The macroeconomic policies are mostly concerned with achieving price stability (more strictly, low inflation rates) and preventing foreign exchange or public debt crises. The cornerstone of macroeconomic stability is fiscal discipline. This need not imply a balanced budget, but rather a fiscal position that does not lead to a rising debt to gross domestic product (GDP) ratio, loss of international currency reserves, or (unacceptably high or rising) inflation (caused by monetary financing of the deficit), and therefore is "sustainable" without major policy adjustments.

Monetary discipline, a second key element of macroeconomic stability, is best achieved when monetary policy instruments (the intervention interest rate, open market operations, etc.) are aimed at controlling the supply of money and/or the price level and not at reaching other objectives such as accelerating growth or reducing unemployment. Central bank independence from government and other sources of political interference is additionally seen as facilitating monetary discipline.

Though no consensus exists in regard to the exchange rate regime most conducive to macroeconomic stability, it is well established that fixed or pegged exchange rate systems make monetary policy instruments ineffective in an environment of international capital mobility. Furthermore, fixed exchange rates insufficiently backed by international reserves may induce speculative attacks that often lead to abrupt exchange rate corrections. Nonetheless, fully floating exchange rates are seldom desirable, as central banks cannot allow exchange rates to freely fluctuate when a large portion of government or private sector debts are denominated in foreign currency and therefore exposed to exchange rate risks, as is the case in most Latin American countries (an attitude known as "fear of floating"). Thus international financial institutions often advocate for strong international reserve positions and limited reliance on external finance as precautionary measures to weather potential external shocks.

Given a sound macroeconomic framework, structural policies are primarily intended to stimulate and sustain growth by facilitating the functioning of markets and minimizing government interference in economic agents' decisions regarding investment, saving, consumption, and work. This entails lifting tariff barriers and other restrictions on international trade (*trade liberalization*); eliminating restrictions on foreign direct investment and on the free movement of funds in and out of the country (*capital account liberalization*); privatizing state-owned en-

terprises and opening to private investment industries previously controlled by the public sector, such as telecommunications, electricity, or mining (*privatization*); reducing bank reserve requirements and dismantling interest rate controls, subsidized loan programs, and directed credit systems (*financial liberalization*); simplifying the tax code, lowering tax rates, and widening tax bases (*tax reform*); facilitating labor hiring and firing, eliminating wage controls, simplifying the labor code, and reducing payroll taxes (*labor deregulation*); and lifting price controls and license requirements, and easing the procedures for entry and exit of firms (*goods markets deregulation*).

The Extent of Policy Reform Little reform had taken place in the developing world before 1989, but the launch of the Brady Plan by the U.S. government (an initiative to convert the nonperforming bank debts of the developing countries into long-term bonds to restore access by those countries to international finance) and the fall of the Berlin Wall that year signaled the beginning of ambitious macroeconomic and structural reforms in Latin America, Eastern Europe, and the former Soviet Union.

The extent of macroeconomic reforms in the following decade and their degree of success were remarkable. The incidence of high inflation rates among developing countries declined sharply, and median inflation rates among medium-income countries declined from 16 percent in 1990 to 6 percent a decade later. The overall fiscal deficit of developing countries, which had reached 7 percent of GDP in the early 1980s, has remained approximately 2–3 percent of GDP since 1990. By the end of the 1990s, the median developing country posted a primary surplus (the fiscal balance excluding interest payments). In addition, the volatility of key macroeconomic variables such as economic growth and real exchange rates declined in the 1990s, though partially in response to a more stable external environment.

The extent of microeconomic, or structural, reform since the late 1980s has also been substantial, especially in Latin America and the countries of the former Soviet bloc, although the effects of this reform remain a matter of intense debate. Aside from Chile, which slashed import tariffs and lifted other restrictions on international trade, liberalized the financial sector, privatized many state-owned enterprises, and streamlined the tax and labor codes under the Pinochet dictatorship (1973–90), no other country in Latin America had fully embraced structural reform until the late 1980s, when the Brady Plan created the opportunity of attracting much-needed external capital by adopting the "right" set of policies in the view of international financial institutions and investors. According to reform indexes computed for Latin America, trade and financial liberalization took off first and advanced furthest in the majority of countries. Privatization and tax reforms were more uneven in depth and timing, while labor reform was timid and erratic. Argentina, Bolivia, and Peru were among the most aggressive reformers, while Costa Rica, Ecuador, Mexico, Uruguay, and Venezuela undertook more cautious but nonetheless substantial reforms. Reform lost momentum in the second half of the 1990s, and major reversals took place after 2000 in Argentina, Bolivia, and Venezuela as governments reintroduced a variety of price controls and international trade restrictions. In some cases entire sectors were expropriated, as in the case of Bolivia's natural gas sector.

The reform process was no less turbulent in the former Soviet bloc countries, where it was part of the larger project of state formation that followed the breakup of the USSR (making it more difficult to judge the success of the new policies). Wage and price deregulation, two of the most important components of labor and goods markets deregulation, were undertaken in most countries at the beginning of the transition process, but then stalled and even reversed in some countries after the mid-1990s. A dozen years after the collapse of the Soviet bloc, domestic markets were still almost as heavily regulated as before in Belarus, Moldova, and Uzbekistan. The liberalization of external trade, investment, and finance, on the other hand, has represented a more gradual but sustained process, although as of the first years of the 21st century that process remained incipient in Azerbaijan, Belarus, Turkmenistan, and Uzbekistan. Although the transition from communist to market

economies offered the former Soviet bloc countries ample opportunities for privatization, the reform indexes available suggest that only a handful of countries (Armenia, Bulgaria, the Czech Republic, Hungary, Macedonia, and Slovakia) have privatized the vast majority of their economic activity. As of 2001, the process had barely progressed in Slovenia and Turkmenistan and had suffered drastic reversals in Russia and Uzbekistan.

The process of microeconomic reform varied even more across time, country, and area of reform among the African countries. In the area of financial liberalization, Africa went from a completely dirigiste stance in the mid-1980s to freely moving interest rates and greater flexibility in bank operations in the late 1990s. State-owned financial institutions still intermediated a sizable portion of domestic credit, however, and restrictions on the allocation of credit abounded. Trade liberalization also advanced substantially, but many countries continued to impose high import tariffs and import and export licensing restrictions in the late 1990s. African countries were likewise reluctant to engage in capital account liberalization during the 1980s. Around the mid-1990s most countries undertook at least partial reforms, but many countries continue to require some form of authorization for the acquisition of firms by foreign investors and for portfolio investments by foreigners. Countries in Africa privatized less and more reluctantly than Latin American or transition countries. Less than 40 percent of Africa's state-owned enterprises were affected by privatization, and only four countries—Ghana, Côte d'Ivoire, Nigeria, and Zambia—accounted for a third of all transactions between 1991 and 2001, worth just $9.1 billion.

Assessment Washington consensus policies have been widely criticized for their ineffectiveness in delivering more macroeconomic stability and higher growth—their two main objectives—as well as for their social and distributional effects.

Although macroeconomic stability vastly improved in the developing world in the 1990s, it failed to reach developed-country levels, and countries remained vulnerable to extreme macroeconomic events such as banking crises, currency crashes, and sudden interruptions in capital flows, or "sudden stops." Argentina, a close follower of the Washington consensus recommendations, nonetheless experienced a severe economic crisis in 2001 and 2002: the exchange rate was devalued by more than 300 percent, the government defaulted on its debt obligations, and economic activity and employment collapsed. The inadequate policy conditions imposed by the IMF on the countries affected by the Asian crisis of 1998 are also offered as evidence of the failure of the Washington consensus to prevent macroeconomic instability.

Among the main shortcomings of the policies advocated are sequencing problems (particularly the premature liberalization of capital flows without adequate financial regulation), excessive reliance on high interest rates to contain aggregate demand, price and exchange rate pressures (at the risk of worsening or precipitating a financial or a debt crisis), and inadequate fiscal adjustment that exacerbates busts and weakens economic recovery. The Washington consensus is further criticized for inadequate international financial architecture to respond to the needs of countries in crisis or facing speculative attacks and to prevent "sudden stops."

All of these objections, however, are subject to intense debate. There is no widespread agreement on whether capital controls are effective in moderating or stabilizing capital flows, or whether financial systems isolated from international competition can be adequately regulated. When fiscal sustainability is at risk (for instance, as a result of a sudden interruption in credit access or a decline in the country's terms of trade), interest rate increases or public expenditure cuts may be necessary in order to prevent further capital outflows, currency depreciation, and inflation. Finally, there is intense debate regarding the role the IMF and other international financial institutions should play in preventing and responding to crises, as bailouts and other forms of support may encourage lack of macroeconomic discipline.

The effects of Washington consensus policies on growth have been a contentious issue since their outset. The lackluster performance of Latin America in relation to other regions, especially the fast-growing countries of East Asia, is often offered as evidence of their modest effect. Econometric evidence for Latin America and the transition economies of the former Soviet bloc suggests that Washington consensus policies had positive, but only weak and transitory, effects on growth. The main explanations for this modest growth effect include insufficient depth and completeness of policies and reforms, excessive use of macroeconomic policies to achieve price stability rather than promote growth, sequencing problems (capital account liberalization, domestic financial liberalization, or privatization prior to the regulatory reforms needed to prevent financial instability and market manipulation), and a host of other implementation problems, due especially to lack of institutional support to administer trade reforms, facilitate resource reallocation, prevent corruption, and implement regulatory reforms. Other critics contend that stimulating and sustaining growth requires removing only the most binding constraints, rather than completing the ambitious list of reforms prescribed by the Washington consensus or its augmented versions, which incorporate a variety of institutional or "second-generation" reforms as well as social policies.

The view that Washington consensus policies have deleterious social effects is presently so widespread as to seem beyond discussion. But the empirical evidence is mixed at best. In many countries in Latin America and Africa, trade liberalization had a negative effect on employment in the sectors affected by import competition, which was not compensated by employment creation in the exporting sectors. Nonetheless trade liberalization and privatization produced both winners and losers among the poor, depending on their sectors of activity and their consumption baskets, and there is virtually no empirical support for the view that aggregate poverty was increased by these reforms.

Much more debate attends the distributional consequences of Washington consensus policies. The fact that trade openness may increase inequality in developing countries seems to go against standard economic theory (or at least theory rooted in the simplest version of the Heckscher-Ohlin model of international trade), since trade should increase the income accruing to the relatively abundant factor, presumably unskilled labor. This effect may be muted or even reversed, however, where trade protection before liberalization was focused on labor-intensive products, as in the case of Mexico, or where the most abundant factor of production is natural resources, as could be the case in Russia or some of the South American countries. Contrary to popular belief, privatizing utilities did not hurt the poor, as the quality and coverage of services improved, while the impact of privatization on income distribution was moderate in Latin American countries, but substantial in some of the ex-communist countries.

An Evolving Concept The terms *Washington confusion* and *Washington contentious*, among others, have been used to convey the state of disarray of the economic, institutional, and social policies advocated by international financial institutions more than a decade after the original Washington consensus. Among the international financial organizations and some Washington-based think tanks, the view prevails that the Washington consensus can deliver growth, stability, and equality if it is "augmented" with a variety of institutional reforms to strengthen state capabilities and with more encompassing and ambitious social policies. In academia, however, as well as in some segments of the World Bank and other organizations, it is argued that a more comprehensive list of policy requirements can hardly be a useful guide for governments short of political support, technical expertise, and administrative capabilities. Furthermore, although no one disputes the importance of macroeconomic stability, secure property rights, market-oriented incentives, outward orientation, and government provision of basic public goods, it is becoming widely accepted that there are no standard prescriptions for achieving these goals. If a new consensus is emerging it is based on the recognition that economic policy reform is always constrained by institutional and political economy factors, which are even harder to reform.

See also capital controls; economic development; evolution of development thinking; financial liberalization;

Heckscher-Ohlin model; import substitution industrialization; International Monetary Fund (IMF); political economy of policy reform; sequencing of financial sector reform; trade and economic development, international; World Bank

FURTHER READING

Birdsall, Nancy, and Augusto de la Torre. 2001. *Washington Contentious. Economic Policies for Social Equity in Latin America*. Washington, DC: Carnegie Endowment for International Peace, Inter-American Dialogue. The best example of the expanded Washington consensus promoted by leading Washington think tanks.

Kuczynski, Pedro-Pablo, and John Williamson, eds. 2003. *After the Washington Consensus: Restarting Growth and Reform in Latin America*. Washington, DC: Institute for International Economics. Puts forward a new economic policy agenda "that the region should be pursuing after a decade that was punctuated by crises, achieved disappointingly slow growth, and saw no improvement in the region's highly skewed income distribution."

Stiglitz, Joseph E. 2002. *Globalization and Its Discontents*. New York: W. W. Norton. This worldwide bestseller should better be titled "The Washington Consensus and Its Discontents." The author is a Nobel Prize laureate who served as economic advisor to the U.S. government and as chief economist of the World Bank during the heyday of the Washington consensus (1993–2000).

Williamson, John, ed. 1990. *Latin American Adjustment: How Much Has Happened*. Washington, D.C.: Institute for International Economics. The book that coined the term and first assessed the extent of policy reform in Latin America and the Caribbean.

World Bank. 2005. *Economic Growth in the 1990s: Learning from a Decade of Reform,* Washington, DC: World Bank. A balanced and comprehensive review of the achievements and shortcomings of the Washington consensus.

EDUARDO LORA

■ West African Economic and Monetary Union

See Economic Community of West African States (ECOWAS)

■ World Bank

The World Bank (henceforth "the bank") is a multilateral institution devoted to the promotion, worldwide, of sustainable economic development and poverty reduction. The bank was established as the International Bank for Reconstruction and Development (IBRD), in Bretton Woods, New Hampshire, in July 1944, and its Articles of Agreement entered into force in December 1945. The International Monetary Fund was set up at the same time: together, the fund and the bank became the "Bretton Woods institutions." The role of the fund in the Bretton Woods system was to administer the international monetary system, initially in the form of a system of fixed but adjustable exchange rates (House, Vines, and Corden 2008). The initial rationale for the bank, in a world where dollars were in short supply and international capital flows were limited, was the provision of low-interest finance for postwar reconstruction.

The rapidity of the postwar recovery, and decolonization in the 1960s, meant that IBRD activities came to be refocused on development and in particular on infrastructure investment. The IBRD operated, as it still does, by borrowing in its own name and then lending on to borrowing governments for public sector projects at a small margin. However it was soon found that, despite evident needs, it was difficult to justify investments on these semicommercial criteria in many developing economies. As a result, the International Development Agency (IDA) was established in 1960 to lend capital from IBRD profits, augmented by funds donated by "Part I" governments to poor "Part II" countries, on an interest-free basis with long grace periods. IDA is a development agency, not a financial institution. The post-1960 bank is therefore a more complex hybrid agency than the one established in 1944.

This more complex bank does three things.

The Bank as a Multilateral Lending Institution. The bank borrows at AAA rates on international markets and then on-lends the funds to countries. This remains the largest of the bank's activities. IBRD lending, financed from this source, averaged $12.8 billion per annum out of a total lending averaging $21.5 billion per year over fiscal years 2002–7. The bank's actual lending (i.e., the total of its disbursed and outstanding loans) stood at $98 billion in 2007; its outstanding IDA development credits amounted to $102 billion, making a total of $200 billion (World Bank 2006).

The bank is able to borrow funds at rates lower than the London interbank offered rate because countries are reluctant to default on loans from an international institution, because the bank is able to provide additional lending to prevent default arising from inability to pay, and also because it has a buffer of "callable capital"—money that member countries have an obligation to contribute if the bank were ever to get into financial difficulties. The bank lends funds to governments with a margin over the cost-of-funds, which makes a contribution to the bank's operational costs. This margin includes a commitment fee and has typically been in the region of 25 to 40 basis points. The bank is able to make this margin because of its advantages, compared with private banks, in having much lower default risk. IDA credits are interest-free but are subject to a commitment fee and a service charge which, in 2007, amounted to 95 basis points.

The Bank as Development Agency. The most basic rationale for development policy is to rectify market failures in the development process. In the early stages of development, these arise particularly because of the complementarity between activities, many of which become profitable only when other activities are already established. As a result of these failures, private sector enterprises may be unable to capture the social returns from potential investments. Governments can assist by undertaking investment projects in which private returns fall short of social returns. This can raise potential returns on private sector projects, thereby stimulating private sector investment.

Undertaking such policies would normally be identified as a role for domestic government. The bank, as a global, multilateral institution, has been involved in these activities partly because its knowledge and experience of development allow it to identify and address these needs more effectively than can governments themselves. In many of the poorest of developing countries governments lack the capacity to operate such policy, and in addition, governments are often constrained by the politics of rent seeking. This government-failure view leads the bank to impose conditions on its loans and to monitor the projects in which it invests.

There are also global public-good aspects of good development policies. "Global commons" problems exist when a situation negatively affects many countries simultaneously. Examples are environmental pollution, the management of global capital flows, and the elimination of drug trafficking. Because the costs of global commons problems are so widespread, they require global solutions. The bank has played a significant role in work of this kind.

The Bank as Provider of Aid. Through its IDA arm, the bank carries out international development assistance directed toward the reduction of poverty. In doing this it provides concessional loans with a large aid component. Arguments for such aid rest on the idea of countries being stuck in a poverty trap from which escape is difficult without assistance from abroad (see Sachs 2005). The use of a multilateral institution such as the bank to provide these funds allows richer countries to give aid to poorer countries without this leading to direct bilateral political power relations with them. Channeling aid through a multilateral agency enables donors to precommit not to impose political conditions or economic conditions such as tying the aid to purchases of the donor country's goods.

The bank's ambition is to promote growth and alleviate the *causes* of poverty, rather than just to alleviate the *symptoms* of poverty. Reduction of poverty in this way came to the fore during the tenure of James Wolfensohn as bank president from 1995 to 2005. It is now widely accepted that poverty reduction through capability building is a necessary precondition for sustainable development.

Criticisms The bank has been heavily criticized by a wide range of people. Their criticisms generally fall into five categories. The first two criticisms are associated with left-wing critics and, more recently, with the anti-globalization movement. The third and

fourth have been associated with professional economists and the right wing of the political spectrum. The final criticism has been voiced by both political scientists and anti-globalization activists.

1. Is the Bank "Neoliberal"? The bank has been accused of imposing "neoliberal" economic policies on countries under the guise of structural adjustment. *Neoliberal* is a label widely attached by international relations scholars to those who see economic development as arising from the pursuance of free market policies (of the kind recommended by neoclassical economics) in conjunction with liberal, democratic political processes. John Williamson coined the term *Washington consensus* to describe those who think about economic development in this way. The majority of professional economists trained in British and U.S. universities over the past two decades would position themselves broadly within such a paradigm, and this is reflected in the bank's staff. Non-economists often see such a position as ideological; professional economists justify their position using both theory and evidence.

These debates are central to an understanding of the structural adjustment policies used by the bank since the 1980s. Prior to that time, the bank had lent almost exclusively for projects, but with the drying up of private flows to developing countries in response to the default by Mexico in 1982, and subsequently elsewhere in Latin America, countries' foreign exchange requirements outstripped the availability of attractive projects. On the "neoliberal" view that countries' abilities to respond were inhibited by over-large public sectors and lack of competition, the bank started to lend to finance reform (see Gilbert and Vines 2000; Mallaby 2004). The critics are correct in arguing that governments were pushed into adopting reforms that they would not otherwise have chosen. But most economists would argue that the critics are incorrect in suggesting that alternative policies might have enabled countries to cope with these problems with greater success or at lower cost. Evidence supporting this position comes, for example, from Tanzania, which attempted to go it alone until the mid-1990s but since reforming has seen much faster growth.

2. Conditionality The bank makes reform of policy a condition for its lending. Hopkins et al. (2000) set out the rationale for the bank's conditionality. The bank's status as a multilateral development agency enables it to impose these conditions, which are designed to improve outcomes. As described earlier, the bank's status allows it to lend at a rate that safeguards its debt servicing and repayment, reducing its risk premium and lowering costs of funds so that they are only marginally above its borrowing rate and less then the rate at which countries would be able to borrow from private markets. The imposition of conditions is a feature of the bank's operations that allows it to lend in circumstances that the private sector avoids.

Critics focus on how these conditions interfere with the sovereignty of the borrowing governments. If the critics' arguments were accepted and the bank was prevented from conditioning its lending on what it regards as appropriate policies, it would be unable to act as a financial intermediary in the way that it does.

But conditionality can lead to policy incoherence, since it results in time inconsistency. Recipient governments may agree ex ante to policy conditions if they see this as a means of attracting future loans or aid support. However, once the aid is disbursed these incentives are diminished, the reforms agreed to in the conditions will not be "owned," resulting in weak implementation, and in certain cases, governments may renege on the conditions to which they had previously agreed. The bank's response to a problem of this type has been to restructure its decisions as a repeated game by designing aid programs that include shorter horizons and more detailed conditions. But governments then have the incentive to hold back from reform and exaggerate its costs. An agile government may be able to sell the same reform several times (see Collier 2000).

As a result, there is a widespread view that bank policy conditionality has been not only undesirable but ineffective as well. Evidence comes in three forms—from case studies, from the bank's own assessments, and from econometric studies (see World Bank 2005 for a concise summary of the large litera-

ature). The failure of conditionality can be put down to a number of difficulties: implementation problems and the impact of external shocks (weather, commodity prices, etc.) that can throw plans off course, the overriding importance of domestic politics in determining policy and a failure of "ownership" of reforms, and the inadequacy of penalties and rewards that the bank can impose in the context of these political imperatives.

These negative findings have prompted the view that the bank should give up on the kind of policy conditionality described above (Burnside and Dollar 2000; Collier 2000). Instead the bank should recognize that there are "good" types and "bad" types of countries, and it should direct aid at the "good" types rather than trying to control the behavior of its clients. The bank should advocate and push for the adoption of policies that are consistent with its accumulated knowledge and practical experience. Governments will have an incentive to pay heed to this advice, because the bank bases its advice on its accumulated knowledge and because following this advice will induce future assistance from the bank: the bank should direct its lending and aid selectively toward countries that have demonstrated that they have good policies. A large component of bank activity in countries with poor policy environments would then become educational.

3. Aid Dependency The aid dependency thesis has been most cogently argued by Easterly (2006) and, in more qualified terms, by Collier (2007). It is an attack on the development agency role of the bank, or at least the way this role has been implemented hitherto. The bank lends to governments but, in Easterly's view, it is individuals and firms who promote development. Lending to governments reinforces the power of groups who have little to gain from development and who in any case can contribute little to that process. Collier particularly focuses on how bad governance and corruption can prevent development. He criticizes the provision of aid, both in countries where it is in danger of being used to further political conflict and in resource-rich countries in which the pursuit of resource rents can come to stifle development.

Both Collier and Easterly seek a substantial redirection of multilateral aid efforts. In part, this might mean a shift of resources within the bank toward the IFC, but it also requires new thought on what aid is effective. Much of the policy debate over the past two decades has been directed toward the question of "Where is aid effective?" We now need to ask, "In those countries in which aid has not hitherto been highly effective, what sort of aid may be effective?"

4. Lending to Emerging Market Economies Critics on the right have argued that the bank should withdraw from lending to middle income countries, because they are now able to access international capital markets on their own. These critics want the bank to retreat to being a development agency concerning itself purely with low-income countries that lack this access (see International Advisory Commission 2000). Ironically, moving in this direction would produce the same effects as those sought by left critics who wish to deny the bank the ability to impose policy conditionalities

The critics of bank lending to emerging markets fail to understand that without its lending to middle income countries, the bank would find its development assistance role in low income countries severely restricted—the bank's current mode of operation depends on this lending. In the absence of a major increase in multilateral funding for development assistance, this financial intermediation function is required to generate the funds for development assistance. For example, in 2007, the bank received about $1 billion in income from its $40 billion of reserves. It also received profits on market-based lending of about $800 million and $800 million from fees charged to countries that borrow from the soft-loan IDA operations. If the bank were to cease market-based lending, then, even if it kept its reserves, it would forgo $800 million or so in annual revenue. According to Mallaby (2004, 409–10), that would not be enough to cover the administrative budget ($1.7 billion) plus the annual transfers that the bank now makes to the IDA ($300 million) and the HIPC debt relief fund ($240 million).

5. Representativeness The final set of criticisms relates to the bank's governance. The bank is governed by a 24-member Executive Board. Although board decisions are almost always consensual, the threat of a vote makes the distribution of votes important. This distribution in part reflects financial contributions to the bank's activities but even more, the status and power of countries in the 1944 Bretton Woods meeting. Uniquely, the United States has veto power on this board. European countries and Japan, together with the United States, make up a significant proportion of the voting strength. Sub-Saharan Africa, which is now the bank's most important client constituency, has the smallest share of votes—19 percent of IDA votes (2007) in relation to 48 percent of IDA credits (2002–7 average). By unwritten convention, the United States has the power to appoint the president, something which proved unpopular both when Paul Wolfowitz was appointed to replace James Wolfensohn in 2005 and when Robert Zoellick was appointed after Wolfowitz was forced to resign in 2007. There is now considerable pressure to reform the governance and voting structure of the organization, to make it more representative (see Woods 2006).

There is general agreement that both the board voting structure and the procedures for appointment of a president need to be overhauled, but as with the similar debates relating to the IMF and the UN Security Council, there is less agreement on the precise reforms, and in particular on which countries should be the beneficiaries of the reforms. The paramount danger in these reform proposals is that, in becoming more representative and democratic, the bank may also become less effective. Concretely, if a reformed bank were to advocate policies that donor country governments considered likely to be ineffective or counterproductive, they would reduce support for multilateral assistance. UNCTAD provides an example of a development institution in which all countries have equal voting power, and which has provided an effective forum in which developing countries can express their views. It has never enjoyed sufficient funding to have a major developmental impact.

The Bank as a "Bundled" Institution The bank has led global development research and has been important in promoting debate, and fostering consensus, on the conditions and policies that will result in sustainable growth. A famous example is the role played by the bank in the early 1980s in the promotion of more open trade policies. This remains true in such diverse areas as poverty reduction strategies, governance, and financial regulation. Although few argue that the bank has originated major new ideas or directions in development economics, bank staff have generated a large volume of empirical research that has been fundamental in the assessment of the scale of problems (e.g., levels and changes in world poverty), the importance of different responses, and the applicability of possible policy reforms (e.g., on aging and HIV/AIDS) (see Squire 2000). World Bank (1998) brings together the results of a large body of important research in the bank on the effectiveness of aid. Gilbert and Vines (2000) refer to this as the "Knowledge Bank."

The bank's operation requires it to "bundle" together this knowledge of development work with its profitable lending to middle-income emerging market economies. This lending enables the bank to generate profits to support its other activities. We can think of the bank as rather like a large private American university, which uses its endowment income and income from lending to subsidize its research and teaching (see Gilbert and Vines 2000).

Squire (2000) clearly describes the value of this bundling: "Without an in-house capacity, integrating the results of research into the World Bank's everyday operations and making those results available to policy-makers in developing countries does not happen. This usually requires an in-house champion, and the best champion is usually the best researcher." Thus the bank brings both research and money. Accountability in relation to the expenditure of public money forces research applicability. And the bank's research culture ensures that projects are directed more closely to developmental and poverty reduction objectives than would otherwise be the case: money carries ideas.

It is hard to see how else this bundling of knowledge and money could be provided. In private banks, or private consulting companies, there will always be cost-minimizing pressures to cut the knowledge overhead, subject merely to satisfactory product (i.e., research) quality. Furthermore private banks have no incentive to disseminate knowledge and make their experience widely available, and consulting firms do so only at a price substantially in excess of the marginal cost of dissemination. By contrast, university research departments produce knowledge, but not necessarily of the kind needed for good policy. In addition knowledge about best-practice development policy is a global public good, requiring a global solution to the provision-problem of the kind that the bank provides. Many reforms of policy that work in one country will tend to work elsewhere; there are significant economies of scale and scope in the development of knowledge about development. It is difficult for individual governments to provide these goods.

Gilbert and Vines (2000) argue that such bundling can also help one to better understand bank conditionality. Conditionality may be necessary if the bank is to be able to lend where commercial banks are unwilling to enter. But the bank's knowledge is necessary to determine what constitutes good development policies and also to identify conditions for the reform of policies of a kind that governments will be willing to "own."

The conception of the bank as a Knowledge Bank is central to this account of what the bank does. The bank's lending provides income from endowment and revenue earned in the provision of loans. This funds the activities of the bank as a development agency, including the production of research that increases the effectiveness of both the lending and the aid that the bank provides.

As emphasized earlier, it is important that countries get the *right* combination of money and knowledge. In the countries with good policies and strong institutions the emphasis should be on money. In countries where the policy environment is poor, either because of an unsatisfactory macroeconomic and trade framework or because of poorly performing public institutions, the emphasis must be on getting these policy and institutional prerequisites right.

See also aid, international; evolution of development thinking; structural adjustment; Washington consensus

FURTHER READING

Burnside, C., and D. Dollar. 2000. "Aid, Growth, the Incentive Regime, and Poverty Reduction." In *The World Bank: Policies and Structure*, edited by C. L. Gilbert and D. Vines. Cambridge: Cambridge University Press, chapter 8. Argues that aid should be directed to countries with good policies.

Collier P. 2000. "Conditionality, Dependence, and Policy Coordination: Three Current Debates in Aid Policy." In *The World Bank: Policies and Structure*, edited by C. L. Gilbert and D. Vines. Cambridge: Cambridge University Press, chapter 12. Critical of the effectiveness of conditionality as practiced by the World Bank.

———. 2007. *The Bottom Billion*. Oxford: Oxford University Press. Examines traps due to conflict, the natural resources "curse," geography, and poor governance, and argues that aid ought to be used to enable countries to escape from these traps.

Easterly, W. 2006. *The White Man's Burden*. Oxford: Oxford University Press. Argues against a view that aid should be used in a big development push and in favor of a smaller amount of carefully targeted aid toward those who might use it best.

Gavin, M., and D. Rodrik. 1995. "The World Bank in Historical Perspective." *American Economic Review, Papers and Proceedings* 85 (2): 329–34. Useful historical account up until the mid-1990s.

Gilbert C. L., and D. Vines, eds. 2000. *The World Bank: Policies and Structure*. Cambridge: Cambridge University Press. An edited volume discussing how the bank's policies could be redirected toward it becoming a "Knowledge Bank" and how the bank's structure could be reformed to assist with this.

Hopkins, R., A. Powell, A. Roy, and C. L. Gilbert. 2000. "The World Bank, Conditionality, and the Comprehensive Development Framework." In *The World Bank: Policies and Structure*, edited by C. L. Gilbert and D. Vines. Cambridge: Cambridge University Press, chapter 11. Sets out the argument for conditionality and examines difficulties with it.

House, B., D. Vines, and W. M. Corden. 2008. "The International Monetary Fund." *New Palgrave Dictionary of Economics*. A discussion of the history of the IMF and its involvement in the resolution of financial crises, international macroeconomics surveillance, and the development of macroeconomic policies in the world's poorest countries.

International Advisory Commission. 2000. *Report of the International Financial Institution Advisory Commission*. Washington, DC: Government Printing Office. The report of a commission, chaired by Allan Meltzer, critical of the IMF and the World Bank and calling for their activities to be scaled back.

Kapur, D., J. Lewis, and R. Webb. 1998. *The World Bank: Its First Half Century*. Washington, DC: Brookings Institution. A careful and thorough history of the bank.

Mallaby, S. 2004. *The World's Banker: A Story of Failed States, Financial Crises, and the Wealth and Poverty of Nations*. New Haven, CT: Yale University Press. A biography of James Wolfensohn, president of the bank from 1995 to 2005, which is at the same time a gripping account of what the bank does and its history.

Sachs, J. 2005. *The End of Poverty*. New York: Penguin. Makes the case for a very large increase in aid in order to help lift the poorest countries out of poverty.

Squire, L. 2000. "Why the World Bank Should Be Involved in Development Research." In *The World Bank: Policies and Structure*, edited by C. L. Gilbert and D. Vines. Cambridge: Cambridge University Press, chapter 4. Argues that involvement in development research is central to the bank's mission of promoting good development policy.

Wolfensohn, J. 1999. "A Proposal for a Comprehensive Development Framework—A Discussion Draft." Washington, DC: World Bank. Available at http://www.worldbank.org/cdf/cdf-text.htm. Written by the former head of the bank, this document describes a set of principles to guide development and poverty reduction.

Woods, N. 2006. *The Globalizers*. Ithaca, NY: Cornell University Press. A revealing study of the relationships between the IMF, the World Bank, and their clients, and of the political processes that lead policies to be adopted.

World Bank. 1998. *Assessing Aid: What Works, What Doesn't, and Why?* Oxford: Oxford University Press. A systematic account of the possibilities and difficulties in the provision of aid.

———. 2005. *Review of World Bank Conditionality: The Theory and Practice of Conditionality, a Literature Review.* Washington, DC: World Bank.

———. 2006. *Annual Report.* Washington, DC: World Bank.

———, Operations Evaluation Department. 2005. *Improving the World Bank's Development Effectiveness: What Does Evaluation Show?* Washington, DC: World Bank.

CHRISTOPHER L. GILBERT AND DAVID VINES

■ World Economic Forum

The World Economic Forum (WEF) is one of the major instances of informal power influencing the world economy. Incorporated as a Swiss not-for-profit foundation whose members are among the world's 1,000 largest companies, the WEF is best known for the annual meetings, attracting around 3,000 participants, that it organizes in Davos, Switzerland, where chief executive officers (CEOs) meet world leaders, government officials, and a broad range of media, cultural, and academic executives identified as opinion leaders. It also organizes yearly meetings with more regional focuses, as well as ad hoc meetings related to the various initiatives it hosts under its Center for Public-Private Partnership.

The WEF has its origins in the Centre d'Etudes Industrielles of Geneva, one of the four executive business schools that had a key role in the managerial revolution following the Marshall Plan in postwar Europe. A junior faculty member, Klaus Schwab, was asked to prepare the 25th anniversary celebration of the institution, which was planned for 1971. He suggested celebrating by organizing a large conference in Davos mingling U.S. experts in management with European businessmen. He also conceived an artful legal artifice to keep control of the event and future initiatives. Thanks to the worldwide reputation of the Centre d'Etudes Industrielles, the conference attracted big names from American business schools and high-profile European industrialists. It is against this background that Klaus Schwab is known as the founder and president of the WEF. The scope of the forum quickly expanded beyond managerial questions to develop an agenda including macroeconomic, political, and strategic issues.

Since the early 1990s, the large increase in the number and prestige, as well as in the geographical and sectoral origins, of the participants has transformed the WEF into the world rallying point for which it is now known. The number of participants grew from fewer than 1,000 in 1971 to around 3,000 by 2007, more than half of whom are invited by the foundation to participate in panels, lend a high profile to the network, and ensure the greatest possible impact. While regular members pay around $20,000 a year to take part in the events, several dozen WEF partners pay more than ten times this amount to be entitled to direct input into the agendas of the meetings by setting up panels, choosing participants, and providing strategic positioning for their industries. Guests include several hundred political leaders and high-ranking officials, including around 20 chiefs of state or government each year; ministers; governors of central banks; directors of international organizations; Forum Fellows chosen from among academic scholars; executive officers of research foundations; some social, religious, and cultural celebrities; as well as around 500 editors and columnists from large press groups around the world. The apogee of the prestige of participants to the forum was probably reached in 2000 when for the first time the president of the United States, William J. Clinton, took part in the event with nine other political leaders of the Organisation for Economic Co-operation and Development (OECD).

Although the WEF advertises itself as an international organization committed to improving the state of the world by engaging leaders in partnerships on key issues to shape global, regional, and industry agendas, critics are prone to identify the WEF as nothing but a meeting place for world masters planning neoliberal globalization behind closed doors. Of course, those closely associated with the forum are inclined to deny its power, while those fiercely opposed are likely to emphasize its overarching influence. More broadly, however, these contrasting views of the influence and power of the WEF in global politics and economy express disagreement on one outstanding feature of the changes associated with globalization: the significance of the power exercised on a global scale by informal and weakly institutionalized nonstate actors.

The WEF presumably reflects the archetype of the most exclusive and powerful transnational elite club. Other groups include the Bildeberg conferences, the Trilateral Commission, the Clinton Global Initiative, or on a more regional basis, the U.S.-based Business Council and the European Round Table of Industrialists. The WEF is an extremely efficient infrastructure for piling up in three days appointments that would otherwise take three months, solving urgent matters among numerous actors, adding up pressure on the public agenda, and ensuring a large impact in elite circles, the media, and wider public opinion. Situated at the interface between economic and political aspects of the world order, it also embodies a strategic function in seeking to find a synthesis between the territorial basis of a legal and political order and the global reach of the world economy. This is why, for instance, key actors in the Middle East conflict such as Mahmoud Abbas, president of the Palestinian Authority, and Simon Peres, top Israeli politician for decades, can mingle with Eric Schmidt, cofounder and CEO of Google, or Matthew J. Cadbury, heir of the British Cadbury Schweppes agribusiness company. The WEF meetings and backup services provided by its secretariat play a crucial role not only in developing common strategies but also in raising collective consciousness among elites from different countries who get better acquainted and influence one another.

The contribution of elite groups like the WEF to the structure of power in the world economy takes two interrelated courses. On the one hand, they reinforce the formation of an overall class consciousness that transcends national and industry-based rivalries and embraces the global dimension of capitalism. On the other hand, they constitute a privileged locus for expanding this worldview to subordinated interests. Media and other dissemination channels target issues easily identified with the general interest. It is against this background that pleas for historic changes from top women and men in Davos should be understood. The WEF, however, faces intrinsic limits to its power. Its actual practices and organizational principles impair its power. It will always lack a recognized institutional basis. The bigger its suggested influence, the greater the problems it faces in legitimizing its informal power. The sheer size of the meetings, the huge media coverage, and the at times better-organized opposition requiring massive security measures have also tarnished the public image of the club atmosphere that made the WEF so successful.

Despite its continued attractiveness to world leaders for reinforcing their class consciousness, shaping the global agenda, and cutting deals, the WEF has tried to overcome these internal and external challenges since the early 2000s. Officials of the foundation have given a twist to its activities in order to bridge the gap between the loose influence of a closed club and a more focused engagement with states, intergovernmental organizations, and society at large in supporting the launch of various initiatives. Foundation officials and guests target a large range of commitments, from health to the digital divide, including education, gender, corruption, religion, energy challenges, and global warming. Although many of the participants drift apart eventually, some of them vie with other initiatives to concretely influence the policy agenda.

One of the self-proclaimed flagships of the WEF in this regard is the GAVI Alliance (Global Alliance for Vaccines and Immunization). Created as a global network of international development organizations, national governments, multilateral development banks, philanthropic organizations, and large corporations involved in vaccines and immunization, it was officially launched at the 2000 annual meeting at the initiative of the former World Health Organization director-general Gro Harlem Brundtland, in association with Bill Gates, CEO of Microsoft and cofounder of the Bill and Melinda Gates Foundation, and other regular participants to the WEF meetings. In December 2006, the amount actually disbursed since its creation reached $1.3 billion.

The Global Competitiveness Report is another well-advertised product of the WEF. It was created in 1979 in conjunction with the International Institute for Management Development, the top European executive business school located in Lausanne, Switzerland. The report uses a large quantity of data to build an index that ranks states according to the environment they provide for supporting the economy. The yearly release of the report in advance of the WEF annual meetings makes headlines. Although not at the same level as the conditionality imposed by international financial institutions on developing countries or the recommendations included in the OECD country and sectoral reports for industrialized countries, WEF competitiveness reports still operate at a distance. By shifting the focus away from management issues related to firm performance to competitiveness concerns in national business environments, they explicitly fulfill an agenda-setting function and contribute to harnessing state capacity to define overall economic orientations.

In conclusion, the WEF has achieved long-standing prominence among the various organizations designed to provide informal platforms for meetings, networking, lobbying, and strategic planning among an impressive list of world leaders. Like other platforms, the WEF claims wide public recognition on various issues as a forum of transnational private governance. Yet its loose and large influence is not without limits, as its so-called club atmosphere has faded away with the growth of its events, and it will always offer a privileged target for protesters and all those contesting its legitimacy. The future of the WEF clearly lies in the narrow path between persisting with its massive communication campaign supporting its public image and returning to a more intimate format that would preserve the discrete atmosphere for business leaders to meet with one another and with government officials.

See also anti-globalization; globalization; Group of Seven/Eight (G7/G8)

FURTHER READING

Berne Declaration. www.publiceye.ch. Web site of a coalition of nongovernmental organizations publicly engaging the WEF.

Graz, Jean-Christophe. 2003. "How Powerful Are Transnational Elite Clubs? The Social Myth of the World Economic Forum." *New Political Economy* 8 (3): 321–40. A scholarly account from an international political economy perspective, which relies on archival material and around 50 interviews.

Lapham, Lewis. 1998. *The Agony of Mammon.* London: Verso. A scathing account of two WEF annual meetings by the editor of *Harper's* magazine.

Pigman, Geoffrey. 2006. *The World Economic Forum.* London: Routledge. The only exhaustive, though uncritical, published monograph on the WEF.

Public Citizen's Global Trade Watch. 2002. *Davos World Economic Forum: Pricey Corporate Trade Association Loses Its Camouflage.* Washington D.C.: Public Citizen. A well-researched report from the division of the U.S. national consumer and environmental group promoting government and corporate accountability in the globalization and trade arena.

World Economic Forum. www.weforum.org. The official Web site of the WEF.

JEAN-CHRISTOPHE GRAZ

■ World Intellectual Property Organization

The World Intellectual Property Organization (WIPO) is the key international organization dealing exclusively with intellectual property rights. As such, and with more than 180 member states, it plays a pivotal role in the negotiation and establishment of intellectual property norms. It was founded in 1970 under the terms of a convention signed in Stockholm in 1967. Under a 1974 agreement, WIPO became a specialized agency of the United Nations.

History The origins of the organization lie in the 1893 merger of the secretariats (or "international bureaus") of the Paris and Berne unions, which made up the contracting parties to the two oldest and most important intellectual property treaties: the 1883 Paris Convention for the Protection of Industrial Property and the 1886 Berne Convention for the Protection of Literary and Artistic Works. The merged organization was known as the Bureaux Internationaux Réunis de la Protection de la Propriété Intellectuelle (BIRPI).

The idea of transforming BIRPI into an international intellectual property organization arose at a 1962 meeting of the Permanent Bureau of the Paris Union and the Berne Union. The meeting recommended the setting up of a Committee of Governmental Experts in order to consider administrative and structural reforms to the Paris and Berne Union systems and prepare for a diplomatic conference.

It is important to note that, during this time, the decolonization process that began just after World War II was gathering pace. Many new, developing countries were becoming independent and seeking to join the United Nations and other international organizations. The United Nations itself was undergoing a period of transformation as it sought to accommodate a rapidly increasing membership with a wide range of interests and concerns. Which parts of the UN system should have jurisdiction over complex and politically contentious matters such as intellectual property rule-making remained unresolved. In consequence, it was obvious that BIRPI could no longer remain as a developed-country "club" and needed a more multilateral character that could attract developing countries, including the newly independent ones.

Some developing nations had their own ideas about international intellectual property norm-setting, however, and were becoming assertive in expressing them. This was cause for concern in some quarters. Indeed, the proposal to establish a new organization based on BIRPI was intended in part to ensure that politicized organizations, including those known for accommodating the specific concerns of the developing countries, would not be chosen as the forum for negotiating intellectual property norms.

According to Stephen P. Ladas (1975), the intent was "to head off any attempt by outsiders, such as the United Nations Economic and Social Council or the United Nations Conference on Trade and Development, to deal with the subject of intellectual property and eventually to form a Specialized Agency of the United Nations in this field."

A second meeting of the committee took place in 1966 and was attended by representatives from 39 nations, of which 9 were developing countries. The rest were developed or European communist countries. The draft convention prepared by BIRPI on the basis of the views expressed by the committee at these two meetings was presented to a diplomatic conference in 1967 in Stockholm, where a final text was approved. The WIPO Secretariat, located in Geneva, Switzerland, is still known as the International Bureau.

Activities, Governance, and Mandate As of late 2007, WIPO administered 24 multilateral agreements. These were of three kinds:

1. *The standard-setting treaties*, which define agreed basic standards of protection for the different intellectual property rights. These include the Paris Convention; the Berne Convention; the 1961 Rome Convention for the Protection of Performers, Producers of Phonograms, and Broadcasting Organizations; the 1996 WIPO Copyright Treaty; and the 2006 Singapore Treaty on the Law of Trademarks.

2. *The global protection system treaties*, which facilitate filing or registering of rights in more than one country. These include the 1970 Patent Cooperation Treaty, the 1891 Madrid Agreement Concerning the International Registration of Marks, and the 1958 Lisbon Agreement for the Protection of Appellations of Origin and their International Registration.

3. *The classification treaties*, which are essentially administrative and concern the management and organization of information concerning patents, trademarks, and

industrial designs. These include the 1957 Nice Agreement Concerning the International Classification of Goods and Services for the Purposes of the Registration of Marks and the 1971 Strasbourg Agreement Concerning the International Patent Classification.

WIPO has three main governing bodies, which are the General Assembly, the Conference, and the Coordination Committee. There are also standing committees and working groups. It is an intergovernmental organization, but official observers are allowed to attend meetings subject to their compliance with certain criteria and procedures. These observers include other intergovernmental organizations and nongovernmental organizations. The latter category comprises not only groups representing business, intellectual property owners, and legal practitioners, which tend to favor intellectual property protection and support WIPO, but also groups whose views range from the very pro–intellectual property to the extremely critical.

What is WIPO's mandate? The organization's two objectives as stated in Article 3 of the convention are: (1) to promote the protection of intellectual property throughout the world through cooperation among states and, where appropriate, in collaboration with any other international organization; and (2) to ensure administrative cooperation among the unions. However, the 1974 agreement between the United Nations and the World Intellectual Property Organization balanced the goal of promoting intellectual property protection by recognizing WIPO's responsibility "for facilitating the transfer of technology related to industrial property to the developing countries in order to accelerate economic, social and cultural development, subject to the competence and responsibilities of the United Nations and its organs."

Recent Challenges WIPO briefly lost influence between 1986, when intellectual property was included in the Uruguay Round of trade negotiations, and 1994, when the Agreement on Trade-Related Aspects of Intellectual Property Rights (TRIPS) became part of the Agreement Establishing the World Trade Organization, and also for a short time afterward. But since then, WIPO has become a high-profile actor, raising levels of intellectual property protection in developing countries and driving the evolution of international intellectual property lawmaking in response to the opportunities and challenges arising from new technologies. For example, WIPO has proffered technical assistance to developing countries implementing TRIPS and provided a forum for the negotiation of new intellectual property treaties, including four since 1996. In addition, it has become a forum for substantive discussion of emerging intellectual property issues, including ones of interest to developing countries, such as protection of traditional knowledge and cultural expressions. Significantly, it is now a well-funded organization on account of the fees charged for services it provides to the private sector.

From time to time, WIPO is criticized for being biased, either in favor of the interests of the developing countries or in favor of those of industry and the developed countries. In the past few years, complaints have been made that it promotes intellectual property protection in ways that benefit transnational corporations but do not suit developing countries. For example, some critics, including governments, claim that WIPO's technical assistance programs for developing countries give insufficient attention to public interest exceptions to intellectual property rights.

Since 2004, 14 developing country WIPO members, led by Brazil and Argentina, have sought to establish a Development Agenda at WIPO to address the perceived bias. These countries, collectively known as the Friends of Development, argue that as a UN agency WIPO should be guided by the Millennium Development Goals, adopted by the UN General Assembly in 2000. To the 14 countries, the agenda should cover such issues as WIPO's mandate and governance, norm-setting, technical cooperation, and transfer of technology. As of late 2007, the agenda had not yet been approved. Nonetheless, the organization has had to position itself publicly as one whose work is dedicated to fostering economic development.

WIPO plays a substantial role in the world economy by dint of its involvement in promoting intellectual property rights internationally. The high commitment of so many governments and businesses to influence negotiations at WIPO is testament to the high economic stakes involved in the regulation of intellectual property rights at the global level. Because of the more obvious economic significance of the World Trade Organization, however, and the huge attention given to the TRIPS Agreement, WIPO tends to receive less attention from trade analysts than it probably should.

See also Agreement on Trade-Related Aspects of Intellectual Property Rights (TRIPS); intellectual property rights

FURTHER READING

Ladas, Stephen P. 1975. *Patents, Trademarks, and Related Rights: National and International Protection*. Vol. 1. Cambridge, MA: Harvard University Press. Contains a useful and informed historical view of the origins and antecedents of WIPO and clarifies the political context for the creation of the organization from the view of a person who was directly involved.

May, Christopher. 2007. *The World Intellectual Property Organization: Resurgence and the Development Agenda*. London: Routledge. The only book written specifically on WIPO. It explains how WIPO operates, describes the role of WIPO within contemporary global politics, and discusses its relationship with the World Trade Organization and the TRIPS Agreement.

Menescal, Andréa K. 2005. "Changing WIPO's Ways?—The 2004 Development Agenda in Historical Perspective." *Journal of World Intellectual Property* 8: 761–96. Well-researched account of WIPO's recent engagement in development-related intellectual property issues from a historical perspective.

Musungu, Sisule F., and Graham Dutfield. 2003. "Multilateral Agreements and a TRIPS-Plus World: The World Intellectual Property Organization." TRIPS Issues Paper No. 3. Geneva: Quaker United Nations Office. Available at http://www.quno.org/geneva/pdf/economic/Issues/Multilateral-Agreements-in-TRIPS-plus-English.pdf. Controversial critical examination of the institutional aspects of WIPO, including the internal architecture of the organization and the allegedly excessive influence of legal practitioner organizations and business associations.

UN Conference on Trade and Development and International Center for Trade and Sustainable Development. 2003. *Intellectual Property Rights: Implications for Development*. Geneva: UNCTAD-ICTSD Capacity Building Project on IPRs. Available at http://www.iprsonline.org/unctadictsd/policyDpaper.htm#policy. Written for an audience with a general interest in the subject, it describes the international intellectual property regulatory system and explains the central position of WIPO within it.

GRAHAM DUTFIELD

■ World Trade Organization

The World Trade Organization (WTO) is *the* international institution governing virtually all trade among its 151 members. As such, it serves two primary functions. First, it provides a set of multilaterally agreed rules that govern policies affecting (1) countries' trade in goods and services and (2) the protection of intellectual property of foreign nationals in member countries. By imposing certain disciplines on countries' trade-related policies, the rules covering trade in goods and services encourage international trade by making future access to foreign markets more predictable. Second, it provides a forum for (1) the day-to-day administration of the various WTO agreements, (2) the settlement of trade disputes among members, and (3) negotiations to further liberalize trade as well as to strengthen and extend the multilateral rules.

Between 1947 and 2007, first under the General Agreement on Tariffs and Trade (GATT), and then under the WTO, world merchandise trade expanded markedly faster than world production (6.2 percent a year on average versus 3.8 percent). It is no coincidence that this period of increasing international specialization, facilitated by the two rules-based multilateral agreements, was also a period of unparalleled prosperity for the world economy, with average per capita income growing more than twice as fast (2.1 percent a year versus 0.9 percent) as in the previous "boom" period of 1820–1913.

Around the time the WTO came into being, the growing share of output traded across national frontiers, coupled with expanded flows of foreign investment and technology, gave rise to what has become the economic catchword of our times: *globalization* (Wolf 2004). With the world's economies progressively more integrated—the essence of globalization— and economic prosperity more and more dependent on developments in world trade, the WTO is both the preeminent international economic organization and, inevitably, the international organization most closely linked in the public's mind with globalization.

Origin of the WTO After more than seven years of often arduous negotiations, the Uruguay Round— the eighth and final round of trade negotiations under the auspices of the GATT—ended successfully in December 1993. In April 1994 trade ministers meeting in Marrakesh, Morocco, signed the Uruguay Round Agreements, including the agreement establishing the WTO, and on January 1, 1995, the WTO came into being. With the subsequent entry of China—an event of major importance for the global economy—Chinese Taipei (Taiwan), and Saudi Arabia, and with the expected entry of Russia, the WTO's members will include all of the major trading nations (at the end of 2007 an additional 28 countries were in various stages of the accession process).

Although the WTO grew out of the GATT and embraces nearly all of the GATT's principles and practices, it is a distinctly different entity. In contrast to GATT's status as a provisional agreement among governments, the WTO is a formal international organization. The rules, which under the GATT covered only trade in goods, were extended to cover trade in services (telecommunications, banking, tourism, etc.) and the protection of intellectual property. Whereas the GATT had included limited membership agreements dating from the Tokyo Round negotiations (1973–79), all the major WTO agreements are binding on all the members.

The GATT, updated by the Uruguay Round, was absorbed by the WTO and became the umbrella treaty for trade in goods (the new agreement is re-ferred to as GATT 1994, the original one as GATT 1947). As noted earlier, the principles that guided the original GATT, along with virtually all of the key rules and procedures of the original GATT, can be found in the WTO.

Basic Principles Five time-tested basic principles carried over from the GATT—some explicit, some implicit—inform the rules and guide the activities of the WTO.

Nondiscrimination. The most-favored-nation (MFN) clause prohibits a WTO member from discriminating between imports of goods or services from other WTO members. By requiring a country to treat imports from all WTO members equally, the MFN rule depoliticizes trade (it also ensures that a country buys its imports from the cheapest foreign source). In the case of services (but not goods), countries could obtain at the inception of the services agreement, or on accession for new members, "MFN exemptions" to cover measures that would otherwise breach the MFN rule.

Some key exceptions to the MFN principle included in the GATT were carried over to the WTO, most notably the provisions for (1) free trade areas and customs unions among small groups of countries and (2) preferential treatment of imports from developing countries. With the rapid spread of preferential trading arrangements—especially free trade areas—beginning in the late 1980s, many trade experts openly question the practical relevance of the MFN rules (see, for example, Srinivasan 2005).

While the MFN clause enforces nondiscrimination at the border, the national treatment principle prohibits discrimination between imported *goods* and domestic products once the imports have entered the country. A retail sales tax applied to imported automobiles but not to domestically produced automobiles, for example, would violate the national treatment principle (however, imposing an import duty on foreign-made automobiles as they enter the country is not a violation of national treatment). For imported *services*, in contrast, application of national treatment is required only to the extent that a country has undertaken an explicit commitment to do so on the service in question.

Tariffs only. The WTO is not a free trade organization. Member countries are not required to participate in trade liberalizing negotiations, and they are free to protect domestic producers by imposing restrictions on imported goods and services. In the case of goods, however, if they do protect they are required to use tariffs only—rather than import quotas or other nontariff restrictions—to provide the protection. This is good economics—tariffs are a less distorting (less inefficient) way of granting protection, and the level of protection provided by a tariff is more transparent than that provided by nontariff barriers.

Consensus decision making. Although there are provisions for majority voting on a one-country, one-vote basis, the WTO has continued the strong tradition, developed under the GATT, of making decisions by consensus—defined as no country present at the meeting when the decision was taken formally objecting to the proposed decision. Although this often slows the decision-making process, it has important advantages, including adding to the intellectual and diplomatic "legitimacy" of the decisions, many of which result in legally binding obligations for all members.

Special treatment for low-income countries. Following a practice that evolved under the GATT, the WTO rules and procedures include special arrangements for developing countries. These include special provisions in WTO agreements (for example, longer implementation periods for new obligations), activities of the Committee on Trade and Development, and technical assistance (mainly training). Responding to a widening income gap among these countries—a number of successful "developing" countries now have per capita incomes approaching those of developed countries, while many others remain very poor—the WTO uses a two-part grouping: developing countries and least-developed countries (a UN grouping of the 50 poorest countries, 32 of which are WTO members), coupled with an increasing focus on helping the latter group of countries (see Part Five of WTO 1999).

Small Secretariat with a limited mandate. The member countries have also continued the tradition, developed under the GATT, of having a Secretariat that is *very* small—in terms of budget and staff—as compared with the other major international economic organizations, such as the World Bank and the International Monetary Fund (IMF). The limited mandate is reflected not only in the limited budget and staff, but also, for example, in the fact that the Secretariat is not allowed to interpret WTO rules, nor can the Director-General initiate a dispute settlement case, no matter how blatant the rule violation. More generally, the head of the WTO has much less authority in relation to both the member countries and the organization's activities than do his counterparts at the World Bank and the IMF.

The result is a Secretariat whose activities are largely limited to servicing meetings and other activities of the member countries. This "member-driven" nature of the WTO, which has become even more pronounced than it was under the GATT, can be traced to the fact that trade policies are highly politicized at the national level. No government—especially no government of a large or medium-size country—can be seen advocating a Secretariat with any real independence and power. (Some analysts argue that the member-driven nature of the GATT was an important factor in its success; see Hudec 1993; Winham 1998.)

Administering the Agreements and Other Day-to-Day Activities Aside from the agreement establishing the WTO, virtually all of the more than 50 agreements, annexes, decisions, and understandings agreed to in the Uruguay Round, as well as the organization's day-to-day activities, fall into one of five broad areas: administering the agreements on trade in goods, on trade in services, and on intellectual property protection, plus dispute settlement and periodic reviews of countries' policies under the Trade Policy Review Mechanism (TPRM). Technical assistance and training activities for officials from low-income countries round out the list of usual activities.

The member-driven nature of the work, plus the fact that all of the nearly 30 councils, committees, working parties, and working groups are open to all WTO members (there are no limited membership "executive groupings"), means that national delegations in Geneva typically have to cope with a heavy schedule of meetings dealing with a variety of often technically complex issues. This can be burdensome for delegations from the smaller developing countries—and especially so for the least-developed countries (Blackhurst, Lyakurwa, and Oyejide 2000).

Dispute Settlement A rules-based agreement can function only if it includes an effective system for resolving disputes between the member countries. Although the GATT's dispute settlement system worked well for much of nearly five decades that the GATT provided the legal framework for world trade, by the early 1980s serious problems were beginning to appear. In particular, there was a noticeable decline in the willingness of countries to "protect" the system by (1) allowing the dispute settlement process to run its course (under GATT rules, any member—including the defendant country—could block the process at any stage) and (2) removing policies that were found to be inconsistent with the country's GATT obligations. Everyone agreed that negotiations to reform the dispute settlement system were a high-priority part of the Uruguay Round agenda.

While most of the GATT's rules and procedures were taken over by the WTO with relatively little or no substantive modification, an important exception to this generalization occurred in the Uruguay Round understanding on dispute settlement. The previous practice of requiring that decisions by the panels that hear cases be adopted by consensus was turned on its head—under the WTO, panel decisions are automatically adopted unless there is a consensus *not* to do so. A second key change was the creation of a new institutional element—the Appellate Body—to which the parties to a dispute can appeal the panel's decision, with the Appellate Body's decision being final. Under the heading "Strengthening of the Multilateral System," the understanding also explicitly prohibits the use of *unilateral* actions in trade disputes between WTO members.

The WTO's dispute settlement system was remarkably successful during its first decade, producing more than 150 panel and Appellate Body reports which, in turn, generated a rich case law. While not disputing that assessment, many countries—especially developing countries—believe the system can be improved and have offered specific proposals for reform (WTO 2004, chapter VI; Sacerdoti, Yanovich, and Bohanes 2006).

Negotiating Rounds The underlying "ethos" of the WTO is that the pursuit of *freer* trade is a desirable goal. During the GATT years that goal was pursued through a series of formal negotiating rounds (eight in total). Despite some support for the view that more progress might be possible through lower profile "continuous" negotiations, during its first decade the WTO embraced the big round approach with the launch—in Doha, Qatar, in November 2001—of the Doha Development Agenda, encompassing both a new round of trade liberalizing negotiations and work on other issues, especially problems many developing countries were encountering in implementing existing commitments agreed to in the Uruguay Round.

At the end of 2007 the outlook for a successful conclusion of the Doha Round remained clouded. This, in turn, has given rise to claims that a failure of the round would seriously, perhaps fatally, harm the WTO. As a ploy to get countries to make the politically difficult decisions needed to conclude the round successfully, there is nothing objectionable about such claims. At the same time, they overlook at least two important sources of strength and stability in the WTO system. First, existing WTO rules and contractual obligations, together with the well-functioning dispute settlement system, impose severe constraints on the ability of countries to *increase* current levels of protection. Of course countries could be tempted to flout the WTO, but then the second source of strength comes into play, namely the fact that politically powerful multinational corporations and other export-oriented firms from many countries, together with their millions of employees, have a very large financial stake in world trade continuing to flow smoothly and be governed by enforceable multilateral rules.

Other Challenges Facing the WTO An international organization with a mandate as broad and complex as that of the WTO is bound to find itself confronting a seemingly endless series of challenges. Very briefly, these include:

- *Dispute settlement.* It was noted earlier that, although the dispute settlement system is working very well, a number of proposals for improving the system are on the table. In addition, there is a fear that a failure of the Doha Round could put additional strains—perhaps very serious strains—on the dispute settlement system if countries sought to obtain through litigation what could not be achieved through negotiation—for example, the reduction or elimination of agricultural subsidies. It is helpful to recall, in this context, that the WTO has no police force and no jails. The dispute settlement system works only if the member countries want it to and are willing to protect it.

- *Preferential trading arrangements.* The continuing proliferation of preferential trading arrangements, in particular free trade areas, is believed by many to be a serious problem for the WTO. However, 20 years of debate and analysis have failed to bring about a consensus among either economists or policymakers on whether, in practice, such agreements—many of which extend to issues not covered by the WTO—support or harm the multilateral trading system (see WTO 2004, chapter II; WTO 1995). It is widely assumed that a failure of the Doha Round would give an added stimulus to the spread of such agreements.

- *Decision making.* The WTO's various councils, committees, and negotiating groups are loosely analogous to what in a national government would be the "parliamentary" branch of government. It is generally accepted in the trade policy community that the practices and procedures in this area—especially the ones surrounding the negotiating activities—are functioning badly and need to be reformed. Along with built-in procedural and structural shortcomings, other factors that have been blamed for the disappointing pace of negotiations and decision making include the increased WTO membership, the increased sensitivity of the issues being considered, the lack of a more regular presence in Geneva of senior policymakers from capitals, and the across-the-board reliance on consensus decision making (see WTO 2004, chapters VII and VIII).

- *Anti-globalization.* The WTO is a major target of the anti-globalization movement—the high point or low point, depending on one's perspective, being the "Battle of Seattle" at the December 1999 Ministerial meeting when an estimated 40,000 to 50,000 people showed up to protest a very wide range of issues (Jones 2004). Aware that such attacks on the WTO can erode public support for further trade liberalization, the WTO has taken a number of steps in the years since 1999 to counter what it believes to be the misconceptions and distortions spread by the anti-globalization movement. These include improving the transparency of WTO activities and the dialogue with nongovernmental organizations (NGOs), expediting the derestriction of documents, providing regular briefings for NGOs in Geneva, holding symposia, and allowing NGO attendance at ministerial meetings (see WTO 2004, especially chapter V; also chapters I and III).

The WTO's Contribution Douglass North shared the 1993 Nobel Prize in economics for his work on the role of institutions in early European and American economic growth and in the experience with postwar growth in developing countries. His focus was on human cooperation that allows societies to capture the gains from specialization and trade stressed by Adam Smith in the *Wealth of Nations* (North 1990). He argues convincingly that an important determinant of a country's rate of economic growth is the extent to which institutions, as they evolve, create—or fail to create—a favorable environment for cooperative solutions to complex economic exchange.

Although North's analysis of differences in growth rates among countries, and within the same country over time, focused on the role of institutions at the subnational and national levels, there is little doubt that global economic integration—spurred by ever more complex production and distribution chains—has progressed to the point that his findings apply with equal force at the international level. If economic growth is a priority, a global economy requires multilateral economic institutions that can perform the essential institutional functions that, in successful economies, are carried out at the national level by national institutions. The WTO is the preeminent example of such a multilateral institution.

See also Agreement on Agriculture; Agreement on Trade-Related Aspects of Intellectual Property Rights (TRIPS); agricultural trade negotiations; anti-globalization; competition policy; customs unions; Doha Round; free trade area; General Agreement on Tariffs and Trade (GATT); General Agreement on Trade in Services (GATS); global public goods; globalization; government procurement; labor standards; multilateralism; nondiscrimination; nontariff measures; quotas; regionalism; sanitary and phytosanitary measures; special and differential treatment; tariffs; technical barriers to trade; trade facilitation; trade in services; Trade Policy Review Mechanism; trade-related capacity building; Uruguay Round; World Trade Organization, accession to; World Trade Organization dispute settlement

FURTHER READING

Barton, John, Judith Goldstein, Timothy Josling, and Richard Steinberg. 2006. *The Evolution of the Trade Regime: Politics, Law, and Economics of the GATT and the WTO.* Princeton, NJ: Princeton University Press. An excellent up-to-date interdisciplinary overview of the WTO regime.

Blackhurst, Richard, Bill Lyakurwa, and Ademola Oyejide. 2000. "Options for Improving Africa's Participation in the WTO." *The World Economy* 23 (4): 491–510. Reprinted in *Developing Countries and the WTO: A Proactive Agenda*, edited by Bernard Hoekman and Will Martin. United Kingdom: Blackwell, 2001. Examines the challenges of WTO participation confronting virtually every WTO member in sub-Sahara Africa (as well as low-income countries elsewhere), including suggestions for reallocating existing budget resources to improve the situation.

Goldstein, Judith, Douglas Rivers, and Michael Tomz. 2006. "Institutions in International Relations: Understanding the Effects of GATT and the WTO on World Trade." *International Organization* 61: 2. Assesses the trade implications of membership in the GATT and the WTO and provides empirical evidence that membership increased trade for both developed and developing countries.

Goode, Walter. 2007. *Dictionary of Trade Policy Terms.* 5th ed. Cambridge: Cambridge University Press. A nearly indispensable guide to terms used in the jargon-filled world of the WTO and other international economic organizations. Also covers various WTO rules, newer issues, and developing country concerns

Hudec, Robert E. 1993. *Enforcing International Trade Law: The Evolution of the Modern GATT Legal System.* Salem, NH: Butterworth Legal Publishers. A standard reference work, by a leading GATT legal scholar, on the GATT legal system as it stood just prior to its major overhaul in 1995 as part of the Uruguay Round Agreements.

Irwin, Douglas A. 2005. *Free Trade under Fire.* 2d ed. Princeton, NJ: Princeton University Press. An excellent review of the case for free (freer) trade that also examines the various arguments for protection. Chapter 2 contains a nontechnical summary of the various ways trade liberalization stimulates economic growth.

Jones, Kent. 2004. *Who's Afraid of the WTO?* Oxford: Oxford University Press. After cataloging a long list of interest groups that have been highly critical of the WTO, the author carefully analyzes and refutes virtually all of the charges leveled against the WTO. The author also provides an excellent overview of the WTO's contribution to economic and noneconomic goals worldwide.

Krueger, Anne O., ed. 1998. *The WTO as an International Organization.* Chicago: University of Chicago Press. A conference volume containing 15 papers by leading WTO scholars from economics, law, and political science covering both institutional and substantive issues and challenges.

North, Douglass. 1990. *Institutions, Institutional Change, and Economic Performance.* Cambridge: Cambridge University Press. Perhaps the best summary of the work that earned him the Nobel Prize in Economics in 1993, this book presents an analytical framework for analyzing how institutions, by influencing the ability of humans to cooperate in the economic sphere, play a key role in economic growth.

Petersmann, Ernst-Ulrich, ed. 2005. *Reforming the World Trading System: Legitimacy, Efficiency, and Democratic Governance.* Oxford: Oxford University Press. A collection of 29 essays by leading WTO specialists from the fields of economics, law, and trade diplomacy covering virtually every issue that has been raised in policy debates over reforming the WTO system as it enters its second decade.

Sacerdoti, Giorgio, Alan Yanovich, and Jan Bohanes, eds. 2006. *The WTO at Ten: The Contribution of the Dispute Settlement System.* Geneva and Cambridge: WTO Secretariat and Cambridge University Press. A collection of articles by a diverse group of experts—including academics, policymakers, judges from a number of international tribunals, and members of the WTO's Appellate Body—written in connection with events commemorating the Appellate Body's 10th anniversary.

Srinivasan, T. N. 2005. "Nondiscrimination in GATT/WTO: Was There Anything to Begin with and Is There Anything Left?" *World Trade Review* 4 (1): 69–95. The author argues that the exceptions to nondiscrimination that were in the GATT from the beginning have become dominant over time to the point that little nondiscrimination remains today. He also considers the relevance of nondiscrimination to the new areas covered by the WTO—services and the protection of intellectual property.

Winham, Gilbert R. 1998. "The World Trade Organization: Institution Building in the Multilateral Trade System." *The World Economy* 21 (3): 349–68. A political scientist's view of the operation of the GATT and its implications for the WTO.

Wolf, Martin. 2004. *Why Globalization Works.* New Haven, CT: Yale University Press. A well-written and detailed analysis of the case for globalization that covers all aspects of the topic. The reference of choice for an in-depth introduction to the forces shaping the world economy.

World Trade Organization. 1995. *Regionalism and the World Trading System.* Geneva: WTO Secretariat. Although the statistics on the number of preferential agreements in existence are not up-to-date (it's a fast moving area), the rest of the study, including the historical part and the analytical parts—which offer a detailed analysis of the many often subtle ways that preferential agreements and the WTO system can interact, for good and for bad—remain fully relevant.

———. 1999. *Guide to the Uruguay Round Agreements.* Geneva: WTO Secretariat. In terms of rhetoric and organization the official legal texts of the Uruguay Round results are virtually incomprehensible to the nonexpert. This book by WTO Secretariat staff members presents the results in an authoritative but understandable way that also makes it easy to get a good sense of the overall package.

———. 2004. *The Future of the WTO: Addressing Institutional Challenges in the New Millennium.* Geneva: WTO Secretariat. The four core chapters of this report by an independent group of eight international experts provide an informed overview of current institutional challenges in the areas of dispute settlement (VI), decision making (VII and VIII), and the role of the Director-General and the Secretariat (IX). A free copy in English may be downloaded from http://www.wto.org/english/thewto_e/10anniv_e/future_wto_e.pdf. Also available in French and Spanish.

———. 2005. *Understanding the WTO.* 3d ed. Geneva: WTO Secretariat. A useful, reasonably detailed introduction to both the WTO system and current challenges confronting the system. At 112 pages it occupies a space between brief descriptions (such as this encyclopedia entry) and detailed academic work on each of the many rules and activities of the GATT/WTO. An up-to-date free version in English may be downloaded from http://www.wto.org/english/thewto_e/whatis_e/tif_e/understanding_e.pdf. Also available in French and Spanish.

———. http://www.wto.org. A comprehensive user-friendly Web site relevant to all aspects of the WTO's history and current activities.

RICHARD BLACKHURST

■ World Trade Organization, accession to

Policymakers give a range of reasons for wanting their countries to join—or accede to—the World Trade

Organization (WTO). For some the rationale is to further integrate their country into the world economy. Here often the hope is that the better access to foreign markets that WTO membership can bring will result in higher exports. Another economic rationale is to encourage greater foreign direct investment and, more generally, to use WTO accession as a seal of approval recognized by the international business community. It is also the case, however, that many nations join the WTO for political reasons. Transition economies, for example, often see WTO membership as a means to join the international community of nations. Some see WTO accession as facilitating both political as well as economic reform processes within their countries.

There is some overlap between these stated rationales and the potential benefits of WTO accession identified in economic research, in particular as they relate to bolstering exports and foreign direct investment inflows. Economists would also point to the benefits that flow from better foreign access to the acceding nation's markets, specifically in terms of lower prices for and a greater variety of imports. By binding national tariffs, committing to eliminate quotas on imports, and reforming other state measures, an acceding nation can enhance the credibility of its policies and reduce the uncertainty facing the private sector. In principle, then, WTO accession can improve important components of the national business environment which, in turn, has sizable domestic payoffs.

The Process of WTO Accession Most WTO members were also contracting parties to the General Agreement on Tariffs and Trade (GATT) and automatically became founder-members of the WTO when it was established on January 1, 1995, because they had either signed the Marrakesh Agreement Establishing the World Trade Organization in April 1994 or because they had joined the GATT after April 1994 but before the WTO was set up. The Marrakesh Agreement also made provision for "any state or customs territory possessing full autonomy in the conduct of its external commercial relations and to the other matters provided for in this Agreement" to accede to the WTO. From January 1, 1995, to

July 2007, 23 new members, including two least-developed countries (LDCs), have acceded to the WTO. At the time of writing, another 28 jurisdictions, 10 of which are LDCs, are in the process of acceding to the WTO.

Article XII.1 of the Marrakesh Agreement permits new members to accede on "terms to be agreed" between the applicant and the WTO. No guidance is given in the Marrakesh Agreement on the "terms to be agreed." However, the WTO Secretariat, in consultation with WTO members, has drawn up a set of procedures for accession that are closely modeled on those followed by contracting parties to the GATT. In brief, these procedures require that:

1. an applicant must send a communication to the Director-General of the WTO indicating its desire to accede to the WTO under Article XII;
2. this communication is then circulated to all WTO members and a decision is made whether to approve the establishment of a working party;
3. once a working party has been established and a chairperson has been appointed, the applicant submits a memorandum on its foreign trade regime;
4. the working party meets to examine the memorandum and the applicant provides further information and answers;
5. a Working Party Report is prepared;
6. at the same time, bilateral negotiations are undertaken on concessions and commitments on market access for goods and services (as well as other specific terms of accession);
7. a goods schedule and a services schedule are prepared;
8. thereafter, a draft decision and a draft Protocol of Accession (containing commitments listed in the Working Party Report and the goods and services schedules) are prepared;
9. the working party, and then the WTO's General Council or the Ministerial Conference, approves the accession package;

10. thereafter, the applicant formally accepts the accession package;

11. the applicant notifies the WTO Secretariat of its formal acceptance; and

12. 30 days later the applicant becomes a member of the WTO.

For the countries that joined the WTO most recently this process took on average 10 years.

The "Price" of WTO Accession Throughout the WTO accession process the onus is on the applicant to satisfy the demands of existing WTO members. This apparently one-sided procedure has given rise to the following perceptions about the accession process (Evenett and Primo Braga 2005):

- The WTO accession process is costly and complex.
- The WTO accession process is taking longer and longer to complete.
- The price of joining the WTO now includes commitments that go beyond the GATT/WTO agreements.
- The price of joining the WTO is steadily rising.
- The WTO accession process takes little account of the specific circumstances of applicant countries or their needs for special and differential treatment.

With respect to the evidence on the "price" of accession, it is important to distinguish between the two broad types of commitments made by acceding countries: those relating directly to market access (for goods and services) and other commitments on rules. Acceding countries may benefit from transition periods or exceptions to existing WTO rules, but these are rarely granted by existing WTO members. Concerning commitments to open national markets to foreign trade, in the areas of agricultural and nonagricultural (typically manufacturing) products there is clear evidence that the price of accession is growing over time. For both agricultural and nonagricultural goods the average tariff binding that acceding countries were allowed has fallen over time (to approximately 15 and 6 percent, respectively) and is now at levels well below those agreed by developing countries in the Uruguay Round (Evenett and Primo Braga 2005). In short, from a mercantilist perspective the relative price of WTO accession is high (in comparison with Uruguay Round commitments made by peer nations) and growing over time.

From the first 20 completed WTO accessions the picture that emerges concerning service sector commitments tells a similar story. Taking the number of services subsectors (of the 160 identified in the WTO's classification list) committed by countries as a proxy for the "price" to be a WTO member, LDCs that were founding members of the WTO committed on average 20 subsectors. The averages for founding members in the developing and industrialized country categories, in turn, were respectively 44 and 108. Countries that have acceded since 1995, in turn, have on average committed around 104 subsectors. Needless to say, this is a crude measure of the "services-related" price of accession as this figure does not capture the depth (e.g., the scheduling of explicit limitations) or the breadth (e.g., the modes of delivery covered) of the commitment. Still, it is illustrative that countries that went through the WTO accession process typically committed a much higher number of subsectors than GATT contracting parties at a similar level of development did in the context of the Uruguay Round negotiations.

Turning to commitments on other policies that countries have adopted when joining the WTO, the picture is more mixed. With the exceptions of China and Taiwan accession countries signed around 25 such commitments. These commitments typically concern a wide range of state measures, some of which are not obviously trade related. Bulgaria, for example, made commitments with respect to domestic price controls, the privatization of state-owned enterprises, and excise taxes on alcohol, as well as many other traditional trade policy–related measures. A controversial question is whether this class of accession obligation goes beyond the commitments agreed during the Uruguay Round (constituting so-called WTO-plus commitments) or involves an accession country agreeing to forgo the rights available to other WTO members (the so-called WTO-minus commitments).

Whether an accession obligation goes beyond an existing WTO agreement depends in large part on how the latter is interpreted, and so it should not be surprising that disagreement is rife on the extent of WTO-plus commitments. Moreover, some WTO-plus obligations may only involve consultation with, or reporting to, existing WTO members and thus are of limited developmental significance. Others may be more significant, such as Jordan's commitment that if any of its laws or state acts are subsequently found to contradict international treaties (not just WTO agreements), then the latter would have precedence. WTO-minus commitments are easier to identify, such as Ecuador's commitment to eliminate all subsidies before the date of accession and its commitment never to introduce them afterward. China's acceptance of product-specific transitional safeguard provisions, which can be more easily triggered than regular WTO safeguards, provides another example. WTO-plus and WTO-minus commitments differentiate WTO members, and they could be interpreted as contributing to a multitier multilateral trade system. This systemic concern is in addition to any of the adverse developmental effects that may result from these specific commitments.

In sum, there is evidence that the accession process is becoming more demanding in terms of market access commitments. In July 2004 WTO members recognized this trend and agreed that less liberalization be demanded of newly acceded members in the agriculture and nonagricultural market access negotiations during the Doha Round. Whether there is a trend increase in WTO-plus or WTO-minus commitments is unclear, but the very fact that existing WTO rules allow for them is a source of concern. Evidence on the latter should be interpreted with care in view of the possibility of a potential bias in the sample of recently acceded countries. After all, most of these countries were transition economies with highly distorted trading regimes to start with. Accordingly it could be argued that the higher demands of WTO members simply reflect this reality rather than a systemic trend.

The Empirical Studies of the Impact of WTO Accession The critical welfare question, however, is not whether the price of WTO accession is rising, but whether the price is worth paying in terms of its developmental impact. If it is, then the demands made by existing WTO members of acceding countries might be characterized as "tough love." Otherwise, the WTO accession process may well be seen as a one-sided power play whereby current WTO members wring commercial advantage out of weaker economic partners.

A comprehensive evaluation of WTO accession should examine postaccession performance on many metrics and should consider the state measures taken before and after the date of WTO accession. At present, few accession countries have five or more years of postaccession data to begin identifying the effect of WTO accession, so the available evidence here is necessarily limited.

The available country-specific research on WTO accession has almost exclusively focused on the case of China, an exception being an analysis of the response of Bulgaria and Ecuador's exports to their accessions (Evenett, Gage, and Kennett 2004). Other country analyses typically refer to countries in the process of accession, and a recent paper by Lissovolik and Lissovolik (2004) on Russia's potential WTO accession is a good example of this type of analysis. These authors found that after controlling for customary determinants of bilateral trade flows Russia's exports to WTO members from 1995 to 2002 were smaller than those to nonmembers. Rather than immediately attribute the export underperformance to Russia's nonmembership in the WTO, Lissovolik and Lissovolik consider four other potential explanations for this finding. Only one such explanation (the nature and extent of Russian export controls) survives scrutiny and the authors qualify their conclusions accordingly.

The second class of relevant literature includes a series of academic studies that have called into question widely held and long-standing views about the economic effects of WTO membership. Having documented numerous claims made by scholars, officials, and international organizations about the beneficial consequences of WTO membership (and of membership in its predecessor, the GATT), Andrew Rose used conventional econometric tools to assess these claims in a series of papers. In one study he found no statistically significant effect of GATT/WTO membership on the value of bilateral trade flows over a 50-year period, a finding he regards as mysterious (Rose 2004). In another study he found that GATT/WTO accession increased the value of bilateral trade flows, but WTO membership itself does not (Rose 2005a). Moreover GATT/WTO membership was found in a third study not to have a statistically significant effect on the volatility of trade flows, as measured by the coefficient of variation of bilateral trade flows over a 25-year period (Rose 2005b). In these three studies GATT/WTO membership is captured in econometric specifications by the use of dummy variables, rather than directly identifying the changes in trade policies that followed from membership or accession.

Rose's findings have prompted others to revisit the questions he posed and the methods he employed. Subramanian and Wei (2003) diverge from Rose's earlier articles in two respects. First, they differentiate between the effects of GATT/WTO membership on industrialized and developing countries. More generally they note that there is no presumption that the effects of GATT/WTO membership are common across all goods and trading partners, hence calling into question the pooling of certain types of trade data. Second, they employ some of the latest techniques for estimating bilateral gravity equations that try to control for country-specific characteristics. These two departures appear to have led to substantially different findings. Subramanian and Wei find that WTO membership raised trade between industrial countries by 40 percent, whereas such membership only increased a developing country's trade if it joined the WTO after the completion of the Uruguay Round. Asymmetric results were found across sectors, and GATT/WTO membership is associated with greater effects on goods trade (which typically faces lower trade barriers than other

sectors). The authors note that these findings are consistent with the reluctance of industrialized economies to liberalize trade in food and clothing under the auspices of the GATT and WTO, and the fact that developing countries were not asked to undertake many liberalizing commitments before the completion of the Uruguay Round.

Noneconomists have also contributed to the literature on the effects of WTO accession. Goldstein, Rivers, and Tomz (2003) draw on the insights of the international relations literature to assess the effects of international institutions on trade patterns. They note that many customs territories (which need not be nations) participated in the GATT and WTO before formally becoming members of these institutions. The date of accession, therefore, may not accurately reflect the point at which a nation begins to align itself with multilateral trade rules. Another interesting observation is that the effects of GATT and WTO membership are likely to be conditional on prevailing preferential trading arrangements and on the nature and history of certain state-to-state ties, such as former colonial links. These authors also undertake a gravity equation analysis and find that, although the GATT/WTO appears to have increased trade among members, these institutions have contributed to faster growth of trade among nonmembers.

To summarize, there is a dearth of empirical evidence on the effects of WTO accession on the developmental prospects of developing countries. This weak evidential base has created a vacuum that has been filled by doubts about the case for opening markets and taking WTO obligations and negotiations seriously. Some have questioned whether developing economies, especially least-developed countries, should be encouraged to use the WTO as a forum to structure national development efforts. Moreover it is difficult to see how technical assistance programs, especially those initiatives that enable firms to capitalize on postaccession export opportunities, can be effectively designed without a better understanding of the economic consequences of WTO accession. One challenge for the scholarly and policymaking communities in the coming years is to fill this knowledge gap.

See also General Agreement on Tariffs and Trade (GATT); political economy of trade policy; trade and economic development, international; World Trade Organization

FURTHER READING

Evenett, Simon J., Jonathan Gage, and Maxine Kennett. 2004. "The Impact of Joining the WTO on Market Access: Detailed Evidence from Bulgaria and Ecuador." Mimeo (September). Oxford University, Saïd Business School. An empirical evaluation of the different potential effects of WTO accession on two nations.

Evenett, Simon J., and Carlos A. Primo Braga. 2005. "WTO Accession: Lessons from Experience." *Trade Note 22*. International Trade Department. Washington, DC: World Bank. A summary of the principal findings on WTO accession taking a deliberately developmental perspective.

Goldstein, Judith, Douglas Rivers, and Michael Tomz. 2003. "How Does the Trade Regime Affect International Trade?" Mimeo. Stanford University, Department of Political Science. An empirical analysis of the effects of different international institutions on international trade flows.

Kennett, Maxine. 2007. *The Principal Legal Obligations of Accession to the World Trade Organization*. Manuscript. Geneva: Ideas Center. A comprehensive analysis of the legal obligations taken on by acceding nations in the first 12 years of the WTO's existence.

Lissovolik, Bodgan, and Yaroslav Lissovolik. 2004. "Russia and the WTO: The 'Gravity' of Outside Status." Mimeo. Washington, DC: International Monetary Fund. An analysis of the potential effect of WTO accession on Russian trading patterns.

Rose, Andrew. 2004. "Do We Really Know that the WTO Increases Trade?" *American Economic Review* 94 (1): 98–114. A much cited paper that finds no statistically significant effect of the WTO or GATT membership on national trade flows.

———. 2005a. "Which International Institutions Promote International Trade?" *Review of International Economics* 13 (4): 682–98. An empirical analysis of the effects of membership of different international institutions on trade flows.

———. 2005b. "Does the WTO Make Trade More Stable?" *Open Economies Review* 16 (1): 7–22. An empirical examination of the effects of WTO membership on the stability of trade flows.

Subramanian, Arvind, and Shang-Jin Wei. 2003. "The WTO Promotes Trade, Strongly but Unevenly." Working Paper No. WP/03/185. Washington, DC: International Monetary Fund. A paper that counters Rose (2005), arguing that a disaggregated empirical analysis generates very different findings.

World Trade Organization. 2005. *Technical Note on the Accession Process*. WT/ACC/10/Rev.3 (28 November). Geneva: WTO. A long, detailed statement of various matters relating to the accession of countries to the WTO.

———. http://www.wto.org/english/thewto_e/acc_e/acc_e.htm. A Web site with the WTO's resources relating to accession.

SIMON J. EVENETT AND CARLOS A. PRIMO BRAGA

■ World Trade Organization dispute settlement

The dispute settlement system of the World Trade Organization (WTO) is the mechanism through which members thought to be in violation of their trade agreement commitments present their cases to a third-party panel for decision. The system evolved from the dispute settlement process of the WTO's predecessor, the General Agreement on Tariffs and Trade (GATT), which first embarked on the process of resolving disputes among its signatories in 1948. GATT's dispute settlement process was initially referred to as a process of "conciliation," not arbitration, and was supervised by a panel of experts that generally consisted of diplomats, not lawyers.

The goal of this process was to reach a solution mutually agreeable to the parties rather than to establish and apply binding legal principles. It did this reasonably well, but there was one major shortcoming. GATT, as its name makes clear, was a multilateral agreement. Indeed, strictly speaking, GATT had no "members." Signatories were known as "Contracting Parties." Since GATT was simply a contract among a group of parties, any action required a consensus of all of those parties. This allowed parties whose practices were challenged to block the establishment of a dispute settlement panel or the adoption of an adverse panel report. There was considerable dissatisfaction with this aspect of the system.

Although some amendments to improve the GATT dispute settlement system were made over the years, it took the establishment of the WTO's dispute settlement system in 1995 to put in place an effective legal system, including an Appellate Body to which panel decisions may be appealed.

The WTO dispute settlement system is governed by the Understanding on Rules and Procedures Governing the Settlement of Disputes, known as the "Dispute Settlement Understanding" or "DSU," and is administered by a Dispute Settlement Body (DSB), which consists of representatives of each WTO member. The DSB is the sole WTO body with authority to establish panels, to adopt their reports and those of the Appellate Body, to maintain surveillance of the implementation of the rulings and recommendations it adopts, and to authorize the suspension of concessions or other obligations under WTO agreements if its rulings and recommendations are not acted on by members in a timely fashion.

The power of the DSB is, perhaps, the biggest difference between the GATT and WTO systems. Consensus is still required, but it is "reverse consensus." Consensus is required *not* to establish a panel when a request is made, reversing the GATT practice of requiring consensus to do so. Since at least one member, the complaining party, always wants the panel to be established, this effectively means there can be no reverse consensus. This reverse consensus rule also applies to the other major functions of the DSB, including the adoption of reports and the authorization of the prevailing member to impose the WTO remedy of suspension of trade concessions or other obligations on a losing member that does not implement the DSB's recommendations.

Jurisdiction The WTO agreements are between governments and impose obligations only on gov-ernments. Therefore access to the dispute settlement system is limited to member governments—private interests have no right of access. Although panels and the Appellate Body sometimes accept amicus curiae submissions from private interests, they have rarely accorded much weight to these submissions in their analysis.

The subject matter jurisdiction of panels and the Appellate Body is limited to the interpretation of the provisions of the WTO agreements cited by the complaining party. Although there is much discussion of whether WTO panels and the Appellate Body should consider other international agreements and principles of public international law as part of their work, they have done so only to assist in interpreting the WTO agreements. The DSU instructs panels to interpret the agreements in accordance with the "customary rules of interpretation of public international law." This has been understood to refer to the Articles 31 and 32 of the Vienna Convention on the Law of Treaties, which places primary emphasis on the role of the ordinary meaning of a treaty's text rather than the history of its negotiation.

The Panel Process The WTO panel process is, unexpectedly, a legalistic one, with rules providing for the establishment and composition of panels and for the procedures they are to follow. The system's diplomatic heritage in GATT is reflected at the outset, however, by the requirement that the process begin with a formal request from one member to another for consultations concerning the subject of the dispute. Only after these are held may a member with a grievance move on to request the establishment of a panel and its procedures to resolve the dispute.

Consultations The consultation requirement concerns those "measures affecting the operation of any covered agreement taken within the territory" of one member that are deemed by another member to contravene WTO commitments. In most cases, however, informal bilateral consultations between the parties have already taken place; consequently, the formal request for consultations is often seen as an effort by the requesting member to signal to the other member that the matter at issue is serious.

The purpose of consultations is to enable the parties to gather relevant, and correct, information—both to assist them in reaching a mutually agreed solution or, failing that, to assist them in presenting accurate information to the panel. Many disputes do not proceed beyond the consultations stage.

The request for consultations plays an important role in defining the jurisdiction of the eventual panel in the dispute. The DSU requires that the complaining party give the reasons for the request, identify the measures at issue, and indicate the legal basis for the complaint. This forms the basis for a subsequent request for the establishment of a panel, although there need not be an exact identity between the measures identified in the request for consultations and those identified in a request for the establishment of a panel. Consultations are confidential and take place bilaterally without any WTO involvement. What transpires during the consultations is not the concern of a panel.

Other WTO members have a limited role in consultations. A complaining member may draft its request for consultations so that even third-party members with a substantial trade interest may not participate. Tactical considerations usually dictate the complaining member's decision on this point. Of course, those third-party members may participate in the panel procedure itself even if they have not been permitted to participate in consultations.

Requests to Establish a Panel The complaining member's request for the establishment of a panel is a fundamental, jurisdictional document. It is incorporated into the panel's terms of reference and, therefore, determines the subject matter jurisdiction of the panel. It also fulfills the due process objective of notifying the responding party—and other WTO members as potential third parties—of the claims at issue. Because of its jurisdictional importance, disagreements over the scope of terms of reference arise frequently.

The formal requirements of a request for the establishment of a panel are set out in the DSU: the request must be in writing, indicate whether consultations were held, identify the objectionable measure taken by the other member, and specify the "legal basis for the complaint." A measure typically is a law or regulation, or an action that applies a law or regulation. The cited measure, together with the legal basis for the complaint, that is, the provisions of the relevant WTO agreement cited in the panel request, constitutes the "matter" over which the panel has jurisdiction.

Composition of Panels Panels normally are composed of three persons, with one serving as chair. Panelists usually are present or former members of nonparty delegations to the WTO or academics who are not paid for their service. Unless the parties agree, panelists may not be nationals of parties or third parties to the dispute. They serve in their individual capacities, not as government representatives or representatives of other organizations. A developing country that is a party to a dispute may request that at least one panelist shall be from a developing country.

Usually panelists are nominated by the WTO Secretariat from member delegations and from a roster of governmental and nongovernmental individuals who are deemed qualified by virtue of their training or experience. If the parties do not agree on panelists within 20 days of the establishment of the panel, either party may request the Director-General of the WTO to name the panelists. Although the DSU instructs members not to oppose nominees of the Secretariat except for compelling reasons, parties frequently have proven unable to agree on the composition of the panel, leaving the Director-General to appoint the panel.

Procedures Panels normally issue their own detailed working procedures soon after their members have been named. These procedures supplement the more general Working Procedures set out in the DSU and may cover topics ranging from the panel's schedule and deadlines to the required format for submissions. Although the DSU sets out some time limits for panels' work, these often prove too short, and panels frequently depart from them, usually with the agreement of the parties and notice to the DSB. Despite these delays, WTO dispute settlement is widely seen as comparatively rapid for litigation as complex as most WTO disputes are.

Although normally all of the relevant information is submitted to a panel by the parties, panels are not confined to the parties as sources of the information they need. They have the right to seek information and technical advice from any source they deem appropriate. They may obtain opinions from experts and, with respect to scientific and technical matters, may request an advisory report from a more formal expert review group.

Other WTO members may participate to a limited extent in panel proceedings as third parties. When a panel is established, the chairman of the DSB usually specifies that members wishing to participate as third parties should file their notifications within 10 days. Third parties are normally entitled to receive only the first submissions of the parties to the panel and to participate in a special session of the first meeting of the panel with the parties. However, members have been granted enhanced third-party rights in several instances.

Meetings of WTO panels with the parties are normally confidential, but, with the agreement of the parties, some panels have opened their meetings to the public or permitted the rebroadcast of portions of the hearings that do not involve confidential information.

Few individuals have served on more than one or two WTO dispute settlement panels. Accordingly, the role of the WTO Secretariat, which provides legal and secretarial advice to panels, cannot be overstated. Not all panelists feel qualified to disagree with the Secretariat on points of law. Although there have been proposals to create a permanent roster of panelists, these proposals have not yet achieved consensus approval.

Panels normally conduct two separate meetings with the parties. At these meetings, the parties present formal statements of their arguments or rebuttals, after which the panel questions them on the details of their arguments. Panels vary greatly in their degree of activity during meetings with the parties. Some will interrupt presentations to ask questions as they arise; others will question after a presentation is concluded; still others do so only after both sides have finished their presentations; and a few present no oral questions at all, but rely entirely on written questions.

Prior to the issuance of their final report, parties are given the opportunity to review an interim report. They may submit comments on this report and may request a meeting with the panel to discuss these comments. In most instances, parties do not request a meeting with the panel, but simply submit written comments on the report. The interim review stage is not intended to present an opportunity to reargue the issues. Generally panels do not revise their substantive findings following the interim review stage, although there have been some exceptions. Although interim reports are supposed to be strictly confidential, their release to the parties provides the first disclosure beyond the Secretariat of the outcome of the proceeding. The gist of the panel's findings frequently makes its way to the press at this point.

The Appellate Process The creation of a standing Appellate Body, staffed by its own secretariat and therefore largely independent of the rest of the WTO, was one of the two most important additions to the GATT dispute settlement system by the WTO. The other, of course, was "reverse consensus." About half of the reports of panels are appealed to the Appellate Body.

The WTO Appellate Body consists of seven members appointed for four-year terms, which may be renewed once. Members serve on a paid, part-time basis. The DSU requires that members be persons of recognized authority and demonstrated expertise in law, international trade, and the subject matter of the WTO agreements. Members may not be affiliated with any government. For the most part, the members have been experienced trade negotiators and lawyers. Generally they have been appointed with a view to ensuring a broad geographic representation on the Appellate Body.

Cases are heard by a Division of three of the seven members of the Appellate Body who are selected on the basis of a rotation system intended to ensure random selection and unpredictability. Unlike panelists, Appellate Body members may serve on any case, including those involving their own country. The Division selects a presiding member, whose responsibilities include coordinating the overall conduct of the proceeding, chairing oral hearings and meetings, and coordinating the drafting of the appellate report. The Appellate Body has adopted its own working procedures, which specify the schedule for each proceeding as well as the required format and content of notices of appeals and other submissions. The Appellate Body's proceedings, like those of panels, are confidential and closed to the public.

Reports of the Appellate Body are signed by all members of the Division. The DSU provides that opinions expressed by individuals shall be anonymous. At the time of this writing (in late 2007), there have been two separate (dissenting) opinions contained in reports of the Appellate Body.

The jurisdiction of the Appellate Body is limited to issues of law covered in a panel report and to legal interpretations developed by a panel. The Appellate Body may uphold, modify, or reverse the legal findings and conclusions of a panel. If it modifies or reverses the findings, however, the Appellate Body may not remand the matter to the panel for further proceedings.

Perhaps the greatest impediment to the work of the Appellate Body is the requirement that it must normally complete the entire appeal process within 60 days and, according to the DSU, in not more than 90 days. Since the panel process normally averages approximately a year to complete, this is an extremely restrictive deadline. On occasion the Appellate Body has found it simply impossible to complete the task within this deadline and the parties have agreed to extend this deadline.

Adoption and Implementation of Reports
Panel reports are formally adopted by the DSB within 60 days of their circulation to all members unless a party gives notice of its decision to appeal the report or the DSB decides by consensus not to adopt the report (which has never happened since the creation of the WTO). Appellate Body reports are normally adopted within 30 days of circulation, again unless the DSB decides by consensus—which must include the prevailing party—not to do so.

Generally, where they find in favor of a complaining party, panels and the Appellate Body simply recommend that the defending party bring its measure into conformity with the relevant WTO Agreement. The defending party must normally state its intentions in this regard at a DSB meeting within 30 days of the adoption of the report. The defending member then has a "reasonable period of time" within which to bring its measure into conformity. Ideally the duration of this "reasonable period of time" is negotiated between the parties to the dispute. If agreement cannot be reached, the DSU provides for an arbitration process, to be completed within 90 days, as to the duration of this period. These arbitrations are conducted by a sole arbitrator agreed on by the parties or, absent agreement, appointed by the WTO Director-General. Arbitrations are relatively infrequent.

In implementing the panel or Appellate Body rulings, the defending member need only ensure that its measures and actions are WTO-consistent with *prospective* effect. There is no obligation to take any action to redress the past effects of any WTO-inconsistent actions.

If the defending member fails to act within the reasonable period of time or the complaining member is not satisfied with the manner in which the defending member has acted, the complaining member may refer the matter back to the original panel. Following a truncated version of the normal process, the reconstituted panel issues a further report—nominally within a 90-day deadline but in practice within about 6 months—as to whether the defending member properly implemented the original panel or Appellate Body's report and is now in compliance with the relevant provisions of the WTO Agreements.

The DSU contains a procedural inconsistency in this area that has led to the so-called sequencing problem. In addition to providing for review of disputes concerning a defending member's compliance with rulings in adopted panel or Appellate Body reports, the DSU also grants complaining members rights (described later) to take certain retaliatory actions in the event of inadequate implementation. The deadline for both actions begins when the time for the defending member to comply has expired, however. The DSU allows, as noted, 90 days for a review of compliance. But it calls for the retaliatory action to be taken within 30 days of the expiration of the time for the defending member to comply—60 days before the members can even know what the compliance ruling will be. In other words, a member wishing to retaliate is called on to do so 60 days before it can know whether it is entitled to do so. This "sequencing" problem has generally been resolved by bilateral agreements between the parties suspending and preserving the retaliatory rights of the complaining member pending the outcome of the review proceedings.

Remedies Where a defending member fails to implement properly an adverse panel ruling, both the GATT and WTO dispute settlement systems provided for remedies in the form of compensation or suspension of concessions. *Compensation*, in GATT/WTO parlance, refers not to monetary compensation, but to a reduction in the defending member's tariff rates or other trade barriers designed to offset the trade harm to the complaining member resulting from the impugned measure. *Suspension of concessions* refers to the imposition by the complaining member of additional tariffs or other trade barriers against imports from the defending member.

The DSU provides that the level of suspension of concessions shall be "equivalent" to the level of nullification or impairment of benefits due to the complaining. This can be difficult to quantify, so the DSU provides the possibility of arbitration, by the original panel or an arbitrator appointed by the WTO Director-General, to determine the appropriate level of retaliation. Economists have frequently pointed out that these "remedies" do not benefit the member taking retaliatory action. Others have pointed out that they also do not benefit the complaining member's exporting industry, which presumably was the intended beneficiary of the action. Both of these points are correct, but they overlook the political statement that retaliatory action, or the credible threat of such action, makes in both the domestic politics of the members concerned and in the internal politics of the WTO. It is also noteworthy that, on several occasions, members have obtained the right to retaliate but have refrained from doing so, presumably because they have realized that not only would such action not benefit their economies but, on the contrary, could harm them.

WTO members continue to negotiate to revise and improve the system. The issues under negotiation largely concern procedural matters, such as the sequencing problem and the panel selection process. Some members see the Appellate Body's lack of authority to remand a dispute back to a panel for further proceedings as a shortcoming. Others see the limited remedies available as a shortcoming, while still others are unwilling to accept a regime with stronger sanctions.

Nevertheless, since its inception the WTO dispute settlement system has been one of the most active forums, if not the most active, in the entire field of public international law. It has produced an extensive body of jurisprudence, and has, for the most part, been highly effective in its stated mission of "providing security and predictability to the multilateral trading system."

See also General Agreement on Tariffs and Trade (GATT); World Trade Organization

FURTHER READING

Hudec, Robert E. 1999. *Essays on the Nature of International Trade Law*. London: Cameron May. A superbly written, nontechnical collection of essays by the dispute settlement system's foremost commentator.

Jackson, John H. 1997. *The World Trading System: Law and Policy of International Economic Relations*. 2d ed. Cambridge, MA: MIT Press. An excellent overview of the workings of the rules governing the international trading system and the tensions those rules create.

Matsushita, Matsuo, Thomas J. Schoenbaum, and Petros C. Mavroidis. 2003. *The World Trade Organization: Law, Practice, and Policy*. Oxford: Oxford University Press. An analysis and commentary on the substantive provisions of the WTO agreements by three of the world's leading international trade law scholars.

Palmeter, David. 2003. *The WTO as a Legal System*. London: Cameron May. A collection of essays on legal and policy issues that have arisen in the WTO.

Palmeter, David, and Petros C. Mavroidis. 2004. *Dispute Settlement in the World Trade Organization: Practice and Procedure.* Cambridge: Cambridge University Press. A practice manual intended for diplomats and lawyers who participate in the WTO dispute settlement process.

Weiss, Friedl, ed. 2000. *Improving WTO Dispute Settlement Procedures: Issues and Lessons from the Practice of Other International Courts and Tribunals.* London: Cameron May. A collection of essays by leading academics looking at the WTO system in light of other international dispute settlement systems.

WTO Secretariat. 2001. *The WTO Dispute Settlement Procedures.* Cambridge: Cambridge University Press. The text of the WTO DSU, as well as the provisions from other WTO agreements relating to dispute settlement, and the texts of the formal decisions taken by the DSB with regard to practices and procedures.

———. 2004. *A Handbook on the WTO Dispute Settlement System.* Cambridge: Cambridge University Press. A general training guide to the system.

NIALL P. MEAGHER
AND DAVID PALMETER

Index

Note: Main entries are indicated by bold type.

626; and Mercosur, 759; natural resource exploitation in, 323; and sovereign wealth funds, 1016; and tariffs, 258;
twin crisis in, 123

Chile tax, 429

China: and agriculture, 28; aid from, 35,
49; and anti-dumping duties, 68; and
bilateral investment treaties, 674; and
brain drain, 135; and brain gain, 137;
and brain waste, 138; and business process outsourcing, 343; and capital account convertibility, 226; and commodity market intervention, 182;
current account surplus of, 214–15;
economic trends in, 151; EPZs in, 402–
3, 455; and exchange rates, 417–18; and
exit tax, 134; and FDI, 462, 741; and
G7/8, 570–71; GDP per capita of, 545;
and global imbalances, 536; immigration in, 766; intraindustry trade in, 710,
710t, 711t; migration from, 765; and
neomercantilism, 758; and processing
trade, 882; reform in, 910, 912–13; reserves of, 704, 1145–47; and shipping,
997; and smuggling, 1002–3; and
South-South trade, 1009–10; and sovereign wealth funds, 1015–16; and steel,
1032, 1034; technology transfer in, 461–
62; and temporary movement of natural
persons, 1083; and textiles/clothing,
1087–90; and toxic waste, 125; as transition economy, 1135; and U.S. bonds,
397; and WTO, 462, 1123

China Investment Corporation, 1015

Chinn, Menzie, 496, 651, 652

Chinoy, Sajjid, 1101

Chirac, Jacques, 796

Christmas Island, 189

Chubais, Anatoly, 913

Chung, Wilbur, 13

Churchill, Winston, 142, 361

cigarette industry, 1003–4

CIS. See Commonwealth of Independent
States

CITES. See Convention on International
Trade in Endangered Species (CITES)

civil society, 840

Clague, Christopher K., 849

Clark, Peter B., 347–48, 1019, 1020

class, democracy and, 267

classical trade theory, and primary products, 934

Clausing, Kimberly A., 707, 1133

Clean Air Act, 926

Clemenceau (ship), 125

Cline, William, 1146

Clinton, Bill, 182, 505, 852, 1034, 1180

Clinton Global Initiative, 48, 1181

closed interest parity, 650

closed regionalism, 61

clothing. *See* **textiles and clothing**

Club of Rome, 371

club NGOs, 840

clustering, 210–11

Coase, Ronald, 475

Cobden-Chevalier Treaty, 521, 799–800,
833

cocaine, 611–13

Code of Hammurabi, 232

Codex Alimentarius, 797, 991

Coe, David, 1078, 1079

coffee, 414

Cohen, Benjamin, 272

Cohen, Daniel, 574

Cold War, 43–44, 361, 369, 1152

Cole, H., 1013

Cole, Matthew A., 588

collective action clauses, 93, 659

collective investment schemes, 862

Collie, David, 237

Collier, P., 48, 1176–77

Collier, Ruth Berins, 267

Collinson, Simon, 211

collusion, 233

Colombia: and Andean Community, 61–
64; and Cairns Group, 1156; and drugs,
612, 613; and Mercosur, 759; and
smuggling, 1003; and Uruguay Round,
1155

colonial America, 948

colonialism: currency and, 189; democracy
and, 266–67; economic development
and, 322; and institutional transfer,
669–70; international aid and, 42

COMESA. *See* **Common Market for
Eastern and Southern Africa**

command economy, 1135

commercial presence, 434, 528

Commission on Global Governance, 771

commitment, in policymaking, 1092

Commitment to Development Index, 49

Committee of Twenty, 1001

commodity chains, 177–81; complementary approaches to, 180–81; defined,
177; future research on, 180–81; governance of, 178–80; history of, 177–78;

modular networks and, 179; producer-
driven vs. buyer-driven, 178–79; and
tariff escalation, 1057–59; textiles and
clothing, 1086–90

commodity money, 243

commodity reserve currency, 183

Commodity Stabilization Fund, 142

commodity terms of trade. *See* **terms of
trade**

commodity-price pegging, 182–83

**Common Agricultural Policy (CAP),
184–88**; common currency and, 190–
91; creation of, 31, 184, 363; Doha
Round and, 27; early features of, 184–
85; evolution of, 185–86; and export
subsidies, 184, 186; future of, 187–88;
and import policy, 17, 186; origins of,
362; Pillars I and II, 187–88; and protectionism, 184–85, 187; reforms of,
186–87; Uruguay Round and, 186

common currency, 188–91; euro as, 190–
91; incentives for, 188–89; incidence of,
189; national vs., 188; and optimum
currency area theory, 189, 870–71;
public finance and, 190; theories of,
189–91

common external tariff (CET): Andean
Community and, 61–63; CACM and,
170–71; customs unions and, 256–58;
regional economic communities and,
10–11

Common Fund, 1152

common market, 191–93; customs union
vs., 192; defined, 191; factor mobility
and, 191–93; limitations of, 191–92

**Common Market for Eastern and South-
ern Africa (COMESA), 194–97**, 961;
and African Union, 9; background of,
194–95; diversity in, 195; and external
actors, 197; impact on members of, 196–
97; institutions of, 195; objective of,
194; provisions of, 195–96; strategy of,
195–96

common preferential tariff, 316

Commonwealth of Independent States
(CIS), 1135–40, 1171–72

communications. *See* **information and
communications technologies**

community indifference curves (CICs),
515

Comoros, and COMESA, 194–97

comparative advantage, 198–204; absolute vs., 199; classical perspectives on,

Hazari, Bharat R., 76, 850

Head, Keith, 13, 14, 722, 742, 751, 752

headquarters services, of MNEs, 409–11, 440, 447–48, 454, 468, 473

health and globalization, 587–90; access to medicines and, 3–5, 588; and economic growth, 588–89; income and inequality and, 587–88; knowledge flows and health technologies, 588; and risks, 589–90

health and safety measures: agriculture and, 32; air transportation reform and, 60; pharmaceutical regulation, 902–3; TRIPS and, 23. *See also* **sanitary and phytosanitary measures**

Hecht, J. E., 1058

Heckscher, Eli, 198, 202, 203, 515, 591

Heckscher-Ohlin model, 591–96; and absolute advantage, 2, 3; and abundant factors, 867; and comparative advantage, 198, 203; factor prices and factor intensities, 592*f*; and FDI, 444; and fragmentation, 499; New Trade Theory vs., 829–30; and nontraded goods, 848–49; North-South trade and, 856; price assumptions of, 568; and primary products, 934; production equilibrium, 593*f*; Ricardian model vs., 591; setting and principal results of, 591–92; specific-factors model and, 1021, 1023–25; theorems of, 592–95; trade and wages in, 595–96; and trade liberalization, 830

Heckscher-Ohlin theorem, 592, 594–95

Heckscher-Ohlin-Samuelson (HOS) general equilibrium framework, 319, 323, 515–16, 918

hedge funds, 597–99; defined, 597; importance of, 597; investment issues for, 598–99; investment strategy for, 597–98; offshore financial centers and, 862; regulatory issues for, 599; role of, 599; types of, 597

hedging, 600–601; emerging economies and, 416; incentives for, 600–601; speculation vs., 600–601

Heller, Robert, 870

Hellman, F. Thomas, 426

Helpman, Elhanan, 410, 411, 447, 449, 473, 475, 479, 655, 832, 836, 910, 920, 921, 940, 981, 1078, 1079, 1098

Henderson, V., 926

Henrekson, Magnus, 632

herding, 217, 1027

Herin, Jan, 981

heroin, 612, 613

Heston, Alan, 665

Hicks, John, 815, 816

Hicks-neutral model of technological differences, 849, 856

Highly Indebted Poor Country Initiative, 933

high-powered money, 787

Hillman, Arye L., 919, 986

Hines, James R., Jr., 707, 715

Hirschman, Albert O., 734, 736

Hirshleifer, Jack, 1131

historical imports, 1062

HIV/AIDS, 601–4; and access to medicines, 4–5, 588, 603; demographics of, 602; economic impact of, 589, 602; epidemiology of, 601–2; informational campaigns on, 588; international response to, 602–4; prevention of, 603

Holmstrom, Bengt, 1131

home country bias, 604–6; in consumption, 3, 423, 606; in equities, 423, 604–6; explanations of, 605–6; in macroeconomics, 606

Home Depot, 402

home market effect, 821, 823–24

Honduras: and CACM, 169–71, 257; and CAFTA-DR, 172–74

Honeywell, 206, 762–64

Hong Kong: and APEC, 82; and currency boards, 241, 382, 993; as financial center, 662–63, 861; financial crisis in, 218; and gender wage gap, 519; human capital in, 320; and South-South trade, 1010; and textiles/clothing, 1090

Hoover Corporation, 1110

Hopkins, R., 1176

Hopkins, Terrence, 177

Horioka, Charles, 164, 421

horizontal foreign direct investment. *See* **vertical versus horizontal foreign direct investment**

Horn, Henrik, 838

Horst, Thomas, 1132

Horstmann, Ignatius, 440, 448, 483, 484, 654, 656

HOS model. *See* Heckscher-Ohlin-Samuelson (HOS) general equilibrium framework

host countries: brain drain and, 132; corruption and FDI in, 636; EPZs and, 401–2; FDI and export performance in,

455; FDI and labor market in, 465–67; FDI and tax revenues of, 471; and intellectual property rights, 648; and joint ventures, 716; and location theory, 740–41; market size and FDI, 753–54; MNEs and, 442–43, 450–53; of temporary migrant workers, 1083

hot money and sudden stops, 607–9; capital account convertibility and, 226; contagion and, 216; defined, 607; FDI and, 608–9; fear of floating and, 417; financial integration and, 703; and output contractions, 607–8

Howitt, Peter, 320

Huberman, G., 605

hubs, 824

Hudec, Robert, 522, 833

Hufbauer, Gary Clyde, 987, 988

human capital: and development, 265; and economic development, 320–21; migration and, 321

human development, 278–79

Human Development Index, 279, 587, 602

human resources, foreign market entry and, 494

Humanitarian Accountability Partnership International, 41

humanitarian aid. *See* **aid, humanitarian**

Hume, David, 103, 199–200, 512, 516, 562, 758, 818

Hummels, David, 569, 1010

Humphrey, John, 179–80

Humphrey, Thomas M., 731

Hungary: and brain use, 139; and Cairns Group, 1156; currency of, 1162; and economic reform, 1171; and EU, 351, 356; and OECD, 872; as transition economy, 1136–39

Hutchison, M., 425, 704

Hymer, Stephen, 481–82

hyperinflation, 947, 992–93

hysteresis. *See* **path dependency**

Iceland: financial problems in, 218; and OECD, 872

ICT. *See* **information and communications technologies**

ideas, and economic growth, 578. *See also* **intellectual property rights**; knowledge

identity: globalization and, 559–60; nation-building and, 672

IFCs. *See* **international financial centers**